THE NEW TESTAMENT
OF
THE JERUSALEM BIBLE

General Editor
ALEXANDER JONES, L.S.S., S.T.L., I.C.B.

The list of all those who have helped in the preparation of the Jerusalem Bible is too long to be given in its entirety. The principal collaborators in translation and literary revision were:

Joseph Leo Alston	Anthony J. Kenny
Florence M. Bennett	D. O. Lloyd James
Joseph Blenkinsopp	James McAuley
David Joseph Bourke	Alan Neame
Douglas Carter	Hubert Richards
Aldhelm Dean O.S.B.	Edward Sackville-West
Illtud Evans, O.P.	Ronald Senator
Kenelm Foster, O.P.	Walter Shewring
Ernest Graf, O.S.B.	Robert Speaight
Prospero Grech, O.S.A.	J. R. R. Tolkien
Edmund Hill, O.P.	R. F. Trevett
Sylvester Houédard, O.S.B.	Thomas Worden
Leonard Johnston	John Wright

Basil Wrighton

THE NEW TESTAMENT OF THE JERUSALEM BIBLE

DOUBLEDAY & COMPANY, INC.
GARDEN CITY, NEW YORK

Nihil Obstat: Lionel Swain, S.T.L., L.S.S.
Imprimatur: ✠ John Cardinal Heenan
Westminster, July 4, 1966

The introductions and notes of this Bible are, with minor variations and revisions a translation of those which appear in *La Bible de Jerusalem* published by Les Editions du Cerf, Paris, (one volume edition, 1961, but modified in the light of the subsequent revised fascicule edition) under the general editorship of Père Roland de Vaux, O.P. The English text of the Bible itself, though translated from the ancient texts, owes a large debt to the work of the many scholars who collaborated to produce *La Bible de Jerusalem*, a debt which the publishers of this English Bible gratefully acknowledge.

FIRST EDITION

Library of Congress Catalog Card Number 67–24835

Printed in the United States of America

CONTENTS

List of principal collaborators . ii
List of abbreviations vii
Explanation of typographical and reference systems . . . ix

Introduction to the Synoptic Gospels 5
The Gospel according to Saint Matthew 15
The Gospel according to Saint Mark 65
The Gospel according to Saint Luke 90
Introduction to the Gospel and Letters of Saint John . . . 139
The Gospel according to Saint John 146
Introduction to the Acts of the Apostles 195
The Acts of the Apostles . . 200
Introduction to the Letters of Saint Paul 251
Romans 267
1 Corinthians 292
2 Corinthians 311
Galatians 322
Ephesians 330
Philippians 338
Colossians 344
1 Thessalonians 350
2 Thessalonians 355
1 Timothy 358
2 Timothy 364
Titus 368
Philemon 371
Hebrews 373
Introduction to the Letters to all Christians 391
Saint James 396
1 Saint Peter 401
2 Saint Peter 407
1 Saint John 411
2 Saint John 420
3 Saint John 421
Jude 422
Introduction to the Book of Revelation 427
The Book of Revelation . . 430

SUPPLEMENTS

Chronological table 455
Genealogical table of the Hasmonaean and Herodian dynasties 463
Table of weights and measures . 465
Maps
Palestine of the New Testament
Jerusalem of the New Testament
The journeys of Saint Paul

LIST OF ABBREVIATIONS

The books of the Bible in biblical order

Genesis	Gn	Jonah	Jon
Exodus	Ex	Micah	Mi
Leviticus	Lv	Nahum	Na
Numbers	Nb	Habakkuk	Hab
Deuteronomy	Dt	Zephaniah	Zp
Joshua	Jos	Haggai	Hg
Judges	Jg	Zechariah	Zc
Ruth	Rt	Malachi	Ml
1 Samuel	1 S		
2 Samuel	2 S		
1 Kings	1 K		
2 Kings	2 K	Matthew	Mt
1 Chronicles	1 Ch	Mark	Mk
2 Chronicles	2 Ch	Luke	Lk
Ezra	Ezr	John	Jn
Nehemiah	Ne	Acts	Ac
Tobit	Tb	Romans	Rm
Judith	Jdt	1 Corinthians	1 Co
Esther	Est	2 Corinthians	2 Co
1 Maccabees	1 M	Galatians	Ga
2 Maccabees	2 M	Ephesians	Ep
Job	Jb	Philippians	Ph
Psalms	Ps	Colossians	Col
Proverbs	Pr	1 Thessalonians	1 Th
Ecclesiastes	Qo	2 Thessalonians	2 Th
Song of Songs	Sg	1 Timothy	1 Tm
Wisdom	Ws	2 Timothy	2 Tm
Ecclesiasticus	Si	Titus	Tt
Isaiah	Is	Philemon	Phm
Jeremiah	Jr	Hebrews	Heb
Lamentations	Lm	James	Jm
Baruch	Ba	1 Peter	1 P
Ezekiel	Ezk	2 Peter	2 P
Daniel	Dn	1 John	1 Jn
Hosea	Ho	2 John	2 Jn
Joel	Jl	3 John	3 Jn
Amos	Am	Jude	Jude
Obadiah	Ob	Revelation	Rv

The books of the Bible in alphabetical order of abbreviations

Ac	Acts	1 Ch	1 Chronicles
Am	Amos	2 Ch	2 Chronicles
Ba	Baruch	1 Co	1 Corinthians

2 Co	2 Corinthians	1 M	1 Maccabees
Col	Colossians	2 M	2 Maccabees
Dn	Daniel	Mi	Micah
Dt	Deuteronomy	Mk	Mark
Ep	Ephesians	Ml	Malachi
Est	Esther	Mt	Matthew
Ex	Exodus	Na	Nahum
Ezk	Ezekiel	Nb	Numbers
Ezr	Ezra	Ne	Nehemiah
Ga	Galatians	Ob	Obadiah
Gn	Genesis	1 P	1 Peter
Hab	Habakkuk	2 P	2 Peter
Heb	Hebrews	Ph	Philippians
Hg	Haggai	Phm	Philemon
Ho	Hosea	Pr	Proverbs
Is	Isaiah	Ps	Psalms
Jb	Job	Qo	Ecclesiastes
Jdt	Judith	Rm	Romans
Jg	Judges	Rt	Ruth
Jl	Joel	Rv	Revelation
Jm	James	1 S	1 Samuel
Jn	John	2 S	2 Samuel
1 Jn	1 John	Sg	Song of Songs
2 Jn	2 John	Si	Ecclesiasticus
3 Jn	3 John	Tb	Tobit
Jon	Jonah	1 Th	1 Thessalonians
Jos	Joshua	2 Th	2 Thessalonians
Jr	Jeremiah	1 Tm	1 Timothy
Jude	Jude	2 Tm	2 Timothy
1 K	1 Kings	Tt	Titus
2 K	2 Kings	Ws	Wisdom
Lk	Luke	Zc	Zechariah
Lm	Lamentations	Zp	Zephaniah
Lv	Leviticus		

Other abbreviations not in common use

Add.	additional words included by some authorities	Lat.	Latin
Arab.	Arabic	LXX	the Greek 'Septuagint'
Ch.	the 'Chronicler' (as well as the Books of Chronicles)	M.T.	Massoretic Text
Ch.	chapter(s)	Om.	words omitted by some authorities
Conj.	conjectural reading	Sam.	Samaritan Pentateuch
Corr.	text has been corrected	Theod.	Theodotian
Hebr.	Hebrew language/text	Var.	variant reading
		Vet. Lat.	Old Latin version
		Vulg.	Vulgate

EXPLANATION OF TYPOGRAPHICAL AND REFERENCE SYSTEMS

Chapter numbers

The beginning of a new chapter is usually marked by a large bold numeral. A smaller bold numeral is used when a new chapter begins inside a paragraph, or to mark a fragment of a chapter separated from the main portion by material of a different chapter.

Verse numbers

In the Old Testament, the division into verses follows the Hebrew. The verse numbers are printed in ordinary roman type. Where the verse-numbering of the Vulgate differs, it is given in addition in italic figures. In a few places, italic verse numbers are also used for some of the passages incorporated from the Septuagint, e.g. Dn 3 (cf. notes), of which the numbering duplicates that of neighbouring Hebrew material.

The beginning of each verse is indicated in the line by a dot • preceding the first word except when a verse starts at the beginning of a line or begins a new chapter. When a Vulgate verse begins at a different point, this is not indicated.

Occasionally verse numbers are given a suffix letter a, b or c. This is generally to mark a rearrangement of parts of the verse, or to relate a reference from elsewhere in the Bible to a specific part of the verse.

Italics in the text

The chief use of italic type in the text is to distinguish words which are quotations from, or close allusions to, another book of the Bible. The origins of such quotations are given as references in the margin. (Conversely, where a passage will be found quoted in a later book, its wording is not printed in italics, but the fact is indicated by a reference in the margin, preceded by a ↗ sign, to the place where the quotation will be found: see explanation of Marginal References below.

Italics are also used (as in Est and Dn) to distinguish supplementary passages brought in from the Septuagint, and the inclusion of such material is always specified in a footnote.

Brackets in the text

In the text, round brackets are never used except to indicate that the words within them are considered to be a gloss.

Footnotes

In each chapter, footnotes are lettered serially. Footnotes are printed on right-hand pages only, and normally the notes relating to the left-hand page are separated by one or more blank lines from those relating to the right-hand page.

The footnotes assume that the reader has already read the Introduction to the book (or group of books) concerned. From time to time there are 'general' notes which explain special biblical terms that recur, or themes which are of importance, e.g. 'remnant' (cf. note on Is 4:3), 'Son of man' (cf. note on Mt 8:20). These general notes are often interconnected, and a note on one passage may refer the reader to a note on the same theme elsewhere. A guide to these general thematic notes is provided by the index of biblical themes included in this volume, and its uses are explained below.

Punctuation of biblical references

Chapter and verse are separated by a colon, e.g. Ex 20:17. In a succession of references, items are separated by a semi-colon, e.g. Ex 20:17; Lv 9:15. The same practice is followed in a succession of references to different chapters of one book, e.g. Ex 20:17; 21:3 or Ex 15; 17; 20.

Marginal References

The marginal references direct the reader's attention to other passages in the Bible (or to footnotes attached to them) which can contribute to an understanding of the text—sources of quotations, earlier use of special terms, phrases, or images and the explanation of allusions whether explicit or implied. The references often occur in groups all relating to one text line; in such cases, the position of the first reference indicates the line to which the whole group applies. The typographical design of this Bible makes it possible to place two marginal reference lines against each line of text; the first reference of a group may therefore appear slightly above or slightly below the text line.

The end of one group of references and the beginning of a new group is normally marked by a space; where this is not possible, the first line of the new group is printed in italic type.

Within a group of references, the order of items is:

1. References to the sources of italicised quotations from other books.
2. References to other passages in the same book; these are *not* preceded by the abbreviated book name.
3. References to passages in other books of the Bible; these are given in biblical order.

References to different books always begin on separate lines. When one reference line cannot accommodate all the references to one book, the references are continued (without repetition of the abbreviated book name) on new lines which are indented slightly away from the text.

Symbols in biblical references

▲ In some cases, a group of marginal references which begins near the foot of a left-hand page has to be continued at the top of the facing page. The references which are thus displaced from a previous page are distinguished by a solid triangle added to each, to show that they do not relate to the lines opposite which they appear.

= or || These symbols are placed in front of references which call attention to the fact that a literary connection exists between two text passages either because one might be called the 'source' of the other or because both have a common source. When the two passages belong to the same book (i.e. are 'doublets') the symbol = is used; where they belong to different books (i.e. are 'parallels') the symbol || is used. However, in the case of those parts of the Bible which are duplications of another part or which, like the synoptic gospels, recount the same events, the references to all the parallels are usually given only in the book which occurs first in order of printing, and references in the other related books guide the reader to the relevant passage in this first book where further references to other parallels will be found. Thus in the synoptic gospels many references useful in the study of Mark or Luke are given once for all in Matthew, but references in Mark or Luke guide the reader to that point in Matthew at which these other references are given.

p This letter at the end of a reference refers the reader not only to the passage indicated but also to doublets or parallels to which references with the symbol = or || will be found at the passage indicated.

↗ The arrow symbol is used before a reference where the text at this point will be used or quoted in a later book to which the reference relates, and particularly where a passage in the Old Testament will be used by a New Testament writer.

\+ The plus symbol used at the end of a reference indicates that, at the point referred to, the reader will find either a note or further references relevant to the passage he is reading. This symbol is the principal means of referring the reader to the general notes on key biblical themes and concepts. For example, in prophetic material which relates to the 'remnant of Israel' references will be found to Is 4:3+ where there is a note explaining this concept.

f This letter at the end of a reference signifies 'and following verses'.

THE
NEW TESTAMENT

THE SYNOPTIC GOSPELS

INTRODUCTION TO

THE SYNOPTIC GOSPELS

Of the four canonical books that record the 'Good News' (*evangelium*, gospel) brought by Jesus Christ, the first three are so alike that they can, in many passages, be placed side by side and viewed as it were at a glance: for this reason they are called 'synoptic' ('with one eye').

Tradition dating from the 2nd century assigns them respectively to Saints Matthew, Mark and Luke. According to the same ecclesiastical tradition Matthew the publican, himself one of the apostles (Mt 9:9; 10:3), was the first to write; he wrote his gospel in Palestine for Christians converted from Judaism. His work, composed in 'the Hebrew tongue', i.e. in Aramaic, was then translated into Greek. John Mark, a disciple from Jerusalem (Ac 12:12) who assisted Paul in his apostolic work (Ac 12:25; 13:5,13; Phm 24; 2 Tm 4:11), and Barnabas his cousin (Ac 15:37,39; Col 4:10) and Peter (1 P 5:13), whose 'interpreter' he was, put Peter's preaching down in writing at Rome. Another disciple, Luke, a medical man (Col 4:14) and, unlike Matthew and Mark, of pagan origin (Col 4:10-14), born at Antioch according to some authorities, accompanied Paul on the latter's second (Ac 16:10f) and third (Ac 20:5f) missionary journeys and was with him during his two Roman captivities (Ac 27:1f; 2 Tm 4:11). For this reason his gospel, the third to be written, could claim the authority of Paul (cf. perhaps 2 Co 8:18) as that of Mark could claim the authority of Peter. Luke composed also a second work—the 'Acts of the Apostles'. The original language of the second and third gospels is Greek.

These traditional data are confirmed and amplified by an internal examination of the three gospels; but before going on with this, it is necessary to say something about the problem of the literary relations between these gospels, i.e. 'The Synoptic Problem'.

All the many solutions offered so far prove inadequate if taken separately, though each contributes an element of truth to the complete solution. In the first place it is highly probable, even certain, that a *common oral tradition* was committed to writing by each of the three Synoptics independently, and consequently with variations. By itself this tradition would never have been able to account for the many striking similarities which exist not only between details in the text but also in the sequence of passages, resemblances which cannot be explained even by the extraordinary memory of people in the ancient Middle East. As for a *written tradition*, in one or many forms, this would be a far better explanation. But even supposing the three evangelists did draw independently on some such written source or sources, that could never explain passages where these likenesses and divergencies show that the evangelists were aware of each other, as is obvious from the fact that at times they copy or correct each other. There must have been some direct interdependence and it is clear that Luke depends on Mark. It is not so clear however that Mark depends on Matthew: though this was held for a long time, a number of indications now suggest the reverse. As for Matthew and Luke, no direct dependence in either direction can be considered probable, and the non-Marcan passages common to these two probably have their common source or sources outside the second gospel.

Starting from these textual considerations modern critics have worked out a '*Two Source Theory*' according to which these sources are: 1. Mark, on whom Matthew and Luke depend for their narrative sections; 2. a source the existence of which is inferred purely from the textual evidence, and which is called 'Q' (initial of the German word *Quelle*, source). From Q, both the first and third gospels draw the 'Sayings' or discourses of Jesus ('Logia'), which in Mark are reduced to a minimum. This hypothesis is a step towards the solution but it involves some grave difficulties. 1. It abandons the traditional belief in the Aramaic origin of the first gospel and in its priority over Mark. Moreover it does not take sufficient account of textual facts which confirm this tradition, facts which suggest that Matthew is not entirely dependent, even in narrative sections, on Mark and that there are times when Matthew appears to represent an even more primitive text than Mark. 2. As for Q, it is hard to see how such a document could have existed at all (at least in any of the many forms suggested) and if it did it would never have accounted sufficiently for all the complicated relationships that can be established between the first and third gospels.

Particularly in Catholic circles, recent criticism has attempted to answer these two difficulties (the evidence of an Aramaic original and the inadequacy of Q). It maintains: 1. that a primitive form of the first gospel in Aramaic existed as distinct from its later Greek form: this, it is claimed, is a far better explanation of the complicated relationship between Matthew and Mark, because it allows Matthew Greek to depend on Mark, and Mark to depend on Matthew Aramaic, which explains how the first gospel, which usually follows Mark, sometimes deserts him and seems to retain a more primitive flavour—the reason being that Matthew Greek is in these cases closer than Mark to Matthew Aramaic, their common source; 2. that Q is an inadequate hypothesis and to help to supply for this inadequacy, in a way that does not conflict with the literary data, it is necessary to distinguish two different sources for the Logia common to Matthew and Luke. a. Matthew Aramaic which, besides narrative matter, contained Logia (of which Mark omitted the greater part) and was therefore a gospel in the true sense of the word; b. the Supplementary Collection of Logia: supplementary, that is, to Matthew Aramaic, because it was meant either to preserve matter omitted from that gospel or to preserve in some different and more desirable form matter which that gospel already contained. To these two sources, both Matthew Greek and Luke are indebted; they are drawing from Matthew Aramaic when the narrative context in which the Logia are grouped is the same in each gospel, and they are drawing from the Supplementary Collection when each makes use of the Logia in its own characteristic way: Luke, keeping them together, inserts them in blocks in his 'great intercalation' (9:51–18:14); Matthew splits them up and distributes them throughout his gospel in his five main sections. One notable result of this complicated literary process is what are called 'doublets': i.e. the same saying or group of sayings occurs twice in Matthew or in Luke because on each occasion they are quoted from the two different sources, i.e. Matthew Aramaic (either immediately or through the medium of Mark) and the Collection. It should be noticed that both Matthew and Luke would have used these two sources not in their primitive Aramaic but in two different Greek translations, which would sometimes agree with each other and sometimes not; this would explain why the parallel texts of the first and third gospels are at times extraordinarily alike, at other times markedly unlike.

Having stated the purely literary considerations of this view, it is now possible to describe each of the steps in *the formation of the first three gospels*. This can be done with some degree of probability, but not with complete certainty.

At the heart of the oral preaching of the apostles lies the 'Kerygma' proclaiming the redemptive death and resurrection of the Lord. Peter's discourses in the Acts of the Apostles provide us with typical summaries of this apostolic preaching which would in practice have included more detailed narratives: principally the story of the Passion which must have assumed its stereotyped pattern very early, as the close similarity of the four gospel accounts shows, but also many anecdotes taken from the Master's life, and throwing light on his person, his mission and his power, or else illustrating his teaching by means of some well-remembered episode, saying, miracle, pronouncement or parable etc. In addition to the apostles themselves there were professional narrators like the evangelists (those who enjoyed a special *charisma* not limited to the writers of our four gospels; cf. Ac 21:8; Ep 4:11; 2 Tm 4:5), who tended to stereotype the anecdotes by constant repetition. Before long, and particularly when the witnesses who had been in touch with the events themselves began to disappear, measures would have been taken to commit this oral tradition to writing. Episodes originally narrated separately and independently of each other would naturally be grouped together either chronologically (e.g. Mk 1:16-39, the Day of Capernaum) or logically (e.g. Mk 2:1–3:6, the Five Disputes); the groupings would be small at first, but would later grow into more extensive collections. This was the stage at which an author intervened who, according to tradition, which there is no reason to doubt, was Matthew the apostle. He was the first to compose a 'gospel' which drew together Christ's deeds and words into a continuous narrative covering the earthly ministry of Jesus from baptism to resurrection. Shortly afterwards a 'Collection', of unknown authorship, appeared side by side with this early gospel; its purpose was to preserve sayings of the Lord which were either not contained in Matthew Aramaic, or were presented there in a different form. This early gospel and this Collection, both written in Aramaic, were soon put into Greek, and eventually various forms of these translations came to exist. Now Peter's preaching of the catechesis (or 'instruction') was probably based on the same Palestinian tradition that Matthew had committed to writing. Consequently, when Peter's disciple Mark set himself to record this catechesis, it was most natural that he should make use of Matthew Aramaic in whatever Greek translation was familiar to him. This would not have prevented Mark from putting into his narratives some of the vivid realism that had come to him from the preaching of his master Peter, which was itself full of that living quality that comes from personal experience of events. It is this realism, loaded with picturesque and true-to-life detail, which endears Mark's narratives to us in spite of his rough Greek style. True to his purpose (of which we shall speak later) Mark decided to put in very few of the Sayings. He shortened or omitted the ones in the early gospel and passed over in silence those in the Collection of which, presumably, he knew nothing. This silence of his was to be remedied by two new gospel editions (though which of them preceded the other it is difficult to say). An anonymous editor, Matthew Greek, decided to rewrite the first Aramaic gospel, which was known to him in one of its Greek translations. This he filled out and made more detailed, using for his narrative parts of the work of Mark his predecessor, to which he added one thing only of importance, i.e. the two chapters of the Infancy Narrative. In general Matthew Greek corrected and followed Mark's text, but at times he went back to the earlier gospel and on these occasions his style, unlike anything in Mark, becomes both original and archaic. For the Sayings, he referred to the earlier gospel in order to record many that Mark omitted, adding to them from the wealth of Sayings in the Supplementary Collection. Hence the impressive blocks of material, each built round some central theme, which make his gospel the remarkable thing it is. But these were not his only sources. The author had access to some information not so generally available, and this not only for his narratives but also for the Sayings: this accounts for the material which is peculiarly his own, notably in the narrative of the Infancy. By setting out to supplement the primitive Aramaic gospel, Matthew Greek clearly did not aim at being a mere translation of it, but at the same time he only developed it according to its own spirit and purpose. The Church has recognised that his work was inspired by accepting his Greek gospel as canonical.

Luke undertook something similar but used a completely different approach. There are three points to notice: 1. like Matthew he also took from the primitive gospel tradition many Sayings that Mark omits, though unlike Matthew he preferred to omit Sayings that would have little interest for his readers who were pagans by birth; moreover, since the Sayings in Luke are derived through channels independent of Matthew Greek they often assume forms in his gospel noticeably different from those they assume in Matthew's. 2. Luke is more careful than Matthew to preserve the order given by his sources: thus, side by side with 'Marcan' sections, in which he follows the second gospel almost exactly (4:31–6:19; 8:4–9:50; 18:15–21:38), he places the Supplementary Collection which he inserts en bloc in a special section that he presents as an ascent to Jerusalem (9:51–18:14). 3. Luke resembles Matthew since, like him, he also has drawn on special sources but he has done this to a greater extent. These special sources of his he discovered by careful enquiry (1:3); to them he owes not only his narrative of the Infancy but many passages that enrich the gospel: the good Samaritan, Martha and Mary, the parables of the prodigal son, of the Pharisee and the publican, etc., which occur for the most part in Luke's Central Section (9:51–18:14), and it is not impossible that this combination of the Collection with the material he has been at pains to find for himself was a stage of Luke's editorial activity independent of, and perhaps prior to, his use of Mark.

The literary process just outlined respects and makes use of the broad data from tradition but is able to fill in details. It does not however make it possible, any more than tradition does, to assign an exact *date* to each of the Synoptics with complete certainty: at a guess however, the interval required for the development of the oral tradition would make it probable that the primitive Aramaic gospel and the later Supplementary Collection were composed between the years 40 and 50. This early date would be definite if it could be proved that Paul's Letters to the Thessalonians, written about 51-52, made use of the first gospel's Apocalyptic Discourse. If Mark wrote towards the end of Peter's life (according to Clement of Alexandria) or shortly after Peter's death (according to Irenaeus) the date of his gospel would be c. 64; in any case it should be dated before 70 as it does not seem from this gospel that Jerusalem has yet been destroyed. Matthew Greek and Luke are later than Mark but their precise date is more difficult to determine. The existence of Luke's gospel is presupposed by the Acts (Ac 1:1) but the date of Acts is itself uncertain (cf. Introduction to Acts) and can provide no criterion. It is true that neither Matthew Greek nor Luke suggests that the destruction of Jerusalem has already taken place (not even Lk 19:42-44; 21:20-24 which employ clichés from the prophetical books to describe an event that cannot have been hard to foresee) but this is not decisive. If neither of them knew of the destruction, then they would have to be put before 70, but if they deliberately aimed at scrupulously preserving the archaic quality of their respective literary sources, then their works might quite well have been composed after the destruction, say about A.D. 80.

In any case, the apostolic origin, direct or indirect, together with their involved literary formation confirm the *historical value* of the Synoptics, and not only that but at the same time help us to understand the nature of that historical value, and since the gospels stem from an oral preaching that goes back to the beginnings of the primitive community, their guarantee in this way would ultimately rest on eyewitness. Neither the apostles themselves, however, nor any of the other preachers of the gospel message and tellers of the gospel story ever aimed at writing or teaching history in the modern technical sense of that word; their concern was sacred and theological: they preached to convert and edify, to infuse faith, to enlighten it and defend it against its opponents. For this purpose they could and did appeal to solid evidence that could be checked, and this appeal was demanded quite as much by their own sincerity as by their anxiety not to leave any loopholes for hostile argument. Those who finally composed the gospels, collecting the evidence and putting it into writing, had the same objective fidelity, and equal respect for their sources of information as is suggested by the simple and archaic quality of their work. In this there are no theological developments characteristic of subsequent decades (cf. Paul for example); much less is there any trace of the sort of extravagant legends that are frequent in the apocryphal gospels. The three Synoptics may not be history books but they do set out to give us historical fact.

This does not mean that each of the events or discourses which they record corresponds exactly to what in fact took place. The laws governing witnesses and the spread of evidence warn us against looking for that material sort of precision. Obvious examples can be found in the gospels themselves where the same events or the same discourses are sometimes recorded in different ways. This is true not only of the content of some episodes, but it is even truer of the order in which these episodes are arranged, which is not the same order in each gospel. This is only to be expected in view of their complex origins.

Their component parts, which at first existed separately, were only gradually collected together into groups; and these groups were later joined together or split up more for reasons of logic or neatness than for anything to do with chronology. In this way many of the gospel events or Sayings have been shifted from their proper time or place. For this reason it is often impossible to take editorial connective phrases like 'then', 'after this', 'on that day', 'at that time', etc., in their literal sense.

The belief of Christians in the authority of these inspired books is not of course affected by this. That there was no perfect agreement in detail among those chosen by the Holy Spirit to speak for him merely implies that he attaches no importance, in the sphere of faith, to that sort of material exactitude; it suggests indeed that he actually willed this difference of evidence. Heraclitus said, 'Implicit agreements are worth more than explicit ones' and it is obvious that a fact which comes to us by a variety of discordant traditions (e.g. the apparitions after the resurrection) appears more real and probable than it would if vouched for by witnesses whose evidence was identical in both detail and vocabulary. It is a further advantage when these discrepancies occur, not just accidentally and unavoidably, but as the result of deliberate correction. It is certain that the gospel writers often presented their material in deliberately different ways, and in any case the earlier oral tradition which they inherited did not only hand down reminiscences of the gospel story passively, but at the same time both interpreted them and adapted them in all sorts of ways to the actual requirements of the living faith they taught. This intervention by the community in forming the tradition was directed by responsible members of that community: there is no reason, therefore, to suspect the fidelity of the tradition. On the positive side, this intervention is instructive: since the community was the Church, its intervention shows how the magisterium was exercised from the beginning. Before inspiring the authors of the gospels, the Holy Spirit supervised the preparation of the material, adapted it to the diffusion of the faith and also secured its inerrancy—i.e. guaranteed as inerrant, not so much the facts and the precise circumstances in which facts occurred, but rather the spiritual meaning conveyed by those facts. All this work of the Spirit was only concerned with the provision of food for the spirit in a form that could be digested by the faithful. In particular it was to the writers of the synoptic gospels that he gave the gift of expressing in completely personal terms the message common to all three of them.

The Gospel according to Saint Mark

The *plan* Mark follows is the least systematic of all the Synoptics. The preaching of John the Baptist plus the baptism and temptation of Jesus make up his prelude (1:1-13); next comes a period of ministry which according to occasional hints was in Galilee (1:14-7:23), then a journey by Jesus and his apostles to the district of Tyre and Sidon, the Decapolis, the neighbourhood of Caesarea Philippi and back to Galilee (7:24–9:50); then lastly the final journey through Peraea and Jericho to Jerusalem where the Passion and resurrection take place (10:1–16:8). Apart from individual sequences of fact, this broad outline itself is purely conventional since it is historically probable, and to judge by the fourth gospel fairly certain, that Jesus visited Jerusalem several times before the last Passover of his life. All the same, this outline, broad as it is, does trace for us an important development which is both factually and theologically significant. The general public received Jesus warmly at first but their enthusiasm waned as they found that his meek and otherworldly conception of the Messiah did not fulfil their hopes. As a result, Jesus left Galilee to devote himself to the instruction of a small group of faithful followers, and the profession of faith at Caesarea Philippi showed that he had secured their absolute allegiance. This was a decisive turning-point: after it Jerusalem became the focus of attention, and it was there that further opposition continued mounting only to end in the drama of the Passion and in the final triumph of the resurrection.

This paradox provides the central interest of the second gospel i.e. how Jesus, while remaining misunderstood and rejected by men, was at the same time God's triumphant envoy. The gospel is not particularly concerned with elaborating the Master's teaching and it records few of his Sayings: the real point of its message is the *manifestation of the crucified Messiah.* On the one hand Jesus is the Son of God, acknowledged as such by the Father (1:11; 9:7), by the devils (1:24; 3:11; 5:7) and even by men (15:39); he is the Messiah claiming divine rank (14:62), higher than the angels (13:32), taking on himself the forgiveness of sin (2:10), vindicating his power and his mission by miracle (1:31; 4:41 etc.) and by exorcism (1:27; 3:23f etc.). On the other hand the gospel puts great emphasis on his apparent frustration at the hands of men: the mockery or refusal of the public (5:40; 6:2f), the antagonism of the Jewish leaders (2:1-3:6 etc.), the lack of understanding even on his disciples' part (4:13+)—all the hostile activities that were to lead to the shame of the cross. It is this 'scandal', this refusal, that the gospel is intent on explaining. This it does not merely by contrasting it with the crowning triumph of the resurrection but also by showing that the hostility was itself an integral part of God's mysterious plan. It was necessary that Christ should suffer and so redeem man (10:45; 14:24), since this had been foretold by the scriptures (9:12; 14:21,49). Both for himself (8:31; 9:31; 10:33f) and for his own followers (8:34f; 9:35; 10:15,24f,29f,39; 13:9-13) Jesus laid down a way of humility and suffering; but the Jews, expecting a victorious warrior-Messiah, were ill prepared for this answer to their hope, and the reason why Jesus wanted silence about his miracles (5:43 etc.) and his identity (7:24; 9:30) was to avoid an enthusiasm which would have been as ill-advised as it would have been mistaken. Rather than call himself Messiah, 8:29f, which would have been too suggestive of human dignity, he took the modest and mysterious title 'Son of Man' (2:10 etc.; cf. Mt 8:20+). This cautionary measure is what is called 'the messianic secret' (Mk 1:34+) and is a basic idea of Mark's gospel. It was not something Mark had invented: it corresponded to that underlying reality in Christ's life of suffering which, in the light of a faith finally and fully established by the Easter event, the evangelist was able to perceive and to place before us for our understanding.

The Gospel according to Saint Matthew

The same light of faith and the same broad outline of Christ's life naturally occur in Matthew as well as in Mark, but with quite a different emphasis. To begin with, the *plan* is not the same and is much more elaborate: Matthew is divided into five books each consisting of a discourse introduced and led up to by painstakingly selected narrative matter; these five books, plus the stories of the Infancy and of the Passion, are combined to form a well-knit whole of seven sections. It is possible that this arrangement, which is so clear in Matthew, goes back to the Aramaic gospel and that it is traceable also in Mark's brief account; but whether this is so or not, it remains true that, as we have already seen, Matthew used his sources with great freedom in order to reach his carefully mapped out ensemble which is so brilliantly adapted for teaching purposes. The fact that this gospel also reports Christ's teaching much more fully than Mark, and stresses specially the theme of 'the kingdom of heaven' (4:17+), makes it a *dramatic account in seven acts of the coming of the kingdom of heaven.* These acts are as follows: 1. The preparation of the kingdom in the person of the child-Messiah, ch. 1-2. 2. The formal proclamation of the charter of the kingdom to the disciples and the public, i.e. the Sermon on the Mount, ch. 3-7. 3. The preaching of the kingdom by missionaries whose credentials (the 'signs' which are to confirm the word) are now hinted at by several miracles done by Jesus himself; the missionaries receive their instructions, ch. 8-10. 4. The obstacles with which the kingdom will meet from men, and which are part of God's deliberate design that the kingdom should come without show, even imperceptibly, as illustrated in the parables of the concluding Instruction, 11:1–13:52. 5. Its embryonic existence in the group of disciples with Peter at their head; the rules for this Church in the making are outlined in the concluding Instruction on the Community, 13:53–18:35. 6. The crisis, provoked by the increasing hostility of the Jewish leaders, which is to prepare the way for the definitive coming of the kingdom and which is the subject of the concluding Eschatological Instruction, ch. 19-25. 7. Lastly, the coming itself, a coming effected through suffering and triumph, through the Passion and resurrection, ch. 26-28.

The kingdom of God (of the 'heavens' in Matthew) is the reassertion of God's dominion as King over men who at last know him, serve him and love him. This kingdom was prepared and foretold in the Old Testament. Matthew therefore, writing among Jews for Jews, makes a special point of demonstrating that *the scriptures are fulfilled* in the person and work of Jesus. In every significant passage of his work he makes use of the Old Testament to prove that Law and prophets are 'fulfilled'—a phrase which means that their hopes have been not only realised but have also been perfected, ennobled, surpassed. As applied to the person of Jesus: he appeals to Old Testament texts for his Davidic descent (1:1-17), for his virgin birth (1:23) at Bethlehem (2:6), for his stay in Egypt and his settling at Capernaum (4:14-16), for his messianic progress into Jerusalem (21:5,16); as applied to the work of Jesus: he appeals to Old Testament texts for cures (11:4-5); and finally as applied to the teaching of Jesus: this 'fulfils' the Law (5:17) while raising it to further heights (5:21-48; 19:3-9, 16-21). Matthew asserts equally strongly that the scriptures are also fulfilled in the lowliness of Christ's person and in what humanly seems to be the frustration of his work. In this way God's plan contains, and the Old Testament foretells: the massacre of the Innocents (2:17f), the hidden life at Nazareth (2:23), the gentle compassion of the 'servant of God' (12:17-21; cf. 8:17; 11:29; 12:7), the disciples' desertion (26:31), the paltry price of betrayal (27:9-10), the arrest (26:54) and the three days' burial (12:40); in this way too the Old Testament foretold the unbelief of the Jews (13:13-15), too tenacious of their man-made traditions (15:7-9), who could be approached only by teaching through the veil of parables (13:14-15,35); Matthew is not the only one of the three Synoptics to make use of arguments from the Old Testament, but even apart from the fact that they might have been copying Matthew Aramaic in this, Matthew relies so heavily on this argument that he has made it one of the chief characteristics of his gospel. Remembering this and recalling the gospel's systematic structure, the work can be aptly described as *the great charter of the new order which, in Christ, completes God's plan.* For Jesus is the Son of God (Matthew emphasises this more than Mark; cf. 14:33; 16:16; 22:2; 27:40,43) and as his teaching is the new Law that fulfils the old, so the Church which he built on Peter (16:18), and of which he is the keystone rejected by the builders (21:42), is the same messianic community as that of the Old Testament, but universalised, since God has allowed those who were first invited to decline (23:34-38; cf. 10:5-6,23; 15:24); this was so that he might throw open the gate of salvation to all nations (8:11-12; 21:33-46; 22:1-10; cf. 12:18,21; 28:19). It is easy to see why a gospel as complete and as neatly arranged as this and written more grammatically (though less attractively) than Mark's should have appealed to the early Church and been used by it in preference to others.

The Gospel according to Saint Luke

The third gospel's distinguishing quality is due to the attractive personality of its author which shines through all his work. Luke is at once a most gifted writer and a man of marked sensibility. He set to work in his own way with an eye to exact information and orderly narrative (1:3), but respect for his sources, together with his method of juxtaposing them, meant that even Luke was not in a position to arrange his traditional material in a more chronological way than Matthew or Mark. His *plan* follows Mark's outline though some episodes are displaced (3:19-20; 4:16-30; 5:1-11; 6:12-19; 22:31-34, etc.). This he did sometimes in the interests of clarity and logical sequence, sometimes under the influence of other streams of tradition including, it should be noted, a tradition traceable also in the fourth gospel. Other episodes are omitted altogether for various reasons: they were not interesting for Luke's non-Jewish readers (Mk 9:11-13), or they were already to be found in the Supplementary Collection (Mk 12:28-34; cf. Lk 10:25-28), or above all (as in the case of Luke's great omission of Mk 6:45–8:26) because it was not in Luke's copy of Mark or because, if it was there, Luke regarded it as unnecessarily repetitive. Luke's most obvious difference from Mark is his great intercalation (cf. 9:51–18:14) which, as has been seen, combines Logia or Sayings from some Collection with information he had found out for himself. This central section uses a journey to Jerusalem for its framework (cf. the reiterated indications, elaborating the datum of Mk 10:1, in Lk 9:51; 13:22; 17:11). But it is not a reminiscence of actual journeys; it is rather a device by which Luke is able to bring out one of his chief theological notions: namely that the Holy City is the predestined stage for the drama of salvation (9:31; 13:33; 18:31; 19:11). Because it is from Jerusalem that the evangelisation of the world must begin (24:47; Ac 1:8), his gospel had to start there (1:5f) and there he will have to bring it to a close (24:52f)—the post-resurrection apparitions and conversations recorded by Luke do not take place in Galilee (cf. 24:13-51 and cf. 24:6 with Mk 16:7; Mt 28:7,16-20).

Comparing Luke and his two sources, a. Mark, the best known, and b. the sources behind the Matthew passages which are parallelled in Luke, it becomes apparent that Luke was a craftsman whose concentration never slackened. His changes are very slight—just small omissions and additions—but through them he gives his work a character peculiarly his own. He avoids or whittles down anything he or his readers found offensive (8:43, cf. Mk 5:26; he omits Mk 9:43-48; 13:32; etc.) or anything they could not be expected to understand (he omits Mt 5:21f,33f; Mk 15:34; etc.). He omits anything derogatory to the dignity of the apostles (Mk 4:13; 8:32f; 9:28f; 14:50) and makes excuses for them (Lk 9:45; 18:34; 22:45). He explains obscure phrases (6:15) and clears up points of topography (4:31; 19:28f,37; 23:51), etc. In these innumerable small corrections, and even more especially in the fresh material he found by personal enquiry, it is possible to see what Luke's preferences were and to see the way his mind worked. Or, to put it more theologically, the Holy Spirit used Luke as his instrument to put the gospel into a completely new shape, packed with doctrine. The originality of Luke is not in his key ideas (they are identical with those of Mark and of Matthew) but in his *religious mentality* which, apart from slight traces of Paul's influence, is overwhelmingly distinctive of Luke's personal temperament. Luke, in Dante's phrase, is the '*scriba mansuetudinis Christi*', the faithful recorder of Christ's lovingkindness. He is anxious to stress his Master's love of sinners (15:1f,7,10); to record his acts of forgiveness (7:36-50; 15:11-32; 19:1-10; 23:34,39-43); and to contrast his tenderness for the lowly and the poor with his severity towards the proud and towards those who abuse their wealth (1:51-53; 6:20-26; 12:13-21; 14:7-11; 16:15,19-31; 18:9-14). But in spite of this severity, the wicked however deserving of punishment will not be condemned till the period set aside for mercy has come to an end (13:6-9; cf. Mk 11:12-14). The one thing necessary is repentance, abdication of self, and on this the gentle, tolerant Luke takes a firm stand, insisting on unflinching and complete detachment (14:25-34), especially from riches (6:34f; 12:33; 14:12-14; 16:9-13). Another group of passages which are also found only in the third gospel is on the necessity of prayer (11:5-8; 18:1-8), of which Jesus set the example (3:21; 5:16; 6:12; 9:28). Finally, Luke is the only one of the Synoptics to give the Holy Spirit the prominence we find in Paul and in Acts (Lk 1:15,35,41,67; 2:25-27; 4:1,14,18; 10:21; 11:13; 24:49). These qualities, combined with that joy in God and that gratitude to him for his gifts which fill the third gospel (2:14; 5:26; 10:17; 13:17; 18:43; 19:37; 24:51f), are the ones that go to make Luke's achievement the warm and human thing it is.

Style

Mark's Greek is rough, strongly Aramaic, and often faulty; but it is fresh, lively and appealing. Matthew's Greek is also rather Aramaic but smoother than Mark's as well as less picturesque and more correct. Luke's is mixed: when writing independently it is excellent but out of respect for his sources he incorporates their imperfections—after polishing them a little. Occasionally he goes out of his way to give a good imitation of Septuagint Greek.

This translation

As far as possible this translation preserves stylistic nuances, and aims at reproducing in detail all similarities and differences between the three Synoptics, which betray their literary relationships.

THE GOSPEL ACCORDING TO
SAINT MATTHEW

I. THE BIRTH AND INFANCY OF JESUS

The ancestry of Jesus ||Lk 3:23-38

1 **1** A genealogy of Jesus Christ, son of David, son of Abraham:[a] 9:27+ Ga 3:16+ Heb 7:14

2 Abraham was the father of Isaac,
Isaac the father of Jacob,
Jacob the father of Judah and his brothers,
3 Judah was the father of Perez and Zerah, Tamar being their mother, Gn 38:29 Rt 4:18 1 S 2:8
Perez was the father of Hezron,
Hezron the father of Ram,
4 Ram was the father of Amminadab,
Amminadab the father of Nahshon,
Nahshon the father of Salmon,
5 Salmon was the father of Boaz, Rahab being his mother, Jos 2:1
Boaz was the father of Obed, Ruth being his mother,
Obed was the father of Jesse;
6 and Jesse was the father of King David.
David was the father of Solomon, whose mother had been Uriah's wife,
7 Solomon was the father of Rehoboam,
Rehoboam the father of Abijah,
Abijah the father of Asa,[b]
8 Asa was the father of Jehoshaphat,
Jehoshaphat the father of Joram,
Joram the father of Azariah,
9 Azariah was the father of Jotham,
Jotham the father of Ahaz,
Ahaz the father of Hezekiah,
10 Hezekiah was the father of Manasseh,
Manasseh the father of Amon,[c]

1 a. Matthew, though stressing the foreign element on the female side, vv. 3,5,6, limits his genealogy to Christ's Israelitic descent. Its aim is to show how Jesus is connected with the leading recipients of the messianic promises, i.e. with Abraham and David and with the latter's royal line. Luke's genealogy is universal in scope and goes back to Adam, head of the human race. The two lists, from David down to Joseph, have only two names in common. There are two possible explanations: either Matthew has preferred dynastic succession to physical descent, or else legal descent (levirate law, Dt 25:5+) has been reckoned equivalent to physical. In Mt, moreover, the systematic nature of the genealogy is brought out by the division of Christ's ancestors into three series of 2 × 7 names (cf. 6:9+), a device which forces the omission of three kings between Joram and Azariah. It also compels the double reckoning of Jeconiah (vv. 11-12); this is made possible by the fact that the same Greek name can translate the two similar Hebr. names Joiaqim and Joiakin. The lists of both Mt and Lk end with Joseph who was Christ's legal father only; the reason is that according to ancient mentality legal paternity (adoption, levirate etc.) is sufficient. by itself, to confer all hereditary rights; the rights here are those of the messianic line. This does not mean that Mary did not belong to that line, though the evangelists do not say that she did.

b. Var. 'Asaph'.

c. Var. 'Amos'.

Amon the father of Josiah;
and Josiah was the father of Jechoniah and his brothers. 11
Then the deportation to Babylon took place.

After the deportation to Babylon: 12
Jechoniah was the father of Shealtiel,
Shealtiel the father of Zerubbabel,
Zerubbabel was the father of Abiud, 13
Abiud the father of Eliakim,
Eliakim the father of Azor,
Azor was the father of Zadok, 14
Zadok the father of Achim,
Achim the father of Eliud,
Eliud was the father of Eleazar, 15
Eleazar the father of Matthan,
Matthan the father of Jacob;
and Jacob was the father of Joseph the husband of Mary; 16
of her was born Jesus[d] who is called Christ.

The sum of generations is therefore: fourteen from Abraham to David; 17
fourteen from David to the Babylonian deportation; and fourteen from the
Babylonian deportation to Christ.

The virginal conception of Christ

Lk 1:27; 2:5,11 This is how Jesus Christ came to be born. His mother Mary was betrothed 18
to Joseph;[e] but before they came to live together she was found to be with child
through the Holy Spirit. •Her husband Joseph, being a man of honour and 19
wanting to spare her publicity, decided to divorce her informally.[f] •He had 20
2:13,19; 28:2 Gn 16:7+ Lk 1:11; 2:9 Jn 5:4 made up his mind to do this when the angel of the Lord[g] appeared to him in
a dream and said, 'Joseph son of David, do not be afraid to take Mary home
Lk 1:35 as your wife, because she has conceived what is in her by the Holy Spirit. •She 21
Lk 1:31 *Ps 130:8* Lk 2:11 will give birth to a son and you must name him Jesus, because he is the one who
is to save[h] his people from their sins.' •Now all this took place to fulfil the words 22
Ac 3:16+; 4:12 spoken by the Lord through the prophet:

Is 7:14

The virgin will conceive and give birth to a son 23
and they will call him Emmanuel,

a name which means 'God-is-with-us'. •When Joseph woke up he did what the 24
angel of the Lord had told him to do: he took his wife to his home •and, though 25
Lk 2:7 he had not had intercourse with her, she gave birth[i] to a son; and he named him
Jesus.

The visit of the Magi

Lk 2:1-17 2 After Jesus had been born at Bethlehem in Judaea during the reign of King 1
Herod,[a] some wise men came to Jerusalem from the east. •'Where is the infant 2
Nb 24:17 king of the Jews?' they asked. 'We saw his star as it rose[b] and have come to do him
homage.' •When King Herod heard this he was perturbed, and so was the whole 3
of Jerusalem. •He called together all the chief priests and the scribes of the people,[c] 4
Jn 7:42 and enquired of them where the Christ was to be born. •'At Bethlehem in Judaea,' 5
they told him 'for this is what the prophet wrote:

Mi 5:1

And you, Bethlehem, in the land of Judah, 6
you are by no means least among the leaders of Judah,
for out of you will come a leader
who will shepherd my people Israel'.

Then Herod summoned the wise men to see him privately. He asked them the 7
exact date on which the star had appeared, •and sent them on to Bethlehem. 8

'Go and find out all about the child,' he said 'and when you have found him,
9 let me know, so that I too may go and do him homage.' •Having listened to
what the king had to say, they set out. And there in front of them was the star
they had seen rising; it went forward and halted over the place where the child
10 11 was.[d] •The sight of the star filled them with delight, •and going into the house
they saw the child with his mother Mary, and falling to their knees they did him Ps 72:10-15 Is 49:23; 60:5f
homage. Then, opening their treasures, they offered him gifts of gold and
12 frankincense and myrrh.[e] •But they were warned in a dream not to go back to
Herod, and returned to their own country by a different way. 1 K 13:9f

The flight into Egypt. The massacre of the Innocents

13 After they had left, the angel of the Lord appeared to Joseph in a dream 1:20+
and said, 'Get up, take the child and his mother with you, and escape into Egypt,
and stay there until I tell you, because Herod intends to search for the child and
14 do away with him'. •So Joseph got up and, taking the child and his mother
15 with him, left that night for Egypt, •where he stayed until Herod was dead. This
was to fulfil what the Lord had spoken through the prophet:

I called my son out of Egypt.[f] Nb 23:22 Ho 11:1

16 Herod was furious when he realised that he had been outwitted by the
wise men, and in Bethlehem and its surrounding district he had all the male
children killed who were two years old or under, reckoning by the date he
17 had been careful to ask the wise men. •It was then that the words spoken
through the prophet Jeremiah were fulfilled:[g]

18 *A voice was heard in Ramah,* Jr 31:15
sobbing and loudly lamenting:
it was Rachel weeping for her children,
refusing to be comforted
because they were no more.

From Egypt to Nazareth

19 After Herod's death, the angel of the Lord appeared in a dream to Joseph in 1:20+
20 Egypt •and said, 'Get up, take the child and his mother with you and go back to
21 the land of Israel, for those who wanted to kill the child are dead'. •So Joseph got Ex 4:19
up and, taking the child and his mother with him, went back to the land of Israel.

d. Several Greek and Lat. authorities, more explicitly 'Joseph, to whom was betrothed the Virgin Mary who gave birth to Jesus'. It is probably due to a misunderstanding of this reading that Syr. Sin. has this text 'Joseph, to whom was betrothed the Virgin Mary, begot Jesus'.

e. The force of Jewish betrothal was such that the fiancé was already called 'husband' and could release himself from the engagement only by an act of repudiation, v. 19.

f. It would appear that Joseph's integrity did not only consist in wanting to withhold his name from a child whose father he did not know, but also, since he was convinced of Mary's virtue, in refusing to expose to the rigour of the Law (Dt 22:20f) a mystery he did not understand.

g. The 'angel of the Lord' in the early texts (Gn 16:7+) means Yahweh himself. With the development of the doctrine of angels (cf. Tb 5:4+) their distinction from God becomes clearer; they retain their function as heavenly messengers and often appear as such in the narratives of the Infancy (Mt 1:20,24; 2:13,19; Lk 1:11; 2:9; cf. also Mt 28:2; Jn 5:4; Ac 5:19; 8:26; 12:7,23).

h. 'Jesus' (Hebr. Yehoshua) means 'Yahweh saves'.

i. Lit. 'and he did not know her until the day she gave birth'. The text is not concerned with the period that followed and, taken by itself, does not assert Mary's perpetual virginity which, however, the gospels elsewhere suppose and which the Tradition of the Church affirms. On the 'brothers' of Jesus, cf. 12:46+.

2 a. About 5 or 4 B.C. Herod was king of Judaea, Idumaea and Samaria from 37-4 B.C. Cf. Lk 2:2+.

b. Alternative translation (Vulg.) 'in the east'. Same alternative for v. 9.

c. Doctors of the Law; usually, but not always, from the ranks of the Pharisees (3:7+). Together with the high priests and the elders they constituted the Great Sanhedrin.

d. Obviously the evangelist is thinking of a miraculous star; it is futile to look for a natural explanation.

e. The wealth and perfumes of Arabia (Jr 6:20; Ezk 27:22). The Fathers see in them symbols of the royalty (gold), divinity (incense), Passion (myrrh) of Christ. The adoration of the Magi fulfils the messianic prophecies of the homage paid by the nations to the God of Israel, cf. Nb 24:17; Is 49:23; 60:5f; Ps 72:10-15.

f. Israel, therefore, the 'son' of the prophet's text, prefigured the Messiah.

g. In its original setting this text means that Rachel, their ancestress, weeps for the men of Ephraim, Manasseh and Benjamin, massacred or deported by the Assyrians. Matthew's application was perhaps suggested to him by a tradition which localised Rachel's tomb in the neighbourhood of Bethlehem (Gn 35:19f).

But when he learnt that Archelaus[h] had succeeded his father Herod as ruler of 22
Judaea he was afraid to go there, and being warned in a dream he left for the
region of Galilee.[i] •There he settled in a town called Nazareth. In this way the 23
words spoken through the prophets were to be fulfilled:

13:54; 26:71 Lk 2:39; 4:34; 18:37; 24:19 Ac 2:22; 3:6; 6:14; 22:8; 24:5; 26:9

He will be called a Nazarene.[j]

II. THE KINGDOM OF HEAVEN PROCLAIMED

A. NARRATIVE SECTION

||Mk 1:1-8 ||Lk 3:1-18

The preaching of John the Baptist

4:17+; 10:7 Ezk 18:32 Ac 2:38+

3 In due course[a] John the Baptist appeared; he preached in the wilderness of 1
Judaea and this was his message: •'Repent,[b] for the kingdom of heaven[c] is 2
close at hand'. •This was the man the prophet Isaiah spoke of when he said: 3

Is 40:3+ Jn 1:23

A voice cries in the wilderness:
Prepare a way for the Lord,
make his paths straight.

11:8-9 2 K 1:8+ Zc 13:4 11:7 21:25,32 Jn 5:35 12:34; 23:33 Is 59:5 Am 5:18+ Jn 8:33-40 Rm 9:7-8 Ga 4:21-31 =7:19p Jn 1:26,33 Jn 1:27,33 Ac 1:5+ *Is 41:16* Jr 15:7 13:42,50

This man John wore a garment made of camel-hair with a leather belt round his 4
waist, and his food was locusts and wild honey. •Then Jerusalem and all Judaea 5
and the whole Jordan district made their way to him, •and as they were baptised 6
by him in the river Jordan they confessed their sins.[d] •But when he saw a 7
number of Pharisees[e] and Sadducees[f] coming for baptism he said to them,
'Brood of vipers, who warned you to fly from the retribution that is coming?[g] 8
But if you are repentant, produce the appropriate fruit, •and do not presume to 9
tell yourselves, "We have Abraham for our father", because, I tell you, God can
raise children for Abraham from these stones. •Even now the axe is laid to the roots 10
of the trees, so that any tree which fails to produce good fruit will be cut down
and thrown on the fire. •I baptise you in water for repentance, but the one who 11
follows me is more powerful than I am, and I am not fit to carry his sandals; he
will baptise you with the Holy Spirit and fire.[h] •His winnowing-fan is in his hand; 12
he will clear his threshing-floor and gather his wheat into the barn; but the chaff
he will burn in a fire that will never go out.'[i]

||Mk 1:9-11 ||Lk 3:21-22

Jesus is baptised

Jn 13:6

Then Jesus appeared: he came from Galilee to the Jordan to be baptised by 13
John. •John tried to dissuade him. 'It is I who need baptism from you' he said 14
'and yet you come to me!' •But Jesus replied, 'Leave it like this for the time being; 15
it is fitting that we should, in this way, do all that righteousness demands'.[j] At this,
John gave in to him.[k]

Is 11:2 Dn 9:24 Jn 1:32-34 *12:18; 17:5* Is 42:1; 49:3

As soon as Jesus was baptised he came up from the water, and suddenly the 16
heavens opened[l] and he saw the Spirit of God descending like a dove and coming
down on him.[m] •And a voice spoke from heaven, 'This is my Son, the Beloved; 17
my favour rests on him'.[n]

||Mk 1:12-13 ||Lk 4:1-13

Temptation in the wilderness[a]

Heb 2:18 Ex 24:18; 34:28 1 K 19:8 *Heb 12:2*

4 Then Jesus was led by the Spirit[b] out into the wilderness to be tempted by the 1
devil. •He fasted for forty days and forty nights, after which he was very 2
hungry, •and the tempter came and said to him, 'If you are the Son of God,[c] tell 3
these stones to turn into loaves'. •But he replied, 'Scripture says: 4

Dt 8:3

Man does not live on bread alone
but on every word that comes from the mouth of God'.

The devil then took him to the holy city and made him stand on the parapet of 5

6 the Temple. •'If you are the Son of God' he said 'throw yourself down; for
scripture says:

He will put you in his angels' charge, Ps 91:11-12
and they will support you on their hands
in case you hurt your foot against a stone'.

h. Son of Herod byMalthake (like Herod Antipas); ethnarch of Judaea from 4 B.C. to 6 A.D

i. Territory of Herod Antipas, cf. Lk 3:1+.

j. Nazoraios: this is the form used by Mt, Jn and Ac (translated 'Nazarene' throughout this version). Nazarenos ('of Nazareth' in this version) is used by Mk. Lk uses both forms. Th..e two synonyms were current transcriptions of an Aramaic adjective *(nasraya)* itself derived from the name of the town 'Nazareth' (Nasrath). Applied to Jesus, whose origin it indicated (26:69,71), and later to his followers (Ac 24:5) the term became common in the semitic world for the disciples of Jesus; the name 'Christian' (Ac 11:26) prevailed in the Graeco-Roman world. It is not clear which prophetic oracles Mt alludes to: possibly to the *nazir* of Jg 13:5,7.

3 a. Lit 'in those days'. Stereotyped expression, merely a formula of transition.

b. *Metanoia* rendered 'repentance', implies a change of heart; 'conversion' in the technical ascetical sense.

c. Instead of 'kingdom of God', cf. 4:17+. The phrase is proper to Mt and reflects the Jewish scruple which substituted metaphor for the divine name.

d. The rite of immersion, symbolic of purification or of renewal, was familiar to the ancient religions and to Judaism (baptism of proselytes, Essene purifications). John's baptism though suggested by these practices is distinct from them for three main reasons: it is directed to moral, not ritual, purification (3:2,6,8,11; Lk 3:10-14); it takes place once only and for this reason appears as a ceremony of initiation; it has an eschatological value in so far as it enrols its recipients among the number of those who professedly and actively prepare themselves for the imminent coming of the Messiah and who are, therefore, the messianic community in anticipation (3:2,11; Jn 1: 19-34). It produces a real effect upon the soul but this effect is not produced sacramentally since it depends on something that has not yet taken place: this future event is God's Judgement embodied in the coming Messiah whose 'fire' will purify or consume according to the good or bad dispositions it meets with; he alone, and not John, will baptise 'in the Holy Spirit' (3:7,10-12). John's baptism continued to be administered by the disciples of Jesus (Jn 4:1-2) until it was absorbed by the new rite which he had instituted (Mt 28:19; Ac 1:5+; Rm 6:4+).

e. A Jewish sect, rigid observers of the Law; undue attachment to the oral tradition of their rabbis led, however, to an extravagant and artificial casuistry

f. In opposition to the outlook of the Pharisees these rejected all tradition not contained in the written Law. They came for the most part from the great priestly families. They were 'ess devout than the Pharisees and more politically minded.

g. The retribution of the day of Yahweh (Am 5:18+), which was to inaugurate the messianic era.

h. In the O.T. fire a purifying element more refined and efficacious than water was already a symbol of God's supreme intervention in history and of his Spirit which comes to purify hearts, cf. Is 1:25; Zc 13:9; Ml 3:2-3; Si 2:5, etc

i. The fire of Gehenna which for ever goes on consuming what has defied purification (Is 66:24; Jdt 16:17; Si 7:17; Zp 1:18; Ps 21:9, etc.).

j. Though sinless (Jn 8:46), Jesus is determined to submit to John's baptism because he sees it as a part of God's design (Lk 7:29-30) and the last act preparatory to the messianic era (Mt 3:6+); by accepting it he expresses his wish to satisfy the saving 'righteousness' of God that governs the whole plan of salvation. Matthew is probably thinking not only of the act of baptism but of the new 'righteousness' which, through Christ, is going to fulfil and perfect that of the old Law, cf. 5:17,20.

k. At this point an apocryphal legend has been inserted into two MSS of Vet. Lat. 'And while he was being baptised a great light came out of the water so that all the bystanders were filled with fear'.

l. Add. 'for him', i.e. before his eyes.

m. The Spirit which hovered over the waters at the first creation (Gn 1:2) now appears at the beginning of the new creation. It has two functions: it anoints Jesus for his messianic mission (Ac 10:38) which it is to guide (Mt 4:1p; Lk 4:14,18; 10:21; Mt 12:18,28), and, according to the patristic view, it sanctifies the water, thus preparing the way for Christian baptism, cf. Ac 1:5+.

n. The immediate purpose of this sentence is to declare that Jesus is in truth the servant foretold by Isaiah but the substitution of 'Son' for 'servant' (made possible by the double sense of the Greek word *pais*) underlines the relationship of Jesus with the Father which is that of anointed Son, cf. 4:3+.

4 a. That these diabolical suggestions were actually made is quite compatible with Christ's sinlessness. Jesus was face.. with the idea of being a material and political Messiah with its accompanying human privileges of wealth, glory, power. He chose instead utter dependence on God, humility, obedience to God's will, cf. Mt 16:21-23; 26:36-46; Heb 5:7-9; 12:2.

b. The Holy Spirit. The temptation was therefore willed by God.

c. The biblical title 'Son of God' does not necessarily mean natural sonship but may imply a sonship which is merely adoptive, i.e. which as a result of God's deliberate choice sets up a very intimate relationship between God and his creature In this sense the title is given to angels (Jb 1:6), to the Chosen People (Ex 4:22; Ws 18:13), to individual Israelites (Dt 14:1; Ho 2:1; cf. Mt 5:9,45 etc.), to their leaders (Ps 82:6). Where therefore it is attributed to the royal Messiah (1 Ch 17:13; Ps 2:7; 89:26) it does not necessarily imply that he is more than man; nor need we suppose that it has any deeper significance when used by Satan (Mt 4:3,6) or by the possessed (Mk 3:11; 5:7; Lk 4:41), still less when used by the centurion (Mk 15:39; cf. Lk 23:47). By itself the sentence at the baptism (Mt 3:17) and at the transfiguration (17:5) suggests no more than the divine predilection for the Messiah-servant, and in all probability the high priest's question (26:63) concerns messiahship only. Nevertheless the title 'Son of God' can bear a further, more profound meaning of sonship in the full sense of the word. Jesus clearly insinuated this meaning when he spoke of himself as 'the Son' (21:37), ranked above the angels (24:36), having God for his 'Father' in a way others had not (Jn 20:17 and cf. 'my Father' in Mt 7:21 etc.), enjoying with the Father an altogether singular relationship of knowledge and love (Mt 11:27). These assertions coupled with others that speak of the Messiah's divine rank (22:42-46), of the heavenly origin of the 'Son of Man' (8:20+), assertions finally confirmed by the triumph of the resurrection, have endowed the expression 'Son of God' with that strictly divine significance which will later be found, e.g. in Paul (Rm 9:5+). During the lifetime of Christ, it is true, his disciples had no clear conception of his divinity—the texts of Mt 14:33 and 16:16 which add the title 'Son of God' to the more primitive text of Mk reflect, in all probability, a later stage in the faith's development. But it is equally true that Jesus expressed with his own lips, and with as much clarity as his audience could support, his own consciousness of being Son of the Father in the fullest sense On these historical utterances the faith of the disciples rested, a faith that reached its perfection after the resurrection with the help of the Holy Spirit.

Jesus said to him, 'Scripture also says: 7

Dt 6:16 *You must not put the Lord your God to the test'.*

Next, taking him to a very high mountain, the devil showed him all the kingdoms 8
of the world and their splendour. •'I will give you all these' he said 'if you fall at 9
16:23 my feet and worship me.' •Then Jesus replied, 'Be off, Satan! For scripture says: 10

Dt 6:13 *You must worship the Lord your God,*
and serve him alone.'

Heb 1:14 Then the devil left him, and angels appeared and looked after him. 11

||Mk 1:14-15 ||Lk 4:14 **Return to Galilee**

Hearing that John had been arrested he went back to Galilee, •and leaving 12 13
Jn 2:12 Nazareth he went and settled in Capernaum, a lakeside town on the borders of
Zebulun and Naphtali. •In this way the prophecy of Isaiah was to be fulfilled: 14

Is 8:23–9:1 *Land of Zebulun! Land of Naphtali!* 15
Way of the sea on the far side of Jordan,
Galilee of the nations! 16
Jn 8:12+ *The people that lived in darkness*
has seen a great light;
on those who dwell in the land and shadow of death
a light has dawned.

3:2+ From that moment Jesus began his preaching with the message, 'Repent, for 17
Dn 7:14 Lk 17:20 the kingdom of heaven[d] is close at hand'.

||Mk 1:16-20 ||Lk 5:1-11 **The first four disciples are called**

As he was walking by the Sea of Galilee he saw two brothers, Simon, who 18
Jn 1:35-42 was called Peter, and his brother Andrew; they were making a cast in the lake
Jn 21:3 *13:47-50* with their net, for they were fishermen. •And he said to them, 'Follow me and I 19
8:19-22,27 will make you fishers of men'. •And they left their nets at once and followed him. 20
Going on from there he saw another pair of brothers, James son of Zebedee 21
and his brother John; they were in their boat with their father Zebedee, mending
their nets, and he called them. •At once, leaving the boat and their father, they 22
followed him.

||Mk 1:39; 3:7-8 ||Lk 4:14-15, 44;6:17-18 **Jesus preaches and heals the sick**

He went round the whole of Galilee teaching in their synagogues, proclaiming 23
=Mt 9:35 the Good News of the kingdom[e] and curing all kinds of diseases and sickness
among the people.[f] •His fame spread throughout Syria,[g] and those who were 24
suffering from diseases and painful complaints of one kind or another, the
possessed, epileptics,[h] the paralysed, were all brought to him, and he cured them.
Large crowds followed him, coming from Galilee, the Decapolis[i], Jerusalem, 25
Judaea and Transjordania.

B. THE EVANGELICAL DISCOURSE[a]

||Lk 6:20-23 **The Beatitudes**

5 Seeing the crowds, he went up the hill.[b] There he sat down and was joined by 1
his disciples. •Then he began to speak. This is what he taught them: 2

19:21,29 2 Co 8:9 'How happy are the poor in spirit;[c] 3
theirs is the kingdom of heaven.
Ps 37:11 Happy *the gentle:*[d] 4
Gn 13:15 Pr 2:21 *they shall have the earth for their heritage.*

5 Happy those who mourn: Ps 126:5 Is 61:2-3
they shall be comforted.
6 Happy those who hunger and thirst for what is right: Pr 21:21 Is 51:1
they shall be satisfied. Am 8:11 *Pr 9:5* Si 24:21
7 Happy the merciful:
they shall have mercy shown them.
8 Happy the pure in heart: Ps 24:3-4 Pr 22:11
they shall see God. *Ex 33:20+*
9 Happy the peacemakers: Ps 34:14 Pr 12:20; 15:18
they shall be called sons of God. Zc 8:16
10 Happy those who are persecuted in the cause of right: ↗1 P 3:14
theirs is the kingdom of heaven.

11 'Happy are you when people abuse you and persecute you and speak all kinds Ws 2:16 Ac 5:41 *23:34*
12 of calumny against you on my account. •Rejoice and be glad, for your reward will Ph 1:29 Col 1:24
be great in heaven; this is how they persecuted the prophets before you.[e] Heb 10:34 Jm 1:2

13 Salt of the earth and light of the world

'You are the salt of the earth. But if salt becomes tasteless, what can make it ||Mk 9:50 ||Lk 14:34-35

d. The sovereignty of God over the Chosen People, and through them over the world is at the heart of Christ's preaching as it was of the theocratic ideal of the O.T It implies a kingdom of 'saints' where God will be truly King because they will acknowledge his royal rights by knowing and loving him. This sovereignty, jeopardised by rebellious sin, is to be reasserted by an act of supreme intervention on the part of God and of his Messiah (Dn 2:28+). This is the intervention which Jesus, following John the Baptist (3:2), declares imminent (4:17,23; Lk 4:43). It is to take the form not, as was commonly expected, of a successful nationalist rising (Mk 11:10; Lk 19:11; Ac 1:6) but of a purely spiritual movement (Mk 1:34+; Jn 18:36). The redemptive work of Jesus as 'Son of Man' (Mt 8:20+) and as 'servant' (Mt 8:17+; 20:28+; 26:28+) sets man free from Satan's rule which opposes God's (4:8; 8:29+; 12:25-26). Before it achieves its final eschatological realisation when the elect will be with the Father in the joy of the heavenly banquet (8:11+; 13:43; 26:29) the kingdom makes an unimpressive entrance (13: 31-33) Its modest beginning is mysterious (13:11) and arouses opposition (13:24-30), it has come unnoticed (12:28; Lk 17:20-21); the development of the kingdom on earth is slow (Mk 4:26-29) and is effected by the Church (Mt 16:18+). By the judgement of God that falls on Jerusalem it is established with power as the kingdom of Christ (Mt 16:28; Lk 21:31) and is preached throughout the world by apostolic missionaries (Mt 10:7; 24:14; Ac 1:3+). When the time comes for the final Judgement (13:37-43,47-50; 25:31-46) the return of Christ in glory (16:27; 25:31) will be the final act that establishes the kingdom which Christ will then present to the Father (1 Co 15:24). Until that time the kingdom appears as a free gift of God (20:1-16; 22:9-10; Lk 12:32) accepted by the humble (Mt 5:3; 18:3-4; 19:14,23-24) and the generous (13:44-46; 19:12; Mk 9:47; Lk 9:62; 18:29f), refused by the proud and selfish (21:31-32,43; 22:2-8; 23:13) There is no entering it without the wedding garment which is the new life (22:11-13; Jn 3:3,5) and not all men are admitted (Mt 8:12; 1 Co 6:9-10; Ga 5:21). One must stay awake so as to be readywhen it comes unexpectedly (Mt 25:1-13). On Matthew's treatment of the kingdom as the guiding idea of his arrangement see Introduction to the Synoptic Gospels.

e. The etymological sense of the word *euanggelion* (gospel) is 'Good News'. The news is of the impending coming of the kingdom of God, cf. v. 17 and 3:2.

f. Miraculous cures are the distinctive sign that the messianic age has dawned, cf. 10:1,7f; 11:4f.

g. The word is not here used in a precise sense and actually means Galilee with its surrounding districts, cf. Mk 1:28.

h. Lit. 'moon-struck, lunatic' (cf. 17:15).

i. The Decapolis was a loose federation of 10 free towns with their surrounding territories, scattered for the most part on the E. side of Jordan and as far N.E. as to include Damascus.

5 a. Jesus sketched the new spirit of the kingdom of God (4:17+) in an inaugural discourse which Mark has omitted (Mk 3:19+) and which Matthew and Luke (6:20-49) present in two different forms. Luke eliminates passages referring to Jewish laws and practices (Mt 5: 17-6:18) which are unlikely to interest his readers; Matthew for his part inserts sayings pronounced on other occasions (cf. their parallels in Lk) to make his programme of the new kingdom more complete. In the resultant composite discourse five main subjects are dealt with: 1. The spirit that should animate the 'children of the kingdom' (5:3-48). 2. The spirit in which they are to 'fulfil' the laws and practices of Judaism, 6:1-18. 3. Detachment from riches, 6:19-34. 4. Relations with one's neighbour 7:1-12. 5. The decisive act of choice that must be made (and the practical consequences thzt must be accepted) in order to enter the kingdom, 7:13-27.

b. One of the hills near Capernaum.

c. Jesus uses the word 'poor' with the moral shade of meaning already noticeable in Zp (2:3+) but here made explicit by the phrase 'in spirit', absent from Lk 6:20. Because they are destitute and oppressed the 'poor', or the 'lowly' are apt subjects for the kingdom of God—this is the theme of the Beatitudes (cf. Lk 4:18; 7:22; Mt 11:5; Lk 14:13; Jm 2:5). 'Poverty' goes hand in hand with the 'spiritual childhood' required for entrance into the kingdom, Mt 18:1f = Mk 9:33f, cf. Lk 9:46f; Mt 19:13fp; 11:25fp—the mystery revealed to 'little ones', *nepioi*, cf. Lk 12,32; 1 Co 1:26f. They are the 'poor', *ptochoi* the 'lowly', *tapeinoi* (Lk 1:48 52; 14:11; 18:14; Mt 23:12; 18:4) and both are the 'last' as opposed to the 'first' (Mk 9: 35), the 'little ones' as opposed to the 'great' (Lk 9:48; cf. Mt 19:30p; 20:26p—cf. Lk 17:10). Although the formula of Mt 5:3 stresses the spirit of poverty for the rich as for the poor, Jesus usually has in mind actual poverty, especially for his disciples (Mt 6:19f, cf. Lk 12 33f; Mt 6:25p; 4:18fp, cf. Lk 5:1f) 9:9p; 19:21p; 19:27; cf. Mk 10:28p; cf. Ac 2:44f; 4:32f. He himself sets the example of poverty (Lk 2:7; Mt 8:20p) and of lowliness (Mt 11:29; 20:28p; 21:5; Jn 13:12f; cf. 2 Co 8:9; Ph 2:7f). He identifies himself with the little ones and the wretched (Mt 25:45, cf. 18:5fp).

d. Or 'the lowly'; the word is taken from the Greek version of the Psalm. V. 4 is possibly only a gloss on v. 3; its omission would reduce the number of Beatitudes to 7, cf. 6:9+.

e. Christ's disciples are the successors of the prophets, cf. 10:41; 13:17; 23:34.

Lv 2:13 Nb 18:19 salty again? It is good for nothing, and can only be thrown out to be trampled
underfoot by men.
Si 20:30 Jn 8:12+ 'You are the light of the world. A city built on a hill-top cannot be hidden. 14
||*Mk 4:21* ||Lk 8:16; No one lights a lamp to put it under a tub; they put it on the lamp-stand where 15
11:33 it shines for everyone in the house. •In the same way your light must shine in the 16
Jn 3:21; 15:8 sight of men, so that, seeing your good works, they may give the praise to your
1 Co 10:31 Father in heaven.

The fulfilment of the Law

Rm 3:31; 10:4 'Do not imagine that I have come to abolish the Law or the Prophets. I have 17
come not to abolish but to complete them.[f] •I tell you solemnly, till heaven 18
||Lk 16:17 and earth disappear, not one dot, not one little stroke, shall disappear from
the Law until its purpose is achieved. •Therefore, the man who infringes even 19
Jm 2:10 one of the least of these commandments and teaches others to do the same will
be considered the least in the kingdom of heaven; but the man who keeps them
and teaches them will be considered great in the kingdom of heaven.

The new standard higher than the old

Rm 10:3 Ph 3:9 'For I tell you, if your virtue goes no deeper[g] than that of the scribes and 20
Pharisees, you will never get into the kingdom of heaven.
Ex 20:13 Si 10:6 'You have learnt[h] how it was said to our ancestors: *You must not kill;* and if 21
anyone does kill he must answer for it before the court. •But I say this to you: 22
Ep 4:26 Jm 1:19-20; anyone who is angry with his brother will answer for it before the court; if a man
3:6 calls his brother "Fool"[i] he will answer for it before the Sanhedrin;[j] and if a man
Si 28:2 Mk 11:25 calls him "Renegade"[k] he will answer for it in hell fire. •So then, if you are bringing 23
your offering to the altar and there remember that your brother has something
against you, •leave your offering there before the altar, go and be reconciled with 24
Pr 17:14 ||Lk 12:58-59 your brother first, and then come back and present your offering. •Come to terms 25
with your opponent in good time while you are still on the way to the court with
him, or he may hand you over to the judge and the judge to the officer, and you
will be thrown into prison. •I tell you solemnly, you will not get our till you have 26
paid the last penny.
Ex 20:14 Jb 31:1 'You have learnt how it was said: *You must not commit adultery.* •But I sad 27 28
Si 9:5 this to you: if a man looks at a woman lustfully, he has already committey
=18:8-9 adultery with her in his heart. •If your right eye should cause you to sin, tear it out 29
and throw it away; for it will do you less harm to lose one part of you than to
have your whole body thrown into hell. •And if your right hand should cause 30
you to sin, cut it off and throw it away; for it will do you less harm to lose one part
of you than to have your whole body go to hell.
Dt 24:1 Ml 2:14-16 'It has also been said: *Anyone who divorces his wife must give her a writ of* 31
=19:9+ ||Mk10:11-12 *dismissal.* •But I say this to you: everyone who divorces his wife, except for the 32
||Lk 16:18 1 Co 7:10 case of fornication, makes her an adulteress; and anyone who marries a divorced
woman commits adultery.
Ex 20:7 Nb 30:3 'Again, you have learnt how it was said to our ancestors: *You must not break* 33
Dt 23:22 *your oath, but must fulfil your oaths to the Lord.* •But I say this to you: do not 34
Ps 11:4 Si 23:9 swear at all, either by *heaven,* since that is God's throne; •or by *the earth,* since 35
Is 66:1 *Ps 48:2* that is *his footstool;* or by Jerusalem, since that is *the city of the great king.* •Do not 36
swear by your own head either, since you cannot turn a single hair white or black.
Si 5:10 2 Co 1:17-19 All you need say is "Yes" if you mean yes, "No" if you mean no; anything more 37
than this comes from the evil one.
Ex 21:24+ 'You have learnt how it was said: *Eye for eye and tooth for tooth.* •But I say 38 39
this to you: offer the wicked man no resistance.[l] On the contrary, if anyone hits
Lm 3:30 ||Lk 6:29 you on the right cheek, offer him the other as well; •if a man takes you to law 40
Rm 12:19,21 and would have your tunic,[m] let him have your cloak as well. •And if anyone 41
Lk 6:30 orders tou to go one mile, go two miles with him. •Give to anyone who asks, 42
and if anyone wants to borrow, do not turn away.

43 'You have learnt how it was said: *You must love your neighbour* and hate your Lv 19:18 Jb 31:29
44 enemy.[n] •But I say this to you: love your enemies[o] and pray for those who ||*Lk 6:27-36;* 23:24
45 persecute you;[p] •in this way you will be sons of your Father in heaven, for he Ac 7:60 Rm 12:20
causes his sun to rise on bad men as well as good, and his rain to fall on honest *Pr 22:2;* 29:13
46 and dishonest men alike. •For if you love those who love you, what right have Si 12:6 *Lk 6:32*
47 you to claim any credit? Even the tax collectors[q] do as much, do they not? •And Lk 3:12
if you save your greetings for your brothers, are you doing anything exceptional?
48 Even the pagans do as much, do they not? •You must therefore be perfect just as Lv 19:2+; 11:44
your heavenly Father is perfect. Jm 1:4 1 P 1:16 1 Jn 3:3

Almsgiving in secret

1 6 'Be careful not to parade your good deeds[a] before men to attract their notice; 23:5 Lk 16:14-15
2 by doing this you will lose all reward from your Father in heaven. •So when *Pr 20:6* Jn 5:44;
you give alms, do not have it trumpeted before you; this is what the hypocrites 12:43 *Am 4:5*
do in the synagogues and in the streets to win men's admiration. I tell you *15:7; 22:18;* 23:13-15
3 solemnly, they have had their reward. •But when you give alms, your left hand
4 must not know what your right is doing; •your almsgiving must be secret, and
your Father who sees all that is done in secret will reward you. Ps 139:2-3

Prayer in secret

5 'And when you pray, do not imitate the hypocrites: they love to say their Pr 20:6 Jm 4:3
prayers standing up in the synagogues and at the street corners for people to see
6 them. I tell you solemnly, they have had their reward. •But when you 2 K 4:33 Tb 3:10f
pray, *go to your private room and, when you have shut your door, pray* to your Is 26:20 Dn 6:11
Father who is in that secret place, and your Father who sees all that is done in
secret will reward you.

How to pray. The Lord's Prayer

7 'In your prayers do not babble as the pagans do, for they think that by using Qo 5:1 Si 7:14
8 many words they will make themselves heard. •Do not be like them; your Father
9 knows what you need before you ask him. •So you should pray like this:[b]

'Our Father in heaven, Tb 13:4 ||Lk 11:2-4
may your name be held holy, *Jn 17:6,26*
10 your kingdom come,
your will be done, Mt26:39,42p
on earth as in heaven.

f. I.e. 'to bring to perfection'. Jesus is speaking not of carrying into effect each single injunction of the old Law but of bestowing on that Law a new and definitive form by raising it to a higher place through the spirit of the gospel, cf. vv. 21-48. It is in this sense that no detail of the Law is to be neglected, vv. 18-19: each has its part to play in the unfolding of the divine plan.

g. Or 'does not greatly surpass'.

h. Lit. 'you have heard' i.e. (normally) in the synagogues where the teachings of tradition were given orally.

i. The Aramaic word *raqa*, transliterated in Mt, translated here, means empty-head, nitwit.

j. Here the Great Sanhedrin which met in Jerusalem, as opposed to the minor courts (vv. 21-22) of the country districts.

k. To the first meaning ('fool') of the Greek word, Jewish usage added the much more insulting one of 'impious'.

l. This deals (cf. the examples in vv. 39-40) with an injustice of which we ourselves are the victims: we are forbidden to resist it by returning evil for evil in the way laid down by the Jewish law of *talio* (v. 38). Christ does not forbid us to resist unjust attack in due measure (Jn 18:22f), still less to strive to eliminate injustice from the world.

m. As a surety, cf. Ex 22:25f; Dt 24:12f. It is clear that the sentence is deliberately hyperbolic, cf. 19:24.

n. The second part of this commandment is not, and could not, be found thus formulated in the Law. It is the brusque expression of a language (the original Aramaic) which has few half-tones and is equivalent to 'There is less obligation to love one's enemy'. Cf. Lk 14:26 with its parallel Mt 10:37.

o. Add. 'do good to those who hate you'.

p. Add. 'and for those who treat you badly', cf. Lk 6:27f.

q. They were employed by the occupying power, and this earned them popular contempt, cf. 9:10.

6 a. Lit. 'perform your righteousness' (var. 'perform almsgiving'), i.e. perform good works which make a man righteous in the sight of God. For the Jews these works were principally: almsgiving (vv. 2-4), prayer (vv. 5-6), fasting (vv. 16-18).

b. The Lord's Prayer in its Matthaean form has 7 petitions The number is a favourite of Matthew's: 2 × 7 generations in the Genealogy (1:17), 7 Beatitudes (5:4+), 7 parables (13:3+), forgiveness not 7 but 77 times (18:22), 7 'alas' for the Pharisees (23:13+), 7 sections into which the gospel is divided (cf. Introduction to the Synoptic Gospels).

Pr 30:8-9 Jn 6:32,35 *18:21-35* Pr 24:29 Si 28:2

Give us today our daily[c] bread. 11
And forgive us our debts, 12
as we have forgiven those who are in debt to us.

26:41p Jn 17:11,15 2 Th 3:3 1 Jn 2:14+

And do not put us to the test, 13
but save us from the evil one.[d]

Si 28:1-5 ||Mk 11:25 *5:7* Pr 21:13 Jm 2:13

Yes, if you forgive others their failings, your heavenly Father will forgive you 14
yours; •but if you do not forgive others, your Father will not forgive your 15
failings either.

Fasting in secret

Pr 20:6 Is 58:3

'When you fast do not put on a gloomy look as the hypocrites do: they pull 16
long faces to let men know they are fasting. I tell you solemnly, they have
had their reward. •But when you fast, put oil on your head and wash your face, 17
so that no one will know you are fasting except your Father who sees all that is 18
done in secret; and your Father who sees all that is done in secret will reward you.

True treasures

Jb 22:24-26 ||Lk 12:33-34 19:21 Ps 62:10 Si 29:8-12 Jm 5:2-3 Tb 4:9

'Do not store up treasures for yourselves on earth, where moths and 19
woodworms destroy them and thieves can break in and steal. •But store up 20
treasures for yourselves in heaven, where neither moth nor woodworms destroy
them and thieves cannot break in and steal. •For where your treasure is, there 21
will your heart be also.

The eye, the lamp of the body

Lk 11:34-35 Pr 20:27

'The lamp of the body is the eye. It follows that if your eye is sound, your 22
whole body will be filled with light. •But if your eye is diseased, your whole body 23
will be all darkness. If then, the light inside you is darkness, what darkness
that will be![e]

God and money

5:3-4; 19:21:26 ||Lk 16:13 *Jb 31:24* Ps 62:10 Ep 5:5

'No one can be the slave of two masters: he will either hate the first and love 24
the second, or treat the first with respect and the second with scorn. You cannot
be the slave both of God and of money.

Trust in Providence

||Lk 12:22-31 Ps 145:15f Si 11:23 Ph 4:6 Ps 147:9 1 K 10:1-29

'That is why I am telling you not to worry about your life and what you are to 25
eat, nor about your body and how you are to clothe it. Surely life means more than
food, and the body more than clothing! •Look at the birds in the sky. They do not 26
sow or reap or gather into barns; yet your heavenly Father feeds them. Are you
not worth much more than they are? •Can any of you, for all his worrying, add 27
one single cubit to his span of life? •And why worry about clothing? Think of the 28
flowers growing in the fields; they never have to work or spin; •yet I assure you 29
that not even Solomon in all his regalia was robed like one of these. •Now if that 30
is how God clothes the grass in the field which is there today and thrown into the
furnace tomorrow, will he not much more look after you, you men of little faith?
So do not worry; do not say, "What are we to eat? What are we to drink? How 31
are we to be clothed?" •It is the pagans who set their hearts on all these things. 32
Your heavenly Father knows you need them all. •Set your hearts on his kingdom 33
first, and on his righteousness, and all these other things will be given you as well.
So do not worry about tomorrow: tomorrow will take care of itself. Each day 34
has enough trouble of its own.

1 K 3:13 2 Ch 1:12 Ws 1:1; 7:11 Is 51:1 Jm 4:3 *Jm 4:13-14*

Do not judge

||Lk 6:37-42 Rm 2:1-2 1 Co 4:5 *Pr 11:25* Ws 12:22 ||Mk 4:24

7 'Do not judge, and you will not be judged;[a] •because the judgements you give 1 2
are the judgements you will get, and the amount you measure out is the

3 amount you will be given. •Why do you observe the splinter in your brother's Ps 36:2
4 eye and never notice the plank in your own? •How dare you say to your brother, Jn 8:7
"Let me take the splinter out of your eye", when all the time there is a plank in
5 your own? •Hypocrite! Take the plank out of your own eye first, and then you
will see clearly enough to take the splinter out of your brother's eye.

6 Do not profane sacred things

'Do not give dogs what is holy;[b] and do not throw your pearls in front of pigs, Pr 23:9 Si 22:9-10
or they may trample them and then turn on you and tear you to pieces.

Effective prayer

||Lk 11:9-13

7 'Ask, and it will be given to you; search, and you will find; knock, and the 18:19 Dt 4:30+
8 door will be opened to you. •For the one who asks always receives; the one who Pr 8:17 Mk 11:24
searches always finds; the one who knocks will always have the door opened to Lk 18:1-8 Jn 14:13
9 him. •Is there a man among you who would hand his son a stone when he asked Jm 1:5+
10
11 for bread? •Or would hand him a snake when he asked for a fish? •If you, then,
who are evil, know how to give your children what is good, how much more will Jm 1:5,17 1 Jn 3:22; 5:14-15
your Father in heaven give good things to those who ask him!

The golden rule

||Lk 6:31 Tb 4:15

12 'So always treat others as you would like them to treat you; that is the Pr 3:27 Rm 13:8-10
meaning of the Law and the Prophets.

The two ways

Dt 30:15f+ Ps 1:1+ ||Lk 13:24

13 'Enter by the narrow gate, since the road that leads to perdition is wide and *Si 21:10*
14 spacious,[c] and many take it; •but it is a narrow gate and a hard road that leads Si 4:17 Jn 10:9-10
to life, and only a few find it. 19:24p

False prophets

Rv 13:11; 19-20

15 'Beware of false prophets[d] who come to you disguised as sheep but underneath 2 P 2:1-3
16 are ravenous wolves. •You will be able to tell them by their fruits. Can people Si 27:6 ||Lk 6:43-44
17 pick grapes from thorns, or figs from thistles? •In the same way, a sound tree *Jm 3:12* *=12:33*
18 produces good fruit but a rotten tree bad fruit. •A sound tree cannot bear bad Ga 5:19-24
19 fruit, nor a rotten tree bear good fruit. •Any tree that does not produce good =3:10p Jn 15:6
20 fruit is cut down and thrown on the fire. •I repeat, you will be able to tell them
by their fruits.

The true disciple

Is 29:13 Am 5:21+ ||Lk 6:46

21 'It is not those who say to me, "Lord, Lord", who will enter the kingdom of Jm 2:14-17 1 Jn 3:18
22 heaven, but the person who does the will of my Father in heaven. •When the day
comes[e] many will say to me, "Lord, Lord, did we not prophesy in your name, 25:11-12 ||Lk 13:26-27
23 cast out demons in your name, work many miracles in your name?" •Then
I shall tell them to their faces: I have never known you; *away from me, you evil men!*' Ps 5:5; 6:8
24 'Therefore, everyone who listens to these words of mine and acts on them Pr 10:8 ||Lk 6:47-49

c. The Greek word is obscure; this traditional rendering is a probable one. Other possibilities: 'necessary for subsistence' or 'for tomorrow'. Whatever the exact translation the sense is that we must ask God for the sustenance we need in this life but for no more—not for wealth or luxury. The Fathers applied this text to the bread of the Holy Eucharist.

d. Or 'from evil'. Add. 'For yours is the kingdom and the power and the glory for ever. Amen' (a reading introduced into text through liturgical influence).

e. According as the eye is sound or diseased it gives or refuses material light to the body; to this light the spiritual light that emanates from the soul is compared; if this light is itself dimmed the blindness is much worse than physical.

7 a. Do not judge others if you do not wish to be judged by God. So also in the following verse.

b. Consecrated meat from animals sacrificed in the Temple, cf. Lv 22:14; Ex 22:30. Similarly sacred teaching of great worth must not be set before those who, incapable of receiving it with profit, may even abuse it. It is not clear whether the reference is to Jews or (cf. 15:26) to pagans.

c. Var. 'the gate that leads to perdition is wide, and the road spacious'.

d. Lying teachers who charm the public by their show of piety while pursuing their own selfish ends, cf. 24:4f,24.

e. The day of the final Judgement.

Pr 10:25; will be like a sensible man who built his house on rock. •Rain came down, floods 25
12:3,7 rose, gales blew and hurled themselves against that house, and it did not fall:
Ezk 33:31 1 Jn 2:17 it was founded on rock. •But everyone who listens to these words of mine and does 26
Jb 8:15 not act on them will be like a stupid man who built his house on sand. •Rain 27
Ezk 13:10-14 came down, floods rose, gales blew and struck that house, and it fell; and what
a fall it had!'

The amazemznt of the crowds

||Lk 7:1 Jn 7:15 Jesus had now finished what he wanted to say, and his teaching made a deep 28
||*Mk 1:22* ||Lk 4:32 impression on the people •because he taught them with authority, and not like 29
their own scribes.[f]

III. THE KINGDOM OF HEAVEN IS PREACHED

A. NARRATIVE SECTION: TEN MIRACLES

||Mk 1:40-45 ||Lk 5:12-16 **Cure of a leper**

8 After he had come down from the mountain large crowds followed him. 1
A leper now came up and bowed low in front of him. 'Sir', he said 'if you want 2
9:25; 11:5; 14:14,36; 15:31,36 to, you can cure me.' •Jesus stretched out his hand, touched him and said, 'Of 3
course I want to! Be cured!' And his leprosy was cured at once.[a] •Then Jesus said 4
Mk 1:34+ to him, 'Mind you do not tell anyone, but go and show yourself to the priest
Lv 14:1-32 Lk 17:14 and make the offering prescribed by Moses, as evidence for them'.

Cure of the centurion's servant

||Lk 7:1-10 ||Jn 4:46-53 When he went into Capernaum a centurion came up and pleaded with him. 5
'Sir,' he said 'my servant is lying at home paralysed, and in great pain.' •'I will 6 7
Lk 5:8 come myself and cure him' said Jesus. •The centurion replied, 'Sir, I am not 8
Ps 33:9; 107:20 worthy to have you under my roof; just give the word and my servant will be
cured. •For I am under authority myself, and have soldiers under me; and I say 9
to one man: Go, and he goes; to another: Come here, and he comes; to my
9:2,22,28 Lk 1:20; 5:5, 20; 7:9,50 servant: Do this, and he does it.' •When Jesus heard this he was astonished and 10
said to those following him, 'I tell you solemnly, nowhere in Israel have I found
Is 25:6+ ||Lk 13:28-29 faith[b] like this. •And I tell you that many will come from east and west to take 11
Rm 11:12 their places with Abraham and Isaac and Jacob at the feast[c] in the kingdom
13:42,50; 22:13; 24:51; 25:30 Jn 8:12+ of heaven; •but the subjects of the kingdom[d] will be turned out into the dark, 12
where there will be weeping and grinding of teeth.'[e] •And to the centurion Jesus 13
said, 'Go back, then; you have believed, so let this be done for you'. And the
servant was cured at that moment.

||Mk 1:29-31 ||Lk 4:38-39 **Cure of Peter's mother-in-law**

And going into Peter's house Jesus found Peter's mother-in-law in bed with 14
9:25p Mk 9:27 Ac 3:7 fever. •He touched her hand and the fever left her, and she got up and began 15
to wait on him.

||Mk 1:32-34 ||Lk 4:40-41 **A number of cures**

That evening they brought him many who were possessed by devils. He cast 16
out the spirits with a word and cured all who were sick. •This was to fulfil the 17
prophecy of Isaiah:

Is 53:4 Jn 5:29 *He took our sicknesses away and carried our diseases for us.*[f]

||Lk 9:57-60 **Hardships of the apostolic calling**

When Jesus saw the great crowds all about him he gave orders to leave for the 18
other side.[g] •One of the scribes then came up and said to him, 'Master, I will 19

20 follow you wherever you go'. •Jesus replied, 'Foxes have holes and the birds Ps 84:3
of the air have nests, but the Son of Man[h] has nowhere to lay his head'. 11:19 2 Co 8:9
21 Another man, one of his disciples, said to him, 'Sir, let me go and bury my *Gn 50:5* Tb 4:3
22 father first'. •But Jesus replied, 'Follow me, and leave the dead to bury their dead'. *4:18f;* 10:37p

The calming of the storm
||Mk 4:35-41 ||Lk 8:22-25

23 24 Then he got into the boat followed by his disciples. •Without warning Ac 27:9f
a storm broke over the lake, so violent that the waves were breaking right over
25 the boat. But he was asleep. •So they went to him and woke him saying, 'Save us, 14:30 Jon 1:6
26 Lord, we are going down!' •And he said to them, 'Why are you so frightened, you
men of little faith?' And with that he stood up and rebuked the winds and the 6:30; 8:10+ Ps 107:29
27 sea; and all was calm again. •The men were astounded and said, 'Whatever kind Ps 65:7+
of man is this? Even the winds and the sea obey him.'

The demoniacs of Gadara
||Mk 5:1-20 ||Lk 8:26-39

28 When he reached the country of the Gadarenes[i] on the other side, two
demoniacs came towards him out of the tombs—creatures so fierce that no one

f. These always sought support for their teaching in the 'tradition' of the ancients. Add. 'and the Pharisees'.

8 a. By his miracles Jesus shows his power over nature (8:23-27; 14:22-33p), especially over sickness (8:1-4, 5-13,14-15; 9:1-8,20-22,27-31; 14:14,36; 15:30; 20:29-34 and p; Mk 7:32-37; 8:22-26; Lk 14:1-6; 17:11-19; Jn 5:1-16; 9:1-41), over death (Mt 9:23-26p; Lk 7:11-17; Jn 11:1-44), over devils (Mt 8:29+). Christ's miracles are not elaborate: in this they differ from the fantastic prodigies reported of the hellenistic world and from those attributed to the Jewish rabbis, but they are most notably different by reason of the spiritual and symbolic significance that Jesus attaches to them. They declare the judgements of the messianic age (21:18-22p) as also the privileges it brings (11:5+; 14:13-21; 15:32-39p; Lk 5:4-11; Jn 2:1-11; 21:4-14); they are the first signs of the triumph of the Spirit over Satan's empire (8:29+) and over all the powers of evil whether sin (9:2+) or disease (8:17+). The motive is sometimes compassion (20:34; Mk 1:41; Lk 7:13) but they are directed principally to the strengthening of faith (8:10+; Jn 2:11+). Thus it is only with great deliberation that Jesus works any miracles at all, demanding secrecy for any he does agree to work (Mk 1:34+), and leaving it for his resurrection to be the miraculous event that was to force decision (12:39-40). When he sent his apostles to preach the kingdom he gave them his own healing power (10:1,8p) and for this reason Matthew recounts before the Missionary Discourse (ch. 10) a series of ten miracles (ch. 8-9) as signs accrediting the missionary (Mk 16:17f; Ac 2:22; cf. 1:8+).

b. The faith that Jesus asks for from the outset of his public life (Mk 1:15) and throughout his subsequent career, is that act of trust and of self-abandonment by which people no longer rely on their own strength and policies but commit themselves to the power and guiding word of him in whom they believe (Lk 1:20,45; Mt 21:25p,32). Christ asks for this faith especially when he works his miracles (8:13; 9:2p,22p,28-29; 15:28; Mk 5:36p; 10:52p; Lk 17:19) which are not so much acts of mercy as signs attesting his mission and witnessing to the kingdom (8:3+, cf. Jn 2:11+); hence he cannot work miracles unless he finds the faith without which the miracles lose their true significance (13:58p; 12:38-39; 16:1-4). Since faith demands the sacrifice of the whole man, mind and heart, it is not an easy act of humility to perform; many decline it, particularly in Israel (8:10p; 15:28; 27:42p; Lk 18:8), or are half-hearted (Mk 9:24; Lk 8:13). Even the disciples are slow to believe (8:26p; 14:31; 16:8; 17:20p) and are still reluctant after the resurrection (28:17; Mk 16:11-14; Lk 24:11,25,41). The most generous faith of all, of the 'Rock' (16:16-18), the disciples' leader, was destined to be shaken by the outrage of the Passion (26:69-75p) though it was to triumph in the end (Lk 22:32). When faith is strong it works wonders (17:20p; 21:21p; Mk 16:17) and its appeal is never refused (21:22p; Mk 9:23) especially when it asks for forgiveness of sin (9:2p; Lk 7:50) and for that salvation of which it is the necessary condition (Lk 8:12; Mk 16:16; cf. Ac 3:16+).

c. Basing their idea on Is 25:6, the Jews often described the joyous messianic era as a banquet (cf. 22:2-14; 26:29p; Lk 14:15; Rv 3:20; 19:9).

d. Lit. 'the sons of the kingdom', that is to say the Jews, natural heirs of the promises. Their place will be taken by the pagans, who prove more worthy.

e. Scriptural image for the dismay and frustration of the wicked at seeing the virtuous rewarded, cf. Ps 35:16; 37:12; 112:10; Jb 16:9. In Mt it is used as a description of damnation.

f. As described by Is the servant 'took' our sorrows on himself in the sense that his own suffering was expiatory. Matthew takes the phrase to mean that Jesus 'took away' these sorrows by his healing miracles. This interpretation, at first sight forced, is in fact profoundly theological. It was to take on himself the expiation of sin that Jesus, the 'servant', came on earth; that is why he could relieve men of their bodily ills which are the consequence and the penalty of sin.

g. The E. bank of Lake Tiberias.

h. With the exception of Ac 7:56; Rv 1:13; 14:14, this title appears only in the gospels. There is no doubt that Jesus used it of himself, and indeed preferred it to others. At times he uses it to express his lowly state, 8:20; 11:19; 20:28, especially the humiliation of the Passion, 17:22 etc. At other times it is used to proclaim the definitive triumph of his resurrection, 17:9, of his return in glory, 24:30, of his coming in judgement, 25:31. That this title, Aramaic in flavour, could bring together these seemingly opposed qualities is clear from the following considerations. The phrase originally meant 'man', Ezk 2:1+, and by reason of its unusual and indirect form it underlined the lowliness of man's state. But the title suggested glory, too. It was used in Dn 7:13+, and later in the Jewish apocalyptic Book of Enoch, to indicate the transcendent figure, heavenly in origin, who was to receive from God's hand the eschatological kingdom (the kingdom 'at the end of times'). In this way therefore the title both veiled and hinted at (cf. Mk 1:34+; Mt 13:13+) the sort of Messiah Jesus was. Moreover, the explicit avowal in the presence of the Sanhedrin, 26:64+, should have removed all ambiguity.

i. The district got its name from the town of Gadara to the S.E. of the Lake. The Var. 'Gerasenes' (Mk, Lk and Vulg. Mt) derives from the name of another town (Gerasa or possibly Chorsia); the variant 'Gergesenes' is the result of a conjecture of Origen.

4:3+; 9:33; 10:1; 12: could pass that way. •They stood there shouting, 'What do you want with us, 29
23,28,43; 15:22; 17: Son of God? Have you come here to torture us before the time?'[j] •Now some 30
18 Lk 4:34,36; distance away there was a large herd of pigs feeding, •and the devils pleaded 31
8:2; 9:2 Ac 8:7; 10: with Jesus, 'If you cast us out, send us into the herd of pigs'. •And he said to them, 32
38; 16:17 Jm 2:19 'Go then', and they came out and made for the pigs; and at that the whole herd
2 P 2:4 charged down the cliff into the lake and perished in the water. •The swineherds 33
ran off and made for the town, where they told the whole story, including what
had happened to the demoniacs. •At this the whole town set out to meet Jesus; 34
and as soon as they saw him they implored him to leave the neighbourhood.

||Mk 2:1-12 ||Lk 5:17-26

Cure of a paralytic

9 He got back in the boat, crossed the water and came to his own town.[a] •Then 1 2
8:10+ some people appeared, bringing him a paralytic stretched out on a bed. Seeing
Lk 7:48 Jn 5:14 their faith, Jesus said to the paralytic, 'Courage, my child, your sins are forgiven'.[b]
Jn 10:33-36 And at this some scribes said to themselves, 'This man is blaspheming'. •Knowing 3 4
Jn 1:48+ what was in their minds Jesus said, 'Why do you have such wicked thoughts in
your hearts? •Now, which of these is easier: to say, "Your sins are forgiven", 5
Dn 7:10, 14,22 or to say, "Get up and walk"? •But to prove to you that the Son of Man has 6
Jn 5:27 *Jn 5:8* authority on earth to forgive sins,'—he said to the paralytic—'get up, and pick up
8:3+ your bed and go off home'. •And the man got up and went home. •A feeling of 7 8
awe came over the crowd when they saw this, and they praised God for giving
such power to men.[c]

||Mk 2:13-14 ||Lk 5:27-28

The call of Matthew

As Jesus was walking on from there he saw a man named Matthew[d] sitting by te 9
4:19 Jn 1:43 customs house, and he said to him, 'Follow me'. And he got up and followed him.

||Mk 2:15-17 ||Lk 5:29-32

Eating with sinners

11:19 Lk 15:1-10; 19:1-10 While he was at dinner in the house it happened that a number of tax collectors 10
and sinners[e] came to sit at the table with Jesus and his disciples. •When the 11
Pharisees saw this, they said to his disciples, 'Why does your master eat with
1 Tm 1:15 tax collectors and sinners?' •When he heard this he replied, 'It is not the healthy 12
who need the doctor, but the sick. •Go and learn the meaning of the words: 13
=12:7 Ho 6:6 *What I want is mercy, not sacrifice.*[f] And indeed I did not come to call the virtuous,
18:11 but sinners.'

Zc 8:19 ||Mk 2:18-22 ||Lk 5:33-39

A discussion on fasting

Then John's[g] disciples came to him and said, 'Why is it that we and the 14
Jn 3:29 Pharisees fast, but your disciples do not?' •Jesus replied, 'Surely the bridegroom's 15
attendants would never think of mourning as long as the bridegroom[h] is still with
them? But the time will come for the bridegroom to be taken away[i] from them,
Jn 1:17 Rm 7:6 and then they will fast. •No one puts a piece of unshrunken cloth on to an old 16
2 Co 5:17 Ga 1:6; 4:9 cloak, because the patch pulls away from the cloak and the tear gets worse. •Nor 17
Jb 32:19 do people put new wine into old wineskins; if they do, the skins burst, the wine
runs out, and the skins are lost. No; they put new wine into fresh skins and both
are preserved.'[j]

||Mk 5:21-43 ||Lk 8:40-56

Cure of the woman with a haemorrhage. The official's daughter raised to life

While he was speaking to them, up came one of the officials,[k] who bowed low 18
1 Tm 4:14+ in front of him and said, 'My daughter has just died, but come and lay your hand
on her and her life will be saved'. •Jesus rose and, with his disciples, followed him. 19
Then from behind him came a woman, who had suffered from a haemorrhage 20
14:36 Nb 15:37 for twelve years, and she touched the fringe of his cloak, •for she said to herself, 21
Ac 19:12 'If I can only touch his cloak I shall be well again'. •Jesus turned round and saw 22
8:10+ her; and he said to her, 'Courage, my daughter, your faith has restored you to
health'. And from that moment the woman was well again.

23 When Jesus reached the official's house and saw the flute-players, with the
24 crowd making a commotion[l] he said, •'Get out of here; the little girl is not dead, Jn 11:11-13
25 she is asleep'. And they laughed at him. •But when the people had been turned
26 out he went inside and took the little girl by the hand; and she stood up. •And the 8:15+
news spread all round the countryside. 8:3+

Cure of two blind men

20:29-34

27 As Jesus went on his way two blind men followed him shouting, 'Take pity 12:23; 15-22; 21:9
28 on us, Son of David'.[m] •And when Jesus reached the house the blind men came Lk 1:32
up with him and he said to them, 'Do you believe I can do this?' They said, 'Sir, 8:10+
29 we do'. •Then he touched their eyes saying, 'Your faith deserves it, so let this
30 be done for you'. •And their sight returned. Then Jesus sternly warned them,
31 'Take care that no one learns about this'. •But when they had gone, they talked Mk 1:34+
about him all over the countryside.

Cure of a dumb demoniac

=12:22-24 ||Lk 11:14-15

32 They had only just left when a man was brought to him, a dumb demoniac.
33 And when the devil was cast out, the dumb man spoke and the people were 8:29+
34 amazed. 'Nothing like this has ever been seen in Israel' they said. •But the Mk 7:37
Pharisees said, 'It is through the prince of devils that he casts out devils'.[n] 10:25

The distress of the crowds

35 Jesus made a tour through all the towns and villages, teaching in their =4:23 Lk 8:1
synagogues, proclaiming the Good News of the kingdom and curing all kinds
of diseases and sickness.
36 And when he saw the crowds he felt sorry for them because they were harassed 14:13 Jr 50:6
37 and dejected, like sheep without a shepherd.[o] •Then he said to his disciples, Zc 10:2 ||Mk 6:34
'The harvest is rich but the labourers are few, so ask the Lord of the harvest to ||*Lk 10:2* *Jn 4:35-38*
send labourers to his harvest'.

j. Until the day of Judgement the demons are to some extent free to work their mischief on earth, Rv 9:5; they do this normally by taking possession of men, 12:43-45+. Such possession often brings disease with it because disease—consequence of sin, 9:2+—is another manifestation of Satan's domination, Lk 13:16. It is for this reason that the gospel exorcisms, though sometimes described simply as expulsions, cf. 15:21-28p; Mk 1:23-28p; Lk 8:2, often take the form of cures, 9:32-34; 12:22-24p; 17:14-18p; Lk 13:10-17. By his power over the devils Jesus destroys Satan's empire, 12:28p; Lk 10:17-19; cf. Lk 4:6; Jn 12:31+, and inaugurates the messianic era of which, according to the prophets, the gift of the Holy Spirit is the distinctive mark, Is 11:2+; Jl 3:1f. Man may refuse to recognise it, 12:24-32, but the demons see it all too well, cf. this passage and Mk 1:24p; 3:11p; Lk 4:41; Ac 16:17; 19:15. This power to exorcise is given by Jesus to his disciples simultaneously with the power of miraculous healing, 10:1,8p, with which it is connected, 8:3+; 4:24; 8:16p; Lk 13:32.

9 a. Capernaum, cf. 4:13.

b. Jesus puts the cure of the soul before that of the body; when he heals the body it is because he has the good of the soul in mind. Nevertheless his words in this verse contain a promise of bodily healing since sickness was regarded as the result of a sin committed either by the sufferer or by his parents, cf. 8:29+; Jn 5:14; 9:2

c. Note the plural: Matthew is probably thinking of the Church's ministers who received this power from Christ, 18:18.

d. Called Levi by Mk and Lk.

e. Those whose moral conduct or disreputable profession, cf. 5:46+, rendered 'unclean' and socially outcast.

f. To the exact performance of the Law's external demands God prefers the inward quality of genuine compassion. It is a favourite theme of the prophets, Am 5:21+.

g. John the Baptist. Like the Pharisees, John's disciples used to observe fasts not prescribed by the Law in the hope that their devotion would hasten the coming of the kingdom.

h. The bridegroom is Jesus. His companions cannot fast because, with his coming, the messianic age has dawned.

i. Christ's death clearly foretold.

j. The old garment and the old wineskins stand for Judaism in so far as it contains elements which (in the scheme of salvation) are to pass away. The new cloth and the new wine represent the new spirit of the kingdom of God. The superadded devotional practices of John's disciples and of the Pharisees, intended to give new life to the old order, in fact are only leading to its downfall. Jesus declines either to add or to patch: his purpose is to produce something quite new—even the spirit of the Law is to be raised to a new plane, cf. 5:17f.

k. The head of the synagogue; called Jairus in Mk and Lk.

l. The loud wailing of the oriental mourner.

m. Messianic title, 2 S 7:1+; cf. Lk 1:32; Ac 2:30; Rm 1:3. It was familiar as such to the Jews, Mk 12:35; Jn 7:42, and Matthew in particular emphasises its application to Jesus (1:1; 12:23; 15:22; 20:30p; 21:9,15) who was slow to welcome the title because it involved a purely human notion of the Messiah, Mt 22:41-46; cf. Mk 1:34+. He preferred the more obscure title 'Son of Man', 8:20+.

n. Verse omitted by representatives of the Western Text.

o. Familiar biblical metaphor: Nb 27:17; 1 K 22:17; Jdt 11:19; Ezk 34:5.

B. THE APOSTOLIC DISCOURSE

The mission of the Twelve

||Mk 3:14; 6:7 ||Lk 9:1 *Mt 8:29+*

10 He summoned his twelve disciples,[a] and gave them authority over unclean 1
spirits with power to cast them out and to cure all kinds of diseases and
sickness.

||Mk 3:16-19 ||Lk 6:13-16 ||Ac 1:13

These are the names of the twelve apostles:[b] first, Simon who is called Peter, 2
and his brother Andrew; James the son of Zebedee, and his brother John; •Philip 3
and Bartholomew; Thomas, and Matthew the tax collector; James the son of
Alphaeus, and Thaddaeus; •Simon the Zealot and Judas Iscariot,[c] the one who 4
was to betray him. •These twelve Jesus sent out, instructing them as follows: 5

15:24 Lk 9:53 Jn 4:9 3:2+; 4:17+ Lk 10:9,11 *Is 55:1* Ac 8:20 ||*Mk 6:8-9* ||Lk 9:3; 10:4 ||*Lk 10:7* ↗1 Co 9:14 3 Jn 8

'Do not turn your steps to pagan territory, and do not enter any Samaritan
town; •go rather to the lost sheep of the House of Israel.[d] •And as you go, 6 7
proclaim that the kingdom of heaven is close at hand. •Cure the sick, raise the 8
dead, cleanse the lepers, cast out devils. You received without charge, give without
charge. •Provide yourselves with no gold or silver, not even with a few coppers 9
for your purses, •with no haversack for the journey or spare tunic or footwear 10
or a staff, for the workman deserves his keep.

||*Mk 6:10-11* ||Lk 9:4-5; 10:5-12 Ac 13:51; 18:6 =11:24 Lk 12:48 ||*Lk 10:3* Jude 7 *7:15* 1 Co 14:20

'Whatever town or village you go into, ask for someone trustworthy and stay 11
with him until you leave. •As you enter his house, salute it,[e] •and if the house 12 13
deserves it, let your peace descend upon it; if it does not, let your peace come back
to you. •And if anyone does not welcome you or listen to what you have to say, 14
as you walk out of the house or town shake the dust from your feet.[f] •I tell you 15
solemnly, on the day of Judgement it will not go as hard with the land of
Sodom and Gomorrah as with that town. •Remember, I am sending you out 16
like sheep among wolves; so be cunning as serpents and yet as harmless as doves.

||Mk 13:9-13 ||Lk 21:12-19

The missionaries will be persecuted[g]

Jn 16:1-4 Ac 5:40 *Jn 15:27* ||Lk 12:11-12 Ex 4:10-12 Jr 1:6-10 Jn 15:26 Ac 4:8,31

'Beware of men: they will hand you over to sanhedrins[h] and scourge you in 17
their synagogues. •You will be dragged before governors and kings for my sake, 18
to bear witness before them and the pagans. •But when they hand you over, do 19
not worry about how to speak or what to say; what you are to say will be given to
you when the time comes; •because it is not you who will be speaking; the Spirit 20
of your Father will be speaking in you.

=24:9 *Jn 15:18-19, 25* =*24:13* 16:28; 24:34

'Brother will betray brother to death, and the father his child; children will 21
rise against their parents and have them put to death. •You will be hated by all 22
men on account of my name; but the man who stands firm to the end will be saved.
If they persecute you in one town, take refuge in the next; and if they persecute 23
you in that, take refuge in another.[i] I tell you solemnly, you will not have gone
the round of the towns of Israel before the Son of Man comes.[j]

||Lk 6:40 ||Jn 13:16; 15:20 9:34; 12:24

'The disciple is not superior to his teacher, nor the slave to his master. •It is 24 25
enough for the disciple that he should grow to be like his teacher, and the slave
like his master. If they have called the master of the house Beelzebul, what will
they not say of his household?

||Lk 12:2-7

Open and fearless speech

||Mk 4:22 ||Lk 8:17 1 Tm 5:25

'Do not be afraid of them therefore. For everything that is now covered will 26
be uncovered, and everything now hidden will be made clear. •What I say to 27
you in the dark, tell in the daylight; what you hear in whispers, proclaim from
the housetops.[k]

Heb 10:31 1 P 3:14 Rv 2:10; 14:7

'Do not be afraid of those who kill the body but cannot kill the soul; fear him 28
rather who can destroy both body and soul in hell. •Can you not buy two 29
sparrows for a penny? And yet not one falls to the ground without your Father
knowing. •Why, every hair on your head has been counted. •So there is no 30 31
need to be afraid; you are worth more than hundreds of sparrows.

'So if anyone declares himself for me in the presence of men, I will declare myself ||Lk 12:8-9
32 for him in the presence of my Father in heaven.[l] •But the one who disowns ||Mk 8:38 ||Lk 9:26
33 me in the presence of men, I will disown in the presence of my Father in 2 Tm 2:12 Rv 3:5
heaven.

Jesus, the cause of dissension[m] ||Lk 12:51-53

34 'Do not suppose that I have come to bring peace to the earth: it is not peace I Lk 2:34
35 have come to bring, but a sword. •For I have come to set *a man against his father,* Lk 22:36 *Mi 7:6*
a daughter against her mother, a daughter-in-law against her mother-in-law.
36 *A man's enemies will be those of his own household.*

Renouncing self to follow Jesus Ex 32:27

37 'Anyone who prefers father or mother to me is not worthy of me. Anyone 8:22 ||Lk 14:26-27 *Dt 33:9*
38 who prefers son or daughter to me is not worthy of me. •Anyone who does not =*16:24-25* ||*Mk 8:34-35*
39 take his cross and follow in my footsteps is not worthy of me. •Anyone who ||Lk 9:23-24; 17:33
finds his life will lose it; anyone who loses his life for my sake will find it.[n] ||Jn 12:25

Conclusion of the apostolic discourse

40 'Anyone who welcomes you welcomes me; and those who welcome me =18:5 ||Mk 9:37 ||Lk 9:48; 10:16
welcome the one who sent me.
41 'Anyone who welcomes a prophet because he is a prophet will have ||Jn 12:44-45; 13:20
a prophet's reward; and anyone who welcomes a holy man because he is a holy 25:40,45
man will have a holy man's reward.[o]
42 'If anyone gives so much as a cup of cold water to one of these little ones[p] Pr 11:25 ||Mk 9:41
because he is a disciple, then I tell you solemnly, he will most certainly not lose
his reward.'

IV. THE MYSTERY OF THE KINGDOM OF HEAVEN

A. NARRATIVE SECTION

1 **11** When Jesus had finished instructing his twelve disciples he moved on from there to teach and preach in their towns.[a]

10 a. Matthew supposes that the reader already knows about the choice of the Twelve; Mark and Luke mention it expressly and distinguish the choice from the mission.

b. Apostle means 'one sent'.

c. 'Thaddaeus' (var. 'Lebbaeus') corresponds to 'Judas (son) of James' in the lists of Lk 6:16 and Ac 1:13. 'Iscariot 'is commonly taken to mean 'man of Kerioth' (a town in Judah, Jos 15:25).

d. Hebraism common in the Bible: the people of Israel. As heirs to the Choice and the Promise, the Jews are to be the first to receive the offer of the Messiah's saving work; but cf. Ac 8:5; 13:5+.

e. The oriental greeting is a wish of peace. In v. 13 this wish is treated in concrete fashion as an entity which, if it fails to secure its effect, nevertheless remains in being and returns to its original owner.

f. The phrase is Jewish in origin. The dust of any country other than the Holy Land is reckoned unclean; in this passage the impurity attaches to any place that refuses the word.

g. The instructions of vv. 17-39 clearly suppose a horizon wider than that of this first mission of the Twelve: they must have been issued at a later date (note their situation in Mk and Lk). Matthew puts them here to complete his missionary's handbook.

h. The small provincial sanhedrins and also the Great Sanhedrin of Jerusalem; cf. 5:21-22.

i. Om. 'and if.......... another'.

j. The coming which is here foretold is not concerned with the world at large but with Israel: it took place at the moment when God 'visited' his now faithless people and brought the O.T. era to an end by the destruction of Jerusalem and of its Temple in 71 A.D., cf. 24:1+.

k. Jesus was obliged to obscure his message: 1. his hearers would have misunderstood a clearer teaching, Mk 1:34+; 2. he himself had not yet completed—by death and resurrection—the work which alone could explain the message. Later on it will be the duty of his disciples to deliver the message in its entirety and without fear. These same words are found in Lk but with an entirely different meaning: the disciples are not to imitate Pharisaic hypocrisy; whatever they may try to hide will certainly come to light eventually; they must therefore speak openly.

l. When the last Judgement takes place and the Son commits the elect to his Father, cf. 25:34.

m. Christ is a 'sign that is rejected', Lk 2:34; his aim is not to provoke dissension, but this becomes inevitable as a result of the strict alternative he offers.

n. In Mt this dictum is given in a more archaic form than in Mk or Lk: 'find' covers the idea of 'winning', 'securing for ones lf', cf. Gn 26:12; Ho 12:9; Pr 3:13; 21:21. See Mt 16:25 +.

o. 'Prophet' and 'holy (or 'righteous') man', cf. also 13:17 and 23:29, are a familiar biblical pair; here they serve to indicate the missionary and the ordinary Christian.

p. The apostles whom Jesus is sending on their mission, cf' Mk 9:41 and Mt 18:1-6,10 14.

11 a. 'their', i.e. the Jews'.

||Lk 7:18-28 **The Baptist's question. Jesus commends him**

Now John in his prison had heard what Christ was doing and he sent his 2
Dt 18:15 disciples[b] to ask him, •'Are you the one who is to come, or have we got to wait for 3
Jn 1:21+ *8:3+* someone else?'[c] •Jesus answered, 'Go back and tell John what you hear and see; 4
Is 16:19; 29: 18f; 35:5f; the blind see again, and the lame walk, lepers are cleansed, and the deaf hear, 5
61:1 and the dead are raised to life and the Good News is proclaimed to the poor;[d]
13:57 Jn 6:61 and happy is the man who does not lose faith in me'. 6

As the messengers were leaving, Jesus began to talk to the people about John: 7
3:1,5-6 Jn 5:33 'What did you go out into the wilderness to see? A reed swaying in the breeze?
No? •Then what did you go out to see? A man wearing fine clothes? Oh no, those 8
who wear fine clothes are to be found in palaces. •Then what did you go out for? 9
16:14+ Lk 1:76-79 To see a prophet? Yes, I tell you, and much more than a prophet: •he is the one 10
of whom scripture says:

Ml 3:1 *Look, I am going to send my messenger before you;*
he will prepare your way before you.

'I tell you solemnly, of all the children born of women, a greater than John 11
the Baptist has never been seen; yet the least in the kingdom of heaven is
greater than he is.[e] •Since John the Baptist came, up to this present time, the 12
||Lk 16:16 kingdom of heaven has been subjected to violence[f] and the violent are taking it
by storm. •Because it was towards John that all the prophecies of the prophets 13
17:11-13 Ml 3:23 and of the Law were leading; •and he, if you will believe me, is the Elijah who 14
was to return.[g] •If anyone has ears to hear, let him listen! 15

||Lk 7:31-35 **Jesus condemns his contemporaries**

'What description can I find for this generation? It is like children shouting to 16
each other as they sit in the market place:

"We played the pipes for you, 17
and you wouldn't dance;
we sang dirges,
and you wouldn't be mourners".

3:4 Lk 1:15 'For John came, neither eating nor drinking, and they say, "He is possessed". 18
8:20+ *9:10:11* The Son of Man came, eating and drinking, and they say, "Look, a glutton and 19
a drunkard, a friend of tax collectors and sinners". Yet wisdom has been proved
Jn 6:35+ right by her actions.'[h]

||Lk 10:13-15 **Lament over the lake-towns**

13:58 Am 3:2 Then he began to reproach the towns in which most of his miracles had been 20
Jn 12:37; 15:24 worked, because they refused to repent.
'Alas for you, Chorazin! Alas for you, Bethsaida! For if the miracles done in 21
you had been done in Tyre and Sidon, they would have repented long ago in
sackcloth and ashes. •And still, I tell you that it will not go as hard on Judgement 22
Is 14:13,15 day with Tyre and Sidon as with you. •And as for you, Capernaum, did you 23
want to be exalted as high as heaven? *You shall be thrown down to hell.* For if the
=10:15 miracles done in you had been done in Sodom, it would have been standing yet.
And still, I tell you that it will not go as hard with the land of Sodom on Judgement 24
day as with you.'

||Lk 10:21-22 **The Good News revealed to the simple. The Father and the Son**

Jn 10:15 13:11 At that time Jesus exclaimed, 'I bless you, Father, Lord of heaven and of 25
Jn 7:48-49 earth, for hiding these things[i] from the learned and the clever and revealing them
1 Co 1:26 *4:3+; 16:17* to mere children. •Yes, Father, for that is what it pleased you to do. •Everything 26 27
Ws 9:17 Jn 1:18; 3: has been entrusted to me by my Father; and no one knows the Son except the
35+; 10:15 *Ws 2:13* Father, just as no one knows the Father except the Son and those to whom the
Jn 3:11+ Son chooses to reveal him.[j]

The gentle mastery of Christ

28 'Come to me, all you who labour and are overburdened,[k] and I will give you Si 24:19 Jr 2:20; 5:5
29 rest. •Shoulder my yoke and learn from me, for I am gentle and humble in heart, *Pr 3:17* Jr 6:16
30 *and you will find rest for your souls.* •Yes, my yoke is easy and my burden light.' Ho 10:11 *Ac 15:10* Ga 5:1 *Ex 20:8+*

Picking corn on the sabbath

||Mk 2:23-28 ||Lk 6:1-5 Jn 7:22

1 **12** At that time Jesus took a walk one sabbath day through the cornfields.
His disciples were hungry and began to pick ears of corn and eat them.
2 The Pharisees noticed it and said to him, 'Look, your disciples are doing
3 something that is forbidden on the sabbath'.[a] •But he said to them, 'Have you
4 not read what David did when he and his followers were hungry—•how he went 1 S 21:4-7
into the house of God and how they ate the loaves of offering which neither he Lv 24:5-9
nor his followers were allowed to eat, but which were for the priests alone?
5 Or again, have you not read in the Law that on the sabbath day the Temple Nb 28:9
6 priests break the sabbath without being blamed for it?[b] •Now here, I tell you,
7 is something greater than the Temple. •And if you had understood the meaning 12:41 Jn 2:20
of the words: *What I want is mercy, not sacrifice,* you would not have condemned *=9:13* 1 S 15:22
8 the blameless. •For the Son of Man is master of the sabbath.'[c] Ho 6:6 *Jn 5:16-17*

Cure of the man with a withered hand

||Mk 3:1-6 ||Lk 6:6-11

9 10 He moved on from there and went to their synagogue, •and a man was there
at the time who had a withered hand. They asked him, 'Is it against the law to Lk 20:20
11 cure a man on the sabbath day?' hoping for something to use against him. •But he Jn 8:6; 9:14
said to them, 'If any one of you here had only one sheep and it fell down a hole ||Lk 14:5 Jn 7:22-23
12 on the sabbath day, would be not get hold of it and lift it out? •Now a man is far
more important than a sheep, so it follows that it is permitted to do good on the
13 sabbath day.' •Then he said to the man, 'Stretch out your hand'. He stretched it Ex 20:8+
14 out and his hand was better, as sound as the other one. •At this the Pharisees Jn 5:18; 11:53
went out and began to plot against him, discussing how to destroy him.

Jesus the 'servant of Yahweh'

15 Jesus knew this and withdrew from the district. Many followed him and he Mk 3:7
16 17 cured them all, •but warned them not to make him known. •This[d] was to fulfil Mk 1:34+; ||3:12
the prophecy of Isaiah:

b. Var. 'two of his disciples'.

c. John the Baptist is not expressing complete doubt about Jesus, but he is surprised to find that he is a very different sort of Messiah from what he had expected, cf. 3:10-12.

d. This allusion to the oracles of Is assures John that the messianic era is being inaugurated, even though Jesus confines himself to beneficent and saving miracles, without resorting to violence and retribution. Cf. Lk 4: 17-21.

e. Simply because he is a member of the kingdom, whereas John, as the Precursor, remains at its gates. The sentence contrasts epochs rather than persons: the era of the kingdom immeasurably transcends that which preceded and prepared for it.

f. Various interpretations have been offered. The 'violence' may be: 1. the praiseworthy violence, the bitter self-sacrifice, of those who would take possession of the kingdom; 2. the misguided violence of those who would establish the kingdom by force (the Zealots); 3. the tyrannical violence of the powers of evil, or of their agents on earth, who seek to maintain their dominion in this world and to thwart the advance of the kingdom of God. 4. A possible translation 'The kingdom of heaven clears a way for itself by violence', i.e. is powerfully establishing itself despite all obstacles.

g. John brings the O.T. era to its close: he carries on where Malachi, the last of the prophets, left off, and fulfils Malachi's last prediction, Ml 3:23.

h. Var. 'by her children', cf. Lk 7:35. Like petulant children who will play none of the games suggested (in this case they refuse to play either at weddings or at funerals), the Jews reject all God's advances whether through the stern penance of John or through the gentle courtesy of Jesus. In spite of this, God's wise design carries through, independently of anything extrinsic to itself, and so its success is its own vindication.

i. Vv. 25-27 are not closely connected with the context in which Matthew has placed the passage (cf. its different position in Lk). Hence, 'these things' refers not to what precedes but to the 'mysteries of the kingdom', 13:11, which are revealed to the 'little ones'—i.e. to the disciples, cf. 10:42—but hidden from the 'wise men'—i.e. from the members and teachers of the Pharisee group.

j. V. 27 has a Johannine flavour: awareness of Christ's divine sonship exists in the deepest stratum of the synoptic tradition as well as in Jn.

k. The burden of the Law and of the additional Pharisaic observances. The 'yoke of the Law' is a current rabbinic metaphor; see also Si 51:26; Zp 3:9 (LXX); Lm 3:27; Jr 2:20; 5:5; cf. Is 14:25.

12 a. The disciples are not attacked for picking the ears as they walked (this was allowed. Dt 23:26) but for doing so on the sabbath. Casuistry saw in this one of the 'works' forbidden by the Law, Ex 34:21.

b. Far from stopping, the work of the sacred ministry actually increased on the sabbath.

c. Jesus here claims authority even over Israel's God-given institutions.

d. I.e. Christ's avoidance of publicity for his work of healing.

Is 42.1-4 *Here is my servant whom I have chosen,* 18
my beloved, the favourite of my soul.
3:16+ *I will endow him with my spirit,*
and he will proclaim the true faith[e] *to the nations.*
He will not brawl or shout, 19
nor will anyone hear his voice in the streets.
Zc 11:16 2 Tm 2:24 *He will not break the crushed reed,* 20
nor put out the smouldering wick
till he has led the truth to victory:
in his name the nations will put their hope. 21

Jesus and Beelzebul

8:29+; =9:32-34 Then they brought to him a blind and dumb demoniac; and he cured him, 22
Tb 8:3 ||Lk 11:14-15 so that the dumb man could speak and see. •All the people were astounded and 23
9:27 said, 'Can this be the Son of David?' •But when the Pharisees heard this they 24
10:25 said, 'The man casts out devils only through Beelzebul,[f] the prince of devils'.
||Mk 3:23-30 ||Lk 11:17-23 Knowing what was in their minds he said to them, 'Every kingdom divided 25
against itself is heading for ruin; and no town, no household divided against
Jb 1:6+ itself can stand. •Now if Satan casts out Satan, he is divided against himself; 26
so how can his kingdom stand? •And if it is through Beelzebul that I cast out 27
devils, through whom do your own experts[g] cast them out? Let them be your
3:16+ Lk 11:20 judges, then. •But if it is through the Spirit of God that I cast devils out, then 28
8:29+ know that the kingdom of God has overtaken you.
Is 49:25 Jn 12:31 'Or again, how can anyone make his way into a strong man's house and 29
burgle his property unless he has tied up the strong man first? Only then can he
burgle his house.
Mk 9:40 Lk 11:23 'He who is not with me is against me, and he who does not gather with me 30
1 Jn 5:16 scatters. •And so I tell you, every one of men's sins and blasphemies will be for- 31
||Lk 12:10 Heb 10:30 given, but blasphemy against the Spirit will not be forgiven. •And anyone who 32
says a word against the Son of Man will be forgiven; but let anyone speak against
the Holy Spirit and he will not be forgiven either in this world or in the next.[h]

=7:16-20 ||Lk 6:43-45 **Words betray the heart**

'Make a tree sound and its fruit will be sound; make a tree rotten and its 33
3:7; 23:33 fruit will be rotten. For the tree can be told by its fruit. •Brood of vipers, how 34
15:11,18 can your speech be good when you are evil? For a man's words flow out of what
Pr 10:14 fills his heart. •A good man draws good things from his store of goodness; a bad 35
man draws bad things from his store of badness. •So I tell you this, that for 36
Jm 3:1-6 every unfounded word[i] men utter they will answer on Judgement day, •since it 37
is by your words you will be acquitted, and by your words condemned.'

||Mk 8:11-12 ||Lk 11:29-32 **The sign of Jonah**

=16:1-4 Ezk 3:7; 5:7 Then some of the scribes and Pharisees spoke up. 'Master', they said 'we 38
Jn 4:48 1 Co 1:22 should like to see a sign[j] from you.' •He replied, 'It is an evil and unfaithful[k] 39
generation that asks for a sign! The only sign it will be given is the sign of the
Jon 2:1 prophet Jonah. •For as Jonah *was in the belly of the sea-monster for three* 40
days and three nights, so will the Son of Man be in the heart of the earth for
three days and three nights.[l] •On Judgement day the men of Nineveh will stand 41
up with this generation and condemn it, because when Jonah preached they
12:6 Rm 2:27 repented; and there is something greater than Jonah here. •On Judgement day 42
1 K 10:1-10 the Queen of the South will rise up with this generation and condemn it, because
Jn 6:35+ she came from the ends of the earth to hear the wisdom of Solomon; and there
is something greater than Solomon here.

8:29+ ||Lk 11:24-26 Tb 8:3 **The return of the unclean spirit**

'When an unclean spirit goes out of a man it wanders through waterless 43

44 country looking for a place to rest,[m] and cannot find one. •Then it says, "I will
return to the home I came from". But on arrival, finding it unoccupied, swept and
45 tidied, •it then goes off and collects seven other spirits more evil than itself, and Mk 5:9
they go in and set up house there, so that the man ends up by being worse than Lk 8:2 *Jn 5:14* 2 P 2:20
he was before. That is what will happen to this evil generation.'

The true kinsmen of Jesus

||Mk 3:31-35 ||Lk 8:19-21

46 He was still speaking to the crowds when his mother and his brothers[n] 13:55-56 1 Co 9:5
appeared; they were standing outside and were anxious to have a word with Lk 2:49-50
48 him.[o] •But to the man who told him this Jesus replied, 'Who is my mother?
49 Who are my brothers?' •And stretching out his hand towards his disciples he said,
50 'Here are my mother and my brothers. •Anyone who does the will of my Father
in heaven, he is my brother and sister and mother.'[p]

B. THE PARABOLIC DISCOURSE

Introduction

||Mk 4:1-2 ||Lk 8:4

1 2 13 That same day,[a] Jesus left the house and sat by the lakeside, •but such
crowds gathered round him that he got into a boat and sat there. The people
3 all stood on the beach, •and he told them many things in parables.[b]

Parable of the sower

||Mk 4:3-9 ||Lk 8:5-8

4 He said, 'Imagine a sower going out to sow. •As he sowed, some seeds fell
5 on the edge of the path, and the birds came and ate them up. •Others fell on
patches of rock where they found little soil and sprang up straight away, because
6 there was no depth of earth; •but as soon as the sun came up they were scorched
7 and, not having any roots, they withered away. •Others fell among thorns, and
8 the thorns grew up and choked them. •Others fell on rich soil and produced their Jn 15:8,16
9 crop, some a hundredfold, some sixty, some thirty. •Listen, anyone who has Is 42:19 Rv 2:7; 13:9
ears!'[c]

Why Jesus speaks in parables

||Mk 4:10-12, 25 ||Lk 8:9-10, 18

10 Then the disciples went up to him and asked, 'Why do you talk to them in
11 parables?' •'Because' he replied 'the mysteries of the kingdom of heaven are
12 revealed to you, but they are not revealed to them. •For anyone who has will be =25:29
given more, and he will have more than enough; but from anyone who has not, ||Lk 19:25

e. 'true faith': this gives the meaning of the Hebr. term *mishpat* (and of its LXX translation *krisis*), often rendered 'judgement', which signifies the divine statute that governs the relationship of God with man in so far as it is known through revelation and the true religion that is founded on it.

f. Canaanite divinity. The name means 'Baal the Prince' (not 'Baal of the dunghill' as is sometimes asserted), and so orthodox monotheism naturally interpreted it as 'Prince of devils'. The form 'Beelzebub' (Syr. and Vulg.) is a contemptuous play on words (already found in 2 K 1:2f) which makes the name mean 'Baal (Lord) of the flies'.

g. Lit. 'your children', a semitism.

h. There is some excuse for not recognising Christ's divine nature since it is hidden under the appearance of an ordinary 'son of man', but there is no excuse for blinding oneself to the manifest works of the Spirit. The man who denies these is resisting God's most direct appeal and putting himself outside the range of God's saving grace, cf. Heb 6:4-6; 10:26-31.

i. Not a merely 'idle' word but a malicious and baseless assertion, a calumny.

j. A miracle that would prove Jesus had authority and show what sort of authority it was, cf. Is 7:11f; Lk 1:18+; Jn 2:11+. He refuses to give any other sign but the decisive one which is his resurrection, here obscurely foretold.

k. Lit. 'adulterous': a biblical metaphor, cf. Ho 1:2+.

l. A ready-made expression borrowed from Jon 2:1 and only approximately indicating the space of time between Christ's death and resurrection.

m. The ancients thought of desert places as inhabited by demons, cf. Lv 16:8+; 17:7+; Is 13:21; 34:14; Ba 4:35; Rv 18:2; Mt 8:28. Nevertheless, the devils much prefer to dwell in man, Mt 8:29+.

n. Not Mary's children but near relations, cousins perhaps, which both Hebr. and Aramaic style 'brothers', cf. Gn 13:8; 14:16; 29:15; Lv 10:4; 1 Ch 23:22f.

o. V. 47 ('Someone said to him: Your mother and brothers are standing outside and want to speak to you') is omitted by some important textual witnesses. It is probably a restatement of v. 46 modelled on Mk and Lk.

p. The claims of physical relationship come after those of spiritual, cf. 8:21f; 10:37.

13 a. A merely transitional cliché of no chronological significance.

b. Making a total of 7, cf. 6:9+. Mt adds 5 parables to the 2 he shares with Mk.

c. Lit. 'He who has ears, let him hear'. As in 11:15 and 13:43 some authorities have 'He who has ears to hear, let...'

Jn 9:39 Rm 11:8 even what he has will be taken away.[d] •The reason I talk to them in parables is 13
that they look without seeing and listen without hearing or understanding.[e] •So in 14
their case this prophecy of Isaiah is being fulfilled:

Is 6:9-10+ Jn 12:40 Ac 28:26 *You will listen and listen again, but not understand,*
see and see again, but not perceive.
For the heart of this nation has grown coarse, 15
their ears are dull of hearing, and they have shut their eyes,
for fear they should see with their eyes,
hear with their ears,
understand with their heart,
and be converted
and be healed by me.

||Lk 10:23,24 Ac 22:15 *Ep 3:5* 1 P 1:12 'But happy are your eyes because they see, your ears because they hear! 16
I tell you solemnly, many prophets and holy men[f] longed to see what you see, and 17
never saw it; to hear what you hear, and never heard it.

||Mk 4:13-20 ||Lk 8:11-15 Jn 12:47

The parable of the sower explained

'You, therefore, are to hear the parable of the sower. •When anyone hears 18 19
the word of the kingdom without understanding, the evil one comes and carries
off what was sown in his heart: this is the man who received the seed on the edge
of the path. •The one who received it on patches of rock is the man who hears 20
the word and welcomes it at once with joy. •But he has no root in him, he does 21
not last; let some trial come, or some persecution on account of the word, and he
falls away at once. •The one who received the seed in thorns is the man who 22
hears the word, but the worries of this world and the lure of riches choke the word
and so he produces nothing. •And the one who received the seed in rich soil is the 23
Jn 15:8,16 Ga 5:22 man who hears the word and understands it; he is the one who yields a harvest
and produces now a hundredfold, now sixty, now thirty.'

Parable of the darnel

He put another parable before them, 'The kingdom of heaven may be 24
compared to a man who sowed good seed in his field. •While everybody was 25
asleep his enemy came, sowed darnel all among the wheat, and made off. •When 26
the new wheat sprouted and ripened, the darnel appeared as well. •The owner's 27
servants went to him and said, "Sir, was it not good seed that you sowed in your
field? If so, where does the darnel come from?" •"Some enemy has done this" 28
he answered. And the servants said, "Do you want us to go and weed it out?"
But he said, "No, because when you weed out the darnel you might pull up the 29
wheat with it. •Let them both grow till the harvest; and at harvest time I shall 30
Jn 15:6 say to the reapers: First collect the darnel and tie it in bundles to be burnt, then
3:12 gather the wheat into my barn." '

||Mk 4:30-32 ||Lk 13:18-19

Parable of the mustard seed

He put another parable before them, 'The kingdom of heaven is like a mustard 31
Si 11:3 seed which a man took and sowed in his field. •It is the smallest of all the seeds, 32
Ezk 17:23 Dn 4:9,18 but when it has grown it is the biggest shrub of all and becomes a tree so that
the birds of the air come and shelter in its branches.'

||Lk 13:20-21

Parable of the yeast

He told them another parable, 'The kingdom of heaven is like the yeast 33
a woman took and mixed in with three measures of flour till it was leavened
all through'.[g]

||Mk 4:33-34 Jn 16:25

The people are taught only in parables

In all this Jesus spoke to the crowds in parables; indeed, he would never speak 34
to them except in parables. •This was to fulfil the prophecy: 35

I will speak to you in parables Ps 78:2
and expound things hidden since the foundation of the world.[h]

The parable of the darnel explained

36 Then, leaving the crowds, he went to the house; and his disciples came to
37 him and said, 'Explain the parable about the darnel in the field to us'. •He said
38 in reply, 'The sower of the good seed is the Son of Man. •The field is the world;
the good seed is the subjects of the kingdom; the darnel, the subjects of the evil 1 Jn 3:10
39 one;[i] •the enemy who sowed them, the devil; the harvest is the end of the world; Jl 4:13 Rv 14:15-16
40 the reapers are the angels. •When then, just as the darnel is gathered up and burnt
41 in the fire, so it will be at the end of time. •The Son of Man will send his angels Zp 1:3
and they will gather out of his kingdom all things that provoke offences and all
42 who do evil, •and throw them into the blazing furnace, where there will be 3:12 Rv 21:8
43 weeping and grinding of teeth. •Then the virtuous will shine like the sun in the *8:12+* *Jg 5:31*
kingdom of their Father.[j] Listen, anyone who has ears! Ws 3:7 Dn 12:3

Parables of the treasure and of the pearl[k]

44 'The kingdom of heaven is like treasure hidden in a field which someone has Pr 2:4 Si 51:28
found; he hides it again, goes off happy, sells everything he owns and buys the *19:21* Pr 4:7
field.
45 'Again, the kingdom of heaven is like a merchant looking for fine pearls;
46 when he finds one of great value he goes and sells everything he owns and buys it.

Parable of the dragnet

47 'Again, the kingdom of heaven is like a dragnet cast into the sea that brings 22:10
48 in a haul of all kinds. •When it is full, the fishermen haul it ashore; then, sitting
down, they collect the good ones in a basket and throw away those that are no
49 use. •This is how it will be at the end of time: the angels will appear and separate
50 the wicked from the just •to throw them into the blazing furnace where there
will be weeping and grinding of teeth. 8:12+

Conclusion

51 52 'Have you understood all this?' They said, 'Yes'. •And he said to them, Mk 4:13+
'Well then, every scribe who becomes a disciple of the kingdom of heaven is like
a householder who brings out from his storeroom things both new and old'.[l]

13 d. For those of good will, what they have learnt from the old covenant will be added to and perfected by the new, cf. 5:17,20. The ill-disposed will even lose what they have, namely, that Jewish Law which, without the perfection Christ brings to it, is destined to become obsolete.

e. A deliberate and culpable insensibility which is both the cause and the explanation of the withdrawal of grace. The preceding narratives, all of which throw light on this 'hardening', 11:16-19,20-24; 12:7,14,24-32, 34,39,45, prepare the way for the parable discourse. Those who saw so dimly could only be further blinded by the light of full revelation, Mk 1:34+. Jesus, therefore, does not reveal with complete clarity the true nature of the messianic kingdom which is unostentatious. Instead he filters the light through symbols, the resulting half-light is nevertheless a grace from God, and invitation to ask for something better and accept something greater.

f. The prophets and holy men of the O.T. Paul speaks more than once of the time when the 'mystery' was not revealed: Rm 16:25; Ep 3:4-5; Col 1:26. Cf. also 1 P 1:11-12.

g. The kingdom, like the mustard seed and the leaven, is unpretentious in its beginnings but destined for enormous growth.

h. Several authorities omit 'of the world'.

i. Lit. 'the children of the kingdom' and 'the children of the evil one', (semitisms).

j. To the kingdom of the Son (the messianic kingdom) of v. 41 there succeeds the kingdom of the Father to whom the Son commits the elect whom he has saved. Cf. Mt 25:34; 1 Co 15:24.

k. If a man discovers the kingdom of heaven he cannot enter unless he leaves all behind, cf. 19:21.

l. The Jewish teacher who becomes a disciple of Christ has at his disposal all the wealth of the Old Testament as well as the perfection of the New, v. 12. This picture of a 'scribe who becomes a disciple' sums up the whole ideal of Matthew the evangelist and may well be a self-portrait.

V. THE CHURCH, FIRST-FRUITS OF THE KINGDOM OF HEAVEN

A. NARRATIVE SECTION

||Mk 6:1-6 ||Lk 4:16-24

A visit to Nazareth

When Jesus had finished these parables he left the district; •and, coming 53 54
2:23 Jn 1:46 to his home town,[m] he taught the people in their synagogue in such a way that
Jn 6:42; 7:46 they were astonished and said, 'Where did the man get this wisdom and these
Mt 27:56 Lk 3:23 miraculous powers? •This is the carpenter's son, surely? Is not his mother the 55
12:46 woman called Mary, and his brothers James and Joseph and Simon and Jude?
His sisters, too, are they not all here with us? So where did the man get it all?' 56
16:14+ Ex 4:1 ||Jn 4:44 And they would not accept him. But Jesus said to them, 'A prophet is only 57
despised in his own country and in his own house', •and he did not work 58
8:10+ many miracles there because of their lack of faith.

||Mk 6:14-16 ||Lk 9:7-9

Herod and Jesus

Lk 3:1+ 14 At that time Herod the tetrarch heard about the reputation of Jesus, •and 1 2
Mt 16:14+ Lk 23:8-12 said to his court, 'This is John the Baptist himself; he has risen from
the dead, and that is why miraculous powers are at work in him'.

||Mk 6:17-29 Lk 3:19-20

John the Baptist beheaded

Now it was Herod who had arrested John, chained him up and put him in 3
Lv 18:16; 20:21 prison because of Herodias, his brother Philip's[a] wife. •For John had told him, 4
'It is against the Law for you to have her'. •He had wanted to kill him but 5
21:26 was afraid of the people, who regarded John as a prophet. •Then, during the 6
celebrations for Herod's birthday, the daughter of Herodias[b] danced before the
company, and so delighted Herod •that he promised on oath to give her anything 7
she asked. •Prompted by her mother she said, 'Give me John the Baptist's head, 8
here, on a dish'. •The king was distressed but, thinking of the oaths he had 9
sworn and of his guests, he ordered it to be given her, •and sent and had John 10
beheaded in the prison. •The head was brought in on a dish and given to the girl 11
who took it to her mother. •John's disciples came and took the body and buried 12
it; then they went off to tell Jesus.

15:32-38p ||Mk 6:31-44 ||Lk 9:10-17 ||Jn 6:1-13

First miracle of the loaves

When Jesus received this news he withdrew by boat to a lonely place where 13
they could be by themselves. But the people heard of this and, leaving the towns,
9:36; 15:32 went after him on foot.[c] •So as he stepped ashore he saw a large crowd; and 14
8:3+ he took pity on them and healed their sick.

When evening came, the disciples went to him and said, 'This is a lonely place, 15
and the time has slipped by; so send the people away, and they can go to the
villages to buy themselves some food'. •Jesus replied, 'There is no need for them 16
to go: give them something to eat yourselves'. •But they answered, 'All we have 17
1 K 19:21 with us is five loaves and two fish'. •'Bring them here to me' he said. •He gave 18 19
orders that the people were to sit down on the grass; then he took the five loaves
Jn 11:41; 17:1 and the two fish, raised his eyes to heaven and said the blessing. And breaking
the loaves he handed them to his disciples who gave them to the crowds.[d] •They 20
all ate as much as they wanted, and they collected the scraps remaining,
16:9 twelve baskets full. •Those who ate numbered about five thousand men, to say 21
nothing of women and children.

||Mk 6:45-52 ||Jn 6:16-21

Jesus walks on the water and, with him, Peter

Directly after this he made the disciples get into the boat and go on ahead 22

23 to the other side while he would send the crowds away. •After sending the crowds
away he went up into the hills by himself to pray. When evening came, he was there Mk 1:35+ Jn 6:15
24 alone, •while the boat, by now far out on the lake,[e] was battling with a heavy *Jn 7:21*
25 sea, for there was a head-wind. •In the fourth watch of the night[f] he went towards
26 them, walking on the lake, •and when the disciples saw him walking on the lake
27 they were terrified. 'It is a ghost' they said, and cried out in fear. •But at once
28 Jesus called out to them, saying, 'Courage! It is I! Do not be afraid.' •It was Peter[g]
who answered. 'Lord,' he said 'if it is you, tell me to come to you across the water.'
29 'Come' said Jesus. Then Peter got out of the boat and started walking towards
30 Jesus across the water, •but as soon as he felt the force of the wind, he took fright
31 and began to sink. 'Lord! Save me!' he cried. •Jesus put out his hand at once and 8:25-26
32 held him. 'Man of little faith,' he said 'why did you doubt?' •And as they got into 8:10+
33 the boat the wind dropped. •The men in the boat bowed down before him and
said, 'Truly, you are the Son of God'. 4:3+; 16:16+

Cures at Gennesaret

||Mk 6:53-56

34 35 Having made the crossing, they came to land at Gennesaret. •When the local
people recognised him they spread the news through the whole neighbourhood
36 and took all that were sick to him, •begging him just to let them touch the fringe 9:20-22
of his cloak. And all those who touched it were completely cured. 8:3+

The traditions of the Pharisees

||Mk 7:1-13

1 2 **15** Pharisees and scribes from Jerusalem then came to Jesus and said, •'Why Rm 14:14 Ga 1:14
do your disciples break away from the tradition of the elders?[a] They do not Col 2:8
3 wash their hands when they eat food.'[b] •'And why do you' he answered 'break Lk 11:38
4 away from the commandment of God for the sake of your tradition? •For God Ex 20:12; 21:17
said: *Do your duty to*[c] *your father and mother* and: *Anyone who curses father or* Lv 20:9 Dt 5:16
5 *mother must be put to death.* •But you say, "If anyone says to his father or mother: Si 3:12
6 Anything I have that I might have used to help you is dedicated to God",[d] •he Pr 20:25
is rid of his duty to father or mother.[e] In this way you have made God's word
7 null and void by means of your tradition. •Hypocrites! It was you Isaiah meant 6:2; 23:13f
when he so rightly prophesied:

8 *This people honours me only with lip-service,* Is 29:13 Ps 78:36f
while their hearts are far from me.
9 *The worship they offer me is worthless;* Col 2:23
the doctrines they teach are only human regulations.'

On clean and unclean[f]

||Mk 7:14-23

10 11 He called the people to him and said, 'Listen, and understand. •What goes

m. Nazareth, where he lived as a child, cf. 2:23.

14 a. Om. (Vulg.) 'Philip'; the omission is due to the difficulty the name seemed to create. But in fact this Philip is not the tetrarch of Ituraea and Trachonitis, Lk 3:1; cf. Mt 16:13; he is another son of Herod the Great by Mariamne II and therefore half-brother of Antipas; Josephus himself calls him Herod. Antipas' fault lay not so much in having married his niece as in having taken her from his brothers who was still living; moreover, he had repudiated his first wife.

b. According to Josephus, the girl's name was Salome.

c. On shore the crowd hurried to the place the boat was making for.

d. This miraculous bread, though not the Holy Eucharist, clearly prefigures and leads up to it. This is the view of the Fathers and indeed of the evangelists before them: cf. v. 19with 26:26, and cf. Jn 6:1-15,51-58.

e. Cf Mk 6:47; var. 'some furlongs from land', cf. Jn 6:19.

f. 3 to 6 a.m.

g. Matthew deliberately punctuates the narrative section of his 'ecclesiastical book' with three episodes featuring Peter: this passage, 16:16-20 and 17:24-27.

15 a. Oral tradition which, to safeguard the observance of the written Law, made many additions to it. According to the rabbis this tradition went back through the 'elders' to Moses himself.

b. Lit. 'eat bread'.

c. Lit. 'Honour', but implying a reverence shown in practical ways.

d. Vulg. interprets 'Every gift I make (to God) is useful to you'.

e. Because property thus made over by vow assumes a sacred character which precludes all claims made by the parents. Such a vow was in fact only a legal fiction involving no sacrifice of ownership; it was no more than a despicable way of escaping the duty of filial piety. Though the rabbis acknowledged its impiety they sustained its validity.

f. The Pharisees had objected to eating with unpurified hands, v. 2, but Jesus passes to the larger question of the legal impurity of certain foods, Lv 11. Legal impurity, he teaches, is secondary to moral which is the only impurity that really matters, Ac 10:9-16,28; Rm 14:14f.

12:34 Ep 4:29 into the mouth does not make a man unclean; it is what comes out of the mouth
1 Tm 4:4 Tt 1:15 that makes him unclean.'
Then the disciples came to him and said, 'Do you know that the Pharisees 12
were shocked when they heard what you said?' •He replied, 'Any plant my 13
23:16,19 ||Lk 6:39 heavenly Father has not planted will be pulled up by the roots. •Leave them 14
Jn 15:2 Ac 5:39 alone. They are blind men leading blind men; and if one blind man leads another,
Jn 9:40 both will fall into a pit.'
At this, Peter said to him, 'Explain the parable for us'. •Jesus replied, 'Do 15 16
Mk 4:13+ even you not yet understand? •Can you not see that whatever goes into the 17
mouth passes through the stomach and is discharged into the sewer? •But the 18
12:34 Tt 1:15 things that come out of the mouth come from the heart, and it is these that make
Jm 3:6 a man unclean. •For from the heart come evil intentions: murder, adultery, 19
fornication, theft, perjury, slander. •These are the things that make a man 20
unclean. But to eat with unwashed hands does not make a man unclean.'

||Mk 7:24-30 **The daughter of the Canaanite woman healed**

Jesus left that place and withdrew to the region of Tyre and Sidon. •Then 21 22
9:27+ out came a Canaanite woman from that district[g] and started shouting, 'Sir, Son
8:29+ of David, take pity on me. My daughter is tormented by a devil.' •But he 23
Lk 11:8 answered her not a word. And his disciples went and pleaded with him. 'Give
her what she wants,'[h] they said 'because she is shouting after us.' •He said in 24
10:6 Rm 15:8 reply, 'I was sent only to the lost sheep of the House of Israel'. •But the woman 25
had come up and was kneeling at his feet. 'Lord,' she said 'help me.' •He replied, 26
'It is not fair to take the children's food and throw it to the house-dogs'.[i] •She 27
retorted, 'Ah yes, sir; but even house-dogs can eat the scraps that fall from their
8:10+ master's table'. •Then Jesus answered her, 'Woman, you have great faith. Let 28
your wish be granted.' And from that moment her daughter was well again.

Cures near the lake

Mk 7:31 Jesus went on from there and reached the shores of the Sea of Galilee, and 29
he went up into the hills. He sat there, •and large crowds came to him bringing 30
the lame, the crippled, the blind, the dumb and many others; these they put
8:3+ *Mk 7:37* down at his feet, and he cured them. •The crowds were astonished to see the 31
dumb speaking, the cripples whole again,[j] the lame walking and the blind with
their sight, and they praised the God of Israel.

14:13-21p ||Mk 8:1-10 **Second miracle of the loaves**

But Jesus called his disciples to him and said, 'I feel sorry for all these people; 32
they have been with me for three days now and have nothing to eat. I do not
want to send them off hungry, they might collapse on the way.' •The 33
disciples said to him, 'Where could we get enough bread in this deserted place
to feed such a crowd?' •Jesus said to them, 'How many loaves have you?' 'Seven' 34
they said 'and a few small fish'. •Then he instructed the crowd to sit down on the 35
ground, •and he took the seven loaves and the fish, and he gave thanks and 36
8:3+ broke them and handed them to the disciples who gave them to the crowds.
They all ate as much as they wanted, and they collected what was left of the 37
16:10 scraps, seven baskets full. •Now four thousand men had eaten, to say nothing 38
of women and children. •And when he had sent the crowds away he got into the 39
boat and went to the district of Magadan.

=12:38-39 ||Mk 8:11-13 ||Lk 11:16,29 *19:3* **The Pharisees ask for a sign from heaven**

16 The Pharisees and Sadducees came, and to test him they asked if he would 1
Jn 6:30-31 show them a sign from heaven. •He replied, 'In the evening you 2
||Lk 12:54-56 say, "It will be fine; there is a red sky", •and in the morning, "Stormy weather 3
today; the sky is red and overcast". You know how to read the face of the sky,
Lk 19:44 but you cannot read the signs of the times.[a] •It is an evil and unfaithful generation 4

that asks for a sign! The only sign it will be given is the sign of Jonah.' And leaving 12:39+ 8:10+
them standing there, he went away.

The yeast of the Pharisees and Sadducees ||Mk 8:14-21 ||Lk 12:1

5 The disciples, having crossed to the other shore, had forgotten to take any food·
6 Jesus said to them, 'Keep your eyes open, and be on your guard against the yeast
7 of the Pharisees and Sadducees'. •And they said to themselves, 'It is because we
8 have not brought any bread'. •Jesus knew it, and he said, 'Men of little faith, 8:10+
9 why are you talking among yourselves about having no bread? •Do you not yet Mk 4:13
understand? Do you not remember the five loaves for the five thousand and the 14:21
10 number of baskets you collected? •Or the seven loaves for the four thousand 15:38
11 and the number of baskets you collected? •How could you fail to understand
that I was not talking about bread? What I said was: Beware of the yeast of the
12 Pharisees and Sadducees.' •Then they understood that he was telling them to be
on their guard, not against the yeast for making bread, but against the teaching
of the Pharisees and Sadducees.[b]

Peter's profession of faith; his pre-eminence ||Mk 8:27-30 ||Lk 9:18-21

13 When Jesus came to the region of Caesarea Philippi he put this question to
14 his disciples, 'Who do people say the Son of Man is?' •And they said, 'Some 8:20+
say he is John the Baptist, some Elijah, and others Jeremiah or one of the 14:2
15 16 prophets'.[c] •'But you,' he said 'who do you say I am?' •Then Simon Peter spoke Jn 6:69
17 up, 'You are the Christ,' he said 'the Son of the living God'.[d] •Jesus replied, 4:3+; 14:33
'Simon son of Jonah, you are a happy man! Because it was not flesh and blood[e] Rm 7:5+ Ep 6:12
18 that revealed this to you but my Father in heaven. •So I now say to you: You Heb 2:14
are Peter[f] and on this rock I will build my Church.[g] And the gates of the under- Is 28:16 Jn 1:42 =*18:18*
19 world[h] can never hold out against it. •I will give you the keys of the kingdom Is 22:22 Lk 22:32 Jn 20:23 Rv 3:7

g. Since the woman has left pagan territory it is in Israel that Jesus grants his favour.

h. Not 'send her away' simply: the Greek verb here means 'let her go with her request granted', as in 18:27; 27:15.

i. Christ must first devote himself to the salvation of the Jews ('children' of God and of the promises) before turning to the pagans who, to the Jewish mind, were 'dogs'. Much of the sting is taken out of the epithet here by the fact that Jesus is using a term blunted by repeated use; moreover, he adopts its diminutive form (little or pet dogs).

j. Om. 'the cripples whole again'.

16 a. Om. 'In the evening. . of the times'. The 'times' are the messianic age; the 'signs' are the miracles worked by Jesus: cf. 11:3-5; 12:28.

b. As leaven ferments the dough, 13:33, but can also make it go bad, cf. 1 Co 5:6; Ga 5:9, so the perverse doctrine of the Jewish leaders threatens to misguide those for whom they are responsible, cf. 15:14.

c. Jesus claimed the title 'prophet' for himself only indirectly and obscurely, Mt 13:57p; Lk 13:33, but the public openly hailed him as such, Mt 16:14p; 21:11,46; Mk 6:15p; Lk 7:16,39; 24:19; Jn 4:19; 9:17. The title had messianic significance because the Jews confidently expected a revival of the spirit of prophecy (extinct since Malachi) as a sign of the messianic era. It was to revive either in the person of Elijah, Mt 17:10-11p, or in the form of a general outpouring of the Spirit, Ac 2:17-18,33. Many (false) prophets did actually arise in Christ's time, Mt 24:11,24p, etc. John the Baptist was himself a prophet, Mt 11:9p; 14:5; 21:26p; Lk 1:76 precisely because he was the Precursor who had come 'in the spirit of Elijah', Mt 11:10p,14; 17:12p. Nevertheless he denied (Jn 1:21+) that he was 'the prophet' foretold by Moses, Dt 18:15. This prophet, the early Christians believed, was Jesus and no other, Ac 3:22-26; Jn 6:14; 7:40. From Pentecost onwards, however, prophecy became a familiar charismatic phenomenon in the early Church Ac 11:27+; for this reason the title prophet as applied to Christ soon dropped out and was replaced by others more suited to his unique function and person.

d. In Mt Peter acknowledges not only that Jesus is the Messiah but also that he is Son of God; this second title is not found in Mk and Lk. Cf. also 14:33 with Mk 6:51f. Cf. Mt 4:3+.

e. The expression indicates man, emphasising his material limited nature as opposed to that of the spirit world, Si 14:18; Rm 7:5+; 1 Co 15:50; Ga 1:16; Ep 6:12; Heb 2:14; cf. Jn 1:13.

f. Neither the Greek word *petros* nor even as it seems, its Aramaic equivalent *kepha* ('rock') was used as a person's name before Jesus conferred it on the apostles' leader to symbolise the part he was to play in the foundation of the Church. This change of name had possibly been made earlier, cf. Jn 1:42; Mk 3:16; Lk 6:14.

g. The Hebr. *qahal* which the Greek renders *ekklesia* means 'an assembly called together'; it is used frequently in the O.T. to indicate the community of the Chosen People, especially the community of the desert period, cf. Ac 7:38. Certain Jewish groups (among them the Essenes of Qumran) regarded themselves as the chosen remnant of Israel (Is 4:3+) which was to survive in 'the latter days'. These had also used the term that Jews now adopts to indicate the messianic community, the community of the 'new alliance' sealed with his blood, Mt 26:28+; Ep 5:25. By using the term 'assembly' side by side with that of 'kingdom of heaven', Mt 4:17+ Jesus shows that this eschatological community (community of the 'end-times') is to have its beginnings here on earth in the form of an organised society whose leader he now appoints. Cf. Ac 5:11+; 1 Co 1:2+.

h. Greek: *Hades*; Hebrew: *Sheol*, the dwelling place of the dead, cf. Nb 16:33+. Here its personified 'gates' suggest the powers of evil which first lead man into that death which is sin and then imprison him once for all in eternal death. The Church's task will be to rescue the elect from death's dominion from the death of the body and above all from eternal death, so that

of heaven: whatever you bind on earth shall be considered bound in heaven;
whatever you loose on earth shall be considered loosed in heaven.'[i] •Then he 20
Mk 1:34+ gave the disciples strict orders not to tell anyone that he was the Christ.[j]

||Mk 8:31-33 ||Lk 9:22

First prophecy of the Passion

17:12,22-23; 20:17-19 From that time[k] Jesus began to make it clear to his disciples that he was 21
Lk 2:38+; 13:33 destined to go to Jerusalem and suffer grievously at the hands of the elders and
Ac 10:40+ chief priests and scribes, to be put to death and to be raised up on the third day.
Then, taking him aside, Peter started to remonstrate with him. 'Heaven preserve 22
you, Lord;' he said 'this must not happen to you'. •But he turned and said to 23
4:10 Peter, 'Get behind me, Satan! You are an obstacle[l] in my path, because the way
Mk 4:13+ you think is not God's way but man's.'

||Mk 8:34–9:1 ||Lk 9:23-27

The condition of following Christ

Then Jesus said to his disciples, 'If anyone wants to be a follower of mine, 24
=10:38-39 let him renounce himself and take up his cross and follow me. •For anyone who 25
||Lk 14:27; 17:33 ||Jn 12:25-26 wants to save his life will lose it; but anyone who loses his life for my sake will
find it.[m] •What, then, will a man gain if he wins the whole world and ruins his 26
life? Or what has a man to offer in exchange for his life?

25:31f 'For the Son of Man is going to come in the glory of his Father with his 27
Jb 34:11 Ps 62:12 angels, and, when he does, he will reward each one according to his behaviour.[n]
Jr 17:10 Zc 14:5 I tell you solemnly, there are some of these standing here who will not taste 28
2 Th 1:7 10:23; 24:30, 34; 26:64 death before they see the Son of Man coming with his kingdom.'[o]

||Mk 9:2-8 ||Lk 9:28-36 2 P 1:16-18

The transfiguration

17 Six days later, Jesus took with him Peter and James and his brother John 1
and led them up a high mountain[a] where they could be alone. •There in 2
their presence he was transfigured: his face shone like the sun and his clothes
28:3 became as white as the light.[b] •Suddenly Moses and Elijah[c] appeared to them; 3
they were talking with him. •Then Peter spoke to Jesus. 'Lord,' he said 'it is 4
wonderful for us to be here;[d] if you wish, I will make[e] three tents here, one for
24:30+ Ex 13:12+; you, one for Moses and one for Elijah.' •He was still speaking when suddenly 5
19:16+ 2 P 1:17 a bright cloud covered them with shadow, and from the cloud there came a voice
which said, 'This is my Son, the Beloved; he enjoys my favour. Listen to him.'
3:17 When they heard this, the disciples fell on their faces, overcome with fear. •But 6 7
Jesus came up and touched them. 'Stand up,' he said 'do not be afraid.' •And 8
when they raised their eyes they saw no one but only Jesus.

||Mk 9:9-13

The question about Elijah

Mk 1:34+ As they came down from the mountain Jesus gave them this order, 'Tell 9
8:20+ no one about the vision until the Son of Man has risen from the dead'. •And the 10
16:14+ Si 48:10 disciples put this question to him, 'Why do the scribes say then that Elijah has
Mi 3:23-24 Lk 1:17 to come first?'[f] •'True;' he replied 'Elijah is to come to see that everything is 11
once more as it should be; •however, I tell you that Elijah has come already and 12
16:21; 17:22-23; 20: they did not recognise him but treated him as they pleased; and the Son of Man
17-19 will suffer similarly at their hands.' •The disciples understood then that he had 13
11:10-14 been speaking of John the Baptist.

||Mk 9:14-29 ||Lk 9:37-43

The epileptic demoniac

As they were rejoining the crowd a man came up to him and went down on 14
his knees before him. •'Lord,' he said 'take pity on my son: he is a lunatic and 15
in a wretched state; he is always falling into the fire or into the water. •I took 16
him to your disciples and they were unable to cure him.' •'Faithless and perverse 17
Ac 2:40 generation!' Jesus said in reply 'How much longer must I be with you? How much
longer must I put up with you? Bring him here to me.' •And when Jesus rebuked 18
8:29+ it the devil came out of the boy who was cured from that moment.

19 Then the disciples came privately to Jesus. 'Why were we unable to cast it
20 out?' they asked. •He answered, 'Because you have little faith.[g] I tell you 8:10+
solemnly, if your faith were the size of a mustard seed you could say to this ||Mk11:22-23 ||Lk 17:6
mountain, "Move from here to there", and it would move; nothing would be =21:22
impossible for you.'[h] 1 Co 13:2

Second prophecy of the Passion

||Mk 9:30-32 ||Lk 9:44-45

22 One day when they were together in Galilee, Jesus said to them, 'The Son 8:20+
23 of Man is going to be handed over into the power of men; •they will put him to 16:21; 17:12; 20:17-19
death, and on the third day he will be raised to life again'. And a great sadness Ac 10:40+
came over them.

The Temple tax paid by Jesus and Peter

24 When they reached Capernaum, the collectors of the half-shekel[i] came to Ex 30:15
25 Peter and said, 'Does your master not pay the half-shekel?' •'Oh yes' he replied,
and went into the house. But before he could speak, Jesus said, 'Simon, what is
your opinion? From whom do the kings of the earth take toll or tribute? From
26 their sons[j] or from foreigners?' •And when he replied, 'From foreigners', Jesus
27 said, 'Well then, the sons are exempt. •However, so as not to offend these
people, go to the lake and cast a hook; take the first fish that bites, open its
mouth and there you will find a shekel; take it and give it to them for me and
for you.'

it may lead them into the kingdom of heaven, cf. Col 1:13; 1 Co 15:26; Rv 6:8; 20:13. In this the Church follows its Master who died, descended into the underworld, cf. 1 P 3:19+, and rose again, Ac 2:27,31.

i. The City of God, like the City of Death, has its gates too; they grant entrance only to those who are worthy of it. Peter has the keys. It is his function, therefore, to open or close to all who would come to the kingdom of heaven through the Church. 'bind' and 'loose' are technical rabbinic terms; primarily they have a disciplinary reference; one is 'bound' (condemned to) or 'loosed' (absolved from) excommunication. Their secondary usage is connected with doctrinal or juridical decisions: an opinion is 'bound' (forbidden) or 'loosed' (allowed). Of the household of God Peter is controller (the keys symbolise this, cf. Is 22:22). In that capacity he is to exercise the disciplinary power of admitting or excluding those he thinks fit; he will also, in his administration of the community, make necessary decisions in questions of doctrinal belief and of moral conduct. The verdicts he delivers and the pronouncements he makes will be ratified by God in heaven. Catholic exegetes maintain that these enduring promises hold good not only for Peter himself but also for Peter's successors. This inference, not explicitly drawn in the text, is considered legitimate because Jesus plainly intends to provide for his Church's future by establishing a régime that will not collapse with Peter's death. Two other texts, Lk 22:31f and Jn 21:15f, on Peter's primacy emphasise that its operation is to be in the domain of faith; they also indicate that this makes him head not only of the Church after the death of Christ but of the apostolic group then and there.

j. Vulg. 'Jesus Christ'.

k. Jesus has just elicited from his disciples the first explicit profession of faith in him as Messiah. At this crucial moment he tells them for the first time of his coming Passion: he is not only the glorious Messiah, he is also the suffering servant. Within the next few days this teaching method will be pursued in a similar situation: the glorious transfiguration will be followed by an injunction to silence and a prediction of Passion, 17:1-12. It is Christ's way of bracing the disciples' faith for the approaching crisis of death and resurrection.

l. By blocking the Messiah's appointed way, Peter becomes an 'obstacle' (primary sense of the Greek *skandalon*) to Christ and becomes, though unwittingly, the tool of Satan, cf. 4:1-10.

m. Paradox. This dictum and those immediately following oscillate between two senses of human 'life': its present stage and its future. The Greek *psyche*, here equivalent to the Hebr. *nephesh* contains all three senses of 'life', 'soul', 'person'.

n. 'his behaviour': var. 'his works'.

o. In vv. 27-28 two sayings of Christ, each dealing with a different event, have been grouped together because they have a common reference to the coming of the kingdom of God: v. 27 refers to the Last Judgement which inaugurates the kingdom of the Father; v. 28 refers to the destruction of Jerusalem which demonstrates the presence of the kingdom of Christ cf. 24:1+.

17 a. Tabor, according to the traditional opinion. Some favour Great Hermon.

b. Var. 'as snow' cf. 28:3.

c. Respectively representing Law and prophets, they do homage to the founder of the 'new alliance', cf. 5:17; Lk 22:20. As once they were privileged at Sinai with God's revelation, Ex 33:20+; cf. 1 K 19: 9-13, so now they are made witnesses of the anticipated revelation of the Son of Man, cf. 24:30.

d. An alternative translation 'It is a good thing for us to be here'

e. Vulg. 'let us make', cf. Mk and Lk.

f. The disciples know that the Messiah has already come 16:16, and have seen him in his glory 17:1-7; they are therefore surprised that Elijah has not played the part of Precursor assigned to him by Malachi. Jesus replies that Elijah has in fact performed that function, though unrecognised, in the humble person of the Baptist.

g. Var. 'no faith'.

h. Add. v. 21 'As for this kind (of devil), it is cast out only by prayer and fasting', cf. Mk 9:29

i. A yearly tax levied on individuals for the upkeep of the Temple.

j. I.e. 'their subjects', cf. 13:38. Christ makes a pun on this semitic metaphorical use of 'son' in order to indicate himself who is the Son, cf. 3:17; 17:5 and 10:32f; 11:25-27, etc., together with his disciples who are his brothers, 12:50, and sons of the same Father, 5:45, etc. Cf. Mt 4:3+.

B. THE DISCOURSE ON THE CHURCH

||Mk 9:33-36 ||Lk 9:46-47 **Who is the greatest?**

18 At this time the disciples came to Jesus and said, 'Who is the greatest in 1
the kingdom of heaven?' •So he called a little child to him and set the child 2
19:14 Ps 131:2 in front of them. •Then he said, 'I tell you solemnly, unless you change and become 3
||Mk 10:15 ||Lk 18:17 like little children you will never enter the kingdom of heaven. •And so, the 4
=n 3:5 *23 12* one who makes himself as little as this little child is the greatest in the kingdom
of heaven.

=10:40 ||Mk 9:37 ||Lk 9:48 *25:40* **On leading others astray**

'Anyone who welcomes a little child like this[a] in my name welcomes me. 5
||Mk 9:42 ||Lk 17:1-2 But anyone who is an obstacle to bring down one of these little ones who have 6
faith in me would be better drowned in the depths of the sea with a great
millstone round his neck. •Alas for the world that there should be such obstacles! 7
Obstacles indeed there must be, but alas for the man who provides them!
=5:29-30 ||Mk 9:43-47 'If your hand or your foot should cause[b] you to sin, cut it off and throw it 8
away: it is better for you to enter into life[c] crippled or lame, than to have two
hands or two feet and be thrown into eternal fire. •And if your eye should cause 9
Lk 12:5 you to sin, tear it out and throw it away: it is better for you to enter into life with
one eye, than to have two eyes and be thrown into the hell of fire.[d]
'See that you never despise any of these little ones, for I tell you that their 10
Heb 1:14 angels in heaven are continually in the presence of[e] my Father in heaven.[f]

Ezk 34:1+ ||Lk 15:3-7 **The lost sheep**

'Tell me. Suppose a man has a hundred sheep and one of them strays; will 12
Ezk 34:4,16 he not leave the ninety-nine on the hillside and go in search of the stray? •I tell 13
you solemnly, if he finds it, it gives him more joy than do the ninety-nine that did
not stray at all. •Similarly, it is never the will of your Father in heaven that 14
one of these little ones should be lost.

||Lk 17:3 **Brotherly correction**

Lv 19:17 Ga 6:1 Tt 3:10 'If your brother does something wrong,[g] go and have it out with him alone, 15
between your two selves. If he listens to you, you have won back your brother.
Dt 19:15 2 Co 13:1 1 Tm 5:19-20 If he does not listen, take one or two others along with you: *the evidence of two* 16
or three witnesses is required to sustain any charge. •But if he refuses to listen to 17
Rm 16:17 1 Co 5:11 these, report it to the community;[h] and if he refuses to listen to the community,
treat him like a pagan or a tax collector.[i]
16:19+ Jn 20:23 'I tell you solemnly, whatever you bind on earth shall be considered bound in 18
heaven; whatever you loose on earth shall be considered loosed in heaven.[j]

Prayer in common

7:7-8 Jn 15:7,16 'I tell you solemnly once again, if two of you on earth agree to ask anything 19
at all, it will be granted to you by my Father in heaven. •For where two or three 20
28:20 1 Co 5:4 meet in my name, I shall be there with them.'

6:12 Si 10:6 ||Lk 17:4 **Forgiveness of injuries**

Col 3:12 Then Peter went up to him and said, 'Lord, how often must I forgive my 21
Gn 4:24 brother if he wrongs me? As often as seven times?' •Jesus answered, 'Not seven, 22
I tell you, but seventy-seven times.[k]

Si 28:4 **Parable of the unforgiving debtor**

25:19 'And so the kingdom of heaven may be compared to a king who decided 23
to settle his accounts with his servants. •When the reckoning began, they 24
brought him a man who owed ten thousand talents;[l] •but he had no means of 25

paying, so his master gave orders that he should be sold, together with his wife
26 and children and all his possessions, to meet the debt. •At this, the servant threw
himself down at his master's feet. "Give me time" he said "and I will pay the
27 whole sum." •And the servant's master felt so sorry for him that he let him go
28 and cancelled the debt. •Now as this servant went out, he happened to meet a fellow
servant who owed him one hundred denarii;[m] and he seized him by the throat
29 and began to throttle him. "Pay what you owe me" he said. •His fellow servant
fell at his feet and implored him, saying, "Give me time and I will pay you".
30 But the other would not agree; on the contrary, he had him thrown into prison
31 till he should pay the debt. •His fellow servants were deeply distressed when
they saw what had happened, and they went to their master and reported the
32 whole affair to him. •Then the master sent for him. "You wicked servant," he
33 said "I cancelled all that debt of yours when you appealed to me. •Were you not
bound, then, to have pity on your fellow servant just as I had pity on you?" 1 Jn 4:11
34 And in his anger the master handed him over to the torturers till he should pay
35 all his debt. •And that is how my heavenly Father will deal with you unless you 6:12 Jm 2:13
each forgive your brother from your heart.'

VI. THE APPROACHING ADVENT OF THE KINGDOM OF HEAVEN

A. NARRATIVE SECTION

The question about divorce Mk 10:1-12

1 **19** Jesus had now finished what he wanted to say, and he left Galilee and Lk 9:51 Jn 10:40
2 came into the part of Judaea which is on the far side of the Jordan. •Large
crowds followed him and he healed them there.
3 Some Pharisees approached him, and to test him they said, 'Is it against the 16:1 Lk 11:54
4 Law for a man to divorce his wife on any pretext whatever?' •He answered, 'Have Jn 8:6
5 you not read that the creator from the beginning *made them male and female* •and Gn 1:27
that he said: *This is why a man must leave father and mother, and cling to his wife,* Gn 2:24 Ep 5:31
6 *and the two become one body?* •They are no longer two, therefore, but one body. 1 Co 6:16; 7:10
So then, what God has united, man must not divide.'[a]
7 They said to him, 'Then why did Moses command that a writ of dismissal Dt 24:1
8 should be given in cases of divorce?' •'It was because you were so unteachable'
he said 'that Moses allowed you to divorce your wives, but it was not like this
9 from the beginning. •Now I say this to you: the man who divorces his wife— =5:32 ||Lk 16:18
I am not speaking of fornication[b]—and marries another, is guilty of adultery.'

18 a. That is to say, one who through the virtue of simplicity becomes a child again, cf. v. 4.

b. Lit. 'a scandal' in the primary sense of the Greek word (something to trip over, cf. 16:23+) not in the common English sense of the word. Vv. 8-9 (already cited in 5:29-30) have been inserted into this passage at the expense of the context and solely because the word 'scandal' (seduction of others) in vv. 6-7 has suggested another dictum on 'scandal' (in the sense of obstacles within oneself).

c. Eternal life.

d. Hebr. Gehinnom, a valley in Jerusalem once polluted by infant sacrifice, Lv 18:21+. Later the name was used for the place of damnation and punishment of the wicked—what we call 'hell'.

e. Lit. 'always gaze on the face' a biblical phrase meaning that the courtier is in the king's presence, cf. 2 S 14:24; 2 K 25:19; Tb 12:15.

f. Add. v. 11 'For the Son of Man has come to save what was lost', cf. Lk 19:10.

g. Many authorities add the specifying phrase 'to you', but it is probably to be omitted. The fault in question is grave and notorious; it has not necessarily been committed against the one whose duty it is to correct it. In v. 21 the case is different.

h. The *ekklesia*, i.e. the *qahal* or gathering of the brethren.

i. I.e. 'outcast', 'excommunicate'.

j. One of the powers conferred on Peter is here conferred on the Church's ministers, to whom this discourse is primarily addressed.

k. Others render 'seventy-times-seven times', cf. 6:9+.

l. About £3,000,000, $9,000,000: the amount is deliberately fantstic.

m. Less than £5, $15.

19 a. Uncomprising assertion of the indissolubility of marriage.

b. This exceptive clause (Mt only) does not mean that Jesus allows full divorce (i.e. with power to remarry) in cases of adultery. If this were so, he would be supporting the very concession he is criticising Attempts have been made to understand 'fornication'

Continence

The disciples said to him, 'If that is how things are between husband and wife, 10
it is not advisable to marry'. •But he replied, 'It is not everyone who can accept 11
what I have said, but only those to whom it is granted. •There are eunuchs born 12
that way from their mother's womb, there are eunuchs made so by men and
1 Co 7:1, 7-8,32-34 there are eunuchs who have made themselves that way for the sake of the kingdom
of heaven. Let anyone accept this who can.'[c]

||Mk 10:13-16 ||Lk 18:15-17
Jesus and the children

Lk 9:47 People brought little children to him, for him to lay his hands on them and 13
1 Tm 4:14+ say a prayer. The disciples turned them away, •but Jesus said, 'Let the little 14
18:3-4 *1 P 2:1-2* children alone, and do not stop them coming to me; for it is to such as these that
the kingdom of heaven belongs'. •Then he laid his hands on them and went on 15
his way.

||Mk 10:17-22 |Lk 18:18-23
The rich young man

And there was a man who came to him and asked, 'Master,[d] what good deed 16
Lk 10:25-28 must I do to possess eternal life?' •Jesus said to him, 'Why do you ask me about 17
what is good? There is one alone who is good.[e] But if you wish to enter into
Ex 20:12-16 Dt 5:16-20 life, keep the commandments.' •He said, 'Which?' 'These:' Jesus replied '*You* 18
must not kill. You must not commit adultery. You must not bring false witness.
Jn 13:34 *Honour your father and mother*, and: *you must love your neighbour as yourself.*' 19
The young man said to him, 'I have kept all these.[f] What more do I need to do?' 20
5:3+ Si 29:8-13 *6:19-21*; 13:44-46 Jesus said, 'If you wish to be perfect, go and sell what you own and give the 21
money to the poor, and you will have treasure in heaven; then come, follow
me'. •But when the young man heard these words he went away sad, for he was 22
a man of great wealth.

||Mk 10:23-27 ||Lk 18:24-27
The danger of riches

Then Jesus said to his disciples, 'I tell you solemnly, it will be hard for a 23
7:14 rich man to enter the kingdom of heaven. •Yes, I tell you again, it is easier 24
1 Co 1:26 for a camel to pass through the eye of a needle than for a rich man to enter the
kingdom of heaven.' •When the disciples heard this they were astonished. 25
'Who can be saved, then?' they said. •Jesus gazed at them. 'For men' he told 26
Gn 18:14 Lk 1:37 them 'this is impossible; for God everything is possible.'

||Mk 10:28-31 ||Lk 18:28-30
The reward of renunciation

4:20,22 Then Peter spoke. 'What about us?' he said to him 'We have left everything 27
and followed you. What are we to have, then?' •Jesus said to him, 'I tell you 28
Dn 7:22 ||Lk 22:30 solemnly, when all is made new[g] and the Son of Man sits on his throne of glory,
1 Co 6:2 Rv 3:21; 20:4 you will yourselves sit on twelve thrones to judge[h] the twelve tribes of Israel.
Lk 14:26 *5:3+* And everyone who has left houses, brothers, sisters, father, mother, children[i] 29
or land for the sake of my name will be repaid a hundred times over, and also
inherit eternal life.
20:16 ||Lk 13:30 'Many who are first will be last, and the last, first. 30

Parable of the vineyard labourers[a]

20 'Now the kingdom of heaven is like a landowner going out at daybreak 1
to hire workers for his vineyard. •He made an agreement with the workers 2
for one denarius a day, and sent them to his vineyard. •Going out at about the 3
third hour he saw others standing idle in the market place •and said to them, 4
"You go to my vineyard too and I will give you a fair wage". •So they went. At 5
about the sixth hour and again at about the ninth hour, he went out and did the
same. •Then at about the eleventh hour he went out and found more men standing 6
round, and he said to them, "Why have you been standing here idle all day?"
"Because no one has hired us" they answered. He said to them, "You go into 7

8 my vineyard too". •In the evening, the owner of the vineyard said to his bailiff, Lv 19:13 Dt 24:14-15
"Call the workers and pay them their wages, starting with the last arrivals and
9 ending with the first". •So those who were hired at about the eleventh hour came
10 forward and received one denarius each. •When the first came, they expected to
11 get more, but they too received one denarius each. •They took it, but grumbled
12 at the landowner. •"The men who came last" they said "have done only one hour,
and you have treated them the same as us, though we have done a heavy day's
13 work in all the heat." •He answered one of them and said, "My friend, I am
14 not being unjust to you; did we not agree on one denarius? •Take your earnings
15 and go. I choose to pay the last-comer as much as I pay you. •Have I no right
16 to do what I like with my own? Why be envious because I am generous?" •Thus Rm 9:19-21
the last will be first, and the first, last.'[b] 19:30 ||Lk 13:30

Third prophecy of the Passion ||Mk 10:32-34 ||Lk 18:31-33

17 Jesus was going up to Jerusalem, and on the way he took the Twelve to one
18 side and said to them, •'Now we are going up to Jerusalem, and the Son of Man 16:21; 17:12 22-23
is about to be handed over to the chief priests and scribes. They will condemn
19 him to death •and will hand him over to the pagans to be mocked and scourged
and crucified; and on the third day he will rise again.' Ac 10:40+

The mother of Zebedee's sons makes her request ||Mk10:35-40

20 Then the mother of Zebedee's sons came with her sons to make a request of
21 him, and bowed low; •and he said to her, 'What is it you want?' She said to
him, 'Promise that these two sons of mine may sit one at your right hand and the 19:28
22 other at your left in your kingdom'.[c] •'You do not know what you are asking' Mk 4:13+
Jesus answered. 'Can you drink the cup[d] that I am going to drink?' They replied, 26:39 Jn 18:11
23 'We can'. •'Very well,' he said 'you shall drink my cup,[e] but as for seats at Ac 12:2
my right hand and my left, these are not mine to grant; they belong to those to
whom they have been allotted by my Father.'[f]

Leadership with service

24 When the other ten heard this they were indignant with the two brothers. ||Mk 10:41-45
25 But Jesus called them to him and said, 'You know that among the pagans the
26 rulers lord it over them, and their great men make their authority felt. •This is ||Lk 22:25-27
not to happen among you. No; anyone who wants to be great among you must Si 3:18
27 be your servant, •and anyone who wants to be first among you must be your Mk 9:35 Jn 13:4-15
28 slave, •just as the Son of Man came not to be served but to serve, and to give his *8:20+*
life as a ransom[g] for many.'[h] 26:28 Rm 5:6-21 1 Tm 2:6

in the sense of an illegitimate union, concubinage, but the severance of such a union is so obvious an obligation as not to deserve mention. The explanation seems rather to be that this text of Mt creates a special category for cases of infidelity in marriage since these require their own solution—but nowhere does he suggest what the solution is. This solution, which was not required at the time when full divorce was allowed, was destined to take shape in the Church and emerge as a 'separation' of the parties that carried with it no permission to remarry, cf. 1 Co 7:11.

c. Christ invites to perpetual continence those who would consecrate themselves entirely to the kingdom of God.

d Var. 'Good Master', cf. Mk and Lk.

e. I.e. God (explicit in Mk and Lk and Vulg. Mt). Another reading, borrowed from Mk and Lk, is 'Why do you call me good? None is good but God alone'.

f Add. 'from my earliest days', cf. Mk and Lk.

g. The reference is to the messianic 'renewal of all things' which is to be revealed when the world ends but which, on the spiritual plane, will already have begun when Christ rises from the dead as *Kyrios* in the Church.

h. In the biblical sense of 'govern'. The 'twelve tribes' stand for the new Israel, the Church.

i. Add. 'wife'.

20 a. The owner of the vineyard goes on into the evening hiring workmen and yet gives all a full day's pay. He is generous to some without being unjust to the others. So God acts. Into his kingdom he brings late-comers—sinners and pagans. Those who were called first (the Jewish people who, from Abraham's time, had been privileged with the covenant) have no right to be offended.

b. Add. 'For many are called, but few are chosen', probably borrowed from 22:14.

c. The apostles expect Christ's kingdom to be manifested very shortly and in all its glory, but this is reserved for Christ's second coming, cf. Mt 4:17+; Ac 1:6+.

d. Biblical metaphor, cf. Is 51:17+ here referring to the approaching Passion.

e. James son of Zebedee was put to death by Herod Agrippa about the year 44, Ac 12:2. His brother John may not indeed have suffered martyrdom but he had no less a share in his Master's sufferings.

f. Christ's mission on earth is not to apportion men's rewards but to suffer for man's salvation, cf. Jn 3:17; 12:47.

g. By sin man incurs, as a debt to the divine justice, the punishment of death demanded by the Law, cf. 1 Co

||Mk 10:46-52 ||Lk 18:35-43

The two blind men of Jericho

9:27 As they left Jericho a large crowd followed him. •Now there were two blind 29 30
men sitting at the side of the road. When they heard that it was Jesus who was
passing by, they shouted, 'Lord! Have pity on us, Son of David.' •And the crowd 31
scolded them and told them to keep quiet, but they only shouted more loudly,
'Lord! Have pity on us, Son of David.' •Jesus stopped, called them over and 32
said, 'What do you want me to do for you?' •They said to him, 'Lord, let us 33
8:3+ have our sight back'. •Jesus felt pity for them and touched their eyes, and immed- 34
iately their sight returned and they followed him.

||Mk 11:1-11 ||Lk 19:28-38 ||Jn 12:12-16

The Messiah enters Jerusalem

21 When they were near Jerusalem and had come in sight of Bethphage on the 1
Mount of Olives, Jesus sent two disciples, •saying to them, 'Go to the village 2
facing you, and you will immediately find a tethered donkey and a colt with her.
Untie them and bring them to me. •If anyone says anything to you, you are to 3
say, "The Master needs them and will send them back directly".' •This took place 4
to fulfil the prophecy:

Is 62:11 Zc 9:9 *Say to the daughter of Zion:* 5
Look, your king comes to you;
11:29 Gn 49:11 *he is humble, he rides on a donkey*
and on a colt, the foal of a beast of burden.[a]

So the disciples went out and did as Jesus had told them. •They brought 6 7
1 K 1:33 the donkey and the colt, then they laid their cloaks on their backs and he sat on
2 K 9:13 them. •Great crowds of people spread their cloaks on the road, while others 8
were cutting branches from the trees and spreading them in his path. •The crowds 9
who went in front of him and those who followed were all shouting:

9:27+ '*Hosanna*[b] to the Son of David!
Ps 118:26 Ac 2:33+ *Blessings on him who comes in the name of the Lord!*
Hosanna in the highest heavens!'

And when he entered Jerusalem, the whole city was in turmoil. 'Who is this?' 10
16:14+ people asked, •and the crowds answered, 'This is the prophet Jesus from Nazareth 11
in Galilee'.

||Mk 11:11.15-17 ||Lk 19:45-46 ||Jn 2:14-16

The expulsion of the dealers from the Temple

Ne 13:8 Jesus then went into the Temple and drove out all those who were selling and 12
buying there; he upset the tables of the money changers and the chairs of those
Is 56:7 who were selling pigeons.[c] •'According to scripture' he said '*my house will be called* 13
Jr 7:11 *a house of prayer;* but you are turning it into a *robbers' den.*' •There were also blind 14
2 S 5:8 LXX and lame people who came to him in the Temple, and he cured them. •At the sight 15
of the wonderful things he did and of the children shouting, 'Hosanna to the
Jn 12:19 Son of David' in the Temple, the chief priests and the scribes were indignant. •'Do 16
you hear what they are saying?' they said to him. 'Yes,' Jesus answered 'have you
never read this:

Ps 8:2 LXX Ws 10:21 *By the mouths of children, babes in arms,*
you have made sure of praise?'

Lk 21:37 With that he left them and went out of the city to Bethany where he spent the 17
night.

||Mk 11:12-14,20-24

The barren fig tree withers. Faith and prayer

Is 5:1 Jr 8:13 As he was returning to the city in the early morning, he felt hungry. •Seeing 18 19
Lk 13:6-9 *8:3+* a fig tree by the road, he went up to it and found nothing on it but leaves.
And he said to it, 'May you never bear fruit again'; and at that instant the fig tree
Ho 9:16 withered.[d] •The disciples were amazed when they saw it. 'What happened to the 20

21 tree' they said 'that it withered there and then?' •Jesus answered, 'I tell you
solemnly, if you have faith and do not doubt at all, not only will you do what 8:10+; =17:20
I have done to the fig tree, but even if you say to this mountain, "Get up and throw ‖Lk 17:6 Jn 14:12
22 yourself into the sea", it will be done. •And if you have faith, everything you ask Jm 1:6 *7:7-11*
for in prayer you will receive.'

The authority of Jesus is questioned ‖Mk 11:27-33 ‖Lk 20:1-8

23 He had gone into the Temple and was teaching, when the chief priests and the
elders of the people came to him and said, 'What authority have you for acting 28:18 Jn 2:18
24 like this?[e] And who gave you this authority?' •'And I' replied Jesus 'will ask you
a question, only one; if you tell me the answer to it, I will then tell you my
25 authority for acting like this. •John's baptism: where did it come from: heaven 3:6 Jn 3:27
or man?' And they argued it out this way among themselves, 'If we say from
26 heaven, he will retort, "Then why did you refuse to believe him?"; •but if we say 21:32
from man, we have the people to fear, for they all hold that John was a prophet'. 14:5; 16:14+
27 So their reply to Jesus was, 'We do not know'. And he retorted, 'Nor will I tell
you my authority for acting like this.

Parable of the two sons

28 'What is your opinion? A man had two sons. He went and said to the first, Si 3:8
29 "My boy, you go and work in the vineyard today". •He answered, "I will not go",
30 but afterwards thought better of it and went. •The man then went and said the
31 same thing to the second who answered, "Certainly, sir", but did not go. •Which
of the two did the father's will?' 'The first' they said. Jesus said to them, 'I tell
you solemnly, tax collectors and prostitutes are making their way into ‖Lk 7:29-30; 18:9-14
32 the kingdom of God before you. •For John came to you, a pattern of true
righteousness,[f] but you did not believe him, and yet the tax collectors and 3:6; 8:10+ Lk 7:37-50; 19:1-10
prostitutes did. Even after seeing that, you refused to think better of it and
believe in him.

Parable of the wicked husbandmen[g] ‖Mk 12:1-12 ‖Lk 20:9-19 Jn 8:37

33 'Listen to another parable. There was a man, a landowner, who planted
a vineyard; he fenced it round, dug a winepress in it and built a tower; then he Is 5:1-7+
34 leased it to tenants and went abroad. •When vintage time drew near he sent his
35 servants to the tenants to collect his produce. •But the tenants seized his servants, 22:3
36 thrashed one, killed another and stoned a third. •Next he sent some more servants, 22:6
37 this time a larger number, and they dealt with them in the same way. •Finally

15:56; 2 Co 3:7,9; Ga 3:13; Rm 8:3-4, with notes. To ransom them from this slavery of sin and death, Rm 3:24+. Christ is to pay the ransom and discharge the debt with the price of his blood, 1 Co 6:20; 7:23; Ga 3:13; 4:5, with notes. By thus dying in place of the guilty, he fulfils the prophesied function of the 'servant of Yahweh' (Is 53). The Hebr. word translated 'many', Is 53:11f, contrasts the enormous crowd of the redeemed with the one Redeemer: it does not imply that the number of redeemed is limited, Rm 5:6-21. Cf. Mt 26:28+.

b. At this point some authorities insert the following passage, derived probably from some apocryphal gospel 'But as for you, from littleness you seek to grow great and from greatness you make yourselves small. When you are invited to a banquet do not take one of the places of honour, because someone more important than you may arrive and then the steward will have to say, "Move down lower", and you would be covered with confusion. Take the lowest place, and then if someone less important than you comes in, the steward will say to you, "Move up higher", and that will be to your advantage.' Cf. Lk 14:8-10.

21 a. In thus describing the messianic king's humble mount the prophet had in mind the unpretentious, unwarlike nature of his rule. Jesus, by performing this action, deliberately took to himself both the words of the prophecy and their deeper meaning.

b. A word of Hebr. origin; its first meaning is 'Pray, save' but it became a mere shout of acclaim.

c. They provided pilgrims with the coinage and sacrificial victims necessary for oblations: a practice which, however legitimate, lends itself to abuse.

d. 'It was not the season for figs', Mk says. But Jesus wished to perform a symbolic action, cf. Jr 18:1+, in which the fig tree represents Israel punished for its fruitlessness.

e. The unusual events that Jesus has just allowed to take place in the very precincts of the Temple: the messianic ovation, expulsion of the merchants, miraculous cures.

f. Lit. 'in the way of righteousness'. Biblical expression: John practised and preached that conformity with the divine will which makes a man 'righteous'.

g. More exactly an 'allegory' because every detail of the story has its own significance: the proprietor is God; the vineyard the Chosen People, Israel, cf. Is 5:1+; the servants the prophets; the son Jesus, put to death outside the walls of Jerusalem; the murderous farmers the faithless Jews; the nation to which the vineyard will be entrusted, the pagans.

Jn 3:16-17 1 Jn 4:9 he sent his son to them. "They will respect my son" he said. •But when the tenants 38
Ga 3:16; 4:7 Heb 1:2 saw the son, they said to each other, "This is the heir. Come on, let us kill him and
Heb 13:12 take over his inheritance." •So they seized him and threw him out of the vineyard 39
and killed him. •Now when the owner of the vineyard comes, what will he do 40
to those tenants?' •They answered, 'He will bring those wretches to a wretched end 41
and lease the vineyard to other tenants who will deliver the produce to him when
the season arrives'. •Jesus said to them, 'Have you never read in the scriptures: 42

Ps 118:22-23 Dn 2:45 Ac 2:33+; 4:11 *Is 28:16* 1 P 2:4-7

It was the stone rejected by the builders
that became the keystone.
This was the Lord's doing
and it is wonderful to see?

Ac 13:5+ Rm 11:11 I tell you, then, that the kingdom of God will be taken from you and given to 43
a people who will produce its fruit.'[h]

When they heard his parables, the chief priests and the scribes realised he was 45
speaking about them, •but though they would have liked to arrest him they were 46
16:14+ afraid of the crowds, who looked on him as a prophet.

8:11+ Pr 9:1-6 ||Lk 14:16-24

Parable of the wedding feast[a]

Ezk 16:1+ Rv 19:9 **22** Jesus began to speak to them in parables once again, •'The kingdom of 1 2
21:34 heaven may be compared to a king who gave a feast for his son's wedding.
He sent his servants to call those who had been invited, but they would not come. 3
Next he sent some more servants. "Tell those who have been invited" he said 4
"that I have my banquet all prepared, my oxen and fattened cattle have been
slaughtered, everything is ready. Come to the wedding." •But they were not 5
21:35 interested: one went off to his farm, another to his business, •and the rest seized 6
his servants, maltreated them and killed them. •The king was furious. He 7
despatched his troops, destroyed those murderers and burnt their town. •Then 8
he said to his servants, "The wedding is ready; but as those who were invited
proved to be unworthy, •go to the crossroads in the town and invite everyone 9
Rv 19:7 you can find to the wedding". •So these servants went out on to the roads and 10
13:38,47 collected together everyone they could find, bad and good alike; and the wedding
hall was filled with guests. •When the king came in to look at the guests he noticed 11
one man who was not wearing a wedding garment, •and said to him, "How did 12
Rv 19:8 you get in here, my friend, without a wedding garment?" And the man was silent.
Then the king said to the attendants, "Bind him hand and foot and throw him 13
8:12+ out into the dark, where there will be weeping and grinding of teeth". •For many 14
are called, but few are chosen.'[b]

||Mk 12:13-17 ||Lk 20:20-26

On tribute to Caesar

Jr 18:18 Lk 11:54 Then the Pharisees went away to work out between them how to trap him 15
Rm 13:1-7 in what he said. •And they sent their disciples to him, together with the 16
Herodians,[c] to say, 'Master, we know that you are an honest man and teach
the way of God in an honest way, and that you are not afraid of anyone, because
a man's rank means nothing to you. •Tell us your opinion, then. Is it permissible 17
to pay taxes to Caesar or not?' •But Jesus was aware of their malice and replied, 18
6:2 'You hypocrites! Why do you set this trap for me? •Let me see the money you 19
pay the tax with.' They handed him a denarius, •and he said, 'Whose head is this? 20
Whose name?' •'Caesar's' they replied. He then said to them, 'Very well, give 21
Rm 13:7 back to Caesar what belongs to Caesar—and to God what belongs to God'.[d]
This reply took them by surprise, and they left him alone and went away. 22

||Mk 12:18-27 ||Lk 20:27-40

The resurrection of the dead

Jn 11:25 Ac 23:8 That day some Sadducees—who deny that there is a resurrection[e]—approached 23
Gn 38:8 Dt 25:5+ him and they put this question to him, •'Master, Moses said that if a man 24
dies childless, his brother is to marry the widow, his sister-in law, to raise

25 children for his brother. •Now we had a case involving seven brothers; the first
26 married and then died without children, leaving his wife to his brother; •the
27 same thing happened with the second and third and so on to the seventh, •and then
28 last of all the woman herself died. •Now at the resurrection to which of those
29 seven will she be wife, since she had been married to them all?' •Jesus answered
them, 'You are wrong, because you understand neither the scriptures nor the
30 power of God. •For at the resurrection men and women do not marry; no, they
31 are like the angels in heaven. •And as for the resurrection of the dead, have you
32 never read what God himself said to you: •*I am the God of Abraham, the God of* Ex 3:6
Isaac and the God of Jacob? God is God, not of the dead, but of the living.'
33 And his teaching made a deep impression on the people who heard it. Ac 13:12

The greatest commandment of all

||Mk 12:28-31 ||Lk 10:25-28 Jn 13:34-35+

34 But when the Pharisees heard that he had silenced the Sadducees they got
35 36 together •and, to disconcert him, one of them[f] put a question, •'Master, which 1 Jn 4:21
37 is the greatest commandment of the Law?' •Jesus said, '*You must love the Lord* Dt 6:5 1 Jn 2:7
38 *your God with all your heart, with all your soul*, and with all your mind. •This is
39 the greatest and the first commandment. •The second resembles it: *You must love* Lv 19:18 Jm 2:8
40 *your neighbour as yourself*. •On these two commandments hang the whole Law, *Rm 13:8-10* Ga 5:14
and the Prophets also.'

Christ not only son but also Lord of David

||Mk 12:35-37 ||Lk 20:41-44

41 While the Pharisees were gathered round, Jesus put to them this question,
42 'What is your opinion about the Christ? Whose son is he?' 'David's' they told him. 9:27+
43 'Then how is it' he said 'that David, moved by the Spirit, calls him Lord, where 2 S 7:1+
he says:

44 *The Lord said to my Lord:* 26:64p Ps 110:1
Sit at my right hand Ac 2:33+, 34f
and I will put your enemies Heb 1:13
under your feet?

45 46 'If David can call him Lord, then how can he be his son?' •Not one could think
of anything to say in reply,[g] and from that day no one dared to ask him any Lk 20:40
further questions.

The scribes and Pharisees: their hypocrisy and vanity

Ws 2:12 Jr 8:8-9 Rm 2:19-20

1 2 **23** Then addressing the people and his disciples Jesus said, •'The scribes and
3 the Pharisees occupy the chair of Moses. •You must therefore do what they

h. Add. v. 44 'He who falls on this stone will be dashed to pieces; anyone it falls on will be crushed', probably a gloss taken from Lk 20:18.

22 a. A parable with allegorical features; in this, as in the lesson it teaches, it resembles the one that precedes it. The king is God; the wedding feast is the happiness of the messianic age and the king's son the Messiah; those sent with invitations are the prophets and the apostles; the invited who ignore them or do them violence are the Jews; those called in from the street are the sinners and the pagans; the burning of the city is the destruction of Jerusalem. At v. 11 the scene changes to that of the Last Judgement. Matthew, it seems, has combined two parables: one akin to Lk 14: 16-24 and another whose concluding verses are found in vv. 11f; these verses explain that the man who accepted the invitation should have been dressed for the occasion —in other words, good works must go with faith, cf. 3:8; 5:20; 7:21f; 13:47f; 21:28f.

b. This sentence appears to refer to the first part of the parable rather than to the second. It is a question not of the elect as a whole but of the Jews, the first to be invited. The parable (of vv. 1-10) neither asserts nor denies that some (a 'few') of the Jewish people have accepted the invitation and are 'chosen', cf. 24:22+.

c. Supporters of the Herodian dynasty, Mk 3:6+, the most suitable people to report to the Roman authorities what they hoped to induce Jesus to say against Caesar.

d. In practice they acknowledge the authority and accept the benefits of Roman government of which this coin is a symbol. Hence it is permissible, indeed it is a duty, for them to pay that government the tribute of their obedience and of their property so long as this does not encroach on what they owe to the overriding authority of God.

e. This sect, 3:7+, adhered rigidly to the written tradition, especially as contained in the Pentateuch; its members were confident that the doctrine of the resurrection of the body, cf. 2 M 7:9+, was not to be found in that tradition. On this point the Pharisees were opposed to the Sadducees. Cf. Ac 4:1+; 23:8+.

f. Add. 'a lawyer', probably borrowed from Lk 10:25.

g. The appropriate answer would have been that though tracing his human origin back to David, cf. 1:1-17, there would be something divine about the Messiah to set him above David.

Dt 17:10 Rm 2:17-24 tell you and listen to what they say;[a] but do not be guided by what they do: since
11:30 ||Lk 11:46 they do not practise what they preach. •They tie up heavy burdens and lay them 4
Ac 15:10 on men's shoulders, but will they lift a finger to move them? Not they! •Everything 5
6:1-8 Nb 15:38 they do is done to attract attention, like wearing broader phylacteries and longer
Am 4:5 ||*Mk 12:38-39* tassels,[b] •like wanting to take the place of honour at banquets and the front 6
||Lk 11:43; 20:46 seats in the synagogues, •being greeted obsequiously in the market squares 7
Lk 14:7 and having people call them Rabbi.[c]
Jm 3:1 'You, however,[d] must not allow yourselves to be called Rabbi, since you have 8
only one Master, and you are all brothers. •You must call no one on earth your 9
father,[e] since you have only one Father, and he is in heaven. •Nor must you allow 10
yourselves to be called teachers, for you have only one Teacher, the Christ.
=20:26 *18:4* The greatest among you must be your servant. •Anyone who exalts himself will 11 12
Lk 1:52-53; ||14:11; 18:14 be humbled, and anyone who humbles himself will be exalted.

6:9+ ||Lk 11:39-48,52

The sevenfold indictment of the scribes and Pharisees

Is 5:8-25 Jr 8:8 Ml 2:8 'Alas for you, scribes and Pharisees, you hypocrites! You who shut up the 13
kingdom of heaven in men's faces, neither going in yourselves nor allowing
others to go in[f] who want to.[g]

'Alas for you, scribes and Pharisees, you hypocrites! You who travel over 15
sea and land to make a single proselyte,[h] and when you have him you make him
twice as fit for hell as you are.

15:14 Jn 9:38-41 Rm 2:19 'Alas for you, blind guides! You who say,[i] "If a man swears by the Temple, 16
it has no force; but if a man swears by the gold of the Temple, he is bound".
Fools and blind! For which is of greater worth, the gold or the Temple that 17
makes the gold sacred? •Or else, "If a man swears by the altar it has no force; 18
15:14 but if a man swears by the offering that is on the altar, he is bound". •You blind 19
men! For which is of greater worth, the offering or the altar that makes the
5:33-37 Si 23:9 offering sacred? •Therefore, when a man swears by the altar he is swearing by 20
that and by everything on it. •And when a man swears by the Temple he 21
is swearing by that and by the One who dwells in it. •And when a man swears 22
by heaven he is swearing by the throne of God and by the One who is seated
there.

Dt 14:22+ Ezk 45:13 'Alas for you, scribes and Pharisees, you hypocrites! You who pay your tithe 23
of mint and dill and cummin[j] and have neglected the weightier matters of the
Am 5:21+ Law—justice, mercy, good faith! These you should have practised, without
neglecting the others. •You blind guides! Straining out gnats and swallowing 24
camels!

Mk 7:4 Lk 11:39-40 Tt 1:15 'Alas for you, scribes and Pharisees, you hypocrites! You who clean the 25
outside of cup and dish and leave the inside full[k] of extortion and intemperance.
Blind Pharisee! Clean the inside of cup and dish first so that the outside may 26
become clean as well.

'Alas for you, scribes and Pharisees, you hypocrites! You who are like 27
Ac 23:3 whitewashed tombs that look handsome on the outside, but inside are full of dead
men's bones and every kind of corruption. •In the same way you appear to people 28
Lk 16:15; 18:9 from the outside like good honest men, but inside you are full of hypocrisy and
lawlessness.

'Alas for you, scribes and Pharisees, you hypocrites! You who build the 29
13:17 Lk 11:47 sepulchres of the prophets and decorate the tombs of holy men, •saying, "We 30
would never have joined in shedding the blood of the prophets, had we lived in
our fathers' day". •So! Your own evidence tells against you! You are the sons of 31
Ac 7:52 *1 Th 2:16* those who murdered the prophets! •Very well then, finish off the work that your 32
fathers began.[l]

Their crimes and approaching punishment

3:7; 12:34 'Serpents, brood of vipers, how can you escape being condemned to hell? 33
2 Ch 36:16 ||Lk 11:49-51 This is why, in my turn, I am sending you prophets and wise men and scribes:[m] 34

some you will slaughter and crucify, some you will scourge in your synagogues 5:12 1 Th 2:14-16 27:25
35 and hunt from town to town; •and so you will draw down on yourselves the blood Gn 4:10
of every holy man that has been shed on earth, from the blood of Abel the Holy Heb 11:4 Rv 16:6; 18:24
to the blood of Zechariah son of Barachiah[n] whom you murdered between the
36 sanctuary and the altar. •I tell you solemnly, all of this will recoil on this
generation.

Jerusalem admonished

||Lk 13:34-35

37 'Jerusalem, Jerusalem, you that kill the prophets and stone those who are 21:35; 22:6
sent to you! How often[o] have I longed to gather your children, as a hen gathers Ps 17:8; 91:4
38 her chicks under her wings, and you refused! •So be it! Your house will be left Jr 7:14; 18: 7; 26:4-6
39 to you desolate,[p] •for, I promise, you shall not see me any more until you say: Ezk 11:23 Jn 2:19-21

Blessings on him who comes in the name of the Lord!'[q] Ps 118:26 Ac 2:33+

B. THE ESCHATOLOGICAL DISCOURSE[a]

Jr 26 ||Mk 13 ||Lk 21:5-33

Introduction

1 24 Jesus left the Temple, and as he was going away his disciples came up to ||Mk 13:1-4 ||Lk 21:5-7
2 draw his attention to the Temple buildings. •He said to them in reply,
'You see all these? I tell you solemnly, not a single stone here will be left

23 a. In so far as they hand on the traditional doctrine that goes back to Moses. Christ in this does not speak of their own interpretations; he has shown elsewhere how these are to be assessed, cf. 15:1-20; 16:6; 19:3-9.

b. The phylactery is a small receptacle containing the most important words of the Law; the Jews attach it to arm or forehead, carrying out the injunction of Ex 13:9,16; Dt 6:8; 11:18 literally. The four tassels were sewn one at each corner of the cloak cf. Nb 15:38+.

c. Aramaic word meaning 'my master', the usual title of the Jewish teacher. Jesus himself was thus addressed by his disciples 26:25,49.

d. Vv. 8-12, addressed to the disciples only, probably did not belong originally to this discourse.

e. *Abba* in Aramaic; another title of honour.

f. The exacting casuistry of the rabbis made observance of the Law impossible.

g. Add. v. 14 'Alas for you, scribes and Pharisees, you hypocrites! You who devour the property of widows though you make a show of lengthy prayers. The more severe will be the sentence you receive'; this is an interpolation taken from Mk 12:40; Lk 20:47 and making eight maledictions instead of the deliberate total of seven, cf. 6:9+.

h. A pagan convert to Judaism. Jewish propaganda was extremely active in the Graeco-Roman world.

i. The question of oaths; to release from those that had been hastily made the rabbis had to invoke tortuous reasoning.

j. The Mosaic Law levied tithe on agricultural produce; the rabbis piously applied the precept to the most insignificant of plants.

k. Var. 'inside you are full'. 'intemperance': var. 'iniquity', 'impurity', 'cupidity'.

l. Allusion to Christ's own death soon to take place, cf. 21:38f.

m. Terms of Jewish origin but here applied to Christian missionaries, cf. 10:41; 13:52.

n. The one referred to is probably the Zechariah of 2 Ch 24:20-22. His murder is the last one to be described in the Bible (2 Ch being the last book of the Jewish Canon) while Abel's, Gn 4:8, is the first. It is possible that 'son of Barachiah' is the result of confusion with another Zechariah, cf. Is 8:2 (LXX); Zc 1:1. Alternatively, the words may be a copyist's gloss.

o. Allusion to repeated visits to Jerusalem on which the Synoptics are silent but which are reported by Jn.

p. Om 'desolate'. In a little while Jesus will be with them no longer, he is to be rejected by his own people; so also will God abandon Jerusalem and its Temple.

q. In Lk 13:35 Christ seems to mean that the Jews will not see him again until the entry into Jerusalem on Palm Sunday (Lk 19:28f). In Mt's context the words probably refer to a later coming than this, perhaps the triumphant coming at the end of time: the reconciled Jews will acclaim this return, cf. Rm 11:25f.

24 a. This discourse operates at two levels: that of the destruction of Jerusalem (in 70 A.D.) and that of the end of the world. In the course of his preaching, Jesus probably distinguished these two levels more clearly (in Lk 17:22-37 there is a separate discourse on Christ's return at the end of time and its elements are inserted here in vv. 26-27,28,37-39,40-41). But in the text of Mt as it stands, as also in Mk 13 and Lk 21, no sharp distinction is drawn between the two levels. Their fusion in this way is a theological expression of truth: though separated in time, these two are inseparable in the sense that the first is the inevitable forerunner and prefiguration of the second. The destruction of Jerusalem marks the end of the Old Covenant—Christ has thus manifestly returned to inaugurate his kingly rule. Such a decisive intervention in the history of salvation will not occur again until the end of time when God will judge the whole human race, now chosen in Christ, with the same judgement he pronounced (in 70 A.D.) upon the first chosen people. For the reason the destruction of Jerusalem is here described in terms of the 'day of Yahweh' foretold by the prophets, cf. Am 5:18+; 8:9+. No other intervention of God in history so involves the whole cosmos or prophesies its end as this one does, and the actual end of the world will be no more than the climax of all this. Since the end of Jerusalem is seen as a divine intervention, there are to be found in this discourse phrases and metaphors characteristic of theophanies, Ex 13:22+, and of the 'visitations' of Yahweh, namely, war, famine, earthquake, unprecedented distress and the 'birthpangs', cosmic catastrophe, the lightning and the 'cloud' (see the references given in the notes). These conventional images are to be interpreted symbolically, as in the prophetic literature from which they are derived. They refer, like the discourse as a whole, both to the destruction of Jerusalem and to the end of the world which follows and is prefigured by it.

on another: everything will be destroyed.' •And when he was sitting on the 3
Mount of Olives the disciples came and asked him privately, 'Tell us, when is
13:39 1 Jn 2:28 this going to happen, and what will be the sign of your coming[b] and of the end
of the world?'

||Mk 13:5-13 ||Lk 21:8-19 **The beginning of sorrows**

2 Tm 3:5 And Jesus answered them, 'Take care that no one deceives you; •because 4 5
Jn 5:43 many will come using my name and saying, "I am the Christ",[c] and they will
Jr 51:46 deceive many. •You will hear of wars and rumours of wars; do not be 6
alarmed, for this is something that must happen, but the end will not be yet.
For nation will fight against nation, and kingdom against kingdom. There will 7
Jn 16:21 Rm 8:22 be famines[d] and earthquakes here and there.[e] •All this is only the beginning of 8
1 Th 5:3 Rv 12:2 the birthpangs.[f]
1 Jn 3:13 'Then they will hand you over to be tortured and put to death; and you will 9
=10:22 be hated by all the nations on account of my name. •And then many will fall 10
10:21,35-36 away; men will betray one another and hate one another. •Many false prophets 11
16:14+ *2 Th 2:3* will arise; they will deceive many, •and with the increase of lawlessness, love in 12
Lk 18:8 *=10:22* most men will grow cold; •but the man who stands firm to the end will be saved. 13
'This Good News of the kingdom will be proclaimed to the whole world[g] as 14
Rm 10:18 a witness to all the nations. And then the end[h] will come.

||Mk 13:14-23 **The great tribulation of Jerusalem**

||Lk 21:20-24 *Dn 9:27; 11:31; 12:11* 'So when you see *the disastrous abomination*, of which the prophet Daniel 15
1 M 1:54 *Ezk 7:15* spoke, set up in the Holy Place[i] (let the reader understand), •then those in 16
Lk 17:31 Judaea must escape to the mountains; •if a man is on the housetop, he must not 17
come down to collect his belongings; •if a man is in the fields, he must not 18
turn back to fetch his cloak. •Alas for those with child, or with babies at the 19
breast, when those days come! •Pray that you will not have to escape in winter 20
Lm 1:12 Dn 12:1 or on a sabbath. •For then there will be *great distress such as, until now, since* 21
Rv 7:14 the world began, there never *has been*, nor ever will be again.[j] •And if that time 22
had not been shortened, no one would have survived; but shortened that time
shall be, for the sake of those who are chosen.[k]
Ps 75:6 Lk 17:23-24 'If anyone says to you then, "Look, here is the Christ" or, "He is there", 23
2 Th 2:3-4,9 2 P 2:1-3 do not believe it; •for false Christs and false prophets will arise and produce great 24
1 Jn 4:1 Rv 13 signs and portents, enough to deceive even the chosen, if that were possible.
There; I have forewarned you. 25

||Lk 17:23-24 **The coming of the Son of Man will be evident**

'If, then, they say to you, "Look, he is in the desert", do not go there; 26
"Look, he is in some hiding place", do not believe it; •because the coming of the 27
Son of Man will be like lightning striking in the east and flashing far into the
Jb 39:30 ||Lk 17:37 west.[l] •Wherever the corpse is, there will the vultures gather. 28

||Mk 13:24-27 **The universal significance of this coming**

||Lk 21:25-27 *Is 13:9-10; 34:4* 'Immediately after the distress of those days[m] the sun will be darkened, the 29
Am 8:9+ Ac 2:20 moon will lose its brightness, the stars will fall from the sky and the powers of
16:28; 17:5 Zc 12:10-12 heaven will be shaken.[n] •And then the sign of the Son of Man will appear 30
Rv 1:7 in heaven;[o] then too all the peoples of the earth will beat their breasts; and they
8:20+; 26:64 Dn 7:13-14 will see the Son of Man coming on the clouds of heaven with power and great
1 Th 4:16 glory.[p] •And he will send his angels with a loud trumpet[q] to gather his chosen 31
from the four winds, from one end of heaven to the other.[r]

||Mk 13:28-32 **The time of this coming**

||Lk 21:29-33 'Take the fig tree as a parable: as soon as its twigs grow supple and its leaves 32
come out, you know that summer is near. •So with you when you see all these 33
10:23; 16:28 Jm 5:8 things: know that he[s] is near, at the very gates. •I tell you solemnly, before 34

35 this generation has passed away all these things will have taken place.[t] •Heaven Is 40:8; 51:6
36 and earth will pass away, but my words will never pass away. •But as for that day *Heb 12:27*
and hour, nobody knows it, neither the angels of heaven, nor the Son,[u] no one Ac 1:7
but the Father only.

Be on the alert
||Lk 17:26-27,34-35

37 38 'As it was in Noah's day, so will it be when the Son of Man comes. •For in Gn 6:5 Heb 11:7
those days before the Flood people were eating, drinking, taking wives, taking
39 husbands, right up to the day Noah went into the ark, •and they suspected nothing Gn 7:11-23 2 P 3:6
till the Flood came and swept all away. It will be like this when the Son of Man *1 Th 5:3*
40 41 comes. •Then of two men in the fields one is taken, one left; •of two women at
the millstone grinding, one is taken, one left.
42 'So stay awake, because you do not know the day[v] when your master is coming. 25:13 Rv 3:3
43 You may be quite sure of this that if the householder had known at what time *||Lk 12:39-40* 1 Th 5:1+
of the night the burglar would come, he would have stayed awake and would
44 not have allowed anyone to break through the wall of his house. •Therefore, you 1 Th 5:2-6 2 P 3:10
too must stand ready because the Son of Man is coming at an hour you do not
expect.

Parable of the conscientious steward[w]
||Lk 12:42-46

45 'What sort of servant, then, is faithful and wise enough for the master to Pr 14:35
place him over his household to give them their food at the proper time?
46 47 Happy that servant if his master's arrival finds him at this employment. •I tell
48 you solemnly, he will place him over everything he owns. •But as for the 19:28; 25:21
49 dishonest servant who says to himself, "My master is taking his time", •and sets

24 b. The Greek word is *parousia;* it means 'presence' and in the Graeco-Roman world was used for official visits by royalty. The Christians adopted it as a technical term for the glorious coming of Christ, cf. 1 Co 15:23+. It is not inevitably linked up with Christ's *final* coming; it can also refer to the power he will display when he comes to establish his messianic kingdom (the Church) on the ruins of Judaism; cf. 16:27-28. In this passage Matthew clearly implies that the has combined the two themes.

c. Before the year 70 several impostors posed as messiahs.

d. Add. 'plagues', cf. Lk 21:11.

e. Cf. Is 8:21; 13:13; 19:2; Jr 21:9; 34:17; Ezk 5:12; Am 4:6-11; 8:8; 2 Ch 15:6.

f. Cf. Is 13:8; 26:17; 66:7; Jr 6:24; 13:21; Ho 13:13; Mi 4:9-10. Jewish literature uses this metaphor to describe the coming of the messianic kingdom.

g. The 'inhabited world' *(oikoumenē)*, i.e. the Graeco-Roman world. All the Jews of the empire are destined to hear the Good News before punishment comes to Israel, cf. Rm 10:18. The earliest 'witness' will be directed against the faithlessness of Judaism, cf. Mt 10:18. Before 70 A.D. the gospel had already reached the main parts of the Roman empire, cf. 1 Th 1:8; Rm 1:5,8; Col 1:6,23.

h. The fall of Jerusalem.

i. Daniel seems to refer to the statue of Zeus set up in the Jerusalem Temple by Antiochus Epiphanes (in 168 B.C.; cf. 1 M 1:54). Jesus applies the prophecy to the siege and capture of the Holy City by the pagan armies from Rome, cf. Lk 21:20.

j. Cf. Ex 10:14; 11:6; Jr 30:7; Ba 2:2; Jl 2:2; Dn 12:1; 1 M 9:27; Rv 16:18.

k. Those among the Jews who are called to enter the kingdom of God: the 'remnant', cf. Is 4:3+; Rm 11:5-7.

l. The coming of the Messiah will be as unmistakable as lightning. Lightning is a characteristic phenomenon that goes with divine judgement, cf. Is 29:6; 30:30; Zc 9:14; Ps 97:4; etc.

m. Join with v. 25; vv. 26-28 are a digression.

n. Cf. Jr 4:23-26; Ezk 32:7f; Am 8:9; Mi 1:3-4; Jl 2:10; 3:4; 4:15 and especially Is 13:9-10; 34:4; the text repeats the phrases of the last two references. The 'powers of heaven' are the stars and all the other celestial forces.

o. For the Fathers this 'sign' was Christ's cross, but possibly it is Christ himself proving by the triumph of his kingdom on earth that he has truly risen and is in glory.

p. In these words Daniel foretold the establishment of the messianic kingdom by a Son of Man coming on the clouds. The cloud is the usual accompaniment of both O.T. and N.T. theophanies: Ex 13:22+; 19:16+; 34:5+; Lv 16:2; 1 K 8:10-11; Ps 18:11; 97:2; 104:3; Is 19:1; Jr 4:13; Ezk 1:4; 10:3f; 2 M 2:8. For N.T. cf. Mt 17:5; Ac 1:9,11; 1 Th 4:17; Rv 1:7; 14:14.

q. Add. 'and a voice'.

r. Lit. 'from the four winds, from the ends of the heavens to their ends', a composite formula from Zc 2:10 and Dt 30:4, texts which treat of the reunion of scattered Israel, cf. Ezk 37:9 and Ne 1:9. See also Is 27:13. Here therefore as in vv. 22 and 24, the 'chosen' are those Jews that Yahweh will rescue from the ruin of their nation in order to admit them, along with the pagans, into his kingdom v. 30.

s. The Son of Man coming to establish his kingdom.

t. This statement refers to the destruction of Jerusalem and not to the end of the world. In the course of his preaching Jesus probably made the distinction between these two things clearer, cf. 24:1+ and 16:28+.

u. Om. (Vulg.) 'nor the Son', probably for theological reasons. Christ as man received from the Father the knowledge of everything that had to do with his mission but, as he explicitly asserts in this passage, he could be ignorant of certain elements in the divine plan.

v. Vulg. 'hour'.

w. After the discourse foretelling the destruction of Jerusalem and the visible coming of the messianic reign in the Church, Matthew adds three parables dealing with the ultimate fate of individuals. The first presents one of Christ's servants who, like the apostles, is given a task to perform in the Church; he is judged on the way he performs it.

about beating his fellow servants and eating and drinking with drunkards, •his 50
master will come on a day he does not expect and at an hour he does not know.
The master will cut him off[z] and send him to the same fate as the hypocrites, where 51
8:12+ there will be weeping and grinding of teeth.

Lk 12:35-38 **Parable of the ten bridesmaids**[a]

Ezk 16:1+ **25** 'Then the kingdom of heaven will be like this: Ten bridesmaids took their 1
lamps and went to meet the bridegroom.[b] •Five of them were foolish and five 2
were sensible: •the foolish ones did take their lamps, but they brought no oil, 3
whereas the sensible ones took flasks of oil as well as their lamps. •The bride- 4 5
groom was late, and they all grew drowsy and fell asleep. •But at midnight there 6
was a cry, "The bridegroom is here! Go out and meet him." •At this, all those 7
bridesmaids woke up and trimmed their lamps, •and the foolish ones said to 8
the sensible ones, "Give us some of your oil: our lamps are going out". •But 9
they replied, " There may not be enough for us and for you; you had better go
to those who sell it and buy some for yourselves". •They had gone off to buy 10
it when the bridegroom arrived. Those who were ready went in with him to the
7:22 Lk 13:25 wedding hall and the door was closed. •The other bridesmaids arrived later. 11
"Lord, Lord," they said "open the door for us." •But he replied, "I tell you 12
24:42 Mk 13:33 solemnly, I do not know you". •So stay awake, because you do not know either 13
the day or the hour.

Lk 19:12-27 **Parable of the talents**[c]

Mk 13:34 'It is like a man on his way abroad who summoned his servants and entrusted 14
his property to them. •To one he gave five talents, to another two, to a third 15
one; each in proportion to his ability. Then he set out. •The man who had received 16
the five talents promptly went and traded with them and made five more. •The 17
man who had received two made two more in the same way. •But the man who 18
had received one went off and dug a hole in the ground and hid his master's
18:23 2 Co 5:10 money. •Now a long time after, the master of those servants came back and went 19
through his accounts with them. •The man who had received the five talents came 20
forward bringing five more. "Sir," he said "you entrusted me with five talents;
here are five more that I have made." •His master said to him, "Well done, good 21
19:28; 24:47 Lk 16:10 and faithful servant; you have shown you can be faithful in small things, I will
trust you with greater; come and join in your master's happiness".[d] •Next the man 22
with the two talents came forward. " Sir," he said "you entrusted me with two
talents; here are two more that I have made." •His master said to him, "Well 23
done, good and faithful servant; you have shown you can be faithful in small
Jn 15:11; 17:24 things, I will trust you with greater; come and join in your master's happiness".
Last came forward the man who had the one talent. "Sir," said he "I had heard 24
you were a hard man, reaping where you have not sown and gathering where
you have not scattered; •so I was afraid, and I went off and hid your talent in 25
the ground. Here it is; it was yours, you have it back." •But his master answered 26
him, "You wicked and lazy servant! So you knew that I reap where I have not sown
and gather where I have not scattered? •Well then, you should have deposited 27
my money with the bankers, and on my return I would have recovered my capital
with interest. •So now, take the talent from him and give it to the man who has 28
=13:12+ Lk 8:18 the five talents. •For to everyone who has will be given more, and he will have more 29
than enough; but from the man who has not, even what he has will be taken away.
As for this good-for-nothing servant, throw him out into the dark, where there 30
8:12+ will be weeping and grinding of teeth."

The Last Judgement

8:20+; 16:27 2 Co 5:10 'When the Son of Man comes in his glory,[e] escorted by all the angels, then 31
he will take his seat on his throne of glory. •All the nations[f] will be assembled 32
Ex 34:17 before him and he will separate men one from another as the shepherd separates

33 sheep from goats. •He will place the sheep on his right hand and the goats
34 on his left. •Then the King will say to those on his right hand, "Come, you whom Is 58:6-8
my Father has blessed, take for your heritage the kingdom prepared for you Rm 8:17 Ep 1:4
35 since the foundation of the world.[g] •For I was hungry and you gave me food; *Tb 4:16* Jb 31:17
I was thirsty and you gave me drink; I was a stranger and you made me welcome; Si 7:34 Ezk 18:7
36 naked and you clothed me, sick and you visited me, in prison and you came to Heb 13:3
37 see me."[h] •Then the virtuous will say to him in reply, "Lord, when did we see
38 you hungry and feed you; or thirsty and give you drink? •When did we see you
39 a stranger and make you welcome; naked and clothe you; •sick or in prison and
40 go to see you?" •And the King will answer, "I tell you solemnly, in so far 10:40; 18:5 Pr 19:17
as you did this to one of the least of these brothers of mine, you did it to me". Lk 10:16 Ac 9:5
41 Next he will say to those on his left hand, "Go away from me, with your curse *Jm 2:14-17*
42 upon you, to the eternal fire prepared for the devil and his angels. •For I was
hungry and you never gave me food; I was thirsty and you never gave me anything Jb 22:7
43 to drink; •I was a stranger and you never made me welcome, naked and you
44 never clothed me, sick and in prison and you never visited me." •Then it will be
their turn to ask, "Lord, when did we see you hungry or thirsty, a stranger or
45 naked, sick or in prison, and did not come to your help?" •Then he will answer,
"I tell you solemnly, in so far as you neglected to do this to one of the 10:41
46 least of these, you neglected to do it to me". •And they will go away to eternal Dn 12:2 Jn 5:29
punishment, and the virtuous to eternal life.'

VII. PASSION AND RESURRECTION

The conspiracy against Jesus ||Mk 14:1-2 ||Lk 22:1-2

1 **26** Jesus had now finished all he wanted to say, and he told his disciples,
2 'It will be Passover, as you know, in two days' time, and the Son of Man
will be handed over to be crucified'.
3 Then the chief priests and the elders of the people assembled in the palace of Ps 2:1-2 Ws 2:12
4 the high priest, whose name was Caiaphas, •and made plans to arrest Jesus by Jn 11:47-53 Ac 4:25-27
5 some trick and have him put to death. •They said, however, 'It must not be during
the festivities; there must be no disturbance among the people'.

The anointing at Bethany[a] ||Mk 14:3-9 ||Jn 12:1-8

6 7 Jesus was at Bethany in the house of Simon the leper, when •a woman came
to him with an alabaster jar of the most expensive ointment, and poured it on his
8 head as he was at table. •When they saw this, the disciples were indignant; 'Why
9 this waste?' they said. •'This could have been sold at a high price and the money
10 given to the poor.' •Jesus noticed this. 'Why are you upsetting the woman?' he
said to them. 'What she has done for me is one of the good works[b] indeed!

x. A word of uncertain meaning; probably to be taken metaphorically: 'he will cut him off', a sort of 'excommunication', cf. 18:17.

25 a. The bridesmaids (lit. 'virgins') represent Christians waiting for Christ. Even if he is slow to come, they must be watchful, i.e. keep their lamps ready.

b. Add. 'and the bride'.

c. Christians are servants expected by Jesus, their master, to make full use of any gifts he has given them so that his kingdom may grow on earth; they must give an account of this administration. The parable of the pounds, Lk 19:12-27, has a similar form but a rather different moral.

d. The happiness of the heavenly banquet, Mt 8:11+. 'I will trust you with greater things' implies an active sharing with Christ in his reign.

e. The perspective changes: it is now a question of Christ's last coming at the end of the world.

f. Every human being of every period of history. The resurrection of the dead is presupposed though not mentioned, cf. 10:15; 11:22,24; 12:41f.

g. Christ, the Messiah-King, ushers the elect from his own kingdom to that of his Father, 13:43+.

h. Men are judged by their works of mercy (here described in O.T. terms, cf. Is 58:7· Jb 22:6f; Si 7:35f. etc.) not by their occasional exploits, cf. 7:22f. In addition to these meritorious acts we find in 10:32f the profession of faith.

26 a. The woman of this episode is Mary the sister of Lazarus (as Jn mentions); the event described in Lk 7:36-50 is not the same.

b. The Jews divided 'good works' into 'almsgiving' and 'charitable deeds'; the latter were reckoned superior and included, among other pious acts, the burial of the dead. The woman therefore, by making provision for Christ's burial has performed a 'work' greater than almsgiving. Jesus seems to suggest, v. 12, that some loving instinct has given her a presentiment of the real significance of her action.

Dt 15:11 You have the poor with you always, but you will not always have me. •When she 11 12
poured this ointment on my body, she did it to prepare me for burial. •I tell you 13
solemnly, wherever in all the world this Good News is proclaimed, what she has
done will be told also, in remembrance of her.'

||Mk 14:10-11 ||Lk 22:3-6

Judas betrays Jesus

Then one of the Twelve, the man called Judas Iscariot, went to the chief priests 14
and said, 'What are you prepared to give me if I hand him over to you?' They 15
27:3f Gn 37:28 Zc 11:12 paid him thirty silver pieces,[c] •and from that moment he looked for an 16
opportunity to betray him.

||Mk 14:12-16 ||Lk 22:7-13 *Jn 13:1; 18:*28; 19:14

Preparations for the Passover supper

Now on the first day of Unleavened Bread[d] the disciples came to Jesus to 17
say, 'Where do you want us to make the preparations for you to eat the
passover?' •'Go to so-and-so in the city' he replied 'and say to him, "The Master 18
Jn 2:4+ says: My time is near. It is at your house that I am keeping Passover with my
disciples." ' •The disciples did what Jesus told them and prepared the Passover. 19

||Mk 14:17-21 ||Lk 22:14, 21-23 ||Jn 13:21-30

The treachery of Judas foretold

When evening came he was at table with the twelve disciples. •And while they 20 21
Ps 55:13-14 were eating[e] he said, 'I tell you solemnly, one of you is about to betray
me'. •They were greatly distressed and started asking him in turn, 'Not I, Lord, 22
Ps 41:9 Jn 13:18 surely?' •He answered, 'Someone who has dipped his hand into the dish with me, 23
will betray me. •The Son of Man is going to his fate, as the scriptures say he 24
Jb 3:3 Jn 17:12 will, but alas for that man by whom the Son of Man is betrayed! Better for that
man if he had never been born!' •Judas, who was to betray him, asked in his 25
turn, 'Not I, Rabbi, surely?' 'They are your own words' answered Jesus.

||Mk 14:22-25 ||Lk 22:19-20 ||1 Co 11:23-25 Jn 6:51-58

The institution of the Eucharist

Now as they were eating,[f] Jesus took some bread, and when he had said the 26
blessing he broke it and gave it to the disciples. 'Take it and eat;' he said 'this is
1 Co 10:16 my body.' •Then he took a cup, and when he had returned thanks he gave it 27
Ex 24:8 Zc 9:11 to them. 'Drink all of you from this,' he said •'for this is my blood, the blood 28
20:28+ Is 53:12 of the[g] covenant, which is to be poured out for many for the forgiveness of
8:11+ sins.[h] •From now on, I tell you, I shall not drink wine until the day I drink 29
the new wine with you in the kingdom of my Father.'[i]

||Mk 14:26-31 ||Lk 22:31-34 ||Jn 13:36-38; 16:32

Peter's denial foretold

After psalms had been sung[j] they left for the Mount of Olives. •Then Jesus said 30 31
to them, 'You will all lose faith in me this night,[k] for the scripture says:
Zc 13:7 *I shall strike the shepherd and the sheep of the flock will be scattered,* •but after my 32
28:7 resurrection I shall go before you to Galilee'. •At this, Peter said, 'Though all 33
lose faith in you, I will never lose faith'. •Jesus answered him, 'I tell you 34
solemnly, this very night, before the cock crows, you will have disowned
26:69-75 me three times'. •Peter said to him, 'Even if I have to die with you, I will never 35
disown you'. And all the disciples said the same.

||Mk 14:32-42 ||Lk 22:40-46 ||Jn 18:1

Gethsemane

Jn 12:27-30 Heb 5:7-10 Then Jesus came with them to a small estate called Gethsemane;[l] and he said 36
to his disciples, 'Stay here while I go over there to pray'. •He took Peter and the 37
two sons of Zebedee with him. And sadness came over him, and great distress.
Then he said to them, 'My soul is sorrowful to the point of death.[m] Wait here and 38
2 Co 12:8 keep awake with me.' •And going on a little further he fell on his face and prayed. 39
6:10 'My Father,' he said 'if it is possible, let this cup pass me by. Nevertheless, let it
Jn 4:34; 6:38 Rm 5:19 Ph 2:8 be as you, not I, would have it.'[n] •He came back to the disciples and found them 40
sleeping, and he said to Peter, 'So you had not the strength to keep awake with

41 me one hour? •You should be awake, and praying not to be put to the test. The Ps 69:20b
42 spirit is willing, but the flesh is weak.' •Again, a second time, he went away and Rm 7:5+ 2 Co 12:8
prayed: 'My Father,' he said 'if this cup cannot pass by without my drinking it, Heb 10:9
43 your will be done!' •And he came again back and found them sleeping, their eyes
44 were so heavy. •Leaving them there, he went away again and prayed for the 2Co 12:8
45 third time, repeating the same words. •Then he came back to the disciples and
said to them, 'You can sleep on now and take your rest.[o] Now the hour has
46 come when the Son of Man is to be betrayed into the hands of sinners. •Get up! Jn 14:30-31
Let us go! My betrayer is already close at hand.'

The arrest

||Mk 14:43-52 ||Lk 22:47-53 ||Jn 18:2-11

47 He was still speaking when Judas, one of the Twelve, appeared, and with him
a large number of men armed with swords and clubs, sent by the chief priests and
48 elders of the people. •Now the traitor had arranged a sign with them. 'The one
49 I kiss,' he had said 'he is the man. Take him in charge.' •So he went straight up to Pr 27:6
50 Jesus and said, 'Greetings, Rabbi', and kissed him. •Jesus said to him, 'My friend, 26:23
do what you are here for'.[p] Then they came forward, seized Jesus and took him in
51 charge. •At that, one of the followers of Jesus grasped his sword and drew it; he
52 struck out at the high priest's servant, and cut off his ear. •Jesus then said, 'Put your
53 sword back, for all who draw the sword will die by the sword. •Or do you think Jn 18:36
that I cannot appeal to my Father who would promptly send more than twelve
54 legions of angels to my defence? •But then, how would the scriptures be fulfilled Lk 24:26-27
55 that say this is the way it must be?' •It was at this time that Jesus said to the
crowds, 'Am I a brigand, that you had to set out to capture me with swords
and clubs? I sat teaching in the Temple[q] day after day and you never laid hands Jn 18:20
56 on me.' •Now all this happened to fulfil the prophecies in scripture. Then
all the disciples deserted him and ran away.

26 c. Thirty shekels—and not thirty *denarii* as is commonly said. It was the price the Law fixed for a slave's life, Ex 21:32.

d. The 'first day' of the week during which unleavened loaves (azymes) were eaten, cf. Ex 12:1+; 23:14+. was normally that which followed the Passover supper, i.e. the 15th of Nisan; the Synoptics however give this title to the preceding day, thus attesting a wider use of the term. Further, if we take account of Jn 18:28 and of other details connected with the Passion, it seems fairly certain that in this particular year the Passover supper was celebrated on the evening of the Friday (or 'Preparation Day', Mt 27:62; cf. Jn 19:14. 31.42). Christ's Last Supper, which the Synoptics put on the day before, i.e. on the Thursday evening, must therefore be explained in one of two ways: either a whole section of the Jewish people thus anticipated the rite, or (and this is preferable) Christ anticipated it on his own initiative. In this second hypothesis Jesus, unable to celebrate the Passover on the Friday (though, indeed, he celebrated it in his own person on the cross, Jn 19:36+; 1 Co 5:7), instituted his new rite in the course of a supper which, in consequence, became endowed with the characteristics of the old Passover. Nisan 14th (the day of the Passover supper) fell on a Friday in 30 and 33 A.D.; interpreters therefore take one or other of these years as the date of Christ's death according as they assign his baptism to 28 or to 29 and reckon a longer or shorter public ministry. Note: The Dead Sea Scrolls have recently revealed a community which, following a solar calendar, always celebrated the Passover supper on a Tuesday evening. It is possible that Jesus did the same. If so, the Synoptics have fitted into a few hours juridical processes which in fact took days.

e. The first course; it preceded the Passover supper properly so called.

f. They have come to the Passover supper itself. The rubrics for this solemn blessing of bread and wine are laid down exactly; on to this ceremony Jesus grafts the sacramental rites of the new religious order of things which he institutes.

g. Add. (Vulg.) 'new', cf. Lk 22:20; 1 Co 11:25.

h. As at Sinai, the blood of victims sealed the covenant of Yahweh with his people, Ex 24:4-8+, so on the cross the blood of Jesus, the perfect victim, is about to seal the 'new' covenant, cf. Lk 22:20, between God and man—the covenant foretold by the prophets, Jr 31:31+. Jesus takes on himself the task of universal redemption that Isaiah assigns to the 'servant of Yahweh', Is 42:6; 49:6; 53:12, cf. 41:8+. Cf. Heb 8:8; 9:15; 12:24.

i. Allusion to the eschatological banquet, cf. 8:11; 22:1f. Jesus and his disciples will never meet at table again.

j. The psalms of the Hallel, Ps 113-118, with which the Passover meal closed.

k. Lit. 'be brought down'; it will be an obstacle for their faith when they see the one they believe to be Messiah, 16:16, and whose approaching triumph they expect, 20:21f, passively yield to his enemies. For a time it will make them lose courage and even faith, cf. Lk 22:31-32.

l. The name means 'oilpress'. It lies in the Kedron valley at the foot of the Mt. of Olives.

m. The turn of phrase recalls Ps 42:5 and Jon 4:9.

n. Jesus feels the full force of the human fear of death; he feels the instinctive urge to escape, gives expression to it and then stifles it by his acceptance of the Father's will.

o. Gently ironical reproach: The hour you should have stayed awake with me has slipped by. Now the testing-time has begun and Jesus must go through it alone; the disciples may go on sleeping if they wish.

p. Lit. 'Friend, for what you are here'. To a question ('Why are you here?') or a reproach ('For what purpose are you here!') one may prefer to see in this a stereotyped phrase meaning 'do what you are here for', 'to your work!' Jesus cuts short the empty show of greeting: it is time for action. Cf. Jn 13:27.

q. Var. (Vulg.) 'I used to sit among you in the Temple', cf. Mk 14:49.

||Mk 14:53-65
Jesus before the Sanhedrin[r]

||Lk 22:54-55,66-71 ||Jn 18:24 The men who had arrested Jesus led him off to Caiaphas the high priest, 57
||*Jn 18:15-16*,18 where the scribes and the elders were assembled. •Peter followed him at 58
a distance, and when he reached the high priest's palace, he went in and sat down
with the attendants to see what the end would be.

Ps 35:11 Jr 26 The chief priests and the whole Sanhedrin were looking for evidence against 59
Ac 25:7 Jesus, however false, on which they might pass the death-sentence. •But they could 60
not find any, though several lying witnesses came forward. Eventually two
stepped forward •and made a statement, 'This man said, "I have power to 61
Jn 2:19 Ac 6:14 destroy the Temple of God and in three days build it up" '.[s] •The high priest 62
then stood up and said to him, 'Have you no answer to that? What is this evidence
27:14 Is 53:7 these men are bringing against you?'[t] •But Jesus was silent. And the high priest 63
4:3+ said to him, 'I put you on oath by the living God to tell us if you are the Christ,
8:20+ the Son of God'. •'The words are your own' answered Jesus. 'Moreover, I tell 64
8:20+;24:30 Ps 110:1 you that from this time onward you will see the *Son of Man seated at the right*
Dn 7:13 Ac 2:33+; *hand of the Power* and *coming on the clouds of heaven*.'[u] •At this, the high priest 65
7:55 tore his clothes and said, 'He has blasphemed.[v] What need of witnesses have
we now? There! You have just heard the blasphemy. •What is your opinion?' 66
They answered, 'He deserves to die'.

Ws 2:19 Is 50:6; Then they spat in his face and hit him with their fists; others said as they 67
52:14 struck him, •'Play the prophet, Christ! Who hit you then?' 68

||Mk 14:66-72
Peter's denials

||Lk 22:56-62 ||Jn 18:17,25-27 Meanwhile Peter was sitting outside in the courtyard, and a servant-girl came 69
up to him and said, 'You too were with Jesus the Galilean'. •But he denied it in 70
8:10+ front of them all. 'I do not know what you are talking about' he said. •When he 71
went out to the gateway another servant-girl saw him and said to the people there,
2:23+ 'This man was with Jesus the Nazarene'.[w] •And again, with an oath, he denied 72
it, 'I do not know the man'. •A little later the bystanders came up and said to 73
Jg 12:6 Peter, 'You are one of them for sure! Why, your accent[x] gives you away.' •Then 74
he started calling down curses on himself and swearing, 'I do not know the man'.
26:34 At that moment the cock crew, •and Peter remembered what Jesus had said, 75
'Before the cock crows you will have disowned me three times'. And he went
outside and wept bitterly.

||Mk 15:1 ||Lk 22:66; 23:1
Jesus is taken before Pilate

26:57+ **27** When morning came, all the chief priests and the elders of the people met 1
Jn 18:28 in council to bring about the death of Jesus. •They had him bound, and 2
Lk 3:1+ led him away to hand him over to Pilate,[a] the governor.

The death of Judas

When he found that Jesus had been condemned, Judas his betrayer was filled 3
26:15 with remorse and took the thirty silver pieces back to the chief priests and elders.
'I have sinned;' he said 'I have betrayed innocent blood.'[b] 'What is that to us?' 4
they replied 'That is your concern.' •And flinging down the silver pieces in the 5
Ac 1:18 sanctuary he made off, and went and hanged himself. •The chief priests picked 6
up the silver pieces and said, 'It is against the Law to put this into the treasury;
it is blood-money'. •So they discussed the matter and bought the potter's field 7
with it as a graveyard for foreigners, •and this is why the field is called the Field 8
of Blood[c] today. •The words of the prophet Jeremiah[d] were then fulfilled: *And* 9
Zc 11:12-13 *they took the thirty silver pieces, the sum at which the precious One was priced*
by children of Israel, •*and they gave them for the potter's field, just as the Lord* 10
directed me.[e]

||Mk 15:2-15 ||Lk 23:2-5,13-25 ||Jn 18:28-40; 19:4-16
Jesus before Pilate

Jesus, then, was brought before the governor, and the governor put to him 11

this question, 'Are you the king of the Jews?' Jesus replied, 'It is you who say 27:29
12 it'.[f] •But when he was accused by the chief priests and the elders he refused to Ws 2:19
13 answer at all. •Pilate then said to him, 'Do you not hear how many charges they
14 have brought against you?' •But to the governor's complete amazement, he 26:63 Is 53:7
offered no reply to any of the charges.
15 At festival time it was the governor's practice to release a prisoner for the Jn 18:39
16 people, anyone they chose. •Now there was[g] at that time a notorious prisoner
17 whose name was Barabbas.[h] •So when the crowd gathered, Pilate said to them,
'Which do you want me to release for you: Barabbas, or Jesus who is called
18 Christ?' •For Pilate knew it was out of jealousy that they had handed him over.
19 Now as he was seated in the chair of judgement, his wife sent him a message,
'Have nothing to do with that man; I have been upset all day by a dream I had
about him'.
20 The chief priests and the elders, however, had persuaded the crowd to demand
21 the release of Barabbas and the execution of Jesus. •So when the governor spoke
and asked them, 'Which of the two do you want me to release for you?' they
22 said, 'Barabbas'. •'But in that case,' Pilate said to them 'what am I to do with Jesus
23 who is called Christ?' They all said, 'Let him be crucified!' •'Why?' he asked 'What
harm has he done?' But they shouted all the louder, 'Let him be crucified!'
24 Then Pilate saw that he was making no impression, that in fact a riot was
imminent. So he took some water, washed his hands[i] in front of the crowd and
25 said, 'I am innocent of this man's blood.[j] It is your concern.' •And the people, Ac 18:6
26 to a man, shouted back, 'His blood be on us and on our children!'[k] •Then he 23:35 Ac 5:28
released Barabbas for them. He ordered Jesus to be first scourged[l] and then
handed over to be crucified.

Jesus is crowned with thorns

||Mk 15:16-20 ||Jn 19:1-3

27 The governor's soldiers took Jesus with them into the Praetorium[m] and
28 collected the whole cohort round him. •Then they stripped him and made

r. The accounts of Luke and of John enable us to distinguish: a preliminary trial before Annas, at night time, and a solemn session of the Sanhedrin on the following morning, Mt 27:1. Matthew and Mark describe the night episode in terms of the morning one which was the only formal and decisive meeting. But for an alternative chronology, cf. 26:17+.

s. What Jesus had in fact foretold was the destruction of the Temple and of the Jewish cult of which it was the symbol, ch. 24. A new temple was to be substituted for the old one, and this was to be, in the first place, his own body risen after three days, 16:21; 17:23; 20:19; Jn 2:19-22, but beyond that, it was to be the Church, 16:18.

t. Vulg. presents this as one question 'Do you make no answer to the evidence these men are bringing against you?'

u. 'The Power' is equivalent to 'Yahweh'. At this critical moment Jesus abandons his policy of the 'messianic secret', cf. Mk 1:34+, and unequivocally acknowledges—as he had already acknowledged to his intimates, Mt 16:16—that he is the Messiah. But he goes further and reveals himself not as the human Messiah of traditional expectation but as the Lord of Ps 110, cf. Mt 22:41f, and the mysterious personage of heavenly origin whom Daniel had seen in vision, cf. Mt 8:20+. Henceforth the Jews will not see him except in his glory which will be manifested first in the victory of the resurrection and subsequently in the victory of the Church. Cf. 23:39 and 24:30.

v. The 'blasphemy' lay not in Jesus' claim to be Messiah but in his claim to divine rank.

w. Nazoraios; var. (cf. Vulg.) Nazarenos.

x. The Galilean accent.

27 a. Var. 'Pontius Pilate'. Cf. Lk 3:1+. In Judaea, as in all the provinces of the Empire, Rome reserved to itself power of life and death; the Jews had to approach this magistrate for confirmation and execution of the sentence they had pronounced.

b. Var. 'righteous blood'. cf. 23:35.

c. In Aramaic Hakeldama (cf. Ac 1:19 and Vulg. in this place). A 4th century tradition, probably reliable, locates it in the Valley of Gehinnom.

d. Om. 'Jeremiah'. Actually this is a free quotation from Zc 11:12-13 combined with the idea of the purchase of a field, an idea suggested by Jr 32:6-15. This, plus the fact that Jeremiah speaks of potters (18:2f) who lived in the Hakeldama district (19:1f), explains how the whole text could by approximation be attributed to Jeremiah.

e. Yahweh complained that, in the person of his prophet Zechariah, he had received from the Israelites a wage that was nothing but an insult. The sale of Jesus for the same paltry sum appeals to Matthew as a fulfilment of this oracle of the prophet.

f. By these words Jesus acknowledges as correct, at least in a sense, what he would never have said on his own initiative. See above 26:25,64; and cf. Jn 18: 33-37+.

g. Vulg. 'he had'.

h. Here and in v. 17, var. 'Jesus Barabbas', which would give peculiar point to Pilate's question but appears to have its origin in an apocryphal tradition.

i. The significance of this gesture must have been well understood by the Jews, cf. Dt 21:6f; Ps 26:6; 73:13.

j. Var. 'of the blood of this just man'.

k. Traditional O.T. phrase, 2 S 1:16; 3:29, cf. Ac 18:6, by which they accept responsibility for the death they demand.

l. In Roman practice the normal prelude to crucifixion.

m. The Praetorium, or residence of the praetor, was probably the former palace of King Herod the Great in which the procurator used to reside whenever he went up from Caesarea to Jerusalem. This palace,

Is 52:14 him wear a scarlet cloak,[n] •and having twisted some thorns into a crown they 29
put this on his head and placed a reed in his right hand. To make fun of him they
27:11 *Is 50:6* knelt to him saying, 'Hail, king of the Jews!' •And they spat on him and took 30
the reed and struck him on the head with it. •And when they had finished making 31
fun of him, they took off the cloak and dressed him in his own clothes and led
him away to crucify him.

||Mk 15:21-27 ||Lk 23:26-34,38 ||Jn 19:17-24

The crucifixion

On their way out, they came across a man from Cyrene, Simon by name, 32
and enlisted him to carry his cross. •When they had reached a place called 33
Ps 69:21 Pr 31:6 Golgotha,[o] that is, the place of the skull, •they gave him wine to drink mixed 34
with gall,[p] which he tasted but refused to drink. •When they had finished 35
Ps 22:18 crucifying him they shared out his clothing by casting lots,[q] •and then sat down 36
and stayed there keeping guard over him.
Above his head was placed the charge against him; it read: 'This is Jesus, 37
Is 53:9,12 Lk 22:37 the King of the Jews'. •At the same time two robbers were crucified with him, 38
one on the right and one on the left.

||Mk 15:29-32 ||Lk 23:35-37 *Ps 22:7* Jr 18:16 Lm 2:15 26:61

The crucified Christ is mocked

The passers-by jeered at him; they shook their heads •and said, 'So you 39 40
would destroy the Temple and rebuild it in three days! Then save yourself! If
you are God's son, come down from the cross!' •The chief priests with the 41
scribes and elders mocked him in the same way. •'He saved others;' they said 42
'he cannot save himself. He is the king of Israel; let him come down from the
Ps 22:8 Ws 2:18-20 cross now, and we will believe in him. •He puts his trust in God; now let God 43
4:3+ rescue him if he wants him. For he did say, "I am the son of God".' •Even the 44
robbers who were crucified with him taunted him in the same way.

||Mk 15:33-41 ||Lk 23:44-49

The death of Jesus

From the sixth hour there was darkness over all the land until the ninth hour.[r] 45
And about the ninth hour, Jesus cried out in a loud voice, 'Eli, Eli, lama sabach- 46
Ps 22:1 thani?' that is, '*My God, my God, why have you deserted me?*'[s] •When some of 47
those who stood there heard this, they said, 'The man is calling on Elijah',[t]
||Lk 23:36 ||Jn 19:29 and one of them quickly ran to get a sponge which he dipped in vinegar[u] and, 48
Ps 69:21 putting it on a reed, gave it him to drink. •'Wait!' said the rest of them 'and 49
see if Elijah will come to save him.' •But Jesus, again crying out in a loud 50
voice, yielded up his spirit.
Heb 6:19 At that, the veil of the Temple[v] was torn in two from top to bottom; the earth 51
1 P 3:19+ quaked; the rocks were split;[w] •the tombs opened and the bodies of many holy men 52
rose from the dead, •and these, after his resurrection, came out of the tombs, 53
entered the Holy City and appeared to a number of people. •Meanwhile the centur- 54
ion, together with the others guarding Jesus, had seen the earthquake and all that
4:3‡ Mk 15:39‡ was taking place, and they were terrified and said, 'In truth this was a son of God.'
Lk 8:2-3 Jn 19:25 And many women were there, watching from a distance, the same 55
women who had followed Jesus from Galilee and looked after him. •Among 56
13:55 them were Mary of Magdala, Mary the mother of James and Joseph, and the
mother of Zebedee's sons.

||Mk 15:42-47 ||Lk 23:50-55 ||Jn 19:38-42

The burial

When it was evening, there came a rich man of Arimathaea, called Joseph, 57
who had himself become a disciple of Jesus. •This man went to Pilate and asked 58
for the body of Jesus. Pilate thereupon ordered it to be handed over. •So Joseph 59
Is 53:9+ took the body, wrapped it in a clean shroud •and put it in his own new tomb 60
which he had hewn out of the rock. He then rolled a large stone across the entrance
of the tomb and went away. •Now Mary of Magdala and the other Mary were 61
there, sitting opposite the sepulchre.

The guard at the tomb

62 Next day, that is, when Preparation Day[x] was over, the chief priests and the
63 Pharisees went in a body to Pilate •and said to him, 'Your Excellency, we
recall that this impostor said, while he was still alive, "After three days I shall 16:21 Jn 7:12
64 rise again". •Therefore give the order to have the sepulchre kept secure until the Ac 10:40+
third day, for fear his disciples come and steal him away and tell the people,
"He has risen from the dead". This last piece of fraud would be worse than what
65 went before.' •'You may have your guard'[y] said Pilate to them. 'Go and make
66 all as secure as you know how.' •So they went and made the sepulchre secure,
putting seals on the stone and mounting a guard.

The empty tomb. The angel's message ||Mk 16:1-8 ||Lk 24:1-10

1 28 After the sabbath,[a] and towards dawn on the first day of the week, Mary of Jn 20:1 1 Co 16:2
2 Magdala and the other Mary[b] went to visit the sepulchre. •And all at once
there was a violent earthquake, for the angel of the Lord, descending from 1:20+
3 heaven, came and rolled away the stone and sat on it. •His face was like lightning, 17:2
4 his robe white as snow. •The guards were so shaken, so frightened of him, that
5 they were like dead men. •But the angel spoke; and he said to the women,
'There is no need for you to be afraid. I know you are looking for Jesus, who was
6 crucified. •He is not here, for he has risen, as he said he would. Come and see
7 the place where he[c] lay, •then go quickly and tell his disciples, "He has risen
from the dead and now he is going before you to Galilee; it is there you will 26:32 Jn 21:1
8 see him". Now I have told you.' •Filled with awe and great joy the women came
quickly away from the tomb[d] and ran to tell the disciples.

Appearance to the women Jn 20:14f

9 And there, coming to meet them, was Jesus. 'Greetings' he said. And the
10 women came up to him and, falling down before him, clasped his feet. •Then Lk 24:9-10 Jn 20:1
Jesus said to them, 'Do not be afraid; go and tell my brothers that they must leave Ac 1:3 1 Co 15:4
for Galilee; they will see me there'.[e]

situated in the W. quarter of the city, was not the family residence of the Hasmonaeans: this was near the Temple and in it Herod Antipas probably received Jesus, sent to him by Pilate, Lk 23:7-12. Some commentators think that the Praetorium was in the fortress called Antonia, to the N. of the Temple.

n. The Roman soldier's cloak *(sagum)*; being red it suggested the imperial purple to the mocking soldiery.

o. Approximate transliteration of the Aramaic word *Gulgoltha*, 'a place of the skull', in Lat. *Calvaria* (whence 'Calvary').

p. A narcotic which sympathetic Jewish women (cf. Lk 23:27f) used to offer the condemned to diminish their sufferings. The wine was mixed with 'myrrh' (cf. Mk 15:23) rather than with 'gall'. The 'gall' in Mt (like the correction of 'wine' to 'vinegar' in the Antiochene recension) is due to a reminiscence of Ps 69:21. Jesus refuses the palliative.

q. Add. 'that the saying of the prophet might be fulfilled: they divided my garments between them and for my robe they cast lots' (Ps 22:18), a gloss taken from Jn 19:24.

r. From noon to three in the afternoon.

s. A cry of real distress but not of despair: this lament which Jesus takes from the scriptures is a prayer to God and is followed in the Psalm by an expression of joyful confidence in final victory.

t. Malicious play on words based on the expectation of Elijah as the Messiah's precursor, cf. 17:10-13+.

u. Sour drink of the Roman soldier. Probably the gesture was sympathetic, cf. Jn 19:28f; the Synoptics regard it as malevolent (Lk 23:36) and describe it in terms that recall Ps 69:21.

v. Either the curtain which hung in front of the Holy Place or, more probably, the one which divided the Holy Place from the Holy of Holies, cf. Ex 26:31f. Following Heb 9:12; 10:20. Christian tradition saw in this tearing of the veil the abrogation of the old Mosaic cult and the way opened up by Christ into the messianic sanctuary.

w. These remarkable phenomena, like the darkness mentioned in v. 45, were foretold by the prophets as unmistakable signs of the 'day of Yahweh', cf. Am 8:9+.

x. Greek *paraskeuē* ('preparation') meaning Friday, i.e. the day when preparations were made for the sabbath.

y. Lit. 'You have a guard', i.e. I now put one at your disposal.

28 a. And not 'On the sabbath evening' (Vulg.). Since the sabbath was the day of rest, the 'first day of the (Jewish) week' corresponds to our Sunday (Rv 1:10), *dies dominica*, or the 'day of the Lord' so named in memory of the resurrection. Cf. Ac 20:7+; 1 Co 16:2.

b. 'Mary of James', Mk 16:1; Lk 24:10; cf. Mt 27:56 and 61.

c. 'he'; var. 'the Lord'.

d. Var. 'came quickly out of the tomb', cf. Mk 16:8.

e. Though they agree in recording the initial apparition of the angel (or angels) to the women (Mt 28:5-7; Mk 16:5-7; Lk 24:5-7; Jn 20:12-13), the four gospels show divergencies when it comes to the appearances of Christ. Setting Mark aside (his abrupt conclusion presents a special problem, cf. Mk 16:8+, and his 'longer ending' recapitulates the data of the other gospels) all the gospels make a clear distinction, both literary and doctrinal, between: 1. Appearances to individuals that help to prove the fact of the resurrection; to Mary Magdalen, either alone (Jn 20:14-17; cf. Mk 16:9), or accompanied (Mt 28:9-10); to the disciples on the road to Emmaus (Lk 24:13-32; cf. Mk 16:12), to Simon (Lk 24:34), to Thomas (Jn 20:26-29). 2. A collective

Precautions taken by the leaders of the people

While they were on their way, some of the guard went off into the city to tell 11
the chief priests all that had happened. •These held a meeting with the elders 12
and, after some discussion, handed a considerable sum of money to the soldiers
with these instructions, 'This is what you must say, "His disciples came during 13
the night and stole him away while we were asleep". •And should the governor 14
come to hear of this, we undertake to put things right with him ourselves and
to see that you do not get into trouble.' •The soldiers took the money and carried 15
out their instructions, and to this day that is the story among the Jews.

Appearance in Galilee. The mission to the world

Meanwhile the eleven disciples set out for Galilee, to the mountain where 16
Jesus had arranged to meet them. •When they saw him they fell down before 17
8:10+ Lk 24:9-10 him, though some hesitated.[f] •Jesus came up and spoke to them. He said, 'All 18
Jn 3:35+ authority in heaven and on earth has been given to me. •Go, therefore, make 19
Mk 16:15-16 Lk 24:47 disciples of all the nations; baptise them in the name of the Father and of the
Ac 1:8+; 2:38+ Son and of the Holy Spirit,[g] •and teach them to observe all the commands I 20
18:20 Ps 125:2 Jn 14:18-21 gave you. And know that I am with you always; yes, to the end of time.'

appearance that is coupled with an apostolic mission (Mt 28:16-20; Lk 24:36-49; Jn 20:19-23; cf. Mk 16:14-18). As well as this distinction there are two traditions as to where the appearances took place: 1. all in Galilee (Mk 16:7; Mt 28:10,16-20); 2. all in Judaea (Lk and Jn 20). By way of appendix, Jn 21 adds an appearance in Galilee which though it bears the character of an appearance to individuals (it is for Peter and John predominantly) is nevertheless coupled with an apostolic mission (given to Peter). The primitive apostolic preaching that Paul reproduces in 1 Co 15:3-7 lists 5 appearances (apart from the appearance to Paul himself) which are not easily harmonised with the gospel accounts; in particular he mentions an appearance to James of which the *Gospel to the Hebrews* also speaks. All this gives the impression that different groups, which cannot now be easily identified, have given rise to different strands of tradition. But these very divergencies of tradition are far better witnesses than any artificial or contrived uniformity to the antiquity of the evidence and the historical quality of all these manifestations of the risen Christ.

28 f. An alternative translation, with less grammatical support: 'those who had hesitated'. On the doubts Mt mentions here cf. Mk 16:11,14; Lk 24:11,41; Jn 20:24-29.

g. It may be that this formula, so far as the fulness of its expression is concerned, is a reflection of the liturgical usage established later in the primitive community. It will be remembered that Ac speaks of baptising 'in the name of Jesus', cf. Ac 1:5+. But whatever the variation in formula, the underlying reality remains the same.

THE GOSPEL ACCORDING TO SAINT MARK

I. PRELUDE TO THE PUBLIC MINISTRY OF JESUS

The preaching of John the Baptist ||Mt 3:1-12 ||Lk 3:3-17

1 2 **1** The beginning of the Good News[a] about Jesus Christ, the Son of God.[b] •It is 10:29 Lk 1:19
written in the book of the prophet Isaiah:

Look, I am going to send my messenger before you; Ml 3:1
he will prepare your way.
3 *A voice cries in the wilderness:* Is 40:3 Jn 1:23
Prepare a way for the Lord,
make his paths straight,

4 and so it was that John the Baptist appeared in the wilderness, proclaiming[c]
5 a baptism of repentance for the forgiveness of sins. •All Judaea and all the people Mt 3:6+
of Jerusalem made their way to him, and as they were baptised by him in the river
6 Jordan they confessed their sins. •John wore a garment of camel-skin,[d] and
7 he lived on locusts and wild honey. •In the course of his preaching he said,
'Someone is following me, someone who is more powerful than I am, and I am Jn 1:27
8 not fit to kneel down and undo the strap of his sandals. •I have baptised you
with water, but he will baptise you with the Holy Spirit.' Jn 1:26,33 Ac 1:5; 11:16

Jesus is baptised Mt 3:13-17 ||Lk 3:21-22

9 It was at this time that Jesus came from Nazareth in Galilee and was baptised
10 in the Jordan by John. •No sooner had he come up out of the water than he
saw the heavens torn apart and the Spirit, like a dove, descending on him. Jn 1:32-34
11 And a voice came from heaven, 'You are my Son, the Beloved; my favour rests
on you'.

Temptation in the wilderness ||Mt 4:1-11 ||Lk 4:1-13

12 13 Immediately afterwards the Spirit drove him out into the wilderness •and he
remained there for forty days, and was tempted by Satan. He was with the wild Jb 1:6+
beasts, and the angels looked after him.

II. THE GALILEAN MINISTRY

Jesus begins to preach ||Mt 4:12-17 ||Lk 4:14-15

14 After John had been arrested, Jesus went into Galilee. There he proclaimed
15 the Good News from God. •'The time has come' he said 'and the kingdom of Rm 1:1 Ep 1:10
God is close at hand. Repent, and believe the Good News.' *Mt 3:2+*; 8:10+

1 a. Good News, Old English 'god-spel', Greek *euaggelion*, hence Lat. *evangelium*. The word is used in the N.T. to mean, not a book, but the Good News of salvation, Jesus himself being both its messenger and its message.

b. Om. 'Son of God'.

c. Var. 'John appeared, baptising in the wilderness and proclaiming...'

d. Var. 'John wore a garment of camel-hair with a leather belt round his waist', cf. Mt 3:4.

||Mt 4:18-22 ||Lk 5:1-11 The first four disciples are called

As he was walking along by the Sea of Galilee he saw Simon and his brother 16
Andrew casting a net in the lake — for they were fishermen. •And Jesus said to 17
them, 'Follow me and I will make you into fishers of men'. •And at once they 18
left their nets and followed him.
Going on a little further, he saw James son of Zebedee and his brother John; 19
they too were in their boat, mending their nets. He called them at once •and, 20
leaving their father Zebedee in the boat with the men he employed, they went
after him.

||Lk 4:31-37 Jesus teaches in Capernaum and cures a demoniac

They went as far as Capernaum, and as soon as the sabbath came he went 21
||Mt 7:28f to the synagogue and began to teach. •And his teaching made a deep impression 22
on them because, unlike the scribes, he taught them with authority.
In their synagogue just then there was a man possessed by an unclean spirit, 23
Mt 8:29+ *Mt 2:23*+ and it shouted, •'What do you want with us,[e] Jesus of Nazareth? Have you come[f] 24
Ac 3:14+ to destroy us? I know who you are: the Holy One of God.'[g] •But Jesus said 25
Mk 1:34+ sharply, 'Be quiet! Come out of him!' •And the unclean spirit threw the man into 26
convulsions and with a loud cry went out of him. •The people were so astonished 27
that they started asking each other what it all meant. 'Here is a teaching that is
4:41 new' they said 'and with authority behind it: he gives orders even to unclean
spirits[h] and they obey him.' •And his reputation rapidly spread everywhere, 28
through all the surrounding Galilean countryside.

||Mt 8:14-15 ||Lk 4:38-39 Cure of Simon's mother-in-law

7:24; 13:3 On leaving the synagogue, he went with James and John straight to the house 29
of Simon and Andrew. •Now Simon's mother-in-law had gone to bed with fever, 30
and they told him about her straightaway. •He went to her, took her by the hand 31
and helped her up. And the fever left her and she began to wait on them.

||Mt 8:16 ||Lk 4:40-41 A number of cures

That evening, after sunset, they brought to him all who were sick and those 32
who were possessed by devils. •The whole town came crowding round the door, 33
3:12; 9:30 Mt 8:4; 9:30; and he cured many who were suffering from diseases of one kind or another; 34
12:16; 17:9 Lk 5:14; 8: he also cast out many devils, but he would not allow them to speak, because they
56; 9:21 knew who he was.[i]

||Lk 4:42-44 Jesus quietly leaves Capernaum and travels through Galilee

Mt 14:23p; In the morning, long before dawn, he got up and left the house, and went 35
26:36p Lk 3:21+ off to a lonely place and prayed there. •Simon and his companions set out in 36
search of him, •and when they found him they said, 'Everybody is looking for 37
you'. •He answered, 'Let us go elsewhere, to the neighbouring country towns, 38
Lk 4:44 Jn 18:37 so that I can preach there too, because that is why I came'.[j] •And he went all 39
||*Mt 4:23* Lk 4:14-15; ||8:1 through Galilee, preaching in their synagogues and casting out devils.

||Mt 8:2-4 ||Lk 5:12-16 Cure of a leper

A leper came to him and pleaded on his knees: 'If you want to' he said 'you 40
5:30+ can cure me'. •Feeling sorry for him, Jesus stretched out his hand and touched 41
him. 'Of course I want to!' he said. 'Be cured!' •And the leprosy left him at once 42
and he was cured. •Jesus immediately sent him away and sternly ordered him, 43
1:34+ Lk 17:14 'Mind you say nothing to anyone, but go and show yourself to the priest, and 44
Lv 14:1-32 make the offering for your healing prescribed by Moses as evidence of your
recovery'. •The man went away, but then started talking about it freely and 45
telling the story everywhere, so that Jesus could no longer go openly into any town,
but had to stay outside in places where nobody lived. Even so, people from
all around would come to him.

Cure of a paralytic

||Mt 9:1-8
||Lk 5:17-26

1 2 When he returned to Capernaum some time later, word went round that he
2 was back; •and so many people collected that there was no room left, even 3:20; 6:31
3 in front of the door. He was preaching the word to them •when some people
4 came bringing him a paralytic carried by four men, •but as the crowd made
it impossible to get the man to him, they stripped the roof over the place where
Jesus was; and when they had made an opening, they lowered the stretcher on
5 which the paralytic lay. •Seeing their faith, Jesus said to the paralytic, 'My child, Mt 8:10+
6 your sins are forgiven'. •Now some scribes were sitting there, and they thought
7 to themselves, •'How can this man talk like that? He is blaspheming. Who can
8 forgive sins but God?' •Jesus, inwardly aware that this was what they were
thinking, said to them, 'Why do you have these thoughts in your hearts?
9 Which of these is easier: to say to the paralytic, "Your sins are forgiven" or to
10 say, "Get up, pick up your stretcher and walk"? •But to prove to you that the
11 Son of Man has authority on earth to forgive sins,'—•he said to the paralytic—
12 'I order you: get up, pick up your stretcher, and go off home.' •And the man
got up, picked up his stretcher at once and walked out in front of everyone, so
that they were all astounded and praised God saying, 'We have never seen Mt 9:33
anything like this'.

The call of Levi

||Mt 9:9
||Lk 5:27-28

13 He went out again to the shore of the lake;[a] and all the people came to him, 4:1
14 and he taught them. •As he was walking on he saw Levi the son of Alphaeus,
sitting by the customs house, and he said to him, 'Follow me'. And he got up and
followed him.

Eating with sinners

||Mt 9:10-13
||Lk 5:29-32

15 When Jesus was at dinner in his house, a number of tax collectors and sinners 7:24
were also sitting at the table with Jesus and his disciples; for there were many of
16 them among his followers. •When the scribes of the Pharisee party saw him eating
with sinners and tax collectors, they said to his disciples, 'Why does he eat with
17 tax collectors and sinners?' •When Jesus heard this he said to them, 'It is not the
healthy who need the doctor, but the sick. I did not come to call the virtuous,
but sinners.'

A discussion on fasting

||Mt 9:14-17
||Lk 5:33-39

18 One day when John's disciples and the Pharisees were fasting, some people
came and said to him, 'Why is it that John's disciples and the disciples of the
19 Pharisees fast, but your disciples do not?' •Jesus replied, 'Surely the bridegroom's
attendants would never think of fasting while the bridegroom is still with them?
As long as they have the bridegroom with them, they could not think of fasting.
20 But the time will come for the bridegroom to be taken away from them, and then,
21 on that day, they will fast. •No one sews a piece of unshrunken cloth on an old
cloak; if he does, the patch pulls away from it, the new from the old, and the tear

e. Lit. 'What is there to us and to you?' cf. Jn 2:4+.

f. Var. 'You have come'.

g. God is the 'Holy One' par excellence, and all that belongs to him is holy, Lv 17:1+; this is pre-eminently true of Jesus who is God's Son and his chosen Messiah, 1:10f, the appointed head of 'the nation of saints', Dn 7:18+, i.e. of the company of the elect, the Christian community, Ac 9:13+. Cf. Lk 1:35; 4:34; Jn 6:69; Ac 3:14+; 4:27, 30; Rv 3:7.

h. Or punctuate 'Here is a teaching that is new; with authority he gives orders even to unclean spirits'.

i. Jesus forbids the news that he is the Messiah to be spread by the devils, 1:25, 34; 3:12, by those he cured, 1:44; 5:43; 7:36; 8:26, even by the apostles, 8:30; 9:9. The silence is not to be broken till after his death, Mt 10:27+. Since the prevailing idea of the Messiah was nationalistic and warlike, in sharp contrast with his own ideal, Jesus had to be very careful, at least on Israelite soil, cf. 5:19, to avoid giving a false and dangerous impression of his mission, cf. Jn 6:15; Mt 13:13+. This policy of silence ('the messianic secret') is not an invention of Mk's, as some have claimed, but is in fact Christ's own, though Mk has given it special emphasis. With the exception of Mt 9:30, Mt and Lk record the injunction to silence only in passages which are parallel with Mk, frequently omitting it even in these cases.

j. Lit. 'came out' i.e. from Capernaum, v. 35. This is the primary sense, but it is possible that another lies behind it, namely, the 'coming forth' of Jesus from God, Jn 8:42; 13:3; 16:27f, 30. Cf. Lk 4:43.

2 a. The 'Sea of Galilee' ('Lake of Tiberias').

gets worse. •And nobody puts new wine into old wineskins; if he does, the wine 22
will burst the skins, and the wine is lost and the skins too. No! New wine, fresh
skins!'

||Mt 12:1-8 ||Lk 6:1-5 **Picking corn on the sabbath**

One sabbath day he happened to be taking a walk through the cornfields, and 23
his disciples began to pick ears of corn as they went along. •And the Pharisees 24
said to him, 'Look, why are they doing something on the sabbath day that is
forbidden?' •And he replied, 'Did you never read what David did in his time of 25
1 S 21:2-7 need when he and his followers were hungry—•how he went into the house of 26
Lv 24:5-9 God when Abiathar[b] was high priest, and ate the loaves of offering which only
the priests are allowed to eat, and how he also gave some to the men with him?'
Dt 5:14 2 M 5:19 And he said to them, 'The sabbath was made for man, not man for the 27
sabbath; •so the Son of Man is master even of the sabbath'. 28

||Mt 12:9-14 ||Lk 6:6-11 **Cure of the man with a withered hand**

3 He went again into a synagogue, and there was a man there who had a withered 1
hand. •And they were watching him to see if he would cure him on the sabbath 2
day, hoping for something to use against him. •He said to the man with the 3
withered hand, 'Stand up out in the middle!' •Then he said to them, 'Is it 4
against the law on the sabbath day to do good, or to do evil; to save life, or to
Lk 14:4 Ep 4:18 kill?' But they said nothing. •Then, grieved to find them so obstinate, he looked 5
angrily round at them, and said to the man, 'Stretch out your hand'. He stretched
it out and his hand was better. •The Pharisees went out and at once began to 6
plot with the Herodians[a] against him, discussing how to destroy him.

||Lk 6:17-19 **The crowds follow Jesus**

||Mt 4:23,25; 12:15-16 Jesus withdrew with his disciples to the lakeside, and great crowds from 7
Galilee followed him. From Judaea,[b] •Jerusalem, Idumaea, Transjordania and 8
the region of Tyre and Sidon, great numbers who had heard of all he was doing
came to him. •And he asked his disciples to have a boat ready for him because 9
of the crowd, to keep him from being crushed. •For he had cured so many that all 10
5:30+ who were afflicted in any way were crowding forward to touch him. •And the 11
Mt 8:29+ ||Lk 4:41 unclean spirits, whenever they saw him, would fall down before him and shout,
1:34+ ||Mt 12:16 'You are the Son of God!' •But he warned them strongly not to make him known. 12

||Mt 10:1-4 ||Lk 6:12-16 **The appointment of the Twelve**

He now went up into the hills and summoned those he wanted. So they came 13
=6:7 to him •and he appointed twelve; they were to be his companions and to be sent 14
Mt 10:2-5 out to preach, •with power to cast out devils. •And so he appointed the Twelve: 15 16
Mt 16:18+ Jn 1:42 Simon to whom he gave the name Peter, •James the son of Zebedee and John 17
Lk 9:54 the brother of James, to whom he gave the name Boanerges or 'Sons of Thunder';
then Andrew, Philip, Bartholomew, Matthew, Thomas, James the son of 18
Alphaeus, Thaddaeus, Simon the Zealot •and Judas Iscariot, the man who 19
was to betray him.[c]

His relatives are concerned about Jesus

2:2; 6:31 He went home again, and once more such a crowd collected that they could 20
not even have a meal. •When his relatives heard of this, they set out to take 21
Jn 10:20 charge of him, convinced[d] he was out of his mind.

||Mt 12:24-32 ||Lk 11:15-23 **Allegations of the scribes**

The scribes who had come down from Jerusalem were saying, 'Beelzebul is 22
in him' and, 'It is through the prince of devils that he casts devils out'. •So he called 23
them to him and spoke to them in parables, 'How can Satan cast out Satan?
If a kingdom is divided against itself, that kingdom cannot last. •And if 24 25

26 a household is divided against itself, that household can never stand. •Now if
Satan has rebelled against himself and is divided, he cannot stand either—it is
27 the end of him. •But no one can make his way into a strong man's house and
burgle his property unless he has tied up the strong man first. Only then can he
burgle his house.
28 'I tell you solemnly, all men's sins will be forgiven, and all their
29 blasphemies; •but let anyone blaspheme against the Holy Spirit and he will never Lk 12:10
30 have forgiveness: he is guilty of an eternal sin.' •This was because they were
saying, 'An unclean spirit is in him'.

The true kinsmen of Jesus
||Mt 12:46-50 ||Lk 8:19-21

31 His mother and brothers now arrived and, standing outside, sent in a message
32 asking for him. •A crowd was sitting round him at the time the message was passed
to him, 'Your mother and brothers and sisters are outside asking for you'.
33 34 He replied, 'Who are my mother and my brothers?' •And looking round at
those sitting in a circle about him, he said, 'Here are my mother and my brothers.
35 Anyone who does the will of God, that person is my brother and sister and
mother.'

Parable of the sower
||Mt 13:1-9 ||Lk 8:4-8

1 **4** Again he began to teach by the lakeside, but such a huge crowd gathered 2:13 Lk 5:1,3
round him that he got into a boat on the lake and sat there. The people were
2 all along the shore, at the water's edge. •He taught them many things in parables,
3 and in the course of his teaching he said to them, •'Listen! Imagine a sower
4 going out to sow. •Now it happened that, as he sowed, some of the seed fell on
5 the edge of the path, and the birds came and ate it up. •Some seed fell on rocky
ground where it found little soil and sprang up straightaway, because there was
6 no depth of earth; •and when the sun came up it was scorched and, not having
7 any roots, it withered away. •Some seed fell into thorns, and the thorns
8 grew up and choked it, and it produced no crop. •And some seeds fell into rich
soil and, growing tall and strong, produced crop;[a] and yielded thirty, sixty,
9 even a hundredfold.' •And he said, 'Listen, anyone who has ears to hear!'

Why Jesus speaks in parables
||Mt 13:10-15 ||Lk 8:9-10

10 When he was alone, the Twelve, together with the others who formed his 7:17
11 company, asked what the parables meant. •He told them, 'The secret of the Rm 16:25 Col 4:3,5
kingdom of God is given to you, but to those who are outside everything comes
12 in parables, •so that[b] *they may see and see again, but not perceive; may hear and* Is 6:9-10+
hear again, but not understand; otherwise they might be converted and be forgiven'.

The parable of the sower explained
||Mt 13:18-23 ||Lk 8:11-15

13 He said to them, 'Do you not understand this parable? Then how will you Jn 12:16
14 15 understand any of the parables?[c] •What the sower is sowing is the word. •Those
on the edge of the path where the word is sown are people who have no sooner

b. The high priest of 1S 21:1-7 was in fact Ahimelech. Either his son Abiathar is named here because, as high priest in David's reign, 2S 20:25, he was the better known, or else Mk is following a different tradition according to which Abiathar was Ahimelech's father (2 S 8:17 Hebr.).

3 a. The term signifies not officials of the court of Herod Antipas, tetrarch of Galilee, cf. Lk 3:1+, but politically minded Jews actively supporting his dynasty and enjoying his favour.

b. Punctuation uncertain. 'From Judaea ... Sidon' may be read with what precedes or with what follows.

c. Here Mk omits the discourse of Mt 5-7 and Lk 6:20-49, evidently assuming that his readers would be interested more in what Christ was and did than in the minutiae of his teaching with regard to the Jewish Law.

d. Lit. 'because they said'. Others translate 'because it was told (them)'.

4 a. Var. (Vulg.) 'produced its crop which grew tall and strong'.

b. The conjunction (Mt avoids it) is equivalent to 'in order that the scripture might be fulfilled that says...'

c. The apostles' incomprehension of Christ's works and words is a favourite theme of Mk: 6:52; 7:18; 8:17-18,21,33; 9:10,32; 10:38. With the exception of certain parallel places (Mt 15:16; 16:9,23; 20:22; Lk 9:45) and of Lk 18:34; 24:25,45, Mt and Lk often pass such remarks over in silence, or even emend them: compare Mt 14:33 with Mk 6:51-52, and see Mt 13:51. Cf. Jn 14:26+.

heard it than Satan comes and carries away the word that was sown in them.
Similarly, those who receive the seed on patches of rock are people who, when 16
first they hear the word, welcome it at once with joy. •But they have no root 17
in them, they do not last; should some trial come, or some persecution on
account of the word, they fall away at once. •Then there are others who receive 18
the seed in thorns. These have heard the word, •but the worries of this world, 19
the lure of riches and all the other passions come in to choke the word, and so
it produces nothing. •And there are those who have received the seed in rich 20
soil: they hear the word and accept it and yield a harvest, thirty and sixty and a
hundredfold.'

||Lk 8:16-17 **Parable of the lamp**

||Mt 5:15 ||Lk 11:33 He also said to them, 'Would you bring in a lamp to put it under a tub or 21
under the bed? Surely you will put it on the lamp-stand? •For there is nothing 22
||Mt 10:26 ||Lk 12:2 hidden but it must be disclosed, nothing kept secret except to be brought to light.
If anyone has ears to hear, let him listen to this.' 23

||Lk 6:38 **Parable of the measure**

||Mt 7:2 He also said to them, 'Take notice of what you are hearing. The amount you 24
||Mt 13:12 ||Lk 8:18; 19:26 measure out is the amount you will be given—and more besides; •for the man 25
who has will be given more; from the man who has not, even what he has will be
taken away.'[d]

Parable of the seed growing by itself

Jm 5:7 He also said, 'This is what the kingdom of God is like. A man throws seed on 26
the land. •Night and day, while he sleeps, when he is awake, the seed is sprouting 27
and growing; how, he does not know. •Of its own accord the land produces first 28
the shoot, then the ear, then the full grain in the ear. •And when the crop is ready, 29
Jl 4:13 Rv 14:15-16 he loses no time: he starts to reap because the harvest has come.'[e]

||Mt 13:31-32 ||Lk 13:18-19 **Parable of the mustard seed**

He also said, 'What can we say the kingdom of God is like? What parable can 30
we find for it? •It is like a mustard seed which at the time of its sowing in the 31
soil is the smallest of all the seeds on earth; •yet once it is sown it grows into the 32
Dn 4:9.18 biggest shrub of them all and puts out big branches so that the birds of the air
can shelter in its shade.'

||Mt 13:34-35 **The use of parables**

Using many parables like these, he spoke the word to them, so far as they were 33
capable of understanding it. •He would not speak to them except in parables, 34
but he explained everything to his disciples when they were alone.

||Mt 8:18. 23-27 ||Lk 8:22-25 **The calming of the storm**

With the coming of evening that same day, he said to them, 'Let us cross over 35
to the other side'. •And leaving the crowd behind they took him, just as he was, 36
in the boat; and there were other boats with him. •Then it began to blow a gale 37
and the waves were breaking into the boat so that it was almost swamped. •But 38
he was in the stern, his head on the cushion, asleep. •They woke him and said 39
to him, 'Master, do you not care? We are going down!' And he woke up and
rebuked the wind and said to the sea, 'Quiet now! Be calm!' And the wind
dropped, and all was calm again. •Then he said to them, 'Why are you so 40
Mt 8:10+ frightened? How is it that you have no faith?'[f] •They were filled with awe and said 41
1:27 to one another, 'Who can this be? Even the wind and the sea obey him.'

||Mt 8:28-34 ||Lk 8:26-39 **The Gerasene demoniac**

5 They reached the country of the Gerasenes[a] on the other side of the lake, •and 1 2
no sooner had he left the boat than a man with an unclean spirit came out

3 from the tombs towards him. •The man lived in the tombs and no one could
4 secure him any more, even with a chain; •because he had often been secured
with fetters and chains but had snapped the chains and broken the fetters, and no
5 one had the strength to control him. •All night and all day, among the tombs
6 and in the mountains, he would howl and gash himself with stones. •Catching
7 sight of Jesus from a distance, he ran up and fell at his feet •and shouted at the
top of his voice, 'What do you want with me, Jesus, son of the Most High God?
8 Swear by God you will not torture me!' •—For Jesus had been saying to him,
9 'Come out of the man, unclean spirit'. •'What is your name?' Jesus asked. 'My
10 name is legion,' he answered 'for there are many of us.' •And he begged him Mt 12:45 Lk 8:2; 11:26
11 earnestly not to send them out of the district. •Now there was there on the
12 mountainside a great herd of pigs feeding, •and the unclean spirits begged
13 him, 'Send us to the pigs, let us go into them'. •So he gave them leave. With that,
the unclean spirits came out and went into the pigs, and the herd of about two
thousand pigs charged down the cliff into the lake, and there they were drowned.
14 The swineherds ran off and told their story in the town and in the country round
15 about; and the people came to see what had really happened. •They came to
Jesus and saw the demoniac sitting there, clothed and in his full senses—the very
16 man who had had the legion in him before—and they were afraid. •And those
who had witnessed it reported what had happened to the demoniac and what had
17 become of the pigs. •Then they began to implore Jesus to leave the neighbourhood.
18 As he was getting into the boat, the man who had been possessed begged to be
19 allowed to stay with him. •Jesus would not let him but said to him, 'Go home 1:34+
to your people and tell them all that the Lord in his mercy has done for you'.
20 So the man went off and proceeded to spread throughout the Decapolis all that Mt 4:25+
Jesus had done for him. And everyone was amazed.

Cure of the woman with a haemorrhage. The daughter of Jairus raised to life ||Mt 9:18-26 ||Lk 8:40-56

21 When Jesus had crossed again in the boat to the other side, a large crowd 2:13
22 gathered round him and he stayed by the lakeside. •Then one of the synagogue
23 officials came up, Jairus by name, and seeing him, fell at his feet •and pleaded
with him earnestly, saying, 'My little daughter is desperately sick. Do come and
24 lay your hands on her to make her better and save her life.' •Jesus went with him
and a large crowd followed him; they were pressing all round him.

25 Now there was a woman who had suffered from a haemorrhage for
26 twelve years; •after long and painful treatment under various doctors, she had Tb 2:10
spent all she had without being any the better for it, in fact, she was getting
27 worse. •She had heard about Jesus, and she came up behind him through the crowd 6:56
28 and touched his cloak. •'If I can touch even his clothes,' she had told herself
29 'I shall be well again.' •And the source of the bleeding dried up instantly, and she
30 felt in herself that she was cured of her complaint. •Immediately aware that
power had gone out from him,[b] Jesus turned round in the crowd and said, 'Who
31 touched my clothes?' •His disciples said to him, 'You see how the crowd is
32 pressing round you and yet you say, "Who touched me?"' •But he continued
33 to look all round to see who had done it. •Then the woman came forward,
frightened and trembling[c] because she knew what had happened to her, and she
34 fell at his feet and told him the whole truth. •'My daughter,' he said 'your faith Mt 8:10+
has restored you to health; go in peace and be free from your complaint.'

35 While he was still speaking some people arrived from the house of the
synagogue official to say, 'Your daughter is dead: why put the Master to any

d. Two proverbs (vv. 24f) are here used to illustrate the attitude required of those who would listen to Christ's word.

e. The kingdom will achieve its full development in virtue of its own hidden, intrinsic power.

f. Var. 'Have you no faith yet?'

5 a. Var. 'Gadarenes', cf. Mt, or 'Gergesenes'.

b. This power is regarded as a physical emanation that heals, cf. Lk 6:19, by contact: cf. Mk 1:41; 3:10; 6:56; 8:22.

c. Not only from a sense of shame but also because the complaint involved legal impurity, Lv 15:25.

further trouble?' •But Jesus had overheard this remark of theirs and he said to 36
Mt 8:10+ the official, 'Do not be afraid; only have faith'. •And he allowed no one to go 37
with him except Peter and James and John the brother of James.[a] •So they came 38
to the official's house and Jesus noticed all the commotion, with people weeping
and wailing unrestrainedly. •He went in and said to them, 'Why all this 39
Ac 20:10 commotion and crying? The child is not dead, but asleep.' •But they laughed 40
Ac 9:40 at him. So he turned them all out and, taking with him the child's father and
mother and his own companions, he went into the place where the child lay.
And taking the child by the hand he said to her, 'Talitha, kum!'[b] which means, 41
'Little girl, I tell you to get up'. •The little girl got up at once and began to walk 42
about, for she was twelve years old. At this they were overcome with astonishment,
1:34+ and he ordered them strictly not to let anyone know about it, and told them 43
to give her something to eat.

||Mt 13:53-58 ||Lk 4:16-30

A visit to Nazareth

6 Going from that district, he went to his home town and his disciples accompa- 1
nied him. •With the coming of the sabbath he began teaching in the synagogue 2
and most of them were astonished when they heard him. They said, 'Where did
the man get all this? What is this wisdom that has been granted him, and these
15:40 miracles that are worked through him? •This is the carpenter, surely, the son 3
Mt 12:46+ Jn 6:42 of Mary, the brother of James and Joset[a] and Jude and Simon? His sisters, too, are
they not here with us?' And they would not accept him. •And Jesus said to them, 4
'A prophet is only despised in his own country, among his own relations and
7:32 1 Tm 4:14+ in his own house'; •and he could work no miracle there, though he cured a few 5
Mt 8:10+ sick people by laying his hands on them. •He was amazed at their lack of faith. 6

||Mt 10:1. 9-14 ||Lk 9:1-6; 10:4-11

The mission of the Twelve

He made a tour round the villages, teaching. •Then he summoned the Twelve 7
=3:14f and began to send them out in pairs, giving them authority over the unclean spirits.
And he instructed them to take nothing for the journey except a staff[b]—no bread, 8
no haversack, no coppers for their purses. •They were to wear sandals but, he 9
added, 'Do not take a spare tunic'. •And he said to them, 'If you enter a house 10
anywhere, stay there until you leave the district. •And if any place does not 11
welcome you and people refuse to listen to you, as you walk away shake off
the dust from under your feet as a sign to them.' •So they set off to preach 12
Jm 5:14f repentance; •and they cast out many devils, and anointed many sick people with 13
oil and cured them.

||Mt 14:1-2 ||Lk 9:7-9

Herod and Jesus

Meanwhile King Herod had heard about him, since by now his name was well- 14
known. Some were saying,[c] 'John the Baptist has risen from the dead, and that
is why miraculous powers are at work in him'. •Others said, 'He is Elijah'; 15
Mt 16:14+ others again, 'He is a prophet, like the prophets we used to have'. •But when 16
Herod heard this he said, 'It is John whose head I cut off; he has risen from the
dead'.

||Mt 14:3-12 Lk 3:19-20

John the Baptist beheaded

Now it was this same Herod who had sent to have John arrested, and had 17
him chained up in prison because of Herodias, his brother Philip's wife whom he
had married. •For John had told Herod, 'It is against the law for you to have 18
your brother's wife'. •As for Herodias, she was furious with him and wanted to 19
Ac 24:25 kill him; but she was not able to, •because Herod was afraid of John, knowing 20
him to be a good and holy man, and gave him his protection. When he had heard
him speak he was greatly perplexed,[d] and yet he liked to listen to him.

An opportunity came on Herod's birthday when he gave a banquet for the 21
nobles of his court, for his army officers and for the leading figures in Galilee.

22 When the daughter of this same Herodias came in and danced, she delighted
Herod and his guests; so the king said to the girl, 'Ask me anything you like
23 and I will give it you'. •And he swore her an oath, 'I will give you anything you Est 5:3
24 ask, even half my kingdom'. •She went out and said to her mother, 'What shall
25 I ask for?' She replied, 'The head of John the Baptist'. •The girl hurried straight
back to the king and made her request, 'I want you to give me John the Baptist's
26 head, here and now, on a dish'. •The king was deeply distressed but, thinking
of the oaths he had sworn and of his guests, he was reluctant to break his word
27 to her. •So the king at once sent one of the bodyguard with orders to bring
28 John's head. •The man went off and beheaded him in prison; then he brought
the head on a dish and gave it to the girl, and the girl gave it to her mother.
29 When John's disciples heard about this, they came and took his body and laid
it in a tomb.

First miracle of the loaves

||Mt 14:13-21 Mk 8:1-10 ||Lk 9:10-17 ||Jn 6:1-13

30 The apostles rejoined Jesus and told him all they had done and taught.
31 Then he said to them, 'You must come away to some lonely place all by yourselves
and rest for a while'; for there were so many coming and going that the apostles 2:2; 3:20
32 had no time even to eat. •So they went off in a boat to a lonely place where they
33 could be by themselves. •But people saw them going, and many could guess where;
and from every town they all hurried to the place on foot and reached it before
34 them. •So as he stepped ashore he saw a large crowd; and he took pity on them Mt 9:36
because they were like sheep without a shepherd, and he set himself to teach them
35 at some length. •By now it was getting very late, and his disciples came up to him
36 and said, 'This is a lonely place and it is getting very late, •so send them away,
and they can go to the farms and villages round about, to buy themselves
37 something to eat'. •He replied, 'Give them something to eat yourselves'. They
answered, 'Are we to go and spend two hundred denarii on bread for them to
38 eat?' •'How many loaves have you?' he asked 'Go and see.' And when they had
39 found out they said, 'Five, and two fish'. •Then he ordered them to get all the
40 people together in groups on the green grass, •and they sat down on the ground
41 in squares of hundreds and fifties. •Then he took the five loaves and the two fish,
raised his eyes to heaven and said the blessing; then he broke the loaves and
handed them to his disciples to distribute among the people. He also shared out
42 43 the two fish among them all. •They all ate as much as they wanted. •They
44 collected twelve basketfuls of scraps of bread and pieces of fish. •Those who had
eaten the loaves numbered five thousand men.

Jesus walks on the water

||Mt 14:22-33 ||Jn 6:16-21

45 Directly after this he made his disciples get into the boat and go on ahead to Lk 9:10
46 Bethsaida,[e] while he himself sent the crowd away. •After saying good-bye to
47 them he went off into the hills to pray. •When evening came, the boat was far out
48 on the lake, and he was alone on the land. •He could see they were worn out
with rowing, for the wind was against them; and about the fourth watch of the
night he came towards them, walking on the lake. He was going to pass them by,
49 but when they saw him walking on the lake they thought it was a ghost and cried
50 out; •for they had all seen him and were terrified. But he at once spoke to them,
51 and said, 'Courage! It is I! Do not be afraid.' •Then he got into the boat with them,
52 and the wind dropped. They were utterly and completely dumbfounded, •because
they had not seen what the miracle of the loaves meant; their minds were closed. 4:13+

d. These are to be privileged witnesses of the transfiguration, 9:2, and of the agony, 14:33; cf. 1:29; 13:3.

e. Aramaic; Christ's native tongue.

6 a. Var. 'Jose' or 'Joseph'.

b. In Mt and Lk the staff is forbidden, but the sense is the same: the missionary must be detached.

c. Var. 'He was saying'.

d. Var. (Vulg.) 'he did many things'. Alternative, but less probable, translation '... gave him his protection. He heard him speak and asked him all kinds of questions and liked to listen to him.'

e. Add. 'on the other side', cf. Mt 14:22.

||Mt 14:34-36 Cures at Gennesaret

Having made the crossing, they came to land at Gennesaret and tied up. •No 53 54
sooner had they stepped out of the boat than people recognised him, •and started 55
hurrying all through the countryside and brought the sick on stretchers to wherever
they heard he was. •And wherever he went, to village, or town, or farm, they 56
5:27-28 Ac 5:15 laid down the sick in the open spaces, begging him to let them touch even the
fringe of his cloak. And all those who touched him were cured.

||Mt 15:1-9 Ac 21:21 The traditions of the Pharisees

7 The Pharisees and some of the scribes who had come from Jerusalem gathered 1
round him, •and they noticed that some of his disciples were eating with 2
Lk 11:38 unclean hands, that is, without washing them. •For the Pharisees, and the Jews 3
Jn 2:6 Ga 1:14 in general, follow the tradition of the elders[a] and never eat without washing their
arms as far as the elbow; •and on returning from the market place they never 4
eat without first sprinkling[b] themselves. There are also many other observances
which have been handed down to them concerning the washing of cups and pots
and bronze dishes. •So these Pharisees and scribes asked him, 'Why do your 5
disciples not respect the tradition of the elders but eat their food with unclean
hands?' •He answered, 'It was of you hypocrites that Isaiah so rightly prophesied 6
in this passage of scripture:

Is 29:13 *This people honours me only with lip-service,*
while their hearts are far from me.
The worship they offer me is worthless, 7
the doctrines they teach are only human regulations.

You put aside the commandment of God to cling to human traditions.' •And 8 9
he said to them, 'How ingeniously you get round the commandment of God
Ex 20:12; 21:17 in order to preserve your own tradition! •For Moses said: *Do your duty to your* 10
Lv 20:9 Dt 5:16 *father and your mother*, and, *Anyone who curses father or mother must be put to*
death. •But you say, "If a man says to his father or mother: Anything I have 11
that I might have used to help you is Corban[c] (that is, dedicated to God), •then 12
he is forbidden from that moment to do anything for his father or mother".
In this way you make God's word null and void for the sake of your tradition 13
which you have handed down. And you do many other things like this.'

||Mt 15:10-20 On clean and unclean

He called the people to him again and said, 'Listen to me, all of you, and 14
understand. •Nothing that goes into a man from outside can make him unclean; 15
it is the things that come out of a man that make him unclean. •If anyone has 16
ears to hear, let him listen to this.'[d]
4:10 When he had gone back into the house, away from the crowd, his disciples 17
4:13+ questioned him about the parable.[e] •He said to them, 'Do you not understand 18
either? Can you not see that whatever goes into a man from outside cannot
Ac 10:9-16 Rm 14 make him unclean, •because it does not go into his heart but through his stomach 19
Col 2:16, 21-22 and passes out into the sewer?' (Thus he pronounced all foods clean.)[f] •And he 20
went on, 'It is what comes out of a man that makes him unclean. •For it is from 21
Jr 17:9 Rm 1:29+ within, from men's hearts, that evil intentions emerge: fornication, theft, murder,
adultery, avarice, malice, deceit, indecency, envy, slander, pride, folly. •All these 22 23
evil things come from within and make a man unclean.'

III. JOURNEYS OUTSIDE GALILEE

||Mt 15:21-28 The daughter of the Syrophoenician woman healed

He left that place and set out for the territory of Tyre.[g] There he went into 24
1:29; 2:15; 9:33; 10:10 a house and did not want anyone to know he was there, but he could not pass

25 unrecognised. •A woman whose little daughter had an unclean spirit heard about
26 him straightaway and came and fell at his feet. •Now the woman was a pagan,
by birth a Syrophoenician, and she begged him to cast the devil out of her Mt 8:29+
27 daughter. •And he said to her, 'The children should be fed first, because it is not
28 fair to take the children's food and throw it to the house-dogs'. •But she spoke
up: 'Ah yes, sir,' she replied 'but the house-dogs under the table can eat the
29 children's scraps'. •And he said to her, 'For saying this, you may go home happy:
30 the devil has gone out of your daughter'. •So she went off to her home and found
the child lying on the bed and the devil gone.

Healing of the deaf man

31 Returning from the district of Tyre, he went by way of Sidon towards the Sea Mt 15:29
32 of Galilee, right through the Decapolis region. •And they brought him a deaf
man who had an impediment in his speech; and they asked him to lay his hand on 6:5; 8:23 1 Tm 4:14+
33 him. •He took him aside in private, away from the crowd, put his fingers into the
34 man's ears and touched his tongue with spittle. •Then looking up to heaven he
35 sighed; and he said to him, 'Ephphatha', that is, 'Be opened'. •And his ears were Mt 8:3+
opened, and the ligament of his tongue was loosened and he spoke clearly.
36 And Jesus ordered them to tell no one about it, but the more he insisted, the 1:34+
37 more widely they published it. •Their admiration was unbounded. 'He has done 9:25 Mt 9:33; 15:31
all things well,' they said 'he makes the deaf hear and the dumb speak.'

Second miracle of the loaves ‖Mt 15:32-39

1 8 And now once again a great crowd had gathered, and they had nothing to eat. 6:30-44
2 So he called his disciples to him and said to them, •'I feel sorry for all these
people; they have been with me for three days now and have nothing to eat.
3 If I send them off home hungry they will collapse on the way; some have come
4 a great distance.' •His disciples replied, 'Where could anyone get bread to feed
5 these people in a deserted place like this?' •He asked them, 'How many loaves
6 have you?' 'Seven' they said. •Then he instructed the crowd to sit down on the
ground, and he took the seven loaves, and after giving thanks he broke them and
handed them to his disciples to distribute; and they distributed them among the
7 crowd. •They had a few small fish as well, and over these he said a blessing and
8 ordered them to be distributed also. •They ate as much as they wanted, and they
9 collected seven basketfuls of the scraps left over. •Now there had been about four
10 thousand people. He sent them away •and immediately, getting into the boat
with his disciples, went to the region of Dalmanutha.[a]

The Pharisees ask for a sign from heaven ‖Mt 12:38-39; 16:1-4

11 The Pharisees came up and started a discussion with him; they demanded Lk 11:16
12 of him a sign from heaven, to test him. •And with a sigh that came straight from
the heart he said, 'Why does this generation demand a sign? I tell you solemnly,
13 no sign shall be given to this generation.' •And leaving them again and re-em-
barking he went away to the opposite shore.

The yeast of the Pharisees and of Herod ‖Mt 16:5-12

14 The disciples had forgotten to take any food and they had only one loaf with
15 them in the boat. •Then he gave them this warning, 'Keep your eyes open; be ‖Lk 12:1
16 on your guard against the yeast of the Pharisees and the yeast of Herod'. •And

7 a. The 'tradition of the elders' comprises the injunctions and practices added by the rabbis to the Mosaic Law.

b. Var. 'bathing'. Or 'they never eat what comes from the market without having sprinkled it'.

c. *Corban*, Aramaic word meaning an offering, especially to God. See Mt 15:6+.

d. Om. v. 16.

e. 'Parable' in the Hebr. sense of *mashal* which includes even brief enigmatic sayings.

f. Lit. 'making all foods clean'; the clause (possibly a gloss) is obscure and variously interpreted.

g. Add. 'and Sidon', cf. Mt 15:21.

8 a. Either a place-name, unidentified like the 'Magadan' of Mt 15:39, or possibly a transliteration of some Aramaic expression.

they said to one another, 'It is because we have no bread'. •And Jesus knew it, 17
and he said to them, 'Why are you talking about having no bread? Do you not
4:13+ yet understand? Have you no perception? Are your minds closed? •Have you 18
Jr 5:21 Ezk 12:2 *eyes that do not see, ears that do not hear?* Or do you not remember? •When 19
I broke the five loaves among the five thousand, how many baskets full of scraps
did you collect?' They answered, 'Twelve'. •'And when I broke the seven loaves 20
for the four thousand, how many baskets full of scraps did you collect?'
And they answered, 'Seven'. •Then he said to them, 'Are you still without 21
perception?'[b]

Cure of a blind man at Bethsaida

5:30+ They came to Bethsaida, and some people brought to him a blind man whom 22
7:33; 9:27 they begged him to touch. •He took the blind man by the hand and led him outside 23
Jn 9:6 1 Tm 4:14+ the village. Then putting spittle on his eyes and laying his hands on him, he asked,
'Can you see anything?' •The man, who was beginning to see,[c] replied, 'I can see 24
people; they look like trees to me, but they are walking about'. •Then he laid 25
Mt 8:3+ his hands on the man's eyes again and he saw clearly; he was cured, and he could
1:34+ see everything plainly and distinctly. •And Jesus sent him home, saying, 'Do 26
not even go into the village'.

||Mt 16:13-20 ||Lk 9:18-21 **Peter's profession of faith**

Jesus and his disciples left for the villages round Caesarea Philippi. On the 27
way he put this question to his disciples, 'Who do people say I am?' •And they 28
told him. 'John the Baptist,' they said 'others Elijah; others again, one of the
prophets.' •'But you,' he asked 'who do you say I am?' Peter spoke up and said 29
1:34+ to him, 'You are the Christ'. •And he gave them strict orders not to tell anyone 30
about him.

||Mt 16:21-23 ||Lk 9:22 **First prophecy of the Passion**

9:9-10, 31-32; 10:32-34 And he began to teach them that the Son of Man was destined to suffer 31
grievously, to be rejected by the elders and the chief priests and the scribes, and
to be put to death, and after three days to rise again; •and he said all this quite 32
openly. Then, taking him aside, Peter started to remonstrate with him. •But, 33
turning and seeing his disciples, he rebuked Peter and said to him, 'Get behind
4:13+ me, Satan! Because the way you think is not God's way but man's.'

||Mt10:38-39; 16:24-28 ||Lk 9:23-27; 14:26-27 **The condition of following Christ**

He called the people and his disciples to him and said, 'If anyone wants to be 34
a follower of mine, let him renounce himself and take up his cross and follow
||Jn 12:25 me. •For anyone who wants to save his life will lose it; but anyone who loses his 35
life for my sake, and for the sake of the gospel, will save it. •What gain, then, is 36
it for a man to win the whole world and ruin his life? •And indeed what can 37
a man offer in exchange for his life? •For if anyone in this adulterous and sinful 38
Mt 10:33 ||Lk 12:8 generation is ashamed of me and of my words, the Son of Man will also be
ashamed of him when he comes in the glory of his Father with the holy angels.'
||Lk 9:27; 21:32 9 And he said to them, 'I tell you solemnly, there are some standing here who 1
Rm 1:4 will not taste death before they see the kingdom of God come with power'.

||Mt 17:1-8 ||Lk 9:28-36 **The transfiguration**

5:37+ Six days later, Jesus took with him Peter and James and John and led them 2
up a high mountain where they could be alone by themselves. There in
16:5 their presence he was transfigured: •his clothes became dazzlingly white, whiter 3
than any earthly bleacher could make them. •Elijah appeared to them with 4
14:40 Moses; and they were talking with Jesus. •Then Peter spoke to Jesus: 'Rabbi,' 5
he said 'it is wonderful for us to be here; so let us make three tents, one for
you, one for Moses and one for Elijah'. •He did not know what to say; they were 6

7 so frightened. •And a cloud came, covering them in shadow; and there came
8 a voice from the cloud, 'This is my Son, the Beloved. Listen to him.' •Then
suddenly, when they looked round, they saw no one with them any more but
only Jesus.

The question about Elijah

||Mt 17:9-13

9 As they came down from the mountain he warned them to tell no one 1:34+
what they had seen, until after the Son of Man had risen from the dead. 8:31
10 They observed the warning faithfully, though among themselves they discussed 4:13+
11 what 'rising from the dead' could mean. •And they put this question to him,
12 'Why do the scribes say that Elijah has to come first?' •'True,' he said 'Elijah Ml 3:23-24
is to come first and to see that everything is as it should be; yet how is it that the
scriptures say about the Son of Man that he is to suffer grievously and be treated
13 with contempt? •However, I tell you that Elijah has come and they have
treated him as they pleased, just as the scriptures say about him.' 1 K 19:2,10

The epileptic demoniac

||Mt 17:14-21
||Lk 9:37-42

14 When they rejoined the disciples they saw[a] a large crowd round them and
15 some scribes arguing with them. •The moment they saw him the whole crowd
16 were struck with amazement and ran to greet him. •'What are you arguing about
17 with them?' he asked. •A man answered him from the crowd, 'Master, I have
18 brought my son to you; there is a spirit of dumbness in him, •and when it Mt 8:29+
takes hold of him it throws him to the ground, and he foams at the mouth and
grinds his teeth and goes rigid. And I asked your disciples to cast it out and
19 they were unable to.' •'You faithless generation' he said to them in reply. 'How
much longer must I be with you? How much longer must I put up with you?
20 Bring him to me.' •They brought the boy to him, and as soon as the spirit
saw Jesus it threw the boy into convulsions, and he fell to the ground and
21 lay writhing there, foaming at the mouth. •Jesus asked the father, 'How
22 long has this been happening to him?' 'From childhood,' he replied •'and it
has often thrown him into the fire and into the water, in order to destroy him.
23 But if you can do anything, have pity on us and help us.' •'If you can?' retorted
24 Jesus. 'Everything is possible for anyone who has faith.' •Immediately the Mt 8:10+
25 father of the boy cried out, 'I do have faith. Help the little faith I have!' •And
when Jesus saw how many people were pressing round him, he rebuked the
unclean spirit. 'Deaf and dumb spirit,' he said 'I command you: come out of him 7:37
26 and never enter him again.' •Then throwing the boy into violent convulsions it
came out shouting, and the boy lay there so like a corpse that most of them
27 said, 'He is dead'. •But Jesus took him by the hand and helped him up, and he 8:23 Mt 8:15+
28 was able to stand. •When he had gone indoors his disciples asked him privately,
29 'Why were we unable to cast it out?' •'This is the kind' he answered 'that can
only be driven out by prayer.'[b]

Second prophecy of the Passion

||Mt 17:22-23
||Lk 9:43-45

30 After leaving that place they made their way through Galilee; and he did Jn 7:1
31 not want anyone to know, •because he was instructing his disciples; he was telling 1:34+
them, 'The Son of Man will be delivered into the hands of men; they will put 8:31+
him to death; and three days after he has been put to death he will rise again'.
32 But they did not understand what he said and were afraid to ask him. 4:13+

Who is the greatest?

||Mt 18:1-5
||Lk 9:46-48

33 They came to Capernaum, and when he was in the house he asked them, 7:24+

b. Jesus asks the disciples to forget their material needs and give their minds to the spiritual nature of his mission to which the miracles point.
c. Others translate 'raising his eyes'.

9 a. Var. 'he saw'.
b. Var. 'by prayer and fasting'.

'What were you arguing about on the road?' •They said nothing because they 34
had been arguing which of them was the greatest. •So he sat down, called the 35
Mt 20:27 Twelve to him and said, 'If anyone wants to be first, he must make himself last
of all and servant of all'. •He then took a little child, set him in front of them, 36
||Mt 10:40+; 18:5 put his arms round him, and said to them, •'Anyone who welcomes one of 37
||Lk 10:16 Jn 13:20 these little children in my name, welcomes me; and anyone who welcomes me
welcomes not me but the one who sent me'.

||Lk 9:49-50 **On using the name of Jesus**

John said to him, 'Master, we saw a man who is not one of us casting out 38
Nb 11:28 devils in your name; and because he was not one of us we tried to stop him'.
Ac 3:16+ 1 Co 12:3 But Jesus said, 'You must not stop him: no one who works a miracle in my name 39
Mt 12:30 is likely to speak evil of me. •Anyone who is not against us is for us. 40

||Mt 10:42 **Charity shown to Christ's disciples**

1 Co 3:23+ 'If anyone gives you a cup of water to drink just because you belong to Christ, 41
then I tell you solemnly, he will most certainly not lose his reward.

||Mt 18:6-9 ||Lk 17:1-2 **On leading others astray**

'But anyone who is an obstacle to bring down one of these little ones who 42
have faith,[c] would be better thrown into the sea with a great millstone round
his neck. •And if your hand should cause you to sin, cut it off; it is better for you 43
to enter into life crippled, than to have two hands and go to hell, into the fire that
cannot be put out.[d] •And if your foot should cause you to sin, cut it off; it is 45
better for you to enter into life lame, than to have two feet and be thrown into
hell. •And if your eye should cause you to sin, tear it out; it is better for you to 47
enter into the kingdom of God with one eye, than to have two eyes and be thrown
Is 66:24+ Si 7:17 into hell •where *their worm does not die nor their fire go out.* •For everyone will 48 49
Lv 2:13+ ||*Mt 5:13* be salted with fire.[e] •Salt is a good thing, but if salt has become insipid, how can 50
||Lk 14:34 Rm 12:18 Col 4:6 you season it again? Have salt in yourselves and be at peace with one another.'

||Mt 19:1-9 **The question about divorce**

Lk 9:51 Jn 10:40-41 **10** Leaving there, he came to the district of Judaea and the far side of the 1
Jordan. And again crowds gathered round him, and again he taught them,
as his custom was. •Some Pharisees approached him and asked, 'Is it against 2
the law for a man to divorce his wife?' They were testing him. •He answered 3
Dt 24:1 them, 'What did Moses command you?' •'Moses allowed us' they said 'to draw 4
up a writ of dismissal and so to divorce.' •Then Jesus said to them, 'It was 5
because you were so unteachable that he wrote this commandment for you.
Gn 1:27 But from the beginning of creation *God made them male and female. •This is why* 6 7
Gn 2:24 *a man must leave father and mother,*[a] •*and the two become one body.* They are no 8
longer two, therefore, but one body. •So then, what God has united, man must not 9
7:24+ divide.' •Back in the house the disciples questioned him again about this, •and 10 11
||Mt 5:32 ||Lk 16:18 he said to them, 'The man who divorces his wife and marries another is guilty of
adultery against her. •And if a woman divorces her husband and marries 12
another she is guilty of adultery too.'

||Mt 19:13-15 ||Lk 18:15-17 **Jesus and the children**

Lk 9:47 People were bringing little children to him, for him to touch them. The 13
disciples turned them away, •but when Jesus saw this he was indignant and said 14
to them, 'Let the little children come to me; do not stop them; for it is to such as
||Mt 18:3 these that the kingdom of God belongs. •I tell you solemnly, anyone who 15
does not welcome the kingdom of God like a little child will never enter it.'
Then he put his arms round them, laid his hands on them and gave them his 16
blessing.

The rich young man

||Mt 19:16-22 ||Lk 18:18-23

17 He was setting out on a journey when a man ran up, knelt before him and
put this question to him, 'Good master, what must I do to inherit eternal life?'
18 Jesus said to him, 'Why do you call me good? No one is good but God alone.
19 You know the commandments: *You must not kill; You must not commit adultery;* Ex 20:12-16 Dt 5:16-20
You must not steal; You must not bring false witness; You must not defraud; Dt 24:14
20 *Honour your father and mother.*' •And he said to him, 'Master, I have kept all
21 these from my earliest days'. •Jesus looked steadily at him and loved him, and
he said, 'There is one thing you lack. Go and sell everything you own and give
the money to the poor, and you will have treasure in heaven; then come, follow
22 me.' •But his face fell at these words and he went away sad, for he was a man
of great wealth.

The danger of riches

||Mt 19:23-26 ||Lk 18:24-27

23 Jesus looked round and said to his disciples, 'How hard it is for those who Pr 11:28
24 have riches to enter the kingdom of God!' •The disciples were astounded by
these words,[b] but Jesus insisted, 'My children,' he said to them 'how hard it is to
25 enter the kingdom of God! •It is easier for a camel to pass through the eye of
26 a needle than for a rich man to enter the kingdom of God.' •They were more
astonished than ever. 'In that case' they said to one another 'who can be saved?'
27 Jesus gazed at them. 'For men' he said 'it is impossible, but not for God: because
everything is possible for God.'

The reward of renunciation

||Mt 19:27-30 ||Lk 18:28-30

28 Peter took this up. 'What about us?' he asked him. 'We have left everything
29 and followed you.' •Jesus said, 'I tell you solemnly, there is no one who has left 1:1+
house, brothers, sisters, father, children or land for my sake and for the sake of
30 the gospel •who will not be repaid a hundred times over, houses, brothers, sisters,
mothers, children and land—not without persecutions—now in this present time
and, in the world to come, eternal life.
31 'Many who are first will be last, and the last first.' ||Lk 13:30

Third prophecy of the Passion

||Mt 20:17-19 ||Lk 18:31-33

32 They were on the road, going up to Jerusalem; Jesus was walking on ahead Jn 11:16
of them; they were in a daze, and those who followed were apprehensive. Once
more taking the Twelve aside he began to tell them what was going to happen 8:31+
33 to him: •'Now we are going up to Jerusalem, and the Son of Man is about
to be handed over to the chief priests and the scribes. They will condemn him
34 to death and will hand him over to the pagans, •who will mock him and spit at
him and scourge him and put him to death; and after three days he will
rise again.'

The sons of Zebedee make their request

||Mt 20:20-23

35 James and John, the sons of Zebedee, approached him. 'Master,' they said
36 to him 'we want you to do us a favour.' •He said to them, 'What is it you want
37 me to do for you?' •They said to him, 'Allow us to sit one at your right hand
38 and the other at your left in your glory'.[c] •'You do not know what you are asking' 4:13+
Jesus said to them. 'Can you drink the cup that I must drink, or be baptised Lk 12:50

c. Add. 'in me'.

d. Omitting, with the best MSS. vv. 44 and 46 (Vulg.), merely repetitions of v. 48.

e. This 'seasoning' fire means either penalties by which the sinner is punished and at the same time preserved, or (preferably) the purifying fire of trials by which the faithful become sacrifices pleasing to God, cf. Lv 2:13 (to this alludes an add. 'and every victim must be salted with salt'). It appears that v. 50, cf. Mt 5:13, has been inserted here for no other reason than the recurrence of the word 'salt'.

10 a. Add. 'and cling to his wife', cf. Gn 2:24 and Mt 19:5.

b. Wealth and prosperity were considered signs of God's favour, cf. Introduction to Wisdom Books.

c. When, as messianic King, your triumph is assured.

with the baptism with which I must be baptised?'[a] •They replied, 'We can'. 39
Jesus said to them, 'The cup that I must drink you shall drink, and with the
baptism with which I must be baptised you shall be baptised, •but as for seats 40
at my right hand or my left, these are not mine to grant; they belong to those
to whom they have been allotted'.

||Mt 20:24-28 ||Lk 22:24-27

Leadership with service

When the other ten heard this they began to feel indignant with James and 41
John, •so Jesus called them to him and said to them, 'You know that among the 42
pagans their so-called rulers lord it over them, and their great men make their
authority felt. •This is not to happen among you. No; anyone who wants to become 43
great among you must be your servant, •and anyone who wants to be first 44
among you must be slave to all. •For the Son of Man himself did not come to 45
be served but to serve, and to give his life as a ransom for many.'

||Mt 20:29-34 ||Lk 18:35-43

The blind man of Jericho

They reached Jericho; and as he left Jericho with his disciples and a large 46
crowd, Bartimaeus (that is, the son of Timaeus), a blind beggar, was sitting at the
side of the road. •When he heard that it was Jesus of Nazareth, he began to shout 47
and to say, 'Son of David, Jesus, have pity on me'. •And many of them scolded 48
him and told him to keep quiet, but he only shouted all the louder, 'Son of David,
have pity on me'. •Jesus stopped and said, 'Call him here'. So they called the 49
blind man. 'Courage,' they said 'get up; he is calling you.' •So throwing off his 50
cloak, he jumped up and went to Jesus. •Then Jesus spoke, 'What do you want 51
Jn 20:16 me to do for you?' 'Rabbuni,'[e] the blind man said to him 'Master, let me see
Mt 8:10 again.' •Jesus said to him, 'Go; your faith has saved you'. And immediately 52
his sight returned and he followed him along the road.

IV. THE JERUSALEM MINISTRY

||Mt 21:1-11 ||Lk 19:28-38 ||Jn 12:12-16

The Messiah enters Jerusalem

11 When they were approaching Jerusalem, in sight of Bethphage and Bethany, 1
close by the Mount of Olives, he sent two of his disciples •and said to them, 2
'Go off to the village facing you, and as soon as you enter it you will find a tethered
colt that no one has yet ridden. Untie it and bring it here. •If anyone says to 3
you, "What are you doing?" say, "The Master needs it and will send
it back here directly".' •They went off and found a colt tethered near a door in 4
the open street. As they untied it, •some men standing there said, 'What are you 5
doing, untying that colt?' •They gave the answer Jesus had told them, and the 6
men let them go. •Then they took the colt to Jesus and threw their cloaks on its 7
back, and he sat on it. •Many people spread their cloaks on the road, others green- 8
ery which they had cut in the fields. •And those who went in front and those who 9
Ps 118:25-26 followed were all shouting, '*Hosanna! Blessings on him who comes in the name*
2 S 7:16 *of the Lord!* •Blessings on the coming kingdom of our father David! *Hosanna* 10
||Mt 21:12 Lk 21:37 in the highest heavens!' •He entered Jerusalem and went into the Temple. He 11
looked all round him, but as it was now late, he went out to Bethany with the
Twelve.

||Mt 21:18-19

The barren fig tree

Next day as they were leaving Bethany, he felt hungry. •Seeing a fig tree in 12 13
leaf some distance away, he went to see if he could find any fruit on it, but when
he came up to it he found nothing but leaves; for it was not the season for figs.
And he addressed the fig tree. 'May no one ever eat fruit from you again' he 14
said. And his disciples heard him say this.

The expulsion of the dealers from the Temple

||Mt 21:12-17
||Lk 19:45-48
||Jn 2:14-16

15 So they reached Jerusalem and he went into the Temple and began driving
out those who were selling and buying there; he upset the tables of the money
16 changers and the chairs of those who were selling pigeons. •Nor would he allow
17 anyone to carry anything through the Temple. •And he taught them and said,
'Does not scripture say: *My house will be called a house of prayer for all* Is 56:7
18 *the peoples?*[a] But you have turned it into *a robbers' den.*' •This came to the ears Jr 7:11
of the chief priests and the scribes, and they tried to find some way of doing
away with him; they were afraid of him because the people were carried away
19 by his teaching. •And when evening came he went out of the city. Lk 21:37

The fig tree withered. Faith and prayer

||Mt 21:20-22

20 Next morning, as they passed by, they saw the fig tree withered to the roots.
21 Peter remembered. 'Look, Rabbi,' he said to Jesus 'the fig tree you cursed has
22 23 withered away.' •Jesus answered, 'Have faith in God. •I tell you solemnly, Mt 8:10+; ||17:20-21
if anyone says to this mountain, "Get up and throw yourself into the sea", with no ||Lk 17:6
hesitation in his heart but believing that what he says will happen, it will be done
24 for him. •I tell you therefore: everything you ask and pray for, believe that you Mt 7:7-8 Jn 11:22
25 have it already, and it will be yours. •And when you stand in prayer, forgive
whatever you have against anybody, so that your Father in heaven may forgive Mt 5:23-24; 6:14-15
your failings too.'[b]

The authority of Jesus is questioned

||Mt 21:23-27
||Lk 20:1-8

27 They came to Jerusalem again, and as Jesus was walking in the Temple, the
28 chief priests and the scribes and the elders came to him, •and they said to him,
'What authority have you for acting like this? Or who gave you authority to do
29 these things?' •Jesus said to them, 'I will ask you a question, only one; answer
30 me and I will tell you my authority for acting like this. •John's baptism: did it
31 come from heaven, or from man? Answer me that.' •And they argued it out
this way among themselves: 'If we say from heaven, he will say, "Then why did
32 you refuse to believe him?" •But dare we say from man?'—they had the people
33 to fear, for everyone held that John was a real prophet. •So their reply to Jesus
was, 'We do not know'. And Jesus said to them, 'Nor will I tell you my authority
for acting like this'.

Parable of the wicked husbandmen

||Mt 21:33-46
||Lk 20:9-19

1 **12** He went on to speak to them in parables, 'A man planted a vineyard; he Is 5:1+
fenced it round, dug out a trough for the winepress and built a tower; then
2 he leased it to tenants and went abroad. •When the time came, he sent a servant
to the tenants to collect from them his share of the produce from the vineyard.
3 4 But they seized the man, thrashed him and sent him away empty-handed. •Next
he sent another servant to them; him they beat about the head and treated
5 shamefully. •And he sent another and him they killed; then a number of others,
6 and they thrashed some and killed the rest. •He had still someone left: his beloved
7 son. He sent him to them last of all. "They will respect my son" he said. •But
those tenants said to each other, "This is the heir. Come on, let us kill him, and the
8 inheritance will be ours." •So they seized him and killed him and threw him out
9 of the vineyard. •Now what will the owner of the vineyard do? He will come and
10 make an end of the tenants and give the vineyard to others. •Have you not read
this text of scripture:

d. To drink the cup, cf. 14:36, and to be baptised are symbols of the approaching Passion: Jesus is to be 'immersed' (Greek: *baptizein*) in suffering.

e. Aramaic 'My master' or 'Master'; cf. Jn 20:16.

11 a. Of the Synoptics only Mk quotes, no doubt deliberately, these last four words of Isaiah's text; they foretell the worldwide worship of the messianic age.

b. Add. v. 26 'But if you do not forgive, your Father in heaven will not forgive your failings either' cf. Mt 6:15.

Ps 118:22-23 *It was the stone rejected by the builders*
that became the keystone.
This was the Lord's doing 11
and it is wonderful to see?

And they would have liked to arrest him, because they realised that the parable 12
was aimed at them, but they were afraid of the crowds. So they left him alone
and went away.

||Mt 22:15-22 ||Lk 20:20-26 Mk 3:6+

On tribute to Caesar

Next they sent to him some Pharisees and some Herodians to catch him out 13
in what he said. •These came and said to him, 'Master, we know you are an honest 14
man, that you are not afraid of anyone, because a man's rank means nothing
to you, and that you teach the way of God in all honesty. Is it permissible to
pay taxes to Caesar or not? Should we pay, yes or no?' •Seeing through their 15
hypocrisy he said to them, 'Why do you set this trap for me? Hand me a
denarius and let me see it.' •They handed him one and he said, 'Whose head 16
is this? Whose name?' 'Caesar's' they told him. •Jesus said to them, 'Give back 17
to Caesar what belongs to Caesar—and to God what belongs to God'. This
reply took them completely by surprise.

||Mt 22:23-33 ||Lk 20:27-40 Dt 25:5f+

The resurrection of the dead

Then some Sadducees—who deny that there is a resurrection—came to 18
him and they put this question to him, •'Master, we have it from Moses in 19
writing, if a man's brother dies leaving a wife but no child, the man must
marry the widow to raise up children for his brother. •Now there were seven 20
brothers. The first married a wife and then died leaving no children. •The second 21
married the widow, and he too died leaving no children; with the third it was
the same, •and none of the seven left any children. Last of all the woman herself 22
died. •Now at the resurrection, when they rise again, whose wife will she be, 23
since she had been married to all seven?'

Jesus said to them, 'Is not the reason why you go wrong, that you understand 24
neither the scriptures nor the power of God? •For when they rise from the dead, 25
men and women do not marry; no, they are like the angels in heaven. •Now 26
about the dead rising again, have you never read in the Book of Moses, in the
Ex 3:6 passage about the Bush,[a] how God spoke to him and said: *I am the God of*
Abraham, the God of Isaac and the God of Jacob? •He is God, not of the dead, 27
but of the living. You are very much mistaken.'

||Mt 22:34-40 ||Lk 10:25-28

The greatest commandment of all

One of the scribes who had listened to them debating and had observed how 28
well Jesus had answered them, now came up and put a question to him, 'Which
Dt 6:4-5 is the first of all the commandments?' •Jesus replied, 'This is the first: *Listen,* 29
Israel, the Lord our God is the one Lord, •and you must love the Lord your God with 30
all your heart, with all your soul, with all your mind and *with all your strength.*
Lv 19:18 The second is this: *You must love your neighbour as yourself.* There is no com- 31
mandment greater than these.' •The scribe said to him, 'Well spoken, Master; 32
Dt 4:35; 6:4 what you have said is true: that he is one and there is no other. •To love him with 33
all your heart, with all your understanding and strength, and to love your
1 S 15:22 Ps 40:6-8 neighbour as yourself, this is far more important than any holocaust or sacrifice.'
Am 5:21+ Jesus, seeing how wisely he had spoken, said, 'You are not far from the kingdom 34
||Mt 22:46 ||Lk 20:40 of God'. And after that no one dared to question him any more.

||Mt 22:41-46 ||Lk 20:41-44

Christ not only son but also Lord of David

Later, while teaching in the Temple, Jesus said, 'How can the scribes maintain 35
Mt 9:27+ that the Christ is the son of David? •David himself, moved by the Holy Spirit, 36
said:

The Lord said to my Lord: Ps 110:1
Sit at my right hand
and I will put your enemies
under your feet.

37 David himself calls him Lord, in what way then can he be his son?' And the
great majority of the people heard this with delight.

The scribes condemned by Jesus ||Mt 23:6-7 ||Lk 11:43; 20:45-47

38 In his teaching he said, 'Beware of the scribes who like to walk about
39 in long robes, to be greeted obsequiously in the market squares, •to take
40 the front seats in the synagogues and the places of honour at banquets; •these
are the men who swallow the property of widows, while making a show of lengthy
prayers. The more severe will be the sentence they receive.'

The widow's mite ||Lk 21:1-4

41 He sat down opposite the treasury and watched the people putting money Jn 8:20
42 into the treasury,[b] and many of the rich put in a great deal. •A poor widow came
43 and put in two small coins, the equivalent of a penny. •Then he called
his disciples and said to them, 'I tell you solemnly, this poor widow has
44 put more in than all who have contributed to the treasury; •for they have all put
in money they had over, but she from the little she had has put in everything
she possessed, all she had to live on'.

The eschatological discourse: introduction ||Mt 24-25

1 13 As he was leaving the Temple one of his disciples said to him, 'Look at the ||Mt 24:1-3 ||Lk 21:5-7
2 size of those stones, Master! Look at the size of those buildings!' •And
Jesus said to him, 'You see these great buildings? Not a single stone will be
left on another: everything will be destroyed.'

3 And while he was sitting facing the Temple, on the Mount of Olives, Peter, 1:29
4 James, John and Andrew questioned him privately, •'Tell us, when is this going 5:37+
to happen, and what sign will there be that all this is about to be fulfilled?'

The beginning of sorrows

5 6 Then Jesus began to tell them, 'Take care that no one deceives you. •Many will ||Mt 24:4-14 ||Lk 21:8-19
7 come using my name and saying, "I am he", and they will deceive many. •When
you hear of wars and rumours of wars, do not be alarmed, this is something that
8 must happen, but the end will not be yet. •For nation will fight against nation,
and kingdom against kingdom. There will be earthquakes here and there; there
will be famines. This is the beginning of the birthpangs.

9 'Be on your guard: they will hand you over to sanhedrins; you will be beaten ||Mt 10:17-22
in synagogues; and you will stand before governors and kings for my sake,
10 to bear witness before them, •since the Good News must first be proclaimed
to all the nations.

11 'And when they lead you away to hand you over, do not worry beforehand ||Lk 12:11-12
about what to say; no, say whatever is given to you when the time comes, because
12 it is not you who will be speaking: it will be the Holy Spirit. •Brother will betray
brother to death, and the father his child; children will rise against their parents
13 and have them put to death. •You will be hated by all men on account of my
name; but the man who stands firm to the end will be saved.

The great tribulation of Jerusalem ||Mt 24:15-25 ||Lk 21:20-24

14 'When you see *the disastrous abomination* set up where it ought not to be Dn 9:27; 11:31; 12:11
(let the reader understand), then those in Judaea must escape to the mountains; 1 M 1:54

12 a. I.e. in which the burning bush incident is narrated.

b. Evidently the treasure chamber inside the Temple enclosure had an alms box outside.

||Lk 17:31 if a man is on the housetop, he must not come down to go into the house to 15
collect any of his belongings; •if a man is in the fields, he must not turn back 16
to fetch his cloak. •Alas for those with child, or with babies at the breast, when 17
Dn 12:1 those days come! •Pray that this may not be in winter. •For in those days there 18 19
||Lk 21:23-24 will be *such distress as, until now, has not been* equalled since the beginning when
Rv 16:18 God created the world, nor ever will be again. •And if the Lord had not shortened 20
that time, no one would have survived; but he did shorten the time, for the sake
of the elect whom he chose.

||Lk 17:23 'And if anyone says to you then, "Look, here is the Christ" or, "Look, he 21
is there", do not believe it; •for false Christs and false prophets will arise and 22
produce signs and portents to deceive the elect, if that were possible. •You 23
Jn 16:4 therefore must be on your guard. I have forewarned you of everything.

The coming of the Son of Man

Mt 24:29-31 Lk 21:25-27

'But in those days, after that time of distress, the sun will be darkened, the 24
moon will lose its brightness, •the stars will come falling from heaven and the 25
14:62 Dn 7:13-14 powers in the heavens will be shaken. •And then they will see the Son of Man 26
Mt 8:20+ coming in the clouds with great power and glory; •then too he will send the angels 27
to gather his chosen from the four winds, from the ends of the world to the ends
of heaven.

The time of this coming

||Mt 24:32-36 ||Lk 21:29-33

'Take the fig tree as a parable: as soon as its twigs grow supple and its leaves 28
come out, you know that summer is near. •So with you when you see these things 29
happening: know that he is near, at the very gates. •I tell you solemnly, 30
before this generation has passed away all these things will have taken
place. •Heaven and earth will pass away, but my words will not pass away. 31
'But as for that day or hour, nobody knows it, neither the angels of heaven, 32
nor the Son; no one but the Father.

Be on the alert

||Mt 24:42; 25:13-15 ||Lk 19:12-13; 12:38, 40

Rv 3:3 'Be on your guard, stay awake, because you never know when the time will 33
Mt 25:14 come. •It is like a man travelling abroad: he has gone from home, and left his 34
servants in charge, each with his own task; and he has told the doorkeeper to
||Lk 12:38,40 stay awake. •So stay awake, because you do not know when the master of the 35
house is coming, evening, midnight, cockcrow, dawn; •if he comes unexpectedly, 36
he must not find you asleep. •And what I say to you I say to all: Stay awake!' 37

V. PASSION AND RESURRECTION

The conspiracy against Jesus

||Mt 26:2-5 ||Lk 22:1-2

Mt 26:17+ **14** It was two days before the Passover and the feast of Unleavened Bread, and 1
the chief priests and the scribes were looking for a way to arrest Jesus by
some trick and have him put to death. •For they said, 'It must not be during 2
the festivities, or there will be a disturbance among the people'.

The anointing at Bethany

||Mt 26:6-13 ||Jn 12:1-8

Jesus was at Bethany in the house of Simon the leper; he was at dinner when 3
a woman came in with an alabaster jar of very costly ointment, pure nard. She
broke the jar and poured the ointment on his head. •Some who were there said 4
to one another indignantly, 'Why this waste of ointment? •Ointment like this 5
could have been sold for over three hundred denarii and the money given to the
poor'; and they were angry with her. •But Jesus said, 'Leave her alone. Why 6
are you upsetting her? What she has done for me is one of the good works.
You have the poor with you always, and you can be kind to them whenever you 7

8 wish, but you will not always have me. •She has done what was in her power to
9 do: she has anointed my body beforehand for its burial. •I tell you solemnly,
wherever throughout all the world the Good News is proclaimed, what she has
done will be told also, in remembrance of her.'

Judas betrays Jesus

||Mt 26:14-16 ||Lk 22:3-6

10 Judas Iscariot, one of the Twelve, approached the chief priests with an offer
11 to hand Jesus over to them. •They were delighted to hear it, and promised to
give him money; and he looked for a way of betraying him when the opportunity
should occur.

Preparations for the Passover supper

||Mt 26:17-19 ||Lk 22:7-13

12 On the first day of Unleavened Bread, when the Passover lamb was sacrificed,
his disciples said to him, 'Where do you want us to go and make the preparations
13 for you to eat the passover?' •So he sent two of his disciples, saying to them,
'Go into the city and you will meet a man carrying a pitcher of water. Follow him, 1 S 10:2-5
14 and say to the owner of the house which he enters, "The Master says: Where
15 is my dining room in which I can eat the passover with my disciples?" •He will
show you a large upper room furnished with couches, all prepared. Make the
16 preparations for us there.' •The disciples set out and went to the city and
found everything as he had told them, and prepared the Passover.

The treachery of Judas foretold

||Mt 26:20-25 ||Lk 22:14, 21-23

17 18 When evening came he arrived with the Twelve. •And while they were at
table eating, Jesus said, 'I tell you solemnly, one of you is about to betray Jn 13:21
19 me, one of you eating with me'. •They were distressed and asked him, one after
20 another, 'Not I, surely?' •He said to them, 'It is one of the Twelve, one who is
21 dipping into the same dish with me. •Yes, the Son of Man is going to his fate,
as the scriptures say he will, but alas for that man by whom the Son of Man
is betrayed! Better for that man if he had never been born!'

The institution of the Eucharist

||Mt 26:26-29 ||Lk 22:15-20 ||1 Co 11: 23-25

22 And as they were eating he took some bread, and when he had said the blessing
23 he broke it and gave it to them. 'Take it,' he said 'this is my body.' •Then he took
a cup, and when he had returned thanks he gave it to them, and all drank from
24 it, •and he said to them, 'This is my blood, the blood of the covenant, which is
25 to be poured out for many. •I tell you solemnly, I shall not drink any more wine ||Lk 22:18
until the day I drink the new wine in the kingdom of God.' Mt 8:11+

Peter's denial foretold

||Mt 26:30-35 ||Lk 22:39, 31-34 ||Jn 13:36-38

26 27 After psalms had been sung they left for the Mount of Olives. •And Jesus Jn 18:1-2
said to them, 'You will all lose faith, for the scripture says: *I shall strike*
28 *the shepherd and the sheep will be scattered,* •however after my resurrection I shall Zc 13:7
29 30 go before you to Galilee'. •Peter said, 'Even if all lose faith, I will not'. •And
Jesus said to him, 'I tell you solemnly, this day, this very night, before
31 the cock crows twice, you will have disowned me three times'. •But he repeated
still more earnestly, 'If I have to die with you, I will never disown you'. And
they all said the same.

Gethsemane

||Mt 26:36-46 ||Lk 22:40-45

32 They came to a small estate called Gethsemane, and Jesus said to his disciples, Jn 18:1
33 'Stay here while I pray'. •Then he took Peter and James and John with him. 5:37+
34 And a sudden fear came over him, and great distress. •And he said to them, 'My
35 soul is sorrowful to the point of death. Wait here, and keep awake.' •And going
on a little further he threw himself on the ground and prayed that, if it were
36 possible, this hour might pass him by. •'Abba (Father)!' he said 'Everything

is possible for you. Take this cup away from me. But let it be as you, not I, would
have it.' •He came back and found them sleeping, and he said to Peter, 'Simon, 37
are you asleep? Had you not the strength to keep awake one hour? •You should 38
Rm 7:5+ be awake, and praying not to be put to the test. The spirit is willing, but the flesh
is weak.' •Again he went away and prayed, saying the same words. •And 39 40
once more he came back and found them sleeping, their eyes were so heavy; and
9:6 they could find no answer for him. •He came back a third time and said to them, 41
'You can sleep on now and take your rest. It is all over. The hour has come. Now
the Son of Man is to be betrayed into the hands of sinners. •Get up! Let us go! 42
My betrayer is close at hand already.'

||Mt 26:47-56 ||Lk 22:47-53 ||Jn 18:2-11

The arrest

Even while he was still speaking, Judas, one of the Twelve, came up with 43
a number of men armed with swords and clubs, sent by the chief priests and
the scribes and the elders. •Now the traitor had arranged a signal with them. 44
'The one I kiss,' he had said 'he is the man. Take him in charge, and see he is
well guarded when you lead him away.' •So when the traitor came, he went 45
straight up to Jesus and said, 'Rabbi!' and kissed him. •The others seized him 46
and took him in charge. •Then one of the bystanders drew his sword and struck 47
out at the high priest's servant, and cut off his ear.

Then Jesus spoke. 'Am I a brigand' he said 'that you had to set out to 48
capture me with swords and clubs? •I was among you teaching in the Temple day 49
after day and you never laid hands on me. But this is to fulfil the scriptures.'
And they all deserted him and ran away. •A young man who followed him had 50 51
nothing on but a linen cloth. They caught hold of him, •but he left the cloth 52
in their hands and ran away naked.[a]

||Mt 26:57-68 ||Lk 22:54, 63-71 ||Jn 18:15-16,18

Jesus before the Sanhedrin

They led Jesus off to the high priest; and all the chief priests and the elders 53
and the scribes assembled there. •Peter had followed him at a distance, right 54
into the high priest's palace, and was sitting with the attendants warming himself
at the fire.

The chief priests and the whole Sanhedrin were looking for evidence against 55
Jesus on which they might pass the death-sentence. But they could not find any.
Several, indeed, brought false evidence against him, but their evidence was 56
conflicting. •Some stood up and submitted this false evidence against him, 57
15:29 2 Co 5:1 'We heard him say, "I am going to destroy this Temple made by human hands, 58
and in three days build another, not made by human hands" '. •But even on 59
this point their evidence was conflicting. •The high priest then stood up before 60
the whole assembly and put this question to Jesus, 'Have you no answer to that?
What is this evidence these men are bringing against you?'[b] •But he was silent 61
and made no answer at all. The high priest put a second question to him, 'Are
you the Christ,' he said 'the Son of the Blessed One?'[c] •'I am,' said Jesus 'and 62
13:26 Dn 7:13 Ps 110:1 you will see *the Son of Man seated at the right hand of the Power* and *coming with*
the clouds of heaven.' •The high priest tore his robes, 'What need of witnesses have 63
we now?' he said. •'You heard the blasphemy. What is your finding?' And they 64
all gave their verdict: he deserved to die.

||Lk 22:63-65 Some of them started spitting at him and, blindfolding him, began hitting 65
him with their fists and shouting, 'Play the prophet!' And the attendants rained
blows on him.

||Mt 26:69-75 ||Lk 22:55-62 ||Jn 18:15-18, 25-27

Peter's denials

While Peter was down below in the courtyard, one of the high priest's 66
servant-girls came up. •She saw Peter warming himself there, stared at him and 67
Mt 2:23+ said, 'You too were with Jesus, the man from Nazareth'. •But he denied it. 68
'I do not know, I do not understand, what you are talking about' he said. And

69 he went out into the forecourt.[d] •The servant-girl saw him and again started
70 telling the bystanders, 'This fellow is one of them'. •But again he denied it.
A little later the bystanders themselves said to Peter, 'You are one of them for
71 sure! Why, you are a Galilean.' •But he started calling down curses on himself
72 and swearing, 'I do not know the man you speak of'. •At that moment the
cock crew for the second time, and Peter recalled how Jesus had said to him,
'Before the cock crows twice, you will have disowned me three times'. And
he burst into tears.

Jesus before Pilate ||Mt 27:1-2, 11-26 ||Lk 22:66; 23:1-5, 13-25

1 **15** First thing in the morning, the chief priests together with the elders and
scribes, in short the whole Sanhedrin, had their plan ready. They had ||Jn 18:28-40; 19:4-16
Jesus bound and took him away and handed him over to Pilate. *Mt 26:57+*

2 Pilate questioned him, 'Are you the king of the Jews?' 'It is you who say it'
3 he answered. •And the chief priests brought many accusations against him.
4 Pilate questioned him again, 'Have you no reply at all? See how many accusations
5 they are bringing against you!' •But, to Pilate's amazement, Jesus made no
further reply.

6 At festival time Pilate used to release a prisoner for them, anyone they asked
7 for. •Now a man called Barabbas was then in prison with the rioters who had
8 committed murder during the uprising. •When the crowd went up and began to
9 ask Pilate the customary favour, •Pilate answered them, 'Do you want me to
10 release for you the king of the Jews?' •For he realised it was out of jealousy that
11 the chief priests had handed Jesus over. •The chief priests, however, had incited
12 the crowd to demand that he should release Barabbas for them instead. •Then
Pilate spoke again. 'But in that case,' he said to them 'what am I to do with the
13 14 man you call king of the Jews?' •They shouted back, 'Crucify him!' •'Why?'Pilate
asked them 'What harm has he done?' But they shouted all the louder, 'Crucify
15 him!' •So Pilate, anxious to placate the crowd, released Barabbas for them and,
having ordered Jesus to be scourged, handed him over to be crucified.

Jesus crowned with thorns ||Mt 27:27-31 ||Jn 19:1-3

16 The soldiers led him away to the inner part of the palace, that is, the Prae-
17 torium, and called the whole cohort together. •They dressed him up in purple,
18 twisted some thorns into a crown and put it on him. •And they began saluting
19 him, 'Hail, king of the Jews!' •They struck his head with a reed and spat on him;
20 and they went down on their knees to do him homage. •And when they had
finished making fun of him, they took off the purple and dressed him in his own
clothes.

The way of the cross ||Mt 27:32-33 ||Lk 23:26 ||Jn 19:17

21 They led him out to crucify him. •They enlisted a passer-by, Simon of Cyrene,
father of Alexander and Rufus,[a] who was coming in from the country, to carry
22 his cross. •They brought Jesus to the place called Golgotha, which means the
place of the skull.

The crucifixion ||Mt 27:34-38 ||Lk 23:33-34 Jn 19:18-24

23 24 They offered him wine mixed with myrrh, but he refused it. •Then they
crucified him, and shared out his clothing, casting lots to decide what each should Ps 22:18
25 26 get. •It was the third hour[b] when they crucified him. •The inscription giving the

14 a. Some commentators identify this young man with the evangelist.

b. Here, and in Mt 26:62, some translate 'Do you make no reply to the charges these men are bringing against you?'

c. 'The Blessed One' (cf. also 'the Power', v. 62) is a substitute for the name 'Yahweh' which the Jews would not pronounce.

d. Add. (Vulg.) 'and a cock crew'.

15 a. Alexander and Rufus were doubtless known to the Roman circle in which Mark wrote his gospel. Cf. Rm 16:13.

b. 9 a.m., or, more vaguely, some time between 9 a.m. and noon.

Is 53:12 Lk 22:37 charge against him read: 'The King of the Jews'. •And they crucified two robbers 27
with him, one on his right and one on his left.[c]

The crucified Christ is mocked
||Mt 27:39-44 ||Lk 23:35-37

The passers-by jeered at him; they shook their heads and said, 'Aha! So you 29
14:58 would destroy the Temple and rebuild it in three days! •Then save yourself: 30
come down from the cross!' •The chief priests and the scribes mocked him among 31
themselves in the same way. 'He saved others,' they said 'he cannot save
himself. •Let the Christ, the king of Israel, come down from the cross now, for 32
Lk 23:39 us to see it and believe.' Even those who were crucified with him taunted him.

The death of Jesus
||Mt 27:45-54 ||Lk 23:44-47 ||Jn 19:28-30

When the sixth hour came there was darkness over the whole land until the 33
ninth hour. •And at the ninth hour Jesus cried out in a loud voice, 'Eloi, Eloi,[d] 34
Ps 22:1 lama sabachthani?' which means, '*My God, my God, why have you deserted me?*'
When some of those who stood by heard this, they said, 'Listen, he is calling on 35
Elijah'. •Someone ran and soaked a sponge in vinegar and, putting it on a reed, 36
gave it him to drink saying, 'Wait and see if Elijah will come to take him down'.
But Jesus gave a loud cry and breathed his last. •And the veil of the Temple was 37 38
torn in two from top to bottom. •The centurion, who was standing in front of 39
Mt 4:3+; ||27:54 him, had seen how he had died, and he said, 'In truth this man was a son of
God'.[e]

The holy women on Calvary
||Mt 27:55-56 ||Lk 23:49 ||Jn 19:25

There were some women watching from a distance. Among them were Mary 40
6:3 Lk 8:2-3 of Magdala, Mary who was the mother of James the younger and Joset, and
Salome.[f] •These used to follow him and look after him when he was in Galilee. 41
And there were many other women there who had come up to Jerusalem with
him.

The burial
||Mt 27:57-61 ||Lk 23:50-55 ||Jn 19:38-42

It was now evening, and since it was Preparation Day (that is, the vigil of the 42
Mt 27:62+ sabbath), •there came Joseph of Arimathaea, a prominent member of the 43
Council,[g] who himself lived in the hope of seeing the kingdom of God, and he
boldly went to Pilate and asked for the body of Jesus. •Pilate, astonished that 44
he should have died so soon, summoned the centurion and enquired if he was
already dead.[h] •Having been assured of this by the centurion, he granted the 45
corpse to Joseph •who bought a shroud, took Jesus down from the cross, 46
wrapped him in the shroud and laid him in a tomb which had been hewn out
of the rock. He then rolled a stone against the entrance to the tomb. •Mary of 47
Magdala and Mary the mother of Joset were watching and took note of where
he was laid.

The empty tomb. The angel's message
||Mt 28:1-8 ||Lk 24:1-12 ||Jn 20:1-10

16 When the sabbath was over, Mary of Magdala, Mary the mother of James, 1
Lk 23:56 and Salome, bought spices with which to go and anoint him. •And very early 2
in the morning on the first day of the week they went to the tomb, just as the
sun was rising.[a]

They had been saying to one another, 'Who will roll away the stone for us 3
from the entrance to the tomb?' •But when they looked they could see that the 4
stone—which was very big—had already been rolled back. •On entering the 5
9:3 tomb they saw a young man in a white robe seated on the right-hand side, and
they were struck with amazement. •But he said to them, 'There is no need for 6
Mt 2:23+ alarm. You are looking for Jesus of Nazareth, who was crucified: he has risen,
he is not here. See, here is the place where they laid him. •But you must go and 7
tell his disciples and Peter, "He is going before you to Galilee; it is there

8 you will see him, just as he told you".' •And the women came out and ran away
from the tomb because they were frightened out of their wits; and they said
nothing to a soul,[b] for they were afraid...

Appearances of the risen Christ[c] Mt 28:10+ ||Jn 20:11-18

9 Having risen in the morning on the first day of the week, he appeared first to
10 Mary of Magdala from whom he had cast out seven devils. •She then went to those Lk 8:2
who had been his companions, and who were mourning and in tears, and told Lk 24:10-11 Jn 20:18
11 them. •But they did not believe her when they heard her say that he was alive Mt 8:10+
and that she had seen him.
12 After this, he showed himself under another form to two of them as they ||Lk 24:13-35
13 were on their way into the country. •These went back and told the others, who
did not believe them either.
14 Lastly, he showed himself to the Eleven themselves while they were at table. ||Lk 24:36-49 ||Jn 20:19-23
He reproached them for their incredulity and obstinacy, because they had refused 1 Co 15:5
15 to believe those who had seen him after he had risen. •And he said to them, 13:10 Is 52:7
16 'Go out to the whole world; proclaim the Good News to all creation. •He who Mt 28:18-20 Lk 24:47
believes and is baptised will be saved; he who does not believe will be condemned. Jn 20:21 Col 1:23
17 These are the signs that will be associated with believers: in my name they will cast *Mt 10:1p* Ac 1:8+;
18 out devils; they will have the gift of tongues;[d] •they will pick up snakes in their 14:3 *Lk 10:19*
hands, and be unharmed should they drink deadly poison; they will lay their Ac 28:3-6
hands on the sick, who will recover.' 1 Tm 4:14+
19 And so the Lord Jesus, after he had spoken to them, was taken up into heaven: 1 Tm 3:16
20 there at the right hand of God he took his place, •while they, going out, preached
everywhere, the Lord working with them and confirming the word by the signs
that accompanied it.

c. Add. v. 28 'And the text of scripture was fulfilled that says: He was taken for a criminal' (Is 53:12). Cf. Lk 22:37.

d. Jesus must have used the Aramaic *Elahi;* the transliteration *Eloi* has probably been influenced by the Hebr. *Elohim.*

e. For the Roman officer, this admission would not have its full Christian content, but Mk clearly sees in it a pagan's acknowledgment that Jesus was more than man.

f. Probably the woman whom Mt (27:56) calls 'the mother of the sons of Zebedee'.

g. I.e. of the Sanhedrin.

h. Var. 'if he had been dead for some time'.

16 a. Var. 'when the sun had risen'.

b. According to Mt 28:8; Lk 24:10,22f; Jn 20:18, they did in fact tell the news. Mark, too, may have said so in a lost ending of his gospel (cf. following note); alternatively, he may have deliberately refrained from speaking of it to avoid having to append an account of the apparitions which he had made up his mind to omit.

c. The 'long ending' of Mark, vv. 9-20, is included in the canonically accepted body of inspired scripture. This does not necessarily imply Marcan authorship which, indeed, is open to question. The manuscript tradition is the main objection. Many MSS (including Vat. and Sin.) omit the present ending. One MS gives, instead, a shorter ending which, proceeding from v. 8, runs 'They reported briefly to Peter's companions what they had been told. Then Jesus himself through their agency broadcast from east to west the sacred and incorruptible message of eternal salvation.' Four MSS give the shorter ending and add the longer. One MS has the longer ending with the following insertion between vv. 14 and 15: 'And they defended themselves thus, "This age of lawlessness and unbelief is under the sway of Satan, who does not allow those under the yoke of unclean spirits to understand God's truth and power. Now, therefore, reveal your righteousness." This is what they said to Christ, and Christ answered, "The number of years allowed for Satan's authority has been reached, but other terrible things draw near. I was handed over to be killed for those who have sinned, so that they might turn to the truth and sin no more, and so inherit the spiritual and incorruptible glory of righteousness which is in heaven..."' The patristic tradition, also, is somewhat uncertain. We may add that the transition from v. 8 to v. 9 is brusque. Moreover, it is difficult to see how the original gospel could have ended so abruptly at v. 8. Hence the hypothesis that, for some unknown reason, the original ending has been lost and the present ending composed to fill the gap. This ending is, in fact, a brief summary of the appearances of the risen Christ, and its style differs notably from the usually concrete and pictorial style of Mark. The present ending, however, was known to Tatian and to Irenaeus in the 2nd century, and is to be found in the vast majority of Greek MSS and of the versions. That Mark was its author cannot be proved; it is, nonetheless, 'an authentic relic of the first Christian generation' (Swete).

d. Var. 'new tongues'.

THE GOSPEL ACCORDING TO
SAINT LUKE

Prologue[a]

1 Seeing that many others[b] have undertaken to draw up accounts of the events 1
15:27 1 Co 15:3 that have taken place among us, •exactly as these were handed down to us by 2
Ac 1:8+ Ep 3:7 those who from the outset were eyewitnesses and ministers of the word, •I in my 3
turn, after carefully going over the whole story from the beginning, have decided
Ac 1:1 to write an ordered account for you, Theophilus, •so that your Excellency may 4
learn how well founded the teaching is that you have received.[c]

I. THE BIRTH AND HIDDEN LIFE OF JOHN THE BAPTIST AND OF JESUS[d]

The birth of John the Baptist foretold

In the days of King Herod of Judaea there lived a priest called Zechariah 5
1 Ch 24:10 who belonged to the Abijah section of the priesthood, and he had a wife,
Elizabeth by name, who was a descendant of Aaron. •Both were worthy in the 6
sight of God, and scrupulously observed all the commandments and observances
Gn 18:11 Jg 13:2-5 1 S 1:5-6 of the Lord. •But they were childless: Elizabeth was barren and they were 7
both getting on in years.

Now it was the turn of Zechariah's section[e] to serve, and he was exercising 8
his priestly office before God •when it fell to him by lot, as the ritual custom 9
was, to enter the Lord's sanctuary and burn incense there.[f] •And at the hour of 10
incense the whole congregation was outside, praying.

Mt 1:20+ Then there appeared to him the angel of the Lord, standing on the right 11
1:65; 4:36; 5:9,26 of the altar of incense. •The sight disturbed Zechariah and he was overcome with 12
2:10 fear.[g] •But the angel said to him, 'Zechariah, do not be afraid, your prayer 13
1:63 has been heard. Your wife Elizabeth is to bear you a son and you must name
1:10,58; 10:17,21 him John.[h] •He will be your joy and delight and many will rejoice[i] at his birth, 14
Nb 6:2-3 Jr 1:5 for he will be great in the sight of the Lord; he must drink no wine, no strong 15
Mt 11:18 Ga 1:15 drink.[j] Even from his mother's womb he will be filled with the Holy Spirit, •and 16
1:76 he will bring back many of the sons of Israel to the Lord their God. •With the 17
Mt 17:10-13+ spirit and power of Elijah,[k] he will go before him *to turn the hearts of fathers*
Ml 3:23-24 Si 48:10-11 *towards their children* and the disobedient back to the wisdom that the virtuous
have, preparing for the Lord a people fit for him.' •Zechariah said to the angel, 18
Gn 15:8 '*How can I be sure of this?*[l] I am an old man and my wife is getting on in years.'
Dn 8:16; 9:21 The angel replied, 'I am Gabriel who stand in God's presence, and I have been 19
Tb 12:15 Mk 1:1+ sent to speak to you and bring you this good news. •Listen! Since you have not 20
Mt 8:10+ believed my words, which will come true at their appointed time, you will be
silenced and have no power of speech until this has happened.' •Meanwhile 21

the people were waiting for Zechariah and were surprised that he stayed in the
22 sanctuary so long. •When he came out he could not speak to them, and they
realised that he had received a vision in the sanctuary. But he could only make
signs to them, and remained dumb.
23 24 When his time of service came to an end he returned home. •Some time later
25 his wife Elizabeth conceived, and for five months she kept to herself. •'The Lord
has done this for me' she said 'now that it has pleased him to take away the
humiliation I suffered among men.'[m]

The annunciation[n]

26 In the sixth month[o] the angel Gabriel was sent by God to a town in Galilee Dn 8:16 Heb 1:14+
27 called Nazareth, •to a virgin betrothed to a man named Joseph, of the House *Mt 1:18*
28 of David; and the virgin's name was Mary. •He went in and said to her, 'Rejoice,
29 so highly favoured![p] The Lord is with you.' •She was deeply disturbed by these Jg 6:12 Rt 2:4
30 words and asked herself what this greeting could mean, •but the angel said Jdt 13:18
31 to her, 'Mary, do not be afraid; you have won God's favour. •Listen! You are Is 7:14+
32 to conceive and bear a son, and you must name him Jesus. •He will be great and 2:21 Mt 1:21+
will be called Son of the Most High. The Lord God will give him the throne *2 S 7:1+* Is 9:6
33 of his ancestor David; •he will rule over the House of Jacob for ever and his reign *Mt 9:27+*
34 will have no end.'[q] •Mary said to the angel, 'But how can this come about, since Dn 2:44; 7:14
35 I am a virgin?'[r] •'The Holy Spirit will come upon you' the angel answered 'and Mt 1:20
the power of the Most High will cover you with its shadow.[s] And so the child
36 will be holy and will be called Son of God. •Know this too: your kinswoman Mk 1:24+ *Mt 4:3+*
Elizabeth has, in her old age, herself conceived a son, and she whom people called Ac 3:14+
37 38 barren is now in her sixth month, •*for nothing is impossible to God.*' •'I am the Gn 18:14 Jr 32:27
handmaid of the Lord,' said Mary 'let what you have said be done to me.' Mt 19:26 Rm 4:21
And the angel left her.

The visitation

39 Mary set out at that time and went as quickly as she could to a town in the
40 hill country of Judah.[t] •She went into Zechariah's house and greeted Elizabeth.
41 Now as soon as Elizabeth heard Mary's greeting, the child leapt in her womb 1:15
42 and Elizabeth was filled with the Holy Spirit. •She gave a loud cry and said,
'Of all women you are the most blessed, and blessed is the fruit of your womb. Jg 5:24 Jdt 13:18

1 a. This prologue uses a classical vocabulary and construction; it is similar to the formal prefaces of historians during the hellenistic age.

b. Hyperbole: understand 'several'. For the narratives known and used by Lk, see Introduction to the Synoptic Gospels.

c. Or possibly 'that has come to your knowledge', in which case Theophilus would not be a Christian to be confirmed in the faith but some distinguished official asking for information.

d. From here to ch. 3 Lk, who possibly has Aramaic sources at his disposal, uses LXX Greek with its semitic tendencies. Biblical allusions and colourings are frequent, and the whole flavour of these chapters is arcnaic and redolent of traditional Israelite messianism.

e. Each section was responsible for a week's service, cf. 1 Ch 24:19; 2 Ch 23:8.

f. It was the priest's duty to keep the brazier burning that stood on the altar of incense in front of the Holy of Holies; he would also supply it with fresh incense, once before the morning sacrifice, again after the evening sacrifice; cf. Ex 30:6-8.

g. Lk is fond of mentioning religious dread and terror: 1:29–30,65; 2:9-10; 4:36; 5:8–10,26; 7:16; 8:25 33–37,56; 9:34,43; 24:37; Ac 2:43; 3:10; 5:5.11; 10:4; 19:17.

h. The name means 'Yahweh-is-gracious'.

i. Joy is the keynote of ch. 1-2;1: 28,46,58; 2:10. Cf. 10:17,20f; 13:17; 15:7,32; 19:6,37; 24:41,52; Ac 2:46+.

j. Several O.T. texts lie behind this remark, especially the law of the nazirite, cf. Nb 6:1+.

k. Ml 3:23 gave rise to the expectation that Elijah would return before the messianic era and pave the way for it. In Mt 17:10-13 John the Baptist is identified with 'the Elijah who has to come'.

l. Zechariah asks for a 'sign', cf. Gn 15:8; Jg 6:17; Is 7:11; 38:7; nevertheless his doubt continues.

m. Lit. 'to take away my shame'. Barrenness was considered a humiliation, Gn 30:23; 1 S 1:5-8, and even a punishment, 2 S 6:23; Ho 9:11.

n. Lk makes the birth and infancy narratives of John parallel to those of Jesus, and gives these latter from Mary's point of view; Matthew tells them from Joseph's.

o. I.e. of John's conception.

p. The translation 'Rejoice' may be preferred to 'Hail' and regarded as containing a messianic reference, cf. Zc 9.9. 'so highly favoured', i.e. as to become the mother of the Messiah. Add. 'Of all women you are the most blessed', cf. 1:42.

q. The angel's words recall several O.T. passages referring to the Messiah.

r. Lit. 'since I do not know man'; this phrase means that Mary is in fact a virgin and perhaps expresses also her intention to remain so.

s. In O.T. this expression is used of the bright cloud which is the sign of God's presence, cf. Ex 13:22+; 19:16+; 24:16+. Cf. Lk 9:34p. The conception of Jesus is effected only by God and his Spirit.

t. Commonly identified with Ain Karim, about 5 m. W. of Jerusalem.

Why should I be honoured with a visit from the mother of my Lord?[u] •For the 43 44
moment your greeting reached my ears, the child in my womb leapt for joy.
Jn 20:29 Yes, blessed is she who believed that the promise made her by the Lord would 45
be fulfilled.'[v]

1 S 2:1-10 Is 29:19

The Magnificat

And Mary[w] said: 46

Is 61:10 'My soul proclaims the greatness of the Lord
1 S 2:1 Hab 3:18 and my spirit *exults in God my saviour;* 47
1 S 1:11 because *he has looked upon his lowly handmaid.* 48
11:27 Gn 30:13 Yes, from this day forward all generations will call me blessed,
Ps 126:3 for the Almighty has done great things for me. 49
Ps 111:9 *Holy is his name,*
Ps 103:17 and *his mercy reaches from age to age for those who fear him.* 50
Ps 89:10; 138:6 He has shown the power of his arm, 51
Si 33:12 Ezk 17:24 he has routed the proud of heart.
Jb 5:11; 12:19 *He has pulled down princes* from their thrones *and exalted the lowly.* 52
Ps 107:9 *The hungry he has filled with good things*, the rich sent empty away. 53
Ps 98:3 Is 41:8-9 *He has come to the help of Israel his servant, mindful of his mercy* 54
Gn 12:3; 13: —according to the promise he made to our ancestors— 55
15; 22:18 of his mercy to Abraham and to his descendants for ever.'

Mary stayed with Elizabeth about three months and then went back home.[x] 56

The birth of John the Baptist and visit of the neighbours

Meanwhile the time came for Elizabeth to have her child, and she gave birth 57
to a son; •and when her neighbours and relations heard that the Lord had shown 58
1:14+ her so great a kindness, they shared her joy.

The circumcision of John the Baptist

Gn 17:10+ Lv 12:3 Now on the eighth day they came to circumcise the child; they were going 59
to call[y] him Zechariah after his father, •but his mother spoke up. 'No,' she 60
said 'he is to be called John.' •They said to her, 'But no one in your family has 61
that name', •and made signs to his father to find out what he wanted him called. 62
1:13 The father asked for a writing-tablet and wrote, 'His name is John'. And they 63
were all astonished. •At that instant his power of speech returned and he spoke 64
1:12+ 2:20+ and praised God. •All their neighbours were filled with awe and the whole affair 65
was talked about throughout the hill country of Judaea. •All those who heard 66
of it treasured it in their hearts. 'What will this child turn out to be?'
1:80+ Ac 11:21 they wondered. And indeed the hand of the Lord was with him.[z]

The Benedictus

His father Zechariah was filled with the Holy Spirit and spoke this prophecy:[aa] 67

Ps 41:13; 72: 18; 106:48 *'Blessed be the Lord, the God of Israel,* 68
Ps 111:9 for he has visited[bb] his people, he has come to their rescue
Ps 132:17 and he has raised up for us a power for[cc] salvation 69
in the House of his servant David,
even as he proclaimed, 70
by the mouth of his holy prophets from ancient times,
Ps 136:24 that he would save us from our enemies 71
and from the hands of all who hate us.
Thus he shows mercy to our ancestors, 72
Lv 26:42 Ps 106:45 thus *he remembers* his holy *covenant,*
the oath he swore 73
Ps 105:8-9 Mi 7:20 to our father Abraham

74 that he would grant us, free from fear,
to be delivered from the hands of our enemies, Gn 22:16-18
75 to serve him in holiness and virtue
in his presence, all our days.
76 And you, little child, Mt 11:10
you shall be called Prophet of the Most High, Mt 16:14+
for you will go before the Lord[aa] 1:16-17
to prepare the way for him. Is 40:3 Ml 3:1 Ac 13:25
77 To give his people knowledge of salvation
through the forgiveness of their sins;
78 this by the tender mercy[ee] of our God
who from on high will bring the rising Sun[ff] to visit us, Ml 3:20+ 2 P 1:19
79 to give light to *those who live* *Is 9:1; 42:7* Jn 8:12+
in darkness and the shadow of death,
and to guide our feet Is 11:6+ Jr 6:14+
into the way of peace.'

The hidden life of John the Baptist

80 Meanwhile the child grew up and his spirit matured.[gg] And he lived out in 1:66; 2:40
the wilderness until the day he appeared openly to Israel. 3:1-18

The birth of Jesus and visit of the shepherds

1 **2** Now at this time Caesar Augustus[a] issued a decree for a census of the whole Mt 2:1
2 world to be taken. •This census—the first[b]—took place while Quirinius was
3 4 governor of Syria, •and everyone went to his own town to be registered. •So Joseph
set out from the town of Nazareth in Galilee and travelled up to Judaea, to the
5 town of David called Bethlehem, since he was of David's House and line, •in 1 S 16:1-13 Jn 7:42
order to be registered together with Mary, his betrothed, who was with child. *Mt 1:18*
6 7 While they were there the time came for her to have her child, •and she gave birth Mt 1:25
to a son, her first-born.[c] She wrapped him in swaddling clothes, and laid him in a
8 manger because there was no room for them at the inn. •In the countryside
close by there were shepherds who lived in the fields and took it in turns to watch
9 their flocks during the night. •The angel of the Lord appeared to them and Ex 24:16+ Tb 5:4+
10 the glory of the Lord shone round them. They were terrified, •but the angel Mt 1:20+
said, 'Do not be afraid. Listen, I bring you news of great joy, a joy to be shared 1:12+

u. 'my Lord', i.e. the Messiah.

v. 'the Lord', i.e. God. Or 'And blessed are you who have believed, because what has been promised to you by the Lord will be fulfilled'.

w. Not 'Elizabeth', a var. with only slight MS support. Mary's canticle is reminiscent of Hannah's, 1 S 2:1-10, and of many other O.T. passages. Apart from the main textual similarities noted in the margin there are two characteristic O.T. ideas: 1. God comes to the help not of the rich and powerful but of the poor and the simple, Zp 2:3+, cf. Mt 5:3+. 2. Ever since Abraham received the promises, Gn 15:1+; 17:1+, Israel has been God's favoured one, cf. Dt 7:6+, etc.

x. It is probable that Mary stayed with Elizabeth until John's birth and circumcision, but Luke's habit is to round off one episode before passing to the next, cf. 1:64 and 67; 3:19-20; 8:37-38.

y. The name was normally given when the child was circumcised, cf. 2:21.

z. I.e. protected him: a biblical expression, Jr 26:24; Ac 11:21.

aa. In the full sense of the term, because Zechariah not only utters a hymn of thanksgiving (vv. 68-75) but also foresees the future (vv. 76-79).

bb. God is said to 'visit' when he intervenes notably in history, Ex 3:16+.

cc. Lit. 'a horn of', cf. Ps 75:4+.

dd. I.e. God, as in 1:16-17, not the Messiah.

ee. 'tender mercy', lit. 'bowels of mercy'. 'will bring'; var. 'has brought'.

ff. I.e. either the messianic era or the Messiah himself.

gg. A kind of refrain: 2:40,52; cf. 1:66 and cf. Ac 2:41+; 6:7+.

2 a. Roman emperor from 30 B.C. to 14 A.D.

b. The first of a series. The translation sometimes given, 'This census preceded that which was held when Quirinius was governor of Syria', is difficult to justify grammatically. The historical circumstances are little known. Most scholars put the census of Quirinius in 6 A.D., but the only authority for this is Josephus who is doubtfully reliable in this matter, cf. Ac 5:37+. The most probable explanation is that the census, which was made with a view to taxation, took place about 8-6 B.C. as part of a general census of the empire, and that it was organised in Palestine by Quirinius who was specially appointed for the purpose. Quirinius might have been governor of Syria, between 4 and 1 B.C., and if so Luke's expression would then be a rough approximation. Jesus was born certainly before Herod's death (4 B.C.), possibly in 8-6 B.C. The 'Christian era', established by Dionysius Exiguus (6th century), is the result of a false calculation, cf. note to Lk 3:1.

c. In biblical Greek, the term does not necessarily imply younger brothers but emphasises the dignity and rights of the child.

1:14+ *Mt 1:21* by the whole people. •Today in the town of David a saviour has been born to 11
1:18+ Is 9:5+ you; he is Christ the Lord.[d] •And here is a sign for you: you will find a baby 12
wrapped in swaddling clothes and lying in a manger.' •And suddenly with the 13
angel there was a great throng of the heavenly host, praising God and singing:

19:38 Ezk 3:12 *Is 9:6* 'Glory to God in the highest heaven, 14
and peace to men who enjoy his favour'.[e]

Now when the angels had gone from them into heaven, the shepherds said 15
to one another, 'Let us go to Bethlehem and see this thing that has happened
which the Lord has made known to us'. •So they hurried away and found 16
Is 1:3 Mary and Joseph, and the baby lying in the manger. •When they saw the child 17
they repeated what they had been told about him, •and everyone who heard 18
2:51 Gn 37:11 it was astonished at what the shepherds had to say. •As for Mary, she treasured 19
all these things and pondered them in her heart. •And the shepherds went 20
1:64; 2:28. 38; 5:26; 7:16; 13:13 back glorifying and praising God[f] for all they had heard and seen; it was exactly
as they had been told.

1:59+ The circumcision of Jesus

Lv 12:3 When the eighth day came and the child was to be circumcised, they gave 21
1:31 Mt 1:21+ him the name Jesus, the name the angel had given him before his conception.

Jesus is presented in the Temple

Lv 12:2-6 And when the day came for them to be purified[g] as laid down by the Law 22
of Moses, they took him up to Jerusalem to present him to the Lord —•observing 23
Ex 13:2; 13:11+ what stands written in the Law of the Lord: *Every first-born male must be con-*
secrated to the Lord—•and also to offer in sacrifice, in accordance with what 24
Lv 5:7; 12:8 is said in the Law of the Lord, *a pair of turtledoves or two young pigeons.*[h] •Now 25
in Jerusalem there was a man named Simeon. He was an upright and devout
Is 40:1+; 42:1 man; he looked forward to Israel's comforting and the Holy Spirit rested on
him. •It had been revealed to him by the Holy Spirit that he would not see death 26
9:29; 23:35 until he had set eyes on the Christ of the Lord.[i] •Prompted by the Spirit he 27
Ex 30:22+ came to the Temple; and when the parents brought in the child Jesus to do for
2:20+ him what the Law required, •he took him into his arms and blessed God; and he 28
said:

The Nunc Dimittis

'Now, Master, you can let your servant go in peace, 29
just as you promised;
Is 52:10 because my eyes have seen the salvation 30
Is 42:6; 46: 13; 49:6 which you have prepared for all the nations to see, 31
Jn 8:12+ a light to enlighten the pagans 32
and the glory of your people Israel'.

The prophecy of Simeon

As the child's father and mother stood there wondering at the things that 33
7:23; 12: 51-53 were being said about him, •Simeon blessed them and said to Mary his mother, 34
Jr 15:10 'You see this child: he is destined for the fall and for the rising of many in Israel,
Jn 19:25-27 Heb 12:3 destined to be a sign that is rejected—•and a sword will pierce your own soul 35
Jn 3:19; 9:39 too—so that the secret thoughts of many may be laid bare'.

The prophecy of Anna

There was a prophetess[j] also, Anna the daughter of Phanuel, of the tribe 36
of Asher. She was well on in years. Her days of girlhood over, she had been
Jdt 8:4-5 1 Tm 5:5 married for seven years •before becoming a widow. She was now eighty-four 37
years old and never left the Temple, serving God night and day with fasting
2:20+ and prayer. •She came by just at that moment and began to praise God; and 38
9:32,51; 13:22,33; she spoke of the child to all who looked forward to the deliverance of Jerusalem.[k]

The hidden life of Jesus at Nazareth 18:31;19:▲ 11,29;24:▲ 21.47▲

39 When they had done everything the Law of the Lord required, they went back
40 to Galilee, to their own town of Nazareth. •Meanwhile the child grew to maturity, 4:16 Mt 2:23
and he was filled with wisdom; and God's favour was with him.

Jesus among the doctors of the Law

41 Every year his parents used to go to Jerusalem for the feast of the Passover. Ex 12:1+ Dt 16:16
42 When he was twelve years old, they went up for the feast as usual. •When they
43 were on their way home after the feast, the boy Jesus stayed behind in Jerusalem
44 without his parents knowing it. •They assumed he was with the caravan, and
it was only after a day's journey that they went to look for him among their
45 relations and acquaintances. •When they failed to find him they went back to
Jerusalem looking for him everywhere.
46 Three days later, they found him in the Temple, sitting among the doctors,
47 listening to them, and asking them questions; •and all those who heard him
48 were astounded at his intelligence and his replies. •They were overcome 4:22 Jn 7:15,46
when they saw him, and his mother said to him, 'My child, why have Ac 3:9
you done this to us? See how worried your father and I have been, looking for
49 you.' •'Why were you looking for me?' he replied 'Did you not know that I must Mt 12:48
50 be busy with my Father's affairs?'[l] •But they did not understand what he meant.

The hidden life at Nazareth resumed

51 He then went down with them and came to Nazareth and lived under their 4:16
52 authority. His mother stored up all these things in her heart. •And Jesus increased 2:19 Gn 37:11
in wisdom, in stature, and in favour with God and men. *1:80+* Pr 3:4

II. PRELUDE TO THE PUBLIC MINISTRY OF JESUS

The preaching of John the Baptist ||Mt 3:1-12 ||Mk 1:1-8

1 **3** In the fifteenth year of Tiberius Caesar's reign,[a] when Pontius Pilate[b] was 1:80 Mt 27:2
governor of Judaea, Herod[c] tetrarch of Galilee, his brother Philip[d] tetrarch
2 of the lands of Ituraea and Trachonitis, Lysanias[e] tetrarch of Abilene, •during
the pontificate of Annas and Caiaphas,[f] the word of God came to John son of Jr 1:2 Ho 1:1

d. He is, therefore, the expected Messiah; but he is also called 'Lord', a title the O.T. reserves for God. A new era is beginning.

e. Lit. 'to men (who are the object) of (God's) benevolence'. The current translation, 'peace to men of good will', based on the Vulg., does not render the usual sense of the Greek term. Another, less certain, reading is 'peace on earth, and among men divine benevolence'.

f. A favourite theme of Lk: 1:64; 2:28,38; 5:25-26; 7:16; 13:13; 17:15,18; 18:43; 19:37; 23:47; 24:53. Cf. Ac 2:47+.

g. Only the mother needed to be purified; the child, however, had to be 'redeemed'. Lk is careful to note that the parents of Jesus, like the Baptist's, observed all that the Law required.

h. Offering of the poor.

i. 'the Christ of the Lord' is the one whom the Lord anoints, cf. Ex 30:22+, i.e. consecrates for a saving mission; the king of Israel, God's chosen prince, is thus consecrated and thus, pre-eminently, the Messiah who is to establish the kingdom of God.

j. A woman dedicated to God and the qualified interpreter of his intentions. Cf. Ex 15:20; Jg 4:4; 2 K 22:14.

k. The messianic deliverance of the Chosen People, 1:68; 24:21, primarily affected their capital city; cf. Is 40:2; 52:9 (and see 2 S 5:9+). For Lk, Jerusalem is God's chosen centre from which will spread his salvation: 9:31,51,53; 13:22,33; 17:11; 18:31; 19:11; 24:47-49,52; Ac 1:8+.

l. Alternative translation 'in my Father's house'. In either case, Jesus is asserting his own personal duty to his Father (Mt 4:3+) and, in the interests of that duty, an absolute independence of creatures. Cf. Jn 2:4; Mt 12:46-50.

3 a. Here, as in 1:5 and 2:1-3, Lk dates his narrative by secular events. Tiberius succeeded Augustus, 2:1, on 19 August 14 A.D. The 15th year, therefore, is from 19 August 28 A.D. to 18 August 29 A.D. Alternatively, if the Syrian method of calculating the year of a reign is being followed, the 15th year is from Sept.-Oct. 27 A.D. to Sept.-Oct. 28 A.D. At that time, Jesus was at least 33 years old, possibly 35 or 36. The indication of v. 23 is approximate, and perhaps it only means that Jesus was old enough to exercise a public ministry. The mistake in calculating the 'Christian era' results from taking 3:23 as an exact figure: the 15th year of Tiberius was 782 'after the foundation of Rome'; Dionysius Exiguus subtracted 29 full years from this, thus arriving at 753 for the beginning of our era. Actually, it should have been 750 or even 746.

b. Procurator of Judaea (including Idumaea and Samaria) 26-36 A.D.

c. The Herod referred to is Herod Antipas, son of Herod the Great and Malthake; he was tetrarch of Galilee and Peraea from 4 B.C. to 39 A.D.

d. Son of Herod the Great and Cleopatra, tetrarch from 4 B.C. to 34 A.D.

e. Known from two inscriptions. Abilene was in Anti-Lebanon.

f. The high priest in office was Joseph, called Caiaphas; he exercised this function from 18-36 A.D. and played a leading part in the plot against Jesus.

Lk 1:80 Zechariah, in the wilderness. •He went through the whole Jordan district pro- 3
Jn 1:23 claiming a baptism of repentance for the forgiveness of sins,[g] •as it is written 4
in the book of the sayings of the prophet Isaiah:

Is 40:3-5
A voice cries in the wilderness:
Prepare a way for the Lord,
make his paths straight.
Every valley will be filled in, 5
every mountain and hill be laid low,
winding ways will be straightened
and rough roads made smooth.
And all mankind shall see the salvation of God. 6

He said, therefore, to the crowds who came to be baptised by him, 'Brood of 7
Ac 26:20 vipers, who warned you to fly from the retribution that is coming? •But if you are 8
repentant, produce the appropriate fruits, and do not think of telling yourselves,
"We have Abraham for our father" because, I tell you, God can raise children for
Abraham from these stones. •Yes, even now the axe is laid to the roots of the 9
trees, so that any tree which fails to produce good fruit will be cut down and
thrown on the fire.'

Ac 2:37 [h]When all the people asked him, 'What must we do, then?' •He answered, 10 11
12:33+ 'If anyone has two tunics he must share with the man who has none, and the
Mt 5:46+ one with something to eat must do the same'. •There were tax collectors too 12
who came for baptism, and these said to him, 'Master, what must we do?' •He 13
said to them, 'Exact no more than your rate'. •Some soldiers asked him in their 14
turn, 'What about us? What must we do?' He said to them, 'No intimidation!
No extortion! Be content with your pay!'

Jn 1:19-20; 3:28 A feeling of expectancy had grown among the people, who were beginning 15
Ac 13:25 to think that John might be the Christ, •so John declared before them all, 'I 16
Jn 1:26, 27, 33; Ac 1:5+ baptise you with water, but someone is coming, someone who is more powerful
than I am, and I am not fit to undo the strap of his sandals; he will baptise
you with the Holy Spirit and fire. •His winnowing-fan is in his hand to clear 17
his threshing-floor and to gather the wheat into his barn; but the chaff he will
burn in a fire that will never go out.' •As well as this, there were many other 18
things he said to exhort the people and to announce the Good News to them.

John the Baptist imprisoned
Mt 14:3-12; Mk 6:17-29

But Herod the tetrarch, whom he criticised for his relations with his brother's 19
wife Herodias and for all the other crimes Herod had committed, •added a further 20
Jn 3:24 crime to all the rest by shutting John up in prison.[i]

Jesus is baptised
||Mt 3:13-17; ||Mk 1:9-11

Now when all the people had been baptised and while Jesus after his own 21
5:16; 6:12; *Jn 1:32-34* baptism was at prayer,[j] heaven opened •and the Holy Spirit descended on him 22
in bodily shape, like a dove. And a voice came from heaven, 'You are my Son,
the Beloved; my favour rests on you'.[k]

The ancestry of Jesus
||Mt 1:1-17

Mt 13:55 When he started to teach, Jesus was about thirty years old, being the son, 23
as it was thought, of Joseph son of Heli, •son of Matthat, son of Levi, son 24
of Melchi, son of Jannai, son of Joseph, •son of Mattathias, son of Amos, son 25
of Nahum, son of Esli, son of Naggai, •son of Maath, son of Mattathias, son 26
of Semein, son of Josech, son of Joda, •son of Joanan, son of Rhesa, son of 27
Zerubbabel, son of Shealtiel, son of Neri, •son of Melchi, son of Addi, son of 28
Cosam, son of Elmadam, son of Er, son of Joshua, •son of Joshua, son of Eliezer, 29
son of Jorim, son of Matthat, son of Levi, •son of Symeon, son of Judah, son 30
of Joseph, son of Jonam, son of Eliakim, •son of Melea, son of Menna, son of 31

32 Mattatha, son of Nathan, son of David, •son of Jesse, son of Obed, son of Boaz,
33 son of Sala, son of Nahshon, •son of Amminadab, son of Admin, son of Arni, Rt 4:18
34 son of Hezron, son of Perez, son of Judah, •son of Jacob, son of Isaac, son Gn 38:29
35 of Abraham, son of Terah, son of Nahor, •son of Serug, son of Reu, son of
36 Peleg, son of Eber, son of Shelah, •son of Cainan, son of Arphaxad, son of
37 Shem, son of Noah, son of Lamech, •son of Methuselah, son of Enoch, son of
38 Jared, son of Mahalaleel, son of Cainan, •son of Enos, son of Seth, son of Adam,
son of God.

Temptation in the wilderness[a]

||Mt 4:1-11 ||Mk 1:12-13

1 **4** Filled with the Holy Spirit,[b] Jesus left the Jordan and was led by the Spirit 10:21
2 through the wilderness, •being tempted there by the devil for forty days.
3 During that time he ate nothing and at the end he was hungry. •Then the devil
4 said to him, 'If you are the Son of God, tell this stone to turn into a loaf'. •But
Jesus replied, 'Scripture says: *Man does not live on bread alone*'. Dt 8:3
5 Then leading him to a height, the devil showed him in a moment of time all
6 the kingdoms of the world •and said to him, 'I will give you all this power and
the glory of these kingdoms, for it has been committed to me and I give it to Jr 27:5 Rv 13:2,4
7 8 anyone I choose.[c] •Worship me, then, and it shall all be yours.' •But Jesus
answered him, 'Scripture says:

You must worship the Lord your God, Dt 6:13
and serve him alone'.

9 Then he led him to Jerusalem and made him stand on the parapet of the
Temple. 'If you are the Son of God,' he said to him 'throw yourself down from
10 here, •for scripture says:

He will put his angels in charge of you Ps 91:11-12
to guard you,

and again:

11 *They will hold you up on their hands*
in case you hurt your foot against a stone'.

12 But Jesus answered him, 'It has been said:

You must not put the Lord your God to the test'. Dt 6:16

13 Having exhausted all these ways of tempting him,[d] the devil left him, to return 22:3,53 Jn 13:2,27
at the appointed time.

III. THE GALILEAN MINISTRY

Jesus begins to preach

||Mt 4:12-17,23 ||Mk 1:14-15,39

14 Jesus, with the power of the Spirit in him, returned to Galilee; and his *4:37; 5:15* Mt 3:16+

cf. Mt 26:3; Jn 11:49; 18:14. His father-in-law, Annas, who had been high priest from 6 (?) to 15 A.D., is associated with him and even named first, cf. Ac 4:6 and Jn 18:13,24, as if his prestige was such that he was high priest in all but name.

g. Probably in the neighbourhood of Jericho.

h. Vv. 10-14 (Lk only) emphasise the practical and positive side of John's teaching. Salvation is for all classes of men but justice and charity are necessary in every walk of life.

i. Lk finishes with John's ministry before passing to that of Jesus, cf. 1:56+. He makes no more than a brief allusion to the Precursor's death, 9:7-9.

j. Jesus at prayer is a favourite theme of Lk, cf. 5:16; 6:12; 9:18,28-29; 11:1; 22:41.

k. Var. 'You are my Son, today I have become your father' (Ps 2:7). In Lk and Mk, unlike Mt, the voice addresses Jesus.

4 a. Lk combines Mk's data (40 days of temptation) with Matthew's (three temptations at the end of 40 days' fast). He changes Matthew's order so as to end with Jerusalem; cf. Lk 2:38+.

b. Luke's interest in the Holy Spirit is evident not only from his first two chapters, 1:15,35,41,67,80; 2:25,26,27, but also from the remainder of the gospel in which, on several occasions, he adds a mention of the Spirit to the other synoptic passages, 4:1,14,18; 10:21; 11:13. In Ac also Lk very frequently speaks of the Spirit, Ac 1:8+.

c. The devil's dominion over the world is one of the key ideas of Jn (12:31; 14:30; 16:11; 1 Jn 3:8+; Rv 13:2,4). See also Mt 8:29+.

d. Rather than 'finished all the temptations'.

=4:44 reputation spread throughout the countryside.[e] •He taught in their synagogues 15
and everyone praised him.[f]

||Mt 13:53-58 ||Mk 6:1-6 Jesus at Nazareth[g]

2:39.51 He came to Nazara,[h] where he had been brought up, and went into the 16
synagogue on the sabbath day as he usually did. He stood up to read,[i] •and they 17
handed him the scroll of the prophet Isaiah. Unrolling the scroll he found the
place where it is written:

Is 61:1-2 Mt 3:16+ *The spirit of the Lord has been given to me,* 18
for he has anointed me.
Zp 2:3+ *He has sent me to bring the good news to the poor,*[j]
to proclaim liberty to captives
and to the blind new sight,
to set the downtrodden free,
to proclaim the Lord's year of favour. 19

He then rolled up the scroll, gave it back to the assistant and sat down. And all 20
eyes in the synagogue were fixed on him. •Then he began to speak to them, 'This 21
2:47; 4:15 text is being fulfilled today even as you listen'. •And he won the approval of all, 22
Jn 7:46 and they were astonished by the gracious words that came from his lips.
They said, 'This is Joseph's son, surely ?' •But he replied, 'No doubt you will 23
quote me the saying, "Physician, heal yourself" and tell me, "We have heard all
that happened in Capernaum,[k] do the same here in your own countryside" '.
And he went on, 'I tell you solemnly, no prophet is ever accepted in his own 24
country.
1 K 17:1; 18:1 'There were many widows in Israel, I can assure you, in Elijah's day, when 25
Jm 5:17 heaven remained shut for three years and six months and a great famine raged
throughout the land, •but Elijah was not sent to any one of these: he was sent 26
1 K 17:9 *to a widow at Zarephath, a Sidonian town.* •And in the prophet Elisha's time 27
2 K 5:14 there were many lepers in Israel, but none of these was cured, except the Syrian,
Naaman.'
Jn 7:30 When they heard this everyone in the synagogue was enraged. •They sprang 28 29
to their feet and hustled him out of the town; and they took him up to the brow
of the hill their town was built on, intending to throw him down the cliff, •but 30
Jn 8:59 he slipped through the crowd and walked away.

Mk 1:21-28 Jesus teaches in Capernaum and cures a demoniac

He went down to Capernaum, a town in Galilee, and taught them on the 31
||Mt 7:28-29 Ac 13:12 sabbath. •And his teaching made a deep impression on them because he spoke 32
with authority.
In the synagogue there was a man who was possessed by the spirit of an 33
Mt 8:29+ unclean devil, and it shouted at the top of its voice, •'Ha! What do you want 34
8:28 Mt 2:23+ with us, Jesus of Nazareth? Have you come to destroy us? I know who you are:
Mk 1:24+ Jn 6:69 the Holy One of God.' •But Jesus said sharply, 'Be quiet! Come out of him!' 35
Ac 3:14+ And the devil, throwing the man down in front of everyone, went out of him
1:12+ without hurting him at all. •Astonishment seized them and they were all saying 36
Mt 8:29+ 4:14+ to one another, 'What teaching! He gives orders to unclean spirits with authority
and power and they come out.' •And reports of him went all through the 37
surrounding countryside.

||Mt 8:14-15 ||Mk 1:29-31 Cure of Simon's mother-in-law

Leaving the synagogue he went to Simon's house. Now Simon's mother-in-law 38
was suffering from a high fever and they asked him to do something for her.
Leaning over her he rebuked the fever and it left her. And she immediately got 39
up and began to wait on them.

A number of cures
Mt 8:16-17 || Mk 1:32-34 ||

40 At sunset all those who had friends suffering from diseases of one kind or Mt 8:16
41 another brought them to him, and laying his hands on each he cured them. •Devils 13:13 1 Tm 4:14+
too came out of many people, howling, 'You are the Son of God'. But he rebuked *Mt 8:29+*
them and would not allow them to speak because they knew that he was the Mk 1:34+
Christ.

Jesus quietly leaves Capernaum and travels through Judaea
||Mk 1:35-39

42 When daylight came he left the house and made his way to a lonely place.
The crowds went to look for him, and when they had caught up with him they
43 wanted to prevent him leaving them, •but he answered, 'I must proclaim the
Good News of the kingdom of God to the other towns too, because that is what 8:1 Ac 10:36
44 I was sent to do'. •And he continued his preaching in the synagogues of Judaea.[l] *4:15; 23:5* Mk 1:38+ Ac 28:21

The first four disciples are called[a]

1 5 Now he was standing one day by the Lake of Gennesaret, with the crowd Mt 4:18 Mk 4:1
2 pressing round him listening to the word of God, •when he caught sight of two *Mk 1:16,19*
boats close to the bank. The fishermen had gone out of them and were washing
3 their nets. •He got into one of the boats—it was Simon's[b]—and asked him to put Mk 4:1-2
out a little from the shore. Then he sat down and taught the crowds from the boat.
4 When he had finished speaking he said to Simon, 'Put out into deep water Jn 21:1-6
5 and pay out your nets for a catch'. •'Master,' Simon replied 'we worked hard all
6 night long and caught nothing, but if you say so, I will pay out the nets.' •And Mt 8:10+
when they had done this they netted such a huge number of fish that their nets Mt 8:3+
7 began to tear, •so they signalled to their companions in the other boat to come
and help them; when these came, they filled the two boats to sinking point.
8 When Simon Peter saw this he fell at the knees of Jesus saying, 'Leave me, 1:12+ Ex 33:20+
9 Lord; I am a sinful man'. •For he and all his companions were completely Mt 8:8
10 overcome by the catch they had made; •so also were James and John, sons of Mk 1:17,19
Zebedee, who were Simon's partners.[c] But Jesus said to Simon, 'Do not be afraid; Jn 21:15-17, 19
11 from now on it is men you will catch'. •Then, bringing their boats back to land,
they left everything and followed him.

Cure of a leper
||Mt 8:1-4 ||Mk 1:40-45

12 Now Jesus was in one of the towns when a man appeared, covered with
leprosy. Seeing Jesus he fell on his face and implored him. 'Sir,' he said 'if you
13 want to, you can cure me.' •Jesus stretched out his hand, touched him and said,
14 'Of course I want to! Be cured!' And the leprosy left him at once. •He ordered
him to tell no one, 'But go and show yourself to the priest and make the offering 17:14 Mk 1:34+
for your healing as Moses prescribed it, as evidence for them'.

e. One of Luke's recurrent motifs: 4:37; 5:15; 7:17: cf., for similar examples, Ac 2:41+; 6:7; Lk 1:80+.

f. Another favourite theme of Lk: the people admiring and praising Jesus: 4:22; 8:25; 9:43; 11:27; 13:17; 19:48; for similar themes, cf. 4:14+ (Christ's growing reputation), 2:20+ (the praise of God), 1:12+ (religious awe).

g. Apparently this passage combines three visits: the first, vv. 16-22 (Jesus is honoured), occurring at the time indicated by Mt 4:13; the second, vv. 23-24 (Jesus astonishing his audience), the visit of which Mt and Mk speak; the third, vv. 25-30 (the life of Jesus threatened), not mentioned by Mt or Mk and to be placed towards the end of the Galilean ministry. In this way Lk presents an introductory tableau which is a summary and symbol of Christ's great offer and of its contemptuous rejection by his own people.

h. Rare form of the name 'Nazareth'.

i. The director of a synagogue could authorise any adult Jew to read the scripture lesson in public.

j. Add. 'to heal the broken-hearted', cf. LXX.

k. i.e. the miracles of which Lk does not speak until after the visit to Nazareth, 4:33, etc.

l. Mk reads 'Galilee'. Lk uses 'Judaea' in the wide sense: the land of Israel. So also in 7:17; 23:5 (?); Ac 10:37; 28:21.

5 a. In this narrative, Lk has combined: 1. A topographical note and an incident about Christ's preaching, vv. 1-3; this section resembles Mk 4:1-2 and 1:16,19; 2. The episode of the miraculous catch, vv. 4-10a, which is like that of Jn 21:1-6; 3. The call of Simon, vv. 10b-11, which is related to Mk 1:17,20. Luke's purpose in placing a period of teaching and miracle before the call of the first disciples was to make their unhesitating response less surprising.

b. In Lk, Simon does not receive the name Peter until 6:14.

c. The 'companions' of v. 7. Andrew is not mentioned because he is in Simon's boat (note the plural pronouns in vv. 5,6,7) which is the central piece in Luke's picture.

4:14+ His reputation continued to grow, and large crowds would gather to hear him 15
and to have their sickness cured, •but he would always go off to some place where 16
3:21+ he could be alone and pray.

||Mt 9:1-8 ||Mk 2:1-12 Cure of a paralytic

6:19 Now he was teaching one day, and among the audience there were Pharisees 17
and doctors of the Law who had come from every village in Galilee, from Judaea
and from Jerusalem. And the Power of the Lord[d] was behind his works of
healing. •Then some men appeared, carrying on a bed a paralysed man whom 18
they were trying to bring in and lay down in front of him. •But as the crowd 19
made it impossible to find a way of getting him in, they went up on to the flat
roof and lowered him and his stretcher down through the tiles into the middle of
Mt 8:10+ the gathering, in front of Jesus. •Seeing their faith he said, 'My friend, your sins 20
are forgiven you'. •The scribes and the Pharisees began to think this over. 'Who is 21
this man talking blasphemy? Who can forgive sins but God alone?' •But Jesus, 22
aware of their thoughts, made them this reply, 'What are these thoughts you have
in your hearts? •Which of these is easier: to say, "Your sins are forgiven you" 23
or to say, "Get up and walk"? •But to prove to you that the Son of Man has 24
authority on earth to forgive sins,'—he said to the paralysed man—'I order you:
get up, and pick up your stretcher and go home.' •And immediately before 25
their very eyes he got up, picked up what he had been lying on and went home
praising God.
2:20+ Ac 19:17 They were all astounded and praised God, and were filled with awe, 26
1:12+ saying, 'We have seen strange things today'.

||Mt 9:9 ||Mk 2:13-14 The call of Levi

When he went out after this, he noticed a tax collector, Levi by name, sitting 27
by the customs house, and said to him, 'Follow me'. •And leaving everything he 28
got up and followed him.

||Mt 9:10-12 ||Mk 2:15-17 Eating with sinners in Levi's house

In his honour Levi held a great reception in his house, and with them at table 29
was a large gathering of tax collectors and others. •The Pharisees and their scribes 30
19:7 complained to his disciples and said, 'Why do you eat and drink with tax collectors
and sinners?' •Jesus said to them in reply, 'It is not those who are well who need 31
the doctor, but the sick. •I have not come to call the virtuous, but sinners to 32
repentance.'

||Mt 9:14-17 ||Mk 2:18-22 Discussion on fasting

They then said to him, 'John's disciples are always fasting and saying prayers, 33
and the disciples of the Pharisees too, but yours go on eating and drinking'.
Jesus replied, 'Surely you cannot make the bridegroom's attendants fast while 34
the bridegroom is still with them? •But the time will come, the time for the bride- 35
groom to be taken away from them; that will be the time when they will fast.'

He also told them this parable, 'No one tears a piece from a new cloak to put 36
it on an old cloak; if he does, not only will he have torn the new one, but the
piece taken from the new will not match the old.

'And nobody puts new wine into old skins; if he does, the new wine will burst 37
the skins and then run out, and the skins will be lost. •No; new wine must be put 38
Jn 3:19 into fresh skins. •And nobody who has been drinking old wine wants new. "The 39
Jn 2:10 old is good" he says.'[e]

||Mt 12:1-8 ||Mk 2:23-28 Picking corn on the sabbath

6 Now one sabbath he happened to be taking a walk through the cornfields, 1
and his disciples were picking ears of corn, rubbing them in their hands
and eating them. •Some of the Pharisees said, 'Why are you doing something 2

3 that is forbidden on the sabbath day?' •Jesus answered them, 'So you have not
4 read what David did when he and his followers were hungry—•how he went into
the house of God, took the loaves of offering and ate them and gave them to his
5 followers, loaves which only the priests are allowed to eat?' •And he said to them,
'The Son of Man is master of the sabbath'.[a]

Cure of the man with a withered hand 13:10-17; 14:1-6 ||Mt 12:9-14 ||Mk 3:1-6

6 Now on another sabbath he went into the synagogue and began to teach, and
7 a man was there whose right hand was withered. •The scribes and the Pharisees
were watching him to see if he would cure a man on the sabbath, hoping to
8 find something to use against him. •But he knew their thoughts; and he said to the Jn 1:48+
man with the withered hand, 'Stand up! Come out into the middle.' And he came
9 out and stood there. •Then Jesus said to them, 'I put it to you: is it against the
10 law on the sabbath to do good, or to do evil; to save life, or to destroy it?' •Then
he looked round at them all and said to the man, 'Stretch out your hand'. He did
11 so, and his hand was better. •But they were furious, and began to discuss the 11:53+
best way of dealing with Jesus.

The choice of the Twelve ||Mt 10:1-4 ||Mk 3:13-19

12 Now it was about this time that he went out into the hills to pray; and he spent
13 the whole night in prayer to God. •When day came he summoned his disciples 3:21+
14 and picked out twelve of them; he called them 'apostles': •Simon whom he ||Mt 10:2-4 ||Ac 1:13
called Peter, and his brother Andrew; James, John, Philip, Bartholomew,
15 16 Matthew, Thomas, James son of Alphaeus, Simon called the Zealot, •Judas son
of James,[b] and Judas Iscariot who became a traitor. Ho 10:8

The crowds follow Jesus ||Mt 4:24-25 ||Mk 3:7-12

17 He then came down with them and stopped at a piece of level ground where
there was a large gathering of his disciples with a great crowd of people from all
parts of Judaea and from Jerusalem and from the coastal region of Tyre and Sidon
18 who had come to hear him and to be cured of their diseases. People tormented
19 by unclean spirits were also cured, •and everyone in the crowd was trying to touch 5:17; 8:46 Mk 5:30+
him because power came out of him that cured them all. *8:45*

The inaugural discourse.[c] The Beatitudes[d] Dt 27:12

20 Then fixing his eyes on his disciples he said: ||Mt 5:1

'How happy are you who are poor: yours is the kingdom of God. ||Mt 5:3
21 Happy you who are hungry now: you shall be satisfied. ||Mt 5:6
Happy you who weep now: you shall laugh. ||Mt 5:5

22 'Happy are you when people hate you, drive you out, abuse you, denounce ||Mt 5:11-12
23 your name as criminal, on account of the Son of Man. •Rejoice when that day
comes and dance for joy, for then your reward will be great in heaven. This was the
way their ancestors treated the prophets.

The curses

24 'But alas for you who are rich: you are having your consolation now. 16:25 Is 5:8-25
25 Alas for you who have your fill now: you shall go hungry. Am 6:1 Jm 5:1
Alas for you who laugh now: you shall mourn and weep. *Pr 14:13*

d. I.e. God.

e. The 'new wine' Jesus provides is not appreciated by those who have drunk the old wine of the Law.

6 a. One MS here adds an interesting, but probably spurious, dictum: 'On the same day, seeing a man working on the sabbath day, he said to him: Friend, if you know what you are doing, you are blessed; but if you do not know, you are accursed as a breaker of the Law'.

b. Lit. 'Judas of James', which could mean 'brother of James'. Cf. Mt 10:4+.

c. Luke's form is shorter than Matthew's because he has not filled out the discourse as Mt has done and has even left out material of a Jewish character which he thought would not interest his readers, cf. Mt 5:1+.

d. Mt has eight beatitudes, Lk four, and four maledictions. Matthew's beatitudes are a formula for the good life, and they promise heavenly rewards; Lk speaks of material conditions in this life to be reversed in the next, cf. 16:25. In Mt, Jesus uses the third person, in Lk he directly addresses his audience.

'Alas for you when the world speaks well of you! This was the way their 26
ancestors treated the false prophets.

Love of enemies

||Mt 5:44 'But I say this to you who are listening: Love your enemies, do good to those 27
1 P 3:9 who hate you, •bless those who curse you, pray for those who treat you badly. 28
||Mt 5:39-40 To the man who slaps you on one cheek, present the other cheek too; to the man 29
Pr 21:26 ||Mt 5:42 who takes your cloak from you, do not refuse your tunic. •Give to everyone who 30
12:33+ asks you, and do not ask for your property back from the man who robs you.
||Mt 7:12 Treat others as you would like them to treat you. •If you love those who love 31 32
||Mt 5:46 you, what thanks can you expect? Even sinners love those who love them. •And if 33
14:12-14 you do good to those who do good to you, what thanks can you expect? For even
Pr 21:26 sinners do that much. •And if you lend to those from whom you hope to receive, 34
what thanks can you expect? Even sinners lend to sinners to get back the same
amount. •Instead, love your enemies and do good, and lend without any hope 35
Si 4:10; 12:6 ||Mt 5:45 of return.[e] You will have a great reward, and you will be sons of the Most High,
for he himself is kind to the ungrateful and the wicked.

Compassion and generosity

15:1f Ex 34:6-7 'Be compassionate as your Father is compassionate. •Do not judge, and you 36 37
||Mt 7:1 Jm 2:13 will not be judged yourselves; do not condemn, and you will not be condemned
Pr 12:14 yourselves; grant pardon, and you will be pardoned. •Give, and there will be 38
gifts for you: a full measure, pressed down, shaken together, and running over,
||Mt 7:2 ||Mk 4:24 will be poured into your lap;[f] because the amount you measure out is the amount
you will be given back.'

Integrity

||Mt 15:14 He also told a parable to them, 'Can one blind man guide another? Surely 39
||Mt 10:24-25 ||Jn 13:16; 15:20 both will fall into a pit?[g] •The disciple is not superior to his teacher; the fully 40
trained disciple will always be like his teacher. •Why do you observe the splinter 41
in your brother's eye and never notice the plank in your own? •How can you say 42
to your brother, "Brother, let me take out the splinter that is in your eye", when
you cannot see the plank in your own? Hypocrite! Take the plank out of your
own eye first, and then you will see clearly enough to take[h] out the splinter
that is in your brother's eye.
||Mt 12:33-35 'There is no sound tree that produces rotten fruit, nor again a rotten tree that 43
||Mt 7:16-18 produces sound fruit. •For every tree can be told by its own fruit: people do not 44
pick figs from thorns, nor gather grapes from brambles. •A good man draws what 45
is good from the store of goodness in his heart; a bad man draws what is bad
from the store of badness. For a man's words flow out of what fills his heart.

The true disciple

||Mt 7:21 'Why do you call me, "Lord, Lord" and not do what I say? 46
||Mt 7:24-27 'Everyone who comes to me[i] and listens to my words and acts on them—I will 47
show you what he is like. •He is like the man who when he built his house dug, 48
and dug deep, and laid the foundations on rock; when the river was in flood it
bore down on that house but could not shake it, it was so well built. •But the one 49
who listens and does nothing is like the man who built his house on soil, with no
foundations: as soon as the river bore down on it, it collapsed; and what a ruin
that house became!'

Cure of the centurion's servant

||Mt 8:5-10, 13 ||Jn 4:46-54 *Mt 7:28* Ac 10:1

7 When he had come to the end of all he wanted the people to hear, he went into 1
Capernaum. •A centurion there had a servant, a favourite of his, who was 2
sick and near death. •Having heard about Jesus he sent some Jewish elders[a] 3
to him to ask him to come and heal his servant. •When they came to Jesus they 4

5 pleaded earnestly with him. 'He deserves this of you' they said •'because he is Ac 10:1,22
friendly towards our people;[b] in fact, he is the one who built the synagogue.' 12:33+
6 So Jesus went with them, and was not very far from the house when the centurion
sent word to him by some friends: 'Sir,' he said 'do not put yourself to trouble;
7 because I am not worthy to have you under my roof; •and for this same reason
I did not presume to come to you myself; but give the word and let my servant
8 be cured.[c] •For I am under authority myself, and have soldiers under me; and I say
to one man: Go, and he goes; to another: Come here, and he comes; to my
9 servant: Do this, and he does it.' •When Jesus heard these words he was
astonished at him and, turning round, said to the crowd following him, 'I tell
10 you, not even in Israel have I found faith like this'. •And when the messengers Mt 8:10+
got back to the house they found the servant in perfect health.

The son of the widow of Nain restored to life[d]

11 Now soon afterwards he went to a town called Nain, accompanied by his
12 disciples and a great number of people. •When he was near the gate of the town
it happened that a dead man was being carried out for burial, the only son of his
mother, and she was a widow. And a considerable number of the townspeople
13 were with her. •When the Lord[e] saw her he felt sorry for her. 'Do not cry' he
14 said. •Then he went up and put his hand on the bier and the bearers stood still,
15 and he said, 'Young man, I tell you to get up'. •And the dead man sat up and Mt 8:3+ Ac 9:41
16 began to talk, and Jesus *gave him to his mother*. •Everyone was filled with awe *1 K 17:23* 1:12+
and praised God saying, 'A great prophet has appeared among us; God has *2:20+* Mt 16:14+
17 visited his people'. •And this opinion of him spread throughout Judaea and all *1:68+*
over the countryside. 4:14+, 44+

The Baptist's question. Jesus commends him ||Mt 11:2-15

18 The disciples of John gave him all this news, and John, summoning two of his
19 disciples, •sent them to the Lord to ask, 'Are you the one who is to come, or must
20 we wait for someone else?' •When the men reached Jesus they said, 'John the
Baptist has sent us to you, to ask, "Are you the one who is to come or have we
21 to wait for someone else?" ' •It was just then that he cured many people of
diseases and afflictions and of evil spirits, and gave the gift of sight to many who
22 were blind. •Then he gave the messengers their answer, 'Go back and tell John
what you have seen and heard: the blind see again, the lame walk, lepers are Is 26:19; 35:5-6; 61:1
cleansed, and the deaf hear, the dead are raised to life, the Good News is pro- Ac 3:8
23 claimed to the poor •and happy is the man who does not lose faith in me'. 2:34
24 When John's messengers had gone he began to talk to the people about John,
25 'What did you go out into the wilderness to see? A reed swaying in the breeze?
No? Then what did you go out to see? A man dressed in fine clothes?
Oh no, those who go in for fine clothes and live luxuriously are to be found at
26 court! •Then what did you go out to see? A prophet? Yes, I tell you, and much
27 more than a prophet: •he is the one of whom scripture says:

See, I am going to send my messenger before you; Ml 3:1
he will prepare the way before you.

28 'I tell you, of all the children born of women, there is no one greater than John;
29 yet the least in the kingdom of God is greater than he is. •All the people who ||Mt 21:31-32

e. The text is difficult and the translation conj. Var. 'driving no one to despair' or 'despairing of no one' or 'not at all despairing'.

f. Folds in the tunic or cloak were used as a pocket or as a bag for provisions.

g. Addressed, in Lk, to the disciples; in Mt 15:14, to the Pharisees. The same applies to vv. 43-45.

h. Or 'and then you will see how to take'.

i. A Johannine expression, cf. Jn 6:35+.

7 a. Local worthies, not to be confused with the Jerusalem 'elders' who were members of the Sanhedrin.

b. Evidently a pagan in sympathy with Judaism, like Cornelius, Ac 10:1-2+.

c. Var. 'and my servant will be cured'.

d. Lk only. The episode leads up to the reply of Jesus to John's disciples, 7:22.

e. For the first time in the gospel narrative, Jesus is given the title hitherto strictly reserved for Yahweh himself. Cf. Ph 2:11+; Ac 2:36+.

heard him, and the tax collectors too, acknowledged God's plan by accepting
baptism from John; •but by refusing baptism from him the Pharisees and the 30
lawyers had thwarted what God had in mind for them.

||Mt 11:16-19 **Jesus condemns his contemporaries**

'What description, then, can I find for the men of this generation? What are 31
they like? •They are like children shouting to one another while they sit in the 32
market place:

Ezk 33:31
"We played the pipes for you,
and you wouldn't dance;
we sang dirges,
and you wouldn't cry".

'For John the Baptist comes, not eating bread, not drinking wine, and you 33
say, "He is possessed". •The Son of Man comes, eating and drinking, and you 34
say, "Look, a glutton and a drunkard, a friend of tax collectors and sinners".
Jn 6:35+ Yet Wisdom has been proved right by all her children.'[f] 35

The woman who was a sinner[g]

11:37; 14:1 One of the Pharisees invited him to a meal. When he arrived at the Pharisee's 36
Mt 21:32 Jn 8:4 house and took his place at table, •a woman[h] came in, who had a bad name in 37
the town. She had heard he was dining with the Pharisee and had brought with her
an alabaster jar of ointment. •She waited behind him at his feet, weeping, and her 38
tears fell on his feet, and she wiped them away with her hair; then she covered
his feet with kisses and anointed them with the ointment.

When the Pharisee who had invited him saw this, he said to himself, 'If this 39
Mt 16:14+ Jn 4:18-19 man were a prophet, he would know who this woman is that is touching him and
what a bad name she has'. •Then Jesus took him up and said, 'Simon, I have 40
something to say to you'. 'Speak, Master' was the reply. •'There was once a 41
creditor who had two men in his debt; one owed him five hundred denarii, the
other fifty. •They were unable to pay, so he pardoned them both. Which of them 42
will love him more?' •'The one who was pardoned more, I suppose' answered 43
Simon. Jesus said, 'You are right'.

Then he turned to the woman. 'Simon,' he said 'you see this woman? I came 44
into your house, and you poured no water over my feet, but she has poured out her
tears over my feet and wiped them away with her hair. •You gave me no kiss, but 45
she has been covering my feet with kisses ever since I came in.[i] •You did not 46
anoint my head with oil, but she has anointed my feet with ointment. •For this 47
reason I tell you that her sins, her many sins, must have been forgiven her, or she
Mt 21:31 would not have shown such great love.[j] It is the man who is forgiven little who
Mt 9:2 shows little love.' •Then he said to her, 'Your sins are forgiven'. •Those who 48 49
were with him at table began to say to themselves, 'Who is this man, that he even
Mt 8:10+ forgives sins?' •But he said to the woman, 'Your faith has saved you; go in peace'. 50

The women accompanying Jesus

||Mt 4:23; 9:35 **8** Now after this he made his way through towns and villages preaching, and 1
||Mk 1:39 *4:43-44* proclaiming the Good News of the kingdom of God. With him went the
Mt 8:29+; 12:45 Twelve, •as well as certain women who had been cured of evil spirits and ailments: 2
Mt 27:55-56 Mk 15:40-41 Mary surnamed the Magdalene, from whom seven demons had gone out,
23:49; 24:10 Jn 19:25 Joanna the wife of Herod's steward Chuza, Susanna, and several others who 3
provided for them out of their own resources.

||Mt 13:1-9 ||Mk 4:1-9 **Parable of the sower**

With a large crowd gathering and people from every town finding their way 4
to him, he used this parable:

'A sower went out to sow his seed. As he sowed, some fell on the edge of the 5

6 path and was trampled on; and the birds of the air ate it up. •Some seed fell on
7 rock, and when it came up it withered away, having no moisture. •Some seed fell
8 amongst thorns and the thorns grew with it and choked it. •And some seed fell
into rich soil and grew and produced its crop a hundredfold.' Saying this he
cried, 'Listen, anyone who has ears to hear!'

Why Jesus speaks in parables ||Mt 13:10-11,13 ||Mk 4:10-12

9 10 His disciples asked him what this parable might mean, •and he said, 'The
mysteries of the kingdom of God are revealed to you; for the rest there are only 10:21
parables, so that

they may see but not perceive, Is 6:9
listen but not understand.

The parable of the sower explained ||Mt 13:18-23 ||Mk 4:14-20

11 12 'This, then, is what the parable means: the seed is the word of God. •Those
on the edge of the path are people who have heard it, and then the devil comes
and carries away the word from their hearts in case they should believe and be Mt 8:10+
13 saved. •Those on the rock are people who, when they first hear it, welcome the
word with joy. But these have no root; they believe for a while, and in time of
14 trial they give up. •As for the part that fell into thorns, this is people who have
heard, but as they go on their way they are choked by the worries and riches and
15 pleasures of life and do not reach maturity. •As for the part in the rich soil, this
is people with a noble and generous heart who have heard the word and take
it to themselves and yield a harvest through their perseverance.

Parable of the lamp ||Mk 4:21-22

16 'No one lights a lamp to cover it with a bowl or to put it under a bed. No, he =11:33 ||Mt 5:15
puts it on a lamp-stand so that people may see the light when they come in. Jn 8:12+
17 For nothing is hidden but it will be made clear, nothing secret but it will be =12:2 ||Mt 10:26
18 known and brought to light. •So take care how you hear; for anyone who has ||*Mt 13:12;* 25:29
will be given more; from anyone who has not, even what he thinks he has will ||Mk 4:24-25 =*19:26*
be taken away.'

The true kinsmen of Jesus[a] Mt 12:46-50 ||Mk 3:31-35

19 His mother and his brothers came looking for him, but they could not get to
20 him because of the crowd. •He was told, 'Your mother and brothers are standing
21 outside and want to see you'. •But he said in answer, 'My mother and my 11:27-28
brothers are those who hear the word of God and put it into practice'. Ezk 33:31

The calming of the storm ||Mt 8:23-27 ||Mk 4:35-41

22 One day, he got into a boat with his disciples and said to them, 'Let us cross
23 over to the other side of the lake'. So they put to sea, •and as they sailed he fell
asleep. When a squall came down on the lake the boat started taking in water and
24 they found themselves in danger. •So they went to rouse him saying, 'Master!
Master! We are going down!' Then he woke up and rebuked the wind and the
25 rough water; and they subsided and it was calm again. •He said to them, 'Where Mt 8:10+
is your faith?' They were awestruck and astonished and said to one another, 1:12+
'Who can this be, that gives orders even to winds and waves and they obey
him?'

f. Var. 'by her actions', cf. Mt 11:19. The children of Wisdom, i.e., of the all-wise God, cf. Pr 8:22+, appreciate and welcome God's works.

g. Lk only. This episode is not the same as the anointing at Bethany, Mt 26:6-13p.

h. Most probably not Mary of Magdala, 8:2, and still less Mary, sister of Martha, 10:39; Jn 11:1,2,5; 12:2-3.

i. Var. 'ever since she came in'.

j. Not, as is usually translated, 'her many sins are forgiven her *because* she has shown such great love'. The context demands the reverse: she shows so much affection because she has had so many sins forgiven.

8 a. Lk has taken this passage out of its context in Mk 3:31-35 to serve as a conclusion to this small section on the parables, hence he modifies v. 21 (cf. Mk 3:35) to match v. 15.

||Mt 8:28-34 ||Mk 5:1-20 **The Gerasene demoniac**

They came to land in the country of the Gerasenes,[b] which is opposite Galilee. 26
He was stepping ashore when a man from the town who was possessed by devils 27
came towards him; for a long time the man had worn no clothes, nor did he
live in a house, but in the tombs.
4:34 Catching sight of Jesus he gave a shout, fell at his feet and cried out at the 28
Mt 4:3+ top of his voice, 'What do you want with me, Jesus, son of the Most High God?
I implore you, do not torture me.' •—For Jesus had been telling the unclean 29
spirit to come out of the man. It was a devil that had seized on him a great many
times, and then they used to secure him with chains and fetters to restrain him,
but he would always break the fastenings, and the devil would drive him out into
the wilds. •'What is your name?' Jesus asked. 'Legion' he said—because 30
many devils had gone into him. •And these pleaded with him not to order them 31
to depart into the Abyss.[c]

Now there was a large herd of pigs feeding there on the mountain, and the 32
devils pleaded with him to let them go into these. So he gave them leave. •The 33
devils came out of the man and went into the pigs, and the herd charged down
the cliff into the lake and were drowned.

When the swineherds saw what had happened they ran off and told their story 34
in the town and in the country round about; •and the people went out to see what 35
had happened. When they came to Jesus they found the man from whom the
10:39 devils had gone out sitting at the feet of Jesus,[d] clothed and in his full
senses; and they were afraid. •Those who had witnessed it told them how the 36
man who had been possessed came to be healed. •The entire population of the 37
1:12+ Gerasene territory was in a state of panic and asked Jesus to leave them. So he
got into the boat and went back.

The man from whom the devils had gone out asked to be allowed to stay with 38
him, but he sent him away. •'Go back home,' he said 'and report all that God has 39
done for you.' So the man went off and spread throughout the town all that
Jesus had done for him.

||Mt 9:18-26 ||Mk 5:21-43 **Cure of the woman with a haemorrhage. Jairus' daughter raised to life**

On his return Jesus was welcomed by the crowd, for they were all there waiting 40
for him. •And now there came a man named Jairus, who was an official of the 41
synagogue. He fell at Jesus' feet and pleaded with him to come to his house,
because he had an only daughter about twelve years old, who was dying. And the 42
crowds were almost stifling Jesus as he went.

Now there was a woman suffering from a haemorrhage for twelve years, 43
Ac 19:12 whom no one had been able to cure.[e] •She came up behind him and touched 44
the fringe of his cloak; and the haemorrhage stopped at that instant. •Jesus said, 45
'Who touched me?' When they all denied that they had, Peter and his companions
5:17; 6:19 said, 'Master, it is the crowds round you, pushing'. •But Jesus said, 'Somebody 46
touched me. I felt that power had gone out from me.' •Seeing herself discovered, the 47
woman came forward trembling, and falling at his feet explained in front of all the
people why she had touched him and how she had been cured at that very moment. 48
'My daughter,' he said 'your faith has restored you to health; go in peace.'

While he was still speaking, someone arrived from the house of the synagogue 49
official to say, 'Your daughter has died. Do not trouble the Master any further.'
Mt 8:10+ But Jesus had heard this, and he spoke to the man, 'Do not be afraid, only have 50
faith and she will be safe'. •When he came to the house he allowed no one to go 51
9:28; 22:8 Jn 13:24-25 in with him except Peter and John and James,[f] and the child's father and mother.
Ac 3:1 They were all weeping and mourning for her, but Jesus said, 'Stop crying; she is 52
not dead, but asleep'. •But they laughed at him, knowing she was dead. •But 53 54
taking her by the hand he called to her, 'Child, get up'. •And her spirit returned and 55
she got up at once. Then he told them to give her something to eat. •Her parents 56
1:12‡ Mk 1:34‡ were astonished, but he ordered them not to tell anyone what had happened.

The mission of the Twelve ||Mt 10:5,8, 9-14 ||Mk 6:7-13

1 **9** He called the Twelve[a] together and gave them power and authority over all
2 devils and to cure diseases, •and he sent them out to proclaim the kingdom of Mt 8:3+; 8:29+
3 God and to heal. •He said to them, 'Take nothing for the journey: neither staff,
nor haversack, nor bread, nor money; and let none of you take a spare tunic.
4 Whatever house you enter, stay there; and when you leave, let it be from there. 10:7 Ac 9:43; 16-
5 As for those who do not welcome you, when you leave their town shake the 15; 17:7; 18:3
6 dust from your feet as a sign to them.' •So they set out and went from village Ac 13:51
to village proclaiming the Good News and healing everywhere.

Herod and Jesus[b] ||Mt 14:1-2 ||Mk 6:14-16

7 Meanwhile Herod the tetrarch had heard about all that was going on; and
he was puzzled, because some people were saying that John had risen from the 9:19
8 dead, •others that Elijah had reappeared, still others that one of the ancient
9 prophets had come back to life. •But Herod said, 'John? I beheaded him. So who
is this I hear such reports about?' And he was anxious to see him. 23:8-12

The return of the apostles. Miracle of the loaves ||Mt 14:13-21 ||Mk 6:30-44 ||Jn 6:1-13

10 On their return the apostles gave him an account of all they had done. Then
he took them with him and withdrew to a town called Bethsaida where they Mk 6:45
11 could be by themselves. •But the crowds got to know and they went after him.
He made them welcome and talked to them about the kingdom of God; and he
cured those who were in need of healing.
12 It was late afternoon when the Twelve came to him and said, 'Send the
people away, and they can go to the villages and farms round about to find lodging
13 and food; for we are in a lonely place here'. •He replied, 'Give them something to eat yourselves'. But they said, 'We have no more than five loaves and two
14 fish, unless we are to go ourselves and buy food for all these people'. •For there
were about five thousand men. But he said to his disciples, 'Get them to sit down
15 16 in parties of about fifty'. •They did so and made them all sit down. •Then he took
the five loaves and the two fish, raised his eyes to heaven, and said the blessing
over them; then he broke them and handed them to his disciples to distribute
17 among the crowd. •They all ate as much as they wanted, and when the scraps
remaining were collected they filled twelve baskets.

Peter's profession of faith[c] ||Mt 16:13-16,20 ||Mk 8:27-30

18 Now one day when he was praying alone in the presence of his disciples he *3:21+*
19 put this question to them, 'Who do the crowds say I am?' •And they answered,
'John the Baptist; others Elijah; and others say one of the ancient prophets come 9:8
20 back to life'. •'But you,' he said 'who do you say I am?' It was Peter who spoke
21 up. 'The Christ of God' he said. •But he gave them strict orders not to tell 2:26+; 23:35
anyone anything about this. *Mk 1:34+*

First prophecy of the Passion[d] ||Mt 16:21 ||Mk 8:31

22 'The Son of Man' he said 'is destined to suffer grievously, to be rejected by the 9:44; 12:50; 17:25; 18:
elders and chief priests and scribes and to be put to death, and to be raised up 31; 24:7, 26,44
on the third day.'

b. Var. 'Gergesenes', 'Gadarenes'.

c. In place of Mark's 'send them out of the district', Mk 5:10. The demons beseech Jesus not to send them back to the depths of the earth, their usual dwelling place and ultimate home, Rv 9:1,2,11; 11:7; 17:8; 20:1,3.

d. As a disciple sits, 8:38; cf. 10:39; Ac 22:3. Lk alone adds this detail.

e. Var. 'a woman who, having spent all she had on doctors, could be cured by no one', cf. Mk 5:26.

f. Cf. Mk 5:37+. Here, however, as in 9:28; Ac 1:13, John is named immediately after Peter. This coupling of John with Peter is common to Lk, 22:8; Ac 3:1,3,11; 4:13,19; 8:14, and the fourth gospel, Jn 13:23-26; 18:15-16; 20:3-9; 21:7,20-23.

9 a. Add. 'apostles'.

b. Lk does not record the Baptist's death; instead, he prepares the reader ('he was anxious to see him') for the subsequent meeting of Herod with Jesus, 23:8-12.

c. Lk has left out a whole section of Mk (6:45–8:26).

d. This prophecy is to be followed by several others, 9:44; 12:50; 17:25; 18:31-33. Cf. 24:7,25-27. Lk omits Peter's protest and his rebuke by Jesus, Mk 8:32f.

||Mt 16:24-27 ||Mk 8:34-38
The condition of following Christ

||Mt 10:38 Then to all he said, 'If anyone wants to be a follower of mine, let him renounce 23
=14:27 Jn 12:26 himself and take up his cross every day and follow me. •For anyone who wants 24
=17:33 ||Mt 10:39 to save his life will lose it; but anyone who loses his life for my sake, that man
||Jn 12:25 will save it. •What gain, then, is it for a man to have won the whole world and to 25
=12:9 ||Mt 10:33 have lost or ruined his very self? •For if anyone is ashamed of me and of my 26
2 Tm 1:8 words, of him the Son of Man will be ashamed when he comes in his own glory
and in the glory of the Father and the holy angels.

||Mt 16:28 ||Mk 9:1
The kingdom will come soon

Mt 16:28+ 'I tell you truly, there are some standing here who will not taste death before 27
they see the kingdom of God.'

||Mt 17:1-9 ||Mk 9:2-10
The transfiguration[e]

8:51+ Now about eight days after this had been said, he took with him Peter and 28
3:21+ John and James and went up the mountain to pray. •As he prayed, the aspect of 29
his face was changed and his clothing became brilliant as lightning. •Suddenly 30
24:4 there were two men there talking to him; they were Moses and Elijah •appearing 31
in glory, and they were speaking of his passing which he was to accomplish in
2:38+ Jerusalem. •Peter and his companions were heavy with sleep, but they kept awake[f] 32
Jn 1:14+ and saw his glory[g] and the two men standing with him. •As these were leaving 33
him, Peter said to Jesus, 'Master, it is wonderful for us to be here; so let us make
three tents, one for you, one for Moses and one for Elijah'.—He did not know
what he was saying. •As he spoke, a cloud came and covered them with shadow; 34
1:12+ and when they went into the cloud the disciples were afraid. •And a voice came 35
Jn 1:34 from the cloud saying, 'This is my Son, the Chosen One.[h] Listen to him.' •And 36
9:21 after the voice had spoken, Jesus was found alone. The disciples kept silence and,
at that time, told no one what they had seen.

||Mt 17:14-18 ||Mk 9:14-27
The epileptic demoniac

Now on the following day when they were coming down from the mountain 37
a large crowd came to meet him. •Suddenly a man in the crowd cried out. 'Master,' 38
he said 'I implore you to look at my son: he is my only child. •All at once a spirit 39
will take hold of him, and give a sudden cry and throw the boy into convulsions
with foaming at the mouth; it is slow to leave him, but when it does it leaves the
boy worn out. •I begged your disciples to cast it out, and they could not.' 40
'Faithless and perverse generation!' Jesus said in reply 'How much longer must I be 41
among you and put up with you? Bring your son here.' •The boy was still moving 42
towards Jesus when the devil threw him to the ground in convulsions. But Jesus
rebuked the unclean spirit and cured the boy and gave him back to his father,
4:15+ and everyone was awestruck by the greatness of God. 43

||Mt 77:22 ||Mk 9:30-32
Second prophecy of the Passion

At a time when everyone was full of admiration for all he did, he said to
his disciples, •'For your part, you must have these words constantly in your 44
9:22+ Mt 17:22 mind: The Son of Man is going to be handed over into the power of men'.
Mk 4:13+ But they did not understand him when he said this; it was hidden from them 45
so that they should not see the meaning of it, and they were afraid to ask him
about what he had just said.

||Mt 18:1-5 ||Mk 9:33-37
Who is the greatest?

=22:24 An argument started between them about which of them was the greatest. 46
Jesus knew what thoughts were going through their minds, and he took a 47
=10:16 ||Mt 10:40 little child and set him by his side •and then said to them, 'Anyone who 48
||Jn 13:20 *22:26* welcomes this little child in my name welcomes me; and anyone who welcomes

me welcomes the one who sent me. For the least among you all, that is the one Mt 18:5▲ *14:11*
who is great.'

On using the name of Jesus

49 John spoke up. 'Master,' he said 'we saw a man casting out devils in your Ac 3:16+; 19:13
50 name, and because he is not with us we tried to stop him.'[i] •But Jesus said
to him, 'You must not stop him: anyone who is not against you is for you'. 11:23

IV. THE JOURNEY TO JERUSALEM[j]

A Samaritan village is inhospitable

51 Now as the time drew near for him to be taken up to heaven,[k] he resolutely 13:22; 17:11 18:31; 19:28; 24:51
52 took the road for Jerusalem •and sent messengers ahead of him. These set out, Mt 19:1
53 and they went into a Samaritan village to make preparations for him, •but the Mk 10:1
54 people would not receive him because he was making for Jerusalem.[l] •Seeing
this, the disciples James and John said, 'Lord, do you want us to call down fire 2 K 1:10
55 56 from heaven to burn them up?'[m] •But he turned and rebuked them,[n] •and they
went off to another village.

Hardships of the apostolic calling ||Mt 8:18-22

57 As they travelled along they met a man on the road who said to him, 'I will
58 follow you wherever you go'. •Jesus answered, 'Foxes have holes and the birds
of the air have nests, but the Son of Man has nowhere to lay his head'.
59 Another to whom he said, 'Follow me', replied,[o] 'Let me go and bury my 14:26,33
60 father first'. •But he answered, 'Leave the dead to bury their dead;[p] your duty
is to go and spread the news of the kingdom of God'.
61 Another said, 'I will follow you, sir, but first let me go and say good-bye 1 K 19:19-21
62 to my people at home'. •Jesus said to him, 'Once the hand is laid on the plough, Ph 3:13
no one who looks back is fit for the kingdom of God'.

The mission of the seventy-two disciples

1 **10** After this the Lord appointed seventy-two[a] others and sent them out ahead 9:1-2
of him,[b] in pairs, to all the towns and places he himself was to visit. Qo 4:9
2 He said to them,[c] 'The harvest is rich but the labourers are few, so ask the Lord ||Mt 9:37-38 Jn 4:36
3 of the harvest to send labourers to his harvest. •Start off now, but remember, ||*Mt 10:16*
4 I am sending you out like lambs among wolves. •Carry no purse, no haversack, =9:3-5; 22:35
5 no sandals. Salute no one on the road. •Whatever house you go into, let your 2 K 4:29 Mt 10:9-15 ||Mk 6:8-11

e. One of the narratives in which Lk most widely differs from Mk. It is clear that Lk had his own source of information (John?).

f. Preferable to 'they woke up'.

g. The glory of his future coming, 9:26.

h. Var. 'the Beloved', cf. Mt and Mk. The titles 'Chosen One', cf. 23:35; Is 42:1, and 'Son of Man' alternate in the *Parables of Enoch.*

i. Var. 'we stopped him'.

j. From 9:51–18:14, Lk deserts Mk. Assembling material he has found in the Collection (cf. Introduction to the Synoptic Gospels) that served Mt also, together with information from his own special source, Lk arranges all within the literary framework of a journey to Jerusalem (9:53,57; 10:1; 13:22,33; 17:11; cf. 2:38+) suggested to him by Mk 10:1.

k. Lit. 'for his taking up'. This 'assumption' of Jesus, cf. 2 K 2:9-11; Mk 16:19; Ac 1:2,10-11; 1 Tm 3:16, refers to the last days of his suffering life (Passion, death) and the beginning of his glory (resurrection, ascension). Jn, thinking more theologically, uses the word 'glorify' in connection with the whole of this period, Jn 7:39; 12:16,23; 13:31f; for him the crucifixion is a 'lifting up', Jn 12:32+.

l. The hatred of the Samaritans for the Jews, Jn 4:9+, would show itself particularly towards those on pilgrimage to Jerusalem; hence it was usual to bypass this territory, cf. Mt 10:5. Only Lk and Jn (4:1-42) mention Christ's presence in this schismatic province, cf. Lk 17:11,16. The early Church was not slow to follow his example, Ac 8:5-25.

m. Add. 'as Elijah did'. Allusion to 2 K 1:10-12. James and John are seen here as 'sons of thunder' indeed, Mk 3:17.

n. Add. 'You do not know what spirit you are made of. The Son of Man came not to destroy souls but to save them.'

o. Add. 'Lord', cf. Mt 8:21.

p. A play on the two meanings of 'death': physical and spiritual.

10 a. Var. 'seventy'.

b. Not, as in 9:52, to arrange for lodgings etc. but to prepare souls for his coming.

c. The collection used by Mt and Lk included a missionary discourse parallel with that of Mk 6:8-11. Lk has made use of both these sources, but separately (9:3-5; 10:2-12), whereas Mt has joined them together 10:7-16. Cf. Lk 11:39+; 17:22+.

first words be, "Peace to this house!" •And if a man of peace[d] lives there, your 6
peace will go and rest on him; if not, it will come back to you. •Stay in the same 7
1 Tm 5:18 house, taking what food and drink they have to offer, for the labourer deserves
his wages; do not move from house to house. •Whenever you go into a town where 8
they make you welcome, eat what is set before you. •Cure those in it who are 9
Mt 3:2+ ||Mt 10:7 sick, and say, "The kingdom of God is very near to you". •But whenever you enter 10
Ac 28:8 a town and they do not make you welcome, go out into its streets and say, •"We 11
Ac 13:51 wipe off the very dust of your town that clings to our feet, and leave it with you.
Yet be sure of this: the kingdom of God is very near." •I tell you, on that day 12
it will not go as hard with Sodom as with that town.

||Mt 11:21-24 'Alas for you, Chorazin! Alas for you, Bethsaida! For if the miracles done 13
in you had been done in Tyre and Sidon, they would have repented long ago, sitting
in sackcloth and ashes. •And still, it will not go as hard with Tyre and Sidon at the 14
Is 14:13,15 Judgement as with you. •And as for you, Capernaum, did you want to be exalted 15
high as heaven? *You shall be thrown down to hell.*

=9:48 Ex 16:8 'Anyone who listens to you listens to me; anyone who rejects you rejects me, 16
||Mt 10:40 ||Mk 9:37 ||Jn 13:20 and those who reject me reject the one who sent me.'

True cause for the apostles to rejoice

1:14+ The seventy-two came back rejoicing. 'Lord,' they said 'even the devils 17
Ac 3:16+ *Is 14:12* submit to us when we use your name.' •He said to them, 'I watched Satan fall 18
Jn 12:31-32 like lightning from heaven. •Yes, I have given you power to tread underfoot 19
Mt 8:29+ *Ps 91:13* serpents and scorpions and the whole strength of the enemy; nothing shall ever
Rv 12:9 *Mk 16:18* hurt you. •Yet do not rejoice that the spirits submit to you; rejoice rather that 20
Rv 20:12+ your names are written in heaven.'

The Good News revealed to the simple. The Father and the Son

||Mt 11:25-27

1:14+; 4:1+ It was then that, filled with joy by the Holy Spirit, he said, 'I bless 21
you, Father, Lord of heaven and of earth, for hiding these things from the learned
8:10 and the clever and revealing them to mere children. Yes, Father, for that is what
it pleased you to do. •'Everything has been entrusted to me by my Father; and 22
Rv 19:12 no one knows who the Son is except the Father, and who the Father is except
the Son and those to whom the Son chooses to reveal him.'

The privilege of the disciples

||Mt 13:16-17

Then turning to his disciples he spoke to them in private, 'Happy the eyes 23
that see what you see, •for I tell you that many prophets and kings wanted to see 24
what you see, and never saw it; to hear what you hear, and never heard it'.[f]

The great commandment

||Mt 22:34-40 ||Mk 12:28-31

2 Ch 28:15 Pr 3:27 There was a lawyer who, to disconcert him, stood up and said to him, 'Master, 25
Mt 19:16 what must I do to inherit eternal life?' •He said to him, 'What is written in the 26
Dt 6:5 Law? What do you read there?' •He replied, '*You must love the Lord your God* 27
with all your heart, with all your soul, with all your strength, and with all your
Lv 19:18 mind, *and your neighbour as yourself*'. •'You have answered right,' said Jesus 28
Lv 18:5 Pr 19:16 'do this and life is yours.'

Parable of the good Samaritan

Jn 4:9 But the man was anxious to justify himself[g] and said to Jesus, 'And who is 29
my neighbour?' •Jesus replied, 'A man was once on his way down from Jerusalem 30
to Jericho and fell into the hands of brigands; they took all he had, beat him
and then made off, leaving him half dead. •Now a priest happened to be travelling 31
down the same road, but when he saw the man, he passed by on the other side.
In the same way a Levite who came to the place saw him, and passed by on the 32
17:16 other side. •But a Samaritan[h] traveller who came upon him was moved with 33
Is 1:6 compassion when he saw him. •He went up and bandaged his wounds, pouring 34

oil and wine on them. He then lifted him on to his own mount, carried him to the
35 inn and looked after him. •Next day, he took out two denarii and handed them
to the innkeeper. "Look after him," he said "and on my way back I will make
36 good any extra expense you have." •Which of these three, do you think, proved
37 himself a neighbour to the man who fell into the brigands' hands?' •'The one
who took pity on him' he replied. Jesus said to him, 'Go, and do the same
yourself'.

Martha and Mary[i]

38 In the course of their journey he came to a village, and a woman named Jn 11:1-2
39 Martha welcomed him into her house. •She had a sister called Mary, who sat 8:35+
40 down at the Lord's feet and listened to him speaking. •Now Martha who was
distracted with all the serving said, 'Lord, do you not care that my sister is leaving 1 Co 7:35
41 me to do the serving all by myself? Please tell her to help me.' •But the Lord 8:3+
answered: 'Martha, Martha,' he said 'you worry and fret about so many things, Mt 6:33
42 and yet few are needed, indeed only one.[j] It is Mary who has chosen the better Jn 6:27
part; it is not to be taken from her.'

The Lord's prayer

1 **11** Now once he was in a certain place praying, and when he had finished 3:21+
one of his disciples said, 'Lord, teach us to pray, just as John taught his
2 disciples'. •He said to them, 'Say this when you pray:[a]

"Father, may your name be held holy, ||Mt 6:9-13
your kingdom come;
3 give us each day our daily bread,[b]
and forgive us our sins,[c]
4 for we ourselves forgive each one who is in debt to us.
And do not put us to the test." '

The importunate friend

18:1-8

5 He also said to them, 'Suppose one of you has a friend and goes to him in
6 the middle of the night to say, "My friend, lend me three loaves, •because a friend
of mine on his travels has just arrived at my house and I have nothing to offer
7 him"; •and the man answers from inside the house, "Do not bother me. The
door is bolted now, and my children and I are in bed; I cannot get up to give
8 it you". •I tell you, if the man does not get up and give it him for friendship's Jg 14:17 Mt 15:23
sake, persistence will be enough to make him get up and give his friend all he
wants.

Effective prayer

||Mt 7:7-11 Jn 14:13-14+

9 'So I say to you: Ask, and it will be given to you; search, and you will find;
10 knock, and the door will be opened to you. •For the one who asks always receives;
the one who searches always finds; the one who knocks will always have the door
11 opened to him. •What father among you would hand his son a stone when he

d. Lit. 'son of peace', a Hebraism for those who deserve 'peace', i.e. all the spiritual and temporal blessings the word implies. Cf. Jn 14:27+.

e. Add. 'and turning to his disciples he said'.

f. Paul emphasises the fact that the 'mystery' was long kept hidden; Rm 16:25+. See also 1 P 1:11-12.

g. For having put the question.

h. An alien and a heretic, Jn 8:48; cf. Lk 9:53+, from whom one might expect hostility, as opposed to those of Israel who should have been most sensitive to the demands of charity.

i. These two sisters reappear, with the same individual characteristics, in the story of the raising of Lazarus, Jn 11:1-44.

j. Var. 'but only one thing is needed', 'but only a few things are needed', readings which make free with the text and deform the sense. In his remark Jesus rises from the material plane ('few things are needed', i.e. for the meal) to the 'one thing necessary', which is to listen to the word of God.

11 a. Matthew's text has seven petitions, Luke's five. There were therefore two traditions of the Lord's prayer. Matthew's form seems the more ancient.

b. Var. (borrowed, perhaps, from a baptismal liturgy) 'may your Holy Spirit come down on us and cleanse us '.

c. 'Debts' in Mt, here correctly interpreted by Lk who, however, does not suppress this juridical aspect (cf. his following line 'each one who is in debt to us').

asked for bread? Or hand him a snake instead of a fish? •Or hand him a 12
scorpion if he asked for an egg? •If you then, who are evil, know how to give 13
your children what is good, how much more will the heavenly Father give
Jn 14:13-16 the Holy Spirit[d] to those who ask him!'

||Mt 12:22-29 ||Mk 3:22-27

Jesus and Beelzebul

Mt 9:32 He was casting out a devil and it was dumb; but when the devil had gone 14
out the dumb man spoke, and the people were amazed. •But some of them 15
=11:29 ||Mt 16:1 ||Mk 8:11 said, 'It is through Beelzebul, the prince of devils, that he casts out devils'. •Others 16
asked him, as a test, for a sign from heaven; •but, knowing what they were 17
thinking, he said to them, 'Every kingdom divided against itself is heading for
ruin, and a household divided against itself collapses. •So too with Satan: if he is 18
divided against himself, how can his kingdom stand?—Since you assert that
it is through Beelzebul[e] that I cast out devils. •Now if it is through Beelzebul 19
that I cast out devils, through whom do your own experts cast them out? Let
Ex 8:15 Mt 12:28 *Lk 17:21* them be your judges, then. •But if it is through the finger of God[f] that I cast 20
Mt 4:17+; 8:29+ out devils, then know that the kingdom of God has overtaken you. •So long as 21
Is 49:25 a strong man fully armed guards his own palace, his goods are undisturbed;
Jr 31:11 but when someone stronger than he is attacks and defeats him, the stronger 22
man takes away all the weapons he relied on and shares out his spoil.

||Mt 12:30

No compromise

9:50 'He who is not with me is against me; and he who does not gather with me 23
scatters.

||Mt 12:43-45

Return of the unclean spirit

Lv 16:22 'When an unclean spirit goes out of a man it wanders through waterless coun- 24
try looking for a place to rest, and not finding one it says, "I will go back to
the home I came from". •But on arrival, finding it swept and tidied, •it then goes 25 26
off and brings seven other spirits more wicked than itself, and they go in and
set up house there, so that the man ends up by being worse than he was before.'

The truly happy

1:48; 4:15+; 23:29 Now as he was speaking, a woman in the crowd raised her voice and said, 27
8:21 'Happy the womb that bore you and the breasts you sucked!' •But he replied, 28
Dt 6:3 Pr 19:16 Rv 1:3 'Still happier those who hear the word of God and keep it!'

||*Mt 12:38-42*

The sign of Jonah

Mt 16:1 The crowds got even bigger and he addressed them, 'This is a wicked genera- 29
Jn 6:30-31 tion; it is asking for a sign.[g] The only sign it will be given is the sign of Jonah.
For just as Jonah became a sign to the Ninevites, so will the Son of Man be to this 30
1 K 10:1-10 generation.[h] •On Judgement day the Queen of the South will rise up with the men 31
of this generation and condemn them, because she came from the ends of the
Jn 6:35+ earth to hear the wisdom of Solomon; and there is something greater than
Jon 3 Solomon here. •On Judgement day the men of Nineveh will stand up with this 32
generation and condemn it, because when Jonah preached they repented; and
there is something greater than Jonah here.

=8:16 ||Mt 5:15 ||Mk 4:21

The parable of the lamp repeated

'No one lights a lamp and puts it in some hidden place or under a tub, but 33
on the lamp-stand so that people may see the light when they come in. •The lamp 34
Mt 6:22-23 of your body is your eye. When your eye is sound, your whole body too is filled with
light; but when it is diseased your body too will be all darkness. •See to it then that 35
the light inside you is not darkness. •If, therefore, your whole body is filled with 36
light, and no trace of darkness, it will be light entirely, as when the lamp shines
on you with its rays.'[i]

The Pharisees and the lawyers attacked

37 He had just finished speaking when a Pharisee invited him to dine at his 7:36; 14:1
38 house. He went in and sat down at the table. •The Pharisee saw this and was Mt 15:2 Mk 7:2,5
39 surprised that he had not first washed before the meal. •But the Lord said to him,[j]
'Oh, you Pharisees! You clean the outside of cup and plate, while inside yourselves ||Mt 23:25-26
40 you are filled with extortion and wickedness. •Fools! Did not he who made the
41 outside make the inside too? •Instead, give alms from what you have[k] and then 12:33+
42 indeed everything will be clean for you. •But alas for you Pharisees! You who pay ||Mt 23:23
your tithe of mint and rue and all sorts of garden herbs and overlook justice and
the love of God! These you should have practised, without leaving the others
43 undone. •Alas for you Pharisees who like taking the seats of honour in the =20:46 ||Mt 23:6-7
44 synagogues and being greeted obsequiously in the market squares! •Alas for ||Mk 12:38-39
you, because you are like the unmarked tombs that men walk on without ||Mt 23:27
knowing it!'[l]

45 A lawyer then spoke up. 'Master,' he said 'when you speak like this you
46 insult us too.' •'Alas for you lawyers also,' he replied 'because you load on men ||Mt 23:4
burdens that are unendurable, burdens that you yourselves do not move a finger
to lift.

47 'Alas for you who build the tombs of the prophets, the men your ancestors ||Mt 23:29-31
48 killed! •In this way you both witness what your ancestors did and approve it; they
did the killing, you do the building.[m]

49 'And that is why the Wisdom of God[n] said, "I will send them prophets and ||Mt 23:34-36
50 apostles; some they will slaughter and persecute, •so that this generation will have
to answer for every prophet's blood that has been shed since the foundation
51 of the world, •from the blood of Abel to the blood of Zechariah, who was
murdered between the altar and the sanctuary". Yes, I tell you, this generation
will have to answer for it all.

52 'Alas for you lawyers who have taken away the key of knowledge! You have ||Mt 23:13
not gone in yourselves, and have prevented others going in who wanted to.'

53 When he left the house, the scribes and the Pharisees began a furious attack 6:11; 19:47; 20:19, 22:2
54 on him[o] and tried to force answers from him on innumerable questions, •setting Mt 19:3; 22:15f
traps to catch him out in something he might say.

Open and fearless speech

1 12 Meanwhile the people had gathered in their thousands so that they were
treading on one another. And he began to speak, first of all to his disciples.[a] ||Mt 16:6, 12 ||Mk 8:15
'Be on your guard against the yeast of the Pharisees—that is, their hypocrisy.
2 Everything that is now covered will be uncovered, and everything now hidden =8:17 Qo 10:20
3 will be made clear. •For this reason, whatever you have said in the dark will ||Mt 10:26-27 ||Mk 4:22
be heard in the daylight, and what you have whispered in hidden places will be
proclaimed on the housetops.

d. Instead of the 'good things' of Mt 7:11. The Holy Spirit is the best of all 'good things'.

e. Var. 'Beelzebul' and 'Beelzebub'.

f. On this phrase, cf. Ex 8:15 and Ps 8:3. This passage and its parallel, Mt 12:28, have combined to provide the title 'finger of God's right hand' for the Holy Spirit.

g. I.e. a miracle in evidence and vindication of Christ's authority, cf. Jn 2:11+; Lk 1:18+. See Mt 8:3+.

h. Jonah showed the Ninevites the way to God; now Jesus points the way, but his hearers, less generous than the Ninevites, have refused to take it. Mt 12:40 offers a different interpretation.

i. The textual tradition of vv. 35-36 is confused, and the text is probably corrupt. But the general meaning is clear: Jesus addresses his message to all, and if the mind is 'healthy', i.e. unclouded by selfish prejudice, cf. Jn 3:19-21, it can be understood by all.

j. Lk depends here on the source he shares with Mt; in 20:45-47 he returns to the same theme, this time depending on Mk. Mt has combined both sources in one discourse (ch. 23). Cf. Lk 10:2+; 17:22+.

k. Interpretation difficult. Others translate 'what is within'.

l. Thus contracting legal impurity, Nb 19:16.

m. Irony. By building the tombs of the prophets they hoped to make amends for their ancestors' sins—yet they have exactly the same mentality as these ancestors.

n. I.e. the divine intention as interpreted by Jesus.

o. The attitude of Christ's enemies continued to harden; Lk traces the process in more detail than Mk; Lk 6:11; 11:53-54; 19:48; 20:19-20; 22:2.

12 a. Or else 'began to say to his disciples: First of all, be on your guard...'

Jn 15:15 ||Mt 10:28-31 'To you my friends I say: Do not be afraid of those who kill the body and 4
after that can do no more. •I will tell you whom to fear: fear him who, after he 5
Jm 4:12 Mt 3:12+; 18:9+ has killed, has the power to cast into hell. Yes, I tell you, fear him. •Can you 6
1 Co 9:9 not buy five sparrows for two pennies? And yet not one is forgotten in God's
21:18 sight. •Why, every hair on your head has been counted. There is no need to be 7
afraid: you are worth more than hundreds of sparrows.
||Mt 10:32-33 ||Mk 8:38 'I tell you, if anyone openly declares himself for me in the presence of men, the 8
Son of Man will declare himself for him in the presence of God's angels. •But 9
=9:26 the man who disowns me in the presence of men will be disowned in the
presence of God's angels.
||Mt 12:32 ||Mk 3:29 'Everyone who says a word against the Son of Man will be forgiven, but he 10
who blasphemes against the Holy Spirit will not be forgiven.
=21:12-15 ||Mt 10:17-20 'When they take you before synagogues and magistrates and authorities, 11
||Mk 13:11 do not worry about how to defend yourselves or what to say, •because when the 12
Jn 14:26+ time comes, the Holy Spirit will teach you what you must say.'

On hoarding possessions

A man in the crowd said to him, 'Master, tell my brother to give me a share 13
Si 5:1f of our inheritance'. •'My friend,' he replied 'who appointed me your judge, or 14
the arbitrator of your claims?' •Then he said to them, 'Watch, and be on your 15
guard against avarice of any kind, for a man's life is not made secure by what he
owns, even when he has more than he needs'.
Si 11:24: 14:4 Then he told them a parable: 'There was once a rich man who, having had 16
Ho 12:9 1 Tm 6:17 a good harvest from his land, •thought to himself, "What am I to do? I have 17
not enough room to store my crops." •Then he said, "This is what I will do: 18
I will pull down my barns and build bigger ones, and store all my grain and my
Pr 27:1 Jm 4:13-15 goods in them, •and I will say to my soul: My soul, you have plenty of good 19
Si 11:19 1 Co 15:33 things laid by for many years to come; take things easy, eat, drink, have a good
Qo 6:2; 9:12 time". •But God said to him, "Fool! This very night the demand will be made 20
for your soul; and this hoard of yours, whose will it be then?" •So it is when 21
Mt 6:19-21 Rv 3:17-18 a man stores up treasure for himself in place of making himself rich in the sight
of God.'

||Mt 6:25-33 **Trust in Providence**

Then he said to his disciples, 'That is why I am telling you not to worry 22
about your life and what you are to eat, nor about your body and how you are
to clothe it. •For life[b] means more than food, and the body more than clothing. 23
1 Co 9:9 Think of the ravens. They do not sow or reap; they have no storehouses and 24
no barns; yet God feeds them. And how much more are you worth than the
birds! •Can any of you, for all his worrying, add a single cubit to his span of 25
life? •If the smallest things, therefore, are outside your control, why worry 26
about the rest? •Think of the flowers; they never have to spin or weave;[c] yet, 27
I assure you, not even Solomon in all his regalia was robed like one of these.
Now if that is how God clothes the grass in the field which is there today and 28
thrown into the furnace tomorrow, how much more will he look after you, you
men of little faith! •But you, you must not set your hearts on things to eat and 29
things to drink; nor must you worry. •It is the pagans of this world who set their 30
hearts on all these things. Your Father well knows you need them. •No; set your 31
hearts on his kingdom, and these other things will be given you as well.
Jn 10; 21: 15-17 'There is no need to be afraid, little flock, for it has pleased your Father to 32
give you the kingdom.

3:11; 6:30 7:5; 11:41 **On almsgiving[d]**

'Sell your possessions and give alms. Get yourselves purses that do not wear 33
Pr 13:7 Ws 7:14 out, treasure that will not fail you, in heaven where no thief can reach it and
||Mt 6:20-21 no moth destroy it. •For where your treasure is, there will your heart be also. 34

On being ready for the Master's return

35 36 ‘See that you are dressed for action and have your lamps lit. •Be like men Si 5:7 1 P 1:13
waiting for their master to return from the wedding feast, ready to open the Mt 25:1-13
37 door as soon as he comes and knocks. •Happy those servants whom the master
finds awake when he comes. I tell you solemnly, he will put on an apron, sit 22:27 Jn 13:4-5
38 them down at table and wait on them. •It may be in the second watch he comes,
39 or in the third, but happy those servants if he finds them ready. •You may be ||Mk 13:35
quite sure of this, that if the householder had known at what hour the burglar ||Mt 24:43-44
would come, he would not have let anyone break through the wall of his house.
40 You too must stand ready, because the Son of Man is coming at an hour you
do not expect.’

41 42 Peter said, ‘Lord, do you mean this parable for us, or for everyone?’ •The
Lord replied, ‘What sort of steward,[e] then, is faithful and wise enough for the ||Mt 24:45-51 1 Co 4:1
master to place him over his household to give them their allowance of food at
43 the proper time? •Happy that servant if his master's arrival finds him at this
44 45 employment. •I tell you truly, he will place him over everything he owns. •But
as for the servant who says to himself, “My master is taking his time coming”,
and sets about beating the menservants and the maids, and eating and drinking
46 and getting drunk, •his master will come on a day he does not expect and at
an hour he does not know. The master will cut him off and send him to the same
fate as the unfaithful.

47 ‘The servant who knows what his master wants, but has not even started to
48 carry out those wishes, will receive very many strokes of the lash. •The one who
who did not know, but deserves to be beaten for what he has done, will receive Mt 10:15
fewer strokes. When a man has had a great deal given him, a great deal will be
demanded of him; when a man has had a great deal given him on trust, even
more will be expected of him.

Jesus and his Passion

49 ‘I have come to bring fire[f] to the earth, and how I wish it were blazing
50 already! •There is a baptism I must still receive, and how great is my distress till 9:22+; 22:14 Mk 10:38+
it is over!

Jesus the cause of dissension

||Mt 10:34-36

51 ‘Do you suppose that I am here to bring peace on earth? No, I tell you, but 22:37
52 rather division. •For from now on a household of five will be divided: three 2:34
53 against two and two against three; •the father divided against the son, son Mi 7:6
against father, mother against daughter, daughter against mother, mother-in-law
against daughter-in-law, daughter-in-law against mother-in-law.’

On reading the signs of the times[g]

54 He said again to the crowds, ‘When you see a cloud looming up in the west 19:44 ||Mt 16:2-3
55 you say at once that rain is coming, and so it does. •And when the wind is from
56 the south you say it will be hot, and it is. •Hypocrites! You know how to
interpret the face of the earth and the sky. How is it you do not know how to
interpret these times? ||Mt 5:25-26

57 58 ‘Why not judge for yourselves what is right? •For example: when you go
to court with your opponent, try to settle with him on the way, or he may drag
you before the judge and the judge hand you over to the bailiff and the bailiff

12 b. Lit. ‘the soul’ in the biblical sense, as in v. 19.

c. Var. ‘work or spin’, cf. Mt 6:28.

d. That riches are a danger and should be given away in alms is characteristic teaching of Lk: cf. 3:11; 6:30; 7:5; 11:41; 12:33-34; 14:14; 16:9; 18:22; 19:8; Ac 9:36; 10:2,4,31.

e. A steward with authority over other servants; Jesus, therefore, is speaking of the apostles (the ‘us’ of Peter's question).

f. This fire symbolises neither the spiritual struggle that the coming of Jesus provokes nor, strictly speaking, the Holy Spirit. It is the fire that is to purify and inflame men's hearts, the fire lit on the cross. Jn 12:32 has the same thought in different words.

g. The messianic era has begun: it is high time for this to be realised, because judgement is coming soon, vv. 57-59.

have you thrown into prison. •I tell you, you will not get out till you have paid 59
the very last penny.'

Examples inviting repentance

13 It was just about this time that some people arrived and told him about 1
the Galileans whose blood Pilate had mingled with that of their sacrifices.[a]
Jn 9:3 At this he said to them, 'Do you suppose these Galileans who suffered like that 2
were greater sinners than any other Galileans? •They were not, I tell you. No; 3
but unless you repent you will all perish as they did. •Or those eighteen on whom 4
the tower at Siloam fell and killed them? Do you suppose that they were more
Jn 7:23;8:24 guilty than all the other people living in Jerusalem? •They were not, I tell you. 5
No; but unless you repent you will all perish as they did.'

Parable of the barren fig tree[b]

Jr 8:13 Mt 21:19-20 He told this parable: 'A man had a fig tree planted in his vineyard, and he 6
came looking for fruit on it but found none. •He said to the man who looked 7
after the vineyard, "Look here, for three years[c] now I have been coming to look
for fruit on this fig tree and finding none. Cut it down: why should it be taking
up the ground?" •"Sir," the man replied "leave it one more year and give me 8
time to dig round it and manure it: •it may bear fruit next year; if not, then 9
you can cut it down." '

6:6-11; 14: 1-6 **Healing of the crippled woman on a sabbath**

Jn 9:14+ One sabbath day he was teaching in one of the synagogues, •and a woman 10 11
Mt 8:29+ was there who for eighteen years had been possessed by a spirit that left her
enfeebled; she was bent double and quite unable to stand upright.[d] •When Jesus 12
saw her he called her over and said, 'Woman, you are rid of your infirmity'
4:40 2:20+ and he laid his hands on her. And at once she straightened up, and she glorified 13
God.
Ex 20:8-10 But the synagogue official was indignant because Jesus had healed on the 14
sabbath,[e] and he addressed the people present. 'There are six days' he said 'when
work is to be done. Come and be healed on one of those days and not on the
14:5 Mt 12:11 sabbath.' •But the Lord answered him. 'Hypocrites!' he said 'Is there one of 15
you who does not untie his ox or his donkey from the manger on the sabbath
Mt 8:29+ and take it out for watering? •And this woman, a daughter of Abraham whom 16
Satan has held bound these eighteen years—was it not right to untie her bonds
1:14+ on the sabbath day?' •When he said this, all his adversaries were covered with 17
4:15+ confusion, and all the people were overjoyed at all the wonders he worked.

||Mt 13:31-32 ||Mk 4:30-32 **Parable of the mustard seed**

He went on to say, 'What is the kingdom of God like? What shall I compare 18
Ezk 17:23 Dn 4:9,18 it with? •It is like a mustard seed which a man took and threw into his garden: 19
it grew and became a tree, and the birds of the air sheltered in its branches.'

||Mt 13:13 **Parable of the yeast**

Another thing he said, 'What shall I compare the kingdom of God with? 20
It is like the yeast a woman took and mixed in with three measures of flour till 21
it was leavened all through.'

The narrow door; rejection of the Jews, call of the gentiles

2:38+; 9:51+ Through towns and villages he went teaching, making his way to Jerusalem. 22
Someone said to him, 'Sir, will there be only a few saved?' He said to them, 23
||Mt 7:13-14 'Try your best to enter by the narrow door, because, I tell you, many will try 24
to enter and will not succeed.
||Mt 25:10-12 'Once the master of the house has got up and locked the door, you may find 25
yourself knocking on the door, saying, "Lord, open to us" but he will answer,

26 "I do not know where you come from". •Then you will find yourself saying, ||Mt 7:22-23
27 "We once ate and drank in your company; you taught in our streets" •but he
will reply, "I do not know where you come from. *Away from me, all you wicked* Ps 6:8
men!"
28 'Then there will be weeping and grinding of teeth, when you see Abraham ||Mt 8:11-12
and Isaac and Jacob and all the prophets in the kingdom of God, and yourselves
29 turned outside. •And men from east and west, from north and south, will come
to take their places at the feast in the kingdom of God.
30 'Yes, there are those now last who will be first, and those now first who will ||Mt 19:30+; 20:16
be last.' ||Mk 10:31

Herod the fox

31 Just at this time some Pharisees came up. 'Go away' they said. 'Leave this
32 place, because Herod[f] means to kill you.' •He replied, 'You may go and give
that fox this message: Learn that today and tomorrow I cast out devils and on
33 the third day[g] attain my end.[h] •But for today and tomorrow and the next day
I must go on, since it would not be right for a prophet to die outside Jerusalem.[i] 2:38+ Mt 16:14+

Jerusalem admonished ||Mt 23:37-39

34 'Jerusalem, Jerusalem, you that kill the prophets and stone those who are 19:41-44
sent to you! How often have I longed to gather your children, as a hen gathers
35 her brood under her wings, and you refused! •So be it! Your house will be left
to you. Yes, I promise you, you shall not see me till the time comes when you Mt 23:39+
say:

Blessings on him who comes in the name of the Lord!' Ps 118:26

Healing of a dropsical man on the sabbath 6:6-11 13:10-17

1 **14** Now on a sabbath day he had gone for a meal to the house of one of the Jn 9:14+
2 leading Pharisees; and they watched him closely. •There in front of him was
3 a man with dropsy, •and Jesus addressed the lawyers and Pharisees. 'Is it
4 against the law' he asked 'to cure a man on the sabbath, or not?' •But they Mk 3:4
5 remained silent, so he took the man and cured him and sent him away. •Then Mt 8:3
he said to them, 'Which of you here, if his son[a] falls into a well, or his ox, will 13:15 ||Mt 12:11
6 not pull him out on a sabbath day without hesitation?' •And to this they could Jn 7:23
find no answer.

On choosing places at table

7 He then told the guests a parable, because he had noticed how they
8 picked the places of honour. He said this, •'When someone invites you to a Pr 25:6-7 Mt 23:6
wedding feast, do not take your seat in the place of honour. A more distinguished
9 person than you may have been invited, •and the person who invited you both
may come and say, "Give up your place to this man". And then, to your em-
10 barrassment, you would have to go and take the lowest place. •No; when you
are a guest, make your way to the lowest place and sit there, so that, when your

13 a. There is no other evidence for this incident or for that mentioned in v. 4. The meaning of both is clear: sin is not the immediate cause of this or that calamity (cf. Jn 9:3), but such disasters as these are providential invitations to repentance.

b. The episode of the withered fig tree in Mt 21:18-22p shows Jesus in a hard light; Lk prefers to substitute this parable of his patience.

c. Possibly an allusion to the length of Christ's ministry as described in the fourth gospel.

d. Or 'unable to hold her head erect'.

e. He takes this act of healing for a 'work' forbidden by the Law.

f. Herod Antipas, cf. Lk 3:1+. If, as is possible, he made this threat to rid himself of Jesus, the term 'fox' refers to that sly trick.

g. The expression signifies a short period of time.

h. A word full of meaning, including both his death and the achievement of his perfection: Jesus was made 'perfect' by his suffering and death, Heb 2:10; 5:9. Cf. Jn 19:30.

i. Meaning apparently 'My work will soon be over, but not yet. I have not finished my work of exorcising and healing; this I shall contrive to do on my way to Jerusalem where my destiny lies', cf. 2:38+. Similarly, in Jn 7:30; 8:20 (cf. 8:59; 10:39; 11:54) the enemies of Jesus have no power over him so long as 'his hour has not yet come'.

14 a. 'his son'; var. 'his donkey'.

host comes, he may say, "My friend, move up higher". In that way, everyone
=18:14 ||Mt 23:12 with you at the table will see you honoured. •For everyone who exalts himself 11
9:48 will be humbled, and the man who humbles himself will be exalted.'

On choosing guests to be invited

6:32-35 Si 12:1-5 Then he said to his host, 'When you give a lunch or a dinner, do not ask 12
12:33+ your friends, brothers, relations or rich neighbours, for fear they repay your
Pr 22:9 courtesy by inviting you in return.[b] •No; when you have a party, invite the poor, 13
the crippled, the lame, the blind; •that they cannot pay you back means that 14
6:35 you are fortunate, because repayment will be made to you when the virtuous
rise again.'

The invited guests who made excuses

On hearing this, one of those gathered round the table said to him, 'Happy 15
Mt 8:11+ the man who will be at the feast in the kingdom of God!' •But he said to him, 16
||Mt 22:2-10 'There was a man who gave a great banquet, and he invited a large number of
people. •When the time for the banquet came, he sent his servant to say to those 17
who had been invited, "Come along: everything is ready now". •But all alike 18
started to make excuses. The first said, "I have bought a piece of land and must
go and see it. Please accept my apologies." •Another said, "I have bought five 19
yoke of oxen and am on my way to try them out. Please accept my apologies."
Yet another said,"I have just got married and so am unable to come". 20
'The servant returned and reported this to his master. Then the householder, 21
in a rage, said to his servant, "Go out quickly into the streets and alleys of the
town and bring in here the poor, the crippled, the blind and the lame". •"Sir," 22
said the servant "your orders have been carried out and there is still room."
Then the master said to his servant, "Go to the open roads and the hedgerows 23
and force people to come in to make sure my house is full; •because, I tell you, 24
not one of those who were invited shall have a taste of my banquet".'

Renouncing all that one holds dear

Great crowds accompanied him on his way and he turned and spoke to 25
Mt 10:37: 19:29 them. •'If any man comes to me without hating[c] his father, mother, wife,[d] children, 26
||*Mt 10:38;* 16:24 brothers, sisters, yes and his own life too, he cannot be my disciple. •Anyone 27
||Mk 8:34 =*9:23* who does not carry his cross and come after me cannot be my disciple.
Jn 12:26

Renouncing possessions

'And indeed, which of you here, intending to build a tower, would not first 28
sit down and work out the cost to see if he had enough to complete it? •Otherwise, 29
if he laid the foundation and then found himself unable to finish the work, the
onlookers would all start making fun of him and saying, •"Here is a man who 30
Pr 24:6 started to build and was unable to finish". •Or again, what king marching to 31
war against another king would not first sit down and consider whether with
ten thousand men he could stand up to the other who advanced against him with
twenty thousand? •If not, then while the other king was still a long way off, he 32
9:59; 12: 33+ would send envoys to sue for peace. •So in the same way, none of you can be 33
my disciple unless he gives up all his possessions.[e]

||Mt 5:13 ||Mk 9:50 **On loss of enthusiasm in a disciple**

'Salt is a useful thing. But if the salt itself loses its taste, how can it be 34
seasoned again? •It is good for neither soil nor manure heap. People throw it 35
out. Listen, anyone who has ears to hear!'

6:36 Ex 34:6+ Ho 2:21+; 11:8-9 **The three parables of God's mercy**

Ps 119:176 15 The tax collectors and the sinners, meanwhile, were all seeking his company 1
19:7 to hear what he had to say, •and the Pharisees and the scribes complained. 2

3 'This man' they said 'welcomes sinners and eats with them.' •So he spoke this Mt 9:10-13
parable to them:

The lost sheep
Ezk 34:1 ||Mt 18:12-14

4 'What man among you with a hundred sheep, losing one, would not leave
the ninety-nine in the wilderness and go after the missing one till he found it? Ezk 34:4,16
5 6 And when he found it, would he not joyfully take it on his shoulders •and then, Is 40:11
when he got home, call together his friends and neighbours? "Rejoice with me,"
7 he would say "I have found my sheep that was lost." •In the same way, I tell you, 19:10
there will be more rejoicing in heaven over one repentant sinner than over 1:14+ Ws 12:2
ninety-nine virtuous men who have no need of repentance. Ezk 18:23; 33:11

The lost drachma

8 'Or again, what woman with ten drachmas would not, if she lost one, light
9 a lamp and sweep out the house and search thoroughly till she found it? •And
then, when she had found it, call together her friends and neighbours? "Rejoice
10 with me," she would say "I have found the drachma I lost." •In the same way, 19:10
I tell you, there is rejoicing among the angels of God over one repentant sinner.' Ezk 18:23; 33:11

The lost son (the 'prodigal') and the dutiful son

11 12 He also said, 'A man had two sons. •The younger said to his father, "Father,
let me have the share of the estate that would come to me". So the father divided
13 the property between them. •A few days later, the younger son got together
everything he had and left for a distant country where he squandered his money Pr 29:3 Si 9:6
on a life of debauchery.
14 'When he had spent it all, that country experienced a severe famine, and now
15 he began to feel the pinch, •so he hired himself out to one of the local inhabitants
16 who put him on his farm to feed the pigs. •And he would willingly have filled
his belly with the husks the pigs were eating but no one offered him anything. Pr 27:7
17 Then he came to his senses and said, "How many of my father's paid servants Zc 10:9
18 have more food than they want, and here am I dying of hunger! •I will leave
this place and go to my father and say: Father, I have sinned against heaven and Ho 2:9
19 against you; •I no longer deserve to be called your son; treat me as one of your
20 paid servants." •So he left the place and went back to his father. Tb 7:6 Jr 3:12f
'While he was still a long way off, his father saw him and was moved with pity. *Is 49:14-16* Jr 31:20
21 He ran to the boy, clasped him in his arms and kissed him tenderly.[a] •Then his
son said, "Father, I have sinned against heaven and against you. I no longer
22 deserve to be called your son."[b] •But the father said to his servants, "Quick!
Bring out the best robe and put it on him; put a ring on his finger and sandals
23 on his feet. •Bring the calf we have been fattening, and kill it; we are going to
24 have a feast, a celebration, •because this son of mine was dead and has come
back to life; he was lost and is found." And they began to celebrate. 19:10
25 'Now the elder son was out in the fields, and on his way back, as he drew
26 near the house, he could hear music and dancing. •Calling one of the servants
27 he asked what it was all about. •"Your brother has come" replied the servant
"and your father has killed the calf we had fattened because he has got him back
28 safe and sound." •He was angry then and refused to go in, and his father came Jon 4:1
29 out to plead with him; •but he answered his father, "Look, all these years
I have slaved for you and never once disobeyed your orders, yet you never
30 offered me so much as a kid for me to celebrate with my friends. •But, for this

b. Or 'for fear they invite you in return and that be your repayment'.

c. Hebraism. Jesus asks, not for hate, but for total detachment now, cf. 9:57-62.

d. 'wife', peculiar to Lk, illustrating his leaning to asceticism, cf. 1 Co 7. So Lk also, 18:29.

e. Applicable to all disciples—Lk seems to make no distinction.

15 a. The father's pity symbolises divine mercy: it contrasts with the son's resentment which is like that of the Pharisees and scribes.

b. Add. 'treat me as one of your paid servants', cf. v. 19.

son of yours, when he comes back after swallowing up your property—he and
his women—you kill the calf we had been fattening."
'The father said, "My son, you are with me always and all I have is yours. 31
1:14+ Ezk 18:23; But it was only right we should celebrate and rejoice, because your brother 32
33:11 19:10 here was dead and has come to life; he was lost and is found."'

The crafty steward

16 [a]He also said to his disciples, 'There was a rich man and he had a steward 1
who was denounced to him for being wasteful with his property. •He called 2
for the man and said, "What is this I hear about you? Draw me up an account of
your stewardship because you are not to be my steward any longer." •Then the 3
steward said to himself, "Now that my master is taking the stewardship from me,
what am I to do? Dig? I am not strong enough. Go begging? I should be too
ashamed. •Ah, I know what I will do to make sure that when I am dismissed 4
from office there will be some to welcome me into their homes."
'Then he called his master's debtors one by one. To the first he said, "How 5
much do you owe my master?" •"One hundred measures of oil" was the reply. 6
The steward said, "Here, take your bond; sit down straight away and write fifty".
To another he said, "And you, sir, how much do you owe?" "One hundred 7
measures of wheat" was the reply. The steward said, "Here, take your bond and
write eighty".
'The master praised the dishonest steward for his astuteness.[b] For the children 8
Jn 8:12+ of this world are more astute in dealing with their own kind than are the children
of light.'

The right use of money

12:33+ Si 29:12 'And so I tell you this: use money, tainted as it is,[c] to win you friends, and 9
thus make sure that when it fails you, they will welcome you into the tents of
‖19:17 ‖Mt 25:21 eternity. •The man who can be trusted in little things can be trusted in great; 10
the man who is dishonest in little things will be dishonest in great. •If then you 11
cannot be trusted with money, that tainted thing, who will trust you with genuine
riches? •And if you cannot be trusted with what is not yours,[d] who will give 12
you what is your very own?[e]
‖Mt 6:24 'No servant can be the slave of two masters: he will either hate the first and 13
love the second, or treat the first with respect and the second with scorn. You
cannot be the slave both of God and of money.'

Against the Pharisees and their love of money

The Pharisees, who loved money, heard all this and laughed at him. •He 14 15
18:9 Mt 6:1; said to them, 'You are the very ones who pass yourselves off as virtuous in
23:28 Pr 21:2 people's sight, but God knows your hearts. For what is thought highly of by men
Ac 1:24 is loathsome in the sight of God.

‖Mt 11:12-13 The kingdom stormed

'Up to the time of John it was the Law and the Prophets; since then, the 16
kingdom of God has been preached, and by violence everyone is getting in.

‖Mt 5:18 The Law remains

'It is easier for heaven and earth to disappear than for one little stroke to drop 17
out of the Law.

‖Mt 5:32; 19:9 Marriage indissoluble

'Everyone who divorces his wife and marries another is guilty of adultery, and 18
the man who marries a woman divorced by her husband commits adultery.

The rich man and Lazarus[f]

'There was a rich man who used to dress in purple and fine linen and feast 19

20 magnificently every day. •And at his gate there lay a poor man called Lazarus,
21 covered with sores, •who longed to fill himself with the scraps that fell from
22 the rich man's table.[g] Dogs even came and licked his sores. •Now the poor man
died and was carried away by the angels to the bosom of Abraham.[h] The rich
man also died and was buried.

23 'In his torment in Hades[i] he looked up and saw Abraham a long way off
24 with Lazarus in his bosom. •So he cried out, "Father Abraham, pity me and
send Lazarus to dip the tip of his finger in water and cool my tongue, for I am
25 in agony in these flames". •"My son," Abraham replied "remember that during
your life good things came your way, just as bad things came the way of Lazarus. 6:24-25
26 Now he is being comforted here while you are in agony. •But that is not all:
between us and you a great gulf[j] has been fixed, to stop anyone, if he wanted
to, crossing from our side to yours, and to stop any crossing from your side to
ours."

27 'The rich man replied, "Father, I beg you then to send Lazarus to my father's
28 house, •since I have five brothers, to give them warning so that they do not
29 come to this place of torment too". •"They have Moses and the prophets," 24:27,44
30 said Abraham "let them listen to them." •"Ah no, father Abraham," said the
31 rich man "but if someone comes to them from the dead, they will repent." •Then
Abraham said to him, "If they will not listen either to Moses or to the prophets, 24:27 Jn 5:46-47
they will not be convinced even if someone should rise from the dead".'

On leading others astray

||Mt 18:6-7 ||Mk 9:42

1 **17** He said to his disciples, 'Obstacles are sure to come, but alas for the one
2 who provides them! •It would be better for him to be thrown into the sea
with a millstone put round his neck than that he should lead astray a single
3 one of these little ones. •Watch yourselves!

Brotherly correction[a]

||Mt 18:15, 21-22

'If your brother does something wrong, reprove him and, if he is sorry,
4 forgive him. •And if he wrongs you seven times a day and seven times comes
back to you and says, "I am sorry", you must forgive him.'

The power of faith

Mt 8:10+

5 6 The apostles said to the Lord, 'Increase our faith'. •The Lord replied, 'Were ||Mt 17:20; 21:21
your faith the size of a mustard seed you could say to this mulberry tree, "Be
uprooted and planted in the sea", and it would obey you. ||Mk 11:23

Humble service

7 'Which of you, with a servant ploughing or minding sheep, would say to him Jn 13:4-5
when he returned from the fields, "Come and have your meal immediately"?[b]
8 Would he not be more likely to say, "Get my supper laid; make yourself tidy
and wait on me while I eat and drink. You can eat and drink yourself afterwards"?

16 a. This chapter is a compilation of two parables and several *logia* of Jesus on the right and wrong use of money. Vv. 16,17,18, each with a different theme, interrupt the literary scheme of the chapter.

b. The steward is commended not for his roguery but for his adroitness in an awkward situation.

c. Money is here called 'tainted' not only because its owner is here presumed to have gained it dishonestly but because great wealth is rarely acquired without some sharp practice.

d. Lit. 'what is outside' i.e. wealth, which is something external to man.

e. 'your very own'; var. 'our very own'. Jesus is speaking of the most intimate possessions a man can have; these are spiritual.

f. Parable in story form without reference to any historical personage.

g. Add. 'but no one offered him a thing'. cf. 15:16.

h. Jewish figure of speech, the equivalent of the old biblical phrase 'gathered to his fathers' i.e. to the patriarchs, Jg 2:10; cf. Gn 15:15; 47:30; Dt 31:16. 'In the bosom of...' implies close intimacy, Jn 1:18, and evokes a picture of the messianic banquet where Lazarus reclines next to Abraham, cf. Jn 13:23; Mt 8:11+.

i. Vulg. has 'in Hades' at the end of v. 22.

j. The 'gulf' is a symbol: the destiny of saved and lost is unalterable.

17 a. Lk, apparently, is thinking of a matter that concerns only two of the community; in Mt the offence is more public. Lk does not mention appealing to the community.

b. With this picture of human relations contrast the gospel paradox, 12:37; 22:27; Jn 13:1-16p.

Jb 22:3; 35:7 Si 10:26 Must he be grateful to the servant for doing what he was told? •So with you: 9 10
when you have done all you have been told to do, say, "We are merely servants:
we have done no more than our duty".'

The ten lepers

9:51+ Jn 4:9 Now on the way to Jerusalem he travelled along the border between Samaria 11
and Galilee.[c] •As he entered one of the villages, ten lepers came to meet him. 12
Lv 13:45-46 They stood some way off •and called to him, 'Jesus! Master! Take pity on us.' 13
5:14 Lv 14:1-32 When he saw them he said, 'Go and show yourselves to the priests'. Now as they 14
Mt 8:4 Mk 1:44 were going away they were cleansed. •Finding himself cured, one of them 15
2:20+ turned back praising God at the top of his voice •and threw himself at the feet 16
9:53+; 10:33+ of Jesus and thanked him. The man was a Samaritan. •This made Jesus say, 17
'Were not all ten made clean? The other nine, where are they? •It seems that no 18
one has come back to give praise to God, except this foreigner.' •And he said to 19
Mt 8:10+ the man, 'Stand up and go on your way. Your faith has saved you.'

The coming of the kingdom of God

Mt 4:17+ Asked by the Pharisees when the kingdom of God was to come, he gave them 20
this answer, 'The coming of the kingdom of God does not admit of observation
and there will be no one to say, "Look here! Look there!" For, you must know, 21
11:20 Mt 3:2 the kingdom of God is among you.'[d]

The day of the Son of Man[e]

He said to the disciples, 'A time will come when you will long to see one of 22
Mt 8:20+ Jn 8:56+ the days of the Son of Man[f] and will not see it. •They will say to you, "Look 23
||*Mt 24:23, 26-27* there!" or, "Look here!" Make no move; do not set off in pursuit; •for as the 24
||Mk 13:21 lightning flashing from one part of heaven lights up the other, so will be the Son
9:22+ of Man when his day comes. •But first he must suffer grievously and be rejected 25
by this generation.
||Mt 24:37-39 'As it was in Noah's day, so will it also be in the days of the Son of Man.[g] 26
Gn 6-8 People were eating and drinking, marrying wives and husbands, right up to the 27
day Noah went into the ark, and the Flood came and destroyed them all. •It 28
Gn 19:1-29 will be the same as it was in Lot's day: people were eating and drinking, buying
and selling, planting and building, •but the day Lot left Sodom, God rained fire 29
and brimstone from heaven and it destroyed them all. •It will be the same when 30
the day comes for the Son of Man to be revealed.
21:21 ||Mt 24:17-18 'When that day comes, anyone on the housetop, with his possessions in the 31
||Mk 13: 15-16 house, must not come down to collect them, nor must anyone in the fields turn
Gn 19:26 back either. •Remember Lot's wife. •Anyone who tries to preserve his life will lose 32 33
9:24 ||Mt 10:39 it; and anyone who loses it will keep it safe. •I tell you, on that night two will be 34
||Jn 12:25 ||*Mt 24:40-41* in one bed: one will be taken, the other left; •two women will be grinding corn 35
together: one will be taken, the other left.'[h] •The disciples interrupted. 'Where, 37
||Mt 24:28 Lord?' they asked. He said, 'Where the body is, there too will the vultures gather'.

The unscrupulous judge and the importunate widow

11:9+ Pr 25:15 *11:5-8* 18 Then he told them a parable about the need to pray continually and never 1
lose heart.[a] •'There was a judge in a certain town' he said 'who had neither 2
fear of God nor respect for man. •In the same town there was a widow who kept 3
on coming to him and saying, "I want justice from you against my enemy!"
For a long time he refused, but at last he said to himself, "Maybe I have neither 4
fear of God nor respect for man, •but since she keeps pestering me I must give 5
this widow her just rights, or she will persist in coming and worry me to death". '
And the Lord said, 'You notice what the unjust judge has to say? •Now will 6 7
Rv 6:9-11 not God see justice done to his chosen who cry to him day and night even when
he delays to help them? •I promise you, he will see justice done to them, and 8
Mt 8:10+; 24:12 done speedily. But when the Son of Man comes, will he find any faith on earth?'

The Pharisee and the publican

9 He spoke the following parable to some people who prided themselves on being 16:15 Pr 21:2;
10 virtuous and despised everyone else, •'Two men went up to the Temple to pray, 28:13 Mt 6:1; 21:
11 one a Pharisee, the other a tax collector. •The Pharisee stood there and said this 31; 23:28 Rm 2:20
prayer to himself, "I thank you, God, that I am not grasping, unjust, adulterous
like the rest of mankind, and particularly that I am not like this tax collector here.
12 13 I fast twice a week; I pay tithes on all I get." •The tax collector stood some
distance away, not daring even to raise his eyes to heaven; but he beat his breast
14 and said, "God, be merciful to me, a sinner". •This man, I tell you, went home
again at rights with God; the other did not. For everyone who exalts himself will ‖Mt 23:12
be humbled, but the man who humbles himself will be exalted.' =14:11

Jesus and the children[b]

9:47 ‖Mt 19:13-15 ‖Mk 10: 13-16

15 People even brought little children to him, for him to touch them; but
16 when the disciples saw this they turned them away. •But Jesus called the children
to him and said, 'Let the little children come to me, and do not stop them; for it
17 is to such as these that the kingdom of God belongs. •I tell you solemnly, anyone
who does not welcome the kingdom of God like a little child will never Mt 18:2
enter it.'

The rich aristocrat

‖Mt 19:16-22 ‖Mk 10: 17-22

18 A member of one of the leading families put this question to him, 'Good
19 Master, what have I to do to inherit eternal life?' •Jesus said to him, 'Why do you 10:25-28
20 call me good? No one is good but God alone. •You know the commandments:
You must not commit adultery; You must not kill; You must not steal; You must Ex 20:12-16 Dt 5:16-20
21 *not bring false witness; Honour your father and mother.*' •He replied, 'I have kept
22 all these from my earliest days till now'. •And when Jesus heard this he said,
'There is still one thing you lack. Sell all that you own and distribute the money 12:33+
23 to the poor, and you will have treasure in heaven; then come, follow me.' •But
when he heard this he was filled with sadness, for he was very rich.

The danger of riches

‖Mt 19:23-26 ‖Mk 10: 23-27

24 Jesus looked at him and said, 'How hard it is for those who have riches to
25 make their way into the kingdom of God! •Yes, it is easier for a camel to pass
through the eye of a needle than for a rich man to enter the kingdom of God.'
26 27 'In that case' said the listeners 'who can be saved?' •'Things that are impossible
for men' he replied 'are possible for God.'

The reward of renunciation

‖Mt 19:27-29 ‖Mk 10: 28-30

28 29 Then Peter said, 'What about us? We left all we had to follow you.' •He said
to them, 'I tell you solemnly, there is no one who has left house, wife, brothers, 14:26+
30 parents or children for the sake of the kingdom of God •who will not be given
repayment[c] many times over in this present time and, in the world to come,
eternal life'.

c. Making for the Jordan valley and so down to Jericho, 18:35; from there he goes up to Jerusalem.

d. As something already present and active. The alternative translation 'within you' would not furnish as direct an answer to the Pharisees' question.

e. The discourse is proper to Lk, who makes a clear distinction between Jesus prophesying the destruction of Jerusalem, 21:6-24, and his own coming in glory at the end of time, 17:22-37. Some of the passages in this discourse are found in the great eschatological discourse of Mt 24:5-41; there, as elsewhere (cf. Lk 10: 2+; 11:39+), Mt has joined together two sources which Lk leaves separate; cf. Mt 24:1+. 'day' is a more biblical term ('day of Yahweh', cf. Am 5:18+) than Matthew's *parousia* ('coming', 24:3) which is hellenistic in origin. Cf. 1 Co 1:8+.

f. Not to experience again one day of the earthly life of Jesus, nor to see the first day of his glorious coming, but to have the joy of even one of the days that are to follow that coming.

g. I.e. at the time of the coming.

h. Add. v. 36 'There will be two men in the fields: one will be taken, the other left', cf. Mt 24:40.

18 a. Pauline in thought and expression: cf. Rm 1:10; 12:12; Ep 6:18; Col 1:3; 1 Th 5:17; 2 Th 1:11, etc., and 2 Co 4:1,16; Ga 6:9; Ep 3:13; 2 Th 3:13.

b. Lk here rejoins Mark's narrative which he deserted in 9:50. Cf. 9:51+.

c. Add. 'in return'.

||Mt 20:17-19 ||Mk 10:28-30
Third prophecy of the Passion

Then taking the Twelve aside he said to them, 'Now we are going up to 31
9:22+; 24:25 2:38+; 9:51+ Ac 3:18 Jerusalem, and everything that is written by the prophets[d] about the Son of Man
is to come true. •For he will be handed over to the pagans and will be mocked, 32
maltreated and spat on, •and when they have scourged him they will put him 33
Mk 4:13+ to death; and on the third day he will rise again.' •But they could make nothing 34
of this; what he said was quite obscure to them, they had no idea what it meant.

||Mt 20:29-34 ||Mk 10:46-52
Entering Jericho: the blind man

Now as he drew near to Jericho there was a blind man sitting at the side of the 35
road begging. •When he heard the crowd going past he asked what it was all about, 36
Mt 2:23+ and they told him that Jesus the Nazarene was passing by. •So he called out, 37 38
Mt 9:27+ 'Jesus, Son of David, have pity on me'. •The people in front scolded him and told 39
him to keep quiet, but he shouted all the louder, 'Son of David, have pity on me'.
Jesus stopped and ordered them to bring the man to him, and when he came up, 40
asked him, •'What do you want me to do for you?' 'Sir,' he replied 'let me see 41
Mt 8:10+ again.' •Jesus said to him, 'Receive your sight. Your faith has saved you.' 42
2:20+ And instantly his sight returned and he followed him praising God, and all the 43
people who saw it gave praise to God for what had happened.

Zacchaeus

Mt 5:46+ **19** He entered Jericho and was going through the town •when a man whose 1 2
name was Zacchaeus made his appearance; he was one of the senior tax
collectors and a wealthy man. •He was anxious to see what kind of man Jesus 3
was, but he was too short and could not see him for the crowd; •so he ran ahead 4
and climbed a sycamore tree to catch a glimpse of Jesus who was to pass that
way. •When Jesus reached the spot he looked up and spoke to him: 'Zacchaeus, 5
come down. Hurry, because I must stay at your house today.' •And he hurried 6
1:14+ down and welcomed him joyfully. •They all complained when they saw what 7
5:30; 15:2 was happening. 'He has gone to stay at a sinner's house' they said. •But Zacchaeus 8
12:33+ Ex 21:37 stood his ground and said to the Lord, 'Look, sir, I am going to give half my
2 S 12:6 property to the poor, and if I have cheated anybody I will pay him back four
Mt 21:31 times the amount'.[a] •And Jesus said to him, 'Today salvation has come to this 9
15:6,9,24,32 house, because this man too is a son of Abraham;[b] •for the Son of Man has come 10
to seek out and save what was lost'.

Parable of the pounds[c]

||Mt 25:14-30 While the people were listening to this he went on to tell a parable, because 11
2:38+ he was near Jerusalem and they imagined that the kingdom of God was going
Mk 13:34 to show itself then and there. •Accordingly he said, 'A man of noble birth went 12
to a distant country to be appointed king and afterwards return.[d] •He summoned 13
ten of his servants and gave them ten pounds. "Do business with these" he told
them "until I get back." •But his compatriots detested him and sent a delegation 14
Ps 2:2f Jn 19:15,21 to follow him with this message, "We do not want this man to be our king".
'Now on his return, having received his appointment as king, he sent for those 15
servants to whom he had given the money, to find out what profit each had made.
The first came in and said, "Sir, your one pound has brought in ten". •"Well done, 16 17
||16:10 my good servant!" he replied "Since you have proved yourself faithful in a very
small thing, you shall have the government of ten cities." •Then came the second 18
and said, "Sir, your one pound has made five". •To this one also he said, "And 19
you shall be in charge of five cities". •Next came the other and said, "Sir, here 20
is your pound. I put it away safely in a piece of linen •because I was afraid of you; 21
for you are an exacting man: you pick up what you have not put down and reap
what you have not sown." •"You wicked servant!" he said "Out of your own 22
mouth I condemn you. So you knew I was an exacting man, picking up what
I have not put down and reaping what I have not sown? •Then why did you not 23

put my money in the bank? On my return I could have drawn it out with
24 interest." •And he said to those standing by, "Take the pound from him and
25 give it to the man who has ten pounds". •And they said to him, "But, sir, he has
26 ten pounds..."[e] •"I tell you, to everyone who has will be given more; but =8:18 ||Mt 13:12 ||Mk 4:25
from the man who has not, even what he has will be taken away.
27 "But as for my enemies who did not want me for their king, bring them here
and execute them in my presence."' Ps 2:9

V. THE JERUSALEM MINISTRY

The Messiah enters Jerusalem
||Mt 21:1-11 ||Mk 11:1-11 ||Jn 12:12-16

28 29 When he had said this he went on ahead, going up to Jerusalem. •Now when 2:38+; 9:51
he was near Bethphage and Bethany, close by the Mount of Olives as it is called,
30 he sent two of the disciples, telling them, •'Go off to the village opposite, and
as you enter it you will find a tethered colt that no one has yet ridden. Untie it
31 and bring it here. •If anyone asks you, "Why are you untying it?" you are to say
32 this, "The Master needs it". ' •The messengers went off and found everything just
33 as he had told them. •As they were untying the colt, its owner said, 'Why are
34 you untying that colt?' •and they answered, 'The Master needs it'.
35 So they took the colt to Jesus, and throwing their garments over its back they
36 helped Jesus on to it. •As he moved off, people spread their cloaks in the road,
37 and now, as he was approaching the downward slope of the Mount of Olives,
the whole group of disciples joyfully began to praise God at the top of their 1:14+ 2:20+
38 voices for all the miracles they had seen. •They cried out: 4:15+

'Blessings on the King who comes, Ps 118:26
in the name of the Lord!
Peace in heaven 2:14
and glory in the highest heavens!'

Jesus defends his disciples for acclaiming him

39 Some Pharisees in the crowd said to him, 'Master, check your disciples', Mt 21:14-16
40 but he answered, 'I tell you, if these keep silence the stones will cry out'.

Lament for Jerusalem

41 42 As he drew near and came in sight of the city he shed tears over it •and said, 13:34-35 Dt 28:36
'If you in your turn had only understood on this day the message of peace![f] Jr 26
43 But, alas, it is hidden from your eyes! •Yes, a time is coming when your enemies
will raise fortifications all round you, when they will encircle you and hem you Is 29:3
44 in on every side; •they will dash you and the children inside your walls to the
ground; they will leave not one stone standing on another within you—and all
because you did not recognise your opportunity when God offered it!'[g] 1:68; 12:54-56

d. Lk often remarks that the Passion was foretold by the prophets: Lk 24:25,27,44; Ac 2:23+; 3:18,24+; 8:32-35; 13:27; 26:22f.

19 a. Fourfold restitution was imposed by the Jewish law (Ex 21:37) for one case only; Roman law demanded it of all convicted thieves. Zacchaeus goes further: he acknowledges the obligation in the case of any injustice he may have been responsible for.

b. Notwithstanding his despised profession. No social rank excludes 'salvation', cf. 3:12-14. All the Jewish privileges follow from 'sonship of Abraham' cf. 3:8; Rm 4:11f; Ga 3:7f.

c. There are notable differences between the parable of the pounds and that of the talents, Mt 25:14-30. Moreover, it seems that in Lk we must distinguish two parables which have been fused into one: that of the pounds, vv. 12-13, 15-26, and that of the royal claimant, vv. 12,14,17,19,27.

d. Probably alluding to the journey of Archelaus to Rome in 4 B.C. to have the will of Herod the Great confirmed in his favour. A deputation of Jews followed him there to thwart the attempt, cf. v. 14.

e. There seems to be a lacuna here.

f. The peace of the messianic age, cf. Is 11:6+; Ho 2:20+.

g. This whole prophecy is made up of O.T. references (especially noticeable in the Greek text for v. 43, cf. Is 29:3; 37:33; Jr 52:4-5; Ezk 4:1-3; 21:27(22); for v. 44, cf. Ho 10:14; 14:1; Na 3:10; Ps 137:9) and suggests the destruction of Jerusalem in 587 B.C. as much as, and more than, that of 70 A.D. of whose distinctive features it says nothing. It cannot, therefore, be concluded from this text that the destruction of 70 A.D. had already taken place.

||Mt 21:12-13 ||Mk 11: 15-17 ||Jn 2:14-16
The expulsion of the dealers from the Temple

Then he went into the Temple and began driving out those who were selling. 45
Is 56:7 'According to scripture,' he said '*my house will be a house of prayer*. But you 46
Jr 7:11 have turned it into *a robbers' den*.'

Jesus teaches in the Temple

21:37; 22:53 He taught in the Temple every day. The chief priests and the scribes, with 47
Jn 18:20 *11:53+* the support of the leading citizens, tried to do away with him, •but they did not 48
||Mk 11:18 *4:15+* see how they could carry this out because the people as a whole hung on his words.

||Mt 21:23-27 ||Mk 11: 27-33
The Jews question the authority of Jesus

20 [a]Now one day while he was teaching the people in the Temple and 1
proclaiming the Good News, the chief priests and the scribes came up,
Ac 4:7 together with the elders, •and spoke to him. 'Tell us' they said 'what authority 2
have you for acting like this? Or who is it that gave you this authority?' •'And 3
I' replied Jesus 'will ask you a question. Tell me: •John's baptism: did it come 4
from heaven, or from man?' •And they argued it out this way among themselves, 5
'If we say from heaven, he will say, "Why did you refuse to believe him?"; •and 6
if we say from man, the people will all stone us, for they are convinced that John
was a prophet'. •So their reply was that they did not know where it came from. 7
And Jesus said to them, 'Nor will I tell you my authority for acting like this'. 8

||Mt 21:33-46 ||Mk 12:1-2
Parable of the wicked husbandmen

And he went on to tell the people this parable: 'A man planted a vineyard 9
and leased it to tenants, and went abroad for a long while. •When the time 10
came, he sent a servant to the tenants to get his share of the produce of the
vineyard from them. But the tenants thrashed him, and sent him away
empty-handed. •But he persevered and sent a second servant; they thrashed 11
him too and treated him shamefully and sent him away empty-handed. •He still 12
persevered and sent a third; they wounded this one also, and threw him out.
Then the owner of the vineyard said, "What am I to do? I will send them my 13
dear son. Perhaps they will respect him." •But when the tenants saw him 14
they put their heads together. "This is the heir," they said "let us kill him so that
the inheritance will be ours." •So they threw him out of the vineyard and killed 15
him.

'Now what will the owner of the vineyard do to them? •He will come and 16
Jn 12:48 make an end of these tenants and give the vineyard to others.' Hearing this they
said, 'God forbid!' •But he looked hard at them and said, 'Then what does this 17
text in the scriptures mean:

Ps 118:22 *It was the stone rejected by the builders*
that became the keystone?

Anyone who falls on that stone will be dashed to pieces; anyone it falls on will 18
be crushed.'

11:53+ But for their fear of the people, the scribes and the chief priests would have 19
liked to lay hands on him that very moment, because they realised that this
parable was aimed at them.

||Mt 22:15-22 ||Mk 12: 13-17
On tribute to Caesar

23:2 So they waited their opportunity and sent agents to pose as men devoted to 20
Mt 12:10 the Law, and to fasten on something he might say and so enable them to hand
him over to the jurisdiction and authority of the governor. •They put to him 21
this question, 'Master, we know that you say and teach what is right; you favour
no one, but teach the way of God in all honesty. •Is it permissible for us to pay 22
taxes to Caesar or not?' •But he was aware of their cunning and said, •'Show 23 24
me a denarius. Whose head and name are on it?' 'Caesar's' they said. •'Well 25

then,' he said to them 'give back to Caesar what belongs to Caesar—and to
God what belongs to God.'
26 As a result, they were unable to find fault with anything he had to say in
public; his answer took them by surprise and they were silenced.

The resurrection of the dead ||Mt 22:23-33 ||Mk 12:18-27

27 Some Sadducees—those who say that there is no resurrection—approached
28 him and they put this question to him, •'Master, we have it from Moses in
writing, that if a man's married brother dies childless, the man must marry the Dt 25:5+
29 widow to raise up children for his brother. •Well then, there were seven brothers.
30 31 The first, having married a wife, died childless. •The second •and then the third
married the widow. And the same with all seven, they died leaving no children.
32 33 Finally the woman herself died. •Now, at the resurrection, to which of them
will she be wife since she had been married to all seven?'
34 35 Jesus replied, 'The children of this world[b] take wives and husbands, •but
those who are judged worthy of a place in the other world and in the resurrection
36 from the dead[c] do not marry •because they can no longer die,[d] for they are the
same as the angels, and being children of the resurrection[e] they are sons of
37 God. •And Moses himself implies that the dead rise again, in the passage
about the bush where he calls the Lord *the God of Abraham, the God of Isaac* Ex 3:6
38 *and the God of Jacob.* •Now he is God, not of the dead, but of the living; for Rm 6:10-11 Ga 2:19
to him all men are in fact alive.'
39 40 Some scribes[f] then spoke up. 'Well put, Master' they said•—because they ||Mt 22:46 ||Mk 12:34
would not dare to ask him any more questions.

Christ, not only son but also Lord of David ||Mt 22:41-45 ||Mk 12:35-37

41 He then said to them, 'How can people maintain that the Christ is son of
42 David? •Why, David himself says in the Book of Psalms:

The Lord said to my Lord: Ps 110:1
Sit at my right hand
43 *and I will make your enemies*
a footstool for you.

44 David here calls him Lord; how then can he be his son?'

The scribes condemned by Jesus ||Mt 23:6-7 ||Mk 12:38-40

45 46 While all the people were listening he said to the disciples, •'Beware of the
scribes who like to walk about in long robes and love to be greeted obsequiously =11:43
in the market squares, to take the front seats in the synagogues and the places
47 of honour at banquets, •who swallow the property of widows, while making
a show of lengthy prayers. The more severe will be the sentence they receive.'

The widow's mite ||Mk 12:41-44

1 **21** As he looked up he saw rich people putting their offerings into the
2 treasury; •then he happened to notice a poverty-stricken widow putting
3 in two small coins, •and he said, 'I tell you truly, this poor widow has put in
4 more than any of them; •for these have all contributed money they had over,
but she from the little she had has put in all she had to live on'.

20 a. Lk omits the symbolic episode of the withered fig tree, Mk 11:12-14,20-25, for which he substitutes the parable of the barren fig tree, Lk 13:6-9; he also omits here the discussion on the first commandment of the Law, Mk 12:28-34, which he has already used, taking it from another source, Lk 10:25-28.

b. 'children': a semitism for 'those who belong to...' Cf. 16:8.

c. Only the resurrection of the just is considered here. Cf. Ph 3:11+.

d. Var. 'they have not to die'.

e. Semitism for those who are actually raised up.

f. The scribes, being Pharisees for the most part, believed in the resurrection of the dead, cf. Ac 23:6-9.

||Mt 24:1-3 ||Mk 13:1-4 Discourse on the destruction of Jerusalem:[a] Introduction

When some were talking about the Temple, remarking how it was adorned 5
with fine stonework and votive offerings, he said, •'All these things you are staring 6
at now—the time will come when not a single stone will be left on another:
everything will be destroyed'. •And they put to him this question: 'Master,' they 7
said 'when will this happen, then, and what sign will there be that this is about
to take place?'

||Mt 24:4-14 ||Mk 13:5-13 The warning signs

'Take care not to be deceived,' he said 'because many will come using my name 8
and saying, "I am he" and, "The time is near at hand". Refuse to join them.
Dn 2:28 And when you hear of wars and revolutions, do not be frightened, for this is some- 9
thing that must happen but the end is not so soon.' •Then he said to them, 'Nation 10
Is 19:2 will fight against nation, and kingdom against kingdom. •There will be great 11
earthquakes and plagues and famines here and there; there will be fearful sights
and great signs from heaven.
12:11-12 ||Mt 10:17-22 'But before all this happens, men will seize you and persecute you; they will 12
Jn 15:20; 16:1-2 hand you over to the synagogues and to imprisonment, and bring you before
Ac 4:13 kings and governors because of my name•—and that will be your opportunity 13
to bear witness. •Keep this carefully in mind: you are not to prepare your defence, 14
Ac 6:10 because I myself[b] shall give you an eloquence and a wisdom that none of your 15
opponents will be able to resist or contradict. •You will be betrayed even by 16
parents and brothers, relations and friends; and some of you will be put to death.
12:7 Mt 10:30 You will be hated by all men on account of my name, •but not a hair of your 17 18
Heb 10:36,39 head will be lost. •Your endurance will win you your lives. 19

||Mt 24:15-20 ||Mk 13:14-18 The siege

'When you see Jerusalem surrounded by armies,[c] you must realise that she will 20
17:31 soon be laid desolate. •Then those in Judaea must escape to the mountains, those 21
inside the city must leave it, and those in country districts must not take refuge
in it. •For this is the time of vengeance when all that scripture says[d] must be 22
fulfilled. •Alas for those with child, or with babies at the breast, when those days 23
come!

||Mt 24:21 ||Mk 13:19 The disaster and the age of the pagans

Ps 81:15 'For great misery will descend on the land and wrath on this people. •They 24
Rm 1:18+ *Dt 28:64* will fall by the edge of the sword and be led captive to every pagan country; and
Rv 11:2 *Dn 12:7* Jerusalem will be trampled down by the pagans until the age of the pagans[e] is
completely over.

||Mt 24:29-30 ||Mk 13:24-26 Cosmic disasters and the coming of the Son of Man

'There will be signs in the sun and moon and stars; on earth nations in agony, 25
bewildered by the clamour of the ocean and its waves; •men dying of fear as they 26
await what menaces the world, for the powers of heaven will be shaken. •And 27
Dn 7:13-14 then they will see the Son of Man coming in a cloud with power and great glory.
Heb 10:37 When these things begin to take place, stand erect, hold your heads high, because 28
your liberation[f] is near at hand.'

||Mt 24:32-35 ||Mk 13:28-31 The time of this coming

And he told them a parable, 'Think of the fig tree and indeed every tree. •As 29 30
soon as you see them bud, you know that summer is now near. •So with you 31
when you see these things happening: know that the kingdom of God is near.[g]
9:27 Mt 16:28 Mk 9:1 I tell you solemnly, before this generation has passed away all will have 32
taken place. •Heaven and earth will pass away, but my words will never pass 33
away.

Be on the alert

34 'Watch yourselves, or your hearts will be coarsened with debauchery and 17:26-30
drunkenness and the cares of life, and that day will be sprung on you suddenly, 1 Th 5:3
35 like a trap. For it will come down[h] on every living man on the face of the earth.
36 Stay awake, praying at all times for the strength to survive all that is going to
happen, and to stand with confidence[i] before the Son of Man.' Rv 6:17

The last days of Jesus

37 In the daytime he would be in the Temple teaching, but would spend the night 19:47+; 22:53
38 on the hill called the Mount of Olives. •And from early morning the people *Mt 21:17* Mk11:11,19
would gather round him in the Temple to listen to him.[j] Jn 8:2

VI. THE PASSION[a]

The conspiracy against Jesus: Judas betrays him

||Mt 26:1-5 ||Mk 14:1-2 Jn 11:47-53

1 **22** The feast of Unleavened Bread, called the Passover, was now drawing near,
2 and the chief priests and the scribes were looking for some way of doing 11:53+ Ac 5:26
away with him, because they mistrusted the people.[b]
3 Then Satan entered into Judas, surnamed Iscariot, who was numbered among 4:13 Jn 13:2,27
4 the Twelve. •He went to the chief priests and the officers of the guard[c] to discuss Ac 5:3
5 a scheme for handing Jesus over to them. •They were delighted and agreed to give ||Mt 26:14-16 ||Mk 14:
6 him money. •He accepted, and looked for an opportunity to betray him to them 10-11
without the people knowing.

Preparation for the Passover supper

||Mt 26:17-19 ||Mk 14: 12-16

7 The day of Unleavened Bread came round, the day on which the passover
8 had to be sacrificed, •and he sent Peter and John, saying, 'Go and make the 8:51+
9 preparations for us to eat the passover'. •'Where do you want us to prepare it?'
10 they asked. •'Listen,' he said 'as you go into the city you will meet a man
11 carrying a pitcher of water. Follow him into the house he enters •and tell the
owner of the house, "The Master has this to say to you: Where is the dining room
12 in which I can eat the passover with my disciples?" •The man will show you a large
13 upper room furnished with couches. Make the preparations there.' •They set off
and found everything as he had told them, and prepared the Passover.

The supper

14 When the hour came he took his place at table, and the apostles with him.
15 And he said to them,[d] 'I have longed to eat this passover with you before I suffer; 12:50+

21 a. In 17:22-37, Lk, following one of his sources, speaks of the coming of Jesus in glory at the end of time. Here he follows Mk where two perspectives merge: that of the final coming and that of the destruction of Jerusalem; cf. Mt 24:1+.

b. Lk, in this place, assigns to Jesus the role reserved by Mt 10:20; Mk 13:11; Lk 12:12 to the Spirit of the Father (Mt), the Holy Spirit (Mk and Lk), Ac 6:10. Cf. Jn 16:13-15.

c. Lk, explaining the obscure 'disastrous abomination', which his source takes from Dn 9:27, foretells the siege. As in 19:43-44, his terms are biblical and do not necessarily suggest a description after the event.

d. Possibly alluding to Dn 9:27.

e. I.e. the period during which the pagans will take the place of the unfaithful Jewish nation; according to Paul, Rm 11:11-32, this period will end with the conversion of all Israel. An age of indefinite duration is, therefore, to elapse between Jerusalem's destruction and the end of time.

f. Or 'redemption', a Pauline term, cf. Rm 3:24+.

g. The kingdom has already come, 17:21, but this refers to the period of its triumphant progress which begins with the destruction of Jerusalem. Cf. 9:27p.

h. Var. 'for it will come down on you like a snare'.

i. Lit. 'and to stand erect'.

j. The literary relationship with Jn 8:1-2 is unmistakable. The adulterous woman passage of Jn 7:53–8:11, for the Lucan authorship of which there are many good arguments, would fit into this context admirably.

22 a. Throughout the Passion narrative, Lk shows himself considerably less dependent on Mk than hitherto; on the other hand, there are many points of contact with Jn.

b. Lk does not record the anointing at Bethany; he has already described a similar incident in 7:36-50.

c. Officers of the Temple police. All of these were Jews, chosen from among the Levites.

d. In Lk, Christ's discourses at the supper play a more important part than in Mt and Mk, preparing us for those of Jn 13:31–17:26.

Mt 8:11+ because, I tell you, I shall not eat it again until it is fulfilled[e] in the kingdom of 16
God'.
Then, taking a cup,[f] he gave thanks and said, 'Take this and share it among 17
||Mt 26:29 ||Mk 14:25 you, •because from now on, I tell you, I shall not drink wine until the king- 18
dom of God comes'.

||Mt 26:26-28 ||Mk 14:22-24 ||I Co 11:23-25 *Jn 6:51*

The institution of the Eucharist[g]

Then he took some bread, and when he had given thanks, broke it and gave it 19
to them, saying, 'This is my body which will be given for you; do this as a memorial
Jr 31:31 Mt 26:28 of me'. •He did the same with the cup after supper, and said, 'This cup is the new 20
covenant in my blood which will be poured out for you.[h]

||Mt 26:20-25 ||Mk 14:17-21 Jn 13:21-30

The treachery of Judas foretold

'And yet, here with me on the table is the hand of the man who betrays me. 21
The Son of Man does indeed go to his fate even as it has been decreed, but alas for 22
that man by whom he is betrayed!' •And they began to ask one another which of 23
them it could be who was to do this thing.

Who is the greatest?

=9:46 A dispute arose also between them about which should be reckoned the 24
||Mt 20:25-27 ||Mk 10:42-44 greatest, •but he said to them, 'Among pagans it is the kings who lord it over them, 25
and those who have authority over them are given the title Benefactor. •This must 26
9:48 not happen with you. No; the greatest among you must behave as if he were the
youngest, the leader as if he were the one who serves. •For who is the greater: 27
12:37 Jn 13:4-15 the one at table or the one who serves? The one at table, surely? Yet here am I
among you as one who serves!

The reward promised to the apostles

Jn 6:66-68; 15:27 'You are the men who have stood by me faithfully in my trials; •and now 28 29
Rv 2:26-28 I confer a kingdom on you, just as my Father conferred one on me: •you will 30
Rv 3:20-21 *||Mt 19:28* eat and drink at my table in my kingdom, and you will sit on thrones to judge the
twelve tribes of Israel.

Peter's denial and repentance foretold

Rv 2:10 [i]'Simon, Simon! Satan, you must know, has got his wish to sift you all like 31
Mt 16:19+ Jn 21:15-17 *Mt 8:10+* wheat; •but I have prayed for you, Simon, that your faith may not fail, and once 32
you have recovered, you in your turn must strengthen your brothers.' •'Lord,' 33
he answered 'I would be ready to go to prison with you, and to death.' •Jesus 34
22:61 ||Mt 26:31-35 ||Mk 14:27-31 ||Jn 13:36-38 replied, 'I tell you, Peter, by the time the cock crows today you will have denied
three times that you know me'.

A time of crisis

10:4 He said to them, 'When I sent you out without purse or haversack or sandals, 35
were you short of anything? •'No' they said. He said to them, 'But now if you have 36
12:51 Mt 10:34 *23:32* a purse, take it; if you have a haversack, do the same; if you have no sword, sell
your cloak and buy one,[j] •because I tell you these words of scripture have to 37
Is 53:12 Mt 27:38 be fulfilled in me: *He let himself be taken for a criminal.* Yes, what scripture says
about me is even now reaching its fulfilment.' •'Lord,' they said 'there are two 38
swords here now.' He said to them, 'That is enough!'[k]

||Mt 26:30, 36-46 ||Mk 14:26, 32-42

The Mount of Olives

He then left to make his way as usual to the Mount of Olives, with the 39
21:37 Jn 18:2 disciples following. •When they reached the place he said to them, 'Pray not to be 40
put to the test'.
Then he withdrew from them, about a stone's throw away, and knelt down 41
3:21+ Jn 12:27-29 and prayed. •'Father,' he said 'if you are willing, take this cup away from me. 42

43 Nevertheless, let your will be done, not mine.' •Then an angel appeared to Ac 21:14▼
44 him, coming from heaven to give him strength. •In his anguish he prayed even
more earnestly, and his sweat fell to the ground like great drops of blood.[l]
45 When he rose from prayer he went to the disciples and found them sleeping
46 for sheer grief. •'Why are you asleep?' he said to them. 'Get up and pray not to
be put to the test.'

The arrest

‖Mt 26:47-56 ‖Mk 14:43-50 ‖Jn 18:3-11

47 He was still speaking when a number of men appeared, and at the head of
them the man called Judas, one of the Twelve, who went up to Jesus to kiss him. Ac 1:16
48 49 Jesus said, 'Judas, are you betraying the Son of Man with a kiss?' •His followers,
50 seeing what was happening, said, 'Lord, shall we use our swords?' •And one of
51 them struck out at the high priest's servant, and cut off his right ear. •But at
this Jesus spoke. 'Leave off!' he said 'That will do!' And touching the man's ear
he healed him.
52 Then Jesus spoke to the chief priests and captains of the Temple guard and
elders who had come for him. 'Am I a brigand' he said 'that you had to set out
53 with swords and clubs? •When I was among you in the Temple day after day 19:47;21:3
you never moved to lay hands on me. But this is your hour; this is the reign of 4:13+ Jn 8:12+
darkness.'

Peter's denials

‖Mt 26:57. 69-75 ‖Mk 14:66-72 ‖Jn 18:15-18. 25-27

54 They seized him then[m] and led him away, and they took him to the high
55 priest's house. Peter followed at a distance. •They had lit a fire in the middle of
56 the courtyard and Peter sat down among them, •and as he was sitting there by
the blaze a servant-girl saw him, peered at him, and said, 'This person was with
57 58 him too'. •But he denied it. 'Woman,' he said 'I do not know him.' •Shortly
afterwards someone else saw him and said, 'You are another of them'. But Peter
59 replied, 'I am not, my friend'.[n] •About an hour later another man insisted,
60 saying, 'This fellow was certainly with him. Why, he is a Galilean.' •'My
friend,' said Peter 'I do not know what you are talking about.' At that instant,
61 while he was still speaking, the cock crew, •and the Lord turned and looked
straight at Peter, and Peter remembered what the Lord had said to him, 'Before 22:34
62 the cock crows today, you will have disowned me three times'. •And he went
outside and wept bitterly.

Jesus mocked by the guards

‖Mt 26:67-68 ‖Mk 14:65

63 Meanwhile the men who guarded Jesus were mocking and beating him.
64 They blindfolded him and questioned him. 'Play the prophet' they said. 'Who
65 hit you then?' •And they continued heaping insults on him.

Jesus before the Sanhedrin[o]

‖Mt 26:57-66; 27:2 ‖Mk 14:53-64; 15:1

66 When day broke there was a meeting of the elders of the people,[p] attended

22 e. The first stage of fulfilment is the Eucharist itself, the centre of spiritual life in the kingdom founded by Jesus; the final stage will be at the end of time when the Passover is to be fulfilled perfectly and in a fashion no longer veiled.

f. Lk distinguishes the Passover and the cup of vv. 15-18 from the bread and the cup of vv. 19-20 in order to draw a parallel between the ancient rite of the Jewish Passover and the new rite of the Christian Eucharist. Some ancient authorities, failing to understand this theological device, and disturbed to find two cups mentioned, quite mistakenly omitted v. 20, or even v. 20 with the second part of v. 19 (i.e. 'which will be given...of me').

g. Note the affinity between Luke's text and Paul's.

h. Or alternatively 'which has to be given' and 'which has to be poured out'.

i. Add. 'And the Lord said'.

j. The purse to buy, the sword to procure by force, the necessities of life. All this is symbolic of a mission in a hostile world.

k. The apostles have taken the words of Jesus too literally and he closes the conversation abruptly.

l. Om. vv. 43-44.

m. In Mt and Mk, Jesus is seized immediately after Judas' greeting; the sword episode follows, and finally the discourse by Jesus. Lk makes the arrest follow the discourse, thus emphasising the control Jesus has over what takes place. Cf., for the same emphasis, Jn 10:18+; 18:4-6.

n. Lit. 'man'.

o. Whereas Mt and Mk have two trials, Lk has only one, and that in the morning, probably held in the 'Tribunal', a building adjacent to the Temple. Cf. Mt 26:57+.

p. 'elders' here means the whole Sanhedrin, not merely one of its three component bodies (the elders);

by the chief priests and scribes. He was brought before their council, •and they 67
Jn 10:24-25 said to him, 'If you are the Christ, tell us'. 'If I tell you,' he replied 'you will not
believe me, •and if I question you, you will not answer. •But from now on, the 68 69
Ps 110:1 Son of Man will be[a] *seated at the right hand* of the Power *of God*.' •Then they 70
Ws 2:14 Mt 4:3+ all said, 'So you are the Son of God then?' He answered, 'It is you who say I am'.
Jn 10:30-33 'What need of witnesses have we now?' they said. 'We have heard it for ourselves 71
Mt 27:1-2 Jn 18:28 from his own lips.' **23** The whole assembly then rose, and they brought him 1
before Pilate.

||Mt 27:11-14 ||Mk 15:2-5 ||Jn 18:29-38a

Jesus before Pilate[a]

They began their accusation by saying, 'We found this man inciting our 2
20:20-26 Ac 17:7; 24:5 people to revolt, opposing payment of the tribute to Caesar, and claiming to be
Christ, a king'. •Pilate put to him this question, 'Are you the king of the Jews?' 3
'It is you who say it' he replied. •Pilate then said to the chief priests and the crowd, 4
'I find no case against this man'. •But they persisted, 'He is inflaming the people 5
4:44+ Ac 3:14 with his teaching all over Judaea; it has come all the way from Galilee, where he
started, down to here'. •When Pilate heard this, he asked if the man were a 6
Galilean; •and finding that he came under Herod's jurisdiction he passed him 7
over to Herod who was also in Jerusalem at that time.

Jesus before Herod[b]

9:9 Mt 14:1-2 Herod was delighted to see Jesus; he had heard about him and had 8
been wanting for a long time to set eyes on him; moreover, he was hoping to see
some miracle worked by him. •So he questioned him at some length; but without 9
Ac 25:7 getting any reply. •Meanwhile the chief priests and the scribes were there, violently 10
pressing their accusations. •Then Herod, together with his guards, treated him 11
with contempt and made fun of him; he put a rich cloak[c] on him and sent him
Ac 4:27+ back to Pilate. •And though Herod and Pilate had been enemies before, they 12
were reconciled that same day.

||Mt 27:15-26 ||Mk 15:6-15 ||Jn 18:38b–19:16

Jesus before Pilate again

Pilate then summoned the chief priests and the leading men and the people. 13
'You brought this man before me' he said 'as a political agitator. Now I have 14
gone into the matter myself in your presence and found no case against the man
in respect of all the charges you bring against him. •Nor has Herod either, since 15
he has sent him back to us. As you can see, the man has done nothing that
deserves death, •so I shall have him flogged and then let him go.'[d] •But as one 16 18
Ac 21:36 man they howled, 'Away with him! Give us Barabbas!' •(This man had been 19
Ac 3:14 thrown into prison for causing a riot in the city and for murder.)
Pilate was anxious to set Jesus free and addressed them again, •but they 20 21
shouted back, 'Crucify him! Crucify him!' •And for the third time[e] he spoke 22
Jn 18:38 Ac 3:13 to them, 'Why? What harm has this man done? I have found no case against
him that deserves death, so I shall have him punished and then let him go.'[f] •But 23
they kept on shouting at the top of their voices, demanding that he should be
crucified. And their shouts were growing louder.
Ac 3:15 Pilate then gave his verdict: their demand was to be granted. •He released 24 25
the man they asked for, who had been imprisoned for rioting and murder, and
handed Jesus over to them to deal with as they pleased.

||Mt 27:31b-34 ||Mk 15:20b-23 ||Jn 19:17

The way to Calvary

As they were leading him away they seized on a man, Simon from Cyrene, 26
who was coming in from the country, and made him shoulder the cross and
carry it behind Jesus. •Large numbers of people followed him, and of women 27
too,[g] who mourned and lamented for him. •But Jesus turned to them and said, 28
'Daughters of Jerusalem, do not weep for me; weep rather for yourselves and for
your children. •For the days will surely come when people will say, "Happy are 29

those who are barren, the wombs that have never borne, the breasts that have 11:27 Ho 9:14
30 never suckled!" •Then they will begin to *say to the mountains,"Fall on us!"*; *to the* *Ho 10:8*
31 *hills, "Cover us!"* •For if men use the green wood like this, what will happen Ezk 21:3,8
32 when it is dry?'[h] •Now with him they were also leading out two other criminals 22:37 Is 53:12
to be executed.

The crucifixion[i]

||Mt 27:35-38 ||Mk 15:24-28 ||Jn 19:17-24

33 When they reached the place called The Skull, they crucified him there and the
34 two criminals also, one on the right, the other on the left. •[j] Jesus said, 'Father,
forgive them; they do not know what they are doing'. Then they cast lots to Ps 22:18 Ac 7:60
share out his clothing.

The crucified Christ is mocked

||Mt 27:39-43 ||Mk 15:29-32a

35 The people stayed there watching him. As for the leaders, they jeered at him.
'He saved others,' they said 'let him save himself if he is the Christ of God, the 2:26+; 9:35+
36 Chosen One.' •The soldiers mocked him too, and when they approached to offer Jn 1:34 *Mt 27:48*
37 38 him vinegar •they said, 'If you are the king of the Jews, save yourself'. •Above
him there was an inscription: 'This is the King of the Jews'. Jn 19:19

The good thief

39 One of the criminals hanging there abused him. 'Are you not the Christ?' Mt 27:44 Mk 15:32b
40 he said. 'Save yourself and us as well.' •But the other spoke up and rebuked him.
'Have you no fear of God at all?' he said. 'You got the same sentence as he did,
41 but in our case we deserved it: we are paying for what we did. But this man has
42 done nothing wrong. •Jesus,' he said 'remember me when you come into your
43 kingdom.'[k] •'Indeed, I promise you,' he replied 'today you will be with me in
paradise.'

The death of Jesus

||Mt 27:45-50 ||Mk 15:33-37 ||Jn 19:25-30

44 It was now about the sixth hour and, with the sun eclipsed, a darkness came
45 over the whole land until the ninth hour. •The veil of the Temple was torn right
46 down the middle; •and when Jesus had cried out in a loud voice, he said, 'Father, Ps 31:5
into your hands I commit my spirit'. With these words he breathed his last. Ac 7:60

After the death

||Mt 27:51-56 ||Mk 15:38-41 ||Jn 19:31-37

47 When the centurion saw what had taken place, he gave praise to God and *Ac 3:14*
48 said, 'This was a great and good man'. •And when all the people who had gathered
for the spectacle saw what had happened, they went home beating their breasts.
49 All his friends stood at a distance; so also did the women who had accompanied 8:2-3; 24:10
him from Galilee, and they saw all this happen.

of these, Lk names the two most influential (chief priests and scribes).

q. Lk omits the 'you will see' of Mt and Mk and also the allusion to Dn.

23 a. Luke's account lies half-way between the less detailed and less dramatic accounts of Mk and Mt, and the prolonged interview in Jn.

b. Lk only. His information comes perhaps from Manaen, 'who had been brought up with Herod the tetrarch', Ac 13:1.

c. The ceremonial dress of princes: Herod's gibe at the royal claim of Jesus, v. 3.

d. Add. v. 17 'He was under obligation to release one man for them every feast day'; this seems to be an explanatory gloss, cf. Mt 27:15p.

e. Lk, like Jn, emphasises Pilate's wish to let Jesus go free, and mentions the procurator's declaration of Christ's innocence three times, cf. Jn 18:38; 19:4,6.

f. Cf. v. 16. Lk does not say what the punishment was; in Mt 27:27-31p it is scourging. Unlike Mt and Mk, but like Jn, Lk regards the punishment as a conciliatory measure designed to avert a sentence not yet pronounced.

g. The Talmud records that noblewomen of Jerusalem were accustomed to give soothing drinks to condemned criminals.

h. If green wood is burnt that is not meant for burning (allusion to Christ's condemnation), what is to happen to the dry wood (the truly guilty)?

i. A comparison with Mk and Mt shows how Lk has softened the harshness of Calvary: Luke's crowd, vv. 27,35,48, is more inquisitive than hostile, and repents in the end, v. 48; Jesus does not utter the seemingly despairing cry, 'My God, my God, why have you deserted me?'; Christ's ministry of forgiveness goes on to the last, vv. 34,39-43; he dies committing his spirit into the hands of his Father, v. 46.

j. This verse is to be retained despite its omission by some good ancient authorities.

k. Or else 'in your kingly power', i.e. to establish your kingdom. Var. 'when you come with (i.e. in possession of) your kingdom'.

||Mt 27:57-61 ||Mk 15:42-47 ||Jn 19:38-42
The burial

Then a member of the council arrived, an upright and virtuous man named 50
Joseph. •He had not consented to what the others had planned and carried out. 51
He came from Arimathaea, a Jewish town, and he lived in the hope of seeing the
kingdom of God. •This man went to Pilate and asked for the body of Jesus. 52
He then took it down, wrapped it in a shroud and put him in a tomb which was 53
hewn in stone in which no one had yet been laid. •It was Preparation Day and 54
the sabbath was imminent.[z]

Meanwhile the women who had come from Galilee with Jesus were following 55
behind. They took note of the tomb and of the position of the body.

Mk 16:1 Then they returned and prepared spices and ointments. And on the sabbath 56
day they rested, as the Law required.

Mt 28:10+
VII. AFTER THE RESURRECTION

||Mt 28:1-8 ||Mk 16:1-8 ||Jn 20:1-2
The empty tomb. The angel's message

24 On the first day of the week, at the first sign of dawn, they went to the 1
tomb with the spices they had prepared. •They found that the stone had 2
been rolled away from the tomb, •but on entering discovered that the body of the 3
9:29 Lord Jesus was not there. •As they stood there not knowing what to think, two 4
Ac 1:10-11 men in brilliant clothes suddenly appeared at their side. •Terrified, the women 5
lowered their eyes. But the two men said to them, 'Why look among the dead
for someone who is alive? •He is not here; he has risen. Remember what he told 6
9:22+ you when he was still in Galilee:[a] •that the Son of Man had to be handed over 7
into the power of sinful men and be crucified, and rise again on the third day?'
And they remembered his words. 8

||Mt 28:10,17 ||Mk 16:10,11,14 ||Jn 20:18,25,29
The apostles refuse to believe the women

When the women returned from the tomb they told all this to the Eleven and 9
8:2-3 to all the others. •The women were Mary of Magdala, Joanna, and Mary the 10
mother of James. The other women with them also told the apostles, •but this 11
Mt 8:10+ story of theirs seemed pure nonsense, and they did not believe them.

||Jn 20:3-10
Peter at the tomb

[b]Peter, however, went running to the tomb. He bent down and saw the binding 12
cloths but nothing else; he then went back home, amazed at what had happened.

||Mk 16:12-13
The road to Emmaus

That very same day, two of them were on their way to a village called Emmaus, 13
seven miles[c] from Jerusalem, •and they were talking together about all that had 14
happened. •Now as they talked this over, Jesus himself came up and walked by 15
24:31 Jn 20:14,20; 21:4 their side; •but something prevented them from recognising him.[d] •He said to 16 17
24:37 them, 'What matters are you discussing as you walk along?' They stopped short,
their faces downcast.[e]

Then one of them, called Cleopas, answered him, 'You must be the only 18
person staying in Jerusalem who does not know the things that have been
happening there these last few days'. •'What things?' he asked. 'All about Jesus 19
Mt 2:23+ *Mt 16:14+* of Nazareth'[f] they answered 'who proved he was a great prophet by the things
Ac 2:22; 7:22 he said and did in the sight of God and of the whole people; •and how our chief 20
priests and our leaders handed him over to be sentenced to death, and had him
1:54,68; 2:38 crucified. •Our own hope had been that he would be the one to set Israel free. 21
And this is not all: two whole days have gone by since it all happened; •and some 22
women from our group have astounded us: they went to the tomb in the early
24:9f morning, •and when they did not find the body, they came back to tell us they 23
had seen a vision of angels who declared he was alive. •Some of our friends[g] 24

went to the tomb and found everything exactly as the women had reported, but
of him they saw nothing.'
25 Then he said to them, 'You foolish men! So slow to believe the full message Mt 8:10+ Mk 4:13+
26 of the prophets! •Was it not ordained that the Christ should suffer and so enter *18:31+* Ac 3:24
27 into his glory?' •Then, starting with Moses and going through all the prophets, *9:22+* 1 P 1:11
he explained to them the passages throughout the scriptures that were about 16:29,31
himself.
28 When they drew near to the village to which they were going, he made as if
29 to go on; •but they pressed him to stay with them. 'It is nearly evening' they said
30 'and the day is almost over.' So he went in to stay with them. •Now while he was
with them at table, he took the bread and said the blessing; then he broke it and
31 handed it to them. •And their eyes were opened and they recognised him; but he 24:16+ Ac 8:39
32 had vanished from their sight. •Then they said to each other, 'Did not our hearts
burn within us as he talked to us on the road and explained the scriptures to us?'
33 They set out that instant and returned to Jerusalem. There they found the
34 Eleven assembled together with their companions, •who said to them, 'Yes, it is
35 true. The Lord has risen and has appeared to Simon.' •Then they told their 1 Co 15:5
story of what had happened on the road and how they had recognised him at the
breaking of bread.[h]

Jesus appears to the apostles

Jn 20:19-23

36 They were still talking about all this when he himself stood among them
37 and said to them, 'Peace be with you!' •In a state of alarm and fright, they thought 1:12+; 24:16+
38 they were seeing a ghost. •But he said, 'Why are you so agitated, and why are
39 these doubts rising in your hearts? •Look at my hands and feet; yes, it is I indeed. 1 Jn 1:1
Touch me and see for yourselves; a ghost has no flesh and bones as you can see
40 41 I have.' •[i]And as he said this he showed them his hands and feet.[j] •Their joy 1:14+ Mt 8:10+
was so great that they still could not believe it, and they stood there dumbfounded;
42 so he said to them, 'Have you anything here to eat?' •And they offered him a piece Tb 12:19 Jn 21:5
43 of grilled fish, •which he took and ate before their eyes. *Jn 21:9-10,13*

Last instructions to the apostles

44 Then[k] he told them, 'This is what I meant when I said, while I was still with 9:22+
you, that everything written about me in the Law of Moses, in the Prophets and 24:25-27
45 in the Psalms, has to be fulfilled'. •He then opened their minds to understand the Mk 4:13+
46 scriptures, •and he said to them, 'So you see how it is written that the Christ would
47 suffer and on the third day rise from the dead, •and that, in his name, repentance Ac 10:40+ *2:38+*
for the forgiveness of sins would be preached to all the nations, beginning Mt 3:2+; 28:19-20
48 from Jerusalem. •You are witnesses to this. Mk 16:15-16 ||*Ac 1:8+*
49 'And now I am sending down to you what the Father has promised. Stay in the ||Ac 1:4
city then, until you are clothed with the power from on high.'

The ascension

||Mk 16:19 ||Ac 1:9,12

50 Then he took them out as far as the outskirts of Bethany, and lifting up his

l. Or possibly 'was shining', alluding to the Jewish custom of lighting lamps when the sabbath began at nightfall.

24 a. Lk does not intend to speak of the Galilean apparitions; he therefore modifies Mk 16:7, just as earlier he omitted Mk 14:28.

b. Om. v. 12.

c. Lit. 'sixty *stadia*' (furlongs); var. (with less support) 'one hundred and sixty'. The identity of the village is disputed.

d. In the apparitions described by Lk and Jn, the disciples do not at first recognise the Lord: they need a word or a sign, Lk 24:30f, 35,37,39-43; Jn 20:14 and 16,20; 21:4 and 6-7; cf. Mt 28:17. This is because the risen body, though the same body that died on the cross, is in a new condition; its outward appearance is therefore changed, Mk 16:12, and it is exempt from the usual physical laws, Jn 20:19. On the condition of glorified bodies, cf. 1 Co 15:44+.

e. Var. 'as you walk along and look sad?'

f. Var. 'the Nazarene'. Cf. Mt 2:23+.

g. Either generalising Peter's experience, v. 12, or alluding to the visit made by Peter with John and described in Jn 20:3-10.

h. In Ac (2:42+) Lk uses this as a technical term for the Eucharist; probably it means the same here.

i. Om. v. 40.

j. Writing for Greeks who scoffed at the idea of bodily resurrection, Lk underlines the physical reality of Christ's risen body, cf. v. 43.

k. The impression given is that all these events took place on the same day, the day of resurrection. See Mt 28:10+.

hands he blessed them. •Now as he blessed them, he withdrew from them and 5
9:51+ was carried up to heaven.[l] •They worshipped him and[m] then went back to 5
1:14‡ 2:20+ Jerusalem full of joy; •and they were continually in the Temple praising God.[n] 5

24 l Om. 'and was carried up to heaven'.
m. Om. 'They worshipped him, and'.

n. Luke's gospel ends where it began, in the Temple; its last word is of joy and praise.

THE GOSPEL ACCORDING TO

SAINT JOHN

INTRODUCTION TO
THE GOSPEL AND LETTERS OF SAINT JOHN

The gospel

The last verse before the Appendix to the fourth gospel (20:31) specifies the book's literary form. It is a 'gospel', just as the preaching of the earlier Church was a 'gospel'; i.e. it proclaims that Jesus is Messiah and Son of God, and its teaching, based on the 'signs' that Jesus gave, aims at bringing men to believe in the Messiah and so to attain life. The fourth gospel, therefore, in spite of all the clues to its late composition, is not unrelated to the most primitive Christian 'kerygma', or message, and in fact it preserves both the structure and the chief points of this message, e.g. the Holy Spirit descends, as the Baptist testifies, to point out Jesus as Messiah, 1:31–34; Christ's 'glory' is manifested in his work and word, 1:35–12:50; his death, resurrection and subsequent apparitions are described, 13:1–20:20; the apostles are sent out with the gift of the Spirit and the power to forgive sins, 20:21–29. The book claims, moreover, to fulfil the condition that (cf. Ac 1:8+) qualifies a witness as 'apostolic': i.e. it offers an (unnamed) eyewitness for its guarantor, 'the disciple Jesus loved', who actually took part in the events of the Passion, 13:23; 19:26,35; cf. 18:15f, saw the empty tomb, 20:2f, and the risen Christ, 21:7,20–24, and was perhaps one of the first two disciples of Jesus, 1:35f.

There are some features peculiar to the fourth gospel that mark it off sharply from the Synoptics. In the first place, its author seems to have been influenced to a considerable extent by ideas current in certain sections of Judaism, ideas that are reflected in the newly discovered Essene documents of Qumran. In this school of thought, the great emphasis laid on 'knowledge' has given its vocabulary the sort of tinge to be found in later Gnostic literature: e.g. the contrasting pairs 'light-darkness', 'truth-lies', 'angel of light-angel of darkness (Beliar)' which all have a dualist flavour. At Qumran—in view of its expectation of an imminent divine Coming—a particular stress was laid both on the need for unity and on the necessity for mutual love. All these ideas which recur in the fourth gospel are characteristic of the Judaeo-Christian milieu in which it must have originated.

In the second place there is this further difference, that the fourth gospel is far more concerned than the Synoptics to bring out the significance of the events of Christ's life and of all that he did and said. The things Christ did were 'signs': their meaning, hidden at first, could be fully understood only after his glorification, 2:22; 12:16; 13:7. The things he said had a deeper meaning not perceived at the time, cf. 2:20+; it was the business of the Spirit who spoke in the name of the risen Christ, to remind the disciples of what Jesus had said, to deepen their understanding of it, and to 'lead' them 'into the whole truth', cf. 14:26+. The fourth gospel is revelation at this stage of development.

Moreover, this gospel is far more interested than the Synoptics in worship and sacraments. It relates the life of Jesus to the Jewish liturgical year, and associates his miracles with the principal feasts: the Temple is often given as the setting both for them and for Christ's discourses. Jesus asserts that he himself is the focus of a religion, restored 'in spirit and in truth', 4:24, but a religion also which is expressed in the very sacraments through which it works. The dialogue with Nicodemus includes all the essentials of a baptismal instruction, 3:1–21, and the narratives of the man born blind and of the paralytic seem to presuppose the ideas of baptism as light, 9:1–39, and new life, 5:1–14; 7:21–24. Ch. 6 by itself is a complete collection of teachings on the Eucharist, but the entire gospel is pervaded by the concept of the Christian Passover, replacing the Jewish Passover, 1:29,36; 2:13; 6:4; 19:36. Jewish purificatory rites, 2:6; 3:25, give way to a purification of the soul by the Word, 15:3, and the Spirit, 20:22f. In this way the life of Christ is seen as directly related to a living liturgical and sacramental Christianity.

The fourth gospel has a complex literary form: it is akin to the earliest Christian preaching, and yet at the same time it gives us the final results of a quest, completed under the guidance of the Holy Spirit, for a deeper and more rewarding apprehension of the mystery of Jesus.

Each of the evangelists has his own approach to Christ's person and mission. For St John he is the Word made flesh, come to give life to men, 1:14, and this, the mystery of the Incarnation, dominates the whole of John's thought. He expresses its theology in concrete terms: Jesus is sent; Jesus bears witness. Christ is God's message, he is the Word sent down to earth by God, to whom he must return when his task is complete, cf. 1:1+. This task of the Word is to declare to men the hidden things of God; and to be witness to all that he has seen and heard from the Father himself, cf. 3:11+. As credentials God has given him certain works or 'signs' which he must perform; these demand more than human power and prove that he has been sent by the God who is active in him, cf. 2:11+; through them is glimpsed his glory which will not be revealed fully till the day of his resurrection, cf. 1:14+, when the Son of Man is to be 'lifted up' as Isaiah foretold, Is 53:12 (LXX), to return to the Father by way of the cross, cf. Jn 12:32+, and to resume the glory he had with God 'before the world was made', 17:5+,24. This is the glory about which the prophets learned through revelation, cf. 5:27; 12:41; 19:37 plus references, and the revealing of this glory is a theophany, or divine self-revelation, that is at once both the culmination and final eclipse of all those other theophanies that had taken place already, whether that given in the act of creation, 1:1, or those given to Abraham, 8:56, Jacob, 1:51, Moses, 1:17, or the prophets. The glory of the 'day of Yahweh', cf. Am 5:18+, is identified with the 'day' of Jesus, 8:56, and more particularly with his hour, 2:4+, which is the hour of his 'lifting up' and of his glorification. In that hour the superhuman majesty of him who was 'sent', cf. 8:24+, the majesty of one who came to the world to give life, cf. 3:35+, to give it to all those whose hearts were opened by faith to the saving message he brought, cf. 3:11+. For this 'salvation' and for this alone the Son was 'sent', and in this way his 'sending' was the supreme manifestation of the Father's love for the world, cf. 17:6+.

In the synoptic gospels the revelation of Christ's glory is associated primarily with his eschatological 'coming', his return at the end of time, Mt 16:27f. The basic elements of traditional eschatology: the expectation of the 'last day', 6:39f; 11:24; 12:48, of the 'coming' of Jesus, 14:3; 21:22f, of the resurrection of the dead, 5:28f; 11:24, and of the last judgement, 5:29,45; 3:36, are all found in the fourth gospel, but in it this eschatology receives a new and double emphasis: both on its presence here and now, and also on its invisible activity in the heart of things. In this way, the 'coming' of the Son of Man is interpreted primarily as the 'coming' of Jesus to this world through his Incarnation, his 'lifting up' on the cross, and his return to his own disciples through the Holy Spirit. In the same way the 'judgement' is presented as something working here and now in the soul, and eternal life (John's counterpart of the Synoptic 'kingdom') is made to be something actually present, already in the possession of those who have faith. That these 'last things' should be seen as present is not surprising, since the salvation of mankind throughout history centres on Christ's historical life and death and resurrection. Beyond the Jews who rejected Jesus looms something more fundamental—the 'world', cf. 1:9–10+, the 'darkness', cf. 8:12+, which is controlled by Satan, the 'prince of this world', cf. 1 Jn 2:13f, who challenges God and his Anointed. There is no one who is not involved in this dramatic conflict of the spirit: the world, face to face with the Word, suffers its 'judgement', 12:31–32, receives its verdict, and admits defeat, 16:7–11,33. Christ gives his life, cf. 10:18+, he is 'lifted up' on the cross, but freely, and only in order to enter into his glory, cf. 12:32+, a glory that is made visible even in this world to the confusion of unbelievers and ending in the defeat of Satan for ever. God's victory over evil, his salvation of the world, is already guaranteed by Christ's resurrection in glory; the return of Jesus at the Last Day will be nothing but its confirmation.

It is difficult to determine the precise scheme adopted by John for this great theme. In the first place, the arrangement of the gospel is not always easy to explain: the sequence of ch. 4, 5, 6, 7:1–24 is awkward; ch. 15–17 are placed after the farewell of 14:31; passages like 3:31–36 and 12:44–50 break into the context. The way the gospel was both written and edited may be responsible for this. It would seem that we have only the end-stage of a slow process that has brought together not only component parts of different ages, but also corrections, additions and sometimes even more than one revision of the same discourse. Finally all this was published not by John himself but by his disciples after his death, 21:24. It is even possible that these disciples had a number of Johannine fragments which they were reluctant to abandon; though uncertain of their place, they worked them into the primitive gospel.

Many ways of dividing the gospel have been suggested. These all satisfy some of the data but are frequently far too rigidly systematic. It is best to follow such clear indications as are given by the evangelist himself. In the first place there is no doubt that he attaches special importance to the Jewish liturgical feasts which he uses to punctuate his narrative. These are: three feasts of Passover, 2:13; 6:4; 11:55, one unnamed feast, 5:1, one feast of Tabernacles, 7:2, and one feast of Dedication, 10:22. Secondly, the evangelist on several occasions very deliberately calculates the number of days with a view to dividing the life of Jesus into set periods. Thus we have the first week of Christ's ministry, 1:19–2:11, the week of the feast of Tabernacles, 7:2,14,37, and the week of the Passion, 12:1,12; 19:31,42, which latter is unified by the symbolic burial that begins it, 12:7, and the actual burial with which it ends, 19:38f; in the same way, 4:45 harks back to the first Passover, cf. 2:13–25, and in this way brackets together a whole section. With the above two points in mind, the following division may be suggested:

Prologue: 'In the beginning...' (1:1–18)

I. *First week* of the messianic ministry: Jesus revealed as Messiah. The week ends with the first miracle at Cana. (1:19–2:11)

II. *First Passover* with its accompanying events, ending with the second miracle at Cana. (2:12–4:54)

III. *Sabbath 'of the paralytic':* Christ cures the man at the Bethzatha pool. (5:1–47)

IV. *The Passover 'of the bread of life':* miracle of the loaves and the subsequent discourse. (6:1–71)

V. *The feast of Tabernacles* with the cure of the man born blind. (7:1–10:21)

VI. *The feast of Dedication* and the resurrection of Lazarus. (10:22–11:54)

VII. *Week of the Passion* and the crucifixion Passover. (11:55–19:42)

VIII. *The resurrection* and week of apparitions. (20:1–29)

IX. *Appendix* concerning the Church and the expectation of Christ's return. (ch. 21)

This division suggests that Christ not only fulfilled the Jewish liturgy but by doing so brought it to an end.

Is the fourth gospel a source of information independent of the three Synoptics? On this problem, and with due caution, the following observations may be made. There are several indications that John was familiar with the traditions behind the Synoptics. At times his omissions would be incomprehensible unless he were presuming that the facts would be known from some other source, but there are also times when he seems anxious to fill out the synoptic tradition and make it more precise. Nevertheless, recent work has been progressively establishing the originality and independence of the Johannine tradition. Even when narrating episodes found in the synoptic gospels, John remains so much himself that literary dependence becomes impossible: the facts must have reached the author by some other route and nowadays he must be considered a source in his own right, an independent witness to the primitive tradition. Between John and Luke the relationship is much closer, close enough to make it possible that when Luke wrote his gospel he made use not perhaps of the fourth gospel as it stands but of the traditions that went to its making, traditions of great antiquity. This applies especially to the Passion and resurrection narratives, but the contrary is also possible, namely, that the final editor of the fourth gospel was influenced by the third.

What then is the historical value of John's gospel? With the growing scholarly appreciation of the independence of the Johannine tradition there has grown also a recognition of its historical significance. On many points, for example, that have to do with Christ's ministry, John improves on the synoptic data; the duration of the ministry and the chronology of the Passion seem to be more precisely defined than in the Synoptics. Indeed, one of the most precise chronological indications in any of the gospels is to be found in John, 2:20, and it is supported by Lk 3:1. Topography in the fourth gospel is also much more detailed than it is in the Synoptics and this information has been confirmed more than once by recent discoveries (e.g. the pool with five porticos, cf. 5:2). Moreover, throughout the gospel we meet with factual detail that displays the author's close familiarity with Jewish religious practice as also with the rabbinic mind and with the casuistry of the doctors of the Law. The portrait of Christ himself as painted by the evangelist represents him as a figure from some other world but nevertheless as someone real and entirely human: simple and humble even in his risen glory. Finally it may be remarked that if John had not been convinced of the truth of all he wrote, his gospel would have to remain an insoluble enigma.

But it is important to realise that 'history' in this context is a very different thing from the concept of modern historians. The absorbing concern of the evangelist is the *meaning* of those historical events which were at once both divine and human, events which were at one and the same time both historical and theological; events which flowered in time but were rooted in eternity. The aim of the evangelist is to make his account a faithful one, something which he intends should be believed; his theme is a supernatural act, carried out in human history by Jesus Christ, the Word who became incarnate for the salvation of the human race. With this in mind, the evangelist has selected his material, carefully choosing events which, it seemed to him, could be presented symbolically. In this way he has deepened their meaning and given them unsuspected overtones. The miracles he describes are 'signs': they not only manifest Christ's glory, they are also symbolic of the gifts (the new purification, the living bread, light and life) he has brought to the world; even non-miraculous events can be presented in a way that brings out their spiritual meaning, a way that makes them vehicles of the divine mysteries (cf. 2:19–21; 9:7; 11:51f; 13:30; 19:31–37 with notes). John can see spiritual depths even in the most material elements of history: when Jesus comes, it is as the light of the world that he comes: his whole life is a battle against darkness; his death is a judgement on the entire world; and in him are realised the types of the Old Testament—he is the lamb of God, 1:29, the new Temple, 2:21, the healing serpent of Moses, 3:14, the bread of life prefigured by manna, 6:35, the perfect shepherd, 10:11, the true vine, 15:1, etc. In John's portrait of him Christ is presented as divine but it is a portrait filled with the details of Christ's true humanity: it records the Christ of history, but Christ as seen in all his depths as saviour of the world: John's symbolism, therefore, does not compromise history but presupposes it; for him there is no tension between the symbolic and the factual: his symbols are the real events of history, and his symbolism is inherent in these events; his symbolism not only explains the inner meaning of these historic events, but to John, the privileged witness of the incarnate Word, all this symbolism would be useless if these events had not taken place.

As for the *author* of this highly rewarding and complex gospel, tradition almost unanimously makes him John the apostle, the son of Zebedee. Even before 150 A.D. the fourth gospel was known and used by Ignatius of Antioch, by the author of the *Odes of Solomon*, by Papias, by Justin, and probably by Clement of Rome, which makes it clear that the work was already considered to have apostolic authority. The first explicit testimony is that of Irenaeus,

c. 180: 'Last of all John, too, the disciple of the Lord who leant against his breast, himself brought out a gospel while he was in Ephesus'. At about the same time, Clement of Alexandria, Tertullian and the Muratorian Canon expressly attribute the fourth gospel to John the apostle, though this authorship was denied in about 200 A.D. by some opponents of the Montanists. These last had used the fourth gospel to bolster their doctrine of the Spirit, and their opponents' reaction, prompted by theological considerations, had no supporting evidence from tradition.

This evidence for its Johannine authorship is confirmed by the gospel itself which claims to be the work of an eye-witness, a beloved disciple of the Lord. Its vocabulary and style betray its semitic origin; it is familiar with Jewish customs and with the topography of Palestine at the time of Christ; its author is apparently a close friend of Peter, 13:23f; 18:15; 20:3–10; 21:20–23, as John the apostle was, according to Luke, Lk 22:8; Ac 3:1–4; 4:13,19; 8:14; and its silence with regard to the sons of Zebedee is best explained on the hypothesis that one of the two wrote it. There is no doubt that 'the disciple Jesus loved... who wrote these things', 21:24, is the one who, with Peter and James, enjoyed Christ's closest friendship, Mk 5:37; 9:2; 13:3; 14:33. One objection which has been urged is that there is some evidence for this apostle's martyrdom at a date anterior to the writing of the gospel. It cannot be denied that an ancient tradition of John's martyrdom did exist, but there is no proof whatever that it has any greater guarantee than the tradition that John died at Ephesus in his old age: if the former tradition is preferred, it still gives no hint of the date of the martyrdom. In any case, as we saw above, the *corpus* of Johannine traditions was certainly in existence at a very early date even though the gospel as we have it may well have been edited and published later, probably by John's disciples. In such circumstances, John's responsibility for the fourth gospel would not be incompatible with the suggestion that he was martyred.

The letters

The three letters we have, and which by tradition bear John's name, are so like the gospel in style and doctrine that it is difficult not to accept the same John as their author. For a time the Johannine authorship of the second and third letters was in doubt, and traces of this uncertainty are to be found in Origen, Eusebius of Caesarea and Jerome, while the church of Antioch and the Syrian churches in general refused for a long time to accept them; however, these brief, incidental letters are of no doctrinal import, and it is hard to see how they could have forced their way into the canon had they not in fact come from John.

The third letter was probably written first: it is an attempt to settle the dispute on jurisdiction which had arisen in one of the churches acknowledging John's authority; the second letter was written to another church in answer to those who publicly denied the reality of the incarnation. The first letter however is by far the most important: its form is that of an encyclical letter to the Christian communities of Asia, threatened with disintegration under the impact of the early heresies. In this letter John summarises the entire content of his religious experience. He successively develops the parallel themes of light, 1:5f, righteousness, 2:29f, love, 4:7–8f, and truth, 5:6f, and then taking these as a basis he goes on to show how we as children of God must necessarily live the life of integrity which, for John, is the only thing which fulfils the twin commandments: faith in Jesus Christ, the son of God, and love of the brethren (cf. notes to 1:3,7). Of John's three letters this is the closest to his gospel both in style and doctrine; it must have been written about the same time, but whether before or after is something that cannot now be determined.

THE GOSPEL ACCORDING TO
SAINT JOHN

PROLOGUE

1:30; 8:24 Gn 1:1-5 1 Jn 1:1-2 **1** In the beginning was the Word:[a] 1
the Word was with God
3:17; 10:30+ and the Word was God.
He was with God in the beginning. 2
Ps 33:9 Col 1:15-20 Heb 1:1-3 Rv 3:14 *3:35+* Through him all things came to be, 3
not one thing had its being but through him.
All that came to be[b] had life in him[c] 4
3:11+ and that life was the light of men,
8:12+ 1 Jn 2:8 a light that shines in the dark, 5
Ws 7:30 a light that darkness could not overpower.[d]

A man came, sent by God. 6
His name was John.[e]
1:19-34 He came as a witness, 7
as a witness to speak for the light,
so that everyone might believe through him.
5:35 He was not the light, 8
only a witness to speak for the light.

3:19; 4:42+; 8:12+; 12:46 Ws 7:26 The Word was the true light 9
that enlightens all men;
and he was coming into the world.[f]
7:7; 8:23; 11:27; 12:26,31; 13:1 2 P 1:4+ 1 Jn 2:15 He was in the world 10
that had its being through him,
and the world did not know him.[g]
He came to his own domain 11
and his own people[h] did not accept him.
10:35 But to all who did accept him 12
3:11+ Ho 2:1 1 Jn 3:2 *1 Jn 5:13* he gave power to become[i] children of God,
to all who believe in the name of him[j]
who was[k] born not out of human stock 13
or urge of the flesh
or will of man
1 Jn 5:18 but of God himself.[l]
Ex 25:8+ Lv 26:11-12 Dt 4:7+ 1 K 8:27 Ps 85:9 Ba 3:38 *17:5+* 1 Jn 1:1-3 *Ex 34:6+* Ho 2:22+ The Word was made flesh,[m] 14
he lived among us,[n]
and we saw his glory,[o]
the glory that is his as the only Son of the Father,
full of grace and truth.[p]

1:19 John appears as his witness. He proclaims: 15
'This is the one of whom I said:

He who comes after me =1:30
ranks before me
because he existed before me'.

16 Indeed, from his fulness we have, all of us, received— Col 2:9-10
yes, grace in return for grace,[q]
17 since, though the Law was given through Moses, 1:21+ Ex 34:10,32 Dt 33:4; 34:10
grace and truth have come through Jesus Christ.
18 No one has ever seen God; *6:46* Ex 33:20+ 1 Jn 4:12
it is the only Son,[r] who is nearest to the Father's heart, *3:11+;* 17:6+ Col 1:15
who has made him known.

I. THE FIRST PASSOVER

A. THE OPENING WEEK

The witness of John 1:7-8,15

19 This is how John appeared as a witness. When the Jews[s] sent priests and 3:28; 5:33
20 Levites from Jerusalem to ask him, 'Who are you?' •he not only declared, but Lk 3:15 Ac 13:25
21 he declared quite openly, 'I am not the Christ'. •'Well then,' they asked 'are you
22 Elijah?'[t] 'I am not' he said. 'Are you the Prophet?'[u] He answered, 'No'. •So they Mt 17:10-13+
said to him, 'Who are you? We must take back an answer to those who sent us. *Mt 16:14+*
23 What have you to say about yourself?' •So John said, 'I am, as Isaiah prophesied:

1 a. The O.T. speaks of the Word of God, and of his Wisdom, present with God before the world was made, cf. Pr 8:22+; Ws 7:22+; by it all things were created; it is sent to earth to reveal the hidden designs of God; it returns to him with its work done, Is 55:10-11; Pr 8:22-36; Si 24:3-22; Ws 9:9-12. On its creative role, cf. also Gn 1:3,6 etc.; Is 40:8,26; 44:24-28; 48:13; Ps 33:6; Jdt 16:14; Si 42:15; on its mission, cf. Ws 18:14-16; Ps 107:20; 147:15-18. For John, too, 13:3; 16:28, the Word existed before the world in God, 1:1,2; 8:24+; 10:30+; it has come on earth, 1:9-14; 3:19; 9:39; 12:46, cf. Mk 1:38+, being sent by the Father, 3:17,34; 5:36,43; 6:29; 7:29; 8:42; 9:7; 10:36; 11:42; 17:3,25, cf. Lk 4:43, to perform a task, 4:34+, namely, to deliver a message of salvation to the world, 3:11+; 1:33+; with its mission accomplished it returns to the Father, 1:18; 7:33; 8:21; 12:35; 13:3; 16:5; 17:11,13; 20:17. The incarnation enabled the N.T., and especially John, to see this separately and eternally existent Word-Wisdom as a person.

b. Alternatively, these words may be joined with the preceding 'not one thing of all that came to be had its being but through him'.

c. Var. 'he is the life'.

d. The Light (Goodness; the Word) cannot be imprisoned by Darkness (Evil; the powers of evil), cf. 7:33f; 8:21; 14:30; 12:31,32; 1 Jn 2:8,14; 4:4; 5:18. Others translate 'could not understand'.

e. John the Baptist, Mt 3:1.

f. Other possible translations 'The true light, that which enlightens every man, was coming into the world', or 'He (the Word) was the true light that enlightens every man who comes into the world'.

g. The 'world' variously means: the cosmos or this earth, the human race, those hostile to God who hate Christ and his disciples, 7:7; 15:18,19; 17:14. This last sense coincides with the contemporary Jewish distinction between 'this world', 8:23 and *passim*, dominated by Satan, 12:31; 14:30; 16:11; 1 Jn 5:19, and 'the world to come' which possibly corresponds to John's 'eternal life', 12:25. The disciples are to remain *in* this world for the present, though not *of* it, 17:11,14f.

h. Probably the Jews.

i. Var. 'to be called'.

j. 'to those who believe in his name' omitted by many of the Fathers.

k. Lit. 'who was born not of blood or the will of the flesh or the will of man'. Var. (the commonly accepted reading) 'those who are born'. 'not of blood...man': the shorter reading 'not of flesh or blood' is perhaps the original one.

l. Allusion to the eternal generation of the Word but also, as it seems, to Christ's virgin birth, cf. Mt 1:16,18-23 and Lk 1:26-38.

m. The 'flesh' is man considered as a frail and mortal being, cf. 3:6; 17:2; Gn 6:3; Ps 56:4; Is 40:6. See Rm 7:5+.

n. Lit. 'pitched his tent among us'. The incarnation of the Word makes God personally and visibly present to mankind; it is no longer a presence unseen and awe-inspiring as in the Tent and Temple of the old régime, Ex 25:8+; cf. Nb 35:34, nor merely the presence of divine Wisdom enshrined in Israel's Mosaic Law, Si 24:7-22; Ba 3:36–4:4.

o. The 'glory' is the manifestation of God's presence, Ex 24:16+. No one could see its brilliance and live, Ex 33:20+, but the human nature of the Word now screens this glory as the cloud once did. Yet at times it pierces the veil, at the transfiguration, for instance, cf. Lk 9:32,35 (alluded to in Jn 1:14?), and when Jesus works miracles—'signs' that God is active in him, 2:11+; 11:40; cf. Ex 14:24-27 and 15:7; 16:7f. The resurrection will reveal the glory fully, cf. Jn 17:5+.

p. 'Grace and truth' recalls the 'grace' (or 'love') and 'faithfulness' of God's self-revelation to Moses, Ex 34:6+, cf. Ho 2:16-22.

q. I.e. 'a grace answering to the grace (that is in Christ)' or 'one grace (that of the New Covenant) in place of (another) grace (that of the Old Covenant)'. An alternative translation is 'grace upon grace'.

r. Var. 'God, only-begotten'.

s. In Jn this usually indicates the Jewish religious authorities hostile to Jesus, cf. 2:18; 5:10; 7:13; 9:22; 18:12; 19:38; 20:19, but occasionally the Jews as a whole.

t. On the expected return of Elijah, see Ml 3:23-24 and Mt 17:10-13.

u. From Dt 18:15,18 (see note) the Jews argued that the expected Messiah would be another Moses (the prophet *par excellence*, cf. Nb 12:7+) who would repeat on a grand scale the prodigies of the Exodus. Cf. Jn 3:14; 6:14,30-31,68; 7:40,52; 13:1+; Ac 3:22-23; 7:20-44; Heb 3:1-11. See also Mt 16:14+.

Is 40:3 ||Mt 3:3+ *a voice that cries in the wilderness:*
Make a straight way for the Lord'.

Now these men had been sent by the Pharisees, •and they put this further 24 25
question to him, 'Why are you baptising if you are not the Christ, and not Elijah,
Mt 3:6+ and not the prophet?' •John replied, 'I baptise with water; but there stands 26
7:27+ among you—unknown to you—•the one who is coming after me; and I am 27
Mk 1:7p *10:40* not fit to undo his sandal-strap'. •This happened at Bethany, on the far side of 28
the Jordan,[v] where John was baptising.

4:42+ Ex 12:1+ The next day, seeing Jesus coming towards him, John said, 'Look, there is 29
Is 53:7,12 the lamb of God[w] that takes away the sin of the world. •This is the one I spoke 30
1:1+; 8:58 of when I said: A man is coming after me who ranks before me because he
existed before me. •I did not know him myself, and yet it was to reveal him to 31
3:34 Is 11:2; 61:1 Israel that I came baptising with water.' •John also declared, 'I saw the Spirit 32
Mt 3:16p coming down on him from heaven like a dove[x] and resting on him. •I did not 33
know him myself, but he who sent me to baptise with water had said to me,
3:5 Mt 3:11+ "The man on whom you see the Spirit come down and rest is the one who is
going to baptise with the Holy Spirit".[y] •Yes, I have seen and I am the witness 34
Is 42:1 Lk 9:35; 23:35 that he is the Chosen One of God.'[z]

Mt 4:18-20p **The first disciples**

On the following day as John stood there again with two of his disciples, 35
19:5 Jesus passed, and John stared hard at him and said, 'Look, there is the lamb of 36
God'. •Hearing this, the two disciples followed Jesus. •Jesus turned round, saw 37 38
them following and said, 'What do you want?' They answered, 'Rabbi,'—which
means Teacher—'where do you live?' •'Come and see' he replied; so they went 39
and saw where he lived, and stayed with him the rest of that day. It was about
the tenth hour.[aa]

One of these two who became followers of Jesus after hearing what John had 40
said was Andrew, the brother of Simon Peter. •Early next morning,[bb] Andrew 41
met his brother and said to him, 'We have found the Messiah'—which means
the Christ—•and he took Simon to Jesus. Jesus looked hard at him and said, 42
Mt 16:18-19+ 'You are Simon son of John; you are to be called Cephas'—meaning Rock.

Mk 3:16 The next day, after Jesus had decided to leave for Galilee, he met Philip and 43
1 Co 1:12+ *Mt 9:9* said, 'Follow me'. •Philip came from the same town, Bethsaida, as Andrew and 44
Jn 12:21 Peter. •Philip found Nathanael[cc] and said to him, 'We have found the one 45
1:21+; 5:39+ Moses wrote about in the Law, the one about whom the prophets wrote: he is
Dt 18:18 Jesus son of Joseph, from Nazareth'. •'From Nazareth?' said Nathanael 'Can 46
Ac 26:22+ *7:41,42,52* anything good come from that place?' 'Come and see' replied Philip. •When 47
Mt 13:54f Jesus saw Nathanael coming he said of him,[dd] 'There is an Israelite who deserves
2:25; 6:61,64 the name, incapable of deceit'. •'How do you know me?' said Nathanael. 48
Mt 9:4 Lk 6:8 'Before Philip came to call you,' said Jesus 'I saw you under the fig tree.'[ee] •Na- 49
6:15; 12:13 thanael answered, 'Rabbi, you are the Son of God,[ff] you are the King of Israel'.
Jesus replied, 'You believe that just because I said: I saw you under the fig tree. 50
You will see greater things than that.' •And then he added, 'I tell you most 51
Gn 28:10-17 solemnly, you will see heaven laid open and, above the Son of Man, the angels
Mt 8:20+ of God ascending and descending'.

The wedding at Cana

21:2; 4:46 **2** Three days later[a] there was a wedding at Cana in Galilee. The mother of 1
Jesus was there,[b] •and Jesus and his disciples had also been invited. •When 2 3
they ran out of wine, since the wine provided for the wedding was all finished,
7:6,30; 8:20; 12:23; 13:1 the mother of Jesus said to him, 'They have no wine'. •Jesus said, 'Woman,[c] why 4
turn to me?[d] My hour[e] has not come yet.' •His mother said to the servants, 5
Gn 41:55 '*Do whatever he tells you*'. •There were six stone water jars standing there, meant 6
Mk 7:3-4 for the ablutions that are customary among the Jews: each could hold twenty or

7 thirty gallons. •Jesus said to the servants, 'Fill the jars with water', and they
8 filled them to the brim. •'Draw some out now' he told them 'and take it to the
9 steward.' •They did this; the steward tasted the water, and it had turned into
wine. Having no idea where it came from—only the servants who had drawn
10 the water knew—the steward called the bridegroom •and said, 'People generally
serve the best wine first, and keep the cheaper sort till the guests have had plenty
to drink; but you have kept the best wine till now'. Mt 26:29p Lk 5:37-39p
11 This was the first of the signs[f] given by Jesus: it was given at Cana in Galilee. *1:14+; 4:54* Ex 4:30-31
12 He let his glory be seen, and his disciples believed in him. •After this he went Nb 16:28
down to Capernaum with his mother and the brothers,[g] but they stayed there 20:17 Mt 4:13
only a few days. Ac 1:15+

B. THE PASSOVER

The cleansing of the Temple ||Mt 21:12-13 ||Mk 11:11, 15-17

13 Just before the Jewish Passover Jesus went up to Jerusalem, •and in the *Ne 13:8*
14 Temple he found people selling cattle and sheep and pigeons, and the money ||Lk 19:45-46
15 changers sitting at their counters there. •Making a whip out of some cord, he Ml 3:1-4
drove them all out of the Temple, cattle and sheep as well, scattered the money
16 changers' coins, knocked their tables over •and said to the pigeon-sellers, 'Take
17 all this out of here and stop turning my Father's house into a market'. •Then his 5:18 Zc 14:21
disciples remembered the words of scripture: *Zeal for your house will devour me.* *Ps 69:9*
18 The Jews intervened and said, 'What sign can you show us to justify what you 4:48; 6:30
19 have done?' •Jesus answered, 'Destroy this sanctuary, and in three days I will Mt 26:61+
20 raise it up'.[h] •The Jews replied, 'It has taken forty-six years to build this Mt 12:6+, 38-40+

v. Not the Bethany near Jerusalem, 11:18.

w. One of the most significant of John's symbols of Christ, cf. Rv 5:6,12, etc. It blends the idea of the 'servant' (Is 53), who takes on himself the sins of men and offers himself as a 'lamb of expiation' (Lv 14), with that of the Passover lamb (Ex 12:1+; cf. Jn 19:36) whose ritual symbolises Israel's redemption. Cf. Ac 8: 31-35; 1 Co 5:7; 1 P 1:18-20.

x. Om. 'like a dove'.

y. This phrase sums up the whole purpose of the Messiah's coming, cf. 1:1+, namely, that mankind might be born again in the Spirit; the O.T. had already foretold it, cf. Ac 2:33+. The Spirit rests on him, Is 11:2; 42:1; Jn 1:33, and so he can confer it on others (baptism in the Spirit, cf. here and Ac 1:5+), but only after his resurrection, 7:39; 16:7,8; 20:22; Ac 2. For Jesus 'came in the flesh', 1 Jn 4:2; 2 Jn 7, flesh that was corruptible, Jn 1:14+, and it is only when he is 'lifted up' and has gone to the Father that his body, glorified now, is fully endowed with divine, lifegiving power. Thenceforward the Spirit flows freely to the world from this body as from an inexhaustible spring: 7:37-39; 19:34; cf. Rm 5:5+. For the water symbolism, cf. 4:1+.

z. Var. 'the Son of God'.

aa. About 4 p.m. The insertion of this detail suggests that the narrative is a personal reminiscence.

bb. Lit. 'early'; var. 'at first' or 'first'.

cc. Probably the Bartholomew of the Synoptics, Mt 10:3p. Cf. Jn 21:2.

dd. 'of him'; var. 'of Nathanael' or 'to him'.

ee. Christ's supernatural knowledge of men and things is one of the features of Jn's portrait of him, cf. 2:24f; 4:17-19,29; 6:61,64,71; 13:1,11,27,28; 16:19, 30; 18:4; 21:17.

ff. In this passage the phrase implies he is Messiah only (like 'king of Israel'). Cf. Mt 4:3+.

2 a. I.e. three days after the meeting with Philip and Nathanael. The opening events of the gospel, therefore, are contained within one week of which almost every day is noticed; it culminates in the manifestation of Christ's glory.

b. Mary is present when Jesus first manifests his glory; she is there again at the cross, 19:25-27. The two descriptions have several details in common, evidently of set purpose.

c. Unusual address from son to mother; the term is used again in 19:26 where there may be a reference to Gn 3:15,20: Mary is the second Eve, 'the mother of the living'.

d. Lit. 'What to me and to thee', a semitic formula not infrequent in O.T., Jg 11:12; 2 S 16:10; 19:23; 1 K 17:18, etc., and in N.T., Mt 8:29; Mk 1:24; 5:7; Lk 4:34; 8:28. It is used to deprecate interference or, more strongly, to reject overtures of any kind. The shade of meaning can be deduced only from the context. Here, Jesus objects that his hour has not yet come.

e. The 'hour' of his glorification and of his return to the Father's right hand. Its approach is noted by the evangelist, 7:30; 8:20; 12:23,27; 13:1; 17:1. This 'hour' is determined by the Father and cannot be anticipated, though the miracle worked through Mary's intervention is a prophetic symbol of it.

f. For credentials, every true prophet must have 'signs', or wonders worked in God's name, Is 7:11, etc.: cf. Jn 3:2; 6:29,30; 7:3,31; 9:16,33; of the Messiah it was expected that he would repeat the Mosaic miracles, 1:21+. Jesus, therefore, works 'signs' in order to stimulate faith in his divine mission, 2:11,23; 4:48-54; 11:15,42; 12:37; cf. 3:11+. And indeed his 'works' show that God has sent him, 5:36; 10:25,37, that the Father is within him, 10:30+, manifesting the divine glory in power, 1:14+; it is the Father himself who does the works, 14:10; 10:38. But many refuse to believe, 3:12; 5:38-47; 6:36,64; 7:5; 8:45; 10:25; 12:37, and their sin 'remains', 9:41; 15:24. Cf. Mt 8:3+.

g. Var. 'and his brothers'; add. 'and his disciples'. The 'brothers' are not blood-brothers of Jesus but the inner circle of his first disciples, cf. Ac 1:15+.

h. In the fourth gospel, Jesus frequently uses terms which, in addition to their obvious meaning appreciated by the audience, possess a metaphorical and higher sense; cf. 2:20 (Temple); 3:4 (new birth); 4:15 (living water); 6:34 (bread of life); 7:35 (to depart); 11:11 (to awaken); 12:34 (to lift up); 13:9 (to wash); 13:36f (to depart); 14:22 (to show oneself). Consequent

sanctuary:[i] are you going to raise it up in three days?' •But he was speaking of 21
1:14+ the sanctuary that was his body,[j] •and when Jesus rose from the dead, his disciples 22
5:39+; 14:26+ remembered that he had said this, and they believed the scripture and the words
he had said.

4:45 During his stay in Jerusalem for the Passover many believed in his name 23
when they saw the signs that he gave, •but Jesus knew them all and did not trust 24
1:48+ Pr 15:11 himself to them; •he never needed evidence about any man; he could tell what 25
a man had in him.

C. THE MYSTERY OF THE SPIRIT REVEALED TO A MASTER IN ISRAEL

The conversation with Nicodemus

7:48,50-52; 12:42-43; 19:39 3 There was one of the Pharisees called Nicodemus, a leading Jew, •who came 1 2
to Jesus by night and said, 'Rabbi, we know that you are a teacher who comes
2:11+; 9:16, 33; 10:21 from God; for no one could perform the signs that you do unless God were with
him'. •Jesus answered: 3

'I tell you most solemnly,
Jm 1:16 1 P 1:23 unless a man is born from above,[a]
he cannot see the kingdom of God'.[b]

2:19+ Nicodemus said, 'How can a grown man be born? Can he go back into his 4
mother's womb and be born again?' •Jesus replied: 5

'I tell you most solemnly,
1:33+ Ezk 36:25 Rm 8:9 Tt 3:5 *Gn 6:3* unless a man is born through water and the Spirit,[c]
he cannot enter the kingdom of God:
what is born of the flesh is flesh; 6
6:63 1 Co 15: 44-50 what is born of the Spirit is spirit.
Do not be surprised when I say: 7
You must be born from above.
Qo 11:5 Ac 2:2 The wind[d] blows wherever it pleases; 8
you hear its sound,
but you cannot tell where it comes from or where it is going.
That is how it is with all who are born of the Spirit.'

'How can that be possible?' asked Nicodemus. •'You, a teacher in Israel, 9 10
and you do not know these things!' replied Jesus.

1:4,12,18; 3:32,34; 5:24,29; 7:16,43 8:14,28,31 Is 50:4,10 Mt 11:27 'I tell you most solemnly, 11
we speak only about what we know
and witness only to what we have seen
and yet you people reject our evidence.[e]
6:60-62 Ws 9:16-17 Ph 3:19f If you do not believe me 12
when I speak about things in this world,
how are you going to believe me
when I speak to you about heavenly things?
20:17+ Pr 30:4 No one has gone up to heaven[f] 13
except the one who came down from heaven,
1:18 Rm 10:6 Ep 4:8,9 the Son of Man who is in heaven;
1:21+; 12:32+ *Nb 21:4-9* Ws 16:5-7 and the Son of Man must be lifted up[g]
as Moses lifted up the serpent in the desert, 14
so that everyone who believes may have eternal life in him.[h] 15
Gn 22 Zc 12:10 Mt 21:37p Rm 8:32 Yes, God loved the world so much 16
that he gave his only Son,

so that everyone who believes in him may not be lost 1 Jn 4:9▲
but may have eternal life.
17 For God sent his Son into the world 1:1+
not to condemn the world,
but so that through him the world might be saved. 4:42+; 12:47 2 Co 5:19
18 No one who believes in him will be condemned;
but whoever refuses to believe is condemned already,
because he has refused to believe Ac 4:12
in the name[i] of God's only Son.
19 On these grounds is sentence pronounced:
that though the light has come into the world 8:12+
men have shown they prefer
darkness to the light Ps 52:3
because their deeds were evil.
20 And indeed, everybody who does wrong Jb 24:13-17
hates the light and avoids it,
for fear his actions should be exposed; Ep 5:13
21 but the man who lives by the truth[j] Tb 4:6 1 Jn 1:6
comes out into the light,
so that it may be plainly seen that what he does is done in God.' Mt 5:14-16

II. JOURNEYS IN SAMARIA AND GALILEE

John bears witness for the last time

22 After this, Jesus went with his disciples into the Judaean countryside and
23 stayed with them there and baptised.[k] •At the same time John was baptising at 4:1-2
Aenon[l] near Salim, where there was plenty of water, and people were going
24 there to be baptised. •This was before John had been put in prison. Mt 3:6+ Lk 3:20
25 Now some of John's disciples had opened a discussion with a Jew about
26 purification,[m] •so they went to John and said, 'Rabbi, the man who was with
you on the far side of the Jordan, the man to whom you bore witness, is baptising
27 now; and everyone is going to him'. •John replied:

misapprehensions provide an opportunity for explanatory developments, cf. 3:11+.

i. Reconstruction work on the Temple began in 19 B.C. This, therefore, is the Passover of 28 A.D.

j. One of the great Johannine symbols. Cf. Rv 21:22. Cf. Paul, 1 Co 12:12+. The body of the risen Christ is to be the focus of worship in spirit and truth, 4:21f, the shrine of the Presence, 1:14, the spiritual temple from which living waters flow, 7:37-39; 19:34.

3 a. To be preferred to 'again'.

b. A phrase common in the Synoptics, Mt 4:17+, but occurring only here (and v. 5) in Jn; its Johannine equivalent is 'life' or 'eternal life'.

c. Allusion to baptism and its necessity, cf. Rm 6:4+.

d. In Greek, as in Hebr., one word serves for both 'wind' and 'spirit'.

e. Jesus does not speak on his own initiative, 7:17-18; he declares what he has seen 'with the Father', 1:18; 3:11; 8:38; cf. 8:24+; it is the Father's words and teaching that he hands on to man, 3:34; 8:28; 12:49,50; 14:24; 17:8,14; he is himself the Word, 1:1,14. This Word is not idle: it calls all things from nothing, 1:1+, it calls the dead from the tomb, 11:43,44; 5:28-29; it gives life to the soul, 5:24; 6:63; 8:51; it confers the Spirit, the source of immortality, 1:33+; 20:22, and so makes men children of God, 10:35; 1:12. It is required only that man should have faith in the Word, 1:12, 'dwell' in it, cf. 8:31, 'keep' it, 8:51,55; 12:47; 14:23; 15:20; 17:6, obey its command which is love, 13:34+. Nevertheless, the Word is enigmatic, 2:20+, and difficult, cf. 6:60; 7:36; it makes its way only into humble hearts. Those who hear it, therefore, respond differently, 7:43; 10:19: some believe, 4:41; 7:40f,46; 8:30, others go away disappointed, 6:66, in spite of the 'signs', 2:11+; this same rejected Word will judge them at the last day, 12:48.

f. Alluding to the ascension, which will both show that Jesus really came from heaven and also establish the Son of Man on his glorious throne.

g. If man would be saved he must turn his eyes to Christ 'lifted up' (12:32+) on the cross, Nb 21:8; Zc 12:10+; Jn 19:37+, as the symbol of his 'lifting up' in the ascension, that is to say, he must believe that Christ is the only-begotten Son, 3:18; Zc 12:10. He will then be washed clean by the water from the pierced side, Jn 19:34; Zc 13:1.

h. Var. 'so that everyone who believes in him may receive eternal life'.

i. Semitism: the 'name' is the person.

j. Lit. 'does the truth', cf. 1 Jn 3:19+.

k. A baptism of the same nature as the Baptist's; baptism 'in the Spirit' is reserved for the period after Christ's resurrection in glory, cf. 1:33+.

l. A tradition locates Aenon ('the Springs') in the Jordan valley about 7 miles S. of Scythopolis. Ain Farah is also a possibility.

m. About baptism probably. 'a Jew'; var. 'Jews'. The text is corrupt. The reading may have been 'Jesus' or 'the disciples of Jesus'.

19:11 Heb 5:4 *1 Co 4:7* 2 Co 3:5 'A man can lay claim
only to what is given him from heaven.

1:19-27 Lk 3:15 'You yourselves can bear me out: I said: I myself am not the Christ; I am 28
the one who has been sent in front of him.

Ezk 16:1+ Mt 9:15+ 'The bride is only for the bridegroom;[n] 29
and yet the bridegroom's friend,
who stands there and listens,
15:11 is glad when he hears the bridegroom's voice.
This same joy I feel, and now it is complete.
He must grow greater, 30
I must grow smaller.
8:23 He who comes from above 31
is above all others;[o]
1 Jn 4:5 he who is born of the earth
is earthly himself and speaks in an earthly way.
He who comes from heaven[p]
3:11 bears witness to the things he has seen and heard, 32
even if his testimony is not accepted;
1 Jn 5:10 though all who do accept his testimony 33
7:28; 8:26 are attesting the truthfulness of God,
1:1+ since he whom God has sent 34
3:11+ speaks God's own words:
1:32 God gives him the Spirit without reserve.[q]
Mt 11:27; 28:18 The Father loves the Son 35
and has entrusted everything to him.[r]
Anyone who believes in the Son has eternal life, 36
9:41 but anyone who refuses to believe in the Son will never see life:
Mt 3:7+ the anger of God stays on him.'

The saviour of the world revealed to the Samaritans[a]

Ps 23:2; 42:1 Jr 31:9 Jl 4:18 4 When Jesus[b] heard that the Pharisees had found out that he was making 1
and baptising more disciples than John—•though in fact it was his disciples 2
Mt 3:6+ who baptised, not Jesus himself—•he left Judaea and went back to Galilee. 3
Lk 9:52-55 This meant that he had to cross Samaria. 4
Gn 33:18-20; 48:21-22 On the way he came to the Samaritan town called Sychar,[c] near the land 5
Jos 24:32 that Jacob gave to his son Joseph. •Joseph's well is there and Jesus, tired by the 6
journey, sat straight down by the well. It was about the sixth hour.[d] •When 7
19:28 a Samaritan woman came to draw water, Jesus said to her, 'Give me a drink'.
His disciples had gone into the town to buy food. •The Samaritan woman said 8 9
Lk 10:29-37; 17:11-19 to him, 'What? You are a Jew and you ask me, a Samaritan, for a drink?'—Jews,
in fact, do not associate with Samaritans.[e] •Jesus replied: 10

3:16 Ac 8:20+ 'If you only knew what God is offering
and who it is that is saying to you:
Give me a drink,
you would have been the one to ask,
6:35 and he would have given you living water'.

'You have no bucket, sir,' she answered 'and the well is deep: how could 11
6:31-32; 8:53 you get this living water? •Are you a greater man than our father Jacob who 12
gave us this well and drank from it himself with his sons and his cattle?' •Jesus 13
replied:

Si 24:21 'Whoever drinks this water
will get thirsty again;
6:35; 7:37-39 but anyone who drinks the water that I shall give 14
will never be thirsty again:

the water that I shall give Ps 36:9 Is 58:11
will turn into a spring inside him, welling up to eternal life'.

15 'Sir,' said the woman 'give me some of that water, so that I may never get 2:19+; 6:34
16 thirsty and never have to come here again to draw water.' •'Go and call your
17 husband' said Jesus to her 'and come back here.' •The woman answered, 'I have
18 no husband'. He said to her, 'You are right to say, "I have no husband"; •for 1:48+
although you have had five, the one you have now is not your husband. You Lk 7:39
19 20 spoke the truth there.' •'I see you are a prophet, sir' said the woman. •'Our Mt 16:14+
fathers worshipped on this mountain,[f] while you say that Jerusalem is the place Dt 12:5+
21 where one ought to worship.'[g] •Jesus said:

'Believe me, woman, the hour is coming
when you will worship the Father
neither on this mountain nor in Jerusalem.
22 You worship what you do not know; 2 K 17:27-33
we worship what we do know; Is 2:3
for salvation comes from the Jews. Rm 9:4-5
23 But the hour will come—in fact it is here already—
when true worshippers will worship the Father in spirit and truth:[h] 2:21+; 17:19
that is the kind of worshipper
the Father wants.
24 God is spirit,
and those who worship[i]
must worship in spirit and truth.'

25 The woman said to him, 'I know that Messiah—that is, Christ—is coming; Dt 18:18-22
26 and when he comes he will tell us everything'. •'I who am speaking to you,' 9:37
said Jesus 'I am he.'
27 At this point his disciples returned, and were surprised to find him speaking
to a woman, though none of them asked, 'What do you want from her?' or, 21:12
28 'Why are you talking to her?' •The woman put down her water jar and hurried
29 back[j] to the town to tell the people, •'Come and see a man who has told me
30 everything I ever did; I wonder if he is the Christ?' •This brought people out of
the town and they started walking towards him.
31 Meanwhile, the disciples were urging him, 'Rabbi, do have something to

n. The O.T. uses the marriage metaphor to express the relationship between God and Israel, Ho 1:2+. Jesus applies it to himself, Mt 9:15p; 22:1f; 25:1f; cf. also Paul in Ep 5:22f; 2 Co 11:2. The Messiah's coming has brought joy to the world, Jn 3:29, cf. 1:29. 36-39; 2:1-11, consequently the marriage feast of the Lamb, Rv 19:7; 21:2, has already begun.

o. Or perhaps 'everything'.

p. Add. 'is above all (others)' (or 'everything').

q. Or 'and gives the Spirit without reserve'.

r. God has communicated his power over life to the Son, 1:4; 5:21; 10:18+, and now the Son gives life to whom he will, 5:26; his gift of the Spirit, 3:5-6; 1:33+; 15:26, establishes 'all flesh' in incorruption, 1:14+; 11:25; 17:2,3. Thus, by the Father's decree, all things are 'in the hand' (or 'power') of the Son, 3:35; 10:28,29; 13:3; 17:2; cf. 6:37-39; Mt 11:27; 28:18; on this is based the sovereignty, 12:13-15; 18:36-37, that he will solemnly assume on the day of his 'lifting up', 12:32+; 19:19; Ac 2:33; Ep 4:8; and on that day, the 'Prince of this world' will forfeit his kingdom, 12:31.

4 a. Meetings at a well are a feature of the patriarchal narratives: Gn 24:10f; 29:1f; Ex 2:15f. Wells and springs play a significant part in the life and religion of the patriarchal and Exodus periods: Gn 26:14-22; Ex 15:22-27; 17:1-7 etc. In the O.T., spring water symbolises the life that God gives, especially that of the messianic age: Is 12:3; 55:1; Jr 2:13; Ezk 47:1f (cf. Ps 46:4 and Zc 14:8); Ps 36:8-9 (and in the N.T.: Rv 7:16-17; 22:17); it symbolises also the life imparted by divine Wisdom and by the Law, Pr 13:14; Si 15:3; 24:23-29. This symbolism is carried further in the gospel narrative: living (i.e. spring) water signifies the Spirit, cf. Jn 7:37-39 and 1:33+.

b. Var. 'the Lord'.

c. Either the ancient Shechem (Sichara in Aramaic) or the present village of Askar at the foot of Mt. Ebal, about 3/4 mile from 'Jacob's Well'. The well is not mentioned in Gn.

d. Noon.

e. Some authorities omit this parenthesis. The Jews hated the Samaritans, Si 50:25-26; Jn 8:48; Lk 9:52-55, cf. Mt 10:5; Lk 10:33; 17:16, and attributed their origin to the importation of five pagan groups, 2 K 17:24-41, who retained some of their loyalty to their old gods; these are symbolised by the 'five husbands' of v. 18.

f. I.e. Gerizim; on this mountain the Samaritans had built a rival to the Jerusalem Temple; it was destroyed by John Hyrcanus in 129 B.C.

g. Lit. 'one ought to worship in Jerusalem'. Var. 'the place (or: house) in which one ought to worship is in Jerusalem'.

h. The Spirit, 14:26+, who makes a new creature of man, 3:5, is also the inspiring principle of the new worship of God. This worship is 'in truth' because it is the only worship that meets the conditions revealed by God through Jesus.

i. Var. 'those who worship him', cf. 12:20.

j. Var. 'went off'.

eat'; •but he said, 'I have food to eat that you do not know about'. •So the 32 33
disciples asked one another, 'Has someone been bringing him food?' •But Jesus 34
said:

'My food
1:1+; 5:30; 6:38-40; is to do the will of the one who sent me,
17:4; 19:30 and to complete his work.
Mt 26:39 Have you not got a saying: 35
Four months and then the harvest?
Well, I tell you:
Mt 9:37-38 Lk 10:2 Rv 14:15 Look around you, look at the fields;
already they are white, ready for harvest![k]
Already •the reaper is being paid his wages, 36
already he is bringing in the grain for eternal life,
Ps 126:5-6 and thus sower and reaper rejoice together.
For here the proverb holds good: 37
one sows, another reaps;
17:18; 20:21 Ac 8:14-17 I sent you to reap 38
a harvest you had not worked for.
Others worked for it;
and you have come into the rewards of their trouble.'[l]

Many Samaritans of that town had believed in him on the strength of the 39
woman's testimony when she said, 'He told me all I have ever done', •so, when 40
the Samaritans came up to him, they begged him to stay with them. He stayed
for two days, and •when he spoke to them many more came to believe; •and 41 42
they said to the woman, 'Now we no longer believe because of what you told us;
1:9-10+, 29; 3:17; 11:52 1 Jn 2:2; 4:15 we have heard him ourselves and we know that he really is the saviour of the
world'.[m]

||Mt 8:5-13 ||Lk 7:1-10 The cure of the nobleman's son

When the two days were over Jesus left for Galilee. •He himself had declared 43 44
Mt 13:57p; 16:14+ that there is no respect for a prophet in his own country, •but on his arrival the 45
Galileans received him well, having seen all that he had done at Jerusalem
Jn 2:23 during the festival which they too had attended.
2:1-11 He went again to Cana in Galilee, where he had changed the water into wine. 46
Mt 8:5 Lk 7:1-10 Now there was a court official there whose son was ill at Capernaum •and, 47
hearing that Jesus had arrived in Galilee from Judaea, he went and asked him
2:18; 20:29 Mt 12:38p to come and cure his son as he was at the point of death. •Jesus said, 'So you will 48
not believe unless you see signs and portents!' •'Sir,' answered the official 'come 49
down before my child dies.' •'Go home,' said Jesus 'your son will live.' The man 50
Mt 8:10+ believed what Jesus had said and started on his way; •and while he was still on 51
the journey back his servants met him with the news that his boy was alive. •He 52
asked them when the boy had begun to recover. 'The fever left him yesterday'
they said 'at the seventh hour.' •The father realised that this was exactly the time 53
when Jesus had said, 'Your son will live'; and he and all his household believed.
2:11+ This was the second sign given by Jesus, on his return from Judaea to Galilee. 54

III. THE SECOND FEAST AT JERUSALEM

The cure of a sick man at the Pool of Bethzatha

5 Some time after this there was a Jewish festival,[a] and Jesus went up to Jeru- 1
salem. •Now at the Sheep Pool in Jerusalem there is a building, called Beth- 2
zatha[b] in Hebrew, consisting of five porticos; •and under these were crowds of 3
sick people—blind, lame, paralysed—waiting for the water to move;[c] •for at 4
Mt 1:20+ intervals the angel of the Lord came down into the pool, and the water was

disturbed, and the first person to enter the water after this disturbance was cured
5 of any ailment he suffered from. •One man there had an illness which had lasted
6 thirty-eight years, •and when Jesus saw him lying there and knew he had been in
7 this condition for a long time, he said, 'Do you want to be well again?' •'Sir,'
replied the sick man 'I have no one to put me into the pool when the water is
disturbed; and while I am still on the way, someone else gets there before me.'
8 9 Jesus said, 'Get up, pick up your sleeping-mat and walk'. •The man was cured Mt 9:6
at once, and he picked up his mat and walked away.

10 Now that day happened to be the sabbath, •so the Jews said to the man who 9:14 Ex 20:8+
had been cured, 'It is the sabbath; you are not allowed to carry your sleeping- Jr 17:21-27
11 mat'. •He replied, 'But the man who cured me told me, "Pick up your mat and
12 walk" '. •They asked, 'Who is the man who said to you, "Pick up your mat and
13 walk"?' •The man had no idea who it was, since Jesus had disappeared into the
14 crowd that filled the place. •After a while Jesus met him in the Temple and said, Mt 9:2+
'Now you are well again, be sure not to sin any more, or something worse may 8:11 Mt 12:45
15 happen to you'.[d] •The man went back and told the Jews that it was Jesus who
16 had cured him. •It was because he did things like this on the sabbath that the Mt 12:8
17 Jews began to persecute Jesus.[e] •His answer to them was, 'My Father goes on 7:23; 9:4
18 working, and so do I'.[f] •But that only made the Jews even more intent on killing 7:1,19,25; 11:53
him, because, not content with breaking the sabbath, he spoke of God as his own *2:16; 10:33* Ws 2:16
Father, and so made himself God's equal. Mt 12:14

19 To this accusation Jesus replied:

'I tell you most solemnly,
the Son can do nothing by himself; 8:28-29
he can do only what he sees the Father doing:
and whatever the Father does the Son does too.
20 For the Father loves the Son 3:35
and shows him everything he does himself,
and he will show him even greater things than these,
works that will astonish you.
21 Thus, as the Father raises the dead and gives them life, Dt 32:39 1 S 2:6 2 K 5:7
so the Son gives life to anyone he chooses; *3:35+ 5:27*
22 for the Father judges[g] no one; Dn 7:10
he has entrusted all judgement to the Son, Ac 10:42+
23 so that all may honour the Son
as they honour the Father.
Whoever refuses honour to the Son 17:6+
refuses honour to the Father who sent him.
24 I tell you most solemnly,
whoever listens to my words, 10:27; 18:37
and believes in the one who sent me, 3:11+ 1 Jn 2:25

k. A harvest of souls: the Samaritans who are coming to Jesus, v. 30, are its first-fruits.

l. The reapers are the apostles, the sowers those who have laboured before them, especially Jesus.

m. Not merely 'King of Israel' as in 1:49. This world-perspective is typical of John, cf. 1:29; 3:16; 11:52; 1 Jn 2:2. Nevertheless, 'salvation comes from the Jews', 4:22.

5 a. Var. 'the festival'. Possibly Pentecost, or Tabernacles.

b. Var. 'Bethesda' (house of mercy), 'Bethsaida' or 'Belsetha'.

c. Probably due to the inflow of fresh water from time to time. The best witnesses omit 'waiting for the water to move' and the whole of v. 4.

d. Jesus does not say that the disease was the result of sin, cf. 9:2f. He warns the man that his cure is a divine favour that must be acknowledged by conversion, cf. Mt 9:2-8; to forget this is to risk something worse than the disease. The miracle is therefore a 'sign' of spiritual resurrection, v. 24.

e. The episode is concluded in 7:19-23. The discourse of 5:19-47 falls into two parts: 1. the Father commits lifegiving power to the Son, vv. 19-30; 2. the Father bears witness to the Son: a. through the Baptist, b. through the works the Father does through Jesus, c. through the scriptures (Moses), vv. 31-47.

f. Jewish theologians reconciled the fact that God 'rested' after the work of creation (the sabbath was the human counterpart of this 'rest', Gn 2:2f) with his unceasing, active government of the world, by distinguishing between God's activity as creator, which is now at an end, and his activity as judge (or 'governor'), which never ends. Jesus claims that what he does and what the Father does are one and the same. Hence the anger of the Jews and Christ's vindication of his claim.

g. Power over life and death expresses the highest judicial function, cf. v. 21.

3:18 has eternal life;
without being brought to judgement
1 Jn 3:14 he has passed from death to life.
I tell you most solemnly, 25
the hour will come—in fact it is here already—
10:16; 11: 25-26 when the dead[h] will hear the voice of the Son of God,
8:51 and all who hear it will live.
6:57 1 Jn 5:11 For the Father, who is the source of life, 26
3:35+ has made the Son the source of life;
Mt 8:20+ and, because he is the Son of Man, 27
5:22 Dn 7:13,22 has appointed him supreme judge.
Mt 9:6 2 Co 5:10 Do not be surprised at this, 28
for the hour is coming
when the dead will leave their graves
3:11+; 11: 43-44 at the sound of his voice:[i]
Mt 25:46 those who did good 29
will rise again to life;
Dn 12:2 Mt 16:27; and those who did evil, to condemnation.
25:46 Ac 24:15 I can do nothing by myself; 30
I can only judge as I am told to judge,[j]
and my judging is just,
4:34; 6:38 because my aim is to do not my own will,
but the will of him who sent me.

8:13-14 'Were I to testify on my own behalf, 31
my testimony would not be valid;
1 Jn 5:9 but there is another witness[k] who can speak on my behalf, 32
and I know[l] that his testimony is valid.
1:19-28 You sent messengers to John, 33
Mt 11:7-11p and he gave his testimony to the truth:
8:18 not that I depend on human testimony; 34
no, it is for your salvation that I speak of this.
1:8 Si 48:1 John was a lamp alight and shining 35
Mt 3:7 and for a time you were content to enjoy the light that he gave.
But my testimony is greater than John's: 36
10:25 the works my Father has given me to carry out,
these same works of mine
1:1+ testify that the Father has sent me.
Besides, the Father who sent me 37
2:11+; 6: 44-45; 8:18 bears witness to me himself.
1 Jn 5:9 You have never heard his voice,
you have never seen his shape,
1 Jn 2:14 and his word finds no home in you 38
8:37 because you do not believe
in the one he has sent.

1:45; 2:22; 5:47; 7:52; 'You study[m] the scriptures, 39
8:56; 12: 16,41; 19: believing that in them you have eternal life;[n]
28; 20:9 Ac 17:12 now these same scriptures testify to me,[o]
and yet you refuse to come to me for life! 40
1:14 1 Th 2:6 As for human approval, this means nothing to me. 41
Besides, I know you too well: 42
1 Jn 2:15; 3:17 you have no love of God in you.
I have come in the name of my Father 43
and you refuse to accept me;
Mt 24:5,24+ if someone else comes in his own name
you will accept him.

4 How can you believe,
since you look to one another for approval 12:43
and are not concerned Mt 6:1 Rm 2:29
with the approval that comes from the one God?[p] 1 Co 4:5 1 Th 2:6
5 Do not imagine that I am going to accuse you before the Father:
you place your hopes on Moses,
and Moses will be your accuser. Dt 31:26
6 If you really believed him
you would believe me too, 5:39+ Dt 18:15
since it was I that he was writing about; Mt 8:10+ Lk 16:31
7 but if you refuse to believe what he wrote,
how can you believe what I say?'

IV. ANOTHER PASSOVER, THE BREAD OF LIFE

The miracle of the loaves

||Mt 14:13-21 ||Mk 6:32-44 ||Lk 9:10-17

1 6 Some time after this, Jesus went off to the other side of the Sea of Galilee—
2 or of Tiberias—•and a large crowd followed him, impressed by the signs he
3 gave by curing the sick. •Jesus climbed the hillside, and sat down there with his
4 disciples. •It was shortly before the Jewish feast of Passover.[a] 11:55
5 Looking up, Jesus saw the crowds approaching and said to Philip, 'Where
6 can we buy some bread for these people to eat?' •He only said this to test Philip;
7 he himself knew exactly what he was going to do. •Philip answered, 'Two hundred
8 denarii would only buy enough to give them a small piece each'. •One of his Nb 11:22
9 disciples, Andrew, Simon Peter's brother, said, •'There is a small boy here
0 with five barley loaves and two fish; but what is that between so many?' •Jesus
said to them, 'Make the people sit down'. There was plenty of grass there, and
1 as many as five thousand men sat down. •Then Jesus took the loaves, gave 21:13
thanks, and gave them out to all who were sitting ready; he then did the same with
2 the fish, giving out as much as was wanted. •When they had eaten enough he
said to the disciples, 'Pick up the pieces left over, so that nothing gets wasted'.
3 So they picked them up, and filled twelve hampers with scraps left over from the 2 K 4:42-44
4 meal of five barley loaves. •The people, seeing this sign that he had given, said,
5 'This really is the prophet who is to come into the world'. •Jesus, who could see 1:21+
they were about to come and take him by force and make him king, escaped[b] 1:49; 12:13; 18:36
back to the hills by himself. Heb 12:2 *Mk 1:34+*

Jesus walks on the waters

||Mt 14:22-33 ||Mk 6:45-52

6 7 That evening the disciples went down to the shore of the lake and •got into
a boat to make for Capernaum on the other side of the lake. It was getting
8 dark by now and Jesus had still not rejoined them. •The wind was strong, and
9 the sea was getting rough. •They had rowed three or four miles when they saw
Jesus walking on the lake and coming towards the boat. This frightened them,
0 1 but he said, 'It is I. Do not be afraid.'[c] •They were for taking him into the boat,
but in no time it reached the shore at the place they were making for.

The discourse in the synagogue at Capernaum[d]

2 Next day, the crowd that had stayed on the other side saw that only one boat

h. The spiritually dead.
i. The reference is to the resurrection of the dead at the last day, cf. Mt 22:29-32.
j. Lit. 'as I hear'. It is the Father whom Jesus 'hears'.
k. The Father.
l. Var. 'you know', wrongly making this verse refer to the Baptist's testimony, v. 33.
m. Alternative translation 'study', imperative.
n. On the scriptures as source of life, cf. Dt 4:1; 8:1,3; 30:15-20; 32:46f; Ba 4:1; Ps 119, etc.
o. The scriptures converge on Jesus who is their focus, cf. 1:45; 2:22; 5:39,46; 12:16,41; 19:28; 20:9.
p. Var. 'from the Only One'.

6 a. The bread Jesus gives is to be the new Passover.
b. Var. 'withdrew'.
c. Om. 'Do not be afraid'.
d. Some interpreters hold that a discourse about the Eucharist (6:51-58: Jesus nourishing the soul with

had been there, and that Jesus had not got into the boat with his disciples, but
that the disciples had set off by themselves. •Other boats, however, had put in 23
from Tiberias, near the place where the bread had been eaten.[e] •When the 24
people saw that neither Jesus nor his disciples were there, they got into those
boats and crossed to Capernaum to look for Jesus. •When they found him on 25
the other side, they said to him, 'Rabbi, when did you come here?' •Jesus ans- 26
wered:

'I tell you most solemnly,
you are not looking for me
2:11+ because you have seen the signs
but because you had all the bread you wanted to eat.
Is 55:2 Lk 10:42 Do not work for food that cannot last, 27
but work for food that endures to eternal life,
Mt 8:20+ the kind of food the Son of Man is offering[f] you,
for on him the Father, God himself, has set his seal.'[g]

Then they said to him, 'What must we do if we are to do the works that God 28
wants?' •Jesus gave them this answer, 'This is working for God:[h] you must 29
Mt 8:10+; 16:1-4 Lk 11:29-32 *1:21+;* *2:11+* *Ex 16:4f* Ps 78:24 believe in the one he has sent'. •So they said, 'What sign will you give to show us 30
that we should believe in you? What work will you do? •Our fathers had manna 31
to eat in the desert; as scripture says: *He gave them bread from heaven to eat.*'
Jesus answered: 32

'I tell you most solemnly,
it was not Moses who gave you bread from heaven,
Mt 6:11 it is my Father who gives you the bread from heaven,
the true bread;
for the bread of God 33
is that which comes down from heaven
and gives life to the world'.

2:19+; 4:15 'Sir,' they said 'give us that bread always.' •Jesus answered: 34 35

4:10+,14 Pr 9:1-6 Si 24:19-22 Is 55:1-3 Mt 11:19 Lk 7:35; 11:31 1 Co 1:24 *2:11+;* 15:24 'I am[i] the bread of life.
He who comes to me will never be hungry;
he who believes in me will never thirst.[j]
But, as I have told you, 36
you can see me and still you do not believe.
4:14 All that the Father gives me will come to me, 37
and whoever comes to me[k]
I shall not turn him away;
4:34; 5:30; 12:27+; 14:31; 15:10 Mt 26:39 Heb 10:9 because I have come from heaven, 38
not to do my own will,
but to do the will of the one who sent me.
Now the will of him who sent me 39
3:35+; 10:28,29; 17:12; 18:9 is that I should lose nothing
of all that he has given to me,
and that I should raise it up on the last day.
Yes, it is my Father's will 40
1 Jn 2:25 that whoever sees the Son[l] and believes in him
shall have eternal life,
and that I shall raise him up on the last day.'

Meanwhile the Jews were complaining[m] to each other about him, because he 41
Mt 13:54-57 Mk 6:1-6 had said, 'I am the bread that came down from heaven'. •'Surely this is Jesus 42
son of Joseph' they said. 'We know his father and mother. How can he now say,
"I have come down from heaven"?' •Jesus said in reply, 'Stop complaining to 43
each other.

4 'No one can come to me
unless he is drawn by the Father who sent me, 5:37 Mt 16:17
and I will raise him up at the last day.
5 It is written in the prophets:
They will all be taught by God, Is 54:13 Jr 31:33f 1 Th 4:9 1 Jn 2:20,27
and to hear the teaching of the Father,
and learn from it,
is to come to me.
6 Not that anybody has seen the Father, 1:18 Ex 33:20+ 1 Jn 4:12
except the one who comes from God:
he has seen the Father. 7:29
7 I tell you most solemnly,
everybody who believes has eternal life.
8 I am the bread of life.
9 Your fathers ate the manna in the desert
and they are dead;
0 but this is the bread that comes down from heaven,
so that a man may eat it and not die.
1 I am the living bread which has come down from heaven. Is 25:6 Mt 26:26f
Anyone who eats this bread will live for ever;
and the bread that I shall give Lk 22:19p
is my flesh,[n] for the life of the world.'[o] 1 Co 11:24

52 Then the Jews started arguing with one another: 'How can this man give
53 us his flesh to eat?' they said. •Jesus replied:

'I tell you most solemnly,
if you do not eat the flesh of the Son of Man 1:14+ Mt 8:20+
and drink his blood,
you will not have life in you.
54 Anyone who does eat my flesh and drink my blood Is 25:6
has eternal life,
and I shall raise him up on the last day.
55 For my flesh is real food
and my blood is real drink.
56 He who eats my flesh and drinks my blood 15:4-5

his flesh and blood, cf. 6:51+) has been inserted into the narrative-discourse which may be summarised as follows: the Jews ask for a 'sign' like that of the manna, vv. 30-31; cf. 1:21+; Jesus tells them, 'The Father's message, which I pass on to man, (cf. 3:11+) makes of me man's true bread, a nourishment that only those with faith can receive', vv. 32f; the Jews do not understand, vv. 60-66; only Peter and the disciples believe, vv. 67-71. (This doctrine is best understood in the light of Dt 8:3; Pr 8:22-24 and 9:1-6; Si 24:3 and 24:17-21; Lk 11:29-32.)

6 e. Add. 'after the Lord had given thanks'.

f. Var. 'will offer'.

g. The 'seal' that Jesus received at his baptism, namely the Spirit, Mt 3:16+, who is the power of God operative in Christ's 'signs'. Cf. Ac 10:38; Mt 12:28; Ep 1:13; 4:30; 2 Co 1:22.

h. For 'works' in the Jewish sense Jesus substitutes faith in God's envoy.

i. The Greek phrase *ego eimi* recalls the name that God revealed to Moses, Ex 3:14+, cf. Jn 8:24+, but here (and frequently elsewhere) it also forms the prelude to the explanation of a parable. In this case the parable is not in words but in action: the gift of the manna and the multiplication of the loaves are explained as parables of Christ's gift of himself, the true bread.

j. As Wisdom invites man to her table, Pr 9:1f, so does Jesus. Jn sees him as the Wisdom of God which, in the O.T. revelation, was already moving towards personification, cf. 1:1+. This perception springs from Christ's own teaching already recorded in the Synoptics, Mt 11:19; Lk 11:31p, but given here much more clearly by Jn. Thus, Christ's origin is mysterious, Jn 7:27-29; 8:14,19; cf. Jb 28:20-28; he alone knows the secrets of God and reveals them to man, 3:11-12,31-32; cf. Mt 11:25-27p; Ws 9:13-18; Ba 3:29-38; he is the living bread that supremely satisfies, 6:35; cf. Pr 9:1-6; Si 24:19-22, if men will only come to him, 3:20,21; 5:40; 6:35,37,44,65; 7:37; cf. Pr 9:4-5; Si 24:19; Mt 11:28; but they must seek him before it is too late, 7:34; 8:21; cf. Pr 1:28. Cf. also Is 55:1-3. For Paul's teaching, cf. 1 Co 1:24+.

k. To 'come to' Jesus is to believe in him.

l. 'Seeing' the Son is perceiving and acknowledging that he is in truth the Son sent by the Father, cf. 12:45; 14:9; 17:6+.

m. As their forefathers did in the desert, cf. Ex 16:2f; 17:3; Nb 11:1; 14:27; 1 Co 10:10.

n. Add. 'that I shall give'; the phrase is, in any case, to be understood.

o. Jesus is the true bread because he is God's Word, vv. 32f, and also because he is a victim whose body and blood are offered in sacrifice for the life of the world, vv. 51-58, cf. 6:22+. The word 'flesh' suggests a connection between Eucharist and incarnation: the Word made flesh, 1:14, is the food of man.

lives in me
and I live in him.
As I, who am sent by the living Father,
myself draw life from the Father,
5:26; 14:19 so whoever eats me will draw life from me.[p] 5
This is the bread come down from heaven;
not like the bread our ancestors ate:[q] 5
they are dead,
but anyone who eats this bread will live for ever.'

He taught this doctrine at Capernaum, in the synagogue. •After hearing it, 5 6
3:11+ many of his followers said, 'This is intolerable language. How could anyone
1:48+ Mt 11:6 accept it?' •Jesus was aware that his followers were complaining about it and 6
12:32+ Mt 8:20+ said, 'Does this upset you? •What if you should see the Son of Man ascend to 6
where he was before?

1:33+; 3:6 'It is the spirit that gives life,
the flesh has nothing to offer. 6
3:11+ The words I have spoken to you are spirit
and they are life.[r]

1:48+ 'But there are some of you who do not believe.' For Jesus knew from the outset 6
those who did not believe, and who it was that would betray him. •He went on, 6
'This is why I told you that no one could come to me unless the Father allows
Lk 22:28 him'. •After this, many of his disciples left him and stopped going with him. 6

||Mt 16:16p **Peter's profession of faith**

Then Jesus said to the Twelve, 'What about you, do you want to go away too?' 6
1:21+ Dt 8:3 Simon Peter answered, 'Lord, who shall we go to? You have the message of 6
Ac 3:14+; 7:38 eternal life, •and we believe; we know that you are the Holy One of God.'[s] 6
10:36; 17:19 Jesus replied, 'Have I not chosen you, you Twelve? Yet one of you is a devil.' 7
13:18 He meant Judas son of Simon Iscariot, since this was the man, one of the Twelve, 7
13:2,27 who was going to betray him.

V. THE FEAST OF TABERNACLES

Jesus goes up to Jerusalem for the feast and teaches there

5:18; 11:54 Mk 9:30p **7** After this Jesus stayed in Galilee; he could not[a] stay in Judaea, because the 1
Jews were out to kill him.
Ex 23:14+ Nb 29:12 As the Jewish feast of Tabernacles drew near, •his brothers[b] said to him, 2 3
Zc 14:16-19 *Mt 5:15* 'Why not leave this place and go to Judaea, and let your disciples[c] see the works
2:11+ you are doing; •if a man wants to be known he does not do things in secret; since 4
you are doing all this, you should let the whole world see'. •Not even his brothers, 5
2:4+ in fact, had faith in him. •Jesus answered, 'The right time[d] for me has not come yet, 6
1:10+ but any time is the right time for you. •The world cannot hate you, but it does 7
3:19; 8:12+ hate me, because I give evidence that its ways are evil. •Go up to the festival 8
yourselves: I am not going[e] to this festival, because for me the time is not ripe
yet.' • Having said that, he stayed behind in Galilee. 9
However, after his brothers had left for the festival, he went up as well, but 10
quite privately, without drawing attention to himself. •At the festival the Jews 11
were on the look-out for him: 'Where is he?' they said. •People stood in groups 12
Mt 27:63 whispering[f] about him. Some said, 'He is a good man'; others, 'No, he is leading
Jn 9:22 the people astray'. •Yet no one spoke about him openly, for fear of the Jews. 13
When the festival was half over, Jesus went to the Temple and began to 14
Mt 7:28; 13:54-57 teach.[g] •The Jews were astonished and said, 'How did he learn to read? He has 15
Lk 2:47 Ac 4:13 not been taught.' •Jesus answered them: 16

'My teaching is not from myself: 3:11+
it comes from the one who sent me;
17 and if anyone is prepared to do his will,
he will know whether my teaching is from God
or whether my doctrine is my own.
18 When a man's doctrine is his own 8:50
he is hoping to get honour for himself;
but when he is working for the honour of one who sent him,
then he is sincere
and by no means an impostor.
19 Did not Moses give you the Law? 8:37-41 Rm 2:17-23
And yet not one of you keeps the Law!

20 'Why do you want to kill me?' •The crowd replied, 'You are mad! Who wants 8:48,52; 10:20
21 to kill you?' •Jesus answered, 'One work I did, and you are all surprised by it. Mt 5:1-9
22 Moses ordered you to practise circumcision—not that it began with him, it goes Gn 17:10+ Ac 7:8
23 back to the patriarchs—and you circumcise on the sabbath. •Now if a man Rm 4:11
can be circumcised on the sabbath so that the Law of Moses is not broken, Mt 12:1-5, 11-12
why are you angry with me for making a man whole and complete on a sabbath?[h] Lk 14:5
24 Do not keep judging according to appearances; let your judgement be according 8:15 Is 11:3
to what is right.' Zc 7:9 Lk 13:5f

The people discuss the origin of the Messiah

25 Meanwhile some of the people of Jerusalem were saying, 'Isn't this the man 5:18
26 they want to kill? •And here he is, speaking freely, and they have nothing to
say to him! Can it be true the authorities[i] have made up their minds that he is
27 the Christ? •Yet we all know where he comes from, but when the Christ appears 1:26 Heb 7:3
no one will know where he comes from.'[j]
28 Then, as Jesus taught in the Temple, he cried out:

'Yes, you know me and you know where I came from. 8:19; 19:9+
Yet I have not come of myself:
no, there is one who sent me and I really come from him,[k] 3:34; 8:26
and you do not know him,
29 but I know him 6:46; 8:55
because I have come from him[l] 1:1+
and it was he who sent me.'

30 They would have arrested him then, but because his time had not yet come 7:44 Lk 4:29f
no one laid a hand on him. *2:4+; 8:20*

p. The life that the Father communicates to the Son passes to the faithful through the Eucharist.

q. Add. 'the manna' or 'in the desert'.

r. Christ's words about the bread from heaven reveal something real and divine of which only the Spirit, cf. 1:33+, can supply understanding, cf. 14:26+, and which is the source of life for men.

s. I.e. the Messiah, God's chosen envoy, consecrated and united in him uniquely, cf. 10:36; 17:19. Var. 'you are the Christ, the Son of God' or 'the Son of the living God', cf. Mt 16:16.

7 a. Var. 'he did not wish to'.

b. In the wide sense: cousins, relations, cf. Mt 12:46+.

c. Those in Jerusalem and Judaea, cf. 2:23; 3:26; 4:1.

d. I.e. 'my hour', cf. 2:4+.

e. Var. 'I am not going yet'.

f. Lit. 'There was whispering (var. much whispering) about him in the crowds'.

g. 7:14-52 is made up of separate passages with a common theme—the uncertainty about Christ's origin. 1. His human origin obscures his divine: he has never been a pupil of the rabbis, what is his knowledge worth? (vv. 14-18); the details of his childhood are known, how can he be the Messiah? (vv. 25-30). 2. His reputed birth at Nazareth shows that he is not the Christ (vv. 40-52). The theme of 'departure', too, (vv. 33-36, cf. 8:21-23) is connected with that of divine origin: the man Christ departs for the place where (in his divine nature, cf. vv. 29 and 34) he has always been. Vv. 19-24 are the conclusion of 5:1-16 and are alien to the present context.

h. The argument is rabbinic in type: circumcision was reckoned the 'healing' of one member; if this 'healing' of one member was allowed on the sabbath, how much more the healing of the whole man?

i. Var. 'the chief priests' or 'the elders' or 'they'.

j. They knew that the Messiah was to be born in Bethlehem, v. 42; Mt 2:5f, but it was commonly believed that he would lie hidden in some secret place, cf. Mt 24:26, (in heaven, according to some) until the day of his coming. This belief was vindicated, though his audience did not recognise it, by Christ's heavenly origin.

k. Lit. 'he who sent me is true' (var. 'truthful').

l. Var. 'because I am at his side'.

Jesus foretells his approaching departure

There were many people in the crowds, however, who believed in him; they 31
2:11+ were saying, 'When the Christ comes, will he give more signs than this man?'
Hearing that rumours like this about him were spreading among the people, 32
the Pharisees[m] sent the Temple police to arrest him.
Then Jesus said: 33

16:16 'I shall remain with you for only a short time now;
1:1+ then I shall go back to the one who sent me.
8:21; 12:21. 26; 14: 3.19 You will look for me and will not find me:[n] 34
where I am
Dt 4:29 Pr 1:28 Is 55:6 Ho 5:6 you cannot come.'

The Jews then said to one another, 'Where is he going that we shan't be 35
Jm 1:1+ 1 P 1:1+ able to find him? Is he going abroad to the people who are dispersed among
the Greeks and will he teach the Greeks? •What does he mean when he says: 36

2:19+ "You will look for me and will not find me:
where I am,
you cannot come"?'

The promise of living water

Nb 29:35 *Pr 1:20; 8:3* On the last day and greatest day of the festival,[o] Jesus stood there and cried 37
out:

4:1+ Nb 20:11 Pr 18:4 Is 55:1.3 'If any man is thirsty, let him come to me![p]
Let the man come and drink •who believes in me!' 38

2:21+; 19:34 As scripture says: From his breast[q] shall flow fountains of living water.[r]
1 Co 10:4+ He was speaking of the Spirit which those who believed in him were to receive; 39
1:33+ Ac5:32;19:2 for there was no Spirit as yet[s] because Jesus had not yet been glorified.

Fresh discussions on the origin of the Messiah

1:21+ Several people who had been listening said, 'Surely he must be the prophet', 40
2 S 7:1-2+ *Mt 9:27+* and some said, 'He is the Christ', but others said, 'Would the Christ be from 41
Rm 1:3 Galilee? •Does not scripture say that the Christ must be descended from David 42
Mi 5:1 Mt 2:5f and come from the town of Bethlehem?'[t] •So the people could not agree about 43
3:11; 7:30 him. •Some would have liked to arrest him, but no one actually laid hands on 44
him.
The police went back to the chief priests and Pharisees who said to them, 45
Mt 13:54-56 Lk 2:47; 'Why haven't you brought him?' •The police replied, 'There has never been 46
4:22 anybody who has spoken like him'. •'So' the Pharisees answered 'you have been 47
3:1 Mt 11:25 led astray as well? •Have any of the authorities believed in him? Any of the 48
9:34 Pharisees? •This rabble knows nothing about the Law—they are damned.' 49
3:1+; 19:39 One of them, Nicodemus—the same man who had come to Jesus earlier—said to 50
Dt 1:16f; 17:4 them, •'But surely the Law does not allow us to pass judgement on a man without 51
5:39 giving him a hearing and discovering what he is about?' •To this they answered, 52
1:46 Mt 16:14+ 'Are you a Galilean too? Go into the matter, and see for yourself: prophets do
not come out of Galilee.'

The adulterous woman[u]

They all went home, 8 and Jesus went to the Mount of Olives. 53 1
At daybreak he appeared in the Temple again; and as all the people came 2
Lk 21:37-38 to him, he sat down and began to teach them.
The scribes and Pharisees brought a woman along who had been caught 3
Lk 7:37-50 committing adultery; and making her stand there in full view of everybody,
Jb 31:11 Dn 13:22 they said to Jesus, 'Master, this woman was caught in the very act of committing 4
Lv 20:10 Dt 22:22-24 adultery, •and Moses has ordered us in the Law to condemn women like this to 5

6 death by stoning. What have you to say?' •They asked him this as a test, looking
for something to use against him. But Jesus bent down and started writing on Mt 12:10; 19:3
7 the ground with his finger.[a] •As they persisted with their question, he looked Lk 20:20
up and said, 'If there is one of you who has not sinned, let him be the first to Dt 17:7 Mt 7:1-5
8 throw a stone at her'. •Then he bent down and wrote on the ground again.
9 When they heard this they went away one by one, beginning with the eldest,
10 until Jesus was left alone with the woman, who remained standing there. •He
looked up and said, 'Woman, where are they? Has no one condemned you?' Ezk 18:32; 33:11
11 'No one, sir' she replied. 'Neither do I condemn you,' said Jesus 'go away, and *Ps 103:8, 13-14*
don't sin any more.' *5:14* Ezk 18:23

Jesus, the light of the world[b]

12 When Jesus spoke to the people again, he said:

'I am the light of the world; Gn 1:5 Ex 13:22
anyone who follows me will not be walking in the dark; Jb 11:17; 18:5
he will have the light of life'. Is 42:6; 58:10 Lm 3:2 Jl 2:2 Am 5:18 Mi 7:8 Mt 5:14

A discussion on the testimony of Jesus to himself

13 At this the Pharisees said to him, 'You are testifying on your own behalf;
14 your testimony is not valid'. •Jesus replied:

'It is true that I am testifying on my own behalf,
but my testimony is still valid, 3:11+; 5:31
because I know
where I came from and where I am going;
but you do not know 14:28
where I come from or where I am going.[c]
15 You judge by human standards;[d] 7:24; 12:47 Rm 7:5
I judge[e] no one,

m. Var. 'Pharisees and chief priests', 'They and the chief priests', 'Chief priests and Pharisees'.

n. Christ, like God himself, must be sought while there is still time to find him. But the Jews will let his 'time' slip by and instead of coming to them, salvation will come to the pagans (the 'Greeks'). Cf. 12:20-21; 12:32+; 19:37+.

o. The day, the 7th or perhaps the 8th, celebrating the end of the festival.

p. Om. 'to me'. Christ's invitation resembles that of divine Wisdom, cf. 6:35+.

q. From Jesus himself, according to the oldest tradition, though another has joined 'the man who believes in me' with what follows, making the 'streams' flow from the believer.

r. The liturgy of the feast of Tabernacles, which formed the background of these words, included prayers for rain, rites which commemorated the Mosaic water-miracle, Ex 17:1-7; cf. 1 Co 10:4, and readings from biblical passages foretelling lifegiving water for Zion, Zc 14:8; Ezk 47:1f. Cf. Jn 4:1+.

s. Var. 'the Spirit had not yet been given'.

t. Add. 'where David was', 'of David', or 'where he was'. Only Christ's intimates knew that he had been born in Bethlehem.

u. The author of this passage, 7:53-8:11, is not John: it is omitted by the oldest witnesses (MSS, versions, Fathers) and found elsewhere in others; moreover, its style is that of the Synoptics and the author was possibly Luke, cf. Lk 21:38+. Nevertheless, the passage was accepted in the canon and there are no grounds for regarding it as unhistorical.

8 a. The significance of the gesture is doubtful.

b. The development in the N.T. of the light-darkness theme can be traced fairly clearly along three main lines: 1. Just as the sun lights man on his way, so anything that shows him his way to God is 'light': of old it was the Law, the Wisdom and Word of God, Qo 2:13; Pr 4:18-19; 6:23; Ps 119:105; cf. Rm 2:19; now it is Christ, Jn 1:9; 9:1-39; 12:35; 1 Jn 2:8-11; cf. 2 Co 4:6, who is compared with the bright cloud that led the Israelites, Jn 8:12; cf. Ex 13:21f; Ws 18:3f; it is also his followers from whom the light of God's own perfections shines on men, Mt 5:14-16; Lk 8:16; Rv 21:24. 2. Light is symbolic of life, contentment, and joy, as darkness is of death, unhappiness, and misery, Jb 30:26; Is 45:7; cf. Ps 17:15+; hence, enslavement is darkness, the deliverance and salvation of the messianic age is light, Is 8:22-9:1; Mt 4:16; Lk 1:79; Rm 13:11-12. This light shines even on the pagan nations, Lk 2:32; Ac 13:47, through Christ who is the Light. Jn (cf. texts just quoted); Ep 5:14; it is at its brightest in the kingdom of heaven, Mt 8:12; 22:13; 25:30; Rv 22:5; cf. 21:3-4. 3. The 'light-darkness' contrast came to be used for the mutually hostile worlds of Good and Evil (cf. the Essene texts of Qumran). Thus in the N.T. there are two 'empires', Christ the lord of one, Satan of the other, 2 Co 6:14-15; Col 1:12-13; Ac 26:18; 1 P 2:9, each striving for the mastery, Lk 22:53; Jn 13:29-30. Men are either 'sons of light' or 'sons of darkness', Lk 16:8; 1 Th 5:5; Ep 5:7-8; Jn 12:36, according as their life is ruled by the light (Christ) or by darkness (Satan), 1 Th 5:4f; 1 Jn 1:6-7; 2:9-10, and what they do shows which they are, Rm 13:12-14; Ep 5:8-11. The coming of the Light makes clear this distinction ('judgement') of man from man, because this coming forces everyone to declare himself either for or against, Jn 3:19-21; 7:7; 9:39; 12:46; cf. Ep 5:12-13. But one day all will be well, and one day the darkness will yield to the light, Jn 1:5; 1 Jn 2:8; Rm 13:12.

c. It is enough for the Son to be his own witness since he alone knows the mystery of his heavenly origin, cf. Mt 11:27p.

d. The Jews judge by what they see: a man like themselves; 'in that flesh they fail to see the glory of God's Son shining' (St Augustine).

e. In the semitic sense of the word, i. e. 'condemn'.

but if I judge, 16
5:30; 8:29 my judgement will be sound,
because I am not alone:
10:30+ the one who sent me is with me;
Dt 17:6; 19:15 Nb 35:30 and in your Law it is written 17
that the testimony of two witnesses is valid.
I may be testifying on my own behalf, 18
5:23,37 but the Father who sent me is my witness too.'

They asked him, 'Where is your Father?' Jesus answered: 19

7:28; 12:45; 15:21 *14:7* 'You do not know me, nor do you know my Father;
if you did know me, you would know my Father as well'.

Mk 12:41 + He spoke these words in the Treasury, while teaching in the Temple. No one 20
2:4+; 7:30 arrested him, because his time had not yet come.

The unbelieving Jews warned

7:33-36 Again he said to them: 21

7:34+; 14-19 'I am going away; you will look for me
Dt 24:16 Ezk 18:20; 33:12-20 Ho 5:6 and you will die in your sin.[f]
Where I am going, you cannot come.'

The Jews said to one another, 'Will he kill himself? Is that what he means by 22
13:33,36 saying, "Where I am going, you cannot come"?' •Jesus went on: 23

'You are from below;
I am from above.
1:10+ You are of this world;
3:31; 17:14; 18:36 I am not of this world.
I have told you already: You will die in your sins. 24
1:1+; 8:28 Ex 3:14+ Is 43:11 Lk 13:5 3 Jn 7+ Yes, if you do not believe that I am He,[g]
you will die in your sins.'

10:24 So they said to him, 'Who are you?' Jesus answered: 25

'What I have told you from the outset.[h]
About you I have much to say 26
and much to condemn;
3:33; 7:28 but the one who sent me is truthful,
and what I have learnt from him
12:48-50 I declare to the world.'

They failed to understand that he was talking to them about the Father. 27
So Jesus said: 28

12:32+ Mt 8:20+ 'When you have lifted up the Son of Man,
8:24+ then you will know that I am He[i]
and that I do nothing of myself:
3:11; 5:19 what the Father has taught me
is what I preach;
8:16; 10:17. 30+; 15:10; 16:3, 32 1 Jn 3:22 he who sent me is with me, 29
and has not left me to myself,
for I always do what pleases him'.

As he was saying this, many came to believe in him. 30

Jesus and Abraham

To the Jews who believed in him Jesus said: 31

3:11+ Rm 9:8 'If you make my word your home
you will indeed be my disciples,

32 you will learn the truth
and the truth will make you free'. Is 42:7 Dn 9:13 Ga 4:25

33 They answered, 'We are descended from Abraham and we have never been Mt 3:9
34 the slaves of anyone; what do you mean, "You will be made free"?' •Jesus replied: Lm 2:17

'I tell you most solemnly, 2:19+ Rm 6:17-19
everyone who commits sin is a slave.[j] 2 P 2:19
35 Now the slave's place in the house is not assured, 14:2 Gn 21:10
but the son's place is assured. Jr 2:14f Ga 4:30f
36 So if the Son makes you free, Ga 5:1
you will be free indeed.
37 I know that you are descended from Abraham; Mt 21:33-46
but in spite of that you want to kill me
because nothing I say has penetrated into you. 5:38; 7:19; 12:48
38 What I, for my part, speak of Rv 2:9+
is what I have seen with my Father; 3:11+
but you, you put into action
the lessons learnt from your father.'

39 They repeated, 'Our father is Abraham'. Jesus said to them:

'If you were Abraham's children,
you would do as Abraham did.[k]
40 As it is, you want to kill me
when I tell you the truth
as I have learnt it from God;
that is not what Abraham did. Gn 15:6; 17:1
41 What you are doing is what your father does.'

'We were not born of prostitution,'[l] they went on 'we have one father: God.' Ex 4:22 Dt 32:6
42 Jesus answered:

'If God were your father, you would love me,
since I have come here from God; yes, I have come from him; Mk 1:38+ 1 Jn 5:1
not that I came because I chose,
no, I was sent, and by him. 1:1+
43 Do you know why you cannot take in what I say?
It is because you are unable to understand my language.[m]
44 The devil is your father, 19:11 Ac 7:51-52; 13:10
and you prefer to do 1 Jn 3:8-15
what your father wants.

8 f. By rejecting Jesus, the Jews are heading for irremediable loss; they are sinning against the truth, vv. 40,45f. It is the sin against the Spirit, Mt 12:31p. Cf. Jn 7:34+.

g. 'I Am' or 'I am He' is the divine name revealed to Moses, Ex 3:14+; it means that the God of Israel is unique, the true God, Dt 32:39. When Jesus appropriates this name, he is claiming to be the one incomparable saviour, the goal of Israel's faith and hope. Cf. Jn 8:28,58; 13:19 and also 6:35; 18:5,8.

h. A very obscure text; it is variously rendered 'Why, in the first place, am I speaking to you?'; 'Why should I speak to you at all?'; 'What I have been telling you from the beginning'; 'Precisely what I am telling you'. Our translation resembles this last but preserves the idea of temporal priority which leads up to the following 'then' of v. 28, thus: as it is, the Jews have the opportunity of knowing Christ from his words; afterwards, when they know him as one 'lifted up' (12:32+), it will be too late. The Vulg. translation '(I am) the Beginning who speak to you' is grammatically impossible.

i. In the O.T. the formula 'you shall know that I am', or 'that I am Yahweh', is a declaration of God's power, cf. 8:24+, or else heralds some notable intervention of God in history, cf. Ex 10:2; Ezk 6:7, 10,13f, etc; Is 43:10 (strikingly like John). This verse foretells the glorification of Jesus through his 'lifting up' on the cross, Jn 12:32+, which is to be the reply to the Jews' question (v. 25) but will be also the condemnation of their unbelief. Cf. 19:37; Rv 1:7; Mt 26:64p; 1 Co 2:8.

j. Add. 'of sin'.

k. Var. 'If you are Abraham's children, do as Abraham did'. Unlike Isaac, the Jews are not 'children' of Abraham because they do not believe; they are merely of his 'race' (like the bondwoman's son, Ishmael, who was cast out, cf. vv. 34-35). On this, cf. Ga 4: 30f+.

l. The prophets call religious infidelity 'prostitution', cf. Ho 1:2+; here, therefore, the Jews are objecting that they have been faithful to God's covenant.

m. Because they have the devil for master, and he is hostile to the truth. Cf. 18:37.

Gn 2:17; 3:1f; Ws 1:13; 2:24; Rm 5:12 He was a murderer from the start;
he was never grounded[n] in the truth;
there is no truth in him at all:
when he lies
he is drawing on his own store,
because he is a liar, and the father of lies.[o]
But as for me, I speak the truth 45
and for that very reason,
you do not believe me.
Heb 4:16; 1 P 2:22; 1 Jn 3:5 Can one of you convict me of sin?[p] 46
If I speak the truth, why do you not believe me?
A child of God 47
10:26+ listens to the words of God;
12:48; 1 Jn 4:6 if you refuse to listen,
it is because you are not God's children.'

4:9+ The Jews replied, 'Are we not right in saying that you are a Samaritan and 48
7:20+ possessed by a devil?' Jesus answered:

'I am not possessed; 49
no, I honour my Father,
but you want to dishonour me.
7:18 Not that I care for my own glory, 50
there is someone who takes care of that and is the judge of it.
3:11+ I tell you most solemnly, 51
5:25-28; 11:25 whoever keeps my word
will never see death.'

7:20+ The Jews said, 'Now we know for certain that you are possessed. Abraham 52
is dead, and the prophets are dead, and yet you say, "Whoever keeps my word
4:12 will never know the taste of death". •Are you greater than our father Abraham, 53
who is dead? The prophets are dead too. Who are you claiming to be?' •Jesus 54
answered:

'If I were to seek my own glory
that would be no glory at all;
my glory is conferred by the Father,
by the one of whom you say, "He is our God"
although you do not know him. 55
7:29 But I know him,
and if I were to say: I do not know him,
I should be a liar, as you are liars yourselves.
But I do know him, and I faithfully keep his word.
5:39+; Gn 17:17+; Mt 13:17f; Lk 17:22 Your father Abraham rejoiced 56
to think that he would see my Day;[q]
he saw it and was glad.'[r]

The Jews then said, 'You are not fifty yet, and you have seen Abraham!' 57
Jesus replied: 58

'I tell you most solemnly,
1:1+,30 before Abraham ever was,
8:24+ I Am'.

10:31,39; 11:8; Lk 4:29f At this they picked up stones to throw at him;[s] but Jesus hid himself and left 59
the Temple.

Is 42:7 **The cure of the man born blind**

9 As he went along, he saw a man who had been blind from birth. •His disciples 1 2
asked him, 'Rabbi, who sinned, this man or his parents, for him to have been

3 born blind?' •'Neither he nor his parents sinned,' Jesus answered 'he was born 5:14+; Lk 13:2
blind so that the works of God[a] might be displayed in him.

4 'As long as the day lasts 11:9-10; 12:35-36
I must[b] carry out the work of the one who sent me; 4:34; 5:16
the night will soon be here when no one can work.[c]
5 As long as I am in the world
I am the light of the world.'[d] 8:12+; 9:37

6 Having said this, he spat on the ground, made a paste with the spittle, put
7 this over the eyes of the blind man, •and said to him, 'Go and wash in the Pool 2 K 5:10
of Siloam[e] (a name that means 'sent'). So the blind man went off and washed Is 8:6
himself, and came away with his sight restored.
8 His neighbours and people who earlier had seen him begging said, 'Isn't
9 this the man who used to sit and beg?' •Some said, 'Yes, it is the same one'.
Others said, 'No, he only looks like him'. The man himself said, 'I am the man'.
10 11 So they said to him, 'Then how do your eyes come to be open?' •'The man called
Jesus' he answered 'made a paste, daubed my eyes with it and said to me, "Go
12 and wash at Siloam"; so I went, and when I washed I could see.' •They asked,
'Where is he?' 'I don't know' he answered.
13 14 They brought the man who had been blind to the Pharisees. •It had been a
15 sabbath day when Jesus made the paste[f] and opened the man's eyes, •so when 5:9 Mt 12:10fp
the Pharisees asked him how he had come to see, he said, 'He put a paste on Lk 13:10f; 14:1f
16 my eyes, and I washed, and I can see'. •Then some of the Pharisees said, 'This
man cannot be from God: he does not keep the sabbath'. Others said, 'How
could a sinner produce signs like this?' And there was disagreement among them. 3:2
17 So they spoke to the blind man again, 'What have you to say about him yourself,
now that he has opened your eyes?' 'He is a prophet' replied the man. Mt 16:14+
18 However, the Jews would not believe that the man had been blind and had
19 gained his sight,[g] without first sending for his parents and •asking them, 'Is this
man really your son who you say was born blind? If so, how is it that he is now
20 able to see?' •His parents answered, 'We know he is our son and we know he
21 was born blind, •but we don't know how it is that he can see now, or who
22 opened his eyes.[h] He is old enough: let him speak for himself.' •His parents
spoke like this out of fear of the Jews, who had already agreed to expel from the 7:13
23 synagogue anyone who should acknowledge Jesus as the Christ. •This was why 12:42
his parents said, 'He is old enough; ask him'.
24 So the Jews again sent for the man and said to him, 'Give glory to God![i]
25 For our part, we know that this man is a sinner.' •The man answered, 'I don't
26 know if he is a sinner; I only know that I was blind and now I can see'. •They
27 said to him, 'What did he do to you? How did he open your eyes?' •He replied,
'I have told you once and you wouldn't listen. Why do you want to hear it all
28 again? Do you want to become his disciples too?' •At this they hurled abuse
29 at him: 'You can be his disciple,' they said 'we are disciples of Moses: •we

n. Var. 'he has no footing in the truth'.

o. Or 'father of the liar'.

p. I.e. of betraying the commission entrusted to him by God.

q. I.e. Christ's coming. Another example of an expression reserved for God in the O.T. (the 'day of Yahweh', cf. Am 5:18+) but adopted for himself by Christ.

r. Abraham saw Christ's 'day' (as Isaiah 'saw his glory', Jn 12:41), but 'from a distance', cf. Heb 11:13; Nb 24:17, because he saw it in the birth of the promised Isaac (at which Abraham 'laughed', Gn 17:17+) which was an event prophetic of Christ. Jesus claims to be the ultimate fulfilment of this promise made to Abraham; he is Isaac according to the spirit.

s. The claim of Jesus to live on the divine plane (v. 58) is, for the Jews, blasphemy, for which the penalty is stoning, Lv 24:16.

9 a. 'Signs', cf. 2:11+.

b. Var. 'we must'.

c. The life of Jesus is compared to a day's work, 5:17, ending with the night of death. Cf. Lk 13:32.

d. Before the miracle takes place its significance is pointed out, cf. 9:37.

e. The water drawn from here during the feast of Tabernacles symbolised the blessings of the messianic age. Henceforth, the source of these blessings is Jesus himself. 'The envoy', or 'the one sent', is one of Jn's favourite names for Christ, cf. 3:17,34; 5:36, etc.

f. Such work was forbidden on the sabbath.

g. Om. 'that the man had been blind and had gained his sight'.

h. Add. 'ask him'.

i. A biblical phrase putting a person under oath to tell the truth and to make reparation for his insult to the divine majesty, cf. Jos 7:19; 1 S 6:5.

know that God spoke to Moses, but as for this man, we don't know where he
comes from'. •The man replied, 'Now here is an astonishing thing! He has 30
10:21 Pr 15:29 opened my eyes, and you don't know where he comes from! •We know that God 31
Is 1:15 doesn't listen to sinners, but God does listen to men who are devout and do his
will. •Ever since the world began it is unheard of for anyone to open the eyes 32
3:2 of a man who was born blind;[j] •if this man were not from God, he couldn't do 33
7:49 a thing.' •'Are you trying to teach us,' they replied 'and you a sinner through 34
and through, since you were born!' And they drove him away.

Jesus heard they had driven him away, and when he found him he said to 35
Mt 8:20+ him, 'Do you believe in the Son of Man?' •'Sir,' the man replied 'tell me who 36
4:26; 9:5+ he is so that I may believe in him.' •Jesus said, 'You are looking at him; he is 37
Mt 8:10+; 23:16 speaking to you'. •[k] The man said, 'Lord, I believe', and worshipped him. 38
Jesus said: 39

8:12+ 'It is for judgement
1:1+ that I have come into this world,
Mt 13:13 2 Th 2:12 so that those without sight may see
and those with sight[l] turn blind'.

Is 5:21 Mt 15:14p Rm 2:19 Hearing this, some Pharisees who were present said to him, 'We are not blind, 40
surely?' •Jesus replied: 41

'Blind? If you were,[m]
you would not be guilty,
but since you say, "We see",
3:36; 12:48 Mt 23:16f your guilt remains.

Jr 23:1-3 Ezk 34:1-31 **The good shepherd**

10 'I tell you most solemnly, anyone who does not enter the sheepfold 1
through the gate, but gets in some other way is a thief and a brigand.
The one who enters through the gate is the shepherd of the flock; •the 2 3
10:26-27 gatekeeper lets him in, the sheep hear his voice, one by one[a] he calls his
own sheep and leads them out. •When he has brought out his flock, he goes 4
Ex 13:22 Mi 2:13 ahead of them, and the sheep follow because they know his voice. •They never 5
follow a stranger but run away from him: they do not recognise the voice of
strangers.'

Jesus told them[b] this parable but they failed to understand what he meant 6
by telling it to them.

So Jesus spoke to them again: 7

'I tell you most solemnly,
I am the gate of the sheepfold.[c]
All others who have come[d] 8
are thieves and brigands;
but the sheep took no notice of them.
Mt 7:14 I am the gate. 9
3:17 Ps 23:1-3 *Is 49:9-10* Anyone who enters through me will be safe:
he will go freely in and out
Ezk 34:14 and be sure of finding pasture.
The thief comes 10
only to steal and kill and destroy.
I have come
10:28 so that they may have life[e]
and have it to the full.
Ezk 34:1+ Heb 13:20 I am the good shepherd:[f] 11
the good shepherd is one who lays down his life for his sheep.
The hired man, since he is not the shepherd 12
and the sheep do not belong to him,

abandons the sheep and runs away Jr 23:1f Ezk 34:3-8 Zc 11:17
as soon as he sees a wolf coming,
and then the wolf attacks and scatters the sheep;
13 this is because he is only a hired man
and has no concern for the sheep.
14 I am the good shepherd; 10:26-27
I know my own
and my own know me,[g] 1 Jn 2:4
15 just as the Father knows me 15:9 Mt11:25-27p
and I know the Father;
and I lay down my life for my sheep.
16 And there are other sheep I have Gn 11:9 Jr 23:3 Ezk 37:24 Ep 2:14f; 4:4f
that are not of this fold,
and these I have to lead as well.[h]
They too will listen to my voice, 5:25; 11:52 18:37
and there will be only one flock,[i]
and one shepherd.
17 The Father loves me,
because I lay down my life 3:35; 8:29 Ezk 34:23; 37:22
in order to take it up again. Ph 2:8-9
18 No one takes it from me; Heb 10:10
I lay it down of my own free will,[j] 13:1; 14:30; 17:19; 19:11,30
and as it is in my power to lay it down,
so it is in my power to take it up again;
and this is the command I have been given by my Father.'

19 20 These words caused disagreement[k] among the Jews. •Many said, 'He is 3:11+
21 possessed, he is raving; why bother to listen to him?' •Others said, 'These are 7:20 Ho 9:7
not the words of a man possessed by a devil: could a devil open the eyes of the *3:2* *9:30-32*
blind?'

VI. THE FEAST OF DEDICATION

Jesus claims to be the Son of God

22 It was the time when the feast of Dedication was being celebrated in Jerusalem. 1 M 4:36+
23 It was winter, •and Jesus was in the Temple walking up and down in the Portico Ac 3:11+
24 of Solomon. •The Jews gathered round him and said, 'How much longer are Lk 22:67
25 you going to keep us in suspense? If you are the Christ, tell us plainly.'[l] •Jesus 8:25
replied:

j. There are many points of resemblance between ch. 9 and 3:1-21, and it is probable that to the evangelist's mind the cure of the man born blind is a symbol of the new birth through water and the Spirit, 3:3-7.

k. Om. all v. 38 and first two words of v. 39.

l. The complacent who trust to their own 'light', cf. vv. 24,29,34, as opposed to the humble, typified by the blind man. Cf. Dt 29:3; Is 6:9f; Jr 5:21; Ezk 12:2.

m. I.e. if you knew you were blind, as blind men do.

10 a. Or possibly 'each by its name'.

b. I.e. to the Pharisees, wilfully blind, 9:40. They fail to realise that the parable refers to them.

c. The gate that gives access to the sheep. Only those who 'go in' by Jesus have authority to guide the flock, 21:15-17.

d. Add. 'before me'. The reference is probably to the Pharisees, cf. Mt 23:1-36; Lk 11:39-52 and Mt 9:36; Mk 6:34.

e. Life eternal. Jesus gives it, 3:16,36; 5:40; 6:33,35,48,51; 14:6; 20:31, with abounding generosity, cf. Rv 7:17; Mt 25:29; Lk 6:38.

f. God, himself the shepherd of his people, was to choose a shepherd for them in the messianic age, cf. Ezk 34:1+. Christ's assertion that he is the good shepherd is a claim to messiahship.

g. In biblical language, cf. Ho 2:22+, 'knowledge' is not merely the conclusion of an intellectual process, but the fruit of an 'experience', a personal contact (cf. Jn 10:14-15 and 14:20; 17:21-22; cf. 14:17; 17:3; 2 Jn 1-2); when it matures, it is love, cf. Ho 6:6+ and 1 Jn 1:3+.

h. Not to take them into the Jewish fold but to gather them into the flock that Jesus 'leads' to eternal life.

i. Var. 'one fold'.

j. Jesus has life in himself, 3:35+, and no one can rob him of it, 7:30,44; 8:20; 10:39; he surrenders it of his own will, 10:18; 14:30; 19:11; hence his perfect control and majestic calm in the face of death, 12:27; 13:1-3; 17:19; 18:4-6; 19:28.

k. Add. 'again'.

l. Not, as hitherto, in the enigmatic language of parable, cf. v. 6; 16:25,29. More urgently than before, 2:18; 5:16; 6:30; 8:25, the Jews press Jesus to say if he is the Messiah. In the Synoptics, the question is put by the high priest before the Passion, Mt 26:63p.

'I have told you,[m] but you do not believe.
2:11+; 5:36 The works I do in my Father's name are my witness;
Pr 28:5 1 Co 2:14 but you do not believe, 26
10:3-4,14 because you are no sheep of mine.[n]
The sheep that belong to me listen to my voice; 27
I know them and they follow me.
10:10 Rm 8:33-39 I give them eternal life; 28
they will never be lost
Dt 33:3 Ws 3:1 and no one will ever steal them from me.
3:35+ The Father who gave them to me is greater than anyone,[o] 29
Dt 32:39 Is 43:13; and no one can steal[p] from the Father.
51:16 *1:1+* The Father and I are one.'[q] 30

8:59 The Jews fetched stones to stone him, •so Jesus said to them, 'I have done 31 32
many good works for you to see, works from my Father; for which of these
Lk 22:70-71 are you stoning me?' •The Jews answered him, 'We are not stoning you for doing 33
5:18; 19:7 Mt 9:3 a good work but for blasphemy: you are only a man and you claim to be God'.
Jesus answered: 34

Rm 3:19 'Is it not written in your Law:
Ps 82:6 Jn 11:4,27; *I said, you are gods*?[r]
12:34; 15:25 So the Law uses the word gods 35
Heb 1:2 *1:12* of those to whom the word of God was addressed,
and scripture cannot be rejected.
1:1+; 17:18 Jr 1:5 Yet you say to someone the Father has consecrated and sent into the world, 36
"You are blaspheming",
6:67-69 because he says, "I am the Son of God".
If I am not doing my Father's work, 37
there is no need to believe me;
but if I am doing it, 38
then even if you refuse to believe in me,
2:11+ at least believe in the work I do;
then you will know for sure
14:11; 17:21 that the Father is in me and I am in the Father.'

8:59 They wanted[s] to arrest him then, but he eluded them. 39

Jesus withdraws to the other side of the Jordan

1:28 Mt 19:1 He went back again to the far side of the Jordan to stay in the district where 40
Mk 10:1 John had once been baptising. •Many people who came to him there said, 'John 41
gave no signs, but all he said about this man was true'; •and many of them 42
believed in him.

The resurrection of Lazarus

12:1-8 **11** There was a man named Lazarus who lived in the village of Bethany with 1
Lk 10:38f the two sisters, Mary and Martha, and he was ill.—•It was the same 2
Mary, the sister of the sick man Lazarus, who anointed the Lord with
ointment and wiped his feet with her hair.[a] •The sisters sent this message to 3
2:11 Jesus, 'Lord, the man you love is ill'. •On receiving the message, Jesus said, 4
1:14+ 'This sickness will end, not in death but in God's glory, and through it the Son
10:34+ of God will be glorified'.[b]

Jesus loved Martha and her sister and Lazarus, •yet when he heard that 5 6
Lazarus was ill he stayed where he was for two more days •before saying to the 7
disciples, 'Let us go to Judaea'.[c] •The disciples said, 'Rabbi, it is not long since 8
8:59; 10:31 the Jews wanted to stone you; are you going back again?' •Jesus replied: 9

9:4 'Are there not twelve hours in the day?
A man can walk in the daytime without stumbling

because he has the light of this world to see by; 8:12+
10 but if he walks at night he stumbles,
because there is no light to guide him.'

11 He said that and then added, 'Our friend Lazarus is resting, I am going to
12 wake him'. •The disciples said to him, 'Lord, if he is able to rest he is sure to get 2:19+
13 better'. •The phrase Jesus used referred to the death of Lazarus, but they thought Mt 9:24p
14 15 that by 'rest' he meant 'sleep', so •Jesus put it plainly, 'Lazarus is dead; •and
for your sake I am glad I was not there because now you will believe.[d] But let 2:11+
16 us go to him.' •Then Thomas—known as the Twin—said to the other disciples, 14:5; 20:24-29
'Let us go too, and die with him'. Mk 10:32
17 On arriving, Jesus found that Lazarus had been in the tomb for four days
18 19 already. •Bethany is only about two miles from Jerusalem, •and many Jews had 11:45; 12:9-11,17-19
20 come to Martha and Mary to sympathise with them over their brother. •When
Martha heard that Jesus had come she went to meet him. Mary remained sitting Lk 10:39f
21 in the house. •Martha said to Jesus, 'If you had been here,[e] my brother would 11:32
22 not have died, •but I know that, even now, whatever you ask of God, he will Mk 11:24p
23 24 grant you'.[f] •'Your brother' said Jesus to her 'will rise again.' •Martha said, 2:19+
25 'I know he will rise again at the resurrection on the last day'. •Jesus said:

'I am the resurrection.[g] 8:51 Mt 22:23+
If anyone believes in me, even though he dies he will live,[h] *5:24*
26 and whoever lives and believes in me 1 Jn 3:14
will never die.
Do you believe this?'

27 'Yes, Lord,' she said 'I believe that you are the Christ, the Son of God, the one 10:34+
who was to come into this world.' 1:9,10+
28 When she had said this, she went and called her sister Mary, saying in a low
29 voice, 'The Master is here and wants to see you'. •Hearing this, Mary got up
30 quickly and went to him. •Jesus had not yet come into the village; he was still
31 at the place where Martha had met him. •When the Jews who were in the house
sympathising with Mary saw her get up so quickly and go out, they followed
her, thinking that she was going to the tomb to weep there.
32 Mary went to Jesus, and as soon as she saw him she threw herself at his
33 feet, saying, 'Lord, if you had been here, my brother would not have died'. •At 11:21
the sight of her tears, and those of the Jews who followed her, Jesus said in great 11:38; 13:21
34 distress, with a sigh that came straight from the heart, •'Where have you put 12:27
35 36 him?' They said, 'Lord, come and see'. •Jesus wept; •and the Jews said, 'See
37 how much he loved him!' •But there were some who remarked, 'He opened the
38 eyes of the blind man, could he not have prevented this man's death?' •Still

m. Christ's previous statements had made it sufficiently clear that he spoke as God's envoy, cf. 2:19; 5:17f,39; 6:32f; 8:24,28f,56f; 9:37.

n. Faith in Jesus implies an inner sympathy with him: man must be 'from above', 8:23, 'of God', 8:47, 'of the truth', 18:37, of his flock, 10:14. Faith presupposes a mind open to truth, 3:17-21. Cf. Ac 13:48+; Rm 8:29f.

o. Var. 'As for my Father, that which he has given me is greater than all'.

p. Var. 'Steal them'.

q. The Son's power is not other than the Father's. The context shows that this is the primary meaning, but the statement is deliberately undefined and hints at a more comprehensive and a profounder unity. The Jews do not miss the implication; they sense a claim to godhead, v. 33. Cf. 1:1; 8:24,29; 10:38; 14:9-10; 17:11,21 and 2:11+.

r. The words were addressed to magistrates whose function made them, in a sense, 'gods' because 'judgement is God's', Dt 1:17; 19:17; Ex 21:6; Ps 58. Christ's argument is a rabbinic *a fortiori*, the conclusion being that blasphemy is a surprising charge to bring when it is God's consecrated envoy who calls himself Son of God. On this title, 'Son of God', v. 36, cf. 5:25; 11:4,27; 20:17,31. Christ's fate is henceforth to turn, cf. 19:7. See Mt 4:3+.

s. Add. 'again'.

11 a. It is unlikely that this is 'the woman who was a sinner' of Lk 7:37.

b. A double meaning here: Jesus will be glorified by the miracle itself, cf. 1:14+, but the miracle will bring about his death, 11:46-54, by which also he will be glorified, 12:32+.

c. Add. 'again'.

d. Had Lazarus not died, there would have been no miracle to confirm their faith.

e. Add. 'Lord'.

f. Martha has faith in Jesus but she stops short as if about to ask an impossibility.

g. Add. 'and the life'.

h. The man of faith has conquered death once and for all; the resurrection of Lazarus is the sign of this victory, cf. 3:11+.

11:33 sighing, Jesus reached the tomb: it was a cave with a stone to close the opening.
Jesus said, 'Take the stone away'. Martha[i] said to him, 'Lord, by now he will 39
smell; this is the fourth day'. •Jesus replied, 'Have I not told you that if you 40
1:14+; 2:11+ believe you will see the glory of God?' •So they took away the stone. Then 41
17:1 Mt 14:19p Jesus lifted up his eyes[j] and said:

'Father, I thank you for hearing my prayer.
I knew indeed that you always hear me, 42
1:1+ but I speak
12:30 for the sake of all these who stand round me,
so that they may believe it was you who sent me.'

5:27-29 When he had said this, he cried in a loud voice, 'Lazarus, here! Come out!' 43
19:40; 20:5-7 The dead man came out, his feet and hands bound with bands of stuff and a 44
cloth round his face. Jesus said to them, 'Unbind him, let him go free'.

The Jewish leaders decide on the death of Jesus

11:19; 12:10 Many of the Jews who had come to visit Mary and had seen what he did 45
Mt 26:3-5p believed in him, •but some of them went to tell the Pharisees what Jesus had 46
12:19 Lk 22:2 done. •Then the chief priests and Pharisees called a meeting. 'Here is this man 47
Ac 4:16 working all these signs' they said 'and what action are we taking? •If we let 48
him go on in this way everybody will believe in him, and the Romans will come
18:13 Lk 3:2+ and destroy the Holy Place[k] and our nation.' •One of them, Caiaphas, the 49
high priest that year, said, 'You don't seem to have grasped the situation at all;
you fail to see that it is better[l] for one man to die for the people, than for the 50
whole nation to be destroyed'. •He did not speak in his own person, it was as 51
high priest[m] that he made this prophecy that Jesus was to die for the nation[n]—
4:42+; 10:16 and not for the nation only, but to gather together in unity the scattered children 52
Gn 11:9 5:18+ of God. •From that day they were determined[o] to kill him. •So Jesus no longer 53 54
Mt 12:14p 7:1 went about openly among the Jews, but left the district for a town called
Ephraim, in the country bordering on the desert, and stayed there with his
disciples.

VII. THE LAST PASSOVER

A. BEFORE THE PASSION

The Passover draws near

2:13; 6:4 The Jewish Passover drew near,[p] and many of the country people who had 55
Nb 9:6-13 gone up to Jerusalem[q] to purify themselves •looked out for Jesus, saying to one 56
another as they stood about in the Temple, 'What do you think? Will he come
to the festival or not?' •The chief priests and Pharisees had by now given their 57
orders: anyone who knew where he was must inform them so that they could
arrest him.

||Mt 26:6-13 ||Mk 14:3-9 **The anointing at Bethany**

12 Six days before the Passover,[a] Jesus went to Bethany, where Lazarus 1
was, whom he had raised from the dead. •They gave a dinner for him 2
11:2+ there; Martha waited on them and Lazarus was among those at table. •Mary 3
brought in a pound of very costly ointment, pure nard, and with it anointed the
feet of Jesus, wiping them with her hair; the house was full of the scent of the
ointment. •Then Judas Iscariot—one of his disciples, the man who was to betray 4
him—said, •'Why wasn't this ointment sold for three hundred denarii, and the 5
money given to the poor?' •He said this, not because he cared about the poor, 6
13:29 but because he was a thief; he was in charge of the common fund and used to
help himself to the contributions. •So Jesus said, 'Leave her alone; she had to 7

8 keep this scent for the day of my burial.[b] •You have the poor with you always,
you will not always have me.'
9 Meanwhile a large number of Jews heard that he was there and came not 11:19
only on account of Jesus but also to see Lazarus whom he had raised from the
10 11 dead. •Then the chief priests decided to kill Lazarus as well, •since it was on his
account that many of the Jews were leaving them and believing in Jesus. 11:45

The Messiah enters Jerusalem ||Mt 21:1-9 ||Mk 11:1-10 ||Lk 19:28-38

12 The next day the crowds who had come up for the festival heard that Jesus
13 was on his way to Jerusalem. •They took branches of palm and went out to 1 M 13:51 Rv 7:9
meet him, shouting, '*Hosanna! Blessings on* the King of Israel,[c] *who comes in the* *1:49; 6:15* Ps 118:26
14 *name of the Lord.*' •Jesus found a young donkey and mounted it—as scripture
15 says: •*Do not be afraid, daughter of Zion; see, your king is coming, mounted on* Zc 9:9f
16 *the colt of a donkey.* •At the time his disciples did not understand this, but later, 14:26+ Mk 4:13+
after Jesus had been glorified, they remembered that this had been written
17 about him and that this was in fact how they had received him. •All who had 5:39+
been with him when he called Lazarus out of the tomb and raised him from the
18 dead were telling how they had witnessed it; •it was because of this, too, that
the crowd came out to meet him: they had heard that he had given this sign.
19 Then the Pharisees said to one another, 'You see, there is nothing you can do; 11:47-48 Mt 21:15-16
look, the whole world is running after him!'

Jesus foretells his death and subsequent glorification

20 Among those who went up to worship at the festival were some Greeks.[d]
21 These approached Philip, who came from Bethsaida in Galilee, and put this 1:44
22 request to him, 'Sir, we should like to see Jesus'. •Philip went to tell Andrew, 7:34+; 12:32+
and Andrew and Philip together went to tell Jesus.
23 Jesus replied to them:

'Now the hour has come 2:4+
for the Son of Man to be glorified. 3:14+ Mt 8:20+
24 I tell you, most solemnly,
unless a wheat grain falls on the ground and dies, 1 Co 15:36
it remains only a single grain; Is 53:10-12
but if it dies,
it yields a rich harvest. Ps 126:6
25 Anyone who loves his life loses it; ||Mt 16:25 ||Mk 8:35 ||Lk 9:24
anyone who hates his life in this world
will keep it for the eternal life.
26 If a man serves me, he must follow me, 1:10+ Mt 16:24
wherever I am,[e] my servant will be there too. *7:34; 14:3;* 17:24
If anyone serves me, my Father will honour him.
27 Now my soul is troubled.[f] 6:38; 11:33; 13:21; 18:4 Mt 26:37 Heb 5:7-8

i. Add. 'the dead man's sister'.

j. Add. 'upwards', 'to heaven', 'upwards to heaven'.

k. Lit. 'our Place'; Jerusalem, the Holy Land, or more probably the holiest of all places, the Temple.

l. Add. 'for you', or 'for us'.

m. Add. 'for that year'.

n. Caiaphas means that Jesus must be executed to save the nation from political extinction; the higher, prophetic sense is that the death of Jesus is necessary for the salvation of the world. Cf. 1:29+.

o. Var. 'they plotted'.

p. Jn repeatedly emphasises the connection between the Passover and Christ's death, 13:1; 18:28; 19:14,42.

q. Add. 'before the Passover'.

12 a. This last week of Christ's life is as carefully punctuated as the first, 12:12; 13:1; 18:28; 19:31; cf. 2:1+. Each of the two weeks culminates in the manifestation of Christ's glory, but the time for 'signs' (cf. Cana, 2:4,11) is now over: 'the hour has come for the Son of Man to be glorified', 12:23; 13:31f; 17:1,5.

b. Christ sees Mary's act as a gesture of respect offered to his dead body before the time; it is a symbol of his actual burial, 19:38f.

c. The Messiah-King.

d. Not Jews by birth but converts to the monotheism of Israel and adopting certain specific Mosaic observances; they are the 'God-fearing men' of Ac 10:2+.

e. In the glory of the Father, cf. 14:3; 17:24.

f. This episode and Gethsemane have many details in common: the anguish as the 'hour' draws near, the appeal to the Father's pity, the acceptance of death, the comfort from heaven (cf. Lk). But we should note the dissimilarities: in Jn, Christ's prayer for pity remains unuttered; nor does he 'fall to the

What shall I say:
Lk 22:40-46p Father, save me from this hour?
18:11 But it was for this very reason that I have come to this hour.
Father, glorify your name!'[g] 28

1:14+; 2:11+; 17:5+ A voice came from heaven, 'I have glorified it, and I will glorify it again'.
People standing by, who heard this, said it was a clap of thunder; others 29
11:42 said, 'It was an angel speaking to him'. •Jesus answered, 'It was not for my sake 30
that this voice came, but for yours.[h]

1:10+; 3:19 1 Jn 3:9 'Now sentence is being passed on this world; 31
Is 14:12 Lk 10:18 now the prince of this world is to be overthrown.[i]
Rv 12:9; 20:1-6 And when I am lifted up from the earth,[j] 32
3:35+ I shall draw all men[k] to myself.'[l]

21:19 By these words he indicated the kind of death he would die. •The crowd 33 34
Rm 3:19+ 1 Col 1:23 answered, 'The Law has taught us that the Christ will remain for ever. How can
2:19+ Mt 8:20+ you say, "The Son of Man must be lifted up"? Who is this Son of Man?' •Jesus 35
then said:

8:12+ 'The light will be with you only a little longer now.
9:4 Jb 5:14 Walk[m] while you have the light,
1 Jn 2:10 or the dark will overtake you;
he who walks in the dark does not know where he is going.
Jr 13:16 While you still have the light, 36
believe in the light
and you will become sons of light.'

Having said this, Jesus left them and kept himself hidden.

Conclusion: the unbelief of the Jews

2:11+; 20:30 Dt 29:1-3 Though they had been present when he gave so many signs, they did not 37
Mt 11:20 believe in him; •this was to fulfil the words of the prophet Isaiah: *Lord, who* 38
Is 53:1 Rm 10:16 *could believe what we have heard said, and to whom has the power of the Lord*
Mt 13:13+ *been revealed?* •Indeed, they were unable to believe because, as Isaiah says 39
Is 6:9f again: •*He has blinded their eyes, he has hardened their heart, for fear they should* 40
see with their eyes and understand with their heart, and turn to me for healing.
5:39+ Is 6:4 Isaiah said this when he saw his glory,[n] and his words referred to Jesus. 41
And yet there were many who did believe in him, even among the leading 42
3:1; 9:22 men, but they did not admit it, through fear of the Pharisees and fear of being
5:44 expelled from the synagogue: •they put honour from men before the honour 43
that comes from God.
Jesus declared publicly: 44

Mt 10:41 'Whoever believes in me
believes not in me
13:20 but in the one who sent me,
8:19; 14:7-9 and whoever sees me, 45
sees the one who sent me.
1:1+,9; 8:12+ I, the light, have come into the world, 46
so that whoever believes in me
need not stay in the dark any more.
3:11+ Mt 13:18-23p If anyone hears my words and does not keep them faithfully, 47
Lk 8:21p; 11:28 it is not I who shall condemn him,
since I have come not to condemn the world,
3:17 but to save the world:
8:26-27 Lk 20:16 he who rejects me and refuses my words 48
has his judge already:
Dt 31:26-29 the word itself that I have spoken

will be his judge on the last day. 8:37,47
49 For what I have spoken does not come from myself; 14:10 Dt 18:18-19
no, what I was to say, what I had to speak,
was commanded by the Father who sent me, 1:1+ 3:11+
50 and I know that his commands mean eternal life.
And therefore what the Father has told me
is what I speak.'

B. THE LAST SUPPER

Jesus washes his disciples' feet

1 **13** It was before the festival of the Passover, and Jesus knew that the hour Mt 26:17+
had come for him to pass from this world to the Father.[a] He had always 1:48+ *10:18+*
loved[b] those who were his in the world, but now he showed how perfect his *1:10+;* 2:4+
love was.[c]
2 They were at supper,[d] and the devil had already put it into the mind[e] of 6:71; 13:27; 14:30
3 Judas Iscariot son of Simon, to betray him. •Jesus knew that the Father had Mt 26:20p Lk 22:3
put everything into his hands, and that he had come from God and was returning *1:1+;* 3:35+
4 to God, •and he got up from table, removed his outer garment and, taking a
5 towel, wrapped it round his waist; •he then poured water into a basin and Lk 12:37; 17:7-10
began to wash the disciples' feet[f] and to wipe them with the towel he was wearing.
6 He came to Simon Peter, who said to him, 'Lord, are you going to wash my Mt 3:13-14
7 feet?' •Jesus answered, 'At the moment you do not know what I am doing, but 12:46+
8 later you will understand'. •'Never!' said Peter 'You shall never wash my feet.'
Jesus replied, 'If I do not wash you, you can have nothing in common with me'.[g]
9 'Then, Lord,' said Simon Peter 'not only my feet, but my hands and my head 2:19+
10 as well!' •Jesus said, 'No one who has taken a bath needs washing,[h] he is clean 15:3
11 all over.[i] You too are clean,[j] though not all of you are.' •He knew who was 1:48+
going to betray him, that was why he said, 'though not all of you are'.
12 When he had washed their feet and put on his clothes again he went back
13 to the table. 'Do you understand' he said 'what I have done to you? •You call

ground' (Mt, Mk) or 'kneel' (Lk). Cf. Jn 18:4-6; 10:18+.

g. Var. 'your Son'. The Father's 'name' is his person. Jesus worked for the Father's glory; his death, now freely offered, is the completion of that work because it shows how great is the Father's love for men, 17:6+.

h. Christ's coming death is thus divinely and publicly sanctioned.

i. Var. 'cast out'. Satan (cf. 14:30; 16:11; 2 Co 4:4; Ep 2:2; 6:12) was lord of the world, 1 Jn 5:19; Christ's death breaks his dominion over men. Cf. Jn 3:35+ and Mt 8:29+; Lk 8:31+; Col 1:12-13.

j. Om. 'from the earth'. Allusion both to the 'lifting up' of Christ on the cross (v. 33) and to his 'lifting up' to heaven, 3:13,14; 8:28, cf. 6:62, on the day of his resurrection, 20:17+; the two events are two aspects of the same mystery, 13:1+. When Christ is raised to the Father's right hand in glory, 12:23; 17:5+, he will send the Spirit, 7:39, through whom his reign will spread over the world, 16:14; cf. 3:35+.

k. Var. 'every man' or 'all things'.

l. The crucified Jesus will be set before the eyes of the world as its saviour, cf. 19:37. This is the answer to the Greeks' request to 'see' Jesus, cf. 6:40+.

m. Jesus urges the Jews to believe in him before it is too late, cf. 7:34+.

n. 'when he saw'; var. 'because he saw'. Alluding to Isaiah's vision in the Temple, Is 6:1-4+. Jn interprets it as a prophetic vision of Christ's glory, cf. 8:56+.

13 a. According to a Jewish tradition the word 'Passover' (*pesah:* cf. Ex 12:11+) meant 'a passing, or crossing over', referring it to the crossing of the Red Sea, Ex 14. Christ (and we with him) will pass from this world, which is enslaved by sin, to the Father's company, the true Land of Promise. Cf. Jn 1:21+.

b. Here, for the first time, Jn clearly states that Christ's life and death are an expression of his love for his disciples. The impression given is one of a secret kept for these last moments, 13:34; 15:9,13; 17:23; 1 Jn 3:16; Ga 2:20; Rm 8:35; Ep 3:19; 5:2,25.

c. Lit. 'he loved them to the end', i.e. utterly.

d. Var. 'Supper was over'.

e. Var. 'the devil having already put in the (his?) heart that Judas Iscariot should betray him', or '...having already put in his heart (i.e. made up his mind)...', or 'Satan having already entered into the heart of Judas in order that he might betray him'. Unseen forces are at work in Christ's Passion: the human agents are tools of the devil. Cf. 6:70f; 8:44; 12:31; 13:27; 16:11; Rv 12:4,17; 13:2; Lk 22:3; 1 Co 2:8.

f. The dress and duty are those of a slave, cf. 1 S 25: 41.

g. Lit. 'you have no share with me', a semitic phrase: Peter is cutting himself off from his Lord and from all share in his ministry and in his glory, because he does not appreciate his Master's outlook.

h. Add. 'except for his feet'.

i. Peter has understood Christ's answer, v. 8, superficially, as if a new rite of purification were being instituted. Jesus replies that his sacrifice has already achieved this purification, cf. 15:2-3; 1 Jn 1:7; Heb 10:22. He explains the meaning of his action in vv. 12-15.

j. The same Greek word is used for 'clean' and 'pure'.

me Master and Lord, and rightly; so I am. •If I, then, the Lord and Master, 14
13:34; 15:1-2 Lk 22:24-30 have washed your feet, you should wash each other's feet.[k] •I have given you 15
Ep 5:2 Ph 2:5,8 1 Tm 5:10 an example so that you may copy what I have done to you.

'I tell you most solemnly, 16
no servant is greater than his master,
15:20 Mt 10:24 Lk 6:40 no messenger is greater than the man who sent him.

Jm 1:25 'Now that you know this, happiness will be yours if you behave accordingly. 17
6:70 I am not speaking about all of you: I know the ones I have chosen; but what 18
Ps 41:9 Lm 1:2 scripture says must be fulfilled: *Someone who shares my table rebels*[l] *against me.*

14:29; 16:4 'I tell you this now, before it happens, 19
so that when it does happen
8:24+ you may believe that I am He.[m]
||Mt 10:40 ||Mk 9:37 ||Lk 9:48 I tell you most solemnly, 20
whoever welcomes the one I send welcomes me,
and whoever welcomes me welcomes the one who sent me.'

||Mt 26:21-25 ||Mk 14:18-21 ||Lk 22:21-23

The treachery of Judas foretold

11:33; 12:27 Having said this, Jesus was troubled in spirit and declared, 'I tell you most 21
solemnly, one of you will betray me'. •The disciples looked at one another, 22
19:26; 20:2; 21:7,20 wondering which he meant. •The disciple Jesus loved was reclining next 23
Lk 8:51+ to Jesus; •Simon Peter signed to him and said, 'Ask who it is he means', •so 24 25
leaning back on Jesus' breast he said, 'Who is it, Lord?' •'It is the one' replied 26
Jesus 'to whom I give the piece of bread[n] that I shall dip in the dish.' He dipped
the piece of bread and gave it to Judas son of Simon Iscariot. •At that instant, 27
13:2+ Lk 22:3 after Judas had taken the bread, Satan entered him. Jesus then said, 'What you
1:48+ are going to do, do quickly'. •None of the others at table understood the reason 28
12:6 he said this. •Since Judas had charge of the common fund, some of them thought 29
Jesus was telling him, 'Buy what we need for the festival', or telling him to give
something to the poor. •As soon as Judas had taken the piece of bread he went 30
8:12+ out. Night had fallen.
When he had gone Jesus said: 31

21:19 Mt 8:20+ 'Now[o] has the Son of Man been glorified,
and in him God has been glorified.
If God has been glorified in him,[p] 32
1:14+ God will in turn glorify him in himself,[q]
and will glorify him very soon.

Farewell discourses

'My little children, 33
16:10 I shall not be with you much longer.
8:21 You will look for me,
and, as I told the Jews,[r]
1:1+ where I am going,
you cannot come.[s]
13:15 1 Jn 2:8 I give you a new commandment:[t] 34
15:12,17 Lv 19:18 love one another;
Mt 19:19; 22:39 just as I have loved you,
Lk 10:26f you also must love one another.
Ac 4:32 By this love you have for one another, 35
everyone will know that you are my disciples.'

2:19+ Mt 26:31f Simon Peter said, 'Lord, where are you going?' Jesus replied, 'Where I am 36
8:21; 21:18-19 going you cannot follow me now; you will follow me later'.[u] •Peter said to him,[v] 37
21:16 ||Lk 22:31-34 'Why can't I follow you now? I will lay down my life for you.' •'Lay down your 38

life for me?' answered Jesus. 'I tell you most solemnly, before the cock crows ||Mt 26:33-35 ||Mk 14: 29-31
you will have disowned me three times.

1 **14** 'Do not let your hearts be troubled.[a] 14:27
Trust in God still, and trust in me. 10:28-30; 16:6,33
2 There are many rooms in my Father's house; 1 Th 4:7
if there were not, I should have told you.[b]
I am going now to prepare a place for you, 8:35
3 and after I have gone and prepared you a place, Heb 6:19-20
I shall return to take you with me;[c]
so that where I am 7:34; 12:26; 17:24
you may be too.
4 You know the way to the place where I am going.'

5 Thomas said, 'Lord, we do not know where you are going, so how can we 11:16; 13:36; 16:5; 20: 24-29
6 know the way?' •Jesus said:

'I am the Way, the Truth and the Life.[d] 1:4 Heb 10:19-20
No one can come to the Father except through me.
7 If you know me,[e] you know my Father too. 8:19; 12:45 2 Co 4:4
From this moment you know him and have seen him.'

8 Philip said, 'Lord, let us see the Father and then we shall be satisfied'. Ex 33:18+
9 'Have I been with you all this time, Philip,' said Jesus to him 'and you still do
not know me?

'To have seen me is to have seen the Father, 1:18; 12:45
so how can you say, "Let us see the Father"? 10:30+; 17:6+
10 Do you not believe[f]
that I am in the Father and the Father is in me?
The words I say to you I do not speak as from myself: 1:1+; 12:49
it is the Father, living in me, who is doing this work. 2:11+
11 You must believe me when I say
that I am in the Father and the Father is in me; 10:38
believe it on the evidence of this work, if for no other reason.
12 I tell you most solemnly,
whoever believes in me Mt 8:10+
will perform the same works as I do myself,
he will perform even greater works, Mt 21:21

k. I.e. serve one another lovingly and humbly.

l. Lit. 'has lifted up his heel against me'.

m. Because it demonstrates Christ's superhuman knowledge and fulfils the scripture, Judas' betrayal and Christ's death will confirm the disciples' faith.

n. Lit. 'morsel'. This particular 'morsel' is not the Holy Eucharist; nevertheless, a comparison of 13:2,18 with 6:64,70 seems to show that there was some connection between the institution and Judas' act of treachery. Cf. Lk 22:21.

o. The Passion has already begun, since Judas has just gone out to do Satan's work: Jesus speaks of his victory as already won, cf. 16:33.

p. Om. 'If God has been glorified in him'.

q. 'himself' refers to God the Father who will glorify the Son of Man by taking him to himself in glory. Cf. 17:5,22,24.

r. Christ's 'departure' and his glorification are intimately connected. The separation will be, for the Jews, final, 8:21; for the disciples, only for a time, 14:2-3.

s. Except by dying, cf. v. 36; 21:19,22f.

t. The reference to Christ's 'departure', v. 33, (which leads up to the prophecy of Peter's denial, vv. 36-38) makes this command, vv. 34-35, a solemn legacy from Christ. Though enunciated in the Mosaic Law, this precept of love is 'new' because Jesus sets the standard so high by telling his followers to love one another as he himself loved them, and because love is to be the distinguishing mark of the 'new' era which the death of Jesus inaugurates and proclaims to the world.

u. A cryptic prophecy of Peter's martyrdom.

v. Add. 'Lord'.

14 a. The apostles are perturbed by the predictions of betrayal, of Christ's departure, and of Peter's denial. Jesus wants to strengthen their faith: this purpose pervades ch. 14.

b. Others translate 'otherwise I would have told you (where I am going)'.

c. This promise keeps the Church's hope alive. Cf. 1 Th 4:16f; 1 Co 4:5; 11:26; 16:22; Rv 22:17,2; 1 Jn 2:28.

d. Jesus is the Way: in him we have our access to the Father; he makes the Father known to the world, 1:18; 12:45; 14:9; he is the Truth: he is the teacher and the personification of worship 'in spirit and truth' which alone pleases the Father, 4:23f; he is the Life: to know the Father, present in the Son, is eternal life, 17:3.

e. Var. 'If you had known me, you would have...'

f. When Philip asks for some marvellous manifestation of the Father, he is falling short of that faith by which alone the Father is seen to be in the Son and the Son in the Father.

because I am going to the Father.[g]
15:7,16; 16:24,26 Mt 7:7-11 Ac 3:16+ 1 Jn 3:22 Whatever you ask for in my name I will do, 13
so that the Father may be glorified in the Son.
If you ask for anything in my name, 14
I will do it.
Dt 6:4-9; 7:11; 11:1 Ws 6:18 1 Jn 2:3; 4:21; 5:3 If you love me you will keep my commandments.[h] 15
I shall ask the Father, 16
and he will give you another Advocate[i]
to be with you for ever,
14:26+ that Spirit of truth[j] 17
1:10+ whom the world can never receive
since it neither sees nor knows him;
1 Jn 4:6 2 Jn 1-2 but you know him,
because he is with you, he is in you.[k]
Mt 28:20 I will not leave you orphans; 18
I will come back to you.
7:34; 8:21 In a short time the world will no longer see me; 19
16:16,22 but you will see me,
6:57 because I live and you will live.[l]
On that day[m] 20
10:30+ you will understand that I am in my Father
17:11,21,22 and you in me and I in you.
1 Jn 2:5; 3:24; 4:21 Anybody who receives my commandments and keeps them 21
will be one who loves me;
16:27; 17:26 Dt 7:12-13 Ws 6:12 Si 4:10,14 and anybody who loves me will be loved by my Father,
and I shall love him and show myself to him.'[n]

2:19+ Judas[o]—this was not Judas Iscariot—said to him, 'Lord, what is all this 22
Ac 10:41 about? Do you intend to show yourself to us and not to the world?' •Jesus 23
replied:

3:11+ 1 Jn 2:5+ *Dt 7:12-13* Si 4:10,14 'If anyone loves me he will keep my word,[p]
and my Father will love him,
and we shall come to him
Ep 3:17 Rv 3:20 and make our home with him.
Those who do not love me do not keep my words. 24
1:1+; 3:11+ And my word[q] is not my own:
it is the word of the one who sent me.
I have said these things to you 25
while still with you;
2:22; 12:16; 13:7; 14:17; 15:26; 16:7,13-15; 20:9 1 Co 2:10 Ep 3:5 1 Jn 2:20,27 *Nb 6:26* but the Advocate, the Holy Spirit, 26
whom the Father will send in my name,
will teach you everything
and remind you of all I have said to you.[r]
Rm 5:1 Ep 2:14-18 2 Th 3:16 Peace[s] I bequeath to you, 27
my own peace I give you,
a peace the world cannot give, this is my gift to you.
14:1-3 Do not let your hearts be troubled or afraid.
You heard me say: 28
8:14 I am going away, and shall return.
If you loved me you would have been glad to know that I am going to the Father,
for the Father is greater than I.[t]
13:19; 16:4 I have told you this now before it happens, 29
so that when it does happen you may believe.
I shall not talk with you any longer,[u] 30
1:10+; 13:2+ because the prince of this world is on his way.

He has no power over me, 10:18+; 16:33
31 but the world must be brought to know that I love the Father
and that I am doing exactly what the Father told me. 6:38+
Come now, let us go. Mt 26:46p

The true vine

1 **15** 'I am the true vine,[a] Is 5:1+ Ph 1:11
and my Father is the vinedresser.
2 Every branch in me that bears no fruit[b]
he cuts away, Mt 15:13
and every branch that does bear fruit he prunes 15:16
to make it bear even more.
3 You are pruned[c] already, 13:10
by means of the word that I have spoken to you. 3:11+
4 Make your home in me, as I make mine in you. 6:56-57
As a branch cannot bear fruit all by itself,
but must remain part of the vine,
neither can you unless you remain in me.
5 I am the vine,
you are the branches.
Whoever remains in me, with me in him,
bears fruit in plenty; 15:16 Dt 8:17
for cut off from me you can do nothing. *1:3* Ps 127:1
6 Anyone who does not remain in me Si 6:3
is like a branch that has been thrown away
—he withers; Ezk 19:12
these branches are collected and thrown on the fire, Ezk 15:1-8 Mt 3:10p; 13:30,40
and they are burnt.
7 If you remain in me
and my words remain in you,
you may ask what you will 14:13 +
and you shall get it. 1 Jn 5:14

g. Christ brought revelation and salvation; his miracles were 'signs' of these things, 2:11+. The 'works' of the disciples will continue this ministry. The Spirit, from whom mighty works will proceed, is to be sent by Jesus seated in glory at the Father's right hand, 7:39; 16:7.

h. Var. 'keep my commandments'. Jesus, like God himself, asserts his right to love and obedience.

i. The Greek word *parakletos* is here translated 'Advocate', but it is difficult to choose between the possible meanings: 'advocate', 'intercessor', 'counsellor', 'protector', 'support'. The parallel between the Spirit's work for the disciples and Christ's brings out powerfully the personal character of the Spirit, cf. 14:26+; 1 Jn 2:1.

j. He who reveals and inspires the true worship of God, 4:23f, as opposed to the prince of this world who is 'the father of lies', 8:44; 1 Jn 4:3f.

k. Var. 'will be in you'.

l. The world has seen its last of Jesus, cf. 7:34; 8:21. The disciples, however, will see him in his risen life, not merely with their eyes but with the inward vision of faith, 20:29.

m. Phrase used by the prophets for the occasions when God notably intervenes in human history, cf. Is 2:17; 4:1f, etc. The 'day' may indicate a whole epoch; here, it is the post-resurrection era.

n. By coming, with the Father, to dwell in him.

o. The 'Judas, brother of James' of Lk 6:16 and Ac 1:13; the Thaddaeus of Mt 10:3 and Mk 3:18.

p. As the world does not: 8:37,43,47.

q. Var. 'the word that you hear'.

r. In place of the departed Christ, the faithful will have the Spirit, 14:16,17; 16:7; cf. 1:33+. He is the *parakletos*, who intercedes with the Father, cf. 1 Jn 2:1, and whose voice is heard in human courts, 15:26,27; cf. Lk 12:11-12; Mt 10:19-20p; Ac 5:32. He is the Spirit of truth, leading men to the very fulness of truth, 16:13, teaching them to understand the mystery of Christ — his fulfilment of the scriptures, 5:39+, the meaning of his words, 2:19+, of his actions, and of his 'signs', 14:26; 16:13; 1 Jn 2:20f,27, all hitherto obscure to the disciples, 2:22; 12:16; 13:7; 20:9. In this way the Spirit is to bear witness to Christ, 15:26; 1 Jn 5:6,7, and shame the unbelieving world, 16:8-11.

s. The customary Jewish greeting and farewell, cf. Lk 10:5p; it means soundness of body but came to be used of the perfect happiness and the deliverance which the Messiah would bring. All this Jesus gives.

t. Though the Son is the Father's equal, 10:30+; 8:24+, his glory is for the moment veiled, 1:14+; his return to the Father will reveal it again, 17:5+. Cf. Ph 2:6-9; Heb 1:3.

u. Var. 'I will not have much more speech with you'.

15 a. On the vine image, cf. Jr 2:21; Is 5:1+. In the Synoptics, Jesus uses the vine as a symbol of the kingdom of God, Mt 20:1-8; 21:28-31, 33-41 and p, and 'the fruit of the vine' becomes the Eucharistic sacrament of the New Covenant, Mt 26:29p. Here he calls himself the true vine whose fruit, the true Israel, will not disappoint God's expectation.

b. The 'fruit' is that of a life of obedience to the commandments, especially that of love, vv. 12-17. Cf. Is 5:7; Jr 2:21.

c. The Greek word seems to be used here in its agricultural sense, but it may also mean 'clean' or 'pure', cf. 13:10.

M t5:16 Rm 6:22; 7:4 It is to the glory of my Father that you should bear much fruit, 8
and then you will be my disciples.[d]
3:35+; 10: 14-15+ As the Father has loved me, 9
so I have loved you.
13:1+; 17:23 Remain in my love,
If you keep my commandments 10
you will remain in my love,
6:38+; 8:29 just as I have kept my Father's commandments
and remain in his love.
I have told you this 11
3:29; 16:21. 22; 17:13 so that my own joy[e] may be in you
1 Jn 1:4 and your joy be complete.
This is my commandment: 12
13:34 love one another,
as I have loved you.
1 Jn 3:16 A man can have no greater love 13
Rm 5:6-8 Ga 2:21 than to lay down his life for his friends.
You are my friends, 14
if you do what I command you.
Rm 8:15 Ga 4:7 I shall not call you servants any more, 15
because a servant does not know
his master's business;
Lk 12:4 I call you friends,
Gn 18:17 Ex 33:11 because I have made known to you
everything I have learnt from my Father.
You did not choose me, 16
Dt 7:6+, 8 1 Jn 4:10 no, I chose you;
and I commissioned you
15:2+, 5 Mt 13:23 to go out and to bear fruit,
Rm 6:20-23 fruit that will last;
14:13+ Mt 18:19 and then the Father will give you
anything you ask him in my name.
What I command you 17
13:34 1 Jn 3:23; 4:21 is to love one another.

The hostile world[f]

Mt 10:22 1 Jn 3:12-13 'If the world hates you, 18
remember that it hated me before you.
If you belonged to the world, 19
the world would love you as its own;
1:10+; 17:14-16 but because you do not belong to the world,
because my choice withdrew you from the world,
therefore the world hates you.
Remember the words I said to you: 20
13:16 Mt 10:24 A servant is not greater than his master.
Lk 6:40 *Mt 10:25* If they persecuted me,
they will persecute you too;
if they kept my word,
they will keep yours as well.
Ac 5:41 But it will be on my account that they will do all this, 21
8:19; 16:3 1 Jn 3:1 because they do not know the one who sent me.
If I had not come, 22
1 Jn 5:16 if I had not spoken to them,
they would have been blameless;
8:21-24+; 16:9 but as it is they have no excuse for their sin.
10:30+ Anyone who hates me hates my Father. 23

24 If I had not performed such works among them
as no one else has ever done, Mt 10:25; 12:24-28
they would be blameless;
but as it is, they have seen all this, 2:11+; 6:36
and still they hate both me and my Father.
25 But all this was only to fulfil the words written in their Law: 10:34 Rm 3:19+
They hated me for no reason. *Ps 35:19; 69:4*
26 When the Advocate comes,
whom I shall send to you from the Father,
the Spirit of truth who issues from[g] the Father, 14:26+
he will be my witness. Mt 10:19-20 Ac 5:32 *1 Jn 1:2*
27 And you too will be witnesses,
because you have been with me from the outset. Mt 10:18 Lk 1:2; 22:28 Ac 1:8+

16

1 'I have told you all this
so that your faith may not be shaken.[a]
2 They will expel you from the synagogues, Mt 10:17 Lk 21:12 Ac 8:1
and indeed the hour is coming
when anyone who kills you will think he is doing a holy duty for God. Ac 26:9-11 1 Tm 1:13
3 They will do these things
because they have never known either the Father or myself. 8:29; 15:21
4 But I have told you all this, 13:19; 14:29
so that when the time for it comes
you may remember that I told you. Mk 13:23

The coming of the Advocate

'I did not tell you this from the outset,
because I was with you; 17:12
5 but now I am going to the one who sent me. 1:1+ Tb 12:20
Not one of you has asked, "Where are you going?" *13:36; 14:5*
6 Yet you are sad at heart because I have told you this. 14:1
7 Still, I must tell you the truth:
it is for your own good that I am going
because unless I go,
the Advocate will not come to you;
but if I do go, 1:33+
I will send him to you. 14:26
8 And when he comes,
he will show the world how wrong it was, 1:10+
about sin,
and about who was in the right,
and about judgement:
9 about sin: 8:21-24; 15:22
proved by their refusal to believe in me;[b]
10 about who was in the right:
proved by my going to the Father 1 Tm 3:16
and your seeing me no more;[c] 13:33

d. Var. 'and so prove to be my disciples'. In this way the Father is 'glorified in the Son', 14:13. Cf. 21:19.

e. The perfect happiness of the messianic era which is communicated by the Son of God.

f. Jesus contrasts the disciples' love for one another with the world's hatred of them. It will be with them as with their Master, and when the world persecutes them, it persecutes Jesus himself. Cf. Ac 9:5; Col 1:24.

g. The sending of the Spirit into the world rather than the eternal 'proceeding' from the Father within the Trinity.

16 a. Lit. 'so that you may not be 'tripped'. To preserve their faith from shock, Jesus forewarns the apostles of coming trials, cf. 13:19.

b. The world's sin is unbelief, 8:21,24,46; 15:22; the Spirit will expose it.

c. The Spirit will demonstrate the right of Jesus to the title 'Son of God', cf. 10:33; 19:7. The 'passing' of Jesus to the Father will prove that he is God's Son, 13:1; 20:17, because it shows that heaven is his true home, 6:62.

about judgement: 11
12:31+ proved by the prince of this world being already condemned.[a]
I still have many things to say to you 12
but they would be too much for you now.
14:26+ But when the Spirit of truth comes 13
he will lead you to the complete truth,
since he will not be speaking as from himself
but will say only what he has learnt;
and he will tell you of the things to come.[e]
He will glorify me, 14
since all he tells you
will be taken from what is mine.
17:10 Everything the Father has is mine; 15
that is why I said:
All he tells you
will be taken from what is mine.[f]

Jesus to return very soon

7:33; 14:19 'In a short time you will no longer see me, 16
and then a short time later you will see me again.'[g]

Then some of his disciples said to one another, 'What does he mean, "In a 17
short time you will no longer see me, and then a short time later you will see me
again" and, "I am going to the Father"? •What is this "short time"?[h] We don't 18
1:48+ know what he means.' •Jesus knew that they wanted to question him, so he 19
16:30 said, 'You are asking one another what I meant by saying: In a short time you
will no longer see me, and then a short time later you will see me again.

'I tell you most solemnly, 20
you will be weeping and wailing
Rv 11:10 while the world will rejoice;
Heb 12:11 you will be sorrowful,
Ps 126:6; 1 P 1:6 but your sorrow will turn to joy.[i]
Is 26:17-18; 66:7-14; Mi 4:9-10 A woman in childbirth suffers, 21
because her time has come;
Si 11:25; Jr 31:13 but when she has given birth to the child she forgets the suffering[j]
in her joy that a man has been born into the world.
So it is with you: you are sad now, 22
14:19; 15:11; 20:20; *Ac 2:46+* but I shall see you again, and your hearts will be full of joy,
and that joy no one shall take from you.
14:20 When that day comes, 23
you will not ask me any questions.
I tell you most solemnly,
14:13+ anything you ask for from the Father
he will grant in my name.
Until now you have not asked for anything in my name.[k] 24
Ask and you will receive,
and so your joy will be complete.
Mt 13:34-35p I have been telling you all this in metaphors, 25
the hour is coming
when I shall no longer speak to you in metaphors;
but tell you about the Father in plain words.[l]
When that day comes 26
14:13 you will ask in my name;
and I do not say that I shall pray to the Father[m] for you,
14:23 because the Father himself loves you 27
for loving me

and believing that I came from God.
28 I came from the Father and have come into the world 1:1+
and now I leave the world to go to the Father.'

29 His disciples said, 'Now you are speaking plainly and not using metaphors!
30 Now we see that you know everything, and do not have to wait for questions to 1:48+;16:19
31 be put into words; because of this we believe that you came from God.' •Jesus
answered them:

'Do you believe at last?
32 Listen; the time will come—in fact it has come already—
when you will be scattered, each going his own way Zc 13:7 Mt 26:31p
and leaving me alone. *Ps 69:20b*
And yet I am not alone, 8:29
because the Father is with me.
33 I have told you all this
so that you may find peace in me. 14:27+
In the world you will have trouble, 1:10+ Ps 129:2
but be brave:
I have conquered the world.' 12:31; 14:30 Ws 7:30 1 Jn 2:14+

The priestly prayer of Christ[a]

17 After saying this, Jesus raised his eyes to heaven and said: 11:41 Mt 14:19

1 'Father, the hour has come: 2:4+;21:19
glorify your Son
so that your Son may glorify you;[b]
2 and, through the power over all mankind[c] that you have given him, 3:35+
let him give eternal life to all those you have entrusted to him. 1 Jn 2:25
3 And eternal life is this: Ws 15:3 Jr 24:7; 31:31-34
to know you,[d]
the only true God, Ezk 36:25-28
and Jesus Christ whom you have sent.[e] 1:1+
4 I have glorified you on earth 14:7-9 1 Jn 5:20-21
and finished the work
that you gave me to do. 4:34+
5 Now, Father, it is time for you to glorify me 12:28 Ph 2:6-11
with that glory I had with you[f] *1:14+;* 17:22,24
before ever the world was.[g] Is 49:4
6 I have made your name[h] known 5:23; 14:9; 17:26 Ex 3:13 Mt 6:10

d. The Spirit will reveal the significance of Christ's death: it is the final sentence pronounced on the prince of this world.

e. The new order of things that is to result from Christ's death and resurrection.

f. By revealing the hidden depths of the mystery of Jesus, the Spirit makes his glory known. Jesus, in his turn, manifests the glory of the Father, 17:4, from whom comes everything he possesses, 3:35; 5:22,26; 13:3; 17:2. The Father is the source of the revelation communicated by the Son and brought to completion by the Spirit who in this way glorifies both Son and Father. There are not three revelations but one.

g. A veiled reference to his approaching death and resurrection. Add. 'because I am going to the Father'.

h. Add. 'he speaks of'.

i. The happiness of seeing the risen Christ after the sad days of his Passion, cf. 20:20.

j. Traditional biblical metaphor for the sufferings which will herald the new, messianic age. Cf. Mt 24:8+.

k. Because Jesus was not yet glorified. Cf. 14:13f.

l. The resurrection and the coming of the Spirit inaugurate the period of more perfect instruction which is to end in the vision of God 'as he is', 1 Jn 3:2.

m. Var. 'and I shall not pray to the Father'. Jesus is still the only mediator, cf. 10:9; 14:6; 15:5; Heb 8:6, but the disciples' faith and love make them one with him and therefore dear to the Father: mediation could not be more perfect.

17 a. The time for the sacrifice draws near: in this prayer Jesus offers himself and intercedes for his disciples.

b. When Jesus asks to be 'glorified', it is not in his own interests, cf. 7:18, 8:50, but the glory of Son and Father are one, cf. 12:28; 13:31.

c. Lit. 'all flesh', cf. 1:14.

d. To 'know' in the biblical sense, cf. 10:14+.

e. Hitherto the Mosaic Law had been the instrument of revelation which now comes to man through Christ.

f. Var. 'the glory which was with you' or 'the glory with which I was' or 'the glory with you'.

g. Either the glory he enjoyed as the pre-incarnate Son, or else the glory predestined for him from eternity by the Father, 1:14+.

h. It was Christ's mission to reveal the 'name', i.e. the person, of the Father, 17:3-6,26; 12:28+; 14:7-11; cf. 3:11+; now love for men is characteristic of the Father, 1 Jn 4:8,16, and he proves this love by

to the men you took from the world to give me.
3:35+ They were yours and you gave them to me,
3:11+ and they have kept your word.
Now at last they know 7
that all you have given me comes indeed from you;
for I have given them 8
3:11+ the teaching you gave to me,
and they have truly accepted this,[i] that I came from you,
and have believed that it was you who sent me.
I pray for them; 9
1:10+ I am not praying for the world
but for those you have given me,
because they belong to you:
16:15 all I have is yours 10
and all you have is mine,
2 Th 1:10,12 and in them I am glorified.
1:10+ I am not in the world any longer, 11
but they are in the world,
1:1+; 14:20 and I am coming to you.
Holy Father,
3:35+ Nb 6:24 Mt 6:13 Ac 4:32 keep those you have given me true to your name,[j]
so that they may be one like us.
While I was with them, 12
16:4; 18:9 I kept those you had given me true to your name.
6:39; 10:28 I have watched over them and not one is lost
13:18,19+ Ps 41:9 Mt 26:24 Ac 1:16,20 except the one who chose to be lost,[k]
and this was to fulfil the scriptures.
But now I am coming to you 13
and while still in the world I say these things
15:11+ to share my joy with them to the full.
3:11+ I passed your word on to them, 14
and the world hated them,
15:19 because they belong to the world
8:23 no more than I belong to the world.
I am not asking you to remove them from the world, 15
Mt 6:13 1 Co 5:10 1 Jn 2:14+; 5:18 but to protect them from the evil one.[l]
They do not belong to the world 16
8:23 any more than I belong to the world.
Ac 9:13+ 1 P 1:22 Consecrate[m] them in the truth; 17
2 S 7:28 your word is truth.
10:36 As you sent me into the world, 18
4:38; 20:21 I have sent them into the world,
10:18+ and for their sake I consecrate myself[n] 19
4:23+; 6:70 1 Th 4:7 Heb 2:11; 5:9; 10:14 so that they too may be consecrated in truth.[o]
I pray not only for these, 20
but for those also
who through their words will believe in me.
10:38; 14:20 Ac 4:32 May they all be one. 21
Father, may they be one in us,
10:30+ as you are in me and I am in you,
so that the world may believe it was you who sent me.
1:14+; 17:5+ I have given them the glory you gave to me, 22
that they may be one as we are one.
With me in them and you in me, 23
may they be so completely one
that the world will realise that it was you who sent me

and that I have loved them[p] as much as you loved me. 15:9
24 Father,
I want those you have given me
to be with me where I am, 12:26; 14:3 1 Th 4:17
so that they may always see the glory *17:5+* Mt 25:23 2 Th 1:12
you have given me
because you loved me
before the foundation of the world. Ep 1:4 1 P 1:20
25 Father, Righteous One,
the world has not known you, 1:10+ 1 Jn 3:1
but I have known you,
and these have known
that you have sent me. 1:1+
26 I have made your name known to them 17:6+ Ex 3:13
and will continue to make it known,
so that the love with which you loved me may be in them, 14:21
and so that I may be in them.'

C. THE PASSION

The arrest of Jesus

1 **18** After he had said all this Jesus left with his disciples and crossed the ||Mt 26:30,36 ||Mk 14:26, 32
Kedron valley. There was a garden there, and he went into it with his ||Lk 23:29
2 disciples. •Judas the traitor knew the place well, since Jesus had often met his
3 disciples there, •and he brought the cohort[a] to this place together with a detach- ||Mt 26:47-56 ||Mk 14: 43-52
ment of guards sent by the chief priests and the Pharisees, all with lanterns and ||Lk 22:47-53
4 torches and weapons. •Knowing everything that was going to happen to him, 1:48+ *12:27+*
5 Jesus then came forward and said, 'Who are you looking for?' •They answered,
'Jesus the Nazarene'. He said, 'I am he'. Now Judas the traitor was standing
6 among them. •When Jesus said, 'I am he', they moved back and fell to the ground. 8:24+
7 He asked them a second time, 'Who are you looking for?' They said, 'Jesus the
8 Nazarene'. •'I have told you that I am he' replied Jesus. 'If I am the one you
9 are looking for, let these others go.' •This was to fulfil the words he had spoken,
'Not one of those you gave me have I lost'. 6:39; 10:28; 17:12
10 Simon Peter, who carried a sword, drew it and wounded the high priest's ser- 18:36
11 vant, cutting off his right ear. The servant's name was Malchus. •Jesus said to
Peter, 'Put your sword back in its scabbard; am I not to drink the cup that the 12:27 Mt 20:22; 26:39p
Father has given me?'

Jesus before Annas and Caiaphas. Peter disowns him

12 The cohort and its captain and the Jewish guards seized Jesus and bound
13 him. •They took him first to Annas, because Annas was the father-in-law of Lk 3:2
14 Caiaphas, who was high priest that year. •It was Caiaphas who had suggested 11:50
to the Jews, 'It is better for one man to die for the people'.
15 Simon Peter, with another disciple,[b] followed Jesus. This disciple, who was ||Mt 26:58, 69-75
16 known to the high priest, went with Jesus into the high priest's palace, •but ||Mk 14:54, 66-72 ||Lk 22:54-62

delivering up his only Son, 3:16-18; 1 Jn 4:9,10,14,16; cf. Rm 8:32; it follows that men must believe that Jesus is the Son, 3:18, if they are to appreciate this love, cf. 1 Jn 2:23; Jn 20:31, and thus 'know' the Father.

i. Add. 'and have known'. Also translated 'they have given them true welcome because I came from you'.

j. Lit. 'Keep those in your name whom (var. which) you have given me'. So also in v. 12.

k. Lit. 'the son of perdition'.

l. Or 'from evil', cf. Mt 6:13.

m. The verb means literally: to set aside for, dedicate to, God; to 'sanctify' (in the original sense of the word), cf. Ac 9:13+.

n. Jesus offers himself in sacrifice for his followers.

o. Dedicated to God's worship 'in spirit and truth'.

p. Var. 'that you have loved them'.

18 a. A detachment from the Roman garrison in Jerusalem.

b. Probably the 'disciple' of 20:2f, 'whom Jesus loved', the evangelist himself.

Peter stayed outside the door. So the other disciple, the one known to the high
priest, went out, spoke to the woman who was keeping the door and brought
21:17 Mt 26:69-70 Peter in. •The maid on duty at the door said to Peter, 'Aren't you another of 17
that man's disciples?' He answered, 'I am not'. •Now it was cold, and the servants 18
and guards had lit a charcoal fire and were standing there warming themselves;
Mt 26:58 so Peter stood there too, warming himself with the others.

The high priest questioned Jesus about his disciples and his teaching. •Jesus 19 20
Is 45:19; 48:16 answered, 'I have spoken openly for all the world to hear; I have always taught
Mt 26:55 Lk 19:47; in the synagogue and in the Temple where all the Jews meet together: I have said
22:53 nothing in secret. •But why ask me? Ask my hearers what I taught: they know 21
Ac 23:2 what I said.' •At these words, one of the guards standing by gave Jesus a slap 22
in the face, saying, 'Is that the way to answer the high priest?' •Jesus replied, 'If 23
there is something wrong in what I said, point it out; but if there is no offence
Mt 26:57 in it, why do you strike me?' •Then Annas sent him, still bound, to Caiaphas 24
the high priest.[c]

21:17 ||Mt 26:69-70 ||Lk 22:54-60 As Simon Peter stood there warming himself, someone said to him, 'Aren't 25
you another of his disciples?' He denied it saying, 'I am not'. •One of the high 26
priest's servants, a relation of the man whose ear Peter had cut off, said, 'Didn't
I see you in the garden with him?' •Again Peter denied it; and at once a cock 27
crew.

Jesus before Pilate

||Mt 27:2, 11:26 They then led Jesus from the house of Caiaphas to the Praetorium.[d] It was 28
||Mk 15:1-15 ||Lk 23:1-7, now morning. They did not go into the Praetorium themselves or they would be
13-25 *11:55* defiled[e] and unable to eat the passover. •So Pilate came outside to them and 29
Mt 26:17+ said, 'What charge do you bring against this man?' They replied, •'If he were 30
not a criminal, we should not be handing him over to you'. •Pilate said, 'Take 31
Ac 18:15 him yourselves, and try him by your own Law'. The Jews answered, 'We are not
allowed to put a man to death'.[f] •This was to fulfil the words Jesus had spoken 32
3:14+ indicating the way he was going to die.

So Pilate went back into the Praetorium and called Jesus to him, 'Are you 33
19:14f, 19-22 the king of the Jews?' he asked. •Jesus replied, 'Do you ask this of your own 34
accord, or have others spoken to you about me?' •Pilate answered, 'Am I a Jew? 35
It is your own people and the chief priests who have handed you over to me:
1:10+; 6:15+ what have you done?' •Jesus replied, 'Mine is not a kingdom of this world; if 36
8:23; 12:32; 18:10-11 my kingdom were of this world, my men would have fought to prevent my being
surrendered to the Jews. But my kingdom is not of this kind.' •'So you are a 37
3:35+ king then?' said Pilate. 'It is you who say it' answered Jesus. 'Yes, I am a king.
3:11+ Si 4:28 I was born for this, I came into the world for this: to bear witness to the truth;
10:26+ 1 Jn 3:19+ and all who are on the side of truth listen to my voice.' •'Truth?' said Pilate 38
'What is that?'; and with that he went out again to the Jews and said, 'I find
Mt 27:15 Lk 23:22+ no case against him. •But according to a custom of yours I should release one 39
prisoner at the Passover; would you like me, then, to release the king of the
Jews?' •At this they shouted: 'Not this man,' they said 'but Barabbas'. Barabbas 40
was a brigand.

||Mt 27:27-31 ||Mk 15: 16-20 19 Pilate then had Jesus taken away and scourged; •and after this, the soldiers 1 2
twisted some thorns into a crown and put it on his head, and dressed him
in a purple robe. •They kept coming up to him and saying, 'Hail, king of the 3
Jews!'; and they slapped him in the face.

Pilate came outside again and said to them, 'Look, I am going to bring 4
Is 52:14 him out to you to let you see that I find no case'.[a] •Jesus then came out wearing 5
1:29,36 the crown of thorns and the purple robe. Pilate said, 'Here is the man'. •When 6
they saw him the chief priests and the guards shouted, 'Crucify him! Crucify him!'
Pilate said, 'Take him yourselves and crucify him: I can find no case against him'.
Lv 24:16 'We have a Law,' the Jews replied 'and according to that Law he ought to die, 7
10:33-36 because he has claimed to be the Son of God.'

8 9 When Pilate heard them say this his fears increased. •Re-entering the Praetorium, he said to Jesus, 'Where do you come from?'[b] But Jesus made no answer. 7:28
10 Pilate then said to him, 'Are you refusing to speak to me? Surely you know I
11 have power to release you and I have power to crucify you?' •'You would have 3:27;10:18+
no power over me' replied Jesus 'if it had not been given you from above; that
is why the one who handed me over to you has the greater guilt.'[c] 8:21,44

Jesus is condemned to death

12 From that moment Pilate was anxious to set him free, but the Jews shouted,
'If you set him free you are no friend of Caesar's; anyone who makes himself Ac 17:7
13 king is defying Caesar'. •Hearing these words, Pilate had Jesus brought out, and
seated himself on the chair of judgement at a place called the Pavement, in
14 Hebrew Gabbatha.[d] •It was Passover Preparation Day,[e] about the sixth hour.[f] 19:31 Mt 26:17+
15 'Here is your king' said Pilate to the Jews. •'Take him away, take him away!' *18:33-37* Lk 19:14
they said.[g] 'Crucify him!' 'Do you want me to crucify your king?' said Pilate.
16 The chief priests answered, 'We have no king except Caesar'. •So in the end Pilate
handed him over to them to be crucified.

||Mt 27:31, 33,37-38 ||Mk 15-20, 22,25-27 ||Lk 23:33,38

The crucifixion

17 They then took charge of Jesus,[h] •and carrying his own cross he went out *Gn 22:6* Lk 23:26
of the city to the place of the skull or, as it was called in Hebrew, Golgotha,
18 where they crucified him with two others, one on either side with Jesus in the Is 53:12
19 middle. •Pilate wrote out a notice and had it fixed to the cross; it ran: 'Jesus
20 the Nazarene, King of the Jews'. •This notice was read by many of the Jews, 3:35+;18:33
because the place where Jesus was crucified was not far from the city, and the Heb 13:12+
21 writing was in Hebrew, Latin and Greek. •So the Jewish chief priests said to
Pilate, 'You should not write "King of the Jews", but "This man said: I am King Lk 19:14
22 of the Jews" '. •Pilate answered, 'What I have written, I have written'.

||Mt 27:35 ||Mk 15:24 ||Lk 23:34

Christ's garments divided

23 When the soldiers had finished crucifying Jesus they took his clothing and
divided it into four shares, one for each soldier. His undergarment was seamless,[i]
24 woven in one piece from neck to hem; •so they said to one another, 'Instead of
tearing it, let's throw dice to decide who is to have it'. In this way the words
of scripture were fulfilled:

They shared out my clothing among them. Ps 22:18
They cast lots for my clothes.

This is exactly what the soldiers did.

||Mt 27:55-56 ||Mk 15: 40-41 ||Lk 23:49

Jesus and his mother

25 Near the cross of Jesus stood his mother[j] and his mother's sister,[k] Mary the *Lk 2:35;* 8:2-3

c. This is all that John has to say about the Jewish trial which, in fact, runs through the whole gospel from the Baptist's cross-examination, 1:19, to the decision to kill Jesus, 11:49-53.

d. The Roman procurator's judicial court.

e. To enter a pagan house was to incur legal impurity, cf. Ac 11:2f.

f. The Romans had withdrawn from the Sanhedrin the power of life and death. Jesus could have been stoned by the Jews, cf. 8:59; 10:31, but not crucified ('lifted up') by them.

19 a. Add. 'in him' or 'against him'.

b. I.e. not 'what district do you come from?' but 'what is the secret of your origin? Who are you?' First, the people of Cana, 2:9, then the Samaritan woman, 4:11, the apostles, the multitude, 6:5, the Jewish leaders, 7:27f; 8:14; 9:29f, and now Pilate, are faced with the mystery of Jesus, 16:28, 17:25, which is the theme of the whole gospel, 1:13.

c. The Jewish leaders, Caiaphas in particular, 11:51f; 18:14, but also Judas who betrayed him to them, 6:71; 13:2,11,21; 18:2,5.

d. Probably meaning 'elevated place', 'mound'.

e. In the course of this day, the Passover supper was made ready (it was to be eaten after sunset, cf. Ex 12:6+) and everything necessary prepared so that the feast could be celebrated without violating the rest prescribed by the Law.

f. About noon, the time by which all leaven had to be removed from the house; during the Passover unleavened bread ('azymes') was to be eaten, cf. Ex 12:15f. It is possible that the evangelist wishes to call attention to this coincidence; cf. 1 Co 5:7.

g. Var. 'shouted' or 'were shouting'.

h. Add. 'and led him away'.

i. Possible allusion to the priesthood of the crucified: the high-priestly robe was without seam.

j. Her presence is mentioned only by John. Cf. 2:1+.

k. Either Salome, mother of the sons of Zebedee

wife of Clopas, and Mary of Magdala. •Seeing his mother and the disciple 26
2:4+; 13:22-23 he loved standing near her, Jesus said to his mother, 'Woman, this is your son'.
Then to the disciple he said, 'This is your mother'.[l] And from that moment the 27
disciple made a place for her in his home.

||Mt 27:48-50 ||Mk 15:36-37 ||Lk 23:46

The death of Jesus

After this, Jesus knew that everything had now been completed, and to 28
4:7; 5:39+ fulfil the scripture perfectly he said:

Ps 22:15 *'I am thirsty'.*

Ps 69:21 A jar full of vinegar stood there, so putting a sponge soaked in the vinegar on 29
a hyssop stick[m] they held it up to his mouth. •After Jesus had taken the vinegar 30
4:34+; 10:18+; 17:4 he said, 'It is accomplished';[n] and bowing his head he gave up his spirit.[o]

Mt 8:20p

The pierced Christ

19:14 Dt 21:23 ||Lk 23:47f Ga 3:13 It was Preparation Day, and to prevent the bodies remaining on the cross 31
during the sabbath—since that sabbath was a day of special solemnity—the Jews
asked Pilate to have the legs broken[p] and the bodies taken away. •Consequently 32
the soldiers came and broke the legs of the first man who had been crucified with
him and then of the other. •When they came to Jesus, they found[q] he was already 33
1:33+ Nb 20:11 dead, and so instead of breaking his legs •one of the soldiers pierced his side 34
Zc 13:1 *7:37-39;* with a lance; and immediately there came out blood and water.[r] •This is the 35
20:27 1 Jn 5:6-8 evidence of one who saw it[s]—trustworthy evidence, and he[t] knows he speaks the
3 Jn 12 truth—and he gives it so that you may believe as well. •Because all this happened 36
to fulfil the words of scripture:

Ex 12:46 Ps 34:20 *Not one bone of his will be broken;*[u]

and again, in another place scripture says: 37

Zc 12:10 Nb 21:9 Rv 1:7 *They will look on the one whom they have pierced.*[v]

||Mt 27:57-60 ||Mk 15:42-46 ||Lk 23:50-54

The burial

After this, Joseph of Arimathaea, who was a disciple of Jesus—though a 38
secret one because he was afraid of the Jews—asked Pilate to let him remove
the body of Jesus. Pilate gave permission, so they[w] came and took it away.
3:1; 7:50 Nicodemus came as well—the same one who had first come to Jesus at night-time 39
—and he brought a mixture of myrrh and aloes, weighing about a hundred
11:44; 20:7 pounds. •They took the body of Jesus and wrapped it with the spices in linen 40
cloths, following the Jewish burial custom. •At the place where he had been 41
crucified there was a garden, and in this garden a new tomb in which no one
had yet been buried. •Since it was the Jewish Day of Preparation and the tomb 42
was near at hand, they laid Jesus there.

VIII. THE DAY OF CHRIST'S RESURRECTION

The empty tomb

||Mt 28:1-8 ||Mk 16:1-8 ||Lk 24:1-11 *Mt 28:10+*

20 It was very early on the first day of the week[a] and still dark, when Mary 1
of Magdala came to the tomb. She saw that the stone had been moved
13:22-23; 18:15 away from the tomb •and came running to Simon Peter and the other disciple, 2
the one Jesus loved. 'They have taken the Lord out of the tomb' she said 'and
we don't know where they have put him.'

So Peter set out with the other disciple to go to the tomb. •They ran together, 3 4
but the other disciple, running faster than Peter, reached the tomb first; •he bent 5
down and saw the linen cloths lying on the ground, but did not go in.[b] •Simon 6
Lk 24:12 Peter who was following now came up, went right into the tomb, saw the linen

7 cloths on the ground, •and also the cloth that had been over his head; this was 11:44; 19:40
8 not with the linen cloths but rolled up in a place by itself. •Then the other disciple 21:7
9 who had reached the tomb first also went in; he saw and he believed. •Till this
moment they had failed to understand the teaching of scripture,[c] that he must 5:39+; 14:26+
10 rise from the dead. •The disciples then went home again.

The appearance to Mary of Magdala

11 Meanwhile Mary stayed outside near the tomb, weeping. Then, still weeping, ‖Mt 28:9-10 ‖Mk 16:9-11
12 she stooped to look inside, •and saw two angels in white sitting where the body
13 of Jesus had been, one at the head, the other at the feet. •They said, 'Woman,
why are you weeping?' 'They have taken my Lord away' she replied 'and I Sg 3:1-3
14 don't know where they have put him.' •As she said this she turned round and
15 saw Jesus standing there, though she did not recognise him. •Jesus said, 'Woman, Lk 24:16
why are you weeping? Who are you looking for?' Supposing him to be the
gardener, she said, 'Sir, if you have taken him away, tell me where you have put
16 him, and I will go and remove him'. •Jesus said, 'Mary!' She knew him[d] then
17 and said to him in Hebrew, 'Rabbuni!'[e]—which means Master. •Jesus said to Mk 10:51
her, 'Do not cling to me,[f] because I have not yet ascended to the Father. But Sg 3:4 *1:1+*
go and find the brothers,[g] and tell them: I am ascending to my Father[h] and your Ac 1:9 *2:12+; 12:32+*
18 Father, to my God and your God.' •So Mary of Magdala went and told the *Lk 24:10*
disciples that she had seen the Lord and that he had said these things to her.

Appearances to the disciples

‖Mk 16:14-18 ‖Lk 24:36-39 21:14

19 In the evening of that same day, the first day of the week, the doors were
closed in the room where the disciples were,[i] for fear of the Jews. Jesus came 16:16
20 and stood among them. He said to them, 'Peace be with you', •and showed 14:27
them his hands and his side. The disciples were filled with joy when they saw Lk 24:16+ 1 Jn 1:1
21 the Lord, •and he said to them again, 'Peace be with you. *15:11; 16:22*

'As the Father sent me, 4:38; 17:18
so am I sending you.' Mt 28:19 Mk 16:15 Lk 24:47f

(cf. Mt 27:56p) or else, if the phrase refers to what follows, 'Mary, the wife of Clopas'.

l. The reference to the O.T. (vv. 24,28,36,37) and the unusual term 'woman' suggest that the evangelist sees more in this than the gesture of a dutiful son: namely, a declaration that Mary, the new Eve, is the spiritual mother of all the faithful, here represented by the beloved disciple.

m. Conj. 'on a spear'.

n. I.e. the Father's work as foretold by the scriptures: the salvation of the world through the sacrifice of Christ. Jn does not record the desolate cry of Mt 27:46 and Mk 15:34: it is the calm majesty of Christ's death that he wishes to emphasise. Cf. Lk 23:46; Jn 12:27+.

o. The last breath of Jesus is a token of the outpouring of the Spirit, 1:33+; 20:22.

p. To hasten death.

q. Var. 'when they saw'.

r. Var. 'water and blood'. The significance of the incident is brought out by two texts of scripture (vv. 36f). The blood shows that the lamb has truly been sacrificed for the salvation of the world, 6:51; the water, symbol of the Spirit, shows that the sacrifice is a rich source of grace. Many of the Fathers, not without good reason, interpret the water and blood as symbols of baptism and the Eucharist, and these two sacraments as signifying the Church which is born like a second Eve from the side of another Adam. Cf. Ep 5: 23-32.

s. The disciple of v. 26, probably the evangelist himself.

t. Referring either to 'the one who saw' or else to God (or Christ) whom 'the one who saw' calls to witness.

u. Two texts are here combined: one from a Psalm describing how God protects the virtuous man persecuted (cf. Ws. 2:18-20), of whom the 'servant of Yahweh' (Is 53) is the ideal example; the other, a ritual instruction for the preparation of the Passover lamb. Cf. Jn 1:29+ and 1 Co 5:7.

v. 'They will look', in the Johannine sense of 'see and understand', cf. 3:14+. For Jn, the Roman soldier symbolises the pagans who will be converted, cf. 12:20-21,32 and notes. Similarly, Mt 27:54+ and Mk 15:39+. Cf. also Lk 23:47,48; Mt 24:30; Rv 1:7.

w. Var. 'he'.

20 a. This was to become 'the Lord's Day', the Christian Sunday; cf. Rv 1:10.

b. The disciple acknowledges that Peter has some title to precedence. Cf. 21:15-17.

c. Cf. Ps 16:8-11; 2:7; Ac 2:24-31; 13:32-37; 1 Co 15:4.

d. Var. 'She turned'.

e. A more solemn address than 'Rabbi', and often used when speaking to God; it therefore approximates to Thomas' profession of faith, v. 28.

f. Mary has fallen at the feet of Jesus to embrace them. Cf. Mt 28:9.

g. Var. 'my brothers'.

h. This assertion does not contradict the account of Ac 1:3f. Christ 'went up' to the Father, that is to say, his body entered into glory, Jn 3:13; 6:62; Ep 4:10; 1 Tm 3:16; Heb 4:14; 6:19f; 9:24; 1 P 3:22; cf. Ac 2: 33+, 36+, on the day he rose fom the tomb, Jn 20:17; Lk 24:51. The significance of the 'ascension', 40 days later, Ac 1:2f,9-11, is that the time of earthly companionship with Christ is over, that he is now 'seated at the right hand of God' and will not return before his final coming (the '*parousia*').

i. Add. 'assembled'.

After saying this he breathed[j] on them and said: 22

1:33+ Ac 1:8+; 2:2 'Receive the Holy Spirit.
For those whose sins you forgive, 23
they are forgiven;
Mt 16:19; 18:18+ for those whose sins you retain,
they are retained.'

11:16; 14:5 Thomas, called the Twin, who was one of the Twelve, was not with them 24
Lk 24:9-10 1 Jn 1:1 when Jesus came. •When the[k] disciples said, 'We have seen the Lord', he ans- 25
wered, 'Unless I see the holes that the nails made in his hands and can put my
finger into the holes they made, and unless I can put my hand into his side,
21:14 I refuse to believe'. •Eight days later the disciples were in the house again and 26
Thomas was with them. The doors were closed, but Jesus came in and stood
14:27 among them. 'Peace be with you' he said. •Then he spoke to Thomas, 'Put 27
1 Jn 1:1 your finger here; look, here are my hands. Give me your hand; put it into my
19:34+ side.[l] Doubt no longer but believe.' •Thomas replied, 'My Lord and my God!' 28
Jesus said to him: 29

'You believe because you can see me.
4:48 Lk 1:45; 24:9-10 Happy are those who have not seen and yet believe.'[m]

CONCLUSION

12:37 There were many other signs that Jesus worked and the disciples saw, but 30
they are not recorded in this book. •These are recorded so that you may believe 31
1 Jn 5:13 that Jesus is the Christ, the Son of God, and that believing this you may have life
Ac 3:16+ through his name.

APPENDIX[a]

Mt 26:32p; 28:7 The appearance on the shore of Tiberias

21 Later on, Jesus showed himself again to the disciples. It was by the Sea 1
11:16; 14:5 of Tiberias, and it happened like this: •Simon Peter, Thomas called the 2
2:1 Twin, Nathanael from Cana in Galilee, the sons of Zebedee and two more of
Mt 4:18 Lk 5:4-10 his disciples were together. •Simon Peter said, 'I'm going fishing'. They replied, 3
'We'll come with you'. They went out and got into the boat but caught nothing
that night.

It was light by now and there stood Jesus on the shore, though the disciples 4
Lk 24:16+. 41 did not realise that it was Jesus. •Jesus called out, 'Have you caught anything, 5
friends?' And when they answered, 'No', •he said, 'Throw the net out to starboard 6
and you'll find something'. So they dropped the net, and there were so many
13:23; 20:8 fish[b] that they could not haul it in. •The disciple Jesus loved said to Peter, 'It is 7
the Lord'. At these words 'It is the Lord', Simon Peter, who had practically
nothing on, wrapped his cloak round him and jumped into the water. •The 8
other disciples came on in the boat, towing the net and the fish; they were only
about a hundred yards from land.

Lk 24:41-43 As soon as they came ashore they saw that there was some bread there, and 9
a charcoal fire with fish cooking on it. •Jesus said, 'Bring some of the fish you 10
have just caught'. •Simon Peter went aboard and dragged the net to the shore,[c] 11
full of big fish, one hundred and fifty-three of them; and in spite of there being
so many the net was not broken. •Jesus said to them, 'Come and have breakfast'. 12
4:27 None of the disciples was bold enough to ask, 'Who are you?'; they knew quite
6:11 Lk 24:42 well it was the Lord. •Jesus then stepped forward, took the bread and gave it 13
20:19-23; 26-29 to them, and the same with the fish. •This was the third time that Jesus showed 14
himself to the disciples after rising from the dead.

15 After the meal Jesus said to Simon Peter, 'Simon son of John, do you love Lk 5:10; 22:32
me more than these others do?' He answered, 'Yes Lord, you know I love you'. Ac 20:28
16 Jesus said to him, 'Feed my lambs'. •A second time he said to him, 'Simon son
of John, do you love me?' He replied, 'Yes, Lord, you know I love you'. Jesus
17 said to him, 'Look after my sheep'. •Then he said to him a third time, 'Simon 13:37,38; 18:17,25-27
son of John, do you love me?' Peter was upset that he asked him the third time,
'Do you love me?' and said, 'Lord, you know everything; you know I love you'. 1:48+ *6:68f*
Jesus said to him, 'Feed my sheep. Mt 16:17-19 Lk 22:31-32

18 'I tell you most solemnly,
when you were young
you put on your own belt
and walked where you liked;
but when you grow old
you will stretch out your hands, 2 P 1:14
and somebody else will put a belt round you
and take you where you would rather not go.'

19 In these words he indicated the kind of death[d] by which Peter would give glory 12:33; 13:31,36; 17:1
to God. After this he said, 'Follow me'. Lk 5:11
20 Peter turned and saw the disciple Jesus loved following them—the one who
had leaned on his breast at the supper and had said to him, 'Lord, who is it that 13:25
21 will betray you?' •Seeing him, Peter said to Jesus, 'What about him, Lord?'
22 Jesus answered, 'If I want him to stay behind till I come,[e] what does it matter
23 to you? You are to follow me.' •The rumour then went out among the brothers
that this disciple would not die. Yet Jesus had not said to Peter, 'He will not die',
but, 'If I want him to stay behind till I come'.[f]

Conclusion

24 This disciple is the one who vouches for these things and has written them 3 Jn 12
down, and we know[g] that his testimony is true.
25 There were many other things that Jesus did; if all were written down, the
world itself, I suppose, would not hold all the books that would have to be
written.

j. The breath of Jesus is a symbol of the Spirit ('breath', in Hebrew); he sends forth the Spirit who will make all things anew, Gn 1:2; 2:7; Ezk 37:9; Ws 15:11. See Jn 19:30+and Mt 3:16+.

k. Add. 'other.'

l. In the closing words of his gospel, John again calls the Christian reader's attention to the wound in Christ's side, cf. 19:34+.

m. On the apostles' witness, cf. Ac 1:8+.

21 a. Added either by the evangelist or by one of his disciples

b. This generosity recalls Cana, 2:6, the loaves miracle, 6:11f, the living water, 4:14; 7:37f, the life which the good shepherd gives, 10:10, and the richness of the Spirit bestowed on Jesus, 3:34.

c. In the Synoptics, this operation is an image of the kingdom's coming, Mt 13:47f, or of the apostles' task, Mt 4:19p. Here, too, it evidently symbolises the apostolic mission under Peter's direction. Cf. Jn 21: 15-17.

d. Martyrdom.

e. I.e. until the *parousia*, cf. 1 Co 11:26; 16:22; Rv 1:7; 22:7,12,17,20.

f. Add. 'what is that to you?'

g. Possibly the words of a group of John's disciples.

THE ACTS
OF THE APOSTLES

INTRODUCTION TO
THE ACTS OF THE APOSTLES

Acts and the third gospel must originally have been two parts of a book that today we should call 'a history of the rise of Christianity'. About 150 A.D., when Christians wanted the four gospels bound in one codex, these two parts were separated. The title 'Acts of the Apostles', or 'Acts of Apostles', which may have been given to the second part at this time, follows normal contemporary hellenistic usage as in, e.g., the 'Acts' of Hannibal and the 'Acts' of Alexander, etc. That these two books of the New Testament were once closely associated is suggested 1. by their Prologues: both are addressed (cf. Lk 1:1-4) to someone called Theophilus and Ac 1:1, having referred to the gospel as an 'earlier work', goes on by way of introduction to say why the gospel was written and to summarise its closing incidents (appearances of the risen Christ, ascension); 2. by their literary affinity: vocabulary, grammar and style are not only consistent all through Acts showing that it is a literary unity, but they are also characteristic of the third gospel, which makes it almost certain that both books are by the same author.

The only identification of the *author* ever suggested by church writers is St Luke, and no critics ancient or modern have ever seriously suggested anyone else. This identification was already known to the churches about the year 175 A.D. as shown by the Roman canon known as the Muratorian Fragment, by the Anti-Marcionite Prologue, by St Irenaeus, Clement and Origen in Alexandria and by Tertullian, and it is supported by internal evidence: the author must have been a Christian of the apostolic age, either a thoroughly hellenised Jew or, more probably, a well educated Greek with some knowledge of medicine and extremely well acquainted with the LXX and Jewish things in general. Lastly, and more significantly, he had accompanied Paul on his journeys judging from his use of the first person plural in Part 2 of Acts, and of all Paul's companions none is more strongly indicated than Luke. According to an ancient tradition Luke was a Syrian from Antioch, a doctor and of pagan origin, Col 4:10-14; Paul describes him as a close friend who stayed by him during his two periods of captivity in Rome, Col 4:14; Phm 24; 2 Tm 4:11. Luke probably accompanied Paul on the second (Ac 16:10f) and third (Ac 20:6f; cf. perhaps 2 Co 8:18) missionary journeys, and the only reason he does not figure in lists like that of Ac 20:4 is because he probably compiled the lists himself.

There is no clear early tradition about either *date* or *place* of writing (Greece, after Paul's death? Rome, before the end of Paul's trial?), and we have to rely on internal evidence. Acts ends with Paul's Roman captivity in 61-63, with reference to which it mentions a period of two years, 28:30+, and this happens to be the legal interval after which a case was dismissed if no evidence had arrived to support the charge. It is possible, therefore, that these lines were written after Paul's release. This ties in with the date of 64 A.D. suggested for Mark, since Acts must be later than Mark. A date as late as 80-100 which has been suggested by some critics is possible, but (as in Luke) there are no positive indications in Acts of a date later than 70 A.D.

The precise date, however, becomes a secondary consideration once the book can establish its primary importance either as an author's eyewitness account for the events that fill a major section or as based on adequate sources at the author's disposal. Analysis of Acts confirms Lk 1:1-4 (meant as prologue to the complete work) by suggesting that Luke must have collected a great deal of detailed evidence from a variety of sources, because in spite of the way Luke has superimposed his own personality in reworking this material he has not succeeded in disguising the various sources he has used. Not only does the flavour of the doctrinal content change according to the context so that in appropriate sections it seems convincingly primitive, but as well as that there is considerable variation in the literary style. In passages where Luke can control the style, when, for example, he is writing up his own travel notes, the Greek is excellent; but in his description of the early history of the Palestinian community we find that the language becomes full of semitisms, clumsy and even inaccurate. In some places this is only because he is trying to copy Old Testament LXX Greek, but mostly it is because he is reproducing his various Aramaic sources as closely as possible. In Luke this can be checked by comparing it with two of its sources (i.e. Mark and the document common to Matthew and Luke), but unfortunately there are no texts with which to compare Acts; it is possible, however, to try to determine what kinds of sources were used. One suggestion was that the whole of 1-15:35 is based on a single Aramaic document, but this is far too sweeping as it does not account for all the editing that Luke has unmistakably done in these chapters. Luke has obviously used not one long source but several short ones, many of which may not even have been written documents, though some probably were. Without being dogmatic about details, it is possible to classify the main kinds of traditions collected by Luke. 1. Those that relate to the *primitive Jerusalem community*, ch. 1-5. 2. Biographical notes about *individuals:* e.g. Peter, 9:32-11:18; ch. 12, or Philip, 8:4-40; these details could have been supplied at first hand by people like Philip, the deacon Luke met at Caesarea, 21:8. 3. Details about the early days of the *community in Antioch* and its foundation by hellenistic Jews: these were obviously provided by that community, 6:1-8:3; 11:19-30; 13:1-3. 4. *Paul's conversion and missionary journeys:* these were things Paul himself could have told Luke, 9:1-30; 13:4-14:28; 15:36f. 5. For *Paul's later journeys* Luke would probably have had his own notes and these he seems to use in the 'we' passages which are precisely the sections where the peculiarities of Luke's own style are most concentrated, 11:28; 16:10-17; 20:5-21:18; 27:1-28:16. Luke managed to organise all this material into a single book by sorting it out chronologically as best he could and linking the episodes together with frequent editorial formulae, e.g. 6:7; 9:31; 12:24; etc.

The unsophisticated nature of this material and the respect with which Luke treats it guarantee the *historical worth* of Acts. It was not easy to put all these sources together, and obviously a certain amount of anticipation, repetition and fusion was unavoidable; thus the events of ch. 12 should come before the visit of Barnabas and Saul to Jerusalem mentioned in 11:30; 12:25, unless this visit is to be identified with that of ch. 15; though the account of the 'council of Jerusalem' (ch. 15) may itself be a conflation of two quite distinct debates (cf. notes). Slight adjustments like this do not affect the basic reliability of the work, as may be seen for example by checking how closely Luke's account of Paul's missionary activities agrees with Paul's epistles, which were quite certainly not among the sources Luke used for Acts. This is even true of Galatians if we make allowances for the conflations in Acts. The earlier events, of course, cannot be checked in this way, but may seem reasonable enough in themselves, and Luke seems to have treated the sources for his account with considerable respect, if we may judge by all the realistic and lifelike details he has left in. Considerable suspicion, however, is aroused by the speeches in Acts since it is maintained that Luke has done what all classical historians did and put his own free compositions into the mouth of his characters. On the other hand it is hard to believe that anyone, however gifted, but least of all a person of Greek culture like Luke, could reproduce so convincingly, after forty years, the archaisms and semitisms of, for example, the speeches by Peter and Stephen. Luke must have had access to records in the sense that the earliest preaching made use of only a very few main themes and supported these with stereotyped arguments set out in standard ways and learnt by heart. Christian Jews had anthologies of scriptural texts; non-Jewish Christians had collections of tags from the accepted philosophers, while both had the essential kerygma (proclamation) of the Messiah who was killed and rose again, together with his invitation to conversion and baptism. Luke must first have come across these outlines of Christian preaching as sermons and from his own researches have been able later on, through his acute sense of psychology, to fill them out authentically with the most important Christian teaching.

Whether Acts is objective is the first question that must be faced when discussing the book's *purpose*. F.C. Baur and his followers thought Acts was a 2nd century attempt to smooth over the quarrel between Petrine and Pauline factions. Such a radical attack on the objectivity of Acts would not be put forward by any exegete today, not only because the date it suggests is far too late, but because its formulation is so obviously influenced by Hegel's philosophy of history. To what extent, however, is Acts a piece of special pleading? To what extent does it twist the facts that it records? Was Luke's purpose in writing Acts to present a portrait of Paul that would convince the Roman authorities that Paul was not a political criminal? This is certainly one aspect of Acts but not the only one, and in any case such a portrait of Paul need not necessarily be tendentious—Luke may have been convinced it was a true portrait, and Luke may have been right. The two things he stresses are the exclusively religious nature of Paul's battle with the Jews, and Paul's loyalty to the Roman authority. These were plain facts and Luke had every right to base his portrait on them. However, as has been said, Luke was not merely interested in giving a portrait of Paul to serve as evidence for the Roman courts: what he aimed at was to write the history of the beginnings of Christianity.

This assertion is based on the *structure* of the book that is summarised in the words of Christ with which it begins: 'You will be my witnesses not only in Jerusalem but throughout Judaea and Samaria, and indeed to the ends of the earth', Ac 1:8. Acts begins with Jerusalem where the faith takes firm root and the first community grows in grace and numbers, ch. 1-5. This community begins to expand, under the stimulus of the world-wide outlook of converts from hellenistic Judaism especially after the martyrdom of Stephen when these converts were expelled, 6:1-8:3. The faith spreads north of Jerusalem to Samaria, 8:4-25, south-west to the coast and north again to Caesarea, 8:26-40; 9:32-11:18. The insertion here of Paul's conversion shows that the faith had already reached Damascus and indicates that it was soon to reach Cilicia, 9:1-30. Refrains like the one that closes this section (9:31, which adds Galilee to the list) draw attention repeatedly to the spread of the faith. Acts turns next to the reception of the Good News in Antioch, 11:19-26, and shows how Antioch became a missionary headquarters, while keeping in touch with Jerusalem, and how Jerusalem and Antioch reached an agreed solution to the main problems connected with the missions, 11:27-30; 15:1-35. This leads on to the spread of the faith to the pagans. After his imprisonment following the conversion of Cornelius, Peter goes off to a place that is not named, ch. 12, and from that point Paul takes over the leading part in Luke's story. His first journey (before the council of Jerusalem) takes the faith to Cyprus and Asia Minor, ch. 13-14; his next two journeys take it as far as Macedonia and Greece, 15:36-18:22; 18:23-21:17. After each one he returns to Jerusalem where eventually he is arrested and later imprisoned at Caesarea, 21:18-26:32. This leads him to Rome, where, still a missionary in spite of being a prisoner in chains, Paul preaches the Good News, ch. 27-28, and since Rome could be taken as 'the ends of the earth' by any one who thought of Jerusalem as the centre, Luke has reached a point where he can stop.

It is a pity that Luke does not write about what the other apostles did, or describe how the Church was founded, for example, in Rome where it had been established before Paul's arrival (cf. Romans, written during Paul's third journey) or in Alexandria. Luke does not even suggest that Peter had an apostolate outside Palestine: there is never any doubt as to who the focus of attention is all through Acts, though only the second half is devoted to Paul exclusively. The sort of things, however, that Luke does not mention and the kind of gaps he leaves are valuable guarantees of the things he does say, since he limits himself to facts that he has acquired either at first hand or from sources he has checked. Luke is not interested in giving *all* the details about the spread of Christianity. What he is interested in is: 1. the spiritual energy inside Christianity that motivates its expansion, and 2. the spiritual doctrine he can deduce from the facts at his disposal. This is what the book is about, and what makes it universal and irreplaceable.

Here it is only possible to list the main points of this elaborate *theology* of Acts. 1. The kerygma (proclamation) of the apostles is centred on faith in Christ, and in Acts this is presented with many slight variations that make it possible for us to recover the history of how this teaching grew more and more precise; e.g. the earliest Christians are shown as feeling no need to go beyond the stage of contemplating the triumph of the human Jesus who has become the *Kyrios* by his resurrection, 2:22-36; but later Paul is made to give him the title 'Son of God', 9:20. 2. From the speeches we know the main scriptural texts that (under the Spirit's guidance) formed the basis both for a systematic Christology and for arguments with the Jews: e.g. the themes of the Servant, 3:13,26; 4:27,30; 8:32-33, and the second Moses, 3:22f; 7:20f; the proof of the resurrection from Ps 16:8-11 (Ac 2:24-32; 13:34-37); and the use of their own history to warn Jews against resisting grace, 7:2-53; 13:16-41. Pagans, of course, needed a more generalised theological argument, 14:15-17; 17:22-31, and though the apostles are primarily 'witnesses', 1:8+ (as such Luke sums up their kerygma, 2:22+, and records their miraculous 'signs') the most urgent problem facing the new Church was the admission of pagans, and Acts provides important details about this. The Jerusalem brotherhood led by James remains faithful to the Jewish Law, 15:1,5; 21:20f; but the Hellenists, for whom Stephen acts as spokesman, want to break away from Temple worship. Peter, but even more so Paul, get the principle of salvation through faith in Christ recognised at the council of Jerusalem. This dispenses the pagans from the need to be circumcised and from obeying the Law of Moses. As it is still true, however, that this salvation comes from Israel, Luke records how Paul always preached to the Jews first, and only turned to the pagans after his fellow Jews had rejected him, 13:5+. 3. Acts also provides important details about life in the earliest Christian communities: e.g. the way of prayer and community of goods known to the church in Jerusalem; the administration of baptism in water and baptism in Spirit, 1:5+; celebration of the Eucharist, 2:42+; early attempts at organisation in e.g. 'prophets' and 'teachers', 13:1+, and the 'elders' who preside in the Jerusalem church, 11:30+, and who are also appointed by Paul in the churches he founds, 14:23. 4. All these developments in community life are attributed to the irresistible guidance of the Spirit. As Lk 4:1+ insists on the importance of the Holy Spirit so Acts (1:8+) attributes the spread of the developing Church to the continuous activity of the Holy Spirit—this is why the book has been called 'the gospel of the Spirit', and why it seems so full of spiritual joy and of wonder at God's works, a fact that can hardly surprise those who understand what the coming of Christianity meant to a world that had never seen anything like it. 5. To this wealth of theology we must add the detailed factual information which we should otherwise lack, the psychological tact with which Luke typically presents his characters, the shrewdness and the craftsmanship of passages like the speech in the presence of Agrippa, ch. 26, and the pathos of scenes like the farewell to the Ephesian elders, 20:17-38. This book, the only one of its kind in the New Testament, is full of treasures. Without it, there would be great gaps in what we know about the beginnings of Christianity.

The texts of the New Testament have come down to us with a great number of minor variants, and for Acts those in the so-called 'Western' Text (Codex Bezae, the old Latin and old Syriac versions, and early ecclesiastical writers) are the most interesting. Because this Western Text has not been critically edited like the Alexandrian recension, it contains many corrupt readings, but many of its concrete and vivid details, absent from the other texts, could be authentic. The most important of these readings have been either mentioned in the footnotes or incorporated in the text.

THE ACTS
OF THE APOSTLES

Prologue

Lk 1:1-4 *1:22* 1 In my earlier work,[a] Theophilus, I dealt with everything Jesus had done and 1
Mt 28:19-20 Lk 24:49 taught from the beginning •until the day he gave his instructions to the 2
Lk 24:51 1 Tm 3:16 apostles he had chosen through the Holy Spirit,[b] and was taken up to heaven.[c]
10:40-41; 13:31 He had shown himself alive to them after his Passion by many demonstrations: 3
Mt 28:10 for forty days he had continued to appear to them and tell them about the
19:8 Lk 24:42-43 kingdom of God.[d] •When he had been at table with them, he had told them not 4
||*Lk 24:49* *2:33+* to leave Jerusalem, but to wait there for what the Father had promised. 'It is'
Ga 3:14 Ep 1:13 he had said 'what you have heard me speak about: •John baptised with water but 5
11:16 Lk 3:16p you, not many days from now, will be baptised[e] with the Holy Spirit.'

The ascension

Now having met together,[f] they asked him, 'Lord, has the time come? Are 6
Dn 2:21 Mt 24:36p you going to restore the kingdom to Israel?'[g] •He replied, 'It is not for you to 7
1 Th 5:1-2 know times or dates[h] that the Father has decided by his own authority, •but 8
Is 43:10 Mt 28:19 you will receive power when the Holy Spirit comes on you,[i] and then you will be
||Lk 24:47-48 my witnesses[j] not only in Jerusalem but throughout Judaea and Samaria, and
indeed to the ends of the earth'.[k]
2 K 2:11 Mk 16:19 As he said this he was lifted up while they looked on, and a cloud[l] took him 9
||Lk 24:50-51 Jn 20:17 from their sight. •They were still staring into the sky when suddenly two men 10
Rm 10:6 Ep 4:8-10 in white were standing near them •and they said, 'Why are you men from Galilee 11
1 P 3:22 *Lk 24:4* standing here looking into the sky? Jesus who has been taken up from you into
3:20 Zc 14:4 heaven, this same Jesus[m] will come back in the same way[n] as you have seen him
go there.'

I. THE JERUSALEM CHURCH

The group of apostles

So from the Mount of Olives, as it is called, they went back to Jerusalem, 12
a short distance away, no more than a sabbath walk; •and when they reached 13
||Lk 6:14-16p the city they went to the upper room where they were staying; there were Peter
and John, James and Andrew, Philip and Thomas, Bartholomew and Matthew,
James son of Alphaeus and Simon the Zealot, and Jude son of James.[o] •All 14
2:42,46; 6:4 Rm 12:12 these joined in continuous prayer, together with several women, including
Lk 23:49 Mary the mother of Jesus, and with his brothers.[p]

The election of Matthias

One day Peter stood up to speak to the brothers[q]—there were about a 15
1:20 hundred and twenty persons in the congregation: •'Brothers, the passage of 16
Ps 41:9 Jn 13:18 scripture had to be fulfilled in which the Holy Spirit, speaking through David,

foretells the fate of Judas, who offered himself as a guide to the men who Lk 22:47
7 arrested Jesus—•after having been one of our number and actually sharing this
8 ministry of ours. •As you know, he bought a field with the money he was paid ||Mt 27:3-10
for his crime. He fell headlong and burst open, and all his entrails poured out. Ws 4:19
19 Everybody in Jerusalem heard about it and the field came to be called the Bloody
20 Acre, in their language Hakeldama. •Now in the Book of Psalms it says:

Let his camp be reduced to ruin, Ps 69:25 Jn 17:12
Let there be no one to live in it.

And again:

Let someone else take his office. Ps 109:8

21 'We must therefore choose someone who has been with us the whole time that
22 the Lord Jesus was travelling round with us, •someone who was with us right
from the time when John was baptising until the day when he was taken up from
us—and he can act with us as a witness to his resurrection.' 1:8+; 10:39
23 Having nominated two candidates, Joseph known as Barsabbas, whose
24 surname was Justus, and Matthias, •they prayed, 'Lord, you can read everyone's 13:9+
25 heart; show us therefore which of these two you have chosen •to take over this 15:8 Jr 11:20+
ministry and apostolate, which Judas abandoned to go to his proper place'. Lk 16:15 Rv 2:23
26 They then drew lots for them, and as the lot fell to Matthias, he was listed as *Ex 33:7+* 1 S 14:41+
one of the twelve apostles.[r]

1 a. The gospel of Luke.

b. This emphasises the part played by the Spirit in the first missionary activities of the apostles, vv. 5,8 and ch. 2, as in the opening of Christ's ministry, Lk 4:1,14,18.

c. The Western Text does not mention the ascension here.

d. The kingdom of God, Mt 4:17+, must be the main subject preached by the apostles, cf. Ac 8:12; 19:8; 20:25; 28:23,31, as it was the main thing preached by Christ, cf. Mt 3:2+.

e. The baptism of the Spirit foretold by John the Baptist, Mt 3:11p, and here promised by Jesus, will be initiated by the outpouring of the Spirit at Pentecost, Ac 2:1-4. Subsequently, the apostles, obedient to Christ's command, Mt 28:19, will continue to make use of baptism in water, Ac 2:41; 8:12,38; 9:18; 10:48; 16:15, 33; 18:8; 19:5, as the ritual initiation into the messianic kingdom, cf. Mt 3:6+, but it will be 'in the name of Jesus', Ac 2:38+, and through belief in Christ as saviour, cf. Rm 6:4+, will be able to absolve from sins and to give the Spirit, Ac 2:38. Connected with this Christian baptism by water there is the companion rite of the imposition of hands, 1 Tm 4:14+, the purpose of which is to give the gifts of the Spirit in as manifest a way as they had been given at Pentecost, Ac 8:16-19; 9:17-18; 19:5-6 (but cf. 10:44-48); this is the origin of the sacrament of confirmation. Side by side with these Christian sacraments the baptism of John was for a time still being administered by certain of the less instructed early Christians, 19:3.

f. Ac 1:6 takes up the narrative broken off in Lk 24:49.

g. The apostles still identified the messianic kingdom with the political restoration of David's dynasty. Cf. Mt 4:17+.

h. Human history is the unfolding of salvation, and it develops through the 'times and dates', cf. Dn 2:21; 1 Th 5:1, that God has always foreseen (Rm 16:25+; 1 Co 2:7; Ep 1:4; 3:9,11; Col 1:26; 2 Tm 1:9; cf. Mt 25: 34): first there are the 'times' of preparation, Heb 1:2; 9:9; 1 P 1:11, and of God's patience, Rm 3:26; Ac 17:30; then follows the appointed time, Ga 4:4+, the moment long foretold for the Messiah to come and begin the era of salvation, Rm 3:26+; after this, the time that is to elapse before the *parousia* or final coming, 2 Co 6:2+; lastly, the great and final 'Day', 1 Co 1:8+ (preceded by the 'last days', 1 Tm 4:1+, and the Last Judgement itself, Rm 2:6+.

i. The Holy Spirit is a favourite theme of Luke (Lk 4:1+); he talks mostly about the Holy Spirit as a Power, Lk 1:35; 24:49; Ac 1:8; 10:38; Rm 15:13,19; 1 Co 2:4,5; 1 Th 1:5; Heb 2:4, sent from God by Christ, Ac 2:33, to broadcast the Good News. 1. The Spirit gives the charismata, 1 Co 12:4f, that guarantee the message: the gift of tongues, Ac 2:4+, of miracles, 10:38, of prophecy, 11:27+; 20:23; 21:11, of wisdom, 6:3,5,10; 2. the Spirit gives strength to proclaim Jesus as Messiah in spite of persecution, 4:8,31; 5:32; 6:10; cf. Ph 1:19, and to bear witness to him, Mt 10:20p; Jn 15:26; Ac 1:8; 2 Tm 1:7f, cf. following note; 3. the Spirit guides the Church in her major decisions: the admission of pagans, Ac 8:29,40; 10:19,44-47; 11:12-16; 15:8, without obligation to observe the Law, 15:28; Paul's mission to the pagan world, 13:2f; 16:6-7; 19:1 (Western Text), cf. Mt 3:16+. Ac also mentions the Spirit as received in baptism and forgiving sins 2:38; cf. Rm 5:5+.

j. The primary function of the apostles is to bear witness: not only to Christ's resurrection, Lk 24:48; Ac 2:32; 3:15; 4:33; 5:32; 13:31; 22:15, but also to the whole of his public life, Lk 1:21; Jn 15:27; Ac 1:22; 10:39f.

k. Nothing can limit the apostolic mission, Is 45: 14+. The progress outlined here follows the geographical plan of Ac: Jerusalem was destined to receive the Good News, to be the centre from which it is now spreading, cf. Lk 2:38+.

l. The cloud is part of theophanies in O.T., Ex 13:22+, and in N.T., Lk 9:34-35p. In particular, Dn 7:13, it marks the coming, or *parousia*, of the Son of Man, Mt 24:30+; v. 11 of this passage; cf. 1 Th 4:17; Rv 1:7; 14:14-16.

m. Thus the Western Text. Text. Rec. 'this Jesus who has been taken up from you into heaven'.

n. The glorious coming, the *parousia*, see notes on Mt 24 and Lk 17:22-37; 21:5-33.

o. 'Son' (of Alphaeus, of James) is not in the Greek. The apostle Jude is not the Jude 'brother' of Jesus, cf. Mt 13:55; Mk 6:3, and brother of James (Jude 1). Nor is it likely that the apostle James son of Alphaeus was James brother of the Lord, Ac 12:17; 15:13, etc.

p. Cousins of Jesus, cf. Mt 12:46+.

q. The term means Christians, usually the laity as distinct from apostles and elders, cf. 11:1; 12:17; 17-18; Rm 1:13, etc.

r. 'he was listed as one of the twelve apostles' Western Text.

Pentecost

Ex 23:14+ **2** When Pentecost day came round, they[a] had all met in one room, •when 1 2
4:31 Ps 33:6; suddenly they heard what sounded like a powerful wind from heaven,[b] the
104:30 Jn 3:8+; noise of which filled the entire house in which they were sitting; •and something 3
20:22 appeared to them that seemed like tongues of fire;[c] these separated and came
1:5+; 19:6 to rest on the head of each of them. •They were all filled with the Holy Spirit, 4
1:8+ Ws 1:7 and began to speak foreign languages as the Spirit[d] gave them the gift of speech.
Lk 24:47 Now there were devout men[e] living in Jerusalem from every nation under 5
Mt 28:19 Col 1:23 heaven, •and at this sound they all assembled, each one bewildered to hear these 6
Gn 11:1-9 men speaking his own language.[f] •They were amazed and astonished. 'Surely' 7
they said 'all these men speaking are Galileans? •How does it happen that each 8
of us hears them in his own native language? •Parthians, Medes and Elamites; 9
people from Mesopotamia, Judaea and Cappadocia, Pontus and Asia, •Phrygia 1
and Pamphylia, Egypt and the parts of Libya round Cyrene; as well as visitors
10:2+ from Rome—•Jews and proselytes[g] alike—Cretans and Arabs; we hear them 1
10:46 preaching in our own language about the marvels of God.' •Everyone was 1
amazed and unable to explain it; they asked one another what it all meant.
1 Co 14:23 Some, however, laughed it off. 'They have been drinking too much new wine' 1
they said.

Peter's address to the crowd

3:4; 4:8; 5:8,29; 10:5 Then Peter stood up with the Eleven[h] and addressed them in a loud voice: 1
'Men of Judaea, and all you who live in Jerusalem, make no mistake about
this, but listen carefully to what I say. •These men are not drunk, as you 1
2:33+ imagine; why, it is only the third hour of the day.[i] •On the contrary, this is 1
what the prophet[j] spoke of:

Jl 3:1-5 Is 2:2 *Rm 7:5+* Si 1:10 *11:27+;* 21:9
In the days to come[k]—it is the Lord who speaks— 1
I will pour out my spirit on all mankind.
Their sons and daughters shall prophesy,
your young men shall see visions,
your old men shall dream dreams.
Even on my slaves, men and women, 1
in those days, I will pour out my spirit.
I will display portents in heaven *above* 1
5:12 and *signs* on earth *below*.
Mt 24:29p The sun will be turned into darkness 2
and the moon into blood
before the great Day of the Lord dawns.[l]
Rm 10:9-13 1 Co 1:2 All who call on the name of the Lord will be saved.[m] 2

Mt 2:23+ 'Men of Israel, listen to what I am going to say:[n] Jesus the Nazarene was a 22
10:38 Lk 24:19 man commended to you by God by the miracles and portents and signs that
God worked through him when he was among you, as you all know. •This 23
4:10 1 Th 2:15 man, who was put into your power by the deliberate intention[o] and foreknowledge
of God, you took and had crucified by men outside the Law.[p] You killed him,
Ps 18:6 but God raised him to life, freeing him from the pangs of Hades;[q] for it was 24
13:34-37 impossible for him to be held in its power since, •as David says of him:[r] 25

Ps 16:8-11
I saw the Lord before me always,
for with him at my right hand nothing can shake me.
So my heart was glad 26
and my tongue cried out with joy;
my body, too, will rest in the hope
that you will not abandon my soul to Hades 27
nor allow your holy one to experience corruption.
You have made known the way of life to me, 28
you will fill me with gladness through your presence.

29 'Brothers, no one can deny that the patriarch David himself is dead and
30 buried: his tomb is still with us. •But since he was a prophet, and knew that
God *had sworn him* an oath *to make one of his descendants succeed him on the* 2 S 7:12 Ps 132:11
31 *throne*, •what he foresaw and spoke about was the resurrection of the Christ: Mt 9:27+
he is the one who was *not abandoned to Hades*, and whose body did not *experience*
32 *corruption*. •God raised this man Jesus to life, and all of us are witnesses to that. 1:8+
33 Now raised to the heights by God's right hand,[s] he has received from the Father 1:4-5+ Ezk 36:27+
the Holy Spirit, who was promised,[t] and what you see and hear is the outpouring Mt 21:9,42
34 of that Spirit. •For David himself never went up to heaven;[u] and yet these Ep 4:8-11
words are his:

The Lord said to my Lord: Ps 110:1
Sit at my right hand
35 *until I make your enemies*
a footstool for you.

36 'For this reason the whole House of Israel can be certain that God has made 2:23+; 9:22; 10:42; 13:33
this Jesus whom you crucified both Lord and Christ.'[v] Rm 10:9 Ph 2:11+

2 a. Not the hundred and twenty, 1:15-26, but the group mentioned in 1:13-14.

b. The Spirit is like the wind, and the same word is used for both 'spirit' and 'breath'.

c. The shape of the flames (Is 5:24; cf. Is 6:6-7) is here associated with the gift of tongues.

d. One element, vv. 4,11,13, of the Pentecost miracle is the gift of *glossolalia* common in the early Church: see 10:46; 11:15; 19:6; 1 Co 12-14; cf. Mk 16:17, cf. early prophecy in Israel, Nb 11: 25-29; 1 S 10:5-6,10-13; 19:20-24; 1 K 22:10. Cf. the promise of Joel, 3:1-5, quoted by Peter, vv. 17f.

e. 'devout men' Sin. Western Text 'Now the Jews who were living in Jerusalem were men from every nation under heaven'. The other texts have both 'devout men' and 'Jews'.

f. A second characteristic of the Pentecost miracle: the apostles speak a universal language: the unity lost at Babel is restored. This symbolises and anticipates the apostles' worldwide mission.

g. Pagan converts to Judaism who joined the chosen race by being circumcised. These proselytes are not the same as the God-fearers, 10:2+, who admire the Jewish religion and attend the synagogue but do not accept circumcision or the ritual prescribed by the Law. Jews and proselytes are not here additional classes of people: the terms qualify the nations just enumerated.

h. Peter speaks as head of the apostolic body and occupies a leading position, cf. 1:15; 2:37; 3:4,6,12; 4:8,13; 5:3,8,9,15,29; cf. 10-11. See Mt 16:19+.

i. About 9 a.m.

j. Add. 'Joel'. Vv. 17-21 quoted as in Western Text; Alexandrian Text favours the LXX.

k. The messianic age.

l. The day of the Lord's coming in glory, the 'day of Yahweh', Am 5:18+. In Christian preaching, this 'day' is that of Christ's return, Mt 24:1+.

m. The Christians style themselves 'those who invoke the name of the Lord', 9:14,21; 22:16; 1 Co 1:2; 2 Tm 2:22; the title 'Lord' no longer indicates Yahweh but Jesus, cf. Ph 2:11; Ac 3:16+. On Judgement day people will be received or rejected according as they have or have not invoked this name, i.e. acknowledged Jesus as Lord: see Ac 4:12 and Rm 10:9.

n. The content of the earliest apostolic preaching (the 'kerygma') is here summarised for the first time; cf. the five discourses of Peter, Ac 2:14-39; 3:12-26; 4:8-12; 5:29-32; 10:34-43, and the discourse of Paul, 13:16-41. The kerygma is 1. a witness, 1:8+, to Christ's death and resurrection, 2:24+, and to his exaltation, 2:33+; 2:36+. 2. It also provides certain details of Christ's ministry; how it was heralded by John the Baptist, 10:37; 13:24, inaugurated by teaching and miracle, 2:22; 10:38, completed by the appearances of the risen Christ, 10:40,41; 13:31, and by the gift of the Spirit, 2:33; 5:32. 3. It places this story in its wider setting: it appeals to the past, adducing the O.T. prophecies, 2:23+; 2:25+, and it surveys the future, the advent of the messianic era, inviting Jews and pagans to repentance, 2:38+, so that Christ's glorious return may come the sooner, 3:20-21. The gospels, which are developments of the primitive preaching, adopt the same scheme.

o. The O.T. prophecies demonstrate this divine plan: Ac 3:18; 4:28; 13:29, cf. 8:32-35; 9:22; 10:43; 17:2-3; 18:5,28; 26:22-23,27; 28:23; Lk 18:31+; 22:22; 24:25-27,44.

p. In this case the Romans. The primitive kerygma accused the Jews in the same way, and confronted them with that act of God which raised up Jesus, 2:32,36; 3:13-17; 4:10; 5:30-31; 7:52; 10:39-40; 13:27-30; 17:31; cf. Rm 1:4+; 1 Th 2:14+.

q. 'of Hades' Western Text; 'of death' Text. Rec. Cf. vv. 27 and 31. 'Hades' in LXX is *sheol*, Nb 16:33+; Mt 16:18+.

r. Quoted according to LXX. In the Hebr. text the psalmist prays only for deliverance from imminent death 'You will not allow your faithful one to see the pit'. Hence the argument presupposes the Greek version which, by translating 'pit' (=grave) as 'corruption', introduces a new idea.

s. Words borrowed from Ps 118 (v. 16 LXX 'The right hand of the Lord has raised me up') used in their preaching by the apostles who took it to be messianic: Ac 4:11; 1 P 2:7; Mt 21:9p,42p; 23:39; Lk 13:35; Jn 12:13; Heb 13:6. But it is possible to translate 'Having been raised up to the right hand of God' and to see in this an introduction to the quotation (v. 34) of Ps 110:1, which is another theme of apostolic preaching: Mt 22:44p; 26:64p; Mk 16:19; Ac 7:55,56; Rm 8:34; 1 Co 15:25; Ep 1:20; Col 3:1; Heb 1:3,13; 8:1; 10:12; 12:2; 1 P 3:22.

t. According to the prophets, the gift of the Spirit would characterise the messianic era, Ezk 36:27+ Peter explains the miracle his hearers have witnessed as the 'pouring out' of this spirit, foretold in Jl 3:1-2, by the risen Christ.

u. The argument is, apparently, that David lies in his tomb and therefore did not ascend into heaven; hence God's summons was addressed not to him but to the one who came out from the tomb. A variant reading 'for he himself says', in place of 'and yet these is words are his' (i.e. it was said by, not to, him), reduces the argument to that of Mt 22:43-45.

v. Conclusion of the argument from scripture: it is by his resurrection that Jesus has been constituted the 'Lord' of whom Ps 110 speaks, and the 'Messiah' (Christ) to whom Ps 16 refers. From Ps 2:7 (Son of God), Ac 13:33+; Heb 1:5; 5:5; Rm 1:4+ develop a similar argument. Cf. also Ac 5:31 (leader and saviour); 10:42 and Rm 14:9 (Judge and Lord of living and dead); Ph 2:9-11 (glorified Lord).

The first conversions

Hearing this, they were cut to the heart and said to Peter and the apostles, 37
16:30 Lk 3:10 'What must we do, brothers?' •'You must repent,'[w] Peter answered 'and every 38
1:5+ Mt 3:2+ one of you must be baptised in the name of Jesus Christ[x] for the forgiveness of
2:33+ your sins, and you will receive the gift of the Holy Spirit. •The promise[y] that was 39
Is 57:19 made is for you and your children, and for all *those who are far away,*[z] *for all*
Jl 3:5 *those whom the Lord* our God *will call to himself*.' •He spoke to them[aa] for a long 40
Dt 32:5 Mt 17:17 time using many arguments, and he urged them, 'Save yourselves from this
Lk 9:41 perverse generation'. •They were convinced by his arguments, and they accepted 41
1:5+; 2:47 what he said and were baptised. That very day about three thousand were added
to their number.[bb]

4:32-35; 5:12-16

The early Christian community[cc]

1:14; 6:4 These remained faithful to the teaching of the apostles,[dd] to the brotherhood,[ee] 42
to the breaking of bread[ff] and to the prayers.[gg]
=5:11-12 The many miracles and signs worked through the apostles made a deep 43
impression on everyone.[hh]
=4:32,34-35 The faithful all lived together and owned everything in common; •they sold 44 45
their goods and possessions and shared out the proceeds among themselves
6:1 according to what each one needed.
5:12; 13:48 Lk 24:53 They went as a body to the Temple every day but met in their houses for the 46
breaking of bread; they shared their food gladly[ii] and generously; •they praised 47
4:21,33; 5:13 God[jj] and were looked up to by everyone. Day by day the Lord added to their
2:41+ community those destined to be saved.[kk]

14:8-10

The cure of a lame man

Lk 8:51 3 Once, when Peter and John were going up to the Temple for the prayers at 1
the ninth hour,[a] •it happened that there was a man being carried past. He 2
was a cripple from birth; and they used to put him down every day near the
Temple entrance called the Beautiful Gate so that he could beg from the people
going in. •When this man saw Peter and John on their way into the Temple he 3
2:14+ begged from them. •Both Peter and John looked straight at him and said, 'Look 4
at us'. •He turned to them expectantly, hoping to get something from them, 5
but Peter said, 'I have neither silver nor gold, but I will give you what I have: 6
3:16+; 4:10 Mt 2:23+ in the name of Jesus Christ the Nazarene, walk!'[b] •Peter then took him by 7
the hand and helped him to stand up. Instantly his feet and ankles became firm,
Is 35:6 Lk 7:22p he jumped up, stood, and began to walk, and he went with them into the Temple, 8
2:47+ walking and jumping and praising God. •Everyone could see him walking and 9
praising God, •and they recognised him as the man who used to sit begging at 10
Lk 1:12+ *5:5; 19:17* the Beautiful Gate of the Temple. They were all astonished and unable to
explain what had happened to him.

Peter's address to the people

Everyone came running towards them in great excitement, to the Portico of 11
5:12 Jn 10:23 Solomon, as it is called, where the man was still clinging to Peter and John.
When Peter saw the people he addressed them, 'Why are you so surprised at 12
10:26; 14:15 this? Why are you staring at us as though we had made this man walk by our
Ex 3:6,15 own power or holiness? •You are Israelites, and it is *the God of Abraham, Isaac* 13
4:27 Is 52:13 *and Jacob, the God of our ancestors, who has glorified his servant*[c] Jesus, the same
2:23+ Jesus you handed over[d] and then disowned[e] in the presence of Pilate after Pilate
Lk 23:22+ *Lk 23:2,5, 19,25,47* had decided to release him. •It was you who accused[f] the Holy One,[g] the Just 14
2:23+ One,[h] you who demanded the reprieve of a murderer •while you killed the prince 15
of life.[i] God, however, raised him from the dead, and to that fact we are the
1:8+ Heb 2:11 witnesses; •and it is the name of Jesus which, through our faith in it, has 16
brought back the strength of this man whom you see here and who is well known

to you. It is faith in that name that has restored this man to health, as you can 3:6; 4:10
all see.[j]
7 'Now I know, brothers, that neither you nor your leaders had any idea what 13:27 1 Co 2:8
8 you were really doing;[k] •this was the way God carried out what he had foretold, 1 Tm 1:13
9 when he said through all his prophets that his Christ would suffer. •Now you Lk 18:31
0 must repent and turn to God,[l] so that your sins may be wiped out, •and so 2:38+ Mt 3:2+
that the Lord may send the time of comfort.[m] Then he will send you the Christ *2 P 3:11-13*
1 he has predestined, that is Jesus,[n] •whom heaven must keep till the universal
restoration[o] comes which God proclaimed, speaking through his holy prophets.[p] Ml 3:23-24 Mt 17:11
2 Moses, for example, said: *The Lord God will raise up a prophet like myself for you,* *7:37* Dt 18:18,19
3 *from among your own brothers; you must listen to whatever he tells you.* •*The* Mt 16:14+ Jn 1:21+

w. Each of the great apostolic discourses closes with a call to repentance (cf. Mt 3:2+) to obtain forgiveness of sins: Ac 3:19,26; 5:31; 10:43; 13:38; cf.17:30; 26:20; Lk 1:77; 3:8; 5:32; 13:3.

x. Baptism is administered 'in the name of Jesus Christ' (cf. 1:5+) and the recipient 'invokes the name of the Lord Jesus' (cf. 2:21+; 3:16+): 8:16; 10:48; 19:5; 22:16; 1 Co 1:13,15; 6:11; 10:2; Ga 3:27; Rm 6:3; cf. Jm 2:7. Such expressions are not necessarily the actual liturgical formulae of baptism, cf. Mt 28:19, they may simply indicate its significance, namely, that the baptised profess their faith in Christ, and Christ adopts those who thenceforth are dedicated to him.

y. The promise is addressed primarily to the Jews, 3:25-26; 13:46; Rm 9:4.

z. I.e. the pagans, alluding to Is 57:19 quoted and explained in Ep 2:13-17; cf. also Ac 22:21.

aa. Or 'he bore witness', cf. 8:25; 28:23.

bb. Luke repeatedly and deliberately notes the Church's numerical growth: v. 47; 4:4; 5:14; 6:1,7; 9:31+; 11:21,24; 16:5; cf. 12:24; 13:48-49; 19:20.

cc. Cf. this passage with 4:32-35 and 5:12-16. These three composite editorial 'summaries' paint similar pictures of life in the first Christian community.

dd. Not the proclamation of the Good News to non-Christians, cf. 15:35, but instructions for the newly converted in which the scriptures were explained in the light of the Christian Event.

ee. What constitutes this 'brotherhood' or 'fellowship' is a united purpose, cf. Ga 2:9; Phm 6; 1 Jn 1:3,6,7, and a care for the poorer members to the extent of holding all goods in common, cf. Rm 15:26; 2 Co 8:4; 9:13; Ph 1:5+. In a word: charity.

ff. See v. 46; 20:7,11; 27:35; Lk 24:30,35. In itself the phrase suggests a Jewish meal at which the one who presides pronounces a blessing before dividing the bread. For Christians, however, it implies the eucharistic ceremony, 1 Co 10:16; 11:24; Lk 22:19p; 24:35+. This, v. 46, was celebrated not in the Temple but in private houses; an ordinary meal would accompany it, cf. 1 Co 11:20-34.

gg. Prayers in common, with the apostles presiding, 6:4; 4:24-30, is one example. Cf. 1:14,24; 12:5. There are many examples in Ac of the constant prayer Jesus recommended (Mt 6:5) and practised (Mt 14:23+). There is the prayer in common presided over by the apostles (1:14; 4:24-30; 6:4) with the breaking of bread as the central ceremony (2:42,46; 20:7,11); the prayer for special occasions like the election and ordination to office in the Church (1:24; 6:6; 13:3; 14:23—accompanied in the last two cases by fasting); the confirmation of the Samaritans (8:15); the prayer in time of persecution (4:24-30; 12:5,12). There are also individual prayers: that of Stephen for himself and his persecutors (7:59-60), the prayer of Paul after his vision (9:5), of Peter and Paul before they work miracles (9:40; 28:8), of Peter when God sends him to Cornelius (10:9; 11:5) who is himself a man of prayer (10:2,4,30-31), of Paul and Silas in prison (16:25), of Paul when he bids farewell at Miletus (20:36) and at Tyre. In most of these cases the prayer is a petition (see also the petition for forgiveness in 8:22-24), but there is also the prayer of praise (16:25) and thanksgiving (28:15). Prayer is evidence of faith: 'to invoke the name of Jesus Christ' is the mark of a Christian (2:21,38; 9:14,21; 22:16).

hh. Add. 'in Jerusalem, and upon all there was great fear'.

ii. Joy is the sequel of faith: 8:8,39; 13:48,52; 16:34; cf. 5:41; Lk 1:14+; Rm 15:13.

jj. Cf. 3:8,9; 4:21; 13:48; 21:20; Lk 2:20+.

kk. When judgement comes the members of the Christian community are assured of salvation, 2:21+, cf. 13:48 and St Paul's letters. The Church is thus identified with 'the remnant of Israel', Is 4:3+. Cf. Rm 9:27.

3 a. The time of evening sacrifice, cf. Ex 29:39,42; Lk 1:8-10+; Ac 10:3,30.

b. Var. 'get up and walk', cf. Lk 5:23-24, etc.

c. The Christians see in Jesus the mysterious 'servant' of Is 52:13–53:12 (quoted in part in Ac 8:32-33), cf. Is 42:1+. See below, v. 26; 4:27,30. His 'glorification' by God is his resurrection, v. 15. Cf. Jn 17:5+.

d. Cf. Is 53:12. Same allusion to the Servant Song in Rm 4:25; 8:32; Ga 2:20; Ep 5:2,25; Ac 7:52.

e. As they disowned Moses, 7:35, himself a figure of Christ.

f. Var. 'disowned'.

g. Cf. with Ac 4:27,30: Jesus is 'the holy servant of God'. He is also 'the holy one of God' and 'the holy one' *par excellence:* Ac 2:27; Lk 1:35; 4:34; Mk 1:24+; Jn 6:69; Rv 3:7.

h. Cf. Is 53:11; Ac 7:52; 22:14. See also Mt 27:19; Lk 23:47; 1 P 3:18; 1 Jn 2:1.

i. The one who leads his subjects to full life, imparting his own life to them. In the Roman liturgy the Easter Sequence borrows the expression *Dux vitae mortuus regnat vivus.* This same title of 'leader' is given, 7:27,35, to Moses who prefigures Christ Cf 5:31+; Heb 2:10.

j. The 'name', according to the ancients, is inseparable from the person and shares his prerogatives, see Ex 3:14+. By invoking the name of Jesus, 2:21+,38+, his power is stirred to action, 3:6; 4:7,10,30; 10:43; 16:18; 19:13; Lk 9:49; 10:17; see also Jn 14:13,14; 15:16; 16:24,26; 20:31. Faith is of course required if this invocation is to be effective, cf. Ac 19:13-17; Mt 8:10+.

k. Apparently an allusion to Lk 23:34; cf. Ac 7:60.

l. By 'repentance' man 'comes back' to God, cf. Mt 3:2+. The pagans must return to God by forsaking idols; see 1 Th 1:9; Ga 4:9; 1 Co 10:7,14; Ac 14:15; 15:19; 26:18,20; the Jews must turn to the Lord by acknowledging Jesus as Lord: cf. 2 Co 3:16; Ac 9:35. The expression of Lk 1:16; Ac 11:21; cf. 1 P 2:25 is somewhat different. Cf. also Is 6:10, quoted in Ac 28:27; Mt 13:15; Mk 4:12; cf. Jn 12:40.

m. This epoch coincides with that of Christ's coming and of 'the restoration of all things', cf. 1:7+; Rm 2:6+, a period which, as the apostles thought, would see the re-establishment of the kingdom in Israel, Ac 1:6-7. Repentance and conversion hasten its coming, cf. 2 P 3:12.

n. Or 'Jesus who has been appointed Christ for you' cf. 2:36+. When the time comes, Christ who became King Messiah through his resurrection will return to establish his kingdom for ever and to make all creation new, v. 21, cf. Rm 8:19+.

o. Term used by the prophets for the return from Exile (foretaste of the messianic age). Jr 15:19, etc.

p. Add. 'from ancient times'.

Mt 17:5p *man who does not listen to that prophet is to be cut off from the people.* •In fact,
Lk 24:25 all the prophets that have ever spoken, from Samuel onwards, have predicted
these days.[q]

Si 44:19-21 Rm 9:4; 15:8 'You are the heirs of the prophets, the heirs of the covenant God made with
Gn 12:3+; 22:18 our ancestors when he told Abraham: *in your offspring all the families of the earth*
2:39+ Ga 3:8-29 *will be blessed.* •It was for you in the first place that God raised up[r] his servant
and sent him to bless you[s] by turning every one of you from your wicked
ways.'[t]

Peter and John before the Sanhedrin

Lk 22:4+ **4** While they were still talking to the people the priests came up to them, accom-
5:17-18,24 panied by the captain of the Temple and the Sadducees.[a] •They were extremely
23:6-8; 24:15,21 annoyed at their teaching the people the doctrine of the resurrection from the
1 Co 15:20-23 dead by proclaiming the resurrection of Jesus. •They arrested them, but as it
was already late, they held them till the next day. •But many of those who had
2:41+ listened to their message became believers, the total number of whom had now
risen to something like five thousand.

The next day the rulers, elders and scribes[b] had a meeting in Jerusalem •with
5:17 Lk 3:2+ Annas the high priest, Caiaphas, Jonathan,[c] Alexander and all the members
of the high-priestly families. •They made the prisoners stand in the middle and
Lk 20:2 began to interrogate them, 'By what power, and by whose name have you men
1:8+; 2:14+, done this?' •Then Peter, filled with the Holy Spirit, addressed them, 'Rulers of
22+ Mt 10:20 the people, and elders! •If you are questioning us today about an act of kindness
to a cripple, and asking us how he was healed, •[d]then I am glad to tell you all,
and would indeed be glad to tell the whole people of Israel, that it was by the
3:6,16+ name of Jesus Christ the Nazarene, the one you crucified, whom God raised
2:23-24+ from the dead, by this name and by no other that this man is able to stand up
Ps 118:22 2:33+ perfectly healthy, here in your presence, today. •This is *the stone rejected* by you
Mt 21:42p 1 P 2:4,7 *the builders, but which has proved to be the keystone.* •For of all the names in the
2:21+ Jl 3:5 world given to men, this is the only one by which we can be saved.'[e]

Lk 12:11-12p; 21:12-15p They were astonished at the asssurance shown by Peter and John, considering
Jn 7:15 they were uneducated laymen; and they recognised them as associates of Jesus;
but when they saw the man who had been cured standing by their side, they could
find no answer. •So they ordered them to stand outside while the Sanhedrin had
Jn 11:47-48 a private discussion. •'What are we going to do with these men?' they asked.
'It is obvious to everybody in Jerusalem that a miracle has been worked through
them in public, and we cannot deny it. •But to stop the whole thing spreading
any further among the people, let us caution them never to speak to anyone in
this name again.'

So they called them in and gave them a warning[f] on no account to make
5:28,40 statements or to teach in the name of Jesus. •But Peter and John retorted, 'You
5:29 must judge whether in God's eyes it is right to listen to you and not to God. •We
1:8+ Jr 20:9 cannot promise to stop proclaiming what we have seen and heard.' •The court
1 Co 9:16 2 Co 13:8 repeated the warnings and then released them; they could not think of any way
2 Tm 1:7-8 *2:47+* to punish them, since all the people were giving glory to God for what
had happened. •The man who had been miraculously cured was over forty years
old.

The apostles' prayer under persecution

As soon as they were released they went to the community and told them
everything the chief priests and elders had said to them. •When they heard it
they lifted up their voice to God all together. 'Master,' they prayed 'it is you
14:15+ who made heaven and earth and sea, and everything in them; •you it is who said
through the Holy Spirit and speaking through our ancestor David, your servant:[g]

Ps 2:1-2 Mt 26:3 *Why this arrogance among the nations,*
these futile plots among the peoples?

26 *Kings on earth setting out to war,*
princes making an alliance,
against the Lord and against his Anointed.[h]

27 'This is what has come true: in this very city Herod and Pontius Pilate[i] *made* Lk 23:12
an alliance with the pagan *nations* and the *peoples* of Israel, against your holy
28 servant Jesus whom you *anointed,*[j] •but only to bring about the very thing that you 3:13+; 10:38
29 in your strength and your wisdom[k] had predetermined should happen. •And 2:23+
now, Lord, take note of their threats and help your servants to proclaim your 18:9-10; 28:31
30 message with all boldness, •by stretching out your hand to heal and to work Ep 6:19 *4:33*
31 miracles and marvels through the name of your holy servant Jesus.' •As they *3:16+*
prayed, the house where they were assembled rocked; they were all filled with 1:8+
the Holy Spirit and began to proclaim the word of God boldly.[l]

The early Christian community[m]

2:42-47; 5:12-16

32 The whole group of believers was united, heart and soul; no one claimed for Jn 17:11,21 Ph 1:27
his own use anything that he had, as everything they owned was held in common. *=2:44-45*
33 The apostles continued to testify to the resurrection of the Lord Jesus with 1:8+
great power,[n] and they were all given great respect.[o] 4:30
34 None of their members was ever in want, as all those who owned land or Dt 15:4
35 houses would sell them, and bring the money from them, •to present it to the Lk 12:33
apostles; it was then distributed to any members who might be in need. 2:44-45

The generosity of Barnabas

36 There was a Levite of Cypriot origin called Joseph whom the apostles surnamed
37 Barnabas (which means 'son of encouragement').[p] •He owned a piece of land 11:22; 13:1 1 Co 9:6
and he sold it and brought the money, and presented it to the apostles. Ga 2:1

The fraud of Ananias and Sapphira

Jos 7

1 5 There was another man, however, called Ananias. He and his wife, Sapphira,
2 agreed to sell a property; •but with his wife's connivance he kept back part of
3 the proceeds, and brought the rest and presented it to the apostles. •'Ananias,' Peter
said 'how can Satan have so possessed you that you should lie to the Holy Spirit Lk 22:3 Jn 13:2,27
4 and keep back part of the money from the land? •While you still owned the land,
wasn't it yours to keep, and after you had sold it wasn't the money yours to do Dt 23:22-24
with as you liked? What put this scheme into your mind? It is not to men that

q. The earliest Christian preaching made a point of showing how Jesus fulfilled O.T. prophecy: he was a descendant of David, 2:30; 13:34, he appeared as a prophet, Moses' successor, 3:22f, cf. Mt 16:14+; Jn 1:21+, he suffered, Ac 2:23+, he was the stone rejected by the builders (the Jews) but now set in a place of honour, 4:11, he rose again, 2:25-31; 13:33-37, and is at God's right hand, 2:34f.

r. Thus implementing the promise recalled in v. 22, because the Greek verb means both 'to raise up' and 'to raise up again'. God by raising Christ from the dead fulfils the promises made to the fathers, 13:32-34; 24:14-15; 26:6-8.

s. Cf. 26:23; 2 Tm 1:10; Ga 3:14. Christ by his resurrection brought to the world the blessing promised to Abraham, v. 25.

t. Others translate 'so long as each of you turns from your wicked ways'.

4 a. The priestly aristocratic faction opposed the Pharisees who were the pious and popular party, see Mt 3:7+. The Sadducees are always represented as denying the doctrine of resurrection, Ac 23:6-8; Lk 20:27-38p. More than once the mutual hostility of these two parties produces an alliance of Pharisees with Christians, cf. Ac 5:34; 23:8-9; 26:5-8; Lk 20:39.

b. The Great Sanhedrin of Jerusalem, Israel's supreme court.

c. Cf. Lk 22:66+. Var. 'John'.

d. For vv. 10-12 we follow the Western Text.

e. 'Jesus' means 'God saves', Mt 1:21.

f. Apparently a solemn legal warning. In matters of this kind the accused (unless they were rabbis) could not be imprisoned except for a second offence (the case in 5:28).

g. Text corrupt, translation uncertain.

h. 'Anointed': the Greek word is 'Christ'; it is explained here, v. 27, according to its etymological sense.

i. Representing respectively the 'kings' and 'princes' the Psalm mentions. For 'Herod', cf. Lk 23:6-16.

j. The 'anointing' that has constituted him King Messiah, 'the Christ', cf. Mt 3:16+.

k. Lit. 'your hand and counsel'.

l. A miniature Pentecost, cf. the earlier one, 2:1f.

m. A summary like that of 2:42-47. The prevailing idea is here the pooling of resources; this preludes two examples: Barnabas, Ananias and Sapphira. The emphasis on sacrificing possessions is characteristic of Luke's religious outlook.

n. A power that showed itself by miracles. Cf. 2:22; 3:12; 4:7; 6:8; 8:13; 10:38; 1 Th 1:5; 1 Co 2:4-5.

o. By the populace: cf. 2:47; 4:21; 5:13.

p. The Greek word means both 'consolation' and 'encouragement'. Cf. 11:23. 'son of', a semitic expression here meaning 'with an aptitude for'. On Barnabas, see 9:27; 11:22-30; 12:25; ch. 13-15; 1 Co 9:6; Ga 2; Col 4:10.

you have lied, but to God.' •When he heard this Ananias fell down dead. This
3:10+ made a profound impression on everyone present. •The younger men got up,
wrapped the body in a sheet, carried it out and buried it.

About three hours later his wife came in, not knowing what had taken place.
2:14+ Peter challenged her, 'Tell me, was this the price you sold the land for?' 'Yes,'
she said 'that was the price.' •Peter then said, 'So you and your husband have
Nb 21:5-6 1 Co 10:9; agreed to put the Spirit of the Lord to the test! What made you do it? You hear
11:30-32 those footsteps? They have just been to bury your husband; they will carry you out,
too.' •Instantly she dropped dead at his feet. When the young men came in they
found she was dead, and they carried her out and buried her by the side of her
20:28 Lk 1:12+ husband.[a] •This made a profound impression on the whole Church[b] and on all
1 Co 1:2 who heard it.

2:42-47; 4:32-35 **The general situation[c]**

=2:46; 3:11 They all[d] used to meet by common consent in the Portico of Solomon. •No one
=2:47 else ever dared to join them, but the people were loud in their praise •and the
2:41 numbers of men and women who came to believe in the Lord increased steadily.[e]
2:19 So many signs and wonders were worked among the people at the hands of the
Mk 6:56 apostles •that the sick were even taken out into the streets and laid on beds and
19:12 sleeping-mats in the hope that at least the shadow of Peter might fall across some
8:6-8; 28:8-9 of them as he went past. •People even came crowding in from the towns round
Lk 4:40-41 about Jerusalem, bringing with them their sick and those tormented by unclean
spirits, and all of them were cured.

The apostles' arrest and miraculous deliverance

4:6 Then the high priest[f] intervened with all his supporters from the party of the
4:1-3 13:45 Sadducees. Prompted by jealousy, •they arrested the apostles and had them put
in the common gaol.

12:7-10; 16:25-26 But at night the angel of the Lord opened the prison gates and said as he led
Mt 1:20+ 13:26,46+ them out, •'Go and stand in the Temple, and tell the people all about this new
Life'.[g] •They did as they were told; they went into the Temple at dawn and
began to preach.

A summons to appear before the Sanhedrin

When the high priest arrived, he and his supporters convened the Sanhedrin
—this was the full Senate[h] of Israel—and sent to the gaol for them to be brought.
But when the officials arrived at the prison they found they were not inside, so
they went back and reported, •'We found the gaol securely locked and the warders
on duty at the gates, but when we unlocked the door we found no one inside'.
4:1+ When the captain of the Temple and the chief priests heard this news they
wondered what this could mean. •Then a man arrived with fresh news.
'At this very moment' he said 'the men you imprisoned are in the Temple.
They are standing there preaching to the people.' •The captain went with his
Lk 20:19p; 22:2p men and fetched them. They were afraid to use force in case the people stoned
them.

When they had brought them in to face the Sanhedrin, the high priest
demanded an explanation. •'We gave you a formal warning' he said 'not to
4:18+ preach in this name,[i] and what have you done? You have filled Jerusalem with
Mt 27:25 your teaching, and seem determined to fix the guilt of this man's death on us.'
2:14+; 4:19 In reply Peter and the apostles said, 'Obedience to God comes before obedience
2:23+ to men; •it was the God of our ancestors who raised up Jesus, but it was you
Ps 118:16 who had him executed by hanging on a tree.[j] •By his own right hand God has
2:33+, 38+; 4:12+ now raised him up to be leader and saviour,[k] to give repentance and forgiveness
1:8+ of sins through him to Israel. •We are witnesses to all this, we and the Holy
Jn 15:27 15:28 Spirit[l] whom God has given to those who obey him.' •This so infuriated them
Jn 7:39 that they wanted to put them to death.

Gamaliel's intervention

34 One member of the Sanhedrin, however, a Pharisee called Gamaliel, who was 22:3
a doctor of the Law and respected by the whole people,[m] stood up and asked
35 to have the men taken outside for a time. •Then he addressed the Sanhedrin,
36 'Men of Israel, be careful how you deal with these people. •There was Theudas 23:9 Jn 7:50f
who became notorious not so long ago. He claimed to be someone important,
and he even collected about four hundred followers; but when he was killed,
37 all his followers scattered and that was the end of them. •And then there was
Judas the Galilean, at the time of the census, who attracted crowds of supporters; Lk 2:2+
38 but he got killed too, and all his followers dispersed.[n] •What I suggest, therefore,
is that you leave these men alone and let them go. If this enterprise, this movement Mt 15:13 Lk 20:4
39 of theirs, is of human origin it will break up of its own accord; •but if it does in
fact come from God you will not only be unable to destroy them, but you might
find yourselves fighting against God.'[o] 2 M 7:19
40 His advice was accepted; •and they had the apostles called in, gave orders
for them to be flogged, warned them not to speak in the name of Jesus and 22:19 Mt 10:17
41 released them. •And so they left the presence of the Sanhedrin glad to have had *4:18* Mt 5:10-11
the honour of suffering humiliation for the sake of the name.[p] 1 Co 4:9f
42 They preached every day both in the Temple and in private houses, and their Ph 2:9-10
proclamation of the Good News of Christ Jesus was never interrupted. 18:5+

II. THE EARLIEST MISSIONS

The institution of the Seven

1 6 About this time, when the number of disciples[a] was increasing, the Hellenists 2:41+
made a complaint against the Hebrews:[b] in the daily distribution their own 2:45

5 a. Prompted by love of money, Ananias and Sapphira tried to deceive the apostles and the Holy Spirit which was leading and directing them; this was their sin.

b. The meaning of this term, adopted from the O.T., cf. Ac 7:38, to signify the messianic community, Mt 16:18+, expanded as Christianity developed. It originally indicated the mother church in Jerusalem, Ac 8:1; 11:22, etc.; later the individual churches throughout Judaea, Ga 1:22; 1 Th 2:14; cf. Ac 9:31, and among the pagans, Ac 13:1; 14:23; 15:41; 16:5; Rm 16:1,4; 1 Co 1:2+, etc.; Jm 5:14; 3 Jn 9; Rv 1:4; 2:1, etc., referring to their 'gatherings', 1 Co 11:18; 14:23,34, etc., cf. Ac 19:32; Phm 2, or to their regions, Rm 16:5; 1 Co 16:19; Col 4:15. Lastly, it stands for the Church united under God, Ac 20:28; 1 Co 10:32; 12:28, etc., for the Church as Body and Bride of Christ, Col 1:18+; Ep 5:23-32, and for the Church as including the whole cosmos, Ep 1:23+.

c. This third 'summary' stresses the miraculous power of the apostles, cf. 2:43; 4:33. Vv. 12b-14 interrupt the development of this theme.

d. Here, it seems, not the apostles but all the faithful.

e. Rather than 'More and more joined (the community) as believers in the Lord'. Cf. 11:24.

f. Var. 'Annas the high priest', cf. 4:6.

g. Lit. 'all the words (cf. v. 32; 10:37) of this Life'. This means the same thing as 'the message of salvation', 13:26. The purpose of Christian preaching is the 'salvation', cf. 4:12; 11:14; 15:11; 16:17,30-31, and 'life', cf. 3:15; 11:18; 13:46,48, promised to those 'who invoke the name of the Lord', 2:21,40,47; 4:12.

h. The terms 'Sanhedrin' and 'Senate' both indicate the same council, the Great Sanhedrin of Jerusalem, cf. Lk 22:66+.

i. Western Text " 'Did we not expressly forbid you to preach in that name? And now...' Then Peter answered, 'Which must we obey? God or man?' 'God' he said. And Peter then replied, 'The God of our ancestors..' "

j. The phrase is repeated in 10:39 (cf. 13:29). It recalls Dt 21:23, quoted in Ga 3:13, cf. 1 P 2:24.

k. The title matches 'Prince of life', 3:15+; it also corresponds to 'Prince and Redeemer' applied to Moses as a prefiguring of Christ, 7:35 (cf. 7:25). See also Heb 2:10; 12:2. There is an implicit comparison of Jesus with Moses.

l. Cf. Mt 10:20p; Jn 15:26-27; Ac 1:8.

m. Gamaliel I, Paul's teacher, 22:3, belonged to the school of Hillel and was the leading exponent of the more liberal and humane interpretation of the Law. The policy he urges here is in line with that of the Pharisaic party, cf. 4:1+.

n. Josephus mentions the revolts of Theudas and of Judas the Galilean but the dates he gives seem improbable. Both must have taken place about the time Jesus was born.

o. A variant introduces the idea of ritual purity '...leave them alone and do not dirty your hands. For if ... God, not only you but kings and tyrants will be powerless to destroy them. Do not therefore touch these men lest you find yourselves at war with God.'

p. The name for whose sake the apostles suffer, cf. 21:13; 1 P 4:14; 3 Jn 7, the name they preach, 4:10,12,17,18; 5:28,40; cf. 3:6,16; 8:12,16; 9:15,16,27,28, and which the Christians invoke, 2:21; 4:12; 9:14,21; 22:16, is the name, i.e. the person, of Jesus, 3:16+, the name he received at his resurrection, 2:36+, 'the name above all other names'. This name was 'Lord', hitherto reserved to God, Ph 2:9-11+.

6 a. 'Disciples': a new use of the term, peculiar to Ac, to indicate the Christians who are thus associated with the small circle of those first adherents of Jesus who are called by this name in the gospels.

b. 'Hellenists': Jews from outside Palestine; in Jerusalem they had their own synagogues where the Bible was read in Greek. The 'Hebrews' were native Palestinian Jews; their language was Aramaic but in their synagogues the Bible was read in Hebr. This distinction made its way into the early Church. Missionary initiative was to come from the hellenistic group.

widows were being overlooked. •So the Twelve called a full meeting of the 2
disciples and addressed them, 'It would not be right for us to neglect the word
Ex 18:17-23 Nb 27:16-18 of God so as to give out food; •you, brothers, must select[c] from among yourselves 3
1:8+ Is 11:2+ seven men of good reputation, filled with the Spirit and with wisdom; we will
1 Tm 3:8-10 hand over this duty to them, •and continue to devote ourselves to prayer and 4
1:14; 2:42 to the service of the word'.[d] •The whole assembly approved of this proposal and 5
8:5; 21:8 elected Stephen, a man full of faith and of the Holy Spirit, together with Philip,
Prochorus, Nicanor, Timon, Parmenas, and Nicolaus of Antioch, a convert to
13:3 1 Tm 4:14+ Judaism.[e] •They presented these to the apostles, who prayed and laid their hands 6
on them.[f]

2:41+; 12: 24; 13:49; The word of the Lord continued to spread:[g] the number of disciples in Jeru- 7
19:20 Rm 1:5+ salem was greatly increased, and a large group of priests made their submission
to the faith.

Stephen's arrest

Stephen was filled with grace and power and began to work miracles and 8
great signs among the people. •But then certain people came forward to debate 9
with Stephen, some from Cyrene and Alexandria who were members of the
synagogue called the Synagogue of Freedmen,[h] and others from Cilicia and Asia.
They found they could not get the better of him because of his wisdom, and 10
1:8+ Lk 21:15 because it was the Spirit that prompted what he said. •So they procured some 11
21:21 men to say, 'We heard him using blasphemous language against Moses and against
God'. •Having in this way turned the people against him as well as the elders 12
and scribes, they took Stephen by surprise, and arrested him and brought him
before the Sanhedrin. •There they put up false witnesses to say, 'This man 13
is always making speeches against this Holy Place and the Law. •We have heard 14
Mt 2:23+ *Mt 26:59-* him say that Jesus the Nazarene is going to destroy this Place and alter the
61p traditions that Moses handed down to us.'[i] •The members of the Sanhedrin all 15
Lk 4:20 looked intently at Stephen, and his face appeared to them like the face of an
angel.[j]

Stephen's speech

7 The high priest asked, 'Is this true?' •He replied,[a] 'My brothers, my fathers, 1
Ps 29:3b listen to what I have to say. The God of glory appeared to our ancestor Abraham, 2
Gn 12:1 while he was in Mesopotamia before settling in Haran,[b] •*and said to him, "Leave* 3
your country and your family and go to the land I will show you". •So he left 4
Chaldaea and settled in Haran; and after his father died God made him leave
Haran and come to this land where you are living today. •God did not give him 5
Gn 12:7+ a single square foot of this land to call his own, yet he promised to *give it to him*
Gn 15:2 *and after him to his descendants, childless* though he was. •The actual words God 6
Gn 15:13 used when he spoke to him are that *his descendants would be exiles in a foreign land,*
Gn 15:14 *where they would be slaves and oppressed for four hundred years*. •"*But I will pass* 7
Ex 3:12 *judgement on the nation that enslaves them*" God said "*and after this they will leave,*
Gn 17:10+ *and worship me in this* place."[c] •Then he made the covenant of circumcision: so 8
Gn 21:4 Jn 7:22 when his son Isaac was born he circumcised him on the eighth day. Isaac did the
same for Jacob, and Jacob for the twelve patriarchs.

Gn 37:11,28 'The patriarchs were *jealous of Joseph and sold him into slavery in Egypt*. But 9
Gn 39:2,3, 21,23 *God was with him*, •and rescued him from all his miseries by making him wise 10
Gn 41:40-41 Ps 105:21 enough to attract the attention of Pharaoh king of Egypt, who *made him governor*
Gn 41:54-55; 42:5 *of Egypt* and put him in charge of the royal household. •*Then a famine came* that 11
caused much suffering *throughout Egypt and Canaan*, and our ancestors could
Gn 42:2 find nothing to eat. •When Jacob *heard that there was grain for sale in Egypt*, 12
he sent our ancestors there on a first visit, •but it was on the second that *Joseph* 13
Gn 45:1 *made himself known to his brothers*, and told Pharaoh about his family. •Joseph 14
Gn 46:27+ then sent for his father Jacob and his whole family, a total of *seventy-five people*.
Jacob went down into Egypt and after he and our ancestors had died there, 15

16 their bodies were brought back to Shechem and buried in the tomb that Abraham Gn 50:13
had bought and paid for from the sons of Hamor, the father of Shechem.[d]
17 ‘As the time drew near for God to fulfil the promise he had solemnly made
18 to Abraham, our nation in Egypt *grew larger and larger,* •*until a new king came* Ex 1:7,8
19 *to power in Egypt who knew nothing of* Joseph. •*He exploited* our race, and ill- Ex 1:10,11
treated our ancestors, forcing them to expose their babies to prevent their Ex 1:22
20 surviving. •It was at this period that Moses was born, *a fine child* and favoured Ex 2:2 Heb 11:23f
21 by God. He was looked after for three months in his father's house, •and after
he had been exposed, *Pharaoh's daughter* adopted him and *brought him up* Ex 2:5,10
22 *as her own son.* •So Moses was taught all the wisdom of the Egyptians and
became a man with power both in his speech and his actions. Lk 24:19
23 24 ‘At the age of forty[e] he decided to visit *his countrymen, the sons of Israel.* •When Ex 2:11
he saw one of them being ill-treated he went to his defence and rescued the man by
25 *killing the Egyptian.* •He thought his brothers realised that through him God Ex 2:12
26 would liberate them, but they did not. •The next day, when he came across
some of them fighting, he tried to reconcile them. ‘Friends,’ he said ‘you are
27 brothers; why are you hurting each other?’ •But *the man who was attacking his* Ex 2:13
fellow countryman pushed him aside. ‘*And who appointed you*’ he said ‘*to be our* Ex 2:14
28 *leader and judge?*[f] •*Do you intend to kill me as you killed the Egyptian yesterday?*’
29 Moses fled when he heard this[g] and *he went to stay in the land of Midian,* where Ex 2:15
he became the father of two sons.
30 ‘Forty years later, *in the wilderness* near Mount Sinai, *an angel appeared to him* Ex 3:1-2
31 *in the flames of a bush* that was on fire. •Moses was amazed by what he saw.
32 *As he went nearer to look at it the voice of the Lord was heard,* •“*I am the God of* Ex 3:4,6
your ancestors, the God of Abraham, Isaac and Jacob”. Moses trembled and *did not*
33 *dare to look any more.* •The Lord said to him, “*Take off your shoes; the place where* Ex 3:5
34 *you are standing is holy ground.* •*I have seen the way my people are ill-treated in* Ex 3:7-8
Egypt, I have heard their groans, and I have come down to liberate them. So come
here and let me send you into Egypt.” Ex 3:10
35 ‘It was the same Moses that they had disowned[h] when they said, “*Who* Ex 2:14
appointed you to be our leader and judge?” who was now sent to be both leader

c. Var. ‘We shall select’.

d. When the community met for public worship the apostles had two functions: they recited the prayers and were responsible also for the *catechesis* (the doctrinal elaboration of the Good News).

e. Luke does not call the chosen seven ‘deacons’, but twice uses the word *diakonia* (‘service’ v. 4; translated ‘distribution’ in v. 1). All seven have Greek names; the last is a proselyte, cf. 2:11+. The hellenistic Christians now have their own organisation independent of the Hebrew group.

f. Lit. ‘and they prayed and laid their hands on them’: possibly a gesture of the community, cf. 13:1-3, more probably (v. 3) of the apostles.

g. A fresh formula, see also 12:24; 19:20; cf. Lk 1:80+, here juxtaposed with the earlier one, see Ac 2:41+.

h. Probably the descendants of Jews carried off to Rome by Pompey in 63 B.C. who were sold into slavery and later released.

i. The ‘false witnesses’ at the trial of Jesus similarly objected that he ‘would destroy the Temple’. There is also a similarity in the climax of the two trials, Ac 7:56-57; Mt 26:62-66. The allegations concerning Mosaic practice will be made in Paul's case also, Ac 15:1,5; 21:21,28; 25:8; 28:17.

j. The sight of an angel induces religious awe, cf. Jg 13:6. The face of Moses, reflecting the glory of God as he came down from Sinai, produced the same effect, Ex 34:29-35; 2 Co 3:7-18; so also the appearance of Jesus was changed, Mt 17:2; Lk 9:29. The members of the Sanhedrin in their turn witness a transfiguration, that of Stephen as he contemplates the glory of God, Ac 7:55-56. The narrative, interrupted by the insertion of Stephen's discourse, 7:1-54, is resumed in 7:55.

7 a. The discourse opens with a summary of the stories of Abraham and Joseph, vv. 2-16; it goes on to expound the history of Moses, vv. 17-43 (cf. the charge made against Stephen, 6:11). With Moses' divine mission of salvation Stephen contrasts the attitude of Israel: rejection, disobedience, faithlessness—traditional themes (cf. Dt) but here elaborated with the Christian Event in mind. When Stephen speaks of Moses he is thinking of Christ whom Moses prefigured: the Jews react now as the Israelites did then. From the subsequent history of Israel Stephen selects only the building of the Temple; his purpose is to point out that God does not dwell in man-made temples, vv. 44-50 (cf. the allegation in 6:13). The speech ends with a fierce diatribe, vv. 51-53, which uses one of the themes of the earliest Christian preaching, cf. 2:23+.

b. According to Gn 11:31 the apparition took place at Haran. Stephen follows a non-biblical tradition.

c. Mt. Horeb, but Stephen says ‘this place’ (i.e. the Jerusalem Temple) instead.

d. ‘father of Shechem’: this detail is taken from Gn 33:19. Var. ‘from the sons of Hemor, son of Shechem’, ‘from the sons of Emmor at Shechem’, ‘from the sons of Emmor (inhabitants) of Shechem’. V. 16 follows a non-biblical tradition.

e. According to Jewish traditions.

f. By raising up Jesus from the dead God has appointed him ‘leader’, cf. 5:31, and ‘judge’, cf. 10:42; 17:31.

g. In Ex 2:15 Moses runs away because he is afraid of Pharaoh; here it is because his compatriots reject him.

h. The Bible does not apply this verb to Moses, but in Ac 3:13-14 it is applied to Jesus. Nor does the Bible give the name ‘redeemer’ to Moses. The image of Christ shades into that of Moses who prefigured him.

and redeemer through the angel who had appeared to him in the bush. •It was 36
Ex 7:3 Moses who, after performing *miracles and signs in Egypt*, led them out across the
Nb 14:33 Am 5:25 Red Sea and *through the wilderness for forty years*. •It was Moses who told the 37
Dt 18:15.18 sons of Israel, "*God will raise up a prophet like myself for you from among*
Dt 4:10; 9:10;18:16 *your own brothers*".[i] •When they held the assembly[j] in the wilderness it was only 38
Jn 1:17 Ga 3:19+ through Moses that our ancestors could communicate with the angel who had
spoken to him on Mount Sinai;[k] it was he who was entrusted with words of life[l]
to hand on to us. •This is the man that our ancestors refused to listen to: they 39
Nb 14:3 pushed him aside, *turned back to Egypt* in their thoughts,[m] •*and said to Aaron*, 40
Ex 32:1.23 "*Make some gods to be our leaders; we do not understand what has come over this*
Ex 32:4.6 *Moses who led us out of Egypt*". •It was then that *they made a bull calf and offered* 41
sacrifice to the idol. They were perfectly happy with something they had made
for themselves. •God turned away from them and abandoned them to the 42
worship of the army of heaven,[n] as scripture says in the book of the prophets:

Am 5:25-27 (LXX)

> *Did you bring me victims and sacrifices in the wilderness*
> *for all those forty years, you House of Israel?*
> *No, you carried the tent of Moloch on your shoulders* 43
> *and the star of the god Rephan,*
> *those idols that you had made to adore.*
> *So now I will exile you even further than Babylon.*

'While they were in the desert our ancestors possessed the Tent of Testimony 44
that had been constructed according to the instructions God gave Moses, telling
Ex 25:40 Heb 8:5 him to *make an exact copy of the pattern* he had been shown. •It was handed 45
down from one ancestor of ours to another until Joshua brought it into the
country we had conquered from the nations which were driven out by God as
we advanced. Here it stayed until the time of David. •He won God's favour and 46
Ps 132:5 asked permission *to have a temple built for* the House[o] of *Jacob*, •though it was 47
1 K 6:2 *Solomon* who actually *built God's house* for him. •Even so the Most High does 48
17:24 Heb 9:11.24 not live in a house that human hands have built: for as the prophet says:

Is 66:1-2

> *With heaven my throne* 49
> *and earth my footstool,*
> *what house could you build me,*
> *what place could you make for my rest?*
> *Was not all this made by my hand?* 50

Ex 33:3+ 2 Ch 30:7-8; 36:14-16 Is 63:10 Jr 4:4+
'You stubborn people, with your pagan hearts and pagan ears. You are always 51
resisting the Holy Spirit,[p] just as your ancestors used to do. •Can you name 52
a single prophet your ancestors never persecuted? In the past they killed those
Mt 23:34-35 Jn 8:44 *2:23+;* 3:14+ *7:38+*
who foretold the coming of the Just One, and now you have become his
betrayers, his murderers. •You who had the Law brought to you by angels are 53
the very ones who have not kept it.'

They were infuriated when they heard this, and ground their teeth at him. 54

The stoning of Stephen. Saul as persecutor

Ex 24:16+ But Stephen, filled with the Holy Spirit, gazed into heaven and saw the glory 55
2:33+ *Mt 26:64p+* of God, and Jesus standing at God's right hand.[q] •'I can see heaven thrown open' 56
Dn 7:13 Mt 8:20+ he said 'and the Son of Man standing at the right hand of God.' •At this all the 57
members of the council shouted out and stopped their ears with their hands; then
Heb 13:12+ they all rushed at him, •sent him out of the city and stoned him. The wit- 58
22:20; 26:10 Ga 1:13+ nesses[r] put down their clothes at the feet of a young man called Saul.[s] •As they 59
Ps 31:5 Lk 23:46 were stoning him, Stephen said in invocation,[t] 'Lord Jesus, receive my spirit'.
Lk 23:34 Then he knelt down and said aloud, 'Lord, do not hold this sin against them'; 60
7:58; 22:20 and with these words he fell asleep. **8** [a]Saul entirely approved of the killing. 1
Jn 16:2 That day a bitter persecution started against the church in Jerusalem, and
everyone[b] except the apostles fled to the country districts of Judaea and Samaria.[c]

There were some devout people, however, who buried Stephen and made
great mourning for him.
Saul then worked for the total destruction of the Church; he went from house 9:1-2; 22:4; 26:10-11
to house arresting both men and women and sending them to prison. 1 Co 15:9 Ga 1:13 Ph 3:6 1 Tm 1:13

Philip in Samaria

4 Those who had escaped went from place to place preaching the Good News. =11:19
5 One of them was Philip who went to a Samaritan town[d] and proclaimed the 6:5; 21:8
Christ to them.[e] •The people united in welcoming the message Philip preached, 18:5+ *5:16*
either because they had heard of the miracles he worked or because they saw
7 them for themselves. •There were, for example, unclean spirits that came shrieking Mt 8:29+
out of many who were possessed, and several paralytics and cripples were cured. 28:8-9
8 As a result there was great rejoicing in that town. 2:46+

Simon the magician

9 Now a man called Simon had already practised magic arts in the town and
astounded the Samaritan people. He had given it out that he was someone
10 momentous, •and everyone believed what he said; eminent iti zens and ordinary
11 people alike had declared, 'He is the divine power that is called Great'.[f] •They
had only been won over to him because of the long time he had spent working
12 on them with his magic. •But when they believed Philip's preaching of the Good
News about the kingdom of God and the name of Jesus Christ, they were
13 baptised, both men and women, •and even Simon himself became a believer. 1:5+
After his baptism Simon, who went round constantly with Philip, was astonished
when he saw the wonders and great miracles that took place.
14 When the apostles in Jerusalem heard that Samaria had accepted the word 11:1,22 Jn 4:38
15 of God, they sent Peter and John to them, •and they went down there, and Lk 8:51+
16 prayed for the Samaritans to receive the Holy Spirit, •for as yet he had not come 1:5+; 19:2,6
down on any of them: they had only been baptised in the name of the Lord Jesus. 10:44
17 Then they laid hands on them, and they received the Holy Spirit. 1:5+ 1 Tm 4:14+

i. A messianic text already cited, 3:22. One other than Moses—the Messiah—is to play a similar part, Mt 16:14+; Jn 1:21+.

j. Lit. 'at the time of the assembly'. The word also means 'church', cf. 5:11+. Dt uses 'day of assembly' to mean the final occasion when the Law was promulgated, Ex 19:10-25. From the earliest days Christians have seen the Church as the successor to this solemn 'assembly' of the chosen people in the desert.

k. Moses acted as mediator between 'the angel, and the people. 'The angel of Yahweh' in the earliest texts is identical with Yahweh as manifesting himself, Gn 16:7+, cf. Mt 1:20+. Later, a distinction was made between Yahweh and his angel in order to emphasise the divine transcendence. Thus Moses is represented as in immediate touch not with God but with one or several angels. There are traces of this idea in Ga 3:19; Heb 2:2.

l. To obey the Law is to live, Dt 4:1; 8:1,3; 30:15-16, 19-20; 32:46-47; Lv 18:5, quoted in Ga 3:12; Rm 10:5; the Law therefore is referred to as 'the statutes of life', Ezk 33:15; Ba 3:9. For the Christian, the gospel preaching is 'the word of life', Ph 2:16; cf. Ac 5:20, i.e. 'the word of salvation', Ac 13:26. Since life springs from God's word, this word is itself 'living': cf. Heb 4:12; 1 P 1:23. And Jesus is himself 'the Word of life': 1 Jn 1:1.

m. Cf. Nb 14:3 and Ex 16:3. Cf. Ezk 20:8-14.

n. Biblical phrase for the stars, often worshipped as gods.

o. Var. 'for the God'.

p. Who spoke through Moses and the prophets.

q. Stephen's vision is to be related to his transfiguration, 6:15+.

r. The false witnesses mentioned in 6:13-14. It was for the hostile witnesses to initiate the execution of the sentence, Dt 17:7.

s. St Paul.

t. A good example of 'invoking the name of the Lord', 2:21+.

8 a. Vv. 1-4 are made up of a number of brief remarks: Stephen's burial (v. 2), the natural conclusion of the foregoing narrative; Saul's campaign against the Christians (vv. 1a and 3) which links the account of the stoning of Stephen, cf. 7:58b, with what appears to be its sequel, namely Paul's conversion, 9:1-30; finally a note on the Church persecuted and scattered (vv. 1b-4) which introduces the narrative of Philip's mission, 8:5-40, and that of Peter, 9:32-11:18; v. 4 is found again in 11:19. We have here, therefore, a preliminary sketch of the various themes developed in the following chapters up to ch. 12.

b. 'everyone': a very general statement. The persecution in fact seems to have been directed principally against the Hellenists, cf. 6:1.5, and it was this group, scattered by persecution, that gave the church its first missionaries, cf. v. 4; 11:19-20.

c. Second stage of the Church's expansion, cf. 1:8. The third begins with the foundation of the church of Antioch, 11:20.

d. Var. 'the town of Samaria', 'the town of Caesarea'. The reference is probably not to the town called Samaria, by this time a hellenistic city and known as Sebaste, but to the province: those who are evangelised are the 'Samaritans' in the Jewish sense of the word, i.e. akin in blood and religion but cut off from Israel's community and living in heresy, cf. Jn 4:9+; Mt 10:5-6+.

e. The Samaritans, too, expected the Messiah, cf. Jn 4:25.

f. Or, less probably, 'that is called Megalleh' (Aramaic for 'Revealing'). Evidently it was thought that Simon's supernatural power issued from some indwelling force of the high God.

When Simon saw that the Spirit was given through the imposition of hands 18
by the apostles, he offered them some money. •'Give me the same power' he said 19
'so that anyone I lay my hands on will receive the Holy Spirit.' •Peter answered, 20
13:10 Jn 4:10 'May your silver be lost forever, and you with it, for thinking that money could
Is 55:1 Mt 10:8 buy what God has given for nothing![g] •You have no share, no rights, in this: 21
God can see how your heart is warped. •Repent of this wickedness of yours, and 22
pray to the Lord; you may still be forgiven for thinking as you did; •it is plain 23
Dt 29:17 Pr 5:22 to me that you are trapped in the bitterness of gall and the chains of sin.'[h]
Jr 4:18 Heb 12:16 'Pray to the Lord for me yourselves' Simon replied 'so that none of the things 24
you have spoken about may happen to me.'[i]
1:8+ Having given their testimony and proclaimed the word of the Lord, they went 25
back to Jerusalem, preaching the Good News to a number of Samaritan villages.

Philip baptises a eunuch

Mt 1:20+ The angel of the Lord[j] spoke to Philip saying, 'Be ready to set out at noon[k] 26
along the road that goes from Jerusalem down to Gaza, the desert road'. •So he 27
1 K 8:41f Ps 68:31 set off on his journey. Now it happened that an Ethiopian[l] had been on pilgrimage
Is 56:3-7 to Jerusalem; he was a eunuch and an officer at the court of the kandake, or
queen, of Ethiopia, and was in fact her chief treasurer. •He was now on his way 28
home; and as he sat in his chariot he was reading the prophet Isaiah. •The 29
1:8+ Spirit said to Philip, 'Go up and meet that chariot'. •When Philip ran up, he 30
heard him reading Isaiah the prophet and asked, 'Do you understand what you
Rm 10:14 are reading?' •'How can I' he replied 'unless I have someone to guide me?' So 31
he invited Philip to get in and sit by his side. •Now the passage of scripture he 32
was reading was this:[m]

Is 53:7-8 Lk 18:31+
Like a sheep that is led to the slaughter-house,
like a lamb that is dumb in front of its shearers,
like these he never opens his mouth.
He has been humiliated and has no one to defend him. 33
Who will ever talk about his descendants,
since his life on earth has been cut short!

The eunuch turned to Philip and said, 'Tell me, is the prophet referring to 34
Lk 24:27 himself or someone else?' •Starting, therefore, with this text of scripture Philip 35
proceeded to explain the Good News of Jesus to him.
Further along the road they came to some water, and the eunuch said, 'Look, 36
10:47; 16:33 there is some water here; is there anything to stop me being baptised?'[n] •He 38
ordered the chariot to stop, then Philip and the eunuch both went down into
1:5+ the water and Philip baptised him. •But after they had come up out of the water 39
1 K 18:12+ Lk 24:31-32 again Philip was taken away by the Spirit of the Lord,[o] and the eunuch never
2:46+ saw him again but went on his way rejoicing. •Philip found that he had reached 40
Azotus and continued his journey proclaiming the Good News in every town as far
21:8 as Caesarea.

=22:5-16 =26:10-18 **The conversion of Saul**[a]

8:3 Ga 1:12-17 9 Meanwhile Saul was still breathing threats to slaughter the Lord's disciples. 1
He had gone to the high priest •and asked for letters addressed to the 2
9:21; 19:9. 23; 22:4; synagogues in Damascus, that would authorise him to arrest and take to Jerusalem
24:14,22 2 P 2:2 any followers of the Way,[b] men or women, that he could find.[c]
Suddenly, while he was travelling to Damascus and just before he reached 3
the city, there came a light from heaven all round him. •He fell to the ground, 4
and then he heard a voice saying, 'Saul, Saul,[d] why are you persecuting me?'
Mt 25:40 1 Co 8:12 'Who are you, Lord?' he asked, and the voice answered, 'I am Jesus, and you 5
are persecuting me.[e] •Get up now and go into the city, and you will be told what 6
you have to do.' •The men travelling with Saul stood there speechless, for 7
Dn 10:7 though they heard the voice they could see no one. •Saul got up from the ground, 8

but even with his eyes wide open he could see nothing at all, and they had to lead
9 him into Damascus by the hand. •For three days he was without his sight, and
took neither food nor drink.
10 A disciple called Ananias who lived in Damascus had a vision in which he 10:3
11 heard the Lord say to him, 'Ananias!' When he replied, 'Here I am, Lord', •the Gn 22:1+
Lord said, 'You must go to Straight Street and ask at the house of Judas for
someone called Saul, who comes from Tarsus. At this moment he is praying,
12 having had a vision[f] of a man called Ananias coming in and laying hands on him 9:17; 28:8 1 Tm 4:14+
to give him back his sight.'
13 When he heard that, Ananias said, 'Lord, several people have told me about 9:41-42; 26:10
14 this man and all the harm he has been doing to your saints[g] in Jerusalem. •He has Rm 1:7; 12:13
only come here because he holds a warrant from the chief priests to arrest 1 Co 1:2; 6:2 2 Co 1:1
15 everybody who invokes your name.' •The Lord replied, 'You must go all the *2:21+ 22:21*
same, because this man is my chosen instrument to bring my name before pagans Rm 1:8 1 Co 9:16-17
16 and pagan kings and before the people of Israel;[h] •I myself will show him how
17 much he himself must suffer for my name'. •Then Ananias went. He entered 15:26; 21:13 Mt 10:22+
the house, and at once laid his hands on Saul and said, 'Brother Saul, I have been 1 Co 4:9-13+
sent by the Lord Jesus who appeared to you on your way here so that you may *22:14; 26:16* 1 Co 9:1;
18 recover your sight and be filled with the Holy Spirit'.[i] •Immediately it was as 15:8
though scales fell away from Saul's eyes and he could see again. So he was Tb 11:10-15
19 baptised there and then, •and after taking some food he regained his strength. 1:5+

Saul's preaching at Damascus
Ga 1:16-17

20 After he had spent only a few days with the disciples in Damascus, •he began
21 preaching in the synagogues, 'Jesus is the Son of God'.[j] •All his hearers were 13:33
amazed. 'Surely' they said 'this is the man who organised the attack in Jerusalem

g. The Holy Spirit is supremely the Gift of God, cf. 2:38; 10:45; 11:17; Lk 11:9,13; the idea recurs in the *Veni Creator.*

h. 'Simony' (trafficking in sacred things) gets its name from this incident.

i. Western Text adds 'and he wept bitterly without ceasing'.

j. Referred to as 'the Spirit' in vv. 29 and 39.

k. Or 'towards the south'.

l. 'Ethiopia' began beyond the first cataract of the Nile: Nubia or the Sudan. It was ruled by queens bearing the generic name 'kandake'.

m. Quoted from the LXX, here somewhat obscure and deriving from a Hebr. text itself obscure and probably corrupt. On the use of Is 53 in early Christian preaching, see 3:13+.

n. V. 37 is a very ancient gloss preserved in the Western Text and suggested by the baptismal liturgy "And Philip said, 'If you believe with all your heart, you may'. And he replied, 'I believe that Jesus Christ is the Son of God'."

o. Var. West. 'the Holy Spirit came down on the eunuch and the angel of the Lord carried Philip away'.

9 a. Crucial event in the Church's history. Luke gives three accounts whose discrepancies of detail are explained by their differing literary forms: the second and third accounts are found in Paul's discourses. See also Ga 1:12-17. The incident took place probably in 36 A.D., about 12 years (14 if we reckon as the ancients did) before the council of Jerusalem', Ga 2:1f; cf. Ac 15, held in 49.

b. The 'Way' is the way of life characteristic of the Christian community; the term is used, by extension, for the community itself. When men follow this 'Way' God is served as he wishes to be served, Mt 22:16p, cf. 7:13-14; 21:32; 1 Co 12:31; 2 P 2:2; Ps 119:1f; Pr 4:10f; Jr 12:16, etc. This unqualified use of the word is peculiar to Ac, 18:25,26; 19:9,23; 22:4; 24:14,22.

c. The Roman authority recognised the high priest's jurisdiction over the members of Jewish communities even outside Palestine; according to 1 M 15:21 this even included right of extradition.

d. Aramaic ('Hebrew', 26:14) form of Saul's name.

e. Whatever is done to the disciples for the sake of the name of Jesus is done to Jesus himself, Mt 10:40+.

f. Lit. 'having seen'; var. 'having seen in a vision'.

g. Since God is the Holy One *par excellence*, Is 6:3, those consecrated to his service are called 'holy', Lv 17:1+. The term, applied originally to the people of Israel, Ex 19:6+, and in particular to the community of the messianic era, Dn 7:18+, is especially apt for the Christians who are the new 'holy race', 1 P 2:5,9, called, Rm 1:7; 1 Co 1:2; Ep 1:4; 2 Tm 1:9, by their baptismal consecration, Ep 5:26f, to a blameless life, 1 Co 7:34; Ep 1:4; 5:3; Col 1:22, which makes them holy as God is holy, 1 P 1:15f, cf. 1 Jn 3:3, and like Jesus himself, 'the Holy One of God', Mk 1:24+. In the early community it becomes the usual term for the Christians, in Palestine first, Ac 9:13,32,41; Rm 15: 26,31; 1 Co 16:1,15; 2 Co 8:4; 9:1,12, and then in all the churches, Rm 8:27; 12:13; 16:2,15; 1 Co 6:1f; 14:33; 2 Co 13:12; Ep 1:15; 3:18; 4:12; 6:18; Ph 4:21f; Col 1:4; 1 Tm 5:10; Phm 5,7; Heb 6:10; 13:24; Jude 3 (and in the introductory formulae of the letters 2 Co 1:1, etc.). In Rv 5:8; 8:3 etc. the word is used more specifically of the Christians who witness by their death. At times its application may be restricted to the leaders, the 'apostles and prophets', Ep 3:5 and Col 1:26; Ep 3:8; 4:12; Rv 18:20. Lastly, as in the O.T., Jb 5:1+, it may indicate the angels, Mk 8:38; Lk 9:26; Ac 10:22; Jude 14; Rv 14:10, and in some cases it is doubtful whether the reference is to angels or to the saints in glory, Ep 1:18; Col 1:12; 1 Th 3:13; 2 Th 1:10.

h. Cf. Jr 1:10. Paul's mission is 'to all men', Ac 22:15, to the pagan nations, 26:17; this agrees with what Paul himself writes in Ga 1:16, cf. Rm 1:5; 11:13; 15:16-18; Ga 2:2,8,9; Ep 3:8; Col 1:27; 1 Tm 2:7. On the 'kings', cf. Ac 26:2+.

i. Characteristic Lucan phrase, Lk 1:15,41,67; Ac 2:4; 4:8,31; 9:17; 13:9. Cf. Lk 4:1+.

j. 'Son of God' corresponds to 'Christ' in v. 22. Cf. Mt 4:3+. We meet the title 'Son of God' only once more in Ac, 13:33. It is characteristic of Pauline Christology, Ga 1:16; 2:20; 4:4,6; Rm 1:3-4,9; 1 Th 1:10; cf. Rm 9:5+.

against the people who invoke this name, and who came here for the sole
9:2 purpose of arresting them to have them tried by the chief priests?' •Saul's power 22
increased steadily, and he was able to throw the Jewish colony at Damascus into
2:36+; 18:5,28 complete confusion by the way be demonstrated that Jesus was the Christ.

Some time passed,[k] and the Jews worked out a plot to kill him, •but news of 23 24
2 Co 11:32-33 it reached Saul. To make sure of killing him they kept watch on the gates day
Jos 2:15 and night, •but when it was dark the disciples[l] took him and let him down from 25
the top of the wall, lowering him in a basket.

Ga 1:18-19
Saul's visit to Jerusalem[m]

22:17 When he got to Jerusalem he tried to join the disciples, but they were all 26
4:36-37 afraid of him: they could not believe he was really a disciple. •Barnabas, 27
however, took charge of him, introduced him to the apostles, and explained how
the Lord had appeared to Saul and spoken to him on his journey, and how he
had preached boldly at Damascus in the name of Jesus. •Saul now started to go 28
13:46+ round with them in Jerusalem, preaching fearlessly in the name of the Lord.
5:41+ But after he had spoken to the Hellenists,[n] and argued with them, they became 29
=22:17-21 determined to kill him. •When the brothers knew, they took him to Caesarea, 30
11:25 and sent him off from there to Tarsus.[o]

A lull

The churches[p] throughout Judaea, Galilee and Samaria were now left in peace, 31
2:41+; 20:32 building themselves up, living in the fear of the Lord, and filled with the consola-
1 Co 8:1 tion of the Holy Spirit.[q]

Peter cures a paralytic at Lydda

Peter visited one place after another and eventually came to the saints living 32
down in Lydda. •There he found a man called Aeneas, a paralytic who had been 33
bedridden for eight years. •Peter said to him, 'Aeneas, Jesus Christ cures you: 34
19:17 get up and fold up your sleeping mat'. Aeneas got up immediately;[r] •everybody 35
who lived in Lydda and Sharon saw him, and they were all converted to the Lord.

Peter raises a woman to life at Jaffa

13:9+ At Jaffa there was a woman disciple called Tabitha, or Dorcas in Greek,[s] 36
Lk 12:33+ who never tired of doing good or giving in charity. •But the time came when she 37
1 K 17:19 got ill and died, and they washed her and laid her out in a room upstairs. •Lydda 38
is not far from Jaffa, so when the disciples heard that Peter was there, they sent
two men with an urgent message for him, 'Come and visit us as soon as possible'.

Peter went back with them straightaway, and on his arrival they took him 39
to the upstairs room, where all the widows stood round him in tears, showing
him tunics and other clothes Dorcas had made when she was with them. •Peter 40
Mk 5:40-41 sent them all out of the room and knelt down and prayed. Then he turned to
the dead woman and said, 'Tabitha, stand up'. She opened her eyes, looked at
Lk 7:15 *3:7;* Peter and sat up. •Peter helped her to her feet, then he called in the saints and 41
9:13+; 20:10 widows and showed them she was alive. •The whole of Jaffa heard about it and 42
19:17 many believed in the Lord.

Lk 9:4 Peter stayed on some time in Jaffa, lodging with a leather-tanner called Simon. 43

15:7
Peter visits a Roman centurion[a]

Lk 7:2,4-5 Ga 2:12 *2:11+* 10 One of the centurions of the Italica cohort stationed in Caesarea was 1
called Cornelius. •He and the whole of his household were devout and 2
Lk 12:33+ *Lk 18:1* God-fearing,[b] and he gave generously to Jewish causes and prayed constantly
to God.

27:23 One day at about the ninth hour he had a vision in which he distinctly saw 3
Mt 1:20+ the angel of God come into his house and call out to him, 'Cornelius!' •He stared 4
9:10+ Lk 1:12+ at the vision in terror and exclaimed, 'What is it, Lord?' 'Your offering of prayers

5 and alms' the angel answered 'has been accepted by God.[c] •Now you must send
6 someone to Jaffa and fetch a man called Simon, known as Peter, •who is lodging 2:14+
7 with Simon the tanner whose house is by the sea.' •When the angel who said
this had gone, Cornelius called two of the slaves and a devout soldier of his staff,
8 told them what had happened, and sent them off to Jaffa.
9 Next day, while they were still on their journey and had only a short distance 16:9
to go before reaching Jaffa, Peter went to the housetop at about the sixth hour
10 to pray. •He felt hungry and was looking forward to his meal, but before it was 11:5-17
11 ready he fell into a trance •and saw heaven thrown open and something like a big
12 sheet being let down to earth by its four corners;[d] •it contained every possible
13 sort of animal and bird, walking, crawling or flying ones. •A voice then said
14 to him, 'Now, Peter; kill and eat!' •But Peter answered, 'Certainly not, Lord;
15 I have never yet eaten anything profane or unclean'. •Again, a second time, the Lv 11 Ezk 4:14
voice spoke to him, 'What God has made clean, you have no right to call Gn 1:31+
16 profane'.[e] •This was repeated three times, and then suddenly the container was
drawn up to heaven again.
17 Peter was still worrying over the meaning of the vision he had seen, when the
men sent by Cornelius arrived. They had asked where Simon's house was and
18 they were now standing at the door, •calling out to know if the Simon known as
19 Peter was lodging there. •Peter's mind was still on the vision and the Spirit[f] had 1:8+
20 to tell him, 'Some men[g] have come to see you. •Hurry down, and do not hesitate
21 about going back with them; it was I who told them to come.' •Peter went down
22 and said to them, 'I am the man you are looking for; why have you come?' •They
said, 'The centurion Cornelius, who is an upright and God-fearing man, highly Lk 7:4-5
regarded by the entire Jewish people, was directed by a holy angel to send for you
23 and bring you to his house and to listen to what you have to say'. •So Peter
asked them in and gave them lodging.
Next day, he was ready to go off with them, accompanied by some of the
24 brothers from Jaffa. •They reached Caesarea the following day, and Cornelius
was waiting for them. He had asked his relations and close friends to be there,
25 and as Peter reached the house Cornelius went out to meet him, knelt at his feet
26 and prostrated himself. •But Peter helped him up. 'Stand up,' he said 'I am only 3:12; 14:15 Rv 19:10
27 a man after all!' •Talking together they went in to meet all the people assembled
28 there, •and Peter said to them, 'You know it is forbidden for Jews to mix with
people of another race and visit them, but God has made it clear to me that 11:3; 15:9 Ga 2:12, 15-16
29 I must not call anyone profane or unclean. •That is why I made no objection

k. Three years, according to Ga 1:17-18; Paul's stay in Arabia belongs to this period. Luke's statement is not detailed.

l. Var. 'his disciples'.

m. Paul mentions this visit, Ga 1:18-19. He observes that at that time the churches in Judaea did not yet know him by sight, but says nothing of the part Barnabas played. He states that, of the apostles, he saw none but Peter, and James the brother of the Lord; Ac, generalising, speaks vaguely of 'the apostles'.

n. Var. 'the Greeks' (i.e. the pagans); same variant in 11:20. The hellenistic Christians (cf. 6:1+) are the most active proselytisers, just as the hellenistic Jews were the most active opponents of Christian propaganda, 6:9f; 7:58; 9:1; 21:27; 24:19.

o. Where Barnabas later finds him, 11:25. Compare this with Ga 1:18-21 and with Ac 22:17-21.

p. 'the churches' Western and Antiochene Texts; 'the Church' Alexandrian Text.

q. Joy in the faith, 2:46+. Others render 'they thrived through the comfort (or: by the help; or: thanks to the encouragement) of the Holy Spirit'.

r. For similar miracles: Lk 5:18-26p; 13:11-13; Jn 5:1-14; Ac 3:1-10 (and 4:22); 14:8-10.

s. I.e. 'gazelle'.

10 a. For Luke, Cornelius' conversion has a wide application. Its significance for the Church at large appears from the narrative itself and from its emphasis on the visions of Peter and of Cornelius, but especially from the way the author deliberately links this incident to the decision of the 'Council of Jerusalem', cf. 15:7-11, 14. There seem to be two separate lessons here. First, God himself has made it clear that the pagans are to be received into the Church without being forced to obey the Law, cf. 10:34-35,44-48a; 11:1,15-18; 15:7-11,14; and Ga 2:1-10. Secondly, God himself has shown Peter that he must accept the hospitality of the uncircumcised. The problem of social relations between Christians converted from Judaism and Christians converted from paganism underlies the narrative, cf. 10:10-16,28-29; 11:2-14; and Ga 2:11-21.

b. The expressions 'fearing God', 10:2,22,35; 13:16,26, and 'worshipping God', 13:43,50; 16:14; 17:4,17; 18:7, are technical terms for admirers and followers of the Jewish religion who stop short of circumcision, cf. 2:11+.

c. Lit. 'has ascended as a memorial before God' The expression recalls the 'memorial' sacrifice, cf. Lv 2:2,9,16, to which Tb 12:12 compares prayer.

d. Following Western Text.

e. Peter is to throw off his scruples of legal purity, 11:9. Cf. Mt 15:1-20p; Rm 14:14,17. The immediate practical conclusion is that Peter must not fear contact with the uncircumcised, Ac 10:27-28.

f. The intervention of the Spirit is like that of the angel of the Lord, cf. 8:26,29.

g. Var. 'Three men', cf. 11:11.

to coming when I was sent for; but I should like to know exactly why you
sent for me.' •Cornelius replied, 'Three days ago I was praying[h] in my house 30
at the ninth hour, when I suddenly saw a man in front of me in shining robes.
He said, "Cornelius, your prayer has been heard and your alms have been 31
accepted as a sacrifice in the sight of God; •so now you must send to Jaffa and 32
fetch Simon known as Peter who is lodging in the house of Simon the tanner, by
the sea". •So I sent for you at once, and you have been kind enough to come. 33
Here we all are, assembled in front of you to hear what message God has given
you for us.'

Peter's address in the house of Cornelius

Then Peter addressed them: 'The truth I have now come to realise' he said 34
Dt 10:17+ Rm 2:11 'is that God does not have favourites, •but that anybody of any nationality who 35
Ga 2:6 1 P 1:17 fears God and does what is right is acceptable to him.[i]

'It is true, God sent his word[j] to the people of Israel, and it was to them that 36
Is 52:7 Na 2:1 *the good news of peace was brought* by Jesus Christ—but Jesus Christ is Lord of
Rm 10:12 *Lk 4:44+* all men. •You must have heard about the recent happenings in Judaea;[k] about 37
Jesus of Nazareth and how he began in Galilee, after John had been preaching
1:8+; 4:27+ Is 61:1 baptism.[l] •*God had anointed him with the Holy Spirit* and with power, and because 38
Mt 3:16+ God was with him, Jesus went about doing good and curing all who had fallen
2:22 Mt 8:29+ into the power of the devil. •Now I, and those with me, can witness to everything 39
1:8+. 22 he did throughout the countryside of Judaea and in Jerusalem itself: and also
2:23+ to the fact that they killed him by hanging him on a tree, •yet three days afterwards 40
God raised him to life[m] and allowed him to be seen, •not by the whole people 41
1:3-4 but only by certain witnesses God had chosen beforehand. Now we are those
Jn 14:22 Lk 24:41-43 witnesses—we have eaten and drunk with him[n] after his resurrection from the
13:31 dead—•and he has ordered us to proclaim this to his people[o] and to tell them 42
2:36+ that God has appointed him to judge everyone, alive or dead.[p] •It is to him that 43
2:23+ all the prophets bear this witness: that all who believe in Jesus will have their sins
2:38+; 3:16+ forgiven through his name.'

15:8
Baptism of the first pagans

1:8+ *8:16* While Peter was still speaking the Holy Spirit came down[q] on all the listeners. 44
Jewish believers who had accompanied Peter were all astonished that the gift 45
2:33 of the Holy Spirit should be poured out on the pagans too, •since they could 46
2:4+.11 hear them speaking strange languages and proclaiming the greatness of God.
8:36; 11:17 Peter himself then said, •'Could anyone refuse the water of baptism to these 47
people, now they have received the Holy Spirit just as much as we have?' •He 48
1:5+; 2:38+; 16:15 then gave orders[r] for them to be baptised in the name of Jesus Christ. After-
18:20 wards they begged him to stay on for some days.[s]

Jerusalem: Peter justifies his conduct

1:15+ *8:14; 15:7* 11 The apostles and the brothers in Judaea heard that the pagans too had 1
accepted the word of God, •and when Peter came up to Jerusalem the 2
10:28.48+ Jews criticised him[a] •and said, 'So you have been visiting the uncircumcised 3
and eating with them, have you?' •Peter in reply gave them the details point by 4
10:10-48 point: •'One day, when I was in the town of Jaffa,' he began 'I fell into a trance as 5
I was praying and had a vision of something like a big sheet being let down from
heaven by its four corners. This sheet reached the ground quite close to me.
I watched it intently and saw all sorts of animals and wild beasts—everything 6
possible that could walk, crawl or fly. •Then I heard a voice that said to me, "Now, 7
Peter; kill and eat!" •But I answered: Certainly not, Lord; nothing profane or 8
unclean has ever crossed my lips. •And a second time the voice spoke from 9
heaven, "What God has made clean, you have no right to call profane". •This 10
was repeated three times, before the whole of it was drawn up to heaven again.

'Just at that moment, three men stopped outside the house where we were 11

12 staying; they had been sent from Caesarea to fetch me, •and the Spirit told me 1:8+
to have no hesitation about going back with them. The six brothers here came
13 with me as well, and we entered the man's house. •He told us he had seen an angel
standing in his house who said, "Send to Jaffa and fetch Simon known as Peter;
14 he has a message for you that will save you and your entire household". 2:47+; 16:15+
15 'I had scarcely begun to speak when the Holy Spirit came down on them 10:44+
16 in the same way as it came on us at the beginning, •and I remembered that the
Lord had said, "John baptised with water, but you will be baptised with the Holy 1:5
17 Spirit". •I realised then that God[b] was giving them the identical thing he gave to us 15:8-9
when we believed in the Lord Jesus Christ; and who was I to stand in God's way?'[c] 10:47; 15:9 Mt 16:23+
18 This account satisfied them, and they gave glory to God. 'God' they said 'can 2:47; 21:20
evidently grant even the pagans the repentance that leads to life.' *13:46f; 14-*27; 17:30; 26:20

Foundation of the church of Antioch

Those who had escaped[d] during the persecution that happened because of 8:1,4
19 Stephen travelled as far as Phoenicia and Cyprus and Antioch,[e] but they usually 21:3
proclaimed the message only to Jews. •Some of them, however, who came from
20 Cyprus and Cyrene, went to Antioch where they started preaching to the Greeks,[f]
proclaiming the Good News of the Lord Jesus[g] to them as well. •The Lord helped Lk 1:66
21 them, and a great number believed and were converted to the Lord. 2:41+; 3:19+
The church in Jerusalem[h] heard about this and they sent Barnabas to Antioch. *4:36+; 8:14*
22 There he could see for himself that God had given grace, and this pleased him,
23 and he urged[i] them all to remain faithful to the Lord[j] with heartfelt devotion; 13:43; 14:22
for he was a good man, filled with the Holy Spirit and with faith. And a large 6:5
24 number of people were won over to the Lord. 2:41+
25
26 Barnabas then left for Tarsus to look for Saul, •and when he found him he 9:30

h. Var. 'I was fasting and praying'.

i. The language of sacrifice (cf. v. 4). The unblemished victim and its offerer are both 'acceptable' to God, Lv 1:3; 19:5; 22:19-27. Isaiah (56:7) had prophesied that when the fulness of time came, the pagans' sacrifices would be 'acceptable' to God; see Ml 1:10-11. Cf. Rm 15:16; Ph 4:18; 1 P 2:5.

j. Var. 'The word that God has sent'.

k. Vv. 37-42 sum up the gospel story, cf. 1:21-22; 2:22+, emphasising the same points as Luke brought out in his own gospel.

l. Lit. 'Jesus from Nazareth, how he began (var. 'how it [all] began') in Galilee after the baptism proclaimed by John'.

m. Lit. 'raised him on the third day': stereotyped formula of the Christian preaching and faith. It appears as early as 1 Co 15:4 (a first stage of the creed) with the addition 'according to the scriptures'. The formula echoes Jon 2:1 (cf. Mt 12:40); see also Ho 6:2. It recurs in Mt 16:21; 17:23; 20:19; 27:64; Lk 9:22; 18:33; 24:7,46.

n. Add. (West.) 'and were his companions for forty days after his resurrection from the dead'.

o. I.e. the Chosen People, Israel, 10:2; 21:28.

p. Those still alive at the glorious coming and those who have died before the coming but then rise for judgement. See 1 Th 4:13–5:10. By raising up Jesus, God has solemnly invested him as supreme Judge, Ac 17:31; Jn 5:22,27; 2 Tm 4:1; 1 P 4:5; to proclaim the resurrection is therefore to invite men to repentance, cf. Ac 17:30-31.

q. 'The Pentecost of the pagans'. As Peter notes, v. 47; 11:15; 15:8, it resembles the first Pentecost.

r. It was not usual for the apostles to administer baptism themselves, cf. 19:5; 1 Co 1:14,17. See also 1 Jn 4:2.

s. That Peter should lodge with the uncircumcised seems to the Jerusalem 'Hebrews' even more shocking and contrary to the Law than that he should authorise their baptism (11:2-3; cf. 10:28). This same question gave rise to the Antioch incident, Ga 2:11f.

11 a. Western Text 'So after some time Peter determined to set out for Jerusalem. After speaking to the brothers and encouraging them, he set out, delivering many sermons throughout the countryside and instructing the people. When he reached them and told them of the favour God had granted, the circumcised brothers remonstrated with him.'

b. 'God' omitted by Western Text (because it is Christ who gives the Spirit).

c. Peter explains why he allowed a pagan to be baptised; he does not answer the objection that he had lodged with the uncircumcised, cf. v. 3, see 10:1+. According to Luke, Peter was considered to have been the first to receive pagans into the Church, in spite of the episode of the Ethiopian eunuch, 8:26-39, and the date of the evangelisation of Antioch to which Luke does not refer till later, vv. 19f. Against this background the council of Jerusalem, 15:5-29, appears as a kind of sequel to, or repetition of, the discussion in 11:1-18.

d. V. 19 takes up from 8:1 and 8:4 and then presents the episode of the Antiochene church's foundation as an immediate sequel to Stephen's martyrdom from which it has been separated by the insertion of the Acts of Philip, 8:5-40, and of Peter, 9:31–11:18. Nevertheless, the narrative presupposes the story of Saul's vocation, 9:1-30, itself concerned with Stephen's martyrdom.

e. Antioch on the Orontes, capital of the Roman province of Syria, third city of the empire after Rome and Alexandria.

f. Var. 'Hellenists', cf. 9:29. 'Greeks', as opposed to 'Jews', v. 19, includes all the uncircumcised.

g. Not 'Christ', a title more suited to a Jewish audience with its messianic expectation; in preaching to pagans Jesus was called 'Lord', cf. 25:26+. He is 'Lord' because, in virtue of his elevation to the Father's right hand, he rules over the kingdom in this fulness of time, cf. 2:21,36; 7:59-60; 10:36; 1 Th 4:15-17; 2 Th 1:7-12; Rm 10:9-13.

h. Which enjoyed right of supervision over the other churches, cf. 8:14; 11:1, and see Ga 2:2+.

i. Apparently a play on the name 'Barnabas', 'son of exhortation', 4:36.

j. Var. 'in the Lord'

brought him to Antioch. As things turned out they were to live together in that
church[k] a whole year, instructing a large number of people. It was at Antioch
1 P 4:16 that the disciples were first called 'Christians'.[l]

Barnabas and Saul sent as deputies to Jerusalem

2:17; 13:1; 15:32; 19:6 While they were there some prophets[m] came down to Antioch from Jerusalem,[n] 27
1:8+; 21:10 and one of them whose name was Agabus, seized by the Spirit, stood up and 28
predicted that a famine would spread over the whole empire. This in fact happened
11:25 before the reign of Claudius came to an end.[o] •The disciples decided to send 29
relief, each to contribute what he could afford, to the brothers living in Judaea.
20:17 Ga 2:1 They did this and delivered their contributions to the elders[p] in the care of 30
Tt 1:5+ 1 P 5:1 Barnabas and Saul.

Peter's arrest and miraculous deliverance[a]

12 It was about this time that King Herod started persecuting certain members 1
Mt 20:22-23 of the Church. •He beheaded James the brother of John, •and when he 2 3
saw that this pleased the Jews he decided to arrest Peter as well. •This was during 4
Ex 12:1+ the days of Unleavened Bread, and he put Peter in prison, assigning four squads
of four soldiers each to guard him in turns. Herod meant to try Peter in public
after the end of Passover week. •All the time Peter was under guard the Church 5
prayed to God for him unremittingly.
5:18-24; 16:25-40 On the night before Herod was to try him, Peter was sleeping between two 6
soldiers, fastened with double chains,[b] while guards kept watch at the main
5:19 Mt 1:20+ entrance to the prison. •Then suddenly the angel of the Lord stood there, and 7
1 K 19:5-7 the cell was filled with light. He tapped Peter on the side and woke him. 'Get up!'
he said 'Hurry!'—and the chains fell from his hands. •The angel then said, 'Put 8
on your belt and sandals'. After he had done this, the angel next said, 'Wrap
your cloak round you and follow me'. •Peter followed him, but had no idea that 9
what the angel did was all happening in reality; he thought he was seeing a vision.
They passed through two guard posts one after the other, and reached the iron 10
gate leading to the city. This opened of its own accord; they went through it[c]
and had walked the whole length of one street when suddenly the angel left him.
It was only then that Peter came to himself. 'Now I know it is all true' he said. 11
'The Lord really did send his angel and has saved me from Herod and from all
that the Jewish people were so certain would happen to me.'
As soon as he realised this he went straight to the house of Mary the mother 12
13:9+; 15:37 Col 4:10 of John Mark,[d] where a number of people had assembled and were praying. •He 13
1 P 5:13 knocked at the outside door and a servant called Rhoda came to answer it. •She 14
recognised Peter's voice and was so overcome with joy that, instead of opening
the door, she ran inside with the news that Peter was standing at the main entrance.
They said to her, 'You are out of your mind', but she insisted that it was true. 15
Then they said, 'It must be his angel!'[e] •Peter, meanwhile, was still knocking, 16
so they opened the door and were amazed to see that it really was Peter himself.
With a gesture of his hand he stopped them talking, and described to them how 17
1:15+; 15:13; the Lord had led him out of prison. He added, 'Tell James[f] and the brothers'.
21:17 1 Co 15:7 Then he left and went to another place.
16:27; 27:42 When daylight came there was a great commotion among the soldiers, who 18
could not imagine what had become of Peter. •Herod put out an unsuccessful 19
search for him; he had the guards questioned, and before leaving Judaea to take
up residence in Caesarea he gave orders for their execution.[g]

2 M 9:5-28 **The death of the persecutor**

Now Herod was on bad terms with the Tyrians and Sidonians. However, they 20
sent a joint deputation which managed to enlist the support of Blastus, the king's
chamberlain, and through him negotiated a treaty, since their country depended
for its food supply on King Herod's territory. •A day was fixed, and Herod, 21

wearing his robes of state and enthroned on a dais, made a speech to them.
22 23 The people acclaimed him with, 'It is a god speaking, not a man!', •and at
that moment the angel of the Lord struck him down, because he had not given Mt 1:20+
the glory to God. He was eaten away with worms and died.[h] 2 M 9:9

Barnabas and Saul return to Antioch

24 25 The word of God continued to spread and to gain followers. •Barnabas and 6:7+; 11:29-30
Saul completed their task and came back from Jerusalem,[i] bringing John Mark 12:12+
with them.

III. THE MISSION OF BARNABAS AND PAUL THE COUNCIL OF JERUSALEM

The mission sent out

1 13 In the church at Antioch the following were prophets and teachers:[a] Bar- 11:27+
nabas, Simeon called Niger, and Lucius of Cyrene, Manaen, who had 4:36+

k. Meaning doubtful. Possibly 'they worked together', 'they were received (by the church)', i.e. were guests of the church.

l. I.e. supporters or followers of Christus (or Chrestus). The nickname shows that the pagans of Antioch took the title 'Christ' (anointed) for a proper name.

m. Like the O.T. prophets, Dt 18:18+; 2 P 1:21; Mt 5:12, those of the N.T. are charismatics, 1 Co 12:1+, who speak in God's name, being inspired by his Spirit. Under the New Covenant this charisma is bestowed even more generously, Ac 2:17-18, and at times it is enjoyed by the faithful at large, Ac 19:6; 1 Co 11:4-5; 14:26,29-33,37. But particular individuals are so specially endowed with the charisma that they are always referred to as 'prophets', Ac 11:27; 13:1; 15:32; 21:9,10. These normally occupy the second place after the apostles in the order of charisma, 1 Co 12:28-29; Ep 4:11; but cf. 1 Co 12:10; Rm 12:6; Lk 11:49; this is because they are the appointed witnesses of the Spirit, Rv 2:7, etc., 1 Th 5:19-20, whose 'revelations' they communicate, 1 Co 14:6,26,30; Ep 3:5; Rv 1:1, just as the apostles are witnesses to the risen Christ, Rm 1:1+; Ac 1:8+, and proclaim the kerygma, Ac 2:22+. They do not simply foretell the future, Ac 11:28; 21:11, or read hearts, 1 Co 14:24-25; cf. 1 Tm 1:18. When they 'edify, exhort, console', 1 Co 14:3; cf. Ac 4:36; 11:23-24, they do so by a supernatural revelation; in this they resemble those who 'speak strange languages', Ac 2:4+; 19:6, but their gift is greater because their speech is intelligible, 1 Co 14. Their chief work was evidently to explain the oracles of scripture under the guidance of the Holy Spirit, especially those of the O.T. prophets, 1 P 1:10-12, and thus expound the 'mystery' of the divine plan, 1 Co 13:2; Ep 3:5; Rm 16:25+. For this reason they are named with the apostles as the foundation of the Church, Ep 2:20+. The Revelation of St John is a typical example of this N.T. 'prophecy', Rv 1:3; 10:11; 19:10; 22:7-10,18-19. For all its dignity, the prophetic charisma communicates knowledge that is imperfect and provisional, being bound up with faith, Rm 12:6, which is itself destined to vanish in face of the beatific vision, 1 Co 13:8-12.

n. Western Text adds 'and there was great rejoicing. While we were together, one of them ...' If this reading is correct, this is the first of the 'We-sections', cf. 16:10.

o. In the reign of Claudius (41-54) famine swept through the empire (49-50), through Greece first, and later Rome. Josephus puts it in the time of Tiberius Alexander the procurator (46-48).

p. The apostles are not mentioned, unlike 15:2, etc.; they had perhaps left Jerusalem. According to Ac 9:26; 11:29f; 15:2, it would seem that Paul made three journeys to Jerusalem before his two visits to Galatia, 16:6; 18:23. Paul himself, however, in Ga 1:18; 2:1f; cf. 4:13, mentions only two. The impression produced by Ac arises perhaps from Luke's method of combining his sources. It may be that the journey of 11:29 is the same as that of 15:2. The 'help' which is the purpose of the journey is probably to be distinguished from that which Paul supplied later, Ac 24:17, when the great collection, made at the appeal of the Jerusalem church, was completed, Ga 2:10; cf. 1 Co 16:1+; 2 Co 8:4; 9:1,12,13; Rm 15:31.

12 a. This episode, which 11:30 and 12:25 seem to place at the same time as the visit of Barnabas and Saul to Jerusalem, must in fact have preceded it, for Herod Agrippa I (called 'king' to distinguish him from his uncle Herod Antipas, the tetrarch of the Passion story, and awarded the royal title by Caligula in 37) was not actually king of Judaea and Samaria until 41; he died in 44. The events here described took place, therefore, between 41 and 44. The narrative has been rather clumsily fitted into its present literary context.

b. Each one to a soldier on either side.

c. Add. 'went down the seven steps'.

d. John Mark is mentioned again in 12:25; 13:5,13; 15:37,39; he was cousin to Barnabas, Col 4:10. During Paul's first Rome captivity Mark was with him, Col 4:10; Phm 24, and shortly before he died Paul asked for Mark's assistance, 2 Tm 4:11. Mark was also a disciple of Peter, 1 P 5:13, and tradition names him as author of the second gospel.

e. It was popularly believed that guardian angels were a kind of spiritual 'double' of their charges.

f. 'James' without qualification means the 'brother of the Lord'. At the time of Paul's first visit to Jerusalem, Ga 1:19 (i.e. in 38-39, cf. Ac 9:1+) and afterwards, James was leader of the 'Hebrew' section of the Jerusalem Christians. After Peter's departure he was in charge of the mother church. See Ac 15:13; 21:18; 1 Co 15:7. The Letter of James appears under his name.

g. Soldiers were liable to the punishment intended for their escaped prisoners, cf. 16:27; 27:42.

h. Var. 'When he had come down from the tribune he became food for worms even while he still lived; and so he died'.

i. Var. 'to Jerusalem', but cf. 11:29.

13 a. On the 'prophets', see 11:27+. The charisma of the teacher, or *didaskalos*, was his ability to instruct others on matters of morality and doctrine, instruction usually based on the scriptures. Cf. 1 Co 12-14+. The five prophets and teachers here named represent the governing body of the church of Antioch; cf. the list of the Twelve, Ac 1:13, and of the Seven, 6:5. Like the latter, the Antiochene Five are, it seems, hellenistic Jews.

13:9+ been brought up with Herod the tetrarch, and Saul. •One day while they were 2
1:8+ offering worship[b] to the Lord and keeping a fast, the Holy Spirit said, 'I want
14:25-26 Barnabas and Saul set apart for the work to which I have called them'. •So it was 3
6:6; 14:23; 15:40 that after fasting and prayer they laid their hands on them[c] and sent them off.

Cyprus: the magician Elymas

So these two, sent on their mission by the Holy Spirit, went down to Seleucia 4
and from there sailed to Cyprus.[d] •They landed at Salamis and proclaimed the 5
12:12+; 13:15,46; word of God in the synagogues of the Jews;[e] John acted as their assistant.
14:1; 16:13; 17:1-2,10,17; They travelled the whole length of the island, and at Paphos they came in 6
18:4,6 contact with a Jewish magician called Bar-jesus. •This false prophet was one 7
of the attendants of the proconsul Sergius Paulus who was an extremely intelligent
man. The proconsul summoned Barnabas and Saul and asked to hear the word
of God, •but Elymas Magos—as he was called in Greek—tried to stop them 8
so as to prevent the proconsul's conversion to the faith. •Then Saul, whose other 9
8:20-23 name is Paul,[f] looked him full in the face •and said, 'You utter fraud, you 10
Jn 8:44 impostor, you son of the devil, you enemy of all true religion, why don't you
stop twisting the straightforward ways of the Lord? •Now watch how the hand 11
of the Lord will strike you: you will be blind, and for a time you will not see the
sun.' That instant, everything went misty and dark for him, and he groped about
to find someone to lead him by the hand. •The proconsul, who had watched 12
Mt 22:33 Lk 4:32 everything, became a believer, being astonished by what he had learnt about
the Lord.

They arrive at Antioch in Pisidia

Paul and his friends went by sea from Paphos to Perga in Pamphylia where 13
15:38 John left them to go back to Jerusalem. •The others carried on from Perga till they 14
reached Antioch in Pisidia. Here they went to synagogue on the sabbath and took
13:5+ their seats. •After the lessons from the Law and the Prophets had been read, 15
28:23 the presidents of the synagogue sent them a message: 'Brothers, if you would
like to address some words of encouragement[g] to the congregation, please do so'.
Paul stood up, held up a hand for silence and began to speak: 16

Paul's preaching before the Jews[h]

2:22+; 10:2+ 'Men of Israel, and fearers of God,[i] listen! •The God of our nation Israel[j] 17
Is 1:2 *Ex 1:7* chose our ancestors, and made our people great when they were living as foreigners
Ex 3-15 in Egypt; then by divine power he led them out, •and for about forty years *took* 18
Dt 1:31 *care of*[k] *them in the wilderness.* •*When he had destroyed seven nations in Canaan,* 19
Dt 7:1+ *Gn 15:13* *he put them in possession* of their land •for about four hundred and fifty years.[l] 20
Ex 12:40-41 *1 S 8-10* After this he gave them judges, down to the prophet Samuel. •Then they 21
demanded a king, and God gave them Saul son of Kish, a man of the tribe of
Benjamin.[m] After forty years, •he deposed him and made David their king, of 22
1 S 13:14 Ps 89:20 whom he approved in these words, "*I have selected David son of Jesse, a man after*
Is 44:28 *13:32* *my own heart, who will carry out my whole purpose*". •To keep his promise, God 23
has raised up[n] for Israel one of David's descendants, Jesus, as Saviour, •whose 24
19:3-4 coming was heralded by John when he proclaimed a baptism of repentance for the
Ml 3:1-2 Lk 1:76 whole people of Israel. •Before John ended his career he said, "I am not the one[o] 25
Mt 3:11p+ Jn 1:20 you imagine me to be; that one is coming after me and I am not fit to undo his
sandal".

'My brothers, sons of Abraham's race, and all you who fear God, this message 26
5:20+ of salvation is meant for you.[p] •What the people of Jerusalem and their rulers 27
2:23+; 3:17+ did, though they did not realise it, was in fact to fulfil the prophecies read on every
Lk 18:31+ *13:14f; 15:21* sabbath.[q] •Though they found nothing to justify his death,[r] they condemned him 28
and asked Pilate to have him executed.[s] •When they had carried out everything 29
5:30+ that scripture foretells about him they took him down from the tree and buried
him in a tomb.[t] •But God raised him from the dead, •and for many days he 30 31

appeared to those who had accompanied him from Galilee to Jerusalem: and 1:3
it is these same companions of his who are now his witnesses before our people. 1:8+
2 'We have come here to tell you the Good News. It was to our ancestors that 2:24-31; 13:23
3 God made the promise but •it is to us, their children,[u] that he has fulfilled it,
by raising Jesus from the dead. As scripture says in the first psalm:[v] *You are my* Ps 2:7
4 *son: today I have become your father.*[w] •The fact that God raised him from the 2:36+; 9: 20+
dead, never to return to corruption, is no more than what he had declared: *To*
5 *you I shall give the sure and holy things promised to David.*[x] •This is explained by Is 55:3
6 another text: *You will not allow your holy one to experience corruption.* •Now when Ps 16:9
David in his own time had served God's purposes he died; he was buried with
7 his ancestors and has certainly *experienced corruption.* •The one whom God has
raised up, however, has not *experienced corruption.*
8 'My brothers, I want you to realise that it is through him that forgiveness of 2:38+ Rm 8:3
your sins is proclaimed. Through him justification from all sins which the Law *15:11* Rm 1:16+; 3:20+
9 of Moses was unable to justify •is offered to every believer.
0 'So be careful—or what the prophets say will happen to you. 28:26-27

1 *Cast your eyes around you, mockers;* Hab 1:5
be amazed, and perish!
For I am doing something in your own days
that you would not believe if you were to be told of it.'[y]

2 As they left they were asked to[z] preach on the same theme the following

13 b. The use of the term for Christian prayer in common puts this on a level with the sacrificial worship of the Old Law, cf. Rm 1:9+.

c. It seems, to judge by 14:26 (cf. 15:40), that by this act the community commends to God's grace the new missionaries chosen, v. 2, and sent, v. 4, by the Holy Spirit. The significance of the rite is not, therefore, exactly the same as that of 6:6 by which the Seven receive their commission from the apostles. Cf. 1 Tm 4: 14+.

d. Barnabas' native country, 4:36.

e. Paul's regular policy, 17:2, is to approach the Jews first, cf. 13:14; 14:1; 16:13; 17:10,17; 18:4,19; 19:8; 28:17,23, on the principle that the Jews have first claim, see 3:26; 13:46; Rm 1:16; 2:9-10; Mk 7:27; only after their refusal does Paul turn to the pagans, cf. Ac 13:46; 18:6; 28:28.

f. The Jews, and the eastern peoples in general, adopted names familiar in the Graeco-Roman world: John took 'Mark', 12:12, Joseph-Barsabbas took 'Justus', 1:23, Simeon 'Niger', 13:1, Tabitha 'Dorcas', 9:36, etc. Luke has given Paul his Roman name for the first time and does not use 'Saul' again. He also gives prominence now to Paul who is no longer a subordinate of Barnabas but the real missionary leader, v. 13.

g. I.e. a sermon based upon the scriptures, cf. Rm 15:4. The synagogue custom mentioned here was followed also when Christians met for worship: the sermons were preached by the 'prophets' or teachers, cf. 1 Co 14:3,31; 1 Tm 4:13; Heb 13:22; Ac 11:23; 14:22; 15:32; 16:40; 20:1,2.

h. The great inaugural discourse of Paul which Luke offers as typical of the apostle's preaching to the Jews. It falls into two parts: vv. 16-25 are a summary of the history of salvation (cf. Stephen's sermon, ch. 7) with an appendix recalling John the Baptist's testimony; vv. 26-39 claim that Jesus who died and has risen is the expected Messiah (thus closely resembling Peter's discourses, though this discourse ends with a suggestion of the Pauline doctrine of justification by faith). The conclusion, vv. 40-41, is a grave warning taken from the scriptures, cf. 28:26-27.

i. The two classes of listeners: Jews by birth and 'God-fearers', 10:2+.

j. Lit. 'the God of this people Israel'.

k. Var. 'upheld' (or: 'bore with').

l. Western (and Antiochene) Text 'For about four hundred and fifty years he gave them judges'. The text is obscure.

m. Paul's own name, and he too was of the tribe of Benjamin, Rm 11:1; Ph 3:5.

n. Or 'raised from the dead'. The Greek verb can mean either, and this ambivalence is exploited in the argument, as in 3:20-26: the 'promise' finds fulfilment in Christ's resurrection, vv. 32-33; see also 26:6-8; moreover, it is by his resurrection that Jesus is established as saviour, cf. 5:31; see also 2:21; 4:12; Rm 5:9-10; Ph 3:20, etc. Thus the verb which means 'raise up' in v. 22 unequivocally means 'raise from the dead' from v. 30 onwards. In v. 23 it is transitional and ambiguous.

o. Var. 'what'.

p. Var. 'for us'.

q. Following Western Text. Current text 'For those who live in Jerusalem and their leaders did not recognise him or (understand) the prophecies read on every sabbath: but they fulfilled the prophecies by condemning him'.

r. A recurring element of the Christian plea: the innocence and unjust condemnation of Jesus, cf. 3:13-14; Lk 23:16,22,47; Mt 27:3-10,19,23-24.

s. 'asked Pilate to have him executed', alternatively (the textual witnesses vary) 'that (he) should be executed'; or 'that (they might) execute him'. Var. 'handed him over to Pilate that he might be executed'.

t. Western Text '... foretells about him, after he had been crucified they asked Pilate for permission to take him down from the tree, and when they received it they took him down and buried him in a tomb'.

u. Var. 'for our children'.

v. 'first psalm' Western reading (following the ancient custom of reading Ps 1 and 2 as one); var. 'second psalm'.

w. By his resurrection Christ was enthroned as Messiah, and from then on his human nature enjoyed all the privileges of the Son of God. Cf. Rm 1:4+.

x. The quotation from Is introduces the reference to Ps 16 (the 'holy things promised to—lit. 'of'—David' are explained as the assurance to David in Ps 16 that 'the holy one of God' would not experience corruption).

y. The disbelief and rejection of the Jews (cf. Mt 21: 33+; 22:1+) are a favourite theme of Luke, cf. Ac 13: 5+; he uses it again as a conclusion to Ac, 28:26-27.

z. Var. 'When they left they felt it appropriate to'.

10:2+; 17:4 sabbath. •When the meeting broke up many Jews and devout converts[aa] joined 43
Paul and Barnabas,[bb] and in their talks with them Paul and Barnabas urged
11:23; 14:22 them to remain faithful to the grace God had given them.[cc]

Paul and Barnabas preach to the pagans

The next sabbath almost the whole town assembled to hear the word of God.[dd] 44
5:17; 17:5 1 Th 2:14+ When they saw the crowds, the Jews, prompted by jealousy, used blasphemies 45
and contradicted everything Paul said. •Then Paul and Barnabas spoke out 46
13:5+; 18:6; 28:24 boldly.[ee] 'We had to proclaim the word of God to you first, but since you have
rejected it, since you do not think yourselves worthy of eternal life, we must turn
1:8 to the pagans. •For this is what the Lord commanded us to do when he said: 47

Is 49:6 Jn 8:12+ *15:14; 26:23* *I have made you a light for the nations,*
so that my salvation may reach the ends of the earth.'[ff]

2:46-47+ Rm 8:28 It made the pagans very happy to hear this and they thanked the Lord for his 48
3:15+ message;[gg] all who were destined for eternal life became believers.[hh] •Thus the 49
6:7+ word of the Lord spread through the whole countryside.
10:2+ But the Jews worked upon some of the devout women of the upper 50
classes and the leading men of the city and persuaded them to turn against Paul
18:6 Lk 9:5; and Barnabas and expel them from their territory. •So they shook the dust 51
10-11p *2:46+* from their feet in defiance and went off to Iconium; •but the disciples were filled 52
Mt 10:14 with joy and the Holy Spirit.

Iconium evangelised

13:5+ 14 At Iconium they went to the Jewish synagogue, as they had at Antioch,[a] 1
and they spoke so effectively that a great many Jews and Greeks became
believers.[b]
17:13 1 Th 2:14+ Some of the Jews, however, refused to believe, and they poisoned the minds 2
of the pagans against the brothers.[c]
4:29-30; 13:46+ Accordingly Paul and Barnabas stayed on for some time, preaching fearlessly 3
20:24,32 for the Lord; and the Lord supported all they said about his gift of grace, allowing
Mk 16:17-20 signs and wonders to be performed by them.
The people in the city were divided,[d] some supported the Jews, others the 4
apostles, •but eventually with the connivance of the authorities a move was 5
2 Tm 3:11 made by pagans as well as Jews to make attacks on them and to stone them.
When the apostles came to hear of this, they went off for safety to Lycaonia where, 6
in the towns of Lystra and Derbe and in the surrounding country,[e] •they preached 7
the Good News.

3:1-10 **Healing of a cripple**

A man sat there[f] who had never walked in his life, because his feet were 8
crippled from birth; •and as he listened to Paul preaching, he managed to catch 9
his eye. Seeing that the man had the faith to be cured,[g] •Paul said in a loud voice, 10
'Get to your feet—stand up', and the cripple jumped up and began to walk.
When the crowd saw what Paul had done they shouted in the language of 11
28:6 Lycaonia, 'These people are gods who have come down to us disguised as men'.
They addressed Barnabas as Zeus, and since Paul was the principal speaker they 12
called him Hermes.[h] •The priests of Zeus-outside-the-Gate,[i] proposing that all 13
the people should offer sacrifice with them, brought garlanded oxen to the gates.
When the apostles Barnabas and Paul heard what was happening they tore their 14
clothes,[j] and rushed into the crowd, shouting, •'Friends, what do you think you 15
3:12; 10:26 are doing? We are only human beings like you. We have come with good news
2:38+; 3:19+ to make you turn from these empty idols to the living God[k] who made heaven
17:22-30+ Ps 147:20 and earth and the sea and all that these hold.[l] •In the past he allowed each nation 16
Ws 13:1 to go its own way; •but even then he did not leave you without evidence of himself 17
Jr 5:24 in the good things he does for you: he sends you rain from heaven, he makes your

18 crops grow when they should, he gives you food and makes you happy.' •Even
this speech, however, was scarcely enough to stop the crowd offering them
sacrifice.

The mission is disrupted

19 Then some Jews arrived from Antioch and Iconium, and turned the people 1 Th 2:14+
against the apostles. They stoned Paul and dragged him outside the town, 2 Co 11:25 2 Tm 3:11
20 thinking he was dead. •The disciples came crowding round him but, as they did
so, he stood up and went back to the town. The next day he and Barnabas went
off to Derbe.
21 Having preached the Good News in that town and made a considerable number
22 of disciples, they went back through Lystra and Iconium to Antioch. •They put
fresh heart into the disciples,[m] encouraging them to persevere in the faith. 'We 15:32,41; 18:23
all have to experience many hardships' they said 'before we enter the kingdom *11:23; 13:43* Mt 10:22; 24:13
23 of God.' •In each of these churches they appointed elders,[n] and with prayer and Rm 5:3-4
fasting they commended them to the Lord in whom they had come to believe. 2 Th 1:4f 2 Tm 2:12; 3:12
24 25 They passed through Pisidia and reached Pamphylia. •Then after proclaiming Heb 10:36
26 the word[o] at Perga they went down to Attalia •and from there sailed for Antioch, *13:3*
where they had originally been commended to the grace of God for the work 13:2-3
they had now completed.
27 On their arrival they assembled the church and gave an account of all that 14:3; 15:4, 12; 21:19
God had done with them, and how he had opened the door of faith[p] to the pagans.
28 They stayed there with the disciples for some time. 15:35

Controversy at Antioch

Ga 2:1-9

1 15 [a]Then some men came down from Judaea[b] and taught the brothers, 'Unless 21:21,25
you have yourselves circumcised in the tradition of Moses you cannot be

aa. 'converts' or 'proselytes', here in the wide sense, is equivalent to 'those who feared God' or 'those who worshipped God', cf. 10:2+.

bb. Add. 'considering it fitting to accept baptism'.

cc. Add. West. 'And in this way the word of God spread through the whole town'.

dd. Var. 'the word of the Lord', or '(to hear) Paul who spoke for a long time about the Lord'.

ee. The 'courage' and 'confidence' of the apostles has been already stressed, 4:13,29,31; Luke repeatedly attributes these qualities to Paul, 9:27-28; 14:3; 19:8; 26:26; 28:31, and Paul himself lays emphasis on them, 1 Th 2:2; 2 Co 3:12; 7:4; Ph 1:20; Ep 3:12; 6:19-20.

ff. LXX text quoted freely. The words may be taken either as referring to Paul himself (cf. 26:17-18), apostle and teacher of the pagans (cf. Rm 11:13; 1 Tm 2:7; Ep 3:8, etc.), or to the risen Christ (see Ac 26:23 which also, it seems, is based on Is 49:6; and see Lk 2:32, dependent on Is 49:6,9): Christ is the light of the pagans, but since only the apostles' witness can spread this light, cf. Ac 1:8+. Paul considers this prophecy as a command that he must carry out.

gg. Var. 'the word of God'.

hh. 'eternal life', cf. v. 46, i.e. the life of the world to come, cf. 3:15+; only those achieve it whose names are 'written in heaven', Lk 10:20, in 'the book of life', Ph 4:3; Rv 20:12+. 'Destined for the life of the world to come' was a common rabbinic expression. In Christian teaching the first prerequisite of this predestination to glory is faith in Christ. See Jn 10:26+; Rm 8:28-30, and earlier in Ac 2:39.

14 a. Lit. 'At Iconium they went to the Jewish synagogue in the same way (or: together)'.

b. V. 1 is continued in v. 3.

c. Refusal to believe becomes in a short time active opposition, cf. 19:9; 28:24 and 9:23; 13:45,50; 17:5-8,13; 18:6,13.

d. Continuation of v. 2.

e. Lystra, a Roman colony, Timothy's home town, cf. 16:1-2. The events of vv. 8-19 take place in Lystra; Paul is not in Derbe until v. 20.

f. All the MSS have 'in Lystra' but this is evidently an addition, cf. v. 20b.

g. Others translate 'to be saved'. The condition for the miracle is faith, cf. Mt 8:10+.

h. Hermes (the Latin 'Mercury') was the gods' mouthpiece.

i. His temple was outside the walls.

j. Sign of displeasure, cf. Mt 26:65.

k. In preaching against polytheism it was customary to contrast the true God with the false, the living God with helpless idols, and to make an appeal for conversion. For a summary of Paul's preaching to the pagans see 1 Th 1:9-10 and Ga 4:9; cf. Ac 15:19; 26:18,20.

l. That God creates the universe shows that he is a living God: this proposition is found in Jewish creeds. Cf. Ex 20:11; Ne 9:6; Ps 146:6; Ac 4:24; 17:24; Rv 10:6; 14:7.

m. Cf. Rm 1:11; 1 Th 3:2,13; Lk 22:32.

n. The elders, cf. 11:30+, are here chosen by the apostles, not by the community; so also Tt 1:5.

o. Add. 'of the Lord' or 'of God'.

p. Paul uses a similar metaphor, 1 Co 16:9; 2 Co 2:12; Col 4:3.

15 a. The events of this chapter raise several difficulties: 1. vv. 5-7a repeat vv. 1-2a as if the author, having two different accounts of how the controversy started, decided to give both as they stood. 2. V. 6 gives the impression that the community leaders held a private meeting, but vv. 12,22 suggest the debate took place before the whole Christian assembly. 3. The meeting issues a decree about how Christian converts from paganism must observe purity rites, and it entrusts this decree to Paul, vv. 22f; later, however (in 21:25), James seems to assume that Paul was then being informed of this decree for the first time. Paul himself does not speak of the decree either in Ga 2:6 (speaking of the Jerusalem meeting) or in 1 Co 8-10; Rm 14 (discussing similar problems). 4. Though the decree of Ac 15:29 was primarily intended for the churches of Syria and Cilicia, 15:23, Luke has nothing to say about Paul publishing it when he travelled through those

saved'. •This led to disagreement, and after Paul and Barnabas had had a long 2
argument with these men it was arranged that Paul and Barnabas and others of
the church[c] should go up to Jerusalem and discuss the problem with the apostles[d]
and elders.

All the members of the church saw them off,[e] and as they passed through 3
Phoenicia and Samaria they told how the pagans had been converted, and this
news was received with the greatest satisfaction by the brothers. •When they 4
arrived in Jerusalem they were welcomed by the church and by the apostles and
21:19 elders, and gave an account of all that God had done with them.

Controversy at Jerusalem

15:1 But certain members of the Pharisees' party who had become believers 5
objected,[f] insisting that the pagans should be circumcised and instructed to keep
the Law of Moses.[g] •The apostles and elders[h] met to look into the matter, •and 6 7
2:14+ after the discussion had gone on a long time, Peter stood up[i] and addressed them.

Peter's speech

10:1–11: 18+ 'My brothers,' he said 'you know perfectly well that in the early days God
made his choice among you: the pagans were to learn the Good News from me
10:44-47; 11:15-17 and so become believers. •In fact God, who can read everyone's heart, showed his 8
approval of them by giving the Holy Spirit to them just as he had to us. •God 9
11:17+ made no distinction between them and us, since he purified their hearts by faith.[j]
Mt 23:4 Ga 5:1 It would only provoke God's anger[k] now, surely, if you imposed on the disciples 10
the very burden that neither we nor our ancestors were strong enough to support?
Rm 7 Ga 3:10-12 Remember, we believe that we are saved in the same way as they are: through 11
the grace of the Lord Jesus.'[l]

This silenced the entire assembly,[m] and they listened to Barnabas and Paul 12
14:3,27; 21:19 describing all the signs and wonders God had worked through them among the
Ga 2:7 pagans.

James' speech

12:17+ When they had finished it was James[n] who spoke. 'My brothers,' he said 13
13:47; 18:10 Rm 9:26; 'listen to me. •Simeon[o] has described how God first arranged to enlist a people 14
15:9-12; 16:26 for his name out of the pagans. •This is entirely in harmony with the words of the 15
2 P 1 prophets, since the scriptures say:[p]

Am 9:11-12

After that I shall return 16
and rebuild the fallen House of David;
I shall rebuild it from its ruins
and restore it.
Then the rest of mankind, 17
all the pagans who are consecrated to my name,[q]
will look for the Lord,
says the Lord who made this •known so long ago.[r] 18

3:19+; 21:25 'I rule, then,[s] that instead of making things more difficult for pagans who 19
turn to God, •we send them a letter telling them merely to abstain from anything 20
polluted by idols,[t] from fornication,[u] from the meat of strangled animals and
from blood.[v] •For Moses has always had his preachers in every town, and is 21
13:27 read aloud in the synagogues every sabbath.'

The apostolic letter

Then the apostles and elders decided to choose delegates to send to Antioch 22
with Paul and Barnabas; the whole church concurred with this. They chose
15:40 1 Th 1 Judas known as Barsabbas[w] and Silas,[x] both leading men in the brotherhood,
2 Th 1:1 1 P 5:12 and gave them this letter to take with them: 23
16:4 'The apostles and elders, your brothers, send greetings to the brothers of pagan

24 birth in Antioch, Syria and Cilicia. •We hear that some of our members have
disturbed you with their demands and have unsettled your minds. They acted Ac 15:1 Ga 2:12
25 without any authority from us, •and so we have decided unanimously to elect
delegates and to send them to you with Barnabas and Paul, men we highly respect
26 27 who have dedicated their lives to the name of our Lord Jesus Christ. •Accord- 9:15-16
ingly we are sending you Judas and Silas, who will confirm by word of mouth
28 what we have written in this letter. •It has been decided by the Holy Spirit and by 1:8+; 5:32; 21:25
29 ourselves not to saddle you with any burden beyond these essentials: •you
are to abstain from food sacrificed to idols, from blood, from the meat of
strangled animals and from fornication. Avoid these, and you will do what is
right.[y] Farewell.'

The delegates at Antioch

30 The party left and went down to Antioch, where they summoned the whole
31 community and delivered the letter. •The community read it and were delighted
32 with the encouragement it gave them. •Judas and Silas, being themselves prophets, 11:27+
33 spoke for a long time, encouraging and strengthening the brothers. •These two 14:22
spent some time there, and then the brothers wished them peace and they went
35 back to those who had sent them.[z] •Paul and Barnabas, however, stayed on in 14:28
Antioch, and there with many others they taught and proclaimed the Good News, 2:42+
the word of the Lord.

provinces, 15:41. Luke does mention it when speaking about Lycaonia, 16:4, but the terms of 15:19-21; 21:25 suggest that the decree was for all regions. All these difficulties may be explained by supposing that Luke has combined two distinct controversies and their varying solutions (Paul distinguishes them more clearly in Ga 2). One controversy was about the obligations of convert pagans to observe the Law, and Peter and Paul both took part, cf. Ga 2:1-10; the other controversy which took place later was about the social relations between the groups of Christian converts, those from Judaism and those from paganism, cf. Ga 2:11-14. In this James, in Peter's absence, took the leading part. Any contact with pagans involved legal impurity for Jews: cf. Ac 15:20+.

15 b. In Ga 2:12 there are several of them and they come from James.

c. Ga 2:1-3 mentions Titus who had pagan blood.

d. The apostles, who are not mentioned either in 11:30 or in 21:18, are grouped here with the elders, cf. Ga 2:2-9 where Peter and John are grouped with James, 'brother of the Lord', as authorities in the Jerusalem church.

e. Others translate 'provided them with all they needed for the journey', cf. 1 Co 16:11; Tt 3:13.

f. In the current text there seems to be no connection between the Pharisees' intervention at Jerusalem and the events that happened at Antioch. The Western Text links them together 'But those who had told them to go up to the elders then stood up...'

g. According to Ga 2:3-5 they are thinking particularly of Titus who had accompanied Paul to Jerusalem.

h. Add. West. 'and the assembly', cf. v. 12.

i. Add. West. '(inspired) by the Spirit'.

j. An interpretation of God's message to Peter, 10:15; 11:9; cf. 10:28; Si 38:10.

k. Lit. 'put God to the test': i.e. to ask God for a miracle to prove his will when this has been made known already—a blasphemous frame of mind. In the present case God had made his attitude clear by sending the Spirit to Cornelius and his family.

l. A straight answer to the assertion in v. 1. The doctrine is that of Ga 2:15-21; 3:22-26; Rm 11:32; Ep 2:1-10; etc. On this score the Jews' position is not privileged, cf. Ac 13:38; Ga 5:6; 6:15.

m. Western Text 'When the elders had expressed their agreement with what Peter had said, this silenced...'

n. Ga 2:9 witnesses to the importance of the part played by James.

o. Simon Peter's semitic name, cf. 2 P 1:1.

p. The text is quoted according to the LXX; the argument depends on variants peculiar to that version and probably comes from hellenistic circles, though here it is ascribed to the leader of the 'Hebrew' party.

q. Lit. 'on whom my name has been invoked' (or 'over whom ... pronounced'). To invoke the name of Yahweh over a people, cf. 2 Ch 7:14, or over a place, cf. 2 Ch 6:34, is to consecrate it to him.

r. Lit. 'says the Lord who makes these things known from of old'. Var. 'says the Lord who does these things. From of old the Lord knows his work.'

s. James settles the discussion, and the terms of the apostolic letter are those of his own pronouncement. Ga 2:9 also suggests that James at this period occupied the first place in the Jerusalem church, cf. Ac 12:17+. A variant reduces this impression 'And so, for my part...'

t. The flesh of animals slain for pagan sacrifice, cf. v. 29 and 21:25. See 1 Co 8-10.

u. This word probably refers to all the irregular marriages listed in Lv 18.

v. Western Text omits 'the meat of strangled animals' and adds, after 'blood': 'and not to do to others what one would not have done to oneself' (so also in v. 29). Another omits 'fornication'. The ritual exceptions mentioned by James show clearly the sort of thing that was at issue and answer the question asked in Ac 11:3 and Ga 2:12-14: what must hellenistic Christians do for Judaeo-Christians to mix with them without incurring legal impurity? James decides to keep only those prescriptions for purity that have a fundamentally religious meaning: 1. to eat idol-meats implies sharing in sacrilegious worship, cf. 1 Co 8-10. 2. Blood symbolises life, and that belongs to God alone. The severity with which the Law forbids it, Lv 1:5+, explains the Jews' reluctance to dispense pagans from this prohibition. 3. As blood remains in strangled animals, this is part of the previous prohibition. 4. The table of irregular marriages is only included here because they involved legal impurity, not by way of moral judgement.

w. Not mentioned elsewhere, cf. 1:23.

x. Silas, missionary companion of Paul, 15:40–18:5, is the same as the Silvanus mentioned in 1 Th 1:1; 2 Th 1:1; 2 Co 1:19; 1 P 5:12.

y. Western Text adds 'under the guidance of the Holy Spirit'.

z. Western Text adds v. 34 'But Silas decided to stay there'. Several MSS further add 'Jude set out by himself'.

IV. PAUL'S MISSIONS

Paul separates from Barnabas and recruits Silas

On a later occasion Paul said to Barnabas, 'Let us go back and visit all the 36
towns where we preached the word of the Lord, so that we can see how
12:12+ the brothers are doing'. •Barnabas suggested taking John Mark, •but Paul was not 37 38
13:13 in favour of taking along the very man who had deserted them in Pamphylia and
had refused to share in their work.
After a violent quarrel they parted company, and Barnabas sailed off with 39
15:22+ Mark to Cyprus. •Before Paul left, he chose Silas to accompany him and was 40
13:3 commended by the brothers to the grace of God.[aa]

Lycaonia: Paul recruits Timothy

14:22+ He travelled through Syria and Cilicia, consolidating the churches.[bb] 41
16 From there he went to Derbe, and then on to Lystra. Here there was a 1
1 Tm 1:2; 2 Tm 1:5; 3:15; Phm 1; Heb 13:23 disciple called Timothy,[a] whose mother was a Jewess who had become a
believer; but his father was a Greek. •The brothers at Lystra and Iconium spoke 2
well of Timothy, •and Paul, who wanted to have him as a travelling companion, 3
had him circumcised. This was on account of the Jews in the locality[b] where
everyone knew his father was a Greek.
15:23-29 As they visited one town after another, they passed on the decisions reached 4
by the apostles and elders in Jerusalem, with instructions to respect them.
2:41+; 14:22+ So the churches grew strong in the faith, as well as growing daily in numbers. 5

The crossing into Asia Minor

Ga 4:13-15 They travelled through Phrygia and the Galatian country,[c] having been told 6
by the Holy Spirit not to preach the word in Asia. •When they reached the frontier 7
Rm 8:9; Ph 1:19; 1 P 1:11 of Mysia they thought to cross it into Bithynia, but as the Spirit of Jesus[d] would
not allow them, •they went through[e] Mysia and came down to Troas. 8
10:9-23 One night Paul had a vision: a Macedonian appeared and appealed to him 9
in these words, 'Come across to Macedonia and help us'. •Once he had seen this 10
vision we[f] lost no time in arranging a passage to Macedonia, convinced that God
had called us to bring them the Good News.

Arrival at Philippi

Sailing from Troas we made a straight run for Samothrace; the next day for 11
Neapolis, •and from there for Philippi, a Roman colony and the principal city 12
of that particular district of Macedonia.[g] After a few days in this city •we went 13
13:5+ along the river outside the gates as it was the sabbath and this was a customary
place for prayer.[h] We sat down and preached to the women who had come to the
10:2+ meeting. •One of these women was called Lydia, a devout woman from the town 14
of Thyatira who was in the purple-dye trade. She listened to us, and the Lord
opened her heart to accept what Paul was saying. •After she and her household 15
1:5+ had been baptised[i] she sent us an invitation: 'If you really think me a true believer
10:48 in the Lord,' she said 'come and stay with us'; and she would take no refusal.[j]

Imprisonment of Paul and Silas

One day as we were going to prayer, we met a slave-girl who was a soothsayer[k] 16
and made a lot of money for her masters by telling fortunes. •This girl started 17
19:15; Mt 8:29+ following Paul and the rest of us and shouting, 'Here are the servants of the Most
High God; they have come to tell you how to be saved!' •She did this every day 18
Mk 16:17 afterwards until Paul lost his temper one day and turned round and said to the
Mk 1:25-26+; *3:16*+ spirit, 'I order you in the name of Jesus Christ to leave that woman'. The spirit
went out of her then and there.
19:24-27 When her masters saw that there was no hope of making any more money 19

out of her, they seized Paul and Silas and dragged them to the law courts in the
market place •where they charged them before the magistrates and said, 'These
1 people are causing a disturbance in our city. They are Jews •and are advocating
2 practices which it is unlawful for us as Romans to accept or follow.'[l] •The crowd
joined in and showed its hostility to them, so the magistrates had them stripped Ph 1:30 1 Th 2:2
3 and ordered them to be flogged. •They were given many lashes and then thrown 2 Co 11:25
4 into prison, and the gaoler was told to keep a close watch on them. •So, following
his instructions, he threw them into the inner prison and fastened their feet in the
stocks.

The miraculous deliverance of Paul and Silas

5 Late that night Paul and Silas were praying and singing God's praises, while Col 3:16
6 the other prisoners listened. •Suddenly there was an earthquake that shook the 4:31
prison to its foundations. All the doors flew open and the chains fell from all the 12:6-11
7 prisoners. •When the gaoler woke and saw the doors wide open he drew his sword 12:18-19; 27:42
8 and was about to commit suicide, presuming that the prisoners had escaped. •But
Paul shouted at the top of his voice, 'Don't do yourself any harm; we are all here'.
9 The gaoler called for lights, then rushed in, threw himself trembling[m] at the
0 feet of Paul and Silas, •and escorted them out, saying, 'Sirs, what must I do to be
1 saved?' •They told him, 'Become a believer in the Lord Jesus, and you will be 2:21+; 16:15+
2 saved, and your household too'. •Then they preached the word of the Lord[n] to
3 him and to all his family. •Late as it was, he took them to wash their wounds,
4 and was baptised then and there with all his household. •Afterwards he took 1:5+; 8:36, 38
them home and gave them a meal, and the whole family celebrated their con- 2:46+
version to belief in God.
5 When it was daylight the magistrates sent the officers with the order: 'Release
6 those men'.[o] •The gaoler reported the message to Paul, 'The magistrates have
7 sent an order for your release; you can go now and be on your way'.[p] •'What!'
Paul replied 'They flog Roman citizens[q] in public and without trial and throw 22:25
us into prison, and then think they can push us out on the quiet! Oh no! They
must come and escort us out themselves.'
8 The officers reported this to the magistrates, who were horrified to hear the
9 men were Roman citizens. •They came and begged them to leave the town.[r] 22:29

aa. Var. 'the grace of the Lord'.

bb. Western Text adds 'passing on to them the injunctions of the elders', cf. 16:4.

16 a. Timothy became Paul's constant companion, cf. 17:14f; 18:5; 19:22; 20:4; 1 Th 3:2,6; 1 Co 4:17; 16:10; 2 Co 1:19; Rm 16:21, and one of his most faithful disciples to the very end (see 1 Tm and 2 Tm which are addressed to him).

b. Paul opposed circumcision for converts from paganism, Ga 2:3; 5:1-12, but Timothy had a Jewish mother and so, by Jewish law, was an Israelite.

c. Galatia strictly so called, cf. Introduction to the Letters of St Paul. When he left Iconium therefore, Paul intended to travel westwards to Ephesus. But the Spirit intervened and he turned N. into Phrygia, then in a north-westerly direction to 'Galatian country', where illness kept him for a time, Ga 4:13-15, preached the gospel in these places and returned later to visit the disciples there, Ac 18:23.

d. Om. 'of Jesus'.

e. Preferable to 'they skirted'.

f. Sudden transition to first person plural: the first 'We-section' of Ac, but see 11:27+. Cf. Introduction.

g. Philippi, a town in the principal district of the province of Macedonia; it had become a Roman colony and was a completely Latin city, its administration modelled on that of Rome.

h. The Jews had no synagogue in Philippi; they met by the side of the river (for ritual ablutions).

i. Lydia's conversion brought her household to the faith; cf. 10:33; 16:31,34; 18:8; 1 Co 1:16.

j. Unusual for Paul: cf. 20:33-35; 1 Th 2:9; 2 Th 3:8; 1 Co 9, though on a later occasion the Philippians persuaded him to accept help again, cf. Ph 4:10-18. He would have accepted it from no one else; it is the greatest compliment to the charity of Lydia and of the other Philippian Christians.

k. Lit. 'who had a Python-spirit', so called from the serpent Python of the ancient Delphic oracle.

l. The practices referred to are Jewish, cf. 6:14; 15:1; 21:21; 26:3; 28:17; Jn 19:40: the accusers make no distinction between Christian and Jew. The precise charge is proselytism: though the Jews were allowed to practise their religion, they had no right to proselytise Romans. Christian propaganda was therefore against the law.

m. This new fear comes from his realising that he has treated as criminals men who are envoys of God.

n. Var. 'the word of God'

o. Var. 'When it was daylight the magistrates met in the market place; remembering the earthquake that had taken place they were afraid and sent the officers to say: Release the men you arrested yesterday.'

p. Add. 'in peace'.

q. The *lex Porcia* forbade (under heavy penalties) the scourging of a Roman citizen.

r. Alex. (and Antiochene) Text 'They came to apologise, and when they had taken them out they asked them to leave the town'. Western Text 'And going with a number of friends to the prison, they urged them to go out, saying: We had not realised what you wanted and that you were holy men. When they had taken them out, they begged them: Get out of this town in case those who shouted against you get another mob together.'

From the prison they went to Lydia's house where they saw all the brothers and
gave them some encouragement; then they left.

Thessalonika: difficulties with the Jews

Ph 4:16 **17** Passing through Amphipolis and Apollonia, they eventually reached
13:5+ Thessalonika, where there was a Jewish synagogue. •Paul as usual intro- 2
duced himself and for three consecutive sabbaths developed the arguments from
Lk 24:25-27, 46-47 scripture for them, •explaining and proving how it was ordained that the Christ
2:23+; 18:5+ should suffer and rise from the dead. 'And the Christ' he said 'is this Jesus whom
13:43 I am proclaiming to you.' •Some of them[a] were convinced and joined Paul and 4
10:2+ Silas, and so did a great many God-fearing people and Greeks,[b] as well as a number
of rich women.

13:45+ 1 Th 2:14+ The Jews, full of resentment, enlisted the help of a gang from the market place, 5
stirred up a crowd, and soon had the whole city in an uproar. They made for
Rm 16:21 Jason's house,[c] hoping to find them there and drag them off to the People's
Assembly; •however, they only found Jason and some of the brothers, and these 6
they dragged before the city council, shouting, 'The people who have been
24:5 turning the whole world upside down have come here now; •they have been 7
Lk 23:2 Jn 19:12-15 staying at Jason's. They have broken every one of Caesar's edicts by claiming
that there is another emperor,[d] Jesus.' •This accusation alarmed the citizens 8
and the city councillors •and they made Jason and the rest give security before 9
setting them free.

Fresh difficulties at Beroea

When it was dark the brothers immediately sent Paul and Silas away to Beroea,[e] 10
13:5+ where they visited the Jewish synagogue as soon as they arrived. •Here the Jews 11
were more open-minded than those in Thessalonika, and they welcomed the word
Jn 5:39 very readily; every day they studied the scriptures to check whether it was true.
Many Jews became believers, and so did many Greek women from the upper 12
classes and a number of the men.

When the Jews of Thessalonika heard that the word of God was being preached 13
14:2+ by Paul in Beroea as well, they went there to make trouble and stir up the people.
1 Th 3:2 So the brothers arranged for Paul to go immediately as far as the coast, leaving 14
Silas and Timothy behind. •Paul's escort took him as far as Athens, and went 15
18:5 back with instructions for Silas and Timothy to rejoin Paul as soon as they could.[f]

Paul in Athens

Paul waited for them in Athens and there his whole soul was revolted at the 16
13:5+ sight of a city given over to idolatry.[g] •In the synagogue he held debates with the 17
10:2+ Jews and the God-fearing, but in the market place he had debates every day with
anyone who would face him.[h] •Even a few Epicurean and Stoic philosophers[i] 18
argued with him. Some said, 'Does this parrot know what he's talking about?'[j]
And, because he was preaching about Jesus and the resurrection,[k] others said,
'He sounds like a propagandist for some outlandish gods'.[l]

1 Co 1:22 They invited him to accompany them to the Council of the Areopagus,[m] where 19
they said to him, 'How much of this new teaching you were speaking about are
we allowed to know? •Some of the things you said seemed startling to us and we 20
2 Tm 3:7 would like to find out what they mean.' •The one amusement the Athenians and 21
the foreigners living there seem to have, apart from discussing the latest ideas,
is listening to lectures about them.

So Paul stood before the whole Council of the Areopagus and made this 22
speech:

Paul's speech before the Council of the Areopagus[n]

'Men of Athens, I have seen for myself how extremely scrupulous you are
in all religious matters, •because I noticed, as I strolled round admiring your 23

sacred monuments, that you had an altar inscribed: To An Unknown God.[o] Well,
the God whom I proclaim is in fact the one whom you already worship without
knowing it.
24 'Since the God who made the world and everything in it[p] is himself Lord of 1 K 8:27 Is 42:5
heaven and earth, he does not make his home in shrines made by human hands. *14:15+*
25 Nor is he dependent on anything that human hands can do for him, since he can 7:48-50
never be in need of anything; on the contrary, it is he who gives everything— 2 M 7:23; 14:35
26 including life and breath—to everyone. •From one single stock[q] he not only Ps 50:12
created the whole human race so that they could occupy the entire earth, but he Gn 10 Dt 32:8
decreed how long each nation should flourish and what the boundaries of its Jb 12:33
27 territory should be.[r] •And he did this so that all nations might seek the deity[s] Dt 4:29 Ps 145:18
and, by feeling their way towards him, succeed in finding him. Yet in fact he is not Ws 13:6 Is 55:6
28 far from any of us, •since it is in him that we live, and move, and exist,[t] as indeed Rm 1:19 *Ps 104*
some of your own writers[u] have said:

"We are all his children".[v] 2 P 1:4

29 'Since we are the children of God, we have no excuse for thinking that the 19:26 Is 40:18
deity looks like anything in gold, silver or stone that has been carved and designed Rm 1:22-23
by a man.[w]
30 'God overlooked that sort of thing when men were ignorant, but now he is Rm 3:25-26
31 telling everyone everywhere that they must repent, •because he has fixed a day
when the whole world will be judged, and judged in righteousness,[x] and he has 2:38+ Lk 24:47
appointed a man to be the judge. And God has publicly proved this by raising
this man from the dead.'[y] 10:42+
32 At this mention of rising from the dead, some of them burst out laughing;
33 others said, 'We would like to hear you talk about this again'.[z] •After that Paul 24:25

17 a. Aristarchus, one of Paul's most faithful companions, cf. 20:4; Col 4:10, was probably one of them.

b. Var. 'Greek worshippers of God'. The reading here preferred distinguishes 'those who worship God', 10:2+, from 'Greeks' not previously influenced by Jewish proselytism. Most of the conversions in Thessalonika were made from paganism, cf. 1 Th 1:9-10, etc.

c. Possibly the Jason of Rm 16:21.

d. Actually, the Christians deliberately avoided calling Jesus by the emperor's title *basileus* ('king'); they preferred 'Christ' (Messiah) and 'Lord'.

e. Despite their departure the persecution at Thessalonika went on, cf. 1 Th 2:14.

f. Luke is summarising and simplifying. Timothy must have gone with Paul because Paul later sends him from Athens to Thessalonika, 1 Th 3:1f.

g. Athens was the intellectual metropolis of pagan hellenism, and to Luke was a symbol. This is evident from the fact that Paul's sermon there, the only sample of his preaching to the pagans, is the only one in which he argues philosophically.

h. The one explicit mention in Ac of this kind of preaching (though cf. 14:7f).

i. The two prevailing philosophical systems.

j. Lit. 'What does this seed-picker want to say?' The local Athenian word *spermologos* was used of birds that peck, crows etc. It came to mean 'beggar', one who picks up food wherever he can find it, and also a garrulous man who speaks in clichés, parrot-wise.

k. Cf. v. 32. They assume *Anastasis* ('Resurrection') is the name of a goddess, consort of Jesus.

l. Socrates was accused of the same thing.

m. A hill to the S. of the Agora. The word means also the Athenian supreme council which held its sessions there. The text may be understood in two ways: either the philosophers lead Paul 'on to (the hill of) the Areopagus', away from the city centre for easier listening, or (preferably) they lead him 'before (the Council of) the Areopagus'.

n. Paul preaches on the knowledge of God, a theme very popular in the propaganda of contemporary hellenistic Judaism. The pagans are accused of not knowing God, v. 23, the proof being that they worship idols v. 29. This ignorance is culpable, v. 30, since all men are capable of knowing God as creator and controller of the cosmos, vv. 24-29. Cf. the same line of argument in 14:15-17; Ws 13-14; Rm 1:19-25; Ep 4:17-19.

o. The pagans used to dedicate altars 'to the unknown gods' lest they provoke the vengeance of gods whose names they did not know. Paul turns the practice to his own purpose and thus parries the charge of preaching 'outlandish gods'.

p. This idea was common in Greek thought and hellenistic Judaism; it is a form of the old biblical theme in Am 5:21f; 1 Ch 29:10f; Ps 50:9-13, etc.

q. Var. 'of one blood', 'of one nation', 'of one race'.

r. Alternative translations 'determining the division of times' or 'determining the order of the seasons (cf. 14:17) and the bounds of human habitation' (man was not to occupy the whole earth but only part of it). The general meaning is the same: the order of the cosmos is enough to lead to a knowledge of God.

s. Var. 'God' or 'the Lord'.

t. Expression suggested by the poet Epimenides of Cnossos (6th c. B.C.).

u. Lit. 'of your people'. Var. 'of your poets' or 'of your sages'.

v. Quotation from the *Phainomena* of Aratus, a poet of Cilician origin (3rd c. B.C.). Cleanthes the Stoic (3rd c.) used almost identical language.

w. This form of attack on idolatry has ancient precedent, cf. Is 40:20+.

x. Cf. Ps 9:8; 96:13; 98:9. The apostles set their appeal for repentance against the background of judgement, cf. especially 10:42-43; 1 Th 1:10.

y. Christ's resurrection justifies belief in his coming as judge and saviour at the end of time, cf. Rm 14:9; 2 Tm 4:1; 1 P 4:5.

z. In the Greek world, even among Christians, the doctrine of the resurrection met stubborn resistance from preconceived ideas, cf. 1 Co 15:12f The Jerusalem Sanhedrists condemned and attacked this Christian dogma; the Athenians of the Areopagus were content to mock. Paul's failure in Athens was all but complete; from now on he refuses to use the devices of Greek philosophy, 1 Co 2:1-5.

left them, •but there were some who attached themselves to him and became
believers, among them Dionysius the Areopagite[aa] and a woman called Damaris,
and others besides.

Foundation of the church of Corinth

Rm 16:3 1 Co 16:19 2 Tm 4:19 **18** After this Paul left Athens and went to Corinth,[a] •where he met a Jew
called Aquila whose family came from Pontus. He and his wife Priscilla[b]
had recently left Italy because an edict of Claudius had expelled all the Jews from
Rome.[c] Paul went to visit them, •and when he found they were tentmakers, of the
20:33-35 1 Co 4:12 same trade as himself, he lodged with them, and they worked together.[d] •Every
13:5+ sabbath he used to hold debates in the synagogues, trying to convert Jews as well
as Greeks.
17:15 1 Th 3:5-7 After Silas and Timothy had arrived from Macedonia,[e] Paul devoted all his
5:42; 8:5; 9:22 time to preaching, declaring to the Jews that Jesus was the Christ.[f] •When they
turned against him and started to insult him, he took his cloak and shook it out
13:51+ Mt 27:24-25 in front of them,[g] saying, 'Your blood be on your own heads; from now on I can
Ac 13:5+; 13:46-47, 51+; 20: go to the pagans with a clear conscience'. •Then he left the synagogue and moved
26; 28:28 to the house next door that belonged to a worshipper of God called Justus.[h]
1 Co 1:14 Crispus, president of the synagogue, and his whole household, all became believers
in the Lord. A great many Corinthians who had heard him became believers and
1:5+ were baptised.[i] •One night the Lord spoke to Paul in a vision, 'Do not be afraid
23:11 Jr 1:8 to speak out, nor allow yourself to be silenced: •I am with you. I have so many 10
1 Co 2:3 *Jn 10:16* people on my side in this city that no one will even attempt to hurt you.' •So Paul 11
stayed there preaching the word of God among them for eighteen months.

The Jews take Paul to court

1 Th 2:14+ But while Gallio was proconsul of Achaia,[j] the Jews made a concerted attack 12
21:27-28 on Paul and brought him before the tribunal. •'We accuse this man' they said 13
'of persuading people to worship God in a way that breaks the Law.'[k] •Before 14
Paul could open his mouth, Gallio said to the Jews, 'Listen, you Jews. If this were
a misdemeanour or a crime, I would not hesitate to attend to you; •but if it is 15
23:29; 25: 18-19 only quibbles about words and names, and about your own Law, then you must
Jn 18:31 deal with it yourselves—I have no intention of making legal decisions about things
like that.' •Then he sent them out of the court, •and at once they all turned on 16 17
Sosthenes,[l] the synagogue president, and beat him in front of the court house.
Gallio refused to take any notice at all.

Return to Antioch and departure for the third journey

After staying on for some time, Paul took leave of the brothers and sailed for 18
Rm 16:1 Syria,[m] accompanied by Priscilla and Aquila. At Cenchreae he had his hair cut
21:23 off, because of a vow he had made.[n]
When they reached Ephesus, he left them, but first he went alone to the 19
13:5+ synagogue to debate with the Jews. •They asked him to stay longer but he declined, 20
10:48 *Jm 4:15* though when he left he said, 'I will come back another time, God willing'. Then 21
he sailed from Ephesus.
He landed at Caesarea, and went up to greet the church.[o] Then he came down 22
to Antioch •where he spent a short time before continuing his journey 23
16:6+; 14:22+ through the Galatian country and then through Phrygia, encouraging all the
followers.

19:1 ### Apollos

1 Co 1:12; 16:12 An Alexandrian Jew named Apollos[p] now arrived in Ephesus. He was an 24
Tt 3:13 eloquent man, with a sound knowledge of the scriptures, and yet, •though he had 25
9:2+ been given instruction in the Way of the Lord and preached with great spiritual
earnestness and was accurate in all the details he taught about Jesus, he had only
19:3-5 experienced the baptism of John. •When Priscilla and Aquila heard him speak 26

boldly in the synagogue, they took an interest in him and gave him further 13:46+ Rm 16:3
instruction about the Way.[q]
When Apollos thought of crossing over to Achaia, the brothers encouraged
him and wrote asking the disciples to welcome him.[r] When he arrived there he was 2 Co 3:1
able by God's grace to help the believers considerably •by the energetic way he
refuted the Jews in public and demonstrated from the scriptures that Jesus was 9:22; 18:5+
the Christ.

The disciples of John at Ephesus

19 While Apollos was in Corinth,[a] Paul made his way overland as far as 18:24
Ephesus,[b] where he found a number of disciples. •When he asked, 'Did
you receive the Holy Spirit when you became believers?' they answered, 'No, 8:15-17 Jn 7:39
we were never even told there was such a thing as a Holy Spirit'.[c] •'Then how
were you baptised?' he asked. 'With John's baptism' they replied. •'John's Mt 3:6+
baptism' said Paul 'was a baptism of repentance; but he insisted that the people 1:5+; 2:38+; 13:
should believe in the one who was to come after him—in other words Jesus.' 24-25+
When they heard this, they were baptised in the name of the Lord Jesus, •and 1:5+
the moment Paul had laid hands on them the Holy Spirit came down on them, 8:15-17+ 1 Tm 4:14+
and they began to speak with tongues and to prophesy.•There were about twelve *Ac 2:4+;* 11:27+
of these men.

Foundation of the church of Ephesus[d]

He began by going to the synagogue, where he spoke out boldly and argued 13:5+,46+
persuasively about the kingdom of God. He did this for three months, •till the 1:3+; 20:25

aa. Luke's readers must have known him. He became the subject of legend, especially since the 5th c. when an author (the 'pseudo-Dionysius') published various mystical writings under his name. Later legend identifies him with St Denys, first Bishop of Paris (3rd c.).

18 a. Corinth, rebuilt by Julius Caesar, became capital of the Roman province of Achaia. Its population was largely Roman and Latin-speaking, but brisk trade had attracted people of all nations. It had a considerable Jewish colony. The immorality of Corinth was proverbial.

b. Also called Prisca, Rm 16:3; 1 Co 16:19; 2 Tm 4:19.

c. This edict, mentioned by Suetonius, was issued in 49 or 50. It was effective for a very short time, cf. Rm 16:3; Ac 28:17.

d. Though Paul acknowledges the missionary's right to sustenance, 1 Co 9:6-14; Ga 6:6; 2 Th 3:9; cf. Lk 10:7, he himself always practised a trade, 1 Co 4:12, not wishing to be a burden on anyone, 1 Th 2:9; 2 Th 3:8; 2 Co 12:13f, and in order to prove his singleness of purpose, Ac 20:33f; 1 Co 9:15-18; 2 Co 11:7-12. Only from the Philippians did he accept help, Ph 4:10-18; 2 Co 11:8f, cf. Ac 16:15+. He recommended his followers to do the same to supply their own needs, 1 Th 4:11f; 2 Th 3:10-12, and those of the poor, Ac 20:35; Ep 4:28.

e. It was after this that Paul wrote his two letters to the Thessalonians.

f. That Jesus was Messiah was the distinctive theme of the preaching to the Jews, cf. 2:36; 3:18,20; 5:42; 8:5,12; 9:22; 17:3; 18:28; 24:24; 26:23.

g. Symbolically breaking off relations. The following sentence is biblical, cf. Lv 20:9-16; 2 S 1:16, and means that the Jews must accept full responsibility for the consequences. Their 'blood', i.e. their punishment, is not Paul's affair; his conscience is clear (lit. 'I am clean').

h. Var. 'Titus Justus' or 'Titius Justus'.

i. Western Text add. 'believing in God through the name of our Lord Jesus Christ', cf. 8:36+. The converts had therefore been pagans.

j. An inscription from Delphi puts Gallio's proconsulate in 52. Paul's arraignment before Gallio must have been towards the end (v. 18) of his eighteen-month stay (v. 11) in Corinth: probably the spring of 52.

k. Ambiguous term capable of meaning the Roman law, cf. 16:21; 17:7, or the Jewish Law which was itself guaranteed by Roman law. Gallio chooses to see the charge as a question of the interpretation of Jewish Law (v. 15) in which he claims no competence.

l. Possibly the Sosthenes of 1 Co 1:1.

m. Back to Antioch, his headquarters.

n. The Greek is obscure, but apparently it was Paul, not Aquila, who took the vow. To take a vow was to be *nazir*, cf. Nb 6:1+, for the period it covered, usually thirty days, and among other obligations it meant leaving the hair uncut during that time. It is not known whether the vow was taken by Paul at Cenchreae or whether it expired there. Cf. Ac 21:23-27 where Paul and four other Jews perform the rites for the fulfilment of a vow.

o. Perhaps the church in Jerusalem.

p. For further information, cf. 1 Co: when he went to Corinth his enormous popularity soon developed into partisanship, cf. 1 Co 1:12; 3:4-11,22; see also Tt 3:13. These remarks about Apollos have something in common with the description of John the Baptist's admirers at Ephesus in the following passage: combining these two descriptions of an imperfectly informed Christianity, we may possibly get some idea of Christianity in the church of Alexandria at this time.

q. Add. 'of God'.

r. On the use of letters of reference in the early Christian communities, cf. Rm 16:1; 2 Co 3:1f; Col 4:10; 3 Jn 9-10,12.

19 a. An editorial link joining two items of information which are inserted in the account of the journey. The Western Text has 'When Paul, pursuing his own plan, wanted to set out for Jerusalem, the Spirit told him to go back to Asia. Consequently, he made his way...'

b. Ephesus at this time was regarded, with Alexandria, as one of the finest cities in the empire; it was a religious, political and commercial centre of mixed population.

c. They were unaware, not that the Spirit existed (evident from the O.T. to the most casual reader) but that the messianic promises had been fulfilled and the Spirit given in abundance, cf. 2:17-18,33.

d. Resumption of the narrative interrupted by the remarks about Apollos and the followers of John the Baptist: 19:8 follows on 18:23 and 19:1.

attitude of some of the congregation hardened into unbelief. As soon as they
9:2+ began attacking the Way in front of the others, he broke with them and took his
disciples apart to hold daily discussions in the lecture room of Tyrannus.[e] •This 10
went on for two years,[f] with the result that people from all over Asia,[g] both Jews
and Greeks, were able to hear the word of the Lord.

The Jewish exorcists

So remarkable were the miracles worked by God at Paul's hands •that 11 12
5:15 Lk 8:44-47p handkerchiefs or aprons which had touched him were taken to the sick, and they
were cured of their illnesses, and the evil spirits came out of them.
3:16+ Lk 9:49p But some itinerant Jewish exorcists[h] tried pronouncing the name of the Lord 13
Jesus over people who were possessed by evil spirits; they used to say, 'I command
you by the Jesus whose spokesman is Paul'. •Among those who did this were 14
16:17 seven sons of Sceva, a Jewish chief priest. •The evil spirit replied, 'Jesus 15
I recognise, and I know who Paul is, but who are you?' •and the man with the 16
evil spirit hurled himself at them and overpowered first one and then another,[i]
and handled them so violently that they fled from that house naked and badly
9:35.42 mauled. •Everybody in Ephesus, both Jews and Greeks, heard about this episode; 17
3:10 Lk 5:26 they were all greatly impressed, and the name of the Lord Jesus came to be held
in great honour.

Some believers, too, came forward to admit in detail how they had used spells[j] 18
and a number of them who had practised magic collected their books and made 19
a bonfire of them in public. The value of these was calculated to be fifty thousand
silver pieces.

6:7+ In this impressive way the word of the Lord spread more and more widely 20
and successfully.[k]

V. A PRISONER FOR CHRIST

Rm 15:22-32 1 Co 16:1-8 **Paul's plans**

11:30+; 23:11 When all this was over Paul made up his mind to go back to Jerusalem through 21
Macedonia and Achaia. 'After I have been there' he said 'I must go on to see
Rm 1:13 1 Co 4:17 Rome as well.' •So he sent two of his helpers, Timothy and Erastus, ahead of 22
him to Macedonia, while he remained for a time in Asia.

Ephesus: the silversmiths' riot[l]

It was during this time that a rather serious disturbance broke out in connection 23
9:2+ with the Way. •A silversmith called Demetrius, who employed a large number 24
16:19 Ws 15:12 of craftsmen making silver shrines of Diana, •called a general meeting of his own 25
men with others in the same trade. 'As you men know,' he said 'it is on this
industry that we depend for our prosperity. •Now you must have seen and heard 26
how, not just in Ephesus but nearly everywhere in Asia, this man Paul has persuaded and converted a great number of people with his argument that gods made
17:29+ by hand are not gods at all. •This threatens not only to discredit our trade, but 27
also to reduce the sanctuary of the great goddess Diana to unimportance.It could
end up by taking away all the prestige of a goddess venerated all over Asia, yes,
and everywhere in the civilised world.' •This speech roused them to fury, and they 28
started to shout,[m] 'Great is Diana of the Ephesians!' •The whole town was in an 29
uproar and the mob rushed to the theatre dragging along two of Paul's
20:4; 27:2 Col 4:10 Macedonian travelling companions, Gaius and Aristarchus.[n] •Paul wanted to 30
make an appeal to the people, but the disciples refused to let him; •in fact, some 31
of the Asiarchs,[o] who were friends of his, sent messages imploring him not to
take the risk of going into the theatre.

By now everybody was shouting different things till the assembly itself had 32
no idea what was going on; most of them did not even know why they had been

33 summoned. •The Jews pushed Alexander to the front, and when some of the
crowd shouted encouragement[p] he raised his hand for silence in the hope of being
34 able to explain things to the people. •When they realised he was a Jew, they all 16:20
started shouting in unison, 'Great is Diana of the Ephesians!' and they kept this
35 up for two hours. •When the town clerk eventually succeeded in calming the
crowd, he said, 'Citizens of Ephesus! Is there anybody alive who does not know
that the city of the Ephesians is the guardian of the temple of great Diana and
36 of her statue that fell from heaven? •Nobody can contradict this and there is no
37 need for you to get excited or do anything rash. •These men you have brought
38 here are not guilty of any sacrilege or blasphemy against our goddess. •If Demetrius and the craftsmen he has with him want to complain about anyone, there are
39 the assizes and the proconsuls; let them take the case to court. •And if you want
40 to ask any more questions you must raise them in the regular assembly. •We could
easily be charged with rioting for today's happenings: there was no ground for it
41 all, and we can give no reason for this gathering.' •When he had finished this
speech he dismissed the assembly.

Paul leaves Ephesus

1 **20** When the disturbance was over,[a] Paul sent for the disciples and, after
speaking words of encouragement to them, said good-bye and set out for 14:22; 16:40 1 Co 16:5
2 Macedonia. •On his way through those areas[b] he said many words of encourage-
3 ment to them and then made his way into Greece, •where he spent three months.[c]
He was leaving by ship for Syria when[d] a plot organised against him by the Jews 9:23; 23:12f 1 Th 2:14+
4 made him decide to go back by way of Macedonia. •He was accompanied[e] by
Sopater, son of Pyrrhus, who came from Beroea; Aristarchus and Secundus who 19:29 Rm 16:21
came from Thessalonika; Gaius from Doberus, and Timothy, as well as Tychicus *16:1+*
5 and Trophimus who were from Asia.[f] •They all went on to Troas where they 19:22+; 21:29
6 waited for us.[g] •We ourselves left Philippi by ship[h] after the days of Unleavened 2 Tm 4:20
Bread[i] and met them five days later at Troas, where we stopped for a week.[j]

Troas: Paul raises a dead man to life

7 On the first day of the week[k] we met to break bread. Paul was due to leave 2:42+

e. Western Text adds 'from the fifth to the tenth hour' (11 a.m. to 4 p.m.).

f. 20:31 says three years. During this stay, Paul wrote the first Letter to the Corinthians, the Letter to the Galatians and, probably, the Letter to the Philippians.

g. Not the whole of proconsular Asia (the W. half of Asia Minor) but the region centred on Ephesus and including the seven towns of Rv 1:11. Epaphras of Colossae had been appointed by Paul to evangelise his own city, and his mission had spread to Laodicea and Hierapolis, Col 1:7; 4:12-13. Paul was also assisted by Timothy and Erastus, Ac 19:22, Gaius and Aristarchus, 19:29, Titus, whom Ac never mentions, and others, cf. 2 Co 12:18. Luke credits Paul with the achievements of his subordinates.

h. On Jewish exorcisms, cf. Mt 12:27. Jesus himself, and his apostles after him, cf. Ac 5:16; 16:18, frequently exorcised, cf. Mt 8:29+.

i. Or 'both' (two of their number).

j. Occult practices for which Ephesus was well-known.

k. Alex. Text 'Thus, through the power of the Lord, the word spread even more widely and impressively'.

l. The literary style of this narrative is unusual in Luke; he has taken it from a special source and linked it with his story of the evangelisation of Ephesus.

m. Western Text adds 'rushing into the street'.

n. Aristarchus, a native of Thessalonika, 20:4, was a companion of Paul during his imprisonment, 27:2; Col 4:10; Phm 24. Gaius is probably the one mentioned in Ac 20:4.

o. Members of the 'Asiatic assembly' which supervised the cult of Rome and the emperor on behalf of the cities of Asia.

p. Others translate 'they made him stand away from the crowd'.

20 a. The narrative is resumed from 19:22.

b. From here he sent his second letter to the Christians in Corinth.

c. Paul was therefore able to carry out the proposal of 1 Co 16:5-6. During this period in Corinth he wrote the Letter to the Romans. Western Text 'When he had been there for three months and the Jews had plotted against him, he intended to set out for Syria, but the Spirit told him to go back through Macedonia'.

d. To take the proceeds of the collection to Jerusalem, cf. 19:21 and Rm 15:25+.

e. Add. 'as far as Asia'. Sopater is perhaps the Jew, Sosipater, of Rm 16:21. 'Doberus'; var. 'Derbe'.

f. Trophimus was an Ephesian, 21:29, cf. 2 Tm 4:20. Tychicus is mentioned several times in the letters, Ep 6:21; Col 4:7; 2 Tm 4:12; Tt 3:12.

g. Narrative in the first person: Paul met Luke again at Philippi; from then on they stayed together, cf. 16:10+.

h. From the port of Neapolis, cf. 16:11.

i. Passover week, cf. Ex 12:1+.

j. On Paul's previous ministry in this town (when on the way from Ephesus to Corinth: vv. 1-2) cf. 2 Co 2:12.

k. The first day of the Jewish week, which had become the Christians' day of assembly, cf. Mt 28:1+; 1 Co 16:2, the 'Lord's day' *(dies dominica)* Rv 1:10. This Sunday meeting was held when the *dies dominica* began, i.e. on the Saturday evening, because the day was reckoned in the Jewish fashion.

the next day, and he preached a sermon that went on till the middle of the night.
A number of lamps were lit in the upstairs room where we were assembled, •and 8 9
as Paul went on and on, a young man called Eutychus who was sitting on the
window-sill grew drowsy and was overcome by sleep and fell to the ground three
9:36-42 1 K 17:17-24 floors below. He was picked up dead. •Paul went down and stooped to clasp the 10
2 K 4:30-37 Mk 5:39p boy to him. 'There is no need to worry,' he said 'there is still life in him.' •Then 11
he went back upstairs where he broke bread and ate and carried on talking till
he left at daybreak. •They took the boy away alive, and were greatly 12
encouraged.

From Troas to Miletus

We were now to go on ahead by sea, so we set sail for Assos, where we were 13
to take Paul on board; this was what he had arranged, for he wanted to go by road.
When he rejoined us at Assos we took him aboard and went on to Mitylene. •The 14 15
next day we sailed from there and arrived opposite Chios. The second day we
touched at Samos and, after stopping at Trogyllium, made Miletus the next day.
Paul had decided to pass wide of Ephesus so as to avoid spending time in Asia, 16
24:11 since he was anxious to be in Jerusalem, if possible, for the day of Pentecost.

Farewell to the elders of Ephesus

11:30+ From Miletus he sent for the elders of the church of Ephesus. •When they 17 18
arrived he addressed these words to them:[l]
1Th 1:5; 2:10-12 'You know what my way of life has been ever since the first day I set foot
Ph 2:3 among you in Asia, •how I have served the Lord in all humility, with all the 19
2 Co 1:8-9; 11:23-31 sorrows and trials that came to me through the plots of the Jews. •I have not 20
hesitated to do anything that would be helpful to you; I have preached to you,
13:5+ 2 Tm 4:2 and instructed you both in public and in your homes, •urging both Jews and 21
Greeks to turn to God and to believe in our Lord Jesus.[m]
'And now you see me a prisoner already in spirit;[n] I am on my way to Jeru- 22
1:8+ salem, but have no idea what will happen to me there, •except that the Holy Spirit, 23
21:4,11 in town after town, has made it clear enough that imprisonment and persecution
Ph 2:16 2 Tm 4:7 await me. •But life to me is not a thing to waste words on,[o] provided that when 24
I finish my race I have carried out the mission the Lord Jesus gave me—and that
26:16-18 was to bear witness to the Good News of God's grace.
'I now feel sure that none of you among whom I have gone about proclaiming 25
19:8; 20:38 the kingdom will ever see my face again.[p] •And so here and now I swear that my 26
18:6+ conscience is clear as far as all of you are concerned, •for I have without faltering 27
20:20 put before you the whole of God's purpose.
5:11+ Jn 21:15-17 'Be on your guard for yourselves and for all the flock of which the Holy Spirit 28
1 Co 1:2+ Ep 1:14+ has made you the overseers, to feed the Church of God[q] which he bought with
1 Tm 4:16 1 P 2:9+; his own blood.[r] •I know quite well that when I have gone fierce wolves will invade 29
5:1-3 you and will have no mercy on the flock. •Even from your own ranks there will 30
Mt 7:15 2 P 2:1-2 be men coming forward with a travesty of the truth on their lips to induce the
1 P 5:8-9 disciples to follow them. •So be on your guard, remembering how night and day 31
19:10+ for three years I never failed to keep you right, shedding tears over each one of
14:23 you. •And now I commend you to God, and to the word of his grace that has 32
9:31 Dt 33:3-4 power[s] to build you up and to give you your inheritance among all the sanctified.
Ep 2:20-22 'I have never asked anyone for money or clothes; •you know for yourselves 33 34
18:3+ that the work I did earned enough to meet my needs and those of my compan-
1 Co 11:1 Ep 4:28 ions. •I did this to show you that this is how we must exert ourselves to support 35
Si 4:31 the weak, remembering the words of the Lord Jesus, who himself said, "There is
more happiness in giving than in receiving".'[t]
21:5 When he had finished speaking he knelt down with them all and prayed. •By 36 37
Rm 16:16+ now they were all in tears; they put their arms round Paul's neck and kissed him;
20:25 what saddened them most was his saying they would never see his face again. 38
Then they escorted him to the ship.

The journey to Jerusalem

21 When we had at last torn ourselves away from them and put to sea, we set
a straight course and arrived at Cos; the next day we reached Rhodes, and
from there went on to Patara.[a] •Here we found a ship bound for Phoenicia, so we
went on board and sailed in her. •After sighting Cyprus and leaving it to port, 11:19; 15:3
we sailed to Syria and put in at Tyre, since the ship was to unload her cargo there.
We sought out the disciples and stayed there a week. Speaking in the Spirit,[b] 20:23; 21:11
they kept telling Paul not to go on to Jerusalem, •but when our time was up we set 20:36-38; 21:12
off. Together with the women and children they all escorted us on our way till we *15:3*
were out of the town. When we reached the beach, we knelt down and prayed;
then, after saying good-bye to each other, we went aboard and they returned
home.

The end of our voyage from Tyre came when we landed at Ptolemais, where
we greeted the brothers and stayed one day with them. •The next day we left and
came to Caesarea. Here we called on Philip the evangelist, one of the Seven, and 6:5; 8:4f,40
stayed with him. •He had four virgin daughters who were prophets. •When we 2:4+,17
had been there several days a prophet called Agabus arrived from Judaea •to see 11:27-28
us. He took Paul's girdle, and tied up his own feet and hands,[c] and said, 'This
is what the Holy Spirit says, "The man this girdle belongs to will be bound like 1:8+; 20:23; 21:33
this by the Jews in Jerusalem, and handed over to the pagans" '.[d] •When we heard
this, we and everybody there implored Paul not to go on to Jerusalem. •To 21:4
this he replied, 'What are you trying to do—weaken my resolution by your tears?
For my part, I am ready not only to be tied up but even to die in Jerusalem for 9:15-16; 20:24+
the name of the Lord Jesus.' •And so, as he would not be persuaded, we gave up
the attempt, saying, 'The Lord's will be done'. Mt 6:10 Lk 22:42p

Paul's arrival in Jerusalem

After this we packed and went on up to Jerusalem. •Some of the disciples
from Caesarea accompanied us and took us to the house of a Cypriot with whom
we were to lodge;[e] he was called Mnason and had been one of the earliest disciples.
On our arrival in Jerusalem the brothers gave us a very warm welcome. •The 1:15+ Rm 15:31
next day Paul went with us[f] to visit James, and all the elders were present. •After *12:17+*
greeting them he gave a detailed account of all that God had done among the 14:27; 15:4, 12
pagans through his ministry. •They gave glory to God when they heard this. *11:18+*
'But you see, brother,' they said 'how thousands of Jews have now become

l. The third great discourse of Paul in Ac. The first, ch. 13, exemplified his preaching to the Jews; the second, ch. 17, his preaching to the pagans; the third, 20:18-35, is as it were the last testament of the departing pastor. Many of the details of this third discourse are found in his letters; its tone is that of the Pastoral Letters. After referring to his mission in Asia, vv. 18-21, he speaks of this as a final parting and seems to hint at his death, vv. 22-27. Paul's last advice to the elders of Ephesus (and through them to all the pastors in every church) is vigilance, vv. 28-32, selflessness, charity, vv. 33-35. In all of this Paul appeals to his own example: the discourse therefore draws a faithful portrait of the apostle himself.

m. Summary of Pauline preaching, to be compared with 17:30-31; 1 Th 1:9-10; 1 Co 8:4-6. Faith and conversion must go together, cf. Mk 1:15.

n. On his way to captivity Paul speaks of himself as a prisoner; in his heart he is one already. Others translate 'a prisoner of the Spirit', i.e. impelled by the Holy Spirit.

o. Cf. 15:26; 21:13; 1 Th 2:8; Ph 1:21-23. Others translate 'But I do not count my life of any value, as if it were precious to me'.

p. Cf. v. 38. From Jerusalem Paul intended to visit Spain, Rm 15:24-28. His long imprisonment affected his plans and he did in fact revisit Ephesus despite the presentiment expressed here, cf. Ac 28:31+.

q. Var. 'the Church of the Lord'. 1 P 2:9-10 speaks of the people which God made his own (following Is 43:21; cf. Ac 18:10+); this people was the 'Congregation (=Church) of God', 5:11, one of Paul's favourite expressions, cf. 1 Co 1:2; 10:32; 11:22, etc.

r. A difficult phrase sometimes rendered 'acquired by him at the price of the blood of his own Son', cf. Rm 8:32; Jn 3:16. But we may see underlying the expression a certain flexibility of thought, since the work of the Father (='God') and of the Son is so inseparably one (cf., for example, Rm 8:31-39). For the doctrine, cf. Ep 5:25-27; Heb 9:12-14; 13:12.

s. 'to God', var. 'to the Lord'. 'that has power', or 'who has power', referring to God, cf. Rm 16:25.

t. The gospels have not recorded this saying.

21 a. Add. 'and Myra'.

b. The command does not come from the Spirit, but the Spirit has revealed to them Paul's fate which their love for him seeks to avert.

c. Prophecy in mime like that used by the prophets in the past, cf. Jr 18:1+.

d. The forecast (cf. 28:17) only approximately corresponds to the narrative of Paul's arrest (cf. 21:31-33) but it resembles the prophecy of Christ's Passion in Lk 18:31-34; cf. Col 1:24; Ph 3:10, etc.

e. The Western Text indicates, perhaps correctly, that this was half-way to Jerusalem.

f. The last 'we' until 27:1 (the departure for Rome): Luke followed Paul as far as Jerusalem and was to accompany him again from Caesarea to Rome.

believers, all of them staunch upholders of the Law,[g] and •they have heard that 21
6:11,14; 15: 1; 28:17 Mk 7:1-13 you instruct all Jews living among the pagans to break away from Moses,[h]
authorising them not to circumcise their children[i] or to follow the customary
practices. •What is to be done? Inevitably there will be a meeting of the whole 22
body, since they are bound to hear that you have come.[j] •So do as we suggest. 23
18:18+; 24:17 We have four men here who are under a vow; •take these men along and be 24
purified with them and pay all the expenses connected with the shaving of their
heads.[k] This will let everyone know there is no truth in the reports they have heard
15:19f,28f about you and that you still regularly observe the Law. •The pagans who have 25
become believers, as we wrote when we told them our decisions, must abstain from
15:1+ things sacrificed to idols, from blood, from the meat of strangled animals and
from fornication.'[l]

So the next day Paul took the men along and was purified with them, and he 26
visited the Temple to give notice of the time when the period of purification would
be over and the offering would have to be presented on behalf of each of them.[m]

Paul's arrest

The seven days were nearly over when some Jews from Asia caught sight of 27
24:18 Rm 15:31 him in the Temple and stirred up the crowd and seized him, •shouting, 'Men of 28
18:13-15; 21:21; 24: Israel, help! This is the man who preaches to everyone everywhere against our
5f,14; 25:8 Lm 1:10 people, against the Law and against this place.[n] Now he has profaned this Holy
Ezk 44:9 Place by bringing Greeks into the Temple.' •They had, in fact, previously seen 29
20:4 Trophimus the Ephesian in the city with him, and thought that Paul had brought
him into the Temple.

This roused the whole city; people came running from all sides; they seized 30
26:21 Paul and dragged him out of the Temple, and the gates were closed behind them.
23:27 They would have killed him if a report had not reached the tribune of the cohort[o] 31
that there was rioting all over Jerusalem. •He immediately called out soldiers 32
and centurions, and charged down on the crowd, who stopped beating Paul when
they saw the tribune and the soldiers. •When the tribune came up he arrested 33
20:23; 21:11; 22:29 Paul, had him bound with two chains and enquired who he was and what he had
done. •People in the crowd called out different things, and since the noise made 34
it impossible for him to get any positive information, the tribune ordered Paul
to be taken into the fortress. •When Paul reached the steps, the crowd became 35
so violent that he had to be carried by the soldiers; •and indeed the whole mob 36
22:22 Lk 23:18 was after them, shouting, 'Kill him!'

Just as Paul was being taken into the fortress, he asked the tribune if he could 37
have a word with him. The tribune said, 'You speak Greek, then? •So you are 38
not the Egyptian who started the recent revolt and led those four thousand cut-
throats[p] out into the desert?' •'I?' said Paul 'I am a Jew and a citizen of the well- 39
known city of Tarsus in Cilicia. Please give me permission to speak to the people.'
The man gave his consent and Paul, standing at the top of the steps, gestured to 40
the people with his hand. When all was quiet again he spoke to them in Hebrew.[q]

Paul's address to the Jews of Jerusalem[a]

7:2 22 'My brothers, my fathers, listen to what I have to say to you in my defence.' 1
When they realised he was speaking in Hebrew, the silence was even greater 2
2 Co 11:22 than before. •'I am a Jew,' Paul said 'and was born at Tarsus in Cilicia. I was 3
26:4-5 5:34 brought up here in this city. I studied under Gamaliel and was taught the exact
26:5 Rm 10:2 observance of the Law of our ancestors. In fact, I was as full of duty towards God
Ga 1:13-14 Ph 3:5-6 as you are today. •I even persecuted this Way[b] to the death, and sent women as 4
8:3; 9:2 well as men to prison in chains •as the high priest and the whole council of elders 5
||9:1-18+; =26:9-18 can testify, since they even sent me with letters to their brothers in Damascus.
When I set off it was with the intention of bringing prisoners back from there
to Jerusalem for punishment.

'I was on that journey and nearly at Damascus when about midday a bright 6

light from heaven suddenly shone round me. •I fell to the ground and heard a voice
saying, "Saul, Saul, why are you persecuting me?" •I answered: Who are you,
Lord? and he said to me, "I am Jesus the Nazarene, and you are persecuting Mt 2:23+
me". •The people with me saw the light but did not hear his voice as he spoke
to me. •I said: What am I to do, Lord? The Lord answered, "Stand up and go
into Damascus, and there you will be told what you have been appointed to do".
The light had been so dazzling that I was blind and my companions had to take
me by the hand; and so I came to Damascus.

'Someone called Ananias, a devout follower of the Law and highly thought
of by all the Jews living there,[c] •came to see me; he stood beside me and said,
"Brother Saul, receive your sight". Instantly my sight came back and I was able
to see him. •Then he said, "The God of our ancestors has chosen you to know 1 Co 9:16-17
his will, to see the Just One[d] and hear his own voice speaking, •because you are 9:17; 26:16 1 Co 9:1
to be his witness before all mankind, testifying to what you have seen and heard.[e] *1:8+* Mt 13:16-17p
And now why delay? It is time you were baptised and had your sins washed away 1 Jn 1:1-3
while invoking his name." *2:38+*

'Once, after I had got back to Jerusalem,[f] when I was praying in the Temple, 9:26 Ga 1:18
I fell into a trance •and then I saw him. "Hurry," he said "leave Jerusalem at *9:29-30*
once; they will not accept the testimony you are giving about me."[g] •Lord,
I answered, it is because they know that I used to go from synagogue to synagogue, imprisoning and flogging those who believed in you; •and that when the 5:40
blood of your witness[h] Stephen was being shed, I was standing by in full agreement 7:58; 8:1; 26:10
with his murderers, and minding their clothes. •Then he said to me, "Go! I am
sending you out to the pagans far away." '[i] 2:39+; 9:15

Paul the Roman citizen

2 So far they had listened to him, but at these words they began to shout, 'Rid
3 the earth of the man! He is not fit to live!' •They were yelling, waving their 21:36; 25:24
4 cloaks and throwing dust into the air, •and so the tribune had him brought into
the fortress and ordered him to be examined under the lash, to find out the reason
5 for the outcry against him. •But when they had strapped him down Paul said
to the centurion on duty, 'Is it legal for you to flog a man who is a Roman citizen 16:37+; 23:27

g. For its observance by others as well as by themselves, cf. 11:2; 15:1,5; Ga 2:12; 5:1f.

h. Paul's doctrine of faith as the one source of justification, cf. Rm 1:16+; 3:22+, did indeed lead to this, since it meant that the Mosaic Law no longer gave the Jew superiority over the gentile. But Paul's purpose in expounding this principle was to leave converts from paganism free of Jewish observance, cf. Ga 2:11f, not to dissuade devout Jews from it.

i. Cf. Rm 2:25-29; 4:9-12; 1 Co 7:17-20.

j. Var. 'What is to be done? They will in any case hear that you have come.'

k. The determination of the nazirite vow had to be celebrated with expensive sacrifices, Nb 6:14-15.

l. Western Text 'Of the pagans who have become believers they have nothing to say to you. For our part, we have sent our decisions, namely that they have no observance to practise but that of abstaining from things sacrificed to idols, from blood, and from fornication.'

m. Text obscure: it seems to presuppose before the nazirite sacrifice a period of seven days devoted to certain rites of purification; there is no other evidence for this practice.

n. Cf. the charges against Stephen, 6:11-14, and against Jesus, Mt 26:61; 27:40.

o. A Roman garrison consisting of an auxiliary cohort was stationed in the Antonia overlooking the Temple area from the N.W. corner.

p. Or 'four thousand Assassins'; the term, *sikarioi*, strictly means extreme nationalists. This revolt is mentioned by Josephus.

q. I.e. Aramaic: Hebrew was not spoken after the Exile.

22 a. After the three discourses which sum up the preaching of Paul, ch. 13, 17, 20, Ac records three apologias: before the Jewish people in Jerusalem, ch. 22, before the procurator Felix, ch. 24, before King Agrippa, ch. 26; each is cleverly adapted to the audience, cf. 9:1+. Before the people Paul defends his conduct as being that of a devout Jew.

b. The Church, cf. 9:2+. On Paul's career as persecutor, cf. 7:58; 8:1,3; 9:1,21; 22:19-20; 26:11; 1 Co 15:9; Ga 1:13,23; Ph 3:6; 1 Tm 1:13.

c. Paul describes Ananias simply as a pious Jew without adding that he was a Christian, 9:10 or mentioning his vision, 9:10-16.

d. Christ, cf. 3:14; 7:52.

e. Cf. 9:15. Ananias here speaks in the name of 'the God of our ancestors', like an O.T. prophet. Paul is to be a witness 'before all mankind', but the pagans are not explicitly mentioned until v. 21.

f. Paul passes over the three years which elapsed before their return, cf. 9:23+. The trance he speaks of is not mentioned elsewhere; it is not to be confused with that of 2 Co 12:1-4.

g. The narrative of Paul's apostolic work emphasises this, cf. 13:46-48; 18:6; 28:25-28.

h. The Greek word, *martyr*, had not yet acquired its restricted meaning but was beginning to: the supreme testimony being that of blood. Cf. Rv 2:13; 6:9; 17:6.

i. Since 'apostle' means 'envoy', Christ's words imply that Paul is now an apostle, cf. Ga 1:1; 1 Co 9:1; 2 Co 12:11-12, and, in particular, an apostle of the pagans, Ga 1:16; 2:7-8, though Ac (with the exception of 14:4,14) reserves the term 'apostle' to the Twelve.

and has not been brought to trial?' •When he heard this the centurion went and 26
told the tribune; 'Do you realise what you are doing?' he said 'This man
is a Roman citizen'. •So the tribune came and asked him, 'Tell me, are you a 27
Roman citizen?' 'I am' Paul said. •The tribune replied, 'It cost me a large sum to 28
acquire this citizenship'. 'But I was born to it' said Paul. •Then those who were 29
16:39; 21:33 about to examine him hurriedly withdrew, and the tribune himself was alarmed
when he realised that he had put a Roman citizen in chains.[j]

His appearance before the Sanhedrin[k]

The next day, since he wanted to know what precise charge the Jews were 30
bringing, he freed Paul and gave orders for a meeting of the chief priests and
the entire Sanhedrin; then he brought Paul down and stood him in front of them.
23 Paul looked steadily at the Sanhedrin and began to speak, 'My brothers, 1
24:16 to this day I have conducted myself before God with a perfectly clear con-
Jn 18:22 science'.[a] •At this the high priest Ananias[b] ordered his attendants to strike him 2
Ezk 13:10-15 Mt 23:27 on the mouth. •Then Paul said to him, 'God will surely strike you, you 3
whitewashed wall! How can you sit there to judge me according to the Law, and
then break the Law by ordering a man to strike me?' •The attendants said, 'It is 4
God's high priest you are insulting!' •Paul answered, 'Brothers, I did not realise 5
Ex 22:27 it was the high priest, for scripture says: *You must not curse a ruler of your
people*'.
4:1-4 Now Paul was well aware that one section was made up of Sadducees and the 6
26:5 Ph 3:5 other of Pharisees, so he called out in the Sanhedrin, 'Brothers, I am a Pharisee
24:15; 26:6f; 28:20 and the son of Pharisees. It is for our hope in the resurrection of the dead that
4:2+ I am on trial.' •As soon as he said this a dispute broke out between the Pharisees 7
and Sadducees, and the assembly was split between the two parties. •For the 8
5:17 Mt 22:23 Sadducees say there is neither resurrection, nor angel, nor spirit,[c] while the
Pharisees accept all three. •The shouting grew louder, and some of the scribes 9
5:34f from the Pharisees' party stood up and protested strongly, 'We find nothing wrong
with this man. Suppose a spirit has spoken to him, or an angel?'[d] •Feeling was 10
running high, and the tribune, afraid that they would tear Paul to pieces, ordered
his troops to go down and haul him out and bring him into the fortress.
18:9-10; 27:24 Next night, the Lord appeared to him and said, 'Courage! You have borne 11
19:21 witness for me in Jerusalem, now you must do the same in Rome.'

The conspiracy of the Jews against Paul

9:23; 20:3; 25:3 When it was day, the Jews held a secret meeting at which they made a vow[e] 12
1 Th 2:14+ not to eat or drink until they had killed Paul. •There were more than forty who 13
took part in this conspiracy, •and they went to the chief priests and elders, and 14
told them, 'We have made a solemn vow to let nothing pass our lips until we have
killed Paul. •Now it is up to you and the Sanhedrin together to apply to the 15
tribune to bring him down to you, as though you meant to examine his case more
closely; we, on our side, are prepared to dispose of him before he reaches you.'
But the son of Paul's sister heard of the ambush they were laying and made 16
his way into the fortress and told Paul, •who called one of the centurions and 17
said, 'Take this young man to the tribune; he has something to tell him'. •So the 18
man took him to the tribune, and reported, 'The prisoner Paul summoned me and
requested me to bring this young man to you; he has something to tell you'. •Then 19
the tribune took him by the hand and drew him aside and asked, 'What is it you
have to tell me?' •He replied, 'The Jews have made a plan to ask you to take Paul 20
down to the Sanhedrin tomorrow, as though they meant to inquire more closely
into his case. •Do not let them persuade you. There are more than forty of them 21
lying in wait for him, and they have vowed not to eat or drink until they have
got rid of him. They are ready now and only waiting for your order to be given.'
The tribune let the young man go with this caution, 'Tell no one that you have 22
given me this information'.

Paul transferred to Caesarea

23 Then he summoned two of the centurions and said, 'Get two hundred soldiers
ready to leave for Caesarea by the third hour of the night with seventy cavalry and
24 two hundred auxiliaries; •provide horses for Paul, and deliver him unharmed
25 26 to Felix the governor'.[f] •He also wrote a letter in these terms: •'Claudius Lysias
27 to his Excellency the governor Felix, greetings. •This man had been seized by the 21:31-33
Jews and would have been murdered by them but I came on the scene with my
troops and got him away, having discovered that he was a Roman citizen. 22:25-29
28 Wanting to find out what charge they were making against him, I brought him
29 before their Sanhedrin. •I found that the accusation concerned disputed points 18:15; 25: 18-19; 26:
of their Law,[g] but that there was no charge deserving death or imprisonment.[h] 31; 28:18
30 My information is that there is a conspiracy against the man, so I hasten to send
him to you, and have notified his accusers that they must state their case against
him in your presence.'[i]

31 The soldiers carried out their orders; they took Paul and escorted him by night
32 to Antipatris. •Next day they left the mounted escort to go on with him and
33 returned to the fortress. •On arriving at Caesarea the escort delivered the letter
34 to the governor and handed Paul over to him. •The governor read the letter
and asked him what province he came from. Learning that he was from Cilicia
35 he said, •'I will hear your case as soon as your accusers are here too'. Then he
ordered him to be held in Herod's praetorium.

The case before Felix

1 24 Five days later the high priest Ananias came down with some of the
elders and an advocate named Tertullus, and they laid information against
2 Paul before the governor. •Paul was called, and Tertullus opened for the
prosecution, 'Your Excellency, Felix, the unbroken peace we enjoy and
3 the reforms this nation owes to your foresight •are matters we accept, always
4 and everywhere, with all gratitude. •I do not want to take up too much of your
5 time, but I beg you to give us a brief hearing. •The plain truth is that we find
this man a perfect pest; he stirs up trouble among Jews the world over, and is a 16:20; 17:6 Lk 23:2
6 ringleader of the Nazarene sect.[a] •He has even attempted to profane the Temple. *Mt 2:23+ 21:28*
7 We placed him under arrest, intending to judge him according to our Law,[b] •but
8 the tribune Lysias intervened and took him out of our hands by force, •ordering
his accusers to appear before you; if you ask him[c] you can find out for yourself
9 the truth of all our accusations against this man.' •The Jews supported him,
asserting that these were the facts.

10 When the governor motioned him to speak, Paul answered:[d]

j. Nevertheless, Paul is left in chains, v. 30; 23:18; 24:27; 26:29. Possibly a distinction is to be made between the heavy chains, a torture in themselves (of which Paul may have been relieved), and the lighter chains to prevent the prisoner from escaping.

k. As Jesus foretold to his disciples, Mt 10:17-18=Mk 13:9-10; Lk 21:12. Paul is to appear before 'councils' Ac 22:30–23:10, 'governors' (Felix, ch. 24), 'kings' (Agrippa, ch. 25-26).

23 a. The 'clear conscience' is a feature of Paul's moral teaching: 1 Co 4:4; 2 Co 1:12; 1 Tm 1:5,19; 3:9; 2 Tm 1:3; cf. Heb 13:18.

b. Ananias son of Nedebaios became high priest in about 47 A.D. He was arrested, sent to Rome and probably deprived of office in 51 or 52, then reinstated; he was assassinated in 66 at the beginning of the Jewish War.

c. The resurrection of the body, cf. 2 M 7:9+, and the doctrine of angels, cf. Tb 5:4+, were not part of Jewish teaching until a comparatively late date. From the text it appears that the Sadducees rejected the latter as well as the former (they certainly denied the doctrine of retribution in the world to come). On both questions Paul and the Pharisees were in agreement, cf. Ac 4:1f+.

d. The conjecture is apparently intended to explain the apparition on the Damascus road.

e. By calling down God's vengeance on themselves should they weaken.

f. Antoninus Felix, a freedman, brother of Pallas, Agrippina's favourite; he was procurator of Judaea from 52 to 59 or 60.

g. Western Text '...points of the Law of Moses, and a man called Jesus'.

h. Luke emphasises such statements which attest Paul's innocence, cf. v. 9; 25:18,25; 26:31; 28:18, as he did in the case of Jesus, cf. 3:13; 13:28; Lk 23:14-15,22.

i. Add. 'Farewell'.

24 a. Christianity was, for its opponents, merely a 'sect', cf. 5:17, within Judaism, cf. v. 14; 28:22.

b. The Jews claim that this is their affair. Cf. 25:9; Jn 18:31+. Alex. Text omits 'intending... before you'.

c. 'him' is Lysias in the text adopted here (cf. v. 22), Paul according to the shorter text.

d. Paul denies the charge of inciting to riot (cf. v. 5), vv. 11-13. He then explains how being a 'Nazarene' (cf. v. 5) in no way prevents him being a faithful Jew, vv. 14-16. He goes on to refute the charge of profaning the Temple, vv. 17-19. Finally he reminds them that it had been found impossible to convict him when he appeared before the Sanhedrin, vv. 20-21.

Paul's speech before the Roman governor

'I know that you have administered justice over this nation for many years,
and I can therefore speak with confidence in my defence. •As you can verify for 11
11:30+; 20:16 yourself, it is no more than twelve days since I went up to Jerusalem on
pilgrimage,[e] •and it is not true that they ever found me arguing with anyone or 12
stirring up the mob, either in the Temple, in the synagogues, or about the town;
neither can they prove any of the accusations they are making against me now. 13
9:2+ 'What I do admit to you is this: it is according to the Way which they describe 14
25:8+ Mt 5:17+ as a sect that I worship the God of my ancestors, retaining my belief in all points
Rm 3:31; 10:4 of the Law and in what is written in the prophets;[f] •and I hold the same hope 15
4:2 Jn 5:29+ in God as they[g] do that there will be a resurrection of good men and bad men
23:1+.6 alike. •In these things, I, as much as they, do my best to keep a clear conscience 16
at all times before God and man.
21:24 'After several years[h] I came to bring alms to my nation[i] and to make offerings;[j] 17
it was in connection with these that they found me in the Temple; I had been 18
21:27 purified, and there was no crowd involved, and no disturbance. •But some Jews 19
from Asia...—these are the ones who should have appeared before you and
accused me of whatever they had against me. •At least let those who are present 20
say what crime they found me guilty of when I stood before the Sanhedrin, •unless 21
it were to do with this single outburst, when I stood up among them and called
4:2; 23:6 out: It is about the resurrection of the dead that I am on trial before you today.'[k]

Paul's captivity at Caesarea

9:2+ At this, Felix, who knew more about the Way than most people, adjourned 22
the case, saying, 'When Lysias the tribune has come down I will go into your
case'. •He then gave orders to the centurion that Paul should be kept under arrest 23
but free from restriction, and that none of his own people should be prevented
from seeing to his needs.[l]
Some days later Felix came with his wife Drusilla who was a Jewess.[m] He sent 24
for Paul and gave him a hearing on the subject of faith in Christ Jesus. •But when 25
Mk 6:17-20 he began to treat of righteousness, self-control and the coming Judgement, Felix
17:32 took fright[n] and said, 'You may go for the present; I will send for you when I find
it convenient'. •At the same time he had hopes of receiving money from Paul, 26
and for this reason he sent for him frequently and had talks with him.
When the two years[o] came to an end, Felix was succeeded by Porcius Festus[p] 27
25:9 and, being anxious to gain favour with the Jews, Felix left Paul in custody.[q]

Paul appeals to Caesar

25 Three days after his arrival in the province,[a] Festus went up to Jerusalem 1
from Caesarea. •The chief priests and leaders of the Jews informed him of 2
23:12-15 the case against Paul,[b] urgently •asking him to support them rather than Paul, 3
and to have him transferred to Jerusalem. They were, in fact, preparing an ambush
to murder him on the way. •But Festus replied that Paul would remain in custody 4
in Caesarea, and that he would be going back there shortly himself. •'Let your 5
authorities come down with me' he said 'and if there is anything wrong about
the man, they can bring a charge against him.'
After staying with them for eight or ten days at the most, he went down to 6
Caesarea and the next day he took his seat on the tribunal and had Paul brought
Mt 26:59-61p; 27: in. •As soon as Paul appeared, the Jews who had come down from Jerusalem 7
12-14p Lk 23:10 surrounded him, making many serious accusations which they were unable to
17:6-7 substantiate. •Paul's defence was this, 'I have committed no offence whatever 8
21:28+; 24:14+ against either Jewish law, or the Temple, or Caesar'. •Festus was anxious to gain 9
favour with the Jews, so he said to Paul, 'Are you willing to go up to Jerusalem
and be tried on these charges before me there?'[c] •But Paul replied, 'I am standing 10
before the tribunal of Caesar and this is where I should be tried. I have done the
Jews no wrong, as you very well know. •If I am guilty of committing any capital 11

crime, I do not ask to be spared the death penalty. But if there is no substance
in the accusations these persons bring against me, no one has a right to surrender
12 me to them. I appeal to Caesar.'[d] •Then Festus conferred with his advisers and 28:19
replied, 'You have appealed to Caesar; to Caesar you shall go'.

Paul appears before King Agrippa

13 Some days later King Agrippa and Bernice[e] arrived in Caesarea and paid
14 their respects to Festus. •Their visit lasted several days, and Festus put Paul's
case before the king. 'There is a man here' he said 'whom Felix left behind in
15 custody, •and while I was in Jerusalem the chief priests and elders of the Jews
16 laid information against him, demanding his condemnation. •But I told them
that Romans are not in the habit of surrendering any man, until the accused
confronts his accusers and is given an opportunity to defend himself against the
17 charge. •So they came here with me, and I wasted no time but took my seat on
18 the tribunal the very next day and had the man brought in. •When confronted
with him, his accusers did not charge him with any of the crimes I had expected;
19 but they had some argument or other with him about their own religion and about 18:15; 23:29
20 a dead man called Jesus whom Paul alleged to be alive. •Not feeling qualified 23:6; 26:6f 1 Co 15:4
to deal with questions of this sort, I asked him if he would be willing to go to
21 Jerusalem to be tried there on this issue. •But Paul put in an appeal for his case
to be reserved for the judgement of the august emperor,[f] so I ordered him to be
22 remanded until I could send him to Caesar.' •Agrippa said to Festus, 'I should
like to hear the man myself'.[g] 'Tomorrow' he answered 'you shall hear him.'
23 So the next day Agrippa and Bernice arrived in great state and entered the
audience chamber attended by the tribunes and the city notables; and Festus
24 ordered Paul to be brought in. •Then Festus said, 'King Agrippa, and all here
present with us, you see before you the man about whom the whole Jewish
community has petitioned me, both in Jerusalem and here, loudly protesting
25 that he ought not to be allowed to remain alive. •For my own part I am satisfied 22:22
that he has committed no capital crime, but when he himself appealed to the
26 august emperor I decided to send him. •But I have nothing definite that I can
write to his Imperial Majesty[h] about him; that is why I have produced him before

e. Lit. 'to worship', cf. 8:27.

f. Christianity is not a different religion, it is Judaism with its ancient hope fulfilled. If the Jews reject Christ, they reject their own religious tradition. Cf. the discourse before Agrippa, ch. 26, the early Christian argument from prophecy, 2:23+; 3:24+, and Paul's own assertions, Rm 1:2; 3:31; 10:4; 16:26; 1 Co 15:3-4; Ga 3, etc.

g. The Pharisees, cf. 23:6+.

h. The visit of 18:22 must have been at least four years earlier, and the 'council of Jerusalem' visit eight or nine years earlier.

i. The only allusion in Ac to the real purpose of the journey, namely to deliver in Jerusalem the collection made among the churches in pagan territory, cf. Rm 15:25+.

j. Sacrifices offered to God, cf. 21:24,26.

k. A doctrine of the Pharisees: Paul shrewdly implies that Christians and Pharisees have something in common.

l. The same conditions as for Paul's imprisonment in Rome.

m. Youngest daughter of Herod Agrippa (12:1+). She had left her first husband, the king of Emesa, to marry Felix.

n. Felix was avaricious, cruel and dissolute. Compare the attitude of John the Baptist before Herod Antipas.

o. Greek: *dietia* (=a period of two years). This term, which recurs in 28:30, here seems to be used in its technical juridical sense: the maximum duration of preventive custody. This would mean that, since sentence had not meanwhile been pronounced, Paul must have been set free when the period expired. This is probably what happened in Rome, cf. 28:30. By detaining Paul, Felix was breaking the law.

p. Appointed probably in 60, died in 62.

q. 'anxious to . . .'; Western Text; 'And he left Paul in prison on account of Drusilla'.

25 a. Or 'after taking office'.

b. Same procedure as in 24:1, cf. 25:15.

c. Festus realises that the dispute is about religious matters, a case not for him but for the Sanhedrin (cf. vv. 19-20). But as a Roman citizen Paul could not be committed to the Sanhedrin without his own consent. To secure this, Festus promises to attend and to preside over the discussion.

d. Since Festus has disclaimed jurisdiction, Paul cannot escape trial before the Sanhedrin except by claiming the Roman citizen's privilege of trial before the imperial tribunal.

e. Agrippa, Bernice and Drusilla (cf. 24:24) were children of Herod Agrippa I, cf. 12:1+. The eldest, later Agrippa II, was born in 27. At this time Bernice was living with her brother and their relationship became matter for gossip; some years later Bernice became the mistress of Titus, the Roman general, later emperor.

f. Lit. 'Augustus'; so also in v. 25. The title 'Augustus', like 'Caesar', was borne by the ruling emperor, in this case Nero (54-68).

g. Just as his great-uncle Herod Antipas had wanted to see Jesus, Lk 9:9; 23:8.

h. Lit. 'to the Lord', term for the emperor considered as a king whose power was absolute and universal, and therefore practically divine.

you all, and before you in particular, King Agrippa, so that after the examination
I may have something to write. •It seems to me pointless to send a prisoner 27
without indicating the charges against him.'

26 Then Agrippa said to Paul, 'You have leave to speak on your own behalf'. 1
And Paul held up his hand and began his defence:

Paul's speech before King Agrippa[a]

'I consider myself fortunate, King Agrippa, in that it is before you I am to 2
answer today all the charges made against me by the Jews, •the more so because[b] 3
you are an expert in matters of custom and controversy among the Jews. So I beg
you to listen to me patiently.
22:3+ Ga 1:14 'My manner of life from my youth, a life spent from the beginning among 4
my own people and in Jerusalem, is common knowledge among the Jews. •They 5
have known me for a long time and could testify, if they would, that I followed
the strictest party in our religion and lived as a Pharisee. •And now it is for my 6
23:6+ hope in the promise made by God to our ancestors that I am on trial, •the promise 7
2 M 7 Dn 12:1-3 that our twelve tribes, constant in worship night and day, hope to attain.[c] For
that hope, Sire, I am actually put on trial by Jews! •Why does it seem incredible 8
to you that God should raise the dead?[d]
=9:1-18; =22:3-16 'As for me, I once thought it was my duty to use every means to oppose the 9
Mt 2:23+ name of Jesus the Nazarene. •This I did in Jerusalem; I myself threw many of the 10
9:13+ saints into prison, acting on authority from the chief priests, and when they were
8:1; 22:20 sentenced to death I cast my vote against them. •I often went round the 11
synagogues inflicting penalties, trying in this way to force them to renounce their
faith; my fury against them was so extreme that I even pursued them into foreign
cities.

'On one such expedition I was going to Damascus, armed with full powers 12
and a commission from the chief priests, •and at midday as I was on my way, 13
your Majesty, I saw a light brighter than the sun come down from heaven. It
shone brilliantly round me and my fellow travellers. •We all fell to the ground, 14
and I heard a voice saying to me in Hebrew, "Saul, Saul, why are you persecuting
me? It is hard for you, kicking like this against the goad."[e] •Then I said: Who 15
are you, Lord? And the Lord answered, "I am Jesus, and you are persecuting
Ezk 2:1 me. •But get up and stand on your feet, for I have appeared to you for this 16
1:8+ reason: to appoint you as my servant and as witness of this vision in which you
Jr 1:5-8 have seen me, and of others in which I shall appear to you. •*I shall deliver you* 17
Is 42:7,16 from the people and *from the pagans, to whom I am sending you* •*to open their* 18
9:17-18 Jn 8:12+ *eyes*, so that they may turn *from darkness to light*,[f] from the dominion of Satan
Col 1:12-14 *Dt 33:3-4* to God, and receive, through faith in me, forgiveness of their sins[g] and a share
in the inheritance of the sanctified."

Ga 1:16 'After that, King Agrippa, I could not disobey the heavenly vision. •On the 19 20
contrary I started preaching, first to the people of Damascus, then to those of
11:18 Jerusalem and all the countryside of Judaea, and also to the pagans, urging them
2:38+ Lk 3:8p to repent and turn to God, proving their change of heart by their deeds. •This 21
21:30-31 was why the Jews laid hands on me in the Temple and tried to do away with me.
But I was blessed with God's help, and so I have stood firm to this day, testifying 22
2:23+ Jn 1:45 to great and small alike, saying nothing more than what the prophets and Moses
himself said would happen: •that the Christ was to suffer and that, as the first 23
1 Co 15:20-23 to rise from the dead, he was to proclaim that light now shone for our people and
13:47 for the pagans too.'

His hearers' reactions

He had reached this point in his defence when Festus shouted out, 'Paul, you 24
are out of your mind; all that learning of yours is driving you mad'.[h] •'Festus, 25
Jn 18:37-38 your Excellency,' answered Paul 'I am not mad: I am speaking nothing but the
sober truth. •The king understands these matters, and to him I now speak with 26

assurance, confident that nothing of all this is lost on him; after all, these things 13:46+
27 were not done in a corner.[i] •King Agrippa, do you believe in the prophets? I know Is 45:19
28 you do.' •At this Agrippa said to Paul, 'A little more, and your arguments would
29 make a Christian[j] of me'. •'Little or more,'[k] Paul replied 'I wish before God
that not only you but all who have heard me today would come to be as I am
—except for these chains.' 28:20
30 At this the king rose to his feet, with the governor and Bernice and those who
31 sat there with them. •When they had retired they talked together and agreed,
32 'This man is doing nothing that deserves death or imprisonment'. •And Agrippa 23:29+
remarked to Festus, 'The man could have been set free if he had not appealed to 28:19
Caesar'.

The departure for Rome

1 27 When it had been decided that we[a] should sail for Italy, Paul and some
other prisoners were handed over to a centurion called Julius, of the
2 Augustan cohort. •We boarded a vessel from Adramyttium bound for ports on the
Asiatic coast, and put to sea; we had Aristarchus with us, a Macedonian of 19:29+
3 Thessalonika. •Next day we put in at Sidon, and Julius was considerate enough
to allow Paul to go to his friends to be looked after.
4 From there we put to sea again, but as the winds were against us we sailed
5 under the lee of Cyprus, •then across the open sea off Cilicia and Pamphylia,
6 taking a fortnight[b] to reach Myra in Lycia. •There the centurion found an Alexandrian ship leaving for Italy and put us aboard.
7 For some days we made little headway, and we had difficulty in making
Cnidus. The wind would not allow us to touch there, so we sailed under the lee
8 of Crete off Cape Salmone •and struggled along the coast until we came to a place
called Fair Havens, near the town of Lasea.

Storm and shipwreck

Jon 1:4-16
Mt 8:23-27p

9 A great deal of time had been lost, and navigation was already hazardous
since it was now well after the time of the Fast,[c] so Paul gave them this warning,
10 'Friends, I can see this voyage will be dangerous and that we run the risk of losing
11 not only the cargo and the ship but also our lives as well'. •But the centurion
took more notice of the captain and the ship's owner than of what Paul was
12 saying; •and since the harbour was unsuitable for wintering, the majority were
for putting out from there in the hope of wintering at Phoenix—a harbour in
Crete, facing south-west and north-west.
13 A southerly breeze sprang up and, thinking their objective as good as reached,
14 they weighed anchor and began to sail past Crete, close inshore. •But it was not

26 a. A flattering address, vv. 2-3; cf. 24:2-3,10, is followed by Paul's assertion that his Christian faith in bodily resurrection is shared by the Pharisees, vv. 4-8; cf. 23:6+. Paul then describes the circumstances of his conversion, vv. 9-18; cf. 9:1-18; 22:3-16, and ends with a summary of his preaching which presents the Christian faith simply as the fulfilment of the scriptures, vv. 19-23; cf. 13:15-41. Behind the immediate quarrel lay the whole question of the relationship of Christianity to Judaism, cf. 24:14+.

b. Others translate 'more than anyone'.

c. The messianic hope takes definite shape in the belief in the resurrection of the virtuous who are to have their place in the kingdom at the end of time, cf. Dn 12:1-3; 2 M 7:9+. This hope has its initial fulfilment in the resurrection of Christ which is the ground of Christian hope, 1 Co 15:15-22; Col 1:18.

d. Var. vv. 7-8 'the promise for which our twelve tribes assiduously worship God day and night in the hope of attaining it; it is for that I am now arraigned by the Jews: namely, that God raises the dead'.

e. Greek proverb for useless resistance: the ox kicking against the goad succeeds only in wounding itself.

f. Paul's missionary vocation is described here in O.T. terms used about two great prophetic figures, Jeremiah and the Servant of Yahweh.

g. In 9:17-18, Paul, his sight restored, passes from darkness to light; in 22:16 (cf. 9:18) Paul is ordered to wash away his sins by baptism. Thus his own experience is a symbol of his mission to others.

h. Festus is taken aback by Paul's biblical erudition and probably by the Jewish method of argument. Agrippa is silent; he is clearly shaken, cf. his evasive reply in v. 28.

i. The scriptures are being fulfilled by events (v. 23: the Passion and death of Christ; the widespread apostolic preaching) which all the world can see.

j. The word is still a nickname, cf. 11:26+. Var. 'In a little while you will persuade me to become a Christian!' or, 'In a little while you will persuade yourself you have made me a Christian!'

k. A play on Agrippa's phrase.

27 a. Luke reappears on the scene. The precision of the narrative suggests a carefully kept diary.

b. Lit. 'for fifteen days', Western Text.

c. Another name for the feast of Atonement, the only fast-day prescribed by the Law, Lv 16:29-31. It was celebrated about the time of the autumn equinox.

long before a hurricane, the 'north-easter' as they call it, burst on them from across
the island. •The ship was caught and could not be turned head-on to the wind, 15
so we had to give way to it and let ourselves be driven. •We ran under the lee of 16
a small island called Cauda and managed with some difficulty to bring the ship's
boat under control. •They hoisted it aboard and with the help of tackle bound 17
cables round the ship; then, afraid of running aground on the Syrtis banks, they
Jon 1:5 floated out the sea-anchor and so let themselves drift. •As we were making very 18
heavy weather of it, the next day they began to jettison the cargo, •and the third 19
day they threw the ship's gear overboard with their own hands. •For a number 20
of days both the sun and the stars were invisible and the storm raged unabated
until at last we gave up all hope of surviving.

27:33 Then, when they had been without food for a long time,[d] Paul stood up among 21
the men. 'Friends,' he said 'if you had listened to me and not put out from Crete,
you would have spared yourselves all this damage and loss. •But now I ask you 22
27:34 not to give way to despair. There will be no loss of life at all, only of the ship.
10:3+ Jon 1:9 Last night there was standing beside me an angel of the God to whom I belong 23
18:9; 23:11 and whom I serve, •and he said, "Do not be afraid, Paul. You are destined to 24
appear before Caesar,[e] and for this reason God grants you the safety of all who
are sailing with you." •So take courage, friends; I trust in God that things will 25
turn out just as I was told; •but we are to be stranded on some island.' 26

On the fourteenth night we were being driven one way and another in the 27
Adriatic,[f] when about midnight the crew sensed that land of some sort was near.
They took soundings and found twenty fathoms; after a short interval they 28
sounded again and found fifteen fathoms. •Then, afraid that we might run 29
aground somewhere on a reef, they dropped four anchors from the stern and
prayed for daylight. •When some of the crew tried to escape from the ship and 30
lowered the ship's boat into the sea as though to lay out anchors from the bows,
Paul said to the centurion and his men, 'Unless those men stay on board you 31
cannot hope to be saved'. •So the soldiers cut the boat's ropes and let it drop 32
away.

27:21 Just before daybreak Paul urged them all to have something to eat. 'For 33
fourteen days' he said 'you have been in suspense, going hungry and eating
27:24 Mt 10:30 nothing. •Let me persuade you to have something to eat; your safety is not in 34
doubt. Not a hair of your heads will be lost.' •With these words he took some 35
bread, gave thanks to God in front of them all, broke it and began to eat.[g] •Then 36
they all plucked up courage and took something to eat themselves. •We were 37
in all two hundred and seventy-six souls on board that ship. •When they had 38
eaten what they wanted they lightened the ship by throwing the corn overboard
into the sea.

When day came they did not recognise the land, but they could make out 39
a kind of bay with a beach; they planned to run the ship aground on this if they
could. •They slipped the anchors and left them to the sea, and at the same time 40
loosened the lashings of the rudders; then, hoisting the foresail to the wind, they
headed for the beach. •But the cross-currents carried them into a shoal and the 41
vessel ran aground. The bows were wedged in and stuck fast, while the stern began
to break up with the pounding of the waves.

12:19+; 16:27 The soldiers planned to kill the prisoners for fear that any should swim off 42
and escape. •But the centurion was determined to bring Paul safely through, and 43
would not let them do what they intended. He gave orders that those who could
swim should jump overboard first and so get ashore, •and the rest follow either 44
on planks or on pieces of wreckage. In this way all came safe and sound to land.

Waiting in Malta

28 Once we had come safely through, we discovered that the island was 12
called Malta. •The inhabitants treated us with unusual kindness. They
made us all welcome, and they lit a huge fire because it had started to rain and

the weather was cold. •Paul had collected a bundle of sticks and was putting
them on the fire when a viper brought out by the heat attached itself to his hand.
When the natives saw the creature hanging from his hand they said to one
another, 'That man must be a murderer; he may have escaped the sea, but divine
5 vengeance[a] would not let him live'. •However, he shook the creature off into the Mk 16:18 Lk 10:19
6 fire and came to no harm, •although they were expecting him at any moment
to swell up or drop dead on the spot. After they had waited a long time without
seeing anything out of the ordinary happen to him, they changed their minds 14:11
and began to say he was a god.

7 In that neighbourhood there were estates belonging to the prefect of the
island, whose name was Publius. He received us and entertained us hospitably
8 for three days. •It so happened that Publius' father was in bed, suffering from
feverish attacks and dysentery. Paul went in to see him, and after a prayer he laid Lk 10:9p
9 his hands on the man and healed him. •When this happened, the other sick 9:12
10 people on the island came as well and were cured;•they honoured us with many 5:15-16; 8:7-8
marks of respect, and when we sailed they put on board the provisions we Lk 4:40 1 Tm 4:14+
needed.

From Malta to Rome

11 At the end of three months·we set sail in a ship that had wintered in the
12 island; she came from Alexandria and her figurehead was the Twins. •We put in
13 at Syracuse and spent three days there; •from there we followed the coast up to
Rhegium. After one day there a south wind sprang up and on the second day we
14 made Puteoli,[b] •where we found some brothers and were much rewarded by
staying a week with them. And so we came to Rome.

15 When the brothers there heard of our arrival they came to meet us, as far as
the Forum of Appius and the Three Taverns. When Paul saw them he thanked
16 God and took courage. •On our arrival in Rome Paul was allowed to stay in
lodgings of his own with the soldier who guarded him.[c]

Paul makes contact with the Roman Jews[d]

17 After three days he called together the leading Jews. When they had assembled,
he said to them, 'Brothers, although I have done nothing against our people or 21:21+; 24:14+
the customs of our ancestors, I was arrested in Jerusalem and handed over to
18 the Romans. •They examined me and would have set me free, since they found
19 me guilty of nothing involving the death penalty; •but the Jews lodged an objec- 23:29+
tion, and I was forced to appeal to Caesar, not that I had any accusation to make 25:11; 26:32
20 against my own nation.[e] •That is why I have asked to see you and talk to you,
for it is on account of the hope of Israel that I wear this chain.' 23:6+; 26:6-8,29

21 They answered,[f] 'We have received no letters from Judaea about you, nor has Lk 4:44+
any countryman of yours arrived here with any report or story of anything to
22 your discredit. •We think it would be as well to hear your own account of 17:19-20
your position; all we know about this sect is that opinion everywhere con- 24:5,14
demns it.'

d. Paul's second speech (vv. 33f) would follow naturally on this observation. This first speech (vv. 21-26) seems to have been rather clumsily introduced into this context and to be partly a repetition of the second.

e. Not before Nero in person but before his tribunal.

f. The name was used for all that part of the Mediterranean between Greece, Italy and Africa.

g. Western Text add. 'giving it to us also'. All Jews pronounced a blessing when about to eat; nevertheless, the terms Luke uses seem to suggest the Eucharist, cf. 2:42+.

28 a. Lit. 'justice', *diké*, the divine justice personified.

b. Pozzuoli on the Gulf of Naples. There was already a Christian colony in this busy port.

c. Western Text (adopted by the Antiochene recension) '...Rome, the centurion handed the prisoners over to the commander. But Paul was allowed to live outside the (Praetorian) camp.' This additional information agrees with what in fact must have happened. By the concession of *custodia militaris* the prisoner had his own lodgings, but his right arm was chained to the left of the soldier in charge.

d. Paul wants to establish good relations with the Jews of Rome as soon as possible. He gives a brief account of his trial, and for the last time protests his loyalty to Judaism.

e. Western Text add. 'but merely wished to escape death'.

f. The reply is cautious.

Paul's declaration to the Roman Jews[g]

So they arranged a day with him and a large number of them visited him at his 23
13:15-41 1:3+ 2:23+ lodgings. He put his case to them, testifying to the kingdom of God and trying
to persuade them about Jesus, arguing from the Law of Moses and the prophets.
13:46-47 This went on from early morning until evening, •and some were convinced by 24
what he said, while the rest were sceptical. •So they disagreed among themselves 25
and, as they went away, Paul had one last thing to say to them,[h] 'How aptly the
Holy Spirit spoke when he told your ancestors through the prophet Isaiah:

13:40 Is 6:9-10 Mt 13:14 *Go to this nation and say:* 26
You will hear and hear again but not understand,
see and see again, but not perceive.
For the heart of this nation has grown coarse, 27
their ears are dull of hearing and they have shut their eyes,
for fear they should see with their eyes,
hear with their ears,
understand with their heart,
and be converted
and be healed by me.

18:6 'Understand, then, that this salvation of God has been sent to the pagans; 28
they will listen to it.'[i]

Epilogue[j]

Paul spent the whole of the two years[k] in his own rented lodging. He welcomed 30
all who came to visit him, •proclaiming the kingdom of God and teaching the 31
4:29 13:46+ truth about the Lord Jesus Christ with complete freedom and without hindrance
from anyone.[l]

---

28 g. In Rome also Paul preaches the gospel first to the Jews, cf. 13:5+. The summary of this preaching should be compared with the opening discourse in Pisidian Antioch, 13:15-41.

h. Paul's words are reminiscent of those following his discourse at Antioch, 13:46-47. They constitute the finale of Ac, and sound its dominant note, cf. 13:41+. They recall the vision of the future offered by Jesus at the end of his discourse in Nazareth, Lk 4:23-27, and in his last words to the apostles, Lk 24:47. The text from Is, 6:9-10 (LXX), is also used in Mt 13:14-15 (cf. Mk 4:12p) and, in part, in Jn 12:40. Both theme and text are commonplaces of early Christianity.

i. The Western Text (followed by the Antiochene recension) adds v. 29 'And when he had said this, the Jews left, arguing hotly between themselves'.

j. Thus Paul arrived in Rome, which brings one period of evangelisation to a close, cf. Lk 24:47; Ac 1:8+, and is presented as the starting-point for a further advance of Christianity. Before Luke had finished his gospel he had opened up wide horizons to the apostolic mission; his Book of Acts ends with the same prospect for the future.

k. The same technical term as in 24:27. Paul, therefore, has been under the *custodia militaris* for the legal period during which his case should have been tried. This suggests that the trial did not in fact take place, probably because there was no one to accuse him. The legal period over, Paul must have been released; Phm 22 looks forward to his approaching liberation. During these two years Paul wrote his letters to the Colossians and to the Ephesians as well as his note to Philemon.

l. Western Text add. 'saying that this is he, Jesus, the son of God, by whom the whole world is destined to be judged', cf. 17:31. On Paul's ministry after his discharge, his second imprisonment, and his death, see the Introduction to the Letters of St Paul.

THE LETTERS OF SAINT PAUL

INTRODUCTION TO
THE LETTERS OF SAINT PAUL

CHRONOLOGY

Through the Acts of the Apostles and through his own letters Saint Paul is more familiar to us than any other figure of the New Testament. These two mutually independent sources confirm and complement each other in spite of certain discrepancies of detail. We are also able to construct a fairly exact chronology of Paul's life from references to dated events such as Gallio's proconsulate in Corinth, Ac 18:12, and the year Festus succeeded Felix, Ac 24:27-25:1.

Paul, born at Tarsus in Cilicia, Ac 9:11; 21:39; 22:3, about 10 A.D. of a Jewish family of the tribe of Benjamin, Rm 11-1; Ph 3:5, was a Roman citizen, Ac 16:37f; 22:25-28; 23:27. As a young man he was educated in Jerusalem by Gamaliel who gave him a thorough grounding in religious doctrine of the school of the Pharisees. He became a bitter persecutor of the infant Church, Ac 22:4f; 26:9-12; Ga 1:13; Ph 3:6, and played some part in Stephen's martyrdom, Ac 7:58; 22:20; 26:10; but on the road to Damascus, c. 34 A.D., a vision of the risen Jesus changed his whole life. The risen Lord opened his mind to the truth of the Christian faith and revealed that he had chosen him to be the apostle of the pagans, Ac 9:3-16p; Ga 1:12,15f; Ep 3:2f. From then on, Paul dedicated his life to serving Christ who had personally chosen him as his follower, Ph 3:12. After spending some time in Arabia he returned to Damascus, Ga 1:17, and began his preaching there, Ac 9:20. In about 39 A.D. after a brief visit to Jerusalem, Ga 1:18; Ac 9:26-29, Paul went to Syria and Cilicia, Ga 1:21; Ac 9:30, till Barnabas fetched him back to Antioch where they preached together, Ac 11:25f and cf. 9:27. During Paul's first missionary journey (45-49) to Cyprus, Pamphilia, Pisidia and Lycaonia, Ac 13-14, he started using his Greek name Paul instead of his Jewish name Saul, Ac 13:9, and, because he preached better, started to become more famous than Barnabas, Ac 14:12. In 49 A.D., fourteen years after his conversion, Ga 2:1, he went to Jerusalem to take part in the apostles' council, and it was partly through his influence that the council agreed that the Jewish Law was not binding on Christian converts from paganism, Ac 15; Ga 2:3-6. His mission as apostle to the pagans was formally sanctioned, Ga 2:7-9, and he set out once more. The dates of his second (50-52; Ac 15:36-18:22) and third missionary journeys (53-58; Ac 18:23-21:17) are discussed later under the letters he wrote at intervals during those journeys. In 58, Paul was arrested in Jerusalem, Ac 21:27-23:22, and imprisoned at Caesarea Palestinae until 60 A.D., Ac 23:23-26:32. In the autumn of 60, Festus the procurator sent him to Rome under escort, Ac 27:1-28:16, where, after the statutory two years (61-63), Ac 28:30, Paul's case was dismissed for want of evidence and he was set free. It is possible that he went to Spain, as he had hoped to do, Rm 15:24,28; but the pastoral letters suggest that he travelled again in the east. A subsequent imprisonment in Rome ended, according to a very ancient tradition, in martyrdom, probably in the year 67.

THE CHARACTER OF PAUL

As well as this chronology, it is possible to recover quite a detailed portrait of Paul from his letters and from Acts.

He was a person of great dedication, capable of pursuing an ideal with a complete disregard for the cost. For him, the only thing that mattered was God, and as God's servant, Paul refused any sort of compromise. It was with equally single-minded determination that he had persecuted those he considered God's enemies, 1 Tm 1:13, cf. Ac 24:5, 14, and later preached Christ as the one, universal saviour. This saviour he served passionately and selflessly for the rest of his life. He knew what work he had been given to do, 1 Co 9:16, and he let nothing stop him doing it: hard work, exhaustion, suffering, poverty, danger of death, 1 Co 4:9-13; 2 Co 4:8f; 6:4-10; 11:23-27. Far from letting these things weaken his love for God or Christ, Rm 8:35-39, he welcomed them, since they helped him to grow into the image of his suffering and crucified Master, 2 Co 4:10f; Ph 3:10f. The knowledge that his vocation was unique gave him an enormous ambition, but it did not make him arrogant. It was with holy humility that Paul felt a personal pride in being responsible for so many churches, 2 Co 11:28, cf. Col 1:24, and claimed to have done more missionary work than others, 1 Co 15:10, cf. 2 Co 11:5, and offered himself as a model to his converts, 2 Th 3:7 +. He never forgot that having persecuted the Church of Christ, he was the unworthiest of all the apostles. All the great things he succeeded in doing he attributed to God's grace working through him, 1 Co 15:10; 2 Co 4:7; Ph 4:13; Col 1:29; Ep 3:7.

Paul had a sensitive temperament that showed itself in his attitude to those he had converted. He had a childlike trust in the converts at Philippi, Ph 1:7f; 4:10-20, a deep affection for those at Ephesus, Ac 20:17-38; he was furious with those in Galatia who were on the verge of apostasy, Ga 1:6; 3:1-3, and deeply upset when he thought that the Christians in Corinth had become vain and unstable, 2 Co 12:11-13:10. When he was being ironical with people he considered superficial, 1 Co 4:8; 2 Co 11:7; 12:13, or when he was outspoken, Ga 3:1-3; 4:11; 1 Co 3:1-3; 5:1-2; 6:5; 11:17-22; 2 Co 11:3f, it was only for their own good, 2 Co 7:8-13, and after these outbursts he soon became tender, 2 Co 11:1-2; 12:14f, and fatherly, 1 Co 4:14f; 2 Co 6:13, cf. 1 Th 2:11; Phm 10, even motherly, 1 Th 2:7; Ga 4:19, and anxious to restore the earlier affection, Ga 4:12-20; 2 Co 7:11-13.

Paul's fiercest outbursts of indignation were directed against everybody who tried to seduce his converts, whether they were Jews, who opposed him wherever he went, Ac 13:45,50; 14:2,19; 17:5,13; 18:6; 19:9; 21:27, or Judaising Christians who wanted all followers of Christ to follow the Law, Ga 1:7; 2:4; 6:12f. He never minced his words with either of these groups, 1 Th 2:15f; Ga 5:12; Ph 3:2, and, however unprepossessing, he felt himself to be an irresistible weapon wielded by divine power against ambitious, arrogant and unspiritual opponents, 2 Co 10:1-12:12. God's weapon was Paul's selfless sincerity, Ac 18:3+. It has been suggested that the people against whom he inveighs were in fact the senior apostles in Jerusalem, but this is impossible. Some of the Judaeo-Christians, who remained faithful to the Law, invoked Peter, 1 Co 1:12, and James, Ga 2:12, in an attempt to discredit Paul, but Paul always respected the authority of these apostles, Ga 1:18; 2:2, though he claimed to be just as much a witness to Christ as they were, Ga 1:11f; 1 Co 9:1; 15:8-11. Even when Paul had his disagreement with Peter, Ga 2:11-14, his attitude was conciliatory, Ac 21:18-26, and he organised a collection for the poor Christians of Jerusalem, Ga 2:10, since he considered this would be the best possible proof that his pagan converts were truly one with the Christians of the mother church, 2 Co 8:14; 9:12-13; Rm 15:26f.

PAUL AS PREACHER

What Paul proclaimed was in all essentials the apostolic 'kerygma', Ac 2:22+, i.e. that Christ had been crucified and had risen from the dead and that this had been foretold in the scriptures, 1 Co 2:2; 15:3-4; Ga 3:1. What he calls 'his' Good News, Rm 2:16; 16:25, was identical with the faith commonly held, Ga 1:6-9; 2:2; Col 1:5-7, but emphasised the conversion of pagans, Ga 1:16; 2:7-9, in line with the missionary policy initiated at Antioch. Paul accepts and sometimes appeals to the apostolic tradition, 1 Co 12:23; 15:3-7, to which he was deeply indebted. Though he probably never met Jesus during his earthly life, cf. 2 Co 5:16+, Paul was familiar with his teaching, 1 Th 4:15; 1 Co 7:10f; Ac 20:35, and confidently claimed to have seen the risen Christ, not only on the Damascus road, Ac 9:17; 22:14f; 26:16; 1 Co 9:1; 15:8, but on several occasions subsequently, Ac 22:17-21; 26:16. He also had revelations and ecstasies, 2 Co 12:1-4, but everything he had received from apostolic tradition he could also attribute, and justly, to direct communication from the Lord, Ga 1:12; 1 Co 11:23.

These mystical experiences have sometimes been attributed to Paul's excitable and morbid temperament, yet this is hardly likely. The disease that detained him in Galatia, Ga 4:13-15, was probably an attack of malaria, and the 'thorn in my side', 2 Co 12:7, may well be the persistent hostility of Jews, his brothers 'according to the flesh', Rm 9:3. Paul does not seem to have had a very vivid imagination judging by his sparing and pedestrian use of imagery: the sports-ground, 1 Co 9:24-27; Ph 3:12-14; 2 Tm 4:7f, and the sea, Ep 4:14. Two images, farming, 1 Co 3:6-8, and building, 1 Co 3:10-17; Rm 15:20; Ep 2:20-22, are so basic that he often mixes them, 1 Co 3:9; Col 2:7; Ep 3:17, cf. Col 2:19; Ep 4:16. His genius was much more intellectual than imaginative, his enthusiasm was never divorced from the rigid logic with which he explains his teaching and adapts it to the needs of his audience. It is to this intellectual need to adapt his teaching to the occasion that we owe the remarkable theological analysis to which he repeatedly submits the kerygma. His logic, which is based on the rabbinical method in which he had been trained, may seem strange to some people today (e.g. Ga 3:16; 4:21-31). His genius, however, was never restricted by these scholastic conventions, so that however unattractive some people may find the method, it does not obscure the profundity of his teaching.

Paul was a Jew with a Greek cultural background which he had possibly begun to acquire when a boy in Tarsus and which was certainly reinforced by repeated contact with the Graeco-Roman world; this influence is obvious not only in his logical method but also in his language and style. He sometimes quotes Greek writers, 1 Co 15:33; Tt 1:12; Ac 17:28, and was familiar with popular Stoic-based philosophy from which he borrows concepts (e.g. of the soul separated from the body and bound for another world, 2 Co 5:6-8; the cosmic *pleroma* in Col and Ep) and clichés (1 Co 8:6; Rm 11:36; Ep 4:6). From the Cynics and Stoics he borrowed the rapid question and answer method (the diatribe), Rm 3:1-9, 27-31, and the rhetorical device of heaping word on word, 2 Co 6:4-10. Even his use of long, packed phrases in wave after wave, Ep 1:3-14; Col 1:9-20, has a precedent in hellenistic religious literature. The Greek that was a second mother tongue to Paul (cf. Ac 21:40), that he was able to use so familiarly with only occasional semitisms, was a cultured form of the *koine*, i.e. the Greek of his own day. Paul never attempted Attic elegance, and he deliberately avoided rhetoric so that his audience would be convinced not by the form but by the content of his message of faith and by the signs the Spirit had promised to provide to confirm it, 1 Th 1:5; 1 Co 2:4f; 2 Co 11:6; Rm 15:18. This is one reason why his grammar is sometimes wrong and his sentences unfinished, 1 Co 9:15; another is that he sometimes thought too fast or too emotionally; a third is that with rare exceptions, Phm 19, he normally dictated his letters, Rm 16:22, (a common practice at the time) and only wrote the final greeting by way of signature, 2 Th 3:17; Ga 6:11; 1 Co 16:21; Col 4:18. Some passages in his letters were obviously written only after long and careful thought, e.g. Col 1:15-20, but mostly his letters suggest spontaneity and lack of revision, and this is why Paul's sentences sound dynamic, and why he seems to pack so much into them. He is not easy to read, 2 P 3:16; profound thoughts expressed by an urgent writer never are; however, some passages have an extraordinary religious and literary power.

It is important to remember that Paul's letters were not meant as theological treatises: they are simply his response to a particular situation in a particular church. They begin according to the usual epistolary convention, Rm 1:1+, but cannot be classed either as private letters, or as literary 'epistles'; they are Pauline dissertations intended for a specific circle of readers and, in a general way, for all the faithful. Paul's letters do not give any systematic and exhaustive exposition of his teaching, they are all commentaries on certain points of sermons that he preached, and the existence of these sermons must always be remembered by the reader. This does not detract from their value: the depth and range of his letters give us all the essentials of Paul's message. No matter what the reason was for writing or who the people were to whom he was writing, his basic teaching remained the same: that Christ died and rose from the dead. The apostle who was all things to all men, 1 Co 9:19-22, adapts this, his one basic doctrine, to the listener; he develops and enriches it. Paul has sometimes been accused of being an eclectic, in the sense of adopting not only different but contradictory opinions according to the circumstances in which he found himself, of being interested less in truth than in persuading people to believe in Christ. He has also been accused of not having an open mind, of being obsessed by the vision that converted him, and of never having allowed his ideas to develop. The truth between these two extremes seems to be that Paul's theology does remain homogeneous but that it did develop under the guidance of the Spirit, who inspired everything he did as an apostle, and that Pauline thought reached its highest development in the letter to the Christians at

Ephesus. To show this development of Paul's thought, his letters have to be read in the same order in which they were written; the order, however, in which they are printed here is the traditional one that arranges them in order of diminishing length.

PAUL'S JOURNEYS AND LETTERS

1 and 2 Thessalonians. 50-51 A.D.

The first letters to be written were to the converts Paul had made in Thessalonika in the summer of 50 A.D. during his second missionary journey, Ac 17:1-10. As a result of the hostility of some Jews he went on to Beroea, and from there to Athens and Corinth where, it seems, he wrote 1 Th during the winter of 50-51. When he wrote this letter, his companions were Silas and Timothy. Timothy had paid a second visit to Thessalonika, and brought back the good news of their faith under persecution, hence the affectionate tone of the opening chapters, 1-3; these are followed by a series of practical recommendations, 4:1-12; 5:12-28, interrupted by an opportune instruction on the destiny of the dead and on Christ's *parousia,* 4:13-5:11. 2 Th was probably written at Corinth a few months later, making further practical recommendations, 1; 2:13-3:15, and offering fresh instruction on the time of the *parousia* and the signs that were to come before it, 2:1-12.

The literary resemblance between 1 and 2 Th is so close that some critics consider 2 Th a forgery made by one who had absorbed Paul's ideas and style, but it is hard to explain why this should have been done; a more obvious explanation is that when, about a year later, Paul had deepened his eschatological thought, he wrote this second letter but repeated various expressions from the first. The two are not contradictory but complementary and the earliest authorities believed that they were both written by Paul.

These two letters are particularly important because of their eschatological teaching, but they also introduce many points elaborated in subsequent letters. At this earlier stage, Paul's ideas were structured around the question of how the resurrection and *parousia* of Christ can bring salvation to his followers whether alive or dead, 1 Th 4:13-18. Paul described this *parousia* in the traditional terms of Jewish and the earliest Christian apocalyptic literature (i.e. the 'eschatological discourse' of the Synoptics, and particularly of Mt). Like Jesus himself he sometimes so emphasised, 1 Th 5:1-11, the unpredictable imminence of the Coming and the necessity for vigilance, as to give the impression that he and his readers would live to see it, 1 Th 4:17; but in 2 Th 2:1-12 he tried to allay the anxiety naturally aroused and reminded his readers that the day could not come till certain signs had preceded it. What these signs were to be is not as clear to us as it must have been to the first readers. Paul seems to consider the 'Adversary' to be an individual person who had to wait till the end of the age before he could appear; some writers consider that by the phrase 'that which at present holds him back', 2 Th 2:6, Paul meant the Roman empire, others that he meant the preaching of the gospel; no conclusion has been reached.

1 and 2 Corinthians. 57 A.D.

Paul wrote the letters to Thessalonika during the eighteen months he spent evangelising Corinth, Ac 18:1-15, from the end of 50 to the middle of 52 A.D. His policy was always to establish the Christian faith in a centre of population, and here he chose the great and populous port of Corinth, so that it could spread from there into the whole of Achaia, 2 Co 1:1; 9:2. The Christian community he established grew strong, and was composed mostly of poor people, 1 Co 1:26-28, but Corinth was not only a great centre of hellenism and a magnet to every sort of philosophy and religion, it was also a notorious centre of immorality; it was a *milieu* that could only create awkward problems for those newly converted to a faith that had only recently been introduced. It was to the solution of these problems that Paul addressed himself when he wrote his two letters to the Christians of Corinth.

How these two letters came to be written now seems clear enough, though some details are still disputed. There had been an earlier letter than these two canonical ones, 1 Co 5:9-13, but the date at which this first letter was written is unknown and it has not survived. Before the end of the two-and-a-half years he spent at Ephesus (54-57) on his third missionary journey, Ac 19:1-20:1, a Corinthian delegation arrived to ask Paul certain questions, 1 Co 16:17; and as he had also received news of Corinth from Apollos, Ac 18:27f; 1 Co 16:12, and from Chloe's household, 1 Co 1:11, he felt obliged to write a second letter. This is 1 Co, and it was written sometime near Easter, 57 (1 Co 5:7f; 16:5-9; compare Ac 19:21). Shortly afterwards, some sort of crisis developed in Corinth and Paul was forced to pay a brief and painful visit, 2 Co 1:23-2:1; 12:14; 13:1-2; while there he promised another and a longer visit, 2 Co 1:15-16, which never in fact took place. Instead, Paul sent a representative to whom he delegated his authority : all that happened was that a second crisis developed; Paul's authority, committed to this delegate, had been flouted, 2 Co 2:5-10; 7:12. Paul still did not pay the promised visit, but sent a severe letter written 'with many tears', 2 Co 2:3f, 9; this third letter had the desired effect, 2 Co 7:8-13. This good news that he heard from Titus only reached Paul after he had gone to Macedonia, 2 Co 2:12f; 7:5-16, after leaving Ephesus as a result of serious disturbances of which we know little, 1 Co 15:32; 2 Co 1:8-10; Ac 19:23-40. At this stage, towards the end of 57, he wrote 2 Co. He must subsequently have travelled via Corinth, Ac 20:1f, cf. 2 Co 9:5; 12:14; 13:1,10, to Jerusalem where he was arrested at Whitsun.

It has been suggested that 2 Co 6:14-7:1 is a fragment of the lost first letter, and 2 Co 10-13 part of the letter written 'in tears'. It would be hard to prove that they were parts of these two particular letters, but it is quite certain that these two sections are not in their original contexts. The first section reads like an insertion, 2 Co 7:2 follows naturally on 6:13, and the whole insertion, 6:14-7:1, has remarkable affinity with some of the Essene literature discovered at Qumran. The vehemence of the second section, 2 Co 10-13, is certainly not in place after the friendly tone of the first nine chapters. To these two dislocations should be added the fact that 9:1 does not make sense after what has been said in ch. 8 about the collection, and is probably part of a completely different note on the subject. These are probably fragments of things Paul wrote on different occasions, that were later put in their present place as part of the process of preserving a collection of the apostle's writings.

In these letters to Corinth, even the details about Paul and the way he treated his converts are important doctrinally. 1 Co in particular contains a great deal of information about urgent problems that faced the church and about the decisions made to meet them : internally there were questions of moral conduct, 1 Co 5:1-13, 6:12-20, of marriage and virginity, 7:1-40, of liturgical and eucharistic meetings, of the charismata, 12:1-14:40; externally, questions of appeals to civil courts, 6:1-11, and eating foods sacrificed to idols, ch. 8-10. It was Paul's religious genius to turn what might have remained cases of conscience or liturgical instruction into a vehicle for the profound doctrine of Christian liberty, the sanctification of the body, the supremacy of love, union with Christ. When forced to defend his apostolate, 2 Co 10-13, he does so in a style of immense power, 2 Co 1:12-6:10; and when he brings up the business of collecting money, 2 Co 8-9, he discusses the collection in the light of the ideal of union between the churches. The eschatological basis of his doctrine is always present in Paul's mind, and provides the perspective in which he explains the resurrection of the body, 1 Co 15; here, however, the apocalyptic imagery of 1 and 2 Th gives place to a philosophical method of justifying a doctrine that the Greek mind found so unsympathetic. As Paul penetrates this new Greek environment, he tries to adapt the Good News he proclaims, and this he does with particular skill when presenting the folly of the cross to Greek wisdom. The apostle's converts at Corinth had split into factions, each proud of its own leader and boasting about his talents; Paul reminded them that there is only one master, Christ, and only one message, the cross, and that there is no wisdom outside that message, 1 Co 1:10-4:13. The importance of this is that quite naturally through the way events had developed, without surrendering anything of the primacy of his eschatological thought, the inner development of Paul's ideas led him to the point where he had to stress how the life we lead here and now is already a life of union between Christ and his followers and that this union is achieved by faith which is the only way to know him. Later, when the Galatian crisis developed, Paul had to relate this teaching to Judaism, and in doing so he explored further depths of this new life into which people are born by faith.

Galatians. Romans. 57-58 A.D.

The letters Paul wrote to the Christians of Galatia and Rome need to be treated together, since both letters analyse the same problem. The first was Paul's immediate reaction to a particular situation, but the second, which is his more considered opinion, is more like a theological treatise than a letter, and in it Paul systematically arranges all his new ideas that had emerged from the argument. This close relationship between the two letters is really the strongest reason against the early dating of Ga (pre-49 A.D., the council of Jerusalem) which some scholars have suggested. They argue that Paul's second visit to Jerusalem, Ga 2:1-10, was the second visit mentioned in Ac 11:30; 12:25, not the third, Ac 15:2-30, since several details here differ from Paul's account, and that, as Paul seems unaware of the decree of the council, Ac 15:20,29 (cf. Ga 2:6), this letter must have been written before it. All difficulties disappear if it is supposed that the 'Galatians' are the Christians of Lycaonia and Pisidia, evangelised by Paul on his first missionary journey when he returned by the way he had come; this would explain the double visit that Ga 4:13 seems to imply. This hypothesis does not have very much to support it apart from the fact that Lycaonia and Pisidia had been part of the province of Galatia in

36-25 B.C.; in the 1st century A.D., however, 'Galatia' normally referred to Galatia properly so called which lay to the north of Lycaonia and Pisidia, and it is unlikely that the inhabitants of each district were *both* called 'Galatians', Ga 3:1. This 'South-Galatia' hypothesis would not even be necessary if the second visit of Ga 2:1-10 could be identified with the third visit of Ac 15; and in fact this third visit of Ac seems to resemble the visit in Ga much more closely than it does the second, Ac 11:30; 12:25, which could have been sufficiently unimportant for Paul to have been justified in leaving it out of the discussion in Ga, in spite of his assurance, Ga 1:20. It is even possible that this second visit of Ac never took place but is simply one of Luke's literary doublets; cf. Introduction to Acts and Ac 11:30+. In this view, then, (that the letter to the Christians of Galatia was probably written eight years after the council of Jerusalem) the reason Paul does not mention the decree could be that the date of the decree was later than that of Ga (cf. Ac 15:1+). This would explain Peter's conduct that Paul says he criticised, Ga 2:11-14. The converts to whom the letter was addressed would then be the inhabitants of the 'Galatian territory' (i.e. North Galatia) through which Paul passed on his second and third journeys, Ac 16:6; 18:23. The letter may have been written at Ephesus, or even in Macedonia, about the year 57.

The letter to the Christians of Rome must, in this case, have been written soon after. In the winter of 57-58 Paul was at Corinth preparing to go to Jerusalem and from there to visit Rome on the way to Spain, Rm 15:22-32; cf. 1 Co 16:3-6; Ac 19:21; 20:3. He had not founded the Roman church, and any information he had about it (from people like Aquila, Ac 18:2) was not considerable: all we learn from occasional allusions in the letter is that it was a mixed community and that there was a danger of Jewish and non-Jewish converts looking down on each other. In view of this danger, Paul thought it would be prudent to pave the way for his visit by sending a letter (through Phoebe the deaconess, Rm 16:1) in which he stated systematically his ideas about the problem of how Judaism and Christianity were related to each other; these ideas were the ones he had been forced to develop by the Galatian crisis. In Rm he reassembled all the ideas he had expressed in Ga and by doing so made them even more precise. Ga has a mixed personal and emotional appeal, 1:12-2:21, with doctrinal argument, 3:1-4:31, and earnest admonition, 5:1-6:18. Rm on the other hand is a carefully planned whole: it has only a few main sections and these are shown to be all parts of one whole by a preliminary section in which Paul outlines all the subjects that are subsequently developed.

Like Co and Ga, the authenticity of the letter to Roman Christians is not seriously disputed though it is suggested that ch. 15 and 16 are later insertions. Chapter 16 has many greetings, and it may quite easily have been a separate note for the church at Ephesus, but in spite of certain MSS ch. 15 cannot be amputated so easily. Critics who keep ch. 16 as part of the original letter suggest that it was quite possible for Paul to have met a great many Christians who, as Jews, had eight years previously been expelled under Claudius and then later on gone back to Rome, and that it was diplomatic for him to mention their names in a letter to a church he had not yet visited. The unusual style of the doxology, 16:25-27, certainly suggests that it could be a later insertion, but this in itself is not sufficient argument against its authenticity.

The letter to Corinth contrasted Christ as the Wisdom of God with the human wisdom of philosophers, but in the letters to Galatia and Rome, Paul contrasted the perfection people can achieve by purely human effort with Christ who is the Perfection of God. What Paul was trying to do was to correct the unbalance of the Greek outlook that relied too exclusively on reason, just as in the earlier letters he had tried to correct the unbalance of the Jewish outlook that relied too heavily on the Law. Judaising Christians who had visited Galatia advised the pagan converts to have themselves circumcised to ensure their salvation. This would have meant adopting all the prescriptions of the Law, Ga 5:2f, the implications of which, to Paul, made nonsense of Christ's redemptive work, Ga 5:4, and it was for this reason that he opposed the circumcision of his converts so violently. He maintained that the true value of the Law could be appreciated only by seeing its place in the development of God's plan, Ga 3:23-25. The Mosaic Law was good and holy, Rm 7:12, because it really did convey God's will to the Jews, but as law it was unable to provide anyone with the spiritual power necessary to obey it: all the Law could do was make people aware of sin and of the need they have for God to help them, Ga 3:19-22; Rm 3:20; 7:7-13. All human beings need this help, and it is necessarily a gift from God: it was promised to Abraham long before the Law was formulated, Ga 3:16-18; Rm 4, and has now been given in Jesus Christ: his death and resurrection have created the human race anew: once polluted by Adam's sin, it now has Christ himself as its prototype, Rm 5:12-21. All human beings united to Christ by faith, and living the new life by sharing the Spirit of Christ, are made perfect gratuitously and so enabled to live in the way God wants human beings to live, Rm 8:1-4. This faith must result in the human person doing 'good works', but these will not be at all the same as those 'good works', commanded by the Law, on which Jews were so proud to rely; they will be works prompted by the presence of the Spirit, Ga 5:22-25; Rm 8:5-13, and they will be open to all who have faith, whether Jew or pagan, Ga 3:6-9, 14. The preparatory or Mosaic stage of religion is over, and Jews who claim they are continuing to fulfil the Law are in fact putting themselves outside the pale of salvation. Had God not permitted their blindness, however, the pagans would not have found themselves invited inside. This cannot be taken as meaning that God has failed to keep his promise to the Jews, it means that their failure to live up to God's original choice will not be permanent: some of them, the 'remnant' foretold by the prophets, have already become believers, and one day all of them will, Rm 9-11. Meanwhile, all converts without exception, whether they are Jews or not, must love and help each other as one family, Rm 12:1-15:13. The general outlines of this thesis were sketched in Ga; the details added in Rm are much deeper insights into mysteries such as the position of the human race as waiting for salvation, Rm 1:18-3:20; the spiritual struggle of each individual to be saved, Rm 7:14-25; God's gift of salvation, Rm 3:24 and *passim*; what the death and resurrection of Jesus actually achieved, Rm 4:24f; 5:6-11, and how Christians share in this by dying and rising in faith and baptism, Ga 3:26f; Rm 6:3-11; the vocation of the whole human race to be children of God, Ga 4:1-7; Rm 8:14-17; the love and wisdom of God who, being perfect and faithful to his promises, only reveals his salvific will stage by stage, Rm 3:21-26; 8:31-39. Paul's thought is still basically eschatological — we are saved 'in hope', Rm 5:1-11; 8:24 — but, as in his letters to Corinth, the stress is on the already present reality of salvation: the Spirit that was promised is already possessed, as 'first-fruits', Rm 8:23, by the Christian who from now on lives in Christ, Rm 6:11, and Christ in him, Ga 2:20.

The letter to the Romans is a magnificent though incomplete synthesis of Paul's theology: it does not exhaust his doctrine. The Lutheran controversy showed it was the most important of Paul's letters, but it would be a pity if this led people to neglect the other letters which are necessary to complete a really adequate review of all Paul's theological ideas.

Philippians. 56-57 A.D.

The Roman colony of Philippi was one of the principal cities of Macedonia; it had been evangelised by Paul in 50 A.D. during his second missionary journey, Ac 16:12-40, and he revisited it twice during his third: in the autumn of 57, Ac 20:1-2, and at Passover 58, Ac 20:3-6. His converts there had proved their affection by contributing to his support first at Thessalonika, Ph 4:16, then at Corinth, 2 Co 11:9, and later still had commissioned Epaphroditus to take further contributions to him, Ph 4:10-20. Paul wrote a letter (Ph) to thank them, and to say that he accepted their gifts. Normally, Paul was afraid of doing anything that might give the impression that he was trying to make money out of his preaching, Ac 18:3+, so it seems he was on terms of special intimacy with his converts at Philippi.

At the time of writing, Paul was under arrest, Ph 1:7, 12-17, and for a long time this was assumed to be the first Roman captivity. Rome, however, was so far away that it seems unlikely that communications between Paul (with whom Epaphroditus was staying) and Philippi could have been as frequent or as easy as they appear to have been, 2:25-30. Nor is it clear why, if Paul were under arrest in Rome or in Caesarea, Ac 23:23, the Philippians should say that the contribution brought by Epaphroditus was the first chance they had had since the second missionary journey (cf. the gifts mentioned in 4:10,16) of helping the apostle, since Paul had visited them twice on his third journey. It may be easier to suppose that Paul actually wrote this letter during the third journey, before reaching Philippi, i.e. while he was at Ephesus, the capital of Roman Asia, in 56-57 hoping to visit Macedonia after his liberation (compare Ph 1:26; 2:19-24 and Ac 19:21f; 20:1; 1 Co 16:5). The 'Praetorium', Ph 1:13, and 'Caesar's household', 4:22, do not necessarily refer to Rome, since there were praetoria in all the major cities and there were most certainly detachments of the praetorian guard in Ephesus. It is true that there is no reference anywhere to an Ephesian captivity; but Luke says very little about Paul's three years there, Ac 19:1-20:1, and Paul himself mentions having fought with beasts at Ephesus, 1 Co 15:32, and troubles and imminent death in Roman Asia, 2 Co 1:8-10.

If we accept this hypothesis we shall have to dissociate Ph from Col, Ep and Phm and group it with the 'great letters', notably with 1 Co. The style and content of the letter are quite consistent with this. It is not particularly doctrinal, it is just a friendly letter, giving some news to his converts at Philippi, warning them against the 'bad workmen' who are ruining his work in other places and might turn on them next, and, above all, appealing for the unity of corporate humility. As part of this appeal Paul gives us, 2:6-11, the poem on the humility of the Messiah; and whether he wrote it or is quoting it, this poem is our chief proof that the early Church believed in the divine pre-existence of Jesus.

The authenticity of the letter is generally accepted, and it is quite possible, as some writers suggest, that it may be made up of several originally separate notes.

Ephesians. Colossians. Philemon. 61-63 A.D.

The letters to the Christians of Ephesus and Colossae (both in Roman Asia) and the letter to Philemon are closely related: the mission on which Onesimus is sent in Col 4:9 is the same as that in Phm 12; the same is true of Tychicus in Col 4:7f and Ep 6:21f; Paul's companions in Col 4:10-14 are the same as in Phm 23-24; Col and Ep are very similar in style and doctrine. All three were written while Paul was under arrest, Phm 1, 9f, 13, 23; Col 4:3,10,18; Ep 3:1; 4:1; 6:20, and this is almost certainly his arrest (61-63) in Rome rather than (58-60) in Caesarea where it would be difficult to account for the presence of Mark and of Onesimus, or (56-57) in Ephesus since there is nothing to suggest that Luke was ever there with Paul. The degree to which Paul's style has changed, and his doctrine developed, suggests some interval between Col, Ep and the 'great letters' Co, Ga, Rm. This interval (57-61) came to an end when Epaphras, Col 1:7, Paul's delegate, arrived from Colossae (a church Paul had not founded) 1:4; 2:1, with disturbing news. Paul promptly wrote a letter to the Christians there, and gave it to Tychicus to deliver. The inherent dangers of this new situation stimulated Paul to rethink things at a deeper level, and just as Rm had systematised the ideas outlined in Ga, so now, at about the same time as Col, Paul wrote another letter in which he restructured his teaching from the new angle that he had been forced to adopt by the recent developments at Colossae. This new synthesis of Paul's thought is referred to as the letter he wrote to the Christians at Ephesus. The title, however, is misleading, and has very scanty MS support, cf. Ep 1:1. This is a general letter in which Paul is speaking to the whole Church and not just to the church at Ephesus where he had spent three years, Ep 1:15; 3:2-4, though it was meant in a special way for Colossae and the other Christian communities of the Lycus valley among whom he asks for it to be circulated, Col 4:16.

Critics have often disputed who the authors are of these two letters: for Col the balance now is in favour of Paul, since not only does it retain his basic ideas but the new ideas in it are such as seem to be satisfactorily explained by the circumstances mentioned above. There is, however, no such agreement that Ep, in the form in which we have it, is a letter of Paul's. Among arguments in favour of Paul are: 1. that Ep is not the work of any derivative thinker like a disciple, but of someone with a genius for creative thinking; 2. that the leisurely, rich and extravagant style of Col and Ep which contrasts so much with the quick, jerky discussions of earlier letters, can probably be explained by these wide new horizons that Paul was opening for himself; 3. that the style of the earlier letters is not at all consistent, and two early examples of this later contemplative, semi-liturgical manner can be found in 2 Co 9:8-14, Rm 3:23-26; 4. that the slavish and awkward borrowing by Ep of phrases from Col might be due to the fact that Paul was not in the habit of composing every word of his letters, and on this occasion he may have allowed a disciple to play a greater part than usual.

The danger at Colossae was due to the basically Jewish (Col 2:16) speculations they had taken up about the celestial or cosmic powers. These were the powers thought to be responsible for the regular movement of the cosmos, and the speculations about them, much influenced by hellenistic philosophy, attached an importance to these powers that threatened the supremacy of Christ. Paul accepts these cosmological premisses and, far from expressing any doubts about these powers, he associates them with the angels of Jewish tradition, 2:15; all he is concerned about is to show their subordinate place in the scheme of salvation. Their task had been to 'mediate' the Law and to administer it and that task is now accomplished: *Christos Kyrios*, Christ the Lord, has established a new order of things and he now governs the cosmos. Raised up to heaven, he is above all the cosmic powers and has stripped them of their ancient dignities, 2:15. Because he is the Son, the Father's image, he was their lord already when the world was made; now in the new creation he is their confirmed and absolute master, for gathered into him is the *pleroma*, the fulness of Being, that is to say the fulness both of God and of all that exists through God's creative power, 1:13-20. Christians have been set free from these 'elements of the world', 2:8,20, through being united with their Master and thus sharing in his fulness, 2:10, Christians must never again accept their tyranny by submitting to an old and now impotent law, 2:16-23. United to the dead and risen Christ by baptism, 2:11-13, they are parts of his Body and live a new life, his life, because as Head of his body he communicates his life to it, 2:19. Paul had always taught that salvation consisted of sharing the life of Christ in this way; the new perspective in which the arguments at Colossae forced him to see things was one in which he saw the effects of Christ's work on the entire cosmos. Since the human race forms part of the cosmos, the cosmos itself must be influenced by the salvific act of the one and only Lord of all creation. In this perspective, Paul is able to widen his whole concept of the 'Body of Christ', which was an idea that, five years or so before in 1 Co 12:12f, he had only touched on. Three aspects of this broader view, which focusses on the function of Christ as Head, are: that the scope of salvation is seen to be cosmic; that Christ, into whom the Church has to structure itself, is this same victor who has triumphed over the whole cosmos; and finally that the concept of the future, eschatological, promise, as already realised, becomes very much more central, cf. Ep 2:6+.

When Paul wrote the letter we know as Ephesians, it was along the same lines, but this time he can assume the conclusions of the previous letter about the subordinate place of the Powers, Ep 1:20-22, and give further thought to how the Church as the Body of Christ embraces the whole of the new Universe, 'the fulness of him who is filled, all in all', 1:23. This concept of the *pleroma* is the innermost depth of Paul's vision, the central statement of everything he wrote. It forms the new focus round which he can synthesise many of his previous insights. In particular he reconsiders some of the problems he had already dealt with in Rm, which is the most important statement of Paul's previous period of thought. In a few phrases he recalls his survey of humanity under the shadow of sin and of how salvation is a gift given by God through Christ, 2:1-10. Next, he re-examines the problem of Jew and pagan that had so troubled him before, Rm 9-11; but this time, in the calm eschatological light of the cosmic Christ, he is aware of the unity of Jews and pagans, who are now reconciled since each is equally part of the New Humanity, and who, together, advance toward the Father, Ep 2:11-22. That it should be the non-Jew who should be benefited by the Messiah who came to save Israel is the 'mystery', 1:9; 3:3-6,9; 6:19; Col 1:27; 2:2; 4:3, which occupies his thoughts for the last five years or so of his life and which he writes about in the inimitable Pauline way. He writes about the infinite wisdom of this 'mystery', 3:9f; Col 2:3, about how it proves Christ's love to be inexhaustible, Ep 3:18f, and about how, out of all possible people, God had made the unexpected choice of Paul, who was 'the least of all', to proclaim this mystery, Ep 3:2-8. That the full truth, about salvation being for the whole human race, was not revealed before, was itself part of the very scheme God had for realising this salvation, Ep 1:3-14, the culmination of which was the salvific act of marriage between Christ and the human race which is his bride, the Church, 5:22-32.

The short letter Paul wrote at about the same time as Col and Ep is to tell Philemon of Colossae, v.19, one of Paul's converts, that Onesimus, a runaway slave belonging to Philemon, and also one of Paul's converts, had returned. It is a very short note, and Paul wrote it in his own handwriting, v. 19. The letter reveals a gentle, affectionate side of the apostle, and also shows how he applies his views on slavery to a particular case, Rm 6:15+: as far as society is concerned, the master still owns his slave, but the two of them should remember that they are brothers serving the same Master, v. 16; cf. Col 3:22; 4:1.

1 Timothy. Titus. 2 Timothy. 65 A.D.

Paul's two letters to Timothy and his letter to Titus are all three of them closely related in substance, form and historical background. 1 Tm and Tt both seem to have been written from Macedonia, Timothy being at that time in Ephesus, 1 Tm 1:3, where Paul hoped to join him in the near future, 3:14; 4:13, while Titus was in Crete where he had been left by Paul, Tt 1:5, who planned to winter at Nicopolis in Epirus where Titus was to join him, Tt 3:12. By the time he wrote 2 Tm, Paul was a prisoner in Rome, 1:8; 16f; 2:9, but had visited Troas, 4:13, and Miletus, 4:20. The position is not hopeful, 4:16, and Paul feels sure he will die soon, 4:6-8,18; he is lonely and would like Timothy to come to him as soon as possible, 4:9-16,21. In spite of certain similarities, this is not the situation either of the Roman captivity, 61-63, or of the journey that preceded it. Some critics have concluded that the letters were written not by Paul, but by a forger who put in these details to make the letter seem more authentic and as Pauline as possible. There is, however, no proof that Paul died at the end of his first captivity, in fact Ac 28:30 suggests he was set free. It is not impossible, therefore, for Paul to have made another journey, not necessarily to Spain as he had once planned seven or eight years before, Rm 15:24,28, but in the east as he had planned a year or so ago, Phm 22. It is possible then that 1 Tm and Tt were written about 65 A.D. on that journey through Crete, Asia Minor, Macedonia and Greece. The background of 2 Tm seems to be a fresh captivity, ending in Paul's death; in that case, this letter would be Paul's last will and testament, and must have been written shortly before his martyrdom in 67.

Paul wrote these letters in order to instruct two of his most loyal followers, Ac 16:1+; 2 Co 2:13+, how to organise and govern the communities he had confided to their care; since the 18th century they have generally been grouped as the 'pastoral letters'. Some critics suggest that they presuppose a stage in the evolution of the Church's hierarchy that only occurred after Paul's death;

others think that the situation they do suppose would not have been at all unlikely towards the end of Paul's lifetime. The titles '*episcopos*' and 'presbyter', Tt 1:5-7, are still, cf. Ac 20:17,28, practically synonymous, as they had been in the earliest communities governed by a college of elders, Tt 1:5+. There is no trace in these letters of the monarchic bishops of whom Ignatius of Antioch writes forty years later. There are signs, however, that this development is taking place: Timothy and Titus are empowered to act as delegates of Paul; they are responsible for several communities though they are not attached to any of them, Tt 1:5; they are living in an interim period when apostolic authority was in the process of being transmitted, since the apostles themselves were dying. Not long after the death of Paul this authority became vested in the head of the college of presbyters, the 'bishop'. To invent the interim period represented in the pastoral letters would seem to be so pointless that its presence is a valuable indication of their authenticity. It should also be noticed that these *episcopoi-presbyteroi* are not just administrative officials; they are that, but they are also primarily responsible for teaching and governing, 1 Tm 3:2,5; 5:17; Tt 1:7,9, and as such they are the ancestors of our 'bishops' and 'priests'.

Many critics have thought the insistence on 'sound teaching', 1 Tm 1:10, etc., and on keeping the deposit of faith, 1 Tm 6:20; 2 Tm 1:14, uncharacteristic of a bold original thinker like Paul. On the other hand it must be remembered that Paul felt his end was near and that he probably felt it his duty to warn his young helpers against the sort of speculation he had seen developing. There were new ideas going round which, if believed in, would make shipwreck of the faith, 1 Tm 1:19. There is no need to assume that these ideas were 2nd century Gnostic teachings being attacked by someone writing under Paul's name. These idle questions, 1 Tm 6:4, empty problems, 'myths and endless genealogies', 1 Tm 1:4, 'Jewish myths', Tt 1:14, 'disputes about the Law', Tt 3:9, and the various ascetical practices they seemed to involve, 1 Tm 4:3, would all appear to belong to those groups of hellenised and syncretistic ideas affecting Judaism, which had formed part of the crisis in Colossae.

These letters are certainly not written in Paul's distinctive style; they flow smoothly without any of the fire and exuberance of the early letters, and the vocabulary used is very different. Some critics have tried to explain this by saying that Paul was getting old, and that being in prison affected him; but Col, Ep, Ph were written less than five years before, and Paul was not under arrest when he wrote 1 Tm and Tt. Attempts have been made to separate the authentic sections from later additions, but these have not proved very satisfactory. The alternative would appear to be that Paul, as in the case of Ep but to a greater degree, must have given someone who was both disciple and secretary an unprecedented amount of freedom. Luke was with Paul at the time, 2 Tm 4:11, and critics have occasionally maintained that they could detect similarities between his style and that of the pastoral letters.

Hebrews. 67 A.D.

The question of who wrote this letter to the Jewish Christians has, unlike the disputed authorship of the pastoral letters, been a subject of debate from the earliest times. Not that its canonical status was often questioned, but up to the end of the 4th century the Western Church denied that Paul had written it, and the Eastern Church only affirmed it with many reservations about its literary composition (Clement of Alexandria; Origen). Its vocabulary and style have a simplicity and a distinction quite uncharacteristic of Paul; the way in which it quotes and uses the Old Testament is different from Paul's; the usual Pauline greetings and introduction are lacking, and though its doctrine has Pauline overtones, it is so original that its immediate attribution to Paul is difficult. Most critics agree that Paul could not have been its author in the same sense as he was author of the other letters, but he is felt to have had sufficient influence, direct or (more likely) indirect, to warrant its inclusion from early times in the *corpus Paulinum.*

No sort of agreement exists as to who actually wrote the letter; Barnabas, Silas, Aristion, etc. have been suggested; perhaps the most likely is Apollos, the Alexandrian Jew who is praised by Luke for his eloquence, apostolic zeal and knowledge of the scriptures, Ac 18:24-28. Not only are these qualities reflected in the letter itself, but its language and thought, by having sufficient affinity with Philo, also suggest Alexandrian culture. The argument of the letter, pleaded with rhetorical skill, is founded entirely on the Old Testament.

The place and date of writing are equally uncertain, and who it was intended for is unknown. But the author seems to be writing from Italy, 13:24, and he speaks as if the Temple were still open for worship, 8:4f, warning his readers against the temptation of going back to it, and, when he emphasises the transitory nature of the Mosaic cult, he makes no reference to the destruction of the Temple. This suggests he was writing before 70 A.D. On the other hand, he certainly makes use of Paul's letters from prison and therefore wrote after 63. If the crisis behind the author's urgent appeal for unshakeable faith, 10:25 etc., is the first threat of the Jewish War, the letter could be dated 67 A.D.

The title 'to the Hebrews' dates from the 2nd century and is well chosen. The letter clearly assumes not only that its readers are thoroughly familiar with the Old Covenant but that they are Jewish Christians, perhaps even Jewish priests, cf. Ac 6:7, to judge by the emphasis on public worship and ceremonial. Having become Christians, they seem to have left Jerusalem and gone for shelter to some coastal town like Caesarea or Antioch. They are tired of exile and think longingly of the splendour of Temple worship and of the part they played in it; their new faith is not very strong, and they have not yet properly understood it; persecution discourages them and they are tempted to go back.

The letter was written to them to try to prevent this happening, 10:19-39. To these exiles the author presents Christian life in the perspective of the Exodus, marching to the Place of Rest, the Promised Land of heaven, an exodus led not by Moses but by Christ, 3:1-6, and led by the same light of faith and hope that had accompanied their ancestors on the Exodus and had illumined all the saints of old, 3:7-4:11; 11 *passim.* Christ himself replaces the old priesthood and, being a priest like Melchisedek, he is higher than Aaron, 4:14-5:10; 7. The ineffectual sacrifices of levitical worship are replaced by the one uniquely efficacious sacrifice of Christ himself, 8:1-10:18. To prove this, the author shows how Jesus Christ, the incarnate Son of God, is, as Leader and Priest, higher than all the angels and ruler of all things, ch. 1-2.

In this letter, strictly theological and exegetical passages alternate with passages of exhortation, but the main themes themselves are interwoven in a very intricate and oriental way, as disconcerting to some modern western readers as its method of using scripture. These are the reasons why this letter can tell us so much about typology, about the way the earliest Christians conceived the harmony of the Old and New Testaments, and about the way they understood the redemptive work of Jesus in terms of God's whole plan of salvation. Add to all that it tells us its deep intuitions into the centre of Christian belief, and it will be clear why this semi-Pauline unsigned document is one of the most important books of the New Testament.

ROMANS

THE LETTER OF PAUL TO THE CHURCH IN ROME

Address[a]

1 1 From Paul, a servant of Christ Jesus who has been called to be an apostle,[b] Ac 26:16-18 Ga 1:10,15
2 and specially chosen to preach the Good News that God •promised long Ph 1:1 Col 1:1
ago through his prophets in the scriptures.
3 This news is about the Son of God who, according to the human nature he 2 S 7:1+ Mt 9:27+
4 took, was a descendant of David: •it is about Jesus Christ our Lord who, in the 1 Tm 3:16 Rv 22:16
order of the spirit, the spirit of holiness that was in him, was proclaimed[c] Son *9:5+; 10:9* 1 Co 6:14
5 of God in all his power through his resurrection from the dead.[d] •Through him
we received grace and our apostolic mission to preach the obedience of faith[e] Heb 11:8
6 to all pagan nations in honour of his name. •You are one of these nations, and Ac 9:15
7 by his call belong to Jesus Christ. •To you all, then, who are God's beloved in
Rome, called to be saints, may God our Father and the Lord Jesus Christ send Ac 9:13+ *1 Co 8:6*
grace and peace.

Thanksgiving and prayer

8 First I thank my God through Jesus Christ for all of you and for the way in 16:19
9 which your faith is spoken of all over the world. •The God I worship[f] spiritually[g] 1 Th 1:8; 2:5
by preaching the Good News of his Son knows that I never fail to mention you 2 Co 1:23 Ph 1:8
10 in my prayers, •and to ask to be allowed at long last the opportunity to visit 2 Tm 1:3 *1 Th 2:17*
11 you, if he so wills. •For I am longing to see you either to strengthen you by Jm 4:15

1 a. Adopting the convention of his time Paul begins letters with an introductory paragraph (names of sender and receiver, good wishes) followed by thanks and a wish. He colours this, however, with his own Christian spirit, and often manages to fit theological ideas into it so as to anticipate the principal themes of each letter. In Rm these themes are: God's freedom to choose his people; the connection between faith and being made holy; salvation through Christ's death and resurrection; the harmony of the two Testaments.

b. A Jewish title that means 'envoy', cf. Jn 13:16; 2 Co 8:23; Ph 2:25, sometimes used in the N.T. for the Twelve chosen by Christ, Mt 10:2; Ac 1:26; 2:37, etc.; 1 Co 15:7; Rv 21:14, to be his witnesses, Ac 1:8+, sometimes in a wider sense for those sent to preach the gospel, Rm 16:7; 1 Co 12:28; Ep 2:20; 3:5; 4:11. Though Paul was not a member of the Twelve, the fact that he had been appointed missionary to the gentiles by God, Ac 26:17; Rm 11:13; 1 Co 9:2; Ga 2:8; 1 Tm 2:7, constitutes him an apostle of Christ, Rm 1:1; 1 Co 1:1; etc., equal to the Twelve, Ac 10:41, because like them he had seen the risen Christ, 1 Co 9:1, and been sent by him, Rm 1:5; Ga 1:16, to be his witness, Ac 26:16. In spite of being 'the least of the apostles', 1 Co 15:9, he is their equal, 1 Co 9:5; Ga 2:6-9, because he did not learn the Good News he preaches from them, Ga 1:1,17,19.

c. Vulg. 'predestined'.

d. For Paul Christ rose only because God raised him, 1 Th 1:10; 1 Co 6:14; 15:15; 2 Co 4:14; Ga 1:1; Rm 4:24; 10:9; Ac 2:24+; cf. 1 P 1:21, thus displaying his 'power', 2 Co 13:4; Rm 6:4; Ph 3:10; Col 2:12; Ep 1:19f; Heb 7:16; and because God raised him to life through the Holy Spirit, Rm 8:11, Christ is established in glory as *Kyrios*, Ph 2:9-11+; Ac 2:36; Rm 14:9, deserving anew, this time in virtue of his messianic work, the name he had from eternity, 'Son of God', Ac 13:33, Heb 1:5; 5:5. Cf. Rm 8:11+; 9:5+.

e. Subjective genitive: the obedience implicit in the virtue of faith. Cf. Ac 6:7; Rm 6:16-17; 10:16; 15:18; 16:19,26; 2 Co 10:5-6; 2 Th 1:8; 1 P 1:22; Heb 5:9; 11:8.

f. Lit. 'I offer worship in my spirit'. The apostolic ministry is an act of worship offered to God, cf. 15:16, like the Christian life itself, since both depend on charity, 12:1; Ph 2:17+; 3:3; 4:18; Ac 13:2; 2 Tm 1:3; 4:6; Heb 9:14; 12:28; 13:15; 1 P 2:5.

g. By spirit *(pneuma)* Paul sometimes means the highest element in a human being, Rm 1:9; 8:16; 1 Co 2:11; 16:18; 2 Co 2:13; 7:13; Ga 6:18; Ph 4:23; Phm 25; 2 Tm 4:22; cf. Mt 5:3; 27:50; Mk 2:8; 8:12; Lk 1:47,80; 8:55; 23:46; Jn 4:23f; 11:33; 13:21; 19:30; Ac 7:59; 17:16; 18:25; 19:21. This he distinguishes from the flesh, the lower element (1 Co 5:5; 2 Co 7:1; Col 2:5; cf. Mt 26:41p; 1 P 4:6; Rm 7:5), from the body (1 Co 5:3f; 7:34; cf. Jm 2:26; Rm 7:24), and from

sharing a spiritual gift with you, •or what is better, to find encouragement 12
among you from our common faith. •I want you to know, brothers, that I have 13
Ac 15:23; 19:21 often planned to visit you—though until now I have always been prevented—
in the hope that I might work as fruitfully among you as I have done among the
other pagans. •I owe a duty to Greeks[h] just as much as to barbarians, to the 14
educated just as much as to the uneducated, •and it is this that makes me want[i] 15
to bring the Good News to you too in Rome.

SALVATION BY FAITH

I. JUSTIFICATION

The theme stated

Ac 13:38; 1 Co 1:18-25; 2:1-5 For I am not ashamed of the Good News: it is the power of God saving all 16
2 Co 12:9f who have faith[j]—Jews first,[k] but Greeks as well—•since this is what reveals the 17
1:16+ justice[l] of God to us: it shows how faith leads to faith,[m] or as scripture says:
Hab 2:4; Ga 3:11; Heb 10:38 *The upright man finds life through faith.*

A. GOD'S ANGER AGAINST PAGAN AND JEW[n]

God's anger against the pagans

Ps 69:24; 85:3-5 The anger of God is being revealed from heaven against all the impiety and 18
Mi 7:9; Zp 1:15 depravity of men who keep truth imprisoned in their wickedness. •For what can 19
be known about God is perfectly plain to them since God himself has made it
Ws 13:1-9; Si 17:8 plain. •Ever since God created the world his everlasting power and deity— 20
Ac 17:24-29; 1 Co 1:21 however invisible—have been there for the mind to see in the things he has
Ws 11:15; Is 5:21; 40:26:28 made. That is why such people are without excuse: •they knew God[o] and yet 21
Ep 4:17-18 refused to honour him as God or to thank him; instead, they made nonsense
1 Co 1:19-20 out of logic and their empty minds were darkened. •The more they called 22
Ps 106:20 themselves philosophers, the more stupid they grew, •until *they exchanged the* 23
Ex 32 *glory* of the immortal God for a worthless imitation, *for the image* of mortal man,
Dt 4:16-18; Ws 11:15; of birds, of quadrupeds and reptiles. •That is why God left them[p] to their filthy 24
12:24; 13:10f enjoyments and the practices with which they dishonour their own bodies,
Jr 2:11; *Ep 4:19* since they have given up divine truth for a lie and have worshipped and served 25
creatures instead of the creator, who is blessed for ever. Amen!

That is why God has abandoned them to degrading passions: why their women 26
have turned from natural intercourse to unnatural practices •and why their 27
menfolk have given up natural intercourse to be consumed with passion for each
other, men doing shameless things with men and getting an appropriate reward
for their perversion.

In other words, since they refused to see it was rational to acknowledge God, 28
God has left them to their own irrational ideas and to their monstrous behaviour.[q]
13:13 And so they are steeped[r] in all sorts of depravity, rottenness, greed and malice,[s] 29
and addicted to envy, murder, wrangling, treachery and spite. •Libellers, 30
slanderers, enemies of God,[t] rude, arrogant and boastful, enterprising in sin,
rebellious to parents, •without brains, honour, love[u] or pity. •They know what 31 32
Ws 14:22 God's verdict is: that those who behave like this deserve to die—and yet they
do it; and what is worse, encourage others to do the same.[v]

The Jews are not exempt from God's anger[a]

Mt 7:1 **2** So no matter who you are, if you pass judgement you have no excuse. 1
In judging others you condemn yourself, since you behave no differently
from those you judge. •We know that God condemns that sort of behaviour 2
Ep 2:3 impartially: •and when you judge those who behave like this while you are 3

4 doing exactly the same, do you think you will escape God's judgement? •Or are
you abusing his abundant goodness, patience and toleration, not realising that Ws 11:23 Si 5:4
5 this goodness of God is meant to lead you to repentance? •Your stubborn refusal 2 P 3:9 *Ac 7:51*
to repent is only adding to the anger God will have towards you on that day of *Zp 1:14-18* 2 Th 1:5-10
6 anger when his just judgements will be made known. •*He will repay each one as* *Ps 62:12* Heb 11:6p
7 *his works deserve.*[b] •For those who sought renown and honour and immortality 1 P 1:7
8 by always doing good there will be eternal life; •for the unsubmissive who
refused to take truth for their guide and took depravity instead, there will be

the *psyche* also (1 Th 5:23+; cf. Heb 4:12; Jude 19); it bears some relationship to *nous* (Rm 7:25; Ep 4:23). Cf. also 'dispositions of the spirit' in 1 Co 4:21; 2 Co 12:18; Ga 6:1; Ph 1:27. By choosing this traditional term (cf. Is 11:2+) instead of the *nous* of the Greek philosophers, the N.T. can suggest a deep affinity between the human spirit and the Spirit of God that stimulates and guides it, Rm 5:5+; Ac 1:8+. There are many texts where it is hard to tell whether it is the natural or supernatural spirit that is referred to, the personal or the indwelling spirit—cf. e.g. Rm 12:11; 2 Co 6:6; Ep 4:3,23; 6:18; Ph 3:3 var.; Col 1:8; Jude 19, etc.

h. In contrast to 'barbarians', 'Greeks' means the inhabitants of the hellenic world (including the Romans, who had adopted the Greek culture); in contrast to 'Jews' it means the pagans in general, 1:16; 2:9-10; 3:10; 10:12; 1 Co 1:22-24, etc.

i. Alternative translation 'And therefore, in so far as it is in my power, I am prepared to...'

j. Faith, which is the response of a human being to God as truth and goodness and so the one source of salvation, relies on the truth of God's promises and on God's faithfulness to them (Rm 3:3f; 1 Th 5:24; 2 Tm 2:13; Heb 10:23; 11:11) and on his power to implement them (Rm 4:17-21; Heb 11:19). After the long O.T. period of preparation (Heb 11) God has spoken through his Son (Heb 1:1). We must believe the Son (cf. Mt 8:10+; Jn 3:11+) and the *kerygma* or proclamation (Rm 10:8-17; 1 Co 1:21; 15:11,14; cf. Ac 2:22+) of the Good News (Rm 1:16; 1 Co 15:1-2; Ph1: 27; Ep 1:13) made by the apostles (Rm 1:5; 1 Co 3:5; cf. Jn 17:20). The *kerygma* proclaims that God raised Jesus from the dead, made him *Kyrios* (Rm 4:24f; 10:9; Ac 17:31; 1 P 1:21; cf. 1 Co 15:14,17), and through him offers life to all who believe in him (Rm 6:8-11; 2 Co 4:13f; Ep 1:19f; Col 2:12; 1 Th 4:14). Faith in the name, or person, of Jesus (Rm 3:26; 10:13; cf. Jn 1:12; Ac 3:16; 1 Jn 3:23) who is the Messiah (Ga 2:16; cf. Ac 24:24; 1 Jn 5:1), the Lord (Rm 10:9; 1 Co 12:3; Ph 2:11; cf. Ac 16:31) and Son of God (Ga 2:20; cf. Jn 20:31; 1 Jn 5:5; Ac 8:37; 9:20) is thus the necessary condition of salvation (Rm 10:9-13; 1 Co 1:21; Ga 3:22; cf. Is 7:9+; Ac 4:12; 16:31; Heb 11:6; Jn 3:15-18). Faith is not only intellectual assent, it is to trust and obey (Rm 1:5; 6:17; 10:16; 16:26; cf. Ac 6:7) the lifegiving truth (2 Th 2:12f). Faith which thus unites a person with Christ (2 Co 13:5; Ga 2:16,20; Ep 3:17) also confers the Spirit on him (Ga 3:2,5,14; cf. Jn 7:38f; Ac 11:17), the Spirit of the sons of God (Ga 3:26; cf. Jn 1:12). Faith is reliance on God and not on self (Rm 3:27; Ep 2:9) and thus contrasts with the old order of the Law (Rm 7:7+) with its vain search (Rm 10:3; Ph 3:9) for holiness by works (Rm 3:20,28; 9:31f; Ga 2:16; 3:11f): only faith can effect true holiness, the saving holiness of God himself (Rm 1:17+; 3:21-26), received as a free gift from him (Rm 3:24; 4:16; 5:17; Ep 2:8; cf. Ac 15:11). Faith relates to the promise made to Abraham (Rm 4; Ga 3:6-18) and so makes salvation accessible to everyone, pagans included (Rm 1:5,16; 3:29f; 9:30; 10:11f; 16:26; Ga 3:8). It is coupled with baptism (Rm 6:4+), calls for public profession (Rm 10:10; 1 Tm 6:12), and expresses itself in charity (Ga 5:6; cf. Jm 2:14+). Faith is obscure (2 Co 5:7; Heb 11:1; cf. Jn 20:29), and involves hope as its concomitant (Rm 5:2+). It must be allowed to grow (2 Co 10:15; 1 Th 3:10; 2 Th 1:3) amid struggles and sufferings (Ph 1:29; Ep 6:16; 1 Th 3:2-8; 2 Th 1:4; Heb 12:2; 1 P 5:9), demanding fortitude (1 Co 16:13; Col 1:23; 2:5,7) and tenacity (2 Tm 4:7; cf. 1:14; 1 Tm 6:20) right up to the vision and possession of God (1 Co 13:12; cf. 1 Jn 3:2).

k. In the actual development of salvation history the Jews come first: 'salvation comes from the Jews' (Jn 4:22). Cf. Rm 2:9-10; Mt 10:5f; 15:24; Mk 7:27; Ac 13:5+. But abuse of this privilege could condemn them.

l. Not 'distributive' justice (reward for deeds) but the saving justice (cf. Is 56:1) of God, 3:26, who fulfils his promise to save by giving salvation as a free gift.

m. The expression probably means that faith is the one necessary condition to ensure this revelation.

n. By way of antithesis, the subject of the Good News being the revelation of God's saving justice, 1:16-17 (resumed in 3:21f), is interrupted by considering what the human race is like before it hears the Good News. In it both pagan, 1:18-32, and Jew, 2:1–3:20, are subject to God's 'anger' which accounts for the increase of sin, and which will reach its climax in the Last Judgement, 2:6+; Mt 3:7+.

o. To know there is one, personal God means to know that one must pray to him and adore him.

p. The traditional biblical phrase 'God abandoned', or 'left them', used three times for emphasis, means that religious error, if blameworthy, results in moral and social ills. Sin produces its own consequences and its own punishment; cf. Ezk 23:28-29; Is 64:6; Ws 11:15-16; 12:23-27. Though Paul judges and condemns pagan society he does not condemn individuals (whose intentions God alone must judge, 2:16; 1 Co 4:5; 5:12-13) since he presupposes, Rm 2, that there are pagans who obey the natural law written in their hearts, 2:14-15. To do that, a human being must admit that he is a sinner.

q. A clever twist here: as a punishment for refusing to use it properly, moral judgement, which goes with knowing about God, v. 21, disappears.

r. Here, as he frequently does elsewhere, Paul uses lists of vices taken from current pagan and (even more so) Jewish literature: 13:13; 1 Co 5:10-11; 6:9-10; 2 Co 12:20; Ga 5:19-21; Ep 4:31; 5:3-5; Col 3:5-8; 1 Tm 1:9-10; 6:4; 2 Tm 3:2-5; Tt 3:3. Cf. also Mt 15:19p; 1 P 4:3; Rv 21:8; 22:15.

s. Add. 'fornication'.

t. Others translate 'hateful to God', but cf. 5:10; 8:7.

u. Add. (Vulg.) 'loyalty', cf. 2 Tm 3:3.

v. The Latin text tradition reads 'They know that God is just, and yet they did not understand that those who behave like this deserve to die, and not only those who do this but those who encourage them'.

2 a. Here Paul turns to the Jews not actually naming them, vv. 1-16, until 2:17–3:20. He is aware, as he condemns others, that he is condemning himself if he behaves in the way they do, vv. 1-5; 17-24. Nothing can take the place of personal virtue: not the Law, vv. 12-16, not circumcision, vv. 25-29, not even the scriptures, 3:1-8. The Jew as well as the pagan will be individually judged by God, 2:6-11, since each is equally liable to sin, 3:9-20.

b. The prophecy of a 'day of Yahweh' which will be a day of anger and salvation, Am 5:18+, will be fulfilled eschatologically in the 'day of the Lord', when Christ returns in glory, 1 Co 1:8+. On this 'day of judgement' (cf. Mt 10:15; 11:22,24; 12:36, 2 P 2:9; 3:7; 1 Jn 4:17) the dead will rise again, 1 Th 4:13-18; 1 Co 15:12-23,51f, and the whole human race will be judged in God's court, Rm 14:10, and in Christ's,

anger and fury. •Pain and suffering will come to every human being who employs 9
himself in evil—Jews first, but Greeks as well; •renown, honour and peace will
Dt 10:17+ Ac 10:34+ come to everyone who does good—Jews first, but Greeks as well. •God has
no favourites.

The Law will not save them

Sinners who were not subject to the Law will perish all the same, without 12
that Law; sinners who were under the Law will have that Law to judge them.
Mt 7:26-27 Lk 8:21 Jm 1:22-25 It is not listening to the Law but keeping it that will make people holy in the 13
sight of God. •For instance, pagans who never heard of the Law but are led 14
by reason[c] to do what the Law commands, may not actually 'possess' the Law,
but they can be said to 'be' the Law. •They can point to the substance of the 15
Law engraved on their hearts—they can call a witness, that is, their own
conscience—they have accusation and defence, that is, their own inner mental
2:6+ 1 Co 4:5 dialogue.[d] •...on the day when,[e] according to the Good News I preach, God, 16
through Jesus Christ, judges the secrets of mankind.

Is 48:1-4 Am 5:21+ If you call yourself a Jew, if you really trust in the Law and are proud of 17
Mt 3:8-9 Jn 8:33f your God, •if you know God's will through the Law and can tell what is right, 18
Jn 9:40-41 if you are convinced you can guide the blind and be a beacon to those in the 19
Mt 23 Lk 18:9-12 dark, •if you can teach the ignorant and instruct the unlearned because your Law 20
Ps 50:16-21 embodies all knowledge and truth, •then why not teach yourself as well as the 21
others? You preach against stealing, yet you steal; •you forbid adultery, yet you 22
commit adultery; you despise idols, yet you rob their temples. •By boasting about 23
the Law and then disobeying it, you bring God into contempt. •As scripture 24
Is 52:5 LXX Ezk 36:20 Jm 2:7 2 P 2:2 says: *It is your fault that the name of God is blasphemed among the pagans.*

Circumcision will not save them

1 Co 7:19 Ga 5:3 It is a good thing to be circumcised if you keep the Law; but if you break the 25
Jr 9:24-25 Law, you might as well have stayed uncircumcised. •If a man who is not 26
circumcised obeys the commandments of the Law, surely that makes up for not
Mt 12:41f being circumcised? •More than that, the man who keeps the Law, even though 27
he has not been physically circumcised, is a living condemnation of the way you
disobey the Law in spite of being circumcised and having it all written down.
Ep 2:11 Ph 3:2f To be a Jew is not just to look like a Jew, and circumcision is more than a physical 28
Jr 4:4+ operation. •The real Jew is the one who is inwardly a Jew, and the real circum- 29
7:6; 8: 2+ 2 Co 3:6 cision is in the heart—something not of the letter but of the spirit. A Jew like that
may not be praised by man, but he will be praised by God.

God's promises will not save them

3 Well then, is a Jew any better off?[a] Is there any advantage in being circum- 1
9:4-5 cised? •A great advantage in every way. First, the Jews are the people to 2
Ps 89:30-37 2 Tm 2:13 whom God's message was entrusted. •What if some of them were unfaithful? 3
Will their lack of fidelity cancel God's fidelity? •That would be absurd. God will 4
Ps 116:11 always be true even though *everyone* proves to be *false*; so scripture says: *In all*
Ps 51:4 LXX *you say your justice shows, and when you are judged you win your case.* •But if our 5
1:18+ Jb 34:12,17 lack of holiness makes God demonstrate his integrity,[b] how can we say God is
unjust when—to use a human analogy—he gets angry with us in return? •That 6
would be absurd, it would mean God could never judge the world. •You might 7
9:19+ as well say that since my untruthfulness makes God demonstrate his truthfulness
and thus gives him glory,[c] I should not be judged to be a sinner at all. •That 8
6:1,15 would be the same as saying: Do evil as a means to good. Some slanderers have
accused us of teaching this,[d] but they are justly condemned.

All are guilty

Well: are we any better off?[e] Not at all: as we said before, Jews and Greeks 9
11:32 Si 8:5 are all under sin's dominion. •As scripture says: 10

There is not a good man left, no, not one; Ps 14:1-3
11 *there is not one who understands,*
not one who looks for God.
12 *All have turned aside, tainted all alike;*
there is not one good man left, not a single one.
13 *Their throats are yawning graves;* Ps 5:9
their tongues are full of deceit.
Vipers' venom is on their lips, Ps 140:3
14 *bitter curses fill their mouths.* Ps 10:7
15 *Their feet are swift when blood is to be shed,* Is 59:7-8
16 *wherever they go there is havoc and ruin.*
17 *They know nothing of the way of peace,*
18 *there is no fear of God before their eyes.* Ps 36:1

19 Now all this that the Law[f] says is said, as we know, for the benefit of those Jn 10:34; 12:34;
who are subject to the Law, but it is meant to silence everyone and to lay the 15:25 Ga 3:22
20 whole world open to God's judgement; •and this is because *no one can be justified* *Ps 143:2* Ga 2:16
in the sight of God by keeping the Law:[g] all that law does is to tell us what is Rm 7:7
sinful.

B. FAITH AND THE JUSTICE OF GOD

The revelation of God's justice

21 God's justice that was made known through the Law and the Prophets has 10:5 1 K 8:46
22 now been revealed outside the Law, •since it is the same justice of God that *1:16+* Ga 2:16;3
comes through faith to everyone, Jew and pagan alike, who believes in Jesus
23 24 Christ. •Both Jew and pagan sinned and forfeited God's glory,[h] •and both are 5:2,13
justified through the free gift of his grace[i] by being redeemed[j] in Christ Jesus Dn 9:24

2 Co 5:10; cf. Mt 25:31f. This trial is inescapable, Rm 2:3; Ga 5:10; 1 Th 5:3, and impartial, v. 11; Col 3:25; cf. 1 P 1:17; it is conducted by God, Rm 12:19; 14:10; 1 Co 4:5; cf. Mt 7:1p. Through Christ, v. 16; 2 Tm 4:1; cf. Jn 5:22; Ac 17:31. God will judge 'the living and the dead', 2 Tm 4:1; cf. Ac 10:42; 1 P 4:5. He examines the heart, v. 16; 1 Co 4:5; cf. Rv 2:23, and his trial is by fire, 1 Co 3:13-15; he will treat everyone according to his works, 1 Co 3:8; 2 Co 5:10; 11:15; Ep 6:8; cf. Mt 16:27; 1 P 1:17; Rv 2:23; 20:12; 22:12. What has been sown will be reaped, Ga 6:7-9; cf. Mt 13:39; Rv 14:15. Angrily he will destroy, Rm 9:22, evil powers, 1 Co 15:24-26; 2 Th 2:8, and evil people, 2 Th 1:7-10; cf. Mt 13:41; Ep 5:6; 2 P 3:7; Rv 6:17; 11:18. But for the chosen, i.e. those who have done good, there will be freedom, Ep 4:30; cf. Rm 8:23, rest, Ac 3:20; cf. 1 Th 1:7; Heb 4:5-11, reward, cf. Mt 5:12; Rv 11:18, salvation, 1 P 1:5, honour, 1 P 5:6, praise, 1 Co 4:5, and glory, Rm 8:18f; 1 Co 15:43; Col 3:4; cf. Mt 13:43.

c. I.e. guided by conscience, not by revealed law. As Jews are not meant to be saved by the Law but guided by it to salvation, so the natural law in his conscience can guide any human being.

d. 'they have . . . dialogue'; lit. 'and the accusing or defending thoughts they have about themselves (or: about each other)'.

e. Anacoluthon: v. 16 follows grammatically on v. 13. Alternative translation 'in the court where God judges . . .', cf. 1 Co 4:3.

3 a. There is one further argument in favour of the Jews: if Israel is the people chosen by God to receive the promise, then how can there be any other way to salvation? Later, ch. 9-11, Paul develops at great length the brief answer he gives here: however much humans are unfaithful to the pact, this cannot abrogate God's promises; indeed the way humans behave only makes the promises more remarkable, a fact however which does not stop God being angry with the sinner (v. 6), or absolve his sin (v. 8). The dialogue used here seems it may echo some of Paul's debates in the synagogues.

b. The argument compares the group: faithfulness truth (truthfulness), integrity, with its anti-group: faithlessness, falsehood, sinfulness.

c. Lit. 'But (var. 'For') if through my untruthfulness God's truthfulness abounds to his glory'.

d. By twisting Paul's words as in Ga 3:22; Rm 5:20; cf. 6:1,15.

e. Disputed translation; some prefer 'what excuse then can we offer?' or 'Are we worse off, then?'

f. 'Law' here means all the O.T., cf. 1 Co 14:34; Jn 10:34, etc.

g. Since Ps 143 says that no human being would ever be forgiven if God judged him by his actions, there must be something else that will account for justification, and Paul finds this in God's promises to save his people: this is God's 'justice' that was promised for the messianic era and that, as Paul says, v. 21, is manifest in Jesus Christ. The Law, which merely regulates behaviour, was not meant by God to eliminate sin but to make sinners aware of the fact, cf. 1:16+; 7:7+.

h. 'Glory' in O.T. sense, Ex 24:16+, that is to say God as present to human beings and communicating himself to them more and more, a process that can only reach its climax in the messianic era, cf. Ps 84:9; Is 40:5, etc.

i. This word *(charis)* when used with reference to human relationships can mean either the quality that makes a person attractive (Ac 2:47), or it can mean thanks for a gift (Lk 6:32-34; 17:9), or it can mean something given free and unearned (Ac 25:3; 1 Co 16:3; 2 Co 8:6-7,19). This last sense predominates in the N.T., and especially in Paul (John uses *agape*) who uses the word to describe the way God saves through Jesus: it is a work of spontaneous love to which no one had any claim. It was an act of 'grace' for Jesus to come on earth (2 Co 8:9; Tt 2:11; Jn 1:14,17), to die (Heb 2:9), for his Father

1 Jn 2:2; 4:10 Heb 2:17 who was appointed by God to sacrifice his life so as to win reconciliation through 25
faith.[k] In this way God makes his justice known; first, for the past, when sins
Ac 17:30 went unpunished because he held his hand,[l] •then, for the present age,[m] 26
5:6; 11:30 Is 53:11 by showing positively that he is just,[n] and that he justifies everyone who believes
1 Tm 2:7 Tt 1:3 in Jesus.

What faith does

1 Co 1:29 So what becomes of our boasts? There is no room for them. What sort of 27
2:17; 4:2-3; 5:2+; 11:18 law excludes them? The sort of law that tells us what to do? On the contrary,
Ga 6:13-14 it is the law of faith,[o] •since,[p] as we see it, a man is justified by faith and not 28
Ep 2:9 by doing something the Law tells him to do. •Is God the God of Jews alone and 29
not of the pagans too? Of the pagans too, most certainly, •since there is only one 30
God, and he is the one who will justify the circumcised because of their faith
8:4 Mt 5:17 and justify the uncircumcised through their faith. •Do we mean that faith makes 31
Ac 24:14 the Law pointless? Not at all: we are giving the Law its true value.[q]

C. THE EXAMPLE OF ABRAHAM

Gn 12:1+; 15:6+ Ga 3:6-9 Jm 2:14+. 20-24

Abraham justified by faith

Si 44:19-21 4 Apply this to Abraham,[a] the ancestor from whom we are all descended.[b] 1
3:27 If Abraham was justified as a reward for doing something, he would really 2
have had something to boast about, though not in God's sight •because scripture 3
Gn 15:6 Ga 3:6 says: *Abraham put his faith in God, and this faith was considered as justifying[c] him.*
Jm 2:23 If a man has work to show, his wages are not considered as a favour but as his 4
due; •but when a man has nothing to show except faith in the one who justifies 5
sinners, then his faith is considered as justifying him.[d] •And David says the same: 6
a man is happy if God considers him righteous, irrespective of good deeds:

Ps 32:1-2 *Happy those whose crimes are forgiven,* 7
whose sins are blotted out;
happy the man whom the Lord considers sinless. 8

Justified before circumcision

Is this happiness meant only for the circumcised, or is it meant for others as 9
well? Think of Abraham again: *his faith,* we say, *was considered as justifying him,*
but when was this done? When he was already circumcised or before he had been 10
circumcised? It was before he had been circumcised, not after; •and when he was 11
Gn 17:11 Jn 7:22 *circumcised* later it was only *as a sign* and guarantee[e] that the faith he had before
Ga 3:7 his circumcision justified him. In this way Abraham became the ancestor of all
1 Co 9:12 uncircumcised believers, so that they too might be considered righteous; •and 12
ancestor, also, of those who though circumcised do not rely on that fact alone,
but follow our ancestor Abraham along the path of faith he trod before he had
been circumcised.

Not justified by obedience to the Law

Gn 12:7+ The promise of inheriting the world was not made to Abraham and his 13
Ga 3:16-18 descendants on account of any law but on account of the righteousness which
consists in faith.[f] •If the world is only to be inherited by those who submit to 14
the Law, then faith is pointless and the promise worth nothing. •Law 15
Ga 3:10 *Rm 5:13; 7:7+* involves the possibility of punishment for breaking the law—only where there
is no law can that be avoided.[g] •That is why what fulfils the promise depends on 16
faith, so that it may be a free gift and be available to all of Abraham's
descendants, not only those who belong to the Law but also those who belong
Gn 17:5 to the faith of Abraham who is the father of all of us. •As scripture says: *I have* 17
made you the ancestor of many nations—Abraham is our father in the eyes of God,

in whom he put his faith, and who brings the dead to life and calls into being what does not exist.[h] Dt 32:39+ Is 48:13 2 Co 1:9 Heb 11:19 Rv 4:11

Abraham's faith, a model of Christian faith

18 Though it seemed Abraham's hope could not be fulfilled, he hoped and he

to give him up as a gift to us, a gift that includes all divine favours (Rm 8:32; cf. 1 Co 2:12; Ep 1:6f): justification, salvation, and the right to inherit by having faith in him without having to perform the works of the Law (Rm 3:24; 4:4f; Ep 2:5,8; Tt 3:7; cf. Ac 15:11); it will also be an act of 'grace' for Christ to come again at the end of the world and for us to receive everlasting glory (1 P 1:13; 2 Th 1:12). It was by grace that Abraham received the promise (Rm 4:16; Ga 3:18) and that a few Israelites were chosen to survive (Rm 11:5f). Since grace is God's love for us, it is inexhaustible (Ep 1:7; 2:7; cf. 2 Co 4:15; 9:8,14; 1 Tm 1:14) and it conquers sin (Rm 5:15,17,20). The one word 'grace' is so useful and full of meaning that it can be used to indicate the entire messianic era (Rm 5:21) that succeeds the era of the Law (Rm 6:14; Ga 2:21; 5:4), the same messianic era that was once proclaimed by the prophets (1 P 1:10) and is now proclaimed as the Good News (Col 1:6; cf. Ac 14:3; 20:24,32). The word sums up the gifts of God so well that Paul begins and ends his letters by wishing 'grace' to all his readers (1 Th 1:1 and 5:28, etc.; cf. 1 P 1:2; 5:10,12; 2 P 1:2; 3:18; 2 Jn 3; Rv 1:4; 22:21). It is by an act of grace that 'the God of all grace' (1 P 5:10) calls men to salvation (Ga 1:6; 2 Tm 1:9; 1 P 3:7), loads them with all spiritual gifts (1 Co 1:4-7; cf. 2 Th 2:16; Ac 6:8), makes Paul an apostle of the pagans (Rm 1:5; 12:3; 15:15f; 1 Co 3:10; Ga 1:15f; 2:9; Ep 3:2,7,8; Ph 1:7) and assigns to each Christian the part he has to play in the life of the Church (Rm 12:6; 1 Co 12:1+; 2 Co 8:1; Ep 4:7; 1 P 4:10); similarly, it is a 'grace' to suffer for Christ (Ph 1:29; 1 P 2:19-20). Mary 'found grace' with God (Lk 1:30; cf. Ac 7:46 and LXX passim); Jesus himself received the 'grace' of the highest name of all (Ph 2:9; cf. Lk 2:40). For human beings to be agreeable to God depends primarily on God's initiative and secondarily on human response. It is possible to receive grace in vain (2 Co 6:1; cf. 1 Co 15:10), to fall from grace (Ga 5:4), to forfeit grace (Heb 12:15), and thus to insult the Spirit of grace (Heb 10:29). Grace obtained must be carefully guarded (Rm 5:2; Heb 12:28; 1 P 5:12) and used wisely (1 P 4:10); it is not enough to remain in grace (Ac 13:43; cf. 14:26; 15:40), it must increase (2 P 3:18), to strengthen us (2 Tm 2:1), and help us to persist in our good intentions (Heb 13:9). This divine help is given to the humble (Jm 4:6; 1 P 5:5) and is obtained by prayer, since this is to approach 'the throne of grace' confidently (Heb 4:26). Grace will be granted and will be found sufficient; it is the power of Christ operating in weak man (2 Co 12:9; cf. 1 Co 15:10), and this grace of Christ triumphs over unspiritual wisdom (2 Co 1:12). The same word *charis* is also used for thanksgiving (Rm 6:17; 7:25; 1 Co 10:30; 15:57; 2 Co 2:14; 8:16; 9:15; Col 3:16; 1 Tm 1:12; 2 Tm 1:3; and cf. the verb *eucharistein*), since gratitude to God is the fundamental and necessary disposition for grace. From all these shades of meaning it is clear that the word *charis* is always used to emphasise that the gift is absolutely free; to bring out its power and its inwardness Paul also uses the word *pneuma* (cf. Rm 5:5+).

j. Yahweh had 'redeemed' Israel by delivering her from the slavery of Egypt, to provide himself with a nation for his 'inheritance', Dt 7:6+. When the prophets spoke of the 'redemption' from Babylon, Is 41:14+, they hinted at a deliverance more profound and less restricted, the forgiveness that is deliverance from sin, Is 44:22; cf. Ps 130:8; 49:7-8. This messianic redemption is fulfilled in Christ, 1 Co 1:30; cf. Lk 1:68; 2:38. God the Father through Christ—and indeed Christ himself—has 'delivered' the new Israel from the slavery of the Law, Ga 3:13; 4:5; and of sin, Col 1:14; Ep 1:7; Heb 9:15, by 'acquiring' her, Ac 20:28, making her his own, Tt 2:14; purchasing her, Ga 3:13; 4:5; 1 Co 6:20; 7:23; cf. 2 P 2:1. The price was the blood of Christ, Ac 20:28; Ep 1:7; Heb 9:12; 1 P 1:18f; Rv 1:5; 5:9. This redemption, begun on Calvary and guaranteed by the present gift of the Spirit, Ep 1:14; 4:30, will be complete only at the *parousia*, Lk 21:28, when deliverance from death is secured by the resurrection of the body, Rm 8:23.

---

k. Lit. 'whom God put forward as (or: destined to be) a propitiatory through faith by his blood'. For the 'propitiatory', or 'throne of mercy', cf. Ex 25:17+; and cf. Heb 9:5. On the Day of Atonement, Lv 16:1+, this was sprinkled with blood, Lv 16:15. The blood of Christ has performed what the ancient ritual could only symbolise: purification from sin. Cf. also the blood of the covenant, Ex 24:8+; Mt 26:28+.

l. A quasi-forgiveness; God declined to attach guilt (a *paresis* or 'passing over'); such 'non-imputation' would be an idle procedure if positive forgiveness were not to follow, i.e. the utter destruction of sin by man's justification. Others translate 'with a view to the remission of sins'.

m. This 'present age' is in God's plan of salvation the 'time appointed', Ac 1:7+, for Christ's redemptive work, Rm 5:6; 11:30; 1 Tm 2:6; Tt 1:3, which comes in the appointed time, Ga 4:4+, once for all, Heb 7:27+, and inaugurates the eschatological era. Cf. Mt 4:17p; 16:3p; Lk 4:13; 19:44; 21:8; Jn 7:6,8.

n. I.e. exercising his (saving, cf. 1:17+) justice, as he had promised, by justifying man.

o. I.e. the 'law' which is faith. Paul contrasts two regimes: of law, 7:7+, and of faith, 1:16+; cf. 4:13.

p. Var. 'Therefore'.

q. Lit. 'we establish (the) Law': it is only by means of the regime of faith that the Law achieves what it was intended to do, viz. to make people holy, cf. 7:7+.

4 a. Lit. 'What then shall we say about Abraham?' Var. (Vulg.) 'What then shall we say that Abraham has gained?'

b. The recurrence of the fatherhood of Abraham theme marks the stages in the argument, vv. 1,12,16-18.

c. Jewish tradition, preoccupied with Abraham's loyalty and his fortitude under trial, had made him the outstanding example of justification by works, Ws 10:5; Si 44:20f; 1 M 2:52 (and cf. especially the Book of Jubilees, ch. 11-12; 16:19f, etc.) cf. also Jm 2:22+, see 2:14+. Paul however finds that this justification and these works have their source in Abraham's faith, Gn 12:1+ and 15:6+. Cf. Heb 11:8f.

d. The words themselves are capable of various interpretations: by reason of his faith Abraham was reckoned a righteous man by God, though in fact he was not so; or, by reason of his faith Abraham had conferred upon him gratuitously by God a righteousness (or 'justice') that was not his when he came to believe; or thirdly, in God's eyes (and hence in fact) faith that is operative is one and the same with righteousness. The first of these interpretations is, however, incompatible with Pauline teaching as a whole, so also, it would seem, is the second; the third is completely consistent with it.

e. This word, *sphragis*, (lit. 'seal' or 'impression of a seal') came very soon to be analogically used of baptism, the sacrament of Christian faith.

f. Lit. 'the righteousness of faith', i.e. that righteousness which is precisely the act of believing with a living faith. The inheritance is conferred not to reward people who respect the clauses of a contract (a law), but to implement promises accepted in a disposition of faith. Cf. 3:27.

g. Lit. 'For law brings anger whereas (var. 'for') where there is no law there is no law-breaking either'.

h. As at the creation. These two most striking manifestations of God's omnipotence prepare the reader for the allusion to Christ's resurrection in v. 24.

believed, and through doing so he did become *the father of many nations* exactly
Gn 15:5 as he had been promised: *Your descendants will be as many as the stars.* •Even
Gn 17:1,17 the thought that his body was past fatherhood—he was about a hundred years
Heb 11:11 old—and Sarah too old to become a mother, did not shake his belief.[i] •Since God 20
Mk 9:23 Heb 11:1f had promised it, Abraham refused either to deny it or even to doubt it, but drew
Jr 32:17 Lk 1:37 strength from faith[j] and gave glory to God, •convinced that God had power 21
to do what he had promised. •This is the faith that was '*considered as justi-* 22
fying him'. •Scripture however does not refer only to him but to us as well 23
1 Co 10:6+ when it says that his faith was thus 'considered'; •our faith too will be 'considered' 24
1:4+ if we believe in him who raised Jesus our Lord from the dead, •Jesus who was 25
Is 53:5,6 1 Co 15:17 *put to death for our sins* and raised to life to justify us.[k]

II. SALVATION

Faith guarantees salvation[a]

Jn 14:27 Ep 3:12 5 So far then we have seen that, through our Lord Jesus Christ, by faith we are 1
judged righteous and at peace[b] with God, •since it is by faith and through 2
3:27+ Jesus that we have entered this state of grace[c] in which we can boast about
3:23+ looking forward to God's glory.[d] •But that is not all we can boast about; we can 3
2 Co 12:9-10 Jm 1:2-4 boast about our sufferings. These sufferings bring patience, as we know, •and 4
1 P 4:13-14 Rv 1:9 patience brings perseverance, and perseverance brings hope, •and this hope is 5
1 Co 13:13+ not deceptive, because the love of God[e] has been poured into our hearts by the
8:14-16 Ga 4:4-6 Holy Spirit which has been given us.[f] •We were still helpless when at his appointed 6
3:26+ 1 P 3:18 moment Christ died for sinful men. •It is not easy to die even for a good man— 7
though of course for someone really worthy, a man might be prepared to die—
8:32 Jn 15:13 but what proves that God loves us is that Christ died for us while we were still 8
1 Jn 4:10,19 sinners. •Having died to make us righteous,[g] is it likely that he would now fail 9
1 Th 1:10 *2 Co 5:18* to save us from God's anger? •When we were reconciled to God by the death of 10
his Son, we were still enemies; now that we have been reconciled, surely we may
count on being saved by the life of his Son? •Not merely because we have been 11
reconciled but because we are filled with joyful trust in God, through our Lord
Jesus Christ, through whom we have already gained our reconciliation.

A. DELIVERANCE FROM SIN AND DEATH AND LAW

Adam and Jesus Christ[h]

Gn 3:1+ Ws 2:24 Well then, sin *entered the world* through one man, and through sin death,[i] and 12
Si 25:24 1 Co 15:21-22 thus death has spread through the whole human race because everyone has
3:23; 6:23 Gn 3:17,19 sinned.[j] •Sin existed in the world long before the Law was given. There was no 13
law and so no one could be accused of the sin of 'law-breaking', •yet death reigned 14
4:15; 7:7+ over all from Adam to Moses, even though their sin, unlike that of Adam, was
not a matter of breaking a law.

Adam prefigured[k] the One to come, •but the gift itself considerably outweighed 15
the fall. If it is certain that through one man's fall so many[l] died, it is even more
certain that divine grace, coming through the one man, Jesus Christ, came to so
many as an abundant free gift. •The results of the gift also outweigh the results of 16
one man's sin: for after one single fall came judgement with a verdict of condemnation, now after many falls comes grace with its verdict of acquittal. •If it is 17
certain that death reigned over everyone as the consequence of one man's fall,
it is even more certain that one man, Jesus Christ, will cause everyone to reign
in life who receives the free gift that he does not deserve, of being made righteous.
Again, as one man's fall brought condemnation on everyone, so the good act of 18
one man brings everyone life and makes them justified. •As by one man's disobed- 19
Is 53:11 ience many were made sinners, so by one man's obedience many will be made

20 righteous.[m] •When law[n] came, it was to multiply the opportunities of falling, 7:7+ Ga 3:19
21 but however great the number of sins committed, grace was even greater; •and 11:32
so, just as sin reigned wherever there was death, so grace will reign to bring 6:23; 7:25
eternal life thanks to the righteousness that comes through Jesus Christ our Lord.

i. Lit. 'Though he considered his own body dead (and that Sarah's womb was dead) it was with unshaken faith'. Text. Rec. and Vulg. 'His faith was not shaken, nor did he give a thought to his own body that was dead already'.

j. Faith is all-powerful, Mk 9:23. It shares in the divine omnipotence itself, cf. 2 Co 12:9-10.

k. 'Justice', or 'righteousness', is in effect the initial sharing in the life of the risen Christ, 6:4; 8:10, etc.; Paul never isolates the death of Jesus from his resurrection.

5 a. The theme of the second section, ch. 5-11: for the Christian who has received justification, cf. ch. 1-4, the love God has for him and the Spirit bestowed on him is a pledge of salvation. After the antithesis of 5:12–7:25 this theme is resumed in ch. 8.

b. Var. 'let us be at peace'.

c. Lit. 'we have access to this grace (i.e. the enjoyment of God's friendship) in which we stand'.

d. Lit. 'about the hope of the glory of God'. For a Christian to hope is to be confident that he will get the eschatological gifts: the resurrection of the body, Rm 8:18-23; 1 Th 4:13f; cf. Ac 2:26; 23:6; 24:15; 26:6-8; 28:20, the rich inheritance of the saints, Ep 1:18; cf. Heb 6:11f; 1 P 1:3f, eternal life, Tt 1:2; cf. 1 Co 15:19, glory, Rm 5:2; 1 Jn 3:2f, in short, salvation, 1 Th 5:8; cf. 1 P 1:3-5, of self and neighbour, 2 Co 1:6f; 1 Th 2:19. Though it means primarily this virtue of expectation, 'hope' is used sometimes for the expected gifts themselves, Ga 5:5; Col 1:5; Tt 2:13; Heb 6:18. Of old, this hope was given to Israel, Ep 1:11-12; cf. Jn 5:45; Rm 4:18, and not to the pagans, Ep 2:12; cf. 1 Th 4:13; but it was a step towards a higher hope, Heb 7:19, offered now to the pagan world also, Ep 1:18; Col 1:27; cf. Mt 12:21; Rm 15:12, through the 'mystery' of Christ, Rm 16:25+. The basis of this hope is God himself, 1 Tm 5:5; 6:17; 1 P 1:21; 3:5, his love, 2 Th 2:16, his invitation, 1 P 1:13-15; cf. Ep 1:18; 4:4, with the power, Rm 4:17-21, truthfulness, Tt 1:2; Heb 6:18, fidelity, Heb 10:23, in implementing the promises declared in the written word, Rm 15:4, and in the gospel message, Col 1:23, promises fulfilled in Christ's person, 1 Tm 1:1; 1 P 1:3,21. The hope is therefore not illusory, Rm 5:5. Since the gifts it expects are in the future, Rm 8:24; Heb 11:1, faith is its prop, Rm 4:18; 5:1f; 15:13; Ga 5:5; Heb 6:11f; 1 P 1:21; charity is its food, Rm 5:5; 1 Co 13:7; hope and faith and charity, the three theological virtues, are closely allied, 1 Co 3:13+. Hope's excelling source is the Holy Spirit, Ga 5:5, greatest of all the eschatological gifts and in part already conferred, Rm 5:5+; Ac 1:8+; this enlightens, Ep 1:17f, and strengthens hope, Rm 15:13, and inspires its prayer, Rm 8:25-27, effecting the unity of the Body, for this hope is common, Ep 4:4. And because hope is built on justification through faith in Christ, Rm 5:1f; cf. Ga 5:5, it is rich in confidence, 2 Co 3:12; Heb 3:6, consolation, 2 Th 2:16; Heb 6:18, joy, Rm 12:12; 15:13; 1 Th 2:19, and is a thing to be proud of, Rm 5:2; 1 Th 2:19; Heb 3:6; the sufferings of this present time cannot dismay it, these cannot compare with the glory to come, Rm 8:18; on the contrary they sustain it, giving it a constancy, Rm 8:25; 12:12; 15:4; 1 Th 1:3; cf. 1 Co 13:7, that tests, Rm 5:4, and fortifies it, 2 Co 1:7.

e. God's love for us; of this the Holy Spirit is a pledge and to this, by his active presence within us, he bears witness: cf. 8:15 and Ga 4:6. Through him we stand before God as sons before their father; the love is mutual. This text therefore, in the light of its parallel passages, asserts that the Christian shares in the life of the Trinity through 'sanctifying grace'.

f. The promised Spirit, Ep 1:13, cf. Ga 3:14; Ac 2:33+, distinctive of the new covenant as contrasted with the old, Rm 2:29; 7:6; 2 Co 3:6; cf. Ga 3:3; 4:29; Ezk 36:27+, is not merely an exhibition of healing or charismatic power, Ac 1:8+; it is also, and especially, an inward principle of new life, a principle that God 'gives', 1 Th 4:8, etc., cf. Lk 11:13; Jn 3:34; 14:16f; Ac 1:5; 2:38 etc.; 1 Jn 3:24, 'sends', Ga 4:6; cf. Lk 24:49; Jn 14:26; 1 P 1:12, 'supplies' Ga 3:5; Ph 1:19, 'pours out', Rm 5:5; Tt 3:5f; cf. Ac 2:33. Received into the Christian by faith, Ga 3:2,14; cf. Jn 7:38f; Ac 11:17, and baptism, 1 Co 6:11; Tt 3:5; cf. Jn 3:5; Ac 2:38; 19:2-6, it dwells within him, Rm 8:9; 1 Co 3:16; 2 Tm 1:14; cf. Jm 4:5, in his spirit, Rm 8:16; cf. Rm 1:9+, and even in his body, 1 Co 6:19. This Spirit, the Spirit of Christ, Rm 8:9; Ph 1:19; Ga 4:6; cf. 2 Co 3:17; Ac 16:7; Jn 14:26; 15:26; 16:7,14; makes the Christian a son of God, Rm 8:14-16; Ga 4:6f, and establishes Christ in his heart, Ep 3:16. For the Christian (as for Christ himself, Rm 1:4+) this Spirit is a principle of resurrection, Rm 8:11+, in virtue of an eschatological gift which even in life signs him as with a seal, 2 Co 1:22; Ep 1:13; 4:30, and which is present within him by way of pledge, 2 Co 1:22; 5:5; Ep 1:14, and of first-fruits, Rm 8:23. It takes the place of the evil principle in man that is 'the flesh', Rm 7:5+, and becomes a principle of faith, 1 Co 12:3; 2 Co 4:13; cf. 1 Jn 4:2f, of supernatural knowledge, 1 Co 2:10-16; 7:40; 12:8f; 14:2f; Ep 1:17; 3:16,18; Col 1:9; cf. Jn 14:26+, of love, Rm 5:5; 15:30; Col 1:8, of sanctification, Rm 15:16; 1 Co 6:11; 2 Th 2:13; cf. 1 P 1:2, of moral conduct, Rm 8:4-9,13; Ga 5:16-25, of apostolic courage, Ph 1:19; 2 Tm 1:7f; cf. Ac 1:8+, of hope, Rm 15:13; Ga 5:5; Ep 4:4, of prayer, Rm 8:26f; cf. Jm 4:3,5; Jude 20. The Spirit must not be quenched, 1 Th 5:19, or grieved, Ep 4:30. It unites men with Christ, 1 Co 6:17, and thus secures the unity of his Body, 1 Co 12:13; Ep 2:16,18; 4:4.

g. Lit. 'Being justified in his blood'.

h. Sin dwells within man, Rm 7:14-24; now death, sin's chastisement, came into the world as a result of Adam's fall, Ws 2:24: from this Paul concludes that sin itself entered into all men through that first fall. We have here the doctrine of original sin. Its interest for Paul lies in the parallel it enables him to draw between the deadly work of the first Adam and the more than sufficient compensation of the 'second Adam', vv. 15-19; 1 Co 15:21f,25. It is as the new head of the human race, the great image in which God remakes his creation, Rm 8:29+; 2 Co 5:17+, that Christ is mankind's saviour.

i. Sin divides man from God. This separation is 'death', death spiritual and eternal; physical death is the symbol of it, cf. Ws 2:24; Heb 6:1+.

j. Meaning disputed. Either by sharing in Adam's sin, ('all have sinned in Adam') or else by their own personal sins, cf. 3:23. In this second interpretation the Greek could be translated 'for this reason that everyone...' a phrase introducing a situation actually occurring which allowed (eternal) death to threaten all mankind. Sin's power which through Adam made its entrance into the world did in fact bring about eternal death by means of personal sin, itself an acquiescence in Adam's rebellion. (Paul is of course speaking of adults.) A further translation is possible 'by reason of which (i.e. of the death-situation brought about by Adam's sin) everyone has sinned'.

k. 'prefigured', cf. 1 Co 10:6+: the likeness, therefore, is not complete—hence the comparison, begun in v. 12 and interrupted by the long parenthesis of vv. 13 and 14, becomes a contrast in v. 15.

l. The word 'many' means all mankind, cf. v. 18; see Mt 20:28+.

m. Not only at the Last Judgement (for Paul regards justification as a present condition, cf. 5:1, etc.) but progressively as each individual becomes reborn in Christ.

n. 'law' without the definite article, i.e. a state of things in which law is the governing factor.

Col 2:12-13 Tt 3:5-7 1 P 3:21-22 *3:8; 6:15*
Baptism

6 Does it follow that we should remain in sin so as to let grace have greater 1
scope? •Of course not. We are dead to sin, so how can we continue to live 2
Ga 3:27 Col 2:12 in it? •You have been taught that when we were baptised in Christ Jesus we were 3
baptised in his death; •in other words,[a] when we were baptised we went into 4
1:4+ the tomb with him and joined him in death,[b] so that as Christ was raised from
Ex 24:16+ the dead by the Father's glory, we too might live a new life.
Ph 3:10-11 If in union with Christ we have imitated his death, we shall also imitate him 5
8:11+ Ep 2:6+ in his resurrection. •We must realise that our former selves have been crucified 6
Col 3:9-10+ Ga 5:24; 6:14 with him to destroy this sinful body and to free us from the slavery of sin. •When 7
Col 3:4-5+ *6:14* a man dies, of course, he has finished with sin.[c]
But[d] we believe that having died with Christ we shall return to life with him: 8
Ac 13:34 1 Co 15:26 Christ, as we know, having been raised from the dead will never die again. Death 9
2 Tm 1:10 Heb 2:14f has no power over him any more. •When he died, he died, once for all, to sin,[e] 10
Rv 1:18 *Heb 7:27+* so his life now is life with God; •and in that way, you too must consider yourselves 11
to be dead to sin but alive for God in Christ Jesus.[f]

Holiness, not sin, to be the master

7:14-24 1 Co 6:15 That is why you must not let sin reign in your mortal bodies[g] or command 12
your obedience to bodily passions, •why you must not let any part of your body 13
turn into an unholy weapon fighting on the side of sin; you should, instead,
offer yourselves to God, and consider yourselves dead men brought back to life;
you should make every part of your body into a weapon fighting on the side of
6:6 God; •and then sin will no longer dominate your life, since you are living by 14
grace and not by law.

The Christian is freed from the slavery of sin[h]

6:1; 14:1 1 Co 6:12; 7:21 Does the fact that we are living by grace and not by law mean that we are 15
free to sin? Of course not. •You know that if you agree to serve and obey a 16
Jn 8:34 2 P 2:19 master you become his slaves. You cannot be slaves of sin that leads to death
and at the same time slaves of obedience that leads to righteousness. •You were 17
1:5+ *16:17* once slaves of sin, but thank God you submitted without reservation to the
Jn 8:36 Ga 5:13 creed you were taught. •You may have been freed from the slavery of sin, but only 18
1 P 2:24 to become 'slaves' of righteousness. •If I may use human terms to help your 19
1 P 1:14-15 natural weakness: as once you put your bodies at the service of vice and immorality, so now you must put them at the service of righteousness for your sanctification.

The reward of sin and the reward of holiness

When you were slaves of sin, you felt no obligation to righteousness, •and 20 21
8:6 Dt 30:15-20 what did you get from this? Nothing but experiences that now make you blush,[i]
Pr 10:16; 12:28 since that sort of behaviour ends in death. •Now, however, you have been set 22
Jn 15:8,16 free from sin, you have been made slaves of God, and you get a reward leading
5:12,21 Gn 2:17 to your sanctification and ending in eternal life. •For the wage paid by sin is 23
Ga 6:7-9 Jm 1:15 death; the present given by God is eternal life in Christ Jesus our Lord.

Ac 15:10-11
The Christian is not bound by the Law[a]

Ga 2:19+ **7** Brothers, those of you who have studied law will know that laws affect 1
1 Co 7:39 a person only during his lifetime.[b] •A married woman, for instance, has legal 2
obligations to her husband while he is alive, but all these obligations come to
an end if the husband dies. •So if she gives herself to another man while her 3
husband is still alive, she is legally an adulteress; but after her husband is dead
her legal obligations come to an end, and she can marry someone else without
6:5-6 becoming an adulteress. •That is why you, my brothers, who through the body 4
of Christ[c] are now dead to the Law, can now give yourselves to another husband,
6:8-11,22 Jn 15:8 to him who rose from the dead to make us productive for God. •Before our 5

conversion[d] our sinful passions, quite unsubdued by the Law, fertilised our 7:7f
6 bodies to make them give birth to death. •But now we are rid of the Law, freed 6:7

6 a. Lit. 'therefore'; var. 'for'.

b. Baptism is not separated from faith but goes with it, Ga 3:26f; Ep 4:5; Heb 10:22; cf. Ac 8:12f,37; 16:31-33; 18:8; 19:2-5, and gives it outward expression by the operative symbolism of the baptismal ceremonial. For this reason Paul ascribes to faith and to baptism the same effects (cf. Ga 2:16-20 and Rm 6:3-9). The sinner is immersed in water (the etymological meaning of 'baptise' is 'dip') and thus 'buried' with Christ, Col 2:12, with whom also he emerges to resurrection, Rm 8:11+, as a 'new creature', 2 Co 5:17+, a 'new man', Ep 2:15+, a member of the one Body animated by the one Spirit, 1 Co 12:13; Ep 4:4f. This resurrection will not be complete or final until the end of time, 1 Co 15:12+ (but cf. Ep 2:6+), but is already taking place in the form of a new life lived 'in the Spirit', vv. 8-11,13; 8:2f; Ga 5:16-24. The death-resurrection symbolism of baptism is particularly Pauline, but this initial rite of the Christian life, Heb 6:2, is also spoken of in the N.T. as a cleansing bath, Ep 5:26; Heb 10:22; cf. 1 Co 6:11; Tt 3:5, a new birth, Jn 3:5; Tt 3:5; cf. 1 P 1:3; 2:2, an enlightenment, Heb 6:4; 10:32; cf. Ep 5:14. On the baptism of water and the baptism of the Spirit, cf. Ac 1:5+: these two aspects of the consecration of the Christian are apparently the 'anointing' and the 'seal' of 2 Co 1:21f. According to 1 P 3:21 the ark of Noah is an antetype of baptism.

c. Possibly in the sense that he no longer has the means to sin, having lost his 'sinful body', v. 6; being no more 'in the flesh', 8:9, he is freed from sin once and for all, cf. 1 P 4:1. Possibly in the sense that in law the death of the accused cancels legal proceedings. Cf. 7:1.

d. Var. 'For'.

e. Christ was sinless, 2 Co 5:21, but having a physical body like our own, Rm 8:3, he belonged to the order of sin; when he became 'spiritual', 1 Co 15:45-46, he belonged only to the divine order. Similarly, though the Christian remains 'in the flesh' for a time, he already lives by the spirit.

f. Text. Rec. and Vulg. 'Christ Jesus our Lord'. Cf. 14:7f; 1 Co 3:23+; 2 Co 5:15; Ga 2:20; 1 P 2:24.

g. Though baptism has destroyed sin in man, as long as his body has not been 'clothed with immortality', 1 Co 15:54, sin can still find a way to reassert itself in a 'mortal' body, i.e. one where concupiscence still has a hold, cf. 7:14f.

h. Christ has freed human beings from evil so as to restore them to God. Paul develops the biblical ideas of 'redemption', 3:24+, and of liberation from death, 7:1+, and in order to bring out their implications makes frequent use of a metaphor that his contemporaries would find impressive: the slave redeemed and set free who can be a slave no longer but must serve his new master freely and faithfully. Christ has paid for our redemption with his life, 1 Co 6:20; 7:23; Ga 3:13; 4:5; and he has made us permanently free, Ga 5:1,13. The Christian must be careful not to let himself be caught again by those who once owned him, Ga 2:4f; 4:9; 5:1, i.e. by sin, Rm 6:18-22; the Law, Rm 6:14; 8:2; Ga 3:13; 4:5; cf. Rm 7:1+, with its ritual observance, Ga 2:4; the principles of the world, Ga 4:3,8, cf. Col 2:20-22; and corruption, Rm 8:21-23. He is a free man, 1 Co 9:1, son of a free mother, i.e. the spiritual Jerusalem, Ga 4:26,31. This liberty is not licence to sin, Ga 5:13; cf. 1 P 2:16; 2 P 2:19. It means serving a new master, God, Rm 6:22; cf. 1 Th 1:9; 1 P 2:16, the Lord Christ, Rm 1:1, etc.; Jm 1:1; 2 P 1:1; Jude 1; Rm 14:18; 16:18, etc., to whom the Christian now belongs, 1 Co 6:19; 3:23, for whom he lives and dies, Rm 7:1+; this obedient service is prompted by faith and leads to righteousness and holiness, Rm 6: 16-19. This is the sort of freedom a son has, Ga 4:7, one who has been one made free by 'the law of the Spirit', Rm 8:2; cf. 7:6; 8:14f; 2Co 3:17 (and cf. Jm 1:25; 2:12), and he must be prepared to surrender it to serve his neighbour in charity, Ga 5:13; cf. 2 Co 4:5, and respect for someone else's scruples require it, 1 Co 10:23-33; Rm 14; cf. 1 Co 6:12-13; 1 Co 9:19. Slavery as a social institution may be tolerated in a society that is, after all, transient, 1 Co 7:20-24,31, it has no real significance in the new order established by Christ, 1 Co 12:13; Ga 3:28; Col 3:11: the Christian slave has been enfranchised by the Lord Christ, and the slave and his master are equally servants of Christ, 1 Co 7:22; cf. Ep 6:5-9; Col 3:22–4:1; Phm 16.

i. Or 'what did you get from actions that now make you blush?'

7 a. Paul now approaches a subject which has been in his mind for some time, 3:20; 4:15; 5:20; 6:14: the emancipation of the Christian from the Law, and this causes him to explain the rôle of the Law as God intended it, cf. 7:7+.

b. Elsewhere Paul refers to the liberation of the Christian either biblically as 'redemption', 3:24+, or, hellenistically, as 'enfranchisement', 6:15+. He also describes it frequently as a deliverance from death, since death frees a man from his past with all its tyrannical demands, 6:7; 7:1-3. The Christian, in union with the dead and risen Christ, 8:11+, and by virtue of faith, 1:16+, and baptism, 6:4+, is now dead to sin, 6:2,11, cf. 1 P 4:1, to the Law, Rm 7:6; Ga 2:19+, to the principles of the world, Col 2:20, and so lives under the new order of grace and the Spirit, Rm 8:5-13. Like an emancipated slave enslaved to a new master, 6:15+, the Christian, risen in Christ, lives no longer for himself but for Christ and for God, 6:11-13; 14:7f; cf. 2 Co 5:15; Ga 2:20.

c. As the Christian is dead to sin, so he is dead to the Law, by virtue of the dead and risen 'body of Christ', cf. 7:1+.

d. Lit. 'While we were in the flesh'. 1. The primary meaning of 'flesh' is the matter of which the body is made, 1 Co 15:39; cf. Lk 24:39; Rv 17:16; 19:18; it is the opposite of spirit, Rm 1:9+; it is the body with its senses, Col 2:1,5, and especially the medium of sexual union, 1 Co 6:16; 7:28; Ep 5:29,31; cf. Mt 19:5p; Jn 1:13; Jude 7, by which people become parents and heirs, Rm 4:1; 9:3,5; 11:14; cf. Heb 12:9. Thus 'flesh', like *basar* in biblical usage, emphasises the weak and perishable side of human beings, Rm 6:19; 2 Co 7:5; 12:7; Ga 4:13f; cf. Mt 26:41p, and their insignificance in comparison with God, Rm 3:20 and Ga 2:16; 1 Co 1:29; cf. Mt 24:22p; Lk 3:6; Jn 17:2; Ac 2:17; 1 P 1:24. This explains the words Paul uses when comparing nature with grace 'according to the flesh', 1 Co 1:26; 2 Co 1:17; Ep 6:5; Col 3:22; cf. Phm 16; Jn 8:15, 'flesh and blood', 1 Co 15:50; Ga 1:16; Ep 6:12; Heb 2:14; cf. Mt 16:17, and 'fleshly', Rm 15:27; 1 Co 3:1,3; 9:11; 2 Co 1:12; 10:4. 2. Since the sending of the Spirit is what gives this eschatological age its character, Paul can use the word 'flesh' to signify the old dispensation as opposed to the new, Rm 9:8; Ga 3:3; 6:12f; Ph 3:3f; Ep 2:11; cf. Heb 9:10,13; Jn 3:6; 6:63; so also the phrase 'according to the flesh', 1 Co 10:18; 2 Co 11:18; Ga 4:23,29; cf. Rm 1:3f; 2 Co 5:16, and 'fleshly', Heb 7:16; but cf. 1 Co 10:3f. 3. For Paul the 'flesh' is especially the sphere in which the passions and sin operate, Rm 7:5,14,18,25; 13:14; 2 Co 7:1; Ga 5:13,19; Ep 2:3; Col 2:13,18,23; cf. 1 P 2:11; 2 P 2:10,18; 1 Jn 2:16; Jude 8,23, condemned to corruption, 1 Co 15:50; Ga 6:8; cf. Jm 5:3; Ac 2:26,31, and to death, Rm 8:6,13; 1 Co 5:5; 2 Co 4:11; cf. 1 P 4:6, so much so that 'flesh' becomes personified as a Power of evil hostile to God, Rm 8:7f, and to the Spirit, Rm 8:4-9,12f; Ga 5:16f. Christ has defeated this Power by assuming 'sinful flesh', Rm 8:3; cf. 1 Tm 3:16; Jn 1:14; 1 Jn 4:2; 2 Jn 7, and putting it to death on the cross, Rm 8:3; Ep 2:14-16; Col 1:22; cf. Heb 5:7f; 10:20; 1 P 3:18; 4:1. Being united with him, Jn 6:51f, Christians are no longer 'in the flesh', Rm 7:5; 8:9, since they have crucified the flesh, Ga 5:24; cf. 1 P 4:1, and cast it off by baptism, Col 2:11; more precisely, they are still 'in the flesh' as long as they remain in this world, Ph 1:22-24; cf. 1 P 4:2, but are not slaves to the flesh any more, 2 Co 10:3; they are its masters through their union with Christ by faith, Ga 2:20, and suffering, Col 1:24.

2:29 Mt 9:16-17 by death from our imprisonment, free to serve in the new spiritual way and not
2 Co 3:6 the old way of a written law.

The function of the Law[e]

3:20; 5:20; 7:5; 8:3 Does it follow that the Law itself is sin? Of course not. What I mean is that 7
Ga 3:10,19 I should not have known what sin was except for the Law. I should not for
Ex 20:17 4:15; 5:13 instance have known what it means to covet if the Law had not said *You shall*
Jm 1:14-15 *not covet*. •But it was this commandment that sin took advantage of to produce 8
1 Co 15:56 all kinds of covetousness in me, for when there is no Law, sin is dead.
Gn 2:17; 3:1f Once, when there was no Law, I[f] was alive; but when the commandment 9
Lv 18:5 Ezk 20:11 came, sin came to life •and I died: the commandment was meant to lead me to 10
life but it turned out to mean death for me, •because sin took advantage of the 11
Gn 3:13 commandment to mislead me, and so sin, through that commandment, killed me.
Dt 4:8 1 Tm 1:8 The Law is sacred, and what it commands is sacred, just and good. •Does 12 13
Jm 1:25 that mean that something good killed me? Of course not. But sin,[g] to show itself
5:20 in its true colours, used that good thing to kill me; and thus sin, thanks to the
commandment, was able to exercise all its sinful power.

The inward struggle[h]

6:12-14 Jb 14:4+ The Law, of course, as we all know, is spiritual; but I am unspiritual; I have 14
Ps 51:5 Ws 9:15 been sold as a slave to sin. •I cannot understand my own behaviour. I fail to carry 15
Ga 5:17 1 P 4:2 out the things I want to do, and I find myself doing the very things I hate. •When 16
I act against my own will, that means I have a self that acknowledges that the
Law is good, •and so the thing behaving in that way is not my self but sin living 17
in me. •The fact is, I know of nothing good living in me—living, that is, in my 18
7:5 unspiritual self—for though the will to do what is good is in me, the performance
is not, •with the result that instead of doing the good things I want to do, I carry 19
Ga 2:20 out the sinful things I do not want. •When I act against my will, then, it is not 20
my true self doing it, but sin which lives in me.[i]
In fact, this seems to be the rule,[j] that every single time I want to do good 21
2 Co 4:16 Ep 3:16 it is something evil that comes to hand. •In my inmost self[k] I dearly love God's 22
Jm 1:14-15; 4:1 Law,[l] but •I can see that my body follows a different law that battles against 23
the law which my reason dictates. This is what makes me a prisoner of that law
of sin which lives inside my body.
8:23 Ws 1:4+ What a wretched man I am! Who will rescue me from this body doomed to 24
5:21; 6:23 death?[m] •Thanks be to God through Jesus Christ our Lord! 25
In short, it is I who with my reason[n] serve the Law of God, and no less I who
serve in my unspiritual self the law of sin.[o]

B. THE CHRISTIAN'S SPIRITUAL LIFE

The life of the spirit

8 The reason, therefore, why those who are in Christ Jesus are not condemned, 1
Ws 1:4+ is that the law of the spirit of life in Christ Jesus has set you[a] free from the 2
7:7+ Ac 13:38-39; law of sin and death.[b] •God has done what the Law, because of our unspiritual 3
15:10-11 *6:10+* nature, was unable to do.[c] God dealt with sin by sending his own Son in a body
Ga 3:13 2 Co 5:21 as physical as any sinful body, and in that body[d] God condemned sin. •He did 4
Heb 2:14-18 *3:31+;* this in order that the Law's just demands[e] might be satisfied in us, who behave
9:30-31+; 10:4 not as our unspiritual nature but as the spirit dictates.
Ga 5:16-23 The unspiritual are interested only in what is unspiritual, but the spiritual 5
6:21 Ga 6:8 are interested in spiritual things. •It is death to limit oneself to what is unspiritual; 6
life and peace can only come with concern for the spiritual. •That is because to 7
limit oneself to what is unspiritual is to be at enmity with God: such a limitation
1 Jn 2:15-16 never could and never does submit to God's law. •People who are interested 8
7:5-6 only in unspiritual things can never be pleasing to God. •Your interests, however, 9

are not in the unspiritual, but in the spiritual, since the Spirit of God has made Ps 51:11 Jn 3:5-6
his home in you. In fact, unless you possessed the Spirit of Christ you would not
10 belong to him. •Though your body may be dead it is because of sin, but if Christ
11 is in you then your spirit is life itself because you have been justified;[f] •and if the
Spirit of him who raised Jesus from the dead is living in you, then he who raised 6:4+ Ezk 37:10
Jesus from the dead will give life to your own mortal bodies through his Spirit *1:4+;* 6:8-11
living in you.[g]

e. In itself the Law is holy and good since it expresses God's will, 7:12-25; 1 Tm 1:8; it is the glorious prerogative of Israel, Rm 9:4; but cf. 2:14f. And yet it seems to have been a failure: in spite of the Law the Jews are sinners like everyone else, Rm 2:21-27; Ga 6:13; Ep 2:3, and obedience to it even makes them so confident, Rm 2:17-20; 3:27; 4:2,4; 9:31f; Ph 3:9; Ep 2:8, that they are shut off by it from the grace of Christ, Ga 6:12; Ph 3:18; cf. Ac 15:1; 18:13; 21:21. In short, the Law is powerless to make any man just, Ga 3:11,21f; Rm 3:20; cf. Heb 7:19. Paul's argument, to which polemic lends a tone of paradox, is that this apparent failure of the Law is due to the nature of the Law itself and to the part it was meant to play in the history of salvation. The Law gives information—it does not give spiritual strength. No law, whether Mosaic or otherwise, not even the primordial command given to Adam, cf. vv. 9-11, can prevent sin, in fact law makes it worse: 1. because though law is not the source of sin it becomes the instrument of sin by arousing concupiscence, Rm 7:7f; 2. because by informing the mind it increases the fault, which becomes a conscious 'transgression', 4:15; 5:13; 3. because the only remedy law can offer is punishment, 4:15, curse, Ga 3:10, condemnation, 2 Co 3:9, death, 2 Co 3:6; hence it can be called 'the law of sin and death', Rm 8:2; cf. 1 Co 15:56; Rm 7:13. Nevertheless God willed this defective system, though as a temporary period of schooling, Ga 3:24, to make people conscious of their sin, Rm 3:19f; 5:20; Ga 3:19, and to teach them to look for justification solely to the grace of God, Ga 3:22; Rm 11:32. Since this state of things is only for a time it has to give way before the fulfilment of the promise made, before the Law, to Abraham and his descendants, Ga 3:6-22; Rm 4. Christ has put an end to the Law, Ep 2:15; cf. Rm 10:4, satisfying its demands by dying a sinner's death, Ga 3:13; Rm 8:3; Col 2:14; but at the same time he 'fulfils', cf. Mt 5:17; 3:15, all that is of positive value in the Law, Rm 3:31; 9:31; 10:4. He emancipates the sons from the guardianship of the tutor, Ga 3:25f. With him they are dead to the Law, Ga 2:19; Rm 7:4-6; cf. Col 2:20, from which he has 'redeemed' them, Ga 3:13, in order to make them sons by adoption, Ga 4:5. Through the promised Spirit he gives to mankind thus renewed, Ep 2:15+, the inward strength to do all the good things prescribed by the Law, Rm 8:4f. This order of grace, superseding that of the old Law, may still be called a law, but it is 'the law of faith', Rm 3:27, 'the law of Christ', Ga 6:2, 'the law of the Spirit', Rm 8:1, and love is its essential precept, Ga 5:14; Rm 13:8f; cf. Jm 2:8.

f. Paul speaks in the person of mankind before the Law was given, cf. 5:13.

g. Sin personified, cf. 5:12, here takes the place of the serpent of Gn 3:1 and the devil of Ws 2:24.

h. Paul now speaks in the person of mankind still under the empire of sin and not yet justified, whereas in ch. 8, he speaks in the name of the justified Christian with the gift of the Spirit who, nevertheless, is conscious of an inward struggle while on earth, Ga 5:17f.

i. Paul is not denying man's personal responsibility for the evil he does, any more than for the good in Ga 2:20.

j. Lit. 'law', in the sense of regular experience.

k. This 'inmost self' is man's rational nature as opposed to the 'outer self', 2 Co 4:16a, which is man's perishable body. This distinction which has its origin in Greek thought is not the same as that between the 'old' and the 'new' self, Col 3:9-10+, which derives from Jewish eschatology. There are texts, however, where Paul speaks of the 'inmost self' in the Christian sense of the 'new self', 2 Co 4:16b; Ep 3:16.

l. Var. 'reason's law' as in v. 23.

m. Lit. 'from the body of this death'. Paul is concerned with the body and its component members, Rm 12:4; 1 Co 12:12,14f, that is to say with the human being as he actually is, a sentient creature, 1 Co 5:3; 2 Co 10:10, with a sexual life, Rm 4:19; 1 Co 6:16; 7:4; Ep 5:28, because it is in the body that man lives morally and religiously. The body, though tyrannised by the 'flesh', Rm 7:5+, by sin, 1:24; 6:12f; 7:23; 8:13; 1 Co 6:18, by death, Rm 6:12; 8:10, and therefore a 'body of flesh', Col 2:11; cf. 1:22, a 'body of sin', Rm 6:6, and a 'body of death', 7:24, is not however doomed to perish, as Greek philosophy would have it, but, in accordance with the biblical tradition, Ezk 37:10+; 2 M 7:9+, destined to live, Rm 8:13; 2 Co 4:10, through resurrection, Rm 8:11+. The principle of this renewal is the Spirit, 5:5+, which takes the place of the *psyche*, 1 Co 15:44+, and transforms the body of the Christian into the likeness of the risen body of Christ, Ph 3:21. Until this ultimate deliverance takes place, Rm 8:23, the body of the Christian, provisionally delivered from the 'flesh' by its union with Christ's death, 6:6; 8:3f, is even now the home of the Holy Spirit, 1 Co 6:19, who produces in it a new life of righteousness and holiness, Rm 6:13,19; 12:1; 1 Co 7:34, which is meritorious, 2 Co 5:10, and gives glory to God, 1 Co 6:20; Ph 1:20.

n. The *nous*, human reason or mind, is a Greek idea very different from the *pneuma* or supernatural Spirit, 5:5+, and even from the spirit in the biblical sense of man's higher self, 1:9+. It is the principle of understanding, 1 Co 14:14,15,19; Ph 4:7; 2 Th 2:2; cf. Lk 24:45; Rv 13:18; 17:9, and of moral judgement, Rm 14:5; 1 Co 1:10. Usually it is reliable, Rm 7:23,25, but is at times perverted, 1:28; Ep 4:17; 1 Tm 6:5; 2 Tm 3:8; Tt 1:15, by the 'flesh', Col 2:18; cf. Rm 7:5+, and has to be renewed, Rm 12:2, within man's own spirit by the Spirit of God, Ep 4:23f; cf. Col 3:10.

o. This sentence, which would come more naturally before v. 24, seems to have been added—perhaps by Paul himself.

8 a. Var. 'me', 'us'.

b. Paul contrasts the order of sin and death with the new order of the Spirit. The word 'spirit' here means either the Holy Spirit in person (as it does more clearly in v. 9) or the spirit of man made new by his presence, cf. 5:5+; 1:9+.

c. The Mosaic Law, imposed from without, could not be an inward principle of salvation, 7:7+. Christ alone, who by his death destroyed our unspiritual nature (lit. 'flesh') in his own person, could destroy sin whose domain the 'flesh' was. Man formerly carnal is now, through union with Christ, spiritual.

d. Lit. 'in the likeness of sinful flesh, and in that flesh...'

e. I.e. the Law's demand for exact punishment of sin.

f. Because of sin, 5:12+, the body is doomed to physical death and is the instrument of spiritual death also; but the Spirit is life, a power of resurrection; see following note.

g. The resurrection of the Christian is intimately dependent on that of Christ, 1 Th 4:14; 1 Co 6:14; 15:20f; 2 Co 4:14; 13:4; Rm 6:5; Ep 2:6; Col 1:18; 2:12f; 2 Tm 2:11. It is by the same power and the same gift of the Spirit, cf. Rm 1:4+, that the Father will raise them to life in their turn. This operation is already being prepared: a new life is making the Christians into sons (v. 14) in the likeness of the Son himself, 8:29+, and they are being incorporated into the risen Christ by faith, 1:16+, and baptism, 6:4+.

So then, my brothers, there is no necessity for us to obey our unspiritual 12
Gn 6:3 Ga 6:8 selves or to live unspiritual lives. •If you do live in that way, you are doomed to 13
Ep 4:22-24 die; but if by the Spirit you put an end to the misdeeds of the body you will live.

Ga 4:4-7 **Children of God**

Ga 5:18 Everyone moved[h] by the Spirit is a son of God. •The spirit you received 14 15
Jn 1:12; 15:15 is not the spirit of slaves bringing fear into your lives again; it is the spirit of
5:5+ 1 Jn 4:18 sons, and it makes us cry out, 'Abba, Father!'[i] •The Spirit himself and our spirit 16
Ga 3:16. 26-29 bear united witness[j] that we are children of God. •And if we are children we 17
Lk 22:28-30; 24:26 are heirs as well: heirs of God and coheirs with Christ, sharing his sufferings
Ph 3:10-11 1 P 4:13 so as to share his glory.

Rv 21:7 **Glory as our destiny**

5:2-5 2 Co 4:17 I think that what we suffer in this life can never be compared to the glory, 18
Col 3:3-4 1 Jn 3:2 as yet unrevealed, which is waiting for us. •The whole creation is eagerly 19
Gn 3:17; 6:20+ waiting for God to reveal his sons.[k] •It was not for any fault on the part of 20
Ho 4:3+ creation that it was made unable to attain its purpose, it was made so by God;[l]
2 P 3:12-13 but creation still retains the hope •of being freed, like us, from its slavery to 21
Rv 21:1 decadence, to enjoy the same freedom and glory as the children of God. •From 22
the beginning till now the entire creation, as we know, has been groaning in
2 Co 5:2-5 one great act of giving birth; •and not only creation, but all of us who possess 23
Ph 3:20 the first-fruits of the Spirit, we too groan inwardly as we wait for[m] our bodies
3:24+; 5:2+; to be set free. •For we must be content to hope that we shall be saved[n]—our 24
7:24+ *2 Co 5:7* salvation is not in sight, we should not have to be hoping for it if it were—•but, 25
Heb 11:1 as I say, we must hope to be saved since we are not saved yet—it is something
we must wait for with patience.

5:5+; 8:15 Ga 4:6 The Spirit too comes to help us in our weakness. For when we cannot choose 26
Jm 4:3,5 words in order to pray properly, the Spirit himself expresses our plea in a way
Jr 11:20+ that could never be put into words, •and God who knows everything in our 27
hearts knows perfectly well what he means, and that the pleas of the saints
expressed by the Spirit are according to the mind of God.[o]

Ep 1:4-14 **God has called us to share his glory**

Gn 50:20 Jm 1:12 We know that by turning everything to their good God co-operates with all 28
Ac 13:48+ those who love him, with all those that he has called according to his purpose.[p]
Jr 1:5 1 Co 15:49 They are the ones he chose specially long ago and intended to become true 29
Ph 3:21 *Col 1:18* images of his Son,[q] so that his Son might be the eldest of many brothers. •He 30
called those he intended for this; those he called he justified, and with those he
justified he shared his glory.[r]

1 Co 13:1+ **A hymn to God's love**

After saying this, what can we add? With God on our side who can be against 31
5:6-11 Gn 22:12,16 us? •Since God did not spare his own Son, but gave him up to benefit us all, 32
Jn 3:16 2 Co 5:14-21 we may be certain, after such a gift, that he will not refuse anything he can give.
1 Jn 4:10 *Is 50:8* Could anyone accuse those that God has chosen? When God acquits, •could 33 34
Ac 2:23 anyone condemn? Could Christ Jesus? No! He not only died for us—he rose
Heb 7:25 from the dead, and there at God's right hand he stands and pleads for us.

Nothing therefore can come between us and the love of Christ, even if we are 35
troubled or worried, or being persecuted, or lacking food or clothes, or being
Ps 44:11 1 Th 3:4 threatened or even attacked. •As scripture promised: *For your sake we are being* 36
2 Tm 3:12 *massacred daily, and reckoned as sheep for the slaughter.* •These are the trials 37
Jn 16:33 through which we triumph, by the power of him who loved us.

For I am certain of this: neither death nor life, no angel, no prince, nothing 38
that exists, nothing still to come, not any power, •or height or depth,[s] nor any 39
created thing, can ever come between us and the love of God made visible in
Christ Jesus our Lord.

C. THE PLACE OF ISRAEL[a]

The privileges of Israel

9 What I want to say now is no pretence; I say it in union with Christ—it is 2 Co 11:29
the truth—my conscience in union with the Holy Spirit assures me of it too.
What I want to say is this: my sorrow is so great, my mental anguish so endless, 2 Co 12:7+
I would willingly be condemned[b] and be cut off from Christ if it could help my Ex 32:32 Ga 1:9
brothers of Israel,[c] my own flesh and blood. •They were adopted as sons, they *Ep 2:12* 1 Th 2:8
were given the glory and the covenants; the Law and the ritual were drawn up *3:1-2*
for them, and the promises were made to them. •They are descended from the
patriarchs and from their flesh and blood came Christ who is above all, God for 1:3 1 Co 15:28
ever blessed![d] Amen. 2 Co 5:16 1 P 4:11

h. 'led' seems inadequate: the Holy Spirit is much more than one who inwardly admonishes, he is the principle of a life truly divine, cf. Ga 2:20.

i. The prayer of Christ in Gethsemane, Mk 14:36.

j. Or (Vulg.)' The Spirit bears witness to our spirit'.

k. Lit. 'waiting for the revelation of the sons of God'. The material world, created for man, shares his destiny. It was cursed for man's sin, Gn 3:17, and is therefore now deformed: impotent and decadent, vv. 19-22. But like man's body, destined to be glorified, it too is to be redeemed, vv. 21,23; it will share the glorious liberty of the children of God, v. 21. For the Greek philosopher matter was evil and the spirit must be delivered from it; Christianity regards matter as itself enslaved and to be set free. In other texts also salvation is extended to creatures (especially angels) other than man, cf. Col 1:20; Ep 1:10; 2 P 3:13; Rv 21:1-5.

l. Lit. 'Creation was subjected to futility; this was not its own fault but the work of him who so subjected it'—i.e. of God who punished man's sin in this way, or of man whose sin was responsible.

m. Add. 'adoptive sonship (and)' which would here have an eschatological sense, but see v. 15.

n. Lit. 'It is through hope that we are saved'. The salvation is eschatological, cf. 5:1-11.

o. Paul insists on the necessity of constant prayer (Rm 12:12; Ep 6:18; Ph 4:6; Col 4:2; 1 Th 5:17; 1 Tm 2:8; 5:5; cf. 1 Co 7:5) taught by Jesus himself (Mt 6:5+; 14:23+) and practised by the early Christians (Ac 2:42+). Paul is always praying for the faithful (Ep 1:16; Ph 1:4; Col 1:3,9; 1 Th 1:2; 3:10; 2 Th 1:11; Phm 4) and asks them to do the same for him (Rm 15:30; 2 Co 1:11; Ep 6:19; Ph 1:19; Col 4:3; 1 Th 5:25; 2 Th 3:1; Phm 22; Heb 13:18), and for each other (2 Co 9:14, Ep 6:18; on prayer for sinners and the sick, cf. 1 Jn 5:16; Jm 5:13-16). These prayers must ask for growth in holiness but also for the removal of all external (1 Th 2:18 and 3:10; Rm 1:10) and internal (2 Co 12:8-9) obstacles to it; we have to pray, too, for the orderly conduct of the country's business (1 Tm 2:1-2). Paul lays special stress on prayers of thanksgiving (Ep 5:4; Ph 4:6; Col 2:7; 4:2; 1 Th 5:18; 1 Tm 2:1) for every gift of God (Ep 5:20; Col 3:17) and particularly for the food God gives us (Rm 14:6; 1 Co 10:31; 1 Tm 4:3-5); he begins all his own letters with a prayer of thanks (Rm 1:8, etc.) and he wants the spirit of gratitude to pervade all the Christians' dealings with each other (1 Co 14:17; 2 Co 1:11; 4:15; 9:11-12). In liturgical gatherings prayers of thanksgiving and praise must predominate (1 Co 11-14) and these sentiments must inspire the hymns that the Christians compose for these occasions (Ep 5:19; Col 3:16). It is the Holy Spirit who inspires the prayer of the Christian, and Paul prefers to emphasise this rather than repeat the traditional Wisdom themes, namely the necessary conditions for prayer and its efficaciousness (cf. Jm 1:5-8; 4:2-3; 5:16-18; 1 Jn 3:22; 5:14-16) which Paul guarantees by the presence of the Spirit of Christ within the Christian, enabling him to pray as a son to his father (Rm 8:15,26-27; Ga 4:6; cf. 6:18; Jude 20), while Christ himself intercedes at the right hand of God (Rm 8:34; cf. Heb 7:25; 1 Jn 2:1). The Father's response is therefore most generous (Ep 3:10). Hence Christians are called 'those who invoke the name of Jesus Christ' (1 Co 1:2; cf. Rm 10:9-13; 2 Tm 2:22; Jm 2:7; Ac 9:14,21; 22:16). On the attitude to be adopted when praying cf. 1 Co 11:14-16; 1 Tm 2:8.

p. Var. (Vulg.) 'We know that for those who love God everything conspires for good, for all those that he has called...'

q. Christ, the image of God in the primordial creation, Col 1:15+, cf. Heb 1:3, has now come, by a new creation, 2 Co 5:17+, to restore to fallen man the splendour of that image which has been darkened by sin, Gn 1:26+; 3:22-24+; Rm 5:12+. He does this by forming man in the still more splendid image of a son of God (Rm 8:29); thus, sound moral judgement is restored to the 'new man', Col 3:10+, and also his claim to glory which he had sacrificed by sin, Rm 3:23+ This glory which Christ as the image of God possesses by right, 2 Co 4:4, is progressively communicated to the Christian, 2 Co 3:18, until his body is itself clothed in the image of the 'heavenly' man, 1 Co 15:49.

r. Everything has been directed by God to the glory of his elect: it was for this they were called to the faith and justified by baptism; with this, it can be said by anticipation, they are already clothed.

s. The 'powers' 'heights' and 'depths' are probably the mysterious cosmic forces which to the mind of antiquity were in general hostile to mankind. Cf. Ep 1:21; 3:18.

9 a. Paul's theme of justification by faith led him to speak of the righteousness of Abraham, ch. 4. Similarly here the theme of salvation lovingly bestowed by God through the Spirit makes it necessary for him to speak about Israel's case, ch. 9-11, a people which remains unbelieving though it has received the promise of salvation. The subject of these chapters, therefore, is not the problem of individual predestination to glory, or even to faith, but of Israel's part in the development of salvation history, the only problem raised by the statements in the O.T.

b. Lit. *anathema*, a thing accursed, under a ban, cf. Jos 6:17+ and Lv 27:28+.

c. Actual descendants of Jacob (called 'Israel', Gn 32:29). All the other privileges derive from this: adoptive sonship, Ex 4:22; cf. Dt 7:6+; the glory of God, Ex 24:16+, who dwells with his people, Ex 25:8+; Dt 4:7+; cf. Jn 1:14+; the covenant with Abraham, Gn 15:1+; 15:17+; 17:1+, with Jacob-Israel, Gn 32:29, with Moses, Ex 24:7-8; the worship of the one true God; the Law which embodies his will; the messianic promises, 2 S 7:1+, and physical relationship with Christ.

d. Both the context and the internal development of the sentence imply that this doxology is addressed to Christ. Paul rarely gives Jesus the title 'God', though cf. Tt 2:13, or addresses a doxology to him, cf. Heb 13:21, but this is because he usually keeps this title for the Father, cf. Rm 15:6, etc., and considers the divine persons not so much with an abstract

3:3+ **God has kept his promise**

Nb 23:19 Is 55:10-11 Does this mean that God has failed to keep his promise? Of course not. 6
2:28-29 Mt 3:9p Not all those who descend from Israel are Israel; •not all the descendants of 7
Gn 21:12 Abraham are his true children. Remember: *It is through Isaac that your name will*
be carried on, •which means that it is not physical descent that decides who are 8
Jn 8:31-44 the children of God; it is only the children of the promise who will count as the
Gn 18:10 true descendants. •The actual words in which the promise was made were: *I shall* 9
visit you at such and such a time, *and Sarah will have a son.* •Even more to the 10
point is what was said to Rebecca when she was pregnant by our ancestor Isaac,
but before her twin children were born and before either had done good or evil. 11
11:5-6 In order to stress that God's choice is free, •since it depends on the one who 12
Gn 25:23 calls, not on human merit, Rebecca was told: *the elder shall serve the younger,*
Ml 1:2-3 or as scripture says elsewhere: *I showed my love for Jacob and my hatred for Esau.* 13

3:5 **God is not unjust**

Dt 32:4 Does it follow that God is unjust? Of course not. •Take what God said to 14 15
Ex 33:19 Moses: *I have mercy on whom I will, and I show pity to whom I please.* •In other 16
Ps 147:10f words, the only thing that counts is not what human beings want or try to do,
Ex 9:16 but the mercy of God. •For in scripture he says to Pharaoh: *It was for this I raised* 17
you up,[e] *to use you as a means of showing my power and to make my name known*
throughout the world. •In other words, when God wants to show mercy he does, 18
and when he wants to harden someone's heart he does so.
3:7 Ws 12:12 You will ask me, 'In that case, how can God ever blame anyone, since no one 19
Mt 20:15 can oppose his will?'[f] •But what right have you, a human being, to cross-examine 20
Is 29:16 God? *The pot has no right to say to the potter: Why did you make me this shape?*
Is 29:16+ Jr 18:6 Surely a potter can do what he likes with the clay? It is surely for him to decide 21
Ws 15:7 Is 45:9; 64:7 whether he will use a particular lump of clay to make a special pot or an ordinary
one?
Or else imagine[g] that although God is ready to show his anger and display 22
2:4; 3:25-26 Pr 16:4 his power, yet he patiently puts up with the people who make him angry,
Ws 12:20-21 however much they deserve to be destroyed. •He puts up with them for the sake 23
of those other people, to whom he wants to be merciful, to whom he wants to
8:29 Ep 2:1-7 reveal[h] the richness of his glory, people he had prepared for this glory long ago.
[i]Well, we are those people; whether we were Jews or pagans we are the ones he 24
has called.[j]

All has been foretold in the Old Testament

Ho 2:25 1 P 2:10 That is exactly what God says in Hosea: *I shall say to a people that was not* 25
Ho 2:1 *mine, 'You are my people', and to a nation I never loved, 'I love you'.* •*Instead of* 26
being told, 'You are no people of mine', they will now be called the sons of the living
Is 10:22-23 Ho 2:1 *God.*[k] •Referring to Israel Isaiah had this to say:[l] *Though Israel should have as* 27
11:5 *many descendants as there are grains of sand on the seashore, only a remnant will*
be saved, •*for without hesitation or delay the Lord will execute his sentence on the* 28
Is 1:9 *earth.*[m] •As Isaiah foretold: *Had the Lord of hosts not left us some descendants we* 29
should now be like Sodom, we should be like Gomorrah.
8:4; 10:4, 20; 11:7 From this it follows[n] that the pagans who were not looking for righteousness 30
found it all the same, a righteousness that comes of faith, •while Israel, looking 31
for a righteousness derived from law failed to do what that law required.[o] •Why 32
did they fail? Because they relied on good deeds instead of trusting in faith. In
Is 8:14 other words, they *stumbled over the stumbling-stone* •mentioned in scripture: 33
Is 28:16 1 P 2:6-8 *See how I lay in Zion a stone to stumble over, a rock to trip men up—only those*
10:11 *who believe in him will have no cause for shame.*

Israel fails to see that it is God who makes us holy

10 Brothers, I have the very warmest love for the Jews, and I pray to God for 1
them to be saved. •I can swear to their fervour for God, but their zeal is 2

3 misguided.[a] •Failing to recognise the righteousness that comes from God, they Mt 5:20 Ph 3:9
try to promote their own idea of it, instead of submitting to the righteousness of
4 God.[b] •But now the Law has come to an end with Christ, and everyone who has 8:4; 9:30, 31+ Mt 5:17
faith may be justified. Ac 24:14 2 Co 3:14 Ga 3:24

The testimony of Moses *3:21; 4*

5 When Moses refers to being justified by the Law, he writes: *those who keep* *Lv 18:5* Ga 3:12+
6 *the Law will draw life from it.* •But the righteousness that comes from faith says
this:[c] Do not tell yourself you have to bring Christ down—as in the text: *Who* Dt 9:4; 30:12f
7 *will go up to heaven?* •or that you have to bring Christ back from the dead—as
8 in the text: *Who will go down to the underworld?*[d] •On the positive side it says: Ps 107:26 1 P 3:19+
The word, that is the faith we proclaim, *is very near to you, it is on your lips and* *Dt 30:14* Si 51:26
9 *in your heart.* •If your lips confess that Jesus is Lord and if you believe in your *Ac 2:36+* 1 Co 12:3
10 heart that God raised him from the dead,[e] then you will be saved. •By believing 1:4
from the heart you are made righteous; by confessing with your lips you are
11 saved. •When scripture says: *those who believe in him will have no cause for shame,* Is 28:16
12 it makes no distinction between Jew and Greek: all belong to the same Lord who 1:16; 32-33; 9:33
13 is rich enough, however many ask his help, •*for everyone who calls on the name* Jl 3:5
of the Lord will be saved. Ac 2:21+

appreciation of their nature as with a concrete appreciation of their functions in the process of salvation. Moreover, he has always in mind the historical Christ in his concrete reality as God made man, cf. Ph 2:5+; Col 1:15+. For this reason he presents Christ as subordinated to the Father, 1 Co 3:23; 11:3, not only in the work of creation, 1 Co 8:6, but also in that of eschatological renewal, 1 Co 15:27f; cf. Rm 16:27, etc. Nevertheless, the title 'Lord', *Kyrios*, received by Christ at his resurrection, Ph 2:9-11; cf. Ep 1:20-22; Heb 1:3f, is the title given by the LXX to Yahweh in the O.T., Rm 10:9,13; 1 Co 2:16. For Paul Jesus is essentially 'the Son of God', Rm 1:3-4,9; 5:10; 8:29; 1 Co 1:9; 15:28; 2 Co 1:19; Ga 1:16; 2:20; 4:4,6; Ep 4:13; 1 Th 1:10; cf. Heb 4:14, etc., his 'own Son', Rm 8:3,32, 'the Son of his love', Col 1:13, who belongs to the sphere of the divine by right, the sphere from which he came, 1 Co 15:47, being sent by God, Rm 8:3; Ga 4:4. The title 'Son of God' became his in a new way with the resurrection, Rm 1:4+; cf. Heb 1:5; 5:5, but it was not then that he received it since he pre-existed not only as prefigured in the O.T., 1 Co 10:4, but ontologically, Ph 2:6; cf. 2 Co 8:9. He is the Wisdom, 1 Co 1:24,30, and the Image, 2 Co 4:4, by which and in which all things were created, Col 1:15-17; cf. Heb 1:3; 1 Co 8:6, and have been re-created, Rm 8:29; cf. Col 3:10; 1:18-20, because into his own person is gathered the fullness of the godhead and of the universe, Col 2:9+. In him God has devised the whole plan of salvation, Ep 1:3f, and he, no less than the Father, is its accomplishment (cf. Rm 11:36; 1 Co 8:6 and Col 1:16,20). The Father raises to life and judges, so does the Son raise to life (cf. Rm 1:4+; 8:11+ and Ph 3:21) and judge (cf. Rm 2:16 and 1 Co 4:5; Rm 14:10 and 2 Co 5:10). In short, he is one of the three persons enumerated in the trinitarian formulae, 2 Co 13:13+.

e. Like the O.T. writers Paul attributes to God as their ultimate cause (stressing the phrase of Ex: I raised you up) the good and bad actions of men, cf. 1:24f.

f. If man's perversity thus becomes part of God's design, how can man be accused of not doing the will of God? Paul replies, as before in a similar case (3:7; 6:1,15), by disallowing the objection. God being the absolute master of what he has made, the question of injustice cannot arise. Cf. Mt 20:15.

g. Lit. 'But if', an obscure phrase here, to be interpreted by the context. Paul is explaining how the hardening of Pharaoh's heart then, and the unbelief of Israel now, are not acts of injustice if regarded as elements in the plan of God. God could destroy the Jewish people, as he could have destroyed Pharaoh, but he patiently tolerates them: thus (while allowing time to repent, 2:4) he 'shows his anger' (by permitting sins to multiply, cf. ch. 1-3, though even this paves the way to conversion); he 'displays his power' by brushing such obstacles aside, v. 17, as the present antagonism of the Jews towards the gospel; but above all he carries out his merciful plan for the pagans, cf. 11:11-12, to whom the gospel is preached once the Jews have rejected it, cf. Ac 13:5+.

h. Lit. 'in order to (reveal)'; var. 'and (revealed)'.

i. In the Greek, vv. 22-24 are a long conditional clause without an apodosis. Supply 'how, if this supposition is correct, could we speak of injustice in God?' In the long run, everything is directed to the salvation of both pagans and Jews, cf. 11:32.

j. Lit. '(namely) to us whom he has called not only from the Jews but from the pagans'.

k. The story of an Israel welcomed back by God despite its unfaithfulness thus becomes the antetype of the invitation to the pagans, who had no claim, to the messianic feast.

l. The texts cited here proclaim both the infidelity of Israel and the return of a 'remnant', cf. Is 4:3+, in which the promises are safeguarded. They are thus a preparation for ch. 11.

m. One var. (Vulg.) makes the quotation follow the LXX text, which Paul abbreviates.

n. Lit. 'Then what shall we say?' This conclusion introduces the argument of the following chapter where the cause of Israel's infidelity is examined not now as in God but as in Israel itself.

o. Only the Christian can do this, 3:31; 8:4; 10:4; cf. 7:7+; Ac 13:39. 'that law': var. (Vulg.) 'that law of righteousness'.

10 a. Like that of Paul before his conversion, Ac 22:3; Ga 1:14; Ph 3:6; cf. 1 Tm 1:13.

b. Righteousness is not something to be won: it is a favour man receives through faith in Christ, cf. 1:16+; 7:7+.

c. The argument is odd at first reading, because the passage of Dt is certainly a eulogy of the righteousness of the Law. But Paul sees in this text, which sums up the whole Law in the precept of love and the 'circumcision of the heart', Dt 30:6,16,20, a presentiment of the new law. The 'word of faith', uttered and made effective by the Spirit of Christ, 8:2,14, is deeper in the heart and sweeter in the mouth than the 'word of the Law' could be.

d. Lit. 'the depths'—of the sea in Dt 30:13, of Sheol in Paul's applied sense. In connection with this text, the Targum had already spoken of the descent of Moses from Sinai and the ascent of Jonah from the depths of the sea.

e. Profession of faith, such as is made at baptism, is the outward expression of the inward commitment of the 'heart'.

Israel has no excuse

Heb 11:6 But they will not ask his help unless they believe in him,[f] and they will not 14
Ac 8:31 believe in him unless they have heard of him, and they will not hear of him unless
they get a preacher, •and they will never have a preacher unless one is sent, but 15
Is 52:7 as scripture says: *The footsteps of those who bring good news is a welcome sound.*[g]
1:5+ Is 53:1 Not everyone, of course, listens to the Good News. As Isaiah says: *Lord, how many* 16
believed what we proclaimed? •So faith comes from what is preached, and what is 17
preached comes from the word of Christ.[h]
Mt 24:14+ Let me put the question: is it possible that they did not hear? Indeed they 18
Ps 19:4 did; in the words of the psalm, *their voice*[i] *has gone out through all the earth, and*
their message to the ends of the world. •A second question: is it possible that Israel 19
11:1,12 Dt 32:21 did not understand? Moses answered this long ago: *I will make you jealous of*
people who are not even a nation; I will make you angry with an irreligious people.[j]
Is 65:1 Isaiah said more clearly: *I have been found by those who did not seek me, and have* 20
9:30 *revealed myself to those who did not consult me;* •and referring to Israel he goes 21
Is 65:2 on: *Each day I stretched out my hand to a disobedient and rebellious people.*[k]

The remnant of Israel

10:19 Ps 94:14 2 Co 11:21+ 11 Let me put a further question then:[a] is it possible that *God has rejected his* 1
people? Of course not. I, an Israelite, descended from Abraham through
the tribe of Benjamin, •could never agree that God had rejected his people, the 2
people he chose specially long ago. Do you remember what scripture says of
1 K 19:10,14 Elijah—how he complained to God about Israel's behaviour? •*Lord, they have* 3
killed your prophets and broken down your altars. I, and I only, remain, and they
1 K 19:18 *want to kill me.* •What did God say to that? *I have kept for myself seven* 4
thousand men who have not bent the knee to Baal. •Today the same thing 5
Is 4:3+ 9:12-17 has happened: there is a remnant, chosen by grace. •By grace, you notice, nothing 6
therefore to do with good deeds, or grace would not be grace at all!
9:30-31 2 Co 3:15 What follows? It was not Israel as a whole that found what it was seeking, 7
but only the chosen few. The rest were not allowed to see the truth; •as scripture 8
Dt 29:3 Is 29:10 says: *God has given them a sluggish spirit, unseeing eyes and inattentive ears, and*
Mt 13:13+ Ps 69:22f *they are still like that today.* •And David says: *May their own table*[b] *prove a trap* 9
for them, a snare and a pitfall—let that be their punishment; •*may their eyes be* 10
struck incurably blind, their backs bend for ever.

The Jews to be restored in the future

11:25,30 Mt 21:43 Ac 13:5+ Let me put another question then: have the Jews fallen for ever, or have they 11
just stumbled?[c] Obviously they have not fallen for ever: their fall, though, has
10:19 Mt 8:11f; 21:43 saved the pagans[d] in a way the Jews may now well emulate. •Think of the extent 12
to which the world, the pagan world, has benefited from their fall and defection—
then think how much more it will benefit from the conversion of them all. •Let 13
me tell you pagans[e] this: I have been sent to the pagans as their apostle, and I am
proud of being sent, •but the purpose of it is to make my own people envious 14
of you, and in this way save some of them. •Since their rejection meant the 15
reconciliation of the world, do you know what their admission will mean? Nothing
less than a resurrection from the dead![f]

The Jews are still the chosen people

A whole batch of bread is made holy if the first handful of dough is made 16
15:27 holy;[g] all the branches are holy if the root is holy. •No doubt some of the branches 17
Ep 2:11-22 have been cut off, and, like shoots of wild olive, you[h] have been grafted among[i]
the rest to share with them[j] the rich sap provided by the olive tree itself, •but still, 18
5:2+; 3:27+ 1 Co 1:31 even if you think yourself superior to the other branches, remember that you do
not support the root; it is the root that supports you. •You will say, 'Those 19
branches were cut off on purpose to let me be grafted in!' True, •they were cut off, 20
but through their unbelief; if you still hold firm, it is only thanks to your faith.

Rather than making you proud, that should make you afraid. •God did not Jr 49:12 Lk 23:31
spare the natural branches, and he is not likely to spare you.[k] •Do not forget
that God can be severe as well as kind: he is severe to those who fell, and he is
kind to you, but only for as long as he chooses to be, otherwise you will find
yourself cut off too, •and the Jews, if they give up their unbelief, grafted back in
your place. God is perfectly able to graft them back again; •after all, if you were
cut from your natural wild olive to be grafted unnaturally on to a cultivated olive,
it will be much easier for them, the natural branches, to be grafted back on the
tree they came from.

The conversion of the Jews

There is a hidden reason for all this, brothers, of which I do not want you 16:25+
to be ignorant, in case you think you know more than you do. One section of
Israel has become blind, but this will last only until the whole pagan world has 11:11+
entered,[l] •and then after this the rest of Israel will be saved as well. As scripture
says:[m] *The liberator will come from Zion, he will banish godlessness from Jacob.* Is 59:20-21
And this is the covenant I will make with them when I take their sins away. Is 27:9

The Jews are enemies of God only with regard to the Good News, and
enemies only for your sake; but as the chosen people, they are still loved by God, 9:6
loved for the sake of their ancestors. •God never takes back his gifts or revokes Nb 23:19 1 S 15:29
his choice. Is 54:10

Just as you changed from being disobedient to God, and now enjoy mercy
because of their disobedience, •so those who are disobedient now—and only 11:11
because of the mercy shown to you—will also enjoy mercy eventually. •God has Ezk 18:23 Ga 3:22
imprisoned all men in their own disobedience only to show mercy to all mankind. *3:9; 5:20*

A hymn to God's mercy and wisdom

How rich are the depths of God—how deep his wisdom and knowledge— Jdt 8:14 Jb 11:6
and how impossible to penetrate his motives or understand his methods! Ps 139:6, 17-18
Who could ever know the mind of the Lord? Who could ever be his counsellor? • *Who* *Is 40:13* 1 Co 2:11

f. The argument, supported by scripture, is clear: if Israel as a people refuses to invoke the name of the Lord, it is because she has been blind to the light that was offered.

g. Lit. 'How beautiful the feet of those who bring good news!'

h. Var. 'word of God'.

i. Of those who preach the gospel.

j. This allusion to Israel's jealousy prepares the way for 11:11,14.

k. In the Hebr. both texts (vv. 20 and 21) refer to the Jewish people, but in the first of these the prophet speaks of Israel 'not invoking the name of Yahweh' and therefore no better than the pagans. Paul's application of v. 20 to the pagans *(ethne)* is the more easily made in that the Greek version uses *ethnos* ('nation') in Is 65:1, and not *laos* (i.e. Israel, the 'people' of God) as in Is 65:2.

11 a. This phrase, used in 10:18,19 to introduce a denunciation of Israel, now prefaces an announcement of its salvation (so also in v. 11). Israel, though unbelieving, 10:21, is still a chosen people, 11:2. The 'remnant', Is 4:3+ its temporary representative, is the pledge of future restoration.

b. This psalm quotation describes the punishment of those who, because they themselves were sated, would not understand the just man's sufferings or his thirst. There may be a reference (as in the Targum) to sacrificial meals; if so, the prophecy is fulfilled to the letter: the Jews are incapable of acknowledging a suffering Messiah precisely because they are so attached to their formal worship.

c. Lit. 'have they stumbled so as to fall (without hope of rising)?'

d. The present unbelief of the Jews is only a false step which God has permitted with a view to the conversion of the pagans, 9:22; 11:12,19,25,30, and ultimately of the Jews themselves: for their own good God will make them 'jealous', 10:19, of the pagans.

e. I.e. the converts to Christianity from paganism. Thus even as apostle of the gentiles Paul is working for the salvation of his own people (lit. his 'flesh').

f. This sentence has been variously interpreted. The meaning seems to be that if a comparison may be drawn between the conversion of the pagans and 'the reconciliation of the world' (the first stage in the redemptive plan), the conversion of Israel will be such a favour from God that it could be compared only with the final resurrection (the second stage). If this is true, Paul is thinking of the general resurrection at the end of time; but he does not say that this is to take place immediately after Israel's conversion. On the other hand some translate 'life from those who were dead'.

g. Even the unbelieving Israelites still belong to the Chosen People and to some degree share its sacred character, just as the first handful of dough (lit. 'the dough offered as first-fruits') makes the whole offering sacred. Nb 15:19-21.

h. The pagan who is now a Christian.

i. Or 'in place of'.

j. Add. 'the root and'.

k. Lit. 'perhaps he will not spare you'; var. 'he will not spare you'.

l. Paul is still speaking of peoples, not of individuals: the Jews *en masse*, and the pagan world as a whole.

m. The O.T. prophesied that as a result of the Messiah's coming Israel would be cleansed of all her sins. Paul teaches (calling it, lit., a 'mystery', v. 25) that this prophecy, partially fulfilled already in the conversion of the pagans, implies the conversion of the Jewish people also.

Jb 41:3 *1 Co 8:6* *could ever give him anything or lend him anything?* •All that exists comes from him; 36
Col 1:16-17 Heb 2:10 all is by him and for him. To him be glory for ever! Amen.

EXHORTATION

Spiritual worship

1 Th 4:1 **12** Think of God's mercy, my brothers, and worship him, I beg you, in a way 1
1:9+ that is worthy of thinking beings,[a] by offering your living bodies as a holy
8:14-16, 26-27 sacrifice, truly pleasing to God. •Do not model yourselves on the behaviour 2
Ep 4:23 of the world around you, but let your behaviour change, modelled by your new
mind. This is the only way to discover the will of God and know what is good,
what it is that God wants, what is the perfect thing to do.

Humility and charity

In the light of the grace I have received I want to urge each one among you 3
Ph 2:3 not to exaggerate his real importance. Each of you must judge himself soberly by
1 Co 12:9; 13:2 the standard of the faith[b] God has given him. •Just as each of our bodies has 4
several parts and each part has a separate function, •so all of us, in union with 5
1 Co 12:12+ Christ, form one body, and as parts of it we belong to each other.[c] •Our gifts 6
Ac 11:27+ 1 Co 12:8- differ according to the grace given us. If your gift is prophecy, then use it as your
10,28-30 Ep 4:7-11 faith suggests; •if administration, then use it for administration; if teaching, 7
1 P 4:10 then use it for teaching. •Let the preachers deliver sermons, the almsgivers give 8
Tt 1:5+ freely, the officials be diligent, and those who do works of mercy do them
cheerfully.

1 Co 12:4 1 P 1:22 Do not let your love be a pretence, but sincerely prefer good to evil. •Love 9 10
Jn 13:34 Ph 2:3 each other as much as brothers should, and have a profound respect for each
1 Co 13:13+ other.[d] •Work for the Lord[e] with untiring effort and with great earnestness of 11
Mk 1:14; 6:4 Col 4:2 spirit. •If you have hope, this will make you cheerful. Do not give up if trials 12
Ac 9:13+ come; and keep on praying. •If any of the saints are in need you must share with 13
them; and you should make hospitality your special care.

Mt 5:38-48+

Charity to everyone, including enemies[f]

1 Co 12:26 Bless those who persecute you: never curse them, bless them. •Rejoice with 14 15
Si 7:34 those who rejoice and be sad with those in sorrow. •Treat everyone with equal 16
Pr 3:7 kindness; never be condescending but make real friends with the poor. Do not
1 Th 5:15 *Pr 20:22* allow yourself to become self-satisfied. •Never repay evil with evil but let everyone 17
Pr 3:4 LXX 2 Co 8:21 see that you are interested only in the highest ideals. •Do all you can to live at 18
1 Co 6:6-7 *Lv 19:18* peace with everyone. •Never try to get revenge; leave that, my friends, to God's 19
Dt 32:35 anger.[g] As scripture says: *Vengeance is mine—I will pay them back,* the Lord
Pr 25:21-22+ promises. •But there is more: *If your enemy is hungry, you should give him food,* 20
and if he is thirsty, let him drink. Thus you heap red-hot coals on his head. •Resist 21
evil and conquer it with good.

Submission to civil authority[a]

1 Tm 2:1-2 Tt 3:1 **13** You must all obey the governing authorities. Since all government comes 1
1 P 2:13-15 *Pr 8:15* from God, the civil authorities were appointed by God, •and so anyone who 2
Jr 27:6 resists authority is rebelling against God's decision, and such an act is bound
to be punished. •Good behaviour is not afraid of magistrates; only criminals 3
have anything to fear. If you want to live without being afraid of authority, you
must live honestly and authority may even honour you. •The state is there to 4
serve God for your benefit. If you break the law, however, you may well have
fear: the bearing of the sword has its significance. The authorities are there to
serve God: they carry out God's revenge by punishing wrongdoers. •You must 5
obey, therefore, not only because you are afraid of being punished,[b] but also
for conscience' sake. •This is also the reason why you must pay taxes, since all 6

government officials are God's officers. They serve God by collecting taxes.
Pay every government official what he has a right to ask—whether it be direct Mt 22:21p
tax or indirect, fear or honour.

Love and law

Mt 22:34-40 Jn 13:34

Avoid getting into debt, except the debt of mutual love. If you love your fellow Col 3:14
9 men you have carried out your obligations.[c] •All the commandments: *You shall* Ex 20:13-17 Dt 5:17-21
not commit adultery, you shall not kill, you shall not steal,[d] *you shall not covet,*
and so on, are summed up in this single command: *You must love your neighbour*[e] Lv 19:18 Ga 5:14
10 *as yourself.* •Love is the one thing that cannot hurt your neighbour; that is why *1 Co 13:4-7*
it is the answer to every one of the commandments.[f]

Children of the light

1 Th 5:4-8

11 Besides, you know 'the time' has come:[g] you must wake up now: our salvation 1 Co 7:26, 29-31
12 is even nearer than it was when we were converted. •The night is almost over, it Ep 5:8-16 Col 4:5
will be daylight soon—let us give up[h] all the things we prefer to do under cover 1 Jn 2:8 Jn 8:12+
13 of the dark; let us arm ourselves and appear in the light. •Let us live decently Ep 6:11+
as people do in the daytime: no drunken orgies, no promiscuity or licentiousness, 1:29+
14 and no wrangling or jealousy. •Let your armour be the Lord Jesus Christ; forget Ga 3:27 Ep 4:24
about satisfying your bodies with all their cravings.

Charity towards the scrupulous

1 Co 8; 10: 14-33

1 **14** If a person's faith is not strong enough,[a] welcome him all the same without 6:15+ 1 Th 5:14
2 starting an argument. •People range from those who believe they may eat
any sort of meat to those whose faith is so weak they dare not eat anything
3 except vegetables. •Meat-eaters must not despise the scrupulous. On the other Col 2:16-21
hand, the scrupulous must not condemn those who feel free to eat anything they
4 choose, since God has welcomed them. •It is not for you to condemn someone Mt 7:1 Jm 4:12
else's servant: whether he stands or falls it is his own master's business; he will
5 stand, you may be sure, because the Lord has power to make him stand. •If
one man keeps certain days as holier than others, and another considers all days Col 2:16
6 to be equally holy, each must be left free to hold his own opinion. •The one who
observes special days does so in honour of the Lord. The one who eats meat also
does so in honour of the Lord, since he gives thanks to God; but then the man
who abstains does that too in honour of the Lord, and so he also gives God thanks.

12 a. Or 'in a spiritual way', as opposed to the ritual sacrifices of Jews or pagans, cf. Ho 6:6. Cf. Rm 1:9+.

b. 'Faith' is used here to mean the spiritual gifts bestowed by God on the members of the Christian community to ensure its life and growth.

c. The sentence emphasises not so much the identification of Christians with Christ, 1 Co 12:27 as their dependence on one another.

d. Or 'outdo each other in mutual esteem'.

e. Lit. 'Serve the Lord'; var. 'Be ready when opportunity arises' (lit. 'Serve the time').

f. The perspective now, particularly from v. 17 onwards, embraces all mankind.

g. Lit. 'give place... to anger', presumably the anger of God waiting to punish sin.

13 a. Paul here enunciates the principle that all authority, supposing it lawful and for the common good, derives from God. Hence the Christian religion, like its morality, 12:1, enters into civil life also, 13:1-7. Paul does not contradict this even after the first persecutions.

b. Lit. 'not only on account of anger'.

c. Lit. 'fulfilled the law'—apparently law in general, not only the Mosaic Law.

d. Add. (Vulg.) 'you shall not bear false witness'.

e. In Lv the 'neighbour' was a fellow countryman, here it is any member of the human family which is made one in Christ, Ga 3:28; Mt 25:40.

f. Lit. 'that is why love is the law in all its fulness'.

g. The thought is a fundamental one in Paul's moral teaching. The 'time' *(kairos)* is apparently the eschatological era, called in the Bible the 'latter days', introduced by Christ's death and resurrection and coextensive with the age of the Church on earth, the age of salvation, 2 Co 6:2+. It is opposed to the era that preceded it by a difference not so much of time as of nature. The Christian, henceforward a 'child of the day', emancipated from the wicked world, Ga 1:4, and from the empire of darkness, belongs to the kingdom of God and of his Son, Col 1:13; he is already a citizen of heaven, Ph 3:20. This entirely new status dominates the whole moral outlook, cf. 6:3f.

h. Lit. 'let us divest ourselves of'; var. 'let us cast away'.

14 a. Christians not sufficiently instructed in the faith and therefore without the firm convictions that would give them a sure conscience, vv. 2,5,22. These considered themselves bound to observe certain days, v. 5, and to abstain from meat or from wine, vv. 2,21, perhaps as a permanent obligation, v. 21. Such ascetical practices were familiar to the pagan world (the Pythagoreans) and the Jewish (the Essenes, John the Baptist). Paul lays down the same general rule as in the similar case of 1 Co 8; 10:14-33: each must act 'for the Lord' as his conscience tells him, vv. 5-6, provided it is not a doubtful conscience, v. 23; but above all, charity must govern the conduct of those 'strong' in the faith, vv. 1,15,19-21 and 15:1-13.

6:10-11 The life and death of each of us has its influence on others; •if we live, we live 7 8
for the Lord; and if we die, we die for the Lord, so that alive or dead we belong
Ac 10:42 2 Co 5:15 to the Lord. •This explains why Christ both died and came to life, it was so that 9
he might be Lord both of the dead and of the living. •This is also why you should 10
never pass judgement on a brother or treat him with contempt, as some of you
2:6+ 2 Co 5:10 have done. We shall all have to stand before the judgement seat of God;[b] •as 11
Is 45:23 Ph 2:10-11 scripture says: *By my life—it is the Lord who speaks—every knee shall bend before*
Ga 6:5 *me, and every tongue shall praise God.* •It is to God, therefore, that each of us 12
must give an account of himself.

Far from passing judgement on each other, therefore, you should make up 13
your mind never to be the cause of your brother tripping or falling. •Now I am 14
Mt 15:1-20p Ac 10:15 perfectly well aware, of course, and I speak for the Lord Jesus, that no food is
1 Tm 4:4 unclean in itself; however, if someone thinks that a particular food is unclean,
1 Co 8:10 then it is unclean for him. •And indeed[c] if your attitude to food is upsetting your 15
1 Co 13:1+ brother,[d] then you are hardly being guided by charity. You are certainly not free
to eat what you like if that means the downfall of someone for whom Christ died.
1 Co 8:8 In short, you must not compromise your privilege,[e] •because the kingdom 16 17
of God does not mean eating or drinking this or that, it means righteousness and
Ga 5:22 1 Th 1:6 peace and joy brought by the Holy Spirit. •If you serve Christ in this way you 18
12:17-18 will please God and be respected by men. •So let us adopt any custom that leads 19
to peace and our mutual improvement; •do not wreck God's work[f] over a 20
Tt 1:15 question of food. Of course all food is clean, but it becomes evil if by eating it
1 Co 8:13; 10:24 you make somebody else fall away.[g] •In such cases the best course is to abstain 21
1 Tm 4:4 from meat and wine and anything else that would make your brother trip or
fall or weaken in any way.

Hold on to your own belief,[h] as between yourself and God[i]—and consider 22
the man fortunate who can make his decision without going against his conscience.
1 Co 8:7 But anybody who eats in a state of doubt is condemned, because he is not in good 23
faith;[j] and every act done in bad faith is a sin.

1 Co 9:22 Ga 6:2 15 We who are strong have a duty to put up with the qualms of the weak 1
1 Co 10:33; 13:5 without thinking of ourselves. •Each of us should think of his neighbours and 2
14:19 1 Co 8:1 help them to become stronger Christians. •Christ did not think of himself: the words 3
Ps 69:9 of scripture—*the insults of those who insult you fall on me*—apply to him. •And 4
1 Co 10:6+ 2 Tm 3:16 indeed everything that was written long ago in the scriptures was meant to teach
1 M 12:9 2 M 15:9 us something about hope from the examples scripture gives of how people who
did not give up were helped by God. •And may he who helps us when we refuse 5
to give up, help you all to be tolerant with each other,[a] following the example
Ph 2:2f of Christ Jesus, •so that united in mind and voice you may give glory to the God 6
and Father of our Lord Jesus Christ.

An appeal for unity

It can only be to God's glory, then, for you to treat each other in the same 7
Mt 15:24 Ac 3:25-26 friendly way as Christ treated you. •The reason Christ became the servant of 8
1 Co 8:7 circumcised Jews was not only so that God could faithfully carry out the promises
Ex 34:6 Ac 15:14-15 made to the patriarchs, •it was also to get the pagans to give glory to God for 9
Ps 18:50 his mercy,[b] as scripture says in one place: *For this I shall praise you among the*
Dt 32:43 LXX *pagans and sing to your name.* •And in another place: *Rejoice, pagans, with his* 10
Ps 117:1 *people*, •and in a third place: *Let all the pagans praise the Lord, let all the peoples* 11
Is 11:10; 11:1 Rv 5:5 *sing his praises.* •Isaiah too has this to say: *The root of Jesse will appear, rising* 12
up to rule the pagans, and in him the pagans will put their hope.

May the God of hope bring you such joy and peace in your faith that the 13
power of the Holy Spirit will remove all bounds to hope.[c]

EPILOGUE

Paul's ministry

14 It is not because I have any doubts about you, my brothers; on the contrary
I am quite certain that you are full of good intentions, perfectly well instructed
15 and able to advise each other. •The reason why I have written to you,[d] and put
some things rather strongly, is to refresh your memories, since God has given me
16 this special position. •He has appointed me as a priest of Jesus Christ, and I am
to carry out my priestly duty[e] by bringing the Good News from God to the pagans, 1:9-10
and so make them acceptable as an offering, made holy by the Holy Spirit.
17 I think I have some reason to be proud of what I, in union with Christ Jesus, 5:2+ Ga 2:7
18 have been able to do for God. •What I am presuming to speak of, of course, is
only what Christ himself has done to win the allegiance of the pagans, using 1:5+
19 what I have said and done •by the power of signs and wonders, by the power of Ac 1:8+ 2 Co 12:12+
the Holy Spirit. Thus, all the way along, from Jerusalem to Illyricum,[f] I have
20 preached Christ's Good News to the utmost of my capacity. •I have always, Col 1:25
however, made it an unbroken rule never to preach where Christ's name has 2 Co 10:15-16
already been heard. The reason for that was that I had no wish to build on other *1 Co 3:10f*
21 men's foundations; •on the contrary, my chief concern has been to fulfil the
text: *Those who have never been told about him will see him, and those who have* Is 52:15
never heard about him will understand.

Paul's plans

22 23 That is the reason why I have been kept from visiting you so long,[g] •though 1:10f Ac 19:21-22
for many years I have been longing to pay you a visit. Now, however, having
24 no more work to do here,[h] •I hope to see you on my way to Spain and, after
enjoying a little of your company, to complete the rest of the journey with your
25 good wishes. •First, however, I must take a present of money to the saints in Ac 19:21
26 Jerusalem, •since Macedonia and Achaia have decided to send a generous 12:13 1 Co 16:1+
27 contribution to the poor among the saints at Jerusalem. •A generous contribution
as it should be, since it is really repaying a debt: the pagans who share the spiritual 11:17f 1 Co 9:11
possessions of these poor people have a duty to help them with temporal posses- Ga 6:6
28 sions. •So when I have done this and officially handed over[i] what has been raised,
29 I shall set out for Spain and visit you on the way. •I know that when I reach you
I shall arrive with rich blessings from Christ.
30 But I beg you, brothers, by our Lord Jesus Christ and the love of the Spirit, 2 Co 1:11 Ep 6:19
31 to help me through my dangers by praying to God for me.[j] •Pray that I may Col 4:3,12 1 Th 5:25

b. Who alone knows the secrets of the heart, cf. 2:16; 1 Co 4:3f.

c. 'And indeed'; var. 'But' or 'Now'.

d. By his taking bad example, or by being scandalised at an action his conscience does not approve.

e. Probably the privilege of Christian liberty of which the 'strong' make use but which may be brought into disrepute, cf. 3:8+.

f. Either the 'weak' man himself or the Christian community, cf. 1 Co 3:9.

g. Lit. 'by eating it with a cause of stumbling' cf. v. 13; that is, according to the context (v. 21 deals with the duties of the 'strong'), while giving 'scandal'. Others interpret while following bad example, cf. v. 14.

h. Var. 'Have you a belief? Hold on to it.'

i. Because it is true and seen as such by God; but charity has a higher claim.

j. 'good faith', lit. 'faith', but here in the sense of right conscience, cf. 14:1+. Other translations 'since he does not act from conviction', or, 'since his action is not prompted by a conviction of faith'.

15 a. I.e. to be thoughtful for each other. Others interpret 'to live in good understanding of each other', 'to live in agreement with each other'.

b. Christ welcomed the pagans, and thus gave glory to God. But by confining his work while on earth to the evangelisation of Israel, cf. Mt 15:24, Christ gave evidence of God's loyalty to his promise, the converted pagans being living evidence rather of God's mercy. Let these in their turn be merciful to their brothers in the faith, cf. 12:1.

c. This blessing resumes the central themes of the doctrinal section of the epistle.

d. Paul once again justifies himself for writing to a church he did not found, cf. 1:5-6,13.

e. The apostolate, even more than the ordinary Christian life, 12:1; cf. Ph 2:12, is a liturgical function, cf. 1:9, the apostle—or rather, through him, Christ, v. 18—makes an offering of men to God.

f. The two extremes of Paul's missionary journeys at the time of writing; whether he had actually entered Illyricum is disputed.

g. Var. 'so many times'.

h. Not that all the pagans there have been converted, but that Paul's task is to lay foundations; he leaves his disciples to build on them, cf. 1 Co 3:6,10; Col 1:7, etc.

i. Lit. 'sealed'.

j. Cf. 2 Co 1:11; Ep 6:19; Col 4:3; 1 Th 5:25; 2 Th 3:1; Heb 13:18.

Ac 20:3,23; 21:10f, 17f,27f escape the unbelievers in Judaea, and that the aid I carry to Jerusalem may be
accepted by the saints. •Then, if God wills, I shall be feeling very happy when 32
I come to enjoy a period of rest among you. •May the God of peace be with you 33
all! Amen.

Greetings and good wishes

16 [a]I commend to you our sister Phoebe,[b] a deaconess of the church at 1
Ac 18:18 Cenchreae. •Give her, in union with the Lord, a welcome worthy of saints, 2
and help her with anything she needs: she has looked after a great many people,
myself included.

Ac 18:2f,26 1 Co 16:19 My greetings to Prisca and Aquila, my fellow workers in Christ Jesus, •who 3 4
2 Tm 4:19 risked death to save my life:[c] I am not the only one to owe them a debt
1 Co 16:19 of gratitude, all the churches among the pagans do as well. •My greetings also 5
Col 4:15 Phm 2 to the church that meets at their house.

1 Co 16:15 Greetings to my friend Epaenetus, the first of Asia's gifts to Christ;[d] greetings 6
to Mary who worked so hard for you; •to those outstanding apostles Andronicus 7
and Junias, my compatriots and fellow prisoners[e] who became Christians before
me; •to Ampliatus, my friend in the Lord; •to Urban, my fellow worker in 8 9
Christ; to my friend Stachys; •to Apelles who has gone through so much for 10
Christ; to everyone who belongs to the household of Aristobulus; •to my 11
compatriot Herodion; to those in the household of Narcissus who belong to the
Lord; •to Tryphaena and Tryphosa, who work hard for the Lord; to my friend 12
Persis who has done so much for the Lord; •to Rufus,[f] a chosen servant of 13
the Lord, and to his mother who has been a mother to me too. •Greetings to 14
Asyncritus, Phlegon, Hermes, Patrobas, Hermas, and all the brothers who are
with them; •to Philologus and Julia, Nereus and his sister, and Olympas and all 15
Ac 20:37 2 Co 13:12+ the saints who are with them. •Greet each other with a holy kiss. All the churches 16
of Christ send greetings.[g]

Ga 6:11

A warning and first postscript

I implore you, brothers, be on your guard against anybody who encourages 17
6:17 Mt 18:17 trouble or puts difficulties in the way of the doctrine you have been taught. Avoid
them.[h] •People like that are not slaves of Jesus Christ, they are slaves of their 18
Ph 3:19 own appetites, confusing the simple-minded with their pious and persuasive
1:5+ arguments. •Your fidelity to Christ, anyway, is famous everywhere, and that 19
1:8 *Mt 10:16* makes me very happy about you. I only hope that you are also wise in what is
1 Co 14:20 *Gn 3:15* good, and innocent of what is bad. •The God of peace will soon crush Satan 20
beneath your feet. The grace of our Lord Jesus Christ be with you.[i]

Last greetings and second postscript

Ac 16:1+ Timothy, who is working with me, sends his greetings; so do my compatriots, 21
Ac 13:1; 17:5; 20:4 Jason and Sosipater. •I, Tertius, who wrote out this letter, greet you in the Lord. 22
1 Co 1:14 Greetings from Gaius, who is entertaining me and from the whole church that 23
meets in his house. Erastus, the city treasurer, sends his greetings; so does our
brother Quartus.

Jude 25

Doxology[j]

11:25 1 Co 2:7 Glory to him who is able to give you the strength[k] to live according to the 25
Ep 1:9; 3:3 Col 1:26 Good News I preach, and in which I proclaim Jesus Christ, the revelation of a
1 Tm 3:9 mystery[l] kept secret for endless ages, •but now so clear that it must be broadcast 26
1:5 Ac 15:14 to pagans everywhere to bring them to the obedience of faith. This is only what
scripture has predicted, and it is all part of the way the eternal God wants things
Ga 1:5 Ep 3:21 to be. •He alone is wisdom;[m] give glory therefore to him through Jesus Christ 27
Ph 4:20 1 Tm 1:17 for ever and ever. Amen.[n]

16 a. This chapter may not have formed part of the original epistle, cf. Introduction to the Letters of St Paul.

b. Probably the bearer of the letter.

c. Presumably in Ephesus, either at the time of the riot described in Ac 19:23f, or during Paul's imprisonment there (cf. v. 7); see Introduction to the Letters of St Paul.

d. Lit. 'the first-fruits of Asia for Christ'. This probably means the first convert in the province of Asia.

e. Paul had been imprisoned several times already, cf. 2 Co 11:23. Andronicus and Junias (var. Julias) are apostles in the wide sense, Rm 1:1+.

f. Possibly the son of Simon of Cyrene, Mk 15:21.

g. This greeting, not found elsewhere in Paul's letters, shows his veneration for the church in Rome.

h. The curt warning is reminiscent of Ga 6:12-17. It probably refers to judaising preachers, cf. Ga 5:7-12 and particularly Ph 3:18-19.

i. Omit 'The grace...' This formula (add. 'all') is placed by some authorities (Vulg.) after v 23 or v. 27.

j. Most authorities place this doxology here, but in some it appears at the end of ch. 15 or 14; others omit. A solemn presentation, cf. Ep 3:20; Jude 24-25, of the main points of the letter.

k. Firmly grounded in doctrine and strong in Christian practice. Cf. 1:11; 1 Th 3:2,13; 2 Th 2:17; 3:3; 1 Co 1:8; 2 Co 1:21; Col 2:7.

l. The idea of a 'mystery' of wisdom, v. 27; 1 Co 2:7; Ep 3:10; Col 2:2-3, long hidden in God and now revealed, v. 25; 1 Co 2:7,10; Ep 3:5,9f; Col 1:26, is borrowed by Paul from Jewish apocalypse, Dn 2:18-19+, but he enriches the content of the term by applying it to the climax of the history of salvation: the saving cross of Christ, 1 Co 2:8; the call of the pagans, v. 26; Rm 11:25; Col 1:26-27; Ep 3:6, to this salvation preached by Paul, v. 25; Col 1:23; 4:3; Ep 3:3-12; 6:19, and finally the restoration of all things in Christ as their one head, Ep 1:9-10. See also 1 Co 4:1; 13:2; 14:2; 15:51; Ep 5:32; 2 Th 2:7; 1 Tm 3:9,16; 2 Tm 1:9-10; Mt 13:11p+; Rv 1:20; 10:7; 17:5,7.

m. Cf. 11:33-36; 1 Co 1:24; 2:7; Ep 3:10; Col 2:3; Rv 7:12.

n. Cf. Ga 1:5; Ep 3:21; Ph 4:20; 1 Tm 1:17; 6:16; 2 Tm 4:18; Heb 13:21; 1 P 4:11; 2 P 3:18; Jude 25; Rv 1:6.

1 CORINTHIANS

THE FIRST LETTER OF PAUL TO THE CHURCH AT CORINTH

INTRODUCTION

Rm 1:1+ **Address and greetings. Thanksgiving**

1 I, Paul, appointed by God to be an apostle, together with brother Sosthenes, 1
10:32 Ac 5:11+ send greetings •to the church of God[a] in Corinth, to the holy people of Jesus 2
Ac 9:13+; 20:28 Christ, who are called to take their place among all the saints everywhere who
Ac 2:21+ pray to our Lord Jesus Christ; for he is their Lord no less than ours. •May God 3
our Father and the Lord Jesus Christ send you grace and peace.
I never stop thanking God for all the graces you have received through 4
2 Co 8:7,9 Jesus Christ. •I thank him that you have been enriched in so many ways, especial- 5
12:8+ ly in your teachers and preachers; •the witness to Christ[b] has indeed been strong 6
2 Th 1:7+ among you •so that you will not be without any of the gifts of the Spirit while 7
3:13; 5:5 2 Co 1:14 you are waiting for our Lord Jesus Christ to be revealed;[c] •and he will keep you 8
Ph 1:6; 2:16 Col 1:22 steady and without blame[d] until the last day, the day[e] of our Lord Jesus Christ,
10:13 2 Co 1:18 because God by calling you has joined you to his Son, Jesus Christ; and God 9
Ph 3:10f 1 Jn 1:3 is faithful.[f]

I. DIVISIONS AND SCANDALS

A. FACTIONS IN THE CORINTHIAN CHURCH

Dissensions among the faithful

All the same, I do appeal to you, brothers, for the sake of our Lord Jesus 10
Rm 15:5 Ph 2:2f Christ, to make up the differences between you, and instead of disagreeing
among yourselves, to be united again in your belief and practice. •From what 11
Chloe's people have been telling me, my dear brothers, it is clear that there are
3:4 2 Co 10:7 serious differences among you. •What I mean are all these slogans that you have, 12
3:22-23 Jn 1:42 like: 'I am for Paul', 'I am for Apollos', 'I am for Cephas',[g] 'I am for Christ'.[h]
Ac 18:24+ Has Christ been parcelled out? Was it Paul that was crucified for you? Were you 13
Ep 4:5 baptised in the name of Paul? •I am thankful that I never baptised any of you 14
Ac 18:8 Rm 16:23 after Crispus and Gaius •so none of you can say he was baptised in my name. 15
16:15-17 Then there was the family of Stephanas, of course, that I baptised too, but no one 16
Ac 16:15+ else as far as I can remember.

The true wisdom and the false

3:18 2 Co 1:12 For Christ did not send me to baptise, but to preach the Good News, and 17
not to preach that in the terms of philosophy[i] in which the crucifixion of Christ
2 Co 2:16 cannot be expressed. •The language of the cross may be illogical to those who 18
Rm 1:16 are not on the way to salvation, but those of us who are on the way see it as God's
Is 29:14 Ps 33:10 power to save. •As scripture says: *I shall destroy the wisdom of the wise and bring* 19
Is 33:18LXX *to nothing all the learning of the learned.* •*Where are the philosophers now? Where* 20

are the scribes? Where are any of our thinkers today? Do you see now how God Is 19:12
21 has shown up the foolishness of human wisdom? •If it was God's wisdom that Rm 1:19-20
human wisdom should not know God, it was because God wanted to save
those who have faith through the foolishness of the message that we preach.
23 22 And so, while the Jews demand miracles and the Greeks look for wisdom, •here Mt 12:38p Jn 2:18+
are we preaching a crucified Christ; to the Jews an obstacle that they cannot Ac 17:19-23 *Jn 12:34*
24 get over, to the pagans madness, •but to those who have been called, whether
25 they are Jews or Greeks, a Christ who is the power and the wisdom of God. •For Jn 6:35+
God's foolishness is wiser than human wisdom, and God's weakness is stronger 2 Co 12:10; 13:14
than human strength.

26 Take yourselves for instance, brothers, at the time when you were called:
how many of you were wise in the ordinary sense of the word,[j] how many were Dt 7:7 Si 10:19f
27 influential people, or came from noble families? •No, it was to shame the wise Rm 7:5 *Jg 7:2*
that God chose what is foolish by human reckoning, and to shame what is strong 1 S 16:7 2 Co 4:7
28 that he chose what is weak by human reckoning; •those whom the world thinks Jm 2:5
common and contemptible are the ones that God has chosen—those who are
29 nothing at all to show up those who are everything. •The human race has nothing Dt 8:17-18+ Rm 3:27
30 to boast about to God, •but you, God has made members of Christ Jesus and by Ep 2:9
God's doing he has become our wisdom, and our virtue, and our holiness, and
31 our freedom. •As scripture says: *if anyone wants to boast, let him boast about* Jr 9:22-23 Si 10:28
the Lord. 2 Co 10:17

1 **2** As for me, brothers, when I came to you, it was not with any show of oratory Rm 1:16 2 Co 1:12;
2 or philosophy, but simply to tell you what God had guaranteed.[a] •During 11:6
my stay with you, the only knowledge I claimed to have was about Jesus, and
3 only about him as the crucified Christ. •Far from relying on any power of my Ga 3:1; 6:14
4 own, I came among you in great 'fear and trembling'[b] •and in my speeches and Ph 2:12
the sermons that I gave, there were none of the arguments that belong to philo-
5 sophy; only a demonstration of the power of the Spirit. •And I did this so that Ac 1:8+ 2 Co 12:12
your faith should not depend on human philosophy but on the power of God. 1 Th 1:5
6 But still we have a wisdom to offer those who have reached maturity:[c] not Col 1:28 Heb 5:14
a philosophy of our age, it is true, still less of the masters of our age,[d] which

1 a. One of Paul's favourite expressions: 10:32; 11:16,22; 15:9; 2 Co 1:1; Ga 1:13; 1 Th 2:14; 2 Th 1:4; 1 Tm 3:5,15; cf. also Ac 20:28. Cf. 'the churches of Christ', Rm 16:16. Cf. Mt 16:18+; Ac 5:11+.

b. I.e. what is said by a witness testifying to Christ. 'among you' or 'in you'.

c. When the hidden plans of God are to be made known, Rm 16:25+. Christ will reveal himself at the end of time, the time of his *parousia*, 1 Co 15:23+, and his Appearing, 1 Tm 6:14+; cf. Lk 17:30; 2 Th 1:7; Heb 9:28; 1 P 1:5,7,13; 4:13. Before this, the Man of Sin will have 'revealed' himsel onlyf, to be destroyed by Christ, 2 Th 2:3-8.

d. Cf. Ph 1:10; 2:15f; Ep 1:4; Col 1:22; 1 Th 3:13; 5:23; Jude 24.

e. This 'day of the Lord', 5:5; 2 Co 1:14; 1 Th 5:2; 2 Th 2:2; cf. 2 P 3:10, called also the 'day of Christ', Ph 1:6,10; 2:16, or simply the 'day', 1 Co 3:13; 1 Th 5:4; cf. Heb 10:25, or 'that day', 2 Th 1:10; 2 Tm 1:12,18; 4:8; cf. Mt 7:22; 24:36; Lk 10:12; 21:34, or 'the day of the Son of Man', Lk 17:24, cf. v. 26, or 'the day of God', 2 P 3:12, or 'the day of visitation', 1 P 2:12, or 'the great day', Jude 6; Rv 6:17; 16:14, or 'the last day', Jn 6:39,40,44,54; 11:24; 12:48, is the fulfilment in the eschatological era, ushered in by Christ, of the 'day of Yahweh' foretold by the prophets, Am 5:18+. The fulfilment begins with the first coming of Christ, Lk 17:20-24, and the punishment of Jerusalem, Mt 24:1+; and this final stage in the history of salvation, cf. Ac 1:7+, will be completed by the glorious second coming, 1 Co 1:7+, 15:23+; 1 Tm 6:14+, of the Sovereign Judge, Rm 2:6+; Jm 5:8-9. A cosmic upheaval and renewal will accompany it (cf. Am 8:9+), Mt 24:29p+; Heb 12:26f; 2 P 3:10-13; Rv 20:11; 21:1; cf. Mt 19:28; Rm 8:20-22. This day of light is coming, Rm 13:12; Heb 10:25; Jm 5:8; 1 P 4:7; cf. 1 Th 5:5,8, but exactly when is uncertain, 1 Th 5:1+, meanwhile we must prepare for it, 2 Co 6:2+.

f. Cf. 10:13; 2 Co 1:18; 1 Th 5:24; 2 Th 3:3; 2 Tm 2:13; Heb 10:23; 11:11.

g. Either because Cephas (Peter) had visited the church of Corinth, or because some members of that church paid special allegiance to Peter's authority acknowledged in other churches.

h. Perhaps these attached themselves to the immediate witnesses of the risen Christ, cf. Ac 1:21f; 10:41, in preference to others, cf. 1 Co 9:1; 2 Co 5:16+; 11:5,23; 12:11; or else they acknowledged no human intermediary between themselves and Christ.

i. Lit. 'wisdom'. This human wisdom (here philosophical speculation and tricks of rhetoric) will be contrasted with the wisdom of God, v. 24 and 2:6f.

j. Lit. 'according to the flesh'. Paul is explaining God's purpose, but at the same time he sardonically reminds the Corinthians that they have no reason to be proud.

2 a. Lit. 'the testimony of God', i.e. to the message of Jesus. Var. 'the mystery of God'.

b. 'fear and trembling': a biblical cliché, cf. Jg 7:3; Ps 2:11; 55:5; Ezk 12:18; Mk 5:33; 1 Co 2:3; 2 Co 7:15; Ep 6:5; Ph 2:12.

c. The 'mature' or 'perfect' *(teleioi)* are not an exclusive group of initiates but those who have reached maturity in Christian life and thought. Cf. 14:20; Ph 3:15; Col 4:12; Heb 5:14.

d. Perhaps human rulers or governments; more probably, the evil powers or demons that control the world, cf. 1 Co 15:24-25; Ep 6:12. See also Lk 4:6 and Jn 12:31+; but the reference is perhaps to both, the latter using the former as their tools.

Rm 16:25+ are coming to their end. •The hidden wisdom of God which we teach in our 7
mysteries is the wisdom that God predestined to be for our glory before the ages
Ep 3:10 1 P 1:12 began. •It is a wisdom that none of the masters of this age have ever known, or 8
Ps 24:8 they would not have crucified the Lord of Glory;[e] •we teach what scripture calls:[f] 9
Is 64:3 Jr 3:16 *the things that no eye has seen and no ear has heard, things beyond the mind of man,*
all that God has prepared for those who love him.

Dn 2:28 These are the very things that God has revealed to us through the Spirit, for 10
Jn 14:26+ 2 Co 13:13+ the Spirit reaches the depths of everything, even the depths of God. •After all, 11
Jdt 8:14 Pr 20:27 the depths of a man can only be known by his own spirit, not by any other man,
Rm 11:33f and in the same way the depths of God can only be known by the Spirit of God
Now instead of the spirit of the world, we have received the Spirit that comes 12
from God, to teach us to understand the gifts that he has given us. •Therefore 13
we teach, not in the way in which philosophy is taught, but in the way that the
15:44+ Spirit teaches us: we teach spiritual things spiritually.[g] •An unspiritual person[h] 14
Pr 28:5 Mt 16:23 is one who does not accept anything of the Spirit of God: he sees it all as nonsense;
Jn 10:26+ it is beyond his understanding because it can only be understood by means of the
15:44+ Spirit. •A spiritual man, on the other hand, is able to judge the value of everything, 15
Is 40:13 Rm 11:34 and his own value is not to be judged by other men.[i] •As scripture says: *Who* 16
Ws 9:13 *can know the mind of the Lord, so who can teach him?* But we are those who have
7:40 the mind of Christ.[j]

3 Brothers, I myself was unable to speak to you as people of the Spirit: I treated 1
1 Th 2:7 Heb 5:12-14 you as sensual men, still infants in Christ. •What I fed you with was milk, 2
1 P 2:2 *Si 37:28* not solid food, for you were not ready for it; and indeed, you are still[a] not ready
Ga 5:19-20 Jm 3:16 for it •since you are still unspiritual. Isn't that obvious from all the jealousy 3
and wrangling[b] that there is among you, from the way that you go on behaving
1:12 like ordinary people? •What could be more unspiritual than your slogans, 'I am 4
for Paul' and 'I am for Apollos'?

The place of the Christian preacher

After all, what is Apollos and what is Paul? They are servants who brought 5
the faith to you. Even the different ways in which they brought it were assigned
2 Tm 2:6 to them by the Lord. •I did the planting, Apollos did the watering, but God 6
made things grow. •Neither the planter nor the waterer matters: only God, who 7
makes things grow. •It is all one who does the planting and who does the watering, 8
and each will duly be paid according to his share in the work •We are fellow 9
Ep 2:20-22 1 P 2:5 workers with God;[c] you are God's farm, God's building
Rm 15:20 By the grace God gave me, I succeeded as an architect and laid the foundations, 10
on which someone else is doing the building Everyone doing the building must
Ps 118:22 Is 28:16 work carefully. •For the foundation, nobody can lay any other than the one 11
Ac 4:11-12 1 P 2:4 which has already been laid, that is Jesus Christ •On this foundation you can 12
build in gold, silver and jewels, or in wood, grass and straw, •but whatever the 13
1:8+ material, the work of each builder is going to be clearly revealed when the day
Mt 3:11-12p 1 P 1:7 comes. That day will begin with fire, and the fire will test the quality of each man's
work. •If his structure stands up to it, he will get his wages; •if it is burnt down, 14 15
Is 43:2 he will be the loser, and though he is saved himself, it will be as one who has gone
through fire.[d]
6:19 2 Co 6-16 Didn't you realise that you were God's temple[e] and that the Spirit of God was 16
Ep 2:20-22 living among you? •If anybody should destroy the temple of God, God 17
will destroy him, because the temple of God is sacred;[f] and you are that temple

Conclusions

1:17-25 Pr 28:26 Make no mistake about it: if any one of you thinks of himself as wise, in the 18
ordinary sense of the word, then he must learn to be a fool before he really can be
wise. •Why? Because the wisdom of this world is foolishness to God As scripture 19
Jb 5:13 says: *The Lord knows wise men's thoughts: he knows how useless they are,*
Ps 94:11 or again: *God is not convinced by the arguments of the wise.* •So there is 20 21

22 nothing to boast about in anything human: •Paul, Apollos, Cephas, the world, 1:12
23 life and death, the present and the future, are all your servants; •but you belong 6:19; 11:3 Rm 8:10
to Christ[g] and Christ belongs to God.

1 **4** People must think of us as Christ's servants, stewards entrusted with the Lk 12:42-44
2 mysteries of God. •What is expected of stewards is that each one should be
3 found worthy of his trust. •Not that it makes the slightest difference to me
whether you, or indeed any human tribunal, find me worthy or not. I will not
4 even pass judgement on myself. •True, my conscience does not reproach me at
all, but that does not prove that I am acquitted: the Lord alone is my judge. 2 Co 5:10-11
5 There must be no passing of premature judgement. Leave that until the Lord Mk 7:1
comes: he will light up all that is hidden in the dark and reveal the secret intentions Lk 12:2-3 Rm 2:16
of men's hearts. Then will be the time for each one to have whatever praise he Jn 5:44
deserves, from God.

6 Now in everything I have said here, brothers, I have taken Apollos and
myself as an example (remember the maxim: 'Keep to what is written');[a] it is not
for you, so full of your own importance, to go taking sides for one man against
7 another. •In any case, brother, has anybody given you some special right? What
do you have that was not given to you? And if it was given, how can you boast Jn 3:27 Ga 6:3
8 as though it were not? •Is it that you have everything you want—that you are *Rv 3:17*
rich already, in possession of your kingdom, with us left outside? Indeed I wish
9 you were really kings, and we could be kings with you! •But instead, it seems to
me, God has put us apostles at the end of his parade, with the men sentenced 2 Co 4:8-12; 6:4-10; 11: 23-33
to death; it is true—we have been put on show in front of the whole universe, 2 Tm 3:10-11
10 angels as well as men. •Here we are, fools for the sake of Christ, while you are
the learned men in Christ; we have no power, but you are influential; you are
11 celebrities, we are nobodies. •To this day, we go without food and drink and 2 Co 11:27
12 clothes; we are beaten and have no homes; •we work for our living with our own Ac 18:3+
hands. When we are cursed, we answer with a blessing; when we are hounded,
13 we put up with it; •we are insulted and we answer politely. We are treated as Ps 116:10
the offal of the world, still to this day, the scum of the earth.

An appeal

14 I am saying all this not just to make you ashamed but to bring you, as my
15 dearest children, to your senses. •You might have thousands of guardians in
Christ, but not more than one father and it was I who begot you in Christ Jesus Ga 4:19 1 Th 2:11
16 17 by preaching the Good News. •That is why I beg you to copy me •and why I have Phm 10 *2 Th 3:7+*
sent you Timothy, my dear and faithful son in the Lord: he will remind you of the *Ac 16:1+*; 19:22
way that I live in Christ, as I teach it everywhere in all the churches.

18 When it seemed that I was not coming to visit you, some of you became self-
19 important, •but I will be visiting you soon, the Lord willing, and then I shall
want to know not what these self-important people have to say, but what they
20 21 can do, •since the kingdom of God is not just words, it is power. •It is for you 2:4+
to decide: do I come with a stick in my hand or in a spirit of love and goodwill? 2 Co 10:2

e. The 'Glory' is the manifestation of Yahweh's power, Ex 24:16+, the incommunicable attribute of God. The title 'Lord of Glory' implies the same dignity for Jesus as that of Yahweh himself.

f. A free combination of Is 64:3 and Jr 3:16, or possibly a quotation from the *Apocalypse of Elijah*.

g. Lit. 'comparing spiritual things with spiritual'. Exact meaning obscure. Other possible renderings 'demonstrating for spiritual men how spiritual truths hold together'; 'spiritual truths being thus suited to spiritual men'; 'submitting spiritual truths to the judgement of men of the Spirit'.

h. *Psychikos:* man left to his own natural resources. Cf. the note on *soma psychikon* of 15:44.

i. A defensive remark: Paul, a 'spiritual' man, is not to be judged by the Corinthians who are 'sensual'. 3:1-3.

j. Var. 'of the Lord'.

3 a. Om. 'still'.

b. Add. 'and dissension'.

c. Or 'fellow workers in God's employment'.

d. This is not a direct reference to purgatory but several Doctors of the Church have taken it as a basis for that doctrine.

e. *Naos:* more precisely the innermost part of the Temple, the 'sanctuary' where God dwells.

f. I.e. consecrated and reserved to God: to lay hands on it is sacrilege.

g. Cf. 1:12; 6:19; 11:3; 2 Co 10:7; Rm 6:11+,15+; 8:9; Mk 9:41.

4 a. Obscure. Perhaps a citation of a proverb familiar to the Corinthian Jews; perhaps a gloss deprecating some insertion by a copyist.

B. INCEST IN CORINTH

Lv 18:8; 20-11 **5** I have been told as an undoubted fact that one of you is living with his father's 1
wife.[a] This is a case of sexual immorality among you that must be unparal-
Dt 27:20 leled even among pagans. •How can you be so proud of yourselves? You should 2
Lv 18:29 Dt 13:6 be in mourning. A man who does a thing like that ought to have been expelled
Col 2:5 from the community. •Though I am far away in body, I am with you in spirit, 3
and have already condemned the man who did this thing as if I were actually
Mt 18:20 present. •When you are assembled together in the name of the Lord Jesus,[b] 4
and I am spiritually present with you, then with the power of our Lord Jesus
2 Th 3:14 1 Tm 1:20 he is to be handed over to Satan so that his sensual body may be destroyed and 5
1:8+ his spirit saved on the day of the Lord.[c]
The pride that you take in yourselves is hardly to your credit. You must know 6
Ga 5:9 how even a small amount of yeast is enough to leaven all the dough, •so get rid 7
Nb 5:3 of all the old yeast, and make yourselves into a completely new batch of bread,
Jn 1:29 1 P 1:19 unleavened as you are meant to be. Christ, our passover, has been sacrificed;
Rv 5:5 let us celebrate the feast, then, by getting rid of all the old yeast of evil and wick- 8
edness, having only the unleavened bread of sincerity and truth.[d]
2 Th 3:14 When I wrote in my letter to you[e] not to associate with people living immoral 9
2 Co 6:17 1 Jn 5:19 lives, •I was not meaning to include all the people in the world who are sexually 10
immoral, any more than I meant to include all usurers and swindlers or idol-
Jn 17:15 worshippers. To do that, you would have to withdraw from the world altogether.
Mt 18:17 Rm 1:29+ What I wrote was that you should not associate with a brother Christian[f] who 11
is leading an immoral life, or is a usurer, or idolatrous, or a slanderer, or a drunkard, or is dishonest; you should not even eat a meal with people like that. •It is 12
Col 4:5 1 Th 4:12 not my business to pass judgement on those outside.[g] Of those who are inside,
1 Tm 3:7 you can surely be the judges. •But of those who are outside, God is the judge. 13
Dt 13:6 *You must drive out this evil-doer from among you.*

C. RECOURSE TO THE PAGAN COURTS

Ac 9:13+ **6** How dare one of your members take up a complaint against another in the 1
Ws 3:8 lawcourts of the unjust[a] instead of before the saints? •As you know, it is the 2
Dn 7:22,26 Mt 19:28 saints who are to 'judge the world';[b] and if the world is to be judged by you, how
Rv 20:4 *Jude 5-6* can you be unfit to judge trifling cases? •Since we are also to judge angels, it follows 3
that we can judge matters of everyday life; •but when you have had cases of that 4
kind, the people you appointed to try them were not even respected in the
Church.[c] •You should be ashamed: is there really not one reliable man among 5
you to settle differences between brothers •and so one brother brings a court 6
case against another in front of unbelievers? •It is bad enough for you to have 7
Mt 5:38-42p Rm 12:17-19 lawsuits at all against one another: oughtn't you to let yourselves be wronged,
1 Th 5:15 and let yourselves be cheated? •But you are doing the wronging and the cheating, 8
and to your own brothers.
Ep 5:5 You know perfectly well that people who do wrong will not inherit the 9
Rm 1:29+ kingdom of God: people of immoral lives, idolaters, adulterers, catamites,
15:50 Jn 3:5 sodomites, •thieves, usurers, drunkards, slanderers and swindlers will never 10
Ga 5:21 Ep 2:1-6 inherit the kingdom of God.[d] •These are the sort of people some of you were 11
Tt 3:3-7 1 Jn 2:12 once, but now you have been washed clean, and sanctified, and justified through
the name of the Lord Jesus Christ and through the Spirit of our God.[e]

D. FORNICATION

10:23 Si 37:28 'For me there are no forbidden things';[f] maybe, but not everything does good. 12
Rm 6:15+ *Gn 4:7* I agree there are no forbidden things for me, but I am not going to let anything
dominate me. •Food is only meant for the stomach, and the stomach for food; 13
Col 2:22 yes, and God is going to do away with both of them. But the body—this is not

14 meant for fornication;[g] it is for the Lord, and the Lord for the body. •God, 10:31
who raised the Lord from the dead, will by his power raise[h] us up too. 15:12f Rm 1:4+;
15 You know, surely, that your bodies are members making up the body of 8:11+ 2:12+
Christ; do you think I can take parts of Christ's body and join them to the body *Rm 6:12-13*
16 of a prostitute? Never! •As you know, a man who goes with a prostitute is one
17 body with her, since *the two,* as it is said, *become one flesh.* •But anyone who is Gn 2:24
joined to the Lord is one spirit with him. Rm 8:9-10
18 Keep away from fornication. All the other sins are committed outside the
19 body; but to fornicate is to sin against your own body. •Your body, you know, 3:16-17
is the temple of the Holy Spirit, who is in you since you received him from God. Rm 5:5+ 1 Th 4:4-8
20 You are not your own property; •you have been bought and paid for.[i] That is *3:23; 7:23*
why you should use your body for the glory of God.[j] Rm 3:24+; 6:15+ Ph 1:20

II. ANSWERS TO VARIOUS QUESTIONS

A. MARRIAGE AND VIRGINITY[a]

Ep 5:22-33+

1 7 Now for the questions about which you wrote. Yes, it is a good thing for Mt 19:12
2 a man not to touch a woman; •but since sex is always a danger, let each
3 man have his own wife and each woman her own husband. •The husband must
give his wife what she has the right to expect, and so too the wife to the husband.
4 The wife has no rights over her own body; it is the husband who has them. In the
5 same way, the husband has no rights over his body; the wife has them. •Do not
refuse each other except by mutual consent, and then only for an agreed time, to
leave yourselves free for prayer; then come together again in case Satan should
6 take advantage of your weakness to tempt you. •This is a suggestion, not a rule:
7 I should like everyone to be like me, but everybody has his own particular gifts
from God, one with a gift for one thing and another with a gift for the opposite.
8 There is something I want to add for the sake of widows and those who are
9 not married: it is a good thing for them to stay as they are, like me, •but if they
cannot control the sexual urges, they should get married, since it is better to be 1 Tm 5:11-14+
married than to be tortured.
10 For the married I have something to say, and this is not from me but from Mt 5:32p; 19:9
11 the Lord: a wife must not leave her husband —•or if she does leave him, she must
either remain unmarried or else make it up with her husband—nor must a husband
send his wife away.

5 a. His stepmother; cf. Lv 18:8.
b. Var. 'of our Lord Jesus Christ'.
c. Not just excommunicated, or expelled from the community, v. 13, but consigned to Satan to be punished. The punishment, however, is intended to convert the man: his 'spirit', that is his soul, is to be saved. Cf. 11:30-32.
d. The Jews removed all yeast from their houses at Passover time, Ex 12:1+, and ate only unleavened bread ('azymes'). Christ crucified (our 'passover', i.e. our paschal lamb) is the one sacrifice for all, cf. Jn 19:36+. The Christian is united with the sacrificed and risen Christ in an unending Passover: he must therefore remove 'the old yeast', i.e. 'evil and wickedness', and use unleavened bread, i.e. 'sincerity and truth', instead.
e. The 'pre-canonical' letter, see Introduction to The Letters of St Paul.
f. Lit. 'a brother'.
g. Those who do not belong to the community, cf. Mk 4:11; Col 4:5; 1 Th 4:12; 1 Tm 3:7. The expression is of Jewish origin, cf. Si, prologue v. 5.

6 a. The pagan magistrates. Not that the Corinthian judges were more corrupt than others but they had not been 'justified' by God through faith in Christ. Hence Paul's play on words: how could they administer 'justice' for those who were 'justified', i.e. the 'saints', or members of the Christian community?
b. Side by side with Christ, the sovereign judge.
c. I.e. the pagan judges, cf. Mt 15:26+; 18:17. An alternative translation 'If therefore you have such everyday cases, set those to try them who are of no account whatever in the Church', that is to say, the least respected of the Christians. The invitation would be then sarcastic: the disputes are so trifling that the most ignorant could deal with them.
d. Cf. 15:50; Ga 5:21; Ep 5:5; Rv 21:8; 22:15.
e. Note the trinitarian formula, cf. 2 Co 13:13+.
f. Probably one of Paul's own sayings the meaning of which has been distorted by the libertines.

g. Against the libertines who maintained that fornication was as necessary for the body as food and drink.
h. Var. 'has raised'.
i. Lit. 'You have been bought for a price'.
j. Lit. 'Glorify (Vulg. adds 'and carry') God in your body'.

7 a. Not a formal treatise on marriage and virginity but a series of replies, probably in the same order as questions were put to Paul. Hence the repetitions and apparent contradictions. The main points are: 1. As a general rule, each should keep the state of life in which his call to the faith found him. 2. Virginity is a higher calling than marriage, and spiritually more profitable. 3. Marriage is a safeguard for those incapable of absolute continence.

1 P 3:1 The rest is from me and not from the Lord. If a brother has a wife who is an 12
unbeliever, and she is content to live with him, he must not send her away;
and if a woman has an unbeliever for her husband, and he is content to live with 13
her, she must not leave him. •This is because the unbelieving husband is made 14
one with the saints through his wife, and the unbelieving wife is made one with
the saints through her husband. If this were not so, your children would be
unclean, whereas in fact they are holy.[b] •However, if the unbelieving partner 15
does not consent, they may separate; in these circumstances, the brother or
sister[c] is not tied:[d] God has called you[e] to a life of peace. •If you are a wife, it 16
may be your part to save your husband, for all you know; if a husband, for all
you know, it may be your part to save your wife.

7:20,24; 11:16 For the rest, what each one has is what the Lord has given him and he should 17
continue as he was when God's call reached him. This is the ruling that I give
in all the churches. •If anyone had already been circumcised at the time of 18
1 M 1:15 his call, he need not disguise it, and anyone who was uncircumcised at
Rm 2:25-29 Ga 5:6; 6:15 the time of his call need not be circumcised; •because to be circumcised or 19
uncircumcised means nothing: what does matter is to keep the commandments
of God. •Let everyone stay as he was at the time of his call. •If, when you were 20 21
Rm 6:15+ Ep 6:5-9 called, you were a slave, do not let this bother you; but if you should have the
Col 3:22-24 chance of being free, accept it. •A slave, when he is called in the Lord, becomes 22
Rm 6:18,22 the Lord's freedman, and a freeman called in the Lord becomes Christ's slave.
6:20 Rm 3:24+ You have all been bought and paid for; do not be slaves of other men.[f] •Each 23 24
1 P 1:18 *7:17* one of you, my brothers, should stay as he was before God at the time of his call.

About remaining celibate, I have no directions from the Lord but give my 25
own opinion as one who, by the Lord's mercy, has stayed faithful. •Well then, 26
Rm 13:11 I believe that in these present times of stress[g] this is right: that it is good for a man
to stay as he is. •If you are tied to a wife, do not look for freedom; if you are 27
free of a wife, then do not look for one. •But if you marry, it is no sin, and it is 28
not a sin for a young girl to get married. They will have their troubles, though,
in their married life,[h] and I should like to spare you that.

2 Co 6:2+ Heb 13:14 Brothers, this is what I mean: our time is growing short. Those who have 29
2 Co 6:8-10 wives should live as though they had none, •and those who mourn should live as 30
though they had nothing to mourn for; those who are enjoying life should live
as though there were nothing to laugh about; those whose life is buying things
should live as though they had nothing of their own; •and those who have to 31
1 Jn 2:16-17 deal with the world should not become engrossed in it.[i] I say this because the
world as we know it is passing away.

Mt 19:12 I would like to see you free from all worry. An unmarried man can devote 32
himself to the Lord's affairs, all he need worry about is pleasing the Lord; •but 33
a married man has to bother about the world's affairs and devote himself to
pleasing his wife: •he is torn two ways. In the same way an unmarried woman, 34
like a young girl, can devote herself to the Lord's affairs; all she need worry
about is being holy in body and spirit. The married woman, on the other hand,
has to worry about the world's affairs and devote herself to pleasing her husband.
I say this only to help you, not to put a halter round your necks, but simply to 35
Lk 10:40 make sure that everything is as it should be, and that you give your undivided
attention to the Lord.

Si 7:25 Still, if there is anyone who feels that it would not be fair to his daughter to 36
let her grow too old for marriage, and that he should do something about it, he
is free to do as he likes: he is not sinning if there is a marriage. •On the other 37
hand, if someone has firmly made his mind up, without any compulsion and
in complete freedom of choice, to keep his daughter as she is, he will be doing
a good thing. •In other words, the man who sees that his daughter is married 38
has done a good thing but the man who keeps his daughter unmarried has done
something even better.[j]

Rm 7:2 A wife is tied as long as her husband is alive. But if the husband dies, she is 39

40 free to marry anybody she likes, only it must be in the Lord.[k] •She would be
happier, in my opinion, if she stayed as she is—and I too have the Spirit of God,[l] 2:16 Ep 3:4
I think.

B. FOOD OFFERED TO IDOLS[a]

General principles Rm 14

1 **8** Now about food sacrificed to idols. 'We all have knowledge'; yes, that is so,
but knowledge gives self-importance—it is love that makes the building grow. Ac 9:31 Rm 15:2
2 A man may imagine he understands something, but still not understand anything
3 in the way that he ought to. •But any man who loves God is known[b] by him.
4 Well then, about eating food sacrificed to idols: we know that idols do not really Ga 4:8
5 exist in the world and that there is no god but the One. •And even if there were Dt 6:4+
things called gods, either in the sky or on earth—where there certainly seem to
6 be 'gods' and 'lords' in plenty[c]—•still for us there is one God, the Father, from Ex 20:2-3+
whom all things come and for whom we exist; and there is one Lord, Jesus Christ, Rm 11:36 Ep 4:5-6 *Jn 1:3*
through whom all things come and through whom we exist. Col 1:16-17 Heb 1:2

The claims of love Rm 14; 15: 1-2,7 1 Th 5:14

7 Some people, however, do not have this knowledge. There are some who
have been so long used to idols that they eat this food as though it really
had been sacrificed to the idol, and their conscience, being weak, is defiled
8 by it. •Food, of course, cannot bring us in touch with God: we lose nothing Rm 14:17 Col 2:21f
9 if we refuse to eat, we gain nothing if we eat. •Only be careful that you Heb 13:9 *Rm 6:15+*
do not make use of this freedom in a way that proves a pitfall for the weak. *Rm 14:15*
10 Suppose someone sees you, a man who understands, eating in some temple Rv 2:18
of an idol; his own conscience, even if it is weak, may encourage him[d]
11 to eat food which has been offered to idols. •In this way your knowledge
could become the ruin of someone weak, of a brother for whom Christ
12 died. •By sinning in this way against your brothers, and injuring their weak Mt 10:40+ Ac 9:5
13 consciences, it would be Christ against whom you sinned. •That is why,
since food can be the occasion of my brother's downfall, I shall never eat meat Rm 14:13, 20-21
again in case I am the cause of a brother's downfall.

Paul invokes his own example[a]

1 **9** I, personally, am free: I am an apostle and I have seen Jesus our Lord. You Ac 9:17+ Rm 1:1+
2 are all my work in the Lord. •Even if I were not an apostle to others, I should *Ac 15:8*

b. 'Sanctification' and 'holiness' here, as frequently in the Bible, mean not so much the perfection of a man's life as its precondition—dedication to God and adoption by him, cf. Ac 9:13+. By marrying one of God's people a pagan is brought into a special relationship with the true God and with his Church.

c. That is, the Christian partner.

d. This is known as 'the Pauline privilege'.

e. Var. 'us'.

f. Spiritually slaves to their outlook and conventions.

g. Lit. 'because of the present (or imminent) distress'.

h. Lit. 'in the flesh', not however referring, as in 7:2,9, to concupiscence.

i. Lit. 'should not use it to the full'.

j. In the classical world a father made what arrangements he thought fit for his daughter. Some interpreters see in this passage a reference to the practice of a man and woman living together under vows of strict chastity, for which there may be some evidence though only from a later date. In this case, read 'virgin' for 'daughter' in vv. 36-38.

k. She must marry a Christian.

l. Var. 'of Christ'.

8 a. The frequent feasts and public ceremonies in antiquity were always accompanied by sacrifice. Portions of the sacrificial food *(eidolytha)* went to the gods, the priests and the donors. What remained was either eaten at a sacred meal or sold in the markets. This situation provided several difficulties for Christians: could they take part in a sacred meal; buy meat that had been sacrificed to idols; accept invitations to eat in a pagan house? Paul answers these specific difficulties, 10:14-22 and 23-30. In principle, enlightened Christians are completely free to decide for themselves, 8:1-6; 10:15,25,29-30, but they must avoid leading astray other Christians who are not yet emancipated from their pre-conversion ideas, 8:7-13; 10:23-24,28-29. Paul makes no reference to the Decree of Jerusalem, Ac 15:20-29, and does not even seem to have heard about it, Ac 15:1+.

b. In the biblical sense, i.e. 'loved'. Cf. Ho 2:22+.

c. Paul is simply stating a fact. The 'gods' are the mythical gods of Olympus, the 'lords' are divinised human beings.

d. Lit. 'be built up'; ironical, cf. 8:1.

9 a. Though free to do whatever he thinks best about food sacrificed to idols a Christian must be guided by charity. Paul himself, as he goes on to say, had given up out of charity some of his rights as an apostle.

2 Co 3:2 still be an apostle to you who are the seal of my apostolate in the Lord. •My 3
answer to those who want to interrogate me is this: •Have we not every right 4
Lk 8:2-3 to eat and drink?[b] •And the right to take a Christian woman[c] round with us, 5
Mt 12:46+ Jn 1:42 like all the other apostles and the brothers of the Lord and Cephas?
Ac 4:36+; 18:3+ Are Barnabas and I the only ones who are not allowed to stop working? •Nobody 6 7
2 Tm 2:6 ever paid money to stay in the army, and nobody ever planted a vineyard and
refused to eat the fruit of it. Who has there ever been that kept a flock and did not
feed on the milk from his flock?

These may be only human comparisons, but does not the Law itself say the 8
Dt 25:4 Lk 12:6,24 1 Tm 5:18 same thing? •It is written in the Law of Moses: *You must not put a muzzle on the* 9
ox when it is treading out the corn. Is it about oxen that God is concerned, •or is 10
10:6+ there not an obvious reference to ourselves? Clearly this was written for our sake
to show that the ploughman ought to plough in expectation, and the thresher to
Rm 15:27 thresh in the expectation of getting his share. •If we have sown spiritual things 11
for you, why should you be surprised if we harvest your material things? •Others 12
are allowed these rights over you and our right is surely greater? In fact we have
4:12 never exercised this right. On the contrary we have put up with anything rather
than obstruct the Good News of Christ in any way. •Remember that the ministers 13
serving in the Temple get their food from the Temple and those serving at the
Mt 10:10p altar can claim their share from the altar itself. •In the same sort of way the Lord 14
directed that those who preach the gospel should get their living from the gospel.

2 Co 11:9 However, I have not exercised any of these rights, and I am not writing all 15
this to secure this treatment for myself. I would rather die than let anyone take
away something that I can boast of.[d] •Not that I do boast of preaching the gospel, 16
Ac 4:20; 9:15-16; 22:14-15; 26:16-18 since it is a duty which has been laid on me; I should be punished if I did not
preach it! •If I had chosen this work myself, I might have been paid for it, but 17
as I have not, it is a responsibility which has been put into my hands. •Do you 18
2 Co 11:7 know what my reward is? It is this: in my preaching, to be able to offer the Good
News free, and not insist on the rights which the gospel gives me.

10:32-33 Mt 20:26p Rm 6:15+ Ga 4:4-5 So though I am not a slave of any man I have made myself the slave of 19
everyone so as to win as many as I could. •I made myself a Jew to the Jews, to 20
win the Jews; that is, I who am not a subject of the Law made myself a subject
of the Law to those who are the subjects of the Law, to win those who are subject
Ga 4:12 to the Law. •To those who have no Law, I was free of the Law myself (though 21
not free from God's law, being under the law of Christ) to win those who have
Rm 15:1 2 Co 11:29 no Law. •For the weak I made myself weak. I made myself all things to all men in 22
order to save some[e] at any cost; •and I still do this, for the sake of the gospel, 23
to have a share in its blessings.

Ga 5:7+ All the runners at the stadium are trying to win, but only one of them gets 24
Ws 5:16 Ph 3:14 2 Tm 4:7-8 Jm 1:12 1 P 5:4 Rv 2:10; 3:11 the prize. You must run in the same way, meaning to win. •All the fighters at 25
the games go into strict training; they do this just to win a wreath that will wither
away, but we do it for a wreath that will never wither. •That is how I run, intent 26
on winning; that is how I fight, not beating the air. •I treat my body hard and 27
make it obey me, for, having been an announcer myself, I should not want to be
disqualified.[f]

Heb 4:2-3 **A warning, and the lessons of Israel's history**[a]

Ex 13:21; 14:22 10 I want to remind you, brothers, how our fathers were all guided by a cloud 1
above them and how they all passed through the sea. •They were all 2
Ex 16:4-35+ baptised into Moses[b] in this cloud and in this sea; •all ate the same spiritual 3
Ex 17:5-6 Nb 20:7-11 Ps 114:8 food •and all drank the same spiritual drink,[c] since they all drank from the 4
spiritual rock that followed them as they went,[d] and that rock was Christ. •In 5
Nb 14:16 Jude 5 spite of this, most of them failed to please God and their corpses littered the
desert.

Nb 11:4,34 Rm 4:23 Heb 9:9,24 These things all happened as warnings[e] for us, not to have the wicked lusts 6
for forbidden things that they had. •Do not become idolaters as some of them 7

did, for scripture says: *After sitting down to eat and drink, the people got up to* Ex 32:6
amuse themselves. •We must never fall into sexual immorality: some of them did, Nb 25:1-9; Ws 10:8
and twenty-three thousand met their downfall in one day. •We are not to put
the Lord[f] to the test: some of them did, and they were killed by snakes. •You Nb 21:5-6; Ac 5:9
must never complain: some of them did, and they were killed by the Destroyer. *Nb 17:6-15; Ex 12:23+*
All this happened to them as a warning, and it was written down to be a lesson 10:6; *Rm 15:4*
for us who are living at the end of the age.[g] •The man who thinks he is safe must *Ga 6:1*
be careful that he does not fall. •The trials that you have had to bear are no
more than people normally have. You can trust God not to let you be tried Si 15:11-20; *1:9+*
beyond your strength, and with any trial he will give you a way out of it and the Jm 1:13-14; *Mt 6:13;* 26:41
strength to bear it.

Sacrificial feasts. No compromise with idolatry

4 This is the reason, my dear brothers, why you must keep clear of idolatry. Rm 14:1
5 6 I say to you as sensible people: judge for yourselves what I am saying. •The
blessing-cup[h] that we bless is a communion with the blood of Christ, and the 11:23-26+; Lv 3:1+
7 bread that we break is a communion with the body of Christ. •The fact that there Mt 26:26-27
is only one loaf means that, though there are many of us, we form a single body 12:12+; Ep 4:4
8 because we all have a share in this one loaf. •Look at the other Israel, the race,[i]
9 where those who eat the sacrifices are in communion with the altar. •Does this
mean that the food sacrificed to idols has a real value, or that the idol itself is
0 real? •Not at all. It simply means that the sacrifices that they offer *they sacrifice to* Dt 32:17; Ps 106:37
demons who are not God. I have no desire to see you in communion with 2 Co 6:14-16
1 demons. •You cannot drink the cup of the Lord and the cup of demons. You
2 cannot take your share at the table of the Lord and at the table of demons. •Do
we want to make the Lord angry; are we stronger than he is? Dt 4:24

Food sacrificed to idols. Practical solutions

23 'For me there are no forbidden things', but not everything does good. True, 6:12+; Si 37:28
there are no forbidden things, but it is not everything that helps the building to
24 grow. •Nobody should be looking for his own advantage, but everybody for the 10:33; Rm 14:19; 15:2
25 other man's. •Do not hesitate to eat anything that is sold in butchers' shops: Ph 2:4
26 there is no need to raise questions of conscience; •for *the earth and everything* *Ps 24:1*
27 *that is in it belong to the Lord.* •If an unbeliever invites you to his house, go if

b. At the expense of the Christian congregations.

c. Lit. 'a sister, a woman (wife?)'. To look after the apostle's needs.

d. Lit. 'I would rather die than... No one shall take away something that I can boast of.' Aposiopesis.

e. Var. (Vulg.) 'all'.

f. In this passage Paul is using contemporary sporting terms.

10 a. Before reverting to the problem of food sacrificed to idols, Paul quotes the O.T. to remind Corinthians about the dangers of idolatry so as to prevent them joining in the actual sacrificial meals, 10:14-22.

b. As Christians are now baptised 'into' Christ (Rm 6:3; Ga 3:27), i.e. to be united with him.

c. Passing through the Red Sea in v. 2 suggests Christian baptism; here manna and water from the rock suggest the Eucharist. Christians took the description in Ex of the liberation from Egypt as a symbol of liberation from sin by Christ, who is symbolised by Moses, cf. Jn 1:21+; 13:1+. This comparison was implied by Jesus when he linked his Eucharist to the Passover-supper, cf. Mt 26:17-29p; 1 Co 5:7. This accounts for the many Exodus references in the Easter liturgy.

d. Allusion to the legend that the rock from which Moses made water flow accompanied the Israelites on their travels through the wilderness. Jewish writers had already tended to identify this rock with Yahweh himself, and had supported this identification with references to Ex 17:6, and to the O.T. use of 'Rock of Israel' as a title for Yahweh, cf. Ps 18:2+. Paul credits the pre-existent Christ with the attributes of Yahweh.

e. Lit. 'types' (*tupoi*). The purpose in the events, intended by God, was to prefigure in the history of Israel the spiritual realities of the messianic age (which are known as 'antitypes', 1 P 3:21, but cf. Heb 9:24). These 'typological' (or less accurately, 'allegorical', Ga 4:24) meanings in the O.T. narrative, though not consciously intended by the authors are nevertheless valid and necessary for the understanding of scripture, since the pattern of God's working on the physical plane does in fact reflect his eternal purposes fulfilled in the incarnation to become the spiritual realities of the messianic age. Typological meanings of O.T. events are often pointed out by the authors of the N.T. as though the sole purpose of Israel's written history had been to provide types for the instruction of Christians. Paul does this, v. 11 and 9:9; Rm 4:23f; 5:14; 15:4; cf. 2 Tm 3:16, and some books like Jn and Heb are largely based on a typological interpretation of the O.T.

f. Var. 'Christ'.

g. Lit. 'unto whom the ends of the ages have reached'.

h. I.e. the cup of wine for which we thank God, like Christ at the Last Supper.

i. Lit. 'the Israel according to the flesh', i.e. the Israel of history, cf. Rm 7:5, as compared with the Israel 'of God', Ga 6:16, the true Israel, the Christian community.

you want to, and eat whatever is put in front of you, without asking questions
just to satisfy conscience. •But if someone says to you, 'This food was offered 2
in sacrifice', then, out of consideration for the man that told you, you should
not eat it, for the sake of his scruples; •his scruples, you see, not your own. Why 2
should my freedom depend on somebody else's conscience? •If I take my share 3
1 Tm 4:4 with thankfulness, why should I be blamed for food for which I have thanked
God?

Conclusion

Col 3:17 1 P 4:11 Whatever you eat, whatever you drink, whatever you do at all, do it for the 3
9:19-23 1:2+ glory of God. •Never do anything offensive to anyone—to Jews or Greeks or to 3
the Church of God; •just as I try to be helpful to everyone at all times, not 3
10:24+ Rm 15:2 anxious for my own advantage but for the advantage of everybody else, so that
11 they may be saved.
2 Th 3:7+ Take me for your model, as I take Christ. 1

C. DECORUM IN PUBLIC WORSHIP

Women's behaviour at services

15:1-3 1 Th 2:13+; You have done well in remembering me so constantly and in maintaining 2
4:1-2 2 Th 2:15 the traditions[a] just as I passed them on to you. •However, what I want you to 3
Ep 5:23 understand is that Christ is the head of every man, man is the head of woman,
3:23 *Ac 11:27+* and God is the head of Christ. •For a man to pray or prophesy with his head 4
covered is a sign of disrespect to his head.[b] •For a woman, however, it is a sign 5
2 Co 3:18 of disrespect to her head[c] if she prays or prophesies unveiled; she might as well
11:15 have her hair shaved off. •In fact, a woman who will not wear a veil ought to have 6
her hair cut off.[d] If a woman is ashamed to have her hair cut off or shaved, she
ought to wear a veil.

Gn 1:26-27 A man should certainly not cover his head, since he is the image of God and 7
reflects God's glory; but woman is the reflection of man's glory. •For man did 8
Gn 2:21-23 1 Tm 2:12-13 not come from woman; no, woman came from man; •and man was not created 9
for the sake of woman, but woman was created for the sake of man. •That is the 10
argument for women's covering their heads with a symbol of the authority[e]
14:34 over them, out of respect for the angels.[f] •However, though woman cannot do 11
without man, neither can man do without woman, in the Lord; •woman may 12
come from man, but man is born of woman—both come from God.

Ask yourselves if it is fitting for a woman to pray to God without a veil; 13
and whether nature itself does not tell you that long hair on a man is nothing 14
11:5 to be admired, •while a woman, who was given her hair as a covering, thinks 15
long hair her glory?

4:17; 7:17; 14:33 To anyone who might still want to argue: it is not the custom with us, nor in 16
1:2+ the churches of God.[g]

The Lord's Supper

Now that I am on the subject of instructions, I cannot say that you have done 17
well in holding meetings that do you more harm than good. •In the first place, 18
I hear that when you all come together as a community, there are separate
factions among you, and I half believe it—•since there must no doubt be separate 19
groups among you, to distinguish those who are to be trusted. •The point is, 20
when you hold these meetings, it is not the Lord's Supper[h] that you are eating,
since when the time comes to eat, everyone is in such a hurry to start his own 21
supper that one person goes hungry while another is getting drunk. •Surely you 22
have homes for eating and drinking in? Surely you have enough respect for the
1:2+ community of God not to make poor people embarrassed? What am I to say to
you? Congratulate you? I cannot congratulate you on this.

23 For this is what I received from the Lord, and in turn passed on to you: that 10:16-17 ||Mt 26:26-29
24 on the same night that he was betrayed, the Lord Jesus took some bread, •and ||Mk 14:22-25
thanked God for it and broke it, and he said, 'This is my body, which is for you;[i] ||Lk 22:14-20 Ex 12:14
25 do this as a memorial of me'. •In the same way he took the cup after supper, Dt 16:3
and said, 'This cup is the new covenant in my blood. Whenever you drink it, do Ex 24:8 Jr 31:31+
26 this as a memorial of me.' •Until the Lord comes, therefore, every time you eat Heb 8:6-13
27 this bread and drink this cup, you are proclaiming his death, •and so anyone
who eats the bread or drinks the cup of the Lord unworthily will be behaving 16:22 Rv 22:17,20
unworthily towards the body and blood of the Lord.
28 Everyone is to recollect himself before eating this bread and drinking this
29 cup; •because a person who eats and drinks[j] without recognising the Body[k]
30 is eating and drinking his own condemnation. •In fact that is why many of you Ac 5:9
31 are weak and ill and some of you have died.[l] •If only we recollected ourselves,
32 we should not be punished like that. •But when the Lord does punish us like that,
it is to correct us and stop us from being condemned with the world. Dt 8:5+ Rv 3:19
33 So to sum up, my dear brothers, when you meet for the Meal, wait for one
34 another. •Anyone who is hungry should eat at home, and then your meeting
will not bring your condemnation. The other matters I shall adjust when I come.

Spiritual gifts[a]

1 12 Now my dear brothers, I want to clear up a wrong impression about 1 Th 5:20
2 spiritual gifts. •You remember that, when you were pagans, whenever Ga 4:8
3 you felt irresistibly drawn,[b] it was towards dumb idols? •It is for that reason that
I want you to understand that on the one hand no one can be speaking under the Jn 14:26+ 1 Jn 4:1-3
influence of the Holy Spirit and say, 'Curse Jesus', and on the other hand, no one
can say, 'Jesus is Lord' unless he is under the influence of the Holy Spirit. Ac 2:21+, 36+ Rm 10:9 Ph 2:11

The variety and the unity of gifts

4 There is a variety of gifts but always the same Spirit; •there are all sorts of Ep 4:5 1 P 4:10
5
6 service to be done, but always to the same Lord; •working in all sorts of different
7 ways in different people, it is the same God who is working in all of them.[c] •The
particular way in which the Spirit is given to each person is for a good purpose. 12:28-30 Ac 1:8+
8 One may have the gift of preaching with wisdom[d] given him by the Spirit; another Rm 12:6-8 *1:5*
9 may have the gift of preaching instruction[e] given him by the same Spirit; •and
another the gift of faith[f] given by the same Spirit; another again the gift of healing, Rm 12:3
10 through this one Spirit; •one, the power of miracles; another, prophecy;[g] Ac 11:27+

11 a. I.e. the teaching of Christ and the apostles.

b. Greek pun on word *kephalē*, 'head', 'leader'. A Christian who prayed with head covered insulted Christ his leader; he should not hide Christ's glory but reflect it 'with uncovered face', cf. 2 Co 3:18.

c. I.e. her husband, since she seemed to be claiming equality with her husband. A woman's veil was a sign of subjection, v. 10.

d. Ironical: having begun by removing the veil, she may as well go all the way and shave her head as well. Cf. v. 15.

e. Lit. 'a power', or 'authority'.

f. Apparently a reference to angels as being guardians of public order in public worship.

g. This puts a stop to any discussion.

h. The supper commemorating Christ's last supper with his disciples during which he instituted the Eucharist. Before the liturgical meal the Corinthians held this ordinary meal, the earliest form of the *agape*. Paul disapproves of this custom v. 34, and condemns its abuses, vv. 21-22.

i. Var. 'This is my body, broken for you'.

j. Add. 'unworthily'.

k. The Body of the Lord.

l. Lit. 'fallen asleep'. Evidently Paul considers the sickness and death of some Corinthians to have been a punishment for irreverence to 'the body and blood of the Lord'.

12 a. The spiritual gifts *(charismata)* granted by the Holy Spirit to some members of the community witnessed to the Spirit's presence and helped the Church to function while its hierarchy was still in a rudimentary state. There were so many gifts, and some were so eccentric and noisy, that they tended to produce disorder. Hence Paul's admonitions: 1. All these gifts come from the Spirit. 2. All are given for the benefit of the community. 3. Their respective values are to be judged by their usefulness to the community. 4. The gift of prophecy *(propheteia)* is vastly superior to the gift of tongues *(glossolalia)* of which the Corinthians are so proud. 5. Finally, it is better to have charity than any of the *charismata*.

b. Allusion to the frenzies and orgies of some pagan cults.

c. Note again the trinitarian formulation, cf. 6:11; 2 Co 13:13+.

d. Probably the gift of preaching the central Christian truths about God and God's life in us: this is the 'perfect teaching' of Heb 6:1. Cf. also 1 Co 2:6-16.

e. The gift of preaching the elementary Christian truths: 'the elementary teaching concerning Christ' of Heb 6:1.

f. An unusually intense faith, cf. 13:2.

g. On 'prophecy' cf. Ac 11:27+.

Ac 2:4+ 1 Jn 4:1-3 another the gift of recognising spirits;[h] another the gift of tongues[i] and another
the ability to interpret them. •All these are the work of one and the same Spirit, 11
who distributes different gifts to different people just as he chooses.

The analogy of the body[j]

6:15; 10:17 Rm 12:4-5 Just as a human body, though it is made up of many parts, is a single unit 12
Ep 4:25 Col 3:15 because all these parts, though many, make one body, so it is with Christ.[k] •In 13
Ga 3:28 Ep 4:4-6 the one Spirit we were all baptised, Jews as well as Greeks, slaves as well as
Col 3:11 citizens, and one Spirit was given to us all to drink.
Nor is the body to be identified with any one of its many parts. •If the foot 14 15
were to say, 'I am not a hand and so I do not belong to the body', would that
mean that it stopped being part of the body? •If the ear were to say, 'I am not 16
an eye, and so I do not belong to the body', would that mean that it was not a part
of the body? •If your whole body was just one eye, how would you hear anything? 17
If it was just one ear, how would you smell anything?
Instead of that, God put all the separate parts into the body on purpose. •If 18 19
all the parts were the same, how could it be a body? •As it is, the parts are many 20
but the body is one. •The eye cannot say to the hand, 'I do not need you', nor can 21
the head say to the feet, 'I do not need you'.
What is more, it is precisely the parts of the body that seem to be the weakest 22
which are the indispensable ones; •and it is the least honourable parts of the 23
body that we clothe with the greatest care. So our more improper parts get
decorated •in a way that our more proper parts do not need. God has arranged 24
the body so that more dignity is given to the parts which are without it, •and so 25
that there may not be disagreements inside the body, but that each part may be
Rm 12:15 equally concerned for all the others. •If one part is hurt, all parts are hurt with 26
it. If one part is given special honour, all parts enjoy it.
12:7-11 Rm 12:6-8 Now you together are Christ's body; but each of you is a different part of it. 27
Ep 4:11 Ac 11:27+ In the Church, God has given the first place to apostles, the second to prophets, 28
Rm 1:1+ Jm 3:1+ the third to teachers;[l] after them, miracles, and after them the gift of healing;
helpers,[m] good leaders,[n] those with many languages. •Are all of them apostles, 29
or all of them prophets, or all of them teachers? Do they all have the gift of
miracles, •or all have the gift of healing? Do all speak strange languages, and 30
all interpret them?

The order of importance in spiritual gifts. Love

Be ambitious for the higher gifts. And I am going to show you a way that is 31
better than any of them.
Rm 8:31; 14:15 Col 1:8 13 If I have all the eloquence of men or of angels, but speak without love,[a] 1
I am simply a gong booming or a cymbal clashing. •If I have the gift of 2
Mt 7:22 prophecy, understanding all the mysteries there are, and knowing everything,
Mt 17:20 Jm 2:14-17 and if I have faith in all its fulness, to move mountains, but without love, then
Mt 6:2 I am nothing at all. •If I give away all that I possess, piece by piece, and if I even 3
let them take my body to burn it,[b] but am without love, it will do me no good
whatever.
Rm 13:8-10 1 Th 5:14-15 Love is always patient and kind; it is never jealous; love is never boastful 4
Rm 12:9-10 or conceited; •it is never rude or selfish; it does not take offence, and is not 5
resentful. •Love takes no pleasure in other people's sins but delights in the truth; 6
Pr 10:12 it is always ready to excuse, to trust, to hope, and to endure whatever comes. 7
13:13+ Ac 11:27+ Love does not come to an end. But if there are gifts of prophecy, the time 8
Ac 2:4+ will come when they must fail; or the gift of languages, it will not continue
for ever; and knowledge—for this, too, the time will come when it must fail.
For our knowledge is imperfect[c] and our prophesying is imperfect; •but once 9 10
perfection comes, all imperfect things will disappear. •When I was a child, I used 11
to talk like a child, and think like a child, and argue like a child, but now I am
2 Co 5:7 a man, all childish ways are put behind me. •Now we are seeing a dim reflection 12

in a mirror; but then we shall be seeing face to face. The knowledge that I have 1 Jn 3:2
now is imperfect; but then I shall know as fully as I am known.[d] Nb 12:8 Ws 3:9
In short,[e] there are three things that last:[f] faith, hope and love; and the *Rm 5:4* Ga 5:6
greatest of these is love. Ep 1:15; 4:2 Col 1:4 Phm 5

Spiritual gifts: their respective importance in the community

Ac 2:4+; 11:27+

14 You must want love more than anything else; but still hope for the spiritual
gifts as well, especially prophecy. •Anybody with the gift of tongues speaks 1 Th 5:20
to God, but not to other people; because nobody understands him when he
talks in the spirit about mysterious things. •On the other hand, the man who
prophesies does talk to other people, to their improvement, their encouragement
and their consolation. •The one with the gift of tongues talks for his own
benefit, but the man who prophesies does so for the benefit of the community. Nb 11:29
While I should like you all to have the gift of tongues, I would much rather you
could prophesy, since the man who prophesies is of greater importance than the

h. The gift of knowing if *charismata* were spiritual, natural, or evil.

i. On the charisma of 'tongues' *(glossolalia)* cf. Ac 2:4+.

j. Paul uses the classical analogy of society as a single body with many parts but his concept of the Body of Christ goes back to the memory of his own conversion, cf. Ac 9:4f; Ga 1:15f, to faith in Jesus whose body, raised from the dead and given life by the Spirit, Rm 1:4+, became the 'first-fruits' of a new creation, 1 Co 15:23. The words spoken by the Lord at Paul's conversion, 'I am Jesus, whom you are persecuting', imply that Christians are identified with the risen Christ. In Paul's writings, Christians are bodily united with the risen body, Rm 8:11, by baptism, 1 Co 12:13; cf. Rm 6:4+, and the Eucharist, 1 Co 10:16f, which make them parts of Christ's body, 1 Co 6:15, united in such a way that he and they together form the Body of Christ (what is now called 'the mystical body'), 1 Co 12:27; Rm 12:4f. This rather realistic teaching of 1 Co is taken up later on and developed in the Letters of the Captivity, where the basic idea remains the same, i.e. humans are reconciled to God by becoming parts of, Ep 5:30, Christ's body which was physically dead but is now spiritually alive, Ep 2:14-18, Col 1:22. The stress however is on the unity of the Body that brings all Christians together in one Spirit, Ep 4:4; Col 3:15, and on the identification of the Body with the Church, Ep 1:22f; 5:23; Col 1:18,24. Having thus personified the body, Ep 4:12f; Col 2:19, Paul asserts that Christ is its Head, Ep 1:22; 4:15f; 5:23; Col 1:18; 2:19 (cf. 1 Co 12:21). This assertion probably developed from the concept of Christ as Head of all Powers, Col 2:10. Eventually, in its widest sense, Paul includes in his concept of the Body the entire cosmos as unified under the Lord Christ, Ep 1:23+. Cf. Jn 2:21+.

k. The way a human body gives unity to all its component parts is the way Christ, as unifying principle of his Church, gives unity to all Christians in his Body.

l. The regular teachers appointed for each separate church, cf. Ac 13:1+.

m. Lit. 'helpings': voluntary gifts to works of charity.

n. Administrators and guides of the churches.

13 a. Love *(agape)* has no possessiveness and is not a desire for satisfaction: it wants to satisfy the other. The supreme charity is God's love for us, 1 Jn 4:19, that made him give his Son so that sinners might be reconciled, Rm 5:8; 8:32-39; 2 Co 5:18-21; Ep 2:4-7; cf. Jn 3:16f; 1 Jn 4:9-10, and become not only God's chosen ones, Ep 1:4, but God's sons, 1 Jn 3:1. This love is attributed to God (the Father), Rm 5:5; 8:39; 2 Co 13:11,13; Ph 2:1; 2 Th 2:16; cf. 1 Jn 2:15, but as it is identical with God's nature, 1 Jn 4:7f,16, it is found in the Son, Rm 8:35,37,39; 2 Co 5:14; Ep 3:19; 1 Tm 1:14; 2 Tm 1:13, so the Son loves the Father as the Son is loved by the Father, Ep 1:6; Col 1:13; cf. Jn 3:35; 10:17; 14:31, and as the Father loves us, so the Son loves the human race, Jn 13:1,34; 14:21; 15:9, which he was sent to save, 2 Co 5:14f; Ga 2:20; Ep 5:2,25; 1 Tm 1:14f; cf. Jn 15:13; 1 Jn 3:16; Rv 1:5. This is the same love that the Holy Spirit, Rm 15:30; Col 1:8, gives Christians, Rm 5:5; cf. Ga 5:22, to help them to carry out, Rm 8:4, the essential commandment of the Law, which is love of God and neighbour, Mt 22:37-40p; Rm 13:8-10; Ga 5:14. To love friends, and enemies, Mt 5:43-48p, is not only the necessary consequence of God's love for us, but actually proves that God loves us, 1 Jn 3:17; 4:20f, and it is the new commandment laid down by Christ, Jn 13:34f; 15:12,17; 1 Jn 3:23; etc., and constantly emphasised by his disciples, Rm 13:8; Ga 5:13f; Ep 1:15; Ph 2:2f; Col 1:4; 1 Th 3:12; 2 Th 1:3; Phm 5:7; cf. Jm 2:8; 1 P 1:22; 2:17; 4:8; 1 Jn 2:10; 3:10f,14; etc. This is how Paul loves the Christians of his own churches, 2 Co 2:4; 12:15; etc., and how they love him, Col 1:8; 1 Th 3:6; etc. Love presupposes sincerity, humility, selflessness and self-sacrifice, Rm 12:9f; 1 Co 13:4-7; 2 Co 6:6; Ph 2:2f, service, Ga 5:13; cf. Heb 6:10, mutual help, Ep 4:2; cf. Rm 14:15; 2 Co 2:7f. Love shows itself in the way we behave, 2 Co 8:8-11,24; cf. 1 Jn 3:18, and the way we obey the Lord's commands, Jn 14:15; 1 Jn 5:2f, etc., and give effect to our faith, Ga 5:6; cf. Heb 10:24. Love holds the community together, Col 3:14; cf. 2 P 1:7, and it 'covers up many sins', 1 P 4:8; cf. Lk 7:47. Since love of neighbour springs from love of God, its motive cannot be fear, Rm 8:28-39; cf. 1 Jn 4:17f. Nor can we be charitable without truth, Ep 4:15, cf. 2 Th 2:10, and it is this that enables us to make moral judgements, Ph 1:9, and gives us spiritual understanding of the divine mystery, Col 2:2; cf. 1 Jn 4:7, and spiritual knowledge of the otherwise unknowable love of Christ, Ep 3:17-19; cf. 1 Co 8:1-3; 13:8-12. Since Christ, Ep 3:17, and the whole Trinity, 2 Co 13:13+; cf. Jn 14:15-23; 1 Jn 4:12, live in the soul that has this love, it fosters the theological virtues, cf. Rm 1:16+; 5:2+, in any person where it is the dominant characteristic, 1 Co 13:13. Love is the only eternal virtue, 1 Co 13:8, and will only be perfect in the vision, 1 Co 13:12; cf. 1 Jn 3:2, when God gives his lovers the gifts he has promised, 1 Co 2:9; Rm 8:28; Ep 6:24; 2 Tm 4:8; cf. Jm 1:12; 2:5.

b. Var. 'I may give all my goods to the poor so that I can boast of it'.

c. Lit. 'in part'.

d. I.e. by God.

e. Or 'Meanwhile'.

f. Or 'In short, then, we are left with these three things'. This association of the three theological virtues, which is found earlier in 1 Th 1:3 and which was probably in use before Paul's time, recurs frequently in his letters, though the order varies: 1 Th 5:8; 1 Co 13:7,13; Ga 5:5f; Rm 5:1-5; 12:6-12; Col 1:4-5; Ep 1:15-18; 4:2-5; 1 Tm 6:11; Tt 2:2. Cf. Heb 6:10-12; 10:22-24; 1 P 1:3-9,21f. Faith and charity are associated in 1 Th 3:6; 2 Th 1:3; Phm 5, faith and fortitude in 2 Th 1:4, love and fortitude in 2 Th 3:5. Cf. 2 Co 13:13

man with the gift of tongues, unless of course the latter offers an interpretation
so that the church may get some benefit.
Now suppose, my dear brothers, I am someone with the gift of tongues, and 6
I come to visit you, what use shall I be if all my talking reveals nothing new, tells
you nothing, and neither inspires you nor instructs you? •Think of a musical 7
instrument, a flute or a harp: if one note on it cannot be distinguished
from another, how can you tell what tune is being played? •Or if no one can 8
be sure which call the trumpet has sounded, who will be ready for the attack?
It is the same with you: if your tongue does not produce intelligible speech, how 9
can anyone know what you are saying? You will be talking to the air. •There are 10
any number of different languages in the world, and not one of them is meaningless,[a] •but if I am ignorant of what the sounds mean, I am a savage to the man 11
who is speaking, and he is a savage to me. •It is the same in your own case: since 12
you aspire to spiritual gifts, concentrate on those which will grow to benefit the
community.
That is why anybody who has the gift of tongues must pray for the power 13
of interpreting them. •For if I use this gift in my prayers, my spirit may be praying 14
but my mind is left barren.[b] •What is the answer to that? Surely I should pray 15
not only with the spirit but with the mind as well? And sing praises not only with
the spirit but with the mind as well? •Any uninitiated person will never be able 16
2 Co 1:20 to say Amen to your thanksgiving, if you only bless God with the spirit, for he
will have no idea what you are saying. •However well you make your thanks- 17
giving, the other gets no benefit from it. •I thank God that I have a greater gift 18
of tongues than all of you, •but when I am in the presence of the community 19
Rm 15:2 I would rather say five words that mean something than ten thousand words
in a tongue.
Rm 16:19 Ep 4:14 Brothers, you are not to be childish in your outlook. You can be babies as 20
Mt 10:16 far as wickedness is concerned, but mentally you must be adult. •In the written 21
Is 28:11-12 Law it says:[c] *Through men speaking strange languages and through the lips of*
foreigners, I shall talk to the nation, and still they will not listen to me, says the
Lord. •You see then, that the strange languages are meant to be a sign not for 22
believers but for unbelievers, while on the other hand, prophecy is a sign not for
unbelievers but for believers. •So that any uninitiated people or unbelievers, 23
Ac 2:4,13 coming into a meeting of the whole church where everybody was speaking in
tongues, would say you were all mad; •but if you were all prophesying and an 24
unbeliever or uninitiated person came in, he would find himself analysed and
judged by everyone speaking; •he would find his secret thoughts laid bare, 25
Is 45:14 Zc 8:23 and then fall on his face and worship God, declaring that *God is among you*
indeed.

Regulating spiritual gifts

So, my dear brothers, what conclusion is to be drawn? At all your meetings, 26
let everyone be ready with a psalm or a sermon or a revelation, or ready to use
his gift of tongues or to give an interpretation; but it must always be for the
common good. •If there are people present with the gift of tongues, let only two or 27
three, at the most, be allowed to use it, and only one at a time, and there must
be someone to interpret. •If there is no interpreter present, they must keep quiet 28
in church and speak only to themselves and to God. •As for prophets, let two 29
or three of them speak, and the others attend to them. •If one of the listeners 30
receives a revelation, then the man who is already speaking should stop. •For 31
you can all prophesy in turn, so that everybody will learn something and
everybody will be encouraged. •Prophets can always control their prophetic 32
spirits, •since God is not a God of disorder but of peace. 33
11:16+ Ac 9:13+ As in all the churches of the saints, •women are to remain quiet at meetings 34
11:3,9 Gn 3:16 since they have no permission to speak; they must keep in the background as
1 Tm 2:11-12 the Law itself lays it down. •If they have any questions to ask, they should ask 35

their husbands at home: it does not seem right for a woman to raise her voice 11:5
at meetings.
36 Do you think the word of God came out of yourselves? Or that it has come
37 only to you? •Anyone who claims to be a prophet or inspired ought to recognise 2:16
38 that what I am writing to you is a command from the Lord. •Unless he recognises 7:40 *15:34*
this, you should not recognise him.[d]
39 And so, my dear brothers, by all means be ambitious to prophesy, do not
40 suppress the gift of tongues, •but let everything be done with propriety and in order.

III. THE RESURRECTION OF THE DEAD[a]

The fact of the resurrection

1 **15** Brothers, I want to remind you of the gospel I preached to you, the gospel 1Th2:13+; 4:14
2 that you received and in which you are firmly established; •because the
gospel will save you only if you keep believing exactly what I preached to you—
believing anything else will not lead to anything.
3 Well then, in the first place, I taught you what I had been taught myself, 11:2+; 23 Lk 1:2
4 namely that Christ died for our sins, in accordance with the scriptures; •that he *Ac 2:23+*
was buried; and that he was raised to life on the third day, in accordance with Mt 28:10+ Lk 24:34f
5 the scriptures; •that he appeared first to Cephas and secondly to the Twelve.
6 Next he appeared to more than five hundred of the brothers at the same time,
7 most of whom are still alive, though some have died; •then he appeared to
8 James, and then to all the apostles; •and last of all he appeared to me too; it was Ac 12:17+ *9:1* Rm 1:1+
as though I was born when no one expected it.[b]
9 I am the least of the apostles; in fact, since I persecuted the Church of God, Ep 3:8 1 Tm 1:15-16
10 I hardly deserve the name apostle; •but by God's grace that is what I am, and *Ac 8:3+* Ga 1:13-14
the grace that he gave me has not been fruitless. On the contrary, I, or rather
11 the grace of God that is with me, have worked harder than any of the others; •but 2 Co 11:23f 1 Tm 1:14
what matters is that I preach what they preach, and this is what you all believed.
12 Now if Christ raised from the dead is what has been preached,[c] how can 6:14
13 some of you be saying that there is no resurrection of the dead? •If there is no
14 resurrection of the dead, Christ himself cannot have been raised, •and if Christ Ac 2:24+
has not been raised then our preaching is useless and your believing it is useless; Ac 25:19
15 indeed, we are shown up as witnesses who have committed perjury before God, Ac 1:8+; 26:16
16 because we swore in evidence before God[d] that he had raised Christ to life. •For
17 if the dead are not raised, Christ has not been raised, •and if Christ has not been Rm 4:24-25; 10:9
18 raised, you are still in your sins. •And what is more serious, all who have died in
19 Christ have perished. •If our hope in Christ has been for this life only, we are
the most unfortunate[e] of all people.
20 But Christ has in fact been raised from the dead, the first-fruits of all who Rm 8:11+ Col 1:18
21 have fallen asleep. •Death came through one man and in the same way the 1 Th 4:14 *Rm5:12-21+*

14 a. Lit. '...sounds in the world but not one soundless'.

b. This prayer of ecstatic utterance is so freed by 'the spirit' that it contains nothing limited enough to be grasped by the 'mind'.

c. The quotation is very free.

d. Or, he is unnoticed by God who does not acknowledge him as his own. Var. 'if he refuses to recognise this, well let him' (Paul losing patience). For a similar way of putting an end to discussion, cf. 11:16; Ph 3:15.

15 a. Christ's resurrection, of which the apostles are witnesses, vv. 2-8, cf. Ac 1:8+, is the decisive proof, vv. 12-28, of the future resurrection of all, which is something the O.T. first of all suspects and hopes for, Ps 16:10+; Jb 19:25+; Ezk 37:10+, but eventually asserts quite plainly, 2 M 7:9+. This is why the resurrection of Christ is the foundation of faith, vv. 12-19. The risen Christ can be called the first-fruit, v. 20, not only heralding but causing the resurrection of all Christians, vv. 20-28, cf. Rm 8:11+.

b. An allusion to the abnormal, sudden and *surgical* nature of Paul's birth into the apostolic family. He makes no distinction between the sort of apparition that took place on the Damascus road and the sort of apparitions of Jesus that took place between the resurrection and the ascension.

c. Paul is talking to those who believe Christ rose from the dead. To believe this and to lead a Christian life necessarily imply belief in the resurrection of the dead.

d. Or 'through God'.

e. 'This life' has become for Christians a state from which life in Christ, through the resurrection, will deliver them. If there is no resurrection, they have lost their deliverance. Note that the possibility of the soul's immortality without the resurrection of the body is not considered.

15:45-49 Si 25:24 resurrection of the dead has come through one man. •Just as all men die in Adam, 22
1 Th 4:16 so all men will be brought to life in Christ; •but all of them in their proper order: 23
Christ as the first-fruits and then, after the coming[f] of Christ, those who belong
Ep 1:22 to him. •After that will come the end, when he hands over the kingdom to God 24
the Father, having done away with every sovereignty, authority and power.[g]
Ps 110:1 Rv 20:14; For he must be king *until he has put all his enemies under his feet* •and the last 25 26
21:4 *Ps 8:6* of the enemies to be destroyed is death, for everything is to be *put under his feet*.
Rm 6:9 —Though when it is said[h] that *everything is subjected*, this clearly cannot include 27
Ph 3:21 the One who subjected everything to him. •And when everything is subjected to 28
Rm 9:5+ Ep 4:6 him, then the Son himself will be subject in his turn to the One who subjected
Col 3:11 all things to him, so that God may be all in all.

If this were not true, what do people hope to gain by being baptised for 29
the dead?[i] If the dead are not ever going to be raised, why be baptised on their
behalf? •What about ourselves? Why are we living under a constant threat? 30
2 Co 4:10-12 Ph 1:26 I face death every day, brothers, and I can swear it by the pride that I take in you 31
Ws 2:6 2 Co 1:8 in Christ Jesus our Lord. •If my motives were only human ones, what good would 32
Is 22:13 Lk 12:19 it do me to fight the wild animals at Ephesus?[j] •You say: *Let us eat and drink* 33
today; tomorrow we shall be dead. You must stop being led astray: 'Bad friends
ruin the noblest people'.[k] •Come to your senses, behave properly, and leave sin 34
14:38 alone; there are some of you who seem not to know God at all; you should be
ashamed.

The manner of the resurrection

Ga 6:8 Someone may ask, 'How are dead people raised, and what sort of body do they 35
Jn 12:24 have when they come back?' •They are stupid questions. Whatever you sow in the 36
ground has to die before it is given new life •and the thing that you sow is not 37
what is going to come; you sow a bare grain, say of wheat or something like that,
and then God gives it the sort of body that he has chosen: each sort of seed gets 38
its own sort of body.

Everything that is flesh is not the same flesh: there is human flesh, animals' 39
flesh, the flesh of birds and the flesh of fish. •Then there are heavenly bodies and 40
there are earthly bodies; but the heavenly bodies have a beauty of their own and
Dn 12:3 the earthly bodies a different one. •The sun has its brightness, the moon a different 41
brightness, and the stars a different brightness, and the stars differ from each
other in brightness. •It is the same with the resurrection of the dead: the thing 42
that is sown is perishable but what is raised is imperishable; •the thing that is 43
sown is contemptible but what is raised is glorious; the thing that is sown is weak
2:14-15+ 2 Co 5:1 but what is raised is powerful; •when it is sown it embodies the soul, when it is 44
Heb 4:12+ Jude 19+ raised it embodies the spirit.[l]

If the soul has its own embodiment, so does the spirit have its own embodiment.
Gn 2:7 The first *man*, Adam, as scripture says, *became a living soul*;[m] but the last Adam 45
15:20-28+ has become a life-giving spirit. •That is, first the one with the soul, not the spirit, 46
and after that, the one with the spirit. •The first man, being from the earth, is 47
Dn 7:13 earthly by nature; the second man is from heaven. •As this earthly man was, so 48
Rm 8:29+ Ph 3:21 are we on earth; and as the heavenly man is, so are we in heaven. •And we, who 49
have been modelled on the earthly man, will be modelled on the heavenly man.

Jn 3:5-6 Or else, brothers, put it this way: flesh and blood cannot inherit the kingdom 50
6:10+ of God: and the perishable cannot inherit what lasts for ever. •I will tell you 51
something that has been secret: that we are not all going to die, but we shall all
1 Th 4:15-17 be changed.[n] •This will be instantaneous, in the twinkling of an eye, when the 52
Nb 10:3+ Jl 2:1+ last trumpet sounds. It will sound, and the dead will be raised, imperishable,
Mt 24:31+ *2 Co 5:1-5* and we shall be changed as well,[o] •because our present perishable nature must 53
put on imperishability and this mortal nature must put on immortality.

A hymn of triumph. Conclusion

When this perishable nature has put on imperishability,[p] and when this 54

mortal nature has put on immortality, then the words of scripture[q] will come
true: *Death is swallowed up in victory.* •*Death, where is your* victory? *Death, where* Is 25:8 *Ho 13:14*
is your sting? •Now the sting of death is sin, and sin gets its power from the Law. Rv 20:14 *Rm 7:7+*
So let us thank God for giving us the victory through our Lord Jesus Christ. Heb 6:1+ *Jn 16:33*
Never give in then, my dear brothers, never admit defeat; keep on working
at the Lord's work always, knowing that, in the Lord, you cannot be labouring
in vain.

CONCLUSION

Commendations. Greetings

16 Now about the collection made for the saints:[a] you are to do as I told the Ac 9:13+ Rm 15:25f
churches in Galatia to do. •Every Sunday,[b] each one of you must put *Ga 2:10* *Mt 28:1*
aside what he can afford, so that collections need not be made after I have come.
When I am with you, I will send your offering to Jerusalem by the hand
of whatever men you give letters of reference to; •if it seems worth while for me Ac 20:4
to go too, they can travel with me.
I shall be coming to you after I have passed through Macedonia—and I am Ac 19:21; 20:1
doing no more than pass through Macedonia—•and I may be staying with you, 2 Co 8:1
perhaps even passing the winter, to make sure that it is you who send me on my
way wherever my travels take me. •As you see, I do not want to make it only
a passing visit[c] to you and I hope to spend some time with you, the Lord permitting. •In any case I shall be staying at Ephesus until Pentecost •because a big 2 Co 2:12 Col 4:3
and important door[d] has opened for my work and there is a great deal
of opposition.
If Timothy comes, show him that he has nothing to be afraid of in you: like 4:17
me, he is doing the Lord's work, •and nobody is to be scornful of him. Send 1 Tm 4:12 2 Tm 1:7

f. *Parousia* (presence), a Greek word adopted by early Christians to indicate the glorious coming of Christ on his 'day', 1 Co 1:8+, at the end of time, Mt 24:3+; cf. also 1 Th 2:19; 3:13; 4:15; 5:32; 2 Th 2:1; Jm 5:7,8; 2 P 1:16; 3:4,12; 1 Jn 2:28. In 2 Th 2:8,9 the same word is used to indicate the coming of the Lawless One. Cf. the similar terms 'revelation', 1 Co 1:7+, and 'appearing', 1 Tm 6:14+.

g. All forces hostile to the sovereignty of God, cf. 1 Co 2:6; Ep 1:21; Col 1:16; 2:15; 1 P 3:22.

h. When the whole cosmos has been subjected to him, Jesus will go to the Father and say his task is complete. The translation '*scripture* says' is incorrect.

i. What this practice was is unknown: Paul does not say if he approved of it or not: he uses it merely for an *ad hominem* argument.

j. What episode Paul is referring to is unknown.

k. Quoted from Menander's *Thais:* it may have become a popular proverb.

l. Lit. It is sown a physical *(psychikon)* body, it is raised a spiritual *(pneumatikon)* body. In Paul, as in the O.T., *psyche* (Hebr. *nephesh;* cf. Gn 2:7) is what gives life to animals, to the human body, 1 Co 15:45; or it is the actual 'life' of the body, Rm 16:4; Ph 2:30; 1 Th 2:8; cf. Mt 2:20; Mk 3:4; Lk 12:20; Jn 10:11; Ac 20:10; etc., its 'living soul', 2 Co 1:23. The term can also mean any human being, Rm 2:9; 13:1; 2 Co 12:15; Ac 2:41,43, etc. As it only gives natural life, 1 Co 2:14, cf. Jude 19, it is less important than *pneuma* by which a human life is divinised by a process that begins through the gift of the Spirit, Rm 5:5+, cf. 1:9+, and is completed after death. Greek philosophers thought of the higher soul (the *nous*) escaping from 'the body', to survive immortally. Christians thought of immortality more in terms of the restoration of the whole person, involving a resurrection of the body effected by the Spirit or divine principle which God withdrew from human beings because of sins, Gn 6:3, but restored to all who are united to the risen Christ, Rm 1:4+; 8:11, who is the 'heavenly' man and life-giving Spirit, 1 Co 15:45-49. The 'body' is no longer *psychikon* but *pneumatikon*, it is incorruptible, immortal, 1 Co 15:53, glorious, 1 Co 15:43; cf. Rm 8:18; 2 Co 4:17; Ph 3:21; Col 3:4, no longer subject to the laws of matter, Jn 20:19,26; it does not even answer the description of matter, Lk 24:16. *Psyche* can be used in a wider sense as the opposite of the body to indicate what it is in a human being that behaves and feels, Ph 1:27; Ep 6:6; Col 3:23; cf. Mt 22:37p; 26:38p; Lk 1:46; Jn 12:27; Ac 4:32; 14:2; 1 P 2:11; etc., or even to indicate the spiritual and immortal soul, Mt 10:28, 39p; Ac 2:27; Jm 1:21; 5:20; 1 P 1:9; Rv 6:9; etc.

m. Something that is alive because it has a *psyche* giving it a merely natural life, subject to decay and corruption.

n. The Vulg. reading 'we all die but we shall not all be changed' is incorrect.

o. I.e. those who will be alive at the time, among whom Paul could theoretically have been included, cf. 1 Th 5:1+.

p. Om. 'When this perishable nature has put on imperishability'.

q. A free quotation.

16 a. On this collection see Rm 15:26-28; Ga 2:10; 2 Co 8:9; Ac 24:17. The 'saints' (cf. 2 Co 8:4) are the Christians in Jerusalem who from the earliest days stood in need of help, Ac 11:29-30. Paul was very anxious to have this collection made, since he regarded it as a sign and a pledge of unity between the churches he had founded and those of the Judaeo-Christians.

b. Lit. 'First day of the week', i.e. 'The Lord's Day'. cf. Ac 20:7; Rv 1:10; Mt 28:1.

c. An alternative translation 'This time, I do not want to pay you a passing visit'; this would presuppose a short visit recently made, which is hardly likely.

d. The same image is used in 2 Co 2:12; Col 4:3; it indicates Paul's missionary opportunities, cf. Rv 3:8.

him happily on his way to come back to me; the brothers and I are waiting for
Ac 18:24+ him.[e] •As for our brother Apollos, I begged him to come to you with the brothers 12
but he was quite firm that he did not want to go yet[f] and he will come as soon
as he can.

Be awake to all the dangers; stay firm in the faith; be brave and be strong. 13
Let everything you do be done in love. 14

1:16 There is something else to ask you, brothers. You know how the Stephanas 15
Rm 16:5-6 family, who were the first-fruits of Achaia, have really worked hard to help the
Ph 2:29-30 1 Th 5:12-13 saints. •Well, I want you in your turn to put yourselves at the service of people 16
Heb 13:17 like this, and anyone who helps and works with them. •I am delighted that 17
Stephanas, Fortunatus and Achaicus[g] have arrived; they make up for your
absence. •They have settled my mind, and yours too; I hope you appreciate men 18
like this.

Ac 18:2+ All the churches of Asia[h] send you greetings. Aquila and Prisca, with the 19
Rm 16:5+ church that meets at their house, send you their warmest wishes, in the Lord.
2 Co 13:12 All the brothers send your their greetings. Greet one another with a holy kiss. 20

Ga 6:11+ This greeting is in my own hand—Paul. 21
Col 4:18 *11:27* Ph 4:5 If anyone does not love the Lord, a curse on him. 'Maran atha.'[i] 22
The grace of the Lord Jesus be with you. 23
My love is with you all in Christ Jesus. 24

16 e. The phrase is ambiguous: either Paul and the 'brothers' of Ephesus are waiting for Timothy, or Paul expects Timothy and the 'brothers' who are his travelling companions (of whom Erastus was one, Ac 19:22).

f. In case his presence aggravated party feeling among his own supporters, 1:12; 3:4-6; 4:6.

g. Probably these had brought the letter from the Corinthians to Paul, 7:1.

h. The Roman province is meant.

i. These Aramaic words ('the Lord is coming') had passed into liturgical use: they expressed the hope that the *parousia* would not be long delayed. An alternative reading is *Marana tha* (Lord, come!), Rv 22:20. Cf. Rm 13:12; Ph 4:5; Jm 5:8; 1 P 4:7.

2 CORINTHIANS

THE SECOND LETTER OF PAUL TO THE CHURCH AT CORINTH

INTRODUCTION

Address and greetings. Thanksgiving Rm 1:1+

1 1 From Paul, appointed by God to be an apostle of Christ Jesus, and from
Timothy, one of the brothers, to the church of God at Corinth and to all the Ac 16:1+ *1 Co 1:2*+
2 saints in the whole of Achaia. •Grace and peace to you from God our Father and Ac 9:13+
the Lord Jesus Christ.
3 Blessed be the God and Father of our Lord Jesus Christ, a gentle Father and
4 the God of all consolation, •who comforts us in all our sorrows, so that we can
offer others, in their sorrows, the consolation that we have received from God
5 ourselves. •Indeed, as the sufferings of Christ overflow to us, so, through Christ, Ph 1:20+ Col 1:24+
6 does our consolation overflow. •When we are made to suffer, it is for your
consolation and salvation. When, instead, we are comforted, this should be a
consolation to you, supporting you in patiently bearing the same sufferings as
7 we bear. •And our hope for you is confident, since we know that, sharing our
sufferings, you will also share our consolations.
8 For we should like you to realise, brothers, that the things we had to undergo[a] Ac 20:19 1 Co 15:32
in Asia were more of a burden than we could carry, so that we despaired of
9 coming through alive. •Yes, we were carrying our own death warrant with us, 4:7 Rm 1:4+; 4:17; 8:11+
and it has taught us not to rely on ourselves but only on God, who raises the
10 dead to life. •And he saved us from dying, as he will save us again; yes, that is our
11 firm hope in him, that in the future he will save us again. •You must all join in the Rm 15:30+
prayers for us: the more people there are asking for help for us, the more will be
giving thanks when it is granted to us. 4:15; 9:12

I. SOME RECENT EVENTS REVIEWED

Why Paul changed his plans

12 There is one thing we are proud of, and our conscience tells us it is true: that 1:17 Jm 3:15
we have always treated everybody, and especially you, with the reverence[b] and
sincerity which come from God, and by the grace of God we have done this
13 without ulterior motives. •There are no hidden meanings in our letters besides 1 Co 1:17; 2:1f
14 what you can read for yourselves and understand. •And I hope that, although
you do not know us very well yet, you will have come to recognise, when the day 1 Co 1:8+
of our Lord Jesus comes, that you can be as proud of us as we are of you. Ph 1:26; 2:16; 4:1
15 Because I was so sure of this, I had meant to come to you first, so that you 1 Th 2:19-20
16 would benefit doubly;[c] •staying with you before going to Macedonia and coming
back to you again on the way back from Macedonia, for you to see me on my way
17 to Judaea.[d] •Do you think I was not sure of my own intentions when I planned

1 a. It is not known what incident this refers to.
b. Var. 'single-mindedness'.
c. Var. 'to give you a double pleasure'.
d. Paul must therefore have changed the plan mentioned in 1 Co 16:5-6.

this? Do you really think that when I am making my plans, my motives are
1:12 Rm 7:5+ ordinary human ones, and that I say Yes, yes, and No, no, at the same time?
Mt 5:37 1 Co 1:9 I swear by God's truth, there is no Yes and No about what we say to you. •The 18 19
Son of God, the Christ Jesus that we proclaimed among you—I mean Silvanus[e]
Ac 16:1+; 18:5 and Timothy and I—was never Yes and No: with him it was always Yes, •and 20
however many the promises God made, the Yes to them all is in him. That is
1 Co 14:16 Rv 3:14+ why it is 'through him' that we answer Amen to the praise of God. •Remember 21
13:13+ it is God himself who assures us all, and you, of our standing in Christ, and has
1 Jn 2:20,27 *Rm 5:5+;* anointed us, •marking us with his seal and giving us the pledge, the Spirit, that 22
6:4+ Ep 1:13-14 we carry in our hearts.

Rm 1:9 By my life, I call God to witness that the reason why I did not come to Corinth 23
after all was to spare your feelings. •We are not dictators over your faith, but are 24
fellow workers with you for your happiness; in the faith you are steady enough.
2 Well then, I made up my mind not to pay you a second distressing visit.[a] 1
I may have hurt you, but if so I have hurt the only people who could give me any 2
pleasure. •I wrote as I did[b] to make sure that, when I came, I should not be dis- 3
tressed by the very people who should have made me happy. I am sure you all
know that I could never be happy unless you were. •When I wrote to you, in deep 4
distress and anguish of mind, and in tears, it was not to make you feel hurt but
to let you know how much love I have for you.

Someone has been the cause of pain; and the cause of pain not to me, but to 5
some degree—not to overstate it—to all of you. •The punishment already imposed 6
by the majority on the man in question[c] is enough; •and the best thing now is to 7
Col 3:13 2 Th 3:14 give him your forgiveness and encouragement, or he might break down from so
much misery. •So I am asking you to give some definite proof of your love for 8
him. •What I really wrote for, after all, was to test you and see whether you are 9
completely obedient. •Anybody that you forgive, I forgive; and as for my 10
forgiving anything—if there has been anything to be forgiven, I have forgiven
it for your sake in the presence of Christ. •And so we will not be outwitted by 11
Ep 4:27 Satan—we know well enough what his intentions are.

From Troas to Macedonia. The apostolate: its importance

1 Co 16:9+ When I went up to Troas to preach the Good News of Christ, and the door 12
was wide open for my work there in the Lord, •I was so continually uneasy in 13
7:6 Ga 2:1 mind at not meeting brother Titus[d] there, I said good-bye to them and went
Tt 1:4 on to Macedonia.

Thanks be to God who, wherever he goes, makes us, in Christ, partners of his 14
Col 2:15 triumph,[e] and through us is spreading the knowledge of himself, like a sweet smell,
everywhere. •We are Christ's incense to God for those who are being saved and 15
1 Co 1:18 for those who are not; •for the last, the smell of death that leads to death, for the 16
first the sweet smell of life that leads to life. And who could be qualified for work
like this? •At least we do not go round offering the word of God for sale, as many 17
other people do. In Christ, we speak as men of sincerity, as envoys of God and
in God's presence.

5:12; 10:12f; 11:18f **3** Does this sound like a new attempt to commend ourselves to you? Unlike 1
Ac 18:27 other people, we need no letters of recommendation either to you or from
1 Co 9:2 you, •because you are yourselves our letter, written in our[a] hearts, that anybody 2
can see and read, •and it is plain that you are a letter from Christ, drawn up by 3
Ex 24:12+ us, and written not with ink but with the Spirit of the living God, not on stone
Jr 31:33 Ezk 11:19; 36:26 tablets but on the tablets of your living hearts.

Before God, we are confident of this through Christ: •not that we are qualified 4 5
Jn 3:27 in ourselves to claim anything as our own work: all our qualifications come from
Ep 3:7 Col 1:23,25 God. •He is the one who has given us the qualifications to be the administrators 6
of this new covenant, which is not a covenant of written letters but of the Spirit:
Rm 2:29; 7:5+ the written letters bring death, but the Spirit gives life. •Now if the administering 7
Ex 32:16; 34:29-35 of death, in the written letters engraved on stones, was accompanied by such a

brightness that the Israelites could not bear looking at the face of Moses, though Heb 3:2
8 it was a brightness that faded, •then how much greater will be the brightness that
9 surrounds the administering of the Spirit! •For if there was any splendour in
administering condemnation, there must be very much greater splendour in
10 administering justification. •In fact, compared with this greater splendour, the
11 thing that used to have such splendour now seems to have none; •and if what
was so temporary had any splendour, there must be much more in what is going
to last for ever.

12 13 Having this hope, we can be quite confident; •not like Moses, who put a veil 1 Th 2:2
over his face so that the Israelites would not notice the ending of what had to
14 fade.[b] •And anyway, their minds had been dulled; indeed, to this very day, that 2 Tm 3:15
same veil is still there when the old covenant is being read, a veil never lifted, since Rm 10:4
15 Christ alone can remove it.[c] •Yes, even today, whenever Moses is read, the veil is Ex 34:34 Rm 11:7-10
16 17 over their minds. •It will not be removed until they turn to the Lord. •Now this
18 Lord is the Spirit, and where the Spirit of the Lord is, there is freedom. •And
we, with our unveiled[d] faces reflecting like mirrors[e] the brightness of the Lord,[f] all 4:6+ Rm 8:29+
grow brighter and brighter as we are turned into the image[g] that we reflect; this 1 Co 11:5+ 2 P 1:4
is the work of the Lord who is Spirit. 1 Jn 3:2 Rv 21:23

1 **4** Since we have by an act of mercy been entrusted with this work of adminis- Rm 1:16
2 tration, there is no weakening on our part. •On the contrary, we will have
none of the reticence of those who are ashamed, no deceitfulness or watering 1 Th 2:4-5
down the word of God; but the way we commend ourselves to every human
3 being with a conscience is by stating the truth openly in the sight of God. •If our
gospel does not penetrate the veil, then the veil is on those who are not on the
4 way to salvation; •the unbelievers whose minds the god of this world[a] has blinded, Ep 2:2 2 Th 2:10
to stop them seeing the light shed by the Good News of the glory of Christ, who *Jn 14:7* Rm 8:29+
5 is the image of God. •For it is not ourselves that we are preaching, but Christ 1 Tm 1:11
6 Jesus as the Lord, and ourselves as your servants for Jesus' sake. •It is the same
God that said, 'Let there be light shining out of darkness', who has shone in our Gn 1:3 Jn 8:12+
minds to radiate the light of the knowledge of God's glory, the glory on the face *Rm 3:23+* Heb 1:3
of Christ.

The trials and hopes of the apostolate

7 We are only the earthenware jars[b] that hold this treasure, to make it clear 1:9; 12:9 1 Co 1:27
8 that such an overwhelming power comes from God and not from us. •We are in
difficulties on all sides, but never cornered; we see no answer to our problems, 6:4-10 1 Co 4:9-13
9 but never despair; •we have been persecuted, but never deserted; knocked down,
10 but never killed; •always, wherever we may be, we carry with us in our body Col 1:24+
the death of Jesus, so that the life of Jesus, too, may always be seen in our body.
11 Indeed, while we are still alive, we are consigned to our death every day, for the 6:9 1 Co 15:31

e. Silvanus is the disciple called Silas in Ac.

2 a. An allusion to a painful visit which Paul must have made to Corinth before writing 2 Co, see Introduction to the Letters of St Paul.

b. An allusion to the 'severe letter' of 2:3,4,9; 7:8,12; see Introduction.

c. The man who had given offence to Paul or to Paul's representative, see Introduction.

d. A Christian of pagan birth, possibly converted by Paul, Tt 1:4, whom he accompanies on Paul's second journey to Jerusalem, Ga 2:1. He was commissioned by Paul to visit Corinth and to settle its problems; in this he was entirely successful, 2 Co 7:5-7. Soon afterwards Paul sent him to Corinth to organise the collection. We meet him again in Crete (63-64) controlling the communities Paul had founded there after his release from the first Roman captivity. It was from there that Paul wrote to Titus asking him to meet him again at Nicopolis in Epirus, Tt 3:12. During Paul's second Roman captivity (66-67) Titus was in Dalmatia, 2 Tm 4:10. Titus with his shrewdness and his strong, well-balanced character, seems to have made an admirable colleague for Paul.

e. Like a victorious general making his solemn entry into Rome, God passes triumphantly through the world with his apostles in his train. Cf. Col 2:15.

3 a. Var. 'your'.

b. Free interpretation, in the rabbinic style, of Ex 34:33-35.

c. Alternative translation 'nor is it revealed to them that this covenant has been abolished by Christ'.

d. As that of Moses had been.

e. Or 'contemplating'.

f. The 'brightness of the Lord' is the glory of Jesus, being 'the glory on the face of Christ', 4:6.

g. The contemplation of God in Christ gives the Christian a likeness to God, Rm 8:29+, cf. 1 Jn 3:2.

4 a. Satan, cf. Ep 2:2. See Lk 4:6, Jn 12:31; 14:30; 16:11.

b. Perhaps 'bodies of clay', cf. 1 Th 4:4, alluding to Gn 2:7.

sake of Jesus, so that in our mortal flesh the life of Jesus, too, may be openly
shown. •So death is at work in us, but life in you. 12
But as we have the same spirit of faith that is mentioned in scripture— 13
Ps 116:10 *I believed, and therefore I spoke*—we too believe and therefore we too speak,
Rm 1:4+; 8:11+ knowing that he who raised the Lord Jesus to life will raise us with Jesus in our 14
turn, and put us by his side and you with us. •You see, all this is for your benefit, 15
1:11 so that the more grace is multiplied among people, the more thanksgiving there
will be, to the glory of God.

Rm 7:22+ That is why there is no weakening on our part, and instead, though this outer 16
man of ours may be falling into decay, the inner man is renewed day by day.
Ws 3:5 Mt 5:11-12 Yes, the troubles which are soon over, though they weigh little, train us for the 17
Rm 8:18 1 P 5:10 carrying of a weight of eternal glory which is out of all proportion to them. •And 18
Rm 8:24-25 Heb 11:1,3 so we have no eyes for things that are visible, but only for things that are
invisible; for visible things last only for a time, and the invisible things are
eternal.

Is 38:12 2 P 1:14 **5** For we know that when the tent that we live in on earth is folded up, there 1
1 Co 15:44-49 is a house built by God for us, an everlasting home not made by human hands,
Ph 3:20 Col 3:3-4 in the heavens. •In this present state, it is true, we groan as we wait with longing 2
Rm 8:23 to put on our heavenly home[a] over the other; •we should like to be found wearing 3
1 Co 15:51-53 clothes and not without them.[b] •Yes, we groan and find it a burden being still 4
1 Th 4:15 in this tent, not that we want to strip it off, but to put the second garment over it
1:22+ Rm 8:23 and to have what must die taken up into life. •This is the purpose for which 5
God made us, and he has given us the pledge of the Spirit.

1 P 1:1+,17 We are always full of confidence, then, when we remember that to live in the 6
body means to be exiled from the Lord, •going as we do by faith and not by sight 7
Rm 8:24 1 Co 13:12 —we are full of confidence, I say, and actually want to be exiled from the body 8
Ph 1:21-23 and make our home with the Lord.[c] •Whether we are living in the body or exiled 9
Mt 25:19,31f Rm 14:10 from it, we are intent on pleasing him. •For all the truth about us will be brought 10
Jn 5:27 out in the law court of Christ, and each of us will get what he deserves for the
Heb 11:6+ things he did in the body, good or bad.

The apostolate in action

And so it is with the fear of the Lord in mind that we try to win people over. 11
God knows us for what we really are, and I hope that in your consciences you
3:1+ Ph 1:26 know us too. •This is not another attempt to commend ourselves to you: we are 12
simply giving you reasons to be proud of us, so that you will have an answer ready
for the people who can boast more about what they seem than what they are.
If we seemed out of our senses, it was for God; but if we are being reasonable 13
Rm 8:32 Ga 2:20 now, it is for your sake.[d] •And this is because the love of Christ overwhelms us 14
Rm 6:4-11 when we reflect that if one man has died for all, then all men should be dead;
Rm 14:9 1 Tm 2:6 and the reason he died for all was so that living men should live no longer for 15
Rm 6:11+; 7:1+ themselves, but for him who died and was raised to life for them.
Rm 7:5+ From now onwards, therefore, we do not judge anyone by the standards of the 16
Rm 1:3; 9:5 flesh. Even if we did once know Christ in the flesh,[e] that is not how we know him
Is 43:19 *Mt 9:16* now. •And for anyone who is in Christ, there is a new creation;[f] the old creation 17
Ep 2:10 Heb 8:13 has gone, and now the new one is here.[g] •It is all God's work. It was God who 18
Rm 5:10 reconciled us to himself through Christ and gave us the work of handing on this
Jn 3:17 reconciliation. •In other words, God in Christ was reconciling the world to 19
himself, not holding men's faults against them, and he has entrusted to us the
news that they are reconciled. •So we are ambassadors for Christ; it is as though 20
God were appealing through us, and the appeal that we make in Christ's name
Is 53:5-8 Rm 8:3 is: be reconciled to God. •For our sake God made the sinless one into sin,[h] so 21
Ga 3:13 1 P 2:24 that in him we might become the goodness of God. **6** As his fellow workers, we 1
1 Jn 3:5 beg you once again not to neglect the grace of God that you have received. •For 2
Is 49:8 he says: *At the favourable time, I have listened to you; on the day of salvation*
I came to your help. Well, now is the favourable time; this is the day of salvation.[a]

3 We do nothing that people might object to, so as not to bring discredit on our 8:21
4 function as God's servants. •Instead, we prove we are servants of God by great 4:8-10 1 Co 4:9-13
5 fortitude in times of suffering: in times of hardship and distress; •when we are
6 flogged, or sent to prison, or mobbed; labouring, sleepless, starving. •We prove
we are God's servants by our purity, knowledge, patience and kindness; by a Ga 5:22
7 spirit of holiness, by a love free from affectation; •by the word of truth and by
the power of God; by being armed with the weapons of righteousness in the right 10:4 Ep 6:11+
8 hand and in the left, •prepared for honour or disgrace, for blame or praise; taken
9 for impostors while we are genuine; •obscure yet famous; said to be dying and 1 Co 7:29-31
10 here are we alive; rumoured to be executed before we are sentenced; •thought 4:11
most miserable and yet we are always rejoicing; taken for paupers though we make
others rich, for people having nothing though we have everything. Rm 8:32

Paul opens his heart. A warning

11 Corinthians, we have spoken to you very frankly;[b] our mind has been opened 7:3
12 in front of you. •Any constraint that you feel is not on our side; the constraint
13 is in your own selves. •I speak as if to children of mine: as a fair exchange, open Ga 4:19
your minds in the same way.
[c]Do not harness yourselves in an uneven team with unbelievers. Virtue is no Dt 22:10
14 companion for crime. Light and darkness have nothing in common. •Christ is Jn 8:12+
15 not the ally of Beliar,[d] nor has a believer anything to share with an unbeliever. Dt 13:14+
16 The temple of God has no common ground with idols, and that is what we[e] 1 Co 3:16-17
are—the temple of the living God. We have God's word for it: *I will make* Lv 26:11-12 Nb 5:3
my home among them and live with them; I will be their God and they shall be my Ezk 37:27
17 *people.* •Then *come away from them and keep aloof, says the Lord. Touch nothing* Is 52:11 Jr 51:45
18 *that is unclean, and I will welcome you* •*and be your father, and you shall be my* *2 S 7:14* Is 43:6
sons and daughters, says the Almighty Lord. Jr 31:9

1 **7** With promises like these made to us, dear brothers, let us wash off all that
can soil either body or spirit, to reach perfection of holiness in the fear of
God.
2 Keep a place for us in your hearts. We have not injured anyone, or ruined
3 anyone, or exploited anyone. •I am not saying this to put any blame on you;
as I have already told you, you are in our hearts—together we live or together 6:11-13

5 a. That is, to be given our 'spiritual body', 1 Co 15:44+, without having to suffer death and corruption, v. 4.

b. That is to say, on the supposition that we are still alive when Christ returns in glory. Paul wants to be of the number of those who will live to see the coming of the Lord and whose bodies will be transformed without having to die. Over the 'natural body' they will, as it were, 'put on' the 'spiritual body', 1 Co 15:44,53,54, which will be 'absorbed' by the former.

c. Here and in Ph 1:23 Paul has in mind a union of Christians with Christ on the death of each individual. This does not contradict the biblical doctrine of the final universal resurrection, Rm 2:6+; 1 Co 15:44+, but this expectation of happiness for the soul that has left the body after death betrays the influence of Greek thought, an influence already making itself felt in the Judaism of the period, cf. Lk 16:22; 23:43; 1 P 3:19+. Cf. also the texts referring to ecstatic states when the soul is 'out of the body', 2 Co 12:2f; cf. Rv 1:10; 4:2; 17:3; 21:10.

d. Paul is taxed with 'folly'; he retorts that this is in God's cause. But he adds that he can be 'reasonable' when he wishes, for the sake of his children in Christ.

e. Paul seems to be protesting against the restriction of the apostolic privilege to those who had known Jesus in his earthly life, cf. Rm 1:1+; 1 Co 1:12+.

f. God who created all things through Christ, cf. Jn 1:3, has restored his work, deformed by sin, by re-creating it in Christ, Col 1:15-20+. The central figure of this 'new creation', here and Ga 6:15—which extends to the whole universe, Col 1:19+; cf. 2 P 3:13; Rv 21:1—is the 'new man' created in Christ, Ep 2:15+, to lead a new life, Rm 6:4, of virtue and holiness, Ep 2:10; 4:24+; Col 3:10+. Cf. the 'new birth' of baptism, Rm 6:4+.

g. Var. 'all is new'.

h. By a kind of legal fiction God identified Jesus with sin so that he might bear the curse incurred by sin, Ga 3:13; Rm 8:3.

6 a. There is an intermediary period, Rm 13:11+, between the time of Christ's coming, Rm 3:26+, and his return, 1 Co 1:8+. This period is the 'day of salvation', a time allowed for conversion, Ac 3:20f; it is granted to the 'remnant', Rm 11:5, and to the pagans, Rm 11:25; Ep 2:12f; cf. 2 Co 8:14; Lk 21:24. Though the duration is uncertain, 1 Th 5:1+, this time of pilgrimage must be regarded as being short, 1 P 1:17; 1 Co 7:26-31; cf. Rv 10:16; 12:12; 20:3, and full of trials, Ep 5:16; 6:13, and sufferings which are a prelude to the glory to come, Rm 8:11. The end is at hand, 1 P 4:7; cf. Rv 1:3+ and 1 Co 16:22; Ph 4:5; Jm 5:8, the day approaches, Rm 13:11, and it is necessary to be on the watch, 1 Th 5:6; cf. Mk 13:33, and to use the time well that remains, Col 4:5; Ep 5:16, for one's own salvation and that of others, Ga 6:10, leaving the final vindication to God, Rm 12:19; 1 Co 4:5.

b. Lit. 'our mouth is open to (or: for) you'.

c. 6:14–7:1 is a warning against the infiltration of pagan practices which would split the church and cut it off from its founder. This section is somewhat alie to the context, cf. Introduction.

d. Var. 'Belial'.

e. Var. 'you'.

we die. •I have the very greatest confidence in you, and I am so proud of you that 4
Col 1:24 in all our trouble I am filled with consolation and my joy is overflowing.

Paul in Macedonia; he is joined by Titus

Even after we had come to Macedonia, however, there was no rest for this 5
body of ours.[a] Far from it; we found trouble on all sides: quarrels outside, mis-
givings inside. •But God comforts the miserable, and he comforted us, by the 6
2:13 arrival of Titus, •and not only by his arrival but also by the comfort which he 7
1 Th 3:6 had gained from you. He has told us all about how you want to see me, how sorry
you were, and how concerned for me, and so I am happier now than I was before.
Heb 12:11 But to tell the truth, even if I distressed you by my letter,[b] I do not regret it. 8
I did regret it before, and I see that that letter did distress you, at least for a time;
but I am happy now—not because I made you suffer, but because your suffering 9
led to your repentance. Yours has been a kind of suffering that God approves,
and so you have come to no kind of harm from us. •To suffer in God's way 10
means changing for the better and leaves no regrets, but to suffer as the world
knows suffering brings death. •Just look at what suffering in God's way has 11
brought you: what keenness, what explanations, what indignation, what alarm!
Yes, and what aching to see me, what concern for me, and what justice done![c]
In every way you have shown yourselves blameless in this affair. •So then, though 12
I wrote the letter to you, it was not written for the sake either of the offender
or of the one offended;[d] it was to make you realise, in the sight of God, your own
concern for us. •That is what we have found so encouraging. 13
With this encouragement, too, we had the even greater happiness of finding
Titus so happy; thanks to you all, he has no more worries; •I had rather boasted 14
to him about you, and now I have not been made to look foolish; in fact, our
boasting to Titus has proved to be as true as anything that we ever said to you.
His own personal affection for you is all the greater when he remembers how 15
1 Co 2:3+ willing you have all been, and with what deep respect you welcomed him. •I am 16
2 Th 3:4 very happy knowing that I can rely on you so completely.

II. ORGANISATION OF THE COLLECTION

Why the Corinthians should be generous

11:8-9 8 Now here, brothers, is the news of the grace of God which was given in the 1
1 Co 16:5 churches in Macedonia; •and of how, throughout great trials by suffering, 2
their constant cheerfulness and their intense poverty have overflowed in a wealth
of generosity. •I can swear that they gave not only as much as they could afford, 3
but far more, and quite spontaneously, •begging and begging us for the favour 4
1 Co 16:1+ of sharing in this service to the saints •and, what was quite unexpected, they 5
offered their own selves first to God and, under God, to us.
Because of this, we have asked Titus, since he has already made a beginning, 6
to bring this work of mercy to the same point of success among you. •You 7
1 Co 1:5 always have the most of everything—of faith, of eloquence, of understanding, of
keenness for any cause, and the biggest share of our affection[a]—so we expect
you to put the most into this work of mercy too. •It is not an order that I am 8
giving you; I am just testing the genuineness of your love against the keenness of
Mt 5:3+; 8:20 others. •Remember how generous the Lord Jesus was:[b] he was rich, but he 9
Ph 2:6-7 *9:15* became poor for your[c] sake, to make you rich out of his poverty. •As I say, I am 10
1 Co 1:5 Heb 12:2 only making a suggestion; it is only fair to you, since you were the first, a year
ago, not only in taking action but even in deciding to. •So now finish the work 11
and let the results be worthy, as far as you can afford it, of the decision you made
so promptly. •As long as the readiness is there, a man is acceptable with whatever 12
he can afford; never mind what is beyond his means. •This does not mean that 13
to give relief to others you ought to make things difficult for yourselves: it is

14 a question of balancing •what happens to be your surplus now against their Rm 15:26-27
present need, and one day they may have something to spare that will supply
15 your own need. That is how we strike a balance: •as scripture says: *The man who* Ex 16:18
gathered much had none too much, the man who gathered little did not go short.

The delegates recommended to the Corinthians

16 I thank God for putting into Titus' heart the same concern for you that I have
17 myself. •He did what we asked him; indeed he is more concerned than ever, and
18 is visiting you on his own initiative. •As his companion we are sending the 12:18
19 brother[d] who is famous in all the churches for spreading the gospel. •More than
that, he happens to be the same brother who has been elected by the churches
to be our companion on this errand of mercy that, for the glory of God, we have
20 undertaken to satisfy our impatience to help. •We hope that in this way there
21 will be no accusations made about our administering such a large fund; •for *we* Pr 3:4 LXX Rm 12:17
22 *are trying to do right* not only *in the sight of God* but *also* in the sight of *men.* •To
accompany these, we are sending a third brother,[e] of whose keenness we have
often had proof in many different ways, and who is particularly keen about this,
23 because he has great confidence in you. •Titus, perhaps I should add, is my own
colleague and fellow worker in your interests; the other two brothers, who are
24 delegates of the churches, are a real glory to Christ. •So then, in front of all the
churches, give them a proof of your love, and prove to them that we are right
to be proud of you.

1 **9** There is really no need for me to write to you[a] on the subject of offering
2 your services to the saints, •since I know how anxious you are to help; in
fact, I boast about you to the Macedonians, telling them, 'Achaia has been ready
3 since last year'. So your zeal has been a spur to many more. •I am sending the
brothers all the same, to make sure that our boasting about you does not prove
to have been empty this time, and that you really are ready as I said you would
4 be. •If some of the Macedonians who are coming with me found you unprepared,
we should be humiliated—to say nothing of yourselves—after being so confident.
5 That is why I have thought it necessary to ask these brothers to go on to you
ahead of us, and make sure in advance that the gift you promised is all ready,
and that it all comes as a gift out of your generosity and not by being extorted
from you.

Blessings to be expected from the collection

6 Do not forget: thin sowing means thin reaping; the more you sow, the more Pr 11:24-25
7 you reap. •Each one should give what he has decided in his own mind, not Tb 4:16
8 grudgingly or because he is made to, for *God loves a cheerful giver.* •And there Pr 22:8 LXX
is no limit to the blessings which God can send you—he will make sure that you
will always have all you need for yourselves in every possible circumstance, and
9 still have something to spare for all sorts of good works. •As scripture says: *He* Ps 112:9
was free in almsgiving, and gave to the poor: his good deeds will never be forgotten.
10 The one who provides *seed for the sower and bread for food* will provide you with Is 55:10
11 all the seed you want and make *the harvest of your good deeds* a larger one, •and, Ho 10:12
made richer in every way, you will be able to do all the generous things which,
12 through us, are the cause of thanksgiving to God. •For doing this holy service
is not only supplying all the needs of the saints, but it is also increasing the

7 a. Emphasising the 'weak' side of Paul, cf. Rm 7:5+.
b. The 'severe letter', cf. 2:3+.
c. I.e. to the guilty man. Paul is enumerating the effects his 'severe letter' had on the Corinthians, cf. 2:5-8.
d. Probably one of Paul's envoys.

8 a. Var. 'the charity towards us which unites us to you'.
b. Lit. 'the generosity (or perhaps 'grace') of the Lord Jesus'.
c. Var. 'our'.
d. Possibly Luke.
e. Identity unknown.

9 a. Since Paul has just written of this at some length, it is possible that ch. 9 was a short note to the churches of Achaia, being inserted here subsequently to follow the instructions on the same subject addressed to the church of Corinth in ch. 8, cf. Introduction.

1:11 amount of thanksgiving that God receives. •By offering this service, you show 13
1 Co 16:1+ them what you are, and that makes them give glory to God for the way you accept
Ac 2:42 and profess the gospel of Christ, and for your sympathetic generosity to them
and to all. •And their prayers for you, too, show how they are drawn to you on 14
8:9 account of all the grace that God has given you. •Thanks be to God for his inex- 15
pressible gift![b]

III. PAUL'S APOLOGIA

Paul's reply to accusations of weakness

Mt 11:29 1 Co 2:3 Ph 2:3 **10** This is a personal matter; this is Paul himself appealing to you by the 1
gentleness and patience of Christ—I, the man who is so humble when he
is facing you, but bullies you when he is at a distance.[a] •I only ask that I do not 2
1 Co 4:21 have to bully you when I come, with all the confident assurance I mean to show
when I come face to face with people I could name who think we go by ordinary
Rm 7:5+ human motives. •We live in the flesh, of course, but the muscles that we fight 3
6:7 1 Co 1:25 with are not flesh. •Our war is not fought with weapons of flesh, yet they are 4
Ep 6:11 strong enough, in God's cause,[b] to demolish fortresses. We demolish sophistries,
Is 2:11-18 and the arrogance that tries to resist the knowledge of God; every thought is 5
our prisoner, captured to be brought into obedience to Christ. •Once you have 6
Rm 1:5+ given your complete obedience, we are prepared to punish any disobedience.
1 Co 1:12 Face plain facts.[c] Anybody who is convinced that he belongs to Christ must 7
11:23 go on to reflect that we all belong to Christ no less than he does. •Maybe I do 8
13:10 Jr 1:10 boast rather too much about our authority, but the Lord gave it to me for building
you up and not for pulling you down, and I shall not be ashamed of it. •I do not 9
want you to think of me as someone who only frightens you by letter. •Someone 10
Si 11:2 said, 'He writes powerful and strongly-worded letters but when he is with you
you see only half a man and no preacher at all'. •The man who said that can 11
remember this: whatever we are like in the words of our letters when we are
absent, that is what we shall be like in our actions when we are present.

His reply to the accusation of ambition

3:1+ We are not being so bold as to rank ourselves, or invite comparison, with 12
Pr 27:2 Ga 6:4 certain people who write their own references. Measuring themselves against
themselves, and comparing themselves to themselves, they are simply foolish.
We, on the other hand, are not going to boast without a standard to measure 13
Rm 15:19f against:[d] taking for our measure the yardstick which God gave us to measure
Col 1:25 with, which is long enough to reach to you. •We are not stretching further than 14
we ought; otherwise we should not have reached you, as we did come all the
Rm 15:20-21 way to you with the gospel of Christ. •So we are not boasting without any measure, 15
about work that was done by other people; in fact, we trust that, as your faith
grows, we shall get taller and taller, when judged by our own standard.[e] •I mean, 16
we shall be carrying the gospel to places far beyond you, without encroaching on
Jr 9:22-23 Si 10:19-24 1 Co 1:31 anyone else's field, not boasting of the work already done. •*If anyone wants to* 17
boast, let him boast of the Lord. •It is not the man who commends himself that 18
can be accepted, but the man who is commended by the Lord.

Paul is driven to sound his own praises

11 I only wish you were able to tolerate a little foolishness from me. But of 1
Dt 4:24+ course: you are tolerant towards me.[a] •You see, the jealousy that I feel 2
Ep 5:27 for you is God's own jealousy: I arranged for you to marry Christ so that I might
Rv 21:2,9 give you away as a chaste virgin to this one husband. •But the serpent, with his 3
Gn 3:1-6 cunning, seduced Eve, and I am afraid that in the same way your ideas may get
corrupted and turned away from simple[b] devotion to Christ. •Because any new- 4
comer has only to proclaim a new Jesus, different from the one that we preached,

or you have only to receive a new spirit, different from the one you have already Ga 1:6-9
received, or a new gospel, different from the one you have already accepted—and
5 you welcome it with open arms. •As far as I can tell, these arch-apostles have 12:11
6 nothing more than I have. •I may not be a polished speechmaker, but as for 1 Co 2:1-5
knowledge, that is a different matter; surely we have made this plain, speaking
on every subject in front of all of you.[c]
7 Or was I wrong, lowering myself so as to lift you high, by preaching the Ac 18:3+ 1 Co 9:18
8 gospel of God to you and taking no fee for it? •I was robbing other churches
9 living on them so that I could serve you. •When I was with you and ran out of 8:1-2 Ph 4:15
money, I was no burden to anyone; the brothers who came from Macedonia
provided me with everything I wanted. I was very careful, and I always shall be,
10 not to be a burden to you in any way, •and by Christ's truth in me, this cause 1 Co 9:15
11 of boasting will never be taken from me in the regions of Achaia. •Would I do that
12 if I did not love you? God knows I do. •I intend to go on doing what I am doing
now—leaving no opportunity for those people who are looking for an opportunity
13 to claim[d] equality with us in what they boast of. •These people are counterfeit Rv 2:2
14 apostles, they are dishonest workmen disguised as apostles of Christ. •There is
nothing unexpected about that; if Satan himself goes disguised as an angel of light,
15 there is no need to be surprised when his servants, too, disguise themselves as the Rv 2:2
servants of righteousness. They will come to the end that they deserve.
16 As I said before, let no one take me for a fool; but if you must, then treat me
17 as a fool and let me do a little boasting of my own. •What I am going to say now
is not prompted by the Lord,[e] but said as if in a fit of folly, in the certainty that
18 I have something to boast about. •So many others have been boasting of their Rm 7:5+
19 worldly achievements, that I will boast myself. •You are all wise men and can 3:1+
20 cheerfully tolerate fools, •yes, even to tolerating somebody who makes slaves of
you, makes you feed him, imposes on you, orders you about and slaps you in the
21 face. •I hope you are ashamed of us for being weak[f] with you instead!
But if anyone wants some brazen speaking—I am still talking as a fool—then
22 I can be as brazen as any of them, and about the same things.[g] •Hebrews, are they? Ac 22:3 Rm 11:1
23 So am I. Israelites? So am I. Descendants of Abraham? So am I. •The servants Ga 1:13-14 Ph 3:4-6
of Christ? I must be mad to say this, but so am I, and more than they: more, *10:7*
because I have worked harder, I have been sent to prison more often, and whipped Ac 20:19 1 Co 15:10
24 so many times more, often almost to death. •Five times I had the thirty-nine 2 Tm 3:11
25 lashes from the Jews; •three times I have been beaten with sticks; once I was Dt 25:2-3 Ac 16:22
stoned; three times I have been shipwrecked and once adrift in the open sea for *Ac 14:19*
26 a night and a day.[h] •Constantly travelling, I have been in danger from rivers and
in danger from brigands, in danger from my own people and in danger from
pagans; in danger in the towns, in danger in the open country, danger at sea and
27 danger from so-called brothers. •I have worked and laboured, often without
sleep; I have been hungry and thirsty and often starving; I have been in the cold 1 Co 4:11
28 without clothes. •And, to leave out much more, there is my daily preoccupation:
29 my anxiety for all the churches. •When any man has had scruples, I have had 1 Co 9:22
scruples with him; when any man is made to fall, I am tortured. Rm 9:1-3
30 31 If I am to boast, then let me boast of my own feebleness. •The God and Father
32 of the Lord Jesus—bless him for ever—knows that I am not lying. •When I was

b. The redemption.

10 a. Allusion to the sarcastic remarks of Paul's opponents, cf. v. 10.

b. Or 'in the sight of God'.

c. Or 'You see only what is superficial'.

d. Var. 'Oh no; by measuring ourselves against ourselves and comparing ourselves with our own selves, we will do no unmeasured boasting'.

e. An alternative translation: 'rather it is our hope that, as your faith grows, we shall more and more increase in your esteem, though always according to the standard laid down for us'.

11 a. Or possibly 'Please be tolerant with me'.

b. Add 'and pure'.

c. Or 'on every subject and in every way'.

d. Paul's selflessness is a guarantee of his apostolic mission; his opponents dare not claim the same for themselves.

e. Var. 'God'.

f. Var. 'I say it to our shame that we are weak'.

g. The needs of controversy oblige Paul on several occasions to appeal, as he does here, to his past life as a faithful Jew: Ga 1:13,14; Rm 11:1; Ph 3:4-6; cf. Ac 22:3f; 26:4-5.

h. For the most part nothing further is known of these hardships.

Ac 9:22-25 in Damascus, the ethnarch of King Aretas put guards round the city to catch
Jos 2:15 me, •and I had to be let down over the wall in a hamper, through a window, in 33
order to escape.

12 Must I go on boasting, though there is nothing to be gained by it?[a] But 1
I will move on to the visions and revelations I have had from the Lord.
I know a man in Christ who, fourteen years ago, was caught up—whether still in 2
the body or out of the body, I do not know; God knows—right into the third
Ex 33:20+ heaven.[b] •I do know, however, that this same person—whether in the body or 3
out of the body, I do not know; God knows—•was caught up into paradise and 4
heard things which must not and cannot be put into human language. •I will 5
boast about a man like that, but not about anything of my own except my weaknesses. •If I should decide to boast, I should not be made to look foolish, because 6
I should only be speaking the truth; but I am not going to, in case anyone should
begin to think I am better than he can actually see and hear me[c] to be.

In view of the extraordinary nature of these revelations, to stop me from 7
Rm 9:2 getting too proud I was given a thorn in the flesh,[d] an angel of Satan to beat me
Mt 26:39, 42,44 and stop me from getting too proud![e] •About this thing, I have pleaded with the 8
4:7 Is 40:29 Lord three times for it to leave me, •but he has said, 'My grace is enough for 9
4:7 Rm 1:16; 5:3 you: my power is at its best in weakness'. So I shall be very happy to make my
weaknesses my special boast so that the power of Christ may stay over me, •and 10
Col 1:24 that is why I am quite content with my weaknesses, and with insults, hardships,
Ph 4:13 persecutions, and the agonies I go through for Christ's sake. For it is when I am
weak that I am strong.

I have been talking like a fool, but you forced me to do it: you are the ones 11
who should have been commending me. Though I am a nobody, there is not
11:5 1 Co 15:10 a thing these arch-apostles have that I do not have as well. •You have seen done 12
Ac 1:8+ Rm 15:19 among you all the things that mark the true apostle, unfailingly produced: the
1 Co 2:4 1 Th 1:5 signs, the marvels, the miracles. •Is there anything of which you have had less than 13
Ac 18:3+ the other churches have had, except that I have not myself been a burden on
you? For this unfairness, please forgive me.[f] •I am all prepared now to come to 14
13:1 you for the third time, and I am not going to be a burden on you: it is you I want,
not your possessions. Children are not expected to save up for their parents, but
parents for children. •I am perfectly willing to spend what I have, and to be 15
expended, in the interests of your souls. Because I love you more, must I be loved
the less?[g]

All very well, you say: I personally put no pressure on you, but like the cunning 16
fellow that I am, I took you in by a trick. •So we exploited you, did we, through 17
8:18-22 one of the men that I have sent to you? •Well, Titus went at my urging, and I sent 18
the brother that came with him. Can Titus have exploited you? You know that
he and I have always been guided by the same spirit and trodden in the same
tracks.

Paul's fears and anxieties

All this time[h] you have been thinking that our defence is addressed to you, 19
but it is before God that we, in Christ, are speaking; and it is all, my dear
brothers, for your benefit. •What I am afraid of is that when I come I may find 20
you different from what I want you to be, and you may find that I am not as you
Rm 1:29+ would like me to be; and then there will be wrangling, jealousy, and tempers
roused, intrigues and backbiting and gossip, obstinacies and disorder. •I am 21
afraid that on my next visit, my God may make me ashamed on your account
and I shall be grieving over all those who sinned before and have still not repented
of the impurities, fornication and debauchery they committed.

12:14 Dt 19:15 13 This will be the third time[a] I have come to you. *The evidence of three, or at* 1
Mt 18:16 1 Tm 5:19 *least two, witnesses is necessary to sustain the charge.* •I gave warning when 2
I was with you the second time and I give warning now, too, before I come, to
those who sinned before and to any others, that when I come again, I shall have

3 no mercy. •You want proof, you say, that it is Christ speaking in me: you have
4 known him not as a weakling, but as a power among you? •Yes, but he was
crucified through weakness, and still he lives now through the power of God. Rm 1:4+
So then, we are weak, as he was, but we shall live with him, through the power Rm 8:11+ 1 Co 1:25
of God, for your benefit.[b]

5 Examine yourselves to make sure you are in the faith; test yourselves. Do
you acknowledge that Jesus Christ is really in you? If not, you have failed the
6 7 test, •but we, as I hope you will come to see, have not failed it. •We pray to God
that you will do nothing wrong: not that we want to appear as the ones who have
8 been successful—we would rather that you did well even though we failed. •We
9 have no power to resist the truth; only to further it. •We are only too glad to be Ac 4:20
weak provided you are strong.[c] What we ask in our prayers is for you to be made
10 perfect. •That is why I am writing this from a distance, so that when I am with
you I shall not need to be strict, with the authority which the Lord gave me for
building up and not for destroying. 10:8 Jr 1:10

CONCLUSION

Recommendations. Greetings. Final good wishes

11 In the meantime, brothers, we wish you happiness; try to grow perfect; help Ph 3:1
one another. Be united; live in peace, and the God of love and peace will be with
you.

12 Greet one another with the holy kiss.[d] All the saints send you greetings. Rm 16:16 1 Co 16:20

13 The grace of the Lord Jesus Christ, the love of God and the fellowship of the *1:21* 1 Co 2:10
Holy Spirit be with you all.[e] Ep 2:18; 4:6 Ph 2:1

12 a. Lit. 'Must there be boasting—there is nothing to be gained by it however'; var. 'There is nothing to be gained by boasting; however, I shall pass on...'

b. That is, to the highest heaven.

c. Or 'about me'.

d. Perhaps a disease with severe and unforeseeable attacks; perhaps the resistance of Israel, Paul's brothers 'according to the flesh', to the Christian faith.

e. Om. 'or I might get too proud'. Possibly also the beginning of v. 7 'and for fear... make me too proud' should be read as the conclusion of v. 6. The clause is awkwardly phrased and the text critically uncertain.

f. A good example of Paul's irony.

g. Var. ' souls, even if, loving you the more, I must be loved the less'.

h. Var. 'Once again'.

13 a. The first time was when the church was founded; the second was the distressing visit referred to in 2 Co 2:1; see Introduction.

b. Lit. 'towards you', omitted by some authorities.

c. When the Corinthians are living a fully Christian life they are 'strong', and Paul, not having to rebuke them, is 'weak': he has no need to exercise his power as an apostle, he as it were 'fails' in the test.

d. The liturgical greeting which symbolises Christian brotherhood, Rm 16:16; 1 Co 16:20; 1 Th 5:26.

e. This trinitarian formula, probably derived from liturgical usage, cf. also Mt 28:19, is echoed in many passages of the epistles where the several functions of the three Persons are referred to as the various contexts suggest: Rm 1:4+; 15:16,30; 1 Co 2:10-16; 6:11,14,15, 19; 12:4-6; 2 Co 1:21f; Ga 4:6; Ph 2:1; Ep 1:3-14; 2:18, 22; 4:4-6; Tt 3:5f; Heb 9:14; 1 P 1:2; 3:18; 1 Jn 4:2; Rv 1:4f; 22:1; cf. Ac 10:38; 20:28; Jn 14:16,18,23. Note in 1 Co 6:11; Ep 4:4-6 the triple formulations emphasising the trinitarian thought. Cf. also the trio of theological virtues in 1 Co 13:13+.

GALATIANS

THE LETTER OF PAUL TO THE CHURCH IN GALATIA

Address[a]

Rm 1:1+ **1** From Paul to the churches of Galatia, and from all the brothers who are here 1 2
1:11f with me, an apostle who does not owe his authority to men or his appointment
to any human being but who has been appointed by Jesus Christ and by God the
Rm 1:4+ Father who raised Jesus from the dead. •We wish you the grace and peace of 3
God our Father and of the Lord Jesus Christ, •who in order to rescue us from 4
1 Tm 2:6 1 Jn 5:19 this present wicked world[b] sacrificed himself for our sins, in accordance with
Rm 16:27+ the will of God our Father, •to whom be glory for ever and ever. Amen. 5

A warning[c]

2 Th 2:2 I am astonished at the promptness with which you have turned away from the 6
Mt 9:16 2 Co 11:4 one who called you and have decided to follow a different version of the Good
5:10 News. •Not that there can be more than one Good News; it is merely that some 7
troublemakers among you want to change the Good News of Christ; •and let 8
me warn you that if anyone preaches a version of the Good News different from
the one we have already preached to you, whether it be ourselves or an angel
Rm 9:3+ from heaven, he is to be condemned.[d] •I am only repeating what we told you 9
1 Co 11:2+ before: if anyone preaches a version of the Good News different from the one
1 Th 2:4 you have already heard, he is to be condemned. •So now whom am I trying to 10
please—man, or God? Would you say it is men's approval I am looking for?[e] If
Rm 1:1 I still wanted that,[f] I should not be what I am—a servant of Christ.

I. PAUL'S APOLOGIA

God's call

1:1 The fact is,[g] brothers, and I want you to realise this, the Good News I 11
preached is not a human message •that I was given by men, it is something 12
Mt 16:17 I learnt only through a revelation of Jesus Christ.[h] •You must have heard of 13
Ac 8:1-3+ 2 Co 11:12+ my career as a practising Jew, how merciless I was in persecuting the Church of
Mk 7:3f Ac 26:4-5 God, how much damage I did to it, •how I stood out among other Jews of my 14
generation, and how enthusiastic I was for the traditions of my ancestors.
Is 49:1 Jr 1:5 Then God, who had specially *chosen* me while I was *still in my mother's* 15
Lk 1:15 *womb*, called me through his grace and chose •to reveal his Son in me,[i] so that 16
Mt 16:17 Ac 9:3-19+ I might preach the Good News about him to the pagans. I did not stop to discuss
Rm 1:1+ this with any human being, •nor did I go up[j] to Jerusalem to see those who were 17
already apostles before me, but I went off to Arabia[k] at once and later went
Ac 9:23-30+ straight back from there to Damascus. •Even when after three years I went up 18
2:9 Ac 12:17+ to Jerusalem to visit Cephas and stayed with him for fifteen days, •I did not see 19
any of the other apostles; I only saw James, the brother of the Lord,[l] •and I 20

1 swear before God that what I have just written is the literal truth. •After that Rm 1:9+
2 I went to Syria and Cilicia, •and was still not known by sight to the churches of Ac 9:30; 11: 25-26
3 Christ in Judaea, •who had heard nothing except that their one-time persecutor
4 was now preaching the faith he had previously tried to destroy; •and they gave
glory to God for me.

The meeting at Jerusalem

Ac 11:30+; 15:1+

1 **2** It was not till fourteen years[a] had passed that I went up to Jerusalem again.
2 I went with Barnabas and took Titus with me. •I went there as the result of Ac 4:36+
a revelation, and privately I laid before the leading men the Good News as I 2 Co 2:13+
proclaim it among the pagans; I did so for fear the course I was adopting or had Ph 2:16
3 already adopted would not be allowed.[b] •And what happened? Even though Titus
4 who had come with me is a Greek, he was not obliged to be circumcised.[c] •The
question came up only because some who do not really belong to the brotherhood
have furtively crept in to spy on the liberty we enjoy in Christ Jesus, and want Rm 6:15+
5 to reduce us all to slavery. •I was so determined to safeguard for you the true
meaning of the Good News, that I refused even out of deference to yield to
6 such people for one moment.[d] •As a result, these people who are acknowledged
leaders—not that their importance matters to me, since God has no favourites— Dt 10:17+ Ac 10:34
7 these leaders, as I say, had nothing to add to the Good News as I preach it.[e] •On
the contrary, they recognised that I had been commissioned to preach the Good Ac 15:3f.12 Rm 15:17-19
News to the uncircumcised just as Peter had been commissioned to preach it to 1 Tm 2:7
8 the circumcised. •The same person whose action had made Peter the apostle of
9 the circumcised had given me a similar mission to the pagans. •So, James, 1:19+ Ac 12:17+
Cephas and John,[f] these leaders, these pillars, shook hands with Barnabas and Ep 3:8 *Rv 3:12*
me as a sign of partnership: we were to go to the pagans and they to the
0 circumcised.[g] •The only thing they insisted on was that we should remember to 1 Co 16:1+
help the poor, as indeed I was anxious to do.

1 a. This opening is shorter and less friendly than in any other letter: there is not a single word of praise for the Galatians. In vv. 1 and 4, Paul brings in the two main themes of his letter: 1. he is a true apostle, ch. 1-2, 2. he brings the Good News that we are saved through faith in Jesus Christ, and that Christians are therefore free, ch. 3-5.

b. The present world as opposed to the 'world to come' of the messianic era. It coincides with the rule of Satan, Ac 26:18, 'god of this world', 2 Co 4:4, cf. Ep 2:2; Jn 12:31, and with the rule of sin and law, Ga 3:19. By dying and rising Christ has freed us from these forces and made us members of his kingdom, of God's kingdom, Rm 14:17; Col 1:13; Ep 5:5, though we will not be completely freed till we also rise from the dead at the *parousia*, cf. Rm 5-8.

c. This warning takes the place of the thanksgiving with which Paul's letters usually begin, Rm 1:1+.

d. Lit. *anathema*, cf. Rm 9:3+.

e. It appears that the Judaisers accused Paul of trying to make the pagans' conversion easier by not insisting on circumcision. But on this occasion at least, he retorts he cannot be suspected of a conciliatory attitude.

f. As once he did, i.e. before his conversion when he preached circumcision.

g. Var. 'But' or 'Now'.

h. The two aspects of revelation, i.e. 'as made by Christ' and 'about Christ', v. 16. This should not be taken as meaning that Paul received all his doctrine without human intermediaries, and much less that on the Damascus road all was revealed to him at once. He is referring to the doctrine that it is not obeying the Law that saves, but having faith: this is the only topic of discussion here.

i. Others translate 'reveal his Son to me'. Paul is not denying that his vision was real, 1 Co 9:1; 15:8; cf. Ac 9:17; 22:14; 26:16, he is stressing the inwardness of this real vision and relating this inwardness to his call as apostle of the gentiles.

j. Var. 'leave for', 'go to'.

k. Probably the kingdom of the Nabataean Arabs to the S. of Damascus, 1 M 5:25+, where Paul took refuge from Aretas, 2 Co 11:32.

l. Lit. 'but only James...' Others translate 'except James', either identifying this James with the son of Alphaeus, Mt 10:3p, and taking him for one of the Twelve, or else understanding 'apostle' in the wider sense, cf. Rm 1:1+.

2 a. Reckoning from the last meeting with Peter or else, preferably from Paul's conversion. It is possible that the 'three years' of 1:18 and the 'fourteen' of 2:1 are no more than one-and-a-half and twelve-and-a-half respectively, since it was customary to count even the last few days or the first few days of a year as a whole year.

b. Lit. 'for fear I was running or had run to no purpose'. Paul is not having second thoughts about the truth of his gospel, he is concerned that when new churches are founded they should keep in touch with the mother church; this is why he felt the collection for the 'poor' in Jerusalem to be important, cf. 1 Co 16:1+; see v. 10.

c. Paul insisted that Timothy be circumcised since his mother was a Jewess, Ac 16:3, cf. 1 Co 9:20: a Jew being defined as one whose mother is Jewish.

d. Lit. 'we did not yield...' By omitting 'not', the Old Latin version makes Paul admit that he gave way for a moment. Om. 'out of deference'.

e. Lit. 'laid down nothing more for me', cf. v. 2.

f. 'James, Cephas and John'; var. 'James, Peter and John', or 'James and John'.

g. This distinction is not racial but geographical: 'the circumcised' (lit. 'the circumcision') refers primarily to the Jews in Palestine, and when Paul went among the gentiles the resident Jews were his first concern, Ac 13:5+.

Ac 15:1
Peter and Paul at Antioch

When Cephas came to Antioch, however, I opposed him to his face, since
Ac 10:1,28; 15:24 he was manifestly in the wrong.[h] •His custom had been to eat with the pagans,[i]
but after certain friends of James arrived he stopped doing this and kept away
from them altogether for fear of the group that insisted on circumcision. •The
other Jews joined him in this pretence, and even Barnabas felt himself obliged
to copy their behaviour.
When I saw they were not respecting the true meaning of the Good News, 1
I said to Cephas in front of everyone, 'In spite of being a Jew, you live like the
pagans and not like the Jews, so you have no right to make the pagans copy
Jewish ways'.

The Good News as proclaimed by Paul[j]

Ac 10:28 Rm 3:22 Ph 3:9 Though we were born Jews and not pagan sinners,[k] •we acknowledge that 1
what makes a man righteous is not obedience to the Law, but faith in Jesus
Christ. We had to become believers in Christ Jesus no less than you had, and
now we hold that faith in Christ rather than fidelity to the Law is what justifies
Ps 143:2 Rm 3:20+ us, and that *no one can be justified* by keeping the Law. •Now if we were to 1
admit that the result of looking to Christ to justify us is to make us sinners like
the rest, it would follow that Christ had induced us to sin, which would be
absurd. •If I were to return to a position I had already abandoned, I should be 1
Rm 6:11+; 7:1+ admitting I had done something wrong. •In other words, through the Law I am 1
dead to the Law,[l] so that now I can live for God. I have been crucified with
Rm 8:10-11 Ph 1:21 Christ, •and I live now not with my own life but with the life of Christ who 2
Col 3:3-4 lives in me.[m] The life I now live in this body[n] I live in faith: faith in the Son of
2 Co 5:14 Ep 5:2,25 God[o] who loved me and who sacrificed himself for my sake. •I cannot bring 2
5:2 Jn 15:13 myself to give up God's gift:[p] if the Law can justify us, there is no point in the
death of Christ.

II. DOCTRINAL MATTERS

Rm 1:16+
Justification by faith

3 Are you people in Galatia mad? Has someone put a spell on you, in spite 1
1 Co 2:2 of the plain explanation you have had of the crucifixion of Jesus Christ?[a]
Let me ask you one question: was it because you practised the Law that you 2
4:6 Rm 5:5+ received the Spirit, or because you believed what was preached to you? •Are you 3
foolish enough to end in outward observances[b] what you began in the Spirit?
Have all the favours you received been wasted?[c] And if this were so, they would 4
Ac 1:8+ most certainly have been wasted. •Does God give you the Spirit so freely and 5
work miracles among you because you practise the Law, or because you believed
what was preached to you?
Gn 15:6 Rm 4:3 Take Abraham for example: *he put his faith in God, and this faith was* 6
Jm 2:23 *Si 44:19-21* *considered as justifying him.* •Don't you see that it is those who rely on faith who 7
are the sons of Abraham? •Scripture foresaw that God was going to use faith 8
to justify the pagans, and proclaimed the Good News long ago when Abraham
Gn 12:3+ Ac 3:25 was told: *In you all the pagans will be blessed.* •Those therefore who rely on 9
faith receive the same blessing as Abraham, the man of faith.

Rm 7:7+
The curse brought by the Law

Ac 15:10 On the other hand, those who rely on the keeping of the Law are under a 1
Dt 27:26 Rm 4:15 curse, since scripture says: *Cursed be everyone who does not persevere in observing*
5:3 Jm 2:10 *everything prescribed in the book of the Law.* •The Law will not justify anyone 1
Hab 2:4 Rm 1:17 in the sight of God, because we are told: *the righteous man finds life through faith.*
Lv 18:5 Rm 3:24 The Law is not even based on faith,[d] since we are told: *The man who practises* 1
Ws 14:7 Is 53:5 *these precepts finds life through practising them.* •Christ redeemed us from the 1

curse of the Law by being cursed for our sake,[e] since scripture says: *Cursed be* Dt 21:23 Ac 5:30+
14 *everyone who is hanged on a tree.* •This was done so that in Christ Jesus the
blessing of Abraham might include the pagans, and so that through faith we might Rm 5:5+ Ep 1:3
receive the promised Spirit.[f] Heb 6:12

The Law did not cancel the promise

15 Compare this, brothers, with what happens in ordinary life. If a will has
16 been drawn up in due form, no one is allowed to disregard it or add to it. •Now
the promises were addressed to Abraham *and to his descendants*—notice, in Gn 12:7+ Mt 1:1+;
passing, that scripture does not use a plural word as if there were several 21:38 Rm 8:16
17 descendants, it uses the singular: to his posterity,[g] which is Christ. •But my
point is this: once God had expressed his will in due form, no law that came
four hundred and thirty years later could cancel that and make the promise Gn 15:13 Ex 12:40
18 meaningless.[h] •If you inherit something as a legal right, it does not come to you
as the result of a promise, and it was precisely in the form of a promise that God Rm 11:6
made his gift to Abraham.

The purpose of the Law

Rm 7:7+

19 What then was the purpose of adding the Law? This was done to specify Rm 5:20
crimes,[i] until the posterity came[j] to whom the promise was addressed. The Law
20 was promulgated by angels,[k] assisted by an intermediary. •Now there can only Ac 7:38,53+ Heb 2:2
21 be an intermediary between two parties, yet God is one.[l] •Does this mean that 4:3+ Col 2:15+
there is opposition between the Law and the promises of God? Of course not.
We could have been justified by the Law if the Law we were given had been Ps 14:1-3 Rm 3:9-20,
22 capable of giving life, •but it is not: scripture makes no exceptions when it says 23
that sin is master everywhere. In this way the promise can only be given through Rm 11:32
faith in Jesus Christ and can only be given to those who have this faith.[m]

h. Peter's conduct was not in itself blameworthy, and in different circumstances Paul was to do the same, Ac 16:3; 21:26; 1 Co 8:13; Rm 14:21; cf. 1 Co 9:20. But on this occasion such a policy suggested that the only true Christians were converted Jews who observed the Law, and threatened to produce two separate communities that could not even meet to celebrate the Eucharist. Peter's behaviour should have advertised his real attitude but instead of that he disguised it, v. 13.

i. Converts from paganism, so also in v. 14, as opposed to the 'circumcised' who are converted Jews.

j. Paul is not only speaking to Peter but more particularly to all the Judaisers, e.g. those of Antioch and still more those of Galatia.

k. This is slightly ironical, though Paul never doubted that Israel kept a privileged position, Rm 1:16; 3:1; 9:4-5, even when unfaithful, Rm 11:12f.

l. So laconic as to be obscure: there have been various explanations: 1. Christians; crucified with Christ, are dead with Christ and therefore, like Christ, dead to the Mosaic Law, cf. Rm 7:1f—and indeed in virtue of that Law, Ga 3:13; this is why Christians already share the life of the risen Christ, Rm 6:4-10; 7:4-6 with notes. 2. Christians only renounced the Law for a deeper obedience to the O.T., Ga 3:19,24; Rm 10:4. 3. Christians are only dead to the Mosaic Law in obedience to a higher law, the law of faith and of the Spirit, Rm 8:2.

m. The living acts of a Christian become somehow the acts of Christ.

n. Lit. 'in the flesh'. Though still physically alive, Rm 7:5+, Christians are already spiritually alive, cf. Ep 3:17; on this paradox, cf. Rm 8.

o. Var. 'faith in God and in Christ'.

p. By returning to the Law, cf. 3:18.

3 a. The foundation of everything Paul teaches is the idea that we are redeemed because Christ died and rose again, cf. 1 Co 15:3f.

b. Reference to being circumcised as urged by Judaising preachers.

c. Others translate 'Have you suffered so much and all to no purpose?'

d. Laws expect to be obeyed in every point, v. 10 and 5:3; cf. Jm 2:10, but do nothing, of themselves, to assure this, cf. Ac 15:10; Rm 7:7+.

e. To free the human race from the curse God laid on it for defying the law, Christ made himself answerable for the curse, cf. Rm 8:3+; 2 Co 5:21+; Col 2:14+. The somewhat remote analogy between the crucified Christ and the criminal of Dt 21:23 is used merely to illustrate this doctrine.

f. Lit. 'the promise of the Spirit'. Var. 'the blessing of the Spirit'.

g. Lit. 'It does not say "And to posterities" as if there were several people, but "And to your posterity" as if there were one'. The use in scripture of a collective capable of indicating an individual enables Paul to illustrate his argument with a verbal pun.

h. God would have contradicted himself had he replaced a scheme of salvation based on a spontaneous promise (compared to a will in v. 15) with one based on a bilateral contract, v. 20. He could not have made the fulfilment of the promise depend on the observance of a law, as this would have been to make the promise a promise no longer, vv. 21f. The Law was given for quite a different purpose, vv. 19,24.

i. On the meaning of this terse statement, lit. 'on account of crimes', cf. Rm 7:7+.

j. Lit. 'Why then the Law? It was added on account of crimes until that posterity came...' Var. 'Why then the law of works? It was added until that posterity came...'

k. In Jewish tradition angels were present at Sinai when the Law was given. The 'intermediary' is Moses, cf. Ac 7:38+.

l. The Law was given through an intermediary; the promise came directly from God.

m. Justification is a free gift; to receive this gift a person must first recognise that it is not the payment of a debt.

The coming of faith

Before faith came, we were allowed no freedom by the Law; we were being 23
Rm 3:22; 10:4 looked after till faith was revealed. •The Law was to be our guardian until the 24
Christ came and we could be justified by faith. •Now that that time has come 25
4:5-7 Jn 1:12 we are no longer under that guardian, •and you are, all of you,[n] sons of God 26
Rm 8:14f,29 *Rm 6:4+;* through faith in Christ Jesus. •All baptised in Christ,[o] you have all clothed 27
13:14+ Ep 4:24 yourselves in Christ, •and there are no more distinctions between Jew and 28
Rm 10:12 1 Co 12:13 Greek, slave and free, male and female, but all of you are one in Christ Jesus.[p]
Col 3:11 *Jn 17:21f* Merely by belonging to Christ you are the posterity of Abraham, the heirs he 29
Heb 6:12 Jm 2:5 was promised.

Sons of God

Rm 4:1+ Heb 9:16 4 Let me put this another way:[a] an heir, even if he has actually inherited 1
everything, is no different from a slave for as long as he remains a child.
He is under the control of guardians and administrators until he reaches the 2
Col 2:8 age fixed by his father. •Now before we came of age we were as good as slaves to 3
Ep 1:10 the elemental principles of this world,[b] •but when the appointed time[c] came, 4
Rm 1:3 God sent his Son, born of a woman, born a subject of the Law, •to redeem the 5
Rm 3:24+ subjects of the Law and to enable us to be adopted as sons.[d] •The proof that you 6
Rm 8:15-17 are sons is that God has sent the Spirit of his Son into our hearts: the Spirit
Jn 15:15 that cries, 'Abba, Father', •and it is this that makes you a son, you are not a 7
slave any more; and if God has made you son, then he has made you heir.
1 Co 12:2 *1 Co 8:4-5* Once you were ignorant of God, and enslaved to 'gods' who are not really 8
1 Th 1:9 *1 Co 13:12* gods at all; •but now that you have come to acknowledge God—or rather, now 9
that God has acknowledged you[e]—how can you want to go back to elemental
Col 2:16,20 things like these, that can do nothing and give nothing, and be their slaves? •You 10
and your special days and months and seasons and years! •You make me feel I 11
Ph 2:16 have wasted my time with you.

A personal appeal

1 Co 9:21 2 Th 3:7+ Brothers, all I ask is that you should copy me as I copied you.[f] You have 12
Ac 16:6+ never treated me in an unfriendly way before; •even at the beginning, when that 13
illness[g] gave me the opportunity to preach the Good News to you, •you never 14
showed the least sign of being revolted or disgusted by my disease that was such
Mt 10:40+ a trial to you; instead you welcomed me as an angel of God, as if I were Christ
Jesus himself. •What has become of this enthusiasm you had? I swear that you 15
would even have gone so far as to pluck out your eyes and give them to me. •Is it 16
telling you the truth that has made me your enemy? •The blame lies in the way 17
they have tried to win you over: by separating you from me, they want to win
you over to themselves. •It is always a good thing to win people over[h]—and 18
I do not have to be there with you—but it must be for a good purpose, •my 19
1 Co 4:14-15 2 Co 6:13 children! I must go through the pain of giving birth to you all over again, until
1 Th 2:7-8 Phm 10 Christ is formed in you. •I wish I were with you now so that I could know exactly 20
what to say; as it is, I have no idea what to do for the best.

The two covenants: Hagar and Sarah

You want to be subject to the Law? Then listen to what the Law says.[i] •It 21 22
Gn 16:15; 21:2 says, if you remember, that Abraham had two sons, one by the slave-girl, and one
by his free-born wife. •The child of the slave-girl was born in the ordinary way;[j] 23
Gn 17:16 the child of the free woman was born as the result of a promise. •This can be 24
1 Co 10:6+ regarded as an allegory: the women stand for the two covenants. The first who
comes from Mount Sinai, and whose children are slaves, is Hagar—•since Sinai 25
Jn 8:32f is in Arabia[k]—and she corresponds to the present Jerusalem[l] that is a slave like
Ps 87:5 Rv 21:2 her children. •The Jerusalem above, however, is free and is our mother, •since 26 27
Is 54:1 scripture says: *Shout for joy, you barren women who bore no children! Break into*
shouts of joy and gladness, you who were never in labour. For there are more sons of

28 *the forsaken one than sons of the wedded wife.* •Now you, my brothers, like Isaac,
29 are children of the promise, •and as at that time the child born in the ordinary Gn 21:9 1 P 3:6
30 way persecuted the child born in the Spirit's way, so also now.[m] •Does not *1 Th 2:14+*
scripture say: *Drive away that slave-girl and her son; this slave-girl's son is not to* Gn 21:10 Jn 8:35
31 *share the inheritance with the son* of the free woman? •So, my brothers, we are
the children, not of the slave-girl, but of the free-born wife.

III. EXHORTATION

Christian liberty

Rm 6:15+

1 **5** When Christ freed us, he meant us to remain free.[a] Stand firm, therefore, Jn 8:36
2 and do not submit again to the yoke of slavery. •It is I, Paul, who tell you Mt 11:29 Ac 15:10
this: if you allow yourselves to be circumcised, Christ will be of no benefit to 2:21
3 you at all. •With all solemnity I repeat my warning: Everyone who accepts
4 circumcision is obliged to keep the whole Law. •But if you do look to the Law 3:10 Jm 2:10
to make you justified, then you have separated yourselves from Christ, and have *Rm 8:23,25*
5 fallen from grace. •Christians are told by the Spirit to look to faith for those 1 Co 7:19
6 rewards that righteousness hopes for,[b] •since in Christ Jesus whether you are 6:15
circumcised or not makes no difference—what matters is faith that makes its
power felt through love. 1 Co 13:13+ Jm 2:14
7 You began your race well:[c] who made you less anxious to obey the truth? 1 Co 9:24 Ph 2:16
8 9 You were not prompted by him who called you! •The yeast seems to be spreading *Qo 10:1* 1 Co 5:6
10 through the whole batch of you. •I feel sure that, united in the Lord, you[d] will *Ph 2:1-5*
agree with me, and anybody who troubles you in future will be condemned, 1 Co 3:17 *1:7*
11 no matter who he is. •As for me, my brothers, if I still preach circumcision,[e]
why am I still persecuted? If I did that now, would there be any scandal of the 1 Co 1:23
12 cross? •Tell those who are disturbing you I would like to see the knife slip.[f] Ph 3:2

Liberty and charity

13 My brothers, you were called, as you know, to liberty; but be careful, or this Rm 6:15+
liberty will provide an opening for self-indulgence. Serve one another, rather, in 1 P 2:16 Jude 4

n. All, i.e. not only 'we', who are Jews, but 'you', who are pagans.

o. Faith and baptism are not being contrasted: one involves the other, cf. Rm 6:4+.

p. Var. 'you are all of Christ Jesus'.

4 a. A further comparison, again taken from the law courts. Though the Jews are chosen as the heir presumptive, yet they are only slaves, v. 3, to the Law; a Christian who wants to submit to this slavery is going back to a state of childhood, cf. v. 9.

b. Reference to the elements that make up the physical universe, cf. v. 9; Col 2:8,20; Paul uses the phrase to indicate both the Law that minutely regulated the use of these elements, v. 10; Col 2:16, and the spirits that used the Law, Ga 3:19+; Col 2:15+, to dominate the universe, Col 2:18+,

c. Lit. 'fullness of time'; the phrase indicates how when the messianic age comes it will fill a need felt for centuries, rather like filling up a jug. Cf. Ac 1:7+ and Mk 1:15; 1 Co 10:11; Ep 1:10; Heb 1:2; 9:26; 1 P 1:20.

d. The two aspects of redemption, negative and positive: the slave attains freedom by becoming a son. First and foremost the adoption to sonship is not simply a legal right to inherit, v. 7, but the real and inward giving of the Spirit, v. 6.

e. The Galatians were converted by God who 'knew' them before they 'knew' him.

f. Probably by refusing to practise the Law's ritual, cf. 1 Co 9:21.

g. This probably prolonged Paul's stay in Galatia, and he took the opportunity to preach the Good News.

h. Var. 'Be won over to what is good'.

i. I.e. the witness of the scriptures, cf. Rm 3:19+; to inherit the promise it is not enough just to be a descendant of Abraham, cf. Mt 3:9; it is not enough to be descended from Abraham like Ishmael, it is necessary to be descended as the result of promise, like Isaac, v. 23; it is necessary to be a spiritual descendant, not just a genealogical one, v. 29; thus Isaac's birth prefigured the rebirth of Christians, v. 28; cf. Rm 9:6f. This basic argument is embellished with other more contrived comparisons.

j. Lit. 'according to the flesh', i.e. in the ordinary course of nature, cf. Rm 7:5+, without God working a miracle to fulfil his promise.

k. 'since Sinai is in Arabia'; var. 'Hagar stands for Sinai in Arabia' (or 'in Arabic').

l. I.e. enslaved to the Law, as opposed to the messianic Jerusalem, cf. Is 2:2, long barren, now a mother, v. 27; cf. Is 54:1-6.

m. Having demonstrated the Ishmael-Jews, Isaac-Christians, parallel, Paul makes two observations, vv. 29 and 30. According to some Jewish traditions Ishmael 'persecuted' Isaac, and according to the sacred text itself, Sarah sees Ishmael as her son's rival and demands Hagar's expulsion. Gn 21:9.

5 a. Human beings must choose either Christ or the Law as author of salvation. Some witnesses (Vulg.) join these words with the preceding verse 'with the freedom by which Christ has made us free'.

b. Or else 'The righteousness that was hoped for'.

c. One of Paul's favourite images, cf. 2:2; 1 Co 9:24-26; Ph 2:16; 3:12-14; 2 Tm 4:7; Heb 12:1.

d. Or else 'I have confidence in the Lord that you'.

e. As Paul's enemies apparently claimed, cf. 1:10; 2:3+.

f. Lit. 'I wish that those who are disturbing you might go even further (than circumcision) and castrate themselves'. Perhaps alluding to castration in the cult of Cybele, the sarcasm resembling that of Ph 3:2.

Rm 13:8-10+ works of love, •since the whole of the Law is summarised in a single command: 14
Lv 19:18 *Love your neighbour as yourself.* •If you go snapping at each other and tearing 15
each other to pieces, you had better watch or you will destroy the whole
community.
Rm 8:5f Let me put it like this: if you are guided by the Spirit you will be in no danger 16
Rm 7:14f Jm 4:1 of yielding to self-indulgence, •since self-indulgence is the opposite of the Spirit, 17
the Spirit is totally against such a thing, and it is precisely because the two are
so opposed that you do not always carry out your good intentions. •If you are 18
Rm 8:14 *Mt 7:17* led by the Spirit, no law can touch you. •When self-indulgence is at work the 19
Rm 1:29+ 1 Co 3:3+ results are obvious: fornication, gross indecency and sexual irresponsibility;
Ep 5:3 Jm 1:21 idolatry and sorcery; feuds and wrangling, jealousy, bad temper and quarrels; 20
disagreements, factions, •envy;[g] drunkenness, orgies and similar things. I warn 21
1 Co 6:10 you now, as I warned you before: those who behave like this will not inherit the
2 Co 6:6 Ep 5:9 kingdom of God. •What the Spirit brings is very different: love, joy, peace, 22
1 Tm 4:12 2 P 1:5-7 patience, kindness, goodness, trustfulness, •gentleness and self-control.[h] There 23
1 Co 13:4-7 1 Tm 1:9 can be no law against things like that, of course. •You cannot belong to Christ 24
Rm 6:6 Col 3:5 Jesus unless you crucify all self-indulgent passions and desires.
Rm 8:14 *Ph 2:3* Since the Spirit is our life, let us be directed by the Spirit. •We must stop 25 26
being conceited, provocative and envious.

On kindness and perseverance

Mt 18:15 2Th 3:14-15 **6** Brothers, if one of you misbehaves, the more spiritual of you who set him 1
2 Tm 2:25 Jm 4:19f right should do so in a spirit of gentleness, not forgetting that you may be
1 Co 10:12 *Jn 13:34* tempted yourselves. •You should carry each other's troubles and fulfil[a] the 2
Rm 8:2 *1 Co 4:7* law of Christ. •It is the people who are not important who often make the 3
mistake of thinking that they are. •Let each of you examine his own conduct; 4
if you find anything to boast about, it will at least be something of your own, not
Rm 14:12 just something better than your neighbour has. •Everyone has his own burden 5
to carry.
Rm 15:27 People under instruction should always contribute something to the support 6
of the man who is instructing them.
Jb 13:9 Ho 8:7 Don't delude yourself into thinking God can be cheated: where a man sows, 7
Dt 30:15-20 Jb 15:35 there he reaps: •if he sows in the field of self-indulgence he will get a harvest of 8
Pr 11:18 Jn 3:6 corruption out of it; if he sows in the field of the Spirit he will get from it a
Rm 6:21-22 1 Co 15:35-49 harvest of eternal life. •We must never get tired of doing good because if we 9
don't give up the struggle we shall get our harvest at the proper time. •While 10
1 Th 5:15 we have the chance,[b] we must do good[c] to all,[d] and especially to our brothers
in the faith.

Rm 16:17
Epilogue

1 Co 16:21 Col 4:18 Take good note of what I am adding in my own handwriting and in large 11
Col 2:18 letters.[e] •It is only self-interest that makes them want[f] to force circumcision on 12
Rm 2:21f you—they want to escape persecution for the cross of Christ—•they accept 13
circumcision but do not keep the Law themselves; they only want you to be
Rm 3:27+ circumcised so that they can boast of the fact. •As for me, the only thing I can 14
boast about is the cross of our Lord Jesus Christ, through whom the world is
5:6+ crucified to me, and I to the world.[g] •[h]It does not matter if a person is circumcised 15
1 Co 7:19 2 Co 5:17+ or not; what matters is for him to become an altogether new creature. •Peace 16
Ps 125:5 and mercy to all who follow this rule, who form the Israel of God.[i]
I want no more trouble from anybody after this; the marks on my body are 17
those of Jesus.[j] •The grace of our Lord Jesus Christ be with your spirit, my 18
brothers. Amen.

g. Add. (Vulg.) 'murders'. Cf. Rm 1:29.

h. Add. 'chastity'.

6 a. 'fulfil'; var. 'you will fulfil'.

b. Possibly alluding to the time that still remains before the *parousia*, cf. 2 Co 6:2+.

c. 'we must do good'; var. 'we do good'.

d. The good act of a Christian is done out of love, and so is concerned with others, 5:14; in this way he gives witness in public, cf. Rm 12:17-18, and as he is specially noticed by Christians, Rm 14:15, he helps to 'build up' the Church, Rm 14:18-19.

e. As usual, Paul adds a few words in his own hand, cf. 2 Th 3:17; 1 Co 16:21-24; Col 4:18, and possibly Rm 16:17-20. Large letters were used for emphasis.

f. Lit. 'It is those who want to make a fair show in the flesh who want...'

g. This present sinful world, cf. 1:4; 4:5; 1 Co 1:20; 2 Co 4:4; Ep 2:2, etc.; Jn 1:10+.

h. Add. 'In Christ Jesus'.

i. The Christian community, the true Israel, cf. 3:29; Rm 9:6-8, as opposed to the Israel 'according to the flesh', 1 Co 10:18

j. The marks of ill-treatment suffered for Christ, cf. 2 Co 6:4-5; 11:23f.

EPHESIANS

THE LETTER OF PAUL TO THE CHURCH AT EPHESUS

Address and Greetings

Rm 1:1+ *Ac 9:13+* 1 From Paul, appointed by God to be an apostle of Christ Jesus, to the saints[a] 1
who are faithful to Christ Jesus: •Grace and peace to you from God our 2
Father and from the Lord Jesus Christ.

I. THE MYSTERY OF SALVATION AND OF THE CHURCH

God's plan of salvation

Tb 13:1 Blessed be God the Father of our Lord Jesus Christ, 3
Ga 3:14 who has blessed us with all the spiritual blessings of heaven in Christ.[b]
Ex 15:16 Jn 17:24 Before the world was made, he chose us, chose us in Christ, 4
1 P 1:20 *5:27* to be holy and spotless, and to live through love[c] in his presence,
1 Co 1:8+ 1 Jn 3:1 determining that we should become his adopted sons,[d] through 5
Jn 1:12 Rm 8:29 Jesus Christ
for his own kind purposes,
to make us praise the glory of his grace,[e] 6
his free gift to us in the Beloved,[f]
Rm 3:24+ ||Col 1:13-14 in whom, through his blood, we gain our freedom, the forgiveness 7
Heb 1:3 of our sins.[g]
2:7 Such is the richness of the grace
which he[h] has showered on us 8
in all wisdom and insight.
Rm 16:25+ He has let us know the mystery of his purpose,[i] 9
the hidden plan he so kindly made in Christ from the beginning
Mk 1:15 Ga 4:4+ to act upon when the times had run their course to the end:[j] 10
that he would bring everything together under Christ, as head,
Col 1:16,20 everything in the heavens and everything on earth.[k]
Dt 7:6+ Col 1:12 And it is in him[l] that we were claimed as God's own,[m] 11
chosen from the beginning,
Is 46:10 under the predetermined plan of the one who guides all things
Rv 4:11 as he decides by his own will;
chosen to be, 12
Ps 66:2 for his greater glory,
the people who would put their hopes in Christ before he came.
Now you too,[n] in him, 13
Ac 1:4 ||Col 1:5; have heard the message of the truth and the good news of your
2:9 Heb 6:12 salvation,
and have believed it;
4:30 2 Co 1:22 and you too have been stamped with the seal of the Holy Spirit
Ac 2:33+ Rm 5:5+ of the Promise,[o]

14 the pledge of our inheritance 2 Co 1:22+
which brings freedom for those whom God has taken for his own,[p] Rm 3:24+
to make his glory praised. Ps 66:2

The triumph and the supremacy of Christ

15 That will explain why I, having once heard about your faith in the Lord Jesus, ||Col 1:3-4,9 Phm 4-5
16 and the love that you show[q] towards all the saints, •have never failed to remember *Ac 9:13+* 1 Co 13:13+
17 you in my prayers and to thank God for you. •May the God of our *3:14,16*
Lord Jesus Christ, the Father of glory, give you a spirit[r] of wisdom and perception Ex 24:16+
18 of what is revealed, to bring you to full knowledge of him. •May he enlighten 1 Jn 5:20
the eyes of your mind[s] so that you can see what hope his call holds for you, what Heb 3:1
19 rich glories he has promised the saints will inherit •and how infinitely great is Ac 9:13+ *3:20*
the power that he has exercised for us believers. This you can tell from the strength 1 P 1:5
20 of his power •at work in Christ, when he used it to raise him from the dead and Is 52:13 Col 2:12
21 to make him sit at his right hand, in heaven, •far above every Sovereignty, *Ac 2:33+* 1 P 3:22
Authority, Power, or Domination,[t] or any other name that can be named, not *Col 1:16;* 2:15
22 only in this age but also in the age to come. •*He has put all things under his feet,* Ph 2:9 *Ps 8:6*
23 and made him, as the ruler of everything, the head of the Church; •which is his 1 Co 15:24-25
body, the fullness of him who fills the whole creation.[u] *Col 1:18+,* 19+

Salvation in Christ a free gift

1/2 2 And you were dead, through the crimes and the sins •in which you used to live ||Col 2:13; 3:7
when you were following the way of this world, obeying the ruler who governs Heb 6:1+ *6:12+*
3 the air,[a] the spirit who is at work in the rebellious. •We[b] all were among them Jn 12:31 2 Co 4:4

1 a. Add. 'who are at Ephesus'. The words 'at Ephesus' were probably not part of the original text. The words 'who are' could be part of a very early addition. Some critics think they are authentic, that they were followed by a blank to be filled in with the name of whichever church was being sent the letter.

b. All the way through the letter, 1:20; 2:6; 3:10; 6:12, Paul reverts to this opening reference to heaven. The spiritual blessings listed in the following verses must wait till the end of the world before they can be fully realised in heaven where they have been formulated since all eternity.

c. First blessing: through their union with the glorified Christ the faithful already enjoy, in a hidden sort of way, the eternal happiness to which the chosen are called. 'Love' here is primarily the love God has for us, and that leads him to 'choose' us and to call us to be 'holy', cf. Col 3:12; 1 Th 1:4; 2 Th 2:13; Rm 11:28, but does not exclude our love for God that results from and is a response to his own love for us, cf. Rm 5:5.

d. Second blessing: Jesus Christ, the only Son, is both the source and the model of the way God has chosen for us to become holy, i.e. by adopting us as his heirs, cf. Rm 8:29.

e. The word 'grace' *(charis)* as it is used here emphasises not so much the interior gift that makes a human being holy, as the gratuitousness of God's favour and the way he manifests his glory, cf. Ex 24:16f. These are the two themes that run through this account of God's blessings: their *source* is God's liberality, and their *purpose* is to make his glory appreciated by creatures. Everything comes from him, and everything should lead to him.

f. Var. (Vulg) 'his beloved Son'.

g. Third blessing: our redemption by an event in time, i.e. the death of Jesus.

h. God the Father.

i. Fourth blessing: the revelation of the 'mystery', Rm 16:25f.

j. Lit. 'for a dispensation of the times' fullness', cf. Ga 4:4f.

k. The main theme of this letter is how the whole body of creation, having been cut off from the Creator by sin, is decomposing, and how its rebirth is effected by Christ reuniting all its parts into an organism with himself as the head, so as to reattach it to God. The human (Jew and pagan) and the angelic worlds are brought together again through the fact that they were saved by a single act, cf. 4:10f.

l. Christ.

m. Fifth blessing: the Jews are chosen to be the human share allotted to God, and are to be his witness until the coming of the Messiah. Paul, being a Jew, here uses 'we'.

n. Sixth blessing: the pagans are called to share the salvation that had, till then, been reserved for the Jews; that they will be saved is proved by the fact that they receive the Spirit as was promised.

o. Paul completes his trinitarian account of God's plan with the Spirit, since the giving of the Spirit shows the plan has reached its final stage. Nevertheless, though this gift has already begun, it is only given in a hidden way while the unspiritual world lasts, and will only be given fully when the kingdom of God is complete and Christ comes in glory.

p. Lit. 'the setting free of that (enslaved people) which has been acquired' i.e. by God, and at the cost of the life of his Son. This is one of the occasions when Paul widens an O.T. concept (like 'blessing', 'saint', 'choice', 'adoption', 'redemption', 'share', 'promise') by applying it to the Church as the new Israel and the body of the saved.

q. Om. 'and the love that you show'.

r. This gift is what technically would be called (actual) grace.

s. Lit. 'heart': used in the Bible for the seat of knowledge as well as of love.

t. Names traditional in Jewish literature for angelic hierarchies.

u. Lit. 'fills all in all'. The Church, as the body of Christ 1 Co 12:12f, can be called the fullness (*pleroma;* cf. *infra* 3:19; 4:13) in so far as it includes the whole new creation that shares (since it forms the setting of the human race) in the cosmic rebirth under Christ its ruler and head, cf. Col 1:15-20f. The adverbial phrase 'all in all' is used to suggest something of limitless size, cf. 1 Co 12:6; 15:28; Col 3:11.

2 a. Air is the habitat of demons and of their ruler Satan.

b. Paul writes as a Jew.

Rm 2;3:9,23 too in the past, living sensual lives, ruled entirely by our own physical desires
5:6 Rm 1:18; 2:8 and our own ideas; so that by nature we were as much under God's anger as the
Ex 34:6+ rest of the world. •But God loved us with so much love that he was generous 4
Rm 5:8 ||*Col 2:13* with his mercy: •when we[c] were dead through our sins, he brought us to life 5
Rm 8:11+ Col 2:12; with Christ[d]—it is through grace that you have been saved—•and raised us up 6
3:1-4 with him and gave us a place with him in heaven, in Christ Jesus.[e]
Dt 9:6 Ps 22:30-31 This was to show for all ages to come, through his goodness towards us in 7
Christ Jesus, how infinitely rich he is in grace. •Because it is by grace that you 8
Dt 8:17-18 Rm 1:16+ have been saved, through faith; not by anything of your own, but by a gift from
God; •not by anything that you have done, so that nobody can claim the credit. 9
2 Co 5:17+ We are God's work of art, created in Christ Jesus to live the good life as from the 10
beginning he had meant us to live it.

Reconciliation of the Jews and the pagans with each other and with God

Do not forget, then, that there was a time when you[f] who were pagans 11
physically, termed the Uncircumcised by those who speak of themselves as the
Circumcision by reason of a physical operation, •do not forget, I say, that 12
Col 1:21,27 you had no Christ[g] and were excluded from membership of Israel, aliens with
Rm 9:4-5 no part in the covenants with their Promise;[h] you were immersed in this world,
2:17 without hope[i] and without God.[j] •But now in Christ Jesus, you that used to be 13
Ps 148:14 so far apart from us have been brought very close, by the blood of Christ.[k]
Is 9:5 For he is the peace between us, and has made the two into one and broken 14
Ga 3:28+ down the barrier which used to keep them apart,[l] actually destroying in his
Col 2:14+ own person the hostility •caused by the rules and decrees of the Law.[m] This 15
was to create one single New Man[n] in himself out of the two of them and by
Col 3:14-15 restoring peace •through the cross, to unite them both in a single Body[o] and 16
reconcile them with God. In his own person he killed the hostility. •Later he 17
Is 57:19 Zc 9:10 came[p] to bring the good news of peace, *peace to you who were far away and peace*
4:4 *to those who were near at hand.* •Through him, both of us have in the one Spirit[q] 18
3:12+ 2 Co 13:13+ our way to come to the Father.
Ex 12:48+ Ps 122:3-4 So you[r] are no longer aliens or foreign visitors: you are citizens like all the 19
Ac 9:13+ *Is 28:16* saints, and part of God's household. •You are part of a building that has the 20
Rm 15:20 1 Co 3:10f apostles and prophets[s] for its foundations, and Christ Jesus himself for its main
2 Co 6:16 *4:11-12* cornerstone. •As every[t] structure is aligned on him, all grow into one holy temple 21
Rv 21:14 *1 Co 3:16+* in the Lord; •and you too, in him, are being built into a house where God lives, 22
1 P 2:5 in the Spirit.

||Col 1:24-29 **Paul, a servant of the mystery**

4:1 Ph 1:13 Col 4:18 2 Tm 2:9 3 So I, Paul, a prisoner of Christ Jesus for the sake of you pagans... •You have 1 2
probably heard how I have been entrusted by God with the grace[a] he meant
for you, •and that it was by a revelation[b] that I was given the knowledge of the 3
Rm 16:25+ mystery, as I have just described it very shortly. •If you read my words, you will 4
1 Co 7:40 2 Co 11:5f have some idea of the depths that I see in the mystery of Christ. •This mystery 5
4:11 Jn 14:26+ that has now been revealed through the Spirit to his holy apostles and prophets[c]
was unknown to any men in past generations; •it means that pagans now share 6
2:12-19 the same inheritance,[d] that they are parts of the same body, and that the same
promise has been made to them, in Christ Jesus, through the gospel. •I have 7
2 Co 3:6 Col 1:23 been made the servant of that gospel by a gift of grace from God who gave it to
1 Th 2:4 *1 Co 15:8f* me by his own power. •I, who am less than the least of all the saints, have been 8
Ga 2:8 Ph 4:13 entrusted with this special grace, not only of proclaiming to the pagans the
Col 1:29 infinite treasure of Christ •but also of explaining[e] how the mystery is to be 9
dispensed. Through all the ages, this has been kept hidden in God, the creator
1 Co 2:7-9+ 1 P 1:12 of everything. Why? •So that the Sovereignties and Powers should learn[f] 10
only now, through the Church, how comprehensive God's wisdom really is,
1:4 exactly according to the plan which he had had from all eternity in Christ Jesus 11
2:18 Rm 5:1 our Lord. •This is why we are bold enough to approach God in complete 12

confidence, through our faith in him; •so, I beg you, never lose confidence just Col 1:22▲ Heb 4:16▲
because of the trials that I go through on your account: they are your glory.[g] 1 P 3:18▲ *Col 1:24* 2 Tm 1:8

Paul's prayer

14 15 This, then, is what I pray, kneeling before the Father,[h] •from whom every 1:17
family,[i] whether spiritual or natural, takes its name:
16 Out of his infinite glory, may he give you the power through his Spirit 2 P 1:3
17 for your hidden self to grow strong, •so that Christ may live in your hearts Ac 1:8+ *Jn 14:23*
18 through faith, and then, planted in love and built on love, •you will with all Rm 7:22+ *Col 1:23; 2:7*
the saints have strength to grasp the breadth and the length, the height and *Ac 9:13+* Col 2:2
19 the depth;[j] •until, knowing the love of Christ,[k] which is beyond all knowledge,[l] you are filled with the utter fullness of God.[m] Col 2:9+
20 Glory be to him whose power, working in us, can do infinitely more[n] than we 1:19f Ph 2:13
21 can ask or imagine; •glory be to him from generation to generation in the Church
and in Christ Jesus for ever and ever. Amen.

c. 'We' here means both the pagans, cf. vv. 1-2, and the Jews, cf. v. 3. V. 3 is a parenthesis.

d. 'with Christ'; var. 'in Christ'. 'it is through grace'; var. (Vulg.) 'through whose grace'.

e. Here as in Col 2:12; 3:1-4, the use of the past tense shows that the resurrection and triumph of Christians in heaven is considered as actually existing, whereas the future tense in Rm 6:3-11; 8:11,17f treats it as something that has still to take place. Treating the eschatological reality as already existing is a characteristic of Paul's letters written from prison.

f. The description of this past that Paul now gives is meant to apply to all pagans in a general way—not specifically to those he is writing to.

g. I.e. you had no Messiah.

h. The successive covenants made by God with Abraham, Isaac, Jacob, Moses, David etc.; cf. Ex 19:1+; Lv 26:42,45; Si 44-45; Ws 18:22; 2 M 8:15; Rm 9:4.

i. Hope of a Messiah, which was hitherto confined to Israel 1:12.

j. The pagans had many gods but not the one true God, 1 Co 8:5f.

k. The crucifixion of Christ that brought together Jews and pagans vv. 14-15, and reconciled both with the Father vv. 16-18.

l. The wall separating the court of the Jews from the court of the pagans in the Temple, cf. Ac 21:28f.

m. The Mosaic Law gave the Jews a privileged status and separated them from pagans. Jesus abolished this Law by fulfilling it once for all on the cross, Col 2:14+.

n. This New Man is the prototype of the new humanity that God recreated (2 Co 5:17+) in the person of Christ, the second Adam (1 Co 15:45), after killing the sinfully corrupt race of the first Adam in the crucifixion (Rm 5:12f; 8:3; 1 Co 15:21). This New Adam has been created in 'the goodness and holiness of the truth' 4:24, and he is unique because in him the boundaries between any one group and the rest of the human race all disappear, Col 3:10f; Ga 3:27f.

o. This 'single Body' is both the physical body of Jesus that was executed by crucifixion, Col 1:22+, and the Church or 'mystical' body of Christ in which, once they are reconciled, all the parts function in their own place, 1 Co 12:12+.

p. Through the apostles who in his name preached the Good News of salvation and peace.

q. The one Spirit that gives life to the single body (of Christ who is one with his Church) is the Holy Spirit who has changed the form of the body now it has risen, and by doing so has come down on each of the parts of which it is made up. The trinitarian structure of this section is repeated in v. 22.

r. Paul inserts vv. 14-18 (how Christ has united pagans and Jews) between his contrasting descriptions of pagans before (vv. 11-13) and after (19-22) conversion.

s. The N.T. prophets, cf. 3:5; 4:11; Ac 11:27+, together with the apostles, are the witnesses to whom the divine plan was first revealed and who were the first to preach the Good News, cf. Lk 11:49; Mt 23:34; 10:41. This is why the Church as well as being founded on Christ, 1 Co 3:10f, is also said to be founded on them.

t. 'every'; var. 'the entire'.

3 a. V. 1 (continued in v. 15) breaks off abruptly, the parenthetical development of vv. 2-14 being suggested by the mention of pagans in v. 1. On the grace of being the apostle of the pagans, cf. 3:7f; Rm 1:5; 15:15f; 1 Co 3:10; Ga 2:9.

b. Cf. 2 Co 12:1,7. The immediate reference is to what was revealed to Paul on the way to Damascus, cf. Ga 1:16; Ac 9:15; 22:21; 26:16-18.

c. The N.T. prophets, cf. 2:20+. The O.T. prophets had only an obscure and imperfect knowledge of the mystery of the Messiah, cf. 1 P 1:10-12; Mt 13:17.

d. I.e. as the Judaeo-Christians, cf. 2:19.

e. Var. (Vulg.) 'showing clearly to all'.

f. The evil spirits were unaware of God's plan for salvation and so they persuaded human beings to crucify Christ, 1 Co 2:8; and it is only the existence of the Church that makes them aware of it now, cf. 1 P 1:12.

g. Var. 'our glory'.

h. Add. (Vulg.) 'of our Lord Jesus Christ'.

i. A play on the Greek words for 'father' and 'family' *(pater: patria)*: *patria* is used for any social group descended from a common ancestor and the one ancestor common to human beings and angels is God, the supreme Father.

j. Stoics used this expression to mean the totality of the cosmos. Paul uses it to suggest the cosmic function of Christ in the rebirth of the world. It could be referred to the size of the mystery of salvation, or preferably to Christ's universal love on which (next verse) the mystery depends. Cf. 1:17-19,23; 2:7; 3:8; Col 2:2f.

k. This love for us that Christ proved by accepting death, 5:2,25; Ga 2:20, is identical with the love the Father has, 2:4,7; 2 Co 5:14,18-19; Rm 8:35,37,39. Cf. 1 Co 13:1+.

l. The love of God cannot be 'grasped' (v. 18, using a philosophical term technical in Greek) but can be 'known' by a mystic's awareness of it through love, cf. 1:17f; 3:3f; Ho 2:22+; Jn 10:14+. This awareness is something deeper than scientific knowledge, cf. 1 Co 13, and is more like knowing that one is loved by the other than knowing the other that one loves, cf. Ga 4:9; even awareness of this sort however can never 'grasp' this sort of love.

m. Lit. 'in order that you may be filled to all the fullness *(pleroma)* of God'. (Var. 'in order that all the fullness of God may be filled'.) Christ who is filled with the divine life fills Christians with it, Col 2:9, and in this way a Christian enters both the Church and the new cosmos which he helps to build and which is the fullness of the total Christ, 1:23; 2:22; 4:12-13; Col 2:10+.

n. Var. (Vulg.) 'can do all'.

II. EXHORTATION

A call to unity[a]

||Col 3:12-14 **4** I, the prisoner in the Lord, implore you therefore to lead a life worthy of your 1
1 Co 13:13+ Ph 1:27 vocation. •Bear with one another charitably, in complete selflessness, 2
Col 3:14-15 gentleness and patience. •Do all you can to preserve the unity of the Spirit by the 3
Rm 12:5 1 Co 10:17; peace that binds you together. •There is one Body, one Spirit, just as you were all 4
12:12+ *1 Co 1:13;* called into one and the same hope when you were called. •There is one Lord, one 5
8:6; 12:4-6 2 Co 13:13+ faith, one baptism, •and one God who is Father of all, over all, through all and 6
within all.[b]

Rm 12:6 Each one of us, however, has been given his own share of grace,[c] given as 7
Christ allotted it. •It was said that he would: 8

Ps 68:18 Ac 2:33
When he ascended to the height, he captured prisoners,
he gave gifts to men.[d]

1 P 3:19+ When it says, 'he ascended', what can it mean if not that he descended[e] right 9
down to the lower regions of the earth?[f] •The one who rose higher than all the 10
heavens to fill all things[g] is none other than the one who descended. •And to 11
1 Co 12:28+ some, his gift was that they should be apostles; to some, prophets; to some,
Tt 1:5+ evangelists; to some, pastors and teachers;[h] •so that the saints together[i] make 12
2:21; 4:16 a unity in the work of service, building up the body of Christ. •In this way we 13
Col 1:23+; 3:11 are all to come to unity in our faith and in our knowledge of the Son of God, until
1:23+ we become the perfect Man,[j] fully mature with the fullness of Christ himself.
1 Co 14:20 Then we shall not be children any longer, or tossed one way and another and 14
carried along by every wind of doctrine, at the mercy of all the tricks men play
Col 2:4,8 Tb 4:6 and their cleverness in practising deceit. •If we live by the truth and in love, we 15
||Col 2:19 shall grow in all ways into Christ, who is the head •by whom the whole body 16
is fitted and joined together, every joint[k] adding its own strength, for each
separate part to work according to its function. So the body grows until it has
built itself up, in love.

The new life in Christ

In particular, I want to urge you in the name of the Lord, not to go on living 17
Rm 1:18-32 ||Col 1:21 the aimless kind of life that pagans live. •Intellectually they are in the dark, 18
1 P 1:18; 4:3 and they are estranged from the life of God, without knowledge because they
have shut their hearts to it. •Their sense of right and wrong once dulled,[l] they 19
have abandoned themselves to sexuality and eagerly pursue a career of indecency
of every kind.[m] •Now that is hardly the way you have learnt from Christ, •unless 20 21
||Col 3:9-10 you failed to hear him properly when you were taught what the truth is in Jesus.
Col 3:5 You must give up your old way of life; you must put aside your old self, which 22
gets corrupted by following illusory desires. •Your mind must be renewed by a 23
2:15+ Col 3:10+ spiritual revolution •so that you can put on the new self that has been created in 24
God's way, in the goodness and holiness of the truth.[n]

Zc 8:16 Col 3:9 So from now on, there must be no more lies: *You must speak the truth to one* 25
1 Co 12:12+ *Ps 4:4* LXX *another*, since we are all parts of one another. •*Even if you are angry, you must not* 26
Mt 5:22 2 Co 2:11 *sin:* never let the sun set on your anger •or else you will give the devil a foothold. 27
Ac 18:3+; 20:34-35 Anyone who was a thief must stop stealing; he should try to find some useful 28
1 Th 4:11 manual work instead, and be able to do some good[o] by helping others[p] that are
Mt 15:11 Jm 3:10-12 in need. •Guard against foul talk; let your words be for the improvement of 29
others, as occasion offers, and do good to your listeners, •otherwise you will 30
Is 63:10 *1:13+* only be grieving the Holy Spirit of God who has marked you with his seal for
Rm 1:29+ Col 3:8 you to be set free when the day comes.[q] •Never have grudges against others, or 31
lose your temper, or raise your voice to anybody, or call each other names,
Mt 6:12, 14-15p or allow any sort of spitefulness. •Be friends with one another, and kind, 32
Col 3:13 forgiving each other as readily as God forgave you[r] in Christ.

5 Try, then, to imitate God, as children of his that he loves, •and follow Christ Mt 5:48; 2 Th 3:7+
2 by loving as he loved you, giving himself up in our place *as a fragrant offering* Ga 2:20; 1 Jn 3:16
3 *and a sacrifice to God.* •Among you there must be not even a mention of Ex 29:18; Ps 40:6
fornication or impurity in any of its forms, or promiscuity: this would Ga 5:19+
4 hardly become the saints! •There must be no coarseness, or salacious talk and Ac 9:13+
5 jokes—all this is wrong for you; raise your voices in thanksgiving instead. •For
you can be quite certain that nobody who actually indulges in fornication Mt 6:24; 1 Co 6:9-10
or impurity or promiscuity—which is worshipping a false god[a]—can inherit Col 3:5; Heb 13:4-5
6 anything of the kingdom of God. •Do not let anyone deceive you with empty Col 2:4,8
arguments: it is for this loose living that God's anger comes down on those who ||Col 3:6
7 8 rebel against him. •Make sure that you are not included with them. •You were 4:18; Jb 24:13
9 darkness once, but now you are light in the Lord; be like children of light, •for Jn 8:12+; 2 Co 4:6; 6:14
the effects of the light are seen in complete goodness and right living and truth. Col 1:12-13
10 11 Try to discover what the Lord wants of you, •having nothing to do with the futile 1 Th 5:4-8
12 works of darkness but exposing them by contrast. •The things which are done
13 in secret are things that people are ashamed even to speak of; •but anything
14 exposed by the light will be illuminated •and anything illuminated turns into Jn 3:20-21
light.[b] That is why it is said:[c]

> Wake up from your sleep,
> rise from the dead, Is 26:19; 60:1
> and Christ will shine on you.[d] *Heb 6:4;* 10:32

15 So be very careful about the sort of lives you lead, like intelligent and not like
16 senseless people. •This may be a wicked age, but your lives should redeem it. Col 4:5
17 18 And do not be thoughtless but recognise what is the will of the Lord. •Do not Col 1:9
drug yourselves with wine, this is simply dissipation; be filled with the Spirit. Pr 23:31 LXX
19 Sing the words and tunes of the psalms and hymns when you are together, ||*Col 3:16-17*
20 and go on singing and chanting to the Lord in your hearts, •so that always and
everywhere you are giving thanks to God who is our Father in the name of our 1 Th 5:18
Lord Jesus Christ.

4 a. Paul lists three different threats to the Church's unity: arguments between Christians vv. 1-3, diversity of service in the Church vv. 7-11, unorthodox teaching vv. 14-15. These threats are all averted by applying the principle of unity in Christ, vv. 4-6,12-13,18.

b. Var. (Vulg) 'within all of us'.

c. Charisms or special graces given to individuals for the benefit of the whole community, cf. 1 Co 12:1+.

d. Following rabbinic practice Paul quotes this text for the sake of two phrases: 'he ascended' vv. 9-10, and 'he gave gifts' v. 11, which he interprets as the ascension of Jesus and the descent of the Spirit.

e. Add. (Vulg) 'first of all'.

f. Lit. 'into the lower parts of the earth'. The most appropriate interpretation is that 'the earth' is itself the 'lower region' to which Christ descended to give 'the gifts' to mankind, and Paul's argument is that 'these gifts can only be from the one who ascended'. But the phrase can be taken to mean the subterranean kingdom of the dead, Nb 16:33f, to which Christ descended before the resurrection, 1 P 3:19f.

g. By ascending through all the cosmic spheres and taking possession of them all one after another, Christ becomes the head of the whole *pleroma* or total cosmos, 1:10+, and makes the entire universe acknowledge him as 'Lord', cf. 1:20-23; Col 1:19; Ph 2:8-11.

h. Paul limits his list to charisms that relate to teaching and which are the only ones that apply in this context, vv. 13-15.

i. The particular 'saints' Paul mentions here seem to be missionaries and other teachers, cf. 3:5, but may include all the faithful in so far as they all help to build up the Church, cf. Ac 9:13+.

j. This does not refer primarily to the individual Christian. The sense is collective. It can be taken as referring to Christ himself, the New Man, the archetype of all who are reborn 2:15+, or else (and this sense is to be preferred) as referring to the total Christ, i.e. the whole body, 1 Co 12:12+, made of head v. 15; 1:22; Col 1:18, and the rest of the body v. 16; 5:30.

k. Var. (Vulg) 'each member'.

l. Var. (Vulg) 'Being devoid of hope'.

m. Or 'sexuality and every kind of indecency and greed'.

n. Each human being should 'put on the New Man', Ep 2:15+ (here, as in v. 22, translated 'self'), so as to be re-created in him, cf. Ga 3:27; Rm 13:14. In some places Paul talks in the same way about the 'new creature', 2 Co 5:17+.

o. Lit. 'working the good thing with his own hand'. 'Good' and '(own) hand' are omitted or interchanged in various readings: the original text may have been ambiguous.

p. Var. (Vulg) 'for building up the faith'.

q. The one Holy Spirit that keeps the one body of Christ united, 4:4; 1 Co 12:13, is 'grieved', cf. 4:30; Is 63:10, by anything that harms the unity of the body.

r. 'you'; var. 'us'. The same in 5:2.

5 a. 'promiscuity'; lit. 'greed', apparently sexual greed in this context. Uncontrolled greed treats all creatures with the worship due to God and so turns them into idols.

b. The wrong sort of way to talk about sexual immorality is the way that leaves the subject in a dangerous obscurity, v. 3. To talk about it in such a way, however, that it is recognised for what it is will lead to its being corrected; this sort of light is the light of Christ that puts an end to darkness.

c. This (like 1 Tm 3:16) seems to be an extract from an early Christian hymn. On baptism as an enlightening, cf. Heb 6:4; 10:32 (cf. Rm 6:4+).

d. Var. 'and you will touch Christ'.

The morals of the home

Ps 87:5 ||Col 3:18 Give way to one another in obedience to Christ. •Wives should regard their 21 22
1 P 3:1-7 husbands as they regard the Lord, •since[e] as Christ is head of the Church and 23
1 Co 11:3 saves the whole body, so is a husband the head of his wife; •and as the Church 24
1:22-23 *5:2* submits to Christ, so should wives to their husbands, in everything. •Husbands 25
||Col 3:19 1 P 3:7 should love their wives just as Christ loved the Church and sacrificed himself
Rm 6:4+ Tt 3:5-7 for her •to make her holy. He made her clean by washing her in water with a form 26
2 Co 11:2 Col 1:22 of words, •so that when he took her to himself she would be glorious, with no 27
Rv 19:7-8; 21:2,9-11 speck or wrinkle or anything like that, but holy and faultless.[f] •In the same way, 28
husbands must love their wives as they love their own bodies; for a man to love
his wife is for him to love himself. •A man never hates his own body, but he feeds 29
it and looks after it; and that is the way Christ treats the Church, •because it is 30
1 Co 12:12+ *Gn 2:24* his body—and we are its living parts.[g] •*For this reason, a man must leave his father* 31
Mt 19:5p *and mother and be joined to his wife, and the two will become one body.* •This 32
Rm 16:25+ mystery has many implications; but I am saying it applies to Christ and the
Church.[h] •To sum up; you too, each one of you, must love his wife as he loves 33
himself; and let every wife respect her husband.

Pr 6:20 Si 3:1-6 **6** Children, be obedient to your parents in the Lord[a]—that is your duty. •The 1 2
||Col 3:20-21 *Ex 20:12* first commandment that has a promise attached to it is: *Honour your father*
and mother, •and the promise is: *and you will prosper and have a long life in the land.* 3
Pr 13:24+ And parents, never drive your children to resentment but in bringing them up 4
correct them and guide them as the Lord does.

||Col 3:22-4:1 Slaves, be obedient to the men who are called your masters in this world, 5
Tt 2:9-10 with deep respect[b] and sincere loyalty, as you are obedient to Christ: •not only 6
Rm 6:15+ 1 P 2:18 when you are under their eye, as if you had only to please men, but because you
are slaves of Christ and wholeheartedly do the will of God. •Work hard and 7
willingly, but do it for the sake of the Lord and not for the sake of men. •You 8
can be sure that everyone, whether a slave or a free man, will be properly rewarded
by the Lord for whatever work he has done well. •And those of you who are 9
employers, treat your slaves in the same spirit; do without threats, remembering
Jb 31:15 that they and you have the same Master in heaven and he is not impressed by one
Dt 10:17+ person more than by another.

The spiritual war

Rm 13:12 2 Co 6:7; 10:4 Finally, grow strong in the Lord, with the strength of his power. •Put God's 10 11
Jm 4:7 armour on[c] so as to be able to resist the devil's tactics. •For it is not against human 12
Mt 16:17+ 1 P 5:8-9 enemies that we have[d] to struggle, but against the Sovereignties and the Powers
who originate the darkness in this world, the spiritual army of evil in the heavens.[e]
That is why you must rely on God's armour, or you will not be able to put up any 13
resistance when the worst happens, or have enough resources to hold your
ground.

Is 11:5; 59:17 So stand your ground, with *truth buckled round your waist*, and *integrity* 14
Ws 5:18 1 Th 5:8 *for a breastplate*, •wearing for shoes on your feet *the eagerness to spread the* 15
Is 40:3,9; 52:7 *gospel of peace* •and always carrying the shield of faith so that you can use it to 16
1 Jn 2:14+ *Is 59:17* put out the burning arrows of the evil one. •And then you must accept *salvation* 17
Heb 4:12 *from God to be your helmet* and receive the word of God from the Spirit to use
as a sword.

Lk 18:1+ ||Col 4:2-4 Pray all the time, asking for what you need, praying in the Spirit on every 18
possible occasion. Never get tired of staying awake to pray for all the saints;
Rm 15:30+ and pray for me to be given an opportunity to open my mouth[f] and speak 19
Rm 16:25+ without fear and give out the mystery of the gospel[g] •of which I am an ambassador 20
in chains; pray that in proclaiming it I may speak as boldly as I ought to.

Personal news and final salutation

I should like you to know, as well, what is happening to me and what I am 21
||Col 4:7 doing; my dear brother Tychicus, my loyal helper in the Lord, will tell you

22 everything. •I am sending him to you precisely for this purpose, to give you
news about us and reassure you.
23 May God the Father and the Lord Jesus Christ grant peace, love and faith to
24 all the brothers. •May grace and eternal life be with all who love our Lord
Jesus Christ.[h]

e. By drawing a parallel between a human marriage and the marriage of Christ to his Church, vv. 23-32, Paul makes these two concepts illumine each other. Christ is the husband of the Church because he is her head and because he loves the Church as much as a man loves his own body when he loves his wife. Having established this, the comparison naturally suggests an ideal for human marriage. The symbol of Israel as the wife of Yahweh is common in the O.T., Ho 1:2+.

f. It was customary in the Middle East, at the time this letter was written, for the 'sons of the wedding' to escort the bride to her husband after she had bathed and dressed. As applied mystically to the Church, Christ washes his bride himself in the bath of baptism, and makes her immaculate (note the mention of a baptismal formula) and introduces her to himself.

g. Add. (Vulg) 'made from his flesh and blood'.

h. Paul makes this Gn text a prophecy of the marriage of Christ and the Church: a mystery, like that of the salvation of the pagans, that has been hidden but is now revealed, cf. 1:9f; 3:3f.

6 a. Om. 'in the Lord'.

b. Lit. 'fear and trembling', cf. 1 Co 2:3+.

c. God in the O.T. arms himself against his enemies, cf. Is 11:4-5; 59:16-18; Ws 5:17-23. These are the arms of Yahweh with which, Paul says, the Christian is to arm himself.

d. Var. 'you have'.

e. These are the spirits who were thought to move the stars and, consequently, the universe. They lived in 'the heavens', 1:20f; 3:10; Ph 2:10, or in 'the air', 2:2, i.e. the space between the surface of the earth and the heaven where God lives. Some of them are among the 'elemental principles of the world', Ga 4:3. They disobeyed God and want to enslave the human race to themselves in sin 2:2. We used to be their slaves but Christ came to free us, 1:21; Col 1:13; 2:15,20, and if Christians are armed with the power of Christ, they will be able to fight them.

f. Lit. 'that I may be given speech in opening of my mouth', Hebraism, cf. Ezk 3:27; 29:21; Ps 51:15; cf. Col 4:3.

g. Om. 'of the gospel'.

h. Or 'May grace be with all who love our Lord Jesus Christ in eternal life'. Add. (Vulg.) 'Amen', cf. Ph 4:23.

PHILIPPIANS

THE LETTER OF PAUL TO THE CHURCH AT PHILIPPI

Address

Ac 16:1+ Rm 1:1+ *Ac 9:13+* 1 From Paul and Timothy, servants of Christ Jesus, to all the saints in Christ 1
Jesus, together with their presiding elders and deacons.[a] •We wish you the 2
grace and peace of God our Father and of the Lord Jesus Christ.

Thanksgiving and prayer

1 Th 1:2 *1:18,25;* I thank my God whenever I think of you; and •every time I pray for all of you, I 3 4
2:2,29; 3:1; 4:1, pray with joy,[b] •remembering how you have helped to spread the Good News[c] 5
4,10 1 Th 5:16 from the day you first heard it[d] right up to the present. •I am quite certain that 6
1:10; 2:16 1 Co 1:8+ the One who began this good work in you will see that it is finished when the Day
of Christ Jesus comes. •It is only natural that I should feel like this towards 7
1:30 you all, since you have shared the privileges which have been mine: both my
Ep 3:2 chains and my work defending and establishing the gospel. You have a permanent
Rm 1:9 place in my heart, •and God knows how much I miss you all, loving you as Christ 8
Col 1:9-10 Phm 6 Jesus loves you. •My prayer is that your love for each other may increase more 9
and more and never stop improving your knowledge and deepening your
perception •so that you can always recognise what is best.[e] This will help you to 10
1:6 Heb 5:14 become pure and blameless, and prepare you for the Day of Christ, •when you 11
3:9+ Jn 15:1 will reach the perfect goodness which Jesus Christ produces in us for the glory
Heb 12:11 Jm 3:18 and praise of God.

Paul's own circumstances

I am glad to tell you, brothers, that the things that happened to me[f] have 12
actually been a help to the Good News.
Ep 3:1 2 Tm 2:9 My chains, in Christ, have become famous not only all over the Praetorium[g] but 13
everywhere, •and most of the brothers have taken courage in the Lord from these 14
chains of mine and are getting more and more daring in announcing the Message[h]
without any fear. •It is true that some of them are doing it just out of rivalry 15
2:20-21 and competition, but the rest preach Christ with the right intention, •out of 16
nothing but love, as they know that this is my invariable way of defending the
gospel. •The others, who proclaim Christ for jealous or selfish motives, do not 17
mind if they make my chains heavier to bear. •But does it matter? Whether 18
from dishonest motives or in sincerity, Christ is proclaimed; and that makes me
1:4+ *Jb 13:16* happy; •and I shall continue being happy, because I know *this will help to save* 19
LXX *me*, thanks to your prayers and to the help which will be given to me by the
Ac 16:7 2 Tm 4:17 Spirit of Jesus. •My one hope and trust is that I shall never have to admit defeat, 20
1 Co 6:20 2 Co 1:5 but that now as always I shall have the courage for Christ to be glorified in my
Ga 2:20 body,[i] whether by my life or by my death. •Life to me, of course, is Christ, but 21
Col 3:3f then death would bring me something more; •but then again, if living in this 22
body means doing work which is having good results—I do not know what

23 I should choose. •I am caught in this dilemma: I want to be gone and be with 2 Co 5:6-9
24 Christ,[j] which would be very much the better, •but for me to stay alive in this
25 body is a more urgent need for your sake. •This weighs with me so much that I feel 2:24
sure I shall survive and stay with you all,[k] and help you to progress in the faith
26 and even increase your joy in it; •and so you will have another reason to give 1:4+; 2:16 1 Co 15:31 2 Co 1:14; 5:12
praise to Christ Jesus on my account when I am with you again. 1 Th 2:19

Fight for the faith

27 Avoid anything in your everyday lives[l] that would be unworthy of the gospel Ep 4:1 Col 1:10
of Christ, so that, whether I come to you and see for myself, or stay at a distance 1 Th 2:12 *Col 2:5*
and only hear about you, I shall know that you are unanimous in meeting the
28 attack with firm resistance, united by your love for the faith of the gospel •and Ac 4:32
quite unshaken by your enemies. This would be the sure sign that they will lose
29 and you will be saved. It would be a sign from God •that he has given you the
30 privilege not only of believing in Christ, but of suffering for him as well. •You and Mt 5:11 2 Th 1:4-7
I are together in the same fight as you saw me fighting before and, as you will *1:7* Col 1:24+
have heard, I am fighting still.[m] 1 Th 2:2

Preserve unity in humility

1 **2** If our life in Christ means anything to you, if love can persuade at all,[a] 2 Co 10:1; 13:13+
2 or the Spirit[b] that we have in common, or any tenderness and sympathy, •then Ga 5:10
be united in your convictions and united in your love, with a common purpose Rm 15:5
and a common mind. That is the one thing which would make me completely 1:4+
3 happy.[c] •There must be no competition among you, no conceit; but everybody Ac 20:19 Rm 12:3,10
is to be self-effacing. Always consider the other person to be better than yourself, 1 Co 1:10f Ga 5:26
4 so that nobody thinks of his own interests first but everybody thinks of other *1 Co 10:24*
5 people's interests instead. •In your minds you must be the same as Christ Jesus:[d] Jn 13:15

6 His state was divine,[e] Jn 1:1f; 17:5 Col 1:15-20
yet he did not cling Heb 1:3
to his equality with God[f]

1 a. The word *'episcopos'* ('overseer', 'supervisor' or 'shepherd') has not yet acquired the same meaning as 'bishop', cf. Tt 1:5f. The 'deacons' are their assistants, Ac 6:1-6.

b. Joy is one of the chief characteristics of this letter; cf. 1:18,25; 2:2,17,28,29; 3:1; 4:1,4,10.

c. Not only by sending money, 4:14-16, but by suffering for the Good News, 1:29-30.

d. Since the day they were converted, cf. Ac 16: 12-40.

e. The ability to see what is morally good is one of the consequences of mutual love.

f. I.e. Paul's arrest and imprisonment awaiting trial.

g. If Paul is writing from his house-arrest in Rome, this must refer to members of the Praetorian Guard (who were quartered just outside the city wall). If Paul is writing from Ephesus or Caesarea, he is referring to the staff of the Praetorium which was the name of the official residence of the governor in each of those cities.

h. Add. 'of God' (Vulg.) or 'of the Lord'.

i. By baptism and Eucharist a Christian is so closely united to Christ, cf. 1 Co 6:15; 10:17; 12:12f,27; Ga 2:20; Ep 5:30, that his life, sufferings and death can be attributed mystically to Christ living in him and being glorified in him, cf. 1 Co 6:20; Rm 14:8. This union would be particularly close in the case of an apostle like Paul, cf. Col 1:24; 2 Co 4:10f.

j. As in 2 Cor 5:8+, this supposes that the (good) Christian who dies is with Christ at once without any temporal gap between death and 'last judgement'.

k. This presentiment (it was no more than that, cf. 2:17) was not mistaken, cf. Ac 20:1-6 and the Pastoral Letters, unlike what he had thought was a last farewell to the Ephesians, Ac 20:25.

l. Lit. 'Live your city-life (i.e. ordinary social life) worthily of the gospel'. The New City of God's kingdom has Christ for its ruler, the gospel for its law, and the Christians as its free citizens, cf. 3:20; Ep 2:19.

m. The first reference is to the persecution Paul had to put up with when he was with them in Philippi, Ac 16:19f; 1 Th 2:2; the second is to his present imprisonment awaiting trial.

2 a. Lit. 'If there is any exhortation in Christ, if there is any incentive in love'; this is a very friendly but a very powerful appeal, in the name of all that is holiest.

b. Almost certainly meant to be taken as a trinitarian reference: in this case 'love' is appropriated to the Father, cf. 2 Co 13:13+.

c. This urgent plea for unity suggests that internal divisions threatened the peace of the church of Philippi, cf. 1:27; 2:14; 4:2. Note how Paul keeps insisting that he is addressing all of them, 1:1,4,7,25; 2:17,26; 4:21.

d. Vv. 6-11 are a hymn, though whether composed or only quoted by Paul is uncertain. Each stanza deals with one stage of the mystery of Christ: divine pre-existence, *kenosis* in the Incarnation, his further *kenosis* in death, his glorification, adoration by the cosmos, new title of Lord. This hymn is concerned solely with the historical Christ in whose personality godhead and manhood are not divided; Paul nowhere divorces the humanity and divinity of Jesus, though he does distinguish his various stages of existence, cf. Col 1:13f.

e. Lit. 'Who subsisting in the form of God': here 'form' means all the attributes that express and reveal the essential 'nature' of God: Christ, being God, had all the divine prerogatives by right.

f. Lit. 'did not deem being on an equality with God as something to grasp' or 'hold on to'. This refers not to his equality by nature 'subsisting in the form of God', and which Christ could not have surrendered, but to his being publicly treated and honoured as equal to God

2 Co 8:9 Rv 5:12 *Mt 20:28* but emptied himself[g] 7
to assume the condition of a slave,[h]
Rm 8:3 Ga 4:4 and became as men are;[i]
Heb 2:17 and being as all men are,[j]
Is 49:4 1 P 5:6 he was humbler yet, 8
Mt 26:39f Rm 5:19 even to accepting death,
Heb 5:8; 12:2 death on a cross.
Is 52:13 Mt 23:12 But God raised him high[k] 9
Jn 10:17f Ep 1:20-23 and gave him the name[l]
which is above all other names[m]
so that *all beings* 10
Ep 4:10+ in the heavens, on earth and in the underworld,[n]
Is 45:23 Rm 14:11 *should bend the knee* at the name of Jesus
and that every tongue should acclaim[o] 11
Ac 2:36+ Rm 1:4; 10:9 Jesus Christ as Lord,[p]
1 Co 12:3 to the glory of God the Father.[q]

Work for salvation

2 Co 7:15 So then, my dear friends, continue to do as I tell you, as you always have; 12
not only as you did when I was there with you, but even more now that I am no
1 Co 2:3+ longer there; and work for your salvation 'in fear and trembling'. •It is God, 13
Ac 17:28 Ep 2:10; for his own loving purpose, who puts both the will and the action into you.
3:20 Heb 13:21 Do all that has to be done without complaining or arguing •and then you will 14 15
Dt 32:5 be innocent and genuine, *perfect children of God among a deceitful and underhand*
Mt 5:14-16 *brood*, and you will shine in the world like bright stars •because you are offering 16
1:26+ 1 Co 1:8+ it the word of life. This would give me something to be proud of for the Day
Ga 2:2; 4: 11; 5:7+ of Christ, and would mean that I had not run in the race and exhausted myself
Rm 1:9+ 2 Tm 4:6 for nothing. •And then, if my blood has to be shed as part of your own sacrifice 17
and offering—which is your faith[r]—I shall still be happy and rejoice with all of
1:4+ you, •and you must be just as happy and rejoice with me. 18

The mission of Timothy and Epaphroditus

Ac 16:1+ I hope, in the Lord Jesus, to send Timothy to you soon, and I shall be 19
reassured by having news of you. •I have nobody else like him here, as whole- 20
1:15-17 heartedly concerned for your welfare: •all the rest seem more interested in 21
themselves than in Jesus Christ. •But you know how he has proved himself by 22
working with me on behalf of the Good News like a son helping his father.
That is why he is the one that I am hoping to send you, as soon as 23
1:25-26 Heb 13:19 I know something definite about my fate. •But I continue to trust, in the Lord, 24
that I shall be coming soon myself.
4:18 It is essential, I think, to send brother Epaphroditus back to you. He was sent 25
as your representative to help me when I needed someone to be my companion
in working and battling, •but he misses you all and is worried because you heard 26
about his illness. •It is true that he has been ill, and almost died, but God took 27
pity on him, and on me as well as him, and spared me what would have been one
grief on top of another. •So I shall send him back as promptly as I can; you will 28
be happy to see him again, and that will make me less sorry. •Give him a most 29
1:4+ 1 Co 16:16 hearty welcome, in the Lord; people like him are to be honoured. •It was for 30
Christ's work[s] that he came so near to dying, and he risked his life to give me the
help that you were not able to give me yourselves.

3

1:4+ 2 Co 13:11 Finally, my brothers, rejoice in the Lord.[a] 1

The true way of Christian salvation

It is no trouble to me to repeat what I have already written to you, and as far
Ga 5:12 as you are concerned, it will make for safety. •Beware of dogs![b] Watch out for 2
2:17+ Jr 4:4+ the people who are making mischief. Watch out for the cutters.[c] •We are the 3

real people of the circumcision, we who worship in accordance with the Spirit Rm 2:25-29▲ 2 Co 11:
of God;[d] we have our own glory from Christ Jesus without having to rely on a 21+▲ Col 2:11▲
4 physical operation.[e] •If it came to relying on physical evidence, I should be fully Rm 7:5+
qualified myself. Take any man who thinks he can rely on what is physical: I am
5 even better qualified. •I was born of the race of Israel and of the tribe of Benjamin, Ac 22:3
a Hebrew born of Hebrew parents,[f] and I was circumcised when I was eight days Gn 17:10+
6 old. As for the Law, I was a Pharisee; •as for working for religion, I was a Mt 3:7+ Ac 23:6
persecutor of the Church; as far as the Law can make you perfect, I was faultless. *Ac 8:1,3+*
7 But because of Christ, I have come to consider all these advantages that I had
8 as disadvantages. •Not only that, but I believe nothing can happen that will
outweigh the supreme advantage of knowing Christ Jesus my Lord. For him I have
accepted the loss of everything, and I look on everything as so much rubbish
9 if only I can have Christ •and be given a place in him. I am no longer trying for
perfection by my own efforts, the perfection that comes from the Law, but I want Rm 10:3
only the perfection that comes through faith in Christ, and is from God and Rm 1:16+ Ga 2:16
10 based on faith.[g] •All I want is to know Christ and the power of his resurrection *Rm 1:4+*
11 and to share his sufferings by reproducing the pattern of his death. •That is the Rm 6:4+; 8:11+17
12 way I can hope to take my place in the resurrection of the dead.[h] •Not that I have
become perfect yet: I have not yet won, but I am still running, trying to capture 2:16 Ga 5:7+
13 the prize for which Christ Jesus captured me.[i] •I can assure you my brothers,
I am far from thinking that I have already won. All I can say is that I forget the Lk 9:62
14 past and I strain ahead for what is still to come; •I am racing for the finish, for 1 Co 9:25+ Heb 3:1
15 the prize to which God calls us upwards to receive in Christ Jesus. •We who are
called 'perfect'[j] must all think in this way.[k] If there is some point on which you
16 see things differently, God will make it clear to you; •meanwhile, let us go forward
on the road that has brought us to where we are.[l]

17 My brothers, be united in following my rule of life. Take as your models 2 Th 3:7+
everybody who is already doing this and study them as you used to study us.

which was a thing that Jesus (unlike Adam, Gn 3:5,22, who wanted to be seen to be like God) could and did give up in his human life.

g. 'He emptied himself': this is not so much a reference to the fact of the incarnation, as to the way it took place. What Jesus freely gave up was not his divine nature, but the glory to which his divine nature entitled him, and which had been his before the incarnation, Jn 17:5, and which 'normally' speaking would have been observable in his human body (cf. the transfiguration, Mt 17:1-8). He voluntarily deprived himself of this so that it could be returned to him by the Father, cf. Jn 8:50,54, after his sacrifice vv. 9-11.

h. 'slave' as opposed to '*Kyrios*' v. 11, cf. Ga 4:1; Col 3:22f. Christ as man led a life of submission and humble obedience, v. 8. This is probably a reference to the 'servant' of Is 52:13-53:12, cf. Is 42:1+.

i. Not just 'a human being' but a human being 'like others', sharing all the weaknesses of the human condition apart from sin.

j. Lit. 'And in fashion found as a man'.

k. Lit. 'super-raised him': by the resurrection and ascension.

l. Named him 'Lord', v. 11; or, at a deeper level, gave him the ineffable and divine name which, through the triumph of the risen Christ, can now be expressed by the title *Kyrios*, Lord: cf. Ac 2:21+; 3:16+.

m. Greater even than the angels, cf. Ep 1:21; Heb 1:4; 1 P 3:22.

n. The three cosmic divisions that cover the entire creation, cf. Rv 5:3,13.

o. Var. 'and every tongue will acclaim'.

p. Om. 'Christ'. This proclamation is the essence of the Christian creed, Rm 10:9; 1 Co 12:3; cf. Col 2:6. The use of Is 45:23 (in which this homage is addressed to Yahweh himself) is a clear indication of the divine character that is meant to be understood by the title *Kyrios*, cf. Jn 20:28; Ac 2:36+.

q. Vulg. interpretation is 'proclaim that Jesus Christ is in the glory of God the Father'.

r. Libations were common to both Greek and Jewish sacrifices: Paul merely applies this custom metaphorically to the spiritual worship of the new creation, cf. 3:3; 4:18; Rm 1:9+.

s. Var. 'the Lord's work', or, 'the work'.

3 a. Paul interrupts the conclusion of the letter to add a long postscript.

b. Term of abuse applied by Jews to pagans, Mt 15:26 and possibly 7:6, and which Paul ironically applies to non-Christian Jews.

c. Lit. 'for the gash'. Paul uses this term *(katatomē)* as a contemptuous pun on 'circumcision' *(peritomē)*, implying a comparison between physical circumcision and the self-inflicted gashes in pagan cults, cf. 1 K 18:28, cf. Ga 5:12.

d. Var. (Vulg.) 'we who worship God in spirit'.

e. Lit. 'without trusting in the flesh', which covers all those outer observances of the old Law, of which circumcision is the most typical example, cf. Rm 7:5+.

f. His parents were Pharisees, Ac 23:6, of the tribe of Benjamin, Rm 11:1. Paul spoke Aramaic, Ac 21:40, unlike the hellenist Jews, Ac 6:1+.

g. The differences between these two sorts of perfection form the entire subject of Paul's letters to the Christians of Galatia and Rome.

h. Paul is not referring to the general resurrection of both saved and damned, Jn 5:29, but to the true resurrection of the saints who are separated from the 'spiritually' dead to life with Christ, Lk 20:35+.

i. Lit. 'but I follow (to see) if indeed I may grasp, inasmuch as I was grasped by Christ Jesus', i.e. the prize which he not only strives to grasp but for which also he was grasped on the road to Damascus.

j. Christians who are mature, cf. 1 Co 2:6+, but who are not totally perfect, v. 12.

k. 'must all think'; var. 'all think'.

l. Var. (Vulg.) 'let us be united in our convictions (cf. 2:2) and let us follow the same rule of life', cf. Ga 6:16.

Ac 20:19 I have told you often, and I repeat it today with tears, there are many who are 18
behaving as the enemies of the cross of Christ. •They are destined to be lost. 19
Rm 16:18 They make foods into their god[m] and they are proudest of something they ought
Jn 3:12 to think shameful;[n] the things they think important are earthly things. •For us, 20
Heb 11:13-16 *1 Tm 1:1+* our homeland is in heaven, and from heaven comes the saviour we are waiting
Ac 3:20-21 Rm 8:23 for, the Lord Jesus Christ, •and he will transfigure these wretched bodies of ours 21
1 Co 15:23-28,47-49 into copies of his glorious body. He will do that by the same power with which
Col 3:1-4 he can subdue the whole universe.

4 So then, my brothers and dear friends, do not give way but remain faithful 1
1:4+ 1 Th 2:19-20 in the Lord. I miss you very much, dear friends; you are my joy and my
crown.

Last advice

I appeal to Evodia and I appeal to Syntyche to come to agreement with each 2
other, in the Lord; •and I ask you, Syzygus,[a] to be truly a 'companion' and to 3
help them in this. These women were a help to me when I was fighting to defend
the Good News—and so, at the same time, were Clement and the others who
Dn 12:1 worked with me. Their names are written in the book of life.
1:4+ I want you to be happy, always happy in the Lord; I repeat, what I want is 4
1 Co 16:22+ Tt 3:2 your happiness. •Let your tolerance be evident to everyone: the Lord is very 5
Mt 6:25-34 near. •There is no need to worry; but if there is anything you need, pray for it, 6
Jn 14:27 Col 3:15 asking God for it with prayer and thanksgiving, •and that peace of God, which 7
is so much greater than we can understand, will guard your hearts and your
thoughts,[b] in Christ Jesus. •Finally, brothers, fill your minds with everything that 8
is true, everything that is noble, everything that is good and pure, everything that
we love and honour,[c] and everything that can be thought virtuous or worthy
1 Th 2:13+ 2 Th 3:7+ of praise. •Keep doing all the things that you learnt from me and have been 9
taught by me and have heard or seen that I do. Then the God of peace will be
with you.

Thanks for help received

1:4+ It is a great joy to me, in the Lord, that at last you have shown some concern 10
for me again; though of course you were concerned before, and only lacked an
opportunity. •I am not talking about shortage of money: I have learnt to manage 11
Heb 13:5 on whatever I have, •I know how to be poor and I know how to be rich too. 12
I have been through my initiation and now I am ready for anything anywhere:
2 Co 12:9-10 Ep 3:8 full stomach or empty stomach, poverty or plenty. •There is nothing I cannot 13
Col 1:29 master with the help of the One[d] who gives me strength. •All the same, it was 14
good of you to share with me in my hardships. •In the early days of the 15
Ac 16:12f 2 Co 11:9 Good News, as you people of Philippi well know, when I left Macedonia, no other
church helped me with gifts of money.[e] You were the only ones; •and twice 16
Ac 17:1 since my stay in Thessalonika you have sent me what I needed. •It is not your 17
1 Tm 6:19 gift that I value; what is valuable to me is the interest that is mounting up in
your account. •Now for the time being I have everything that I need and more: 18
2:25 I am fully provided now that I have received from Epaphroditus the offering
Gn 8:21+ *2:17* that you sent, *a sweet fragrance*—the sacrifice that God accepts and finds
Heb 13:16 pleasing. •In return my God will fulfil[f] all your needs, in Christ Jesus, as lavishly 19
Rm 16:27+ as only God can. •Glory to God, our Father, for ever and ever. Amen. 20

Greetings and final wish

Ac 9:13+ My greetings to every one of the saints in Christ Jesus. The brothers who are 21
with me send their greetings. •All the saints[g] send their greetings, especially those 22
of the imperial household.[h] •May the grace of the Lord Jesus Christ be with 23
your spirit.[i]

m. The dietary laws loomed large in the Jewish practice of religion, Lv 11, cf. Rm 14; 16:18; Ga 2:12; Col 2:16,20f; Mt 15:10-20p; 23:25-26; Ac 15:20.

n. Lit. 'they glory in their shame', where 'shame' may be only the traditional euphemism for the circumcised member.

4 a. 'Syzygus' means yoke-fellow, mate, second of a pair, colleague, companion, cf. Phm 10-11.

b. Var. 'your bodies'.

c. Add. 'everything there is of knowledge', or 'of discipline' (Vulg.).

d. 'the One', var. 'Christ'.

e. Paul always refused all payments however legitimate; the one exception was what he received from his beloved Christians of Philippi, cf. Ac 16:15; 18:3+; 2 Co 11:8.

f. Var. (Vulg.) 'may my God fulfil'.

g. All the Christians of the place from which Paul is writing.

h. The 'household' of Caesar was a wide term that covered anybody employed in the service of the emperor, either in Rome or in any of the chief towns of the empire.

i. Add. 'Amen'.

COLOSSIANS

THE LETTER OF PAUL TO THE CHURCH AT COLOSSAE

PREFACE

Address

Rm 1:1+ 1 From Paul, appointed by God to be an apostle of Christ Jesus, and from our 1
Ac 9:13+ brother Timothy •to the saints in Colossae, our faithful brothers in Christ: 2
Grace and peace to you from God our Father.[a]

Thanksgiving and prayer

||Ep 1:15-16 ||Phm 4-5 We have never failed to remember you in our prayers and to give thanks for 3
you to God, the Father of our Lord Jesus Christ, •ever since we heard about 4
1 Co 13:13+ your faith in Christ Jesus and the love that you show towards all the saints
1 P 1:3 because of the hope which is stored up for you in heaven. It is only recently that 5
1:23 ||Ep 1:13 you heard of this, when it was announced in the message of the truth. The Good
Ac 14:3; 20:24,32 News •which has reached you is spreading all over the world and producing the 6
2 Co 6:1 same results as it has among you ever since the day when you heard about God's
grace and understood what this really is. •Epaphras, who taught you, is one of 7
our closest fellow workers and a faithful deputy for us as Christ's servant,[b] •and 8
1 Co 13:1+ it was he who told us all about your love in the Spirit.
||Ep 1:15 That will explain why, ever since the day he told us, we have never failed to 9
Ep 5:17 Ph 1:9 pray for you, and what we ask God is that through perfect wisdom and spiritual
Phm 6 *3:10+* understanding you should reach the fullest knowledge of his will. •So you will 10
Ph 1:27 be able to lead the kind of life which the Lord expects of you, a life acceptable
to him in all its aspects; showing the results in all the good actions you do and
increasing your knowledge of God. •You will have in you the strength, based on 11
Ws 5:5+ Ep 1:11-13; his own glorious power, never to give in, but to bear anything joyfully, •thanking 12
5:8 1 P 1:4; 2:9 the Father who has made it possible for you to join the saints and with them
Ac 26:18 to inherit the light.[c]
Jn 8:12+ Because that is what he has done: he has taken us out of the power of darkness 13
||Ep 1:6-7 and created a place for us in the kingdom of the Son that he loves, •and in him, 14
Rm 3:24+ Heb 1:3+ we gain our freedom,[d] the forgiveness of our sins.

I. FORMAL INSTRUCTION

Christ is the head of all creation[e]

1:18+ Gn 1:1-2 He is the image of the unseen God 15
Ps 89:27 Ws 7:26 and the first-born of all creation,
Zc 12:10 Jn 1:3,18 for in him were created 16
Rm 8:29 Heb 1:3,6 all things in heaven and on earth:
everything visible and everything invisible,
Ep 1:10,21+ Thrones, Dominations, Sovereignties, Powers—
Rm 11:36 1 Co 8:6 all things were created through him and for him.

17 Before anything was created, he existed,
and he holds all things in unity.
18 Now the Church is his body, 1:15,24 Ep 1:22-23;
he is its head.[f] 5:23f

As he is the Beginning,
he was first to be born from the dead, 1 Co 15:20 Rv 1:5
so that he should be first in every way; *Rm 8:29*
19 because God wanted all perfection 2:9+
to be found in him[g] Ep 1:23
20 and all things to be reconciled through him and for him,[h] Ep 1:10; 2:14,16
everything in heaven and everything on earth,[i]
when he made peace
by his death on the cross.

The Colossians have their share in salvation

21 Not long ago, you were foreigners and enemies,[j] in the way that you used to Ep 2:1f; 4:18-19
22 think and the evil things that you did; •but now he has reconciled you, by his *2:13* Ep 2:14-16
death and in that mortal body.[k] Now you are able to appear before him holy, 1 Co 1:8+
23 pure and blameless—•as long as you persevere and stand firm on the solid base Ep 5:27+
of the faith, never letting yourselves drift away from the hope promised by the 1:5f Mk 16:15
Good News, which you have heard, which has been preached to the whole human Ac 2:5 2 Co 3:6
race,[l] and of which I, Paul, have become the servant. Ep 3:17 *Ep 3:7*

Paul's labours in the service of the pagans

24 It makes me happy to suffer for you, as I am suffering now, and in my own 2:1 Mt 5:11
body to do what I can to make up all that has still to be undergone by Christ for *1:18+* 2 Co 1:5
25 the sake of his body, the Church.[m] •I became the servant of the Church when God *Rm 15:19* 2 Co 3:6

1 a. Add. (Vulg.) 'and the Lord Jesus Christ'.

b. Lit. 'A faithful servant of Christ on behalf of us'; var. (Vulg.) 'on behalf of you'.

c. Lit. 'Thanking the Father (for) having made you (var. 'us') fit for the part of the lot of the saints in the light'; var. 'for having called you (var. 'us') to...' The 'lot of the saints' is what all holy people are to inherit, i.e. the 'salvation' that had been thought of as a bequest made exclusively to Israel. Now, non-Jews are called to share it, cf. Ep 1:11-13. The word 'saints' (lit. 'holy ones') here can mean either Christians, i.e. people called to live the 'life of light' while still living on earth, Rm 1:7f, cf. Jn 8:12f, or it can mean the angels who live with God in the eschatological 'light', cf. Ac 9:13+.

d. Lit. 'In whom we have the redemption'. Add. (Vulg.) 'by blood', cf. Ep 1:7.

e. In this poem Paul introduces two ways in which Christ can claim to be the 'head' of everything that exists: 1. he is the head of creation, of all that exists naturally, vv. 15-17; 2. he is head of the new creation and of all that exists supernaturally through having been saved, vv. 18-20. The subject of the poem is the pre-existent Christ, but considered only in so far as he was manifest in the unique historic person that is the son of God made man, cf. Ph 2:5+. It is as the incarnate God that Jesus is the 'image of God', i.e. his human nature was the visible manifestation of God who is invisible, cf. Rm 8:29+, and it is as such, in this concrete human nature, and as part of creation, that Jesus is called the 'first-born of creation'—not in the temporal sense of having been born first, but in the sense of having been given the first place of honour.

f. On the Church as Christ's body, cf. 1 Co 12:12f; he is called the 'head' of his own body both in a temporal sense (v. 18, i.e. he was the first to rise from the dead) and in a spiritual sense (v. 20, i.e. he is the leader of all the saved).

g. Lit. 'because (God) wanted the *pleroma* to dwell in him'. The exact meaning of the word *pleroma* (i.e. the thing that fills up a gap or hole, like a patch, cf. Mt 9:16) is not certain here. Some writers have thought it must mean the same as in 2:9 (the fullness of divinity that filled Jesus), but since vv. 15-18 have already dealt with the divinity of Jesus, it seems likely that the reference here is to the biblical concept of the entire cosmos as filled with the creative presence of God, cf. Is 6:3; Jr 23:24; Ps 24:1; 50:12; 72:19; Ws 1:7; Si 43:27 etc. This concept was also widespread in the Graeco-Roman world. Paul teaches that the incarnation and resurrection make Christ head not only of the entire human race, but of the entire created cosmos, so that everything that was involved in the fall is equally involved in the salvation, cf. Rm 8:19-22; 1 Co 3:22f; 15:20-28; Ep 1:10; 4:10; Ph 2:10f; 3:21; Heb 2:5-8. Cf. 2:9+.

h. I.e. through and for Christ, cf. the parallel 'through him and for him' of v. 16. Alternatively, it could read 'God wanted everything... to be reconciled to himself, through him who made peace...', cf. Rm 5:10; 2 Co 5:18f.

i. This reconciliation of the whole universe (including angels as well as human beings) means, not that every single individual will be saved, but that all who are saved will be saved by their collective return to the right order and peace of perfect submission to God. Any individuals who do not join this new creation through grace will be forced to join it, cf. 2:15; 1 Co 15:24-25 (the heavenly spirits) and 2 Th 1:8-9; 1 Co 6:9-10; Ga 5:21; Rm 2:8; Ep 5:5 (men).

j. The context suggests that there is a closer parallel with Ep 4:18f (foreigners to God and therefore God's enemies) than with Ep 2:12 (foreigners in Israel).

k. 'he', i.e. the Father. The human, mortal body is that of his Son (lit. 'flesh body'); this provides the locus where the reconciliation takes place. Into this body the entire human race is effectively gathered, cf. Ep 2:14-16, because Christ has assumed its sin, 2 Co 5:21. The 'flesh' body is the body as affected by sin, 2 Co 5:21; cf. Rm 8:3; 7:5+; Heb 4:15.

l. Lit. 'to all creation under the sky'.

m. Lit. 'all that is lacking from the sufferings of Christ... Church'. Jesus suffered in order to establish the

made me responsible for delivering God's message to you, •the message which 26
Rm 16:25+ was a mystery hidden for generations and centuries and has now been revealed to
his saints. •It was God's purpose to reveal it to them and to show all the rich glory 27
3:4 Ep 2:12 of this mystery to pagans. The mystery is Christ among you, your hope of glory:[n]
1 Th 4:13 *1 Co 2:6* this is the Christ we proclaim, this is the wisdom in which we thoroughly train 28
Ep 4:13+ everyone and instruct everyone, to make them all perfect in Christ. •It is for 29
Ph 4:13 2 Th 1:11 this I struggle wearily on, helped only by his power driving me irresistibly.

Paul's concern for the Colossians' faith

1:24 2 Yes, I want you to know that I do have to struggle hard for you, and for 1
1 Th 2:17 those in Laodicea, and for so many others who have never seen me face to
face. •It is all to bind you together in love and to stir your minds, so that your 2
Ep 3:18-19 understanding may come to full development, until you really know God's
Pr 2:4-5 Is 45:3 secret[a] •in which[b] all the jewels of wisdom and knowledge are hidden. 3
Ep 4:14; 5:6 I say this to make sure that no one deceives you with specious arguments.[c] 4
1 Co 5:3-4 Ph 1:27 I may be absent in body, but in spirit I am there among you, delighted to find you 5
1 Th 2:17 all in harmony and to see how firm your faith in Christ is.

II. A WARNING AGAINST SOME ERRORS

Live according to the true faith in Christ, not according to false teaching

Ep 4:21 Heb 2:9 You must live your whole life according to the Christ you have received— 6
Ac 2:22+ Ep 3:17 Jesus the Lord; •you must be rooted in him and built on him and held firm by the 7
1 Th 2:13+ faith you have been taught, and full of thanksgiving.
Mt 15:2 Ga 4:3+ Make sure that no one traps you and deprives you of your freedom[d] by some 8
Ep 4:14; 5:6 secondhand, empty, rational philosophy based on the principles of this world
instead of on Christ.

Christ alone is the true head of men and angels

1:19+ Jn 1:16 In his body lives the fullness of divinity,[e] and in him you too find your own 9
Ep 1:13; 3: 19; 4:12-13 fulfilment, •in the one who is the head of every Sovereignty and Power.[f] 10
Jr 4:4+ In him you have been circumcised, with a circumcision not performed by 11
Rm 2:25-29 Ph 3:3 human hand, but by the complete stripping of your body of flesh.[g] This is cir-
Rm 6:3-4+ cumcision according to Christ.[h] •You have been buried with him, when you 12
Rm 1:4+; 8:11+ were baptised; and by baptism, too, you have been raised up with him through
Ep 1:19f; 2:6+ your belief in the power of God who raised him from the dead. •You were dead, 13
1:22 because you were sinners and had not been circumcised: he[i] has brought you[j]
||Ep 2:1,5f to life with him, he has forgiven us[k] all our sins.
Ep 2:15 He has overridden the Law, and cancelled every record of the debt that we 14
had to pay; he has done away with it by nailing it to the cross;[l] •and so he got 15
Is 53:12 1 P 3:22 rid of the Sovereignties and the Powers, and paraded them in public, behind him
2 Co 2:14 in his triumphal procession.[m]

Against the false asceticism based on 'the principles of this world'

Rm 14:3-4 Ga 4:3+ From now onwards, never let anyone else decide what you should eat or drink, 16
1 Tm 4:3 Heb 9:10 or whether you are to observe annual festivals, New Moons or sabbaths. •These 17
Heb 10:1 were only pale reflections of what was coming: the reality is Christ.[n] •Do not be 18
taken in by people who like grovelling[o] to angels and worshipping them;[p] people
Ga 6:12 like that are always going on about some vision they have had,[q] inflating themselves to a false importance with their worldly outlook. •A man of this sort 19
||Ep 4:15-16 is not united to the head,[r] and it is the head that adds strength and holds the
whole body together, with all its joints and sinews—and this is the only way in
which it can reach its full growth in God.
Ga 4:3+ If you have really died with Christ to the principles of this world, why do you 20
still let rules dictate to you, as though you were still living in the world? •'It is 21

forbidden to pick up this, it is forbidden to taste that, it is forbidden to touch
2 something else'; •all these prohibitions are only concerned with things that 1 Co 6:13; 8:8
perish by their very use—an example of *human doctrines and regulations*! *Is 29:13* Mt 15:9
3 It may be argued that true wisdom is to be found in these, with their self-imposed
devotions, their self-abasement, and their severe treatment of the body; but once 2 Tm 3:5
the flesh starts to protest, they are no use at all.[s]

Life-giving union with the glorified Christ

1 3 Since you have been brought back to true life with Christ, you must look for Ep 2:6+ Ph 3:20
the things that are in heaven, where Christ is, sitting at God's right hand. *Ac 2:33+*
2 Let your thoughts be on heavenly things, not on the things that are on the earth,
3 because you have died, and now the life you have is hidden with Christ in God. 2:12 Ph 1:21
4 But when Christ is revealed—and he is your[a] life—you too will be revealed in all *1:27* 1 P 5:1
your glory with him.[b] 1 Jn 3:2 *Rm 8:19*

reign of God, and anyone who continues his work must share this suffering. Paul is not saying that he thinks his own sufferings increase the value of the redemption (since that value cannot be increased) but that he shares by his sufferings as a missionary in those that Jesus had undergone in his own mission, cf. 2 Co 1:5; Ph 1:20+. These are the sufferings predicted for the messianic era, Mt 24:8+; Ac 14:22+; 1 Tm 4:1+, and are all part of the way in which God had always intended the Church to develop; Paul feels that being the messenger Christ has chosen to send to the pagans, he has been specially called on to experience these sufferings.

n. Previously, when it had seemed (to the Jews) that pagans could never be saved, as salvation was restricted to 'Israel', pagans had seemed to be without a Messiah and consequently to be deprived of all hope, Ep 2:12. The 'mystery' or secret of God that had now been revealed was that the pagans too were, and had been, all called to be saved through union with Christ, and so to reach eternal glory, cf. Ep 2:13-22; 3:3-6.

2 a. Var. 'the mystery of Christ', cf. 4:3; Ep 3:4; or 'God's mystery of Christ', or 'the mystery of God the father of Christ', or 'the mystery of God the Father, and of Christ', etc.

b. 'in which' i.e. in the 'mystery' that revealed what till then had been 'hidden', namely the 'infinite wisdom' of God, cf. Rm 16:25+; 1 Tm 3:16+. That it is Christ who is revealed in the mystery, 1:27, is of course true, and he himself is also the Wisdom of God, 1 Co 1:24.30, and he is also the Mystery, 1 Co 2:7, that is hard to understand, Ep 3:8.19.

c. This will be developed in v. 8f.

d. To deny Christ after he has liberated them from the tyranny of 'darkness' 1:13f, by going back to error, would be nothing but a new slavery, cf. Ga 4:8f; 5:1.

e. The word *pleroma* here cf. 1:19+, is defined as the 'divinity' that is actually 'filling' Christ now in his body: in other words, the risen Christ, through his incarnation and resurrection, unites the divine and the created. The former is what he is by his pre-existence and his present glory; the latter is, as human, what he has assumed directly, and, as cosmic, what he assumed indirectly through being human. In this way he himself is the *pleroma* of all possible categories of being.

f. A Christian shares this *pleroma* of Christ by being part of it, i.e. part of Christ's body, cf. (text and notes) 1:19; Ep 1:23; 3:19; 4:12-13 and as a consequence of this he is raised to be higher than even the highest grade of angel. The following verses develop these two ideas: disciples of Christ share his triumph, vv. 11-13, over even the highest grade of angel, vv. 14-15.

g. Surgical circumcision removes only a piece of skin.

h. The 'circumcision' instituted by Christ, i.e baptism.

i. God the Father.

j. 'you'; var. 'us'.

k. 'us'; var 'you'.

l. The Law was able to do nothing about a sinner except condemn him to death, Rm 7:7+: this death sentence is what God had carried out on his own Son in order to suppress it for the rest of the world, and it was for this very reason that God's Son was 'made sin' 2 Co 5:21, 'subject to the Law', Ga 4:4, and 'cursed' by the Law, Ga 3:13. In the person of his Son, whom he allowed to be executed, God nailed up and destroyed our death warrant, as well as all the charges it made against us.

m. The tradition is that the Law was brought down to Moses by angels, Ga 3:19+, and by honouring them as the lawgivers, cf. v. 18, people have been distracted from the true creator. Now that God has brought the régime of that Law to an end, by means of the crucifixion, these angelic powers have lost the one thing that had given them power, and so they too must acknowledge that Christ has triumphed over them.

n. Lit. 'but the body is Christ'—a pun on the word *soma* ('body') as being both that which is more real than any shadow or reflection, and the body of the risen Christ which is what gives reality to our eschatological hope, and which is the first evidence that the new creation has already begun.

o. Or 'Do not let people take the liberty of looking down on you just because they grovel...'

p. Dietary and cultic practices, v. 16, are only superstitious worries about material things and the 'spirits' that are supposed to control them, cf. Ga 4:3f.

q. Var. (Vulg.) 'they have not (in fact) had'. Paul is explaining where the teachers at Colossae have gone wrong, which is either because they attach a false importance to their 'visions' or, at a more general level, because they think their own completely unspiritual ideas are what religion is about.

r. Christ, Ep 4:15.

s. Lit. these things 'are not in any honour for satisfaction of the flesh': this may mean either that they are of no real value in subduing 'the flesh', or else 'they are of no value and only help to satisfy the flesh'.

3 a. Var. 'our'.

b. Through union with Christ in baptism, 2:12, his followers already live the identical life he lives in heaven, cf. Ep 2:6+, but this spiritual life is not manifest and glorious as it will be at the *parousia*.

III. EXHORTATION

General rules of Christian behaviour

Rm 6:11f; Ga 5:24; Ep 4:22; *Rm 1:29+*; ||*Ep 5:6*; Rm 1:18+; ||*Ep 2:2-3*; Tt 3:3; *Ep 4:31*; Ep 4:25; *Rm 6:6*; ||Ep 4:22-24; Gn 1:26-27; Gn 11:1; 1 Co 12:13; 15:28; Ga 3:27-28; Ep 4:13

That is why you must kill everything in you that belongs only to earthly life:[c] fornication, impurity, guilty passion, evil desires and especially greed, which is the same thing as worshipping a false god; •all this is the sort of behaviour that makes God angry.[d] •And it is the way in which you used to live when you were surrounded by people doing the same thing, •but now you, of all people, must give all these things up: getting angry, being bad-tempered, spitefulness, abusive language and dirty talk; •and never tell each other lies. You have stripped off your old behaviour with your old self, •and you have put on a new self which will progress towards true knowledge the more it is renewed in the image of its creator;[e] •and in that image there is no room for distinction between Greek and Jew, between the circumcised or the uncircumcised, or between barbarian and Scythian, slave and free man. There is only Christ: he is everything and he is in everything.[f]

||Ep 4:1-2,32; *1 Th 5:15*; *Mt 6:14*; 18:21-35; 2 Co 2:7; Ep 4:32+; *Rm 13:8-10+*; 1 Co 13:1+; Ep 2:16; 4:3-4; Ph 4:7; *1 Co 12:12+*

You are God's chosen race, his saints; he loves you, and you should be clothed in sincere compassion, in kindness and humility, gentleness and patience. •Bear with one another; forgive each other as soon as a quarrel begins. The Lord has forgiven you; now you must do the same. •Over all these clothes, to keep them together and complete them, put on love. •And may the peace of Christ reign in your hearts, because it is for this that you were called together as parts of one body. Always be thankful.

Ep 4:29; Ac 16:25; ||Ep 5:19-20; 1 Co 10:31

Let the message of Christ,[g] in all its richness, find a home with you. Teach each other, and advise each other, in all wisdom. With gratitude in your hearts sing psalms and hymns and inspired songs to God;[h] •and never say or do anything except in the name of the Lord Jesus, giving thanks to God the Father through him.

||Ep 5:21-6:9; 1 P 3:1-7

The morals of the home and household[i]

Tt 2:5; Ep 6:1

Wives, give way to your husbands, as you should in the Lord. •Husbands, love your wives and treat them with gentleness. •Children, be obedient to your parents always, because that is what will please the Lord. •Parents, never drive your children to resentment or you will make them feel frustrated.

Rm 6:15+; 1 Co 7:21-23; Ep 6:5; 1 Tm 6:1; Tt 2:9-10; Phm 16; 1 P 2:18; Jb 31:15; Ep 6:5; Phm 16

Slaves, be obedient to the men who are called your masters in this world; not only when you are under their eye, as if you had only to please men, but wholeheartedly, out of respect for the Master.[j] •Whatever your work is, put your heart into it as if it were for the Lord and not for men, •knowing that the Lord will repay you by making you his heirs.[k] It is Christ the Lord that you are serving; •anyone who does wrong will be repaid in kind and he does not favour
one person more than another. **4** Masters, make sure that your slaves are given 1
what is just and fair, knowing that you too have a Master in heaven.

The apostolic spirit

Rm 12:12; ||Ep 6:18-20; 1 Th 5:6; *Rm 15:30+*; 1 Co 16:9+; 2 Th 3:1; Heb 13:18

Be persevering in your prayers and be thankful as you stay awake to pray. 2
Pray for us especially, asking God to show us opportunities for announcing the 3
message and proclaiming the mystery of Christ,[a] for the sake of which I am in
chains; •pray that I may proclaim it as clearly as I ought. 4

1 Co 5:12+; ||Ep 5:15; *2 Co 6:2+*; Ep 5:16

Be tactful with those who are not Christians and be sure you make the best 5
use of your time with them. •Talk to them agreeably and with a flavour of wit,[b] 6
and try to fit your answers to the needs of each one.

Personal news

Ac 20:4+; ||Ep 6:21

Tychicus will tell you all the news about me. He is a brother I love very much, 7

8 and a loyal helper and companion in the service of the Lord. •I am sending him
to you precisely for this purpose: to give you news about us[c] and to reassure you.
9 With him I am sending Onesimus, that dear and faithful brother who is a fellow Phm 10f
citizen of yours. They will tell you everything that is happening here.

Greetings[d] and final wishes

Phm 23f

10 Aristarchus, who is here in prison with me, sends his greetings, and so does Ac 19:29
Mark, the cousin of Barnabas—you were sent some instructions about him; Ac 12:12+ 2 Tm 4:11
11 if he comes to you, give him a warm welcome—•and Jesus Justus adds his greetings. Of all those who have come over from the Circumcision, these are the only
ones actually working with me for the kingdom of God. They have been a great
12 comfort to me. •Epaphras, your fellow citizen, sends his greetings; this servant
of Christ Jesus never stops battling for you, praying that you will never lapse but Rm 15:30
13 always hold perfectly and securely to the will of God. •I can testify for him that
14 he works hard for you, as well as for those at Laodicea and Hierapolis. •Greetings
from my dear friend Luke, the doctor, and also from Demas. 2 Tm 4:10-11
15 Please give my greetings to the brothers at Laodicea and to Nympha and the
16 church which meets in her house. •After this letter has been read among you, Rm 16:5 *1 Th 5:27*
send it on to be read in the church of the Laodiceans; and get the letter[e] from
17 Laodicea for you to read yourselves. •Give Archippus this message, 'Remember Phm 2
the service that the Lord wants you to do, and try to carry it out'.
18 Here is a greeting in my own handwriting—PAUL. Remember the chains I 1 Co 16:21 Ga 6:11 Ep 3:1+ 2 Th 3:17 Phm 19 *Phm 9*
wear. Grace be with you.[f]

c. At the mystical level of union with Christ in heaven, participation in his death and resurrection through baptism is instantaneous and total, 2:12f,20; 3:1-4; Rm 6:4+, but at the practical level of life on earth, this union has to be grown into gradually. Already 'dead' in theory, the Christian must experience death and rebirth daily, constantly, by 'killing' the old and sinful self.

d. Add. (Vulg.) 'with those who resist him', cf. Ep 5:6.

e. The human race, that was to have been the 'image of God', Gn 1:26+, lost its way trying to locate the 'knowledge of good and evil' outside and apart from the will of God, Gn 2:17+, and became the slave of sin and sinful urges, Rm 5:12+. This is the 'old self (man)' that must die, Rm 6:6; Ep 4:22; the 'new self' is reborn in Christ, Ep 2:15+, who is the true image of God, Rm 8:29+. In this way the human race can both recover its original purity and reach true moral certitude, 1:9; Heb 5:14.

f. The new creation will not be divided into races and religions and cultures and social classes in the way the present creation has been since the Fall: the whole world will be reunited in Christ.

g. Var. 'of the Lord', or 'of God': possibly the text originally read 'the Word', cf. Ph 1:14; 2:30.

h. These 'inspired songs' could be charismatic improvisations suggested by the Spirit during liturgical assembly; cf. 1 Co 12:7f; 14:26.

i. Paul christens these simple precepts of ordinary morality by introducing his phrase 'in the Lord' which must be taken here as meaning 'according to the Christian way of life'. These Christian applications are further developed in Ep 5:22f.

j. 'your masters... the Master': Paul uses the same word each time, i.e. Christ is the master equally of both slave and slave-owner.

k. That a master should name a slave as his heir, cf. Mt 21:35-38; Lk 15:19; Ga 4:1-2, is one of the most impressive proofs of how different the new creation 'in Christ' is, cf. Rm 8:15-17; Ga 4:3-7; Phm 16.

4 a, Var. 'of God', cf. 2:2.

b. Lit. 'seasoned with salt', a classical Greek cliché. Cf. Mk 9:50.

c. Var. (Vulg.) 'to get your news'.

d. On Aristarchus, cf. Ac 19:29. On Mark, cf. Ac 12:12+. 'Jesus Justus' is not mentioned anywhere else; his surname was quite common among Jews and Jewish converts, cf. Ac 1:23; 18:27. Epaphras, born at Colossae (and therefore not the same person as Epaphroditus who came from Philippi, Ph 2:25; 4:18) had been sent by Paul to evangelise Colossae, his own native town, Col 1:7. Luke is the evangelist and author of Ac: he had joined Paul towards the end of his third journey, Ac 20:5f, had been with him till they reached Rome, Ac 27:1f, and now, with Paul under arrest, he is still by his side, cf. Phm 24, as he will be again after Paul has been arrested a second time, 2 Tm 4:11. On Demas, cf. Phm 24; 2 Tm 4:10. Who the woman called Nympha was (or man, if the correct spelling is Nymphas) is unknown. Archippus, v. 17, is probably the son of Philemon, Phm 2; what the service was the Lord wanted him to do is not known.

e. Paul expected his letters to be read in public to the assembled brothers, 1 Th 5:27, and then passed on to neighbouring churches, cf. 2 Co 1:1. The letter that was to be brought back from Laodicea to Colossae was probably the one that Paul wrote to Ephesus.

f. Add. (Vulg.) 'Amen', cf. Ph 4:23.

1 THESSALONIANS

THE FIRST LETTER OF PAUL TO THE CHURCH IN THESSALONIKA

Rm 1:1+ 2 Th 1:1-2 **Address**

Ac 15:22+; 16:1+ 1 From Paul, Silvanus and Timothy, to the Church in Thessalonika which is in 1
God the Father and the Lord Jesus Christ; wishing you grace and peace.[a]

2 Th 1:3 **Thanksgiving and congratulations**

Ph 1:3 We always mention you in our prayers and thank God for you all, •and 2 3
5:8 1 Co 13:13+ constantly remember before God our Father how you have shown your faith in
Rv 2:2 action, worked for love and persevered through hope, in our Lord Jesus Christ.
2 Th 2:13 We know, brothers, that God loves you and that you have been chosen, 4
Ac 20:18 1 Co 2:4 because when we brought the Good News[b] to you, it came to you not only as 5
2 Co 12:12 *Ac 1:8+* words, but as power and as the Holy Spirit and as utter conviction. And you
observed the sort of life we lived when we were with you, which was for your
Ac 17:1-9 2 Th 3:7+ instruction, •and you were led to become imitators of us, and of the Lord; and 6
3:3 Rm 14:17 it was with the joy of the Holy Spirit that you took to the gospel, in spite of the
Ga 5:22 *2 Th 1:4* great opposition all round you. •This has made you the great example to all 7
believers in Macedonia and Achaia •since it was from you that the word of the 8
Rm 1:8 Lord started to spread—and not only throughout Macedonia and Achaia, for
the news of your faith in God has spread everywhere. We do not need to tell other
people about it: •other people tell us how we started the work among you, how 9
Ac 3:19+ Ga 4:8 you broke with idolatry when you were converted to God and became servants
2:19-20; 4:16-17; of the real, living God; •and how you are now waiting for Jesus, his Son, whom 10
5:9 *Mt 3:7+* he raised from the dead, to come from heaven to save us from the retribution[c]
Rm 2:5f; 5:9 which is coming.

Paul's example in Thessalonika

2 You know yourselves, my brothers, that our visit to you has not proved 1
ineffectual.
Ac 16:19-40 We had, as you know, been given rough treatment and been grossly insulted 2
Ph 1:30 *Ac 13:46+* at Philippi, and it was our God who gave us the courage to proclaim his Good
2 Co 3:12 News to you in the face of great opposition. •We have not taken to preaching 3
Ep 3:7 because we are deluded, or immoral, or trying to deceive anyone; •it was God 4
1 Tm 1:11 who decided that we were fit to be entrusted with the Good News, and when we
Jr 11:20 2 Co 4:2; 5:9 are speaking, we are not trying to please men but God, *who can read* our *inmost*
Ga 1:10 *Rm 1:9* *thoughts*. •You know very well, and we can swear it before God, that never at 5
any time have our speeches been simply flattery, or a cover for trying to get money;
Jn 5:41,44 nor have we ever looked for any special honour from men, either from you or 6
anybody else, •when we could have imposed ourselves on you with full weight, 7
as apostles of Christ.[a]
1 Co 3:2 Ga 4:19 Instead, we were unassuming.[b] Like a mother feeding and looking after her own
Rm 9:3 Ga 2:20+ children, •we felt so devoted and protective towards you, and had come to love 8

you so much, that we were eager to hand over to you not only the Good News
9 but our whole lives as well. •Let me remind you, brothers, how hard we used to 4:11 Ac 18:3+
work, slaving night and day so as not to be a burden on any one of you while 2 Th 3:7-9
10 we were proclaiming God's Good News to you. •You are witnesses, and so Ac 20:18 2 Co 4:4
is God, that our treatment of you, since you became believers, has been impeccably
11 right and fair. •You can remember how we treated every one of you as a father 1 Co 4:15 Phm 10
12 treats his children, •teaching you what was right, encouraging you and appealing *Ph 1:27*
to you to live a life worthy of God, who is calling[c] you to share the glory of his Mt 4:17+ 2 Tm 2:10
kingdom. 1 P 5:10

The faith and the patience of the Thessalonians

13 Another reason why we constantly thank God for you is that as soon as you
heard the message that we brought you as God's message, you accepted it for what 1 Co 11:2+; 15:1
it really is, God's message[d] and not some human thinking; and it is still[e] a living *Ep 1:13* Ph 4:9
14 power among you who believe it. •For you, my brothers, have been like the *Rm 1:16* Heb 4:12
churches of God in Christ Jesus which are in Judaea, in suffering the same *1 Co 1:2+* 2 Th 3:7+
15 treatment from your own countrymen as they have suffered from the Jews,[f] •the
people who put the Lord Jesus to death, and the prophets too. And now they have Mt 23:29-37 Ac 2:23-24+
been persecuting us, and acting in a way that cannot please God and makes them
16 the enemies of the whole human race, •because they are hindering us from
preaching to the pagans and trying to save them. They never stop trying *to finish* Gn 15:16 2 M 6:14
off the sins they have begun, but retribution[g] is overtaking them at last. Mt 23:32

Paul's anxiety

17 A short time after we had been separated from you—in body but never in 3:10 Col 2:1,5
thought, brothers—we had an especially strong desire and longing to see you face Rm 1:10-11
18 to face again, •and we tried hard to come and visit you; I, Paul, tried more than
19 once, but Satan prevented us. •What do you think is our pride and our joy? You 2 Th 2:9+
are; and you will be *the crown* of which we shall be *proudest* in the presence of our Ezk 16:12; 23:42 Pr 16:31
20 Lord Jesus when he comes; •you are our pride and our joy. 1 Co 9:25+ Ph 2:16 *1:10+* 1 Co 15:23+ 2 Co 1:14+

Timothy's mission to Thessalonika

1 **3** When we could not bear the waiting any longer, we decided it would be best
2 to be left without a companion at Athens, and •sent our brother Timothy, Ac 17:14-16+
who is God's helper[a] in spreading the Good News of Christ, to keep you firm and *1 Co 3:9* 2 Co 6:1
3 strong in the faith •and prevent any of you from being unsettled by the present *1:6*
4 troubles. As you know, these are bound to come our way: •when we were with
you, we warned you that we must expect to have persecutions to bear, and that Mt 16:24p Ac 14:22
5 is what has happened now, as you have found out. •That is why, when I could Rm 8:36 2 Th 1:5
not stand waiting any longer, I sent to assure myself of your faith: I was afraid 2 Tm 3:12 Heb 10:32,36

1 a. Add. 'from God our Father and the Lord Jesus Christ', cf. 2 Th 1:2.

b. Var. 'the Good News of God', or 'of our God'. The Good News is more than a proclamation, it is the whole new economy of salvation.

c. Lit. 'wrath'. Vv. 9-10 seem to give an extremely condensed summary of Paul's characteristic 'proclamation'. The two main elements of the Good News as preached by Paul were: his emphasis on monotheism, and the prominence he gives to the return of the risen Lord, cf. Rm 1:1-4,20f; 1 Co 1:18,21; Ga 1:3f; 3:1; Ac 14:15-17; 17:21-31, etc.

2 a. Lit. 'being able to be with weight as apostles of Christ': interpreted morally, this can mean that Paul could have insisted on his own dignity and prestige, or that materially he could have expected to have been fed and kept at their expense, cf. 2:9; 2 Th 3:8; 2 Co 11:9.

b. Lit. 'babies'; var. 'gentle'.

c. Var. 'called you'.

d. A brief summary of the apostolic tradition: the message is first 'received', 4:1; 2 Th 3:6; 1 Co 15:1; Ga 1:9; Ph 4:9; Col 2:6, or 'heard', Rm 10:17+; Ep 1:13; Ac 15:7, etc. It then penetrates the mind or heart, Rm 10:8-10, where if it is welcomed, 1:6; 2 Th 2:10; 2 Co 11:4; Ac 8:14, etc. Mk 4:20, it proves that the hearer acknowledges that God has been speaking through his missionary, 4:1f; 2 Co 3:5; 15:3.

e. Or 'has become'; God acts through his message that has been welcomed by the believer, cf. 1:8; 2 Th 3:1.

f. The harsh tone of vv. 15-16 gives a good idea of how bitter the atmosphere was in Jerusalem, Mt 5:12; 21:33-46; 23:29-37; Ac 2:23+, owing to the way Paul upset the Jewish community by preaching to pagans v. 16; cf. Ac 13:5+. Later on Paul was able to take a more balanced attitude than he takes here, by frequent references to the special position of God's chosen people, cf. Rm 9:11; Ga 4:21-31. He tried hard to reconcile convert pagan with Jewish Christian, cf. 1 Co 16:1+; Ep 2:11-22.

g. Lit. 'the wrath'; add 'of God'.

3 a. Om. 'who is God's helper', var. 'who is God's slave' or 'God's slave and our helper'.

the Tempter[b] might have tried you too hard, and all our work might have been
wasted.

Paul thanks God for good reports of the Thessalonians

2 Th 1:3; 2:15+ *2 Co 7:7* 2 Th 2:15 Rv 2:9-10 2:17

However, Timothy is now back from you and he has given us good news of 6
your faith and your love, telling us that you always remember us with pleasure
and want to see us quite as much as we want to see you. •And so, brothers, your 7
faith has been a great comfort to us in the middle of our own troubles and sorrows;
now we can breathe again, as you are still holding firm in the Lord. •How can we 8 9
thank God enough for you, for all the joy we feel before our God on your account?
We are earnestly praying night and day to be able to see you face to face again and 10
make up any shortcomings[c] in your faith.

2 Th 2:16-17 5:15 Rm 12:17 Ga 6:10 2 Th 1:3 Tt 3:2 *5:23* *Zc 14:5* 1 Co 1:8+; 15:23+

May God our Father himself, and our Lord Jesus Christ, make it easy for us 11
to come to you. •May the Lord be generous in increasing your love and make you 12
love one another and the whole human race[d] as much as we love you. •And may 13
he so confirm your hearts in holiness that you may be blameless in the sight of our
God and Father when our Lord Jesus Christ comes *with all his saints*.[e]

Live in holiness and charity

2 Th 3:6 2:13+ Rm 12:1-2 1 Co 11:2+

4 Finally, brothers, we urge you and appeal to you in the Lord Jesus[a] to make 1
more and more progress in the kind of life that you are meant to live: the life
that God wants, as you learnt from us, and as you are already living it.[b] •You 2
have not forgotten the instructions we gave you on the authority of the Lord Jesus.

5:18 Mt 6:10 Ep 1:4 *1 Co 6:12-20* Jr 10:25 Ps 79:6 *Dt 32:35* Ps 94:1-2 Jn 17:19 Lk 10:16 *Ezk 37:14* 2 Th 2:13

What God wants is for you all to be holy.[c] He wants you to keep away from 3
fornication, •and each one of you to know how to use the body that belongs to 4
him[d] in a way that is holy and honourable, •not giving way to selfish lust like *the* 5
pagans who do not know God. •He wants nobody at all ever to sin by taking advan- 6
tage of a brother in these matters; the Lord always punishes sins of that sort, as
we told you before and assured you. •We have been called by God to be holy, 7
not to be immoral; •in other words, anyone who objects is not objecting to a 8
human authority, but to God, *who gives you his* Holy *Spirit*.[e]

Is 54:13 Jr 31:33-34 Jn 6:45; 13:34+ 1 Jn 4:7 2 Th 1:3 2:9 Ac 18:3+ Ep 4:28 2 Th 3:6-12 *1 Co 5:12+*

As for loving our brothers, there is no need for anyone to write to you about 9
that, since you have learnt from God yourselves to love one another, •and in fact 10
this is what you are doing with all the brothers throughout the whole of
Macedonia. However, we do urge you, brothers, to go on making even greater
progress •and to make a point of living quietly, attending to your own business 11
and earning your living, just as we told you to, •so that you are seen to 12
be respectable by those outside the Church, though you do not have to depend
on them.

The dead and the living at the time of the Lord's coming[f]

Ep 2:12 Col 1:27 Rm 1:4+; 8:11+; 10:9+ 1 Co 15: 1+,20 *1 Co 15:51* *1 Co 15:23* Mt 24:30-31+ 1 Co 15:52+ 2 Th 1:7f

We want you to be quite certain, brothers, about those who have died,[g] to make 13
sure that you do not grieve about them, like the other people who have no hope.
We believe that Jesus died and rose again, and that it will be the same for those 14
who have died in Jesus: God will bring them with him. •We can tell you this from 15
the Lord's own teaching,[h] that any of us[i] who are left alive until the Lord's coming
will not have any advantage over those who have died. •At the trumpet of God, 16
the voice of the archangel will call out the command and the Lord himself will
come down from heaven;[j] those who have died in Christ will be the first to rise,
and then those of us who are still alive[k] will be taken up in the clouds, together 17
with them, to meet the Lord in the air. So we shall stay with the Lord for ever.[l]
With such thoughts as these you should comfort one another. 18

Watchfulness while awaiting the coming of the Lord[a]

Dn 2:21 Ac 1:8+ *Mt 24:36,43* 2 P 3:10

5 You will not be expecting us to write anything to you, brothers, about 'times 1
and seasons',[b] •since you know very well that the Day of the Lord is going to 2

come like a thief in the night. •It is when people are saying, 'How quiet and Rv 3:3▲ *Jr 6:14*
peaceful it is' that the worst suddenly happens, as suddenly as labour pains come Jr 4:31+
on a pregnant woman; and there will be no way for anybody to evade it. Mt 24:8+ Lk 21:34-35
But it is not as if you live in the dark, my brothers, for that Day[c] to overtake Ep 5:8-9
you like a thief. •No, you are all sons of light and sons of the day: we do not belong *Jn 8:12+*
to the night or to darkness, •so we should not go on sleeping, as everyone else Mt 24:42+ Rm 13:12-13
does, but stay wide awake and sober. •Night is the time for sleepers to sleep and 1 P 1:13; 4: 7; 5:8
drunkards to be drunk, •but we belong to the day and we should be sober; let us *Ep 6:11*
put on faith and love for a *breastplate*, and the hope of *salvation* for a *helmet*. 1:3 Is 59:17
God never meant us to experience the Retribution, but to win salvation through 1 Co 13:13+ *1:10+*
our Lord Jesus Christ, •who died for us so that, alive or dead,[d] we should still live 4:14+
united to him. •So give encouragement to each other, and keep strengthening one Ep 2:20
another, as you do already.

Some demands made by life in community

We appeal to you, my brothers, to be considerate to those who are working 1 Co 16:16 1 Tm 5:17
amongst you and are above you in the Lord as your teachers. •Have the greatest Tt 1:5+ Heb 13:17
respect and affection for them because of their work. *Ga 6:6*
Be at peace among yourselves. •And this is what we ask you to do, brothers:
warn the idlers, give courage to those who are apprehensive, care for the weak and Rm 14:1 2 Th 3:6-12
be patient with everyone. •Make sure that people do not try to take revenge; *Ex 21:25+* Mt 5:38f
you must all think of what is best for each other and for the community. •Be Rm 12:17 Col 3:12-13
happy at all times; •pray constantly; •and for all things give thanks to God, *Ph 1:4+* *Ep 5:20*
because this is what God expects you to do in Christ Jesus. 4:3

b. 'Tempter', i.e. 'Satan' as in 2:18, cf. Mk 1:13.

c. This would refer to gaps in their knowledge of Christian doctrine, as well as gaps in their code of Christian behaviour, cf. Rm 14:1; 2 Co 10:15; Ph 1:25.

d. Brotherly love of one another in the Christian community is only the beginning of charity; it has to spread to love for the whole human race.

e. Add. 'Amen'. Holiness, 4:3+, begins with brotherly love but will not be perfect till the *parousia*. In this context 'saints' can refer to the chosen, the saved or the angels, Ac 9:13+.

4 a. Paul speaks 'in' (v.1) 'by' (v.2) or 'in the name of' Christ, cf. 4:15; 2 Th 3:6,12. His doctrine on moral behaviour which is based on the earliest Christian teaching invests ordinary day-to-day life with a new depth: it has the seal of Christ on it, Col 3:18+.

b. Om. 'and as you are already living it'.

c. It is the will of God, cf. Mt 6:10, that makes people holy, vv. 3,7; 2 Th 2:13; Ep 1:4. It is God who makes them holy, 5:23; 1 Co 6:11. Christ has made himself our 'holiness', 1 Co 1:30. The Holy Spirit is involved in making us holy, v.8; 2 Th 2:13; 1 Co 6:11.

d. Lit. 'each one of you to 'know' (or 'be able') to possess the vessel of himself in sanctification and honour'. 'Vessel' means 'wife' in 1 P 3:7 and many rabbinic texts, but it means 'body' in 5:23; cf. Rm 12:1; 1 Co 6:19.

e. Ezekiel foretold that the Spirit would be given to the messianic people: this reference draws attention to the continuity between the church of Thessalonika and the giving of this gift to the early Christian community, Ac 2:16f,33,38 etc. On the gift of the Spirit to the spirit of each believer, cf. Rm 5:5+.

f. The converts in Thessalonika had obviously been worried about this and uncertain what the Christian position was. Replying to their questions Paul affirms the fundamental doctrine of the resurrection so as to strengthen the faith and hope of all the converts.

g. Lit. 'we do not wish you to be ignorant, brothers, concerning the sleeping'. The euphemism was common in the O.T., the N.T., and in Greek literature: the natural concomitant was to call the resurrection (to new life or from death) an 'awakening'.

h. No precise reference in the written gospels can be given for this saying of Jesus, but cf. Mt 24 with vv. 15-17. Perhaps Paul is relying here on the authority he had been given by the vision on the Damascus road, cf. Dn 7:1,13,16.

i. 'us'; Paul includes himself among those who will be present at the *parousia:* more by aspiration, however, than by conviction, cf. 5:1+.

j. The trumpet, voice and clouds were traditional signs that accompanied manifestations of God, cf. Ex 13:32+; 19:16+, and they were adopted as conventional elements of apocalyptic literature, cf. Mt 24:30f+; 2 Th 1:8+.

k. Om. '(we) who are still alive'.

l. Of all the details given here: that the dead will answer the summons by returning to life, that they and the living will be taken to meet the Lord, and that they will accompany him to the judgement with which the eternal kingdom begins, the essential one is the last: eternal life with Christ, cf. 5:10; 2 Th 2:1. That is to be the 'salvation', the 'glory', the 'kingdom' that Jesus shares among his chosen followers.

5 a. Paul asserts that he has no idea when the Last Day will come, and he merely repeats what the Lord said, Mt 24:36p; Ac 1:7, about having to stay awake till it comes, Mt 24:42p,50; 25:13. The Day of the Lord, 1 Co 1:8+, will come like a thief, cf. Mt 24:43p, so it is necessary to stay awake, v.6, cf. Rm 13:11; 1 Co 16:13; Col 4:2; 1 P 1:13; 5:8; Rv 3:2f; 16:15. It will come soon, 2 Co 6:2+. At first Paul expected he would live to see the Last Day, 1 Th 4:17; cf. 1 Co 15:51; he later realised he might die before it, 2 Co 5:3; Ph 1:23, and he warns people it will not come as soon as they thought, 2 Th 2:1f. More than anything, the prospect of how long it would take to convert the pagans, Rm 11:25, made it certain that the Last Day would not come for a very long time, cf. Mt 25:19; Lk 20:9; 2 P 3:4.

b. 'about times and seasons': a cliché, cf. Ac 1:7+, underlying which is the idea of God as outside time and yet as controlling it and its divisions, Ac 17:26.

c. Mention of 'the Day' without further qualification, 1 Co 1:8+, helps Paul to introduce the mention of light and day and contrast 'wakefulness' with the dark, night and sleep (in a different sense from 4:13f), and also make the contrast between Christians (sons of the light) and others (sons of darkness), cf. Jn 8:12+.

d. Lit. 'awake or asleep' in same sense as 4:14-17: all the faithful will share in the final salvation.

1 Co 12:1+ *1 Co 12:10+* Never try to suppress the Spirit •or treat the gift of prophecy with contempt; 1 2
Jb 1:1,8; 2:3 think before you do anything—hold on to what is good •and *avoid every* form of 2 2
evil.

Closing prayer and farewell

Is 11:6+ 2 Th 3:16 May the God of peace make you perfect and holy; and may you all be kept 2
3:13+ safe and blameless, spirit, soul and body,[e] for the coming of our Lord Jesus Christ.
1 Co 1:9+ 2 Th 3:3 God has called you and he will not fail you. 2
2 Th 3:1 Pray for us, my brothers. 2
Rm 15:30+ 2 Co 13:12+ Greet all the brothers with the holy kiss. •My orders, in the Lord's name, 2 2
Col 4:16 are that this letter is to be read to all the[f] brothers.
The grace of our Lord Jesus Christ be with you.[g] 2

5 e. Paul seems to have developed no coherent system of anthropology: this is the only place he mentions a tripartite division of body (cf. Rm 7:24+), soul (cf. 1 Co 15:44+) and spirit (which can be taken in two ways: as the divine presence in a human being, giving him new life in union with Christ, Rm 5:5+, or more probably as the innermost depths of the human being, open and awake to the Spirit, cf. Rm 1:9+).

f. Vulg. inserts 'holy'.

g. Add. (Vulg.) 'Amen'.

2 THESSALONIANS

THE SECOND LETTER OF PAUL
TO THE CHURCH IN THESSALONIKA

Address 1 Th 1:1

1 **1** From Paul, Silvanus and Timothy, to the Church in Thessalonika which is in Ac 15:22+; 16:1+
2 God our Father and the Lord Jesus Christ; •wishing you grace and peace
from God the Father and the Lord Jesus Christ.

Thanksgiving and encouragement. The Last Judgement

3 We feel we must be continually thanking God for you, brothers; quite rightly, 1 Th 1:2
because your faith is growing so wonderfully and the love that you have for one 1 Th 3:6-12 *1 Th 3:12;* 4:9-10
4 another never stops increasing; •and among the churches of God we can take *Ac 14:22*
special pride in you for your constancy and faith under all the persecutions and 1 Co 1:2+ 1 Th 1:7-8; 2:19-20
5 troubles you have to bear. •It all shows that God's judgement is just, and the
purpose of it is that you may be found worthy of the kingdom of God; it is for the Mt 4:17+ 1 Th 2:14; 3:4+
sake of this that you are suffering now.
6 7 God will very rightly repay with injury those who are injuring you, •and reward Ph 1:28 *Rv 14:13*
you, who are suffering now, with the same peace as he will give us,[a] when the Lord
8 Jesus appears from heaven with the angels of his power. •He will come *in flaming* 1 Co 1:7+ *Ex 3:2*
fire[b] to impose the penalty on *all who do not acknowledge God* and *refuse to accept* Is 66:15 *Jr 10:25*
9 the Good News of our Lord Jesus.[c] •It will be their punishment to be lost eter- *Is 66:4* Rm 1:5+
nally, excluded *from the presence of the Lord and from the glory of his strength* Is 2:10
10 *on that day* when he comes *to be glorified among his saints* and *seen in his glory* *Is 2:11-17;* 49:3; 66:5
by all who believe in him;[d] and you are believers, through our witness.[e] Ps (LXX) 68: 34; 89:7
11 Knowing this, we pray continually that our God will make you worthy of his
call, and by his power fulfil all your[f] desires for goodness and complete all that Ph 2:13
12 you have been doing through faith; •because in this way *the name* of our Lord Is 66:5; 24:15
Jesus Christ *will be glorified* in you and you in him, by the grace of our God and the *Jn 17:10.24*
Lord Jesus Christ.

The coming of the Lord and the prelude to it[a]

1 **2** To turn now, brothers, to the coming of our Lord Jesus Christ and how we Mt 24:31+ 1 Co 15:23
2 shall all be gathered round him: •please do not get excited too soon or 1 Th 4:15-17
alarmed by any prediction or rumour or any letter claiming to come from us, 3:17

1 a. Paul often compares his own situation with that of the churches he is writing to, cf. 1 Th 2:3; 1 Co 4:8; Ph 1:30, etc.

b. Heaven, cf. 1 Th 4:16, the angels, cf. Mt 13:39, 41,49; 16:27p; 24:31; 25:31; Lk 12:8f (and probably the 'saints' of 1 Th 3:13), the 'fire' of various theophanies, cf. Ex 13:22+; 19:16+, are all conventional elements of apocalyptic literature, cf. 1 Th 4:16+.

c. I.e. both pagans, 1 Th 4:5, and Jews, Rm 10:16.

d. Paul here seems to be thinking of angels (the 'saints', cf. Ac 9:13+) and Christians ('those who believe').

e. Vv.6-10 form a parenthesis, v.11 follows on from v.5.

f. Or 'his'

2 a. In 1 Th 4:13-5:11 Paul avoided suggesting anything that would indicate when the *parousia* would take place, cf. 1 Th 5:1+. Obviously replying to further questions, Paul does not now repeat all he said, about what would happen to the living and the dead: all he is concerned with is to emphasise that the coming is not imminent, and that it cannot take place till certain specific signs have preceded it.

1 Co 1:8+ Ga 1:6 implying that the Day of the Lord has already arrived. •Never let anyone 3
deceive you in this way.
Rv 13:1-8 It cannot happen until the Great Revolt[b] has taken place and the Rebel, the
Lost One, has appeared. •This is the Enemy,[c] the one who claims to be so much 4
Dn 11:36 *greater than all* that men call 'god', so much greater than anything that is worship-
Is 14:13 Ezk 28:2 ped, that *he enthrones himself* in *God's* sanctuary and claims that he is God.
Surely you remember me telling you about this when I was with you? •And you 5 6
Rv 20:3 know, too, what is still holding him back[d] from appearing before his appointed
Rv 17:5 time. •Rebellion is at its work already, but in secret,[e] and the one who is holding 7
it back has first to be removed •before the Rebel appears openly.[f] The Lord[g] 8
Is 11:4 Ps 33:6 Rv 19:11-21 *will kill him with the breath of his mouth* and will annihilate him with his glorious
appearance at his coming.
Ep 2:2 Rv 13:13-17 But when the Rebel comes, Satan will set to work:[h] there will be all kinds of 9
Mt 24:12 miracles and a deceptive show of signs and portents, •and everything evil that 10
Jn 8:44 Heb 3:13 can deceive those who are bound for destruction because they would not grasp
1 K 22:22 Is 6:10 the love of the truth which could have saved them. •The reason why God 11
is sending a power to delude them and make them believe what is untrue •is 12
Jn 3:19; 9:39 to condemn all who refused to believe in the truth and chose wickedness
instead.[i]

Encouragement to persevere[j]

But we feel that we must be continually thanking God for you, brothers whom 13
1 Th 1:4-5 the Lord loves, because God chose you from the beginning[k] to be saved by the
1 Th 4:3+,8 1 P 1:2 sanctifying Spirit and by faith in the truth. •Through the Good News that we 14
brought he called you to this so that you should share the glory of our Lord Jesus
1 Th 3:6,8 *1 Co 11:2+* Christ. •Stand firm, then, brothers, and keep the traditions that we taught you, 15
1 Th 3:11-13 whether by word of mouth or by letter.[l] •May our Lord Jesus Christ himself, and 16
God our Father who has given us his love and, through his grace, such inexhaustible comfort and such sure hope, •comfort you and strengthen you in everything 17
good that you do or say.

Ps 147:15 Ep 6:19f 3 Finally, brothers, pray for us; pray that the Lord's message may spread 1
Col 4:3 1 Th 5:25 quickly, and be received with honour as it was among you; •and pray that we 2
Heb 13:18 *Rm 10:16* may be preserved from the interference of bigoted and evil people, for faith is not
Mt 6:13 1 Th 5:24 given to everyone. •But the Lord is faithful, and he will give you strength and 3
1 Jn 2:14+ *2 Co 7:16* guard you from the evil one,[a] •and we, in the Lord, have every confidence that 4
you are doing and will go on doing all that we tell you. •May the Lord turn your 5
1 Co 13:13+ hearts towards the love of God and the fortitude of Christ.

Against idleness and disunity

1 Th 4:1,11-12; 5:14 In the name of the Lord Jesus Christ, we urge you, brothers, to keep away from 6
2:15+; 3:14 any of the brothers who refuses to work or to live according to the tradition we
passed on to you.
Ac 18:3+ 1 Co 11:1 You know how you are supposed to imitate us:[b] now we were not idle when 7
Ga 4:12 1 Th 2:9+ we were with you, •nor did we ever have our meals at anyone's table without 8
Mt 6:11 paying for them; no, we worked night and day, slaving and straining, so as not to
Mt 10:10 be a burden on any of you. •This was not because we had no right to be, but in 9
order to make ourselves an example for you to follow.
We gave you a rule when we were with you: not to let anyone have any food if 10
he refused to do any work.[c] •Now we hear that there are some of you who are 11
living in idleness, doing no work themselves but interfering with everyone else's.
Gn 3:19 In the Lord Jesus Christ, we order and call on people of this kind to go on quietly 12
working and earning the food that they eat.
Ga 6:9 *3:6* My brothers, never grow tired of doing what is right. •If anyone refuses to obey 13 14
1 Co 5:5,9-11 2 Co 2:7 what I have written in this letter, take note of him and have nothing to do with
Ga 6:1 1 Th 5:14 him, so that he will feel that he is in the wrong; •though you are not to regard him 15
Mt 18:15-18 as an enemy but as a brother in need of correction.

Prayer and farewell wishes

16 May the Lord of peace himself give you peace all the time and in every way.[d] Jn 14:27 1 Th 5:23
The Lord be with you all.
17 From me, PAUL, these greetings in my own handwriting, which is the mark Ga 6:11+ Col 4:18
18 of genuineness in every letter; this is my own writing. •May the grace of our Lord 2:2
Jesus Christ be with you all.[e]

b. The way this Revolt *(apostasia)* is mentioned here shows that the Thessalonians had already been told something about it. The word is used here in its usual sense of 'secession' or 'defection' but with a specifically religious reference, Ac 5:37; 21:21; Heb 3:12. It seems that the rebels are not only those who have never belonged to Christ but also those who have given up the faith, cf. 1 Tm 4:1; 2 Tm 3:1; 4:3f; etc.

c. The apostasy will be due to a being who is given three names. He is the 'Rebel' (lit. 'man of lawlessness' or 'man of sin'). He is a being destined to be lost (lit. 'son of perdition') v.10; Jn 17:12; cf. 1 Th 5:5. He is the enemy of God and is described here in terms reminiscent of the description of Antiochus Epiphanes in Dn 11:36. Later on in Christian tradition, based on Dn, he is called the Antichrist, cf. 1 Jn 2:18; 4:3; 2 Jn 7. Unlike Satan, whose tool he is, and who is already at work in 'secret' (lit. 'the mystery') v.7, the lawless one is represented as a person who will be revealed at the 'end of time', and whose power will persecute and seduce Christians. On the final 'test', that will only come to an end with the *parousia* of Christ, cf Mt 24:24; Rv 13:1-8.

d. We do not know what Paul refers to when he talks about a cause that delays the *parousia* of Christ. All he says is that it is something, v.6, or someone, v.7, that can 'delay' it. This person or power blocks the coming of Christ by preventing the manifestation of the Messiah's enemy who must precede the coming of the Messiah himself.

e. Rebellion (lit. 'lawlessness') is going on, but it is underground, secretly preparing for the great revolt. When the obstacle, whatever it is, is removed, lawlessness (or the lawless one) will work unmasked.

f. The revealing of the Rebel, vv. 6-8, is the counterpart of the revealing of Christ, 1:7; 1 Co 1:7, in the same way as his *parousia* is the counterpart of Christ's *parousia*, v.8. The enemy of God becomes the enemy of Christ, but Christ will conquer his enemy.

g. Add. 'Jesus'

h. The Rebel is the instrument through which Satan works, cf. 1 Th 2:18, and whom he endows with superhuman power rather as Christ endows his followers with his own Spirit. Cf. the Dragon and the Beast, Rv 13:2,4.

i. Truth and untruth here have a religious as well as an intellectual reference because they involve the whole of human life and activity, cf. 1 Jn 3:19.

j. This passage, 2:13-3:5, is very closely linked to the description of the *parousia*. Having corrected the false ideas of the Thessalonians, Paul goes on to describe the positive consequences of his conception.

k. Var. 'as first-fruits'.

l. What Paul taught them when he was in Thessalonika and what he had written to them since he returned from there, 2:2,5; 1 Th 3:4; 4:2,6; 5:27, include, in the message of the Good News, cf. 1 Th 2:13+, the principles on which a Christian should lead his life, cf. 1 Th 4:1; 1 Co 11:2,23-25.

3 a. Or perhaps 'from evil'. Christians will be tempted but not beyond their powers of resistance, 1 Co 10:13.

b. By imitating Paul, 1 Co 4:16; Ga 4:12; Ph 3:17, Christians will be imitating Christ, 1 Th 1:6; Ph 2:5; cf. Mt 16:24; 1 P 2:21; 1 Jn 2:6, who is himself the one that Paul is imitating, 1 Co 11:1. Christians must also imitate God, Ep 5:1 (cf. Mt 5:48), and they must imitate each other, 1 Th 1:7; 2:14; Heb 6:12. Behind this community of life is the idea of a model of doctrine, Rm 6:17, that has been received by tradition, v.6; 1 Co 11:2+; 1 Th 2:13+. The leaders who transmit the doctrine must themselves be 'models' v.9; Ph 3:17; 1 Tm 1:16; 4:12; Tt 2:7; 1 P 5:3, whose faith and life are to be imitated, Heb 13:7.

c. This may have been laid down by Jesus, but it may have been a proverb: it has been called the golden rule for Christian work.

d. Var. (Vulg.) 'everywhere'.

e. Add. 'Amen', cf. 1 Th 3:13; 5:28.

1 TIMOTHY

THE FIRST LETTER FROM PAUL TO TIMOTHY

Address

Rm 1:1 Ph 3:20 1 From Paul, apostle of Christ Jesus appointed by the command[a] of God our 1
Tt 1:3 *Ac 16:1* saviour[b] and of Christ Jesus our hope, •to Timothy, true child of mine in the 2
faith; wishing you grace, mercy and peace from God the Father and from Christ
Jesus our Lord.

Suppress the false teachers

As I asked you when I was leaving for Macedonia, please stay at Ephesus, to 3
insist that certain people stop teaching strange doctrines •and taking notice of 4
4:7; 6:4,20 2 Tm 2:14, myths and endless genealogies;[c] these things are only likely to raise irrelevant
16,23; 4:4 Tt 1:14; 3:9 doubts instead of furthering the designs of God[d] which are revealed in faith.
The only purpose of this instruction is that there should be love, coming out 5
of a pure heart, a clear conscience and a sincere faith. •There are some people 6
who have gone off the straight course and taken a road that leads to empty
speculation; •they claim to be doctors of the Law but they understand neither 7
the arguments they are using nor the opinions they are upholding.

The purpose of the Law

Rm 7:7, 12f+ We know, of course, that the Law[e] is good, but only provided it is treated 8
Ga 5:23 like any law,[f] •in the understanding that laws are not framed for people who 9
Rm 1:29+ are good.[g] On the contrary, they are for criminals and revolutionaries, for the
irreligious and the wicked, for the sacrilegious and the irreverent; they are for
people who kill their fathers or mothers and for murderers, •for those who are 10
Rv 18:13 immoral with women or with boys or with men, for liars and for perjurers—and
6:3 Tt 1:9,13 for everything else that is contrary to the sound teaching[h] •that goes with the 11
Jn 1:14 2 Co 4:4 Good News of the glory of the blessed God, the gospel that was entrusted to me.
1 Th 2:4 Tt 1:3; 2:13

Paul on his own calling

I thank Christ Jesus our Lord, who has given me strength, and who judged 12
me faithful enough to call me into his service •even though I used to be 13
Ac 8:3+ a blasphemer and did all I could to injure and discredit the faith. Mercy, however,
Ac 3:17+ was shown me, because until I became a believer I had been acting in ignorance;
Jn 16:2 1 Co 15:10 and the grace of our Lord filled me with faith and with the love that is in Christ 14
3:1; 4:9 Mt 9:13p Jesus. •Here is a saying that you can rely on[i] and nobody should doubt: that 15
Tt 3:8 2 P 3:15 Christ Jesus came into the world to save sinners. I myself am the greatest of them;
1 Co 15:9 and if mercy has been shown to me, it is because Jesus Christ meant to make 16
2 Th 3:7+ me the greatest evidence of his inexhaustible patience for all the other people
6:16 Tb 13:6 who would later have to trust in him to come to eternal life. •To the eternal 17
Ps 145:13 Rm 16:27+ King, the undying,[j] invisible and only God, be honour and glory for ever and
Col 1:15 ever. Amen.

Timothy's responsibility

18 Timothy, my son, these are the instructions that I am giving you: I ask you
to remember the words once spoken over you by the prophets,[k] and taking them 4:14+
19 to heart to fight like a good soldier •with faith and a good conscience for your 2 Tm 4:7
weapons. Some people have put conscience aside and wrecked their faith in
20 consequence. •I mean men like Hymenaeus and Alexander, whom I have handed 2 Tm 2:17; 4:14
over to Satan to teach them not to be blasphemous. 1 Co 5:5+

Liturgical prayer

1 **2** My advice is[a] that, first of all, there should be prayers offered for everyone Ba 1:11
2 —petitions, intercessions and thanksgiving—•and especially for kings and Rm 13:1-7+ Tt 3:1
others in authority,[b] so that we may be able to live religious and reverent lives
3 4 in peace and quiet. •To do this is right, and will please God our saviour: •he 1:1+
5 wants everyone to be saved[c] and reach full knowledge of the truth. •For there Ezk 18:23+ Jn 8:32
is only one God, and there is only one mediator between God and mankind, 2 Tm 3:7 *Heb 8:6+*
6 himself a man, Christ Jesus, •who sacrificed himself as a ransom for them all. *6:13+* Mt 20:28p
7 He is the evidence of this, sent at the appointed time,[d] and •I have been named 2 Co 5:15 Ga 1:4
a herald and apostle of it and—I am telling the truth and no lie—a teacher of Ep 5:2 *Rm 3:26*
the faith and the truth to the pagans. 2 Tm 1:11 *Ac 9:15*
8 In every place, then, I want the men to lift their hands up reverently Ga 2:7
in prayer, with no anger or argument.

Women in the assembly

9 Similarly, I direct that women are to wear suitable clothes and to be dressed 1 P 3:2-4
quietly and modestly, without braided hair or gold and jewellery or expensive Is 3:16f
10 clothes; their adornment is •to do the sort of good works that are proper for
11 women who profess to be religious. •During instruction, a woman should be 1 Co 14:34-35
12 quiet and respectful. •I am not giving permission for a woman to teach or to *Gn 3:16*
13 tell a man what to do. A woman ought not to speak, •because Adam was Si 25:24 1 Co 11:3, 8-12
14 formed first and Eve afterwards, •and it was not Adam who was led astray but *Gn 2:18,21f;* 3:12-13
15 the woman who was led astray and fell into sin. •Nevertheless, she will be saved
by childbearing,[e] provided she lives a modest life and is constant in faith and
love and holiness. 1 Co 13:13+

The elder-in-charge

Tt 1:6-9

1 **3** Here is a saying that you can rely on: To want to be a presiding elder[a] is to 1:15+
2 want to do a noble work. •That is why the president must have an impeccable 2 Tm 2:24

1 a. Var. 'the promise'

b. Paul hardly ever uses the title 'saviour' in his other letters, Ep 5:23; Ph 3:20, but in the Pastoral Letters he makes use of it both when referring to the Father, 1 Tm 2:3; 4:10; Tt 1:3; 2:10; 3:4, and when referring to Christ, 2 Tm 1:10; Tt 1:4; 3:6.

c. Genealogies of O.T. patriarchs and heroes constructed by Jewish writers in the same style as those in the *Book of Jubilees*.

d. Var. (Vulg.) 'the building-up of God's house'.

e. The 'Law of Moses'.

f. Lit. 'Now the Law is good if anyone uses it lawfully', i.e. without asking it to be more than it claims to be.

g. Seen as a penal code, the aim of the Law is to make provision not for the righteous, but for offenders, by threatening, accusing and punishing them.

h. One characteristic of the Pastoral Letters is this insistence on 'sound doctrine', cf. 6:3; 2 Tm 1:13; 4:3; Tt 1:9,13; 2:1,8.

i. Lit. 'faithful is the word (or 'saying')': this is one of the characteristic phrases of the Pastoral Letters, cf. 3:1; 4:9; 2 Tm 2:11; Tt 3:8.

j. Lit. 'incorruptible' or 'imperishable'; var. (Vulg.) 'immortal'.

k. Here and in 4:14 Paul reminds Timothy of the part played by the 'prophets' when the college of elders laid their hands on his head, Ac 13:1-3; 11:27+.

2 a. 'My advice is'; var. 'Advise'.

b. Nero was emperor when this was written: the end of the verse probably reflects Paul's apprehensions about what the future would bring. On Paul's political loyalty, cf. Rm 13:1-7.

c. This is a statement with enormous theological implications, and it provides the correct interpretation of some passages in the letter to the Christians at Rome, cf. Rm 9:18,21.

d. Cf. 6:13. By his willingness to die for the whole human race Christ showed the human race that God wanted everybody to be saved. He was the Father's 'witness' all through his life, but never so supremely as at the moment of his execution. (The Greek word for 'witness' is the same as for 'martyr'.)

e. It is not clear whether Paul is implying that women are saved by the 'one-body' relationship with their marriage partners or whether childbearing itself, as the mediation of life and the bringing up of children, constitutes a vocation. He may quite easily have been thinking specifically of the 'false teachers' who condemned marriage, 4:3.

3 a. The word '*episcopos*' ('overseer', 'supervisor' or 'president') has not yet acquired the same meaning as 'bishop', cf. Tt 1:5f+.

3:12 Tt 2:6+ character. He must not have been married more than once, and he must be
temperate, discreet and courteous, hospitable and a good teacher; •not a heavy 3
drinker, nor hot-tempered, but kind and peaceable. He must not be a lover of
3:12 money. •He must be a man who manages his own family well and brings his 4
children up to obey him and be well-behaved: •how can any man who does not 5
1 Co 1:2+ understand how to manage his own family have responsibility for the church
of God? •He should not be a new convert, in case pride might turn his head 6
and then he might be condemned as the devil was condemned. •It is also 7
1 Co 5:12+ necessary that people outside the Church should speak well of him, so that he
never gets a bad reputation and falls into the devil's trap.

Ac 6:1-6 **Deacons**

In the same way, deacons must be respectable men whose word can be 8
1 P 5:2 trusted, moderate in the amount of wine they drink and with no squalid greed
Rm 16:25+ for money. •They must be conscientious believers in the mystery of the faith. 9
They are to be examined first, and only admitted to serve as deacons if there 10
is nothing against them. •In the same way, the women[b] must be respectable, 11
3:2,4 not gossips but sober and quite reliable. •Deacons must not have been married 12
more than once, and must be men who manage their children and families
well.• Those of them who carry out their duties well as deacons will earn a 13
high standing for themselves and be rewarded with great assurance in their
work for the faith in Christ Jesus.

The Church and the mystery of the spiritual life

At the moment of writing to you, I am hoping that I may be with you soon; 14
Tt 1:7 but in case I should be delayed, I wanted you to know how people ought to behave 15
1 Co 1:2+ Ep 2:20+ in God's family—that is, in the Church of the living God, which upholds the
Heb 3:6 *Rm 16:25+* truth and keeps it safe. •Without any doubt, the mystery of our religion is very 16
deep indeed:

Jn 1:14 Rm 1:3-4 He[c] was made visible in the flesh,
attested by the Spirit,
Jn 16:10 Ep 3:10 1 P 1:12 seen by angels,
proclaimed to the pagans,
believed in by the world,
Mk 16:19 Ac 1:2,11 taken up in glory.[d]

False teachers

Mt 24:23-24 Ac 20:29-30 **4** The Spirit has explicitly said that during the last times[a] there will be some 1
2 Tm 3:1; 4:3 who will desert the faith and choose to listen to deceitful spirits and doctrines
Tt 1:10 Heb 1:1-2 that come from the devils; •and the cause of this is the lies told by hypocrites 2
2 P 2:1; 3:3 1 Jn 2:18; whose consciences are branded as though with a red-hot iron:[b] •they will say 3
4:1 *Col 2:16-23* marriage is forbidden, and lay down rules about abstaining from foods which
2:4 Gn 9:3 God created to be accepted with thanksgiving by all who believe and who know
Gn 1:31+ 1 Co 10:25f, the truth.[c] •Everything God has created is good, and no food is to be rejected, 4
30f *Mt 15:11f* provided grace is said for it: •the word of God and the prayer make it holy. 5
Rm 14:14,20 If you put all this to the brothers, you will be a good servant of Christ Jesus and 6
2 Tm 2:15 show that you have really digested the teaching of the faith and the good doctrine
1:4+ which you have always followed. •Have nothing to do with godless myths and 7
old wives' tales. Train yourself spiritually. •'Physical exercises are useful enough, 8
but the usefulness of spirituality is unlimited, since it holds out the reward of
1:15+ life here and now and of the future life as well'; •that is a saying that you can 9
rely on and nobody should doubt it. •I mean that the point of all our toiling and 10
1:1+ battling is that we have put our trust in the living God and he is the saviour of
the whole human race but particularly of all believers. •This is what you are to 11
enforce in your teaching.

12 Do not let people disregard you because you are young, but be an example 1 Co 16:11 Ga 5:22
to all the believers in the way you speak and behave, and in your love, your faith 2 Th 3:7+ Tt 2:7-8,15
13 and your purity. •Make use of the time until I arrive by reading to the people, *6:11* Ga 5:22+
14 preaching and teaching. •You have in you a spiritual gift which was given to 1:18+
you when the prophets spoke and the body of elders laid their hands on you;[d] Mt 9:18; 19:13
15 do not let it lie unused. •Think hard about all this, and put it into practice, and Lk 4:40 Ac 6:6; 8:17;
16 everyone will be able to see how you are advancing. •Take great care about what 9-12; 19:6; 28:8
you do and what you teach; always do this, and in this way you will save both 2 Tm 1:6; 2:2
yourself and those who listen to you. Heb 6:2

Pastoral practice

1 **5** Do not speak harshly to a man older than yourself, but advise him as you Lv 19:32 Tt 2:2
2 would your own father; treat the younger men as brothers •and older women
as you would your mother. Always treat young women with propriety, as if they
were sisters.

Widows

3 Be considerate to widows; I mean those who are truly widows.[a] •If a widow
4 has children or grandchildren, they are[b] to learn first of all to do their duty to
their own families and repay their debt to their parents, because this is what
5 pleases God. •But a woman who is really widowed and left without anybody
can give herself up to God and consecrate all her days and nights to petitions Lk 2:37
6 and prayer. •The one who thinks only of pleasure is already dead while she Rv 3:1
7 is still alive: •remind them of all this, too, so that their lives may be blameless.
8 Anyone who does not look after his own relations, especially if they are living
with him, has rejected the faith and is worse than an unbeliever.
9 Enrolment as a widow is permissible only for a woman at least sixty years
10 old who has had only one husband. •She must be a woman known for her good
works and for the way in which she has brought up her children, shown hospi-
tality to strangers and washed the saints' feet,[c] helped people who are in trouble Jn 13:14 Ac 9:13+
11 and been active in all kinds of good work. •Do not accept young widows because 1 Co 7:8
if their natural desires get stronger than their dedication to Christ, they want
12 to marry again, •and then people condemn them for being unfaithful to their
13 original promise.[d] •Besides, they learn how to be idle and go round from house
to house; and then, not merely idle, they learn to be gossips and meddlers in
other people's affairs, and to chatter when they would be better keeping quiet.
14 I think it is best for young widows to marry again[e] and have children and a home

b. This instruction is probably intended for the deaconesses, cf. Rm 16:1, rather than for the wives of deacons.

c. He, i.e. Christ: many authorities (e.g. Vulg.) read 'It', i.e. the 'mystery', cf. Col 2:3+. Paul is quoting part of an early Christian hymn, cf. 6:15-16; 2 Tm 2:11-13; Ph 2:6-11. Also cf. Ep 1:3-14; 5:14; Col 1:15-20.

d. 'attested (lit. 'justified') by the Spirit': the holiness and divinity of Christ were proved by the fact that he rose in glory, cf. Rm 1:4+. 'Taken up in glory', i.e. at the ascension.

4 a. On the crisis that will characterise the 'last times' cf. 2 Th 2:3-12; 2 Tm 3:1; 4:3-4; 2 P 3:3; Jude 18. Also cf. Mt 24:6fp; Ac 20:29-30. As, eschatologically, the 'last times' have already begun, Rm 3:26+, we are already living in this final epoch of crisis, cf. 1 Co 7:26; Ep 5:6; 6:13; Jm 5:3; 1 Jn 2:18; 4:1,3; 2 Jn 7; Mt 26:41.

b. Lit. 'Having been marked with a red-hot branding iron on their own conscience', i.e. branded like runaway slaves.

c. The rejection of marriage was to be one of the hallmarks of Gnosticism: dietary regulations were more specifically Jewish.

d. Lit. 'a spiritual gift given by means of prophecy with imposition of hands by the body of elders'. The 'imposition of hands' can be the rite for transmitting grace or a charism, Heb 6:2, or it can be the gesture used when blessing, Mt 19:15, or curing, Mt 9:18p; Mk 6:5; 7:32; 8:23-25; 16:18; Lk 4:40; 13:13; Ac 9:12, 17; 28:8, or imparting the Holy Spirit to the newly baptised, Ac 1:5+. It can also be the rite for consecrating a person for a particular public function, Ac 6:6; 13:3, as in this passage and 5:22+; 2 Tm 1:6. Since the day on which he received the imposition of hands, Timothy has had a permanent charism ('grace-gift') that consecrates him to his ministry. For the part played by the 'prophets', cf. 1 Tm 1:18.

5 a. Three categories of widows are mentioned here: those who do not need assistance from the Church since they have relations to look after them, v. 4; those who are 'true widows' because they have no one to look after them, and whom the Church is obliged to help, vv. 3-5,16; and those who (whether helped by the Church or not) are called by the Church to fulfil certain official functions. Widows in this third category have to satisfy quite severe regulations, vv. 9-15.

b. Var. (Vulg.) 'she is'.

c. The normal courtesy then shown to guests.

d. Lit. 'for setting aside (their) first faith', i.e. their vow or promise to consecrate themselves to God.

e. Made wiser by experience, Paul modifies what he had said, 1 Co 7:8,40.

Tt 2:8 to look after, and not give the enemy any chance[f] to raise a scandal about them;
there are already some who have left us to follow Satan. •If a Christian woman 15 16
has widowed relatives, she should support them and not make the Church bear
the expense but enable it to support those who are genuinely widows.

Tt 1:5+ **The elders**

The elders who do their work well while they are in charge are to be given 17
1 Th 5:12+ double consideration,[g] especially those who are assiduous in preaching and
Dt 25:4 Lk 10:7 teaching. •As scripture says: *You must not muzzle an ox when it is treading out* 18
1 Co 9:9 3 Jn 8 *the corn;* and again: *The worker deserves his pay.*[h] •Never accept any accusation 19
Dt 19:15 Mt 18:16 brought against an elder unless it is supported *by two or three witnesses.* •If any 20
2 Co 13:1 of them are at fault, reprimand them publicly, as a warning to the rest. •Before 21
God, and before Jesus Christ and the angels he has chosen, I put it to you as a
duty to keep these rules impartially and never to be influenced by favouritism.
Do not be too quick to lay hands on any man,[i] and never make yourself an 22
accomplice in anybody else's sin; keep yourself pure.
Si 31:28 You should give up drinking only water and have a little wine for the sake 23
of your digestion and the frequent bouts of illness that you have.
The faults of some people are obvious long before anyone makes any 24
complaint about them, while others have faults that are not discovered until
Mt 5:16 afterwards. •In the same way, the good that people do can be obvious; but even 25
Mt 10:26p when it is not, it cannot be hidden for ever.

Slaves

Rm 2:24+; 6:15+ 6 All slaves 'under the yoke' must have unqualified respect for their masters, 1
1 Co 7:21-22 so that the name of God and our teaching are not brought into disrepute.
Ep 6:5-8 Col 3:22-25 Slaves whose masters are believers are not to think any the less of them because 2
Tt 2:6+, 9-10 they are brothers; on the contrary, they should serve them all the better,
since those who have the benefit of their services are believers and dear to
God.[a]

The true teacher and the false teacher

This is what you are to teach them to believe and persuade them to do.
1:10+ Anyone who teaches anything different, and does not keep to the sound teaching 3
which is that of our Lord Jesus Christ, the doctrine which is in accordance with
1:4+ true religion, •is simply ignorant and must be full of self-conceit—with a craze 4
for questioning everything and arguing about words. All that can come of this
Rm 1:29+ is jealousy, contention, abuse and wicked mistrust of one another; •and unending 5
disputes by people who are neither rational nor informed and imagine that
religion is a way of making a profit. •Religion, of course, does bring 6
Tb 4:21 Jb 1:21 large profits, but only to those who are content with what they have. •We brought 7
Qo 5:14 *Ps 49:17* nothing into the world, and we can take nothing out of it; •but as long as we 8
have food and clothing, let us be content with that. •People who long to be rich 9
are a prey to temptation; they get trapped into all sorts of foolish[b] and dangerous
ambitions which eventually plunge them into ruin and destruction. •'The love 10
Mt 6:24 Tt 1:11 of money is the root of all evils'[c] and there are some who, pursuing it, have
wandered away from the faith, and so given their souls any number of fatal
wounds.

2 Tm 4:1 **Timothy's vocation recalled**

2 Tm 2:22 But, as a man dedicated to God, you must avoid all that. You must aim to 11
1 Co 13:13+ Ga 5:22+ be saintly and religious, filled with faith and love, patient and gentle. •Fight the 12
Tt 2:2 *2 Tm 4:7* good fight of the faith and win for yourself the eternal life to which you were
called when you made your profession and spoke up for the truth[d] in front of
many witnesses. •Now, before God the source of all life and before Jesus Christ, 13
2:6+ Jn 18:36-37 who spoke up as a witness for the truth in front of Pontius Pilate,[e] I put to you

14 the duty •of doing all that you have been told, with no faults or failures, until
the Appearing[f] of our Lord Jesus Christ, 2 Tm 4:1,8 Heb 9:28

15 who at the due time will be revealed
by God, the blessed and only Ruler of all,
the King of kings and the Lord of lords, Dt 10:17 2 M 13:4 *Ps 136:3*
16 who alone is immortal, Rv 17:14
whose home is in inaccessible light, *1 Jn 1:5+*
whom no man has seen and no man is able to see: Ex 33:20+ Jn 1:17-18+
to him be honour and everlasting power. Amen. 1:17

Rich Christians

17 Warn those who are rich in this world's goods that they are not to look down
on other people; and not to set their hopes on money, which is untrustworthy, Lk 12:17-21 Jm 1:10
but on God[g] who, out of his riches, gives us all that we need for our happiness.
18 Tell them that they are to do good, and be rich in good works, to be generous
19 and willing to share—•this is the way they can save up a good capital sum for Mt 6:20 Ph 4:17
the future if they want to make sure of the only life that is real.

Final warning and conclusion

20 My dear Timothy, take great care of all that has been entrusted to you.[h] Have 1:4+ 2 Tm 1:12,
nothing to do with the pointless philosophical discussions and antagonistic 14; 2:2; 3:14
21 beliefs of the 'knowledge' which is not knowledge at all; •by adopting this, some Tt 2:1
have gone right away from the faith. Grace be with you.[i]

f. Lit. 'so as to give no occasion for reviling to the one who opposes'; this could refer to Satan, but Paul may be referring to unfriendly, anti-Christian neighbours.

g. Lit. 'let them be deemed worthy of being paid double honour' (or 'doubly paid').

h. Var. 'his keep', cf. Mt 10:10.

i. I.e. to confer a function in the Church, cf. 4:14+. Some writers have considered this a reference to a gesture made when absolving sinners.

6 a. Or 'and dear brothers'.

b. 'trapped', var. (Vulg.) 'trapped by the devil in their own temptations'. 'foolish'; Vulg. 'useless'.

c. A contemporary proverb.

d. When had Timothy 'spoken up for the truth'? Perhaps at his baptism, or possibly when he was consecrated to the ministry.

e. When he declared himself to be the messianic King and the revealer of Truth, Jn 18:36-37. This is the great example of how a follower of Christ should proclaim his faith, whether at his baptism or when faced with persecution.

f. The word 'epiphany' ('appearing', used in 2 Th 2:8 with reference to the Great Rebel) is adopted in the Pastoral Letters in preference to *'parousia'* ('Coming', 1 Co 15:23+), or 'apocalypse' ('revealing', 1 Co 1:7+), as the technical term here; 2 Tm 4:1,8; Tt 2:13; Heb 9:28, both for the manifestation of Christ in his eschatological triumph, and also, 2 Tm 1:10; cf. Tt 2:11; 3:4, for his manifestation in the results of his action as saviour.

g. Var. (Vulg.) 'the living God'.

h. The faith that has been entrusted to him: this is one of the main themes of the Pastoral Letters.

i. 'you', plural; var. (Vulg.) 'you' singular. Add. (Vulg.) 'Amen'.

2 TIMOTHY

THE SECOND LETTER FROM PAUL TO TIMOTHY

Greeting and thanksgiving

Rm 1:1+ **1** From Paul, appointed by God to be an apostle of Christ Jesus in his design 1
Ac 16:1+ to promise life in Christ Jesus; •to Timothy, dear child of mine, wishing you 2
grace, mercy and peace from God the Father and from Christ Jesus our Lord.
Rm 1:9+ Ph 3:5 Night and day I thank God, keeping my conscience clear and remembering 3
my duty to him as my ancestors did, and always I remember you in my prayers;
4:9,21 I remember your tears[a] •and long to see you again to complete my happiness. 4
Then I am reminded of the sincere faith which you have; it came first to live in 5
Ac 16:1 your grandmother Lois, and your mother Eunice, and I have no doubt that it
3:14-15 is the same faith in you as well.

The gifts that Timothy has received

That is why I am reminding you now to fan into a flame the gift that God 6
Ac 4:20-21 Rm 8:15 gave you when I laid my hands on you. •God's gift was not a spirit of timidity, 7
1 Tm 4:14+ *1:16* but the Spirit of power, and love, and self-control. •So you are never to be 8
Lk 9:26 Rm 1:16; ashamed of witnessing to the Lord, or ashamed of me for being his prisoner;
5:3f Ep 3:13 but with me, bear the hardships for the sake of the Good News, relying on the
Tt 3:5 power of God •who has saved us and called us to be holy[b]—not because of 9
Rm 8:28 anything we ourselves have done but for his own purpose and by his own grace.
This grace had already been granted to us, in Christ Jesus, before the beginning
Rm 16:25 Tt 2:11; 3:4 of time, •but it has only been revealed by the Appearing[c] of our saviour Christ 10
Rm 6:9; 8:2 Heb 2:14-15 Jesus. He abolished death, and he has proclaimed life and immortality through
1 Tm 2:7 the Good News; •and I have been named its herald, its apostle and its teacher.[d] 11
It is only on account of this that I am experiencing fresh hardships here 12
now;[e] but I have not lost confidence, because I know who it is that I have put
1 Tm 6:20+ my trust in, and I have no doubt at all that he is able to take care of all that
1 Co 1:8+ I have entrusted to him[f] until that Day.
1 Tm 1:10+ Keep as your pattern the sound teaching you have heard from me, in the 13
1 Tm 6:20+ faith and love that are in Christ Jesus. •You have been trusted to look after 14
Rm 5:5+ something precious; guard it with the help of the Holy Spirit who lives in us.
As you know, Phygelus and Hermogenes and all the others from Asia refuse 15
4:19 to have anything more to do with me. •I hope the Lord will be kind to all the 16
family of Onesiphorus, because he has often been a comfort to me and has never
1:8+ been ashamed of my chains. •On the contrary, as soon as he reached Rome, he 17
really searched hard for me and found out where I was. •May it be the Lord's 18
will that he shall find the Lord's mercy on that Day.[g] You know better than
anyone else how much he helped me at Ephesus.

How Timothy should face hardships

3:14 1 Tm 4:14; 6:12 **2** Accept the strength, my dear son, that comes from the grace of Christ Jesus. 1
You have heard everything that I teach in public; hand it on to reliable 2
people so that they in turn will be able to teach others.

3 Put up with your share of difficulties, like a good soldier of Christ Jesus.[a]
4 In the army, no soldier gets himself mixed up in civilian life, because he must 4:8
5 be at the disposal of the man who enlisted him; •or take an athlete—he cannot 1 Co 9:25+
6 win any crown unless he has kept all the rules of the contest; •and again, it is
7 the working farmer who has the first claim on any crop that is harvested. •Think 1 Co 3:6-9 Heb 6:7
over what I have said, and the Lord will show you how to understand it all. *1 Co 9:7.10*
8 Remember the Good News that I carry, 'Jesus Christ risen from the dead, Ac 13:22-23 Rm 1:3,4
9 sprung from the race of David'; •it is on account of this that I have my own
hardships to bear, even to being chained like a criminal—but they cannot chain Ep 3:1 Ph 1:13-18
10 up God's news. •So I bear it all for the sake of those who are chosen, so that *Col 1:24+*
in the end they may have the salvation that is in Christ Jesus and the eternal 1 Th 2:12
glory that comes with it.
11 Here is a saying that you can rely on:[b] 1 Tm 1:15+

If we have died with him, then we shall live with him. Rm 6:5+
12 If we hold firm, then we shall reign with him. Ac 14:22 Rm 8:17
If we disown him, then he will disown us. *Mt 10:33*
13 We may be unfaithful, but he is always faithful, Rm 3:3 1 Co 1:9+
for he cannot disown his own self. *Nb 23:19+* Tt 1:2 Heb 6:18

The struggle against the immediate danger from false teachers

14 Remind them of this; and tell them in the name of God[c] that there is to be
no wrangling about words: all that this ever achieves is the destruction of those 1 Tm 1:4+
15 who are listening. •Do all you can to present yourself in front of God as a man
who has come through his trials, and a man who has no cause to be ashamed 1 Tm 4:6-7
of his life's work and has kept a straight course with the message of the truth.
16 Have nothing to do with pointless philosophical discussions—they only lead
17 further and further away from true religion. •Talk of this kind corrodes like
18 gangrene, as in the case of Hymenaeus and Philetus, •the men who have gone 1 Tm 1:20
right away from the truth and claim that the resurrection has already taken
place.[d] Some people's faith cannot stand up to them.
19 However, God's solid foundation stone is still in position, and this is the Ep 2:20+
inscription on it: '*The Lord knows those who are his own*' and 'All who *call on* Nb 16:5,26 *Is 26:13*
the name of the Lord must avoid sin'.[e]
20 Not all the dishes in a large house are made of gold and silver; some are
made of wood or earthenware: some are kept for special occasions and others Is 29:66+ Rm 9:21
21 are for ordinary purposes. •Now, to avoid these faults that I am speaking about
is the way for anyone to become a vessel for special occasions, fit for the Master
himself to use, and kept ready for any good work.
22 Instead of giving in to your impulses like a young man, fasten your attention 1 Tm 6:11
on holiness, faith, love and peace, in union with all those who call on the Lord Ga 5:22+
23 with pure minds. •Avoid these futile and silly speculations, understanding that 1 Tm 1:4+
24 they only give rise to quarrels; •and a servant of the Lord is not to 1 Tm 3:2f Tt 1:7
engage in quarrels, but has to be kind to everyone, a good teacher, and patient.

1 a. When Paul left Timothy at Ephesus, 1 Tm 1:3.

b. Lit. 'and called us with a holy call': this may be taken in two ways here: the calling of Christians to salvation, cf. Rm 1:6-7; 8:28; 1 Co 1:2,24; Col 3:15; Ep 1:18; 4:4; Ph 3:14; etc., or (by metonymy) the state ('vocation') to which Christians have been called.

c. The 'Appearing' ('epiphany'), cf. 1 Tm 6:14+, here refers to the incarnation and redemption.

d. Add. (Vulg.) 'to the pagans'.

e. The second imprisonment at Rome.

f. Either Christian doctrine (by keeping it intact, 1 Tm 6:20+) or the good that Paul has done and his consequent merit, cf. 1 Tm 6:19; 2 Tm 4:7f.

g. 'Lord' can be taken in either case as a reference either to the Father or to the Son.

2 a. Vv. 4-6 are three short parables: the soldier, the athlete, the farm labourer.

b. Vv. 11-13 are part of a Christian hymn, cf. 1 Tm 3:16+.

c. Var. (Vulg.) 'the Lord'.

d. The Greek mind found the resurrection particularly hard to accept, Ac 17:32; 1 Co 15:12. Hymenaeus and Philetus may well have given it a purely spiritual interpretation by analogy with the mystical resurrection that occurs in baptism, Rm 6:4+; Ep 2:6+.

e. Details about a building were often inscribed on its foundation stone: as the building here is the Church, the foundation stone could be either Christ himself, 1 Co 3:11, or the apostles, Ep 2:20, cf. Rv 21:14, or faith in the unbreakable promise of God, cf. 2 Tm 2:13.

Is 42:3 Mt 12:20 He has to be gentle when he corrects people who dispute what he says, never 25
Ga 6:1 forgetting that God may give them a change of mind so that they recognise the
1 Jn 2:14+ truth and •come to their senses, once out of the trap where the devil caught 26
them and kept them enslaved.

The dangers of the last days

1 Tm 4:1+ **3** You may be quite sure that in the last days there are going to be 1
Rm 1:29+ some difficult times. •People will be self-centred and grasping; boastful, 2
arrogant and rude; disobedient to their parents, ungrateful, irreligious; •heartless 3
and unappeasable; they will be slanderers, profligates, savages and enemies of
everything that is good; •they will be treacherous and reckless and demented 4
by pride, preferring their own pleasure to God. •They will keep up the outward 5
Mt 7:15; 24:4f,24 appearance of religion but will have rejected the inner power of it.[a] Have nothing
Col 2:23 to do with people like that.
Tt 1:11 Of the same kind, too, are those men who insinuate themselves into families 6
in order to get influence over silly women who are obsessed with their sins and
Ac 17:21 follow one craze after another •in the attempt to educate themselves, but can 7
Jn 8:32 1 Tm 2:4 never come to knowledge of the truth. •Men like this defy the truth just as 8
Jannes and Jambres defied Moses:[b] their minds are corrupt and their faith
spurious.•But they will not be able to go on any longer: their foolishness, like 9
that of the other two, must become obvious to everybody.
1 Co 4:9 You know, though, what I have taught, how I have lived, what I have aimed 10
1 Co 13:13+ at; you know my faith, my patience and my love; my constancy •and the 11
Ac 14:5,22 2 Co 11:23f persecutions and hardships that came to me in places like Antioch, Iconium and
Lystra—all the persecutions I have endured; and the Lord has rescued me from
Ac 14:22+ Rm 8:36 every one of them. •You are well aware, then, that anybody who tries to live 12
1 Th 3:4-5 *Tt 1:10* in devotion to Christ is certain to be attacked; •while these wicked impostors 13
will go from bad to worse, deceiving others and deceived themselves.
2:2 1 Tm 6:20+ You must keep to what you have been taught and know to be true; remember 14
1:5 who your teachers were,[c] •and how, ever since you were a child, you have known 15
Ac 16:1 *2 Co 3:14-18* the holy scriptures—from these you can learn the wisdom that leads to salvation
Rm 15:4 through faith in Christ Jesus. •All scripture is inspired by God and can[d] profit- 16
1 Co 10:6+ 2 P 1:20-21 ably be used for teaching, for refuting error, for guiding people's lives and
teaching them to be holy. •This is how the man who is dedicated to God 17
becomes fully equipped and ready for any good work.

1 Tm 6:11f **A solemn charge**

Ac 10:42+ 1 P 4:5 **4** Before God and before Christ Jesus who is to be judge of the living and the 1
1 Tm 6:14+ dead, I put this duty to you, in the name of his Appearing and of his kingdom:
proclaim the message and, welcome or unwelcome, insist on it. Refute falsehood, 2
Ac 20:21 correct error, call to obedience—but do all with patience and with the intention
1 Tm 4:1+ of teaching. •The time is sure to come when, far from being content with sound 3
1 Tm 1:10+ teaching, people will be avid for the latest novelty and collect themselves a whole
series of teachers according to their own tastes; •and then, instead of listening 4
1 Tm 1:4+ to the truth, they will turn to myths. •Be careful always to choose the right 5
course; be brave under trials; make the preaching of the Good News your life's
work, in thoroughgoing service.

Paul in the evening of his life

Ph 2:17+ As for me, my life is already being poured away as a libation,[a] and the time 6
Ac 20:24 1 Co 9:24 has come for me to be gone. •I have fought the good fight to the end; I have run 7
1 Tm 1:18; 6:12 the race to the finish; I have kept the faith; •all there is to come now is the 8
2:4-5 crown of righteousness reserved for me, which the Lord, the righteous judge,
1 Co 9:25+ will give to me on that Day; and not only to me but to all those who have longed
1 Tm 6:14+ for his Appearing.

Final advice

9 10 Do your best to come and see me as soon as you can. •As it is, Demas has 1:4 *Phm 24*
deserted me for love of this life and gone to Thessalonika, Crescens has gone Col 4:14
11 to Galatia[b] and Titus to Dalmatia; •only Luke[c] is with me. Get Mark[d] to come Col 4:10
12 and bring him with you; I find him a useful helper in my work. •I have sent
13 Tychicus to Ephesus. •When you come, bring the cloak I left with Carpus in Tt 3:12+
14 Troas, and the scrolls, especially the parchment ones. •Alexander the copper- 1 Tm 1:20
smith has done me a lot of harm; *the Lord will repay him for what he has done.* Ps 28:4; 62:12
15 Be on your guard against him yourself, because he has been bitterly contesting Pr 24:12
everything that we say.

16 The first time I had to present my defence,[e] there was not a single witness to
support me. Every one of them deserted me—may they not be held accountable
17 for it. •But the Lord stood by me and gave me power, so that through me the Mt 10:19f Ph 1:19f
whole message might be proclaimed for all the pagans to hear; and so I was Col 4:3f
18 *rescued from the lion's mouth.* •The Lord will rescue me from all evil attempts Ps 22:21 Dn 6:17
on me, and bring me safely to[f] his heavenly kingdom. To him be glory for ever Rm 16:27+
and ever. Amen.

Farewells and final good wishes

19 20 Greetings to Prisca and Aquila, and the family of Onesiphorus. •Erastus 1:16 Ac 18:2+; 19:22; 20:4
21 remained at Corinth, and I left Trophimus ill at Miletus.•Do your best to come Rm 16:23
before the winter. 1:4
Greetings to you from Eubulus, Pudens, Linus, Claudia and all the brothers.
22 The Lord[g] be with your spirit. Grace be with you.

3 a. This is reminiscent of the 'false prophets' foretold in Mt 7:15; 24:4-5,24. A fresh outbreak of irreligion is one of the characteristics of the 'last times', cf. 1 Tm 4:1+.

b. Paul gets the names that he gives these magicians (who are mentioned in Ex 7:11-13,22, etc.) from Jewish tradition in which Jannes and Jambres (or 'Mambres'), represented as the leaders of the Egyptian magicians, are said to be the disciples (or even sons) of Balaam, Nb 22:2+.

c. Var. (Vulg.) 'who your teacher was'. These teachers were Lois, Eunice, 1:5, and, above all, Paul himself.

d. Or (less probably) 'all scripture that is inspired by God can...' (Vulg.). This important affirmation about the inspiration of the O.T., cf. 2 P 1:21, probably includes some Christian writings also, 1 Tm 5:18.

4 a. Libations of wine, water or oil were poured over the victims not only in pagan sacrifices but also in Jewish ones, cf. Ex 29:40; Nb 28:7.

b. Var. 'Gaul'. At that time the name 'Galatia' was still given both to the Roman province in Asia, and to the country of the Gauls.

c. Luke the evangelist, cf. Col 4:14.

d. Mark the evangelist, Ac 12:12+. His old quarrel with Paul, Ac 15:37-39, seems to have been forgotten.

e. At some recent hearing of his case.

f. Or 'and keep me safe for'.

g. Add. (Vulg.) 'Jesus Christ', and (at end) 'Amen'.

TITUS

THE LETTER FROM PAUL TO TITUS

Address

Rm 1:1+ **1** From Paul, servant of God, an apostle of Jesus Christ to bring those whom 1
1 Tm 2:4+ God has chosen to faith and to the knowledge of the truth that leads to true
Nb 23:19 Heb 6:18+ religion; •and to give them the hope of the eternal life that was promised so long 2
2 Tm 2:13 *Ac 1:7+* ago by God. He does not lie •and so, at the appointed time, he revealed his 3
Rm 3:26 *1 Tm 1:1+*, 11 decision, and, by the command of God our saviour, I have been commissioned to
2 Co 2:13+ proclaim it. •To Titus, true child of mine in the faith that we share, wishing you 4
grace and peace from God the Father and from Christ Jesus our saviour.

1 Tm 3:1-7
The appointment of elders

Ac 11:30+ Rm 12:8 The reason I left you behind in Crete was for you to get everything organised 5
Ep 4:12+ 1 Th 5:12 there[a] and appoint elders[b] in every town, in the way that I told you: •that is, each 6
1 Tm 5:17+ Heb 13:7+ of them must be a man of irreproachable character; he must not have been married
Jm 5:14+ more than once, and his children must be believers and not uncontrollable or
1 Tm 3:15 Heb 3:2f liable to be charged with disorderly conduct. •Since, as president, he will be God's 7
representative, he must be irreproachable: never an arrogant or hot-tempered
2 Tm 2:24 1 P 5:2 man, nor a heavy drinker or violent, nor out to make money; •but a man who 8
is hospitable and a friend of all that is good; sensible, moral, devout and
self-controlled; •and he must have a firm grasp of the unchanging message of the 9
1 Tm 1:10+ tradition, so that he can be counted on for both expounding the sound doctrine
and refuting those who argue against it.

Opposing the false teachers

1 Tm 4:1 2 Tm 3:13 And in fact you have there a great many people who need to be disciplined, 10
who talk nonsense and try to make others believe it, particularly among those
2 Tm 3:6 of the Circumcision. •They have got to be silenced: men of this kind ruin whole 11
1 Tm 6:10 families, by teaching things that they ought not to, and doing it with the vile motive
of making money. •It was one of themselves, one of their own prophets, who 12
said,[c] 'Cretans were never anything but liars, dangerous animals and lazy': •and 13
that is a true statement. So you will have to be severe in correcting them, and
1 Tm 1:4+. 10 make them sound in the faith •so that they stop taking notice of Jewish myths 14
and doing what they are told to do by people who are no longer interested in the
truth.
Mt 15:11, 18-20p;23: 25-26p To all who are pure themselves, everything is pure; but to those who have been 15
Rm 14:14-20 corrupted and lack faith, nothing can be pure—the corruption is both in their
minds and in their consciences. •They claim to have knowledge of God but the 16
things they do are nothing but a denial of him; they are outrageously rebellious
and quite incapable of doing good.

Some specific moral instruction

1 Tm 6:20+ **2** It is for you, then, to preach the behaviour which goes with healthy doctrine. 1
1 Tm 5:1-2; 6:11 The older men should be reserved, dignified, moderate, sound in faith and 2

3 love and constancy. •Similarly, the older women should behave as though they 1 Co 13:13+
were religious, with no scandalmongering and no habitual wine-drinking—they
4 are to be the teachers of the right behaviour •and show the younger women how
5 they should love their husbands and love their children, •how they are to be Ep 5:22 Col 3:18
sensible and chaste, and how to work in their homes, and be gentle, and do as 1 Tm 2:12
6 their husbands tell them, so that the message of God is never disgraced. •In the
7 same way, you have got to persuade the younger men to be moderate •and in 1 Tm 6:1
everything you do[a] make yourself an example to them of working for good: when 2 Th 3:7+ 1 Tm 4:12
8 you are teaching, be an example to them in your sincerity and earnestness •and 1 P 5:3+
in keeping all that you say so wholesome that nobody can make objections to it; 1 Tm 1:10+
and then any opponent will be at a loss, with no accusation to make against us. 1 Tm 5:14+
9 Tell the slaves that they are to be obedient to their masters and always do what Ep 6:5-8 Col 3:22+
10 they want without any argument; •and there must be no petty thieving—they 1 Tm 6:1+ *Phm 18-19*
must show complete honesty at all times, so that they are in every way a credit
to the teaching of God our saviour. 1 Tm 1:1+

The basis of the Christian moral life

11 You see, God's grace has been revealed, and it has made salvation possible for 3:4 2 Tm 1:10+
12 the whole human race •and taught us that what we have to do is to give up everything that does not lead to God, and all our worldly ambitions; we must be 1 Jn 2:16
13 self-restrained and live good and religious lives here in this present world, •while
we are waiting in hope for the blessing which will come with the Appearing of the 1 Tm 1:11+
14 glory of our great God and saviour Christ Jesus.[b] •He sacrificed himself for 1 Tm 2:6+
us in order to *set us free from all wickedness* and *to purify a people so that it could* Ps 130:8 Rm 3:24+
be his very own and would have no ambition except to do good. *Ex 19:5* Dt 7:6+
15 Now this is what you are to say, whether you are giving instruction or Ep 5:25-27
correcting errors; you can do so with full authority, and no one is to question it. 1 Tm 4:12

General instruction for believers

1 3 Remind them that it is their duty to be obedient to the officials and represent- Rm 13:1-7 1 Tm 2:2+
2 atives of the government; to be ready to do good at every opportunity; •not 1 P 2:13-14
to go slandering other people or picking quarrels, but to be courteous and always Ph 4:5 1 Th 3:12
3 polite to all kinds of people. •Remember, there was a time when we too were *Rm 1:29+;* 3:21-26 1 Co 6:11 Ep 2:3-10 Col 3:7 1 P 4:3

1 a. As usual, Paul had begun the work of evangelisation and then left it to be completed by others, cf. 1 Co 3:6,10; Col 1:7+; Rm 15:23+.

b. In the earliest days each Christian community was governed by a body of elders ('presbyters', whence English word 'priests') or prominent people. This was the case both in Jerusalem (Ac 11:30; 15:2f; 21:18) and in the Dispersion (Ac 14:23; 20:17; Tt 1:5) and it merely continued both the ancient practice of the O.T., Ex 18:13f; Nb 11:16; Jos 8:10; 1 S 16:4; Is 9:14; Ezk 8:1, 11 etc., and the more recent practice of the Jews, Ezr 5:5; 10:14; Jdt 6:16; Lk 7:3; 22:66; Ac 4:5 etc., cf. Josephus, Philo etc. These '*episcopoi*' (supervisors, overseers, watchers, guardians) who are not yet 'bishops' and who are mentioned in connection with the '*diaconoi*' (servants, attendants, assistants, deputies, ministers: 'deacons': Ph 1:1; 1 Tm 3:1-13; the Apostolic Fathers) seem in some passages, Tt 1:5 7; Ac 20:17,28, to be identical with the elders. The Greek word *episcopos*, taken over from the pagan world probably as an equivalent for a semitic title (cf. the *Mebaqqer* of the Essenes, and cf. Nb 4:16; 31:14; Jg 9:28; 2 K 11:15,18; 12:11, etc.) indicated the duty of an officer, while *presbyteros* indicated the status or dignity of the same officer. The *episcopoi* in the college of presbyters may have taken turns to carry out their official duties, cf. 1 Tm 5:17. It is quite certain that Christian *presbyteroi* or *episcopoi* were not merely concerned with the practical side of organising things: they had to teach, 1 Tm 3:2; 5:17; Tt 1:9, and govern, 1 Tm 3:5; Tt 1:7. They were appointed by the apostles, Ac 14:23, or their representatives, Tt 1:5, by the imposition of hands, 1 Tm 5:22, cf. 1 Tm 4:14+; 2 Tm 1:6; their powers derived from God, Ac 20:28, and were charismatic, 1 Cor 12:28. The word *episcopos* eventually replaced analogous titles like '*proistamenos*' (official) Rm 12:8; 1 Th 5:12, *poimen* (pastor, shepherd) Ep 4:11, '*hegoumenos*' (guide, leader) Heb 13:7,17,24. These heads of the local community who developed into our priests (*presbyteroi*) and bishops (*episcopoi*) were helped by *diaconoi* (deacons). The transformation of a local assembly ruled by a body of bishops or presbyters, into an assembly ruled by a single bishop set over a number of priests (a stage reached by the time of Ignatius of Antioch, died c. 107 A.D.) must have involved the intermediate stage when a single *episcopos* in each community was given the same powers over that local community which had previously been exercised over several communities by the apostles or their representatives like Timothy or Titus.

c. Quotation attributed to the Cretan poet Epimenides of Knossos (6th c. B.C.): first half quoted by Callimachus of Alexandria (early 3rd c. B.C.).

2 a. Or '... to be moderate in everything they do; make...' The virtue of being 'sensible' or 'moderate', cf. 1:8, was extremely Greek: here it sums up all the possible virtues of young people, but Paul urges moderation frequently all through the Pastoral Letters, cf. 1 Tm 2:9,15; 3:2; 2 Tm 1:7; Tt 2:2,5,12.

b. This verse is regularly accepted by the Fathers as a statement of the divinity of Christ, cf. Rm 9:5+, but possibly translate '... God, and of our saviour Christ Jesus'. For Christ as 'the brightness of the glory of the Father', cf. Heb 1:3+.

ignorant, disobedient and misled and enslaved by different passions and luxuries;
we lived then in wickedness and ill-will, hating each other and hateful ourselves.
2:11 1 Tm 1:1+ But when the kindness and love of God our saviour for mankind were revealed, 4
2 Tm 1:10+ *Rm 6:1* it was not because he was concerned with any righteous actions we might have 5
2 Tm 1:9 *Jn 3:5* done ourselves; it was for no reason except his own compassion that he saved us,
Rm 5:5; 6:4+ by means of the cleansing water of rebirth and by renewing us with the Holy Spirit
2 Co 13:13+ Ep 5:26 which he has so generously poured over us through Jesus Christ our saviour. 6
1 Tm 1:1+ *Rm 3:24;* He did this so that we should be justified by his grace, to become heirs looking 7
8:17,24 forward to inheriting eternal life.[a] •This is doctrine that you can rely on. 8

Personal advice to Titus

1 Tm 1:15+ I want you to be quite uncompromising in teaching all this, so that those who
now believe in God may keep their minds constantly occupied in doing good
works. All this is good, and will do nothing but good to everybody. •But avoid 9
1 Tm 1:4+ pointless speculations, and those genealogies, and the quibbles and disputes about
the Law—these are useless and can do no good to anyone. •If a man disputes 10
Mt18:15-17p what you teach, then after a first and a second warning, have no more to do with
him:[b] •you will know that any man of that sort has already lapsed and condemned 11
himself as a sinner.

Practical recommendations, farewells and good wishes

Ac 20:4+ 2 Tm 4:12 As soon as I have sent Artemas or Tychicus to you, lose no time in joining 12
me at Nicopolis, where I have decided to spend the winter. •See to all the travelling 13
Ac 18:24+ arrangements for Zenas the lawyer and Apollos, and make sure they have everything they need. •All our people are to learn to occupy themselves in doing good 14
works for their practical needs as well,[c] and not to be entirely unproductive.
All those who are with me send their greetings. Greetings to those who love 15
us in the faith. Grace[d] be with you all.

3 a. The effects of baptism are: rebirth, free forgiveness by Christ, reception of his Holy Spirit, cf. Rm 5:5+, and the immediate enjoyment of all rights as heir to eternal life (the presence of the Holy Spirit being a pledge of this, cf. 2 Co 1:22).

b. Lit. 'Avoid any heretical man after one or two warnings'; Paul uses a contemporary philosophical term; etymologically a 'heretic' is someone who instead of being open to all truth chooses what truths he will believe: groups of people who agree on the same choice are 'sects' (offshoots of parent bodies).

c. Lit. 'for urgent needs' or 'for the necessities of life'. This is perhaps a postscript to 3:8: they must learn to do good works not only for the good of their souls but also for a living: they are not to be parasites on society.

d. Add. 'of the Lord', or (Vulg.) 'of God'. Vulg. adds 'Amen' at the end.

PHILEMON

THE LETTER FROM PAUL TO PHILEMON

Address Rm 1:1+

1 From Paul, a prisoner of Christ Jesus and from our brother Timothy; to our Ac 16:1+
2 dear fellow worker Philemon, •our sister[a] Apphia, our fellow soldier Archippus Col 4:17 2 Tm 2:3
3 and the church that meets in your house; •wishing you the grace and the peace Rm 16:5+
of God our Father and the Lord Jesus Christ.

Thanksgiving and prayer ||Ep 1:15-16 ||Col 1:3f

4 5 I always mention you in my prayers and thank God for you, •because I hear
of the love and the faith which you have for the Lord Jesus and for all the saints. 1 Co 13:13+ *Ac 9:13+*
6 I pray that this faith will give rise to a sense of fellowship that will show you all Ph 1:9-11
7 the good things that we are able to do for Christ.[b] •I am so delighted, and com- Col 1:9-11 *2 Jn 4-6*
forted, to know of your love; they tell me, brother, how you have put new heart
into the saints.

The request about Onesimus

8 Now, although in Christ I can have no diffidence about telling you to do
9 whatever is your duty, •I am appealing to your love instead, reminding you that
this is Paul writing, an old man now and, what is more, still a prisoner of Christ Ep 3:1; 4:1 Col 4:18
10 Jesus. •I am appealing to you for a child of mine, whose father I became[c] while 1 Co 4:16
11 wearing these chains: I mean Onesimus. •He was of no use to you before, but he Ga 4:19 Col 4:9
12 will be useful[d] to you now, as he has been to me. •I am sending him back to you, 1 Th 2:11
13 and with him—I could say—a part of my own self.[e] •I should have liked to keep
him with me; he could have been a substitute for you, to help me while I am in the
14 chains that the Good News has brought me. •However, I did not want to do
anything without your consent; it would have been forcing your act of kindness,
15 which should be spontaneous. •I know you have been deprived of Onesimus for
16 a time,[f] but it was only so that you could have him back for ever, •not as a slave Rm 6:15+ Ep 6:5-9
any more, but something much better than a slave, a dear brother; especially Col 3:22-4:1
dear to me, but how much more to you, as a blood-brother as well as a brother
17 in the Lord.[g] •So if all that we have in common means anything to you, welcome
18 him as you would me; •but if he has wronged you in any way or owes Tt 2:10
19 you anything,[h] then let me pay for it. •I am writing this in my own handwriting: Col 4:18+

a. Var. 'our beloved Apphia', or 'our beloved sister Apphia'.

b. Lit. 'that the fellowship of your faith may become effectual in a full knowledge of every good thing in us for Christ'; i.e. faith unites a person not only to Christ but to all who are his brothers through their union with Christ. Faith and love go together, v. 5, and Paul expects that faith will produce practical results. 'effectual'; var. (Vulg.) 'manifest'. 'we are able'; var. (Vulg.) 'you are able'.

c. He became his 'father' by converting him, cf. 1 Co 4:15; Ga 4:19.

d. A pun: 'Onesimus' means 'useful', cf. Ph 4:3.

e. 'And with him . . .'; var. (Vulg.) 'and I ask you to welcome him as though he were myself', cf. v. 17.

f. 'Deprived' of him by God who allowed the slave to escape only so that everyone might subsequently benefit.

g. Lit. 'as a brother both in the flesh and in the Lord'.

h. It seems that Onesimus had not only run away but had stolen something from Philemon as well.

I, Paul, shall pay it back—I will not add any mention of your own debt to me,
which is yourself.[i] •Well then, brother, I am counting on you, in the Lord; put 2
new heart into me, in Christ. •I am writing with complete confidence in your 2
compliance, sure that you will do even more than I ask.

A personal request. Good wishes

There is another thing: will you get a place ready for me to stay in? I am hoping 2
Heb 13:19 through your prayers to be restored to you.
Col 4:10+ Epaphras, a prisoner with me in Christ Jesus, sends his greetings; •so do my 2 2
2 Tm 4:10 colleagues Mark, Aristarchus, Demas and Luke.
May the grace of our Lord Jesus Christ be with your spirit.[j] 2

i. Philemon must have been one of Paul's converts. j. Add. 'Amen', cf. Ph 4:23.

THE LETTER TO THE HEBREWS

A LETTER ADDRESSED TO A JEWISH-CHRISTIAN COMMUNITY

PROLOGUE

The greatness of the incarnate Son of God

1 1 At various times in the past and in various different ways, God spoke to our 2 Ch 36:15 Jn 1:3
2 ancestors through the prophets; but •in our own time, the last days, he has *Ga 4:4+* 1 Tm 4:1+
spoken to us through his Son, the Son that he has appointed to inherit everything[a] *Mt 4:3+* Jn 1:18+; 10:34
3 and through whom he made everything there is.[b] •He is the radiant light of God's *Ws 7:22+*
glory and the perfect copy of his nature,[c] sustaining the universe by his powerful 2 Co 4:6,18 *Col 1:15+.* 17
command; and now that he has destroyed the defilement of sin, he has gone to *Ep 1:7*
4 take his place in heaven at the right hand of divine Majesty. •So he is now as far Col 1:14 *Ac 2:33+*
above the angels as the title which he has inherited is higher than their own name. Ph 2:9-11+

I. THE SON IS GREATER THAN THE ANGELS

Proof from the scriptures

5 God has never said to any angel: *You are my Son, today I have become your* Ps 2:7 Ac 13:33+
6 *father;* or: *I will be a father to him and he a son to me.* •Again, when he brings the *2 S 7:14*
7 First-born into the world,[d] he says: *Let all the angels of God worship him.* •About Col 1:15+ Dt 32:43
8 the angels, he says: *He makes his angels winds and his servants flames of fire,*[e] •but Ps 97:7 *Ps 104:4*
to his Son he says: *God, your throne shall last for ever and ever;* and: *his*[f] *royal* *Ps 45:6-7*
9 *sceptre is the sceptre of virtue; •virtue you love as much as you hate wickedness.*
This is why God, your God, has anointed you with the oil of gladness, above all your
10 *rivals.*[g] •And again: *It is you, Lord, who laid earth's foundations in the beginning,* Ps 102:25-27
11 *the heavens are the work of your hands; •all will vanish, though you remain, all*
12 *wear out like a garment; •you will roll them up like a cloak, and* like a garment[h]
they will be changed. But yourself, you never change and your years are unending.

1 a. To be a son implies having the right to inherit, cf. Mt 21:38, Ga 4:7. Here, however, God is credited with the handing over of the whole creation because the inheritance in question is messianic and eschatological.

b. Lit. the 'aeons', hebraism for the whole of creation.

c. These two metaphors are borrowed from the *sophia* and *logos* theologies of Alexandria, Ws 7:25-26; they express both the identity of nature between Father and Son, and the distinction of person. The Son is the brightness, the light shining from its source, which is the bright glory, cf. Ex 24:16+, of the Father ('Light from Light'). He is also the replica, cf. Col 1:15+, of the Father's substance, like an exact impression made by a seal on clay or wax, cf. Jn 14:9.

d. Either at the *parousia* or, more probably, at the incarnation.

e. The author, thinking perhaps of the theophany on Sinai, 2:2+, takes this LXX text as a description of the nature of angels, subtle and changeable and therefore inferior to that of the Son reigning from his eschatological throne.

f. Var. 'your', cf. Ps 45 LXX.

g. Following Middle Eastern custom the psalm attributes divinity to the King-Messiah by hyperbole: here it is attributed literally, cf. v. 3. The divine Messiah is to reign for ever.

h. Vulg. omits. 'like a garment'.

Ps 110:1 Ac 2:33-35+ God has never said to any angel: *Sit at my right hand and I will make your enemies* 13
Tb 5:4+ *a footstool for you.* •The truth is they are all spirits whose work is service, sent to 14
Ps 91:11 Mt 4:11; help those who will be the heirs of salvation.[i]
18:10; 26:53 Lk 1:26

An exhortation

2 P 3:17 2 We ought, then, to turn our minds more attentively than before to what we 1
12:25 Ac 7:38,53+ have been taught, so that we do not drift away. •If a promise that was made 2
Ga 3:19+; 4:3+ through angels[a] proved to be so true that every infringement and disobedience
brought its own proper punishment, •then we shall certainly not go unpunished 3
Ac 10:37 if we neglect this salvation that is promised to us. The promise was first announced
by the Lord himself, and is guaranteed to us by those who heard him;
Ac 1:8+ God himself confirmed their witness with signs and marvels and miracles of all 4
kinds, and by freely giving the gifts of the Holy Spirit.

Redemption brought by Christ, not by angels

Col 2:15+ He did not appoint angels to be rulers of the world to come, and that world is 5
what we are talking about. •Somewhere there is a passage that shows us this. It 6
Ps 8:4-6 LXX runs: *What is man that you should spare a thought for him, the son of man that you*
should care for him? •*For a short while you made him lower than the angels; you* 7
crowned him with glory and splendour.[b] •*You have put him in command of every-* 8
1 Co 15:25 Ep 1:20-23 *thing*. Well then, if he has *put him in command of everything*, he has left nothing
Ph 3:21 which is not under his command. At present, it is true, we are not able to see that
Ph 2:6-11 *everything has been put under his command*,[c] •but we do see in Jesus one who was 9
for a short while made lower than the angels and is now *crowned with glory and*
splendour because he submitted to death;[d] by God's grace[e] he had to experience
death for all mankind.

As it was his purpose to bring a great many of his sons into glory, it was appro- 10
Rm 11:36 1 Co 8:6 priate that God, for whom everything exists and through whom everything exists,
12:2 Is 53:4 should make perfect, through suffering, the leader who would take them to their
5:9+ *Jn 17:19* salvation.[f] •For the one who sanctifies, and the ones who are sanctified, are of the 11
Ac 3:15+ *Ps 22:22* same stock;[g] that is why he openly calls them *brothers* •in the text: *I shall announce* 12
Jn 17:6 *Is 8:17* *your name to my brothers, praise you in full assembly*; or the text: •*In him I hope*; 13
Is 8:18 or the text: *Here I am with the children whom God has given me.*
Mt 16:17+ Since all the *children* share the same blood and flesh, he too shared equally 14
Jn 12:31+ Rm 6:9 in it, so that by his death he could take away all the power of the devil,[h] who had
Rm 5:12f power over death, •and set free[i] all those who had been held in slavery all their 15
lives by the fear of death. •For it was not the angels that he took to himself; he 16
Is 41:8-9 took to himself *descent from Abraham.* •It was essential that he should in this way 17
Rm 8:3,29 Ph 2:7 become completely like his brothers so that he could be a compassionate and
3:1+; 4: 15; 5:7+ trustworthy high priest of God's religion, able to atone for human sins. •That is, 18
Mt 4:1 Rm 3:25 because he has himself been through temptation he is able to help others who are
1 Jn 2:2; 4:10 tempted.

II. JESUS THE FAITHFUL AND MERCIFUL HIGH PRIEST

Christ higher than Moses

2:17; 7:26; 8:1; 10:21; 3 That is why all you who are holy brothers and have had the same heavenly 1
11:16; 12: 22 call should turn your minds to Jesus, the apostle and the high priest[a] of our
Ep 1:18 Ph 3:14 religion. •He was *faithful* to the one who appointed him, just like *Moses*, who 2
4:14; 10:23 Nb 12:7 LXX stayed faithful *in all his house;* •but he has been found to deserve a greater glory 3
2 Co 3:7f than Moses. It is the difference between the honour given to the man that built
the house and to the house itself. •Every house is built by someone, of course; 4
but God built everything that exists. •It is true that Moses was *faithful in the* 5
house of God, as a servant, acting as witness to the things which were to be
1:2+; 10:21 1 Co 3:9 divulged later; •but Christ was faithful as a son, and as the master in the house. 6

And we are his house, as long as we cling to our hope with the confidence that we Ep 2:19f▲ 1 Tm 3:15▲
glory in.[b]

How to reach God's land of rest

7 8 The Holy Spirit says: *If only you would listen to him today;* •*do not harden* Ps 95:7-11
your hearts, as happened in the Rebellion, on the Day of Temptation in the
9 *wilderness,* •*when your ancestors challenged me and tested me, though they had*
10 *seen what I could do* •*for forty years. That was why I was angry with that generation*
11 *and said: How unreliable these people who refuse to grasp my ways!* •*And so, in* Nb 14:21-23
12 *anger, I swore that not one would reach the place of rest I had for them.* •Take care,
brothers, that there is not in any one of your community a wicked mind, so unbe- 2 Th 2:3
13 lieving as to turn away from the living God. •Every day, as long as this 'today'
lasts, keep encouraging one another so that none of you is *hardened* by the lure of 10:25 *2 Th 2:10*
14 sin, •because we shall remain co-heirs with Christ only if we keep a grasp on our
15 first confidence right to the end. •In this saying: *If only you would listen to him*
16 *today; do not harden your hearts, as happened in the Rebellion,* •those who
rebelled after they had *listened* were all the people who were brought out of Egypt
17 by Moses. •And those who made God *angry for forty years* were the ones who
18 sinned and whose *dead bodies were left lying in the wilderness.* •Those that he Nb 14:29 1 Co 10:10
swore would never reach the place of rest he had for them were those who had been
19 disobedient. •We see, then, that it was because they were unfaithful that they
were not able to reach it.

1 **4** Be careful, then: the promise of *reaching the place of rest he had for them* still Ex 33:14
2 holds good, and none of you must think that he has come too late for it.[a] •We
received the Good News exactly as they did; but hearing the message did them no 1 Co 10:1-3
3 good because they did not share the faith of those who listened.[b] •We, however,[c]
who have faith, shall reach a place of rest, as in the text: *And so, in anger, I swore* Ps 95:11
that not one would reach the place of rest I had for them. God's work was undoubt-
4 edly all finished at the beginning of the world; •as one text says, referring to the
5 seventh day: *After all his work God rested on the seventh day.* •The text we are Gn 2:2
6 considering says: *They shall not reach the place of rest I had for them.* •It is estab- Ps 95:11
lished, then, that there would be some people who would reach it, and since those
7 who first heard the Good News failed to reach it through their disobedience, •God
fixed another day when, much later, he said 'today' through David in the text Ps 95:7f
already quoted: *If only you would listen to him today; do not harden your hearts.*
8 If Joshua had led them into this place of rest, God would not later on have spoken Dt 31:7 Jos 22:4
9 so much of another day. •There must still be, therefore, a place of rest reserved Rv 14:13

i. Compared with the Son, angels are only servants employed to save human beings.

2 a. The Law, given through the intermediary of angels, cf. Gn 3:19+, and sanctioned by severe penalties.

b. Vulg. adds 'You have made him lord over the work of your hands'.

c. The first Christians, despised and persecuted, were still waiting for the coming of God's reign on earth, 2 P 3:4. Although Christ had already entered his glory, his reign on earth has to continue in time till he has conquered all his enemies (1:13) before his full and final triumph.

d. Christ is glorified because he has suffered and this triumph shows that God accepts the redemptive nature of his death.

e. 'God's grace'; rare var. 'without God' which may have been a gloss meant to emphasise that the Messiah could suffer only in his human, not in his divine, nature; but it could be an allusion to what Jesus cried out from the cross (Mt 27:46), or it could be taken as meaning that Christ died for all, but not for God, cf. 1 Co 15:27.

f. By dying and fulfilling the will of God, Christ becomes the one perfect saviour, responsible for the entry of human beings into the glory of God.

g. From the context, the translation could read 'form a single whole'.

h. Sin and death are related because both derive from Satan whose reign is the opposite of the reign of Christ.

i. By his resurrection, which is the guarantee to believers that they will rise, Rm 8:11+.

3 a. Christ is both 'apostle', i.e. someone 'sent' by God to the human race, cf. Jn 3:17,34; 5:36; 9:7; Rm 1:1+; 8:3; Ga 4:4, and high priest representing the human race before God, cf. 2:17; 4:14; 5:5,10; 6:20; 7:26; 8:1; 9:11; 10:21.

b. Add. 'unwavering right till the end'.

4 a. This 'comparison between Moses and Jesus, 3:1f; cf. Ac 7:20-44+; Jn 1:21+, can be extended to the relationship between Israelites and Christians. Since the Israelites refused to believe God's promise and so never reached the peace of the promised land, 3:7-19, this promise (which cannot be empty, because it was made by God) is still open to Christians who are invited to reach the peace of the spiritual promised land, of which the earthly promised land was only a type.

b. E.g. Joshua and Caleb, cf. Nb 13-14. Var. 'because (the message) was not accompanied by faith in what they heard'.

c. 'however'; var. 'therefore'. 'a place of rest', var. 'the place of rest'.

for God's people,[a] the seventh-day rest, •since to *reach the place of rest* is to *rest* 10
after your work, as God did after his. •We must therefore do everything we can 11
to *reach this place of rest*, or some of you might copy this example of disobedience
and be lost.

The word of God and Christ the priest

Is 49:2; 1 Th 2:13+ The word of God[e] is something alive and active: it cuts like any double-edged 12
1 P 1:23; Rv 1:16 sword but more finely: it can slip through the place where the soul is divided from
Rm 1:9+; 1 Co 15:44+ the spirit, or joints from the marrow; it can judge the secret emotions and
Ep 6:17; *Jb 34:21-22* thoughts. •No created thing can hide from him; everything is uncovered and open 13
Ps 139:2-3; Ws 1:6 to the eyes of the one to whom we must give account of ourselves.
3:1; 9:11. 24; 10:22 Since in Jesus, the Son of God, we have the supreme high priest who has gone 14
Dn 13:42 through to the highest heaven, we must never let go of the faith that we have
2:17-18; 5:7+ professed. •For it is not as if we had a high priest who was incapable of feeling 15
Jn 8:46; Rm 8:3 our weaknesses with us; but we have one who has been tempted in every way that
2 Co 5:21; *10:19+* we are, though he is without sin. •Let us be confident, then, in approaching the 16
Ep 3:12 throne of grace, that we shall have mercy from him and find grace when we are in
need of help.

Jesus the compassionate high priest

8:3 **5** Every high priest has been taken out of mankind and is appointed to act for 1
men in their relations with God, to offer gifts and sacrifices for sins; and so
he can sympathise with those who are ignorant or uncertain because he too lives 2
7:27; Lv 9:7; 16:6 in the limitations of weakness. •That is why he has to make sin offerings for 3
Jn 3:27 himself as well as for the people. •No one takes this honour on himself, but each 4
Ex 28:1 one is called by God, as Aaron was. •Nor did Christ give himself the glory of 5
Ps 2:7 becoming high priest, but he had it from the one who said to him: *You are my*
Ps 110:4 *son, today I have become your father*, •and in another text: *You are a priest of* 6
5:7; 4:15 *the order of Melchizedek, and for ever*. •During his life on earth,[a] he offered up 7
Mt 26:36fp; Jn 12:27 prayer and entreaty, aloud and in silent tears, to the one who had the power to
save him out of death,[b] and he submitted so humbly that[c] his prayer was heard.
Ph 2:8 Although he was Son, he learnt to obey through suffering; •but having been 8 9
2:10+; 7:28; Jn 17:19 made perfect,[d] he became for all who obey him the source of eternal salvation
Rm 1:5+; *6:20* and was acclaimed by God with the title of high priest *of the order of Melchizedek*. 10

III. THE AUTHENTIC PRIESTHOOD OF JESUS CHRIST

Christian life and theology

On this subject we have many things to say, and they are difficult to explain 11
Si 37:28; 1 Co 3:1-3 because you have grown so slow at understanding. •Really, when you should by 12
this time have become masters, you need someone to teach you all over again the
elementary principles of interpreting God's oracles; you have gone back to needing
1 P 2:2 milk, and not solid food. •Truly, anyone who is still living on milk cannot digest 13
1 Co 2:6+ the doctrine of righteousness[e] because he is still a baby. •Solid food is for mature 14
Ph 1:10+; Col 3:10+ men with minds trained by practice to distinguish between good and bad.

The author explains his intention

6 Let us leave behind us then[a] all the elementary teaching about Christ and 1
concentrate on its completion, without going over the fundamental doctrines
9:14; Ep 2:1+ again: the turning away from dead actions[b] and towards faith in God; •the teaching 2
Mt 3:2+; Ac 2:38+ about baptisms[c] and the laying-on of hands; the teaching about the resurrection
Rm 1:16+; 2:6+ of the dead and eternal judgement. •This, God willing, is what we propose to do. 3
1 Tm 4:14+; *10:32+* As for those people who were once brought into the light, and tasted the gift 4
Ep 5:14; *Rm 5:5+* from heaven, and received a share of the Holy Spirit, •and appreciated the good 5
10:26-31; 12:17 message of God and the powers of the world to come •and yet in spite of this 6

have fallen away[d]—it is impossible for them to be renewed a second time. They 1 Jn 5:16▲
cannot be repentant if they have wilfully crucified the Son of God and openly
7 mocked him. •A field that has been well watered by frequent rain, and gives the
crops that are wanted by the owners who grew them, is given God's blessing; 2 Tm 2:6
8 but one that grows brambles and thistles is abandoned, and practically cursed. Gn 3:17-18
It will end by being burnt.

Words of hope and encouragement

9 But you, my dear people—in spite of what we have just said, we are sure you
10 are in a better state and on the way to salvation. •God would not be so unjust
as to forget all you have done, the love that you have for his name or the services 10:32-34
11 you have done, and are still doing, for the saints.[e] •Our one desire is that every Ep 1:15p
one of you should go on showing the same earnestness to the end, to the perfect
12 fulfilment of our hopes, •never growing careless, but imitating those who have the 2 Th 3:7
faith and the perseverance to inherit the promises. Ga 3:14,29 Ep 1:13-14
13 When God made the promise to Abraham, he *swore by his own self*, since it Gn 22:16f
14 was impossible for him to swear by anyone greater: •*I will shower blessings on*
15 *you and give you many descendants.* •Because of that, Abraham persevered and Rm 4:20
16 saw the promise fulfilled. •Men, of course, swear an oath by something greater
than themselves, and between men, confirmation by an oath puts an end to all
17 dispute. •In the same way, when God wanted to make the heirs to the promise
thoroughly realise that his purpose was unalterable, he conveyed this by an oath;
18 so that there would be two unalterable things[f] in which it was impossible for God Nb 23:19+ 2 Tm 2:13
to be lying, and so that we, now we have found safety, should have a strong Tt 1:2
19 encouragement to take a firm grip on the hope that is held out to us. •Here we
have an anchor for our soul,[g] as sure as it is firm, and reaching right *through* Lv 16:2 Mt 27:51p
20 *beyond the veil* •where Jesus has entered before us and on our behalf, to become *9:3; 10:20* Jn 14:3
a high *priest of the order of Melchizedek, and for ever.* *5:10* Ps 110:4

d. God's people, resting in Canaan after the Exodus, is taken as a figure of God resting in heaven after the creation: the new covenant calls those who are faithful to its terms to share God's beatitude.

e. All that God has revealed through the prophets or through his Son, 1:1-2; 2:1-4; 3. Since the promises and threats of the message are still 'alive' and in force, they make it impossible for human beings to avoid declaring their true intentions, i.e. they 'judge' them.

5 a. Lit. 'in the days of his flesh' (on the word 'flesh' cf. Rm 7:5+). The emphasis of this section is on humanity: a priest must be human since he represents human beings and he must share their sufferings since he must feel compassion for them, cf. 2:17-18; 4:15. Jesus suffered in this way all through his life on earth, and especially in his agony and death.

b. Not saved from dying, since that was the whole purpose of his life, Jn 12:27f, but rescued from death after dying, Ac 2:24f. God transformed his death by raising him to glory after it, Jn 12:27f; 13:31f; 17:5; Ph 2:9-11; Heb 2:9.

c. Lit. 'because of his *eulabeia*' (i.e. religious awe). It was because the prayer of Christ in Gethsemane was a prayer of total submission to the will of his Father, Mt 26:39,42, that it was heard and answered.

d. Having totally succeeded in his task of being priest and victim.

e. 'The doctrine of righteousness' like 'God's oracles' can mean either the O.T., cf. 2 Tm 3:16, or the whole body of doctrine. Here it seems to mean all that Christ taught about the righteousness of God as applied to mankind, Rm 3:21-26, and especially about his own priesthood of mediation, prefigured by Melchizedek, the 'king of righteousness', 7:2.

6 a. In spite of the difficulties his readers will have, the author is going to try and stimulate them by formulating the difficult doctrine already mentioned in 5:11.

b. Anything done without faith and the divine life is called a 'dead' action because it is done in the context of sin, Rm 1:18-3:20, which leads to death, Rm 5:12,21; 6:23; 7:5; 1 Co 15:56; Ep 2:1; Col 2:13; cf. Jm 1:15; Jn 5:24; 1 Jn 3:14.

c. Not only Christian baptism, cf. Ac 1:5+; Rm 6:4+, but all the washings, lustrations and purificatory rites then practised, including the 'baptism of John' Ac 18:25; 19:1-5.

d. The irreparable apostasy of rejecting Christ and not believing in the power of his sacrifice to save.

e. The same phrase is used, Rm 15:25,31; 2 Co 8:4; 9:1,12, about a collection for the church in Jerusalem. The 'saints' are all Christians, but especially members of the mother church at Jerusalem and in particular the apostles, cf. Ac 9:13+.

f. I.e. the promise and the oath of God who 'does not lie', Tt 1:2.

g. Anchor: symbol of stability in the classical world, adopted in Christian iconography of 2nd c. as a symbol of hope.

A. CHRIST'S PRIESTHOOD HIGHER THAN LEVITICAL PRIESTHOOD

Gn 14:18+ Ps 110:4+ **Melchizedek**[a]

Gn 14:17-20 7 You remember that *Melchizedek, king of Salem, a priest of God Most High,* 1
went to meet Abraham who was on his way back after defeating the kings, and
blessed him; •and also that it was to him that Abraham gave *a tenth of all that* 2
he had. By the interpretation of his name, he is, first, 'king of righteousness' and
also *king of Salem,* that is, 'king of peace'; •he has no father, mother or ancestry, 3
1:2+ and his life has no beginning or ending; he is like the Son of God. He remains
Jn 7:27 a priest for ever.

Melchizedek accepted tithes from Abraham

Gn 14:20 Now think how great this man must have been, if the patriarch *Abraham paid* 4
him a tenth of the treasure he had captured.[b] •We know that any of the descendants 5
Dt 14:22+ of Levi who are admitted to the priesthood are obliged by the Law to take tithes
from the people, and this is taking them from their own brothers although they
too are descended from Abraham. •But this man, who was not of the same 6
descent, took his tenth from Abraham, and he gave his blessing to the holder of
the promises. •Now it is indisputable that a blessing is given by a superior to an 7
inferior. •Further, in the one case it is ordinary mortal men who receive the 8
tithes, and in the other, someone who is declared to be still alive. •It could be said 9
that Levi himself, who receives tithes, actually paid them, in the person of
Gn 14:17 Abraham, •because he was still in the loins of his ancestor when *Melchizedek* 10
came to meet him.

From levitical priesthood to the priesthood of Melchizedek[c]

Now if perfection had been reached through the levitical priesthood because 11
the Law given to the nation rests on it, why was it still necessary for a
Ps 110:4 new priesthood to arise, one *of the same order as Melchizedek* not counted as being
8:6f 'of the same order as' Aaron? •But any change in the priesthood must mean a 12
change in the Law as well.
8:4 So our Lord, of whom these things were said, belonged to a different tribe, 13
Gn 49:10 Mt 1:1f; 2:6 the members of which have never done service at the altar; •everyone knows he 14
Rm 1:3 Rv 5:5 came from Judah, a tribe which Moses did not even mention when dealing with
priests.

The abrogation of the old Law

This[d] becomes even more clearly evident when there appears a second 15
Rm 1:4+ Melchizedek, who is a priest •not by virtue of a law about physical descent,[e] but 16
Jr 33:18 by the power of an indestructible life. •For it was about him that the prophecy 17
Ps 110:4 was made: *You are a priest of the order of Melchizedek, and for ever.* •The 18
earlier commandment is thus abolished, because it was neither effective nor useful,
10:1; 11:40 Rm 7:7+ since the Law could not make anyone perfect; but now this commandment is 19
10:19+ replaced by something better—the hope that brings us nearer to God.

Christ's priesthood is unchanging

What is more, this was not done without the taking of an oath. The others, 20
indeed, were made priests without any oath; •but he with an oath sworn by the 21
Ps 110:4 one who declared to him: *The Lord has sworn an oath which he will never retract:*
8:6-13 *you are a priest, and for ever.*[f] •And it follows that it is a greater covenant for 22
which Jesus has become our guarantee. •Then there used to be a great number of 23
those other priests, because death put an end to each one of them; •but this one, 24
9:24; 10:19+ Nb 18:1 because he remains *for ever,* can never lose his priesthood. •It follows, then, that 25

his power to save is utterly certain, since he is living for ever to intercede for all Rm 8:34▲ 1 Jn 2:1▲
who come to God through him. Rv 1:18▲

The perfection of the heavenly high priest

26 To suit us, the ideal high priest would have to be holy, innocent and 3:1+ Ex 29:1
uncontaminated, beyond the influence of sinners, and raised up above the 1 Jn 3:5-6 *9:25-28*
27 heavens; •one who would not need to offer sacrifices every day, as the other high *5:3; 9:7,12; 10:11-14*
priests do for their own sins and then for those of the people, because he has done Rm 6:10
28 this once and for all[g] by offering himself. •The Law appoints high priests who are
men subject to weakness; but the promise on oath, which came after the Law,[h]
appointed the Son who is made perfect *for ever.* 5:9

B. THE SUPERIORITY OF THE WORSHIP, THE SANCTUARY AND THE MEDIATION PROVIDED BY CHRIST THE PRIEST

The new priesthood and the new sanctuary

1 **8** The great point of all that we have said is that we have a high priest 3:1+
of exactly this kind. He has his place *at the right* of the throne of divine Ps 110:1 Ac 2:33+
2 Majesty in the heavens, •and he is the minister of the sanctuary and of the true
3 *Tent* of Meeting which *the Lord,* and not any man, *set up.*[a] •It is the duty of every Nb 24:6 LXX
high priest to offer gifts and sacrifices, and so this one too must have something *5:1*
4 to offer. •In fact, if he were on earth, he would not be a priest at all, since there 7:13f
5 are others who make the offerings laid down by the Law •and these only maintain 9:23; 10:1 Ac 7:44
the service of a model or a reflection of the heavenly realities. For Moses, when Rv 11:19
he had the Tent to build, was warned by God who said: *See that you make* Ex 25:40
everything according to the pattern shown you on the mountain.

Christ in the mediator of a greater covenant

6 We have seen that he has been given a ministry of a far higher order, and to 7:12,22; 9:15; 12:24
the same degree it is a better covenant of which he is the mediator,[b] founded on 1 Tm 2:5 1 Jn 2:1

7 a. Melchizedek the priest-king: an O.T. type of Christ. Gn 14 is oddly silent about any ancestors or descendants of Melchizedek and this suggested the idea that he represented the eternal priesthood, vv. 1-3, cf. vv. 15-17 and Ps 110:4+. He was superior to Abraham in so far as Abraham offered him, Gn 14:20, a tithe of everything that had been captured, so *a fortiori,* the argument goes, he was superior to all the descendants of Abraham, including the Levites, v. 4f.

b. The tithe paid to levitical priests, Dt 14:22+, was both the stipend for their ministry at the altar and acknowledgement that as priests they were members of a higher class than those who paid. Levi (in the person of Abraham) could only have paid his tithe if Melchizedek were a priest of an even higher class than himself.

c. The argument here is based on Ps 110:4. This text prophesies that the King-Messiah will not be descended from Levi, but will be an eternal priest in the same sense as Melchizedek. This implies that when Christ comes, his sort of priesthood will replace the levitical priesthood, and this in turn will necessitate a new law since the old one was only concerned with the levitical priesthood, vv. 12, 16f, 21.

d. What has been said in v. 12.

e. Lit. 'a law of a carnal commandment', namely the law that restricted the priesthood of Levi to his physical descendants, cf. Nb 1:47f; 3:5f; Dt 10:8f; 18:1f; 33:8f.

f. Add 'of the order of Melchizedek'.

g. The one and only sacrifice of Christ is the centre of salvation history, Ac 1:7+. It closes a long epoch of preparation, 1:1f; cf. Rm 10:4; it occurs at 'the appointed time', Ga 4:4+, Rm 3:26+, and it begins the eschatological epoch. Though the Last Day, 1 Co 1:8+; Rm 2:6+, will follow, 2 Co 6:2+, only at some unspecified, 1 Th 5:1+, time in the future; salvation for the human race has been in essence certain from the moment when, in the person of Christ, it died to sin and rose to live again. Heb makes a special point of how the whole of this hope flows from the absolutely unique, unrepeatable sacrifice of Christ, 7:27; 9:12,26, 28; 10:10; cf. Rm 6:10; 1 P 3:18. Being unrepeatable, 10:12-14, this sacrifice is different from all others in the O.T. that had to be repeated again and again because they were unable actually to save anyone.

h. Cf. the promise made before the Law was given, Ga 3:17.

8 a. The argument so far has been to prove that what Christ is, i.e. an eternal and perfect priest, is superior to what the levitical priests are, since they are all mortals and sinners, ch. 7; now the argument goes on to show that what Christ does is equally superior to what the levitical priests do: Christ's sanctuary is better because it is in heaven, 8:1-5, cf. 9:11f, while the one on earth is only a copy of it, Ex 25:40; and the covenant brought by the mediation of Christ is a better covenant, vv. 6-13, cf. 9:15f.

b. Technically Christ is the one and only true mediator: he is true man and true God, Col 2:9, and so the one and only intermediary, Rm 5:15-19; 1 Tm 2:5, cf. 1 Co 3:22-23; 11:3, between God and the human race. He unites them and reconciles them, 2 Co 5:14-20. Through him come grace, Jn 1:16-17; Ep 1:7, and complete revelation, Heb 1:1-2. In heaven he continues to intercede for those who are faithful to him, 7:25+.

better promises. •If that first covenant had been without a fault, there would have 7
been no need for a second one to replace it. •And in fact God does find fault with 8
them; he says:

Jr 31:31-34 *See, the days are coming—it is the Lord who speaks—*
Mt 26:28+ 1 Co 11:25 *when I will establish a new covenant*
with the House of Israel and the House of Judah,
but not a covenant like the one I made with their ancestors 9
on the day I took them by the hand
to bring them out of the land of Egypt.
They abandoned that covenant of mine,
and so I on my side deserted them. It is the Lord who speaks.
10:16-17 *No, this is the covenant I will make* 10
with the House of Israel
when those days arrive—it is the Lord who speaks.
I will put my laws into their minds
and write them on their hearts.
Then I will be their God
and they shall be my people.
There will be no further need for neighbour to try to teach neighbour, 11
or brother to say to brother,
'Learn to know the Lord'.
No, they will all know me,
the least no less than the greatest,
since I will forgive their iniquities 12
10:17 *and never call their sins to mind.*

2 Co 5:17 Rv 21:4-5 By speaking of a *new* covenant, he implies that the first one is already old. Now 13
anything old only gets more antiquated until in the end it disappears.

Christ enters the heavenly sanctuary

Ex 25-26+; 26:31 9 The first covenant also[a] had its laws governing worship, and its sanctuary, 1
a sanctuary on this earth. •There was a tent which comprised two 2
compartments: the first, in which the lamp-stand, the table and the presentation
6:19 loaves were kept, was called the Holy Place;[b] •then beyond the second veil, an 3
innermost part which was called the Holy of Holies •to which belonged the gold 4
Ex 30:1+ *Ex 25:10+* altar of incense,[c] and the ark of the covenant, plated all over with gold. In this
Ex 16:1+ *Nb 17:25* were kept the gold jar containing the manna, Aaron's branch that grew the buds,
Ex 24:12+ and the stone tablets of the covenant. •On top of it was the throne of mercy, and 5
Ex 25:17+, 18+ outspread over it were the glorious cherubs. This is not the time to go into
greater detail about this.
Lv 16:1 Under these provisions, priests are constantly going into the outer tent to 6
Ex 30:10 carry out their acts of worship, •but the second tent is entered only once a year, 7
7:27+ Lv 17:11+ and then only by the high priest who must go in by himself and take the blood to
offer for his own faults and the people's. •By this, the Holy Spirit is showing that 8
10:20 no one has the right to go into the sanctuary as long as the outer tent remains
1 Co 10:6+ standing; •it is a symbol for this present time.[d] None of the gifts and sacrifices 9
11:40+ offered under these regulations can possibly bring any worshipper to perfection
Col 2:16-17 in his inner self; •they are rules about the outward life, connected with foods and 10
drinks and washing at various times, intended to be in force only until it should
be time to reform them.
But now Christ has come, as the high priest of all the blessings which were to 11
4:14; 9:24; 10:20 come.[e] He has passed through the greater, the more perfect tent, which is better
Ac 7:48 than the one made by men's hands because it is not of this created order; •and he 12
7:27+ has entered the sanctuary[f] once and for all, taking with him not the blood of goats
Mt 26:28 Rm 3:24+ and bull calves, but his own blood, having won an eternal redemption for us.
10:4 Nb 19:2-10, The blood of goats and bulls and the ashes of a heifer are sprinkled on those who 13

have incurred defilement and they restore the holiness of their outward lives; 17-20▲ Ps 51:7▲
how much more effectively the blood of Christ, who offered himself as the *10:10+* 2 Co 13:13+
perfect sacrifice to God through the eternal Spirit,[g] can purify our inner self from 1 P 1:18-19 *6:1+*
dead actions so that we do our service to the living God. *12:28* Rm 1:9+

Christ seals the new covenant with his blood[h]

He brings a new covenant, as the mediator, only so that the people who were 8:6+
called to an eternal inheritance may actually receive what was promised: his death Ga 4:1-7
16 took place to cancel the sins that infringed the earlier covenant. •Now wherever
17 a will is in question, the death of the testator must be established; •indeed, it only
becomes valid with that death, since it is not meant to have any effect while the
18 testator is still alive. •That explains why even the earlier covenant needed
19 something to be killed in order to take effect, •and why, after Moses had
announced all the commandments of the Law to the people, he took the calves' Ex 24:6-8+
blood, the goats' blood and some water, and with these he sprinkled the book
20 itself and all the people, using scarlet wool and hyssop; •saying as he did so: *This* 10:29 Ex 24:8
21 *is the blood of the covenant that God has laid down for you.* •After that, he sprinkled Mt 26:28p
22 the tent and all the liturgical vessels with blood in the same way. •In fact, Lv 17:11+
according to the Law almost everything has to be purified[i] with blood; and if
23 there is no shedding of blood, there is no remission. •Obviously, only the copies 8:5
of heavenly things can be purified in this way, and the heavenly things themselves
24 have to be purified[j] by a higher sort of sacrifice than this. •It is not as though 4:14; 7:25; 9:11f
Christ had entered a man-made sanctuary which was only modelled on the real Ac 7:48 *1 Co 10:6+*
one; but it was heaven itself, so that he could appear in the actual presence of God 7:25+
25 on our behalf. •And he does not have to offer himself again and again, like the
high priest going into the sanctuary year after year with the blood that is not his
26 own, •or else he would have had to suffer over and over again since the world
began. Instead of that, he has made his appearance once and for all,[k] now at the 7:27+ Jn 1:29
27 end of the last age, to do away with sin by sacrificing himself. •Since men only Ga 4:4+ 1 P 3:18+
28 die once, and after that comes judgement, •so Christ, too, offers himself only once *10:10* 1 Tm 6:14+
to take the faults of many on himself, and when he appears a second time, it will *Is 53:12* Ac 3:20-21
not be to deal with sin but to reward with salvation those who are waiting for Ph 3:20-21
him.[l]

9 a. Om. 'also'.

b. In the desert Tent-Sanctuary, Ex 25-26 (cf. the Temple of Solomon, 1 K 6) a curtain hung between the Holy Place and the Holy of Holies, Ex 26:33. Only the high priest ever went into the Holy of Holies and he did so only once a year on *yom kippur*, the Day of Atonement. Cf. Lv 16:1+.

c. Ex 30:6; 40:26 says that the incense altar, Ex 30:1+, was in the Holy Place: Heb may be following a different liturgical tradition, or the sense may be that the place of the altar of incense was immediately in front of the curtain of the inner sanctuary.

d. The spiritual meaning of this ceremonial arrangement is that under the old covenant the people had no access to God. Under the new covenant, Christ himself is the way to the Father, Jn 14:6; cf. Heb 10:19+. The abrogation of the old worship can thus be appropriately symbolised by the Temple curtain splitting wide open at the death of Jesus, Mt 27:51p.

e. Var. 'blessings already won'.

f. In his ascension Christ 'passed through' all the successive heavenly spheres that form the 'Holy Place' of the celestial Tent, and so came into the presence of God in the celestial 'Holy of Holies'.

g. Var. 'the Holy Spirit', cf. Rm 1:4+.

h. This section is parallel to 8:6-13: it shows that the death of Christ was essential for him to act as mediator. It does this by making use of a pun: the Greek word *diathēkē* can mean 'pact', as in vv. 15. 18-20, or 'last will and testament', as in vv. 16-17; this makes it possible for the author to argue that a 'pact' or covenant suggests the death of a 'testator'. All pacts were sealed with the shedding of blood, Ex 24:6-8.

i. E.g. the altar, Lv 8:15; 16:19; the priests, Lv 8:24-30; the Levites, Nb 8:15; the sinful people, Lv 9:15-18; a mother, Lv 12:7-8, etc.; one exception, cf. Lv 5:11.

j. The 'purification' of the sanctuary, whether the earthly or the heavenly one, does not necessarily imply any previous 'impurity': it is a consecratory and inaugural rite.

k. The sacrifice of Christ is unique, 7:27+: being offered 'at the end of the last age' (lit. 'at the completion of the aeons'), i.e. the end of human history, there is no need for it to be repeated, since it wipes out sin, not with non-human ('alien') blood, but with Christ's own blood, cf. 9:12-14, so its effect is unconditional.

l. The first coming of Christ gave him a direct relationship to sin, Rm 8:3; 2 Co 5:21. The second coming of Christ will, since the redemption is complete, have no connection with sin. Christians wait for this *parousia* that will take place at the Judgement, 1 Co 1:8+; Rm 2:6+.

SUMMARY: CHRIST'S SACRIFICE SUPERIOR TO THE SACRIFICES OF THE MOSAIC LAW

The old sacrifices ineffective

8:5; 10:11 Col 2:17 **10** So, since the Law has no more than a *reflection* of these realities, and no 1
7:19 Rm 7:7+ finished picture of them, it is quite incapable of bringing the worshippers to
10:19+; 11:40+ perfection, with the same sacrifices repeatedly offered year after year. •Otherwise, 2
the offering of them would have stopped, because the worshippers, when they had
been purified once, would have no awareness of sins. •Instead of that, the sins are 3
9:13 recalled year after year in the sacrifices. •Bulls' blood and goats' blood are useless 4
for taking away sins, •and this is what he said, on coming into the world: 5

Ps 40:6-8 LXX
> *You who wanted no sacrifice or oblation,*
> *prepared a body for me.*
> *You took no pleasure in holocausts or sacrifices for sin;* 6
> *then I said,* 7
> *just as I was commanded in the scroll of the book,*
> *'God, here I am! I am coming to obey your will.'*

Notice that he says first: *You did not want* what the Law lays down as the things 8
to be offered, that is: *the sacrifices, the oblations, the holocausts and the sacrifices*
1 S 15:22 Jn 6:38 *for sin,* and *you took no pleasure* in them; •and then he says: *Here I am! I am* 9
Mt 26:39; 42p *coming to obey your will.* He is abolishing the first sort to replace it with the
9:14,28; 10:12,14 second. •And this *will* was for us to be made holy by the *offering* of his *body* made 10
Jn 10:17-18 Ep 5:2 *7:27+* once and for all by Jesus Christ.

The efficacy of Christ's sacrifice

10:1-4 All the priests stand at their duties every day, offering over and over again 11
the same sacrifices which are quite incapable of taking sins away. •He, on the 12
7:27+; 10:10+ other hand, has offered one single sacrifice for sins, and then taken his place for
Ps 110:1 Ac 2:33+ ever, *at the right hand of God,* •where he is now waiting *until his enemies are made* 13
10:10; 11:40+ *into a footstool for him.* •By virtue of that one single offering, he has achieved 14
Jn 17:19+ the eternal perfection of all whom he is sanctifying. •The Holy Spirit assures us 15
of this; for he says, first:

8:10 Jr 31:33-34
> *This is the covenant I will make with them* 16
> *when those days arrive;*

and the Lord then goes on to say:

8:12
> *I will put my laws into their hearts*
> *and write them on their minds.*
> *I will never call their sins to mind,* 17
> or their offences.

When all sins have been forgiven, there can be no more sin offerings. 18

IV. PERSEVERING FAITH

The Christian opportunity

4:16; 7:19, 25; 10:1 In other words, brothers, through the blood of Jesus we have the right to enter 19
6:19-20; 9:8,11-12 the sanctuary,[a] •by a new way which he has opened for us, a living opening 20
Jn 14:6 *3:1+,6; 4:14* through the curtain, that is to say, his body. •And we have the *supreme high priest* 21
Zc 6:11-12 Rm 6:4+ over all *the house of God.* •So as we go in, let us be sincere in heart and filled with 22
1 P 3:21 faith, our minds sprinkled and free from any trace of bad conscience and our
bodies washed with pure water. •Let us keep firm in the hope we profess, because 23

24 the one who made the promise is faithful. •Let us be concerned for each other, 3:2; 4:14; 11:11
25 to stir a response in love and good works. •Do not stay away from the meetings 1 Co 1:9+
of the community, as some do, but encourage each other to go; the more so as you 3:13
see the Day[b] drawing near. 1 Co 1:8+

The danger of apostasy

26 If, after we have been given knowledge of the truth, we should deliberately 6:4-6; 12:17
27 commit any sins, then there is no longer any sacrifice for them.[c] •There will be
left only the dreadful prospect of judgement and of *the raging fire* that is to *burn* Is 26:11 LXX
28 *rebels.* •Anyone who disregards the Law of Moses is ruthlessly *put to death on the* Dt 17:6
29 *word of two witnesses or three;* •and you may be sure that anyone who tramples
on the Son of God, and who treats *the blood of the covenant* which sanctified him 6:6; 9:20 Ex 24:8
as if it were not holy, and who insults the Spirit of grace, will be condemned to a
30 far severer punishment. •We are all aware who it was that said: *Vengeance is* Dt 32:35-36
31 *mine; I will repay.* And again: *The Lord will judge his people.* •It is a dreadful thing Mt 12:31-32p
to fall into the hands of the living God. Mt 10:28p

Motives for perseverance

32 Remember all the sufferings that you had to meet after you received the 6:4,10 Ep 5:14
33 light,[d] in earlier days; •sometimes by being yourselves publicly exposed to insults 1 Co 4:9
and violence, and sometimes as associates of others who were treated in the same
34 way. •For you not only shared in the sufferings of those who were in prison,[e] but 13:3
you happily accepted being stripped of your belongings, knowing that you owned Mt 5:11,40
35 something that was better and lasting. •Be as confident now, then, since the reward Mt 6:20
36 is so great. •You will need endurance to do God's will and gain what he has Lk 21:19 Ac 14:22+ 1 Th 3:4
promised.

37 Only *a little while now, a very little while,* Is 26:20 LXX
and the one that is coming will have come; he will not delay. *Lk 21:28*
38 *The righteous man will live by faith,* Hab 2:3-4 LXX
but if he draws back, my soul will take no pleasure in him. Rm 1:17

39 You and I are not the sort of people who *draw back*, and are lost by it; we are
the sort who keep *faithful* until our souls are saved. Lk 21:19 1 P 1:9

The exemplary faith of our ancestors Si 14

1 **11** Only faith can guarantee the blessings that we hope for, or prove the Rm 1:16+; 4:20; 8:24-25
2 existence of the realities that at present remain unseen.[a] •It was for faith 2 Co 4:18
that our ancestors were commended.
3 It is by faith that we understand that the world was created by one word from Gn 1 Rm 1:20
God, so that no apparent cause can account for the things we can see.[b]
4 It was because of his faith that Abel offered God a better sacrifice than Cain, 12:24
and for that he was declared to be righteous when *God* made acknowledgement Gn 4:4
of *his offerings.* Though he is dead, he still speaks by faith. Gn 4:10 Jb 16:18+ Mt 23:35

10 a. Only the high priest could enter the Holy of Holies, and he could do so only once a year. From now on, all who are faithful will be able to reach God through Christ. Cf. 4:16; 7:19,25; 10:1; Rm 5:2; Ep 1:4; 2:18; 3:12; Col 1:22.

b. When Christ returns at the end of history, cf. 1 Co 1:8+. This verse may refer to the signs preceding the *parousia*, particularly to the disturbances that prelude the destruction of Jerusalem, itself one of the 'visitations' of the Lord.

c. The sin of apostasy or deliberate revolt against God, cf. 6:6+. The fire, v. 27, is the traditional weapon God uses in anger, Is 26:11; Mt 3:11-12; Mk 9:48-49+; Rv 11:5.

d. 'Enlightenment' or 'illumination' in N.T. as in patristic writers always refers to baptism, 6:4; Ep 5:14 (cf. Rm 6:4+).

e. Var. 'of my chains', referring to Paul's imprisonment, Ph 1:7; Col 4:18.

11 a. Var. 'Faith is the assurance of things hoped for (heaven) and the conviction of things unwanted (hell)'. The Jewish Christians to whom he is writing have been discouraged by persecution, so the author emphasises that it is only what is future and what is invisible that concerns hope. This verse was adopted as a theological definition of faith, i.e. the anticipated and assured possession of heavenly realities, cf. 6:5; Rm 5:2; Ep 1:13f. The examples taken from the lives of O.T. saints are meant to illustrate how faith is the source of patience and strength.

b. Creation seen with the eye of faith reveals 'unseen reality': before creation everything real existed in God from whom everything comes.

Si 44:16 It was because of his faith that Enoch was taken up and did not have to 5
Gn 5:24 experience death: *he was not to be found because God had taken him.* This was
because before his assumption it is attested that *he had pleased God.* •Now it is 6
Rm 2:7; 10:14 impossible to please God without faith, since anyone who comes to him must
Ex 3:14 + Jr 29:12-14 believe that he exists and rewards those who try to find him.[c]
Gn 6:8-22 Mt 24:37-39 It was through his faith that Noah, when he had been warned by God of 7
1 P 3:20 2 P 2:5 something that had never been seen before, felt a holy fear and built an ark to save
his family. By his faith the world was convicted,[d] and he was able to claim the
Rm 1:16+ righteousness which is the reward of faith.
Gn 12:1-4 Rm 1:5+ It was by faith that Abraham obeyed the call to *set out* for a country that was 8
the inheritance given to him and his descendants, and that *he set out* without
Gn 23:4; 26:3; 35:12 knowing where he was going. •By faith he arrived, *as a foreigner*, in the Promised 9
Land, and lived there as if in a strange country, with Isaac and Jacob, who were
13:14 Rv 21:10-22 heirs with him of the same promise. •They lived there in tents while he looked 10
forward to a city founded, designed and built by God.
10:23 Gn 17:19; 21:2 It was equally by faith that Sarah, in spite of being past the age, was made able 11
Rm 4:19-21 to conceive, because she believed that he who had made the promise would be
faithful to it. •Because of this, there came from one man, and one who was 12
Gn 22:17 Ex 32:13 already as good as dead himself, *more descendants than could be counted, as many*
Dn 3:36 LXX *as the stars of heaven or the grains of sand on the seashore.*
All these died in faith, before receiving any of the things that had been 13
Jn 8:56 promised, but they saw them in the far distance and welcomed them, recognising
Gn 23:4 Ps 39:12; 119:19 that they were only *strangers and nomads on earth.* •People who use such terms 14
about themselves make it quite plain that they are in search of their real homeland.
They can hardly have meant the country they came from, since they had the 15
13:14 Ph 3:20 opportunity to go back to it; •but in fact they were longing for a better homeland, 16
their heavenly homeland. That is why God is not ashamed to be called their God,
3:1 Rv 21:2 since he has founded the city for them.
Gn 22:1-14 Si 44:20-21 It was by faith that Abraham, *when put to the test, offered up Isaac.* He offered 17
Jm 2:21-22 to sacrifice his only son even though the promises had been made to him •and he 18
Gn 21:12 had been told: *It is through Isaac that your name will be carried on.* •He was 19
Rm 4:17-21 *1 Co 10:6* confident that God had the power even to raise the dead; and so, figuratively
speaking,[e] he was given back Isaac from the dead.
Gn 27:27f, 39f It was by faith that this same Isaac gave his blessing to Jacob and Esau for the 20
Gn 48:15f still distant future. •By faith Jacob, when he was dying, blessed each of Joseph's 21
Gn 47:31 sons, *leaning on the end of his stick as though bowing to pray.* •It was by faith that, 22
when he was about to die, Joseph recalled the Exodus of the Israelites and made
Gn 50:24-25 the arrangements for his own burial.
Ex 2:2 Ac 7:20 It was by faith that Moses, when he was born, *was hidden by his parents for* 23
three months; they defied the royal edict when they *saw* he was such a *fine* child.[f]
Ex 2:11 It was by faith that, *when he grew to manhood*, Moses refused to be known as the 24
son of Pharaoh's daughter •and chose to be ill-treated in company with God's 25
people rather than to enjoy for a time the pleasures of sin. •He considered that 26
13:13 Ps 89:50f the insults offered to the Anointed[g] were something more precious than all the
treasures of Egypt, because he had his eyes fixed on the reward. •It was by faith 27
Ex 2:15 that he left Egypt and was not afraid of the king's anger; he held to his purpose
Ex 12:11, 22:23 like a man who could see the Invisible. •It was by faith that he kept *the Passover* 28
and sprinkled *the blood* to prevent *the Destroyer* from touching any of the first-
Ex 14:22,27 born sons of Israel. •It was by faith they crossed the Red Sea as easily as dry land, 29
while the Egyptians, trying to do the same, were drowned.
Jos 6:20 It was through faith that the walls of Jericho fell down when the people had 30
Jos 2:11; 6:17 been round them for seven days. •It was by faith that Rahab the prostitute 31
Jm 2:25 welcomed the spies and so was not killed with the unbelievers.
Is there any need to say more? There is not time for me to give an account 32
Jg 4:6; 13:24 of Gideon, Barak, Samson, Jephthah, or of David, Samuel and the prophets.
These were men who through faith conquered kingdoms, did what is right and 33

34 earned the promises. They could keep a lion's mouth shut, •put out blazing fires Dn 6:23 *Dn 3:49-50*
and emerge unscathed from battle. They were weak people who were given
35 strength, to be brave in war and drive back foreign invaders. •Some came back
to their wives from the dead, by resurrection; and others submitted to torture, 1 K 17:23 2 K 4:36
36 refusing release so that they would rise again to a better life. •Some had to bear *2 M 6:18–7:42*
37 being pilloried and flogged, or even chained up in prison. •They were stoned, Jr 20:2; 37:15f
or sawn in half,[h] or beheaded; they were homeless, and dressed in the skins of
sheep and goats; they were penniless and were given nothing but ill-treatment.
38 They were too good for the world and they went out to live in deserts and
39 mountains and in caves and ravines. •These are all heroes of faith, but they did 1 P 1:10-12
40 not receive what was promised, •since God had made provision for us to have 7:19; 9:9; 10:1,14; 12:23+
something better, and they were not to reach perfection except with us.[i] 1 P 3:19+

The example of Jesus Christ

1 **12** With so many witnesses in a great cloud on every side of us, we too, then,
should throw off everything that hinders us, especially the sin that clings
2 so easily, and keep running steadily in the race we have started. •Let us not lose Ga 5:7+
sight of Jesus, who leads us in our faith and brings it to perfection: for the sake of 2:10 Mt 4:3-11p
the joy which was still in the future, he endured the cross, disregarding the Jn 6:15 2 Co 8:9
shamefulness of it, and *from now on has taken his place at the right* of God's throne. Ph 2:6-8 Ps 110:1
3 Think of the way he stood such opposition from sinners[a] and then you will not Ac 2:33+ Lk 2:34
4 give up for want of courage. •In the fight against sin, you have not yet had to
keep fighting to the point of death. 10:32f

God's fatherly instruction

5 Have you forgotten that encouraging text in which you are addressed as sons?
My son, when the Lord corrects you, do not treat it lightly; but do not get discouraged Pr 3:11-12 LXX
6 *when he reprimands you.* •*For the Lord trains the ones that he loves and he punishes* Rv 3:19
7 *all those that he acknowledges as his sons.* •Suffering is part of your *training;*[b]
God is treating you as his *sons.* Has there ever been any *son* whose father did not
8 *train* him? •If you were not getting this training, as all of you are, then you would
9 not be *sons* but bastards. •Besides, we have all had our human fathers who
punished us, and we respected them for it; we ought to be even more willing to
10 submit ourselves to our spiritual Father, to be given life. •Our human fathers
were thinking of this short life when they punished us, and could only do what
they thought best; but he does it all for our own good, so that we may share his Lv 17:1+
11 own holiness. •Of course, any punishment is most painful at the time, and far 2 P 1:4 *Jn 16:20*
from pleasant; but later, in those on whom it has been used, it bears fruit in peace 2 Co 7:8-11 1 P 1:6-7
12 13 and goodness. •So *hold up your limp arms and steady your trembling knees* •and Jm 1:2-4 *Is 35:3*
smooth out the path you tread; then the injured limb will not be wrenched, it will Pr 4:26 LXX
grow strong again.

c. The faith that is essential for salvation has two objects; belief in the existence of one personal God, Ws 13:1, who by his very nature cannot be seen, Jn 1:18; Rm 1:20; Col 1:15; 1 Tm 1:17; 6:16; Jn 20:29; 2 Co 5:7, and belief that God will pay a just wage for all effort spent in searching for him; cf. Mt 5:12p; 6:4,6,18; 10:41fp; 16:27; 20:1-16; 25:31-46; Lk 6:35; 14:14; Rm 2:6; 1 Co 3:8,14; 2 Co 5:10; Ep 6:8; 2 Tm 4:8,14; 1 P 1:17; 2 Jn 8; Rv 2:23; 11:18; 14:13; 20:12-13; 22:12.

d. Noah's confidence in what God had said 'convicts' a sinner, cf. Ws 4:16; Mt 12:41.

e. Lit. 'by a parable'. The saving of Isaac from death prefigures the resurrection of all humans and, according to traditional exegesis, the death and resurrection of Christ.

f. Some authorities insert the story of the murdered Egyptian here, cf. Ex 2:11-12; Ac 7:24.

g. In the psalm, God's 'Anointed' who is 'insulted' refers to the people of God, v. 25, consecrated to Yahweh, Ex 19:6+. The author of Heb applies the text to Christ himself on whose account Moses (through faith, since the Messiah was still in the future) suffered. Cf. 10:33; 13:13.

h. Some apocryphal books say this was how king Manasseh had Isaiah executed. Add. 'tempted' (put through ordeals).

i. The eschatological epoch of 'perfection' was inaugurated by Christ, 2:10; 5:9; 7:28; 10:14, and access to the divine life has been made available only by him, 9:11f; 10:19f. The O.T. saints, who could not be 'perfected' by the Law, 7:19; 9:9; 10:1, had thus to wait till the resurrection of Christ before they could enter the perfect life of heaven, 12:23; cf. Mt 27:52f; 1 P 3:19+.

12 a. Lit. 'endured contradictions of sinners against himself'; var. '...against themselves'.

b. To the eyes of faith, the various trials of life are all part of the way God is bringing us up. The argument depends on the biblical concept of education, *mûsar, paideia,* mean 'teaching through hitting, punishing', cf. Jb 5:17; 33:19; Ps 94:12; Si 1:27; 4:17; 23:2.

Unfaithfulness is punished

Ps 34:14 Rm 12:18 *Always be wanting peace* with all people, and the holiness without which no 14
Mt 5:8-9 1 Jn 3·2 one can ever see the Lord. •Be careful that no one is deprived of the grace of God 15
Dt 29:17 LXX and that no *root of bitterness should begin to grow and make trouble;* this can poison
Ac 8:23 a whole community. •And be careful that there is no immorality, or that any of 16
Gn 25:33 you does not degrade religion like Esau,[c] *who sold his birthright* for one single
meal. •As you know, when he wanted to obtain the blessing afterwards, he was 17
Gn 27:30-40 rejected and, though he pleaded for it with tears, he was unable to elicit a change
of heart.

The two covenants

Ex 19:16,18 What you have come to is nothing known to the senses:[d] not a *blazing fire,* 18
or a *gloom* turning to *total darkness,* or a *storm;* •or *trumpeting thunder* or the 19
Dt 4:11 *Ex 20:19* *great voice speaking* which made everyone that heard it beg that no more should
Ex 19:12f be said to them.[e] •They were appalled at the order that was given: *If even an animal* 20
touches the mountain, it must be stoned. •The whole scene was so terrible that 21
Dt 9:19 Moses said: *I am afraid,* and was trembling with fright. •But what you have come 22
Rv 14:1; 21:10 to is Mount Zion and the city of the living God, the heavenly Jerusalem where the
millions of angels have gathered for the festival, •with the whole Church in which 23
everyone is a 'first-born son' and a citizen of heaven. You have come to God
Rm 2:6+ himself, the supreme Judge, and been placed with spirits of the saints who have
11:40+ been made perfect; •and to Jesus, the mediator who brings a new covenant and a 24
8:6+; 11:4+ blood for purification which pleads more insistently than Abel's. •Make sure that 25
Gn 4:10 you never refuse to listen when he speaks. The people who refused to listen to the
warning from a voice on earth could not escape their punishment, and how shall
2:2-3 we escape if we turn away from a voice that warns us from heaven? •That time 26
Hg 2:6 Ex 19:18 his voice made the earth shake, but now he has given us this promise: *I shall make*
Jg 5:4-5 Ps 68:8 *the earth shake once more and* not only the earth but *heaven as well.* •The words 27
once more show that since the things being shaken are created things, they are
Mt 24:35p 2 P 3:12-13 going to be changed, so that the unshakeable things will be left.[f] •We have 28
Rv 21:1 been given possession of an unshakeable kingdom. Let us therefore hold on to the
9:14 Rm 1:9+ grace that we have been given and use it to worship God in the way that he finds
Dt 4:24 Is 33:14 acceptable, in reverence and fear.[g] •For our *God* is a *consuming fire.* 29

APPENDIX

Final recommendations

Rm 12:13 *Gn 18:2f;* 19:1f **13** Continue to love each other like brothers, •and remember always to 1 2
Jg 6:11-24; 13:3-23 welcome strangers, for by doing this, some people have entertained angels
Tb 5:4f without knowing it. •Keep in mind those who are in prison, as though you were 3
10:34 in prison with them; and those who are being badly treated, since you too are in
Mt 25:36 the one body. •Marriage is to be honoured by all, and marriages are to be kept 4
Ws 3:13 Ep 5:5-6 undefiled, because fornicators and adulterers will come under God's judgement.
Ph 4:12 Put greed out of your lives and be content with whatever you have; God himself 5
Dt 31:6 has said: *I will not fail you or desert you,* •and so we can say with confidence: 6
Ps 118:6; 27:1-3 Rm 8:31-39 *With the Lord to help me, I fear nothing: what can man do to me?*

Faithfulness

Tt 1:5+ Remember your leaders,[a] who preached the word of God to you, and as you 7
2 Th 3:7+ *Ps 102:27* reflect on the outcome of their lives, imitate their faith. •Jesus Christ is the same 8
Ep 4:14 today as he was yesterday and as he will be for ever.[b] •Do not let yourselves 9
be led astray by all sorts of strange doctrines: it is better to rely on grace for inner
1 Co 8:8+ strength than on dietary laws which have done no good to those who kept them.
Lv 3:1+ We have our own altar[c] from which those who serve the tabernacle have no right 10
Lv 16:27 to eat. •The bodies of the animals *whose blood is brought into the sanctuary* by the 11

12 high priest *for the atonement of sin are burnt outside the camp*, •and so Jesus too Nb 19:3 *10:14*
13 suffered outside the gate to sanctify the people with his own blood.[d] •Let us go to Mt 21:39p Jn 19:20
14 him, then, *outside the camp*, and share his degradation. •For there is no eternal Ac 7:58 *11:26*
15 city for us in this life but we look for one in the life to come. •Through him,[e] *11:10,14-16* 1 Co 7:29-31
let us offer God an unending *sacrifice of praise*, a verbal sacrifice that is offered Ph 3:20 *Ps 50:14,23*
16 every time we acknowledge his name. •Keep doing good works and sharing your Ho 14:3 Ac 2:21+
resources, for these are sacrifices that please God. Rm 1:9+; 10:9 *Ph 4:18*

Obedience to religious leaders

17 Obey your leaders and do as they tell you, because they must give an account Ezk 3:18 1 Co 16:16
of the way they look after your souls; make this a joy for them to do, and not a 1 Th 5:12f
18 grief—you yourselves would be the losers. •We are sure that our own conscience Rm 15:30 Ep 6:19
is clear and we are certainly determined to behave honourably in everything we Col 4:3 1 Th 5:25
19 do; pray for us. •I ask you very particularly to pray that I may come back to you 2 Th 3:1 *Ph 2:24*
all the sooner. Phm 22

EPILOGUE

News, good wishes and greetings

20 I pray that the God of peace, *who brought* our Lord Jesus *back* from the dead Is 63:11
to become the great Shepherd of the sheep by the blood that sealed an eternal Zc 9:11 *Ezk 34:1+;* 37:26
21 *covenant*, •may make you ready to do his will in any kind of good action; and Jn 10:11
turn us all into whatever is acceptable to himself through Jesus Christ, to whom 1 P 2:25; 5:4 *Ph 2:13*
be glory for ever and ever, Amen. Rm 16:27+
22 I do ask you, brothers, to take these words of advice kindly; that is why I have
written to you so briefly.
23 I want you to know that our brother Timothy has been set free. If he arrives Ac 16:1+
24 in time, he will be with me when I see you. •Greetings to all your leaders and to
25 all the saints. The saints of Italy send you greetings. •Grace be with you all.

c. Lit. 'or be profane like Esau'. This refers to the sin committed by Esau when he surrendered the position that was his by birth, of being heir to the messianic promises.

d. Lit. 'You have not approached something that can be touched', var. '...a mountain that can be touched', cf. v. 22.

e. As at the theophany on Sinai, when the old covenant was made. The new covenant replaces fear with peace.

f. Cosmic upheavals are traditional metaphors in apocalypses for the time when God intervenes to introduce a new regime, cf. Am 8:9+; 1 Co 1:8+; Mt 24:1+.

g. This is the real conclusion, and an apt one for a letter that lays such emphasis on the liturgy. The 'unshakeable' kingdom summarises vv. 22-24. God reigns over both his angels and his saints in the kingdom of heaven, the eternal and spiritual Jerusalem. From now on Christians are able to enter this kingdom and live there a life that is a eucharistic liturgy.

13 a. The heads of the community.

b. Christ Jesus was the central theme on which the heads of the community preached. They may die but Christ remains, and so it is to him that Christians owe their allegiance.

c. Not the table used for the Eucharist, but either the cross on which Christ was sacrificed, or Christ himself through whom we offer the sacrifice of prayer to God. Non-Christian Jews who still 'served the tabernacle' cannot participate.

d. On the Day of Atonement the high priest went into the Holy of Holies and sprinkled it with the blood of animals that had been killed, and the bodies of these animals were burnt outside the camp. This prefigured how Jesus as expiatory victim was to be killed outside the walls of Jerusalem. The lesson drawn from this is that Christians should break with Judaism and think of themselves as exiles from the world.

e. 'Through him', add. 'therefore'.

THE LETTERS
TO ALL CHRISTIANS

INTRODUCTION TO THE LETTERS TO ALL CHRISTIANS

There are seven New Testament letters which are not Pauline and which, in spite of having no other obvious connection, were very soon grouped together. Three of these letters are attributed to John, two to Peter and the other two to James and Jude. They were already given the title 'universal' or 'catholic' by the end of the 2nd century; it is not certain why, possibly because most are addressed to the whole Christian Church and not to particular communities or individuals.

The letter of *James* was generally accepted as canonical in the Church from the 2nd century onwards. Its author is usually identified with the James, 'brother of the Lord', Mt 13:55p; cf. 12:46+, who played an important part in the earliest Christian community in Jerusalem, Ac 12:17+; 15:13-21; 21:18-26; 1 Co 15:7; Ga 1:19; 2:9,12, and who was put to death by Jews about the year 62 (Josephus, Hegesippus). He is obviously not the apostle James, son of Zebedee, Mt 10:2p, martyred by Herod in 44, Ac 12:2, though he could theoretically be identified with the apostle James, son of Alphaeus, Mt 10:3p; even early writers, however, were doubtful and most critics nowadays reject it. Paul's turn of phrase in Ga 1:19 is ambiguous. But even without being one of the Twelve, James, as 'the brother of the Lord', was sufficiently prominent for the apostolic authority of his letter to be accepted from the beginning.

The traditional attribution of the letter to James, 'the brother of the Lord', leader of the Judaeo-Christian community in Jerusalem, is supported by internal evidence. The author was familiar with the Old Testament and with the teachings of Jesus, yet his letter, though it is full of Hebraisms and makes use of parallelism, and is in a didactic style that is characteristically semitic, was obviously written in Greek. It is written, moreover, with such elegance, such a rich vocabulary and with such a skilful use of the 'diatribe', that many critics have found it hard to believe the author was a Galilean. No accurate estimate, however, can be made as to how competent first-century Palestinians were in writing Greek, and James may have been helped by a disciple familiar with the hellenistic world and its culture.

The letter is addressed to the 'twelve tribes of the Dispersion', 1:1, i.e. to the Jewish Christians scattered all over the Graeco-Roman world but concentrated in countries near Palestine like Syria and Egypt. The whole tone of the letter shows that it was intended for Jewish converts and presumes that the readers are familiar with the Old Testament since, unlike Paul and the author of the Hebrews, James hardly ever makes use of direct quotations but argues from the imprecise and rather general allusions that underlie the whole text.

His two chief sources are the Old Testament wisdom literature, on which he bases his moral lessons, and the teaching found in the gospels. Some critics have thought of the letter as an exclusively Jewish product, but, on the contrary, ideas and even characteristic expressions of Jesus can be detected all through it, not so much by explicit quotations from written texts, as by reference to a living, oral tradition. James is a Judaeo-Christian sage who has rethought the maxims of the Jewish Wisdom tradition in the light of his Master's teachings, and is able to re-present them in an original way.

More a sermon than a letter, it probably reflects the regular teaching of Judaeo-Christian assemblies and consists of a series of moral exhortations linked either by a common theme or sometimes by nothing more than verbal assonances. The sort of subjects dealt with are: how to behave in time of trial, 1:1-12; 5:7-11; the origin of temptation, 1:13-18; how to control the tongue, 1:26; 3:1-18; good relations and sympathy with one's neighbour, 2:8,13; 3:13–4:2; 4:11f; the power of prayer, 1:5-8; 4:2f; 5:13-18 etc. In 5:14f is the *locus classicus* on the sacramental (cf. Council of Trent) anointing of the sick.

There are two main themes. The first praises the poor and threatens the rich, 1:9-11; 1:27–2:9; 4:13–5:6, showing a concern for the lowly, God's favoured ones, that follows one Old Testament tradition but particularly the Beatitudes, Mt 5:3+. The second insists that Christians must do good and not be content with a faith that produces nothing, 1:22-27; 2:10-26; this leads on to a section, 2:14-26, that ridicules the preaching of faith completely unrelated to good works, and some have seen this as aimed against Paul. James and Galatians-Romans have many significant points of contact, particularly noticeable in the different ways they interpret Old Testament texts on Abraham. James may be opposing Paul himself or, more probably, certain Christians who drew pernicious conclusions from Paul's teaching. Two points are worth remembering: first, that beneath the clash between their different positions, Paul and James agree on essentials, cf. 2:14+; secondly, that the problem of relating faith to works is inherent in the data of Jewish religion and may have been a traditional topic that James and Paul dealt with independently of each other.

The dating of the letter depends on how the problem just mentioned is solved. If James is thinking of what Paul taught in Galatians-Romans, it must be dated after 57/58; if not, it could be dated before the judaising crisis (about 49), which would account for its primitive Christology. In either case it must be dated before the First Letter of Peter which is indebted to James.

Jude who calls himself 'brother of James', v. 1, is also, it appears, one of the 'brothers of the Lord', Mt 13:55p. There is no reason to identify him with the apostle of the same name, Lk 6:16; Ac 1:13; cf. Jn 14:22, especially as he refers to himself as being outside the apostolic body, v. 17. Nor is it likely that an anonymous author would have adopted the name, since Jude was not sufficiently prominent to lend authority to a letter. Our hypothesis is that after his brother James had been executed in 62 A.D., Jude followed his example and warned the Jewish Christians against new threats to their faith. If this is so, his anonymous readers are those for whom James wrote, and his Greek, which is accurate, with semitic turns of phrase, may be accounted for as in the case of James. The letter was accepted as canonical by many of the churches as early as 200, though its use of two apocryphal sources, the Book of Enoch in vv. 6,14f, and the Assumption of Moses in v. 9, had prompted certain hesitations; but to quote contemporary Jewish writings is hardly equivalent to recognising their inspiration.

Jude's purpose in writing this letter is to denounce the false teachers who are a danger to Christian faith. He threatens them with the divine punishments familiar from Jewish tradition, vv. 5-7, and also seems to base his description of their false teaching on the same traditions, v. 11. He nowhere states precisely what these doctrines were, so they cannot be identified with second-century Gnosticism. He accuses them of irreligion and immorality, in particular of blasphemies against the Lord Christ and the angels, vv. 4,8-10. These may have been part of the syncretistic tendencies denounced in Colossians, the Pastoral Letters and Revelation.

The letter must be dated fairly late in the 1st century: the apostles are quoted as belonging to the past, vv. 17f; the faith is now something fixed and 'handed on once for all', v. 3; and the author appears to be acquainted with Paul's letters. It is true that 2 Peter borrows from Jude and is therefore later, but the 'Second Letter of Peter' could have been written after Peter's death (cf. *infra*). The limits seem to be between 70 and 80.

Two of these 'universal' letters are attributed to *Peter*. 1 Peter introduces the name of the apostle in the opening verse, 1:1, and has never been doubted in any part of the Church. Clement of Rome seems to have used it; Polycarp certainly did, and since the time of Irenaeus it has been expressly attributed to Peter. The apostle writes from Rome (Babylon, 5:13), and calls Mark, who is with him, his 'son'. Very little is known about Peter's last years; according to tradition he went to Rome and was martyred there under Nero (in 64 or possibly 67). His letter is addressed to the Christians 'of the Dispersion', and names five provinces, 1:1, which represent practically the whole of Asia Minor. From what he says, 1:14,18; 2:9f; 4:3, it seems that most of them were converted pagans, though there may have been some Judaeo-Christians among them. He was obviously obliged to send them a letter in Greek—James had done the same with less reason—and though Peter's Greek is unsophisticated it is too accurate and unforced for a fisherman from Galilee. Unlike the letter from James, the name of a disciple and secretary is mentioned who may have helped: this is Silvanus, 5:12, usually identified with the Silvanus who had been a companion of Paul, Ac 15:22+.

The purpose of the letter is to help its readers' faith in a time of trial. Some critics think this may refer to a persecution under Domitian or Trajan, which would date the letter much later than Peter; but the allusions in the letter are not strong enough to make this conclusion inevitable, since it seems that this 'time of trial' could refer rather to the personal malice and spiteful calumnies caused by the strictly moral life led by converts among those whose sins they no longer shared, 2:12; 3:16; 4:4,12-16.

Another argument against Petrine authorship is based on the liberal use the letter makes of John, Romans and Ephesians, and on the surprisingly little direct use it makes of the gospel. There are, however, many reminiscences of the gospel but these are so implicit as to constitute an argument against the idea that the author merely wanted to pretend the apostle had written it. There is a tendency perhaps to exaggerate the number of points of contact with James and Paul. Specifically Pauline themes, e.g. the abolition of the Jewish Law, the Body of Christ, etc., do not appear at all, and though some themes appear that are best known from Paul's letters, yet these are themes common to all early Christian theology, e.g. the redemptive nature of the death of Jesus; faith and baptism, etc. Certain formulae used in primitive preaching and certain items in anthologies of Old Testament quotations are being increasingly identified by critics, and any early writings could well have drawn on these independently. Even the remaining cases where 1 Peter is dependent on Romans or Ephesians need not militate against Petrine authorship, since Peter, feeling his lack of theological gifts, may well have had recourse to Paul's writings, especially as he was writing to people who had felt Paul's influence. It is also worth remembering that Silvanus was a disciple of both apostles and that some scholars detect affinities not only between 1 Peter and Paul but also between 1 Peter and two groups of writings whose climate is Petrine: i.e. Mark and the discourses of Peter in Acts.

If the substance of the letter were in existence before Peter's death in 64 or 67, Silvanus could still have given it its present form many years later. This hypothesis would be more likely if it could be proved that the letter was made up of fragments. It is suggested that, for example, a baptismal homily, 1:13–4:11, is one such fragment, but these identifications remain very tentative.

Though a very practical letter, it is also a valuable summary of apostolic theology. The dominating theme is fortitude in trial, for which Christ himself is the model, 2:21-25; 3:18; 4:1. Christians must suffer patiently like him when their trials are due to their faith and to their saintly lives, 2:19f; 3:14; 4:12-19; 5:9, i.e. if, in return for evil, they offer: charity, obedience to civil authority, 2:13-17, and gentleness to all, 3:8-17; 4:7-11,19. There is one obscure passage, 3:19f, cf. 4:6; the 'preaching' of Christ can be taken as an announcement either of salvation or of punishment; the 'spirits in prison' can be taken either as the wicked who were drowned in the Flood or as the fallen angels of biblical and apocalyptic tradition. On either view, this passage refers the 'preaching' to the moment Jesus died and is the chief source for the doctrine of the Descent into Hell.

The Second Letter of Peter claims to have been written by the apostle himself. He is named in the opening address, 1:1, the prediction of Peter's death is made by Jesus to the author himself, 1:14, who also claims to have witnessed the transfiguration, 1:16-18, and who alludes to a former letter that is obviously meant to be 1 Peter.

The purpose of the letter is twofold: to warn against false teachers, ch. 2, and to allay anxiety due to the delay of the *parousia*, ch. 3. It is possible that both these difficulties existed before Peter's death, but other considerations make Petrine authorship doubtful and suggest a later date. The vocabulary is notably different from 1 Peter; the whole of ch. 2 is obviously a free repetition of Jude; an accepted Pauline corpus seems to be already in existence, 3:15f; the apostolic body is referred to, with the prophets, as a thing of the past and as if the author did not belong to it. These difficulties caused early writers to hesitate, and there is no sure evidence that the letter was accepted at all before the 3rd century, and some, according to Origen, Eusebius and Jerome, explicitly refused to accept it. Most critics nowadays also reject the Petrine authorship, though the writer may have had some claim to represent Peter: perhaps he belonged to a group of Peter's disciples, perhaps he filled out one of Peter's writings with ideas from the letter of Jude. This is what we should call forgery but what in those days literary convention found admissible.

The letter has been definitely accepted by the Church as canonical, and Christians accept it as an authoritative document from the apostolic age. The doctrine it teaches supports this: note especially the vocation of all Christians to the 'share in the divine nature', 1:4; the way scriptural inspiration is defined, 1:20f; the assurance that eventually the *parousia* will come though no one can know when; the prediction of a new world free of all injustice after the old world has been destroyed by fire, 3:3-13.

For the three letters of *John* cf. the Introduction to the Gospel and Letters of Saint John.

THE LETTER OF JAMES

Address and greetings

Ac 12:17+ *Ac 26:7* 1 P 1:1 *Jn 7:35*
1 From James, servant of God and of the Lord Jesus Christ. Greetings[a] to the 1
twelve tribes of the Dispersion.[b]

Trials a privilege

Mt 5:11+ 1 P 4:13-14 *Heb 12:11* 1 P 1:6-7 *Rm 5:3-5*
My brothers, you will always have your trials but, when they come, try to treat 2
them as a happy privilege; •you understand that your faith is only put to the 3
test to make you patient, •but patience too is to have its practical results[c] so that 4
Mt 5:48 you will become fully-developed, complete, with nothing missing.
1 K 3:7f Pr 2:6+ Ws 8:21f *Mt 7:7;* 21:21p
If there is any one of you who needs wisdom, he must ask God, who 5
gives to all freely[d] and ungrudgingly; it will be given to him. •But he must ask 6
with faith, and no trace of doubt, because a person who has doubts is like the
Is 57:20 waves thrown up in the sea when the wind drives. •That sort of person, in two 7 8
minds, wavering between going different ways, must not expect that the Lord
will give him anything.
Jr 9:22-23 It is right for the poor brother to be proud of his high rank,[e] •and the rich 9 10
one to be thankful that he has been humbled, because riches last no longer than
Is 40:6-7 *the flowers in the grass;* •the scorching sun comes up,[f] and *the grass withers, the* 11
flower falls; what looked so beautiful now disappears. It is the same with the rich
man: his business goes on; he himself perishes.
Dn 12:12 Rm 8:28 *Happy the man who stands firm* when trials come. He has proved himself, 12
Ws 5:15-16 1 Co 9:25+ and will win the prize of life, the crown that the Lord[g] has promised to those who
love him.

Temptation

Pr 19:3 Si 15:11-20 1 Co 10:13
Never, when you have been tempted, say, 'God sent the temptation'; God 13
cannot be tempted to do anything wrong, and he does not tempt anybody.
Rm 7:8-10. 23 Everyone who is tempted is attracted and seduced by his own wrong desire. 14
Rm 5:12; 6:23 Then the desire conceives and gives birth to sin, and when sin is fully grown, it too 15
Heb 6:1+ has a child, and the child is death.
Mt 7:11 Jn 3:3,27 Make no mistake about this, my dear brothers: •it is all that is good, 16 17
everything that is perfect, which is given us from above; it comes down[h] from the
Jn 8:12+ 1 Jn 1:5 Father of all light;[i] with him there is no such thing as alteration, no shadow of a
Jn 1:12-13 1 P 1:23+ change. •By his own choice he made us his children by the message of the truth[j] 18
Rv 14:4 so that we should be a sort of first-fruits of all that he had created.

True religion

Pr 10:19; 14:17 Si 5:11
Remember this, my dear brothers: be *quick to listen* but *slow* to speak and 19
Mt 5:22 slow to rouse your temper; •God's righteousness is never served by man's anger; 20
1 P 2:1-2 *Ga 5:19+* so do away with all the impurities and bad habits that are still left in you—accept 21

and submit to the word which has been planted in you and can save your souls. Jn 3:11+
22 But you must do what the word tells you, and not just listen to it and deceive Mt 7:24-27p Lk 8:21
23 yourselves. •To listen to the word and not obey is like looking at your own features Rm 2:13 1 Jn 3:17f
24 in a mirror and then, •after a quick look, going off and immediately forgetting
25 what you looked like. •But the man who looks steadily at the perfect law of Ps 19:7 Mt 5:17
freedom[k] and makes that his habit—not listening and then forgetting, but actively Jn 13:17 Rm 7:12; 6: 15+; 8:2
putting it into practice—will be happy in all that he does.
26 Nobody must imagine that he is religious while he still goes on deceiving
himself and not keeping control over his tongue; anyone who does this has the 3:2f
27 wrong idea of religion. •Pure, unspoilt religion, in the eyes of God our Father[l]
is this: coming to the help of orphans and widows when they need it, and keeping Ex 22:21+
oneself uncontaminated by the world.

Respect for the poor

1 **2** My brothers, do not try to combine faith in Jesus Christ, our glorified Lord,[a]
2 with the making of distinctions between classes of people. •Now suppose a man
comes into your synagogue,[b] beautifully dressed and with a gold ring on, and at
3 the same time a poor man comes in, in shabby clothes, •and you take notice of the
well-dressed man, and say, 'Come this way to the best seats'; then you tell the
4 poor man, 'Stand over there' or 'You can sit on the floor by my foot-rest'. •Can't
you see that you have used two different standards in your mind, and turned
yourselves into judges, and corrupt judges at that?
5 Listen, my dear brothers: it was those who are poor according to the world 1 Co 1:26-29 *Zp 2:3+*
that God chose, to be rich in faith[c] and to be the heirs to the kingdom which he Rv 2:9 *1:12*
6 promised to those who love him. •In spite of this, you have no respect for anybody Mt 4:17+ Ga 3:29
who is poor. Isn't it always the rich who are against you? Isn't it always their
7 doing when you are dragged before the court? •Aren't they the ones who insult Is 52:5
8 the honourable name to which you have been dedicated?[d] •Well, the right thing Rm 13:8-10
to do is to keep the supreme law of scripture: *you must love your neighbour as* Lv 19:18 Mt 22:39p
9 *yourself;* •but as soon as you make distinctions between classes of people, you are *Pr 24:23+*
committing sin, and under condemnation for breaking the Law. Dt 1:17
10 You see, if a man keeps the whole of the Law, except for one small point Dt 27:26 Mt 5:19
11 at which he fails, he is still guilty of breaking it all. •It was the same person who Ga 3:10; 5:3
said, '*You must not commit adultery*' and '*You must not kill*'. Now if you commit *Ex 20:13-14* Dt 5:17-18
murder, you do not have to commit adultery as well to become a breaker of the

1 a. Lit. 'Be joyful' or 'Rejoice', a normal Greek greeting. 'Happy privilege' v. 2 (lit. 'all joy deem it') is in Greek a pun on the greeting formula.

b. In O.T. days the 'Dispersion' (*diaspora*) was used to describe the Jews who had emigrated from their country, cf. Ps 147:2; Jdt 5:19; cf. Jn 7:35. Here the reference is to the Jewish Christians living in the Graeco-Roman world, cf. Ac 2:5-11.

c. James, in the tradition of the Jews, believes the essence of religion is its practical value in actions, cf. 2:14+.

d. Lit. 'uncompoundedly' i.e. simply, or unreservedly.

e. It is a theme of the O.T. that the poor, cf. Zp 2:3+, will be rewarded, 1 S 2:7-8; Ps 72:4,12, etc., and this theme is developed in the gospels, cf. Lk 1:52, Lk 6:20, etc., to show their reward in terms of the kingdom of heaven. This privilege of the poor is recognised in the early Church; it is barred to the rich unless they reduce themselves to the same humble state, cf. Mt 5:3+.

f. Or 'As soon as the sun, with a scorching wind'.

g. Om. 'the Lord'. Vulg. reads 'God'.

h. Om. (Vet. Lat.) 'from above'.

i. Lit. 'the Father of the lights', i.e. the maker of the stars, Gn 1:14-18, and source of spiritual light, cf. 1 P 2:9; 1 Jn 1:5. The imagery following this phrase is suggested by astronomy. Var. 'no such thing as alteration due to the movement of a shadow'.

j. Lit. 'He deliberately teemed us forth by a word of truth'. This 'word of truth' is everything God has revealed to the human race, it is also called the law of freedom or the supreme Law, cf. 1:21-25; 2:8.

k. This reflects the Jewish concept of human freedom as flowing from obedience to the Law; Paul, however, had a different concept of Christian freedom as something flowing from the Christian's release from obedience to the Law, cf. Rm 6:15+; 7:1+.

l. Cf. Mt 6:9; 1 Co 15:24; Ep 5:20. The O.T. uses the phrase in Dt 32:6; cf. Is. 63:16; Si 23:1,4; Ws 2:16.

2 a. Lit. 'our Lord Jesus Christ of glory', cf. 1 Co 2:8+.

b. James is writing to Jewish Christians; it is possible they may even have still been attending Jewish synagogues, or it may be his word for the Christian 'assembly' for liturgical services.

c. I.e. poor in money, rich in faith, cf. 1:9+; this letter is not concerned to advocate social reform since it emphasises that the poor already have the truest wealth.

d. Lit. 'blaspheming the good name invoked over you (or: that you bear)'. In the O.T. the name of Yahweh pronounced over someone dedicated him to the divine protection, Am 9:12; Is 43:7; Jr 14:9. In the N.T. the only means of salvation is the name of Jesus invoked, e.g. at baptism, Ac 2:21+.

Law. •Talk and behave like people who are going to be judged by the law of 12
Mt 6:14-15; 18:35 freedom, •because there will be judgement without mercy for those who have 13
Lk 6:36f Rm 6:15+ 1 Jn 4:18 not been merciful themselves;[e] but the merciful need have no fear of judgement.

Faith and good works[f]

2:24 Rm 4:1 Take the case, my brothers, of someone who has never done a single good 14
Ga 5:6 *Mt 25:41-45* act but claims that he has faith. Will that faith save him? •If one of the brothers 15
1 Co 13:3 1 Jn 3:17 or one of the sisters is in need of clothes and has not enough food to live on,
Mt 7:21 and one of you says to them, 'I wish you well; keep yourself warm and 16
eat plenty', without giving them these bare necessities of life, then what good is
that? •Faith is like that: if good works do not go with it, it is quite dead.[g] 17
This is the way to talk to people of that kind:[h] 'You say you have faith and I 18
have good deeds; I will prove to you that I have faith by showing you my good
deeds—now you prove to me that you have faith without any good deeds to show.
Mt 8:29+ You believe in the one God—that is creditable enough, but the demons have the 19
same belief, and they tremble with fear. •Do realise, you senseless man, that faith 20
Rm 4:1+ without good deeds is useless.[i] •You surely know that Abraham our father was 21
Gn 22:9 Heb 11:17 justified by his deed, because he *offered his son Isaac on the altar*? •There you see 22
it: faith and deeds were working together; his faith became perfect by what he did.[j]
Gn 15:6 Rm 4:3 This is what scripture really means when it says: *Abraham put his faith in God,* 23
Ga 3:6 *and this was counted as making him justified;* and that is why he was called 'the
friend of God'.
2:14+ You see now that it is by doing something good, and not only by believing, 24
that a man is justified. •There is another example of the same kind: Rahab the 25
Jos 2:4f Heb 11:31 prostitute, justified by her deeds because she welcomed the messengers[k] and
showed them a different way to leave. •A body dies when it is separated from the 26
spirit, and in the same way faith is dead if it is separated from good deeds.

Uncontrolled language

Mt 12:36; 23:8 1 Co 12:28+ 3 Only a few of you, my brothers, should be teachers, bearing in mind that 1
those of us[a] who teach can expect a stricter judgement.
1:26 Pr 10:19; After all, every one of us does something wrong, over and over again; the 2
13:3;18:21 Si 14:1 only man who could reach perfection would be someone who never said anything
Si 5:9-15; 28:13-26 wrong—he would be able to control every part of himself. •Once[b] we put a bit 3
into the horse's mouth, to make it do what we want, we have the whole animal
under our control. •Or think of ships: no matter how big they are, even if a gale 4
is driving them, the man at the helm can steer them anywhere he likes by
controlling a tiny rudder. •So is the tongue only a tiny part of the body, but it can 5
proudly claim that it does great things. Think how small a flame can set fire to a
Pr 16:27; 26:18-21 huge forest; •the tongue is a flame like that. Among all the parts of the body, the 6
Si 5:13; 28:22 tongue is a whole wicked world in itself:[c] it infects the whole body; catching fire
Mt 5:22+; 15:18 itself from hell, it sets fire to the whole wheel of creation.[d] •Wild animals and birds, 7
Gn 1:26+; 9:2 reptiles and fish can all be tamed by man, and often are; •but nobody can tame the 8
Ps 140:3 tongue—it is a pest that will not keep still, full of deadly poison. •We use it to 9
Gn 1:27+ bless the Lord and Father,[e] but we also use it to curse men who are made in God's
image: •the blessing and the curse come out of the same mouth.[f] My brothers, 10
Ep 4:29 this must be wrong—•does any water supply give a flow of fresh water and salt 11
Mt 7:16 water out of the same pipe? •Can a fig tree give you olives, my brothers, or a 12
vine give figs? No more can sea water give you fresh water.

Real wisdom and its opposite

Ep 4:1-2 If there are any wise or learned men among you, let them show it by their good 13
lives, with humility and wisdom in their actions. •But if at heart you have the 14
bitterness of jealousy, or a self-seeking ambition, never make any claims for
yourself or cover up the truth with lies —•principles of this kind are not 15
2 Co 1:12 *1 Co 3:3* the wisdom that comes down from above: they are only earthly, animal and

6 devilish. •Wherever you find jealousy and ambition, you find disharmony, and
7 wicked things of every kind being done; •whereas the wisdom that comes down 1:5+ Ws 7:22
from above is essentially something pure; it also makes for peace, and is kindly 1 Co 13:4-7
and considerate;[g] it is full of compassion and shows itself by doing good; nor is
8 there any trace of partiality or hypocrisy in it. •Peacemakers, when they work for Mt 5:9 Ph 1:11
peace, sow the seeds which will bear fruit in holiness. Heb 12:11

Disunity among Christians

1 4 Where do these wars and battles between yourselves first start? Isn't it precisely
2 in the desires fighting inside your own selves? •You want something and you Rm 7:23 Ga 5:17
haven't got it; so you are prepared to kill. You have an ambition that you cannot 1 P 2:11
satisfy; so you fight to get your way by force.[a] Why you don't have what you
3 want is because you don't pray for it; •when you do pray and don't get it, it Ps 66:18 Mt 6:5-13, 33
is because you have not prayed properly, you have prayed for something to indulge Rm 8:26
your own desires.

4 You are as unfaithful as adulterous wives;[b] don't you realise that making
the world your friend is making God your enemy? Anyone who chooses the world Mt 6:24p 1 Jn 2:15-17
5 for his friend turns himself into God's enemy. •Surely you don't think scripture *Rm 8:26*
is wrong when it says: the spirit which he sent to live in us wants us for himself Gn 2:7
6 alone?[c] •But he has been even more generous to us, as scripture says: *God opposes* 1 P 5:5-9 *Pr 3:34*
7 *the proud but he gives generously to the humble.* •Give in to God, then; resist the LXX *Ep 6:11*
8 devil, and he will run away from you. •The nearer you go to God, the nearer he *Zc 1:3* Ml 3:7
will come to you. Clean your hands, you sinners, and clear your minds, you *1:8*
9 waverers. •Look at your wretched condition, and weep for it in misery; be
10 miserable instead of laughing, gloomy instead of happy.[d] •Humble yourselves Mt 23:12
before the Lord and he will lift you up.

11 Brothers, do not slander one another. Anyone who slanders a brother, or Lv 19:6 Mt 7:1-5
condemns him, is speaking against the Law and condemning the Law. But if you
condemn the Law, you have stopped keeping it and become a judge over it.
12 There is only one lawgiver[e] and he is the only judge and has the power to acquit Dt 32:39+ Mt 10:28p
or to sentence. Who are you to give a verdict on your neighbour?[f] Lk 12:5 Rm 14:4

e. 'Judgement' (i.e. 'condemnation') is merciless to anyone who does not show mercy. 'the merciful ... judgement'; lit. 'mercy triumphs over judgement'. Cf. Mt 18:35.

f. The different points of view of James and Paul, Rm 3:20-31; Ga 2:16; 3:2,5,11f; Ph 3:9, are not wholly irreconcilable. Paul is anxious to rule out the view that a human being can earn salvation without having faith in Christ, since such a reliance on self-made sanctity would be contradicted by the radical sinfulness of unredeemed man, Rm 1:18-3:20; Ga 3:22, and would make faith in Christ superfluous, Ga 2:17; cf. Rm 1:16+. But Paul does not deny that the saint who has been made holy by grace must show his faith by actually loving, Ga 5:6; cf. 1 Th 1:3; 2 Th 1:11; Phm 6, and in this way obeying the Law, Rm 8:4, i.e. the Law or commandment of Christ and his Spirit, Ga 6:2; Rm 8:2, which is the commandment to love, Rm 13:8-10; Ga 5:14. It is perfectly true, however, that in order to teach the same truth as Paul, James in a different context and under different circumstances explains the case of Abraham in a completely different way from Paul.

g. Lit. 'it is dead by itself'.

h. The same opponents as in vv. 14 and 16.

i. Var. (Vulg.) 'dead', cf. vv. 17 and 26.

j. Unlike most Jews, James does not consider Abraham's faith (trust in God) as constituting a 'good deed' in itself: however closely he relates the two things, James makes a clear distinction between having faith and doing something as a result of that faith.

k. 'messengers'; var. 'spies', cf. Heb 11:31.

3 a. Var. (Vulg.) 'you'.

b. Lit. 'Now if (var. 'Behold' as, lit. in v. 4) we put bits into horses' mouths'.

c. Lit. 'the tongue... is the *kosmos* of wickedness' i.e. 'it is the world of wickedness', or alternatively 'it is the ornament of wickedness'.

d. Lit. 'inflaming the wheel (var. course) of nature' (i.e. of the world) 'and being inflamed by Gehenna'.

e. 'Lord and Father', var. (Vulg.) 'God and Father'.

f. The antithesis 'bless-curse' is common in the O.T., Gn 12:3; 27:29; Nb 23:11; 24:9; Jos 8:34.

g. Vulg. adds 'in harmony with good'.

4 a. Alternative translation (corr.) 'You crave things you don't have, you are envious and jealous of things you cannot have, you squabble and fight' (lit. 'fight and go to war'). 'War' here is not the internal spiritual struggle of a Christian, cf. Rm 7:23; 1 P 2:11, and it seems to be more than just a heated argument between Christians, it seems to mean coming to real blows.

b. Lit. 'You adulteresses, don't you know that friendship of the world is enmity of God?' The imagery of Israel the unfaithful wife of Yahweh is traditional in the O.T., Ho 1:2+, cf. Mt 12:39; Mk 8:38; 2 Co 11:2.

c. Lit. 'the spirit he has made to dwell in us yearns for our love'; or 'he yearns intensely over the spirit he has made to dwell in us'. This text, now lost, seems to have inspired Rm 8:26-27 as well. It is because God has shared his Spirit with us, that we want what God wants and that God answers our prayers, cf. Mt 18: 19-20; Jn 14:13+.

d. Cf. Is 32:11f; Mi 2:4; Jr 4:13f; Zc 11:2f.

e. Var. 'There is only one: the lawgiver...'

f. Lit. 'And who are you the one judging your neighbour?' cf. 2:4. To believe yourself qualified to judge (=punish) a neighbour breaks the golden rule, 2:8, of love. Cf. Rm 2:1.

A warning for the rich and the self-confident

Pr 27:1 Mt 6:34 Here is the answer for those of you who talk like this: 'Today or tomorrow, 13
Lk 12:19-20 we are off to this or that town; we are going to spend a year there, trading, and
make some money'. •You never know what will happen tomorrow: you are no 14
Jb 14:2+ more than a mist that is here for a little while and then disappears. •The most 15
Ac 18:21 Rm 1:10 you should ever say is: 'If it is the Lord's will, we shall still be alive to do this or
1 Jn 2:16+ that'. •But how proud and sure of yourselves you are now! Pride of this kind is 16
always wicked. •Everyone who knows what is the right thing to do and doesn't 17
do it commits a sin.

Lk 6:24 5 Now an answer for the rich. Start crying, weep for the miseries that are 1
coming to you. •Your wealth is all rotting, your clothes are all eaten up by 2
Si 29:10-12 Mt 6:19-21 moths. •All your gold and your silver are corroding away, and the same corrosion 3
Pr 16:27 *Pr 11:4,28* will be your own sentence, and eat into your body. It was a burning fire that you
Lv 19:13 stored up as your treasure for the last days.[a] •Labourers mowed your fields, and 4
Dt 24:14-15 you cheated them—listen to the wages that you kept back, calling out; realise
Ex 22:22 that the cries of the reapers have reached the ears of the Lord of hosts. •On earth 5
you have had a life of comfort and luxury; in the time of slaughter[b] you went
Ws 2:10-20 on eating to your heart's content. •It was you who condemned the innocent and 6
killed them; they offered you no resistance.

A final exhortation

1Co 15:23+ 1 P 2:19+ Now be patient, brothers, until the Lord's coming. Think of a farmer: how 7
Dt 11:14 patiently he waits for the precious fruit of the ground until it has had the autumn
Mt 24:33p Rm 2:6+ rains[c] and the spring rains! •You too have to be patient; do not lose heart, 8
2 Co 6:2+ Rv 1:3 because the Lord's coming will be soon. •Do not make complaints against one 9
another, brothers, so as not to be brought to judgement yourselves; the Judge is
already to be seen waiting at the gates. •For your example, brothers, in sub- 10
Mt 5:11-12p mitting with patience, take the prophets who spoke in the name of the Lord;
1:2-3,12 remember it is those who had endurance that we say are the blessed ones. You 11
Jb 42:10-17 have heard of the patience of Job, and understood the Lord's purpose, realising
Ps 103:8 that *the Lord is kind and compassionate.*

Si 5:10; 23:9 Above all, my brothers, do not swear by heaven or by the earth, or use any 12
Mt 5:34-37 oaths at all. If you mean 'yes', you must say 'yes'; if you mean 'no', say 'no'.
Otherwise you make yourselves liable to judgement.

If any one of you is in trouble, he should pray; if anyone is feeling happy, he 13
Tt 1:5+ should sing a psalm. •If one of you is ill, he should send for the elders 14
Mk 6:13 of the church, and they must anoint him with oil in the name of the Lord[d] and
Ac 3:16+ pray over him. •The prayer of faith will save the sick man and the Lord will raise 15
Gn 18:16 Ps 32 him up again; and if he has committed any sins, he will be forgiven. •So confess 16
Pr 28:13+ Si 4:26 your sins to one another, and pray for one another, and this will cure you;[e] the
1 Jn 1:8-10 *Ex 32:11+* heartfelt[f] prayer of a good man works very powerfully. •Elijah was a human 17
1 K 17:1; 18:1,42 being like ourselves—he prayed hard for it not to rain, and no rain fell for
Lk 4:25 Rv 11:6 three-and-a-half years; •then he prayed again and the sky gave rain and the earth 18
gave crops.

Mt 18:15 Ga 6:1 My brothers, if one of you strays away from the truth, and another brings 19
him back to it, •he may be sure[g] that anyone who can bring back a sinner from 20
Pr 10:12 1 P 4:8 the wrong way that he has taken will be saving a soul from death and *covering*
up a great number of sins.

5 a. Eschatologically the misfortunes of the rich will be apparent only at the Judgement, 5:7-9. We however are already living in the last days, cf. 2 Co 6: 2+.

b. Not a reference to Judgement day, but to the extreme violence to which, once, the innocent had been subjected, v. 6, while the rich were living at ease, v. 5.

c. 'rains', var. 'fruits'.

d. Om. 'of the Lord'. The tradition that these prayers and this anointing with oil in the name of the Lord, and for the purpose of helping the sick and forgiving their sins, are the origin of the Church's 'sacrament of the sick' (or Holy Unction), was endorsed by the Council of Trent.

e. This mutual confession and prayer for each other, instead of being only recommendations to the sick, v. 15. are here urged on all Christians. Nothing special however may be deduced about sacramental confession.

f. Var. (Vulg.) 'assiduous'.

g. Var. 'you can be sure'.

1 PETER

THE FIRST LETTER OF PETER

Address. Greetings

1 **1** Peter, apostle of Jesus Christ, sends greetings to all those living among
foreigners[a] in the Dispersion of Pontus, Galatia, Cappadocia, Asia and Jn 7:35; 2 Co 5:6
2 Bithynia, who have been chosen, •by the provident purpose of God the Father, Jm 1:1+; *Rm 8:29*
to be made holy by the Spirit, obedient to Jesus Christ and sprinkled with his Ep 1:4; 2 Th 2:13
blood.[b] Grace and peace be with you more and more. *Ex 24:8*; Mt 26:28+

Introduction. The salvation of Christians

3 Blessed be God the Father of our Lord Jesus Christ, who in his great mercy 1:23
has given us a new birth as his sons, by raising Jesus Christ from the dead, so that Jn 3:5; 1 Jn 2:29; 3:9
4 we have a sure hope •and the promise of an inheritance that can never be spoilt Mt 6:19-20p
or soiled and never fade away, because it is being kept for you in the heavens. Rm 1:4+; Col 1:5,12; 3:3-4
5 Through your faith, God's power will guard you until the salvation which has *Ep 1:19f*
6 been prepared is revealed at the end of time.[c] •This is a cause of great joy for you, 1 Jn 3:2; *Jn 16:20*
even though you may for a short time have to bear being plagued by all sorts of Jm 1:2-3; Heb 12:11
7 trials; •so that, when Jesus Christ is revealed, your faith will have been tested and
proved like gold—only it is more precious than gold, which is corruptible even Ml 3:2-3; 1 Co 3:13
though it bears testing by fire—and then you will have praise and glory and *Rm 2:7*
8 honour. •You did not see him, yet you love him; and still without seeing him, 1 Jn 4:20
you are already filled with a joy so glorious that it cannot be described, because
9 you believe; •and you are sure of the end to which your faith looks forward, that
is, the salvation of your souls. Heb 10:39

The hope of the prophets

10 It was this salvation that the prophets were looking and searching so hard for; Ac 11:27+; Heb 11:39
11 their prophecies were about the grace which was to come to you. •The Spirit of 2 P 1:20; *Is 52:13-53:12*
Christ which was in them[d] foretold the sufferings of Christ and the glories that Lk 18:31+
would come after them, and they tried to find out at what time and in *Ac 1:7+*; 2:23+
12 what circumstances all this was to be expected. •It was revealed to them that the
news they brought of all the things which have now been announced to you, by Mt13:16-17p
those who preached to you the Good News through the Holy Spirit sent from Rm 16:25+
heaven, was for you and not for themselves. Even the angels long to catch a Ep 3:10+
glimpse of these things.

1 a. They are in an alien environment that does not make the practice of religion easy. This is also true of Christians in general. The Christian's city is heaven, Ph 3:20; Col 3:1-4; Heb 13:14; he is an exile on earth, 2 Co 5:6; 1 P 1:17; he is a foreigner here, Ps 39:12; 119:19; Heb 11:13; 1 P 1:1; 2:11, on an exodus to the heavenly promised land, Heb 3:1-4:11.

b. Trinitarian formula, cf. 2 Co 13:13+.

c. Lit. 'at the last time', cf. 1:20.

d. By saying the prophets are inspired by the pre-existing Christ, cf. 1 Co 10:4,9, the author makes clear the unity of the O.T. and the N.T.

A call to sanctity and watchfulness

Lk 12:35-40 1 Th 5:6 Free your minds, then, of encumbrances; control them, and put your trust 13
in nothing but the grace that will be given you when Jesus Christ is revealed.
Rm 6:19 Do not behave in the way that you liked to before you learnt the truth; make 14
Mt 5:48 Ac 9:13+ a habit of obedience: •be holy in all you do, since it is the Holy One who has 15
1 Jn 3:3 *Lv 17:1+; 19:2* called you, •and scripture says: *Be holy, for I am holy.* 16
Dt 10:17+ Heb 11:6+ If you are acknowledging as your Father one who has no favourites and judges 17
everyone according to what he has done, you must be scrupulously careful as long
2 Co 5:6 *Is 52:3* as you are living away from your home. •Remember, the ransom that was *paid* 18
1 Co 6:20; 7:23 *to free you* from the useless way of life your ancestors handed down was not paid
in anything corruptible, neither in *silver* nor gold, •but in the precious blood of a 19
Jn 1:29+ *Jn 17:24* lamb without spot or stain, namely Christ;[e] •who, though known since before 20
Ga 4:4 the world was made, has been revealed only in our time, the end of the ages, for
Rm 1:16+ your sake. •Through him you now have faith in God, who raised him from the 21
Rm 1:4+ *Rm 8:11+* dead and gave him glory for that very reason—so that you would have faith and
hope in God.

Love

Rm 1:5+ You have been obedient to the truth and purified your souls until you can 22
Jn 17:17 Rm 12:9 love like brothers, in sincerity; let your love for each other be real and from the
Jn 3:11+ Jm 1:18 heart[f]—•your new birth was not from any mortal seed but from the everlasting 23
1 Jn 3:9; 5:1 1 P 1:3 word of the living and eternal God.[g] •*All flesh is grass and its glory like the wild* 24
Is 40:6-8 *flower's. The grass withers, the flower falls,* •*but the word of the Lord remains for* 25
ever. What is this word? It is the Good News that has been brought to you.

Integrity

Mt 19:14 Jm 1:21 2 Be sure, then, you are never spiteful, or deceitful, or hypocritical, or envious 1
1 Co 3:2 Heb 5:12 and critical of each other. •You are new born, and, like babies, you should 2
be hungry for nothing but milk—the spiritual honesty which will help you to
Ps 34:8 grow up to salvation—•now that you have *tasted the goodness of the Lord.* 3

The new priesthood

Mt 21:42p Ac 4:11 He is the living stone, rejected by men but chosen by God and precious to him; 4
Ep 2:20-22 *Ex 19:6+* set yourselves close to him •so that you too, the holy priesthood that offers the 5
Rm 1:9+ spiritual sacrifices which Jesus Christ has made acceptable to God, may be living
Is 28:16 Rm 9:33; 10:11 stones making a spiritual house. •As scripture says: *See how I lay in Zion a precious* 6
cornerstone that I have chosen and *the man who rests his trust on it will not be disap-*
pointed. •That means that for you who are believers, it is precious; but for 7
Ps 18:22 unbelievers, *the stone rejected by the builders has proved to be the keystone,* •*a* 8
Is 8:14f *stone to stumble over, a rock to bring men down.* They stumble over it because they
do not believe in the word; it was the fate in store for them.[a]
Is 43:20-21 *Ex 19:5-6+* But you are *a chosen race, a royal priesthood, a consecrated nation, a people set* 9
Rm 3:24+ Ep 1:14+ *apart* to sing the praises of God who called you out of the darkness into his
Ac 26:18 Col 1:12-13 wonderful light. •Once you were *not a people* at all and now you are the People 10
Ho 1:6-9; 2:3,25 of God; once you were *outside the mercy* and now *you have been given mercy.*

The obligations of Christians: towards pagans

Ps 39:12 I urge you, my dear people, while you are *visitors and pilgrims*, to keep your- 11
Ga 5:24 selves free from the selfish passions that attack the soul. •Always behave 12
Jm 4:1 honourably among pagans so that they can see your good works for themselves
Is 10:3 and, when the day of reckoning comes, give thanks to God for the things which
Mt 5:16 now make them denounce you as criminals.

Towards civil authority

Rm 13:1-7 Tt 3:1

For the sake of the Lord, accept the authority of every social institution: the 13
emperor, as the supreme authority, •and the governors as commissioned by him 14

15 to punish criminals and praise good citizenship. •God wants you to be good
16 citizens, so as to silence what fools are saying in their ignorance. •You are slaves
of no one except God, so behave like free men, and never use your freedom as an Ga 5:13
17 excuse for wickedness. •Have respect for everyone and love for our community; Jude 4 *Pr 24:21*
fear God and honour the emperor. Mt 22:21p

Towards masters

18 Slaves must be respectful and obedient to their masters, not only when they Ep 6:5-8+
19 are kind and gentle but also when they are unfair. •You see, there is some merit[b] 3:14; 4:14 Jm 5:7-11
in putting up with the pains of unearned punishment if it is done for the sake of
20 God •but there is nothing meritorious in taking a beating patiently if you have
done something wrong to deserve it. The merit, in the sight of God, is in bearing
it patiently when you are punished after doing your duty.
21 This, in fact, is what you were called to do, because Christ suffered[c] for you Mt 16:24 2 Th 3:7+
22 and left an example for you to follow the way he took. •He had not done anything Jn 8:46
23 wrong, and *there had been no perjury in his mouth.* •He was insulted and did not *Is 53:9* *Mt 5:39*
retaliate with insults; when he was tortured he made no threats but he put his
24 trust in the righteous judge. •He was *bearing our faults* in his own body on the Rm 12:19 *Is 53:12*
cross, so that we might die to our faults and live for holiness; *through his wounds* *Rm 6:11,18* 2 Co 5:21
25 *you have been healed.* •You had *gone astray like sheep*[d] but now you have come *Is 53:5,6*
back to the shepherd and guardian[e] of your souls. Ezk 34:1+

In marriage

1 **3** In the same way, wives should be obedient to their husbands. Then, if there Ep 5:22-24 Col 3:18
are some husbands who have not yet obeyed the word, they may find them- 1:25 1 Co 7:12-16
2 selves won over, without a word spoken, by the way their wives behave, •when
3 they see how faithful and conscientious they are. •Do not dress up for show: Is 3:16f+ 1 Tm 2:9-15
4 doing up your hair, wearing gold bracelets and fine clothes; •all this should be
inside, in a person's heart,[a] imperishable: the ornament of a sweet and gentle
5 disposition—this is what is precious in the sight of God. •That was how the holy
women of the past dressed themselves attractively—they hoped in God and were
6 tender and obedient to their husbands; •like Sarah, who was obedient to Abraham, Gn 18:12 LXX
and called him her *lord.* You are now her children, as long as you live good lives Ga 4:28
and do not give way to fear or worry.
7 In the same way, husbands must always treat their wives with consideration Ep 5:25-33 Col 3:19
in their life together, respecting a woman as one who, though she may be the
weaker partner, is equally an heir[b] to the life of grace. This will stop anything
from coming in the way of your prayers.

Towards the brothers

8 Finally: you should all agree among yourselves and be sympathetic; love the Rm 12:14-18 Mt 5:39,44
9 brothers, have compassion and be self-effacing.[c] •Never pay back one wrong
with another, or an angry word with another one; instead, pay back with a
blessing. That is what you are called to do, so that you inherit a blessing yourself. Lk 6:28
10 Remember: *Anyone who wants to have a happy life and to enjoy prosperity must* Ps 34:12-16
11 *banish malice from his tongue, deceitful conversation from his lips; •he must never*
12 *yield to evil but must practise good; he must seek peace and pursue it. •Because the*

e. Or 'by the precious blood of the Christ, this spotless lamb'.

f. Var. 'from a pure heart'.

g. Or 'the living and eternal Word of God'.

2 a. Lit. 'to this indeed they were appointed'. By rejecting the Good News the Jews have lost their prerogatives which have been transferred to Christians, 3:9. The O.T. quotations in vv. 6-10 reflect the need of the earliest Christians to find scriptural explanations for the unbelief of Israel.

b. Add. 'in the sight of God'.

c. Var. 'died', cf. 3:18.

d. Var. 'you were like stray sheep'.

e. The '*episcopos*', i.e. the inspector or overseer, cf. Tt 1:5+.

3 a. Lit. 'should be the hidden man (self) of the heart'.

b. '(she) is equally an heir', var. 'you are equally heirs'. 'the life of grace', lit. 'the grace of life'; var. 'her own form of the grace of life', cf. 4:10.

c. 'be self-effacing' (lit. 'have a humble disposition'); Vulg. 'be modest and humble'.

face of the Lord frowns on evil men, but the eyes of the Lord are turned towards the virtuous.

In persecution

No one can hurt you if you are determined to do only what is right; •if you 13 14
Mt 5:10 Is 8:12-13 do have to suffer for being good, you will count it a blessing. *There is no need to*
LXX Mt 10:26-31 *be afraid or to worry about them.*[d] •Simply *reverence*[e] *the Lord*[f] Christ in your 15
Pr 3:25 hearts, and always have your answer ready for people who ask you the reason for
the hope that you all have. •But give it with courtesy and respect and with a clear 16
conscience, so that those who slander you when you are living a good life in Christ
may be proved wrong in the accusations that they bring. •And if it is the will of 17
God that you should suffer, it is better to suffer for doing right than for doing
wrong.

The resurrection and 'the descent into hell'

Rm 5:6; 6:10 Why, Christ himself, innocent though he was, had died once for sins,[g] died for 18
2:21-24 Is 53:11 the guilty, to lead us to God. In the body he was put to death, in the spirit he was
Ac 3:14+ Rm 1:3-4+ raised to life, •and, in the spirit, he went to preach to the spirits in prison.[h] 19
Heb 9:26-28 2 P 3:9 Now it was long ago, when Noah was still building that ark which saved only a 20
Gn 7:7 2 P 2:5 small group of eight people 'by water', and when God was still waiting patiently,
Col 2:12-13 that these spirits refused to believe. •That water is a type of the baptism[i] which 21
Rm 6:4+ saves you now, and which is not the washing off of physical dirt[j] but a pledge[k]
made to God from a good conscience, through the resurrection of Jesus Christ,
Ac 2:33+ Ep 1:20-21 who has entered heaven and is at God's right hand,[l] now that he has made the 22
Col 2:15+ angels and Dominations and Powers his subjects.

2:21 4 Think of what Christ suffered in this life, and then arm yourselves with the 1
Rm 6:2.7 same resolution that he had: anyone who in this life has bodily suffering has
Rm 7:14f 1 Jn 2:16-17 broken with sin, •because for the rest of his life on earth he is not ruled by human 2
passions but only by the will of God. •You spent quite long enough in the past 3
Ep 4:17-18 Tt 3:3 living the sort of life that pagans live, behaving indecently, giving way to your
Rm 1:29+ passions, drinking all the time, having wild parties and drunken orgies and
degrading yourselves by following false gods. •So people cannot understand why 4
you no longer hurry off with them to join this flood which is rushing down to
Ac 10:42 2 Tm 4:1 ruin,[a] and then they begin to spread libels about you. •They will have to answer 5
for it in front of the judge who is ready to judge the living and the dead. •And 6
3:19+ because he is their judge too, the dead had to be told the Good News as well,[b] so
that though, in their life on earth, they had been through the judgement that
Rm 1:9+ 2 Co 5:5+ comes to all humanity, they might come to God's life in the spirit.

The revelation of Christ is close

1:5-7; 4:17 2 Co 6:2+ Everything will soon come to an end, so, to pray better, keep a calm and sober 7
Pr 10:12 Jm 5:20 mind. •Above all, never let your love for each other grow insincere, since *love* 8
covers over many a sin. •Welcome each other into your houses without grumbling. 9
Rm 12:6-8 1 Co 12:4-11 Each one of you has received a special grace, so, like good stewards responsible 10
for all these different graces of God, put yourselves at the service of others. •If 11
you are a speaker, speak in words which seem to come from God;[c] if you are a
1 Co 10:31 helper,[d] help as though every action was done at God's orders; so that in
Rm 9:5 everything God may receive the glory, through Jesus Christ, since to him alone
Rm 16:27+ belong all glory and power for ever and ever. Amen.

Recapitulation

3:14 My dear people, you must not think it unaccountable that you should be tested 12
1:7 by fire. There is nothing extraordinary in what has happened to you. •If you can 13
Mt 5:11-12 Rm 5:3-5 have some share in the sufferings of Christ, be glad, because you will enjoy a much
1:21 Col 3:4 greater gladness when his glory is revealed. •It is a blessing for you when they 14
Jm 1:2-3 insult you for bearing the name of Christ, because it means that you have the

15 Spirit of glory,[e] the Spirit of God resting on you. •None of you should ever deserve
16 to suffer for being a murderer, a thief, a criminal or an informer; •but if anyone
of you should suffer for being a Christian, then he is not to be ashamed of it; he Ac 11:26+
17 should thank God that he has been called one. •The time has come for the judgement to begin at the household of God; and if what we know now is only the Jr 25:29 Lk 23:31
beginning, what will it be when it comes down to those who refuse to believe God's
18 Good News? •*If it is hard for a good man to be saved, what will happen to the wicked* Pr 11:31 LXX
19 *and to sinners?* •So even those whom God allows to suffer must trust themselves
to the constancy of the creator and go on doing good.

Instructions: to the elders

1 **5** Now I have something to tell your elders:[a] I am an elder myself, and a witness[b] Ac 11:30+ 20:28+
to the sufferings of Christ, and with you I have a share in the glory that is Col 3:4
2 to be revealed.[c] •Be the shepherds of the flock of God that is entrusted to you:
watch over it, not simply as a duty but gladly, because God wants it;[d] not for 1 Tm 3:8 Tt 1:7
3 sordid money, but because you are eager to do it. •Never be a dictator over any
group that is put in your charge, but be an example that the whole flock can 1 Co 4:16+ Tt 2:7-8
4 follow.[e] •When the chief shepherd appears, you will be given the crown of *Ezk 34:1+* 1 Co 9:25+
unfading glory.

To the faithful

5 To the rest of you I say: do what the elders tell you,[f] and all wrap yourselves 1 Jn 2:12-14
in humility to be servants of each other, because *God refuses the proud and will* Jn 13:14 *Pr 3:34* LXX
6 *always favour the humble.* •Bow down, then, before the power of God now, and he *Jb 22:29*
7 will raise you up on the appointed day;[g] •*unload* all *your worries on to him,* since Ph 2:8-9 Jm 4:6-10
8 he is looking after you. •*Be calm but vigilant,* because your enemy the devil[h] is *Ps 55:22* Mt 6:25f
9 prowling round like a roaring lion, looking for someone to eat. •Stand up to him, *Ps 22:13* Ep 6:11
strong in faith and in the knowledge that your brothers all over the world are
10 suffering the same things. •You will have to suffer only for a little while: the God Rm 8:18 2 Co 4:17

d. Om. 'or to worry about them'.

e. Lit. 'sanctify'.

f. 'The lord'; var. 'God'. 'hope', add. 'and faith'. The allusion is to local persecutions.

g. 'sins', Vulg. 'our sins'. Om. 'to God'.

h. Probably alludes to the descent of Christ to Hades, cf. Mt 16:18+, between his death and resurrection, Mt 12:40; Ac 2:24,31; Rm 10:7; Ep 4:9; Heb 13:20. He went there 'in spirit', cf. Lk 23:46, or (better) 'according to the spirit', Rm 1:4+, his 'flesh' being dead on the cross, Rm 8:3f. The 'spirits in prison' to whom he 'preached' (or 'proclaimed') salvation are identified by some writers as the chained demons mentioned in the *Book of Enoch* (some texts are corrected so as to make Enoch, and not Christ, preach to them). These spirits have thus been put under the authority of Christ as *Kyrios* v. 22, cf. Ep 1: 21f; Ph 2:8-10, and this subjection to him is to be confirmed later on, 1 Co 15:24f. Other writers suggest these were the spirits of people drowned in the Flood as a punishment but who are now summoned by God's 'patience' to eternal life, cf. 4:6. Mt 27:52f is a similar episode of liberation by Christ between his death and resurrection, only here it is the saints, the holy ones who were waiting for him, that are liberated, cf. Heb 11:39f; 12:23, and are given the freedom of the holy (the heavenly) city. The descent of Christ to Hades is one of the articles in the 'Apostles' Creed'.

i. Lit. 'by water, to which the antitype is the baptism' i.e. that which was prefigured by the 'type' (cf. 1 Co 10:6+). Here the 'type' of baptism is Noah's Flood.

j. As so few were saved from drowning, the Flood is taken to symbolise the O.T. purificatory rites that were, almost without exception, limited to an *external* 'bodily', purity, whereas the baptism by which a person is reborn can have no limits to its efficacy.

k. The 'pledge' (alternative translation 'the request') made by a convert at his baptism.

l. Add. (Vulg.) 'submitting to death so that we might inherit eternal life'.

4 a. Lit. 'rush with them to the same "unsafe up-pouring" (i.e. "flood of no-salvation" or "flood of debauchery")'; this dangerous flood destroys the good, unlike Noah's Flood that destroyed the wicked, cf. 3:20.

b. For the proclamation of the Good News to the dead cf. 3:19+. Some exegetes interpret this as meaning the 'spiritually dead' e.g. those who are persecuting the Christians to whom the letter is being written.

c. As in impromptu spiritual prophecies and in *glossolalia*, cf. 1 Co 14:2-19; Ac 11:27+ with Ac 2:4+.

d. This could possibly refer to liturgical service.

e. Add. 'and power'. Add. at end of verse '(the Spirit) blasphemed by them but honoured by you'.

5 a. These elders are to be identified with the 'presbyters' of Tt 1:5+, cf. note on 5:5 where 'elders' means 'older people'.

b. This can mean either that as an apostle, 1:1, he witnessed the Passion of Jesus, or that through his own sufferings he is a witness to Christ.

c. At the *parousia*, cf. 1:5,13; 4:7,17; 5:10.

d. Om. 'watch over it' and 'because God wants it'.

e. Lit. 'Nor as lording it over those allocated (i.e. to you) but becoming examples of the flock'; var. 'Be examples to the flock'. Add. (Vulg.) 'with all your heart'.

f. Lit. 'Likewise younger people submit yourselves to older people'; the 'younger people' here are not adolescents as opposed to 'older people', cf. Tt 2:6, but the body of the faithful as opposed to the 'presbyters' or elders, 5:1+.

g. Add. (Vulg.) 'of his coming', cf. 2:12.

h. The word *diabolos* (lit. 'one who passes to another information against a third party') may be translated 'accuser'; it is applied to the devil in its legal sense of 'prosecutor'.

1 Th 2:12; 5:24 of all grace who called you to eternal glory in Christ will see that all is well again:
4:11 he will confirm, strengthen and support you.[i] •His[j] power lasts for ever and ever. 11
Amen.

Last words. Greetings

Ac 15:22+ I write these few words to you through Silvanus, who is a brother I know I can 12
trust, to encourage you never to let go this true grace of God to which I bear
witness.
Rv 17:5 2 Jn 1+ Your sister in Babylon, who is with you among the chosen,[k] sends you 13
Ac 12:12+ greetings; so does my son, Mark.
2 Co 13:12+ Greet one another with a kiss of love.[l] 14
Peace to you all who are in Christ.[m]

5 i. 'called you', var. (Vulg.) 'called us'. 'in Christ', add. (Vulg.) 'Jesus'. Om. (Vulg.) 'strengthen'.
j. Add. 'glory and'.
k. Lit. 'the co-chosen *(feminine)* in Babylon greets you'; var. (Vulg.) 'The co-chosen church'. The reference is to the church at Rome.
l. Var. (Vulg.) 'holy kiss', cf. Rm 16:16; 1 Co 16:20.
m. Add. (Vulg.) 'Jesus. Amen.'

2 PETER

THE SECOND LETTER OF PETER

Greetings

1 1 From Simeon Peter, servant and apostle of Jesus Christ; to all who treasure Ac 15:14+
the same faith as ourselves, given through the righteousness of our God and
2 saviour Jesus Christ.[a] •May you have more and more grace and peace as you ||Jude 2
come to know our Lord[b] more and more. 1:8 Ph 3:10 Col 2:6

A call to Christian living, and its reward

3 By his divine power, he has given us all the things that we need for life and for Ep 3:16-19
true devotion, bringing us to know God himself, who has called us by his own
4 glory and goodness.[c] •In making these gifts, he has given us[d] the guarantee of Jn 1:14+
something very great and wonderful to come: through them[e] you will be able to Ws 2:33 Jn 1:10+,12
share the divine nature and to escape corruption in a world that is sunk in vice.[f] Ac 17:28+ 2 Co 3:18
5 But to attain this,[g] you will have to do your utmost yourselves, adding goodness 1 Jn 2:15f; 5:19
6 to the faith that you have, understanding to your goodness, •self-control to your Ga 5:22+
understanding, patience to your self-control, true devotion to your patience,
7 kindness towards your fellow men to your devotion, and, to this kindness, love.
8 If you have a generous supply of these, they will not leave you ineffectual or
unproductive: they will bring you to a real knowledge of our Lord Jesus Christ. 1:2
9 But without them[h] a man is blind or else short-sighted; he has forgotten how
10 his past sins were washed away. •Brothers, you have been called and chosen: work
all the harder to justify it.[i] If you do all these things there is no danger that you will 2 Th 1:11 1 Jn 3:6+
11 ever fall away. •In this way you will be granted admittance into the eternal
kingdom[j] of our Lord and saviour Jesus Christ.

The apostolic witness

12 That is why I am continually recalling the same truths to you, even though you ||Jude 5
13 already know them and firmly hold them. •I am sure it is my duty, as long as 1 Jn 2:21 *Ws 9:15*
14 I am in this tent, to keep stirring you up with reminders, •since I know the time Is 38:12 2 Co 5:1
for taking off this tent is coming soon, as our Lord Jesus Christ foretold to me. *Jn 21:18-19*
15 And I shall take great care that after my own departure you will still have a
means to recall these things to memory.

1 a. Or 'of our God and of the saviour Jesus Christ'.

b. Lit. 'through knowing our Lord'; var. 'through knowing God and Jesus (or Jesus Christ) our Lord'. All through this letter it is Christ who is proposed as the object of a Christian's knowledge, 1:3,8; 2:20; 3:18.

c. 'glory' here refers to the miracles done by Jesus as a sign of his divinity, cf. Jn 1:14+, but in particular it refers to the transfiguration, 2 P 1:16-18. 'goodness' could refer to his powers both natural and miraculous.

d. 'us', var. 'you'. What has been promised is something that concerns the 'Day of the Lord', cf. 3:4,9-10,12-13.

e. I.e. as a result of the glory and goodness of Christ. Var. (Vulg.) 'through it'.

f. Var. (Vulg.) 'the corruption of the vice that is in the world'.

g. Lit. 'For this very reason'; var. (Vulg.) 'But you'.

h. This is the same sort of warning against Gnosticism that is given in the Johannine letters, cf. 1 Jn 1:8+. Gnostics claimed to know God without keeping his commandments.

i. Add. (Vulg.) 'by good deeds'.

j. This, like 1:4; 3:4,9-10, looks forward to the *parousia*.

3:4+ Mt 17:1+ It was not any cleverly invented myths that we were repeating[k] when we 16
1 Co 15:23+ brought you the knowledge of the power and the coming of our Lord Jesus Christ;
Lk 9:31-32p Jn 1:14 we had seen his majesty for ourselves.[l] •He was honoured and glorified by God 17
Mt 17:5p the Father, when the Sublime Glory itself spoke to him and said,[m] 'This is my Son,
the Beloved; he enjoys my favour'. •We heard this ourselves, spoken from heaven, 18
when we were with him on the holy mountain.[n]

The value of prophecy

So we have confirmation of what was said in prophecies;[o] and you will be 19
right to depend on prophecy and take it as a lamp for lighting a way
Lk 1:78 Rv 2:28+ through the dark until the dawn comes and the morning star rises in your minds.
At the same time, we must be most careful to remember that the interpretation 20
of scriptural prophecy is never a matter for the individual. •Why? Because no 21
2 Tm 3:16 1 P 1:10-12 prophecy ever came from man's initiative. When men spoke for God it was the
Ac 3:21 Holy Spirit that moved them.

False teachers

3:3+ Dt 13:2-6 2 As there were false prophets in the past history of our people, so you too will 1
Mt 24:24 ||Jude 4 have your false teachers, who will insinuate their own disruptive views and
Rm 3:24+ disown the Master who purchased their freedom. They will destroy themselves
Is 52:5 Ac 9:2+ very quickly; •but there will be many who copy their shameful behaviour and the 2
Rm 2:24 Way of Truth will be brought into disrepute on their account. •They will eagerly 3
try to buy you for themselves with insidious speeches, but for them the Condem-
nation, pronounced so long ago, is at its work already, and Destruction is not
Gn 6:1-2 Mt 8:29 asleep.[a] •When angels sinned, God did not spare them: he sent them down to the 4
||Jude 6 underworld and consigned them to the dark underground caves to be held there
Gn 6:17 Si 44:17 till the day of Judgement. •Nor did he spare the world in ancient times:[b] it was 5
Heb 11:7 1 P 3:20 only Noah he saved, the preacher of righteousness, along with seven others, when
he sent the Flood over a disobedient world. •The cities of Sodom and Gomorrah, 6
Gn 19 Ws 10:6 these too he condemned and reduced to ashes; he destroyed them completely,[c] as
Mt 10:15p ||Jude 7 a warning to anybody lacking reverence in the future; •he rescued Lot, however, 7
a holy man who had been sickened by the shameless way in which these vile people
behaved— •for that holy man, living among them, was outraged in his good soul 8
by the crimes that he saw and heard of every day. •These are all examples of how 9
2 Th 1:5-10 the Lord can rescue the good from the ordeal, and hold the wicked for their
Rm 2:6+ ||Jude 8 punishment until the day of Judgement, •especially those who are governed by 10
their corrupt bodily desires and have no respect for authority.[d]

The punishment to come

Such self-willed people with no reverence are not afraid of offending against
||Jude 9-10 the glorious ones,[e] •but the angels in their greater strength and power make no 11
complaint or accusation against them in front of the Lord.[f] •All the same, these 12
Ps 49:12-14 people who only insult anything that they do not understand are not reasoning
beings, but simply animals born to be caught and killed, and they will quite
certainly destroy themselves by their own work of destruction, •and get their 13
reward of evil for the evil that they do. They are unsightly blots on your society:
men whose only object is dissipation all day long,[g] and they amuse themselves
||Jude 12 deceiving you even when they are your guests at a meal; •with their eyes always 14
looking for adultery,[h] men with an infinite capacity for sinning, they will seduce
any soul which is at all unstable. Greed is the one lesson their minds have learnt.
Nb 22:2+ ||Jude 11 They are under a curse. •They have left the right path and wandered off to follow 15
Rv 2:14-15 the path of Balaam son of Beor,[i] who thought he could profit best by sinning,
Nb 22:28-33 until he was called to order for his faults. The dumb donkey put a stop to that 16
||Jude 12-13 prophet's madness when it talked like a man. •People like this are dried-up rivers, 17
fogs swirling in the wind, and the dark underworld is the place reserved for them.
||Jude 16 With their high-flown talk, which is all hollow, they tempt back the ones who 18

have only just escaped from paganism,[j] playing on their bodily desires with
19 debaucheries. •They may promise freedom[k] but they themselves are slaves, slaves
to corruption; because if anyone lets himself be dominated by anything, then Jn 8:34 Rm 6:16-17
20 he is a slave to it; •and anyone who has escaped the pollution of the world once
by coming to know our Lord and saviour Jesus Christ, and who then allows
himself to be entangled[l] by it a second time and mastered, will end up in a worse Mt 12:45p
21 state than he began in. •It would even have been better for him never to have Ezk 3:20
learnt the way of holiness, than to know it and afterwards desert the holy rule
22 that was entrusted to him. •What he has done is exactly as the proverb rightly 1 Co 11:2+
says: *The dog goes back to his own vomit* and: When the sow has been washed, it Pr 26:11
wallows in the mud.

The Day of the Lord; the prophets and the apostles

1 **3** My friends, this is my second[a] letter to you, and in both of them I have tried
2 to awaken a true understanding in you by giving you a reminder: •recalling to ||Jude 17
you what was said in the past by the holy prophets and the commandments of the
Lord and saviour which you were given by the apostles.

3 We must be careful to remember[b] that during the last days[c] there are bound Ezk 12:22 1 Tm 4:1+
to be people who will be scornful, the kind who always please themselves what ||Jude 18
4 they do, and they will make fun of the promise •and ask, 'Well, where is this 1:16; 2:1
coming? Everything goes on as it has since the Fathers[d] died, as it has since it Is 5:19
5 began at the creation.' •They are choosing to forget[e] that there were heavens Gn 1:2,6-9
at the beginning, and that the earth was formed by the word of God out of
6 water and between the waters, •so that the world of that time was destroyed by Gn 7-9 Mt 24:38-39
7 being flooded by water. •But by the same word, the present sky and earth are
destined for fire, and are only being reserved until Judgement day so that all Is 51:6 Mt 3:12+ Rm 2:6+
sinners may be destroyed.

8 But there is one thing, my friends, that you must never forget: that with the
Lord, 'a day' can mean a thousand years, and *a thousand years is like a day.* Ps 90:4
9 The Lord is not being slow to carry out his promises, as anybody else might be Hab 2:2-3
called slow; but he is being patient with you all, wanting nobody to be lost and Ezk 18:23 Rm 2:4-5
10 everybody to be brought to change his ways.[f] •The Day of the Lord will come 1 P 3:20 *Mt 24:43p*
like a thief, and then with a roar the sky will vanish, the elements will catch fire 1 Th 5:2 *Mt 24:29+*
and fall apart, the earth and all that it contains will be burnt up.[g] Rv 20:11

Conclusion and doxology

11 Since everything is coming to an end like this, you should be living holy and Ac 3:19-20

k. Lit. 'not following myths that have been cleverly devised'; this is another warning against Gnostics who had a doctrine of the *parousia* based not on logical proofs, but on an elaborate mythological system, cf. 3:4f.

l. At the transfiguration.

m. Lit. 'For receiving from God (the) Father honour and glory such a voice being borne to him by the magnificent glory'; var. (Vulg.) '...out of the magnificent glory'.

n. 'holy mountain' should perhaps be taken as a suggestion that the mountain of transfiguration was the antitype of Sinai.

o. Lit. 'We have more firm the prophetic word'. The transfiguration is a preliminary glimpse of scripture prophecy being fulfilled.

2 a. These false teachers have already been condemned, cf. Jude 4.

b. The antediluvian world.

c. Lit. 'he reduced to ashes and condemned them to extinction'; om. 'to extinction'.

d. The authority of Christ, cf. 2:1; Jude 4,8.

e. Lit. 'glories'; the angels.

f. 'in front of the Lord'; om. (Vulg.).

g. Lit. 'deeming daytime luxury to be pleasure', var. 'happy to give themselves up to debauchery in broad daylight'.

h. Lit. 'eyes full of adultery'; var. (Vulg.) '...of an adulteress'.

i. 'Beor', misspelt in most MSS Bosor or even Beorsor.

j. Lit. 'from those who live in error'. The reference is to the 'unstable souls' of 2:14; many of them copy the shameful behaviour of the false teachers, 2:2.

k. Liberty, for the Gnostics, included freedom from any moral restrictions, cf. Jude 4.

l. This refers to those who have been seduced by the false teachers not to the teachers themselves.

3 a. Alludes probably to 1 P.

b. The prediction that follows seems to be based more on the teaching of the apostles than on O.T. prophecy, cf. Ac 20:29; 2 Tm 3:1-5. If fits into Jude 18 better than it fits in here.

c. That heretics should exist is itself a proof that the last days are near.

d. Either the patriarchs or the Christians of the first generation.

e. The inference is that the false teachers proved the impossibility of the *parousia* from the unchangeableness of the universe.

f. God's mercy is an alternative explanation for the alleged delay of the *parousia*, cf. Ws 11:23f; 12:8+.

g. 'burnt up', corr.; 'uncovered' (Greek). This destruction of the world by fire was, in Graeco-Roman times, a common topic for philosophers.

Is 34:4; 51:6+ saintly lives •while you wait and long for the Day of God to come, when the sky 12
Rm 8:21 Heb 12:27+ will dissolve in flames and the elements melt in the heat. •What we are waiting 13
Rv 20:11+ *Is 65:17; 66:22* for is what he promised: the new heavens and new earth, the place where right-
Rv 21:1,27 eousness will be at home. •So then, my friends, while you are waiting, do your 14
Is 60:21 Rm 8:19+ best to live lives without spot or stain so that he will find you at peace. •Think of 15
||Jude 24 *1 Tm 1:15-16* our Lord's patience as your opportunity to be saved: our brother Paul, who is so
dear to us, told you this when he wrote to you with the wisdom that is his special
gift. •He always writes like this when he deals with this sort of subject, and this 16
makes some points[h] in his letter hard to understand; these are the points that
uneducated and unbalanced people distort, in the same way as they distort the rest
Heb 2:1 of scripture[i]—a fatal thing for them to do. •You have been warned about this, 17
my friends; be careful not to get carried away by the errors of unprincipled
people, from the firm ground that you are standing on. •Instead, go on growing 18
in the grace and in the knowledge of our Lord and saviour Jesus Christ. To him
Rm 16:27+ be glory, in time and in eternity. Amen.

3 h. About the *parousia*, presumably, since that is the subject under discussion.

i. This implies that the letters of Paul were considered canonical.

1 JOHN

THE FIRST LETTER OF JOHN

INTRODUCTION

The incarnate Word

1 **1** Something which has existed since the beginning, 2:13 Jn 1:1-5 Ac 22:15+
that we have heard,
and we have seen with our own eyes; Jn 20:20,25, 27
that we have watched
and touched with our hands: Lk 24:39
the Word, who is life— Jn 1:1+; 3:11+
this is our subject.
2 That life was made visible:
we saw it and we are giving our testimony, Jn 1:14+; 15:27 *5:20*
telling you of the eternal life
which was with the Father and has been made visible to us.
3 What we have seen and heard 2:3,19,24,29 Ac 4:20; 26:16
we are telling you
so that you too may be in union[a] with us, Ac 2:42f
as we are in union
with the Father
and with his Son Jesus Christ. 1 Co 1:9 Jn 15:11; 16:22-24
4 We are writing this to you to make our own[b] joy complete. 2 Jn 12

I. WALK IN THE LIGHT

5 This is what we have heard from him, 3:11
and the message that we are announcing to you:
God is light; there is no darkness in him at all. Dn 2:22 Jn 8:12+ 1 Tm 6:16
6 If we say that we are in union with God[c] Jm 1:17
while we are living in darkness,
we are lying because we are not living the truth. Jn 3:21
7 But if we live our lives in the light,
as he is in the light,
we are in union with one another,[d]

1 a. Lit. 'have fellowship' (so also in v. 7). This union is the idea most central to John's mysticism, Jn 14:20; 15:1-6; 17:11,20-26; union between all Christians results from the union created by Christ between each Christian and God. This union is referred to in different ways: a Christian lives 'in' God and God lives 'in' him, 1 Jn 2:5,6,24,27; 3:6,24; 4:12,13,15,16; a Christian is begotten by God, has new life from him, 2:29; 3:9; 4:7; 5:1,18; the Christian is from God, is his child, 2:16; 3:10; 4:4-6; 5:19; the Christian knows God, 2:3,13,14; 3:6; 4:7,8 (on knowledge and presence cf. Jn 14:17; 2 Jn 1-2). This union with God shows itself in a person's faith and in his love for the brothers, cf. 1:7+.

b. 'our own', var. (Vulg.) 'your'.

c. Lit. 'him'. In this translation the pronoun has been rendered 'God', or 'Christ', where it seemed necessary for the sense.

d. God is in Christians, 1:3+, as the principle of their new life. Since God is light, 1:5, virtue, 2:29, and love, 4:8,16, whoever lives in union with God must live a life of light, virtue and love, and keep God's commandments, especially the commandment to love all human beings, 2:10,11; 3:10; 4:8,16. Faith and love are thus the visible evidence of true union with God, 1:6,7; 2:3,6; 3:6,10,17,24; 4:6,8,13,16,20.

Mt 26:28p Rm 3:24-25+ Rv 1:5 and the blood of Jesus, his Son,
purifies us from all sin.

First condition: break with sin

Pr 20:9 Qo 7:20 Si 8:5 If we say we have no sin in us, 8
we are deceiving ourselves
and refusing to admit the truth;[e]
Pr 28:13+ Jm 5:16+ but if we acknowledge our sins, 9
then God who is faithful and just
Ps 32:1+ Mt 6:12p will forgive our sins and purify us
from everything that is wrong.
To say that we have never sinned 10
is to call God a liar
and to show that his word is not in us.

2

I am writing this, my children, 1
3:6+ to stop you sinning;
but if anyone should sin,
Heb 7:25; 8:6+ *Jn 14:16* we have our advocate with the Father,
Ac 3:14+ Jesus Christ, who is just;
4:10 Rm 3:25+ he is the sacrifice that takes our sins away, 2
and not only ours,
Jn 4:42+ but the whole world's.

Second condition: keep the commandments, especially the law of love

1:3+,7+ Jn 10:14+ We can be sure that we know God 3
only by keeping his commandments.
4:20 Anyone who says, 'I know him', 4
and does not keep his commandments,
is a liar,
refusing to admit the truth.[a]
Jn 14:21,23 But when anyone does obey what he has said, 5
3:17 God's love comes to perfection in him.[b]
We can be sure
that we are in God
Jn 13:15,34 Ep 5:2 2 Th 3:7+ only when the one who claims to be living in him 6
is living the same kind of life as Christ[c] lived.
My dear people, 7
this is not a new commandment that I am writing to tell you,
3:11 Dt 6:5 Mt 22:37-40 2 Jn 5 but an old commandment
that you were given from the beginning,
the original commandment which was the message brought to you.
Jn 13:34+ Yet in another way, what I am writing to you, 8
and what is being carried out in your lives as it was in his,
is a new commandment;
Rm 13:12 because the night is over
Jn 1:5; 8:12 and the real light is already shining.
Anyone who claims to be in the light 9
but hates his brother
is still in the dark.
Jn 12:35-36 But anyone who loves his brother is living in the light 10
Pr 4:19 Qo 2:14 and need not be afraid of stumbling;
unlike the man who hates his brother and is in the darkness, 11
not knowing where he is going,
Mt 15:14p because it is too dark to see.

Third condition: detachment from the world

12 I am writing to you, my own children, 1 P 5:5+
whose sins have already been forgiven through his name; 1:7; 2:2 Ac 3:16+ 1 Co 6:11
13 I am writing to you, fathers,
who have come to know the one
who has existed since the beginning; 1:1 Jn 1:1
I am writing to you, young men,
who have already overcome the Evil One; Ep 6:16
14 I have written[d] to you, children,
because you already know the Father;
I have written to you, fathers,
because you have come to know the one
who has existed since the beginning;
I have written to you, young men,
because you are strong and God's word has made its home in you, Jn 3:11+
and you have overcome the Evil One.[e] Mt 6:14+ Jn 5:38
15 You must not love this passing world Jn 1:10+
or anything that is in the world.
The love of the Father cannot be Jn 5:42+
in any man who loves the world, Rm 8:7-8 2 P 1:4+
16 because nothing the world has to offer
—the sensual body, Mt 6:24p Jm 4:4 *Pr 27:20*
the lustful eye,
pride in possessions—[f] Jm 4:16
could ever come from the Father
but only from the world;
17 and the world, with all it craves for, 1 Co 7:31 1 P 4:2
is coming to an end;
but anyone who does the will of God Pr 10:25 Is 40:8 Mt 7:21
remains for ever.

Fourth condition: be on guard against the enemies of Christ

18 Children, these are the last days; 1 Tm 4:1+
you were told that an Antichrist[g] must come, 2 Th 2:4+
and now several antichrists have already appeared; 4:1 2 Jn 7
we know from this that these are the last days.
19 Those rivals of Christ came out of our own number, but they had never really belonged;[h] 2 Co 6:14-18
if they had belonged, they would have stayed with us; 1:3+
but they left us, to prove that not one of them
ever belonged to us.
20 But you have been anointed[i] by the Holy One, Lv 17:1+ Is 6:3+ Jn 14:26+ 2 Co 1:21
and have all received the knowledge.[j]

e. This is possibly an allusion to the sect that called themselves 'spirituals', *pneumatikoi*, and who were the forerunners of the Gnostics of the 2nd c. who looked down on other people as being either *psychikoi* or *hylikoi*, i.e. either incompletely or not at all liberated from matter.

2 a. Add. 'of God'.

b. Lit. 'in him the love of God has been perfected (reached its goal)': this refers more to God's love for us than to our love for him.

c. Lit. 'as That One': Jesus is repeatedly referred to in this way, 3:3,5,7,16; 4:17, cf. Jn 2:21; 19:35.

d. Var. (Vulg.) 'I am writing to you (now)'. The second clause ('I have written to you, fathers ... beginning') is omitted by Vulg.

e. The devil is still the Tempter as in Gn 3:1-6; Jb 1:6+, who incites human beings to wickedness, 1 Jn 3:8+. Christians, however, having 'known' the Son, the Son lives in them, 1:3+, and 'clothes' them in light, virtue and love, 1:7+; and as this protects them from the devil, 5:18; Jn 17:15, and prevents them from sinning, 3:6,9, it constitutes their victory over the devil, 2:13,14, and over this transient world, 4:4; 5:4,5; cf. Jn 12:31; 14:30; 16:33; Mt 6:13.

f. Lit. 'the ostentation of living'.

g. 'an Antichrist' var. 'The Antichrist'.

h. Though they seemed to belong to the community, they lacked the spirit of Christ.

i. In the O.T. the chrism that was to anoint the Messiah (the 'anointed') was identified, Is 11:2; 61:1, with the (holy) Spirit or Breath of Yahweh. Christians share in this anointing that teaches them the true *gnosis* or knowledge.

j. Var. 'you know all things'.

2 P 1:12 It is not because you do not know the truth that I am writing to you 21
2 Jn 1:2 but rather because you know it already
3:19+ and know that no lie can come from the truth.[k]
The man who denies that Jesus is the Christ— 22
he is the liar,
2 Th 2:4+ 2 Jn 7 he is Antichrist;
and he is denying the Father as well as the Son,[l]
because no one who has the Father can deny the Son, 23
Jn 14:7-9; 17:6+ and to acknowledge the Son is to have the Father as well.
Keep alive in yourselves what you were taught in the beginning:[m] 24
as long as what you were taught in the beginning is alive in you,
1:3+ you will live in the Son
and in the Father;
Jn 5:24; 6:40,68; 17:2 and what is promised to you by his own promise 25
is eternal life.
This is all that I am writing to you about the people who are trying to lead you astray. 26
22:20 But you have not lost the anointing that he gave you, 27
and you do not need anyone to teach you;[n]
Jr 31:34 Jn 14:26+ the anointing he gave teaches you everything;
you are anointed with truth, not with a lie,
and as it has taught you, so you must stay in him.
Live in Christ, then, my children, 28
4:17 so that if he appears, we may have full confidence,
2 Th 1:9 and not turn from him in shame
Mt 24:3+ 1 Co 15:23+ at his coming.
You know that God is righteous— 29
1:3+,7+ then you must recognise that everyone whose life is righteous
has been begotten by him.

II. LIVE AS GOD'S CHILDREN

3 Think of the love that the Father has lavished on us, 1
Jn 1:12 Rm 8:14-17, 37-39 by letting us be called God's children;
Ep 1:5 and that is what we are.[a]
Jn 15:21; 16:3; 17:25 Because the world refused to acknowledge him,
therefore it does not acknowledge us.
My dear people, we are already the children of God 2
but what we are to be in the future has not yet been revealed;
Rm 8:29 Ph 3:21 all we know is, that when it is revealed
Col 3:4 we shall be like him
because we shall see him as he really is.

First condition: break with sin

Surely everyone who entertains this hope 3
2:6 Mt 5:48+ must purify himself, must try to be as pure as Christ.[b]
Anyone who sins at all 4
breaks the law,
because to sin is to break the law.
Jn 1:29+ Now you know that he appeared in order to abolish sin,[c] 5
Jn 8:46 Heb 7:26 and that in him there is no sin;
1:3+; 2:14+ Mt 7:18 anyone who lives in God does not sin,[d] 6
and anyone who sins
has never seen him or known him.
My children, do not let anyone lead you astray: 7

to live a holy life
is to be holy just as he is holy;
8 to lead a sinful life is to belong to the devil,[e] 3:12
since the devil was a sinner from the beginning. Gn 3:15 Jn 8:44
It was to undo all that the devil has done
that the Son of God appeared. 3:5 Jn 12:31-32
9 No one who has been begotten by God sins; 3:6+
because God's seed[f] remains inside him,
he cannot sin when he has been begotten by God. 2:14+

Second condition: keep the commandments, especially the law of love

10 In this way we distinguish the children of God 1:7+; 4:6
from the children of the devil: 3:8+
anybody not living a holy life
and not loving his brother 3:23
is no child of God's.
11 This is the message 1:5
as you heard it from the beginning: 2:7
that we are to love one another; Jn 13:34
12 not to be like Cain, who belonged to the Evil One 3:8+ Gn 4:8
and cut his brother's throat; Jn 8:44 Jude 11
cut his brother's throat simply for this reason,
that his own life was evil and his brother lived a good life.
13 You must not be surprised, brothers, when the world hates you; Mt 24:9 Jn 15:18-21
14 we have passed out of death and into life, Jn 5:24; 11:26
and of this we can be sure
because we love our brothers.
15 If you refuse to love, you must remain dead; Heb 6:1+
to hate your brother is to be a murderer,
and murderers, as you know, do not have eternal life in them.
16 This has taught us love— 2:6 Mt 20:28
that he gave up his life for us; Jn 15:12-13 Ep 5:2
and we, too, ought to give up our lives for our brothers.
17 If a man who was rich enough in this world's goods Dt 15:7,11 Jm 2:16
saw that one of his brothers was in need,
but closed his heart to him,
how could the love of God be living in him? 2:5; 4:12 Jn 5:42
18 My children,
our love is not to be just words or mere talk, Mt 7:21 Jm 1:22
but something real and active;
19 only by this can we be certain[g]

k. Or 'and because you know that the lies cannot have come from truth'.

l. Probably a reference to Cerinthus who taught that Jesus was an ordinary human being who was 'possessed' by the Messiah at his baptism in the Jordan; this Messiah ascended before the Passion of Jesus. Another possible reference to his teaching is in 5:6—the belief in baptism ('water') but not the sacrificial death ('blood').

m. The apostolic teaching concerning the mystery of Christ.

n. Christians are taught by the apostles, 1:3,5; 2:7,24, but merely hearing what is said is not enough, the message must penetrate them and this it cannot do except through the grace of the Holy Spirit, cf. 2:20+.

3 a. Om. 'and that is what we are'; var. (Vulg.) 'and may we become precisely that'.

b. Lit. 'as That One'.

c. Lit. 'sins'; var. 'our sins'.

d. Because God, living in the Christian, is present with all his divine power for life. John is talking in general terms, ignoring people's momentary lapses, 1:7—2:1; all he is giving is a schematic contrast between the two 'worlds', cf. 3:9; 5:18.

e. Having used expressions like: of God, from Truth, child of God, to show how a Christian lives under the influence of God living in him, John now uses expressions like: of the devil, 3:8; of the Evil One, 3:12, from, or of, the impermanent world, 2:16; 4:5, children of the devil, to indicate those who live under the influence of the devil and allow themselves to be seduced by him.

f. The 'seed' of God could be a reference to Christ, cf. Ga 3:16; 1 Jn 5:13, but some commentators take it as a reference to the Spirit, cf. 2:20-27, or to the seed of divine life introduced into us by God.

g. Lit. 'we shall be certain'; var. (Vulg.) 'we are certain'.

2:21+ Jn 18:37 2 Jn 4 that we are children of the truth[h]
and be able to quieten our conscience in his presence,
whatever accusations it may raise against us, 20
4:4 because God is greater than our conscience and he knows everything.[i]
My dear people, 21
if we cannot be condemned by our own conscience,
we need not be afraid in God's presence,
5:15 Mt 7:7-11p Jn 14:13-14 and whatever we ask him, 22
we shall receive,
because we keep his commandments
Jn 8:29 and live the kind of life that he wants.
His commandments are these: 23
that we believe in the name of his Son Jesus Christ
5:3 and that we love one another
Jn 13:34; 15:17 as he told us to.
Whoever keeps his commandments 24
1:3+ lives in God and God lives in him.
1:7+ Jn 14:21-23 *4:13* We know that he lives in us
by the Spirit that he has given us.

Third condition: be on guard against the enemies of Christ and against the world

4 It is not every spirit, my dear people, that you can trust; 1
1 Co 12:10+ test them, to see if they come from God,
2:18 Mt 24:24 1 Tm 4:1+ Jude 4 *1 Co 12:3* 1 Th 5:21 there are many false prophets, now, in the world.
You can tell the spirits that come from God by this: 2
every spirit which acknowledges that Jesus the Christ has come in the flesh
is from God;
but any spirit which will not say this of Jesus[a] 3
is not from God,
2:22 2 Th 2:4+ but is the spirit of Antichrist,
whose coming you were warned about.
Well, now he is here, in the world.
Children, 4
2:14+ you have already overcome these false prophets,
because you are from God and you have in you
3:20 one who is greater than anyone in this world;
3:8+ as for them, they are of the world, 5
and so they speak the language of the world
and the world listens to them.
1:3+ Jn 8:47; 10:26+ But we[b] are children of God, 6
and those who know God listen to us;
those who are not of God refuse to listen to us.
3:10 Jn 14:17 This is how we can tell
the spirit of truth from the spirit of falsehood.[c]

III. LOVE AND FAITH

Love

My dear people, 7
let us love one another
1 Th 4:9 since love comes from God
1:3+ and everyone who loves is begotten by God and knows God.
1:7+ Anyone who fails to love can never have known God, 8

because God is love.[d] 4:16
9 God's love for us was revealed
when God sent into the world his only Son Gn 22:12 Mt 21:37
so that we could have life through him; Jn 3:16
10 this is the love I mean: Dt 7:8 Ws 6:16
not our love for God, Rm 8:31f
but God's love for us when he sent his Son Rm 5:8
to be the sacrifice that takes our sins away. 2:2 Rm 3:25+
11 My dear people,
since God has loved us so much, Mt 18:33
we too should love one another.
12 No one has ever seen God;[e] Ex 33:20+ Jn 1:18; 6:46
but as long as we love one another
God will live in us 1:3+
and his love will be complete in us.
13 We can know that we are living in him 1:7+
and he is living in us
because he lets us share his Spirit.[f] 3:24 Rm 5:5+
14 We ourselves saw and we testify
that the Father sent his Son Jn 3:17
as saviour of the world. Jn 4:42+
15 If anyone acknowledges that Jesus is the Son of God,
God lives in him, and he in God.
16 We ourselves have known and put our faith in
God's love towards ourselves. Jn 17:6+
God is love 4:7-8
and anyone who lives in love lives in God, 1:3+
and God lives in him.
17 Love will come to its perfection in us
when we can face the day of Judgement without fear; 2:28 Rm 8:15
because even in this world Jm 2:13
we have become as he is. 2:6+; 3:2-3
18 In love there can be no fear, 2 Th 3:7+
but fear is driven out by perfect love: 2 Tm 1:7
because to fear is to expect punishment,
and anyone who is afraid is still imperfect in love.[g]
19 We are to love, then,
because he loved us first. 4:9-10
20 Anyone who says, 'I love God', 2:4
and hates his brother,

h. In the O.T. 'truth' (contrasting with unrighteousness and evil) often means the rightness of a life morally well lived in accordance with the will of Yahweh, in fidelity to Yahweh. This is the way John uses the word. As there is a double commandment to fidelity and love, 3:23, people are said to 'belong to truth' if they believe, 2:21,22, and love, 3:19; they are said to live 'in union with (walk according to) truth' 2 Jn 4-6, 3 Jn 3-6, to 'do the truth', Jn 3:21 (to perform or act it, as opposed to committing sin, doing wrong), cf. Jn 18:37; 4:24.

i. The person whose conscience (lit. 'heart') reproaches him will find that God as a judge is both more acute and more lenient than his conscience, providing (it is understood) that charity has been practised. Another translation could be 'In the presence of God we shall prove to our conscience, if it has been accusing us, that God is greater than our conscience is, and that he knows everything'.

4 a. Var. (Vulg.) and strongly supported 'which dissolves (or breaks, splits, divides) Jesus'.

b. 'we' i.e. the authorised preachers, and particularly the apostles.

c. Lit. 'From this we know the spirit of truth and the spirit of error'; the theme of the two spirits, which also occurs in Essene (Qumran) literature, was destined to have a considerable influence on early Christian thought. All people are torn between the two 'worlds', cf. 3:8+; 3:19+, and in varying degrees all are inspired by the spirit of each of these 'worlds'. For John the spirit of truth comes from God, 3:24; 4:13, cf. Jn 14:26+.

d. The idea that God loves Israel was one of the great poetic inspirations of the O.T., cf. Is 54:8+. The fact that God sent his only Son to save the world proves that God is love.

e. This is directed against the *pneumatikoi* who held that by intuition a human being can 'reach' God.

f. It is God himself who through his Spirit produces charity in us.

g. It is impossible to combine the love of a son with the fear of a slave.

is a liar,
since a man who does not love the brother that he can see
1 P 1:8 cannot love God, whom he has never seen.
Mt 22:36-40 Jn 14:15,21; 15:17 So this is the commandment that he has given us, 21
that anyone who loves God must also love his brother.

5

Whoever believes that Jesus is the Christ 1
1:3+ has been begotten by God;
Jn 8:42 1 P 1:23 and whoever loves the Father that begot him
loves the child whom he begets.[a]
We can be sure that we love God's children 2
Rm 13:9 Ga 5:14 if we love God himself and do what he has commanded us;
this is what loving God is— 3
3:23 2 Jn 6 keeping his commandments;
Dt 30:11 Mt 11:30 and his commandments are not difficult, 4
because anyone who has been begotten by God
Jn 16:33 has already overcome the world;
2 14+ this is the victory over the world—
our faith.

Faith

Who can overcome the world? 5
Only the man who believes that Jesus is the Son of God:[b]
Jn 19:34 Jesus Christ who came by water and blood,[c] 6
Jn 4:1+ not with water only,
but with water and blood;
Jn 1:33+ with the Spirit as another witness—
2:20,27 Jn 14:26+ since the Spirit is the truth—
so that there are three witnesses,[d] 7
the Spirit, the water and the blood, 8
and all three of them agree.[e]
We accept the testimony of human witnesses, 9
Jn 5:32,37 but God's testimony is much greater,
and this is God's testimony,
given as evidence for his Son.
Everybody who believes in the Son of God 10
has this testimony inside him;
Jn 3:33 and anyone who will not believe God
is making God out to be a liar,
because he has not trusted
the testimony God has given about his Son.
Jn 3:11+ This is the testimony: 11
1:2; 5:20 Jn 1:4; 5: 21,26 God has given us eternal life
and this life is in his Son;
anyone who has the Son has life, 12
anyone who does not have the Son does not have life.

Conclusion

I have written all this to you 13
so that you who believe in the name of the Son of God
Jn 1:12; 20:31 may be sure that you have eternal life.

ENDING[f]

Prayer for sinners

Mt 7:7p We are quite confident that if we ask him for anything, 14

and it is in accordance with his will, 3:22 Jn 14:13-14; 15:7
he will hear us;
15 and, knowing that whatever we may ask, he hears us,
we know that we have already been granted what we asked of him.
16 If anybody sees his brother commit a sin
that is not a deadly sin,
he has only to pray, and God will give life to the sinner
—not those who commit a deadly sin; Jn 15:22-24
for there is a sin that is death,[g] Mt 12:31
and I will not say that you must pray about that.
17 Every kind of wrong-doing is sin,
but not all sin is deadly.[h]

Summary of the letter

18 We know that anyone who has been begotten by God 1:3+,13+
does not sin, 3:6+
because the begotten Son of God[i] protects him, Jn 1:13
and the Evil One does not touch him. 2:14+ Jn 17:15
19 We know that we belong to God,
but the whole world lies in the power of the Evil One.
20 We know, too, that the Son of God has come,
and has given us the power Jr 24:7 Ep 1:17
to know the true God.[j]
We are in the true God, Jn 17:3
as we are in his Son, Jesus Christ. 5:12
This is the true God,
this is eternal life. 1:2
21 Children, be on your guard against false gods.[k]

5 a. To believe the truth is to be begotten by God and to love God as Father and so also to love all God's other children.

b. This argument is based on two previous ones; whoever believes is begotten by God, v. 1, and to be begotten by God is to be the conqueror of the 'world', v. 4.

c. The water and the blood that came from his side when Jesus was pierced on the cross, cf. Jn 19:34 and note. These were the 'evidence', for the original eyewitnesses, but they are also the witness for all Christians as the type of the baptism and the sacrificial death of Jesus which are operative in their own lives. The three components of the new life 'in Christ' are: the death (the blood), the resurrection, baptism (the water) and the gift of the Spirit.

d. Vulg. vv. *7-8* read as follows 'There are three witnesses *in heaven: the Father the Word and the Spirit, and these three are one; there are three witnesses on earth:* the Spirit the water and the blood'. The words in italics (not in any of the early Greek MSS, or any of the early translations, or in the best MSS of the Vulg. itself) are probably a gloss that has crept into the text.

e. See note c on v. 6. The three witnesses support each other; the water of baptism is accompanied by the Spirit, and the Spirit came through the 'blood' of the death of Jesus. The writer probably intends another warning here, against the doctrine of Cerinthus—that the Spirit which came on Jesus at his baptism (water) left him before his death (blood).

f. As in the gospel, cf. Jn 21, the conclusion is followed by a postscript.

g. The sin against the Spirit, against truth, cf. Mt 12:31+.

h. Lit. 'and there is a sin that is not to death'; Vulg. omits 'not'.

i. Jesus, cf. Jn 1:13,18.

j. Lit. 'the True'; he is the only true God and the only one known for what he is in truth, i.e. Life and Love.

k. Lit. 'idols', as in paganism, but also the 'idols of the heart' (Qumran) that deflect human beings from their faith and true love. Vulg. adds 'Amen'.

2 JOHN

THE SECOND LETTER OF JOHN

1 P 5:13 From the Elder:[a] my greetings to the Lady, the chosen one,[b] and to her 1
3 Jn 1 children, she whom I love in the truth—and I am not the only one, for so do all
1 Jn 2:21 *Jn 14:17* who have come to know the truth— •because of the truth that lives in us and will 2
be with us for ever. •In our life of truth and love, we shall have grace, mercy and 3
peace from God the Father and from Jesus Christ, the Son of the Father.

The law of love

Phm 7 3 Jn 3 It has given me great joy to find that your children have been living the life of 4
1 Jn 3:19+ truth[c] as we were commanded by the Father. •I am writing now, dear lady, not to 5
1 Jn 2:7-11 give you any new commandment, but the one which we were given at the beginning, and to plead: let us love one another.
1 Jn 5:3 To love is to live according to his commandments: this is the commandment 6
which you have heard since the beginning,[d] to live a life of love.

The enemies of Christ

1 Jn 2:18 *1 Jn 4:2-3* There are many deceivers about in the world, refusing to admit that Jesus 7
1 Jn 2:22 Christ has come in the flesh. They are the Deceiver; they are the Antichrist.
Watch yourselves, or all our work[e] will be lost and not get the reward it deserves. 8
If anybody does not keep within the teaching of Christ[f] but goes beyond it,[g] he 9
1 Jn 2:23-24 cannot have God with him: only those who keep to what he taught can have the
Jude 4 Father and the Son with them. •If anyone comes to you bringing a different 10
doctrine, you must not receive him in your house or even give him a greeting.
To greet him would make you a partner in his wicked work. 11
3 Jn 13f There are several things I have to tell you, but I have thought it best not to 12
trust them to paper and ink. I hope instead to visit you and talk to you personally,
1 Jn 1:4 so that our joy[h] may be complete.
Greetings to you from the children of your sister,[i] the chosen one. 13

a. The elders were the leaders in each community, cf. Tt 1:5+. Here the title refers to John the apostle, the outstanding leader of the communities of Asia Minor.

b. The 'Chosen Lady' or 'Sovereign Lady', figurative reference to one of the local churches under the jurisdiction of the Elder.

c. Lit. 'walk in the truth'.

d. Or 'you must obey that commandment as you learnt it at the beginning'.

e. Var. (Vulg.) 'your work'.

f. Teaching either by, or about, Christ.

g. Teaching pure speculation as apostolic doctrine, cf. Tt 3:9; 1 Tm 2:16, etc.

h. Var. (Vulg.) 'your joy'.

i. The church (perhaps Ephesus) from which the letter is being written.

3 JOHN

THE THIRD LETTER OF JOHN

1 From the Elder: greetings to my dear friend Gaius, whom I love in the truth. 2 Jn 1+
2 My dear friend, I hope everything is going happily with you and that you are as
3 well physically as you are spiritually. •It was a great joy to me when some brothers 2 Jn 4
came and told of your faithfulness to the truth, and of your life in the truth.
4 It is always my greatest joy[a] to hear that my children are living according to 1 Jn 3:19+
the truth.
5 My friend, you have done faithful work in looking after these brothers, even
6 though they were complete strangers to you.[b] •They are a proof to the whole
Church of your charity and it would be a very good thing if you could help them
7 on their journey in a way that God would approve. •It was entirely for the sake
of the name[c] that they set out, without depending on the pagans for anything; Mt 18:5p Jn 8:24+
8 it is our duty to welcome men of this sort and contribute our share to their work *Mt 10:10,41* 1 Tm 5:18
for the truth.

Beware of the example of Diotrephes

9 I have written a note[d] for the members of the church, but Diotrephes, who
10 seems to enjoy being in charge of it, refuses to accept us.[e] •So if I come, I shall
tell everyone how he has behaved, and about the wicked accusations he has been
circulating against us. As if that were not enough, he not only refuses to welcome
our brothers, but prevents the other people who would have liked to from doing
11 it, and expels them from the church. •My dear friend, never follow such a bad
example, but keep following the good one; anyone who does what is right is a 1 Jn 1:3+. 7+
child of God, but the person who does what is wrong has never seen God.

Commendation of Demetrius

12 Demetrius[f] has been approved by everyone, and indeed by the truth itself. 1 Jn 5:6
We too will vouch for him and you know that our testimony is true. Jn 19:35; 21:24

Epilogue

13 There were several things I had to tell you but I would rather not trust them 2 Jn 12
14 to pen and ink. •However, I hope to see you soon and talk to you personally.
15 Peace be with you; greetings from your friends; greet each of our friends by name.

a. 'Joy', var. (Vulg.) 'privilege'.

b. Probably missionaries sent by the apostle to the communities of Asia Minor.

c. The name of the Lord; i.e. the Good News or gospel which carries the name of Jesus Christ to the pagans.

d. Perhaps 2 Jn.

e. Lit. 'Diotrephes loving being (or anxious to be) their leader is not receiving us'; by rejecting John's missionaries they reject John himself.

f. Either a leading member of that community or one of the missionaries recommended to Gaius.

THE LETTER OF
JUDE

Address

Ac 12:17+ From Jude, servant of Jesus Christ and brother of James; to those who are 1
called, to those who are dear to[a] God the Father and kept safe for Jesus Christ,
2 P 1:2 wishing you all mercy and peace and love. 2

The reason for this letter

My dear friends, at a time when I was eagerly looking forward to writing to 3
you about the salvation that we all share,[b] I have been forced[c] to write to you
Ac 9:13+ now and appeal to you to fight hard for the faith which has been once and for all
||2 P 2:1 entrusted to the saints. •Certain people have infiltrated among you, and they 4
are the ones you had a warning about, in writing, long ago, when they were
Ga 5:13 1 P 2:16 condemned[d] for denying all religion, turning the grace of our God into immorality,
1 Jn 4:1 2 Jn 10 and rejecting our only Master and Lord, Jesus Christ.[e]

The false teachers: the certainty of their punishment

1 Co 6:3 ||2 P 1:12 I should like to remind you—though you have already learnt it once and for 5
Nb 14:26-35 1 Co 10:5 all[f]—how the Lord[g] rescued the nation from Egypt, but afterwards he still
||*2 P 2:4* destroyed the men who did not trust him. •Next let me remind you of the angels 6
Gn 6:1-2 who had supreme authority but did not keep it and left their appointed sphere;[h]
he has kept them down in the dark, in spiritual chains, to be judged on the great
Gn 19 2 P 2: 6-9 day. •The fornication of Sodom and Gomorrah and the other nearby towns was 7
Mt 10:15p equally unnatural,[i] and it is a warning to us that they are paying for their crimes
in eternal fire.

Their violent language

||2 P 2:10-12 Nevertheless, these people[j] are doing the same: in their delusions they not 8
only defile their bodies and disregard authority,[k] but abuse the glorious angels
Dt 34:6+ Dn 10:13+ as well. •Not even the archangel Michael, when he was engaged in argument 9
Zc 3:2+ with the devil about the corpse of Moses,[l] dared to denounce him in the language
of abuse; all he said was, 'Let the Lord correct you'. •But these people abuse 10
anything they do not understand; and the only things they do understand—just
by nature[m] like unreasoning animals—will turn out to be fatal to them.

Their vicious behaviour

Gn 4:8 ||2 P 2:15 May they get what they deserve, because they have followed Cain; they have 11
1 Jn 3:12 *Nb 22:2+* rushed to make the same mistake as Balaam and for the same reward; they have
Rv 2:14 *Nb 16* rebelled just as Korah did—and share the same fate. •They are a dangerous 12
Pr 25:14 ||2 P 2:13, 17-18 obstacle[n] to your community meals, coming for the food and quite shamelessly
only looking after themselves. They are like clouds blown about by the winds and
bringing no rain, or like barren trees which are then uprooted in the winter and so

13 are twice dead; •like wild sea waves capped with shame as if with foam; or like Is 57:20
14 shooting stars[o] bound for an eternity of black darkness. •It was with them in
mind that Enoch, the seventh patriarch from Adam, made his prophecy when he
said, 'I tell you, the Lord will come with his saints in their tens of thousands, Dn 7:10 Rv 5:11
15 to pronounce judgement on all mankind and to sentence the wicked for all the
wicked things they have done, and for all the defiant things said against him by
16 irreligious sinners'.[p] •They are mischief-makers, grumblers governed only by ||2 P 2:18
their own desires,[q] with *mouths full of boastful talk*, ready with flattery for other Dn 7:8,20
people when they see some advantage in it. Lv 19:15

A warning

17 But remember, my dear friends, what the apostles of our Lord Jesus Christ ||2 P 3:2-3
18 told you to expect. •'At the end of time,' they told you 'there are going to be 1 Tm 4:1+
people who sneer at religion and follow nothing but their own desires for
19 wickedness.' •These unspiritual and selfish people are nothing but mischief- 1 Co 15:44+
makers.[r]

The duties of love

20 But you, my dear friends, must use your most holy faith as your foundation 1 Co 3:9-17 Ep 2:20-22
21 and build on that, praying in the Holy Spirit; •keep yourselves within the love
of God and wait for the mercy of our Lord Jesus Christ to give you eternal life.
22 23 When there are some who have doubts, reassure them; •when there are some
to be saved from the fire, pull them out; but there are others[s] to whom you must
be kind with great caution, keeping your distance even from outside clothing
which is contaminated by vice.

Doxology

24 Glory be to him who can keep you from falling and bring you safe to his ||2 P 3:14
25 glorious presence, innocent and happy.[t] •To God, the only God, who saves us
through Jesus Christ our Lord, be the glory, majesty, authority and power, which Rm 16:25-27+
he had before time began, now and for ever. Amen. Rv 5:13

a. 'To those who are', var. 'to the nations who are'. 'dear to'; var. 'made holy by'.

b. 'the salvation that we all share'; Vulg. 'your salvation'.

c. By the danger these heretics represent.

d. Lit. 'For certain men crept in who long ago have been written beforehand for this judgement'; var. 'for this sin'.

e. Var. 'rejecting God, the only Master and our Lord Jesus Christ'.

f. The faith entrusted 'once and for all', v. 3, to the saints must never be changed.

g. God the Father, cf. 2 P 2:4. Var. (Vulg.) 'Jesus', i.e. a reference to Christ in his divine pre-existence, cf. 1 Co 10:4.

h. They let themselves be seduced by the 'daughters of men', Gn 6:1-2; the subject is elaborated in the *Book of Enoch*.

i. Lit. 'Like Sodom...in the same way fornicating and going after alien flesh'. They lusted not after human beings, but after the strangers who were angels, Gn 19:1-11. The apocryphal *Testament of the Twelve Patriarchs*, like Jude 6-7, also compares the sin of the angels with the sin of the Sodomites.

j. The heretics living at the same time as Jude. Om. (Vulg.) 'in their delusions'.

k. 'disregard authority', lit. 'despise sovereignty'; var. 'sovereignties', i.e. the angels, cf. Ep 1:21; Col 1:16.

l. Almost certainly a reference to the apocryphal *Assumption of Moses*.

m. Their lack of knowledge results from the fact that they do not possess the Spirit, they know nothing except what they have learnt through their unaided natural powers.

n. Lit. 'They are reefs to your agapēs' (cf. 1 Co 11: 20+). 'reefs': var. (Vulg.) 'blots'. 'agapēs': var. 'deceits', cf. 2 P 2:13. These heretics were still taking part in the life of the Church; all that had happened to them so far was that they had been noticed.

o. In Jewish apocrypha, e.g. the *Book of Enoch*, 'stars' often stand for 'angels'.

p. *Enoch* 1:9, probably quoted from memory.

q. Suggested by *Enoch* 5:5.

r. Lit. 'There are the ones who make divisions (Vulg. 'who separate themselves', i.e. from the Church), *psychikoi* not having the Spirit'. The heretics are like 'animals' because they act irrationally or on impulse, v. 10; the central human quality they lack is openness to the Spirit, cf. Rm 1:9+.

s. 'When there are some who have doubts, be kind to them, save them, pull them out of the fire; but there are others...'

t. Vulg. adds 'at the coming of our Lord Jesus Christ'.

THE BOOK OF
REVELATION

INTRODUCTION TO THE BOOK OF REVELATION

The Greek title of this book is 'Apocalypse of John', and the word 'apocalypse' is a transliteration of the Greek word for revelation: any writing under this title claims to include a revelation of hidden things, imparted by God, and particularly a revelation of events hidden in the future. It is not easy to draw an exact dividing line between prophecy and apocalypse, and the writers of apocalyptic are in some ways the successors of the prophets; but we can at least make the distinction that the Old Testament prophets characteristically received the message by 'hearing the word of God' and passed it on by word of mouth, whereas the author of a written apocalypse was given his revelation in a vision and passed it on in writing.

The language of apocalyptic writing is richly symbolic, and the importance of the visions which are described is never in their immediate literal meaning. It can be taken as a rule that every element in this kind of writing has symbolic value—persons, places, animals, actions, objects, parts of the body, numbers and measurements, stars, constellations, colours and garments—and if we are not to misunderstand or distort the writer's message, we must appreciate the imagery at its true value and do our best to translate the symbols back into the ideas which he intended them to convey. There are parts of the text in which this will involve our distinguishing a direct allegorical interpretation of the images that are used. There are other parts, however, in which no single interpretation can be confidently adopted, since a single group of images will be found to draw its meaning from various different associations.

Apocalyptic writing became very popular in some Jewish circles (including the Essenes of Qumran) in the two centuries before Christ. The visions of prophets like Ezekiel and Zechariah paved the way, and apocalypse as a literary form was already fully developed by the time of Daniel and in the many apocryphal writings about the beginning of the Christian era. The New Testament includes only one apocalypse; its author says he was called John, 1:9, and that at the time of writing he was an exile for his Christian faith on the island of Patmos. A tradition as early as Justin and widespread by the end of the 2nd century (Irenaeus, Clement of Alexandria, Tertullian, the Canon of Muratori) identified this John with the apostle, author of the fourth gospel. On the other hand, it is almost certain that the churches of Syria, Cappadocia and even Palestine did not include the Revelation in the canon of scripture until the 5th century; evidently they did not believe it to be the work of an apostle. At the beginning of the 3rd century a priest of Rome, Caius by name, attributed it to Cerinthus the heretic, though this may have been merely an attempt to justify his attack on it. Internal evidence shows that the Revelation of John has some affinity with the other Johannine writings, but as it is so sharply distinguished from them by language, style, and some theological positions, notably its view of the *parousia*, it is impossible to identify the author of Revelation as it stands with the author of the rest of the Johannine literature. In spite of that, Revelation is clearly Johannine in inspiration: it was written inside the apostle's immediate circle and is pervaded by his doctrine. Of its canonicity there can be no doubt; as for its date the most common opinion is that it was written in the reign of Domitian, about 95; others, with some justification, believe that parts of it at least were composed as early as Nero's time, shortly before 70.

Whatever its precise date, we cannot understand the Revelation without taking into account the historical conditions that gave birth to it. It is first and foremost a tract for the times, like the apocalypses (particularly Daniel) that preceded it and on which it draws. It was written during a period of disturbance and bitter persecution to increase the hope and determination of the infant Church. Jesus had said, 'Be brave: I have conquered the world', Jn 16:33; how therefore could God permit this mortal attack on his own Church? John's answer begins by recalling the classical themes of the prophets, notably that of the 'Great Day' of Yahweh (cf. Am 5:18+). When the Chosen People had been enslaved to the Assyrians, Chaldaeans, and Greeks, when they had been scattered abroad and nearly annihilated by persecution, the prophets had promised: the day is coming, and soon, when God will liberate his people from their oppressors, and restore their independence, and help them to conquer their enemies after he has punished them and brought them to the point of extinction. When John wrote the Revelation, the Church, the new chosen race, had just been decimated by persecution, ch. 13; 6:10-11; 16:6; 17:6; Rome and its empire (the Beast) was only a tool, but a tool wielded by Satan, ch. 12; 13:2,4, the great and only real enemy of Christ and his people. In the opening vision John describes God as emperor, enthroned in heaven; he is master of human destiny, ch. 4, and to the Lamb he gives the scroll that foretells the doom of the persecutors, ch. 5; the vision then proclaims a foreign invasion (the Parthians) and its familiar concomitants, war, famine, plague, ch. 6. During this, God's faithful will be preserved, 7:1-8; cf. 14:1-5, and eventually rejoice triumphantly in heaven, 7:9-17; cf. 15:1-5. God, however, wants to save their enemies as well, so instead of destroying them immediately, he warns them, as he had warned Egypt and its Pharaoh, by a series of plagues, ch. 8-9; cf. 16. The persecutors are only hardened in their evil determination, and God is forced to destroy them, ch. 17. Their aim was to corrupt the world and get it to worship Satan (an allusion to emperor-worship in pagan Rome). After this comes a lament over fallen Babylon (Rome), ch. 18, and hymns of victory in heaven, 19:1-10. There is a second vision of the destruction of the Beast (persecuting Rome), this time by Christ in glory, 19:11-21, that begins an era of prosperity for the Church, 20:1-6, which is to end in a new assault by Satan, 20:7f, followed by the annihilation of the Enemy, the resurrection and judgement of the dead, 20:11-15, and ultimately by the definitive establishment of the kingdom of perfect happiness in heaven when death itself has been destroyed, 21:1-8. A final vision glances back to the period just before this consummation, and describes the beauty of the new Jerusalem, or Church, on earth, 21:9f.

The significance of the Revelation is wider than this primary, basic, meaning derived by historical interpretation: the book is interested in the unchanging realities, to which faith is always open in any period of history. God's promise to be 'with his people', cf. Ex 25:8+, protecting them and saving them, had always been the foundation of their confidence in him in the Old Testament, and it is this presence that has now been perfected by the marriage of God and his new chosen people in the person of his Son, Immanuel (God-with-us). The promise of the risen Christ, 'I shall be with you always, yes, to the end of time', is what gives life to the Church, Mt 28:20. As a result, those who are faithful to Jesus have nothing to fear: they may suffer a while for him but in the end they will triumph over Satan and his schemes. The Revelation is an epic of Christian hope, the victory song of the persecuted Church.

As it stands, the text of Revelation presents many difficulties: repetitions, interruptions in the sequence of visions, and passages obviously divorced from their context. Many explanations for this have been suggested: that Revelation was compiled from diverse sources, that whole chapters have been accidentally misplaced, etc. The following hypothesis was first suggested in 1949 (cf. *Revue Biblique*, 1949, 507-541); it is that the strictly prophetic part of Revelation, ch. 4-22, is made up of two different apocalypses written by the same author at different times and later fused into one by some author. It is suggested that the two originally separate texts are as follows:

	Text I	Text II
Prologue: The small book		10:1-2a,3-4,8-11
Satan attacks the Church	12:1-6,13-17	12:7-12
The Beast attacks the Church		13
Proclamation and preludes of the Great Day of wrath	4-9; 10:1-2b,5-7; 11:14-18	14-16
The Great Day of wrath:		
Babylon's wickedness described	17:1-9,15-18	17:10,12-14
Babylon's fall	18:1-3	(cf. 14:8)
The elect preserved		18:4-8
Lament for Babylon	18:9-13,15-19,21,24	18:14,22-23
Canticles of triumph	19:1-10	18:20 (cf. 16:5-7)
The messianic kingdom	20:1-6	
The eschatological war	20:7-10	19:11-21
The Judgement	20:13-15	20:11-12
The Jerusalem to be	21:9-22:2 and 22:6-15	21:1-4; 22:3-5; 21:5-8
Appendix: The two witnesses		11:1-13,19

The letters to the seven churches, ch. 1-3, which were certainly intended to be read as an introduction to the two prophecies, must originally also have existed as separate text.

THE BOOK OF REVELATION

Prologue

1 This is the revelation given by God to Jesus Christ[a] so that he could tell his 1
Dn 2:28 servants[b] about the *things which are* now *to take place* very soon; he sent his
22:6f.16 angel to make it known[c] to his servant John, •and John has written down 2
19:10+ everything he saw and swears it is the word of God guaranteed by Jesus Christ.[d]
22:7 Lk 11:28 Happy[e] the man who reads this prophecy, and happy those who listen to him, if 3
2 Co 6:2+ they treasure all that it says, because the Time[f] is close.

I. THE LETTERS TO THE CHURCHES OF ASIA

Address and greeting[g]

From John, to the seven churches of Asia: grace and peace to you from him 4
1:8; 4:8; 11:17; 16:5 who is, who was, and who is to come,[h] from the seven spirits in his presence before
Ex 3:14+ Ps 89:27,37 his throne, •and from Jesus Christ, *the faithful witness, the First-born* from the 5
Is 55:4 dead, *the Ruler of the kings of the earth.*[i] He loves us and has washed away[j] our
Ex 19:6 1 P 2:9 sins with his blood, •and made us a *line of kings, priests to serve*[k] his God and 6
Rm 16:27+ Father; to him, then, be glory and power for ever and ever. Amen. •It is he who 7
Dn 7:13 Zc 12:10,14 *is coming on the clouds;* everyone will see him, even *those who pierced*
Mt 24:30+ Jn 19:37 *him,* and *all the races of the earth will mourn over him.* This is the truth. Amen.
1:4; 21:6; 22:13 'I am the Alpha and the Omega'[l] says the Lord God, who is, who was, and who 8
is to come, the Almighty.

The beginning of the vision

My name is John, and through our union in Jesus I am your brother and share 9
Rm 5:3 2 Tm 2:12 your sufferings, your kingdom, and all you endure. I was on the island of Patmos[m]
for having preached God's word and witnessed for Jesus; •it was the Lord's day 10
and the Spirit possessed me, and I heard a voice behind me, shouting like
a trumpet, •'Write down all that you see in a book, and send it to the seven 11
churches of Ephesus, Smyrna, Pergamum, Thyatira, Sardis, Philadelphia and
Laodicea'. •I turned round to see who had spoken to me, and when I turned 12
1:20 Dn 7:13 I saw seven golden lamp-stands •and, surrounded by them, a figure *like a Son* 13
Dn 10:5 *of man,*[n] dressed in a long robe tied at the waist with a *golden girdle.* •*His head* 14
Dn 7:9 and *his hair* were *white as white wool* or as snow, *his eyes* like a *burning* flame,
Dn 10:6 *his feet like burnished bronze* when it has been refined in a furnace, and *his voice* 15
Ezk 43:2 2:1,12; *like the sound of the ocean.* •In his right hand he was holding seven stars, out of 16
3:1; 19:15 Heb 4:12 his mouth came a sharp sword, double-edged, and his face was like the sun
shining with all its force.
Jg 13:20 Ezk 1:28+ When I saw him, I fell in a dead faint at his feet, but he touched me with his 17
Dn 8:18; 10:15-19 right hand and said, 'Do not be afraid; it is I, *the First* and *the Last;* I am the

18 Living One,[o] •I was dead and now I am to live for ever and ever, and I hold the *1:8+* Is 44:6;
19 keys of death and of the underworld.[p] •Now write down all that you see of present 48:12 Heb 7:25
20 happenings[q] and *things that are still to come.* •The secret of the seven stars you *Dn 2:28* Hab 2:2
have seen in my right hand, and of the seven golden lamp-stands is this: the seven 1:12; 16:5
stars are the angels[r] of the seven churches, and the seven lamp-stands are the
seven churches themselves.

1. Ephesus

1 2 'Write to the angel of the church in Ephesus[a] and say, "Here is the message
of the one who holds the seven stars in his right hand and who lives 1:16
2 surrounded by the seven golden lamp-stands: •I know all about you: how hard 1:12 *1 Th 1:3*
you work and how much you put up with. I know you cannot stand wicked men,
and how you tested the impostors who called themselves apostles[b] and proved 2 Co 11:13, 15
3 they were liars. •I know, too, that you have patience, and have suffered for my
4 name[c] without growing tired. •Nevertheless, I have this complaint to make;
5 you have less love now than you used to. •Think where you were before you fell;
repent, and do as you used to at first, or else, if you will not repent, I shall come
6 to you and take your lamp-stand from its place.[d] •It is in your favour, nevertheless,
7 that you loathe as I do what the Nicolaitans are doing. •If anyone has ears 2:15+ *13:9*
to hear, let him listen to what the Spirit is saying to the churches: those who Mt 13:9
prove victorious I will feed *from the tree of life set in* God's *paradise.*"[e] 22:2 Gn 2:9 Pr 3:18

2. Smyrna

8 'Write to the angel of the church in Smyrna and say, "Here is the message of

1 a. Lit. 'A revelation of Jesus Christ which God gave to him'.

b. 'His servants' may possibly be the prophets in the early Church, cf. 10:7; 11:18; 22:6; Ac 11:27+; and Am 3:7, among whom John includes himself, cf. 19:10 and 22:9; but the same word is regularly used for all followers and disciples of Christ and 19:10 suggests that no firm distinction is made between 'prophets' and other 'witnesses to Jesus' such as evangelists and martyrs.

c. Lit. 'He conveyed through signs sent by his messenger': ambiguous, the angel could be sent by Jesus, cf. 19:10; 22:6-20, or by God, in which case the angel would be the Messiah himself, cf. 14:14,15 and 1:13.

d. Lit. 'the Word of God and the witness of Jesus Christ'.

e. First of the seven beatitudes in the Apocalypse, cf. 14:13; 16:15; 19:9; 20:6; 22:7,14.

f. When Jesus returns; cf. 3:11; 22:10,12,20 and 1:7.

g. This section makes use of many O.T. allusions to suggest the King-Messiah's glorious return, solemn enthronement and future reign over God's people in fulfilment of the promise made to David. This is basically what the whole book is about.

h. Common title in Jewish literature, developed from the name revealed to Moses: 'I am who am', Ex 3:14+.

i. The Messiah is the 'witness' to the promise that was made to David, 2 S 7:1+; Ps 89; Is 55:3-4; Zc 12:8, both in his person and in his work; as he fulfils this promise he is the efficacious Word, God's 'Yes', Rv 3:14; 19:11,13; 2 Co 1:20. Not only is he heir to David, Rv 5:5; 22:16, but by his resurrection he is the 'First-born', Col 1:18, who will reign over the universe when his enemies have been destroyed. Dn 7:14; Rv 19:16.

j. Var. 'released us from'.

k. Lit. 'He made us a kingdom and priests for': those who turn to the Messiah and whose sins he forgives, vv. 5 and 7, will be a family of king-priests, Ex 19:6+; kings because they will rule over all the nations, Dn 7:22,27; Is 54:11-17; Zc 12:1-3; cf. Rv 2:26; 5:10; 20:6; 22:5; priests because in union with Jesus the messianic Priest they will consecrate the universe to God in a sacrifice of praise.

l. The beginning and end, originator and goal, of all things: Is 41:4; 44:6; Rv 21:6; 22:13. 'the Almighty': '*pantokrator*' lit. 'the All-Ruler', a stock rendering of 'Lord of Hosts' ('Yahweh Sabaoth').

m. Deported there for being a Christian proselytiser. Patmos (10 miles x 5 miles) was used by Romans as a penal colony.

n. The Messiah as eschatological Judge (cf. Dn 7:13, also 10:6). The long robe symbolises his priesthood (cf. Ex 28:4; 29:5; Zc 3:4), the golden girdle his royalty, cf. 1 M 10:89, the white hair his eternity (cf. Dn 7:9), the burning eyes (to probe minds and 'hearts', cf. Rv 2:23) his divine knowledge, the feet of bronze (cf. Dn 2:31-45) his permanence; the brightness of his legs and face, and the strength of his voice symbolise the fear inspired by his majesty. In his power (his 'right hand') he holds the seven churches (the 'stars', cf. v. 20); he is prepared to sentence faithless Christians to death (the 'double-edged sword'), cf. 19:15+; 2:16; and Is 49:2; Ep 6:17; Heb 4:12. One or other of his attributes as Judge is used, at the beginning of each of the seven letters, to suggest the situation of the particular church addressed.

o. The one who has life 'in himself', cf. Jn 5:21,26; 1:4.

p. Lit. 'death and Hades'. Hades was the place of the dead, the Gk word corresponding to the *sheol* of the O.T., cf. Nb 16:33+. Christ has the power to release souls from Hades, Jn 5:26-28.

q. 'present happenings' refers to the letters of ch. 2 and 3; 'things that are still to come': the revelations of ch. 4-22.

r. Jews held that not only the physical universe was controlled by angels, cf. Rv 7:1; 14:18; 16:5, but also human beings (both individuals and communities), cf. Ex 23:20+. Each church here is thought of as under the control of an angel appointed to be responsible for it.

2 a. Metropolis of the province of Asia; the other six churches of the letters that follow were located in the same province.

b. Probably the Nicolaitans of v. 6, see 2:15+. Cf. 2 Co 11:5,13.

c. Allusion to some previous persecution.

d. Ephesus will cease to be the religious capital.

e. Var. (Vulg.) 'the paradise of my God'.

1:17-18+ Is 44:6; *the First* and *the Last*, who was dead and has come to life again: •I know the trials 9
48:12 Jm 2:5 you have had, and how poor you are—though you are rich[f]—and the slanderous
accusations that have been made by the people who profess to be Jews[g] but are
3:9 Jn 8:37-44 really members of the synagogue of Satan. •Do not be afraid of the sufferings 10
Si 2:1 that are coming to you: I tell you, the devil is going to send some of you to prison
Dn 1:12,14 Lk 22:31-33 *to test you*, and you must face an ordeal for *ten days*.[h] Even if you have to die,
1 Co 9:25+ keep faithful, and I will give you the crown of life for your prize. •If anyone has 11
ears to hear, let him listen to what the Spirit is saying to the churches: for those
20:6,14; 21:8 who prove victorious there is nothing to be afraid of in the second death."

3. Pergamum

'Write to the angel of the church in Pergamum and say, "Here is the message 12
1:16; 19:15 of the one who has the sharp sword, double-edged: •I know where you live, 13
in the place where Satan is enthroned, and that you still hold firmly to my name,
and did not disown your faith in me even when my faithful witness, Antipas, was
killed in your own town, where Satan lives.[i]

Nevertheless, I have one or two complaints to make: some of you are 14
Nb 22:2+ followers of Balaam, who taught Balak to set a trap for the Israelites[j] so that
Nb 25:1-2 1 Co 8:10 they committed adultery[k] by eating food that had been sacrificed to idols; •and 15
2 P 2:1 2:6 among you, too, there are some as bad who accept what the Nicolaitans teach.[l]
You must repent, or I shall soon come to you and attack these people with the 16
sword out of my mouth. •If anyone has ears to hear, let him listen to what the 17
Spirit is saying to the churches: to those who prove victorious I will give the
3:12+; 19:12 Is 62:2; 65:15 hidden manna and a white stone[m]—a stone with *a new name* written on it,
known only to the man who receives it."

4. Thyatira

'Write to the angel of the church in Thyatira and say, "Here is the message 18
1:14-15 of the Son of God who has eyes like a burning flame and feet like burnished
bronze: •I know all about you and how charitable you are; I know your faith and 19
devotion and how much you put up with, and I know how you are still making
progress. •Nevertheless, I have a complaint to make: you are encouraging the 20
woman Jezebel[n] who claims to be a prophetess, and by her teaching she is luring
my servants away to commit the adultery of eating food which has been sacrificed
2:14 to idols. •I have given her time to reform but she is not willing to change her 21
adulterous life. •Now I am consigning her to bed, and all her partners in adultery 22
to troubles that will test them severely, unless they repent of their practices;[o]
and I will see that her children[p] die, so that all the churches realise that it is I who 23
Jr 11:20+; 17:10 *search heart and loins and give each one of you what your behaviour deserves.*
Ps 62:12 Ac 1:24 But on the rest of you in Thyatira, all of you who have not accepted this teaching 24
3:8-11 or learnt the secrets of Satan,[q] as they are called, I am not laying any special
duty; •but hold firmly on to what you already have[r] until I come. •To those who 25 26
12:5; 19:5 Ps 2:8-9 prove victorious, and keep working for me until the end, *I will give* the
authority over *the pagans* •which I myself have been given by my Father, *to rule* 27 28
1:6+; 19:15 *them with an iron sceptre and shatter them like earthenware.* And I will give him
22:16 Is 14:12 2 P 1:19 the Morning Star.[s] •If anyone has ears to hear, let him listen to what the Spirit 29
is saying to the churches."

5. Sardis

3 'Write to the angel of the church in Sardis and say, "Here is the message 1
1:16 of the one who holds the seven spirits[a] of God and the seven stars: I know all
1 Tm 5:6 about you: how you are reputed to be alive and yet are dead. •Wake up; revive 2
what little you have left: it is dying fast. So far I have failed to notice anything in
the way you live that my God could possibly call perfect, •and yet do you 3
remember how eager you were when you first heard the message? Hold on to that.
Mt 24:42-44p Repent. If you do not wake up, I shall come to you like a thief, without telling

4 you at what hour to expect me. •There are a few in Sardis, it is true, who have Mk 13:33▲ 1 Th 5:2▲
kept their robes from being dirtied, and they are fit to come with me, dressed *7:14*
5 in white. •Those who prove victorious will be dressed, like these, in white robes;[b]
I shall not blot their names out of the book of life, but acknowledge their names 20:12+ 1 S 25:29+
6 in the presence of my Father and his angels. •If anyone has ears to hear, let him Ps 69:28 Mt 10:32
listen to what the Spirit is saying to the churches." Lk 9:26

6. Philadelphia

7 'Write to the angel of the church in Philadelphia and say, "Here is the message Lv 17:1+
of the holy and faithful one who *has the key of David*, so that *when he opens*, Is 6:3+ *1:18*
8 *nobody can close, and when he closes, nobody can open*: •I know all about you; Is 22:22 Mt 16:19
and now I have opened in front of you a door that nobody will be able to close[c]—
and I know that though you are not very strong, you have kept my commandments
9 and not disowned my name. •Now I am going to make the synagogue of 2:9+
Satan—those who profess to be Jews, but are liars, because they are no such
thing—I will make them come and *fall at your feet* and admit that *you are* the Is 45:14; 60:14
10 people *that I love*. •Because you have kept my commandment to endure trials, *Is 43:4*
I will keep you safe in the time of trial which is going to come for the whole world, 2 P 2:9
11 to test the people of the world.[d] •Soon I shall be with you:[e] hold firmly to what 2:25+ 1 Co 9:24-27
12 you already have, and let nobody take your prize away from you. •Those who 2 Co 6:2+
prove victorious I will make into pillars in the sanctuary of my God, and they 2:17 Ga 2:9
will stay there for ever; I will inscribe on them the name of my God[f] and the 1 Tm 3:15 *7:4*
name of the city of my God, the new Jerusalem which comes down from my God *Ezk 48:35* *21:2f*
13 in heaven, and my own new name as well.[g] •If anyone has ears to hear, let him 2:17+
listen to what the Spirit is saying to the churches."

7. Laodicea

14 'Write to the angel of the church in Laodicea and say, "Here is the message of 1:5+; 19:11
the Amen,[h] the faithful, the true witness, the ultimate source of God's creation:[i] 2 Co 1:20 Jn 1:3
15 I know all about you: how you are neither cold nor hot. I wish you were one or
16 the other, •but since you are neither, but only lukewarm, I will spit you out of my
17 mouth. •You say to yourself, 'I am rich, I have made a fortune, and have Pr 13:7 Ho 7:9; 12:9
everything I want', never realising that you are wretchedly and pitiably poor, and Lk 12:21

f. Smyrna's spiritual wealth contrasts with her poverty.

g. Henceforth the Church of Christ is the true Israel, cf. Ga 6:16; Rm 9:8.

h. I.e. of short duration.

i. Emperor-worship, as well as other forms of paganism, flourished in Pergamum, and is always represented in Rv as the worship of Satan, 'the prince of this world'.

j. According to one Jewish tradition, cf. Nb 31:16, Balaam suggested to Balak that he should persuade Israel to idolatry with the help of the women of Moab, Nb 25:1-3.

k. The prophets used this as a common figure of speech for idolatry, religious infidelity, cf. Ho 1:2+.

l. This doctrine had some affinity with the errors already attacked by Paul in the Captivity Letters (notably in Col); it heralded the gnostic speculations of the 2nd cent., but also tolerated a measure of compromise with pagan cults, e.g. participation in sacred banquets, cf. v. 14.

m. The perspective, as in the other six letters, is eschatological. The manna (hidden, together with the ark, by Jeremiah, 2 M 2:4-8) will be brought out as the food of those who are saved in the heavenly kingdom, cf. 15:8+. The white stone (white is the colour of triumph and joy) alludes to various ancient usages (badges of honour, tablets of discharge or admission) and symbolises entry into the kingdom. The 'new name' signifies the Christian's spiritual rebirth.

n. 'Jezebel'; var. 'your wife Jezebel'. A self-styled prophetess of the Nicolaitan sect; her name is symbolic, cf. 2 K 9:22.

o. Var. 'her practices'.

p. Those who follow her teaching.

q. The doctrine of the Nicolaitans, so called either by the heretics themselves, or, sarcastically, by their opponents, cf. 1 Co 2:10.

r. The true faith in Christ.

s. In Eastern literature the Morning Star is both the symbol of dominion and power and also, as apparently here, of resurrection and triumphant glory. Christ reigns because he rose from the dead, cf. Ac 2:36+; Rm 1:4+; Rv 1:5+, and his faithful will share his reign as they share the glory of his resurrection, on which his worldwide empire is based. In the Roman liturgy, this theme is introduced into the *Exultet* of the Easter Vigil.

3 a. These seven spirits of God are seven angels.

b. A symbol of purity but also of victory and joy.

c. Perhaps the opportunity of spreading the Good News in fresh areas, for which this is a common metaphor, cf. Ac 14:27+, and Paul's letters.

d. Lit. 'all living on the earth', i.e. the pagan world, as always in Rv. This 'testing' is therefore the plagues of 8-9 and 16, from which God's servants will be preserved, cf. 7:1f.

e. The return of Christ in glory.

f. Cf. 2:17; 14:1; 19:12,13; and Is 56:5; 62:2; 65:15. Cf. Is 1:26+.

g. Either a name that will not be known until the *parousia*, or the name 'Word', cf. 19:13.

h. Reference to Is 65:16 where 'God of truth' is literally 'God of Amen'. Cf. Rv 1:5+.

i. Cf. Pr 8:22; Ws 9:1f; Jn 1:3; Col 1:16f; Heb 1:2.

Is 55:1 blind and naked too.[j] •I warn you, buy from me the gold that has been tested in 18
the fire[k] to make you really rich, and white robes to clothe you and cover your
shameful nakedness, and eye ointment to put on your eyes so that you are able
Pr 3:12 1 Co 11:32 to see.[l] •I *am* the one *who reproves and disciplines all those he loves:* so repent 19
Heb 12:4-11 *Jn 14:23* in real earnest. •Look, I am standing at the door, knocking. If one of you hears 20
Lk 22:29-30 me calling and opens the door, I will come in to share his meal, side by side with
1:6+; 20:4 him. •Those who prove victorious I will allow to share my throne, just as I was 21
Si 2:3 Mt 19:28 victorious myself and took my place with my Father on his throne. •If anyone has 22
ears to hear, let him listen to what the Spirit is saying to the churches." '

II. THE PROPHETIC VISIONS

A. THE PRELUDE TO THE GREAT DAY

God entrusts the future of the world to the Lamb[a]

1:10 4 Then, in my vision, I saw a door open in heaven and heard the same voice 1
speaking to me, the voice like a trumpet, saying, 'Come up here: I will show
Dn 2:28 you *what is to come* in the future'. •With that, the Spirit possessed me and I saw 2
Is 6:1 Ezk 1:26-28 a throne standing in heaven, and the *One* who was *sitting on the throne,* •and 3
Ex 24:10 Gn 9:12-17 the Person sitting there looked like a diamond and a ruby. There was a rainbow
encircling the throne, and this looked like an emerald.[b] •Round the throne in a 4
Is 24:23 circle were twenty-four thrones, and on them I saw twenty-four elders[c] sitting,
8:2,5; 11:19; 16:18 dressed in white robes with golden crowns on their heads. •Flashes of lightning 5
were coming from the throne, and the sound of peals of thunder,[d] and in front
of the throne there were seven flaming lamps burning, the seven Spirits[e] of
Ex 24:10 God. •Between the throne and myself was a sea[f] that seemed to be made of glass, 6
Ezk 1:5-21 like crystal. *In the centre,* grouped round the throne itself,[g] were *four animals*[h]
Ezk 10:14 *with many eyes,* in front and behind. •*The first* animal was like *a lion, the second* 7
like *a bull, the third* animal had *a human face,* and *the fourth* animal was like
Is 6:2 *Ezk 1:18;* 10:12 a flying *eagle.* •*Each* of the four animals had *six wings* and *had eyes all the way* 8
round as well as inside; and day and night they never stopped singing:

Is 6:3 *'Holy, Holy, Holy*
is the Lord God, the Almighty;
1:4+ he was, he is and he is to come'.[i]

Every time the animals glorified and honoured and gave thanks to the One sitting 9
Dn 4:31 on the throne, *who lives for ever and ever,* •the twenty-four elders prostrated 10
themselves before him to worship the One *who lives for ever and ever,* and threw
down their crowns in front of the throne,[j] saying, •'You are our Lord and our 11
14:7 Ps 115:3 God, you are worthy of glory and honour and power, because you made all the
Rm 4:17 Ep 4:11 universe and it was only by your will that everything was made and exists'.[k]

Is 29:11 Ezk 2:9 5 I saw that in the right hand of the One sitting on the throne there was *a scroll* 1
Dn 12:4,9 *that had writing on back and front* and was sealed with seven seals.[a] •Then 2
I saw a powerful angel who called with a loud voice, 'Is there anyone worthy
5:13 to open the scroll and break the seals of it?' •But there was no one, in heaven 3
or on the earth or under the earth,[b] who was able to open the scroll and read it.
I wept bitterly because there was nobody fit to open the scroll and read it, •but 4 5
Lk 7:13-15 *Gn 49:9* one of the elders said to me, 'There is no need to cry: *the Lion* of the tribe *of*
Is 11:1,10 Rm 15:12 *Judah, the Root* of David, has triumphed,[c] and he will open the scroll and the
1 Co 5:8 Heb 7:14 seven seals of it'.

Then I saw, standing between the throne with its four animals and the circle 6
Jn 1:29+ of the elders, a Lamb that seemed to have been sacrificed;[d] it had seven horns,
4:5+ *Zc 4:10* and it had seven eyes,[e] which are the seven Spirits God has *sent out all over the*
world. •The Lamb came forward to take the scroll from the right hand of the 7
One sitting on the throne, •and when he took it, the four animals prostrated 8

themselves before him and with them the twenty-four elders; each one of them
was holding a harp and had a golden bowl full of incense made of the prayers 8:3
9 of the saints. •They sang a new hymn: 9:13+

'You are worthy to take the scroll 14:3+
and break the seals of it,
because you were sacrificed, and with your blood 14:4
you bought[f] men for God
of every race, language, people and nation[g] 1:6+
10 and made them *a line of kings and priests*, Is 61:6 Ex 19:6
to serve our God and to rule the world'.[h] 20:4

11 In my vision, I heard the sound of an immense number of angels gathered
round the throne and the animals and the elders; there were *ten thousand times* Dn 7:10 Jude 14-15
12 *ten thousand of them* and *thousands upon thousands*, •shouting, 'The Lamb that
was sacrificed is worthy to be given power, riches,[i] wisdom, strength, honour, Dn 2:20 Ph 2:7-9
13 glory and blessing'. •Then I heard all the living things in creation—everything
that lives in the air, and on the ground, and under the ground, and in the sea, 5:3 Ps 150:6
crying, 'To the One who is sitting on the throne and to the Lamb, be all praise, *Jude 25*
14 honour, glory and power, for ever and ever'. •And the four animals said, 'Amen';
and the elders prostrated themselves to worship.

The Lamb breaks the seven seals[a]

1 6 Then I saw the Lamb break one of the seven seals, and I heard one of the Jr 15:2-4 Ezk 5:17; 14:13-21
2 four animals shout in a voice like thunder, 'Come'. •Immediately a white *Zc 1:8-10;* 6:1-3

j. Unlike Smyrna,2:9, Laodicea was rich in worldly goods, but spiritually poor.

k. The true riches that are of the spirit.

l. The clothing and the eye ointment are, of course, needed to repair the 'blindness and nakedness' of v.17; but there may be a special point in this as an allusion to the local products for which Laodicea was known.

4 a. God delegates to the Lamb the power of carrying out his decrees against persecuting pagans. The 'Great Day' of God's anger is about to dawn. The vision begins with a view of God's throne and widens to a view of the whole universe.

b. Lit. 'the Enthroned One looked like a jasper stone (diamond) and a *sardion* (ruby) and a rainbow round the throne looked like a *smaragdos* (emerald)'. John is careful not to describe God anthropomorphically; he prefers to give an impression of light. The whole scene draws heavily on Ezk 1 and 10; cf. also Is 6.

c. The elders have a priestly function: they praise and worship God, 4:10; 5:9; 11: 16, 17; 19:4, and offer him the prayers of the faithful, 5:8. The number twenty-four suggests the twenty-four priestly classes of 1 Ch 24:1-9; the thrones indicate that the elders are 'judges' in the New Israel which is the redeemed world; the crowns are the sign that they share God's royal power. It is to be noted that the thrones of the elders make the outer ring of the heavenly court, and in the New Jerusalem which comes down from heaven, ch. 21, the outer walls are composed of twelve foundation stones of apostles and twelve gates which are the twelve tribes of Israel.

d. Thunder is frequently associated with theophanies, cf. Ex 19:16+; Ezk 1:4,13.

e. Not the sevenfold Spirit of mediaeval tradition but the seven 'angels of the presence', cf. 3:1+; 8:2; Tb 12:15, God's messengers, cf. Zc 4:10; Tb 12:14; Lk 1:26; Rv 5:6 and *passim*.

f. Either the 'upper waters' of Gn 1:7; Ps 104:3, or the 'Sea' of 1 K 7:23-26.

g. Lit. 'In the centre of the throne and round the throne'; the text is obscure. 'In the centre of the throne and' is possibly a gloss from Ezk 1:5.

h. The symbolism derives from Ezk 1:5-21. The 'animals' are the four angels responsible for directing the physical world. 'Four' symbolises the universe; their many eyes symbolise God's omniscience and providence. They give unceasing glory to God for his creation. The figures of lion, bull, man, eagle suggest all that is noblest, strongest, wisest, most swift, in the created world. Since Irenaeus, these four creatures have been used as symbols of the four evangelists.

i. The liturgical *Trisagion* or *Sanctus* echoes this doxology. It is said that the Church thus shares in the worship of the heavenly court, but it is also possible that John's vision of heaven reproduces the worship of the Church on earth.

j. The crowns symbolise the government of the world, entrusted to the 'elders' by God. This power comes from God and must go back to him.

k. Lit. 'Through your will they were (var. 'they were not') and they were created': text uncertain.

5 a. A roll of papyrus in which God's hitherto secret decrees are written. The contents are made known in ch. 6-9.

b. In Hades, 1:18+.

c. Over Satan and the world, cf. Jn 3:35+; 1 Jn 2:14+.

d. The Messiah, the Passover lamb sacrificed for the salvation of the Chosen People, cf. Jn 1:29+. The wounds that caused the death of the Lamb are visible, but the Lamb has risen from death, and therefore stands upright. The Messiah, who became a lamb in order to submit as sacrifice, to suffer and to die, is a lion because he conquered death.

e. Symbolising the fulness (number seven) of the Messiah's power (horns) and knowledge (eyes).

f. Var. 'you bought us', 'you bought us for God'. The reading 'us' supposes that the elders are human beings, possibly the O.T. patriarchs. Lit. 'you were killed and you bought for God by your blood'.

g. Cliché for 'the whole world'. Cf. Dn 3:4,7,96.

h. Lit. 'you made them into a kingdom and priests for our God and they will reign on earth' (or 'over pagans'); Vulg. 'you have made us... we shall reign...'

i. Vulg. 'divinity'.

6 a. Ch. 6-9 plus 11:14-18 make one homogeneous whole—a series of symbolic visions heralding and preluding the destruction of the Roman empire. The four horsemen of this first vision are modelled on Zc 1:8-10 and 6:1-3; but they further symbolise the four scourges with which God, through the prophets,

horse appeared, and the rider on it was holding a bow; he was given the victor's
crown and he went away, to go from victory to victory.[b]
When he broke the second seal, I heard the second animal shout, 'Come'. 3
And out came another horse, bright red, and its rider was given this duty: to take 4
Ezk21:14-16 away peace from the earth and set people killing each other. He was given a huge
sword.[c]
When he broke the third seal, I heard the third animal shout, 'Come' 5
Immediately a black horse appeared, and its rider was holding a pair of scales;[d]
Lv 26:26 Ezk 4:16f and I seemed to hear a voice shout from among the four animals and say, 'A ration 6
of corn for a day's wages, and three rations of barley for a day's wages, but do not
tamper with the oil or the wine'.
When he broke the fourth seal, I heard the voice of the fourth animal shout, 7
'Come'. •Immediately another horse appeared, deathly pale, and its rider was 8
1:18+ called Plague,[e] and Hades followed at his heels.[f]
Ezk 14:21 They were given authority over a quarter of the earth, *to kill by the sword,*
by famine, by plague and wild beasts.
8:3; 14:18; 16:7; 19:2 When he broke the fifth seal, I saw underneath the altar[g] the souls of all the 9
people who had been killed on account of the word of God,[h] for witnessing to it.
Lk 18:7 *Dt 32:43* They shouted aloud, 'Holy, faithful Master, how much longer will you wait 10
Jb 16:18+; 24:12 before you pass sentence and take vengeance for our death on the inhabitants
Zc 1:12-13 of the earth?'[i] •Each of them was given a white robe,[j] and they were told to be 11
patient a little longer, until the roll was complete and their fellow servants and
brothers had been killed just as they had been.
Jl 3:4 Mt 24:29 In my vision, when he broke the sixth seal, there was a violent earthquake 12
and the sun went as black as coarse sackcloth; the moon turned red as blood all
Is 34:4 over, •and *the stars of the sky fell* on to the earth *like figs* dropping from a fig 13
tree when a high wind shakes it; •the *sky disappeared like a scroll rolling up* and all 14
16:20 the mountains and islands were shaken from their places.[k] •Then all the earthly 15
rulers, the governors and the commanders, the rich people and the men of
Is 2:10,19 influence, the whole population, slaves and citizens, took to the mountains *to hide*
Ho 10:8 *Is 2:10,18,19* *in caves and among the rocks.* •*They said to the mountains* and the rocks, '*Fall on us* 16
Lk 23:30 and hide us away from the One who sits on the throne and from the anger of
Jl 2:11; 3:4 Rm 1:18 the Lamb. •For *the Great Day of his anger*[l] has come, *and who can survive it*?' 17
1 Co 1:8+

21:12 **God's servants will be preserved**

Ezk 7:2 7 Next I saw four angels, standing at *the four corners of the earth,* holding the 1
Jr 49:36 Zc 6:5 four winds of the world back to keep them from blowing over the land or the
sea or in the trees. •Then I saw another angel rising where the sun rises, carrying 2
the seal of the living God; he called in a powerful voice to the four angels[a]
3:12; 9:4; 13:16; 22:4 whose duty was to devastate land and sea, •'Wait before you do any damage on 3
Is 44:5+ Ezk 9:4 land or at sea or to the trees, until we have put the *seal on the foreheads* of the
=*14:1* Ex 12:7-14 servants of our God'. •Then I heard how many were sealed: a hundred and forty- 4
four thousand,[b] out of all the tribes of Israel.
From the tribe of Judah, twelve thousand had been sealed; from the tribe of 5
Reuben, twelve thousand; from the tribe of Gad, twelve thousand; •from the 6
tribe of Asher, twelve thousand; from the tribe of Naphtali, twelve thousand;
from the tribe of Manasseh, twelve thousand; •from the tribe of Simeon, twelve 7
thousand; from the tribe of Levi, twelve thousand; from the tribe of Issachar,
twelve thousand; •from the tribe of Zebulun, twelve thousand; from the tribe of 8
Joseph, twelve thousand; and from the tribe of Benjamin, twelve thousand were
sealed.

The rewarding of the saints

=15:2-5 Gn 15:5 After that I saw a huge number, impossible to count, of people from every 9
Dn 3:4 nation, race, tribe and language;[c] they were standing in front of the throne and in
Jn 12:13 front of the Lamb, dressed in white robes and holding palms in their hands.[d]

10 They shouted aloud, •'Victory to our God, who sits on the throne, and to the
11 Lamb!' •And all the angels who were standing in a circle round the throne,
surrounding the elders and the four animals, prostrated themselves before
the throne, and touched the ground with their foreheads, worshipping God
12 with these words, 'Amen. Praise and glory and wisdom and thanksgiving and
honour and power and strength to our God for ever and ever. Amen.'
13 One of the elders then spoke, and asked me, 'Do you know who these people
14 are, dressed in white robes, and where they have come from?' •I answered him,
'You can tell me, my lord'. Then he said,[e] 'These are the people who have been =15:2 Mt 24:21
through the great persecution,[f] and because they have washed their robes white 1:5; 3:4; 22:14
15 again in the blood of the Lamb, •they now stand in front of God's throne and
serve him day and night in his sanctuary; and the One who sits on the throne will
16 spread his tent over them. •*They will never hunger or thirst* again; *neither the* Is 4:5-6; 25:4-5
17 *sun nor scorching wind will ever plague them*, •because the Lamb who is at the *Is 49:10*
throne *will be their shepherd and will lead them to springs of living water*; and God Is 49:10
will wipe away all tears from their eyes.'[g] =21:3-4; 22:3-5 Is 25:8

The seventh seal

1 **8** The Lamb then broke the seventh seal, and there was silence in heaven for Hab 2:20 Zp 1:7
about half an hour.[a] Zc 2:17

The prayers of the saints bring the coming of the Great Day nearer

2 Next I saw seven trumpets being given to the seven angels who stand in the 4:5+ Tb 12:15
3 presence of God. •Another angel, who had a golden censer,[b] came and stood
at the altar.[c] A large quantity of incense was given to him to offer with the prayers 16:7 5:8; 6:9
4 of all the saints on the golden altar that stood in front of the throne; •and so Tb 12:12 Ps 141:2
from the angel's hand the smoke of the incense went up in the presence of God
5 and with it the prayers of the saints. •Then the angel took the censer and *filled* Lv 16:12 Ps 11:6
it with the fire from the altar, which he then threw down on to the earth; Ezk 10:2
immediately there came peals of thunder and flashes of lightning, and the earth 4:5; 11:19
shook.

The first four trumpets

=16:1-9

6 The seven angels that had the seven trumpets now made ready to sound them. Jl 2:1+
7 The first blew his trumpet and, with that, hail and fire, mixed with blood, were Ex 9:24 Jl 3:3
dropped on the earth; a third of the earth was burnt up, and a third of all trees,
8 and every blade of grass was burnt.[d] •The second angel blew his trumpet, and it
was as though a great mountain, all on fire, had been dropped into the sea: a third Jr 51:25
9 of the sea turned into blood, •a third of all the living things in the sea were Ex 7:20

threatened a faithless Israel: wild animals, war, famine, plague, cf. Lv 26:21-26; Dt 32:24; Ezk 5:17; 14:13-21; and also Ezk 6:11-12; 7:14-15; 12:16; 33:27.

b. The rider on the white horse (symbol of victory) represents the Parthians, identified by the bow, their favourite weapon. They were the terror of the Roman world in the 1st cent. These are the 'wild beasts' of v. 8 (i.e. victorious pagan nations, cf. Dt 7:22; Ezk 34:28; Jr 15:2-4; 50:17). The Parthian invasion is described in the vision of 9:13f. One tradition identified the rider with the Messiah, as in 19:11-16.

c. Symbol of war.

d. Symbol of famine: food is rationed and sold at a prohibitive price.

e. Lit. 'death', but this word (as in 'the black death') signifies an endemic plague.

f. To swallow up the victims.

g. The altar of holocaust, 1 K 8:64+.

h. The martyrs.

i. The pagan nations.

j. Symbolising triumphant joy.

k. In prophetic writings, these cosmic phenomena are the concomitants of the Day of Yahweh, cf. Am 8:9+. They are to be interpreted therefore not as physical realities but as symbols of God's anger, cf. Mt 24:1+.

l. Var. 'their anger'.

7 a. The angels of v. 1.

b. Twelve (the sacred number) squared and multiplied by one thousand represents the totality of all who have been faithful to Christ (the new Israel, cf. Ga 6:16).

c. All the Christian martyrs now in heaven, v. 14.

d. Palms symbolise victory.

e. For this form of dialogue cf. Zc 6:4-5 and also 4:4-13.

f. Nero's persecution.

g. Common metaphors in the prophetic tradition, used to symbolise eschatological bliss, cf. Ho 2:20+; Is 11:6+; they recur in 21:4.

8 a. The 'coming of Yahweh' is often preceded and heralded by silence, in prophetic literature.

b. This was in the shape of a scoop or shovel, and was also used for carrying the live coals from the altar of holocaust to the altar of incense.

c. The altar of incense, cf. Ex 30:1; 1 K 6:20-21.

d. For the symbolism of these disasters see 6:14+.

killed, and a third of all ships were destroyed. •The third angel blew his trumpet, 10
Is 14:12 and a huge star fell from the sky, burning like a ball of fire, and it fell on a third
Jr 9:14 of all rivers and springs; •this was the star called Wormwood, and a third of all 11
water turned to bitter wormwood, so that many people died from drinking it.
The fourth angel blew his trumpet, and a third of the sun and a third of the moon 12
Ex 10:21-23 and a third of the stars were blasted, so that the light went out of a third of them
and for a third of the day there was no illumination, and the same with the night.
14:6 *Ezk 7:5,26* In my vision, I heard an eagle, calling aloud as it flew high overhead, 'Trouble, 13
Hab 2:6 trouble, trouble, for all the people on earth at the sound of the other three
trumpets which the three angels are going to blow'.

The fifth trumpet

20:1 *Is 14:12* 9 Then the fifth angel blew his trumpet, and I saw a star[a] that had fallen from 1
heaven on to the earth, and he was given the key to the shaft leading down
Gn 19:28 Ex 19:18 to the Abyss.[b] •When he unlocked the shaft of the Abyss, *smoke poured up* out of 2
the Abyss *like the smoke from a* huge *furnace* so that the sun and the sky were
Ex 10:12,15 Ws 16:9 darkened by it, •and out of the smoke dropped locusts which were given the 3
Jl 1-2 powers that scorpions have on the earth:[c] •they were forbidden to harm any 4
7:3 Ezk 9:6 fields or crops or trees[d] and told only to attack any men who were without God's
seal on their foreheads. •They were not to kill them, but to give them pain for 5
five months, and the pain was to be the pain of a scorpion's sting. •When this 6
Jb 3:21 happens, *men will long for death and not find it anywhere*; they will want to die
and death will evade them.
Jl 2:4 To look at, these locusts were *like horses armoured for battle*; they had things 7
that looked like gold crowns on their heads, and faces that seemed human, •and 8
Jl 1:6 hair like women's hair, and *teeth like lions' teeth.* •They had body-armour like 9
Jl 2:5 iron breastplates, and the noise of their wings sounded like a great charge of
horses and chariots into battle. •Their tails were like scorpions', with stings, 10
and it was with them that they were able to injure people for five months.[e] •As 11
their leader they had their emperor, the angel of the Abyss, whose name in
Hebrew is Abaddon, or Apollyon[f] in Greek.
8:13; 11:14 Ezk 7:5 That was the first of the troubles; there are still two more to come. 12

The sixth trumpet

The sixth angel blew his trumpet, and I heard a voice come out of the four 13
Ex 30:1-3 horns of the golden altar[g] in front of God. •It spoke to the sixth angel with the 14
=16:12 trumpet, and said, 'Release the four angels that are chained up at the great river
1 Co 1:8 Euphrates'.[h] •These four angels had been put there ready for this hour of this 15
day of this month of this year,[i] and now they were released to destroy a third of
the human race. •I learnt how many there were in their army: twice ten thousand 16
times ten thousand mounted men. •In my vision I saw the horses, and the riders 17
Jb 41:10-13 with their breastplates of flame colour, hyacinth-blue and sulphur-yellow; the
horses had lions' heads, and fire, smoke and sulphur were coming out of their
mouths. •It was by these three plagues, the fire, the smoke and the sulphur coming 18
out of their mouths, that the one third of the human race was killed. •All the 19
horses' power was in their mouths and their tails: their tails were like snakes,
Am 4:6+ and had heads that were able to wound. •But the rest of the human race, who 20
16:9 Is 17:8 escaped these plagues, refused either to abandon *the things they had made with*
Dn 5:4 Ps 135:15-17 *their own hands*—the *idols made of gold, silver, bronze, stone and wood* that can
neither see nor hear nor move—or to stop worshipping devils. •Nor did they give 21
up their murdering, or witchcraft, or fornication or stealing.

The imminence of the last punishment

10 Then I saw another powerful angel coming down from heaven, wrapped in 1
a cloud, with a rainbow over his head; his face was like the sun, and his legs
Ezk 2:10 were pillars of fire. •In his hand he had a small scroll, unrolled; he put his right foot 2

3 in the sea and his left foot on the land •and he shouted so loud, it was *like a lion* Am 3:8 Ps 29:3-9
4 *roaring*. At this, seven claps of thunder made themselves heard[a] •and when the Jr 25:30
seven thunderclaps had spoken, I was preparing to write, when I heard a voice
from heaven say to me, 'Keep the words of the seven thunderclaps secret and do 22:10 Dn 8:26; 12:4,9
5 not write them down'.[b] •Then the angel that I had seen, standing on the sea
6 and the land, *raised his right hand to heaven,*[c] •and *swore by the One who lives* Dn 12:7 *Dt 32:40*
for ever and ever, *and made heaven and all that is in it*, and *earth and all it bears,* Ne 9:6
7 and *the sea and all it holds*, 'The time of waiting is over; •at the time when the Ex 20:11 Ezk 12:28
seventh angel is heard sounding his trumpet, God's secret intention[d] will be *Rm 16:25+*
fulfilled, just as he announced in the Good News told to *his servants the prophets*'. Am 3:7

The seer eats the small scroll

8 Then I heard the voice I had heard from heaven speaking to me again. 'Go,'
it said 'and take that open scroll out of the hand of the angel standing on sea
9 and land.' •I went to the angel and asked him to give me the small scroll, and Zc 5:2
he said, 'Take it and eat it; it will turn your stomach sour, but in your mouth it
10 will taste as sweet as honey'. •So I took it out of the angel's hand, and swallowed Ezk 3:1-3
it; it was as sweet as honey in my mouth, but when I had eaten it my stomach
11 turned sour.[e] •Then I was told, 'You are to prophesy again, this time about
many different nations and countries and languages and emperors'.

The two witnesses

1 **11** Then I was given a long cane as a measuring rod, and I was told,[a] 'Go and Ezk 40:1-5 Zc 2:5-9
measure God's sanctuary, and the altar, and the people who worship there;[b]
2 but leave out the outer court and do not measure it, because it has been handed
3 over to pagans—they will trample on the holy city for forty-two months.[c] •But Lk 21:24
I shall send my two witnesses to prophesy for those twelve hundred and sixty days, 12:6,14; 13:5 Dn 7:25+
4 wearing sackcloth. •These are the *two olive trees* and the two lamps *that stand* Zc 4:3,14
5 *before the Lord of the world.*[d] •Fire can come from their mouths and consume *2 K 1:10* Jr 5:14
their enemies if anyone tries to harm them; and if anybody does try to harm
6 them he will certainly be killed in this way. •They are able to lock up the sky so 1 K 17:1 Jm 5:17
that it does not rain as long as they are prophesying; they are able to turn water *Ex 7:17;* 11:10
into blood and strike the whole world with any plague as often as they like.

9 a. One of the fallen angels, possibly Satan himself, cf. v. 11 and Lk 10:18.

b. Where the fallen angels are imprisoned pending their ultimate punishment.

c. The vision of locusts is suggested by Jl 1-2 which, according to Jerome, the Jews interpreted historically: the four armies of locusts being successive invaders, Assyrian, Persian, Greek, Roman; cf. Jr 51:27. Here the locusts probably indicate the Parthians. Another suggestion is that the locusts symbolise spiritual torments inflicted by demons.

d. Possibly symbols of upright, faithful Christians, cf. 7:1f.

e. Lit. 'They have scorpion-like tails and stings and their authority (power) is to harm people for five months with their tails'; Var. 'they have tails like scorpions, and stings, and in their tails (lies) their power...'

f. Destruction, or ruin.

g. This shows that the pagans are punished in answer to the martyrs' prayer of 6:9,10 (cf. 8:2f).

h. The Parthians lived east of the Euphrates; the sixth plague represents Parthian cavalry. Cf. 6:2+.

i. Lit. 'for the hour and day and month and year'. For the 'Great Day' of wrath, cf. 6:17.

10 a. The voice of God.

b. Because the time of their fulfilment has not yet come. Cf. 22:10.

c. The angel, in contact with air, sea and land, the three regions of the universe, is about to swear by him who made them. Cf. Gn 14:22; Ezk 20:6,15,28; Dt 32:40.

d. The definitive establishment of the kingdom; the sign of this is the destruction of the enemies of God's people, i.e. Babylon, ch. 17, Satan, and the pagan nations, 20:7-10. On the 'mystery' or 'secret' of God in the eschatological sense, cf. Rm 11:25; 2 Th 2:6f and Rm 16:25+. Cf. 2:24, the 'secrets of Satan'.

e. The news is sweet because it announces the Church's victory, bitter because it foretells her suffering.

11 a. Lit. 'A reed like a rod was given to me saying'; var. 'and the angel stood (there) saying'.

b. The Holy City, Jerusalem, symbolises the Church, cf. 20:9, which is about to be persecuted by the Beast (the Roman empire, cf. ch. 13). The Temple of God, which is measured as a sign that it will be spared, symbolises those who will remain faithful to Christ (cf. 14:1-5), the new 'remnant' of Israel, cf. Is 4:3+.

c. This period (three-and-a-half years) taken from Dn, had become the symbol for any persecution, cf. Lk 4:25; Jm 5:17. Here it is the Roman persecution.

d. In Zc the two olive trees symbolise Joshua and Zerubbabel, the religious and the civil leaders of the repatriated community who restored Temple and city after the Exile. Here they probably symbolise the two leaders appointed to build the new Temple, the Church of Christ, namely Peter and Paul, probably martyred in Rome under Nero, v. 8. They are described in terms of Moses and Elijah, the two witnesses of the transfiguration.

When they have completed their witnessing, the beast that comes out of the 7
Dn 7:21 Abyss[e] *is going to make war on them and overcome them* and kill them. •Their 8
corpses will lie in the main street of the Great City[f] known by the symbolic
names Sodom and Egypt, in which their Lord was crucified. •Men out of every 9
people, race, language and nation will stare at their corpses, for three-and-a-half
Jn 16:20 days, not letting them be buried, •and the people of the world will be glad about 10
Est 9:19 it and celebrate the event by giving presents to each other, because these two
prophets have been a plague to the people of the world.'
Ezk 37:5,10 After the three-and-a-half days, *God breathed life into them and they stood up*, 11
and everybody who saw it happen was terrified; •then they heard[g] a loud voice 12
from heaven say to them, 'Come up here', and while their enemies were watching,
2 K 2:11 they went up to heaven in a cloud. •Immediately, there was a violent earthquake, 13
and a tenth of the city collapsed; seven thousand persons[h] were killed in the
earthquake, and the survivors, overcome with fear, could only praise the God
of heaven.

The seventh trumpet

8:13; 9:12 Ezk 7:5 That was the second of the troubles; the third is to come quickly after it.[i] 14
Then the seventh angel blew his trumpet, and voices could be heard shouting 15
1:5+; 12:10 Ps 2; 22:28 in heaven, calling, 'The kingdom of the world has become the kingdom of our
Dn 7:14,27 Zc 14:9 Lord and his Christ, and he will reign for ever and ever'. •The twenty-four elders, 16
enthroned in the presence of God, prostrated themselves and touched the ground
1:4+; with their foreheads worshipping God •with these words, 'We give thanks to 17
16:5; 19:6 you, Almighty Lord God, He-Is-and-He-Was,[j] for using your great power and
Ps 2:1,5 beginning your reign. •*The nations were seething with rage* and now the time has 18
19:2 Am 3:7 come for your own anger, and for the dead to be judged, and for your servants
19:5 Ps 115:13 the prophets, for the saints and for all who worship you, small or great, to be
rewarded. The time has come to destroy those who are destroying the earth.'
Ex 25:8-10+ 2 M 2:5-8 Then the sanctuary of God in heaven[k] opened, and the ark of the covenant 19
Heb 8:5 *4:5; 8:5* could be seen inside it. Then came flashes of lightning, peals of thunder and an
earthquake, and violent hail.

The vision of the woman and the dragon[a]

22:14 Gn 37:9 Sg 6:10 **12** Now a great sign appeared in heaven: a woman,[b] adorned with the sun, 1
standing on the moon, and with the twelve stars on her head for a crown.
Gn 3:16 Mi 4:9-10 She was pregnant, and in labour, crying aloud in the pangs of childbirth. •Then 2 3
Dn 7:7 a second sign appeared in the sky, a huge red dragon which had seven heads
and ten horns, and each of the seven heads crowned with a coronet.[c] •Its tail 4
Dn 8:10 dragged a third of *the stars from the sky and dropped them to the earth*,[d] and the
dragon stopped in front of the woman as she was having the child, so that he could
Is 66:7 eat it as soon as it was born from its mother. •The woman brought *a male child* 5
2:27 Ps 2:9 *into the world*,[e] the son who was *to rule all the nations with an iron sceptre*, and the
1:6+ child was taken straight up to God and to his throne,[f] •while the woman escaped 6
into the desert,[g] where God had made a place of safety ready, for her to be
11:3+; 12:14 looked after in the twelve hundred and sixty days.
20:2 Dn 10:13+; 12:1 And now war broke out in heaven, when Michael with his angels attacked the 7
dragon. The dragon fought back with his angels, •but they were defeated and 8
driven out of heaven. •The great dragon, the primeval serpent, known as the 9
20:2-3 Gn 3:1-4 devil or Satan, who had deceived all the world, was hurled down to the earth
Lk 10:19 Jn 12:31 and his angels were hurled down with him. •Then I heard a voice shout from 10
11:15 heaven, 'Victory and power and empire for ever have been won by our God, and
all authority for his Christ, now that the persecutor, who accused our brothers
day and night before our God, has been brought down. •They have triumphed 11
over him by the blood of the Lamb and by the witness of their martyrdom,
because even in the face of death they would not cling to life. •Let the heavens 12
rejoice and all who live there; but for you, earth and sea, trouble is coming—

because the devil has gone down to you in a rage, knowing that his days are 20:3 2 Co 6:2+
numbered.'
13 As soon as the devil found himself thrown down to the earth, he sprang
14 in pursuit of the woman, the mother of the male child, •but she was given a huge Gn 3:15
pair of eagle's wings to fly away from the serpent into the desert, to the place Ex 19:4 Is 40:31
where she was to be looked after for *a year and twice a year and half a year.*[h] *11:3+; 12:6* Dn 7:25+
15 So the serpent vomited water from his mouth, like a river, after the woman,
16 to sweep her away in the current,[i] •but the earth came to her rescue; it opened
17 its mouth and swallowed the river thrown up by the dragon's jaws. •Then the
dragon was enraged with the woman and went away to make war on the rest of Gn 3:15
her children, that is, all who obey God's commandments and bear witness for 14:12
Jesus.[j]

The dragon delegates his power to the beast[k] Dn 7 2 Th 2:3-12

18 1 I was standing[l] on the seashore. **13** Then I saw *a beast emerge from the sea:* =17:3,8 Dn 7:3
it had seven heads and ten horns, with a coronet on each of its ten horns, and its
2 heads were marked with blasphemous titles. •I saw that the beast *was like* Dn 7:4-6
a leopard, with paws like *a bear* and a mouth like *a lion*; the dragon had handed
3 over to it his own power and his throne and his worldwide authority.[a] •I saw that Jr 27:6 Lk 4:6
one of its heads seemed to have had a fatal wound but that this deadly injury had
healed[b] and, after that, the whole world had marvelled and followed the beast.
4 They prostrated themselves in front of the dragon because he had given the beast 17:8; 18:18 Jr 27:6
his authority; and they prostrated themselves in front of the beast, saying, 'Who
5 can compare with the beast?[c] How could anybody defeat him?' •For forty-two 11:3+
months the beast was allowed *to mouth its boasts* and blasphemies and to do Dn 7:8,11; 11:36+
6 whatever it wanted; •and it mouthed its blasphemies against God, against his
7 name, his heavenly Tent and all those who are sheltered there. •It was allowed

e. The emperor Nero, type of Antichrist, cf. 13:1,18; 17:8 with notes.

f. The Great City here is Babylon i.e. Rome, cf. 16:19; 17:18; 18:10,16,18,19; it is called Sodom and Egypt for its two great crimes: refusing God's messengers and oppressing the people of Christ, cf. 17:4-6. The words 'in which their Lord was crucified', identifying the Great City with Jerusalem, are probably a gloss suggested by Mt 23:37, or can be justified by the responsibility of Roman authority for the crucifixion.

g. Var. 'I heard'.

h. The figure symbolises people of all classes of society (seven) and in great numbers (thousands).

i. The second disaster was described (the sixth trumpet) in 9:15-19. The third is to be the fall of Babylon (Rome) in ch. 17-18.

j. Add. (Vulg.) 'and he is to come'.

k. As opposed to the Jerusalem Temple referred to in vv. 1 and 2.

12 a. This chapter is made up of two separate visions: the attack of the dragon on the woman and her children, vv. 1-6 and 13-17; the attack of Michael on the dragon, vv. 7-12.

b. The woman is essentially an image of Israel as the mother of the messianic saviour, cf. Mi 4:9-10; Is 66:7; the son born to her is, like Moses, snatched from the dragon of water (in whom Leviathan of the Nile-Pharaoh can be seen) and taken up to the throne, while she herself escapes into the desert for a time of 42 months which recalls the 42 years of Israel's desert wanderings; the earth's swallowing of the dragon's river can be associated with the miraculous crossing of the Red Sea. The Messiah is here seen under the type of Moses. The woman's pain in travail may recall the curse of Eve, whose offspring would ultimately wound the serpent, so that Israel is seen as representing all humanity. It does not seem probable that John had Mary in mind or intended any allusion to the physical birth of the Messiah in the incarnation; cf. note to v. 5.

c. I.e. Satan, cf. v. 9 and 20:2; this Hebr. word, rendered diabolos by LXX, in its primary sense means 'Accuser', cf. v. 10 and Zc 3:1-2 and see Jb 1:6+. In Jewish tradition the snake and the dragon symbolised the power of evil, the enemy of God and his people which God is to destroy at the end of time, cf. Jb 3:8+ and 7:12+.

d. Allusion to the fall of the angels seduced by Satan.

e. The Messiah considered simultaneously as an individual person and as head or leader of the new Israel, cf. the 'Son of Man' of Dn 7:13, and the 'Servant of Yahweh' of Is 42:1+.

f. Allusion to the ascension and the triumph of the Messiah that will result in the dragon's fall.

g. Traditional O.T. refuge for the persecuted, cf. Ex 2:15; 1 K 17:2f; 19:3f; 1 M 2:29,30. To exist, the Church must depend not on paganism but on her own divine life, cf. Ex 16; 1 K 17:4,6; 19:5-8; Mt 14:13,19.

h. Lit. 'a time and times and half a time'. Three-and-a-half years, cf. 11:3+.

i. The Roman empire, like a flood let loose by Satan, cf. Is 8:7-8, will try to engulf the Church, cf. Rv 13.

j. All faithful Christians.

k. This vision is inspired by Dn 7 (persecution of Antiochus Epiphanes). According to Rv 17:10,12-14, the Beast symbolises the Roman empire, type of all forces that are to oppose the Church. The seven heads are a series of successive emperors; the ten crowned horns are ten subject kings.

l. Var. 'he stood', which would join v. 18 to the preceding passage.

13 a. Satan, 'prince of this world', Jn 12:31+, can give imperial power to anybody he chooses, cf. Lk 4:6+.

b. Allusion to the empire recovering after some temporary setback; possibly Julius Caesar's assassination or the disturbances after Nero's death. The risen beast is a caricature of the risen Christ.

c. A parody of the name Michael, 12:7, which means 'Who-can-compare-with-God?'

Dn 7:21 *Dn 7:6* *to make war against the saints and conquer them, and given power* over every race,
people, language and nation; •and all people of the world will worship it, that 8
is, everybody whose name has not been written down since the foundation of
20:12+ 2:7 the world in the book of life of the sacrificial Lamb. •If anyone has ears to hear, 9
Mt 13:9 *Jr 15:2* let him listen: •*Captivity for those who are destined for captivity; the sword for* 10
those who are to die[d] *by the sword.*[e] This is why the saints must have constancy
and faith.

The false prophet as the slave of the beast

Then I saw a second beast; it emerged from the ground;[f] it had two horns 11
Mt 7:15 like a lamb, but made a noise like a dragon. •This second beast was servant to 12
the first beast, and extended its authority everywhere, making the world and
all its people worship the first beast, which had had the fatal wound and had
Dt 13:2-4 Mt 24:24 been healed. •And it worked great miracles, even to calling down fire from 13
2 Th 2:9-10 heaven on to the earth while people watched. •Through the miracles which it 14
was allowed to do on behalf of the first beast, it was able to win over the people
of the world and persuade them to put up a statue in honour of the beast that
15:2 had been wounded by the sword and still lived. •It was allowed to breathe 15
life into this statue, so that the statue of the beast was able to speak, and to have
Dn 3:5-7,15 *anyone who refused to worship the statue of the beast* put to death.[g] •He compelled 16
7:3; 14:9. 11; 16:2; everyone—small and great, rich and poor, slave and citizen—to be branded on
19:20; 20: 4 the right hand or on the forehead, •and made it illegal for anyone to buy or sell 17
anything unless he had been branded with the name of the beast or with the
the number of its name.
17:9 There is need for shrewdness here: if anyone is clever enough he may interpret 18
the number of the beast: it is the number of a man, the number 666.[h]

=7:1-8+ The companions of the Lamb[a]

2 K 19:30-31 Jl 3:5 **14** Next in my vision I saw Mount Zion, and standing on it a Lamb[b] who 1
Ob 17 Zp 3:12-13 had with him a hundred and forty-four thousand people, all with his name
Ac 2:21+ and his Father's name written on their foreheads. •I heard a sound coming 2
out of the sky like the sound of the ocean or the roar of thunder; it seemed to be
5:9; 15:3 the sound of harpists playing their harps. •There in front of the throne they were 3
Ps 33:3; 98:1 Is 42:10; 43: 19 singing a new hymn[c] in the presence of the four animals and the elders, a hymn
that could only be learnt by the hundred and forty-four thousand who had been
redeemed from the world.[d] •These are the ones who have kept their virginity[e] 4
Jr 2:2-3 Jm 1:18 and not been defiled with women; they *follow* the Lamb wherever he goes;[f]
they have been redeemed from amongst men to be *the first-fruits for God* and
Zp 3:13 for the Lamb. •They never *allowed a lie*[g] *to pass their lips* and no fault can be 5
found in them.

Angels announce the day of Judgement[h]

8:13 Then I saw another angel, flying high overhead, sent to announce the Good 6
Dn 3:4 News of eternity to all who live on the earth, every nation, race, language and
4:11 Mt 10:28p tribe. •He was calling, 'Fear God and praise him, because the time has come for 7
Ex 20:11 him to sit in judgement; worship *the maker of heaven and earth and sea* and every
water-spring'.
=18:2-3 Is 21:9 A second angel followed him, calling, '*Babylon has fallen, Babylon the Great has* 8
Is 51:17+ Jr 25:15 *fallen*,[i] Babylon which gave the whole world *the wine of* God's *anger* to drink'.[j]
13:15-17+ A third angel followed, shouting aloud, 'All those who worship the beast and 9
his statue, or have had themselves branded on the hand or forehead, •will be made 10
16:19; 19: 20+; 20: 14+ to drink the wine of God's fury which is ready, undiluted, in his cup of anger;
Gn 19:28 in *fire and brimstone*[k] they will be tortured in the presence of the holy angels and
19:3 Is 34:9-10 the Lamb •and *the smoke* of their torture *will go up for ever* and ever. There will 11
be no respite, *night or day*, for those who worshipped the beast or its statue
or accepted branding with its name.' •This is why there must be constancy in the 12

13 saints who keep the commandments of God and faith in Jesus. •Then I heard 12:17 Ac 9:13+
a voice from heaven say to me, 'Write down: Happy are those who die in the *1:3+* Si 14:19
Lord! Happy indeed, the Spirit says; now they can rest for ever after their work, 2 Th 1:7 *Mt 11:28-29*
since their good deeds go with them.' Heb 4:10

The harvest and vintage of the pagans[l] Jl 4:12-13

14 Now in my vision I saw a white *cloud* and, *sitting on it, one like a son of man* 1:7 Dn 7:13
15 with a gold crown on his head and a sharp sickle in his hand. •Then another angel
came out of the sanctuary, and shouted aloud to the one sitting on the cloud,
'*Put your sickle in* and reap: harvest time has come and *the harvest* of the earth Jl 4:13 Am 8:2
16 *is ripe*'. •Then the one sitting on the cloud set his sickle to work on the earth, and *Mt 13:36-43* Jn 4:35
the earth's harvest was reaped. Rm 2:6+
17 Another angel, who also carried a sharp sickle, came out of the temple in
18 heaven, •and the angel in charge of the fire left the altar[m] and shouted aloud to 6:9-10; 8:3-5
the one with the sharp sickle, 'Put your sickle in and cut all the bunches off the
19 vine of the earth; all its grapes are ripe'. •So the angel set his sickle to work on 19:15 Is 63:1-6
the earth and harvested the whole vintage of the earth and put it into a huge
20 winepress, the winepress of God's anger, •outside the city,[n] where it was trodden
until the blood that came out of the winepress was up to the horses' bridles as 19:14,21
far away as sixteen hundred furlongs.

The hymn of Moses and the Lamb[a]

1 **15** What I saw next, in heaven, was a great and wonderful sign: seven angels
were bringing the seven plagues that are the last of all, because they
2 exhaust the anger of God. •I seemed to see a glass lake suffused with fire, and =7:9,14; 13:15-18
standing by the lake of glass, those who had fought against the beast and won,
and against his statue and the number which is his name. They all had harps
3 from God, •and they were singing the hymn of Moses,[b] the servant of God, 14:3+ Ex 15
and of the Lamb:

d. Var. 'he who kills by the sword must die...'

e. This seems to mean that God's decrees against the persecutors will be carried out inexorably; their punishment is at hand; cf. 14:11,12; Mt 26:52.

f. This second beast is later called the 'false prophet', 16:13; 19:20; 20:10. Before describing the return of the Son of Man, 14:14-21; cf. 19:11f and Mt 24:30, John describes the activities of the false messiahs (first beast) and false prophets (second beast) foretold by Christ himself, Mt 24:24; cf. 2 Th 2:9.

g. The second beast mimics the Spirit who works miracles in the Church to encourage faith in Christ. Similarly, the first beast had imitated the risen Messiah, 13:3. The Dragon, the first beast and the second beast form a caricature of the Trinity.

h. Var. '616'. In both Greek and Hebr., letters are used for numbers, the value corresponding to the place in the alphabet; by adding up the values of component letters the total 'number of a person's name' is obtained. Some commentators point out that in Hebr. the letters of Caesar Nero add up to 666, and that in Greek the letters of Caesar-God add up to 616 (the alternative reading).

14 a. The followers of the beast who are branded with his name and number, 13:16-17, are now contrasted with the followers of the Lamb marked with his name and the name of his Father. This is the 'remnant' of the new Israel, Is 4:3+, the faithful Christians who have survived persecution and who are to begin the restoration of God's kingdom when its enemies have been destroyed.

b. Var. 'the Lamb'.

c. Moses had celebrated the deliverance from Egypt, Ex 15:1-21; cf. Rv 15:3-5; the new hymn celebrates the new deliverance of God's people and of the new order introduced by the Lamb that was sacrificed.

d. Lit. 'the earth', which is here equivalent to the 'world' of the fourth gospel, cf. Jn 1:10+, i.e. the pagan world, cf. 5:9.

e. Metaphorically. In the O.T. marital infidelity is a metaphor for idolatry, cf. Ho 1:2+, in this case the worship of the beast.

f. Just as Israel followed Yahweh at the Exodus, so the new Israel, newly redeemed, follows the Lamb into the desert, cf. Jr 2:2-3, where the marriage rites are renewed (Ho 2:16-25).

g. I.e. they have not invoked false gods, the beast.

h. Before God's vengeance strikes, the angels appear to exhort the persecutors to repentance by proclaiming the hour of judgement; but the appeal goes unheeded, cf. 16:2,9,11,21. See 15:5+.

i. The tense is the prophetic perfect.

j. Lit. 'who has made all nations drink the wine of anger' corr. 'drink the wine of the anger of her adultery' Greek, as in 18:3. The 'wine of anger' is a familiar image, cf. Is 51:17+, for the divine anger to which Babylon (Rome) has exposed all nations by making them worship her idols.

k. The lake of burning sulphur is where the wicked are punished, cf. 19:20; 20:10; 21:8.

l. The destruction of the pagan nations. The fulfilment of this prophecy is described in 19:11f.

m. Persecutors are annihilated in answer to the martyrs' prayers which are carried to God by the angel who tends the altar fire.

n. The pagans are to be destroyed outside Jerusalem according to Zc 14:2f,12f; Ezk 38-39; cf. Heb 13:11; Lv 4:12+. See also Is 63.

15 a. The hymn of Moses, vv. 2-4, interrupts the development of the vision of the seven cups, just as the symbolic liturgy of 8:3-5 interrupted the vision of the seven trumpets. The severity of the divine punishment is thus vindicated before it is described.

b. The hymn of Ex 15 which celebrated Israel's triumph over Pharaoh. Here the conquerors of the

Ps 92:5; 98:1 'How great and wonderful are all your works,
Lord God Almighty;
Dt 32:4 Ps 145:17 just and true are all your ways,
King of nations.
Jr 10:7 *Who would not revere* and *praise your name, O Lord?* 4
You alone are holy,
Ps 86:9 *and all the pagans will come and adore you*
for the many acts of justice you have shown.'

The seven bowls of plagues[c]

Ex 25:22+ After this, in my vision, the sanctuary, the Tent of the Testimony, opened 5
in heaven, •and out came the seven angels with the seven plagues, wearing pure 6
19:8 white linen, fastened round their waists with golden girdles. •One of the four 7
14:8+ animals gave the seven angels seven golden bowls filled with the anger of God
1 K 8:10-11 Is 6:4 who lives for ever and ever. •*The smoke from the glory* and the power *of God* 8
filled the temple so that no one could go into it[d] until the seven plagues of the
seven angels were completed.

=8:6-12 16 Then I heard a voice from the sanctuary shouting to the seven angels, 1
'Go, and empty the seven bowls of God's anger over the earth'.
The first angel went and emptied his bowl over the earth; at once, on all the 2
13:15-17 people who had been branded with the mark of the beast and had worshipped
Ex 9:8-11 its statue, there came disgusting and virulent sores.
The second angel emptied his bowl over the sea, and it turned to blood, like 3
the blood of a corpse, and every living creature in the sea died.
Ex 7:14-24 The third angel emptied his bowl into the rivers and water-springs and they 4
1:20+ turned into blood. •Then I heard the angel of water say, 'You are the holy 5
1:4+ *11:17* He-Is-and-He-Was, the Just One, and this is a just punishment: •they spilt the 6
=*18:24* Ezk 35:6 blood of the saints and the prophets, and blood is what you have given them
Mt 23:35 *6:9; 8:3-4* to drink; it is what they deserve'. •And I heard the altar itself say, 'Truly, Lord 7
Dn 3:27 =*19:2* God Almighty, the punishments you give are true and just'.
The fourth angel emptied his bowl over the sun and it was made to scorch 8
people with its flames; •but though people were scorched by the fierce heat of it, 9
9:20 Am 4:6+ they cursed the name of God who had the power to cause such plagues, and
they would not repent and praise him.
The fifth angel emptied his bowl over the throne of the beast[a] and its whole 10
Ex 10:21-23 Is 8:22 empire was plunged into darkness. Men were biting their tongues for pain,
Jr 5:3 but instead of repenting for what they had done, they cursed the God of heaven 11
because of their pains and sores.
=9:14 The sixth angel emptied his bowl over the great river Euphrates; all the water 12
dried up so that a way was made for the kings of the East[b] to come in. •Then 13
from the jaws of dragon and beast and false prophet I saw three foul spirits come;
Ex 8:2-3 they looked like frogs •and in fact were demon spirits, able to work miracles, 14
17:13-14; 19:19 going out to all the kings of the world to call them together for the war of the
1 Co 1:8+ *3:3-4,18* Great Day of God the Almighty.[c]—•This is how it will be: I shall come like 15
1:3+ a thief. Happy is the man who has stayed awake and not taken off his clothes
=20:8 so that he does not go out naked and expose his shame.—•They called the 16
kings together at the place called, in Hebrew, Armageddon.[d]
18:4 Is 66:6 The seventh angel emptied his bowl into the air, and a voice shouted from 17
21:6 *4:5* the sanctuary,[e] 'The end has come'. •Then there were flashes of lightning and 18
Dn 12:1 Mk 13:19 peals of thunder and the most violent earthquake *that anyone has ever seen since*
there have been men *on the earth.* •The Great City was split into three parts 19
14:8,10 and the cities of the world collapsed; Babylon the Great was not forgotten:
God made her drink the full winecup of his anger. •Every island vanished and 20
6:14 *Ex 9:22-26* the mountains disappeared;[f] •and hail, with great hailstones weighing a talent 21
each,[g] fell from the sky on the people. They cursed God for sending a plague
of hail; it was the most terrible plague.

B. THE PUNISHMENT OF BABYLON

The famous prostitute Ezk 16:23

1 17 One of the seven angels that had the seven bowls came to speak to me,
and said, 'Come here and I will show you the punishment given to the
2 famous prostitute[a] *who* rules *enthroned beside abundant waters,*[b] •the one with Jr 51:13
whom all the kings of the earth have committed fornication, and who has made 18:3+ Is 23:17
3 all the population of the world drunk with the wine of her adultery'.[c] •He took Jr 51:7
me in spirit to a desert,[d] and there I saw a woman riding a scarlet beast which Is 21:1f
had seven heads and ten horns[e] and had blasphemous titles written all over it. =13:1
4 The woman was dressed in purple and scarlet, and glittered with gold and jewels 18:16
and pearls, and she was holding a gold winecup filled with the disgusting filth Jr 51:7
5 of her fornication; •on her forehead was written a name, a cryptic name:
'Babylon the Great,[f] the mother of all the prostitutes and all the filthy practices 2 Th 2:7 1 P 5:13+
6 on the earth'. •I saw that she was drunk, drunk with the blood of the saints,
and the blood of the martyrs of Jesus;[g] and when I saw her, I was completely
7 mystified. •The angel said to me, 'Don't you understand? Now I will tell you
the meaning of this woman, and of the beast she is riding, with the seven heads
and the ten horns.

The symbolism of the beast and the prostitute

8 'The beast you have seen once was and now is not; he is yet to come up =13:3,4
from the Abyss, but only to go to his destruction.[h] And the people of the world,
whose names have not been written since the beginning of the world in the book 20:12+
of life, will think it miraculous when they see how the beast once was and now
9 is not and is still to come. •Here there is need for cleverness, for a shrewd mind; 13:18
the seven heads are the seven hills, and the woman is sitting on them.
10 'The seven heads are also seven emperors.[i] Five of them have already gone,
one is here now, and one is yet to come; once here, he must stay for a short while.
11 The beast, who once was and now is not, is at the same time the eighth and one of
the seven, and he is going to his destruction.
12 '*The ten horns are ten kings*[j] who have not yet been given their royal power Dn 7:24
but will have royal authority only for a single hour and in association with the
13 beast. •They are all of one mind in putting their strength and their powers at the 16:14

beast celebrate the justice of God in punishing the wicked persecutors.

c. Before finally destroying Babylon (Rome), 16:18-19, God sends a series of plagues on the wicked (several are reminiscent of the Egyptian plagues, Ex 7-10) to bring them to repentance; but, like Pharaoh, the wicked are obstinate.

d. According to 2 M 2:4-8 the reappearance of the sacred tent and the manifestation of God's glory as in the time of Moses, Ex 40:34-35, and of Solomon, 1 K 8:10, were to herald the coming of the messianic age and the renaissance of the chosen people. The 'glory' (cf. Ex 24:16+) is the sign of God's presence (cf. the 'silence' of 8:1, and the appearance of the ark of the covenant in 11:19).

16 a. Rome, type of all pagan powers hostile to God.

b. The Parthian kings, dreaded by the Roman world.

c. The work of these evil spirits is foreordained to bring the pagan nations to judgement.

d. I.e. 'the mountains of Megiddo'. The defeat of King Josiah near this town, 2 K 23:29f, made the place symbolise disaster for any armies assembling there, cf. Zc 12:11.

e. Add. '(proceeding) from the throne' or 'from God'.

f. These cosmic phenomena symbolise the powers of this world withering under God's anger.

g. Lit. 'about one talent'.

17 a. Rome, type of any place where evil is supreme. Prostitution symbolises idolatry as in Ezk 16 and 23, cf. Ho 1:2+. See also Rv 14:4+.

b. A literal description of Babylon, metaphorically explained in v. 15.

c. All pagan nations and their kings who have adopted the imperial cult.

d. Where unclean beasts live, cf. Lv 16:8+; 17:7+.

e. The seven heads are Rome's seven hills, v. 9, and the horns ten subject kings, v. 16. The beast, v. 8, is Nero himself; he is dead but will return as the ruler of the subject peoples to avenge himself on Rome, vv. 16-17—a reflection of popular belief that the dead Nero would return, at the head of a Parthian army. This return figures as a parody of Christ's resurrection just as the formula of v. 8, 'he once was and now is not (and he is to come)' echoes the divine name, 'He was, he is, and he is to come'.

f. Babylon is the symbolic name for Rome.

g. Allusion to Nero's persecutions. Like Jerusalem (Ezk 16:36-38 and 23:37-45) Rome is guilty of a double crime: idolatry, v. 4, and murder, v. 6.

h. Two different interpretations of the beast's symbolism are combined, vv. 8,9,15-18 and vv. 10,12-14; these correspond to the two originally distinct texts of Rv (see Introduction).

i. Seven Roman emperors; the sixth, Nero, is now on the throne.

j. The kings of the satellite nations.

19:11-21 beast's disposal, •and they will go to war against the Lamb; but the Lamb is 14
14:4 Dt 10:17 *the Lord of lords and the King of kings*, and he will defeat them and they will
2 M 13:4 1 Tm 6:16 be defeated by his followers, the called, the chosen, the faithful.'
Jr 51:13 Dn 3:4 The angel continued, 'The waters you saw, beside which the prostitute was 15
sitting, are all the peoples, the populations, the nations and the languages. •But 16
the time will come when the ten horns and the beast will turn against the
Ezk 16:37-41; 23:25-29 prostitute, and *strip off her clothes and leave her naked*; then they will eat her
flesh and burn the remains in the fire. •In fact, God influenced their minds to do 17
what he intended, to agree together to put their royal powers at the beast's
11:8+ disposal until the time when God's words should be fulfilled. •The woman you 18
saw is the great city which has authority over all the rulers on earth.'

An angel announces the fall of Babylon

Jr 50 **18** After this, I saw another angel come down from heaven, with great 1
Ezk 43:2 authority given to him; *the earth was lit up with his glory*. •At the top of 2
=14:8 Is 21:9 his voice he shouted, '*Babylon has fallen*, Babylon the Great has fallen, and has
Jr 50:15 *Is 13:21-22;* 34:11,14 become *the haunt of devils* and a lodging for every foul spirit and dirty, loathsome bird. •All the nations have been intoxicated by the wine of her prostitution;[a] 3
17:2 Jr 51:7 every king in the earth has committed fornication with her, and every merchant
grown rich through her debauchery.'

The people of God summoned away

16:17 Is 48:20; A new voice spoke from heaven; I heard it say, 'Come out, my people, away 4
52:11 Jr 50:8; from her, so that you do not share in her crimes and have the same plagues
51:6 *Jr 51:9* to bear. •*Her sins have reached up to heaven*, and God has her crimes in mind: 5
Gn 18:20 *Jr 50:15* *she is to be paid in her own coin.* She must be paid double the amount she exacted. 6
Jr 16:18 She is to have a doubly strong cup of her own mixture. •Every one of her shows 7
Is 47:8 and orgies is to be matched by a torture or a grief. *I am the queen on my throne,*
she says to herself, and *I am no widow* and shall never be in mourning. •For that, 8
Is 47:9 *within a single day*, the plagues will fall on her: disease and mourning and famine.
She will be burnt right up. The Lord God has condemned her, and he has great
power.'

Ezk 27-28 **The people of the world mourn for Babylon**

Ezk 26:17 There will be mourning and weeping for her by the kings of the earth who 9
have fornicated with her and lived with her in luxury. They see the smoke as she
burns, •while they keep at a safe distance from fear of her agony. They will 10
say:

'Mourn, mourn for this great city,
Babylon, so powerful a city,
doomed as you are within a single hour'.

There will be weeping and distress over her among all the traders of the earth 11
when there is nobody left to buy their cargoes of goods; •their stocks of gold 12
and silver, jewels and pearls, linen and purple and silks and scarlet; all the
sandalwood, every piece in ivory or fine wood,[b] in bronze or iron or marble; •the 13
cinnamon and spices, the myrrh and ointment and incense; wine, oil, flour and
1 Tm 1:10+ corn; their stocks of cattle, sheep, horses and chariots, their slaves, their human
cargo...
Ho 10:5 Am 6:7 'All the fruits you had set your hearts on have failed you; gone for ever, never 14
to return, is your life of magnificence and ease.'
The traders who had made a fortune out of her will be standing at 15
a safe distance from fear of her agony, mourning and weeping. •They will be 16
saying:

'Mourn, mourn for this great city;
for all the linen and purple and scarlet that you wore,

for all your finery of gold and jewels and pearls; 17:4
17 your riches are all destroyed within a single hour'.

All the captains and seafaring men,[c] sailors and all those who make a living Ezk 27:27-29
18 from the sea will be keeping a safe distance, •watching the smoke as she burns,
19 and crying out, 'Has there ever been a city as great as this!' •They will throw dust
on their heads and say, with tears and groans:

'Mourn, mourn for this great city
whose lavish living has made a fortune
for every owner of a sea-going ship;
ruined within a single hour.

20 'Now heaven, celebrate her downfall, and all you saints, apostles and prophets: =19:1-2 Dt 32:43 Is 44:23
God has given judgement for you against her.' Jr 51:48
21 Then a powerful angel picked up a boulder like a great millstone, and as he *Ex 15:5* Jr 51:63-64
hurled it into the sea, he said, 'That is how the great city of Babylon is going Ezk 26:21
to be hurled down, never to be seen again.[d]

22 'Never again in you, Babylon, Is 24:8 Jr 7:34; 16:9 Ezk 26:13
will be heard the song of harpists and minstrels,
the music of flute and trumpet;
never again will craftsmen of every skill be found
or *the sound of the mill* be heard; Jr 25:10
23 never again will shine *the light of the lamp*,
never again will be heard
the voices of bridegroom and bride.
Your traders were the princes of the earth,
all the nations were under your spell.

24 In her you will find the blood of prophets and saints, and all the blood that was =16:5-7 Mt 23:35-37
ever shed on earth.'

Songs of victory in heaven

1 **19** After this I seemed to hear the great sound of a huge crowd in heaven,
2 singing, 'Alleluia! Victory and glory and power to our God! •He judges 18:20+ Jr 51:48
fairly, he punishes justly, and he has condemned the famous prostitute who *=16:7* Dn 3:27
corrupted the earth with her fornication; he has avenged his servants that she *6:9; 11:8*
3 killed'. •They sang again, 'Alleluia! *The smoke* of her *will go up for ever* and 14:11 Is 34:10
4 ever.' •Then the twenty-four elders and the four animals prostrated themselves
and worshipped God seated there on his throne, and they cried, 'Amen, Alleluia'.
5 Then a voice came from the throne; it said, 'Praise our God, you servants 11:18 *Ps 115:13*
6 of his and *all who, great or small, revere him*'. •And I seemed to hear the voices
of a huge crowd, like the sound of the ocean or the great roar of thunder,
7 answering, 'Alleluia! The reign of the Lord our God Almighty has begun; •let us 11:17
be glad and joyful and give praise to God, because this is the time for the marriage Mt 22:9 Ep 5:27+
8 of the Lamb.[a] •His bride is ready, and she has been able to dress herself in dazzling *15:6* Is 61:10
9 white linen,[b] because her linen is made of the good deeds of the saints.' •The Mt 22:12
angel said, 'Write this: Happy are those who are invited to the wedding feast of 1:3+ Mt 8:11+; 22:1-14
the Lamb', and he added, 'All the things you have written are true messages *Dn 8:26*
10 from God'. •Then I knelt at his feet to worship him, but he said to me, 'Don't 1:1; 22:8-9
do that: I am a servant just like you and all your brothers who are witnesses to 20:4

18 a. 'her prostitution'; var. 'the anger of her prostitution', cf. 14:8. 'have been intoxicated', lit. 'have drunk deep'; var. 'have fallen' or 'she has drunk deep'.
b. Lit. 'very valuable wood'; Vulg. 'precious stone'.
c. Lit. 'Everyone who steers, everyone sailing to a place'; Vulg. 'who sail the sea'.
d. V. 21 is continued in v. 24. The description of 18:1-3 is completed here: Babylon is to be destroyed for its idolatry, 18:1-3, cf. 17:4, and for persecuting the Christians, 18:21.
19 a. The wedding of the Lamb symbolises the beginning of the heavenly kingdom described in 21:9f. See Ho 1:2+ and Ep 5:22-23+.
b. Symbol of victorious purity, a gift from God.

Jesus. It is God that you must worship.' The witness Jesus gave is the same as
the spirit of prophecy.[c]

C. THE DESTRUCTION OF THE PAGAN NATIONS

=20:7-10 **The first battle of the End**[d]

1:5; 3:7,14 2 Th 2:8 And now I saw heaven open, and a white horse[e] appear; its rider was called 11
Is 11:4 1:14; 2:18 Faithful and True; he is *a judge with integrity*, a warrior for justice. •His eyes 12
were flames of fire, and his head was crowned with many coronets;[f] the name
Lk 10:22 Is 63:1 written on him was known only to himself; •*his cloak was soaked in blood.*[g] He is 13
Jn 1:1+ known by the name, The Word of God.[h] •Behind him, dressed in linen of dazzling 14
1:16; 14:20 white, rode the armies of heaven[i] on white horses. •From his mouth came a sharp 15
Ps 2:9 sword[j] to strike the pagans with; he is the one *who will rule them with an iron*
2:27+; 14:19 *sceptre*, and tread out the wine of Almighty God's fierce anger.[k] •On his cloak and 16
Is 63:3 Dt 10:17 on his thigh[l] there was a name written: *The King of kings and the Lord of lords.*
2 M 13:4 Ezk 39:17 I saw an angel standing in the sun, and he shouted aloud to all the birds that 17
were flying high overhead in the sky, 'Come here. *Gather together at the great*
feast that God is giving. •*There will be the flesh* of kings for you, and the flesh of 18
great generals and heroes, the flesh of horses and their riders and of all kinds of
men, citizens and slaves, small and great.'

17:12-14 Ps 2:2 Then I saw the beast, with all the kings of the earth and their armies, gathered 19
Dn 7:11 together to fight the rider and his army. •But the beast was taken prisoner, 20
Mt 7:15 together with the false prophet who had worked miracles on the beast's behalf
13:16 and by them had deceived all who had been branded with the mark of the beast
and worshipped his statue.[m] These two were thrown alive into the fiery lake
14:10+; 20:10,14 of burning sulphur. •All the rest were killed by the sword of the rider, which 21
Ezk 39:20 came out of his mouth, and *all the birds were gorged with their flesh.*

Jn 12:31 **The reign of a thousand years**

9:1+ 20 Then I saw an angel come down from heaven with the key of the Abyss 1
12:7,9 Gn 3:1 in his hand and an enormous chain. •He overpowered the dragon, that 2
Mt 12:28-29 primeval serpent which is the devil and Satan, and chained him up for a thousand
12:12 2 Co 6:2+ years. •He threw him into the Abyss, and shut the entrance and sealed it over him, 3
2 Th 2:6-8+ to make sure he would not deceive the nations again until the thousand years
had passed. At the end of that time he must be released, but only for a short
while.

Dn 7:22 Mt 19:28 Then I saw some thrones, and I saw *those who are given the power to be judges* 4
19:10+ take their seats on them. I saw the souls of all who had been beheaded for having
witnessed for Jesus and for having preached God's word,[a] and those who refused
13:15-17 to worship the beast or his statue and would not have the brand-mark on their
5:10 foreheads or hands; they came to life, and reigned with Christ for a thousand
years.[b] •This is the first resurrection; the rest of the dead did not come to life 5
1:3+ until the thousand years were over. •Happy and blessed are those who share 6
2:11+ in the first resurrection; the second death cannot affect them[c] but they will be
1:6+ priests of God and of Christ and reign with him for a thousand years.[d]

=19:11-21 **The second battle of the End**

When the thousand years are over, Satan will be released from his prison 7
and will come out to deceive all the nations in the four quarters of the earth, 8
Ezk 38:2,9,15 *Gog and Magog*,[e] and mobilise them for war. His armies will be as many as the
16:14-16 Lk 21:24 sands of the sea; •they will come swarming over the entire country[f] and besiege 9
Ac 9:13+ Ezk 38:22 the camp of the saints, which is the city that God loves.[g] But *fire will come down*
on them from heaven and consume them. •Then the devil, who misled them, will 10
19:20 be thrown into the lake of fire and sulphur, where the beast and the false prophet
are, and their torture will not stop, day or night, for ever and ever.

The punishment of the pagans

Rm 2:6+

11 Then I saw a great white throne and the One who was sitting on it. In his
12 presence, earth and sky vanished, leaving no trace.[h] •I saw the dead, both great 21:1 2 P 3:7,10,12
and small, standing in front of his throne, while the book of life was opened, and *3:5; 13:8;* 17:8
other books opened which were the record of what they had done in their lives, *Dn 7:10+* Lk 10:20
by which the dead were judged.[i]
13 14 The sea gave up all the dead who were in it; •Death and Hades were emptied 1:18+
of the dead that were in them; and every one was judged according to the way
in which he had lived. Then Death and Hades were thrown into the burning 19:20; 21:4 1 Co 15:26, 54
15 lake.[j] This burning lake is the second death; •and anybody whose name could
not be found written in the book of life was thrown into the burning lake. 2:11+; 14:10+

D. THE JERUSALEM OF THE FUTURE

The heavenly Jerusalem[a]

=7:15-17

1 **21** Then I saw *a new heaven and a new earth;*[b] the first heaven and the first Is 65:17 2 P 3:13
2 earth had disappeared now, and there was no longer any sea.[c] •I saw the *Jb 7:12+* Rm 8:19-23
holy city, and the new Jerusalem, coming down from God out of heaven, as 19:7-8
3 beautiful as a bride all dressed for her husband.[d] •Then I heard a loud voice call
from the throne, 'You see this city? Here God lives among men. He will make 7:15-17
his home among them; they shall be his people, and he will be their God; his name Ezk 37:27

c. Lit. 'the witness of Jesus'; this is the word of God to which Jesus testifies and which is implanted in every Christian, cf. 1:2; 6:9; 12:17, and which inspires the prophets.

d. After the fall of Babylon, foretold in 14:8 and described in 16:19,20, Christ comes from heaven at the beginning of the Great Day of Yahweh on which all evil will be destroyed, as had been proclaimed in 14:14-20 and 17:12-14.

e. The colour symbolises victory.

f. Because he is King of kings, cf. v. 16.

g. Alluding (cf. v. 15) to Is 63:1. Symbol of the mortal ruin he deals his enemies, cf. Rv 5:5.

h. The rider comes from heaven: God's Word destroying the first-born of Egypt, Ws 18:14-18.

i. The angels, cf. Mt 26:53, or preferably, following 14:5 and 17:14, the white-robed martyrs, cf. 19:8; 3:5,18; 6:11; 16:15 and also Mt 22:11f.

j. Lit. 'a sharp blade issues out of his mouth', symbol of the destroying Word; cf. Is 11:4; Ws 18:16 and also Ho 6:5; Rv 1:16; 2 Th 2:8.

k. The winepress is a common image in prophetic literature for God's destruction of his people's enemies on the Great Day of his revenge; cf. Gn 49:9-12; Jr 25:30; Is 63:1-6; Jl 4:13. On the 'wine of anger', cf. 14:8+ and Is 51:17+.

l. Possibly meaning 'on his sword'; it has also been suggested that we should read 'on his standard', since the similarity of the two words in Hebr. could be responsible for the present reading.

m. This long parenthesis echoes the events described in ch. 13.

20 a. Lit. 'I saw thrones, they sat on them, judgement was given to them, and I saw the souls of those beheaded for the witness of Jesus and the Word of God'. This verse, scarcely intelligible as it stands, must have begun 'I saw the souls...' and must have been completed '...Word of God: they came to life and reigned...' The remainder ('And I saw thrones on which all those took their seats who would not worship the beast and his image or be sealed on their foreheads or their hands') must have belonged to Text II (see Introduction) and should be read between vv. 11 and 12. Cf. Mt 19:28; 1 Co 6:2-3.

b. One interpretation makes this 'resurrection' of the martyrs (cf. Is 26:19; Ezk 37) symbolise the recovery of the Church after the Roman persecution; the 'reign of a thousand years' is then the period of the kingdom of Christ on earth from the end of persecution (the fall of Rome) to the Last Judgement (in 20:11f). According to Augustine and others who follow him, the 'reign of a thousand years' is to be reckoned from Christ's resurrection, and the 'first resurrection' is baptism, cf. Rm 6:1-10; Jn 5:25-28. A literal interpretation of this verse was widespread in the early Church: after the first resurrection, of the martyrs, Christ was to return to reign on earth with his faithful for a thousand years. This literal millenarianism was censured.

c. The first death is on earth, the second 'death' is failure to win eternal life

d. The messianic rule of Christians on earth is foretold in 5:9-10, and under the symbol of the New Jerusalem, in 21:9-22 and 22:6-15; this second passage has been inserted so that it follows the mention of the Last Judgement, 20:13-15.

e. Ezk 38-39 (see notes) mentions 'Gog, king of Magog', here the two names symbolise all the pagan nations leagued against the Church at the end of time. This is the eschatological combat of Text I and it corresponds to the war of Text II described in 19:11.

f. Palestine.

g. Jerusalem, symbol of the Church, cf. Lk 21:24.

h. At this point part of v. 4 should be inserted (see note to v. 4).

i. The first scrolls unrolled list human deeds, the scroll of life opened last is the list of the predestined, cf. Dn 7:10+; 12:1+; Ac 13:48+.

j. After the Last Judgement death itself will lose its power.

21 a. A vision of heaven, cf. 7:15-17. The opening is suggested by Is (51 and 65 especially).

b. In Is 51:16; 65:17; 66:12, the phrase is merely a symbol of the new messianic age. St Paul, following the lead of Jesus, cf. Mt 19:28, is more realistic: the whole of creation will one day be freed from the dominance of corruption, renewed and transformed by the glory of God, Rm 8:19+.

c. The sea symbolises evil because it was the home of the dragon, cf. Jb 7:12+; it will vanish as it did at the Exodus, but this time for ever, before the triumphant advance of the new Israel, cf. Is 51:9-10; Ps 74:13,14; Jb 26:12-13; Is 27:1.

d. The new and joyful wedding of Jerusalem and her God has taken place, cf. Is 65:18; 61:10; 62:4-6; the Exodus ideal has at last been achieved, cf. Ho 2:16+.

Is 8:8 *Is 25:8* is *God-with-them.*[e] •*He will wipe away all tears from their eyes;* there will be no 4
Is 35:10 more death, and no more mourning or sadness. The world of the past has gone.'
2 Co 5:17 Then the One sitting on the throne spoke: 'Now I am making the whole of 5
Dn 8:26 creation new' he said. 'Write this: that what I am saying is sure and will come
1:8+ true.' •And then he said, 'It is already done. I am the Alpha and the Omega, the 6
22:17 Is 55:1 Beginning and the End. I will give water from the well of life free to anybody
who is thirsty;[f] •it is the rightful inheritance of the one who proves victorious; 7
2 S 7:14 and *I will be his God* and *he a son to me.*[g] •But the legacy for cowards, for those 8
=22:15 Rm 1:29+ who break their word, or worship obscenities, for murderers and fornicators, and
for fortune-tellers, idolaters or any other sort of liars, is the second death[h] in
the burning lake of sulphur.'

Ep 5:27 **The messianic Jerusalem**[i]

One of the seven angels that had the seven bowls full of the seven last plagues 9
2 Co 11:2 came to speak to me, and said, 'Come here and I will show you the bride that the
Ezk 40:2 Heb 11:10 Lamb has married'. •*In the spirit, he took me to the top of an enormous high* 10
21:2 *mountain*, and showed me Jerusalem, the holy city, coming down from God out
Is 60:1-2 of heaven.[j] •It *had all the radiant glory of God* and glittered like some precious 11
jewel of crystal-clear diamond. •The walls of it were of a great height, and had 12
twelve gates; at each of the twelve gates there was an angel, and over the gates
7:1-8 Ezk 48:31-35 were written the names *of the twelve tribes of Israel;* •*on the east there were three* 13
gates, on the north three gates, on the south three gates, and on the west three gates.
Ep 2:20 The city walls stood on twelve foundation stones, each one of which bore the 14
name of one of the twelve apostles of the Lamb.

The angel that was speaking to me was carrying a gold measuring rod 15
to measure the city and its gates and wall. •The plan of the city is perfectly 16
square, its length the same as its breadth.[k] He measured the city with his rod and
it was twelve thousand furlongs in length and in breadth, and equal in height.[l]
He measured its wall, and this was a hundred and forty-four cubits high—the 17
Is 54:11-12 angel was using the ordinary cubit. •The wall was built of diamond, and the city 18
of pure gold, like polished glass. •The foundations of the city wall were faced 19
with all kinds of precious stone: the first with diamond, the second lapis lazuli,
the third turquoise, the fourth crystal, •the fifth agate, the sixth ruby, the seventh 20
gold quartz, the eighth malachite, the ninth topaz, the tenth emerald, the eleventh
sapphire and the twelfth amethyst. •The twelve gates were twelve pearls, each 21
gate being made of a single pearl, and the main street of the city was pure gold,
transparent as glass. •I saw that there was no temple in the city[m] since the Lord 22
Jn 2:19-21 God Almighty and the Lamb were themselves the temple, •and the city did not 23
Is 60:1-2, 19-20 need the sun or the moon for light, since it was lit by the radiant glory of God
2 Co 3:18 *Is 60:3* and the Lamb was a lighted torch for it. •*The pagan nations will live by its light* 24
Is 60:11 and the kings of the earth will bring it their treasures. •*The gates of it will never* 25
Is 60:3,11 *be shut by day*—and there will be no night there—•and *the nations will come,* 26
Is 35:8; 52:1 Zc 13:1-2 *bringing their treasure* and their wealth. •Nothing unclean may come into it: no 27
2 P 3:13 one who does what is loathsome or false, but only those who are listed in the
Lamb's book of life.

Ezk 47:1-12 Jn 4:1+ 22 Then the angel showed me the river of life, rising from the throne of God 1
and of the Lamb[a] and flowing crystal-clear •down the middle of the city 2
2:7; 22:14 Ezk 47:12 street. *On either side*[b] *of the river were the trees of life, which bear twelve crops*
of fruit in a year, one in each month, and the leaves of which are the cure for the
pagans.
=7:15 Zc 14:11 *The ban will be lifted.*[c] The throne of God and of the Lamb will be in its place 3
1 Co 13:12 1 Jn 3:2 in the city; his servants will worship him, •they will see him face to face, and his 4
name will be written on their foreheads. •It will never be night again and they 5
will not need lamplight or sunlight, because the Lord God will be shining on them.
They will reign for ever and ever.
19:9; 21:5 Dn 8:26 The angel said to me, 'All that you have written is sure and will come true: 6

the Lord God who gives the spirit to the prophets has sent his angel to reveal 1:1; 22:16 Dn 2:28
7 to his servants *what is soon to take place.* •Very soon now, I shall be with you
again.' Happy are those who treasure the prophetic message of this book. 1:3+
8 I, John, am the one who heard and saw these things. When I had heard
and seen them all, I knelt at the feet of the angel who had shown them to me, 19:10
9 to worship him; •but he said, 'Don't do that: I am a servant just like you and
like your brothers the prophets and like those who treasure what you have written
in this book. It is God that you must worship.'
10 This, too, he said to me, 'Do not keep the prophecies in this book a secret, 10:4
11 because the Time is close. •Meanwhile let the sinner go on sinning, and Dn 12:10
the unclean continue to be unclean; let those who do good go on doing good,
12 and those who are holy continue to be holy.[d] •Very soon now, I shall be with you Is 40:10
again, *bringing the reward to be given to every man according to what he* Ps 62:12
13 *deserves.* •I am the Alpha and the Omega, *the First and the Last*, the Beginning 1:8+ *Is 41:4;* 44:6
14 and the End. •Happy are those who will have washed their robes clean, so that
they will have the right to feed on the tree of life and can come through the gates 7:14; 12:1+; 22:2
15 into the city.[e] •These others must stay outside: dogs, fortune-tellers, and =*21:8* Nb 5:1-4
fornicators, and murderers, and idolaters, and everyone of false speech and false Rm 1:29+
life.'

EPILOGUE

16 I, Jesus, have sent my angel to make these revelations to you for the sake of 1:1,11f; 22:6
the churches. I am of David's line, the root of David and the bright star of the 2:28+
morning.
17 The Spirit and the Bride[f] say, 'Come'. Let everyone who listens answer,
'Come'.[g] *Then let all who are thirsty come:* all who want it may *have the water* Is 55:1
of life, *and have it free.* 21:6 1 Co 11:26
18 This is my solemn warning to all who hear the prophecies in this book: if Dt 4:2
anyone adds anything to them, God will add to him every plague mentioned in the
19 book; •if anyone cuts anything out of the prophecies in this book, God will cut
off his share of the tree of life and of the holy city, which are described in the
book.
20 The one who guarantees these revelations repeats his promise: I shall indeed Ac 3:20-21 1 Co 15:23+
be with you soon. Amen; come, Lord Jesus.
21 May the grace of the Lord Jesus be with you all.[h] Amen.

e. Lit. 'and he, God with them, will be their God' Vulg.; var. 'and God himself will be their God' or 'and God himself will be with them'. The *shekinah*, or presence, is an essential part of God's covenant with his people, cf. Ex 25:8 and Jn 1:14+, and is to be real and total after the end of the world, cf. Jl 4:17,21; Zc 2:14; Zp 3:15-17; Is 12:6.

f. In the O.T., fresh, drinking water is a symbol of life, and as such is to be a feature of the messianic age. In the N.T. it is a symbol of the Spirit, cf. Jn 4:1+.

g. The title 'Son of God' was to be conferred on King-Messiah, David's heir, on the day of his enthronement, 2 S 7:14+; hence Jesus was proclaimed 'Son of God' in virtue of his resurrection, Ac 2:36+; Rm 1:4+.

h. Eternal death. The fire, like the water of v. 6, is symbolic.

i. This is Jerusalem on earth during the last or messianic days since the pagan nations have not yet been destroyed, 21:24, and have a chance of conversion, 22:2; but it foreshadows the heavenly Jerusalem that develops from it. The details of the description are mostly from Ezk 40-47.

j. I.e. renewal in these present, messianic times; the transformation of humanity by an act of God.

k. The symbol of (terrestrial) perfection.

l. Symbolic number: twelve (for the new Israel) multiplied by one thousand (for immensity).

m. The destruction of the Jerusalem Temple symbolises the end of the old covenant; there is now a new temple, the Body of Christ; cf. Jn 2:19-21.

22 a. Allusion to the Trinity, since the river of living water is a symbol of the Spirit (Jn 4:1+), cf. Rv 21:6+.

b. Or punctuate 'Down the middle ... on either side'.

c. Vv. 3-5 (Text II) should be inserted after 21:4. Cf. Introduction.

d. God pursues his design whatever man may do.

e. The Jerusalem described in 21:9f.

f. The Church, wife of the Messiah, cf. 21:10.

g. The appeal is addressed to the Messiah; it is the *Marana tha* refrain of the liturgical assemblies, 1 Co 16:22, expressive of the Christians' longing for the *parousia*, see 1 Th 5:1+.

h. Lit. 'with all'; var. 'with the saints' or 'with all the saints'.

SUPPLEMENTS

CHRONOLOGICAL TABLE

The columns to the right of the date column deal with Palestinian and biblical history; those to the left deal with general history. In the right-hand column extra-biblical writings are in *italics.*

The names of rulers, kings, governors and high priests are in SMALL CAPITALS or CAPITALS according to their importance. The names of biblical books, when mentioned at the time of their composition, are in **bold type;** other important personages, places and items are also in **bold type.**

ROMAN PALESTINE TO THE TIME OF HADRIAN 63 B.C.-135 A.D.

63, Pompey at Damascus. Arrogance of Aristobulus and incapacity of Hyrcanus		Summer or autumn 63, **Pompey takes Jerusalem,** names Hyrcanus high priest and sends Aristobulus and his son Antigonus to Rome
		The Idumaean ANTIPATER, minister of Hyrcanus, is the real ruler of Judaea. Rebellion of the last of the Hasmonaeans
CLEOPATRA VII, queen of Egypt: 51-30	50	About 50, in Alexandria, **Wisdom**
		The Psalms of Solomon
48, JULIUS CAESAR defeats Pompey at Pharsalia. Pompey killed in Egypt		
		47, Caesar names HYRCANUS ethnarch (47-41). Herod son of Antipater is named *strategos* of Galilee; the revolt of Hezekiah is suppressed
44, Caesar is assassinated		
41-30, ANTONY in the East		41, Anthony names Herod and his brother Phasael as tetrarchs
40, **Parthians** in Syria and Palestine		
End of 40, the Senate declares Herod king		ANTIGONUS: king and high priest, 40-37. Herod flees to Rome. Hyrcanus is mutilated
38, Parthians driven from Syria and Palestine		39-37, struggle between Herod and Antigonus
		Early 37, Herod marries MARIAMNE I, granddaughter of Aristobulus II and Hyrcanus II
	B.C.	
SOSIUS governor of Syria: 38-37		June(?) 37, **capture of Jerusalem by Sosius and Herod**
31, OCTAVIAN defeats Antony at naval battle of **Actium**		HEROD THE GREAT effectively king: 37-4 B.C.
30, suicide of Antony and Cleopatra. Egypt a Roman province		Herod builds the Antonia, and in 23 the Palace in the upper city. Founds or rebuilds Antipatris, Phaselis, Samaria (Sebaste), the Herodion and Caesarea
29, Octavian, Imperator for life and, in 27, named AUGUSTUS		
Syria an imperial province with a legate from Augustus		Numerous wives: in 23, Mariamne II, daughter of the High Priest Simon, son of Boethos. (Mariamne I was put to death in 29 and, some time after 30, her grandfather Hyrcanus)
Herod 'rex socius'		
25, Galatia a Roman province		
24, Herod is given Trachonitis, Batanaea and Auranitis and later Paneas		Winter of 20-19, start of the rebuilding of the Temple
13-11, M. TITIUS legate in Syria. His successor is not known		The Pharisees Hillel and Shammai and their rival schools

	B.C.	
About 10(?), SULPICIUS QUIRINIUS (as legate of Syria?) subdues the Homonades of Taurus. Several indications of a census throughout the empire		The census of Lk 2:1f? Cf. the *lapis Venetus* inscription, undated, giving evidence of a census in Apamea (Syria) by order of Quirinius 'legate in Syria'. Cf. Lk 2:2
ARETAS IV succeeds his father Obodas II as king of Nabataea and reigns until 39		9-8, Herod violates the territory of the Nabataeans to capture the brigands of Trachonitis sheltered by the minister Syllaios, who complains to Augustus. Temporary disgrace of Herod
Sentius Saturninus, legate in Syria: 9-6		About the year 7, Herod has Alexander and Aristobulus, his two sons by Mariamne I, strangled
According to Tertullian, it is Saturninus who initiates the census of Judaea		More than 6000 Pharisees refuse to take the oath to Augustus on the occasion of a census (?) (which continues that of Quirinius?)
QUINTILIUS VARUS, legate in Syria: 6-4		Birth of JESUS, about 7-6(?)
		March of the year 4, the affair of the golden eagle in the Temple. Execution of Antipater, eldest son of Herod. Herod's will in favour of the sons of Malthake the Samaritan (Archelaus and Herod Antipas) and the son of Cleopatra (Philip)
		End of March, beginning of April, 4 B.C., **death of Herod** at Jericho. Archelaus takes his body to the Herodion
SABINUS, procurator for Augustus in Syria		4, at the Passover (11th April) Archelaus puts down a rebellion at Jerusalem, then goes to Rome to appeal to Augustus for the title of king.
End of year 4, Augustus confirms Herod's last will, but omits the title of king for Archelaus		Sabinus comes to Jerusalem to make an inventory of the resources of the kingdom of Herod: sharp opposition and trouble throughout the country. At this time, possibly, the rebellion of Judas the Galilean, cf. Ac 5:37, and of the Pharisee Saddok who urged disobedience to Rome and refusal to pay taxes. (Origin of the **Zealots,** cf. Mt 22:17) Sabinus appeals to Varus who pursues the rebels; 2000 are crucified
ARCHELAUS ethnarch of Judaea and Samaria: 4 B.C.-6 A.D.		
HEROD ANTIPAS tetrarch of Galilee and Peraea: 4 B.C.-39 A.D.		
PHILIP tetrarch of Gaulanitis, Batanaea, Trachonitis, Auranitis and the district of Paneas (Ituraea): 4 B.C.-34 A.D.		The *Assumption of Moses* (apoc.)
3-2 B.C., the successor to Varus is unknown. Some here place Quirinius as legate		If Quirinius was in fact legate 3-2, he could have continued the census begun by Sabinus and ordered the census of Apamea (the undated *lapis Venetus*)
	A.D.	
1/2 A.D.-4, Quirinius is counsellor to young GAIUS CAESAR, grandson of Augustus, during his mission to the East	1	Philip the tetrarch builds Julias (Bethsaida). He enriches the shrine of Pan (Paneas, the *Paneion*), which he names Caesarea in honour of Augustus
VOLUSIUS SATURNINUS, legate in Syria: 4-5 A.D.		
6, Augustus deposes Archelaus who is exiled to Vienne (Gaul)		
6-41, **Judaea a procuratorial province** (with Caesarea as the capital)		
6-8, COPONIUS procurator		
6, according to Josephus, QUIRINIUS legate in Syria(?)		6, according to Josephus, Quirinius comes to Judaea to make an inventory of possessions of Archelaus; this could have provoked the rebellion of Judas and Saddok. But for the year 6 Josephus repeats events he has described for the year 4

	A.D.
	ANNAS, son of Seth, high priest: 6(?)-15
	Between 5 and 10, birth of Paul at Tarsus; pupil of Gamaliel the Elder, Ac 22:3, cf. 5:34
14 (19th August), death of Augustus. TIBERIUS emperor: 14-37	
VALERIUS GRATUS procurator: 15-26	Valerius Gratus deposes Annas. Three other high priests follow, then JOSEPH CALLED CAIAPHAS: 18-36
17-19, GERMANICUS, adopted son of Tiberius, in the East	About 17, foundation of Tiberias by Antipas. Under Tiberius, LYSANIAS tetrarch of Abilene, Lk 3:1 *and inscriptions*
18, Cappadocia a Roman province	
26-36, PONTIUS PILATE procurator	
	About 27, Herod Antipas, married to the daughter of Aretas, marries Herodias, the wife of his brother Herod (son of Mariamne II)
The 15th year of Tiberius, Lk 3:1: 19th August 28 or 18th August 29, but according to the Syrian calculation: Sept.-Oct. 27 to Sept.-Oct. 28	Autumn of 27, the preaching of JOHN THE BAPTIST and the beginning of the ministry of Jesus. Cf. Lk 3:2 +
	28, Passover. Jesus in Jerusalem, Jn 2:13. The 46 years of Jn 2:20 begin from 20/19 B.C.
	Beginning of 29, John, imprisoned at Machaerus (Josephus), is beheaded, Mt 14:3
	29, shortly before the Passover, the multiplication of the loaves, Jn 6:1; Mt 14:13
	Feasts of Tabernacles and of the Dedication: Jesus in Jerusalem, Jn 7-10
'(The) Christ condemned to death by Pontius Pilate, under the Emperor Tiberius' (Tacitus, *Annals*)	30, on the eve of the Passover, i.e. 14th Nisan, a Friday, death of Jesus, Jn 19:31f. (The Passover fell on the Saturday, 8th April in 30 and 4th April in 33: the second date is too late, cf. Jn 2:20). Cf. Mt 26:17 +
	30, **Pentecost,** outpouring of the Spirit on the Church, Ac 2. The first community, Ac 2:42, etc.
33-34, Philip dies without an heir and Tiberius joins his tetrarchy with the province of Syria	Pontius Pilate has difficulties with the Jews: the incidents of the standards and shields (Philo). Pilate's aqueduct
	Election of the seven hellenist deacons, Ac 6:1f
L. VITELLIUS, legate in Syria: 35-39. The father of the emperor Vitellius	About 35, Pontius Pilate orders the massacre of the Samaritans at Gerizim
He is given full powers in the East	36, Passover. Vitellius in Jerusalem. He replaces Caiaphas with JONATHAN, son of Annas
36, on the Euphrates, he concludes a pact with Artaban, king of the Parthians. Antipas is with him	36, the troops of Aretas defeat those of Antipas. Tiberius orders Vitellius to attack Aretas
	Autumn of 36, Pontius Pilate is sent to Rome by Vitellius to justify his conduct. He dies a violent death (execution or suicide)

	A.D.	
36-37, winter. Vitellius concentrates the legions at Ptolemais		36-37, winter (?), **martyrdom of Stephen** and **dispersion** of part of the community. A little later, **conversion** of PAUL. Cf. Ac 9:1 +
37, March. Death of Tiberius. Vitellius breaks off his campaign against Aretas		37, Passover. Vitellius, on his way to Petra, stops at Jerusalem. He replaces Jonathan with his brother THEOPHILUS, high priest from 37-41
CALIGULA emperor: 37-41		
MARCELLUS procurator		Paul in 'Arabia', then in Damascus, Ac 9:19f; Ga 1:17f
37, Caligula gives AGRIPPA I, son of Aristobulus, the tetrarchies of Philip and Lysanias, with the title of king. (37-44)		
38, persecution of the Jews in Alexandria. 39, embassy of the Jewish philosopher Philo to Rome (he dies after 41)		
39-42, P. PETRONIUS legate in Syria		About 39, Paul escapes from Damascus, 2 Co 11:32f, and makes a first visit to the elders of the Church, Ga 1:18f (Cephas and James the brother of the Lord); Ac 9:25f
39, Caligula exiles Antipas to the Pyrenees and gives his tetrarchy to Agrippa I		39, Caligula orders the erection of his statue in the Temple. Thanks to Petronius and Agrippa I the affair drags on until the assassination of Caligula
41-54, CLAUDIUS emperor. Agrippa I, now in Rome, contributes to his success; Claudius concedes him Judaea and Samaria. His brother Herod becomes king of Chalcis (41-48) and marries Berenice (daughter of Agrippa)		The kingdom of Herod the Great is reconstituted. Agrippa builds the 3rd wall of Jerusalem, but at his death it is unfinished. Many buildings, in particular at Berytus (Beirut)
41, Claudius' edict and letter to the Alexandrians		
42-44, VIBIUS MARSIUS legate in Syria		About 43, Paul and Barnabas at **Antioch** which becomes the centre for the hellenistic Christians. PETER in Samaria (Simon the magician) and in the coastal plain (the centurion Cornelius)
44, spring. On the death of Herod Agrippa I, Judaea again becomes a procuratorial province, 44-66		43 or 44, before the Passover, Agrippa I orders the beheading of JAMES, BROTHER OF JOHN (James the Great); during the feast he imprisons Peter. Ac 12
CUSPIUS FADUS procurator 44-46		28th June 45, a rescript of Claudius gives the Jews the custody of the priestly vestments. Herod of Chalcis is named inspector of the Temple, with the right to nominate the high priest. In 47 he nominated Ananias, son of Nebadios (47-59), cf. Ac 23:2f
CASSIUS LONGINUS, the lawyer, legate in Syria: 45-50		
		Fadus and the false prophet Theudas, cf. Ac 5:36
46-48, TIBERIUS ALEXANDER procurator. Nephew of Philo, but an apostate. At this time, several famines throughout the empire		Between 45 and 49, **1st mission by Paul:** Antioch, Cyprus, Antioch in Pisidia, Lystra, . . .Antioch, Ac 13:1f
48-52, VENTIDIUS CUMANUS procurator		About 48, famine in Judaea, worsened by the sabbatical year 47/48. Visit to Jerusalem, by HELEN, queen of Adiabene, a convert to Judaism; she brings relief to the population
AGRIPPA II, son of Agrippa I, king of Chalcis 48-53. In 49 he is named inspector of the Temple, with the right to nominate the high priest		

	A.D.	
49, Claudius 'drives from Rome the Jewish agitators stirred up by Chrestos' (Suetonius), cf. Ac 18:2		48-49, prophecy of Agabus and the aid given to the community at Jerusalem by that of Antioch. The **council of Jerusalem:** converts from paganism exempt from the Law, Ac 15:5f; Ga 2:1f
	50	About the year 50, the oral tradition of the gospel is put into written form: the **Aramaic Matthew,** and the complementary **collection.** The **Letter of James** (or about 58)
50-60, UMMIDIUS QUADRATUS legate in Syria		50-52, 2nd mission by Paul: Lystra (Timothy), Phrygia, Galatia, Philippi, Thessalonika, Athens (sermon on the Areopagus)
52 (rather than 51), GALLIO, brother of Seneca, proconsul of Achaia		
		Winter of 50 to summer of 52, Paul in Corinth: the **Letters to the Thessalonians;** and, in the spring of 52, summoned to appear before Gallio. Summer 52, he goes to Jerusalem, Ac 18:22, and then to Antioch
Agrippa II in favour at Rome. Claudius exiles Cumanus		The Jews in their struggle against the Samaritans are supported by Cumanus. He is sent to Rome by Quadratus, who visits Jerusalem, Passover of 52
ANTONIUS FELIX procurator: 52-60. Brother of the freedman Pallas. Marries DRUSILLA, sister of Agrippa II, already married to Aziz, king of Emesa, cf. Ac 24:24		Felix checks brigandage
53, Claudius gives the tetrarchies of Philip and Lysanias to Agrippa II, in exchange for Chalcis, (53-93)		53-58, 3rd mission by Paul; APOLLOS at Ephesus and then at Corinth
54-68, NERO emperor		54-57, after passing through Galatia and Phrygia, Paul stays at Ephesus for 2¼ years. After 56(?), **Letter to the Philippians.** About Passover 57, **1 Corinthians.** Then a quick visit to Corinth, 2 Co 12:14. Return to Ephesus and **Letter to the Galatians**
55, Nero adds a part of Galilee and Peraea to the kingdom of Agrippa		
		End of 57, passes through Macedonia. **2 Corinthians**
		Winter 57-58, at Corinth, Ac 20:3, cf. 1 Co 16:6; **Letter to the Romans**
		Passover 58, at Philippi, Ac 20:6, then, by sea, to Caesarea (Philip and Agabus)
		Summer 58, in Jerusalem. JAMES THE BROTHER OF THE LORD heads the Judaeo-Christian community; his **Letter** to the Jews of the Dispersion (or possibly before 49)
		About 58, Felix disbands the followers of the Egyptian false prophet on the Mount of Olives, cf. Ac 21:38. He has the former High Priest Jonathan assassinated, in spite of the fact that he owed his position to Jonathan
		58, Pentecost. Paul arrested in the Temple and brought before Ananias and the Sanhedrin. Taken to Caesarea, he is brought before Felix
Between 59 and 67, Agrippa II nominates six high priests, among whom ANAN SON OF ANNAS (62)		58-60, Paul a captive at Caesarea, the scene of serious troubles between Jews and Syrians
60-63, CORBULO legate in Syria		60, Paul appears before Festus and appeals to Caesar. He pleads his cause before Agrippa and his sister Berenice
PORCIUS FESTUS procurator: 60-62		

	A.D.
	Autumn of 60, Paul's voyage to Rome, the storm, he winters in Malta
	61-63, Paul in Rome under military guard. His apostolate, **Letters to Colossians, Ephesians, Philemon** (and **to Philippians?**)
LUCCEIUS ALBINUS procurator: 62-64	62, the High Priest Anan has **James** the brother of the Lord **stoned to death** (after the death of Festus and before the arrival of Albinus). SIMEON, son of Cleophas and of Mary (sister-in-law of the mother of Jesus), succeeded James as head of the church of Jerusalem (Eusebius)
	Anan deposed by Agrippa II
CESTIUS GALLUS legate in Syria: 63-66	63, Paul is set free, and possibly goes to Spain, Rm 15:24f
64, July, burning of Rome and persecution of the Christians	About 64, **I Peter and the gospel of Mark**
	64 (or 67), **martyrdom of Peter in Rome**
64-66, GESSIUS FLORUS procurator. Nominated by influence of Poppaea, the Jewish wife of Nero	About 65, Paul at Ephesus, 1 Tm 1:3; in Crete, Tt 1:5; in Macedonia, whence he sends his **1st Letter to Timothy,** 1 Tm 1:3; and probably **Titus**
	The **Greek gospel of Matthew;** the **gospel of Luke** and the **Acts of the Apostles:** before 70? or about 80?
66, rising of the Alexandrian Jews. Tiberius Alexander, at that time prefect in Egypt, massacres several thousands	Summer 66, in Jerusalem, Florus crucifies some Jews, but a rising compels him to leave the city. Troubles in Caesarea and throughout the country
66-67, spectacular tour of Greece by Nero: he appoints VESPASIAN and his son TITUS to restore order in Palestine	Sept. 66, Jerusalem attacked by Cestius Gallus. He retires with heavy losses. Rebel government
	Exodus of people of importance and doubtless some Christians, cf. Lk 21:20f, who take refuge in Pella (Eusebius)
MUCIANUS legate in Syria: 67-69	67, Vespasian, with 60,000 men, reconquers Galilee (JOSEPHUS, its rebel governor, is taken prisoner)
	About 67, **Letter to the Hebrews.** Paul, a prisoner in Rome, writes **2 Timothy.** A little later he is beheaded
68, March, in Gaul the revolt of the legate VINDEX	67-68, the Zealots of JOHN OF GISCHALA, escaped from Galilee, are masters of Jerusalem with the Idumaeans. Anan and the leading people are massacred
68, April, GALBA emperor	68, Vespasian occupies the maritime plain and the Valley of the Jordan (destruction of Qumran). On Nero's death the siege of Jerusalem is broken off
68, June, suicide of Nero	
69, January, OTHO proclaimed Emperor by the Praetorians and VITELLIUS by the legions in Germany	69, SIMON BARGIORA and the *sicarii* in Jerusalem. Vespasian subdues the rest of Judaea; the *sicarii* hold out in Jerusalem, and in the Herodion, Masada and Machaerus
69, July, Tiberius Alexander supports Vespasian. His lead is followed by all the East	

	A.D.	
69-79, VESPASIAN emperor. He entrusts the siege of Jerusalem to Titus		70, Passover. Many pilgrims in Jerusalem. **Titus** lays siege to the city with four legions. Tiberius Alexander is second in command
End of 69, Vespasian in sole command of the empire		
		Capture of the 3rd wall, then of the 2nd. Circumvallation. Capture of the Antonia. Famine
		Beginning of August, sacrifices cease
		70, 29th August, capture of the Inner Court and **burning of the Temple** (the 10th of Loos, i.e. the 10th of the 5th month, the day when Nebuzaradan set fire to the first Temple, Jr 52:12 and Josephus)
		Sacrifice to the standards, in front of the Temple, cf. Mt 24:15. Titus hailed as Imperator
		70, Sept., capture of the Upper City and the palace of Herod. The inhabitants killed, sold into slavery or condemned to hard labour
70, end of the year, Judaea an imperial province; under the rule of the legate of the Xth Legion based in Jerusalem. Caesarea a Roman colony		Titus in Syria; many Jews killed in the gladiatorial games
		71, summer, triumph of Vespasian and Titus in Rome (with the Temple furnishings): execution of Simon Bargiora. The Arch of Titus
71-72, LUCILIUS BASSUS legate in Judaea		The didrachma formerly subscribed to the Temple is now given to Jupiter Capitolinus
72, foundation of **Flavia Neapolis** (Naplus)		Capture of the Herodion and Machaerus, by L. Bassus
73, FLAVIUS SILVA legate in Judaea		Siege of **Masada** by F. Silva: Eleazar (descendant of Judas the Galilean) and his *sicarii* commit suicide rather than yield (Passover, 73)
A number of *sicarii* take refuge in Egypt, but are handed over to the Romans. Closing of the temple founded by Onias at Leontopolis		**Return** to Jerusalem of a group of **Judaeo-Christians** (Epiphanius). Rabbi Eleazar re-opens the synagogue of the Alexandrians
		Rabbi Johanan ben-Zakkai founds the **Academy of Yabneh** (Jamnia), successor to the Sanhedrin. GAMALIEL II succeeds him; origins of the Mishna
79-81, TITUS emperor		70-80, the **Letter of Jude,** then **2 Peter.** *2 Esdras* (apocryphal). About 78, the *Jewish War* (Josephus)
81-96, DOMITIAN emperor. Brother of Titus		About 93, *The Antiquities of the Jews* (Josephus)
95, has his cousin FLAVIUS CLEMENS condemned to death as a Christian. Exiles his wife, Domitilla, to Pandataria		About 95, John exiled to Patmos. Final text of **Revelation.** *Letter of St. Clement,* bishop of Rome, to the Corinthians
96-98, NERVA emperor		**Gospel of John;** then **1 John** (**3 John** and **2 John** are possibly earlier). He opposes Cerinthus and his Docetism
98-117, TRAJAN emperor		
		The *Didache* (end of 1c.?)
CORNELIUS PALMA, legate in Syria, occupies the kingdom of Nabataea, which becomes the **province of Arabia,** capital Bostra (Bozra) (106)	100	At the beginning of Trajan's reign, **death of John at Ephesus**

	A.D.
Claudius Atticus Herodes governor of Judaea in 107	107, **martyrdom of Simeon,** 2nd bishop of Jerusalem. From now until the Second Revolt there are 13 other bishops, likewise Judaeo-Christians
111-113, PLINY THE YOUNGER legate in Bithynia. His letter on the persecution of the Christians and the **rescript of Trajan**	About 110, the seven *letters* of Ignatius, bishop of Antioch, and his martyrdom at Rome
114-116, annexation of Armenia, of Assyria and Mesopotamia. **The Roman empire at the height of its power**	A little later, the *Letter to the Philippians* of Polycarp, bishop of Smyrna and disciple of John († 156)
	The *Odes of Solomon* (apocryphal)
117, **rising of the Jews** throughout the East and revolt of the new provinces. These are recaptured by the Moor LUSIUS QUIETUS; he is named legate of Judaea	
117-138, HADRIAN emperor. Establishes the frontier of the empire on the Euphrates	Quietus erects the statue of Trajan in front of the altar of the Temple (Hippolytus). He is deposed and subsequently put to death by Hadrian
Hadrian's second tour of the empire, 128-134. At Athens the completion of the temple of the Olympian (or 'Capitoline') Zeus. Antiochus Epiphanes had contributed to its construction	About 130, the *Letter of Barnabas* (apocryphal). At Hierapolis in Phrygia, the bishop Papias. In Alexandria, the gnostic Basilides
Tineius Rufus legate in Judaea and Publicius Marcellus legate in Syria	130, Hadrian in Jerusalem. He decides to rebuild the city (Aelia Capitolina) and the Temple, now dedicated to Jupiter
	132-135, **second Jewish rebellion**
	Simeon Ben Koseba (*letters of Murabbaat*) seizes Jerusalem; Eleazar high priest. Ben Koseba acknowledged by Rabbi Akiba as Messiah and as the Star of Nb 24:17, whence his name of Bar Kokeba (Son of the Star). He persecutes the Christians because they refuse to join the revolt
	In spite of the reinforcements of Marcellus, Rufus is overrun by the rebels: Hadrian sends the legate in Britain, Julius Severus, and arrives in person
	Beginning of 134, **capture of Jerusalem**
	After the conquest of nearly 50 strongholds, Severus seizes **Bether,** where Bar Kokeba perishes (August, 135)
	The captives are sold at Mamre and Gaza
The province of Judaea becomes the **province of Syria-Palestine.** Jerusalem a Roman colony, forbidden to the Jews	135, Rufus builds Aelia (the temple of Jupiter, Juno and Venus on the site of Calvary and the tomb of Christ). **The Temple is made into a sanctuary of Zeus and Hadrian**
	The temple of Zeus Hypsistos at Gerizim and the sacred grove of Adonis around the Cave at Bethlehem
	The bishop Mark (about 135-155) and the new Christian community. The Judaeo-Christians, dispersed in Transjordania and Syria, in time form the sect of the **Ebionites** (the 'Poor'), with the *Gospel of the Hebrews;* they do not accept the divinity of the Messiah and reject the Pauline Letters

THE HASMONAEAN AND HERODIAN DYNASTIES

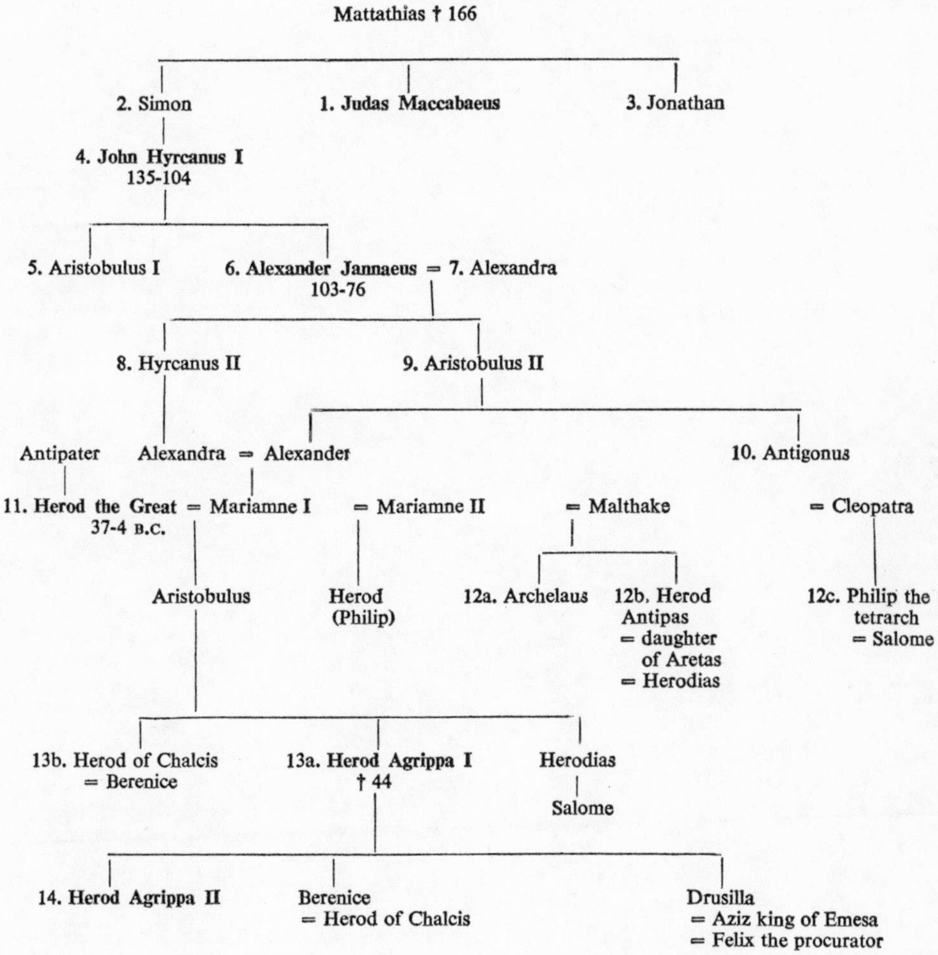
Mattathias † 166
2. Simon
1. Judas Maccabaeus
3. Jonathan
4. John Hyrcanus I
135-104
5. Aristobulus I
6. Alexander Jannaeus = 7. Alexandra
103-76
8. Hyrcanus II
9. Aristobulus II
Antipater
Alexandra = Alexander
10. Antigonus
11. Herod the Great = Mariamne I
37-4 B.C.
= Mariamne II
= Malthake
= Cleopatra
Aristobulus
Herod
(Philip)
12a. Archelaus
12b. Herod
Antipas
= daughter
of Aretas
= Herodias
12c. Philip the
tetrarch
= Salome
13b. Herod of Chalcis
= Berenice
13a. Herod Agrippa I
† 44
Herodias
Salome
14. Herod Agrippa II
Berenice
= Herod of Chalcis
Drusilla
= Aziz king of Emesa
= Felix the procurator

= indicates marriages

MEASURES AND MONEY

TABLES OF APPROXIMATE EQUIVALENTS

I. DISTANCE

	RATIO	INCHES	CENTIMETRES
amma (cubit)	1	18	45
zereth (span)	1/2	8.8	22
tofah (palm)	1/6	3	7.2
esba (finger)	1/24	0.8	2

The old cubit of Ezekiel measured 7 palms or handbreadths (= 21 ins/52.5 cms), cf. Ezk 40:5 note f; the man's measuring rod was 6 old cubits = 10 ft 4 ins/315 cms. The N.T. has, besides the cubit, the arm-span of approximately 6 ft/1.84 metres, and the *stadion* of approximately 202 yds/185 metres. The Roman mile was 8 stadia or some 1616 yds/1.48 km. The *schoinos* of 2 M 11:5 equals 30 stadia, or about 3½ modern miles/5.55 km.

II. CAPACITY (Dry)

	RATIO	BUSHELS/GALLONS	LITRES
homer/cor	10	12½ bus.	450
lethech	5	6¼ bus.	225
ephah	1	1¼ bus.	45
seah (measure)	1/3	3⅓ U.K. gal. 4 U.S. gal.	15
issaron (tenth of a measure)	1/10	1 U.K. gal. 1¼ U.S. gal.	4.5

(Liquid)

	RATIO	GALLONS U.K.	GALLONS U.S.A.	LITRES
cor	10	100	120	450
bath	1	10	12	45
hin	1/6	1⅔	2	7.5
		pints	quarts	
kab	1/18	4½	2½	2.5
			fl. ozs	
log	1/72	1	20	0.6

The *art abē* in Dn 14:3 (LXX) is a Persian measure of about 12⅓ (U.K.)/14¾ (U.S.) gallons or 56 litres In the N.T. there are: the 'measure' *(metrētē)* of 8⅔ (U.K.)/10½ (U.S.) gallons or 39.4 litres which is equivalent to *bath*; the 'sixth' *(sextarius* or *xestes)* of ¾ (U.K.) pint/15 (U.S.) fl. ozs or 0.46 litres as an equivalent to the *log*; the *modion* in 2 (U.K.)/2⅓ (U.S.) gallons or 8.75 litres which is two thirds of the *seah*; and the *choinix* of Rv 6:6 which is 2 (U.K.) pints/1⅛ (U.S.) quarts or 1.1 litres. The N.T. also uses the words *seah, cor,* and *bath* in Greek forms.

III. WEIGHT

	RATIO	LBS/OZS	KILOGRAMS
kikkar (talent)	3000	75 lbs	34.272
maneh (mina)	50	1¼ lbs	0.571
shekel	1	0.39 ozs	0.0114
beqa (half-shekel)	1/2	0.19 ozs	0.0057
gerah	1/20	0.02 ozs	0.0006

The mina of Ezk 45:12 is 60 shekels (1½ lbs or 0.685 kg.). The N.T. has the Roman pound (Lat. *libra* = Gr. *litra*) of approximately 11½ ozs/0.326 kg.

IV. MONEY

1. Before Darius I. Coinage first appeared in the 7c. B.C. in Anatolia and then in Greece. Prior to this date the value of metal was gauged only by its weight. The *gold drachmas* of Ne 7:69 = Ezr 2:69, are probably the Attic half-staters (see table of monetary equivalents). The *silver mina* mentioned at the same place was only money of account, and was possibly the Babylonian *maneh* of about 1 lb or 0.505 kg.

2. Darius, soon after 515 B.C., issued the *gold daric* having the weight of the Babylonian shekel of ⅓ oz. or 8.41 grams (Ezr 8:27), and a *silver shekel* one twentieth of the value of the gold coin and thus weighing ⅕ oz. or 5.60 grams, since gold was valued at 13.3 times as much as silver. It is this shekel that is mentioned in Ne 5:15, whereas the shekel of Ne 10:33 is regarded only in terms of weight[a]. The minting of silver coinage seems to have been permitted throughout the Persian empire; silver coins have been found in Palestine with the inscription YHD = Judah.

3. Hellenistic and Roman period. Alexander extended the Attic system throughout his empire, with a gold to silver value ratio of 10 to 1. Later the Romans introduced their currency; they reckoned large sums in *sesterces* (see table). In the East, reckonings continued to be made in talents and minas i.e. in equivalents of 6000 and 100 drachmas.

MONETARY EQUIVALENTS

GREEK MONEY	WEIGHT		VALUE RATIO		WEIGHT		ROMAN MONEY
	OZS	GRAMS	GR.	RM.	GRAMS	OZS	
Attic stater (= gold standard). Weight = two silver drachmas:	0.3	8.6	20[b]	25	7.8	0.27	gold aureus[c], under Augustus
Attic silver tetradrachma:	0.6	17.4	4				
In Syria, under the empire:	±0.5[a]	±14.	3				
Sometimes called stater, Mt 21:27; 26:15 (D), cf. Zc 11:12							
Attic silver didrachma:	0.3	8.6	2				
Under the empire, Mt 17:24	±0.25	±7.	1½				
Attic drachma (= silver standard):	0.15	4.36	1		4.55	0.16	silver denarius[c], appears 269 B.C.; good quality alloy up to 3c.
Under Antiochus IV, 2 M 12:43:	±0.14	±4.					
Under the empire:	0.12	3.5	3/4		3.85	0.13	From 216 B.C. up to Nero.
					3.41	0.12	From Nero onwards.
				1/4	25.4	0.9	latten alloy sesterce; under Augustus = 4 as (weight one ounce).
Attic silver obol:	0.025	0.72	1/6	1/8	12.4	0.44	latten alloy dipondium; under Augustus = 2 as (Lk 12 and Vulg)
							as or assarius (= bronze standard) originally a Roman pound i.e. 12 ounces or 327 grams.
				1/16	10.8	0.38	Under Augustus.
Attic bronze chalkos:	0.3	8.6	1/48	1/32	4.5	0.16	bronze semis, under Augustus.
Under Antiochus IV	±0.21	±6.					
Attic bronze lepton: one seventh of the chalkos; sometimes called obol, chalkos, etc. Mk 12:42; Lk 12:59 = Mt 5:26			1/336	1/64	3.1	0.11	bronze quadrans, under Augustus. In the East, coinage of small values was locally minted by the ruling dynasty, by procurators or by cities, in rough conformity with the chalkos and as.

Silver coinage in Palestine during the Graeco-Roman Period (issued only during the First and Second Revolts):

FIRST REVOLT, 66-70 A.D.:

tetradrachmas	0.49 oz./14 gr.	inscribed 'shekel of Israel'
didrachmas	0.25 oz./7 gr.	inscribed 'half shekel'
drachmas	0.12 oz./3.35 gr.	inscribed 'quarter shekel'

SECOND REVOLT, 133-135 A.D.:

tetradrachmas	0.49 oz./14 gr.
denarii	restruck

NOTES

a. The tetradrachma represents a unit of the same order as the ancient shekel-pound. The didrachma annual levy for the Temple corresponds to the half-shekel of Ex 30:13 and to the third-of-a-shekel of Ne 10:33. The rabbis stipulated that these should conform to the standard of Tyre whose staters (tetradrachmas) had a high reputation.

b. Before Alexander.

c. This gold coin was the equivalent of 0.3225 grams of gold.